# The Coming of
# Managerial Capitalism
### A Casebook on the
### History of
### American Economic Institutions

**THE IRWIN SERIES IN MANAGEMENT
AND THE
BEHAVIORAL SCIENCES**
L. L. CUMMINGS AND E. KIRBY WARREN
*CONSULTING EDITORS*

# The Coming of
# Managerial Capitalism

## A Casebook on the
## History of
## American Economic Institutions

**Professor Alfred D. Chandler, Jr.**
Graduate School of Business Administration
*Harvard University*

**Assistant Professor Richard S. Tedlow**
Graduate School of Business Administration
*Harvard University*

1985

RICHARD D. IRWIN, INC.
Homewood, Illinois   60430

Case material of the Harvard Graduate School of Business
Administration is made possible by the cooperation of business firms and other organizations which may wish to
remain anonymous by having names, quantities and other
identifying details disguised while maintaining basic
relationships. Cases are prepared as the basis for class
discussion rather than to illustrate either effective
or ineffective handling of administrative solutions.

ISBN 0-256-03285-8

Library of Congress Catalog Card No. 84–82470

*Printed in the United States of America*

1 2 3 4 5 6 7 8 9 0 MP 2 1 0 9 8 7 6 5

*To the Business Historians at the Harvard Business School—*
*our colleagues past, present, and future.*

# *Preface to Students*

This book is a compilation of the materials which we use in teaching the course on "The Coming of Managerial Capitalism" to students in the second year of the MBA program at the Harvard Business School. This course and its predecessors in business and economic history have been an important part of the curriculum at Harvard for over half a century, and this book represents our effort to make the course available to students, both undergraduate and graduate, at other institutions. In these introductory remarks, we would like to explain first what a case is and how to prepare it and second the overall structure of the book.

Cases have been used in business education for many years. If you, the student reading this preface, are enrolled in a bachelors or masters degree program in business administration, you probably have encountered numerous cases already. If, on the other hand, you are concentrating in history or economics, cases will probably be less familiar to you.

The goal of each of our cases is to act as a vehicle for an intensive discussion of a key issue in the history of American economic institutions. Our book is not a conventional narrative history text. Our goal has not been to be comprehensive, to touch every base so to speak. Rather, we have sought to be intensive. We have focused on what we believe to be the most important issues and critical turning points and have provided you a lot of information on them.

Our hope is that you will not spend your time memorizing facts but rather that you will use the data in the cases to form opinions about the issues which they present. A case discussion must be more than merely a regurgitation of the facts that the case presents. It demands that students take an active and aggressive stance in developing and presenting their views based on those facts. Facts are the means, not the end. You must think beyond the data provided. The instructor may supply you with study questions to encourage this process. You will discover that many of these questions have no one right answer and present problems as controversial today as when they first arose.

Before outlining the content of this book, we would like to say a word about the phrase "economic institutions," which appears in the subtitle. This book is not only concerned with the growth of the large corporation. Big business is such an integral part of modern society that it cannot be studied without also exploring the history of government and of organized labor. Thus we also include considerable material on those two subjects.

Let us now proceed to a discussion of the book's structure.

The book begins by setting forth the approach and framework to be used in analyzing the cases. The first cases take a look at the social and political context that helped define the rules for economic behavior in the 18th century. Our attention then turns to the increasing specialization that occurred within commerce and industry as the American people grew in numbers and moved west and as the output of their farms, shops, and mills expanded. This examination is carried out by reviewing the career of John Jacob Astor, the most successful of the American merchants; the rise of the port of New York, the nation's leading commercial center; the Second Bank of the United States, its most powerful business institution; and the early New England factory systems.

The analysis of the economic revolution of the 19th century begins with the railroads, the nation's first big business, which provided (with the telegraph) the high-speed, high-volume, and widely available transportation and communication so necessary to the beginnings of modern mass production and mass distribution. The readings examine how entrepreneurs responded to new challenges and needs by creating new business methods and procedures required to build, finance, and operate the nation's transportation and communication infrastructure.

The book next focuses on the great transformation of production and distribution, particularly as carried out by the large industrial enterprises that integrated mass production with mass distribution. The cases deal with why and how business enterprise responded to new technologies and rapidly expanding markets, how it developed new ways of management and competition, as well as how modern big business altered the structure of American industries and the economy as a whole.

The next section of the book deals with the broader political and institutional response to the growth of the large transportation and industrial enterprises that spearheaded the drive to industrialism. First comes a review of the response of the working force—organized and unorganized. Special emphasis is given to the rise of the industrial union in the 1930s that became the workers' most effective organization for bargaining with the managers of the large business enterprises. Next the book explores the role of government in dealing with issues of antitrust in the early 20th century. We then see the role of government expand with the collapse of economic stability in the 1930s. With the Great Depression and the resulting New Deal, the Federal Government became responsible for regulating the economy as well as regulating business enterprise.

The final phase of the book focuses on the ways business enterprises continued to grow in number and size in the new institutional environment, continuing to exploit modern technology and expanding markets. Several cases analyze the coming of a new strategy of product diversification and the concomitant decentralized, multidivisional structure. They examine the energetic expansion of American business enterprises overseas after World War II largely through use of the new strategy and structure, and the coming of a modified version of the multidivisional form—the comglomerate—in the merger movement of the late 1960s. The final case provides a vehicle for students to discuss future challenges to business management in light of its history.

# ACKNOWLEDGMENTS

Many people at the Harvard Business School have helped make this book a reality, and it is a pleasure here to express our appreciation for their contributions.

John H. McArthur, Dean of the Harvard Business School, has vigorously supported all the activities of its business historians, among which this book is an example. So has Professor E. Raymond Corey, Director of the School's Division of Research. Their support has helped keep the institution the leading center for this discipline.

We have profited from the contributions of numerous historians who have taught at the School in the past or are there at present. These include (in alphabetical order): James P. Baughman, the late N.S.B. Gras, the late Ralph W. Hidy, Arthur M. Johnson, the late Henrietta Larson, Thomas K. McCraw, Albro Martin, Thomas R. Navin, Glenn Porter, Stephen Salsbury, Barry Supple, and Richard H. K. Vietor. We have also benefitted from the interest of a number of Harvard/Newcomen Fellows, including James E. Fell, Jr.; Katherine D. Hughes, who wrote the last case in the book; Daniel A. Pope; and Leonard S. Reich.

In order to reach its potential, the work of business historians must be informed by a knowledge of how business is conducted in the present day. We are especially fortunate to have as colleagues numerous professors who have that current perspective and who have generously contributed their insights. (We are reproducing the research of some of these individuals in our book.) These professors are (also in alphabetical order): Francis J. Aguilar, Kenneth R. Andrews, Christopher A. Bartlett, Norman A. Berg, C. Roland Christensen, J. Ronald Fox, Richard G. Hamermesh, Robert S. Kaplan, Warren A. Law, George C. Lodge, D. Quinn Mills, Michael G. Rukstad, Bruce R. Scott, Jeffrey A. Sonnenfeld, and David B. Yoffie.

We have also had the valuable help of four research assistants: Gordon Hylton, who contributed a case; Richard R. John, Jr.; Josepha M. Perry; and David B. Sicilia.

Few people who have not had first-hand experience with a manuscript of this size appreciate the extent of the staff assistance it necessitates. We are particularly fortunate to have had the benefit of the efforts of efficient and hard-working individuals in this regard. Our secretaries, Violette G. Crowe and Kenjalin Ogata, were very helpful to us. We are particularly indebted to Kenje Ogata, who kept meticulous records of the progress of the manuscript, spent a great deal of time with other people on the Harvard Business School staff to pilot it through its various phases, and proofread part of it. Typing and the bulk of the proofreading were handled by Rose M. Giacobbe and her staff at the School's Word Processing Center. They labored long and hard, through seemingly endless revisions. Finally,

Patricia A. North, Business Manager of the *Business History Review*, did not actually work on this project, but the skill with which she has handled her responsibilities on the *Review* freed up time for us to devote to it.

This is a better book because of the generous help of all those named above. Needless to say, the responsibility for any shortcomings it may possess rests solely with us.

Alfred D. Chandler, Jr.
Richard S. Tedlow

# Contents

# PART ONE

# *The Agrarian, Commercial Economy*

## INTRODUCTION

## FORGING A NATIONAL ECONOMY

# CASE 1

# *Benjamin Franklin and the Definition of American Values**

*All that has happened to you is also connected with the detail of the manners and situation of a rising people.*[1]

*Nothing but money is sweeter than honey.*[2]

Benjamin Franklin, who through versatile talents became internationally the most widely known American of his time, was born in Boston in 1706. His father, Josiah, had left England about 1685, partly to better his economic condition and partly because of his dissension from the Church of England. He had settled with his wife and children in Boston, then a town of 5,000 or 6,000 inhabitants, and finding no demand for his skill as a dyer of cloth, had turned to making and selling candles and soap to support a growing family. Within a few years, his wife died and Josiah soon married Abiah Folger, the daughter of one of the early English settlers on Nantucket. She bore him 10 children; Benjamin was the youngest of the 6 boys.

*This case was originally prepared from published sources by Josepha M. Perry under the direction of Dr. Barry E. Supple. This revised and expanded version has been prepared by Assistant Professor Richard S. Tedlow, as a basis for class discussion rather than to illustrate either effective or ineffective handling of an administrative situation.

Copyright © 1983 by the President and Fellows of Harvard College.

Harvard Business School case 383–160, rev. 6/84.

[1]Benjamin Vaughan to Benjamin Franklin, January 31, 1783.

[2]*Poor Richard's Almanack*, 1735.

Benjamin's father contemplated educating him for the ministry and to this end sent him to a classical grammar school at the age of eight. But a few months later when the full impact of the expense involved in such training, including four years at Harvard, came to Josiah, Benjamin entered a more practical academic environment where the chief subjects were writing and arithmetic. Thus his acquisition of Latin was postponed until he himself decided to tackle it some 20 years later, along with French, Italian, Spanish, and German.

His father took him at the age of 10 into his chandler's shop. Ben did not like the work and betrayed a restless interest in going to sea. Seeking to place him in a more congenial occupation, Josiah apprenticed him to his half brother James, a printer, who shortly thereafter started to publish the weekly *New England Courant*.

This newspaper was spokesman for a group of liberal minds frequently at odds with the city government, and Ben worked in a stimulating intellectual atmosphere. He had been an avid reader of such books as he could lay hands on, notably essays and the *Spectator*, which served as inspiration for his own writings. His first published pieces were the "Silence Dogood Papers," slipped anonymously under the door of his brother's office and printed in the *Courant* on their own merit with no suspicion of their authorship.

After five years, Ben quarreled with James and, heedless of family attempts to effect a reconciliation, ran away to New York and then on to Philadelphia in search of work in a printing office. This he found with Samuel Keimer before he had quite spent the Dutch dollar and copper shilling that comprised his entire financial resources on arrival. At 17 he was a well-trained printer, capable of handling plain typesetting and presswork. Just as important, he had already acquired the ability to make friends and attract favorable attention that later smoothed his path in public life.

The first patron he attracted, however, proved a feeble support. Sir William Keith, governor of Pennsylvania, heard of Ben through Ben's brother-in-law and encouraged him to set up his own printing business. Ben's father refused to supply the capital for such a precocious venture, so Keith sent Ben off to London to buy equipment, promising him letters of credit to finance the project. But Keith was not a man to keep promises, and Franklin found himself in London with no money for equipment or for passage home. He was, however, sufficiently expert at his trade to earn a good living.

In spite of his now-famous veneration of thrift as the chief virtue, Franklin seems to have been vulnerable to the claims of improvident friends, and in London he laid out a considerable amount of money for James Ralph, who had come with him from Philadelphia full of literary aspirations and with small ability to get a livelihood. Moreover, in company with Ralph, Franklin took advantage of metropolitan attractions such as the theater and other amusements. In consequence, he saved nothing for transportation back to America. But life in London in 1725 was a stimulating experience. It was an "age of intellect" influenced by the presence of Hogarth, Fielding, Defoe, and Isaac Newton. Franklin wrote and printed a pamphlet entitled *A Dissertation on Liberty and Necessity, Pleasure and Pain*, partly a rationalization of his own pleasure-seeking existence at the time. This publication brought him to the notice of interesting and companionable people. And withal, he worked diligently at his job, perfecting his typographical skill.

After 19 months, however, Franklin was ready to accept a proposition that he return to Philadelphia with Thomas Denham, a wealthy Quaker merchant who had met him on the ship to England and who now wanted him to go back and assist in a store Denham was going to open. After less than a year, Denham's death ended Franklin's career as clerk and bookkeeper, and he went back to run the printing house for Keimer, his first Philadelphia employer.

Relationships were rather strained at Keimer's; and Hugh Meredith, a fellow worker, persuaded Franklin to take him as a partner and start a printing office with capital supplied by Meredith's father. The father sent to London for the necessary equipment and early in 1728 Meredith and Franklin took a house on Market Street for £24 a year. They rented part of it to a family with whom they boarded and set up their printing paraphernalia in the rest.

Competition was keen at first with three printers in the city. Keimer, however, was not long a threat since he failed in 1729. Franklin bought the newspaper he had recently started and issued it as the *Pennsylvania Gazette*. Andrew Bradford was a stronger rival; as government printer for Pennsylvania, he had a backlog of lucrative jobs. Franklin made short work of this advantage of Bradford's by printing an "Address from the Assembly to the Governor" in his own paper and giving a copy to every Assembly member. The workmanship was so superior that in 1730 Franklin obtained the government contract. Later he became public printer for New Jersey and Maryland.

Meredith was proving an unstable partner and his father had not completed payments on the imported equipment. Franklin finally agreed to assume his partner's personal debts as well as those of the firm and pay back £100 of the elder Meredith's capital, whereupon the partnership was dissolved.

Established independently, Franklin set out by industriousness and thrift to acquire a competence. He was becoming well known in the city; he had an enthusiastic group of friends; and he was the best writer in America at that time. Columns of his worldly wise humor increased the circulation of his *Gazette*. In his *Autobiography* he wrote:

> In order to secure my credit and character. . .I took care not only to be in reality industrious and frugal but to avoid all appearance to the contrary. I dressed plainly; I was seen at no places of idle diversion. I never went a-fishing or shooting; a book, indeed, sometimes debauched me from my work, but that was seldom, snug, and gave no scandal; and, to show that I was not above my business, I sometimes brought home the paper I purchased at the stores through the streets on a wheelbarrow.[3]

In 1730, he married Deborah Read, a woman incapable of sharing his intellectual interests but a devoted and patient wife. They lived in the house where the

---

[3]Leonard W. Labaree et al., eds., *The Autobiography of Benjamin Franklin* (New Haven: Yale University Press, 1975), pp. 125–26.

printing office was, and she helped with the shop he set up there to sell stationery and books imported from England. Over a period of years his stock expanded to include, as occasion offered, foodstuffs such as coffee, Rhode Island cheese, codfish, and mackerel in barrels, as well as cloth, stockings, spectacles, maps, compasses, and a multitude of other goods. He could without expense apprise the public of items on hand by advertisements in his *Gazette*. In 1737, he became postmaster of Philadelphia with the legal right to send his newspaper out by the postriders. He published books and pamphlets as well as doing job printing. Capital began to accumulate to a point where he felt ready to invest it.

Apparently with two purposes in mind—to make money and to encourage the spread of printing—Franklin became a silent partner in several enterprises, usually setting up a protegé with presses, paying one third of the going expenses, and receiving one third of the profits. In Charleston, South Carolina, in Antigua and Jamaica, and in Lancaster, Pennsylvania, printing houses were started with his participation. In Philadelphia he had two or three partners publishing German books and papers. The most enduring of these ventures was with one of his journeymen, James Parker, whom he sent to New York. Upon the retirement of the only other printer there, Parker took over the *New York Gazette* and became public printer for the province. He also established in partnership with Franklin an office in New Haven, procured the printing business of Yale College, and established the *Connecticut Gazette*.

With modest financial success achieved, Franklin took a partner into his own printing office and retired from active operation of the business to a life of leisure for the writing, study, and scientific experimentation that his inquiring mind craved. From England in 1743 he had, upon the recommendation of a friend, hired David Hall, who proved a satisfactory manager. In 1748 at the age of 42, Franklin wrote that he had put his printing house under the care of his partner, absolutely left off bookselling, and removed to a quieter part of town. Until 1766 the business was known as Franklin and Hall, and, according to agreement, Hall paid Franklin £1,000 a year from the partnership during that period.

In addition to Hall's payments, Franklin had, when he retired, a small salary as postmaster of Philadelphia and an income estimated at about £700 a year from invested savings. Some part of his wealth was in houses and lots in Philadelphia. After the Revolution this property increased in value to perhaps three times its original cost to him. From the public positions he later held, he received varying stipends.

Franklin's fame as well as his fortune were enhanced by the publication of *Poor Richard's Almanack*, the first number of which was for the year 1733. Almanacs had a ready market in the eighteenth century; they circulated far outside of towns in peddlers' packs, sometimes the only bit of reading matter that a family purchased. Calendars, tide tables, phases of the moon, weather prophecies, and scraps of astrology were supplemented by recipes, poems, and jottings of wit and wisdom. In this latter field, Franklin's almanac outdid its rivals. In the person of Richard Saunders, he created a mouthpiece for old sayings, frequently with a new and pithy twist, and original quips for the edification and amusement of a solid colonial citizenry.

Under the title of "The Way to Wealth," the preface to the 1758 edition contained a compilation of these sayings, particularly the ones dealing with thrift and wise enterprise, purporting to be an old man's speech to a crowd attending an auction (reproduced as Exhibit 1). It was widely reprinted and translated into 15 languages. It was published in broadsides and posted on walls in England; it was handed to parishioners by the clergy in France.

*Poor Richard's Almanack* was an immediate success, selling 10,000 copies within the first three months of publication. Franklin's partners stocked it in their bookshops and advertised it in the various *Gazettes* they published.

Franklin's creative talents had a practical turn, and as is well known, he invented a number of useful contrivances. The "Pennsylvania fireplace," an open-front stove with doors, allowed all the cheer of a crackling fire in a grate and gave good circulation of heat besides, since it could be set well out from the wall. Bifocal spectacles and a "long arm" for reaching and clasping books or merchandise on high shelves are credited to his ingenuity. His most famous invention was the lightning rod, an outgrowth of experiments with flying a kite in a thunderstorm to prove a connection between lightning and electricity. Such a connection was being studied by many scientists in Europe, and Franklin's independent proof added luster to the reputation he was already achieving abroad. His lightning rod was widely and enthusiastically adopted in this country as a protective device. Franklin took out no patents on any of his inventions. The model for his stoves he turned over to a friend with an iron foundry who manufactured them on his own account. A concern for human welfare seems to have been a genuine motive in much that Franklin did.

Among other public services, Franklin established a circulating library, organized the first fire brigade in Philadelphia, helped to start a hospital, and also the Academy of Philadelphia, which eventually grew into the University of Pennsylvania.

From 1750 to 1764, Franklin was annually elected to the Assembly of Pennsylvania by the popular, or progressive, party. Through many of those years, he was in London as Colonial Agent for Pennsylvania. The friends he made there in political and fashionable circles stood him in good stead when he went back again in 1764 and faced not only Pennsylvania's problems but the whole question of relations between England and the Colonies. His influence was felt in the repeal of the Stamp Act in 1766. Georgia, New Jersey, and Massachusetts also appointed him as agent, so great was his prestige. He traveled on the continent during this period and was enthusiastically welcomed in France and Germany by economists, philosophers, and scientists who had read his pamphlets or heard of his work, again widening his reputation in a way that later strengthened his diplomatic influence.

On his return to Philadelphia in 1775, all efforts to keep the peace having failed, his public position in America was firm. He was elected to the Congress and was on the committee that framed the Declaration of Independence. In September, 1776, he crossed the Atlantic again as the most important of three commissioners to France, seeking aid for the American cause. He remained after the fighting stopped to arrange terms of peace with England, a touchy mission that involved relations with France as well. After the signing of the treaty in 1783, Franklin stayed on as minister to France for two years.

His life in France was a diplomatic and personal triumph. Among scientists and philosophers, at a time when "philosophy was the fashion" in France, he already had friends and cultivated more. His ability to charm both men and women seems to have flowered, and since women were socially important in France, his popularity with them enhanced his public renown. The King and Queen received him graciously. French monetary aid, as gifts and loans, flowed to the new nation. Franklin contributed political articles to French papers and also wrote for distribution among his friends a series of short and pleasant essays called *Bagatelles*, which had a wide vogue.

In 1785, Franklin resigned his post and went back to Philadelphia. At home he continued political activities as President of the Commonwealth of Pennsylvania until ill health in 1788 forced his retirement.

Printer, author, philanthropist, inventor, statesman, diplomat, scientist, Benjamin Franklin died on April 17, 1790, full of years and honors. His name was known throughout the Western world, and his influence was felt in the lives of men as diverse as George Washington and Johann Wolfgang von Goethe. In his own life, he seemed to personify the strivings of many of his contemporaries and also of Americans who came after him. From penniless vagabondage, he accumulated an estate valued at about a quarter of a million dollars at the time of his death. Despite only two years of formal schooling, he received honorary degrees from Harvard, Yale, and Oxford and was a founder of the University of Pennsylvania. The commonest of common men, he became the honored guest of statesmen and royalty.

Many an entrepreneur has been inspired by Franklin's example and precepts. One example was Thomas Mellon, founder of one of America's great fortunes, who wrote that "the reading of Franklin's *Autobiography* was the turning point in my life." It prompted him to leave the family farm and enter finance. Mellon later had a thousand copies of the *Autobiography* printed to be distributed to young men asking for advice. In a recent 2,600-page collection of business documents from ancient times to the present compiled by three scholars from the Harvard Business School, Franklin's name appears more often than that of any other individual.[4] In 1983, a new biography of Franklin merited a review on *The Wall Street Journal*'s editorial page, where he was described as a man who "can still enthrall. . .us."[5]

And Franklin's influence has been felt amongst the nation's leading intellects. Wrote Jared Sparks, who rose from a poor Connecticut farm to the presidency of Harvard, Franklin's *Autobiography* "first roused by mental energies. . .prompted me to resolutions, and gave me strength to adhere to them. . . . It taught me that

---

[4]Edward C. Bursk; Donald T. Clark; and Ralph W. Hidy, eds., *The World of Business* (New York: Simon and Schuster, 1962), II, p. 1070.

[5]*The Wall Street Journal*, January 25, 1983, p. 32.

circumstances have not a sovereign control over the mind."[6] In the words of his greatest biographer:

> In any age, in any place Franklin would have been great. Mind and will, talent and art, strength and ease, wit and grace met in him as if nature had been lavish and happy when he was shaped. Nothing seems to have been left out except a passionate desire, as in most men of genius, to be all ruler, all soldier, all saint, all poet, all scholar, all some one gift or merit or success. Franklin's powers were from first to last in a flexible equilibrium. Even his genius could not specialize him. He moved through his world in a humorous mastery of it.[7]

Franklin, however, has always been a figure of controversy. His numerous critics have attacked him for what they viewed as his hypocrisy, his delight in manipulation, and his neglect of the spirit. Franklin's vision of the wise man, they felt, was that of one who did indeed live by bread alone.

Among the most brilliant and imaginative uses of Franklin's life and work was that of Max Weber, who saw in Franklin the very incarnation of "the spirit of capitalism" which had swept away the world view of previous ages. Reviewing aphorisms such as those reproduced in Exhibit 1, Weber observed:

> The peculiarity of this philosophy of avarice appears to be. . .above all the idea of a duty of the individual toward the increase of his capital, which is assumed as an end in itself. Truly what is here preached is not simply a means of making one's way in the world, but a peculiar ethic. The infraction of its rules is treated not as foolishness but as forgetfulness of duty. That is the essence of the matter. It is not mere business astuteness, that sort of thing is common enough, it is an ethos. *This* is the quality which interests us.
>
> When Jacob Fugger, in speaking to a business associate who had retired and who wanted to persuade him to do the same, since he had made enough money and should let others have a chance, rejected that as pusillanimity and answered that "he (Fugger) thought otherwise, he wanted to make money as long as he could," the spirit of his statement is evidently quite different from that of Franklin. What in the former case was an expression of commercial daring and a personal inclination morally neutral, in the latter takes on the character of an ethically coloured maxim for the conduct of life. The concept spirit of capitalism is here used in this specific sense, it is the spirit of modern capitalism.
>
> The spirit of capitalism, in the sense in which we are using the term, had to fight its way to supremacy against a whole world of hostile forces. A state of mind such as that expressed in the passages we have quoted from Franklin, and which called forth the applause of a whole people, would both in ancient times and in the Middle Ages have been proscribed as the lowest sort of avarice and as an attitude entirely lacking in self-respect. It is, in fact, still regularly thus looked upon by those social groups which are least involved in or adapted to modern capitalistic conditions.[8]

---

[6]See Labaree, *Franklin*, pp. 10–11.

[7]Carl Van Doren, *Benjamin Franklin* (New York: Garden City Publishing Co., 1941), p. 782.

[8]Max Weber, *The Protestant Ethic and the Spirit of Capitalism* (New York: Charles Scribner's Sons, 1958), pp. 48–57.

# EXHIBIT 1

*Franklin on Business Values: The Way to Wealth, as Clearly Shown in the Preface of an Old Pennsylvania Almanack, Intitled, Poor Richard Improved (1758)*

Courteous Reader,

I have heard, that nothing gives an author so great pleasure, as to find his works respectfully quoted by others. Judge, then, how much I must have been gratified by an incident I am going to relate to you. I stopped my horse lately, where a great number of people were collected, at an auction of merchants goods. The hour of the sale not being come, they were conversing on the badness of the times; and one of the company called to a plain clean old man, with white locks, 'Pray, Father Abraham, what think you of the times? Will not these heavy taxes quite ruin the country? How shall we ever be able to pay them? What would you advise us to?' Father Abraham stood up, and replied, 'If you would have my advice, I will give it you in short, "for a word to the wise is enough," as Poor Richard says.' They joined in desiring him to speak his mind, and gathering round him, he proceeded as follows:

'Friends,' says he, 'the taxes are, indeed, very heavy, and, if those laid on by the government were the only ones we had to pay, we might more easily discharge them; but we have many others, and much more grievous to some of us. We are taxed twice as much by our idleness, three times as much by our pride, and four times as much by our folly; and from these taxes the commissioners cannot ease or deliver us, by allowing an abatement. However, let us hearken to good advice, and something may be done for us; "God helps them that help themselves," as Poor Richard says.

'I.  It would be thought a hard government that should tax its people one-tenth part of their time, to be employed in its service; but idleness taxes many of us much more; sloth, by bringing on diseases, absolutely shortens life. "Sloth, like rust, consumes faster than labour wears, while the used key is always bright," as Poor Richard says. "But dost thou love life, then do not squander time, for that is the stuff life is made of," as Poor Richard says. How much more than is necessary do we spend in sleep! forgetting, that "the sleeping fox catches no poultry, and that there will be sleeping enough in the grave," as Poor Richard says.

' "If time be of all things the most precious, wasting time must be," as Poor Richard says, "the greatest prodigality;" since, as he elsewhere tells us, "lost time is never found again; and what we call time enough always proves little enough:" Let us then up and be doing, and doing to the purpose; so by diligence shall we do more with less perplexity. "Sloth makes all things difficult, but industry all easy; and he that riseth late, must trot all day, and shall scarce overtake his business at night; while laziness travels so slowly, that poverty soon overtakes him. Drive thy business, let not that drive thee; and early to bed, and early to rise, makes a man healthy, wealthy, and wise," as Poor Richard says.

## EXHIBIT 1 (*continued*)

'So what signifies wishing and hoping for better times? We may make these times better, if we bestir ourselves. "Industry need not wish, and he that lives upon hope will die fasting. There are no gains without pains; then help hands, for I have no lands," or, if I have, they are smartly taxed. "He, that hath a trade, hath an estate; and he, that hath a calling, hath an office of profit and honour," as Poor Richard says; but then the trade must be worked at, and the calling well followed, or neither the estate nor the office will enable us to pay our taxes. If we are industrious, we shall never starve; for, "at the working man's house, hunger looks in, but dares not enter." Nor will the bailiff or the constable enter, for "industry pays debts, while despair increaseth them." What though you have found no treasure, nor has any rich relation left you a legacy, "diligence is the mother of good luck, and God gives all things to industry. Then plow deep, while sluggards sleep, and you shall have corn to sell and to keep." Work while it is called to-day, for you know not how much you may be hindered to-morrow.

' "One to-day is worth two to-morrows," as Poor Richard says; and farther, "never leave that till to-morrow, which you can do to-day." If you were a servant, would you not be ashamed that a good master should catch you idle? Are you then your own master? Be ashamed to catch yourself idle, when there is so much to be done for yourself, your family, your country, and your king. Handle your tools without mittens; remember, that "the cat in gloves catches no mice," as Poor Richard says. It is true, there is much to be done, and perhaps you are weak-handed; but stick to it steadily, and you will see great effects, for "constant dropping wears away stones; and by diligence and patience the mouse ate in two the cable; and little strokes fell great oaks."

'Methinks I hear some of you say, "must a man afford himself no leisure?" I will tell thee, my friend, what Poor Richard says; "employ thy time well, if thou meanest to gain leisure; and since thou art not sure of a minute, throw not away an hour." Leisure is time for doing something useful; this leisure the diligent man will obtain, but the lazy man never; for "a life of leisure and a life of laziness are two things. Many, without labour, would live by their wits only, but they break for want of stock;" whereas industry gives comfort, and plenty, and respect. "Fly pleasures, and they will follow you. The diligent spinner has a large shift; and now I have a sheep and a cow, every body bids me good-morrow."

'II.   But with our industry we must likewise be steady, settled, and careful, and oversee our own affairs with our own eyes, and not trust too much to others; for, as Poor Richard says,

> "I never saw an oft' removed tree,
> Nor yet an oft-removed family,
> That throve so well as those that settled be."

And again, "three removes is as bad as a fire;" and again, "Keep thy shop, and thy shop will keep thee;" and again, "if you would have your business done, go, if not, send." And again,

# EXHIBIT 1 (*continued*)

> "He that by the plough would thrive,
> Himself must either hold or drive."

And again, "the eye of a master will do more work than both his hands;" and again, "want of care does us more damage than want of knowledge;" and again, "not to oversee workmen, is to leave them your purse open." Trusting too much to other's care is the ruin of many; for, "in the affairs of this world, men are saved, not by faith, but by the want of it;" but a man's own care is profitable; for, "if you would have a faithful servant, and one that you like, serve yourself. A little neglect may breed great mischief; for want of a nail the shoe was lost, and for want of a shoe the horse was lost, and for want of a horse the rider was lost," being overtaken and slain by the enemy; all for want of a little care about a horse-shoe nail.

'III.   So much for industry, my friends, and attention to one's own business; but to these we must add frugality, if we would make our industry more certainly successful. A man may, if he knows not how to save as he gets, "keep his nose all his life to the grind-stone, and die not worth a groat at last. A fat kitchen makes a lean will;" and

> "Many estates are spent in the getting,
> Since women for tea forsook spinning and knitting,
> And men for punch forsook hewing and splitting."

"If you would be wealthy, think of saving, as well as of getting. The Indies have not made Spain rich, because her outgoes are greater than her incomes."

'Away then, with your expensive follies, and you will not then have so much cause to complain of hard times, heavy taxes, and chargeable families; for

> "Women and wine, game and deceit,
> Make the wealth small, and the want great."

And farther, "what maintains one vice, would bring up two children." You may think, perhaps, that a little tea, or a little punch now and then, diet a little more costly, clothes a little finer, and a little entertainment now and then, can be no great matter; but remember, "many a little makes a mickle." Beware of little expences "a small leak will sink a great ship, as Poor Richard says; and again, "who dainties love, shall beggars prove;" and moreover, "fools make feasts, and wise men eat them."

'Here you are all got together to this sale of fineries and nicknacks. You call them *goods,* but if you do not take care, they will prove *evils* to some of you. You expect they will be sold cheap, and perhaps they may, for less than they cost; but, if you have no occasion for them, they must be dear to you. Remember what Poor Richard says, "buy what thou hast not need of, and ere long thou shalt sell thy necessaries." And again, "at a great penny-worth pause a while." He means, that perhaps the cheapness is apparent only, and not real; or the bargain, by straitening thee in thy business, may do thee more harm than good. For in another place

## EXHIBIT 1 (*continued*)

he says, "Many have been ruined by buying good pennyworths." Again, "it is foolish to lay out money in a purchase of repentance;" and yet this folly is practised every day at auctions, for want of minding the almanack. Many a one, for the sake of finery on the back, have gone with a hungry belly, and half starved their families; "silks and sattins, scarlet and velvets, put out the kitchen fire," as Poor Richard says. These are not the necessaries of life, they can scarcely be called the conveniences; and yet, only because they look pretty, how many want to have them? By these and other extravagancies, the genteel are reduced to poverty, and forced to borrow of those whom they formerly despised, but who, through industry and frugality, have maintained their standing; in which case it appears plainly, that "a ploughman on his legs is higher than a gentleman on his knees," as Poor Richard says. Perhaps they have had a small estate left them, which they knew not the getting of; they think "it is day, and will never be night;" that a little to be spent out of so much is not worth minding; but "always taking out of the meal-tub, and never putting in soon comes to the bottom," as Poor Richard says; and then, "when the well is dry, they know the worth of water." But this they might have known before, if they had taken his advice: "if you would know the value of money go and try to borrow some; for he that goes a borrowing goes a sorrowing," as Poor Richard says; and indeed so does he that lends to such people, when he goes to get it in again. Poor Dick farther advises, and says,

> "Fond pride of dress is sure a very curse,
> Ere fancy you consult, consult your purse."

And again, "pride is as loud a beggar as want, and a great deal more saucy." When you have bought one fine thing, you must buy ten more, that your appearance may be all of a piece; but Poor Dick says, "it is easier to suppress the first desire than to satisfy all that follow it:" and it is as truly folly for the poor to ape the rich, as for the frog to swell, in order to equal the ox.

> "Vessels large may venture more,
> But little boats should keep near shore."

It is, however, a folly soon punished; for, as Poor Richard says, "pride that dines on vanity, sups on contempt; pride breakfasted with plenty, dined with poverty, and supped with infamy." And, after all, of what use is this pride of appearance, for which so much is risked, so much is suffered? It cannot promote health, nor ease pain; it makes no increase of merit in the person; it creates envy, it hastens misfortune.

'But what madness must it be to *run in debt* for these superfluities! We are offered, by the terms of this sale, six months credit; and that, perhaps, has induced some of us to attend it, because we cannot spare the ready money, and hope now to be fine without it. But ah! think what you do when you run in debt; you give to another power over your liberty. If you cannot pay at the time, you will be ashamed to see your creditor, you will be in fear when you speak to him, you will make poor pitiful sneaking excuses, and, by degrees, come to lose your veracity, and sink into

# EXHIBIT 1 (*continued*)

base, downright lying; for, "the second vice is lying, the *first* is running in debt," as Poor Richard says; and again, to the same purpose, "lying rides upon debt's back;" whereas a free-born Englishman ought not to be ashamed nor afraid to see or speak to any man living. But poverty often deprives a man of all spirit and virtue. "It is hard for an empty bag to stand upright." What would you think of that prince, or of that government, who should issue an edict, forbidding you to dress like a gentleman or gentlewoman, on pain of imprisonment or servitude? Would you not say, that you were free, have a right to dress as you please, and that such an edict would be a breach of your privileges, and such a government tyrannical? And yet you are about to put yourself under that tyranny, when you run in debt for such dress! Your creditor has authority, at his pleasure, to deprive you of your liberty, by confining you in gaol for life, or by selling you for a servant, if you should not be able to pay him. When you have got your bargain, you may, perhaps, think little of payment; but, as Poor Richard says, "creditors have better memories than debtors; creditors are a superstitious sect, great observers of set-days and times." The day comes round before you are aware, and the demand is made before you are prepared to satisfy it; or, if you bear your debt in mind, the term, which at first seemed so long, will, as it lessens, appear extremely short: Time will seem to have added wings to his heels as well as his shoulders. "Those have a short Lent, who owe money to be paid at Easter." At present, perhaps, you may think yourselves in thriving circumstances, and that you can bear a little extravagance without injury; but

"For age and want save while you may,
No morning sun lasts a whole day."

Gain may be temporary and uncertain, but ever, while you live, expence is constant and certain; and, "it is easier to build two chimneys than to keep one in fuel," as Poor Richard says: so "rather go to bed supperless than rise in debt."

"Get what you can, and what you get hold, 'Tis the stone that
Will turn all your lead into gold."

And when you have got the philosopher's stone, sure you will no longer complain of bad times, or the difficulty of paying taxes.

'IV.   This doctrine, my friends, is reason and wisdom: but, after all, do not depend too much upon your own industry, and frugality, and prudence, though excellent things; for they may all be blasted, without the blessing of heaven; and therefore ask that blessing humbly, and be not uncharitable to those that at present seem to want it, but comfort and help them. Remember Job suffered, and was afterwards prosperous.

'And now, to conclude, "experience keeps a dear school, but fools will learn in no other," as Poor Richard says, and scarce in that; for, it is true, "we may give advice, but we cannot give conduct:" however, remember this, "they that will not be counselled cannot be helped;" and farther, that "if you will not hear reason she will surely rap your knuckles," as Poor Richard says.'

## EXHIBIT 1 (*concluded*)

Thus the old gentleman ended his harangue. The people heard it and approved the doctrine; and immediately practised the contrary, just as if it had been a common sermon, for the auction opened and they began to buy extravagantly. — I found the good man had thoroughly studied my almanacks, and digested all I had dropt on those topics during the course of twenty-five years. The frequent mention he made of me must have tired any one else; but my vanity was wonderfully delighted with it, though I was conscious, that not a tenth part of the wisdom was my own, which he ascribed to me, but rather the gleanings that I had made of the sense of all ages and nations. However, I resolved to be the better for the echo of it; and, though I had at first determined to buy stuff for a new coat, I went away, resolved to wear my old one a little longer. Reader, if thou wilt do the same, thy profit will be as great as mine.

I am, as ever, Thine to serve thee,

Richard Saunders.

Source: *The Complete Works of the Late Dr. Benjamin Franklin in Philosophy, Politics, and Morals, Now First Collected and Arranged with Memoirs of His Early Life, Written by Himself,* 3 (London: J. Johnson, 1806), pp. 453–68.

## EXHIBIT 2

### *Franklin on "Moral Perfection"*

The following is a famous passage from Franklin's *Autobiography.*

It was about this time I conceiv'd the bold and arduous project of arriving at moral perfection. I wish'd to live without committing any fault at any time; I would conquer all that either natural inclination, custom, or company might lead me into. As I knew, or thought I knew, what was right and wrong, I did not see why I might not always do the one and avoid the other. But I soon found I had undertaken a task of more difficulty than I had imagined. While my care was employ'd in guarding against one fault, I was often surprised by another; habit took the advantage of inattention; inclination was sometimes too strong for reason. I concluded, at length, that the mere speculative conviction that it was our interest to be completely virtuous, was not sufficient to prevent our slipping; and that the contrary habits must be broken, and good ones acquired and established, before we can have any dependence on a steady, uniform rectitude of conduct. For this purpose I therefore contrived the following method.

In the various enumerations of the moral virtues I had met with in my reading, I found the catalogue more or less numerous, as different writers included more or fewer ideas under the same name. Temperance, for example, was by some confined to eating and drinking, while by others it was extended to mean the

# EXHIBIT 2 (*continued*)

moderating of every other pleasure, appetite, inclination, or passion, bodily or mental, even to our avarice and ambition. I propos'd to myself, for the sake of clearness, to use rather more names, with fewer ideas annex'd to each, than a few names with more ideas; and I included under thirteen names of virtues all that at that time occurr'd to me as necessary or desirable, and annexed to each a short precept, which fully express'd the extent I gave to its meaning.

These names of virtues, with their precepts, were:

1. **Temperance.** Eat not to dullness; drink not to elevation.
2. **Silence.** Speak not but what may benefit others or yourself; avoid trifling conversation.
3. **Order.** Let all your things have their places; let each part of your business have its time.
4. **Resolution.** Resolve to perform what you ought; perform without fail what you resolve.
5. **Frugality.** Make no expense but to do good to others or yourself; i.e., waste nothing.
6. **Industry.** Lose no time; be always employ'd in something useful; cut off all unnecessary actions.
7. **Sincerity.** Use no hurtful deceit; think innocently and justly, and, if you speak, speak accordingly.
8. **Justice.** Wrong none by doing injuries, or omitting the benefits that are your duty.
9. **Moderation.** Avoid extremes; forbear resenting injuries so much as you think they deserve.
10. **Cleanliness.** Tolerate no uncleanliness in body, cloths, or habitation.
11. **Tranquillity.** Be not disturbed at trifles, or at accidents common or unavoidable.
12. **Chastity.** Rarely use venery but for health or offspring, never to dulness, weakness, or the injury of your own or another's peace or reputation.
13. **Humility.** Imitate Jesus and Socrates.

My intention being to acquire the *habitude* of all these virtues, I judg'd it would be well not to distract my attention by attempting the whole at once, but to fix it on one of them at a time; and, when I should be master of that, then to proceed to another, and so on, till I should have gone thro' the thirteen; and, as the previous acquisition of some might facilitate the acquisition of certain others, I arrang'd them with that view, as they stand above . . . .

I made a little book, in which I allotted a page for each of the virtues. I rul'd each page with red ink, so as to have seven columns, one for each day of the week, marking each column with a letter for the day. I cross'd these columns with thirteen red lines, marking the beginning of each line with the first letter of one of the virtues, on which line, and in its proper column, I might mark, by a little black spot, every fault I found upon examination to have been committed respecting that virtue upon that day.

## EXHIBIT 2 (*continued*)

**Form of the Pages**

**TEMPERANCE**

*Eat not to dullness; drink not to elevation*

|        | Sun. | M. | T. | W. | Th. | F. | S. |
|--------|------|----|----|----|-----|----|----|
| Tem.   |      |    |    |    |     |    |    |
| Sil.   | *    | *  |    | *  |     | *  |    |
| Ord.   | *    | *  |    |    | *   | *  | *  |
| Res.   |      | *  |    |    |     | *  |    |
| Fru.   |      | *  |    |    |     | *  |    |
| Ind.   |      |    | *  |    |     |    |    |
| Sinc.  |      |    |    |    |     |    |    |
| Jus.   |      |    |    |    |     |    |    |
| Mod.   |      |    |    |    |     |    |    |
| Clea.  |      |    |    |    |     |    |    |
| Tran.  |      |    |    |    |     |    |    |
| Chas.  |      |    |    |    |     |    |    |
| Hum.   |      |    |    |    |     |    |    |

I determined to give a week's strict attention to each of the virtues successively. Thus, in the first week, my great guard was to avoid every the least offence against *Temperance*, leaving the other virtues to their ordinary chance, only marking every evening the faults of the day. Thus, if in the first week I could keep my first line, marked T, clear of spots, I suppos'd the habit of that virtue so much strengthen'd, and its opposite weaken'd, that I might venture extending my attention to include the next, and for the following week keep both lines clear of spots. Proceeding thus to the last, I could go thro' a course compleat in thirteen weeks, and four courses in a year. . . .

[Franklin provides a discussion of how he fared with regard to various of these virtues. What follows is part of his discussion concerning "Order."]

The precept of *Order* requiring that *every part of my business should have its allotted time*, one page in my little book contain'd the following scheme of employment for the 24 hours of a natural day.

I enter'd upon the execution of this plan for self-examination, and continu'd it with occasional intermissions for some time. I was surpris'd to find myself so much fuller of faults than I had imagined; but I had the satisfaction of seeing them diminish. To avoid the trouble of renewing now and then my little book, which, by scraping out the marks on the paper of old faults to make room for new ones in a new course, became full of holes, I transferr'd my tables and precepts to the ivory leaves of a memorandum book, on which the lines were drawn with red ink, that made a durable stain, and on those lines I mark'd my faults with a black-lead

# EXHIBIT 2 *(concluded)*

| | | |
|---|---|---|
| The Morning.<br>Question:<br>What good shall I do this day? | 5<br>6<br>7 | Rise, wash and address *Powerful Goodness*! Contrive day's business, and take the resolution of the day; prosecute the present study, and breakfast. |
| | 8<br>9<br>10<br>11 | Work. |
| Noon. | 12<br>1 | Read, or overlook my accounts, and dine. |
| | 2<br>3<br>4<br>5 | Work. |
| Evening.<br>Question:<br>What good have I done to-day? | 6<br>7<br>8<br>9 | Put things in their places. Supper. Music or diversion, or conversation. Examination of the day. |
| Night. | 10<br>11<br>12<br>1<br>2<br>3<br>4 | Sleep. |

pencil, which marks I could easily wipe out with a wet sponge. After a while I went thro' one course only in a year, and afterward only one in several years, till at length I omitted them entirely, being employ'd in voyages and business abroad, with a multiplicity of affairs that interfered; but I always carried my little book with me.

My scheme of ORDER gave me the most trouble; and I found that, tho' it might be practicable where a man's business was such as to leave him the disposition of his time, that of a journeyman printer, for instance, it was not possible to be exactly observed by a master, who must mix with the world, and often receive people of business at their own hours. *Order*, too, with regard to places for things, papers, etc., I found extremely difficult to acquire. I had not been early accustomed to it, and, having an exceeding good memory, I was not so sensible of the inconvenience attending want of method. This article, therefore, cost me so much painful attention, and my faults in it vexed me so much, and I made so little progress in amendment, and had such frequent relapses, that I was almost ready to give up the attempt, and content myself with a faulty character in that respect.

Source: *The Autobiography of Benjamin Franklin* (New York: Collier, 1976), pp. 82–87.

# EXHIBIT 3

## *Franklin on National Growth*

Franklin wrote the following tract in 1751 and it was published in 1754. The occasion for its composition was the Iron Act of 1750, by which Parliament prohibited the construction of additional slitting and rolling mills, plating forges, and steel furnaces in the Colonies.

This essay provides a glimpse of Franklin as an analyst rather than as an epigrammatist.

OBSERVATIONS concerning the Increase of Mankind, Peopling of Countries, & c.

**1.** Tables of the proportion of Marriages to Births, of Deaths to Births, of Marriages to the Numbers of Inhabitants, &c. form'd on Observations made upon the Bills of Mortality, Christnings, &c. of populous Cities, will not suit Countries; nor will Tables form'd on Observations made on full settled old Countries, as Europe, suit new Countries, as America.

**2.** For People increase in Proportion to the Number of Marrriages, and that is greater in Proportion to the Ease and Convenience of supporting a Family. When Families can be easily supported, more Persons marry, and earlier in Life.

**3.** In Cities, where all Trades, Occupations and Offices are full, many delay marrying, till they can see how to bear the Charges of a Family; which Charges are greater in Cities, as Luxury is more common: many live single during Life, and continue Servants to Families, Journeymen to Trades, &c. hence Cities do not by natural Generation supply themselves with Inhabitants; the Deaths are more than the Births.

**4.** In Countries full settled, the Case must be nearly the same; all Lands being occupied and improved to the Heighth: those who cannot get Land, must Labour for others that have it; when Labourers are plenty, their Wages will be low; by low Wages a Family is supported with Difficulty; this Difficulty deters many from Marriage, who therefore long continue Servants and single. Only as the Cities take Supplies of People from the Country, and thereby make a little more Room in the Country; Marriage is a little more incourag'd there, and the Births exceed the Deaths.

**5.** Europe is generally full settled with Husbandmen, Manufacturers, &c. and therefore cannot now much increase in People: America is chiefly occupied by Indians, who subsist mostly by Hunting. But as the Hunter, of all Men, requires the greatest Quantity of Land from whence to draw his Subsistence, (the Husbandman subsisting on much less, the Gardner on still less, and the Manufacturer requiring least of all), the Europeans found America as fully settled as it well could be by Hunters; yet these having large Tracks, were easily prevail'd on to part with

EXHIBIT 3 (*continued*)

Portions of Territory to the new Comers, who did not much interfere with the Natives in Hunting, and furnish'd them with many Things they wanted.

6. Land being thus plenty in America, and so cheap as that a labouring Man, that understands Husbandry, can in a short Time save Money enough to purchase a Piece of new Land sufficient for a Plantation, whereon he may subsist a Family; such are not afraid to marry; for if they even look far enough forward to consider how their Children when grown up are to be provided for, they see that more Land is to be had at Rates equally easy, all Circumstances considered.

7. Hence Marriages in America are more general, and more generally early, than in Europe. And if it is reckoned there, that there is but one Marriage per Annum among 100 Persons, perhaps we may here reckon two; and if in Europe they have but 4 Births to a Marriage (many of their Marriages being late) we may here reckon 8, of which if one half grow up, and our Marriages are made, reckoning one with another at 20 Years of Age, our People must at least be doubled every 20 Years.*

8. But notwithstanding this Increase, so vast is the Territory of North America, that it will require many Ages to settle it fully; and till it is fully settled, Labour will never be cheap here, where no Man continues long a Labourer for others, but gets a Plantation of his own, no Man continues long a Journeyman to a Trade, but goes among those new Settlers, and sets up for himself, &c. Hence Labour is no cheaper now, in Pennsylvania, than it was 30 Years ago, tho' so many Thousand labouring People have been imported.

9. The Danger therefore of these Colonies interfering with their Mother Country in Trades that depend on Labour, Manufacturers, &c. is too remote to require the Attention of Great Britain.

10. But in Proportion to the Increase of the Colonies, a vast Demand is growing for British Manufactures, a glorious Market wholly in the Power of Britain, in which Foreigners cannot interfere, which will increase in a short Time even beyond her Power of supplying, tho' her whole Trade should be to her Colonies: Therefore Britain should not too much restrain Manufactures in her Colonies. A wise and good Mother will not do it. To distress, is to weaken, and weakening the Children, weakens the whole Family.

11. Besides if the Manufactures of Britain (by Reason of the American Demands) should rise too high in Price, Foreigners who can sell cheaper will drive her Merchants out of Foreign Markets; Foreign Manufacturers will thereby be

---

*The population of the Colonies as a whole and of Franklin's home, Pennsylvania, was:

|  | 1730 | 1750 | 1770 |
|---|---|---|---|
| All Colonies | 629,000 | 1,170,000 | 2,148,000 |
| Pennsylvania | 51,000 | 119,000 | 240,000 |

## EXHIBIT 3 *(continued)*

encouraged and increased, and consequently foreign Nations, perhaps her Rivals in Power, grow more populous and more powerful; while her own Colonies, kept too low, are unable to assist her, or add to her Strength.

12. 'Tis an illgrounded Opinion that by the Labour of Slaves, America may possibly vie in Cheapness of Manufactures with Britain. The Labour of Slaves can never be so cheap here as the Labour of working Men is in Britain. . . . Why then will Americans purchase Slaves? Because Slaves may be kept as long as a Man pleases, or has Occasion for their Labour; while hired Men are continually leaving their Master (often in the midst of his Business,) and setting up for themselves.

13. As the Increase of People depends on the Encouragement of Marriages, the following Things must diminish a Nation, viz. 1. The being conquered; for the Conquerors will engross as many Offices, and exact as much Tribute or Profit on the Labour of the conquered, as will maintain them in their new Establishment, and this diminishing the Subsistence of the Natives discourages their Marriages, and so gradually diminishes them, while the Foreigners increase. 2. Loss of Territory. Thus the Britons being driven into Wales, and crowded together in a barren Country insufficient to support such great Numbers, diminished 'till the People bore a Proportion to the Produce, while the Saxons increas'd on their abandoned Lands; 'till the Island became full of English. And were the English now driven into Wales by some foreign Nation, there would in a few Years be no more Englishmen in Britain, than there are now People in Wales. 3. Loss of Trade. Manufactures exported, draw Subsistence from Foreign Countries for Numbers; who are thereby enabled to marry and raise Families. If the Nation be deprived of any Branch of Trade, and no new Employment is found for the People occupy'd in the Branch, it will also be soon deprived of so many People. 4. Loss of Food. Suppose a Nation has a Fishery, which not only employs great Numbers, but makes the Food and Subsistence of the People cheaper; If another Nation becomes Master of the Seas, and prevents the Fishery, the People will diminish in Proportion as the Loss of Employ, and Dearness of Provision, makes it more difficult to subsist a Family. 5. Bad Government and insecure Property. People not only leave such a Country, and settling Abroad incorporate with other Nations, lose their native Language, and become Foreigners; but the Industry of those that remain being discourag'd, the Quantity of Subsistence in the Country is lessen'd, and the Support of a Family becomes more difficult. So heavy Taxes tend to diminish a People. 6. The Introduction of Slaves. The Negroes brought into the English Sugar Islands, have greatly diminish'd the Whites there; the Poor are by this Means depriv'd of Employment, while a few Families acquire vast Estates; which they spend on Foreign Luxuries, and educating their Children in the Habit of those Luxuries; the same Income is needed for the Support of one that might have maintain'd 100. The Whites who have Slaves, not labouring, are enfeebled, and therefore not so generally prolific; the Slaves being work'd too hard, and ill fed, their Constitutions are broken, and the Deaths among them are more than

## EXHIBIT 3 (*continued*)

the Births; so that a continual Supply is needed from Africa. The Northern Colonies having few Slaves increase in Whites. Slaves also pejorate the Families that use them; the white Children become proud, disgusted with Labour, and being educated in Idleness, are rendered unfit to get a Living by Industry.

**14.** Hence the Prince that acquires new Territory, if he finds it vacant, or removes the Natives to give his own People Room; the Legislator that makes effectual Laws for promoting of Trade, increasing Employment, improving Land by more or better Tillage; providing more Food by Fisheries; securing Property, &c. and the Man that invents new Trades, Arts or Manufactures, or new Improvements in Husbandry, may be properly called *Fathers* of their Nation, as they are the Cause of the Generation of Multitudes, by the Encouragement they afford to Marriage.

**15.** As to Privileges granted to the married . . . , they may hasten the filling of a Country that has been thinned by War or Pestilence, or that has otherwise vacant Territory; but cannot increase a People beyond the Means provided for their Subsistence.

**16.** Foreign Luxuries and needless Manufactures imported and used in a Nation, do, by the same Reasoning, increase the People of the Nation that furnishes them, and diminish the People of the Nation that uses them. Laws therefore that prevent such Importations, and on the contrary promote the Exportation of Manufactures to be consumed in Foreign Countries, may be called (with Respect to the People that make them) *generative Laws,* as by increasing Subsistence they encourage Marriage. Such Laws likewise strengthen a Country, doubly, by increasing its own People and diminishing its Neighbours.

**17.** Some European Nations prudently refuse to consume the Manufactures of East-India. They should likewise forbid them to their Colonies; for the Gain to the Merchant, is not to be compar'd with the Loss by this Means of People to the Nation.

**18.** Home Luxury in the Great, increases the Nations's Manufacturers employ'd by it, who are many, and only tends to diminish the Families that indulge in it, who are few. The greater the common fashionable Expence of any Rank of People, the more cautious they are of Marriage. Therefore Luxury should never be suffer'd to become common.

**19.** The great Increase of Offspring in particular Families, is not always owing to greater Fecundity of Nature, but sometimes to Examples of Industry in the Heads, and industrious Education; by which the Children are enabled to provide better for themselves, and their marrying early, is encouraged from the Prospect of good Subsistence.

**20.** If there be a Sect therefore, in our Nation, that regard Frugality and In-

## EXHIBIT 3 (*concluded*)

dustry as religious Duties, and educate their Children therein, more than others commonly do; such Sect must consequently increase more by natural Generation, than any other Sect in Britain.

**21.** The Importation of Foreigners into a Country that has as many Inhabitants as the present Employments and Provisions for Subsistence will bear; will be in the End no Increase of People; unless the New Comers have more Industry and Frugality than the Natives, and then they will provide more Subsistence, and increase in the Country; but they will gradually eat the Natives out. Nor is it necessary to bring in Foreigners to fill up any occasional Vacancy in a Country; for such Vacancy (if the Laws are good, §14, 16) will soon be filled by natural Generation. Who can now find the Vacancy made in Sweden, France or other Warlike Nations, by the Plague of Heroism 40 Years ago; in France, by the Expulsion of the Protestants; in England, by the Settlement of her Colonies; or in Guinea, by 100 Years Exportation of Slaves, that has blacken'd half America? The thinness of Inhabitants in Spain is owing to National Pride and Idleness, and other Causes, rather than to the Expulsion of the Moors, or to the making of new Settlements.

**22.** There is in short, no Bound to the prolific Nature of Plants or Animals, but what is made by their crowding and interfering with each others Means of Subsistence. Was the Face of the Earth vacant of other Plants, it might be gradually sowed and overspread with one Kind only; as, for Instance, with Fennel; and were it empty of other Inhabitants, it might in a few Ages be replenish'd from one Nation only; as, for Instance, with Englishmen. Thus there are suppos'd to be now upwards of One Million English Souls in North America, (tho' 'tis thought scarce 80,000 have been brought over Sea) and yet perhaps there is not one in the fewer in Britain, but rather many more, on Account of the Employment the Colonies afford to Manufacturers at Home. This Million doubling, suppose but once in 25 Years, will in another Century be more than the People of England, and the greatest Number of Englishmen will be on this Side the Water. What an Accession of Power to the British Empire by Sea as well as Land! What Increase of Trade and Navigation! What Numbers of Ships and Seamen! We have been here but little more than 100 Years, and yet the Force of our Privateers in the late War, united, was greater, both in Men and Guns, than that of the whole British Navy in Queen Elizabeth's Time. How important an Affair then to Britain, is the present Treaty for settling the Bounds between her Colonies and the French, and how careful should she be to secure Room enough, since on the Room depends so much the Increase of her People?

Source: Leonard W. Labaree, ed., *The Papers of Benjamin Franklin,* 4 (New Haven: Yale University Press, 1961), pp. 225–34.

# APPENDIX A

## *Chronology of Franklin's Life*

| | |
|---|---|
| 1/17/1706: | Born in Boston |
| 1718: | Apprenticed to his brother James, a printer. |
| 4/2/1722: | First "Silence Dogood" paper published in *New England Courant*. |
| 1723: | Runs away to Philadelphia. Enters employ of Samuel Keimer, a printer, soon after arrival. |
| 11/5/1724: | Sails to England, where he works as a printer. |
| 1726: | Returns to Philadelphia. |
| 1726–1727: | Works as a clerk in a merchant's shop and then once again as a printer for Keimer. |
| 1727: | Organizes the Junto, a society for the discussion of issues of the day. |
| 1728: | Forms a printing partnership with Hugh Meredith. |
| 10/2/1729: | Franklin and Meredith take over *The Pennsylvania Gazette*. |
| 1/29/1730: | Franklin and Meredith become printers to the Assembly. |
| 7/14/1730: | Franklin buys Meredith out. |
| 11/8/1731: | Organizes subscription library. |
| 12/19/1732: | First edition of *Poor Richard's Almanack*. |
| 12/7/1736: | Forms Union Fire Company, Philadelphia's first. |
| 10/5/1737: | Becomes postmaster of Philadelphia, serving until 1753. |
| 1739–1740: | Invents "Franklin stove." |
| 5/14/1743: | Publishes *Proposal for Promoting Useful Knowledge* which leads to the formation of the American Philosophical Society. |
| 1/1/1748: | Forms 18-year partnership with David Hall, retires from active printing business. |
| 11/13/1749: | Elected president of trustees of Academy of Philadelphia, later the University of Pennsylvania. |
| 1751–1754: | *Experiments and Observations on Electricity* published. |
| 5/11/1751: | Influential in chartering the Pennsylvania Hospital. |

| | |
|---|---|
| 3/25/1752: | Becomes president of Philadelphia's first fire insurance company. |
| 10/19/1752: | Publishes account of kite experiment. |
| 1754: | Albany Congress adopts Plan of Union, based largely on Franklin's proposals. |
| 1755–1756: | Active in defense against Indians. Builds forts and is commissioned colonel of a Philadelphia militia regiment. |
| 4/29/1759: | Elected Fellow of the Royal Society. |
| 1757–1762: | First mission to England to represent the assembly in its dispute with Thomas and Richard Penn. Receives many honors, including an honorary D.C.L. from Oxford on April 30, 1762. |
| 1762–1764: | Philadelphia. Various political activities and pamphleteering including *A Narrative of the Late Massacres* denouncing Indian haters. |
| 1764–1775: | Second mission to England as agent for the Pennsylvania Assembly. Also appointed agent for Georgia (1768), New Jersey (1769), and Massachusetts (1770). During these tumultuous years, he became the most important colonial representative in Britain. He committed his greatest political blunder in 1765 in underestimating American opposition to the Stamp Act, yet succeeded in ameliorating his standing at home. |
| 1775–1776: | Helps draft and signs the Declaration of Independence. Involved in diplomatic activities and military provisioning. |
| 1776–1785: | Mission to France. Purpose: to secure French alliance and aid and take other actions to strengthen America's international position. On March 12, 1781, Franklin asked Congress to relieve him of his duties as minister, pleading age and ill health. Not only is no action taken on this request, but three months later he is appointed one of the commissioners to negotiate peace with Great Britain. |
| 1785–1790: | Philadelphia. |
| 4/23/1787: | Pennsylvania Society for Promoting the Abolition of Slavery reorganized with Franklin elected president. |
| 1787: | Participates in Constitutional Convention and is one of the signers of the Constitution itself. |
| 10/14/1788: | Ends service as president of the Supreme Executive Council of Pennsylvania, thus bringing his career as holder of public office to a close. |
| 2/3/1790: | In his final public document, he signs a Pennsylvania Abolition Society petition to Congress against slavery and the slave trade. |
| 4/17/1790: | Benjamin Franklin dies. |

Source: Leonard W. Labaree *et al., The Autobiography of Benjamin Franklin* (New Haven: Yale University Press, 1975), pp. 303–22.

# CASE 2

# *Establishing the Political Base**

*"We looked for danger on the same side where we had been used to look."*

*Federalist Politician*

**Fisher Ames**

The continental colonies won their independence from Great Britain by military victories in a war of revolution. Yet military success in itself assured neither the formation of a viable polity nor a viable economy. To fight the war and to deal with foreign nations, the colonies, after transforming themselves into sovereign states, joined together in a confederation. Essential as such an alliance was to the ultimate success of the American cause, the states had great difficulty in agreeing to the nature of this loose alliance. The Articles of Confederation were not ratified by all the states until March, 1781, five years after the signing of the Declaration of Independence and a few months before the Revolution's final major battle at Yorktown.

The central government under the Articles proved very weak, politically and economically. As early as 1783, Robert Morris, the Confederation's able finance

---

*This case was originally compiled by Assistant Professor P. Glenn Porter under the supervision of Professor Alfred D. Chandler, Jr. Some material has been added by Assistant Professor Richard S. Tedlow.

Harvard Business School case 374–348, rev. 6/84.

minister, had announced that "our public credit is gone." By the mid-1780s the Confederation was without funds and, after the disbanding of Washington's army, without military force.

Merchants and planters, the two groups who had engineered the break from England, then turned to strengthening the central government. Conflicts among Maryland, Virginia, Delaware, and Pennsylvania over commercial matters led to the calling of a convention at Annapolis "to take into consideration the trade of the United States." As the delegates of only five states came to Annapolis, the convention decided to extend its representation and mission. It urged the Congress to ask the states to send delegates to a second convention, this time to be held in Philadelphia "for the sole and express purpose of revising the Articles of Confederation," to "render the federal constitution adequate to the exigencies of government, and the preservation of the Union." That convention, which met in Philadelphia, drafted the Constitution.

The Constitution makers were, it must be remembered, not wise men—founding fathers—who met in the hallowed chambers of Independence Hall to set up some sort of ideal state. They were merchants, planters, and lawyers who were trying to solve very real and complex political, economic, and business problems. And their solutions to these problems made possible the development of a national economy.

The Constitution created the institutional framework for a national economy as well as a national polity. But it provided only the bare bones of such a framework. The actions taken by the new government during the first years of President Washington's administration were equally critical to the formation of a national economy. In creating the instruments and procedures essential to the existence of a viable economy, no man played a more significant role than did Alexander Hamilton. Hamilton had convinced his fellow delegates at the Annapolis Convention to issue the call for a constitutional convention. He campaigned vigorously to obtain the Constitution's ratification. Then, as Washington's first Secretary of the Treasury, he was responsible for formulating the economic policies of the strengthened central government. In formulating and carrying out these policies he met increasing opposition from Thomas Jefferson, the new nation's first Secretary of State. The resulting conflict led to the formation of the first political parties in the United States.

The following set of readings documents the initial creation of the national economy of the United States. Part A gives the provisions of the Articles of Confederation and those of the Constitution which deal with economic matters. (The provisions of the Constitution are not given in full because it is a much longer document than the Articles and because its provisions setting up the nation's basic political organization are well known.) A comparison between the two documents reveals clearly the economic and business concerns of the Constitution makers.

Part B consists of a report on the state of American commerce preepared in the summer of 1792 by Thomas Jefferson at the request of the House of Representatives. The report emphasizes the critical weaknesses in American trade and shipping the prosperity of which was essential to the nation's economic well-being.

Part C focuses on Alexander Hamilton. A brief biographical sketch is followed by excerpts from his famous "Report on Manufactures" written in December 1791. That report was the capstone to the economic program Hamilton had presented to Congress during the preceding year. In it Hamilton suggests the reasons for developing a strong economy, outlines his plans to achieve it, and indicates the role he expects the new federal government to play in assuring continuing economic stability and growth.

# Part A: Confederation and Constitution

The Articles of Confederation, drafted initially in November 1777, were not ratified until March 1781. The Articles basically legalized what Congress had been doing since it met in May 1775 as the Second Continental Congress. Each state was represented in Congress by a single delegation. The central or federal government included little more than Congress itself. It had no executive nor judicial branch. The Articles gave Congress the power to appoint executive departments and to create a Committee of States to operate between sessions of Congress. They further made a vote of 9 of the 13 states binding on most important matters. Nevertheless, the guiding principle of the Confederation remained that of the preservation of the independence and the sovereignty of the individual states.

Articles of Confederation
March 1, 1781

TO ALL TO WHOM THESE PRESENTS SHALL COME, WE THE UNDER SIGNED DELEGATES OF THE STATES AFFIXED TO OUR NAMES, SEND GREETING.

Whereas the Delegates of the United States of America, in Congress assembled, did, on the 15th day of November, in the Year of Our Lord One Thousand Seven Hundred and Seventy Seven, and in the Second Year of the Independence of America, agree to certain articles of Confederation and perpetual Union. . .in the words following, viz. "Articles of Confederation and perpetual Union between the states of Newhampshire, Massachusetts-bay, Rhodeisland and Providence Plantations, Connecticut, New-York, New-Jersey, Pennsylvania, Delaware, Maryland, Virginia, North-Carolina, South-Carolina and Georgia."

### ARTICLE I
The Stile of this confederacy shall be "The United States of America."

### ARTICLE II
Each state retains its sovereignty, freedom, and independence, and every Power, Jurisdiction and right, which is not by this confederation expressly delegated to the United States, in Congress assembled.

### ARTICLE III
The said states hereby severally enter into a firm league of friendship with each other, for their common defence, the security of their Liberties, and their mutual and general

welfare, binding themselves to assist each other, against all force offered to, or attacks made upon them, or any of them, on account of religion, sovereignty, trade, or any other pretence whatever.

### ARTICLE IV

The better to secure and perpetuate mutual friendship and intercourse among the people of the different states in this union, the free inhabitants of each of these states, paupers, vagabonds and fugitives from justice excepted, shall be entitled to all privileges and immunities of free citizens in the several states; and the people of each state shall have free ingress and regress to and from any other state, and shall enjoy therein all the privileges of trade and commerce, subject to the same duties, impositions and restrictions as the inhabitants thereof respectively, provided that such restriction shall not extend so far as to prevent the removal of property imported into any state, to any other state, of which the Owner is an inhabitant; provided also that no imposition, duties or restriction shall be laid by any state, on the property of the united states, or either of them. . . .

Full faith and credit shall be given in each of these states to the records, acts and judicial proceedings of the courts and magistrates of every other state.

### ARTICLE V

. . .No state shall be represented in Congress by less than two, nor by more than seven Members; and no person shall be capable of being a delegate for more than three years in any term of six years; nor shall any person, being a delegate, be capable of holding any office under the united states, for which he, or another for his benefit receives any salary, fees or emolument of any kind.

Each state shall maintain its own delegates in a meeting of the states, and while they act as members of the committee of the states.

In determining questions in the united states in Congress assembled, each state shall have one vote. . . .

### ARTICLE VI

No state, without the Consent of the united states in congress assembled, shall send any embassy to, or receive any embassy from, or enter into any conference, agreement, alliance or treaty with any king, prince or state; nor shall any person holding any office of profit or trust under the united states, or any of them, accept of any present, emolument, office or title of any kind whatever from any king, prince or foreign state; nor shall the united states in congress assembled, or any of them, grant any title of nobility.

No two or more states shall enter into any treaty, confederation or alliance whatever between them, without the consent of the united states in congress assembled, specifying accurately the purposes for which the same is to be entered into, and how long it shall continue.

No state shall lay any imposts or duties, which may interfere with any stipulations in treaties, entered into by the united states in congress assembled, with any king, prince or state, in pursuance of any treaties already proposed by congress, to the courts of France and Spain.

No vessels of war shall be kept up in time of peace by any state, except such number only, as shall be deemed necessary by the united states in congress assembled, for the defence of such state, or its trade; nor shall any body of forces be kept up by any state, in time of peace, except such number only as in the judgment of the united states, in congress assembled, shall be deemed requisite to garrison the forts necessary for the defence of such state; but every state shall always keep up a well regulated and disciplined militia, sufficiently armed and accoutred, and shall provide and constantly have ready for use, in public stores, a due number of field pieces and tents, and a proper quantity of arms, ammunition, and camp equipage.

No state shall engage in any war without the consent of the united states in congress assembled unless such state be actually invaded by enemies, or shall have received certain advice of a resolution being formed by some nation of Indians to invade such state, and the danger is so imminent as not to admit of a delay till the united states in congress assembled can be consulted. . . .

## ARTICLE VIII

All charges of war, and all other expences that shall be incurred for the common defence or general warfare, and allowed by the united states in congress assembled, shall be defrayed out of a common treasury, which shall be supplied by the several states in proportion to the value of all land within each state, granted to or surveyed for any Person, as such land and the buildings and improvements thereon shall be estimated according to such mode as the united states in congress assembled, shall from time to time direct and appoint.

The taxes for paying that proportion shall be laid and levied by the authority and direction of the legislatures of several states within the time agreed upon by the united states in congress assembled.

## ARTICLE IX

The united states in congress assembled, shall have the sole and exclusive right and power of determining on peace and war, except in the cases mentioned in the sixth article—of sending and receiving ambassadors—entering into treaties and alliances, provided that no treaty of commerce shall be made whereby the legislative power of the respective states shall be restrained from imposing such imposts and duties on foreigners as their own people are subjected to, or from prohibiting the exportation or importation of any species of goods or commodities, whatsoever. . . .

The united states in congress assembled shall also have the sole and exclusive right and power of regulating the alloy and value of coin struck by their own authority, or by that of the respective states—fixing the standard of weights and measures throughout the united states—regulating the trade and managing all affairs with the Indians, not members of any of the states, provided that the legislative right of any state within its own limits be not infringed or violated—establishing or regulating post-offices from one state to another, throughout all the united states, and exacting such postage on the papers passing thro' the same as may be requisite to defray the expences of the said office—appointing all officers of the land forces, in the service of the united states, excepting regimental officers—appointing all the officers of the naval forces, and commissioning all officers whatever in the service of the united states—making rules for the government and regulation of the said land and naval forces, and directing their operations.

The united states in congress assembled shall have authority to appoint a committee, to sit in the recess of congress, to be denominated "A Committee of the States," and to consist of one delegate from each state; and to appoint such other committees and civil officers as may be necessary for managing the general affairs of the united

states under their direction—to appoint one of the number to preside, provided that
no person be allowed to serve in the office of president more than one year in any term
of three years; to ascertain the necessary sums of money to be raised for the service of
the united states, and to appropriate and apply the same for defraying the public expences—to borrow money, or emit bills on the credit of the united states, transmitting
every half year to the respective states an account of the sums of money so borrowed or
emitted,—to build and equip a navy—to agree upon the number of land forces, and to
make requisitions from each state for its quota, in proportion to the number of white
inhabitants in such state; which requisition shall be binding, and thereupon the legislature of each state shall appoint the regimental officers, raise the men and cloath, arm
and equip them in a soldier like manner, at the expence of the united states; and the officers and men so cloathed, armed and equipped shall march to the place appointed,
and within the time agreed on by the united states in congress assembled. . . .

The united states in congress assembled shall never engage in a war, nor grant letters of marque and reprisal in time of peace, nor enter into any treaties or alliances,
nor coin money, nor regulate the value thereof, nor ascertain the sums and expences
necessary for the defence and welfare of the united states, or any of them, nor emit
bills, nor borrow money on the credit of the united states, nor appropriate money, nor
agree upon the number of vessels of war, to be built or purchased, or the number of
land or sea forces to be raised, nor appoint a commander in chief of the army or navy,
unless nine states assent to the same: nor shall a question on any other point, except for
adjourning from day to day be determined, unless by the votes of a majority of the
united states in congress assembled. . . .

## ARTICLE X

The committee of the states, or any nine of them, shall be authorized to execute, in
the recess of congress, such of the powers of congress as the united states in congress
assembled, by the consent of nine states, shall from time to time think expedient to vest
them with; provided that no power be delegated to the said committee, for the exercise
of which, by the articles of confederation, the voice of nine states in the congress of the
united states assembled is requisite. . . .

## ARTICLE XII

All bills of credit emitted, monies borrowed and debts contracted by, or under the
authority of congress, before the assembling of the united states, in pursuance of the
present confederation, shall be deemed and considered as a charge against the united
states, for payment and satisfaction whereof the said united states, and the public faith
are hereby solemnly pledged.

## ARTICLE XIII

Articles of this Confederation shall be inviolably observed by every state, and the
union shall be perpetual; nor shall any alteration at any time hereafter be made in any
of them; unless such alteration is agreed to in a congress of the united states, and be
afterwards confirmed by the legislatures of every state.

\*       \*       \*       \*       \*

The Constitution of the United States, signed in September 1787 and ratified
in the following year, extended and expanded the powers of Congress and set up
new executive and judicial branches in the government. The instrument first

spelled out the qualifications and the methods of election or appointment for the members of each branch of government as well as outlining their duties and functions and the prohibitions placed on their actions. Nearly all the provisions of the Constitution concerning economic and business matters were listed in Article I, which dealt with the legislative branch.

## The Constitution of the United States

We the people of the United States, in order to form a more perfect union, establish justice, ensure domestic tranquility, provide for the common defense, promote the general welfare, and secure the blessings of liberty to ourselves and our posterity, do ordain and establish this Constitution for the United States of America.

## ARTICLE I
### Section 1

All legislative power herein granted shall be vested in a Congress of the United States which shall consist of a Senate and a House of Representatives.

### Section 7

**1.** All bills for raising revenue shall originate in the House of Representatives; but the Senate may propose or concur with amendments as on the other bills.

**2.** Every bill which shall have passed the House of Representatives and the Senate, shall, before it becomes a law, be presented to the President of the United States; if he approves he shall sign it, but if not he shall return it, with his objections to that House in which it shall have originated, who shall enter the objections at large on their journal, and proceed to reconsider it. If after such reconsideration two thirds of that House shall agree to pass the bill, it shall be sent, together with the objections, to the other House, by which it shall likewise be reconsidered, and if approved by two thirds of that House, it shall become a law.

**3.** Every order, resolution, or vote to which the concurrence of the Senate and the House of Representatives may be necessary (except on a question of adjournment) shall be presented to the President of the United States; and before the same shall take effect, shall be approved by him, or being disapproved by him, shall be passed by two thirds of the Senate and House of Representatives, according to the rules and limitations prescribed in the case of a bill.

### Section 8

The Congress shall have the power,

1. To lay and collect taxes, duties, imposts, and excises, to pay the debts and provide for the common defense and general welfare of the United States; but all duties, imposts, and excises shall be uniform throughout the United States;
2. To borrow money on the credit of the United States;
3. To regulate commerce with foreign nations, and among the several States, and with the Indian tribes;
4. To establish a uniform rule of naturalization, and uniform laws on the subject of bankruptcies throughout the United States;
5. To coin money, regulate the value thereof, and of foreign coin, and fix the standard of weights and measures;

6. To provide for the punishment of counterfeiting the securities and current coin of the United States;
7. To establish post offices and post roads;
8. To promote the progress of science and useful arts, by securing for limited times to authors and inventors the exclusive right to their respective writings and discoveries;
9. To constitute tribunals inferior to the Supreme Court;
10. To define and punish piracies and felonies committed on the high seas, and offenses against the law of nations;
11. To declare war, grant letters of marque and reprisal, and make rules concerning captures on land and water;
12. To raise and support armies, but no appropriation of money to that use shall be for a longer term than two years.
13. To provide and maintain a navy;
14. To make rules for the government and regulation of the land and naval forces;
15. To provide for calling forth the militia to execute the laws of the Union, suppress insurrections and repel invasions;
16. To provide for organizing, arming, and disciplining the militia, and for governing such part of them as may be employed in the service of the United States, reserving to the States respectively, the appointment of the officers, and the authority of training the militia according to the discipline prescribed by Congress;
17. To exercise exclusive legislation in all cases whatsoever, over such district (not exceeding ten miles square) as may, by cession of particular States, and the acceptance of Congress, become the seat of the government of the United States. . . .
18. To make all laws which shall be necessary and proper for carrying into execution the foregoing powers, and all other powers vested by this Constitution in the government of the United States, or in any department or officer thereof.

## Section 9

1. The migration or importation of such persons as any of the States now existing shall think proper to admit, shall not be prohibited by the Congress prior to the year 1808, but a tax or duty may be imposed on such importation, not exceeding 10 dollars for each person.
2. The privilege of the writ of habeas corpus shall not be suspended, unless when in cases of rebellion or invasion the public safety may require it.
3. No bill of attainder or ex post facto law shall be passed.
4. No capitation, or other direct, tax shall be laid, unless in proportion to the census or enumeration hereinbefore directed to be taken.[1]
5. No tax or duty shall be laid on articles exported from any State.
6. No preference shall be given by any regulation of commerce or revenue to the ports of one State over those of another: nor shall vessels bound to, or from, one State be obliged to enter, clear, or pay duties in another.

---

[1]Revised by the 16th Amendment.

7. No money shall be drawn from the treasury, but in consequence of appropriations made by law; and a regular statement and account of the receipts and expenditures of all public money shall be published from time to time.

8. No title of nobility shall be granted by the United States and no person holding any office of profit or trust under them, shall, without the consent of the Congress, accept of any present, emolument, office, or title, of any kind whatever, from any king, prince, or foreign State.

## Section 10

1. No State shall enter into any treaty, alliance, or confederation; grant letters of marque and reprisal; coin money; emit bills of credit; make anything but gold and silver coin a tender in payment of debts; pass any bill of attainder, ex post facto law, or law impairing the obligation of contracts, or grant any title of nobility.

2. No State shall, without the consent of Congress, lay any imposts or duties on imports or exports, except what may be absolutely necessary for executing its inspection laws: and the net produce of all duties and imposts laid by any State on imports or exports, shall be for the use of the treasury of the United States; and all such laws shall be subject to the revision and control of the Congress.

3. No State shall, without the consent of the Congress, lay any duty of tonnage, keep troops, or ships of war in time of peace, enter into any agreement or compact with another State, or with a foreign power, or engage in war, unless actually invaded, or in such imminent danger as will not admit of delay.

## ARTICLE II
## Section 1

1. The executive power shall be vested in a President of the United States of America. He shall hold his office during the term of four years, and, together with the Vice President, chosen for the same term, be elected as follows:

2. Each State shall appoint, in such manner as the legislature thereof may direct, a number of electors, equal to the whole number of senators and representatives to which the State may be entitled in Congress; but no senator or representative, or person holding an office of trust or profit under the United States, shall be appointed an elector. . . .

## Section 2

1. The President shall be the commander in chief of the army and navy of the United States, and of the militia of the several States, when called into the actual service of the United States. . .and he shall have power to grant reprieves and pardons for offenses against the United States, except in cases of impeachment.

2. He shall have power, by and with the advice and consent of the Senate, to make treaties, provided two thirds of the senators present concur; and he shall nominate, and by and with the advice and consent of the Senate, shall appoint ambassadors, other

public ministers and consuls, judges of the Supreme Court, and all other officers of the United States, whose appointments are not herein otherwise provided for, and which shall be established by law: but the Congress may by law vest the appointment of such inferior officers, as they think proper, in the President alone, in the courts of law, or in the heads of departments.

3. The President shall have the power to fill up all vacancies that may have happened during the recess of the Senate, by granting commissions which shall expire at the end of their next session.

Article III dealt with the Supreme Court. Article IV began by repeating one of the Articles of Confederation which read: "Full faith and credit shall be given in each State to the public acts, records, and judicial proceedings of every other State." It added that "The citizens of each State shall be entitled to all the privileges and immunities of the citizens of the several States." Article IV also included provisions for the returning of runaway slaves, admitting new states, and governing territories belonging to the federal union. Article V outlined methods of amending the Constitution.

### ARTICLE VI

1. All debts contracted and engagements entered into, before the adoption of this Constitution, shall be as valid against the United States under this Constitution, as under the Confederation.

2. This Constitution, and the laws of the United States, which shall be made in pursuance thereof; and all treaties made, or which shall be made, under the authority of the United States, shall be the Supreme Law of the land; and the judges in every State shall be bound thereby, any thing in the Constitution or laws of any State to the contrary notwithstanding.

3. The Senators and Representatives before mentioned, and the Members of the several State legislatures, and all executive and judicial officers, both of the United States and of the several States, shall be bound by oath or affirmation, to support this Constitution; but no religious test shall ever be required as a qualification to any office or public trust under the United States.

The final article, Article VII, stated that the Constitution would go into effect after nine states had ratified it.

The fact that the Constitution as originally drafted contained no enumeration of fundamental individual rights prompted considerable criticism. Supporters of the Constitution believed such an enumeration unnecessary in both theory and practice. In theory, they held that it was superfluous since the Anglo-American common law tradition assumed such rights to be inalienable. In practice, they contended that the powers of the central government, while greater than those of the central government under the Articles, were so limited as to pose no conceivable threat to the individual. Critics feared that the central government did, at least potentially, pose such a threat, and that, therefore, an enumeration would help to preserve liberties fought for in the Revolution. Such an enumeration, consisting of the first ten amendments to the Constitution, was ratified by the states in 1791. Including guarantees of freedom of speech, religion, and due process of law, these amendments are generally known today as the "Bill of Rights."

# Part B: Jefferson's Report on the Restrictions on American Commerce, Summer 1792

Although the ratification of the Constitution provided the United States with the institutional framework necessary to forge a national economy, its provisions were not effective enough to revive the nation's foreign trade. Nor did they protect the employment of American ships and seamen. Jefferson's report to the House of Representatives, prepared in the summer of 1792, reviewed the oppressive regulations other nations had placed on American trade and shipping. In outlining the new nation's most serious economic problem, Jefferson's report reveals much about the nature of American commerce—goods carried, markets reached, and services provided. Jefferson concluded this report by saying:[2]

To sum up these restrictions, so far as they are important:

First.   In Europe—

Our bread stuff is at most times under prohibitory duties in England, and considerably dutied on reexportation from Spain to her colonies.

Our tobaccoes are heavily dutied in England, Sweden and France, and prohibited in Spain and Portugal.

Our rice is heavily dutied in England and Sweden, and prohibited in Portugal.

Our fish and salted provisions are prohibited in England, and under prohibitory duties in France.

Our whale oils are prohibited in England and Portugal.

And our vessels are denied naturalization in England, and of late in France.

Second.   In the West Indies—

All intercourse is prohibited with the possessions of Spain and Portugal.

Our salted provisions and fish are prohibited by England.

Our salted pork and bread stuff (except maize) are received under temporary laws only, in the dominions of France, and our salted fish pays there a weighty duty.

Third.   In the article of navigation—

Our own carriage of our own tobacco is heavily dutied in Sweden, and lately in France.

We carry no article, not of our own production, to the British ports in Europe. Nor even our own produce to her American possessions.

Such being the restrictions on the commerce and navigation of the United States; the question is, in what way may they best be removed, modified or counteracted?

As to commerce, two methods occur. (1) By friendly arrangements with the several nations with whom these restrictions exist; or, (2) By the separate act of our own legislatures for countervailing their effects.

---

[2]Paul L. Ford, ed., *The Works of Thomas Jefferson* VIII (New York: Putnam, 1904), pp. 110–13.

There can be no doubt but that of these two, friendly arrangements is the most eligible. Instead of embarrassing commerce under piles of regulating laws, duties, and prohibitions, could it be relieved from all its shackles in all parts of the world, could every country be employed in producing that which nature has best fitted it to produce, and each be free to exchange with others mutual surplusses for mutual wants, the greatest mass possible would then be produced of those things which contribute to human life and human happiness; the numbers of mankind would be increased, and their condition bettered.

Would even a single nation begin with the United States this system of free commerce, it would be advisable to begin it with that nation; since it is one by one only that it can be extended to all. Where the circumstances of either party render it expedient to levy a revenue, by way of impost, on commerce, its freedom might be modified, in that particular, by mutual and equivalent measures, preserving it entire in all others.

Some nations, not yet ripe for free commerce in all its extent, might still be willing to mollify its restrictions and regulations for us, in proportion to the advantages which an intercourse with us might offer. Particularly they may occur with us in reciprocating the duties to be levied on each side, or in compensating any excess of duty by equivalent advantages of another nature. Our commerce is certainly of a character to entitle it to favor in most countries. The commodities we offer are either necessaries of life, or materials for manufacture, or convenient subjects of revenue; and we take in exchange, either manufactures, when they have received the last finish of art and industry, or mere luxuries. Such customers may reasonably expect welcome and friendly treatment at every market. Customers, too, whose demands, increasing with their wealth and population, must very shortly give full employment to the whole industry of any nation whatever, in any line of supply they may get into the habit of calling for from it.

But should any nation, contrary to our wishes suppose it may better find its advantages by continuing its system or prohibitions, duties and regulations, it behooves us to protect our citizens, their commerce and navigation, by counter prohibitions, duties and regulations, also. Free commerce and navigation are not to be given in exchange for restrictions and vexations; nor are they likely to produce a relaxation of them.

Our navigation involves still higher considerations. As a branch of industry, it is valuable, but as a resource of defence, essential.

Its value, as a branch of industry, is enhanced by the dependence of so many other branches on it. In times of general peace it multiplies competitors for employment in transportation, and so keeps that at its proper level; and in times of war, that is to say, when those nations who may be our principal carriers, shall be at war with each other, if we have not within ourselves the means of transportation, our produce must be exported in belligerent vessels, at the increased expence of war-freight and insurance, and the articles which will not bear that, must perish on our hands.

But it is as a resource of defence that our navigation will admit neither negligence nor forbearance. The position and circumstances of the United States leave them nothing to fear on their land-board, and nothing to desire beyond their present rights. But on their seaboard, they are open to injury, and they have there, too, a commerce which must be protected. This can only be done by possessing a respectable body of citizen-seamen, and of artists and establishments in readiness for shipbuilding.

# Part C: The Role of Alexander Hamilton

### Brief Review of Hamilton's Career

Alexander Hamilton was born in Nevis, one of the Leeward Islands, on January 11, 1757. He came to New York in 1772 and entered King's College (now Columbia University) the next year. His college career interrupted by the Revolution, he entered into the pamphlet wars of the day with a series of brilliant expressions of a moderate point of view.

Commissioned to command an artillery company in 1776, he fought in the campaigns on Long Island and at Harlem Heights, White Plains, Trenton, and Princeton. He became secretary and aide-de-camp to General George Washington on March 1, 1777, with the rank of lieutenant-colonel. He became the general's trusted advisor and did much to systematize the handling of business at the headquarters of the Continental Army. He also drafted a series of important reports on the defects of the military system.

Between 1777 and 1781, Hamilton developed an extensive correspondence with various colonial leaders and became widely noted for his political ideas and the incisiveness of his thought. He was a staunch believer in representative government, but insisted that it must act through a highly centralized authority. In a letter of 1780 to James Duane, he made the first proposal for a national American constitutional convention. Also, in 1780, he married Elizabeth Schuyler, daughter of General Philip Schuyler which linked him to one of New York's oldest and most influential families.

After a quarrel with General Washington in February 1781, he resigned from the staff but was appointed to command an infantry regiment. At Yorktown, the final campaign of the war, he conducted a crucial and brilliant attack on one of the key British fortifications.

Following the British surrender, Hamilton retired to Albany to read law and was admitted to the New York Bar. In 1783, after one term in the Continental Congress, he opened a law office in New York City and increased his support of the movement for creation of a strong federal government. As a New York delegate to a seemingly routine commercial convention in Annapolis in 1786, he secured the adoption of a resolution recommending a constitutional convention to meet in Philadelphia the following May.

Named a delegate from New York to the Philadelphia Constitutional Convention, his most important role in those proceedings was as a participant in the fierce newspaper war over ratification. He planned and published the "Federalist" series, a magnificent sequence of expository and argumentative articles written in collaboration with James Madison and John Jay. Almost single-handedly, his articles and speeches secured New York's crucial ratification of the Philadelphia document, and he sat again in the Continental Congress until the new federal government was organized in April 1789.

On September 11, 1789, Hamilton was appointed Secretary of the Treasury in the Washington administration and worked arduously to organize and give direction to that department of the government. At the request of Congress, he devised a plan for establishing the nation's credit on a sound basis which was presented to the House of Representatives on January 14, 1790. He argued that the new federal government should fund its foreign and domestic debts at par, even though many holders of public securities had bought them cheaply for speculation. He also argued that the federal government should assume all debts contracted during the Revolution by the states and offered several means of deferring interest charges. He proposed to provide annual operating revenue by levying import duties and an excise. He carried his points over fierce opposition led by Thomas Jefferson and saw his funding and assumption proposals become law on August 4, 1791.

Meanwhile, Hamilton had presented Congress with plans to improve further the credit of the United States, to assure the soundness of its currency, and to facilitate financial transactions and the accumulation of investment capital within its borders. On December 17, 1790, he recommended the placing of an excise tax on whiskey and other distilled spirits to supplement the tariff passed in 1789 to provide revenue for the operation of the federal government. (That first tariff, providing a 5% rating on most imports, was thus passed primarily to raise revenue rather than for the protection of American manufacturing.) On December 18, Hamilton proposed the creation of a federally chartered bank. A month later he sent to Congress a report on coinage and the establishment of a mint. Congress finally accepted all three of these proposals, but that for a bank led to a debate as bitter as that on the funding and assumption bills.

The bank bill proposed the incorporation of a central bank similar to the Bank of England which could provide financial services to the merchants and manufacturers, as well as to the state and federal governments. The bank would have branches in all the country's larger towns and would provide services that were still unavailable or had just become available in America, for in 1790 there were only three banks in the country, the oldest of which was less than 10 years old.

Opposition to Hamilton's bank bill was led by Thomas Jefferson, who argued against the proposal on constitutional rather than economic grounds. Jefferson's "strict constructionist" position was that the Constitution did not specifically authorize Congress to incorporate banks. In his reply, Hamilton elaborated what became the "loose constructionist" view of the Constitution. The creation of the bank was implied, he maintained, in the congressional power to collect taxes and regulate trade for the "general welfare" of the nation. Hamilton wrote President Washington, "If the *end* be critically comprehended within any of the specified powers, and if the measure has an obvious relation to that *end*, and is not forbidden by any particular provision of the Constitution, it may safely be deemed to come within the compass of the national authority." The debate on the bank continued until Congress adjourned, and so the bill was not passed until the following session.

Before that session had met, Hamilton prepared the capstone to his economic program—the "Report on Manufactures" which he presented to Congress in December 1791. By that time the issues raised by his early proposals had helped to create the nation's first political parties. The Jeffersonian opposition prevented the passage of the measures outlined in the "Report on Manufactures" in that session in Congress. They would not be enacted until after the close of the War of 1812, many years after Hamilton's death.

Hamilton's aggressive arrogance and his belief that he was the prime minister of Washington's cabinet led him to improper interference with other departments and accentuated the growing party divisions. His natural antagonist remained Secretary of State Thomas Jefferson, and their philosophical and political arguments culminated in Jefferson's resignation in December 1793. Hamilton resigned in January 1795 because of personal financial pressures, but remained a close adviser of Washington and helped draft the final form of the latter's famous Farewell Address.

Hamilton remained out of civil office thereafter, busying himself with an eminently successful legal practice. He nonetheless remained active politically, harassing John Adams's administration continually and waging a relentless and successful campaign against his fellow New Yorker Aaron Burr's quest for the presidency and the governorship. These activities so infuriated Burr that he challenged Hamilton to a duel, which occurred at Weehawken, New Jersey, on July 11, 1804. Mortally wounded, Hamilton died the next day.

## Excerpts from Hamilton's Report on Manufactures

Of all his writings, Hamilton's famous "Report on Manufactures"[3] most cogently expressed the breadth and imagination of his economic philosophy. Delivered to the House of Representatives on December 5, 1791, the report was the first attempt ever made to survey the industrial resources and activities of the United States and the first formulation of a broad theoretical basis for what had previously been measures of expediency. The passages that follow are typical of Hamilton's analytical style and suggestive of his philosophy. They should be read with particular attention to the economic ends and means proposed.

### INDUSTRY AND COMMERCE

1.  *As to the Division of Labor*

It has justly been observed, that there is scarcely any thing of greater moment in the economy of a nation than the proper division of labor. The separation of occupations causes each to be carried to a much greater perfection than it could possibly acquire if they were blended. This arises principally from three circumstances:

1st. The greater skill and dexterity naturally resulting from a constant and undivided application to a single object. It is evident that these properties must increase in proportion to the separation and simplification of objects, and the steadiness of the attention devoted to each; and must be less in proportion to the complication of objects, and the number among which the attention is distracted.

---

[3]Henry Cabot Lodge, ed., *Works of Alexander Hamilton* III (New York: Houghton, Mifflin, 1885), pp. 310–21, 364–79.

2d. The economy of time, by avoiding the loss of it, incident to a frequent transition from one operation to another of a different nature. This depends on various circumstances: the transition itself, the orderly disposition of the implements, machines, and materials employed in the operation to be relinquished, the preparatory steps to the commencement of a new one, the interruption of the impulse which the mind of the workman acquires from being engaged in a particular operation, the distractions, hesitations, and reluctances which attend the passage from one kind of business to another.

3d. An extension of the use of machinery. A man occupied on a single object will have it more in his power, and will be more naturally led to exert his imagination, in devising methods to facilitate and abridge labor, than if he were perplexed by a variety of independent and dissimilar operations. Besides this the fabrication of machines, in numerous instances, becoming itself a distinct trade, the artist who follows it has all the advantages which have been enumerated, for improvement in his particular art; and, in both ways, the invention and application of machinery are extended.

And from these causes united, the mere separation of the occupation of the cultivator from that of the artificer, has the effect of augmenting the productive powers of labor, and with them, the total mass of the produce or revenue of a country. In this single view of the subject, therefore, the utility of artificers or manufacturers, towards promoting an increase of productive industry, is apparent.

2. *As to an Extension of the Use of Machinery, a Point which, Though Partly Anticipated, Requires to Be Placed in One or Two Additional Lights.*
It shall be taken for granted, and the truth of the position referred to observation, that manufacturing pursuits are susceptible in a greater degree, of the application of machinery, than those of agriculture. If so, all the difference is lost to a community which, instead of manufacturing for itself, procures the fabrics requisite to its supply from other countries. The substitution of foreign for domestic manufactures is a transfer to foreign nations of the advantages of accruing from the employment of machinery, in the modes in which it is capable of being employed with most utility and to the greatest extent.

The cotton-mill, invented in England, within the last twenty years, is a signal illustration of the general proposition which has been just advanced. In consequence of it, all the different processes for spinning cotton are performed by means of machines, which are put in motion by water, and attended chiefly by women and children—and by a smaller number of persons, in the whole, than are requisite in the ordinary mode of spinning. And it is an advantage of great moment, that the operations of this mill continue with convenience during the night as well as through the day. The prodigious effect of such a machine is easily conceived. To this invention is to be attributed, essentially, the immense progress which has been so suddenly made in Great Britain, in the various fabrics of cotton.

3. *As to the Additional Employment of Classes of the Community Not Originally Engaged in the Particular Business*
This is not among the least valuable of the means by which manufacturing institutions contribute to augment the general stock of industry and production. In places where those institutions prevail, besides the persons regularly engaged in them, they afford

occasional and extra employment to industrious individuals and families, who are willing to devote the leisure resulting from the intermissions of their ordinary pursuits to collateral labors, as a resource for multiplying their acquisitions or their enjoyments.

The husband-man himself experiences a new source of profit and support from the increased industry of his wife and daughters, invited and stimulated by the demands of the neighboring manufactories.

Besides this advantage of occasional employment to classes having different occupations, there is another, of a nature allied to it, and of a similar tendency. This is the employment of persons who would otherwise be idle, and in many cases a burthen on the community, either from the bias of temper, habit, infirmity of body, or some other cause, indisposing or disqualifying them for the toils of the country. It is worthy of particular remark that, in general, women and children are rendered more useful, and the latter more early useful, by manufacturing establishments, than they would otherwise be. Of the number of persons employed in the cotton manufactories of Great Britain, it is computed that four sevenths, nearly, are women and children, of whom the greatest proportion are children, and many of them of a tender age. . . .

#### 4. *As to the Promoting of Emigration from Foreign Countries*

Men reluctantly quit one course of occupation and livelihood for another, unless invited to it by very apparent and proximate advantages. Many who would go from one country to another, if they had a prospect of continuing with more benefit the callings to which they have been educated, will often not be tempted to change their situation by the hope of doing better in some other way. Manufacturers who, listening to the powerful invitations of a better price for their fabrics or their labor, of greater cheapness of provisions and raw materials, of an exemption from the chief part of the taxes, burthens, and restraints which they endure in the Old World, of greater personal independence and consequence, under the operation of a more equal government, and of what is far more precious than mere religious toleration, a perfect equality of religious privileges, would probably flock from Europe to the United States, to pursue their own trades or professions, if they were once made sensible of the advantages they would enjoy, and were inspired with an assurance of encouragement and employment, will, with difficulty, be induced to transplant themselves, with a view to becoming cultivators of land. . . .

*　　*　　*　　*　　*

#### 7. *As to the Creating, in Some Instances, a New, and Securing, in All, a More Certain and Steady Demand for the Surplus Produce of the Soil*

This is among the most important of the circumstances which have been indicated. It is a principal means by which the establishment of manufactures contributes to an augmentation of the produce or revenue of a country, and has an immediate and direct relation to the prosperity of agriculture.

It is evident that the exertions of the husbandman will be steady or fluctuating, vigorous or feeble, in proportion to the steadiness or fluctuation, adequateness or inadequateness of the markets on which he must depend for the vent of the surplus which may be produced by his labor; and that such surplus, in the ordinary course of things, will be greater or less in the same proportion.

For the purpose of this vent, a domestic market is greatly to be preferred to a foreign one; because it is, in the nature of things, far more to be relied upon. . . .

Considering how fast and how much the progress of new settlements in the United States must increase the surplus produce of the soil, and weighing seriously the tendency of the system which prevails among most of the commercial nations of Europe, whatever dependence may be placed on the force of natural circumstances to counteract the effects of an artificial policy, there appear strong reasons to regard the foreign demand for that surplus as too uncertain a reliance, and to desire a substitute for it in an extensive domestic market.

To secure such a market, there is no other expedient than to promote manufacturing establishments. Manufacturers, who constitute the most numerous class, after the cultivators of land, are for that reason the principal consumers of the surplus of their labor. . . .

A full view having now been taken of the inducements to the promotion of manufactures in the United States, accompanied with an examination of the principal objections which are commonly urged in opposition, it is proper, in the next place, to consider the means by which it may be effected, as introductory to a specification of the objects, which in the present state of things, appear the most fit to be encouraged, and of the particular measures which it may be advisable to adopt, in respect to each.

In order to [reach] a better judgment of the means proper to be resorted to by the United States, it will be of use to advert to those which have been employed with success in other countries. The principal of these are:

### 1. *Protecting Duties—or Duties on Those Foreign Articles which Are the Rivals of the Domestic Ones Intended to Be Encouraged*

Duties of this nature evidently amount to a virtual bounty on the domestic fabrics; since, by enhancing the charges on foreign articles, they enable the national manufacturers to undersell all their foreign competitors. The propriety of this species of encouragement need not be dwelt upon, as it is not only a clear result from the numerous topics which have been suggested, but is sanctioned by the laws of the United States, in a variety of instances; it has the additional recommendation of being a resource of revenue. Indeed, all the duties imposed on imported articles, though with an exclusive view to revenue, have the effect, in contemplation, and, except where they fall on raw materials, wear a beneficent aspect toward the manufacturers of the country.

### 2. *Prohibitions of Rival Articles, or Duties Equivalent to Prohibitions*

This is another and an efficacious means of encouraging national manufacturers; but, in general, it is only fit to be employed when a manufacture has made such progress, and is in so many hands, as to insure a due competition, and an adequate supply on reasonable terms. Of duties equivalent to prohibitions, there are examples in the laws of the United States; and there are other cases to which the principle may be advantageously extended, but they are not numerous.

Considering a monopoly of the domestic market to its own manufacturers as the reigning policy of manufacturing nations, a similar policy, on the part of the United States, in every proper instance, is dictated, it might almost be said, by the principles of distributive justice; certainly, by the duty of endeavoring to secure to their own citizens a reciprocity of advantages.

### 3. *Prohibitions of the Exportation of the Materials of Manufactures*

The desire of securing a cheap and plentiful supply for the national workmen, and where the article is either peculiar to the country, or of peculiar quality there, the jealousy of enabling foreign workmen to rival those of the nation with its own materials, are the leading motives to this species of regulation. It ought not to be affirmed that it is in no instance proper; but is, certainly, one which ought to be adopted with great circumspection, and only in very plain cases.

### 4. *Pecuniary Bounties*

This has been found one of the most efficacious means of encouraging manufactures, and is, in some views, the best. Though it has not yet been practised upon by the Government of the United States (unless the allowance on the exportation of dried and pickled fish and salted meat could be considered as a bounty), and though it is less favored by public opinion than some other modes, its advantages are [clear]. . . .

Bounties are, sometimes, not only the best but the only proper expedient for uniting the encouragement of a new object of agriculture with that of a new object of manufacture. It is the interest of the farmer to have the production of the raw material promoted by counteracting the interference of the foreign material of the same kind. It is the interest of the manufacturer to have the material abundant and cheap. If, prior to the domestic production of the material, in sufficient quantity to supply the manufacturer on good terms, a duty be laid upon the importation of it from abroad, with a view to promote the raising of it at home, the interest both of the farmer and manufacturer will be disserved. By either destroying the requisite supply, or raising the price of the article beyond what can be afforded to be given for it by the conductor of an infant manufacture, it is abandoned or fails, and there being no domestic manufactories to create a demand for the raw material, which is raised by the farmer, it is in vain that the competition of the like foreign article may have been destroyed. . . .

The continuance of bounties on manufactures long established must almost always be of questionable policy; because a presumption would arise, in every such case, that there were natural and inherent impediments to success. But, in new undertakings they are as justifiable as they are oftentimes necessary.

There is a degree of prejudice against bounties, from an appearance of giving away the public money without an immediate consideration, and from a supposition that they serve to enrich particular classes at the expense of the community.

But neither of these sources of dislike will bear a serious examination. There is no purpose to which public money can be more beneficially applied than to the acquisition of a new and useful branch of industry; no consideration more valuable than a permanent addition to the general stock of productive labor.

As to the second source of objection, it equally lies against other modes of encouragement, which are admitted to be eligible. As often as a duty upon a foreign article makes an addition to its price, it causes an extra expense to the community for the benefit of the domestic manufacturer. A bounty does no more. But it is the interest of the society, in each case, to submit to the temporary expense—which is more than compensated by an increase of industry and wealth, by an augmentation of resources and independence, and by the circumstances of eventual cheapness, which has been noticed in another place. . . .

### 5. *Premiums*

There are various societies, in different countries, whose object is the dispensation of premiums for the encouragement of agriculture, arts, manufactures, and commerce; and though they are, for the most part, voluntary associations, with comparatively slender funds, their utility has been immense. Much has been done, by this means, in Great Britain. Scotland, in particular, owes, materially to it, a prodigious amelioration of condition. From a similar establishment in the United States, supplied and supported by the Government of the Union, vast benefits might, reasonably, be expected. Some further ideas on this head shall, accordingly, be submitted in the conclusion of this report.

6.  *The Exemption of the Materials of Manufactures from Duty.*
The policy of that exemption, as a general rule, particularly in reference to new establishments, is obvious. It can hardly ever be advisable to add the obstructions of fiscal burthens to the difficulties which naturally embarrass a new manufacture; and where it is matured, and in condition to become an object of revenue, it is, generally speaking, better that the fabric, than the material, should be the subject of taxation. . . .

8.  *The Encouragement of New Inventions and Discoveries at Home, and of the Introduction into the United States of Such As May Have Been Made in Other Countries; Particularly Those which Relate to Machinery.*
This is among the most useful and unexceptionable of the aids which can be given to manufactures. The usual means of that encouragement are pecuniary rewards, and, for a time, exclusive privileges. The first must be employed according to the occasion and the utility of the invention or discovery. For the last, so far as respects "authors and inventors," provision has been made by law. But it is desirable, in regard to improvements, and secrets of extraordinary value, to be able to extend the same benefit to introducers, as well as authors and inventors; a policy which has been practised with advantage in other countries. Here, however, as in some other cases, there is cause to regret that the competency of the authority of the National Government to the good which might be done, is not without a question. Many aids might be given to industry, many internal improvements of primary magnitude might be promoted, by an authority operating throughout the Union, which cannot be effected as well, if at all, by an authority confined within the limits of a single State.

But, if the Legislature of the Union cannot do all the good that might be wished, it is, at least, desirable that all may be done which is practicable. . . .

It is customary with manufacturing nations to prohibit, under severe penalties, the exportation of implements and machines which they have either invented or improved. There are already objects for a similar regulation in the United States; and others may be expected to occur from time to time. The adoption of it seems to be dictated by the principle of reciprocity. Greater liberality, in such respects, might better comport with the general spirit of the country; but a selfish and exclusive policy, in other quarters, will not always permit the free indulgence of a spirit which would place us upon an unequal footing. As far as prohibitions tend to prevent foreign competitors from deriving the benefit of the improvements made at home, they tend to increase the advantages of those by whom they may have been introduced, and operate as an encouragement to exertion.

9.  *Judicious Regulations for the Inspection of Manufactured Commodities*
This is not among the least important of the means by which the prosperity of manufactures may be promoted. It is, indeed, in many cases, one of the most essential. Contributing to prevent frauds upon consumers at home and exporters to foreign countries, to improve the quality and preserve the character of the national manufactures, it cannot fail to aid the expeditious and advantageous sale of them, and to serve as a

guard against successful competition from other quarters. The reputation of the flour and lumber of some States, and of the potash of others, has been established by an attention to this point. And the like good name might be procured for those articles, wheresoever produced, by a judicious and uniform system of inspection throughout the ports of the United States. A like system might also be extended with advantage to other commodities.

### 10. *The Facilitating of Pecuniary Remittances from Place to Place*

It is a point of considerable moment to trade in general, and to manufacturers in particular, by rendering more easy the purchase of raw materials and provisions, and the payment for manufactured supplies. A general circulation of bank paper, which is to be expected from the institution lately established, will be a most valuable means to this end. But much good would also accrue from some additional provisions respecting inland bills of exchange. If those drawn in one State, payable in another, were made negotiable everywhere, and interest and damages allowed in case of protest, it would greatly promote negotiations between the citizens of different States, by rendering them more secure, and with it the convenience and advantage of the merchants and manufacturers of each.

### 11. *The Facilitating of the Transportation of Commodities*

Improvements favoring this object intimately concern all the domestic interests of a community; but they may, without impropriety, be mentioned as having an important relation to manufactures. There is, perhaps, scarcely any thing which has been better calculated to assist the manufacturers of Great Britain than the melioration of the public roads of that kingdom, and the great progress which has been of late made in opening canals. Of the former, the United States stand much in need; for the latter, they present uncommon facilities.

The symptoms of attention to the improvements of inland navigation which have lately appeared in some quarters, must fill with pleasure every breast warmed with a true zeal for the prosperity of the country. These examples, it is to be hoped, will stimulate the exertions of the government and citizens of every State. There can certainly be no object more worthy of the cares of the local administrations; and it were to be wished that there was no doubt of the power of the National Government to lend its direct aid on a comprehensive plan. This is one of those improvements which could be prosecuted with more efficacy by the whole than by any part or parts of the Union. There are cases in which the general interests will be in danger to be sacrificed to the collision of some supposed local interests. Jealousies, in matters of this kind, are as apt to exist as they are apt to be erroneous.

# APPENDIX A

## Estimated Population of American Colonies/States, 1610 to 1800

### 1610–1700

| Colony/State | 1610 | 1620 | 1630 | 1640 | 1650 | 1660 | 1670 | 1680 | 1690 | 1700 |
|---|---|---|---|---|---|---|---|---|---|---|
| Maine[b] | — | — | 400 | 900 | 1,000 | — | — | — | — | 4,958 |
| New Hampshire[c] | — | — | 500 | 1,055 | 1,305 | 1,555 | 1,805 | 2,047 | 4,164 | — |
| Vermont[c] | — | — | — | — | — | — | — | — | — | — |
| Plymouth[d] | — | 102 | 390 | 1,020 | 1,566 | 1,980 | 5,333 | 6,400 | 7,424 | — |
| Massachusetts[b,c,d] | — | — | 506 | 8,932 | 14,037 | 20,082 | 30,000 | 39,752 | 49,504 | 55,941 |
| Rhode Island[c] | — | — | — | 300 | 785 | 1,539 | 2,155 | 3,017 | 4,224 | 5,894 |
| Connecticut[c] | — | — | — | 1,472 | 4,139 | 7,980 | 12,603 | 17,246 | 21,645 | 25,970 |
| New York[c] | — | — | 350 | 1,930 | 4,116 | 4,936 | 5,754 | 9,830 | 13,909 | 19,107 |
| New Jersey[c] | — | — | — | — | — | — | 1,000 | 3,400 | 8,000 | 14,010 |
| Pennsylvania[c] | — | — | — | — | — | — | — | 680 | 11,450 | 17,950 |
| Delaware[c] | — | — | — | — | 185 | 540 | 700 | 1,005 | 1,482 | 2,470 |
| Maryland[c] | — | — | — | 583 | 4,504 | 8,426 | 13,226 | 17,904 | 24,024 | 29,604 |
| Virginia[c] | 350 | 2,200 | 2,500 | 10,442 | 18,731 | 27,020 | 35,309 | 43,596 | 53,046 | 58,560 |
| North Carolina[c] | — | — | — | — | — | 1,000 | 3,850 | 5,430 | 7,600 | 10,720 |
| South Carolina[c] | — | — | — | — | — | — | 200 | 1,200 | 3,900 | 5,704 |
| Georgia[c] | — | — | — | — | — | — | — | — | — | — |
| Kentucky | — | — | — | — | — | — | — | — | — | — |
| Tennessee | — | — | — | — | — | — | — | — | — | — |
| Alabama | — | — | — | — | — | — | — | — | — | — |
| Mississippi | — | — | — | — | — | — | — | — | — | — |
| District of Columbia | — | — | — | — | — | — | — | — | — | — |
| Ohio | — | — | — | — | — | — | — | — | — | — |
| Total | 350 | 2,302 | 4,646 | 26,634 | 50,368 | 75,058 | 111,935 | 151,507 | 210,372 | 250,888 |

1710–1800

| Colony/State | 1710 | 1720 | 1730 | 1740 | 1750 | 1760 | 1770 | 1780 | 1790[a] | 1800[a] |
|---|---|---|---|---|---|---|---|---|---|---|
| Maine[b] | — | — | — | — | — | 20,000 | 31,257 | 49,133 | 97,000 | 152,000 |
| New Hampshire[c] | 5,681 | 9,375 | 10,755 | 23,256 | 27,505 | 39,093 | 62,396 | 87,802 | 142,000 | 184,000 |
| Vermont[d] | — | — | — | — | — | — | 10,000 | 47,620 | 85,000 | 154,000 |
| Plymouth[d] | — | — | — | — | — | — | — | — | — | — |
| Massachusetts[b,c,d] | 62,390 | 91,008 | 114,116 | 151,613 | 188,000 | 202,600 | 235,308 | 268,627 | 379,000 | 423,000 |
| Rhode Island[c] | 7,573 | 11,680 | 16,950 | 25,255 | 33,226 | 45,471 | 58,196 | 52,946 | 69,000 | 69,000 |
| Connecticut[c] | 39,450 | 58,830 | 75,530 | 89,580 | 111,280 | 142,470 | 183,881 | 206,701 | 238,000 | 251,000 |
| New York[c] | 21,625 | 36,919 | 48,594 | 63,665 | 76,696 | 117,138 | 162,920 | 210,541 | 340,000 | 589,000 |
| New Jersey[c] | 19,872 | 29,818 | 37,510 | 51,373 | 71,393 | 93,813 | 117,431 | 139,627 | 184,000 | 211,000 |
| Pennsylvania[c] | 24,450 | 30,962 | 51,707 | 85,637 | 119,666 | 183,703 | 240,057 | 327,305 | 434,000 | 602,000 |
| Delaware[c] | 3,645 | 5,385 | 9,170 | 19,870 | 28,704 | 33,250 | 35,496 | 45,385 | 59,000 | 64,000 |
| Maryland[c] | 42,741 | 66,133 | 91,113 | 116,093 | 141,073 | 162,267 | 202,599 | 245,474 | 320,000 | 342,000 |
| Virginia[c] | 78,281 | 87,757 | 114,000 | 180,440 | 231,033 | 339,726 | 447,016 | 538,004 | 748,000 | 887,000 |
| North Carolina[c] | 15,120 | 21,270 | 30,000 | 51,760 | 72,984 | 110,442 | 197,200 | 270,133 | 394,000 | 478,000 |
| South Carolina[c] | 10,883 | 17,048 | 30,000 | 45,000 | 64,000 | 94,074 | 124,244 | 180,000 | 249,000 | 346,000 |
| Georgia[c] | — | — | — | 2,021 | 5,200 | 9,578 | 23,375 | 56,071 | 83,000 | 163,000 |
| Kentucky | — | — | — | — | — | — | 15,700 | 45,000 | 74,000 | 221,000 |
| Tennessee | — | — | — | — | — | — | 1,000 | 10,000 | 36,000 | 106,000 |
| Alabama | — | — | — | — | — | — | — | — | — | 1,000 |
| Mississippi | — | — | — | — | — | — | — | — | — | 8,000 |
| District of Columbia | — | — | — | — | — | — | — | — | — | 8,000 |
| Ohio | — | — | — | — | — | — | — | — | — | 45,000 |
| Total | 331,711 | 466,185 | 629,445 | 905,563 | 1,170,760 | 1,593,625 | 2,148,076 | 2,780,369 | 3,391,000 | 5,304,000 |

[a]The statistics for 1790 and 1800 were drawn from a different set of tables which provided numbers rounded to thousands.

[b]For 1660–1750, Maine counties included with Massachusetts. Maine was a part of Massachusetts until it became a separate state in 1820.

[c]One of the original 13 States.

[d]Plymouth became a part of the Province of Massachusetts in 1691.

Source: *Historical Statistics of the United States, Colonial Times to 1970.*

# APPENDIX B

*Value of Exports to and Imports from England by American Colonies and States: 1700 to 1791 (in pounds sterling)*

| Year | Total Exports | Imports |
|------|--------|---------|
| 1791 | 1,011,313 | 4,014,416 |
| 1790 | 1,043,389 | 3,258,238 |
| 1789 | 893,296 | 2,306,529 |
| 1788 | 883,618 | 1,709,928 |
| 1787 | 780,444 | 1,794,214 |
| 1786 | 743,644 | 1,431,255 |
| 1785 | 775,892 | 2,078,744 |
| 1784 | 701,190 | 3,418,407 |
| 1783 | 314,058 | 1,435,229 |
| 1782 | 28,676 | 256,325 |
| 1781 | 99,847 | 847,883 |
| 1780 | 18,560 | 825,431 |
| 1779 | 20,579 | 349,797 |
| 1778 | 17,694 | 33,986 |
| 1777 | 12,619 | 57,295 |
| 1776 | 103,964 | 55,415 |
| 1775 | 1,920,950 | 196,162 |
| 1774 | 1,373,846 | 2,590,437 |
| 1773 | 1,369,229 | 2,079,412 |
| 1772 | 1,258,515 | 3,012,635 |
| 1771 | 1,339,840 | 4,202,472 |
| 1770 | 1,015,535 | 1,925,571 |
| 1769 | 1,060,206 | 1,336,122 |
| 1768 | 1,251,454 | 2,157,218 |
| 1767 | 1,096,079 | 1,900,923 |
| 1766 | 1,043,958 | 1,804,333 |
| 1765 | 1,151,698 | 1,944,114 |
| 1764 | 1,110,572 | 2,249,710 |
| 1763 | 1,106,161 | 1,631,997 |
| 1760 | 761,099 | 2,611,764 |
| 1750 | 814,768 | 1,313,083 |
| 1740 | 718,416 | 813,382 |
| 1730 | 572,585 | 536,860 |
| 1720 | 468,188 | 319,702 |
| 1710 | 249,814 | 293,659 |
| 1700 | 395,021 | 344,341 |

Source: *Historical Statistics of the United States: Colonial Times to 1970.*

# APPENDIX C

## *Number of Urban Places by Size of Place in 1790*

| Population Class | |
|---|---|
| 25,000 –49,999 | 2 |
| 10,000 –24,999 | 3 |
| 5,000 – 9,999 | 7 |
| 2,500 – 4,999 | 12 |
| Total | 24 |

Source: *Historical Statistics of the United States: Colonial Times to 1970.*

# APPENDIX D

 *Population in Urban and Rural Territory by Size of Place, 1790*

### Urban Territory

| *Population Class* | *Number of Inhabitants* |
|---|---|
| 25,000 – 49,999 | 62,000 |
| 10,000 – 24,999 | 48,000 |
| 5,000 – 9,999 | 48,000 |
| 2,500 – 4,999 | 44,000 |
| Total | 202,000 |

### Rural Territory

| | |
|---|---|
| Places of under 2,499 | 3,728,000 |

Note: The figure for total population in 1790 provided here differs from that in Appendix A. These differences occur in the respective tables of the authoritative *Historical Statistics*.

Source: *Historical Statistics of the United States: Colonial Times to 1970.*

# APPENDIX E

 *Private Physical Wealth per Free Person, 1774 (in pounds sterling)*

|  | New England | Middle Colonies | Southern Colonies | Total 13 Colonies |
|---|---|---|---|---|
| Land | 27 | 28 | 55 | 38 |
| Servants and slaves | 0 | 2 | 58 | 21 |
| Livestock | 3 | 5 | 9 | 6 |
| Farm tools and household equipment | 1 | 1 | 3 | 2 |
| Crops and perishables | 1 | 3 | 5 | 3 |
| Consumer durables | 4 | 4 | 6 | 5 |
| Other | 2 | 3 | 1 | 2 |
| Total | 38 | 46 | 137 | 76 |

Note: All figures have been rounded to the nearest pound sterling. Components may not add to total due to rounding.

Source: Gary M. Walton, "The Colonial Economy" in Glenn Porter, ed., *Encyclopedia of American Economic History* (New York: Scribner's, 1980).

# APPENDIX F

 *Chronology, 1750–1800*

| | |
|---|---|
| 1750 | Iron Act passed by Parliament limiting production of finished iron goods in colonies. |
| 1751 | Currency Act passed by Parliament restricting issuance and currency of paper money in New England colonies. |
| 1754–63 | French and Indian War (colonial phase of Europe's Seven Years War, 1756–63). |
| 1760 | George III succeeds to throne. |
| 1763 | Treaty of Paris ends Seven Years War between Great Britain and France and Spain. Proclamation line drawn along Appalachians by British forbids settlement in West by whites. |
| 1764 | Sugar Act passed by Parliament, reducing duty on foreign molasses. Currency Act prohibits issues of legal-tender currency in the colonies. |
| 1765 | Stamp Act passed. Stamp Act Congress meets in New York. |
| 1766 | Stamp Act repealed by Parliament, which adopts Declaratory Act asserting its authority to bind the colonies "in all cases whatsoever." |
| 1767 | Townshend Duties passed. |
| 1768 | Secretary of State for the Colonies established in England—first executive department with exclusively colonial concerns. John Hancock's sloop *Liberty* seized. British troops sent to Boston. |
| 1770 | Lord North's ministry formed. Townshend Duties repealed, except for duty on tea. Boston Massacre. |
| 1772 | Boston Committee of Correspondence formed. |
| 1773 | Tea Act imposed. Boston Tea Party. |
| 1774 | Coercive Acts. Continental Congress meets in Philadelphia. |
| 1775 | Battle of Lexington and Concord. Second Continental Congress meets in Philadelphia. George Washington appointed commander in chief of Continental Army. George III proclaims colonists in open rebellion. |

| | |
|---|---|
| 1776 | Thomas Paine's *Common Sense*. British troops evacuate Boston. Congress calls on colonies to suppress all crown authority and establish governments under authority of the people. Declaration of Independence. British take New York City. New Hampshire, New Jersey, Pennsylvania, Delaware, Maryland, Virginia, North Carolina, and South Carolina write state constitutions. Rhode Island and Connecticut change their colonial charters. |
| 1777 | Battle of Monmouth, New Jersey. Although outcome indecisive, Washington's troops stand up to British regulars. British occupy Philadelphia. Burgoyne surrenders at Saratoga. Articles of Confederation adopted by Continental Congress but not ratified by all states until 1781. Washington retires to Valley Forge for winter. New York and Georgia write state constitutions. |
| 1778 | United States concludes military alliance and commercial treaty with France: first and only military alliance by United States until North Atlantic Treaty Organization, 1949. British evacuate Philadelphia. British seize Savannah, Georgia. |
| 1779 | Spain enters the war against Britain. |
| 1780 | Americans surrender 5,500 men and the city of Charleston, South Carolina. |
| 1781 | Cornwallis surrenders to Washington at Yorktown, Virginia. Articles of Confederation ratified. Congress establishes Bank of North America. |
| 1783 | Newburgh conspiracy of American army officers. Treaty of Peace with Britain signed. |
| 1785 | Land Ordinance for Northwest Territory adopted by Congress. |
| 1786 | Shays' Rebellion in western Massachusetts. Annapolis Convention adopts plan to meet in Philadelphia to revise Articles of Confederation. |
| 1787 | Federal Constitutional Convention meets in Philadelphia and drafts Constitution. Northwest Ordinance enacted by Congress. *The Federalist* papers begun by Madison, Hamilton, and Jay. |
| 1788 | Ratification of United States Constitution by all states except Rhode Island and North Carolina. |
| 1789 | First session of Congress meets. Washington inaugurated as first President. |
| 1790 | Hamilton's Report on Public Credit; Funding bill; Assumption bill. |
| 1791 | Bank of the United States established. |
| 1792 | First 10 amendments to Constitution (Bill of Rights) adopted. |
| 1793 | Washington inaugurated for second term. Proclamation of Neutrality by Washington. Samuel Slater erects first cotton mill at Pawtucket, Rhode Island. Eli Whitney applies for patent on cotton gin. Yellow fever epidemic in Philadelphia. |

1794    Whiskey Rebellion in western Pennsylvania. Battle of Fallen Timbers, Ohio; General Anthony Wayne defeats Indians. Philadelphia-Lancaster turnpike completed.

1796    Washington's Farewell Address, warning against foreign entanglements and domestic factionalism. John Adams elected President.

1798    Quasi-war with France on high seas. Alien and Sedition acts enacted by Federalists in Congress. Virginia and Kentucky resolutions.

1799    Fries uprising in Pennsylvania.

1800    Washington, D.C., becomes capital. Thomas Jefferson elected President.

Source: Bernard Bailyn, David Brion Davis, David Herbert Donald, John L. Thomas, Robert H. Wiebe, and Gordon S. Wood, *The Great Republic*, 2d ed. (Lexington, Mass.: D. C. Heath, 1977).

# CASE 3

# John Jacob Astor, 1763–1848*

## Introduction

John Jacob Astor was one of the last of the great general merchants and one of the first of the great specialists. Beginning in a small way as a retailer of musical instruments, he soon became one of America's foremost merchants, combining foreign trade, both European and Oriental, and the fur trade. His business reached from the leading markets of the Old World and the Orient to the Indian villages and the camps of the lone trappers of the great American wilderness. A typical general merchant, Astor at first engaged in a wide variety of business functions, but he later felt strongly the impact of the revolution that came in American business after 1815 and became more specialized.

From the earliest part of his career, Astor had been investing in real estate in a small way, particularly in New York City. The great internal development of the United States resulting from the swift expansion of population into the Mississippi Valley and the rapid growth of the cotton trade created new opportunities for profitable investment. Astor, more than most New York merchants, appreciated the

*Much of the material for this case has been taken from Kenneth Wiggins Porter, *John Jacob Astor, Business Man* (Cambridge, Mass.: Harvard University Press, 1931). An earlier version of this case appeared in N.S.B. Gras and Henrietta M. Larson, *Casebook in American Business History* (New York: Appleton-Century-Crofts, 1939), pp. 76–97. This revised and expanded version has been prepared by Professor Alfred D. Chandler, Jr.

impact which the growth of the city's hinterland would have on real estate values on Manhattan Island. The man who had been known as one of America's outstanding foreign merchants was, at the time of his death, the greatest landlord of New York.

## Astor, the Man

From a portrait of John Jacob Astor painted in his fifties, his biographer, Kenneth W. Porter, has drawn the following impressions. Astor was of medium height and somewhat heavy and unwieldy of body. He had a high and broad forehead, a prominent and strongly arched nose, a straight and thin-lipped mouth, and a jaw of iron. His eyes, deeply set, had a characteristically shrewd and keen expression. His countenance reveals a nature that was good-humored but at the same time aggressive and inflexible. The portrait gives the general impression that Astor was a man of intense mental activity and strong self-confidence.

In his relations with those who were close to him, Astor showed both kindness and indulgence—there was much of the patriarch in him. With his family he was affectionate and generous; and he was comparatively liberal with those of his agents with whom he had close personal contact. Some of his people stayed with him for twenty or more years.

Astor's imagination was limited by the practices of his own class and generation. The lack of contact with the distant parts of his empire gave him little feeling of responsibility for the many people whose interest he touched, such as the Indians or *engagés* in the fur country or the commoners cutting Hawaiian sandalwood. Indeed, his attitude toward the people with whom he did not come in personal contact was inevitably similar to that which he had toward bales of fur.

Astor's life was business. He had a passion for profits and an abhorrence of waste or loss. Vincent Nolte, the international merchant on whose reminiscences Hervey Allen based his novel *Anthony Adverse*, tells of an incident which occurred when Astor was under observation of a Parisian doctor. One day, when Astor and the doctor were out for a ride, Astor acted as if he were "suffering from some secret pain or trouble." When the doctor urged him to tell what was wrong, Astor replied: "Look ye! Baron. How frightful this is! I have here in the hands of my banker, at Paris, about 2,000,000 francs, and cannot manage, without great effort, to get more than 2½ percent per annum on it. Now, this very day I have received a letter from my son in New York, informing me that there the best acceptances are from 1½ to 2 percent per month. Is it not enough to enrage a man?"

Many contemporary stories point to Astor's seeming niggardliness. It was characteristic of him to pretend that times were hard and profits low. On one occasion he subscribed to Audubon's *Birds of America*, the price of which was $1,000. But, so the story runs, when Audubon asked him to pay, he would not because "money is very scarce; I have nothing in the bank; I have invested all my funds." On the author's sixth visit to Astor, he found the father and son together. Again pleading the scarcity of funds, Astor turned to his son, who had not followed the conversation, and asked if they had any money in the bank. On the son's enumeration of $220,000 in one bank, $120,000 in another, and so on, Astor interrupted him with orders to write a check for $1,000.

Astor was a man of regularity and decision. It is said that, in spite of the multiplicity of his interests and personal attention he gave to details, he "did not bestow at his countinghouse more than half the time most merchants feel compelled to give their concerns." He went to his office early in the morning, transacted the necessary business, and left at two in the afternoon.

A contemporary's characterization is significant in this connection: "Astor possessed marked executive ability. He was quick in his perceptions. He came rapidly to his conclusions. He made a trade or rejected it at once. . . . He made distinct contracts. These he adhered to with inflexible purpose." "In trade," it was said, he was an "autocrat in bearing," yet withal "he was represented as being a pleasant man to do business with, seldom being ruffled in temper or intemperate in speech."

Astor's efficiency in conducting business gave him time for other interests. After business was over in the early afternoon he had dinner. This, it is said, was followed by exactly three games of checkers and a glass of beer. Then came a ride around Manhattan on his horse, Astor keeping lookout for promising pieces of land for sale. In the evening he frequently went to the theater or had musicales at home.

This stolid man of business had many cultural interests. Astor could not write the English language without marvelous errors in grammar and spelling, but he enjoyed reading literature and history; and he gave aid to several men following a literary career and became a close friend of a few. Fitz-Greene Halleck, the poet, was Astor's confidential secretary from 1832 until Astor's death, and Washington Irving, who wrote *Astoria* about Astor's western enterprise, became a close friend. It was no doubt Astor's interest in literature and history and his friendship with writers which led him to endow the Astor Library in New York City (now the New York City Public Library).

Astor also had many friends among important public men. He seems always to have been on good terms with the dominant party. Those of his associates who were active in political life were predominantly Federalists before 1800, Jeffersonian Republicans until about 1824, and Jacksonian Democrats until about the time of his retirement. "He aroused no enmity among any group by conspicuous advocacy of the claims of some other, and so had little difficulty in securing favorable consideration from whatever party was in power."

No definite connection can be traced between Astor's religion and his business life. "In most respects he seemed, and doubtless was, a perfectly orthodox if somewhat inactive churchman." His philosophy was definitely secular: "Make the best of things" was his motto in adversity. Astor supported the church and assisted missionaries where he traded. This was good business, but he was no hypocrite and made no claims of "Christianizing the savage." In his later years he took a considerable interest in the question of immortality which he discussed at length with one of his secretaries. "Cogswell did not seem altogether sure of Astor's final decision upon the principal subject of their doctrinal discussions, but we can be confident that if he ever formed an opinion it was upon arguments tested and found valid by his own reasons."

On the death of Astor, James Gordon Bennett, the leading journalist of his time, wrote in the April 5, 1848, edition of his *New York Herald*:

> We give in our columns, an authentic copy of one of the greatest curiosities of the age—the will of John Jacob Astor, disposing of the property amounting to about twenty million dollars, among his various descendants of the first, second, third and fourth degrees. . . . If we had been an associate of John Jacob Astor,. . .the first idea we should have put into his head would have been that *one-half of his immense property—ten million, at least—belonged to the people of the city of New York*. During the last fifty years of the life of John Jacob Astor, his property has been augmented and increased in value by the aggregate intelligence, industry, enterprise and commerce of New York, fully to the amount of one-half of its value. The farms and lots of ground which he bought forty, twenty, ten and five years ago, have all increased in value entirely by the industry of the citizens of New York. Of course, it is as plain as that two and two make four, that the half of his immense estate, in its actual value, has accrued to him by the industry of the community.

## Astor's Early Business Career, 1784–1800

In 1784, John Jacob Astor, aged 20, landed in the United States with seven flutes and about five guineas in his possession. Born in the German Rhine country, the youngest son of a none-too-prosperous butcher, John Jacob, after attending school until 14 and then helping his father for a time, had at the age of 16 set out for London, where an older brother was a maker of musical instruments. Young Astor had remained in London for four years, during which time he had probably worked for his brother and a musical instrument firm, had learned English, and had saved money. On the long passage across the ocean—so it is told—he had learned much about the American fur trade from some passengers who were in that business.

Astor arrived in New York in 1784, where he had another brother who was in the "horse and cart" stage of the butcher's business. Putting his flutes out to be sold on commission, the young immigrant worked at a number of occupations. He began by peddling bakery products. But it was not long before he found employment with a furrier, Robert Browne. He not only helped Browne to process pelts but acted as his agent in buying and selling furs. Before the year was out, Astor was back in London marketing furs for Browne and himself and investing the proceeds in merchandise to sell in New York on his return to the United States.

Shortly after his return, there occurred an event which was of great significance to Astor's business career. In 1785, he married Sarah Todd, the daughter of a sea captain. She had excellent connections in New York, a dowry of $300, and a great talent for business.

In 1786, Astor opened a shop of his own in a room in his mother-in-law's house. Tradition says he first sold German toys, but newspaper advertisements reveal that he had for sale different musical instruments and other articles in the music line. It is probable that Sarah Astor tended the shop while John Jacob tended to his fur business, but Mrs. Astor also helped with the furs. One contemporary, Scoville, remarks that Mrs. Astor knew more about the market value of furs than her husband, and that "when they became very affluent, she used to make him pay her $500 an hour for using her judgment and knowledge of furs to promote his commercial plans."

By 1788, the fur business had attained primacy over the trade in musical instruments. Astor was then making regular fur-buying excursions into the back country of New York. Going out with Indian goods, at first with a pack on his back and later on a horse, he returned with furs. Through forest and swamp he sought out the Indians and the white trappers.

Early in the 1790s, he seems to have ceased his personal purchase of furs in the backwoods. By then he had agents and correspondents such as Peter Smith of Utica, who collected peltries for him on commission. A few years later he was sending young men out to represent him. A letter to Peter Smith, introducing a young Frenchman whom Astor was sending upstate to buy furs, shows something of how he tried out a young agent:

> Acting Causiously I Gave him about 500$ a Cridet of 500 or 1000 more at Albany now it appears he is gone your way & without making use of the Cridet at Albany So that he has but abaut 500$ with him with which you know he Can not purshas much furr. I would there for be glad if in Case he should Lay aut his Little money if you would eighter pay him for my account from five to ten hundred Dollars—or pass his Bill on me for that amount this hawever youil observe is to be done only in Case that you have no reason to belive that he maks any bade use of the money.

By 1788, Astor had his annual fur-buying trips to Montreal, which was at that time the capital of the American fur trade. In Montreal Astor established connections with a merchant who shipped furs for him to London, to be reshipped to Rotterdam and New York. (British mercantile policy did not allow direct shipment from Montreal to New York.) It is significant that only four years after his arrival in America, Astor had sufficient funds or credit to purchase furs in Montreal worth $3,000.

In 1789, describing himself for the first time under the resounding title of "John Jacob Astor of New York. . .Merchant," Astor was again in Montreal. This time he reached further westward by an agreement with a Detroit merchant to furnish him 15,000 "Good and Merchantable Musquash Skins." Astor continued his trips to Montreal, leaving New York in the summer, staying in the fur city about two months buying and shipping furs, and returning to New York City in October or November.

The center of Astor's operations was New York. There he prepared the furs for shipping and managed their sale. He also had a considerable importing business. To his import of pianos and music supplies were soon added Indian goods for use in the purchase of furs and manufactured goods for the use of his merchant-correspondents in the backwoods. By 1800, Astor's chief European imports were arms, ammunition, and blankets purchased principally through London merchants.

John Jacob Astor fell a victim to a common ailment of the time, the frontier real estate fever. He tried to buy a large tract of land in Canada but failed; he succeeded, however, in upstate New York. There he, another New York merchant, and Peter Smith of Utica bought 37,200 acres on joint account in 1794. This proved not to be a very profitable venture. For several years there were disputes over the title to the lands, and not until the late 1820s did Astor dispose of his share.

The management of these lands remained in the hands of Peter Smith for about 30 years. For his work Smith received no remuneration from his partners in the venture. On one occasion Astor collected Smith's share of a small attorney's fee of 20 years' standing with compound interest; but, when the latter asked for some compensation for his years of work, Astor wrote in reply, "I believe the agreement was that you were not to charge any."

Occasional glimpses are seen of Astor's finances in those early years. Though his business was steadily growing, he was not without his difficulties. In 1792, commenting on the number of bankruptcies, he wrote that they had caused him great loss and had "affaceted my property but not So as to Affacet my business." Probably referring to the Duer Panic of 1792, Scoville remarks that "those who suppose Mr. Astor had an easy time in money matters are greatly mistaken. He has often paid old Prime, in Wall Street, very large interest and a large commission to get long paper discounted."

In the fall of 1795, on returning from Europe, Astor said that he found his business "very mush Derangd So that I Shall am afraid fall short of Cash Even to Comply with my Engagements." Early in September he was still in the same condition, according to a letter to Peter Smith: "I Can not Describe to you on Black and white how much I am in want of Cash theare for If you Can Sent me any it will oblige me mush be the Sum ever So Smale."

Though Astor was at times hard pressed, he was making a success of his business. By 1800, he is said to have been worth "something like $250,000." In that year he established a residence apart from his business, and there is evidence to suggest that he was not without some standing socially.

## Expansion of Astor's Business, 1800–1815

In 1799 and 1800, Astor began to advertise such eastern goods as India silks, "very excellent Hyson and Souchong Tea," nankeens and black India lutestrings. At that time no stock-in-trade of a general merchant was considered complete without a line of oriental goods. Furthermore, it was logical to add Canton to London and Continental ports as a market for furs.

In 1800, Astor became the principal owner of a vessel to carry his furs to China and to return with Chinese goods. By 1805, Astor began to have ships built especially for the China trade. This trade was checked in 1807 and 1808 by the

American embargo on foreign trade, but in 1809 Astor had five ships engaged in the trade with the Orient.

During his first decade of participation in the China trade, Astor's commercial policy was simple, straightforward, and unoriginal. His ships, the *Severn* until 1805 and then the *Beaver* and the *Magdalen* in the following years, would normally leave for Canton in May and return immediately, making the round-trip within less than a year. As his biographer points out: "The China goods would be advertised in the New York press, some sold over the counter of his store, a part disposed of by some well-known auction firm, another part, perhaps, shipped to some other eastern city for sale, to Canada, or even to Europe."

The following account of a cargo bound for China illustrates the rather uncomplicated nature of Astor's early shipping ventures. The cargo went aboard the *Severn* and left New York for Canton in May 1804:

> First, there were 51 "Keges" of "Specia," valued at $140,000; next in value were 7 casks of furs, containing 2,570 rabbit skins, 1,322 otter skins, 166 beaver skins, and some seal and fox skins, invoiced at $8,000; 53 casks of ginseng containing 117-1/2 piculs were valued at $6,000 but of these only 38 bore Astor's unmistakable mark (HA). Eighteen bales of cotton, estimated at $1,000, formed another feature of the cargo. To the above must be added some additional kegs and boxes of specie to the value of $11,000, none of which, however, bore Astor's personal mark. The entire value of the outward cargo, then, was $166,100, of which something over $153,000 is known to have been on Astor's account.
>
> We have a pretty good idea, also, of the source of these goods. The furs were doubtless the choicest of those purchased by Astor at Montreal the previous autumn or secured by his agents in the backcountry of New York. The ginseng, too, probably came from New York State, collected by the same agents who were there engaged in purchasing peltries. In July 1799, Astor had informed Peter Smith that, "Gensang will Sell 3/6 to 4/prlb if not too large aquantey is Caured." The cotton, of course, had come up from Charleston, Baltimore, or other southern ports on some of the coasting vessels which occasionally brought goods consigned to Astor. It was not always easy to acquire enough specie for a China voyage. Astor seems to have had an arrangement with Garrit W. Van Schaick, cashier of the Bank of Albany, by which Astor took up the notes of that bank which appeared in New York City and transmitted them to Albany, receiving payment in dollars.

During 1807–08, the embargo on American trade, which was intended to protect American interests from becoming involved in the Napoleonic struggles in Europe, led to an important incident with respect to Astor's business career. Instead of dismissing the captains, laying up his ships with tar barrels over the mastheads, and philosophically settling down to wait for the inevitable repeal of the repressive acts or besieging Congress and the president with threats and petitions directed against the embargo and its supporters, Astor, by a stroke of ingenious trickery, actually caused the president to suspend the embargo in his favor.

The idea seemed perfectly innocent to President Jefferson. A Chinese mandarin, who had been to America on business and had suddenly been called home, "where the affairs of his family and particularly the funeral obsequies of his grandfather, require his solemn attention," applied to President Jefferson for permission to "depart for his own country with his property in a vessel to be engaged by himself." The president granted the mandarin's request both as an act of courtesy and a "means of making our nation known advantageously as the source of power in China." Certain merchants of Philadelphia challenged the mandarin story, but their warnings to government officials were disregarded. John Jacob Astor's *Beaver* was the ship that undertook the mission.

The *Beaver*'s outbound cargo consisted of only 3,000 otter skins and five piculs of cochineal. But, though she had been granted permission to bring back merely the proceeds of goods shipped by citizens of the United States before the embargo went into effect, the *Beaver* returned, it was alleged, with "two hundred thousand dollars more than she left with," a cargo which was unusually large and was made up of a variety of China goods. The result was that Astor was able to import China goods when other merchants could not do so. As for the mandarin, there can be no doubt that he was a Chinese commoner elevated in rank only by the active and scheming imagination of John Jacob Astor.

Astor's China trade continued to grow but eventually ran into a serious snag, the War of 1812. Before the war Astor had sent at least one ship a year to the Orient. During the war years 1812–14, he was able to commence and complete not a single voyage. During the first year of the war, however, he had the good fortune to receive two cargoes of tea from China despite the British cruisers. His principal connection with the China trade during the war was the sale of goods brought by those ships. Since Chinese goods were scarce during the war, they brought very attractive prices.

In 1807, shortly before the embargo went into effect, Astor began to conceive of a grand plan that would assure him of a cheaper supply of furs and at the same time bring American control over furs trapped and traded on American soil. At the time two Canadian companies completely dominated the fur trade of the American West. Of the two, the North West Company was the older and more powerful, having been formed in the 1780s by leading Montreal merchants to compete with the ancient and formidable Hudson's Bay Company, which operated further to the north. By 1800, the North West Company was capitalized at $1,200,000. The second enterprise, the Michilimackinac Company had been formed in 1806 with a capital of $800,000 by a group of Montreal traders, some of whom were already connected with the North West Company, and all of whom felt the need for stronger mutual protection. After its formation the Michilimackinac Company signed a noninterference agreement with the North West Company, assigning areas of influence and providing for mutual assistance against outsiders. This arrangement, by assuring the continued exploitation of the Mississippi and Missouri Valleys by the Canadians, meant that Astor and other Americans would have to buy their pelts in Montreal as they had done in the past.

Astor devised two strategies for breaking the dominance of the Canadian companies. He would move into the recently opened area of the Pacific Northwest, where the Canadians had only begun to penetrate. And he would use his growing supply of capital to organize systematically the American fur trade in the interior of the continent, which in 1803 had come into the possession of the United States with the purchase of the Louisiana Territory from France. In this way he would divert the trade from Montreal to New York, assure himself of an ample supply of furs, and at the same time profit from the production as well as the marketing of furs.

The instrument to carry out these strategies was the American Fur Company, which was incorporated in 1808 in New York State with a capital of $1 million. The preamble of the charter read as follows:[1]

> Whereas John Jacob Astor has presented his petition to the legislature, representing, among other things, that he is desirous of forming a trading company, for the purpose of carrying on an extensive trade with the native Indian inhabitants of America, but that an undertaking of such magnitude would require a greater capital than any individual or unincorporated association could well furnish, and who would be less able to support a fair competition with foreigners who are at present almost in the exclusive possession of the fur trade; and has prayed that he and such other persons as may be associated with him, may be incorporated, the better to enable them to carry into effect this design: *And whereas*, such an establishment may be of great public utility, by serving to conciliate and secure the good will and affections of the Indian tribes toward the government and people of the United States, and may conduce to the peace and safety of our citizens inhabiting the territories bordering on the native Indian tribes.

The preamble notwithstanding, the American Fur Company was in reality John Jacob Astor. As Washington Irving, the official historian for this part of Astor's life, wrote, "Capital was furnished by himself—he, in fact, constituted the company, for though he had a board of directors, they were really nominal; the whole business was conducted on his plans, and with his resources but he preferred to do so under the imposing and formidable aspect of a corporation, rather than in his individual name, and his policy was sagacious and effective." Having secured for the project the blessings of President Jefferson, to whom he had explained the beneficial effects which it would have for the United States, Astor was ready to go ahead.

The first part of Astor's plan, that of moving into the Pacific Northwest, involved a deal with the Russians. The Russians had been the first to explore and the Russian American Fur Company the first to exploit that area. In the late 18th century, the Russians claimed the territory, and the company set up trading posts as far south as San Francisco Bay. Soon it was sending seal and sea otter pelts to China, where the furs brought astonishingly high prices. The British had only learned of the region after Captain Cook's explorations were followed up by those of George Vancouver and others in the early 1790s. Americans who were opening the China trade in the same decade also discovered the value in the Orient of the furs in the Pacific Northwest. After the purchase of the Louisiana Territory in 1803, President Jefferson had sent an exploratory expedition under two army officers, the famed Lewis and Clark, to find a possible route across the continent to

---

[1]*Private Laws of the State of New York, passed at the Thirty-First Session of the Legislature*, pp. 160–61, as quoted in Porter, *Astor* 1, pp. 413–14.

the Pacific Northwest. The reports of the expedition, which returned to St. Louis in September 1806, indicated the feasibility of the overland route and emphasized the abundance of furs. Meriwether Lewis in his journal particularly praised the pelt of the sea otter as "the richest and most delicious fur in the world that least I cannot form an idea of any more so. It is deep silkey in the extreem and strong." The news of the success of the Lewis and Clark expedition was probably as important as was the formation of the Michilimackinac Company in that same year in stimulating Astor's grand strategy. Astor's plans called for setting up a network of posts along the route taken by Lewis and Clark, which provided Americans with more of a direct access to the new regions than was available to the Canadians.

Astor's first move after the formation of the American Fur Company was to begin negotiations with the Russian consul general in the United States. That diplomat enthusiastically supported a proposal that Astor supply the Russian posts. In return Astor's company would procure furs from the Russians and be permitted to set up a trading post of its own. In November 1809, Astor sent the ship *Enterprise* with Captain Ebbits as master with a cargo for the Russians. Ebbits was to return with the cargo of West Coast furs. A letter of instruction to the captain shows something of Astor's attention to details:

'New york 13 Nav^r. 1809

Dear Sir:

I give you note of furrs as I am in hopes you will find Some Land furrs which will be worth bringing here at all events beso good & bring with you from every port you Stop at Some few Skins of easch kind & keep a memrandum of where thy cam from also particular acoount of where easch kind are the most plenty Henry Merschel Whom you have on Board has Some knowlage of the quality as also how to preserve tham all kind of skins Should be put in Cask Say rum punchions to be /s/ crew /?/ but not to hard except Deer & Muss Skins which are to Large for Casks & Should beput in Bales—at foot you have price &c all Skins are the better for being keept from the air in a cole place & where it is not Damp as other wise thy grow Mauldy Do not omit to writ to me as often as you can if you find many Land Furrs of good quality it may well be worth while to trade for tham & bring tham here Say Minck & Martin Skins as also fisher & Silver fox and Musrat Skins if any all these take Little Room and will Sell here Say Martin Skins from 4 to 8/—Minck from 2/ to 4/ Fischer from 4 to 8/—Mush Depends on the coller of the Martin and Mink the Darker the better & profidd thy are taking in Season wild Catts are worth from 4 to 8/—gray fox 2 to 4/—wolf from 4 to 8/—Beare Skins black are worth from 8 to 40/—thy aught to be thick and Long fine haire—Deer Skins in red haire of the wight of 2 lb to 2 1/2 lbs are worth 6 to 7/ pr Skin those in gray Blue haire wighting 3 lbs are worth 6/—those of long gray haire & thin Lether are not worth anything Dear Skins Should have thick Lether & thin haire—furrs and Skins should be thin & the furr thick—Racown Skins if well furred & Large are worth 4/—Muss Skins if thick 16/—Musrat Skins 3/ if very good you may find Still Same ather Skins & if So bring Some

"and ob/li/ge Dear Sir your
Hbl Svt" J. J. Astor

To carry on his West Coast business, Astor organized the Pacific Fur Company, an affiliate of the American Fur Company. For his associates in the new undertaking Astor sought experienced western fur men. These included Wilson Price Hunt of St. Louis, and Ramsay Crooks, Robert McClelan, and Joseph Miller, who had all been engaged in the fur trade on the Missouri when it was still under French rule. Crooks had also been connected with one of the Canadian companies. From Canada came David and Robert Stuart and the veteran North Westers, Alexander McKay, Donald McKenzie, and Duncan McDougall.

One of the objectives of the Pacific Fur Company was the establishment of a trading post on the Columbia River. The post was to be known as Astoria. Astor was to manage the business and furnish the necessary funds, not in excess of $400,000; he was to bear all the loss for five years, though any profit should be apportioned according to the shares. Astor through the American Fur Company took 50 of the 100 shares. Others took two and one half to seven shares with an average of five. Hunt was to reside on the coast as agent.

Astoria proved an unfortunate undertaking. The *Tonquin*, sent out to establish the post, was badly captained and, after unloading some of the partners and goods at the mouth of the Columbia River, was destroyed by Indians. The War of 1812 interfered greatly with the operations of the post by cutting off communications. But it was the opposition of the Canadian North West Company which finally broke the enterprise. That company effectively used the threat of bringing in British naval forces to get the partners of the Pacific Fur Company who were then on the Coast to sell the company's property to the Canadians. Thus for all practical purposes came to an end the career of both the Pacific Fur Company and Astoria as well as Astor's hopes of creating a great fur empire on the Pacific Coast.

The second part of Astor's plan, originally devised in 1807, was to organize systematically the fur trade in the vast interior valleys of the Mississippi and Missouri. Here he moved initially against the newer and weaker of his Canadian rivals, the Michilimackinac Company. He was confident of success even to informing Jefferson that once the American Fur Company got under way that Canadian enterprise would withdraw. The Canadians, however, refused Astor's offer to buy them out. In turn they proposed having him take a minority share in their enterprise. This he immediately rejected. The Michilimackinac Company responded by enlarging its partnership and capital.

Its partners, however, soon decided to come to terms. Astor's aggressive moves impressed them, as did his obvious resources. Moreover, they realized that, as British subjects carrying on nearly all their trading on American soil, they could be at the mercy of American legislation.

Early in 1811, the senior partners of the Michilimackinac Company and representatives of the North West Company traveled to New York to negotiate an all-embracing agreement for the fur trade on the continent of North America south of the areas controlled by the Hudson's Bay Company. Astor and the Michilimackinac Company then formed the South West Company with headquarters at Mackinac Island at the juncture of Lake Michigan and Lake Huron. The new company was to last for five years, unless earlier dissolved by mutual consent. The trade was to be conducted on the joint account of Astor and the Montreal firm, each bearing half the expense and sharing the profit and loss equally. The representatives of the North West Company then agreed that after 1811 their company would stay out of the United States east of the Missouri and the Rockies. In return the South West Company promised to keep out of Canada except in a small area in the Lake Huron region.

The coming of the War of 1812 disarranged Astor's fur interests in the interior of the continent almost as badly as it did those on the Pacific Coast. At first Astor was primarily concerned with salvaging his property, particularly the furs at Mackinac Island, from seizure by the British. His actual fur trading was confined principally to the regions where he had been for some time established. Even there he met many difficulties, "including lack of transportation facilities, great scarcity of some kinds of furs, an oversupply of others, and a general lack of funds for purchasing those which were available." Astor, however, did take advantage of the war to establish closer connection with traders in the Missouri River region. Still, not much was accomplished in St. Louis, where the established traders, fearful of the growth of the New Yorkers' activities, remained strong enough to keep out Astor and his associates.

Astor's fur trade suffered in two other respects during the war. His importation of goods from Europe to be used in the Indian trade and the shipment of furs to European markets were almost stopped by the war. The result was scarcity on the one hand and a glutted fur market on the other. Between March 1813 and late 1814, no ships arrived at New York with goods for Astor.

To relieve this condition, Astor tried every device for getting his vessels to Europe. His ingenuity may be illustrated by one case. On the pretext that the *Hannibal* was to carry back to France the anti-Napoleonic general, Moreau, permission was gained from the British for the ship to pass unmolested. A cargo was carried for Astor worth $60,000 and goods for others which brought more than $27,000 in freight. Astor's object in dispatching the vessel was probably that it would be advantageous to have a ship in Europe in the event of peace. That Astor was not always so fortunate as in the case of *Hannibal* is proved by the capture and condemnation of another of his ships, the *Caroline*.

Any intention Astor might have had of sending additional ships would probably have been dissolved by the very effective British blockade of 1813 and 1814 and the embargo laid by Congress from December 1813 to April 1814. It was not surprising, then, that Astor should write Peter Smith in February 1814 that he was to "withdraw from almost every kind of business & I mean to remain so."

While the war brought difficulties to Astor, it also opened up new business. With idle funds on hand, he was in a position to take advantage of other opportunities. He bought sterling bills on London and Amsterdam guilders to hold for a rise, but his biggest operations were in government loans.

When the government loan of 1813 failed to sell through popular subscription, Astor, Girard of Philadelphia, and Parish of Hamburg took the remainder, of which Astor subscribed for $2,056,000 at 88 with a commission of one quarter of one percent. Since the expected peace and rise in price of the bonds failed to come soon, Astor began to dispose of his portion through his own countinghouse and agents in Boston, Philadelphia, and Baltimore. The bonds held up well for several months but then fell, reaching 75 during the year. Astor, therefore, ceased selling and began buying government bonds of both 1813 and 1814. When the bonds were low, he ordered a Boston broker to borrow funds at 2 percent a month to invest in governments. That Astor profited by this operation is seen from the fact that, as he wrote, "My losses at Sea are made up in the peace by the rise on my Stocks of which I have something more than 800m$."

Astor came out of the war in a very good condition, comparatively speaking. His losses had been large, but gains from his government securities were to be considerable. He had avoided greater loss by keeping himself "practically withdrawn from business," "doing nothing. . .ever since the unhappy war," avoiding commercial ventures involving any considerable element of risk, and abstaining from speculation as much as was possible under the abnormal conditions then prevalent. In May 1814, he wrote, "it will be well for men who wish to live in comfort to be out of debt, I am more so than I have been for many years, of notes I have scarse any out, I owe some on acct. of Stock [United States bonds] & to the customhouse."

Astor welcomed peace. He was not one to choose the speculative risks of war times—he preferred peace as it "puts every thing on safe ground & I can always make money if I will be prudent."

## The Height of Astor's China and Fur Trade, 1815–1834

At the end of the war, Astor, with his capital practically unimpaired and his vigor at its height, was ready for his last and crowning score of years in business. With a large capital, a fleet of nine vessels mostly purchased at the low prices prevailing during the war, a firm position in the American fur trade and in the New York-Europe and New York-Canton trade, and with a beginning in the Pacific trade, Astor was in a position to do a large business when peace and order were again established.

The prospects of a great business made Astor look about for a partner. His choice was Albert Gallatin, a Swiss-American distinguished for his political service to his adopted country. On offering Gallatin a partnership, Astor explained that he had a capital of about $800,000 engaged in trade from which he expected net profits of from $50,000 to $100,000 a year. Gallatin refused the offer. His 18-year-old son could not visualize his father as a partner of Astor, who "ate his ice cream and peas with a knife!" Perhaps Gallatin was too much aware of Astor's commercial tricks—he had been Secretary of the Treasury at the time of the *Beaver* affair. Probably Gallatin was not interested in entering business. At any rate, the fact that he was offered a position of minister to France gave him an excellent pretext for refusing Astor's offer.

Astor thereupon decided to make his son, William B., his assistant partner. Young Astor was then still in Europe as a student, having as a tutor the famous Baron von Bunsen, inventor of the Bunsen burner, and as a friend, Schopenhauer, the philosopher. He was in Paris studying French literature when he received a peremptory order from his father to return home. A few days later he was at Liverpool ready to sail. The scholar soon became the businessman.

Two general policies dominated Astor's business in the decade after the war: the building up of a very complicated foreign trade and a continued drive towards dominance in the fur trade. Both were intimately interrelated and both reflected the fruition of his earlier business strategies.

Astor greatly extended his foreign trade after the war. Canton and New York were no longer the only ports concerned, for various European ports as well as the Pacific Coast of America came to be closely associated with the Orient. Sometimes three fleets of vessels belonging to Astor would be operating simultaneously: one between New York and Europe, another between New York and China, and a third in the Pacific Ocean.

In this complicated trade, in which a ship might be gone several years on a trading voyage, it was necessary to have efficient, resourceful ship captains. "It was Astor's policy to take into consideration every situation which might conceivably arise and give minute instructions as to his captains' conduct in each contingency, but he also strove to secure shipmasters who would not only follow his instructions to the letter in all cases for which he had made provision, but could also, when the need arose, take measures on their own initiative and carry these to a successful conclusion."

A significant product added to Astor's trade in the Pacific at this time was the sandalwood of the Hawaiian Islands, which was much in demand for incense burning in Chinese temples. Sandalwood was a royal monopoly and was cut on shares for the Hawaiian king by his chiefs, the work being done by the commoners for little or no compensation. An ingenious captain and an unscrupulous chief could sometimes get together on the trade to their mutual profit, in that way bypassing the king. Indeed, Astor recommended this as more expeditious, though "clandestine."

In exchange for wood, the king and the chiefs bought quantities of goods. Astor's large capital enabled him to sell superior goods at a low price, so that his captains had a distinct advantage over their rivals. Those low prices were conditioned on receiving payment in wood at once, and thus a minimum of time was expended by Astor's ships at the Islands. The result was that the ships would arrive in Canton early in the season, secure the best prices in the market, and get back to New York before the market was flooded.

The complicated nature of the foreign trade of Astor, in contrast to the voyage of the *Severn* a few years earlier, and the place of the Pacific in that trade can best be indicated by an excerpt quoted from Porter's biography of Astor:

> Let us imagine, then, that in some particular year after the end of the War of 1812 Astor finds himself in possession of a considerable quantity of assorted furs. Some of these are sold in the fur market of New York; a few are shipped to other ports in the United States. Those in which we are particularly interested are, however, sent as freight to various ports in England and on the Continent, of which London, Hamburg, and Le Havre are typical examples.

In return for these furs, from London come dry goods and hardware, such as blankets, cutlery and muskets. From Hamburg, perhaps are received iron, lead and gin. Le Havre gives dry goods of a somewhat finer quality than those furnished by London. At New York some of these goods are, perhaps, offered in the open market. Some of the blankets, cutlery, muskets, lead, iron, gin and other suitable articles are sent into the interior to be sold to the Indians for furs. But those which we are especially concerned in following are loaded on a vessel, intended for the Pacific Ocean. This vessel, perhaps, touches first at one of the Hawaiian Islands, where a miscellaneous assortment of goods from her cargo is sold on short credit because of the low prices made possible by Astor's large capital. Rum is popular, as are the fine textiles from Le Havre. Leaving the natives to collect the sandalwood for which the goods are exchanged, the vessel sails next for Norfolk Sound to trade with the Russians for seal skins and the fur of the sea otter. At Norfolk Sound, also, rum is popular, but there is a demand for general merchandise of all kinds. Perhaps some muskets and ammunition will be sold to the natives, if this can be done without arousing the suspicions of the Russians. Then the vessel may drop down to the vicinity of the Columbia River and sell guns, powder, shot, knives, rum and all sorts of metalwork to the natives. On the coast of California general merchandise again meets a ready market among the inhabitants, though before 1818 one must be on the lookout for the Spanish authorities. Having pretty well disposed of the cargo they took on board at New York, the captain and supercargo decide to return to the Islands. Here they take on the sandalwood which has been cut for them in their absence on the Coast, and with this and the furs from Norfolk Sound, Columbia River and California—perhaps some silver and pearl-shell from the last-named place—they sail to Canton.

Here sandalwood and furs are bartered for teas, silks, nankeens, chinaware, sugar, spices, etc.—a cargo sure to meet with a ready sale at New York. But there are markets nearer to Canton than any city of the United States. Back to the Hawaiian Islands they head. The wives of the chiefs are impressed by the beautiful Chinese silks. What matter that their store-houses are already piled with goods sufficient to last a generation? There is plenty of sandalwood on the mountains, plenty of commoners to cut and carry it to the seashore free of charge. Soon a part of the Canton cargo has been sold and the ship's sails are again set for the coast of the Americas. This time the cargo is not so suitable for the Indian trade, but the Russians at New Archangel and the Spaniards of California are ready to purchase teas, silks, and nankeens in exchange for seal skins, sea otter furs, silver, and pearl-shell. Moreover, farther to the south are Ecuador, Peru and Chile, which have recently cast off the Spanish yoke and thrown open their ports to the trade of the whole world. So ho for Guayaquil, for Callao, for Coquimbo, where the rest of the cargo taken on board at Canton may be sold for red copper and white specie. Then back to the Islands to stow away odorous sandalwood beside the bales of glossy skins of the seal and the otter, the copper ingots, and the kegs of specie.

Once again at Canton, a China cargo is taken on board, but this time the vessel at last clears for her home port from which she sailed three or four years ago. At New York the China cargo is unloaded. Some of the goods are sold at auction, some over the counter of Astor's own shop, some are shipped as freight to other ports in the United States and to the West Indies. Some, perhaps in company with furs from the Great Lakes and the Missouri, are shipped to Hamburg and Le Havre. We, however, shall devote our attention to those which are loaded on brigs and schooners, sometimes belonging to John Jacob Astor or to the Astor firm. The vessels clear for the Mediterranean, and sail away through the Straits of Gibraltar and on to the eastern end of the great inland sea. Here at Smyrna part of the China cargo is exchanged for Turkey opium. The brig then turns back on her course to Gibraltar, where the remainder of her China cargo is exchanged for quicksilver, specie and lead, and the vessel clears once more for her home port.

At New York the vessels are unloaded. Some of the opium and quicksilver may be advertised for sale in the New York newspapers, but a large proportion of the products of this Mediterranean cruise—opium, quicksilver, lead and specie—is loaded on board an Astor vessel. Beneath the hatches are also stowed away bales of the choicest furs from the interior of North America, red fox skins, beaver, and land otter furs, much inferior in value to the sea otter and seals of the North West Coast, but still of a type to meet with a ready sale in the Canton fur market. There are also a number of kegs of ginseng and perhaps a little cotton and cochineal. This time the vessel proceeds directly to Canton, sells her cargo for the usual teas, nankeens, silks, chinaware and cassia, and returns at once to New York, having been gone for less than a year. There her cargo is dispensed in much the same way as the cargo of the ship which we followed on her return from the Pacific.

. . .Is it surprising, in view of the number of times that goods are turned over between the departure and the return to New York, and the unsophisticated character [from a commercial point of view] of at least two of the nationalities from which Astor obtained the most important types of the commodities utilized in this commerce— from the Indians furs and from the Hawaiians sandalwood—that Astor became a multimillionaire of commerce at a time when simple millionaires were a rarity? Of course we must not forget that all this process was not as simple as it may sound. This program itself required careful planning based on long and hazardous experience, wise selection of subordinates, and a large capital which had been amassed from literally nothing by means of hard labor and the same foresight and willingness to venture on a small scale which he was now exhibiting in a large field. Otherwise Astor would not have emerged from the ruck of China merchants.[2]

After the war Astor's fur trade grew along the lines which he had planned at the time of the organization of the American Fur Company in 1808. Though the Astoria enterprise had proved a failure at the hands of the Canadians, the Treaty of Ghent and an act of 1816 requiring the licensing of alien traders on the soil of the United States made it easier to get the North West Company to agree in that same year to the extension of the 1811 agreement for another five years. In the following year when a gigantic struggle broke out between North West and the Hudson's Bay Company, Astor was able to buy out the Canadian interest in the South West Company. After 1817, the American Fur Company's major remaining competitors were the veteran trading firms that operated out of St. Louis.

Astor had two policies with respect to his rivals in the fur trade. First, individual traders and small, weak companies would be speedily and ruthlessly crushed by means of the force of his financial and political power. The more efficient of the vanquished might be employed by Astor or allowed to trade on shares. But if a company put up a stubborn fight, rather than waste time and money, Astor usually bought out or admitted the concern to the American Fur Company on fairly generous terms.

---

[2]Porter, *Astor* 2, pp. 662–665.

Second, it was always the object of Astor and the American Fur Company to stand well with the government. Astor's friendship with President Monroe was close, and Governor Cass of Michigan Territory did much to help keep out alien competition and otherwise to assist in the Northern Department. Significant is the fact that Senator Benton of Missouri was at one and the same time attorney for the American Fur Company and leader of the opposition which destroyed the government factory system, a system of government trading posts which carried on trade with the Indians and therefore competed with Astor.

Astor has especially been accused of flaunting the law in debauching the Indians with whiskey. As a matter of fact, however, there is some evidence to support the conclusion that Astor at first was opposed to selling liquor to the Indian trappers. Possibly he believed that liquor lowered their efficiency and therefore their usefulness to him. Possibly also, he believed that he could outcompete his rivals so long as barter was carried on with the imported goods which he could obtain so cheaply. But the very fact that Astor had such a competitive advantage made other traders depend on liquor as a tool in the trade. Astor at first urged strict enforcement of the law that forbade the sale of intoxicants to Indians, but, when enforcement appeared impossible, he set out to beat his rivals at rum selling.

It was Astor's policy to secure the most efficient men for his organization. When he revived the American Fur Company in 1815, he brought in two veterans of the fur company, Ramsay Crooks and Robert Stuart. Both were given positions of great responsibility. Crooks became Astor's general assistant with particular responsibility for the Western Department, which had its headquarters in St. Louis, and Stuart headed the Northern Department with its base at Mackinac Island. Both became partners in the American Fur Company, with Crooks receiving 5 and then 20 of the 100 shares outstanding, and Stuart getting 5. As others came into the partnership they normally took either 2 1/2 or 5 shares. In addition the partners received salaries up to $2,000 a year.

For the subordinate positions the most successful traders were chosen, men who knew the business, who had influence with the Indians, and who were unscrupulous as traders. Some of the agents of the company were notorious for their lawlessness and their ruthless methods. Life on the frontier was rough and rugged and held particular attraction for the hard-bitten type of man.

By the force of its strength, the American Fur Company drove toward monopoly. Its first victory was in the region of the Great Lakes, which in 1822 became the Northern Department with Stuart as its head. In the same year the Western Department was organized with headquarters at St. Louis. In 1827, the last serious rival at St. Louis, Bernard Pratte & Company, became a partner in the Western Department, sharing equally with the American Fur Company in the profits or losses on the Mississippi below Prairie du Chien (Wisconsin) and on the Missouri and its tributaries. Also, in that same year the Columbia Fur Company, veteran and ruthless traders operating in both the Northern and Western Departments, became partners in the American Fur Company in establishing the Upper Missouri Outfit (to be managed by the leading partner in the Columbia Fur Company).

When opposition to the American Fur Company had been driven off in a given area, the territory was organized as a part of a department, and responsibility was definitely allocated. As heads of departments, Stuart, Crooks, and to some extent the St. Louis partners were responsible to Astor. The head of each outfit, or subdivision, was responsible to those in charge of the department, the clerks at trading posts were under the trader who managed the outfit, and the *engagés*, who went out for furs, were the humble servitors of the trading post clerk.

Astor profited from the fur trade in several ways. As a partner in the American Fur Company, he participated in its profits. As a partner in John Jacob Astor & Son, he purchased goods to be used in the fur trade and sold furs for the American Fur Company in the large markets, for which he received a commission and expenses. As an individual, he furnished capital to the fur company, on which he received interest.

The returns to Astor were respectable. From 1817 to 1823, when the competitive war was on, his profits from the American Fur Company were not great. But for over a decade beginning in 1823, the company made good profits. It is estimated that from the operations of the fur company in the years 1817–1834 Astor "cleared in dividends, interest, commissions, etc., not less than a million dollars, and probably nearer two million."

These profits were apparently made mostly in the Indian country. As the Astor concern acquired strength, it virtually subjected the traders and made them purchase goods at whatever prices the former thought proper. Credit terms were dictated and furs purchased on the same principle.

It must not be gathered that Astor's success came only from bludgeoning his competitors. "It had been," says Porter, "through sheer perseverance, foresight, and a process of profiting by the mistakes of himself and of others that Astor had become the wielder of this tremendous capital which now made him king of the fur trade." Those very qualities served him well in that trade. No one excelled him as a buyer of goods or as a seller of furs. He dominated the fur market in New York and Canton; and even in London, where he met the competition of the powerful Hudson's Bay Company, his position was a commanding one.

One of the significant things about Astor's career is the fact that on several occasions, when a certain business seemed still to be profitable, he withdrew from it. In 1823, he began to withdraw from the China trade conducted in his own vessels, and by 1825, his withdrawal was practically complete. In the very next year there was a heavy fall in the tea market. Had he foreseen the results of overexpansion in the China trade? His withdrawal from the Pacific trade came only a short time later; in fact, the Pacific trade could hardly exist alone. The exhaustion of sandalwood, following a period of reckless cutting of the wood to meet the king's heavy debts, caused a collapse of that trade in Hawaii and struck a mortal blow to the business.

In 1834, Astor withdrew from the American Fur Company. He had for some time talked of retiring. Though he complained of the state of the fur business, the fact that he had passed three score and ten and was in ill health probably accounted sufficiently for his retirement. His interest in the Western Department was sold to Pratte, Chouteau & Co. of St. Louis, and the Northern Department was taken over by a group headed by Ramsay Crooks. By 1835, after a short period of liquidation, Astor had ended his connection with the fur trade and with commerce, the business in which he had been engaged for fifty years. It is worth noting that within seven years the Northern Department, under Ramsay Crooks, was in bankruptcy.

## Astor's Investments, Principally Real Estate

In his fur trade and foreign trade, Astor was a business man of the old order. In his interest in railroads, banks, insurance companies, hotels, theaters, and real estate in general, he was making a transition to the new order by investing in the many specialized ventures that were growing out of the industrial revolution.

Astor seems to have followed closely the rise of new investment opportunities. From his purchase of a share in the Tontine Coffee House in 1792 in New York until late in his life, he is known to have invested in a number of insurance companies. From 1816 to 1838, he was sufficiently interested in insurance at various times to hold directorships in one or more of four companies, but he was never heavily interested in this field as compared with some of his other types of investments.

Like most moneyed men of his time, Astor was interested in banking. As early as 1791, he held shares in New York's first bank. He took an active part in the organization of the Second Bank of the United States and became one of its directors, representing the government as well as president of the New York branch. From 1819 to 1826, he took little part in American banking since he spent most of his time in Europe. At some time or other after 1829, he purchased stock of more than a dozen banking institutions. A large part of his investment was in banks in Albany, Utica, Oswego, and Rochester, but he also invested heavily in the banks of New York City. In his will were mentioned from 500 up to 1,604 shares in such corporations as the Bank of North America, the Manhattan Co., the Merchants Bank, and the Mechanics Bank, the first named a Philadelphia bank and the other three of New York.

About the same time that Astor retired from shipping, he became interested in advancing inland transportation, at first canals but principally railroads. He participated in 1828 in financing the Mohawk & Hudson Railroad, taking 500 out of 3,000 shares and serving as a director. In the next 20 years his investments in transportation were few but not small—for instance, 70 shares of the Camden & Amboy, investment in the Philadelphia & Trenton, and a loan to the Delaware-Raritan Canal of $150,000. For some time after the panic of 1837, he was not particularly interested in railroads, but by 1847, he was convinced that they had good promise and started to invest heavily in them shortly before his death.

Another form of investment in which Astor became interested was the bonds of municipalities, states, and the federal government. In the 30s he purchased United States securities in Europe below par to hold till they were to be redeemed shortly thereafter. The retirement of the United States debt during Jackson's administration ended Astor's investment in the early federal loans. The Mexican War loans again placed federal securities on the market, and Astor bought heavily, probably for trust funds for his heirs.

Astor similarly invested in state "stocks." In 1826 and 1828, he bought $1,100,000 of Ohio 6 percent bonds. These rose considerably after he had acquired them. He also invested heavily in Pennsylvania loans and took smaller amounts of loans of Louisiana, Massachusetts, Indiana, and other states.

The outstanding investment interest of Astor was real estate. In this he was following the general practice of the general merchant, who in earlier times, since there were few (if any) bonds available for investment, had characteristically turned to land for the investing of his surplus capital. During his whole business career, Astor invested in lands. At first, this was merely a side interest, he purchased land when he thought an especially good opportunity presented itself, or he acquired it on mortgage. In the last years of his life, real estate came to be Astor's dominating interest, partly because his son and business heir, William B. Astor, was very successful in that area.

Two interests closely related to Astor's activities in lands need be noted. In 1806, in company with another New Yorker, he bought the Park Street Theatre for $50,000, and in 1828, he bought the City Hotel, the largest in New York. Even more important was the erection in 1834 of the Astor Hotel (at first the Park). The hotel contained 300 rooms and was valued at $750,000.

Astor's real estate interest was, however, chiefly in lands and not in improvements on them. Indeed, it is notable that he rarely improved the lands which he owned and was sometimes accused of holding lots that were an eyesore to their neighbors.

The real estate ventures which made Astor a rich and famous landlord were those which took place on Manhattan Island. Up to 1820, the bulk of Astor's real estate was purchased with profits from his commercial business. There is a close correlation between the rise and fall in land investments and changes in income from the China and fur trades. From 1820 to 1834, however, another source of funds for land investments became of much greater importance, that is, the income from real estate. During that period Astor's income from land investments was sufficient to finance the $445,000 that he put into property. Then, from 1835 until his death, Astor's income from rents alone was more than the amount invested in land.

It has been said that Astor secured his lands at unreasonably low cost through foreclosures, through purchases from indigent heirs, and through the acquisition of tidewater lots from New York City at a low valuation. In fact most of Astor's real estate on Manhattan was acquired by purchase in fee simple, although he did acquire property in all of the above-mentioned ways. During his entire career Astor became owner of 70 pieces of property by foreclosure, but these foreclosures were only 70 out of the 500 mortgages held by Astor at one time or another. Most of Astor's foreclosures followed the depression of 1837. Frequently Astor carried mortgages beyond the time agreed upon, provided the mortgagor maintained his interest payments; if the mortgagor failed to pay interest, Astor foreclosed promptly.

Astor also acquired land worth well over $100,000 from George Clinton of New York, who had spent himself into insolvency through his political activities, and from Clinton's more or less distressed heirs. There is some truth in the statement that Astor bought much of his land during the depressed periods. In the three depression years 1837–39, he invested in Manhattan real estate an annual average of $160,000, which was four times as much as the annual average of the other two periods when he was active in the real estate market—1800–09 and 1826–34. One statement that is frequently made in connection with Astor's real estate ventures is pure fiction, however. This is the assertion that once having bought, he never sold. During his lifetime Astor spent $1,788,342.44 on property purchases; some of this property he in turn sold for a total of $986,129.36, though no doubt at a substantial profit.

Two types of leases also figure in Astor's real estate ventures. In 1803–05, he purchased the Trinity Church leases from Aaron Burr, who was forced to sell because of debt. The parcel of somewhat over 241 lots was purchased at approximately $120,000, the lease to expire in 1866. The other was the lease of water lots from the city; that is, Astor was given the right to reclaim land under water which bordered on land owned by him. In 1806–29, he received 12 or 15 grants, for which he usually agreed to pay $32.50 annually. The understanding was that Astor should fill up the lots and otherwise improve them; but he did not do as agreed, and sometimes the lots became public nuisances.

In acquiring Manhattan real estate, Astor had a definite policy as to the location of his lands. He did not generally buy the highest priced lands in the heart of the city, but he chose rather to buy far enough out so that prices were still low and yet in a location close enough to the center so that the land would soon be in greater demand.

When Astor died in 1848, his property was estimated to be worth from $20,000,000 to $30,000,000. He was the first American to leave a fortune valued in eight figures (Stephen Girard of Philadelphia left about $7,500,000 on his death in 1831), and the Astor family remained the richest in the country until the Vanderbilt fortune was established.

All agreed that the greatest source of Astor's wealth was to be found in the increase in value of his lands on Manhattan Island. It was through his almost unique vision of the future of New York City that he was able to invest his profits from trade so that with little personal exertion he became the richest man in America. Just before he died, Astor is said to have made the statement, "Could I begin life again, knowing what I know, and had the money to invest, I would buy every foot of land on the Island of Manhattan."

# APPENDIX A

 *A Discussion of Accounting in the Mercantile World of the Early National Period*

What follows is a discussion of how accounts were kept in the firm of the wealthy Baltimore merchant, Robert Oliver. In its essentials, Oliver's system is probably typical of that of other major merchants such as Astor.

## Accounting

Price and market information came to the Oliver countinghouse from outside sources. Inside the office, however, lay thick Journals and Ledgers and other bookkeeping records of the firm's transactions. Meticulously kept by the double-entry system of bookkeeping, these records were indispensable to the routine management of business. They informed the Olivers how much they owed, and to whom; how much others owed them, and when the payments were due. They showed the firm where its capital was, and in what forms: how much was in goods of various kinds, in claims against debtors at home and abroad, in the counting-house and warehouse, in stocks, cash, and in the bank; and they showed changes in form and value wrought by daily business . . .

The accounts also constituted a record of past investments and their results. Did information on past gains and losses help Oliver decide what goods to buy and where to ship them?

The question must be answered in the negative. In the first place, a very large number of "Adventure" accounts, the type of account usually employed to record the costs and sales proceeds of shipments did not show the net outcome of a voyage. Whenever the Olivers imported or exported in a vessel they owned wholly or in part — and such shipments were very numerous — some of the costs of the voyage were recorded in other types of accounts. The value of the cargo, costs of loading it on board, and insurance on the goods, were charged the Adventure account. But the cost of the vessel and her outfits, insurance, and expenditures for repairs were entered in an account erected in the name of the vessel. And to a Vessel Expense account were charged the wages of captain and crew, costs of stores and supplies, and such miscellaneous expenses as consular fees and fees paid harbor masters to stow the cargo. These various costs were sometimes consolidated. In general, vessel expenses were transferred from the Vessel Expense account to the Vessel account as soon as voyage costs were known. And sometimes the balance of gain or loss from the Adventure account was transferred to the Vessel account. But as a rule, Adventure and Vessel accounts were independently closed to Profit & Loss. The net result of the voyage emerged only after the latter was itself closed to the partners' Capital accounts: but it almost never emerged as a separate entry.

The number of instances is also large where even the gross profit or loss of what is essentially one venture is found partly in one account, and partly in another. When the Olivers bought flour, for example, they charged the purchase price to a Flour account. But when they exported it they sometimes valued it at a figure higher than cost. When they did so, part of the profit was in the Flour account, and the other part in the Adventure account. Sometimes the article sold for less than the value assigned to it at the time of export. In either case the actual gross gain or loss emerged only after both the Commodity and Adventure accounts had been closed to Profit & Loss, and the latter to Capital.

The difficulty in determining the gross profit of a voyage becomes insoluble in many of the instances in which the Olivers imported a cargo and later re-exported all or most of it. The Olivers preferred selling their imports in Baltimore, but it was often necessary to go into new ventures to get clear of them. In one instance they were obliged to sell a cargo by making eight reshipments to different ports. Examples of multiple re-exports are numerous. The cost of the cargo was entered in the Adventure-of-import account. The value of reshipped parcels was entered in the Adventure-of-re-export accounts. Frequently it is impossible, in the first place, to determine whether or not the re-exports were valued at cost. And in the second place it is frequently impossible to determine the prices at which they were sold abroad. For they were often re-exported along with other goods, and no record kept on the proceeds of the separate parcels.

Consider the case of the ship *Harmony*, which brought a coffee cargo from Batavia. Its cost was charged to the "Adventure to the East Indies" account. After her arrival in Baltimore in March 1798 a very small quantity of coffee was sold locally. Almost all of it was re-shipped to Rotterdam in April 1798, and to Emden in October 1798. At the time of these re-exports the Olivers apparently valued the coffee at the rate they were then selling it for in Baltimore, crediting the East Indian account for these sums. Having thus disposed of the *Harmony's* inward cargo they calculated they had made a "gain on her . . . Voyage" of $23,839. But in truth it was a gain not on the voyage, but on the East Indian Adventure account. The gain from the importation cannot in logic be calculated apart from the results of the re-exports, for these were the means by which almost all the incoming cargo was sold. It is impossible to determine the amount of this gain because the coffee was sent to Emden along with other cargo, and while the net proceeds of the entire cargo is a matter of record, the proceeds of the Batavian coffee alone were unknown.

In sum, many Adventure accounts reveal the gross profit of a voyage, but in many instances the gross profit is found partly in a Commodity account and partly in an Adventure account. Often the gross profit is in two or more Adventure accounts; often it cannot be determined at all. These complexities are compounded by the Olivers' practice of using an Adventure account to record the costs and sales proceeds not of one voyage, but of two or more. Their "Adventure to Vera Cruz" account ran for three and a half years before being closed to Profit & Loss, and the resulting gain came from a very large number of shipments. In view of the uncertainties generated by the interrelationships of accounts pertaining to a single investment, one can often refer with confidence not to the profit or loss of a particular venture, but only to the gross result of a particular account . . .

## Investment Decisions

Very frequently, then, Oliver could not have consulted any single account to ascertain the net result of a particular venture. This is sufficient reason to believe that he did not base his investment decisions on bookkeeping records of past gain or loss. But this is quite a distinct matter from his desire to assemble, at the time he was considering an investment decision, the various factors of cost that would affect the net profit of a voyage. That he wished to know the net profit a contemplated venture would yield is clearly shown by a detail calculation made for the benefit of John Craig in May 1797. He planned to send the *Harmony* to Batavia for a return cargo, a voyage he expected would require nine months, and to send out $24,000 in specie which to purchase it. Inviting Craig to take a one-third interest in the venture, he proceeded to outline "the actual profits of such a voyage." The *Harmony* would carry 500,000 pounds of either coffee or sugar, on the assumption that the return cargo would consist of 250,000 pounds of each, the costs in Batavia and expected sales price in Baltimore would leave the net profit shown in Table IX. (Oliver figured on $60,000 in insurance because the cost of the sugar, coffee, vessel and outfits, and of the insurance itself, amounted approximately to that total.)

Oliver also made alternative calculations on the assumption that the return cargo would consist entirely of sugar, or entirely of coffee. In these calculations all rates of cost and sales remained the same. A sugar cargo would cost double the sum given in the table, or $16,666, and one of coffee would cost $45,000. While sugar alone would cost less than a combined cargo, and the cost of insurance would be less, the sales proceeds would also be less, with the result that the cargo would yield only $23,662. Exactly opposite conditions would obtain in the case of a cargo solely of coffee, and the profit would amount to $33,600.

In sum, we have on the one hand a merchant who calculated the net profit of a contemplated venture, and on the other a set of records so kept that it was frequently difficult or impossible to determine the amount of it. From the point of view of the bases of Oliver's investment decisions the inconsistency is unimportant. Common sense suggests, and no evidence negates the view that gains or loss from a past investment could not be considered in the light of changed conditions. Gain or loss in the past had derived from the difference between purchase and sales prices. What mattered was not past prices and their results, but present and future prices: not past, but current market information, and sound judgment. In

## TABLE IX

**Oliver's Calculation of Net Profits From a Cargo of Batavian Sugar and Coffee (May 1797)**

| *Costs* | | *Sales Proceeds* | |
|---|---|---|---|
| $22,500 — | 250,000 lbs. coffee @ 9¢ p. lb. "on board" [i.e., charges included] | $55,000 — | of coffee (@ 27¢ p lb. or 22¢ "clear of duty") |
| 8,333 — | 250,000 lbs sugar @ 3-1/3¢ p lb. "inclug.g charges" at Batavia. | 32,364 — | of sugar (@ $16 p 112 lbs, or $14.50 minus duty). |
| 10,000 — | cost of vessel | 10,000 — | of the vessel. |
| 8,000 — | outfits "including Coppering." | | |
| 12,000 — | insurance on $60,000 out & home, @ 20%. | | |
| 2,000 — | wages of supercargo. | | |
| 1,200 — | expenses at Batavia. | | |
| 4,800 — | wages of crew, @ $400 p month. | | |
| $68,633 — | [sic] Total Costs. | $97,364 | Total Proceeds |
| | Net Profit: | $28,731 | |

1804 the Olivers wrote houses in London and Liverpool: "Experience having satisfied us that England is generally a bad Market for our exports we determin'd many years ago to make no more Shipments to that quarter. . . . It is not likely that we shall ever make any Shipments to England. . . . " At the same time, they acknowledged that "circumstances" might "induce us to change our minds." Two years later they exported cochineal to London. Experience was of far less importance than fresh news.

Source: Stuart W. Bruchey, *Robert Oliver, Merchant of Baltimore* (Baltimore: The Johns Hopkins University Press, 1956), pp. 135–41.

# APPENDIX B1

 *Chronology of Astor's Life and Career*

| | |
|---|---|
| 1763 | Born in Waldorf, Germany, in the Rhineland. |
| 1777 | Confirmed in Lutheran Church; left school to help father. |
| 1779–83 | Worked in London. |
| 1784 | In April came to New York. Returned to London to sell furs he had bought. |
| 1785 | Married Sarah Todd in New York. |
| 1786 | Set up small shop for sale of musical instruments and carried on fur business. |
| 1788 | Fur trade became Astor's leading business interest. Bought furs in Montreal to ship to London and Rotterdam. |
| 1789 | Made his first two purchases of New York real estate. |
| 1794 | Bought land in New York's back country. |
| 1795 | Jay's Treaty opened direct trade with Canada and required the British to give up frontier posts on United States territory. |
| 1797 | Astor's importing business included dry goods, cutlery, powder, and shot. |
| 1799 | Began to advertise sale of Oriental goods. |
| 1800 | Said to be worth $250,000. Owned share in vessel sent to China. Began to invest more heavily in New York City real estate. |
| 1807–08 | Foreign trade checked by international difficulties and embargo. |
| 1808 | American Fur Company organized by Astor with capital of $1 million. |
| 1808–09 | Astor's *Beaver* sent to China despite embargo, returning with cargo of teas, silks, and nankeens. |
| 1810 | Pacific Fur Company with capital of $400,000 organized to establish Astoria on the Northwest Coast. |
| 1811 | Post established at Astoria. The South West Company organized by Astor and partners of the Michilimackinac Company. |
| 1812–14 | Astor's business badly damaged by the war. |

| | |
|---|---|
| 1813 | Bought $2 million of a United States loan. Astoria and Pacific Fur Company gave way to British. |
| 1816 | Act passed giving Americans monopoly on fur trade in United States. Astor gained foothold in St. Louis and extended his interests in the Pacific. |
| 1817 | Astor purchased full control of the South West Company. |
| 1819–48 | Astor left work of management chiefly to son, who had become his partner in 1815. |
| 1822 | United States "factories" for trade with Indians closed. |
| 1825 | Astor discontinued using his own ships in the China trade, except for a brief period in 1827. |
| 1828 | Astor's Pacific trade brought to a close. Had monopoly of fur trade in United States. |
| 1834 | Withdrew from American Fur Company. |
| 1834–48 | Interested exclusively in investments and lending money on real estate security. |
| 1848 | Died, leaving a fortune of about $20 million. |

# APPENDIX B2

## *Chronology of Selected World Events in This Period*

| | |
|---|---|
| 1763 | Peace of Paris. Complete British victory in French and Indian War. Tightening of imperial economic system. |
| 1775–83 | American Revolution. |
| 1787 | Constitution ratified. |
| 1787–91 | Completion of the process of ratification by the original thirteen states. |
| 1790–91 | Hamilton presents his economic program. |
| 1792 | Establishment of the Republic of France. |
| 1792 to 1815 | Wars of the French Revolution and Napoleon. Worldwide impact on trade patterns. The United States becomes the great neutral carrier. |
| 1795 | Jay's Treaty with Britain makes possible direct trade with Canada. |
| Mar. 1802 to May 1803 | Temporary peace in the French wars. |
| 1803 | Louisiana Purchase. |
| 1803–06 | Lewis and Clark Expedition. |
| 1807–10 | Embargo and other trade restrictions. |
| 1811 | Trade with Britain stopped. |
| 1812–15 | War of 1812 with Britain. |
| 1815 to 1914 | No great international wars. |

# CASE 4

# *The Rise of New York Port* *

*I have listened with some degree of grief and surprise to opinions expressed in this House in deprecation of the favors claimed to be showered upon the locality which I in part represent. Sir, nothing which conduces to the advantage of the commerce of that great metropolis is or can be local in its nature; it is as important and general as commerce itself, universally absorbing. . . . Sir, it is nature and not art that constitutes the great emporium of trade. You might as well try to dip up and roll back Niagara with the hand as to turn aside the natural currents of commerce. New York enjoys her advantages, not by reason of the artificial influences of legislation, but because she sits enthroned, the queen of the seas. Into her lap flow the tides of commerce, because commerce follows the avenues and obeys the impulses of profit.*

**John Cochrane of New York speaking in
the House of Representatives in favor
of a renewal of the federal subsidy to
the financially troubled Collins
Packet Line, 1858.**

*This case was prepared by Assistant Professor Richard S. Tedlow, as a basis for class discussion rather than to illustrate either effective or ineffective handling of an administrative situation.

Harvard Business School case 384–023, rev. 6/84.

*[T]he direct trade which was her own by every law of commerce and nature, and which should have grown and increased every year, grew less and less until it almost disappeared, being by this unpropitious policy transferred to the northern ports and people. . . . The importing merchants of the South became almost an extinct race, and her direct trade, once so great, flourishing and rich, dwindled down to insignificance. . . . The South thus stands in the attitude of feeding from her own bosom a vast population of merchants, shipowners, capitalists, and others, who without the claims of her progeny drink up the life-blood of her trade.*

**Report of a Commercial Convention at Charleston, South Carolina in 1839.**

## Introduction: Cities in the Wilderness

Large cities were slow to grow in North America. In 1790, only 24 places could boast a population of greater than 2,500, and only one out of 20 citizens of the new nation lived within their limits. In 1700, when there were more than a half million people living in London, the largest city in North America was Boston, with about 6,000. Blessed with a fine harbor, which was accessible to a variety of products including agricultural produce, lumber, and fish, Boston developed into the leading colonial entrepôt. Its shrewd merchants took care to maintain their credit with English exporters while developing trade relations with a variety of places.

By 1720, Boston with its 10,000 inhabitants had nearly twice the population of the next two largest cities. Its urban preeminence persisted into the third quarter of the 18th century, when it was relinquished to Philadelphia, which was able to exploit its location near the rich agricultural regions of the Middle Atlantic states. Table 1 provides population statistics for five cities from 1750 to 1790.

In the Revolutionary era, it was Philadelphia which seemed to be the city of destiny in North America. Its "unchallenged commercial supremacy" on the continent was surpassed in the British Empire as a whole by only London and Bristol.

Among Philadelphia's strengths was its merchant population. Many were Quakers, a sect which placed great emphasis on truthful dealing. This bias toward honesty was a particularly important asset in an age in which communications from ship to shore were virtually nonexistent, and expensive vessels with valuable cargos might be absent from their home port for two to three years. Philadelphia's

**TABLE 1**

Urban Population: 1750–1790

| Year Founded | Philadelphia 1682 | New York 1624 | Boston 1630 | Charleston 1680 | Baltimore 1730 |
|---|---|---|---|---|---|
| 1750 | 13,400 | 13,300 | 15,731 | 8,000 | c.100 |
| 1770 | 28,000 | 21,000 | 15,520 | 10,863 | c.5,000 |
| 1790 | 42,444 | 33,131 | 18,038 | 16,359 | 13,503 |

Source: Richard B. Morris, *Encyclopedia of American History* (New York: Harper & Row, 1976), p. 648.

Quaker merchants were in effect one branch of a worldwide network of adherents to their denomination. Many in this network were members of large extended families, and thus ties of blood and those of faith operated together to create a relationship of trust which facilitated the pursuit of commercial transactions.

The advantage of Philadelphia's location close to the heartland of the continent has already been mentioned. The city itself was (and, of course, still is) located about a hundred miles up the Delaware River from the open sea, thus providing plentiful protection from ocean gales for the ships in its harbor.

This location was not, however, without problems. First, a bar just below the city cut the depth of water to 18 feet even at high tide. As ships grew larger during the pre-Civil War period, some of the largest found access to the port problematical. Neither Boston nor Portland, Maine, suffered any constraints in this regard while the main ship channel into New York Harbor provided 23 feet of clearance even at low tide. Depth of clearance was, however, a problem for various other ports. Baltimore's controlling clearance was 18 feet. Charleston's varied with the tides from 12 to 17 feet; Savannah's from 7 to 14 feet; Mobile's from 10 to 11 feet; and New Orleans's from 13 to 14 feet.

Fog was not a severe problem for Philadelphia, but ice was. Due to its slow current, the Delaware froze more often than the Hudson or East Rivers. The port was closed, for example, for 50 days in 1817 and 52 in 1822, during which periods marine notices such as the following were not uncommon: "Ship *Nautilus,* 65 days from Liverpool, belonging to Philadelphia, put in here [New York City] on account of ice."

Despite such problems, it is highly questionable whether at the time of independence, the dispassionate observer would have declared it "inevitable" that New York rather than Philadelphia, Boston, or the awakening Baltimore, at the head of the Chesapeake, would become America's "great commercial emporium." The Revolutionary War itself had had a cataclysmic effect on New York City and the state of which it was a part:

> No other state suffered more for the cause of independence than did New York. Its frontiers blazed constantly in guerilla warfare. Armies marched and countermarched through its principal river valleys, strewing death and destruction behind them. Nearly one-third of the engagements of the war were fought on New York soil. New York City, which controlled most of the commerce of the state, was continuously in enemy hands from 1776 until 1783. Two major fires destroyed many buildings in the great seaport.
>
> No history can adequately portray the cost of independence in terms of human suffering. The conclusion of hostilities brought little respite. Roads, factories, farms and business houses essential to the economy had been destroyed or damaged. Many of the old trade connections enjoyed by New York City had been lost. The currency was unstable and inflation stalked the land. Mistrust and hatred of the loyalists who remained in the state ran high. New Yorkers who found their courage and resourcefulness heavily taxed during the Revolution faced equally serious problems at the war's end.[1]

---

[1]David M. Ellis, James A. Frost, Harold C. Syrett, and Harry J. Carman, *A History of New York State* (Ithaca, N.Y.: Cornell University Press, 1967), p. 118.

From this prostrate condition, far more characteristic of the vanquished in war rather than the victorious, New York City became the greatest urban center of the United States and one of the greatest of the world. Its population surpassed that of Philadelphia by 1810, and by 1860, it contained 36,000 more inhabitants than Philadelphia and Baltimore (the nation's third city) combined. (See Exhibit 1.) Its total registered tonnage in 1860 amounted to 1,464,000, accounting for 27 percent of the nation's total, over three times as great as that of its nearest rival, Boston. In that year, tonnage entered at New York was 1,973,000, 24 percent of the national total and about two and three quarters that of runner-up Boston. Tonnage cleared for foreign ports was 1,678,000, 19 percent of the national total and almost twice that of runner-up New Orleans. In dollar terms, New York's leadership became no less impressive. It accounted in 1860 for more than two thirds of the nation's imports, while over one third of exports passed through its wharves. (See Exhibit 2.) The last indicator of commercial supremacy deserving note is immigration. An estimated 5,457,914 aliens chose to come to the United States from 1820 to 1860. Of this number, 3,742,532 came through New York. New Orleans, the next leading entrepôt, accounted for 555,322.

What explains this remarkable performance? Indeed, what makes a great port?

The characteristics of the geographic location of a port are a good place to begin in discussing inter-port competition for America's international trade. In the age of sail, when an "average" vessel on an "average" day might cover 100 miles (but far less than that near shore),[2] proximity to other trading ports and to the open sea was important. Mileage data are provided in Exhibit 3, and marine insurance rates in Exhibit 4.

The characteristics of the site itself are critically important also. Problems of ice, fog, and shelter have already been noted. In addition, a port needed not only sufficient depth of water but relative ease in locating the channel where that depth lay. Furthermore, the port needed space which would enable it to expand as its business did.

Superb on some of these dimensions, New York was seriously deficient on none of them. Most remarkable was the site of the port itself. (See Exhibit 5.) New York was virtually landlocked, yet it was accessible to the open sea from two directions: Lower New York Bay and Long Island Sound. It was thus a rare day that ill winds and tides would keep all ships out of the harbor. Furthermore, the fact that Manhattan was a narrow island meant that there was a lot of wharf space available near a central business district. Lastly, the channels into the port were relatively easy to locate. An indication of these great natural characteristics is that of the $800 million spent in national river and harbor appropriations up to 1911, only $21 million was allocated to New York.

---

[2]Speed, of course, depended on wind and current, especially the former. Prevailing winds were west to east, north of 30° latitude and east to west, south of it.

# National Growth

In order to facilitate an understanding of how New York City attained its commercial preeminence, this case will present a discussion of developments in international and domestic trade. First, however, these developments should be placed in context through a very brief discussion, supplemented by exhibits, of the nation's expansion in terms of population and area.

From 1700 to 1860, America's population grew at a rate of approximately 3 percent per year. Probably no other country in the history of the world has sustained such a high growth rate over such an extended period of time. (For population statistics by region, see Exhibit 6.) In addition, the physical size of the nation increased more than threefold from the Revolution to the Civil War (see Exhibits 7A and B).

In his first inaugural address, delivered in 1801 prior to this territorial expansion, Thomas Jefferson exhorted his fellow citizens to rejoice in "possessing a chosen country, with room enough for our descendants to the thousandth and thousandth generation. . . ." In an era in which it took 75 days for a wagon loaded with cotton cards and pulled by a team of four horses to journey from Worcester, Massachusetts, to Charleston, South Carolina; an era in which it was more expensive to send freight 30 miles inland by road (as opposed to by river) than to London; an era in which, in the words of an 1816 report by a United States Senate Committee, "A coal mine may exist in the United States not more than 10 miles from valuable ores of iron and other materials, and both of them be useless until a canal is established between them, as the price of land carriage is too great to be borne by either"; an era in which grain grown in the Old Northwest had to make a 3,000-mile trip down the Ohio and Mississippi and thence by coasting vessel to market in the seacoast cities in the Northeast; an era in which, to quote a leading historian of the period, "travel and transportation [were carried on] by methods surprisingly little changed from the days of the Phoenicians";[3] in such an era, Jefferson's observation was more than understandable. As a distinguished British historian once observed, however, one must always remember that events which are now in the past were once in the future. No one could have foreseen the dramatic growth which took place, growth driven by the Industrial Revolution, demography, technological innovation, and entrepreneurship.

# International Trade

The most important factor in international trade between the Revolution and the Civil War and indeed a development of world-historical importance in the charting of pathways to the present was the Industrial Revolution in Britain. Ever since Adam took a bite from the apple, the problem of clothing the human race had

---

[3]George Rogers Taylor, *The Transportation Revolution, 1815–1860* (New York: Harper & Row, 1951), p. 5.

been a major one. Transforming sheep fleece or balls of cotton from raw material to finished product was a laborious, many-faceted task which was often quite unpleasant. Through the Middle Ages to the early modern era, this manufacture had been carried on in cottages and on farms where individuals spun yarn and wove cloth independent of centralized supervision. Toward the end of the 18th century in Britain, however, a series of seminal inventions brought mechanization to these processes. In 1769, Arkwright's water frame was patented, as were Hargreaves' spinning jenny and Crompton's mule in the following decade. In 1784, the power loom was invented and greatly improved in the two decades that followed. Meanwhile, an instrument maker to the University of Glasgow named James Watt scored a breakthrough in harnessing steam power, and he patented his steam engine in 1769. By 1782, a rotary steam engine was being used to power machinery. The results were vast economies in textile manufacture which made England the workshop of the world.

To feed its hungry mills, Britain needed many raw materials, of which cotton was perhaps the most important. About three million pounds were imported in 1751 and somewhat under five million 20 years later. In 1861, imports had skyrocketed to 1,261.4 billion pounds. At the same time, exports of British manufacturers of all descriptions rose from £45,000 in 1751 to £46,800,000 110 years later.

America's role in that segment of the Industrial Revolution falling between the War of 1812 and the Civil War was twofold. First, its rapid growth meant increasing demands for imports. Second, it provided cotton, the commodity which fueled the industry of the 19th century as oil did of the 20th. For data on the importance of cotton to the American export trade in comparison to other items, see Exhibit 9.

The end of the Napoleonic Wars in 1815 marked the end of more than two decades of disruption in world trade. At this time, New York, Boston, Philadelphia, and the rapidly growing Baltimore "were more evenly matched than they were ever to be again."[4] New York's strengths up to this point, in addition to matters of location already touched upon, included:

■ Greater social mobility: While the mercantile leadership of other major ports tended to be rather homogeneous, New York had a reputation for providing a career open to talents. The city proved hospitable to English merchants such as Jeremiah Thompson, whose uncle owned woolen mills in Yorkshire, and Benjamin Marshall, another Yorkshire native, who exported raw cotton and imported manufactured cotton goods from Lancashire.

■ A superior medium in specie and paper money for both domestic and foreign exchange: Better domestic exchange meant that merchants could take payment in money rather than in goods they would have to resell; better foreign exchange meant that merchants could pay for English

---

[4]Robert G. Albion, "New York Port and Its Disappointed Rivals, 1815–1860," *Journal of Economic and Business History* III (1931), p. 608.

goods by buying a bill of exchange instead of seeking foreign exchange by dealing with other foreign markets.

■ The Hudson River: Navigable for 150 miles upstream, the Hudson provided a means of tapping a rich hinterland. The Hudson and Mohawk Valleys provided the only sea level route to the West, a route which was blocked by the Iroquois until the War of 1812.

With the coming of peace, a veritable "flotilla" of British and later American ships flooded the American market with woolen and cotton cloth, hardware, cutlery, and various other items of British manufacture.[5] New York was apparently selected for this "dumping" of goods because of its central location and because of the presence of Thompson, Marshall, Isaac Wright, and other Quaker merchants with close connections to Britain.

The arrival of British goods in 1815 sparked an explosion of commercial activity. In order to process this flood of merchandise, new marketing methods had to be developed. Traditionally, the British manufacturer would sell his goods to a British exporter, who would then sell them to an American importer. This latter would await the best price and sell to American retailers. Now, however, the glut of manufactures was such that British producers were retaining title until their products reached New York auction houses. Auctions were nothing new in New York or in other American ports. But they now were becoming far more important in the movement of goods.

By early in 1817, some New Yorkers began to voice concern that British manufacturers might shift their emphasis to other ports. In order to prevent this occurrence, a leading auctioneer, Abraham Thompson, was asked by his colleagues to propose special legislation to the governor which would strengthen the auction system. Thompson boasted that the legislation he proposed would "cause all the Atlantic cities to become tributary to New York." This legislation had two major features. First, duties collected by the state were slashed, on the average, from 3 percent to 1.5 percent. Second, as Thompson explained:

> Every piece of goods offered at auction should be positively sold, and to ensure a sale, the duty should always be paid upon every article offered at auction. . . . The truth was, that both in Boston and Philadelphia, the free and absolute sale of goods by auction was not encouraged. (It did not seem to be understood.) In Philadelphia, goods were allowed to be offered, and withdrawn, free from state duty, and the purchaser went to the auction rooms of that city with no certainty of making his purchases. He was not certain that the goods would be sold to the highest bidder.[6]

The right to run an auction house was a monopoly, restricted to a small group by appointment of the governor. Some large fortunes were made as a result.

---

[5]Robert G. Albion, *The Rise of New York Port* (New York: Charles Scribner's Sons, 1939), p. 12. Much of this case is drawn from Professor Albion's writings.

[6]Robert G. Albion, "New York Port and Its Disappointed Rivals, 1815–1860," *Journal of Economic and Business History* III (1931), p. 609.

The long-term effect of this auction policy is not easy to determine. It is known that in the 1820s, 44 percent of New York's imports passed through auction houses. The following decade, that percentage dropped to 21, although the dollar volume was virtually the same. By the 1840s, the attack on auctioneering by conventional merchants had taken a heavy toll, and the great bulk of New York's goods moved through the traditional channels, making it possible to do business without the violent fluctuations in price which were an inescapable part of the auction system. Nevertheless, some scholars do believe that New York's manipulation of its auction system served to wed to itself British trade at a strategic moment.

A second major postwar development, spurred on by Jeremiah Thompson, in New York's foreign commerce was the establishment of liners which sailed on a regular basis between two ports. Prior to the inauguration of the Black Ball Line in January 1818, ocean shipping had been carried on by transients and regular traders. Transients, or "tramps," sailed from one port to the next picking up and delivering whatever cargos were to be had. Regular traders specialized in a single sea lane between two or perhaps three ports. These ships usually made two round trips per year and were often owned by merchants who used them to move their own goods and filled remaining space with the cargos of others. While operating with more regularity than the transients, the regular traders did not feature coordinated sailings or punctuality. A regular trader departed when its hold was sufficiently filled. This often meant later than (but sometimes before, in special circumstances) the date advertised. As a result, expensive cargos, and passengers as well, would simply have to wait. The lack of coordinated sailings meant that many ships might leave one port for another in a single week while none others would clear for that port for two months.

The sailing packets of the Black Ball Line and those established after it added an important element of predictability to the Atlantic trade. They also added a third sailing, thus providing contact between ports in the winter months, during which regular traders had traditionally lain idle. Very soon, the liners garnered the lion's share of passengers who could afford them and of expensive freight. By 1822, there were four packet lines from New York to Liverpool alone.

Other American ports attempted to establish packet lines of their own, but none met with great success. Philadelphia began liner service to Liverpool in 1821, but while New York had dozens of ships plying this trade only four sailed from Philadelphia through the 1820s. Other ports met with even less success, largely because of the problems of securing sufficient eastbound cargos.

## Domestic Trade

Two major initiatives helped make New York Port the leader in domestic commerce. The first of these was a great engineering achievement, the Erie Canal. The second was less dramatic but no less important, the capture of the cotton trade.

Astute observers had long understood the rewards to be won by the tidewater port which could win the trade of the West. Writing in 1784, George Washington observed:

> The western settlers . . . stand as it were upon a pivot. The touch of a feather would turn them any way. They have looked down the Mississippi . . . for no other reason than because they could glide gently down the stream; without considering, perhaps, the difficulties of the voyage back again, and the time necessary to perform it in; and because they have no other means of coming to us but by long land transportations and unimproved roads. These causes have hitherto checked the industry of the present settlers. . . . But smooth the road, and make easy the way for them, and then see what an influx of articles will be poured upon us; how amazingly our exports will be increased by them, and how amply we shall be compensated for any trouble and expense we may encounter to effect it.[7]

Washington was anxious to win this trade for the Potomac, on the banks of which Mount Vernon stood. This route had the advantage, he wrote, of having tidewater closer to Detroit than the St. Lawrence and the Hudson by 168 miles and 176 miles, respectively. He noted, however, that plans were already afoot in Philadelphia to build a canal which would facilitate transportation to Fort Pitt. Furthermore, that New York would also reach out for western trade as soon as the British finally evacuated its territory, "no person, who knows the temper, genius, and policy of those people as well as I do can harbor the smallest doubt, any more than they will of the difficulty of diverting trade after connections are once formed, and it has flowed for any length of time in one channel, to that of another."[8]

The state of New York did indeed move first. In 1810, the legislature authorized a study of the possibilities of building a canal from Albany to Buffalo. Such a route offered an advantage possessed by neither Boston nor Philadelphia nor Baltimore. By following the Mohawk Valley to Utica and Rome and then running almost due west, through Syracuse, north of the Finger Lakes, and just south of Rochester and Lake Ontario, the canal could reach Lake Erie on a route far closer to water level than any other. At its highest point, near Buffalo, the route rose only 650 feet above the Hudson.

The problems, however, were daunting. The project was unprecedented from every point of view. At the time of the passage of the bill proclaiming that New York State would finance, build, and operate the canal, only three canals in the whole country were more than two miles in length, and the largest of these stretched 27.25 miles. There were about 100 miles of canals in the nation. In an era before the invention of the steam shovel and when there were few trained engineers in America, endless miles of earth had to be excavated, forests to be cleared, more than seven dozen locks 90 feet long to be built, and numerous other feats such as the building of a 750-foot aqueduct to be accomplished.

---

[7]W. C. Ford, ed., *The Writings of George Washington* X (New York: G. P. Putnam's Sons, 1891), pp. 402–14.

[8]Ibid.

The cost was also without precedent. Seven million dollars was so large a sum that, when the federal government refused help, it was clear that the state had to use its credit. Private financing was never seriously contemplated.

The canal was opened in sections, and every city on its route experienced a freshening of economic activity. It was November 4, 1825—a date which lives in the history of New York City along with that marking the completion of the Brooklyn Bridge on May 24, 1883—that the canal boat *Seneca Chief* was hailed by New York City's leaders, "Whence came you and where are you bound?" The reply, "From Lake Erie—bound for Sandy Hook!" DeWitt Clinton, one-time mayor of New York City, now governor of the state for the second time, and the man most responsible for pushing the canal through, poured a keg of unpolluted Lake Erie water into Upper New York Bay, and the city celebrated with fireworks and festivities. Everyone knew this was an event of national importance. The President of the United States, John Quincy Adams, was on hand, as was the man who would succeed him, the war hero General Andrew Jackson, and four of John Quincy Adam's predecessors, John Adams, Thomas Jefferson, James Madison, and James Monroe. Data on the canal are presented in Exhibit 8.

Philadelphia and Baltimore moved to establish their own trans-Appalachian routes to the Ohio Valley and to expand their trade in other directions as well. In 1829, Philadelphia opened the Chesapeake & Delaware Canal, providing access to the Susquehanna and to the southern coasting trade. Its great effort to rival New York to the west was, however, less than successful. The city fathers decided upon a combination railroad/canal over the mountains to Pittsburgh. At one point, the route rose 2,200 feet above sea level. Such heights were considered excessive for the era's rudimentary locomotives, so stationary engines were used to hoist cars up and down steep inclined planes. Though a triumph of engineering, the canal/rail route contained too many bottlenecks and transshipments. It never effectively competed against the Erie.

The rising port of Baltimore chose to build an all-rail route to the Ohio River at Wheeling. Construction began in 1828, and by 1835, Baltimore had won for itself the rich wheat fields of the Shenandoah Valley by reaching Harpers Ferry. Political problems plagued the route constantly, however. The Chesapeake and Ohio Canal, with its terminus near Washington, D.C., wanted to use the same route and garnered some support in Maryland. Not only did the Baltimore and Ohio have to scale heights in western Virginia steeper than those between Philadelphia and Pittsburgh, it also had to deal with the state government of Virginia, whose legislators were in the habit of referring to Baltimore as a "foreign port." The state of Pennsylvania also threw up road blocks, which were only finally cleared when the Wheeling Bridge Case was litigated before the Supreme Court. The B&O finally reached Wheeling in 1852, after three other railroads had already penetrated the west.

Of the major ports, Boston's challenge to New York was the most significant. The city's leaders realized that the Berkshires were too great a barrier for canals. In the 1830s, they initiated a rail link to Albany by way of which they hoped to lure the Erie Canal traffic from the Hudson. Completed in 1841, it immediately found much traffic. The following year, seven railroads were combined paralleling the

Erie, thus providing a rail link for Boston with Buffalo. The Hudson River Railroad, linking New York to Albany, was not completed until 1851. A summary of these developments is presented as Exhibit 10.

Meanwhile, steam travel had come to the Atlantic, threatening New York's sailing packet hegemony. In 1839, Samuel Cunard won a coveted subsidy of £60,000 to carry the mails from Liverpool to Halifax, Nova Scotia, to the United States. The admiralty had at first thought that New York should be the line's eastern terminus; but Cunard's personal connections were with the Boston business community, and he selected that port.

For eight years, Boston thus enjoyed the best connection with England. In 1848, however, Cunard extended his service to New York. That city was simply too well established to be bypassed. With this development and the completion of the Hudson River Railroad, Boston's challenge had been met.

One more development in domestic trade deserves attention. Less dramatic than those discussed above, it was not commemorated by fireworks and gala celebrations; but it was nonetheless important. This was the capture of a large share of the cotton trade for New York.

A great deal of the cotton exported to Europe arrived by way of New York. The city had always needed return freight for the ships which brought European merchandise to America, and the market for northern goods was insufficient. This was the role that cotton was to play. Northerners led by New Yorkers "penetrated every nook and cranny of the field where a dollar was to be made." Even when bales were shipped directly to Europe via the cotton ports instead of transshipped via the Northeast, there were Northerners living in southern towns who acted as factors advancing credit and Northerners in the cotton ports arranging for shipment. The ships themselves were often New York owned. A wide variety of commissions, insurance premiums, and other charges were also involved in this trade. So essential was the North in bringing cotton to market that it has been estimated that four cents out of every ten paid for the commodity wound up in northern pockets.[9]

## The Changing Mercantile World

The leading merchants of colonial America were generalists. The merchant "was not only exporter and importer, wholesaler and retailer, a trader on his own account and a commission man, but money lender, insurer, owner of shares in vessels, and freighter of space as well."[10] There were numerous reasons for the breadth of this economic activity. A general shortage of circulating currency and the absence of commercial banks meant that barter was the order of the day. The resulting pace of economic activity was so slow (as we saw in the previous case on John Jacob Astor) that numerous fields of activity were required to generate vol-

---

[9]Robert G. Albion, *Square-Riggers on Schedule* (Princeton: Princeton University Press, 1938), pp. 49–76.

[10]Stuart Bruchey, *The Roots of American Economic Growth, 1607–1861* (New York: Harper & Row, 1965), p. 54.

ume. Transactions were risky, and merchants felt that diversification protected them from disaster. Finally, merchants sought to service the multitudinous demands of their domestic customers and overseas correspondents.

The developments discussed in this case both facilitated and demanded commercial specialization. Canals and railroads greatly increased commercial contact with the hinterland; and larger ships, smaller crews, and faster turnaround times, not to mention the coming of steam, improved the efficiency of shipping. The heightened pace of commercial activity meant that product/market specialization became possible to an undreamt of degree. Risk reduction could be accomplished through the growing commercial insurance industry, while the development of banking and government issued securities meant that more investments were now available to protect against business failures.[11]

Of the nation's commercial centers, it was New York City which through attracting and developing specialists of all sorts became the general business center of the nation. It was New York where the insurance was available, where banking and security transactions flourished, and where credit could be had; New York where the widest variety of products could find a market; New York, where shipbuilding and repair were most advanced; New York where the bargains were to be found. And it was to New York that people of all sorts wanted to go. It became the center of entertainment and of the high life and low life in what was still an overwhelmingly rural nation.

During the first six decades of the 19th century, New York cemented its position as America's commercial emporium, a position it has never relinquished. George Washington turned out to be right: "[D]iverting trade after connections are all formed [and have flowed] for any length of time in one channel is difficult indeed."

## EXHIBIT 1

**Population of the Leading Seaports, 1790–1860 (*in thousands*)**

|  | 1790 | 1800 | 1810 | 1820 | 1830 | 1840 | 1850 | 1860 |
|---|---|---|---|---|---|---|---|---|
| New York | 33 | 60 | 96 | 123 | 202 | 312 | 515 | 813 |
| Philadelphia | 42 | 69 | 91 | 112 | 161 | 220 | 340 | 565 |
| Baltimore | 13 | 26 | 35 | 62 | 80 | 102 | 169 | 212 |
| Boston | 18 | 24 | 33 | 43 | 61 | 93 | 136 | 177 |
| New Orleans | — | — | 17 | 27 | 46 | 102 | 116 | 168 |
| Charleston | 16 | 20 | 24 | 24 | 30 | 29 | 42 | 40 |
| Savannah | — | 5 | 5 | 7 | 7 | 7 | 15 | 22 |
| Mobile | — | — | — | 1 | 3 | 12 | 20 | 29 |
| Portland | 2 | 3 | 7 | 8 | 12 | 15 | 20 | 26 |

Source: Robert G. Albion, *The Rise of New York Port*, p. 419. The reader should be aware that discrepancies will sometimes be found among the various authoritative sources for population statistics in early American history. Despite such discrepancies, the basic trends which these sources present are similar.

---

[11]For a good discussion of these issues, see Thomas M. Doerflinger, "Commercial Specialization in Philadelphia's Merchant Community, 1750–1791," *Business History Review* 57, no. 1 (Spring 1983).

## EXHIBIT 2

**Commerce Statistics by States, 1791–1860\*** *(in millions of dollars)*

|  | 1791 | 1801 | 1811 | 1821 | 1831 | 1841 | 1851 | 1860 |
|---|---|---|---|---|---|---|---|---|
| | | | *Imports* | | | | | |
| United States | 29 | 111 | 53 | 62 | 103 | 127 | 220 | 362 |
| New York | 6* | 26* | 12* | 23 | 57 | 75 | 141 | 248 |
| Massachusetts | 4* | 24* | 14* | 14 | 14 | 30 | 32 | 41 |
| Pennsylvania | 6* | 20* | 12* | 8 | 12 | 10 | 14 | 14 |
| Maryland | 2* | 11* | 5* | 4 | 4 | 6 | 6 | 9 |
| South Carolina | 2* | 11* | 1* | 3 | 1 | 1 | 2 | 1 |
| Louisiana | — | — | 1* | 3 | 9 | 10 | 12 | 22 |
| | | | *Exports* | | | | | |
| United States | 19 | 94 | 61 | 64 | 81 | 121 | 218 | 400 |
| New York | 2 | 19 | 12 | 13 | 25 | 33 | 86 | 145 |
| Massachusetts | 2 | 14 | 11 | 12 | 7 | 11 | 12 | 17 |
| Pennsylvania | 3 | 17 | 9 | 7 | 5 | 5 | 5 | 5 |
| Maryland | 2 | 12 | 6 | 3 | 4 | 4 | 5 | 9 |
| South Carolina | 2 | 14 | 4 | 7 | 6 | 8 | 15 | 21 |
| Louisiana | — | — | 2 | 2 | 16 | 34 | 54 | 108 |
| | | | *Combined Imports and Exports* | | | | | |
| United States | 48 | 205 | 114 | 127 | 184 | 249 | 439 | 762 |
| New York | 8* | 45* | 24* | 36 | 82 | 108 | 227 | 393 |
| Massachusetts | 6* | 38* | 25* | 26 | 21 | 31 | 45 | 58 |
| Pennsylvania | 9* | 37* | 21* | 15 | 17 | 15 | 19 | 19 |
| Maryland | 4* | 23* | 18* | 7 | 9 | 11 | 12 | 19 |
| South Carolina | 4* | 25* | 6* | 10 | 7 | 9 | 17 | 22 |
| Louisiana | — | — | 3* | 10 | 26 | 44 | 66 | 130 |

\*The starred figures are approximate, since there are no definite statistics for the value of imports by states until 1821. These starred figures are based upon the amount of duties collected in each state, multiplied by the proportion of the total duties to the total imports of the nation. The apparent discrepancy in certain totals of combined imports and exports arises from the adding of the fractional parts of the separate figures. Adequate figures are not obtainable for all the separate seaports as distinct from the states, but in all cases except Massachusetts, the principal seaports (New York, Philadelphia, Baltimore, Charleston, and New Orleans) monopolized most of the trade of their respective states. Roughly 10 percent of the Massachusetts figures before 1820 represent Maine commerce, while Salem represents a similar amount. By 1851, Boston's total commerce was 40 out of 45 million for the state.

Source: Robert G. Albion, "New York Port and Its Disappointed Rivals," *Journal of Economic and Business History* 3 (1931), p. 607.

**EXHIBIT 3**

Distances between Selected Seaports (*in nautical miles, by shortest natural routes*)

| | Mont. | Port. | Bost. | N.Y. | Phil. | Balt. | Norf. | Char. | Sav. | N.O. | Liverpool | Gibraltar | Havana | Rio |
|---|---|---|---|---|---|---|---|---|---|---|---|---|---|---|
| Montreal | — | 1205 | 1247 | 1459 | 1608 | 1768 | 1653 | 1939 | 2012 | 3049 | 2785 | 3188 | 2472 | 5356 |
| Portland | 1205 | — | 98 | 349 | 521 | 686 | 564 | 891 | 964 | 1986 | 2927 | 2999 | 1456 | 4772 |
| Boston | 1247 | 98 | — | 290 | 475 | 640 | 518 | 845 | 918 | 1940 | 2964 | 3036 | 1415 | 4741 |
| New York | 1459 | 349 | 290 | — | 235 | 413 | 292 | 627 | 700 | 1711 | 3137 | 3209 | 1227 | 4770 |
| Philadelphia | 1608 | 521 | 475 | 235 | — | 381 | 260 | 597 | 670 | 1681 | 3280 | 3352 | 1156 | 4817 |
| Baltimore | 1768 | 686 | 640 | 413 | 381 | — | 172 | 548 | 621 | 1632 | 3418 | 3490 | 1107 | 4844 |
| Norfolk | 1653 | 564 | 518 | 292 | 260 | 172 | — | 426 | 499 | 1510 | 3367 | 3369 | 985 | 4723 |
| Charleston | 1939 | 891 | 845 | 627 | 597 | 548 | 426 | — | 99 | 1171 | 3557 | 3619 | 646 | 4721 |
| Savannah | 2012 | 964 | 918 | 700 | 670 | 621 | 499 | 99 | — | 1133 | 3630 | 3689 | 606 | 4753 |
| New Orleans | 3049 | 1986 | 1940 | 1711 | 1681 | 1632 | 1510 | 1171 | 1133 | — | 4614 | 4577 | 602 | 5186 |

Source: U.S. Hydrographic Office, *Table of Distances Between Ports*, as reproduced in Robert G. Albion, *The Rise of New York Port*, p. 416.

## EXHIBIT 4

**New York Marine Insurance Rates, 1816–1860, Compiled from Shipping and Commercial List***

The rates for the "round voyage" were generally less than double the one-way rate. Unless otherwise specified, these rates permitted a stop at only one port; there was an additional charge for extra ports. The figures below are one-way rates unless otherwise indicated.

| *By the Trip* | *1835* |
|---|---|
| British Isles | 1–1 1/4 |
| France | 1–1 1/4 |
| North Sea | 1–1 1/4 |
| Lisbon or Cadiz | 1–1 1/4 |
| Gibraltar or Malaga | 1–1 1/4 |
| Mediterranean | 1–1 1/2 |
| Madeira, Canaries, etc. | 1–1 1/4 |
| Canton direct | 1 1/4–1 1/2 |
| Batavia or Indian Ocean | 1 1/2 |
| Brazil | 1– |
| Buenos Aires–Montevideo | –1 1/2 |
| "Spanish Main" | 1 1/4–1 1/2 |
| Vera Cruz, Tampico | 1 3/4–2 |
| West Indies, general | |
| additional ports | 1/4–1/2 |
| Windward Islands | 1–1 1/2 |
| Cuba | 1 1/4–1 1/2 |
| Santo Domingo | 1 1/4–1 1/2 |
| New Orleans, Mobile, to | 1 1/2–2 |
| New Orleans, Mobile, from | 1 1/4 |
| Charleston, Savannah | 5/8–3/4 |
| Wilmington, N.C. | 5/8–3/4 |
| N.C. "over Ocracoke Bar" | 1 1/4–1 1/2 |
| Chesapeake Bay, 1 port | 1/2–3/4 |
| Delaware River, 1 port | 1/2– |
| Rhode Island–Connecticut | 3/8 |
| Massachusetts | 1/2 |
| Maine–New Hampshire | 1/2 |
| Halifax | 1 1/4–1 1/2 |

*Three different kinds of insurance were sold in the shipping industry: (1) for the ship itself, (2) for the cargo, and (3) for prospective freight earnings. The rates presented here are for prospective freight earnings.

Source: Robert G. Albion, *The Rise of New York Port*, p. 412.

## EXHIBIT 5

### The Port of New York

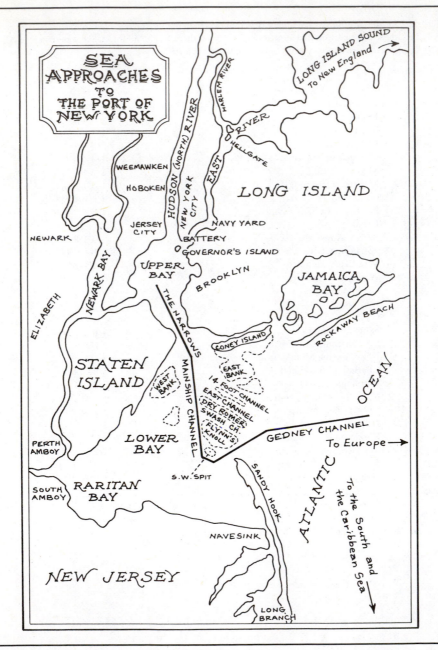

Source: Robert G. Albion, *The Rise of New York Port*, p. 18.

## EXHIBIT 6

### United States Population Distribution by Regions 1810–1860

| | South* | | West* | | Northeast* | | Total U.S. Population (does not include territories) |
|---|---|---|---|---|---|---|---|
| Year | Population | Total Population | Population | Total Population | Population | Total Population | |
| 1810 | 2,314,556 | 32.1% | 961,407 | 13.3% | 3,939,895 | 54.6% | 7,215,858 |
| 1820 | 2,918,198 | 30.4 | 1,845,863 | 19.2 | 4,836,722 | 50.4 | 9,600,783 |
| 1830 | 3,774,405 | 29.4 | 2,980,294 | 23.2 | 6,066,169 | 47.3 | 12,820,868 |
| 1840 | 4,749,875 | 27.9 | 4,960,580 | 29.1 | 7,309,186 | 42.9 | 17,019,641 |
| 1850 | 6,271,237 | 27.2 | 7,494,608 | 32.5 | 9,301,417 | 40.3 | 23,067,262 |
| 1860 | 7,993,531 | 25.6 | 11,796,680 | 37.8 | 11,393,533 | 36.5 | 31,183,744 |

*South—Alabama, Arkansas, Florida, Georgia, Louisiana, Mississippi, North Carolina, South Carolina, Texas and Virginia; West—Illinois, Indiana, Iowa, Kansas, Kentucky, Michigan, Minnesota, Missouri, Nebraska, Ohio, Tennessee, Wisconsin, California, Nevada and Oregon; Northeast—Connecticut, Delaware, Maine, Maryland, Massachusetts, New Hampshire, New Jersey, New York, Pennsylvania, Rhode Island, and Vermont.

Source: Douglas C. North, *The Economic Growth of the United States, 1790–1860* (New York: Norton, 1966), p. 257.

## EXHIBIT 7A

### Territorial Growth of the United States

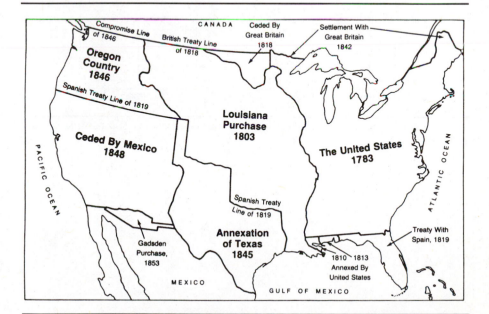

Source: Richard B. Morris, *Encyclopedia of American History* (New York: Harper & Row, 1976), p. 587.

## EXHIBIT 7B

United States Territorial Expansion: 1790–1860 (*in millions of square miles*)

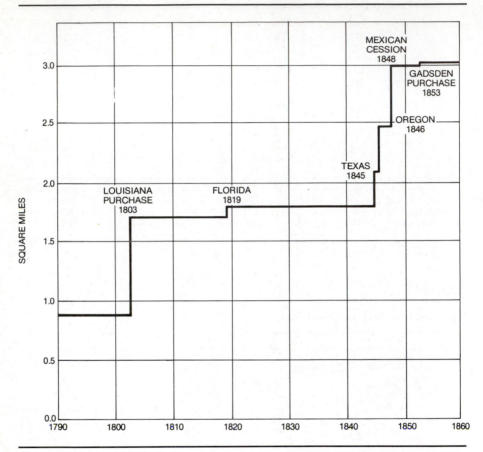

Source: Douglas C. North, *The Economic Growth of the United States, 1790–1860* (New York: Norton, 1966), p. 49.

# EXHIBIT 8

## New York State Canal Traffic

Figures refer to both the Erie and Champlain Canals, including feeders. "East" means eastbound traffic to tidewater; "West" means westbound traffic from tidewater.

| Year | Tolls ($ 000) | Total Traffic East & West Including Local Tonnage (000 tons) | Value ($) | Erie Canal Rates (per ton) State Tolls West: Albany to Buffalo | East: Buffalo to Albany |
|------|------|------|------|------|------|
| 1821 | 2 | — | — | — | — |
| 1822 | 44 | — | — | — | — |
| 1823 | 119 | — | — | — | — |
| 1824 | 289 | — | — | — | — |
| 1825 | 521 | — | — | — | — |
| 1826 | 841 | — | — | — | — |
| 1827 | 880 | — | — | — | — |
| 1828 | 827 | — | — | — | — |
| 1829 | 797 | — | — | — | — |
| 1830 | 1,017 | — | — | 10.22 | 5.11 |
| 1831 | 728 | — | — | 10.22 | 5.11 |
| 1832 | 1,083 | — | — | 10.22 | 5.11 |
| 1833 | 1,349 | — | — | 8.76 | 3.65 |
| 1834 | 1,338 | — | — | 6.57 | 3.28 |
| 1835 | 1,430 | — | — | 6.57 | 3.28 |
| 1836 | 1,539 | 1,310 | — | 6.57 | 3.28 |
| 1837 | 1,273 | 1,171 | 67 | 6.57 | 3.28 |
| 1838 | 1,400 | 1,333 | 55 | 6.57 | 3.28 |
| 1839 | 1,576 | 1,435 | 65 | 6.57 | 3.28 |
| 1840 | 1,534 | 1,417 | 73 | 6.57 | 3.28 |
| 1841 | 1,892 | 1,521 | 66 | 6.57 | 3.28 |
| 1842 | 1,705 | 1,236 | 92 | 6.57 | 3.28 |
| 1843 | 1,863 | 1,513 | 60 | 6.57 | 3.28 |
| 1844 | 2,258 | 1,816 | 76 | 6.57 | 3.28 |
| 1845 | 2,214 | 1,977 | 90 | 6.57 | 3.28 |
| 1846 | 2,606 | 2,268 | 100 | 4.80 | 2.92 |
| 1847 | 3,257 | 2,869 | 115 | 4.80 | 2.92 |
| 1848 | 2,883 | 2,796 | 151 | 4.80 | 2.92 |
| 1849 | 3,062 | 2,894 | 140 | 4.80 | 2.92 |
| 1850 | 3,055 | 3,076 | 144 | 4.80 | 2.92 |
| 1851 | 3,308 | 3,582 | 156 | 4.40 | 2.19 |
| 1852 | 2,915 | 3,863 | 159 | 2.92 | 2.19 |
| 1853 | 2,928 | 4,247 | 196 | 2.92 | 2.19 |
| 1854 | 2,754 | 4,165 | 207 | 2.92 | 2.19 |
| 1855 | 2,436 | 4,022 | 210 | 2.92 | 2.19 |
| 1856 | 2,498 | 4,116 | 204 | 2.92 | 2.19 |
| 1857 | 2,310 | 3,344 | 218 | 2.92 | 2.19 |
| 1858 | 1,882 | 3,665 | 136 | 1.46 | 1.46 |
| 1859 | 1,652 | 3,781 | 138 | .70 | 1.41 |
| 1860 | 2,169 | 4,650 | 132 | 1.40 | 1.41 |

Source: Robert G. Albion, *The Rise of New York Port*, p. 411.

# EXHIBIT 9

## Value of Leading American Exports, 1815–1860

| Year | Cotton* Unmanufactured | | Tobacco* Unmanufactured | | Wheat* and Flour | | Corn and* Corn Meal | | Rice* | |
|---|---|---|---|---|---|---|---|---|---|---|
| | *Value* | *Percent of Total* | *Value* | *Percent of Total* | *Value* | *Percent of Total* | *Value* | *Percent of Total* | *Value* | *Percent of Total* |
| 1816–20 | $121.5 | 39% | $47.5 | 15% | $ 50.6 | 16% | $ 7.6 | 2% | $13.1 | 4% |
| 1821–25 | 123.4 | 48 | 28.1 | 11 | 25.4 | 10 | 4.1 | 2 | 8.7 | 3 |
| 1826–30 | 133.1 | 49 | 27.8 | 10 | 25.6 | 9 | 4.4 | 2 | 11.4 | 4 |
| 1831–35 | 207.6 | 56 | 31.5 | 8 | 30.1 | 8 | 4.5 | 1 | 11.2 | 3 |
| 1836–40 | 321.2 | 63 | 43.0 | 8 | 29.0 | 6 | 4.3 | 1 | 11.0 | 2 |
| 1841–45 | 256.8 | 55 | 42.6 | 9 | 33.9 | 7 | 4.8 | 1 | 9.9 | 2 |
| 1846–50 | 296.6 | 46 | 39.0 | 6 | 82.2 | 13 | 40.3 | 6 | 13.7 | 2 |
| 1851–55 | 491.5 | 53 | 55.3 | 6 | 97.5 | 10 | 21.9 | 2 | 10.7 | 1 |
| 1856–60 | 744.6 | 54 | 86.5 | 6 | 157.7 | 11 | 24.7 | 2 | 11.3 | 1 |

| Year | Beef,* Tallow, Hides, and Horned Cattle | | Pork (Pickled),* Bacon Lard, and Live Hogs | | Dried,* Smoked, or Pickled Fish | | Staves, Shingles,* Boards, and Hewn Timber | | Domestic† Manufactures | |
|---|---|---|---|---|---|---|---|---|---|---|
| | *Value* | *Percent of Total* | *Value* | *Percent of Total* | *Value* | *Percent of Total* | *Value* | *Percent of Total* | *Value* | *Percent of Total* |
| 1816–20 | $ 3.7 | 1% | $ 4.2 | 1% | $6.8 | 2.0% | $15.5 | 5% | $ 21.1 | 7% |
| 1821–25 | 3.9 | 2 | 7.3 | 3 | 5.1 | 2.0 | 7.6 | 3 | 27.9 | 11 |
| 1826–30 | 3.6 | 1 | 7.8 | 3 | 4.7 | 2.0 | 8.7 | 3 | 32.8 | 12 |
| 1831–35 | 4.0 | 1 | 9.2 | 2 | 4.8 | 1.0 | 9.5 | 3 | 36.2 | 10 |
| 1836–40 | 2.8 | 1 | 7.7 | 2 | 4.1 | 1.0 | 10.7 | 2 | 46.4 | 9 |
| 1841–45 | 6.9 | 1 | 13.6 | 3 | 3.9 | 1.0 | 9.4 | 2 | 50.9 | 11 |
| 1846–50 | 10.5 | 2 | 36.3 | 6 | 3.4 | 1.0 | 10.8 | 2 | 70.1 | 11 |
| 1851–55 | 12.6 | 1 | 37.1 | 4 | 2.4 | 0.3 | 17.6 | 2 | 126.4 | 14 |
| 1856–60 | 21.8 | 2 | 53.9 | 4 | 3.9 | 0.3 | 29.3 | 2 | 167.3 | 12 |

*House Miscellaneous Document No. 49, Pt. 2, 48 Cong., I Sess., Vol. XXIV.

†House Document No. 15, Pt. 10, 57 Cong., 2 Sess., XLII, 3242.

Source: Stuart W. Bruchey, *Cotton and the Growth of the American Economy* (New York: Harcourt Brace Jovanovich, 1967), p. 23.

## EXHIBIT 10

Principal Canals and Railroads from Major Seaports to the West

|  | *From* | *To* | *Length (miles)* | *Begun (year)* | *Finished (year)* | *Cost (millions)* |
|---|---|---|---|---|---|---|
| Erie Canal | Albany | Buffalo | 363 | 1817 | 1825 | 7 |
| Pa. "Main Line" (canal and rail) | Philadelphia | Pittsburgh | 395 | 1827 | 1835 | 14 |
| Chesapeake & Ohio Canal | Georgetown | Cumberland | 184 | 1828 | 1850 | 10 |
| Baltimore & Ohio Railroad | Baltimore | Wheeling | 379 | 1828 | 1852 | 20 |
| 7 Roads (later New York Central) | Albany | Buffalo | 298 | 1830 | 1842 | 6 |
| Western, etc. (later Boston & Albany) | Boston | Albany | 200 | 1832 | 1841 | 11 |
| Erie Railroad | Piermont | Dunkirk | 446 | 1836 | 1851 | 24 |
| Hudson River Railroad | New York | Albany | 144 | 1847 | 1851 | 10 |
| Pennsylvania Railroad | Philadelphia | Pittsburgh | 331 | 1847 | 1852 | 25 |

Source: Robert G. Albion, *The Rise of New York Port,* p. 417.

# CASE 5

# *The Second Bank of the United States**

## Banks and Banking before the Second United States Bank

Although by 1816 the national economy was becoming highly complex requiring extensive credit, an adequate circulating medium, and the easy transfer of funds from one section to another and abroad, American banking was still in its infancy. In 1791, there were only three banks in the entire country. By 1816, the date of the chartering of the Second Bank of the United States, the number had increased to nearly 250; but banking was chaotic, techniques were primitive, and administration was unspecialized. It is necessary to evaluate the Second Bank's success and failure as a business enterprise against this background.

---

*This case was prepared by Barbara Shapiro under the supervision of Arthur M. Johnson. It is based upon material to be found in the following works: N. S. B. Gras and Henrietta Larson, *Casebook in American Business History* (New York: Appleton-Century-Crofts, 1939); Thomas P. Govan, *Nicholas Biddle, Nationalist and Public Banker, 1786–1844* (Chicago: University of Chicago Press, 1959); Bray Hammond, *Banks and Politics in America from the Revolution to the Civil War* (Princeton: Princeton University Press, 1957); Arthur M. Schlesinger, Jr., *The Age of Jackson* (Boston: Little, Brown, 1945); Walter B. Smith, *Economic Aspects of the Second Bank of the United States* (Cambridge: Harvard University Press, 1958); Peter Temin, *The Jacksonian Economy* (New York: W. W. Norton, 1969); and various journal articles.

Harvard Business School case 307–094, rev. 6/84.

Throughout the first four decades of the 19th century, the lack of specie[1] plagued the American financial world. Although the dollar in theory represented a specified quantity of gold or silver, all commercial and industrial development would have stopped dead had merchants and capitalists depended solely upon gold and silver dollars. In point of fact, there was never enough specie to serve as a circulating medium, let alone pay for America's frequent unfavorable foreign trade balances.

Indeed, the first banks arose in the great commercial centers of Philadelphia, New York, Boston, and Baltimore with the specific purpose of overcoming the specie shortage. Alexander Hamilton, writing in 1791, described a bank as a "deposit of coin or other property as a fund for *circulating a credit* upon it which is to answer the purpose of money." Thus a typical bank at that time issued notes based on coin, real property, promissory notes, commercial paper, and accommodation paper.[2] The bank notes took the place of gold and silver dollars.

Banks proved a boon to foreign trade. A person holding a draft on an overseas bank or commercial house could sell this paper to his local bank for bank notes which would satisfy local creditors. At the same time a merchant who owed money abroad could use bank notes to purchase foreign exchange. By the mid-1820s many private banks and the Second Bank were purchasing large quantities of foreign exchange due the cotton sellers of the South and were using it to satisfy the North's debt for imported goods. Thus banking became a vital link in the ever-growing flow of goods between Europe and the United States. In the same manner banks facilitated trade between cities and regions within the United States.

Besides aiding merchants in trading activities, banks stood behind America's growing internal improvement boom. Boston financial institutions, for example, exchanged their notes for state guaranteed railroad bonds. In this manner railroad corporations received money which could be used to pay workers, contractors, and other local creditors. Even farmers benefited, for they often received notes in return for mortgages on their land.

Key to the whole banking operation was the creation of money, or purchasing power, which evaded the use of scarce gold and silver. Most banks kept only a small quantity of specie. Paradoxically, however, the value of a bank's notes depended upon how easily they could be converted into gold or silver. In theory each bank agreed to exchange its notes for specie on demand. In practice banks hoped that such demands would be few. Indeed, no institution maintained enough specie on hand to redeem more than a fraction of its outstanding notes. Thus a banker's major task was to maintain public confidence in his ability to convert notes on demand. Lack of confidence could start an embarrassing run on the bank.

By 1816, the nation's monetary system was highly confused. Over 250 state-chartered banks issued paper. Since there was always a question as to the convert-

---

[1]Coin, usually gold or silver. Hard money.

[2]Accommodation paper is a negotiable instrument on which one places one's name for the benefit of another person, with the intention of lending the credit of one's name to the document so that it can circulate more freely.

ibility of bank notes, gold and silver dollars commanded a premium. To make matters worse, each bank's notes had a different value, which often fluctuated, depending upon the public's confidence in the institution's ability to redeem its notes in specie. In the case of large banks in the commercial cities, confidence was generally high and their notes were often worth close to face value. Out-of-town paper, which was hard to send back for redemption, often sold at a substantial discount. This was especially true with notes of rural and Western banks which sometimes issued paper backed by little or no specie.

Outside of New England, where the Boston banks banded together and established a forerunner of the modern clearing house to ease the exchange of notes between banks in Massachusetts, there was no effective central control or regulation of banks. Each institution was free to issue as much or as little paper as it wanted, limited mainly by the integrity of its management or the gullibility of the public.

There was one important exception to this picture—the First Bank of the United States. This pioneering institution had been chartered by the federal government in 1791. Alexander Hamilton, the first Secretary of the Treasury, saw this new institution as an aid to the commercial and propertied classes, and he also viewed it as an arm of the federal government which would aid tax collection, administer public finances, and serve as a source of loans to the Treasury.

The federal charter created a joint public-private institution. It required that one fifth of the bank's shares be government-owned, the remainder to be held by private individuals. The new bank served the business and mercantile community, and it acted as the government's fiscal agent: It transferred federal funds, and it stored government deposits. Its notes, unlike those of any other bank, were used throughout the country. As the custodian of federal revenue collections, the bank always held substantial quantities of state bank notes, for which it could demand specie payment. Thus the First Bank came to exercise a degree of control over the state institutions, since it could and did demand gold and silver dollars from those which it considered unsound.

Despite the First Bank's obvious benefits, it encountered strong opposition. It was chartered at a time when there were only three banks in the entire country, and the economic significance of banking was not generally recognized or appreciated. The whole project soon became identified with Hamilton's scheme to centralize power in the hands of the federal government. Hence the bank was attacked by the Jeffersonian Republicans, many of whom were Southern agrarians who mistrusted both a strong central government and the commercial classes of the North. In 1800, the Federalist Party, of which Hamilton was a member, lost control of the government to Jefferson. In 1811, the Republicans, reacting largely against Hamilton's interpretation of the Constitution, failed to renew the charter and thus killed the bank.

The demise of the bank, coming in a period of inflation and impending war, added to the strains that disrupted banking and imperiled the money supply. The number of state-chartered banks shot upwards—from 88 to 246 in five years. There was no longer control over note issues, and these banks were free to expand loans without limits. The circulation of bank notes grew accordingly—from $28 million in 1811 to $68 million in 1816—without a corresponding increase in specie. The result of unchecked accommodations was the suspension of specie payment in 1814, except in New England. Bank notes plummeted in value and were discounted everywhere. Lack of knowledge of the real as distinguished from the face value of such notes limited their acceptance to areas of issue. Inflation was rampant.

Government finances were also adversely affected by these developments. Financing the War of 1812 proved extremely difficult without a United States bank. State banks paid the government in depreciated notes of limited acceptability. Transfer of funds became difficult. Government credit sank low, and its balances shrank alarmingly. In fact, during the war federal bonds went to new lows, and such important private merchants as David Parish, John Jacob Astor, and Stephen Girard had to step in and help to market bonds even when they were offered at a 30 percent discount. Treasury efforts to resume specie payments failed. Such was the situation when the nation emerged from the war and returned to the task of developing the land and resources that beckoned beyond the Appalachians.

The financial and monetary chaos of the war years was a strong argument for reviving a national bank. Although there continued to be opposition to such a step, many who had opposed recharter of the First Bank of the United States in 1811 now supported a new one. The national administration was favorable because a national bank could help to restore specie payment, create a sound currency, and aid the Treasury's fiscal operations. Constitutional objections did not loom as large in 1816 as in 1791 because of the position taken by the administration. Most arguments heard in Congress revolved about details: the proper location of the bank's headquarters, the proportion of specie to government obligations, the amount of the bank's capital, and the degree of government interest and participation. Nevertheless, it was clear that the economy needed a national bank and that it would get one.

# Organization of the Second Bank of the United States

The Second Bank of the United States was established on lines very similar to those of the First Bank. Under the 20-year charter, one fifth of the bank's $35 million capital was to be provided by the government, the remaining four fifths to be open to public subscription. Since the charter conveyed an important franchise, the corporation was required to pay the government $1.5 million for it. To protect the government's interest, five of the bank's 25 directors were to be selected by the president with the consent of Congress. The board, which was forbidden to have other banking interests, was to select a president annually. Various provisions were aimed at preventing foreigners or even a small group of American stockholders from dictating bank policy.

Although the Second Bank was authorized to engage in most normal banking activities, others were specifically prohibited by the charter. The bank could not own real estate or engage in the trading of goods except in connection with defaulted mortgages or forfeited collateral. It was also prohibited from purchasing any public debt and could not charge more than 6 percent per year for loans or discounts.

In connection with the Second Bank's public responsibilities, numerous controls and restraints were imposed. While it was to hold the principal Treasury deposits and transfer and disburse government funds without charge, the bank could make no loans to the federal government exceeding $500,000. It could not loan any state more than $50,000, and loans to foreign states were prohibited unless Congress approved. Both the bank's notes and deposits were to be redeemable in specie on penalty of 12 percent annual interest on unredeemed items. The Treasury was to exercise continuing supervision over the bank, and provided Congress was informed, the Secretary of the Treasury was authorized to remove the government's deposits if he felt them to be unsafe. Congress could initiate action leading to forfeiture of the charter if wrongdoing were uncovered. The government, however, was not entitled to inspect private accounts and could not charter other national banks for the duration of the charter.

In both its public and private capacities the Second Bank was launched on a stormy sea. As a national enterprise it had to establish a system of branches which would cover the country in the most effective manner possible and then staff them with reliable and competent personnel. In an age of uncertain communication and slow transportation, this was a serious challenge which was not greatly different from that faced by the Medici in the 15th century. Furthermore, it was inevitable that the branches should reflect and respond to local pressures. Only determined and able administrators could make 16 or more different branches, as distant as New Orleans and Chillicothe, Ohio, act in harmony with one another and the Philadelphia headquarters, even on a limited number of issues. Under such conditions there were temptations for speculation and disregard of bank policies that could—and did—disrupt the plans of the bank's top officials. To the extent that this group was itself weak, these problems were compounded.

To the problems of internal organization and control were added those of an economy shaken by war and a crazy-quilt financial structure. The Second Bank commenced its operations in a period of depreciated state bank notes and suspended specie payment; the government itself was teetering on the brink of insolvency. One justification for the bank's existence, in fact, was the expectation that it could help bring order out of this chaos and give the nation a semblance of financial stability. On the other hand, there were hostile elements, such as the mushrooming state banks which profited from the chaos and had political influence to use against the new bank. Its management therefore not only had to overcome the problems of any new organization but also had to solve those uniquely associated with its activities as a national financial institution. Further, their decisions had to be made in an environment where any misstep would strengthen an already powerful opposition.

## The Second Bank under William Jones, 1816–1819

Those who thought that the Second Bank would provide an easy solution to the nation's financial woes were in for a rude shock. For one thing, two hostile forces jousted for control of the new institution. One group, headed by a leading Philadelphia merchant-capitalist, Stephen Girard, viewed the bank as an instrument of federal fiscal policy designed to assist the entrenched mercantile class. Girard demanded a moderate note issue; he wanted the bank to use its power to curb the printing of inflated paper by state banks and hoped that such policies would initiate a sound national banking system.

Opposing the conservative merchant class was a rising and aggressive new generation of capitalists. These were typified by William Jones, the first president of the Second Bank, and by James W. McCulloch, cashier of the Baltimore branch, both of whom saw banks as a way to create money and credit to be used in new industrial and transportation ventures. In contrast to Girard, the new capitalists had little cash of their own; they hoped to use the bank as an institution which would lend them money for their schemes.

At the initial stockholders' meeting, the speculative capitalists triumphed; and William Jones, backed by a sympathetic board, took the bank's reins for the first years.

The bank's first task was to bring about the resumption of specie payments and to transfer the public deposits from the state banks to itself. By making agreements which favored the associated banks of New York, Philadelphia, Baltimore, and Richmond, the national bank was able in February of 1817 to exact promises of specie resumption from these banks. This strategy, however, failed, and specie not only continued to command a premium over bank currency, but the premium even increased. In 1820, the Secretary of the Treasury complained that throughout the greater portion of the time since the "specie resumption" of 1817, the "convertibility of bank notes into specie has been rather nominal than real in the largest portion of the Union."

Similar difficulties plagued the transfer of funds from the state banks to the national banks. According to a mutual agreement this transfer was to take place on July 1, with interest, though the bank assumed in February the burden of paying government drawings up to $8.8 million. The bank extended further concessions to interior banks, but even then some Pennsylvania, Virginia, and Ohio institutions could not see that any advantages would result to them from the arrangement. Their resistance made it clear from the start that certain state banks would use their power and influence to thwart the national bank and its policies.

The earliest and most important decisions made by the Jones administration concerned branches. Soon after the main office in Philadelphia opened in January 1817, the directors selected 16 cities as sites for branch offices: Boston, New York, Baltimore, Charleston (South Carolina), New Orleans, Washington, D.C., Richmond (Virginia), Savannah (Georgia), Norfolk (Virginia), Lexington (Kentucky), Cincinnati, Portsmouth (New Hampshire), Providence, Middletown

(Connecticut), Chillicothe (Ohio), and Pittsburgh. By July of 1818, the number of active branches had increased to 19.

The effectiveness and strength of the Second Bank depended upon branches which would work in concert with the main office. The Philadelphia management had the power to control branches through the appointment of directors. Early appointments followed two patterns. First, they favored the aggressive new capital groups. And second, in an attempt to placate hostile local political elements, the Philadelphia officials often selected as branch officers men prominent in local banking. The branch directors, therefore, instead of acting conservatively, often abused their power, issuing notes in conflict with the aims of the central office.

The eager rising capitalists at the Baltimore branch involved themselves in a serious scandal. Several of the branch officers formed a company to speculate in bank stock. They abused their power by making noninterest bearing loans to one another, using bank stock as security or with no security at all. They constantly renewed these loans and concealed them from Philadelphia. They falsified records to prevent suspicion. By the time the fraud was discovered, the bank's loss exceeded $1.5 million and the damage to its reputation was even more serious.

While the Baltimore scandal rocked the bank, it ran into even more serious trouble because Philadelphia seemed to lack the power to control branch offices. For all practical purposes the branches were independent. Although they had no fixed capital, they could and did print bank notes. Slow transportation and communication made it possible for branch officers to flout directives from Philadelphia with relative impunity.

Since one of the main aims of the national bank was to establish a sound, uniform currency, William Jones found it necessary to order the redemption of notes issued by one branch at all other offices. The western officers used this policy to their advantage; they overexpanded their note issue, knowing that redemption would fall in the East. This created hostility between eastern and other branches and led to a directive restricting redemption to the office of issue. This attempt to control the branches brought on a storm of public criticism, for it seemed that the bank was repudiating its own notes. The Secretary of the Treasury suggested that unless the bank honored the notes of one branch at all offices, the institution might forfeit its charter. This, together with congressional pressure, forced a return to the old policy. Clearly, the bank officials had to walk a narrow line to maintain both solvency and the charter.

Beginning in the fall of 1818, a downturn in the economy that deepened into a national crisis made the bank's position even more precarious. With immediate demand liabilities of over $22 million and a specie reserve of only 10 percent of that amount, the bank began a drastic curtailment of loans and discounts. Interior branches were instructed to send specie east, and eastern offices were told to refuse notes of nonspecie paying state banks. These and other measures failed to stem the panic. The bank simply did not have the power to force the contraction necessary to remedy the situation, and it acted too late. As it was, businesses failed, and numerous banks, particularly those in the South and West, were forced to suspend specie payment. The public was outraged and blamed the bank. A congressional committee investigated the situation, and Jones was forced to resign. Although the bank did not cause the panic of 1819, as many contemporaries claimed, it helped to precipitate it and thereby won a legacy of public hatred.

### Rescuing the Second Bank, 1819–1822

While Jones's major problem had been to organize the bank and to restore the currency, the bank's new president, Langdon Cheves, had to save the bank from collapse. The former speaker of the House of Representatives was a self-confident, uncompromising man of considerable administrative ability. He seemed admirably qualified for the task at hand.

Cheves quickly instituted a series of reform measures. Interior branches were forbidden to issue notes, directed to send most of their specie and two thirds of their government deposits east, and instructed to insist on the payment of adverse balances by state banks. The purchase or collection of bills of exchange in the interior was also forbidden, and Jones's policy of curtailment was continued. Loans were reduced by as much as 50 percent in some areas. Incompetent officers and directors were dismissed, salaries and operating expenses were cut, and investigations on all phases of bank operation were carried out. Branch organization and control were improved, but Cheves's effort to improve the quality of branch officers was relatively unsuccessful. It was impossible to find able men willing to devote their full energies to the bank on its meager salaries.

The bank continued to pursue conservative and restrictive policies even after the emergency had passed. Its funds were put in conservative investments. Specie reserves were built up. Loan policy was altered to decrease loans on personal security. Credit was expanded very gradually. By comparison to earlier and later administrations, the bank at this time had a very small commercial business. The currency situation improved but was not solved, efforts in this area being impaired by antibank state legislation. By January 1, 1821, however, the capital of the bank had been restored, and a dividend of 1.5 percent was declared.

Since Cheves felt that overexpansion was the bank's major problem, he sought to control it, particularly by limiting branch activity. The extension of credit by branch offices was held to a minimum. Branches were forbidden to issue notes unless they were creditors and were to stop issuing when notes were used as substitutes for bills of exchange. They were instructed to operate so they could meet note redemption demands and pay their debts to other branches. As a result branch note circulation dropped sharply. Cheves even asked the Treasury for permission to refuse western branch notes in the East when tendered for government payments. The Treasury replied that this would not only be illegal but would convert branch issue into local currencies. Cheves, however, was more concerned with control of the branches than the condition of the currency.

The bank as a private institution was saved by policies which conflicted with its public responsibilities. The limitations placed on credit forced state banks to press their clients, causing many businesses to fail. Bills of exchange could not be sold, and bank credit dried up. At a time when the loosening of credit would have helped the nation's recovery from depression, the stringency imposed by Cheves led to the popular assertion that he had saved the bank but ruined the country. His administration was also criticized from within the bank by stockholders angered at the loss of dividends occasioned by the deliberate reduction of bank business and by directors who felt that the president's credit policies were too restrictive. Having done a disagreeable job that he thought had to be done, Cheves gladly resigned in 1822.

# The Second Bank of the United States as a Central Bank, 1823–1832

## Nicholas Biddle, Central Banker

In January 1823, Nicholas Biddle was elected president of the Bank of the United States. This 37-year-old lawyer came from a distinguished Philadelphia family. A graduate of Princeton, he had lived abroad, served in the state senate, and had been a director of the bank since 1819. His avocation was literature; he wrote poetry as well as prose and had edited Lewis and Clark's *Journal* on their exploration of the Northwest. He was also a student of economics and had more than a passing familiarity with the works of Adam Smith, David Ricardo, and the French economists. The new bank president was also well acquainted with contemporary economic theory pertaining to banking and monetary questions. Ambitious, able, hard-driving though somewhat vain and autocratic, Biddle was better qualified for the job of central banker than his predecessors had been. Furthermore, he had the advantage of inheriting a going concern that they had steered through its baptism of fire.

Biddle was not, as Cheves had been, afraid of credit and debt. This view was important in making the bank a factor in the expansion of the economy rather than a drag on it. On the other hand, he proceeded in this direction only after he had combined better control of branches with latitude for local decisions and centralization of major policy decisions in Philadelphia.

The new president removed Cheves's allocation of specific amounts of capital to each branch and set aside restrictions on the circulation of notes. To insure that this freedom would not be abused, directors from the head office sat on local boards in an advisory capacity, and branch cashiers were selected from the Philadelphia staff. Since the cashiers were now dependent on Philadelphia for advancement, they were no longer so subject to the temptation to respond to local demands. Inspection techniques were developed further and supplemented unofficial reports by Biddle's trusted confidants.

These steps were possible because Biddle dominated the bank completely, sharing authority with no one. He frequently did not even consult with the board but simply asked it to ratify his decisions on important policy matters. His influence over the election of private directors permitted such autocratic behavior, which extended to impatience with any governmental intervention. Though he was a government appointee up to 1832, once the other government directors were appointed as required by the charter, they were ignored. As Biddle put it in 1824, "No officer of the government from the president downwards, has the least right, the least authority, the least pretence, for interference in the concerns of the bank."[3]

Sometimes there was good reason for Biddle's hostility to public officials. One such example occurred in connection with the issuance of branch drafts. As note circulation increased, it became physically impossible to comply with the charter stipulation that all bank notes be signed by the president and cashier. Congress obstinately refused to change this provision, and Biddle devised a means of circumventing it. Beginning in 1827, branch drafts, drawn on one branch by another, were circulated together with regular bank notes. The bank's enemies seized upon this apparent violation of the federal charter. Although President Jackson declared that branch drafts would not be accepted for payments to the government, they continued to be widely used in business transactions.

In other situations where Biddle was on less firm ground, the characteristics that made him an effective bank administrator handicapped him in fighting political adversaries. As a result, his many actions taken in the public interest quietly and unspectacularly did not offset the public portrait of a powerful, unbending, and selfish financier that emerged from his conflicts with the people's representatives.

During the 1820s Biddle put the Second Bank on a sound basis, developed its potentialities as a central bank, and made it a profitable enterprise in the process. Criticism died away for a time, and the bank became decidedly popular in many formerly hostile camps. Such accomplishments reflected a sophisticated approach to banking and entitles Nicholas Biddle to be called the nation's first central banker.

## Central Banking

The Federal Reserve System, created in 1913, executes the functions of a modern central bank. By its role in monetary policy, it can help to smooth the peaks and valleys from the business cycle. It serves as fiscal agent for the government, adjusts currency circulation to seasonal needs, and performs similar routine functions. However, its chief influence is on the supply of credit, which is far more important than currency in our money supply. By raising or lowering the reserves that member banks are required to keep, the "Fed" can affect the availability of bank credit. It is, in fact, the bank of last resort. The purchase or sale of government securities on the open market is another way of affecting the reserves of member banks and therefore their ability to extend credit. Changes in the rediscount rate[4] are a third device for encouraging or discouraging commercial bank loans. Moral suasion is perhaps as important a weapon as any of the others. In

---

[3]Arthur M. Schlesinger, Jr., *Age of Jackson*, p. 76.

[4]The "rediscount rate" is the rate of discount applied when commercial paper is resold.

particularly difficult periods, such as wartime, the Federal Reserve System has been authorized to limit directly specific types of credit, such as that extended in retail sales. In these and other ways, our central banking system has an important effect on the money supply, though the effectiveness tends to be greater on up-swings of the business cycle when demands for credit are large than on down-swings when credit is abundant.

The Second Bank of the United States did not follow all the policies, nor did it have all the means, of our modern central banking system. Nevertheless, under Nicholas Biddle the Second Bank developed a variety of surprisingly sophisticated devices for regulating the supply of money and credit and for mitigating the effects of international and domestic financial disturbances.

### Reserves

Although the reserve requirements of banks are now a key feature of credit control, they did not play as significant a role in the 1820s and 1830s. Reserves in those days took the form of specie, and there was no attempt to maintain a specific ratio of reserves to liabilities. Specie holdings of the Second Bank and of other banks varied with the amount of credit they individually extended and also with the balance of payments between the United States, Europe, and East Asia. Since this balance frequently ran against the United States, the country's supply of specie was always somewhat precarious. Prior to 1819, the Second Bank was relatively short of specie partly as a result of speculative activity in its notes which could be bought at a discount and then exchanged for their face value in specie. After 1819, the bank's specie reserves generally proved ample to meet demands on them, and they remained so until 1836.

With the largest specie reserves in the country, the bank was in a position to make loans to banks in need. Thus it served as a lender of last resort, although not legally required to do so. At times the bank delayed collecting balances owed by banks in difficulty, in effect making them short-term loans. In addition, particularly under Biddle, the bank devised various means of stemming the flow of specie to Europe and East Asia, thereby improving both its own and the state bank's specie positions.

### Currency and Credit Control

Specie reserves were intimately connected with currency and credit control. By keeping state banks in its debt, the Second Bank could demand payment of outstanding balances in specie. State banks were thus forced to keep sufficient reserves to maintain convertible note issues. Lending and note issue policies had to be adjusted accordingly.

The bank's creditor position, largely obtained in its capacity as government fiscal agent, was maintained during most of its lifetime. The bank watched note circulation carefully and instructed its branches to require weekly redemption of their state bank-note holdings. Thus the clearing system could be used to implement control of state bank-note circulation. The bank's own notes, and later branch drafts, circulated nationally and were such a stable medium of exchange they were sometimes preferred to specie. Control over note issue was carefully exercised and pressure was gently applied when necessary.

Biddle took considerable pride in these achievements. He wrote in 1826:

> The Bank of the United States was established for the purpose of restoring the currency. It went into operation amidst a great number of institutions whose movements it was necessary to control and often to restrict, and it has succeeded in keeping in check many institutions which might otherwise have been tempted into extravagant and ruinous excesses. This necessary and salutary control could never be completely established until the Bank carried into complete execution the system of issuing only its own notes and receiving from the community the notes of other solvent banks. This system is now universal, and the general scheme of administering the Bank is to preserve a mild and gentle but efficient control over the monied institutions of the United States so as rather to warn than to force them into a scale of business commensurate with their real means.[5]

## Loan Policy

The Second Bank's loan policy, like the rediscount rate today, served as a barometer watched by the commercial banks. Although the discount rate in Biddle's time was not regarded as a control device, the size and type of the bank's loans had a direct effect on the loan policies of other banks. On occasion loan policy was used directly as a control device. For example, when business transactions of a certain type endangered the economy, the bank sometimes simply refused to make loans to people engaged in these enterprises. In 1828, when specie was leaving the country in large quantities in consequence of an extreme excess of imports over exports, the bank refused loans to business houses engaged in exporting specie.

## The Bank and Government Debt Redemption

By buying or selling government securities on the open market, the Federal Reserve System can affect the market for governments as well as member bank reserves. The Second Bank under Biddle had somewhat the same role. Acting as the government's agent in debt operations, it consciously developed methods to mitigate their unsettling effects.

During the 1820s most of these operations involved redemption of securities in connection with the federal government's effort to retire the debt as rapidly as possible. Since much of the debt was held abroad, redemption could easily have resulted in a serious loss of specie to Europe and general financial upheaval. Bank policy was therefore directed at averting such results.

Plans for redemption were made far in advance. For example, knowing that it would have to retire or refinance two government loans in 1825 and 1826, the

---

[5]Bray Hammond, *Banks and Politics,* p. 307.

bank began preparations as early as 1823. In the absence of such planning, sharp curtailment of the bank's loans to meet the government's demands would have caused a very tight money situation until the day of debt repayment; then the money market would have been suddenly flooded. To avoid such a disturbance, the bank persuaded holders of government securities who planned reinvestment to take loans from the bank on the collateral of their governments prior to the redemption date.

But these preparations were not sufficient. In 1824, Biddle induced the Treasury to pressure Congress into permitting the bank to bid on loans being floated to pay off the debt. Two entire loans were sold to the bank, which then disposed of them in England and at home. In the latter case the securities brought in state bank notes, which allowed the bank to maintain its creditor position with little impairment. To complete payments abroad, the bank increased its purchase of foreign exchange and drew on its credit with Baring Brothers in England. Redemption was accomplished so smoothly that the public was almost completely unaware that it had occurred.

Although the bank was able to mitigate or eliminate the potentially disturbing effects of debt redemption, it could not go as far in this direction as it might have wished, for its charter prohibited the purchase of government bonds without special congressional approval. However, as in 1824, it occasionally bought whole issues directly from the Treasury. It is doubtful that such operations were actually regarded as control devices, though they had somewhat that effect.

## Domestic Exchange

The Second Bank under Biddle became a major factor in the exchange business, both domestic and foreign. A bill of exchange is an order for payment drawn by one party on another, generally at a distance, for the benefit of a third. Bills could thus circulate as a form of money, with their exchange value determined by such factors as the length of time they had to run and the interest rates involved. Bills of exchange were typically handled by state banks and by merchants who collected their own bills.

The bank entered the exchange picture to end the drain on its specie reserves which were flowing westward to redeem the notes issued by its branches. To correct this situation, the bank limited discounts on personal security in the West and required western branches to purchase bills of exchange (on agricultural products) payable in northern or eastern cities or in Europe. These bills had a ready market in the East, and the proceeds from their sale could then be used to redeem the bank's southern and western issues. Whenever possible, the western branches were to accommodate borrowers by offering the newly purchased bills instead of issuing more bank notes. In this way relatively fewer notes would move eastward for redemption. Furthermore, the bank could enlarge its loans in the South and West, where capital was in greatest demand, while ending the transfer of its own reserves to the West.

The bank soon became the nation's major dealer in domestic exchange. From purchases of about $9 million of inland bills in 1823, the amount rose to over $46 million in 1831. The majority of these operations were in the West and Southwest. By 1835, domestic exchange accounted for one third of the bank's total discounts and bills. Earnings from this source were substantial and were estimated at $150,000 to $200,000 for the year 1830 alone.

Despite the benefit to the West and to the security of farmers and business people throughout the nation, the bank was criticized for these operations. State banks were displeased because they were driven out of the domestic exchange business by the bank's lower rate. Speculators who had gained advantage from wide fluctuations were also angered. It was charged, probably with some justice, that the bank forced customers to accept bills because the bank could thus make larger profits than the 6 percent charter limitation on regular discounts.

Although the impetus for bank activity in this area arose from difficulties with its own note issue, the development of a stable domestic exchange was one of the bank's outstanding achievements. The improved domestic exchange system was not only profitable to the bank but helped to market the country's staples, facilitated the interregional movement of funds, prevented curtailment of credit in areas where it was most needed, and even increased credit in these areas. In other words, it facilitated economic growth, especially in the newer regions of the country. The fact that over the years an increasing proportion of the bank's stock was held abroad meant that imported capital was aiding these operations.

## Foreign Exchange

The Second Bank was also active in foreign exchange. Foreign trade in this period was closely linked to the volatile cotton market. Cotton bills, drawn on European buyers, originated in the South but were often sold in the North, where they were used to pay for imported manufactured goods. They were also used by American foreign exchange bankers and the Bank of the United States to build up their British and French balances.

As the largest dealer in foreign exchange in America after 1826, the Second Bank had a major influence on exchange rates. In order to stabilize exchange, the bank built up foreign balances when the rates were low and went into debt when the rates were high. This activity was profitable for the bank and helped to prevent violent fluctuations of the exchange market. To facilitate its foreign exchange dealings, the bank had revolving credits[6] with Baring Brothers of London and other financial houses in Paris and Amsterdam.

As already noted, government debt redemptions handled by the bank involved large payments to foreign bondholders and sometimes threatened this country's specie holdings. In 1832, for example, the bank had to pay $13 million

---

[6]A revolving credit is a credit established by a bank permitting a borrower to make new withdrawals equal to payments made on prior accounts.

to holders of government bonds, $7.5 million of the amount outside the United States. When such payments were due, the bank drew on its foreign credit and built up its foreign balances by increasing its purchase of cotton bills, which could be used to pay off the debt in Europe. In this way domestic and foreign exchange dealings functioned as two parts of one stabilizing operation which protected domestic specie reserves.

Since outflow of specie was the product of an excess of demand for foreign exchange over the supply, the bank was frequently able to prevent the exchange rate from reaching specie shipment level by making more exchange available. If the bank could not prevent the specie outflow, it tried to make the necessary curtailments of domestic credit as gradual as possible. The bank also kept a close watch over import inventories, since they were particularly sensitive to changes in credit conditions. When it felt conditions warranted action, the bank tried to influence and alter the amount of foreign indebtedness.

Prior to Biddle's assumption of the bank's leadership, trade with East Asia as well as Europe resulted in serious specie outflow. Annually China merchants called for large sums of specie to use in East Asian ports. To prevent this drain, the bank in the mid-1820s developed the long-dated bill of exchange (180-days sight[7]) on London which proved quite acceptable in the Orient and helped to keep specie at home.

Critics charged the bank with manipulating foreign exchange to further its own rather than the public interest. Although profits from foreign exchange were considerable, Biddle claimed this field was less important as a source of profit than as a means for protecting the currency from ruinous fluctuations. Certainly in an economy extremely sensitive to both intersectional and international specie flow, the bank's exchange activities—foreign and domestic—had an important stabilizing effect.

## The Second Bank in Times of Crises

Under Biddle's guidance the Second Bank developed a variety of techniques with which to play the role of a central bank. Although they were employed with ingenuity, there were significant limitations on their effectiveness. First, the American money market was a satellite of the London market; American business was closely tied to world trade. Consequently, domestic controls had to deal with the effects of foreign as well as American business and financial crises. Second, problems of communication and control of branches could not be completely overcome. As long as time and distance separated Philadelphia headquarters from branch offices, the best available organizational techniques and personnel policies could not insure uniform implementation of centrally determined policies. Third, the Second Bank and its branches were superimposed on state banks over which they had no direct authority as the Federal Reserve does today over member banks. Finally, as a private enterprise operating under public auspices, the bank inevitably made

---

[7]A sight bill is a bill of exchange payable immediately on demand.

political enemies who could handicap its effectiveness as a central bank. In executing public responsibilities, the Treasury's lack of coordination with the bank's activities was a perennial problem. These factors, over which the bank's management could exercise little or no control, conditioned the exercise of central bank functions in times of crises such as 1825, 1827–1828, and 1831.

The difficulties of 1825 originated in England and reached panic proportions as a result of speculation, particularly in cotton. Several English financial houses failed and caused severe economic strain throughout Great Britain. Fear of similar panic spread to the United States. At first the bank could do little because panic conditions unfortunately coincided with the $7 million debt redemption operation already described. In connection with it, the bank temporarily had to go into debt to state banks in Philadelphia and New York. As soon as payment was made, the bank strengthened its own position by selling government securities and its own stock in order to regain its creditor position vis-à-vis the state banks.

The crisis caused bank credit across the country to be curtailed and also led to the hoarding of reserves against anticipated specie demands. In order to restore confidence, the bank lent a portion of its government securities to banks which were under pressure. If called upon for specie, these banks could instead agree to pay interest on interbank balances, using the bank's government stock as security. The bank was able to pursue this policy because it correctly surmised that specie was not needed for export but was being demanded by panicky state banks.

The bank also attempted to dispel the lack of confidence by expanding its own loans. The New York branch made a small increase in loans. Although the amount was only $50,000, the move proved successful. Timing rather than quantity was decisive. The policies of the bank and their skillful application averted the spread of the English crisis to the United States.

The bank again prevented widespread financial difficulties in 1827–1828. A monetary crisis had been precipitated by a great increase in the importation of manufactured goods financed largely on credits advanced by Anglo-American merchant bankers and stimulated by the impending rise in the tariff. At the same time the price and volume of American agricultural products, whose export usually helped to pay for imports, dropped sharply. The combination of these two movements resulted in an adverse balance of payments, a rapid rise in the rate of exchange, and the shipment of specie to pay these debts. The bank could not apply immediate remedies because it had to expand loans to prepare for a payment on the national debt. Once the debt payment had been made, however, the bank contracted its loans to firms exporting specie, sold government securities in New York with the hope of absorbing funds which would otherwise be devoted to the purchase of foreign goods, and used the funds from bond sales to replenish its specie supply by making demands on state banks. This warning that the period of easy credit had passed was not immediately heeded. The crisis continued to mount, but the bank maintained pressure on state banks. Gradually they responded by reducing discounts, and the situation returned to normal. The bank had again softened the blow of financial readjustment and provided time for such readjustment to take place.

The bank once more attempted to avert a national financial crisis in 1831. Early that year exchange rates were very low, encouraging Americans to stock up on European goods. At first the bank encouraged these imports because Americans held high balances abroad resulting from large European purchases of foodstuffs in anticipation of war. When danger of war passed, the price of American agricultural products dropped sharply. Holders of American staples refused to ship at the new prices while imported goods ordered earlier flowed into the country. Measures to halt imports proved unsuccessful, and the demand for exchange raised the exchange rate to the point where specie began to leave the country. When this occurred, the bank went into action. It refused to make loans to importers, expanded its use of credits with the Barings, and lowered its foreign exchange rate below the specie shipment point so that bills of exchange would be used for foreign payments instead of silver. These efforts were undermined when the Treasury, without prior consultation with the bank, announced almost immediate redemption of $6 million in government bonds. The bank now had no choice but to curtail its own loans; the exchange rate rose and specie again flowed to Europe. But as soon as preparation for repayment of the debt had been made, relief measures were again instituted by the bank. Within a week dangers of panic had passed, although a tight money and credit situation remained for some time. Thus the Second Bank in both domestic and foreign exchange operations exerted a stabilizing influence in a highly volatile economy closely tied to world trade and foreign money markets.

## The Bank and Politics

The Second Bank could not avoid politics. Indeed its very charter resulted from the concerted political action of its friends in Congress. From the first the bank's enemies used political pressure to attack it, but the institution was not helpless—it had many supporters in all sections of the country.

Foremost among the bank's friends were the entrenched and wealthy merchant and industrial groups of the northeastern states. People like Boston's Nathan Appleton or Philadelphia's Stephen Girard appreciated the bank's effort to build a sound national currency. Their trading ventures required an institution which could facilitate the transfer of funds between regions and nations. Their manufacturing interests did not depend upon the creation of capital through manipulated bank credit.

But the bank's support did not come solely from the Northeast. The planters of the South and Southwest also needed an institution which could make it possible to receive the money due from their cotton sales in New and Old England. Thus it is not surprising that Nashville, Andrew Jackson's home city and the commercial center of Tennessee, broke with President Jackson and supported the bank. Indeed, between 1836 and 1844, many a Tennessee politician rode to a statewide election victory upon a platform which included as a major plank a national bank on the model of the Bank of the United States.

Without doubt, however, the bank's enemies outnumbered its friends. But these opponents found themselves agreed solely on their hostility to the Bank of the United States; they had radically different views about national monetary policy.

Certain of the state bankers worked ceaselessly to destroy the federal bank. Typical was Boston's David Henshaw. Unlike Nathan Appleton, Henshaw started life in poverty. By 1830, he controlled three state-chartered Boston banks. He saw that the end of Biddle's bank could benefit him in two ways. First, it would remove a force which hindered his banks from expanding their loans. Second, with the federal bank out of the picture, government specie would become available for deposit in state banks. Significantly, when Jackson removed the federal money from Biddle's institution in 1833, Henshaw's Commonwealth Bank became one of Boston's depositories. Unfortunately for Henshaw, the Commonwealth Bank overextended its loans, and despite its prestige as a federal depository, it failed in 1838.

Henshaw and those who shared his views attacked Biddle's institution as a government-sponsored monopoly which hindered private initiative. They linked themselves with Jefferson and supported the idea that the "government which governs best, governs least."

New York bankers had a special grievance against the Second Bank. By 1825, their city had become America's undisputed commercial center, and they resented the fact that the huge federal tariff revenues collected at the port of New York passed into the hands of a bank controlled from Philadelphia.

In the West many small farmers opposed all banks, state as well as federal. Led by people like Missouri's Senator Thomas Hart Benton, these western agrarians viewed themselves as victims of the banking system. They had been cheated with worthless bank notes or had been hurt when the national bank contracted credit. They saw bankers as people who lived by manipulating paper, people who produced nothing yet grew wealthy—speculators who exercised control over the truly productive element of society. The small farmer yearned for a return to "honest" gold and silver dollars. He little appreciated the complexity of the national economy or the creative role which banks played in it. And he had no realization that the destruction of the national bank accompanied by lack of control of state banks would result in more—not less—paper money.

Allied in their monetary views with the small farmers of the West were a group of urban workers, tradesman, and craftsmen. They resented banks because unscrupulous employers and business firms often took advantage of the workingman by dealing in depreciated paper. The bank's urban opponents, like the farmers, saw Biddle's institution not as a regulator which built sound and honest currency but as the chief and largest issuer of paper.

Finally, some influential people, especially in the South, opposed the national bank on constitutional grounds. More and more Southerners saw a narrow interpretation of the Constitution as a safeguard against unwanted interference with their peculiar institution, slavery. The bank, of course, represented a triumph of Hamilton's doctrine, which saw in the Constitution broad implied powers. Many

Southerners felt that the destruction of Biddle's bank would be a victory for states' rights.

Initially, political opposition to the bank centered in the states. It reached a peak during the panic of 1819, when critics blamed the financial distress on the bank's rapid contraction of credit. Smarting from the deflationary effect of Cheves's policies, voters and hard-hit state banks demanded aid. Several state legislatures responded by passing stay laws and other measures to aid debtors. Six legislatures passed statutes taxing the bank's branches. Such moves threatened the bank's destruction until the Supreme Court in *McCulloch* v. *Maryland* (1819) declared such taxes to be unconstitutional. Further Supreme Court decisions invalidated other types of antibank legislation. These rulings made it clear that any successful attack on the bank would have to be made at the federal rather than at the state level.

Biddle's sound management and the return of national prosperity tended to remove the bank from politics during the years between 1822 and 1828. The administrations of James Monroe (1817–1825) and John Quincy Adams (1825–1829) favored the bank, and its enemies in Congress were too disunited to present a serious challenge.

But Andrew Jackson's election in 1828 posed a new threat. The bank's charter was to expire in 1836, and if Jackson were elected to a second term, he would be able to block a recharter bill by the use of the presidential veto. Thus it was vital for Biddle to ascertain Jackson's views.

Banking had not been a political issue in 1828, and although several of Jackson's advisors were well-known enemies of the bank, Jackson's Secretary of the Treasury, Louis McLane, assured Biddle that in the end the president could be persuaded to approve a new bank charter. At first, therefore, Biddle considered recharter merely a matter of strategy. He knew that he had ample votes to pass the measure in Congress, but he realized that there was not enough support to override a presidential veto. Jackson, hoping to evade taking a public stand on a controversial issue, suggested that the whole question be put off until after the 1832 election. This suited Biddle, provided Jackson gave some indication that he would sign a new bank charter.

The plan to postpone recharter until after 1832 did not please everyone. Biddle's main congressional support came from a group led by Daniel Webster and Henry Clay, who were forming a new party to oppose Andrew Jackson. Clay planned to run for president in 1832, and he seized upon the bank as an issue which could fatally injure Jackson.

Thus Biddle found himself in a trap. Not to press recharter alienated his strongest friends in Congress. But introduction of the bank bill risked Jackson's ire. Biddle's decision had to rest upon an analysis of Jackson's intentions. Biddle did not make his decision carelessly. Late in 1831, working with Jackson's pro-bank Secretary of the Treasury, Biddle thought he had reached an agreement whereby McLane would persuade Jackson to sign a recharter bill, which would be delayed until after the 1832 election. During these negotiations Biddle made it clear that he would approve of virtually any modifications which the president might suggest. But public statements made in December of 1831 convinced Biddle that Jackson would never agree to recharter. Reluctantly Biddle took the only path that remained open—he embraced Henry Clay. The bank bill passed Congress early in 1832, and to no one's surprise Jackson vetoed it. As expected, Congress sustained the president, thereby throwing the whole issue into the coming presidential election.

It should be noted that Jackson's two chief advisors, Attorney General Roger B. Taney and Martin Van Buren, both hated Biddle's institution. Taney owned stock in a Baltimore state bank which became a federal depository after the Second Bank's destruction; Van Buren represented New York's financial institutions which hoped to increase their power by liquidating the Philadelphia-controlled national bank.

Jackson himself had strong feelings about banks. In his early years he had suffered a severe financial reverse by accepting the notes of a Philadelphia speculator. As a creditor in Tennessee during the panic of 1819, Jackson had opposed the creation of a state bank which had the purpose of lending notes to those hard-hit by the crisis. Jackson saw paper money as a swindle. He demanded a return to "honest" gold and silver dollars, and he clearly believed that destroying the Second Bank would further the cause of hard money. He did not appreciate the economic complexity which made banks necessary, nor did he see the regulatory role which the Second Bank played. In addition, Jackson had substantial constitutional objections to any federal bank. He believed that the government's monetary obligations had been met when Congress fixed the quantity of gold and silver to be contained in the dollar.

When Biddle allied himself with Clay, Jackson's hatred of banks in the abstract focused upon the "Chestnut Street monster." "The bank," he told Van Buren, "is trying to kill me, *but I will kill it!*"[8] Biddle joined the fray with vigor. He contributed heavily to Clay's campaign, and he did the same for congressional candidates who supported the bank.

But it was a losing cause. Biddle showed little skill as a politician. In the height of the 1832 campaign, he committed what Bray Hammond terms as "the most profound descent into indiscretion he ever made." When asked by a congressional committee whether the bank ever oppressed the state banks, Biddle replied, "Never." He could have stopped there, but instead he continued: "There are very few banks which might not have been destroyed by an exertion of the power of the bank. None have ever been destroyed by an exertion of the power of the bank. None have ever been injured. Many have been saved. And more have been and are, constantly relieved when it is found that they are solvent but are suffering under temporary difficulty."[9] Thus from Biddle's own mouth came the unnecessary assertion that he had the power to ruin most state banks! His opponents never let him forget this blunder.

In reality the bank proved a very poor political issue. Although its opponents had widely different aims, they could unite on opposing recharter and on the sup-

[8]Arthur M. Schlesinger, Jr., *Age of Jackson,* p. 89.
[9]Bray Hammond, *Banks and Politics,* p. 297.

port of Jackson. Biddle's enemies conjured up the image of a greedy monopoly thwarting opportunity and oppressing the people. Typical was this statement by the Boston state banker, David Henshaw: "The nation . . . owes a new debt of gratitude to its venerable Head for bringing this subject to its notice thus early, thus fearlessly and directly. It has called down upon him the vindictive hatred of a MONIED OLIGARCHY; but the people will sustain him. And if in his second official term he can exterminate this aristocratic monster—this bank hydra—and rear upon its ruins a people's bank, an institution of which the people can reap the profits . . . they will give greater lustre to his character as a statesman than the battle of New Orleans to his fame as a warrior."[10]

In the ensuing election Jackson won a decisive victory, which he interpreted as a mandate to destroy the bank. Although the charter still had several years to run, the government and the bank could be effectively separated by removing the federal funds. This Jackson did in September 1833 through the action of a newly appointed Secretary of the Treasury, Roger B. Taney.

Bank policy responded to the pressures of administration attack. To protect itself against the threat of deposit removal, the bank as early as 1832 began converting discounts to more liquid assets. Although the administration used its power to damage the bank's reputation and impair the value of its stock, Biddle thwarted the attempts of new government directors to use their position to gain information about the bank's practices. Vindictiveness increasingly characterized bank-administration relations. For example, Jackson attempted to end the payment of pensions by the bank, and the bank in turn purposely embarrassed the administration over a protested draft on France.

Prior to 1832, critics had concentrated on the dangers attributed to the institution, not its officers; now they claimed the bank was improperly run and that Biddle was dishonest. At this critical juncture the bank added fuel to the fires of controversy. Its agent, Thomas Cadwalader, had been sent to England to make arrangements with Baring Brothers & Co. for payment of a public bond issue. Bondholders there were encouraged to sell their holdings to the Barings. Cadwalader knew that the bank could not legally purchase the bonds but thought indirect purchase by the bank's London agent was permissible. When Biddle was informed, he repudiated the agreement; but public announcement by the Barings had already been made. A tremendous public outcry ensued, and this episode helped to condition public attitudes toward the bank in its time of crisis.

Despite the government's promise of gradual withdrawal of its deposits, large demands were made on the bank. Biddle decided to curtail loans in preparation for meeting these demands. This curtailment, which was rapid, unfortunately came during a recession in 1833–1834 at the very time when business needed more—not less—credit. A financial crisis resulted. It was widely believed that the bank was using contraction as a means to force recharter and that it had purposely created panic conditions. Although the bank was soon "safe," it instituted further

---

[10]Bray Hammond, *Banks and Politics,* p. 409.

curtailment, causing more failures. State banks suffered, and suspension of specie payment seemed imminent. Even the conservative business community felt that restriction had been prolonged longer than necessary. Seemingly the bank's power, which had been previously used constructively, was now being wielded for spite. Biddle finally yielded, credit restrictions were relaxed, and the crisis passed.

Once withdrawal had been completed and government funds had been deposited with "pet" state banks, the Second Bank ceased to exercise regulatory functions, and Biddle felt that its public responsibility had ended. Initially the directors decided to liquidate the bank's assets in preparation for closing, but in 1836, a decision was made to continue as a state-chartered bank. Under a Pennsylvania charter the bank shifted its emphasis from central banking to avowed profit-making, and it became an inflationary rather than a conservative force in the economy.

The wide disparity among the forces which had united to destroy the bank became apparent after its disappearance from the financial scene. Victory belonged in the end to the new commercial and agricultural classes that wanted easy money and easy credit to exploit the business opportunities and resources of the nation whatever the costs in boom and bust. Banks were no longer held in check and could expand loans without limit. The currency again became chaotic, and a uniform national currency disappeared. The economy was left to work itself out as best it would without the restraining and regulating force of the Bank of the United States.

## The Bank of the United States, of Pennsylvania

On March 3, 1836, the state-chartered bank of the United States came into existence. Nicholas Biddle, central banker, had been forced by the turn of events to work from a smaller base and without the resources and prestige that the bank had earlier enjoyed. The new incarnation of the bank inherited major obligations from the old and paid heavily for a new lease on life. Embittered by political trials but still hopeful that the bank might be restored to political favor, Biddle turned to the task of keeping his institution at the forefront of American banking. Freed of public responsibilities, he essayed the role of investment banker.

Unfortunately the environment that soon confronted Biddle was more like the one which Jones and Cheves had faced in the early days of the Second Bank than the one under which he had first assumed power. In 1837, a panic of major proportions swept over the country. The preceding few years had for the most part been boom times; capital had flowed into the country from abroad; western land sales rose; internal improvements financed by private and public credit assumed major importance. The enthusiasm for still more expansion was partially checked by the issuance of a government circular in 1836 requiring payment for public lands in specie. The impact of this form of restraint on credit was heightened by such developments as a curtailment of foreign credits, a slowing of foreign trade, a drop in the price of cotton, and new caution by European investors. Western bank credit was contracted; eastern as well as western banks engaged in financing agricultural production were forced to suspend specie payment. Liquidations and collapse snowballed. The reversal of economic gears turned a boom into a sharp depression.

Biddle was caught in this situation and lacked the means to avoid suspension of specie payment. With heavy obligations and collateral rapidly depreciating in value, the bank faced the prospect of liquidation. But Biddle proved as resourceful as ever. In a private capacity he undertook to rescue not only his own bank but the banking system from collapse.

Biddle's strategy resembled that of the central banker. It was designed primarily to liquidate the immediate obligations of the United States abroad and thereby to end the external pressure on American specie reserves. This was achieved, with the cooperation of New York and Philadelphia banks, by issuing "post notes" (short-term interest-bearing notes). The largest issue was by Biddle's bank, but others followed his lead. These notes proved acceptable in England, but their value depended on the price of cotton, since this staple was the chief means of settling America's foreign trade balances, and post notes were exchanged for cotton bills.

Biddle's tactics therefore became quite different from those of a responsible central banker. To maintain the price of cotton, he set about "rigging" it—maintaining the price at as high a rate as possible as long as possible. Through Bevan & Humphries, Philadelphia merchants, cotton was bought in the South by means of notes on the Bank of the United States and consigned at first to Baring Brothers and shortly to a new firm, Humphries & Biddle of Liverpool. Baring Brothers having withdrawn their open credit granted to the Bank of the United States, Biddle had established Samuel Jaudon as his financial agent in London. When the cotton bills on Humphries & Biddle became due, that house drew on Jaudon instead of selling at low prices. To cover payments, Jaudon issued post notes of the Bank of the United States, which were redeemed when due by the proceeds from the sale of recently acquired state securities.

The scheme worked. At the end of eighteen months, the cotton pool had made $800,000 for its operators, chiefly officials of the Bank of the United States, while the rise in cotton brought the desired improvement in the cotton industry and in American credit abroad. Thinking he had accomplished his aims, Biddle resigned in March 1839.

The very success of the bank in pegging American credit abroad, however, led to further complications. While the bank weathered the panic and the subsequent recession, the tactics employed kept it from making use of a possible chance to strengthen its own position by the liquidation of its assets, especially state bonds, and the contraction of its business.

Adverse circumstances broke cotton prices in England in 1839, and the credit of the Bank of the United States no longer sufficed to hold up the price. A second cotton pool failed in September to the amount of $900,000, much of the loss falling on the Bank of the United States. Its credit practically disappeared. European shareholders came to the rescue temporarily. This assistance was later covered by loans from the Paris Rothschilds and the Amsterdam Hopes on bonds of Mississippi, Illinois, Indiana, and Pennsylvania as security.

As the head of a state-chartered institution, Biddle seemed unwilling or unable to exercise the careful judgment that had distinguished his moves as a central banker. In addition he became heavily involved in the marketing of securities issued by states and corporations to finance the construction of canals and recently invented steam railroads. For a brief period Biddle became the nation's foremost, indeed its first, modern investment banker. Not only did his bank sell securities on commission, it often bought large blocks of them on its own account. Often, too, it guaranteed payment of interest on securities sold on commission. And it made short- and long-term loans that were settled by the delivery of securities. Through a connection with the Morris Canal and Bank Company, for example, the bank was dragged into guaranteeing unsalable Michigan bonds. When the bank finally closed its doors, it had over $30 million of state and railroad securities of dubious market value (see Exhibit 2).

The unhappy situation in which the bank found itself was symbolized by the charter requirement that it make loans to the Pennsylvania state government and that it buy the state's canal and railroad securities. This was a high price for survival as a banking institution, and the demands made under these provisions, in addition to unwise investment decisions, helped to topple the bank. In October 1839, the bank was forced to suspend specie payment for the second time. The collapse of the cotton pool merely delivered the *coup de grace*. Somehow the bank staggered on until February 1841 when it closed its doors forever.

# EXHIBIT 1

**Selected Items from the General Statements of the Bank of the United States, January 1823–1832 (*000 omitted*)**

| Date | Discounts on | | | Domestic Exchange[4] | Real Estate | Funded Debt | Balances with European Bankers |
|---|---|---|---|---|---|---|---|
| | Personal Security[1] | Bank Stock[2] | Other Securities[3] | | | | |
| 1823 | $22,597 | $6,149 | $ 50 | $ 1,940 | $ 626 | $11,018 | $(− 1,268) |
| 1824 | 24,324 | 6,708 | 75 | 2,323 | 1,302 | 10,874 | 414 |
| 1825 | 23,170 | 5,655 | 258 | 2,727 | 1,495 | 18,422 | − 2,383 |
| 1826 | 27,104 | 3,131 | 69 | 3,118 | 1,848 | 18,303 | 170 |
| 1827 | 24,330 | 2,933 | 326 | 3,347 | 2,039 | 17,764 | 180 |
| 1828 | 26,452 | 1,928 | 280 | 5,022 | 2,295 | 17,624 | (− 1,111) |
| 1829 | 29,854 | 1,375 | 298 | 7,689 | 2,345 | 16,099 | 482 |
| 1830 | 30,654 | 1,002 | 315 | 8,691 | 2,886 | 11,610 | 1,530 |
| 1831 | 32,827 | 665 | 83 | 10,456 | 2,629 | 8,674 | 2,383 |
| 1832 | 48,852 | 731 | 18 | 16,691 | 2,136 | 2 | (− 1,356) |

| Date | Balances with State Bank | Specie | Circulation[5] | Public Deposits[6] | Other Deposits | Profits | |
|---|---|---|---|---|---|---|---|
| | | | | | | On Discounts | On Exchange |
| 1823 | $ 1,407 | $ 4,424 | $ 4,361 | $ 4,275 | $3,347 | $ 573 | $ 49 |
| 1824 | 1,287 | 5,813 | 4,647 | 10,181 | 3,520 | 678 | 67 |
| 1825 | 2,130 | 6,746 | 6,068 | 6,702 | 5,330 | 558 | 78 |
| 1826 | 747 | 3,960 | 9,474 | 5,769 | 5,444 | 711 | 107 |
| 1827 | 1,683 | 6,457 | 8,549 | 8,982 | 5,337 | 721 | 101 |
| 1828 | (− 1,697) | 6,170 | 9,855 | 8,354 | 6,142 | 697 | 190 |
| 1829 | 1,723 | 6,098 | 11,901 | 10,697 | 6,364 | 823 | 274 |
| 1830 | 1,199 | 7,608 | 12,924 | 9,654 | 6,391 | 876 | 372 |
| 1831 | (− 734) | 10,808 | 16,251 | 9,131 | 8,165 | 889 | 401 |
| 1832 | 1,993 | 7,088 | 21,355 | 12,589 | 8,107 | 1,254 | 584 |

[1]Mortgages.

[2]Of the Second Bank of the United States.

[3]Discounts on notes of American Banks other than the Second Bank of the United States.

[4]Loans made to state banks.

[5]Note issue.

[6]Deposits by the United States treasurer and other public officials.

## EXHIBIT 1 (*concluded*)

**Selected Items from Semiannual Statements of the Bank of the United States, 1833–1836 (*000 omitted*)**

| Date | | Personal Security | Bank Stock | Other Securities | Domestic Exchange | Real Estate |
|------|--|------------------|-----------|-----------------|------------------|-------------|
| | | | *Discounts on* | | | |
| 1833 | January | $40,085 | $ 687 | $ 2,854 | $18,069 | $1,855 |
| | July | 37,032 | 827 | 3,833 | 21,676 | 1,809 |
| 1834 | January | 33,703 | 912 | 3,993 | 16,302 | 1,741 |
| | July | 29,932 | 1,031 | 3,459 | 16,601 | 1,741 |
| 1835 | January | 29,933 | 1,006 | 3,686 | 17,183 | 1,760 |
| | July | 32,132 | 1,860 | 6,228 | 24,976 | 1,758 |
| 1836 | January | 31,356 | 3,043 | 5,961 | 19,824 | 1,486 |
| | March 3 | 20,148 | 3,060 | 17,385 | 17,750 | 2,570 |

| Date | | Balances with European Bankers | Balances with State Banks | Specie | Circulation | Public Deposits | Other Deposits |
|------|--|-------------------------------|---------------------------|--------|-------------|-----------------|----------------|
| 1833 | January | $3,106 | $ 1,596 | $ 8,951 | $17,518 | $12,752 | $7,518 |
| | July | 1,911 | 485 | 10,098 | 19,366 | 6,512 | 9,868 |
| 1834 | January | 1,801 | 1,536 | 10,031 | 19,208 | 4,230 | 6,734 |
| | July | 3,827 | 408 | 12,823 | 16,641 | 2,675 | 6,735 |
| 1835 | January | 1,922 | 1,490 | 15,708 | 17,339 | 2,621 | 7,844 |
| | July | 2,378 | (−2,065) | 13,429 | 25,332 | 1,686 | 9,558 |
| 1836 | January | 73 | 1,427 | 8,417 | 23,075 | 627 | 4,369 |
| | March 3 | 1 | 2,653 | 5,595 | 21,109 | 324 | 3,390 |

# EXHIBIT 2

### Selected Items from a Statement of Assets (*December 21, 1840*)

|  (1) Stocks and Bonds | Amount | Total |
|---|---|---|
| On hand at Bank of United States | | |
| State loans | | $    380,988 |
| City loans | | 172,625 |
| Bank stock: | | |
| Morris Canal and Banking Co. | $   961,380 | |
| Banks in Natchez, Mississippi | 465,700 | |
| Grand Gulf, Mississippi | 205,300 | |
| Vicksburg, Mississippi | 120,855 | |
| Other places, Mississippi | 48,800 | |
| New Orleans | 333,800 | |
| Louisiana | 99,200 | |
| Tennessee | 228,100 | |
| Other states | 169,865 | |
| | | 2,633,000 |
| Texas bonds and Treasury notes | | 137,015 |
| Incorporated companies: | | |
| Located in Pennsylvania: | | |
| Loan to Cumberland Valley Railroad | $   441,000 | |
| Danville & Pottsville Railroad | 647,011 | |
| Sandy & Beaver Canal | 647,011 | |
| Philadelphia, Wilmington & Baltimore Railroad | 152,500 | |
| Williamsport & Elmira Railroad | 350,000 | |
| Union Canal | 247,300 | |
| Stock of Reading Railroad | 208,800 | |
| Stock and loan to Little Schuylkill Navigation, | | |
| Railroad and Coal Co. | 960,792 | |
| Other companies | 871,346 | |
| | | 3,995,834 |
| Located in other states: | | |
| Loan to New York, Boston & Providence Railroad | $   501,592 | |
| Delaware & Chesapeake Canal | 375,893 | |
| Other companies | 370,350 | |
| | | $ 1,247,836 |
| Bank of United States stock—balance unsold, 24,714 shares | | 2,471,400 |
| On hand at agency, New Orleans | | 56,774 |
| On hand at agency in London: | | |
| Indiana 5 per cents | $   162,000 | |
| Maryland 5 per cents | 179,000 | |
| Illinois 6 per cents | 33,000 | |
| Michigan 6 per cents | 272,000 | |
| Other state bonds | 4,000 | |
| Ohio Life and Trust Co. bonds | 1,000,000 | |
| Farmers' Loan and Trust | 234,000 | |
| American Life and Trust | 527,555 | |
| Reading Railroad | 411,111 | |
| Texas bonds | 184,204 | |
| | | 3,106,871 |

# EXHIBIT 2 (*concluded*)

| (1) Stocks and Bonds | Amount | Total |
|---|---|---|
| Deposited as security for loans in Europe: | | |
| Pennsylvania 5 per cents | $5,117,906.16 | |
| Mississippi 5 per cents | 3,086,000.00 | |
| Maryland 5 per cents | 400,000.00 | |
| Indiana 5 per cents | 596,000.00 | |
| Michigan 6 per cents | 3,583,000.00 | |
| Illinois 6 per cents | 1,368,000.00 | |
| Farmers Loan and Trust bonds | 300,000.00 | |
| | | 14,450,906.16 |
| | | |
| On hand with R. Alsop and J.A. Brown, special agents: | | |
| Pennsylvania 5 per cents | $1,160,000.00 | |
| Camden & Amboy Railroad bonds | 522,222.22 | |
| Hazleton Coal Company bonds | 231,481.48 | |
| Philadelphia, Wilmington & Baltimore Railroad bonds | 811,111.11 | |
| | | 2,724,814.81 |
| Pennsylvania 5 per cents | | 16,487.21 |
| Special loan to Commonwealth | | 271,000.00 |
| Total | | $31,665,553.66 |

| (2) Due by State Banks* | | |
|---|---|---|
| To Bank of the United States: | | |
| North American Trust and Banking Co. | | $    357,000.00 |
| Bank in Natchez, Mississippi | | 2,683,982.32 |
| Banks in Vicksburg, Mississippi | | 1,429,166.74 |
| Gas Light and Banking Co. | | 2,151,799.44 |
| Banks in Florida | | 436,298.86 |
| Other banks | | 395,425.89 |
| Bonds of Planters' Bank | | 550,000.00 |
| To offices and agencies | | 711,126.98 |
| | | $ 8,714,800.23 |

*Most of these banks were weak.

## EXHIBIT 3

**Federal Government Finances, 1830–1840** (*millions of dollars*)

|      |         | Revenue |       |              | Surplus or |
|------|---------|---------|-------|--------------|------------|
|      | Customs | Public Lands | Other | Expenditures | Deficit (−) |
| 1830 | 21.9    | 2.3     | .6    | 15.1         | 9.7        |
| 1831 | 24.2    | 3.2     | 1.1   | 15.2         | 13.3       |
| 1832 | 28.5    | 2.6     | .8    | 17.3         | 14.6       |
| 1833 | 29.0    | 4.0     | .9    | 23.0         | 10.9       |
| 1834 | 16.2    | 4.9     | .7    | 18.6         | 3.2        |
| 1835 | 19.4    | 14.8    | 1.3   | 17.6         | 17.9       |
| 1836 | 23.4    | 24.9    | 2.5   | 30.9         | 20.0       |
| 1837 | 11.2    | 6.8     | 7.0   | 37.2         | (−12.3)    |
| 1838 | 16.2    | 3.1     | 7.1   | 33.9         | ( −7.6)    |
| 1839 | 23.1    | 7.1     | 1.3   | 26.9         | 4.6        |
| 1840 | 13.5    | 3.3     | 2.7   | 24.3         | ( −4.8)    |

Source: Peter Temin, *The Jacksonian Economy* (New York: Norton, 1969), p. 168.


## EXHIBIT 4

**Comparison of 1839–1843 with 1929–1933** (*percent*)

|                                           | 1839–43 | 1929–33 |
|-------------------------------------------|---------|---------|
| Change in money stock                     | − 34    | − 27    |
| Change in prices                          | − 42    | − 31    |
| Change in number of banks                 | − 23    | − 42    |
| Change in real gross investment           | − 23    | − 91    |
| Change in real consumption                | + 21    | − 19    |
| Change in real gross national product     | + 16    | − 30    |

Notes: The 1839–43 data are taken from peak to trough of the respective series, and dates differ somewhat. Data on money and banks are from late 1838 to late 1842; data on prices, from calendar-year 1839 to calendar-year 1843; data on GNP, etc., from census-year 1839 (year ending May 31, 1839) to census-year 1843.

Source: Peter Temin, *The Jacksonian Economy* (New York: Norton, 1969), p. 167.

# EXHIBIT 5

## *President Jackson's Bank Veto Message*

The present corporate body, denominated by the president, directors, and company of the Bank of the United States, will have existed at the time this act is intended to take effect twenty years. It enjoys an exclusive privilege of banking under the authority of the General Government, a monopoly of its favor and support, and, as a necessary consequence almost a monopoly of the foreign and domestic exchange. The powers, privileges, and favors bestowed upon it in the original charter, by increasing the value of the stock far above its par value, operated as a gratuity of many millions to the stockholders . . . .

The act before me proposes another gratuity to the holders of the same stock, and in many cases to the same men, of at least seven millions more . . . . It is not our own citizens only who are to receive the bounty of our Government. More than eight millions of the stock of this bank are held by foreigners. By this act the American Republic proposes virtually to make them a present of some millions of dollars. For these gratuities to foreigners and to some of our own opulent citizens the act secures no equivalent whatever. They are the certain gains of the present stockholders under the operation of this act, after making full allowance for the payment of the bonus.

Every monopoly and all exclusive privileges are granted at the expense of the public, which ought to receive a fair equivalent. The many millions which this act proposes to bestow on the stockholders of the existing bank must come directly or indirectly out of the earnings of the American people . . . .

It is not conceivable how the present stockholders can have any claim to the special favor of the Government. The present corporation has enjoyed its monopoly during the period stipulated in the original contract. If we must have such a corporation, why should not the Government sell out the whole stock and thus secure to the people the full market value of the privileges granted? Why should not Congress create and sell twenty-eight millions of stock, incorporating the purchasers with all the powers and privileges secured in this act and putting the premium upon the sales into the Treasury?

But this act does not permit competition in the purchase of this monopoly. It seems to be predicated on the erroneous idea that the present stockholders have a prescriptive right not only to the favor but to the bounty of Government. It appears that more than a fourth part of the stock is held by foreigners and the residue is held by a few hundred of our own citizens, chiefly of the richest class. For their benefit does this act exclude the whole American people from competition in the purchase of this monopoly and dispose of it for many millions less than it is worth. This seems the less excusable because some of our citizens not now stockholders petitioned that the door of competition might be opened, and offered to take a charter on terms much more favorable to the Government and country.

But this proposition, although made by men whose aggregate wealth is believed to be equal to all the private stock in the existing bank, has been set aside,

## EXHIBIT 5 (*continued*)

and the bounty of our Government is proposed to be again bestowed on the few who have been fortunate enough to secure the stock and at this moment wield the power of the existing institution. I cannot perceive the justice or policy of this course. If our Government must sell monopolies, it would seem to be its duty to take nothing less than their full value, and if gratuities must be made once in 15 or 20 years let them not be bestowed on the subjects of a foreign government nor upon a designated and favored class of men in our own country. It is but justice and good policy, as far as the nature of the case will admit, to confine our favors to our own fellow-citizens, and let each in his turn enjoy an opportunity to profit by our bounty. In the bearings of the act before me upon these points I find ample reasons why it should not become a law . . . .

Is there no danger to our liberty and independence in a bank that in its nature has so little to bind it to our country? The president of the bank has told us that most of the State banks exist by its forbearance. Should its influence become con-centered, as it may under the operation of such an act as this, in the hands of a self-elected directory whose interests are identified with those of the foreign stock-holders, will there not be cause to tremble for the purity of our elections in peace and for the independence of our country in war? Their power would be great whenever they might choose to exert it; but if this monopoly were regularly re-newed every 15 or 20 years on terms proposed by themselves, they might seldom in peace put forth their strength to influence elections or control the affairs of the nation. But if any private citizen or public functionary should interpose to curtail its powers or prevent a renewal of its privileges, it cannot be doubted that he would be made to feel its influence.

Should the stock of the bank principally pass into the hands of the subjects of a foreign country, and we should unfortunately become involved in a war with that country, what would be our condition? Of the course which would be pursued by a bank almost wholly owned by the subjects of a foreign power, and managed by those whose interests, if not affections, would run in the same direction there can be no doubt. All its operations within would be in aid of the hostile fleets and ar-mies without. Controlling our currency, receiving our public moneys, and hold-ing thousands of our citizens in dependence, it would be more formidable and dangerous than the naval and military power of the enemy.

If we must have a bank with private stockholders, every consideration of sound policy and every impulse of American feeling admonishes that it should be *purely American*. Its stockholders should be composed exclusively of our own citi-zens, who at least ought to be friendly to our Government and willing to support it in times of difficulty and danger . . . .

The bank is professedly established as an agent of the executive branch of the Government, and its constitutionality is maintained on that ground. Neither upon the propriety of present action nor upon the provisions of this act was the Ex-ecutive consulted. It has had no opportunity to say that it neither needs nor wants an agent clothed with such powers and favored by such exemptions. There is nothing in its legitimate functions which makes it necessary or proper. Whatever

## EXHIBIT 5 (*concluded*)

interest or influence, whether public or private, has given birth to this act, it cannot be found either in the wishes or necessities of the executive department, by which present action is deemed premature, and the powers conferred upon its agent not only unnecessary, but dangerous to the Government and country.

It is to be regretted that the rich and powerful too often bend the acts of government to their selfish purposes. Distinctions in society will always exist under every just government. Equality of talents, of education, or of wealth cannot be produced by human institutions. In the full enjoyment of the gifts of Heaven and the fruits of superior industry, economy, and virtue, every man is equally entitled to protection by law; but when the laws undertake to add to these natural and just advantages artificial distinctions, to grant titles, gratuities, and exclusive privileges, to make the rich richer and the potent more powerful, the humble members of society—the farmers, mechanics, and laborers—who have neither the time nor the means of securing like favors to themselves, have a right to complain of the injustice of their Government. There are no necessary evils in government. Its evils exist only in its abuses. If it would confine itself to equal protection, and, as Heaven does its rains, shower its favors alike on the high and the low, the rich and the poor, it would be an unqualified blessing. In the act before me there seems to be a wide and unnecessary departure from these just principles.

Nor is our Government to be maintained or our Union preserved by invasions of the rights and powers of the several States. In thus attempting to make our general government strong we make it weak. Its true strength consists in leaving individuals and States as much as possible to themselves—in making itself felt, not in its power, but in its beneficence; not in its control, but in its protection; not in binding the States more closely to the center, but leaving each to move unobstructed in its proper orbit.

Experience should teach us wisdom. Most of the difficulties our Government now encounters and most of the dangers which impend over our Union have sprung from an abandonment of the legitimate objects of Government by our national legislation, and the adoption of such principles as are embodied in this act. Many of our rich men have not been content with equal protection and equal benefits, but have besought us to make them richer by act of Congress. By attempting to gratify their desires we have in the results of our legislation arrayed section against section, interest against interest, and man against man, in a fearful commotion which threatens to shake the foundations of our Union. It is time to pause in our career to review our principles, and if possible revive that devoted patriotism and spirit of compromise which distinguished the sages of the Revolution and the fathers of our Union. If we cannot at once, in justice to interests vested under improvident legislation, make our Government what it ought to be, we can at least take a stand against all new grants of monopolies and exclusive privileges, against any prostitution of our Government to the advancement of the few at the expense of the many, and in favor of compromise and gradual reform in our code of laws and system of political economy.

# APPENDIX A

## *Chronology, 1800–1850*

| | |
|---|---|
| 1800 | Washington, D.C., becomes capital. Thomas Jefferson elected president. |
| 1801 | John Marshall becomes chief justice. |
| 1803 | *Marbury* v. *Madison*; Supreme Court upholds right of judicial review. Louisiana Purchase. War resumed in Europe. |
| 1804 | Hamilton killed by Vice-President Aaron Burr in duel. Lewis and Clark expedition organized. Jefferson elected for second term. |
| 1805 | *Essex* decision by British prize court increases British seizures of American neutral ships. |
| 1807 | Embargo Act. Robert Fulton's steamboat *Clermont* travels on Hudson River from Albany to New York in 30 hours. |
| 1808 | Congress prohibits Americans from participating in African slave trade. James Madison elected president. Embargo repealed; Non-Intercourse Act passed, prohibiting trade with Britain and France. |
| 1810 | Macon's Bill No. 2 passed, restoring trade with Britain and France, but providing for trade restrictions to be reimposed on one of the powers if other should abandon its seizure of American ships. West Florida annexed by Madison. |
| 1811 | Madison, believing Napoleon has removed restrictions on American commerce, prohibits trade with Britain. Charter of the Bank of the United States allowed to lapse by Congress. |
| 1812 | Congress declares war against Britain. Americans surrender Detroit to British. Madison elected for second term. |
| 1814 | British burn Washington, D.C. British turned back at Plattsburg, New York. Hartford Convention of Federalist delegates from New England states meets. Treaty of Ghent signed between United States and Great Britain. |

| | |
|---|---|
| 1815 | Battle of New Orleans; Jackson defeats British. |
| 1816 | Second Bank of the United States chartered by Congress. Protective tariff passed. James Monroe elected president. |
| 1818 | Rush-Bagot convention between Britain and United States establishes American fishing rights and boundary between United States and Canada. |
| 1819 | Commercial panic with many bank failures. Langdon Cheves becomes president of the Second Bank of the United States. Adams-Onis Treaty signed between United States and Spain; Spain cedes Florida to the United States and recognizes the western limits of the Louisiana Purchase. |
| 1820 | Missouri Compromise. James Monroe reelected president. |
| 1822 | Denmark Vesey's conspiracy to lead massive slave uprising in South Carolina exposed. |
| 1823 | President Monroe issues the Monroe Doctrine. Nicholas Biddle becomes president of the Second Bank of the United States. |
| 1824 | Congress enacts higher protective tariff. Supreme Court, in *Gibbons* v. *Ogden*, extends power of Congress to regulate commerce. John Quincy Adams elected president by House of Representatives after failure of any candidate to win electoral majority. |
| 1825 | Completion of Erie Canal. |
| 1828 | John C. Calhoun's anonymous *South Carolina Exposition and Protest*. Congress passes "Tariff on Abominations." Election of Andrew Jackson as President brings triumphant victory to new Democratic party. |
| 1830 | Jackson vetoes Maysville Road bill. Congress passes bill authorizing Indian removal. Webster-Hayne debate on land policy and nature of the union. Peter Cooper builds first American locomotive. |
| 1831 | Nat Turner's slave insurrection in Virginia. McCormick invents reaper. |
| 1832 | Jackson declares war on the Second Bank of the United States and issues a ringing veto of its recharter. Special convention in South Carolina nullifies new protective tariff. Jackson reelected president. |
| 1833 | Removal of government deposits from the Second Bank. These funds are placed in the so-called "pet" banks. Congress provides for a gradual lowering of tariffs, but passes Force bill authorizing Jackson to enforce federal law in South Carolina. Emergence of Whig party, formed by Jackson's opponents. |
| 1835 | Jackson calls for suppression of abolitionist propaganda. Roger B. Taney succeeds Marshall as chief justice. |
| 1836 | The Bank of the United States, of Pennsylvania receives its charter from the state of Pennsylvania. Jackson's Specie Circular. Congress |

adopts the Gag Rule, automatically tabling antislavery petitions. Texas proclaims independence from Mexico. Martin Van Buren elected president.

1837    Financial panic brings many bank failures and suspension of specie payment. Biddle manages the first cotton pool. Supreme Court, in *Charles River Bridge* v. *Warren Bridge*, places community rights above special privileges guaranteed by contract.

1838    John Quincy Adams's filibuster defeats move to annex Texas by joint resolution.

1839    A major depression begins, leading to widespread bankruptcies and default of several states. The failure of the second cotton pool of the Bank of the United States of Pennsylvania.

1840    Congress passes Van Buren's Independent Treasury Act. William H. Harrison elected; Whigs in power.

1841    The failure of the Bank of the United States, of Pennsylvania. Harrison's death makes John Tyler president. Congress passes general preemption law allowing squatters to purchase 160 acres of public land at minimum $1.25 per acre.

1842    Webster-Ashburton Treaty settles disputed U.S.-Canadian boundary; provides for extradition of fugitives. Tyler agrees to higher tariff after Whigs abandon demands for a distribution to the states of surplus federal revenue.

1843    Economic recovery begins. Duff Green, Calhoun, and others begin planning imperial expansion to thwart British plots to undermine American slavery.

1844    Senate rejects Calhoun's Texas annexation treaty. Calhoun, as secretary of state, incorporates defense of slavery as part of America's foreign policy. Slavery issue splits Methodist Episcopal Church into northern and southern camps. James K. Polk elected president.

1845    Before Tyler retires, Texas annexed by joint resolution of Congress. Polk gives an aggressive reformulation to the Monroe Doctrine. Polk risks war with England by asserting America's right to "All Oregon" and terminating joint-occupation agreement. Failure of Ireland's potato crop marks beginning of mass emigration to United States. Sectional division of the Baptists.

1846    Beginning of Mexican War. General Zachary Taylor invades Mexico from the north. U.S.-British dispute over Oregon settled. Wilmot Proviso fuses question of slavery's expansion with consequences of Mexican War. Walker tariff adopted for revenue only, eliminates principle of protection. Elias Howe patents sewing machine.

1847    General Winfield Scott captures Vera Cruz and Mexico City. Mormons arrive in Great Salt Lake Valley. Calhoun's resolutions in Senate, affirming right to take slaves into any United States territory.

1848        Treaty of Guadalupe Hidalgo ends Mexican War. Gold discovered on
            American River in California. Van Buren, running for president on
            Free-Soil ticket, receives 10 percent of popular vote. Zachary Taylor
            elected president.

1850        In Congress, violent sectional debate culminates in Compromise of
            1850. Taylor's death makes Millard Filmore president. Nashville
            convention considers the South's stake in the Union.

Source: Bernard Bailyn, et al., *The Great Republic*, pp. 422–23 and 644–45.

# CASE 6

# *Samuel Slater, Francis Cabot Lowell, and the Beginnings of the Factory System in the United States* *

## Introduction

In nearly every country, the first factories have produced cotton cloth. As a nation industrializes, textiles lead the way. This has been true in the 20th century in such relatively underdeveloped countries as Mexico and India. It was the case in the 18th century for Great Britain, the first industrial nation.

Britain had been, for centuries, a major producer of hand-spun and woven woolen yarn and cloth. In the last decades of the 18th century, however, a series of mechanical inventions made possible the production of cloth from raw cotton by water- and then steam-powered machines. The invention of these machines not only set off the industrial revolution in Britain but also had a powerful impact on the American economy by creating a massive, wholly new demand for cotton. As a result, cotton was first grown commercially in the United States in 1786. After the invention of the cotton gin in 1793 made possible the exploitation of upland cotton, that crop, and with it the slave-manned plantation, spread rapidly inland and westward.

---

*This case was prepared by Alfred D. Chandler, Jr., as a basis for class discussion rather than to illustrate either effective or ineffective handling of an administrative situation. Other contributors to the case have been Thomas R. Navin and Glenn Porter. The section on Slater is based on a case entitled "Samuel Slater and the American Textile Industry" that first appeared in N. S. B. Gras and Henrietta Larson, *Casebook in American Business History* (New York: Appleton-Century-Crofts, 1939), pp. 209–30 and was revised in 1974.

Harvard Business School case 377-222, rev. 6/84.

In addition, cotton textile machinery soon found its way to the United States. Samuel Slater, a skilled British mechanic, came in 1789 to Rhode Island. There, financed by members of an established mercantile family, the Browns, he established the first spinning mill in this country. Because weaving was more complex than spinning, it was mechanized more slowly. In 1813, Francis Cabot Lowell, of a prominent Boston mercantile clan, brought from England to the United States the plans for a power loom. Lowell's achievement was, however, more than just introducing the new weaving machines; by placing these looms in the same building with improved spinning machinery, he built the first integrated textile mill in the United States. This was the nation's first modern factory.

The following two selections tell of the beginnings of the textile industry in the United States and the coming of the factory system. The first has been compiled from the records of Samuel Slater and his associates, particularly the records of the partnership of Almy and Brown, which financed Slater's activities and marketed the output of his mills. The second selection is from a memoir written by Nathan Appleton in 1858. Appleton, a close friend and ally of Lowell, assisted in financing the latter's venture and in marketing his goods, and then in setting up the first industrial city in the United States—one that was named for Lowell.

# Samuel Slater and Almy & Brown

### Innovations in Spinning

Before the coming of the innovations in spinning and weaving, four of the five basic operations involved in the production of cotton goods were performed by women and children. Only the fifth operation, weaving, was performed by men. Women *picked* out of the cotton the seeds and seed pods that had not been removed in the cotton field. They then *carded* the cotton by brushing it with something that resembled a wire dog brush. Next, they shaped it into a *roving* or a loose strand of roughly parallel fibers. Then finally they *spun* the cotton into a filament or "yarn." The yarn was then sent to the weavers, who *wove* it into cloth.

One of the devices by which the cotton manufacturing process was gradually mechanized was the invention of a "jenny" which permitted the production of not one, but several, strands of cotton yarn simultaneously. The output of the spinner was thereby increased somewhat, but the machine still had to be operated by hand power, and the quality of the output was still so poor that it continued to be necessary to use cotton yarn running in only one direction of the cloth, with linen or wool running in the other direction to provide strength and durability.

The invention which simultaneously solved the problem both of quality and of output was the spinning machine patented by Richard Arkwright in 1769 (the same year in which Watt secured the first patent on his steam engine; together, the Watt and Arkwright patents were the most famous and the most important in England in the 18th century). The Arkwright spinning frame was designed to be used with central power, but because of lack of capital, Arkwright's first "central power" had to be a blindfolded horse, led around a rotating shaft in the basement of his mill. By 1771, however, Arkwright had secured the financial assistance of a merchant named Jedediah Strutt and had built a mill that was driven by water power.

Arkwright went on to make a fortune for himself, and Jedediah Strutt augmented his own estate by engaging independently in cotton manufacture on license from Arkwright. But it is doubtful whether either man would have made the success he did had it not been for the rotary-motion steam engine put on the market by the firm of Boulton & Watt after 1782. This engine freed the manufacturer from dependence on water power, of which England was particularly short, and made possible the amazing growth of the English cotton textile industry between 1782 and 1800.

### Samuel Slater Leaves England for America

One of the employees of Jedediah Strutt in his independent cotton mill ventures was Samuel Slater, who began his career as a clerk for Strutt at the age of 14 and who later became an overseer (foreman). Slater was a steady, persevering, self-contained, blunt young man with a capability for enterprise and an infinite concern for detail. As the cotton mill fever swept through England, he became convinced that prosperous mill conditions could not continue, and he began to toy with the idea of emigrating to America. American papers were carrying advertisements encouraging young Englishmen to bring their knowledge of the new types of textile machinery to the United States, and Slater believed that a fortune might lie in wait for him across the seas.

In those days it was not easy for a skilled mechanic to leave his homeland, however. For a century, the British government had been following a restrictive policy wherever there was danger or threat to England's world supremacy in economic affairs; and with the textile machinery revolution, this policy was extended to cover the exportation of any machinery and of models or diagrams and even was interpreted to prohibit the emigration of any trained personnel. In 1789, the 21-year-old Slater evaded these restrictions by disguising himself as a farm boy and departing by way of London. It was his conscious intention to secure the advantages, financial and otherwise, of being the first to introduce into the United States the improved textile machinery with which he had become, by personal association, so thoroughly familiar. (A few years later—in 1805—a worker named Lievin Bauwens managed to smuggle out of England a set of machinery drawings with which he was able to launch a cotton textile industry on the continent of Europe.)

Upon arriving in New York, Slater made inquiries regarding possible sources of financial support and was advised to get in touch with the Brown family of Providence. The Browns were known to be wealthy merchants who had interested themselves in cotton manufacture, partly as a speculative investment and partly because there was abroad in the country at the time a patriotic fervor that made people want to advance the industrial prosperity of their new republic.

## The Firm of Almy & Brown

The four Brown brothers had inherited a mercantile fortune, which had been made in the wholesaling of English manufactured goods, the exchange of goods with the West Indies (especially Rhode Island and Connecticut tobacco for West Indian molasses) and the trade in African slaves. Under the astute management of the brothers, the family business had branched into manufacturing, especially the production of high-grade candles made from spermaceti (whale) wax and the operation of an iron works at which were made some of the cannon used during the Revolutionary War. Moses Brown, the youngest of the brothers, had interested himself also in cotton manufacture and, after retirement, had experimented with some textile machinery, which proved to be imperfectly made. Moses had also followed with interest the unsuccessful cotton manufacturing venture of the Cabot family, wealthy merchants of Beverly, Massachusetts, north of Boston.

In Slater's correspondence with the Browns, he received a letter in which Moses described at some length the unproductive cotton manufacturing experiment with which he had been associated:[1]

> We have two spinning machines. . .one of 32 spindles,[2] the other of 24. They have been worked, and spun about one hundred and fifty skeins of cotton yarn, from 5 to 8 skeins[3] of 15 lays[4] around a reel of 2 yards to the pound; but the person whom we let the mill to, being unacquainted with the business, and the mills probably not perfected, he could not make wages in attending them, and therefore they are at present, still. We then wrought hand roping and the carding machine was not in order. We have since got a jenny, and are putting on fine cards to the machines: these with an eight-four and a sixty spinning jenny, and a doubling and twisting jenny, compose the principal machinery about our manufactory. We have from Ireland a man and his wife who are spinners on the jennies, but we are destitute of a person acquainted with the frames. We shall be glad to be informed what quantity of yarn your mills spin in a day on one spindle. What number of spindles a lad can, or does attend, and at what age? How your roping is made, what fineness, whether twisting harder or softer than for jennies? Whether the cotton is soaped before carding, as that for the jenny, or not at all? What the wooden rollers in the mills are covered with? Ours have been done with calf skin. How the taking up is regulated? Ours is by leather string. Or what the spools play and run; on irons?

In January 1790, Slater accepted the invitation of Moses Brown to visit Providence to discuss the manufacture of cotton goods by the English method. Moses was quickly impressed by Slater's obvious command of the cotton manufacturing business, but the older man knew from experience that the establishment of an op-

---

[1]George S. White, *Memoir of Samuel Slater* (Philadelphia: Kelley, 1836), pp. 64–65.

[2]A spindle is a slender tapered rod, probably made of wood or iron at this time, set in vertical position along the side of a ring-spinning frame upon which a bobbin (a spool-like device) revolves to receive yarn as it is spun.

[3]A skein is a quantity of thread or yarn wound in a coil.

[4]As can be seen from the context, a certain number of lays of yarn make up a skein. Thus, a lay is a thinner strand than a skein.

erating mill would take considerable time, especially since Slater's equipment consisted only of the knowledge he carried in his head and did not include either drawings or scale models. Brown therefore proposed that the mercantile firm of Almy & Brown (consisting of William Almy, a son-in-law of Moses, and Smith Brown, a kinsman) contract with Slater to build a pilot battery of machines—cards, roving machines, and spinning frames. (Picking and carding were to continue by hand, and weaving was to be by hand-operated looms in homes or in separate establishments.)

A new partnership was formed to be known as Almy, Brown & Slater, and a contract was drawn as of April 5, 1790:[5]

> The following agreement, made between William Almy and Smith Brown of the one part, and Samuel Slater of the other part, Witnesseth that the said parties have mutually agreed to be concerned together in, and carry on, the spinning of cotton by water, (of which the said Samuel professes himself a workman, well skilled in all its branches;) upon the following terms, viz: that the said Almy and Brown, on their part, are to turn in the machinery, which they have already purchased, at the price they cost them, and to furnish materials for the building of two carding machines, viz: a breaker and a finisher; a drawing and roving frame; and to extend the spinning mills, or frames, to one hundred spindles. And the said Samuel, on his part, convenants and engages, to devote his whole time and service, and to exert his skill according to the best of his abilities, and have the same effected in a workmanlike manner, similar to those used in England, for the like purposes. And it is mutually agreed between the said parties, that the said Samuel shall be considered an owner and proprietor in one-half of the machinery aforesaid, and accountable for one-half of the expense that hath arisen, or shall arise, from the building, purchasing, or repairing, of the same, but not to sell, or in any manner dispose of any part, or parcel thereof to any other person or persons, excepting the said Almy and Brown; neither shall any others be entitled to hold any right, interest, or claim, in any part of the said machinery, by virtue of any right which the said Slater shall or may derive from these presents, unless by an agreement, expressed in writing from the said Almy and Brown, first had and obtained—unless the said Slater has punctually paid one-half of the cost of the said machinery with interest thereon; nor then, until he has offered the same to the said Almy and Brown in writing upon the lowest terms; that he will sell or dispose of his part of the said machinery to any other person, and instructed the said Almy and Brown, or some others by them appointed, in the full and perfect knowledge of the use of the machinery, and the art of water spinning. And it is further agreed, that the said Samuel, as a full and adequate compensation for his whole time and services, both whilst in constructing and making the machinery, and in conducting and executing the spinning, and preparing to spin upon the same, after every expense arising from the business is defrayed, including the usual commissions of two and one-half percent for purchasing of the stock, and four percent for disposing of the yarn, shall receive one half of the profits, which shall be ascertained by settlement from time to time, as occasion may require; and the said Almy and Brown the other half—the said Almy and Brown to be employed in the purchasing of stock, and disposing of the yarn. And it is further covenanted, that this indenture shall make void and supersede the former articles of agreement, made between the

---

[5]White, *Slater,* p. 65.

said Almy and Brown and the said Slater, and that it shall be considered to commence, and the conditions mentioned in it be binding upon the parties, from the beginning of the business; the said Samuel to be at the expense of his own time and board from thence forward. And it is also agreed that if the said Almy and Brown choose to put in apprentices to the business, that they have liberty so to do. The expense arising from the maintenance of whom, and the advantages derived from their services during the time the said Almy and Brown may think proper to continue them in the business, shall be equally borne and received as is above provided for in the expenses and profits of the business. It is also to be understood, that, whatever is advanced by the said Almy and Brown, either for the said Slater, or to carry on his part of the business, is to be repaid them with interest thereon, for which purpose they are to receive all the yarn that may be made, the one-half of which on their own account, and the other half they are to receive and dispose of, on account of the said Slater, the net proceeds of which they are to credit him, towards their advance, and stocking his part of the works, so that the business may go forward.

In witness whereof the parties to these presents have interchangeably set their hands, this fifth day of the fourth month, seventeen hundred and ninety.

Wm. Almy<br>
Smith Brown<br>
Samuel Slater

Witnesses—
Oziel Wilkinson, Abraham Wilkinson

## Early Years of Almy, Brown & Slater

Slater found that the old machines were not worth improving—the spinning frame made very poor yarn. He therefore set about building new machines with capital furnished by Almy & Brown. He would not, however, begin building the Arkwright machine until he had been promised a man to work on wood who should be under bond not to steal the patterns nor disclose the nature of the work. When he had been satisfied on this point, he at once set to work behind closed shutters and drawn blinds to build carding engines, roving frames, and spinning machines.

Slater found that he had settled in a thoroughly Quaker community. His partners were Quakers and so were the Wilkinsons, the family with which he boarded. And when he encountered difficulty with the insertion of carding wires into the leather strips that were to form the covering of his carding cylinders, his partners invited consultation with another Quaker, Pliny Earle, who had made a business of manufacturing leather-set hand cards.

The Wilkinson family figured prominently from the first. Oziel Wilkinson was the operator of a blacksmith shop and in his shop made many of the metal parts needed by Slater for his machines. Oziel's son, David Wilkinson, was a clever designer and helped Slater to improve on many of his first rough efforts. Later Slater was to marry one of the daughters of the Wilkinson family.

Initially, the machinery was powered by hand. Later water power was installed. On wintry nights the water wheel frequently froze, and the impatient Slater, irked by delays, sometimes spent two or three hours before breakfast, it is said, breaking the ice.[6] The effects of this exposure are believed to have stayed with him the rest of his life.

By December 1790, two spinning machines were completed, and Slater was ready to begin commercial production, though admittedly on a limited scale.[7] There is no definite information available as to the amount of yarn produced or the profits made, if any, by the mill, but two years later there appeared in the records of Almy & Brown two entries which may have been intended to summarize the cotton-manufacturing venture to date. If so, it would seem that the scale of operations had been moderate indeed. The first entry is credited to Slater's account and the second is debited.[8]

> Nov. 25, 1792. By the one-half of the proceeds from the sale of yarn spun at the mills, and of credit taken to our account, and accounted for by us as sold—£882 4s 11 1/2d.
>
> To the one-half of our account against spinning mills for machinery, & c. up to Feb. 11, 1792, £252 1 6.
>
> To one-half of do. for stock (raw materials?) up to same date, 210 19 1 3/4.

Apparently, Slater's pilot efforts were regarded as successful, for in 1793, Slater's partners agreed to finance the construction, at Pawtucket Falls, on the Blackstone River north of Providence, of a mill, which was to be completely equipped with Slater machinery. This mill, handsomely constructed of native stone, came to be known later as the "Old Mill." (It still stands and is now open to the public as a museum.)

The commercial success of the "Old Mill" must have been considerable. Not only was it widely imitated, but in at least one year for which we have accounts (1803), it would appear that the amount and rate of the return were considerable.[9]

## Labor

The first record of employees begins with Monday, December 20, 1790, though some say that the new machinery began producing yarn as early as October. During the first week, four boys, Turpin and Charles Arnold, Smith Wilkinson, and Jabez Jenks, were employed full time. On the next Monday (December 27), Eunice Arnold, on Wednesday of the same week Otis Borrows, and on Thursday, John and Sylvanus (Varnus) Jenks commenced work. On the following Monday (January 3), Ann Arnold was added to the list, and during that week, all the nine

---

[6]Perry Walton, *The Story of Textiles* (Boston: J. S. Lawrence, 1925), pp. 172–73.

[7]The larger of Slater's two original spinning frames is on display in the Smithsonian Institute. The only metal parts are the gears and rollers; the rest is made of wood.

[8]White, *Slater*, p. 76.

[9]*Almy & Brown's Account with Spinning Mills,* 1793–1833, Slater Papers, Baker Library, Harvard University.

operatives, seven boys and two girls, worked the full time of six days. The same operatives also continued in the fourth week, though either "Varnus" Jenks or Smith Wilkinson (there is an error in the record, which makes this point uncertain) worked only five days, while Turpin Arnold was absent two half-days.

All these workers were children of from seven to twelve, according to Smith Wilkinson, Slater's brother-in-law, who began work for Almy, Brown & Slater at the age of ten "by tending the breaker."[10] The family basis of this employment is shown by the fact that among these nine early workers, only four family names were represented, there being four Arnolds, three Jenkses, a Wilkinson, and a Borrows.

Since Pawtucket at that time contained only about a dozen houses, at first it was difficult to secure operatives for the mills. On this account, Slater was obliged to persuade families to emigrate to Pawtucket. His son, H. N. Slater, explains that the Arnolds, with a dozen children, lived in a lean-to cabin of slabs with a stone chimney. Mrs. Arnold, on being consulted about moving to Pawtucket, stipulated that the family should be provided with as good a house as the one they would be leaving.[11]

We have some information about working and living conditions among Slater's workers. Wages ranged from 80 cents to $1.30 and $1.40 per week. There was neither school nor church in Pawtucket, so Slater established in 1793 a Sunday school in his own house for the children working in the mills and for those of the adult employees who had not received an elementary education. At first he taught school himself, but he later hired students from Rhode Island College, now Brown University. Slater's strict paternal discipline was not always well received. He attempted to introduce the English apprenticeship system, but it did not suit the American temperament and had to be abandoned.

Before being spun into yarn in the mills constructed by Slater and his associates, raw cotton was put out to poor families to be cleansed and whipped at from 4 to 6 cents per pound, the rate depending on the cleanliness of the cotton. The raw cotton was delivered in bags of about 100 pounds each and was carried sometimes for many miles, usually on horseback, and gave employment to many women and children at their homes.[12]

## Marketing (through Almy & Brown)

The firm of Almy, Brown & Slater did no weaving. It produced only yarn and expected that the yarn would be woven into cloth either by the customer or by someone hired by him to do the work. The firm did not market the yarn directly, but rather turned it over to be sold by the mercantile firm of Almy & Brown. Slater

---

[10]William R. Bagnall, *Samuel Slater* (Middletown, Connecticut: 1890), pp. 44–45; White, *Slater,* p. 99. According to Moses Brown, the work was done by children of from 8 to 14, not a material discrepancy.

[11]*Slater Mills at Webster,* 1812–1912 (Worcester, Massachusetts: 1912), p. 18.

[12]*The Two Samuels, Slater and Batchelder,* Scrapbook (Boston, 1791), p. 5.

consequently had nothing to do with the sale of the goods he produced beyond ensuring their marketable quality. This complete separation of the production and
marketing functions came to be typical of manufacturing enterprises wherever
they were established by mercantile interests, and it continued in existence in the
United States for nearly a hundred years.

The first machine-spun yarn went to market in June 1791, about six months
after the spinning had started. The initial lot of 116 pounds brought £35 3s 4d. It
was sold principally near Providence, but in some instances, as far away as Nor-
wich, Connecticut.

By 1798, as we see in a letter of January 9 to Hussey, Faber & Co.,[13] a Boston
firm with a branch in Lynn, the market must have been extended at least to Boston, since Almy & Brown promised to send this firm an invoice of yarn in care of
Joseph Hussey, Boston, to be forwarded to them. This letter acknowledged the receipt of a payment and granted the firm the privilege of selling yarn on credit for
commission, accounting with Almy & Brown semiannually. Almy & Brown promised to keep the firm well supplied with yarn and urged that its sale be vigorously
promoted.

A letter of January 22 to John B. Cockray (address not given in copy) indicates the sending of a consignment of yarn on six-months' settlement. But, wrote
Almy & Brown, "being Desirous to spread the use of the yarn We matter not so
much as to the punctual payment of the same, unless sold, provided it be in safe
Hands."

On March 19, 1798, Almy & Brown wrote to "Oziell Wilkenson" mention-
ing that they had sent him something over $400 worth of cotton goods and cotton
yarn, which they wished him to sell for money or barter for grain or, failing to do
so, leave in the hands of Harris and Peter Colt, Hartford, or some other responsible person who would handle their sale. The yarn was invoiced at the wholesale
price so that Wilkinson would receive the ordinary retail profit. He was authorized to sell on a credit of 90 days, "with good security, such as on enquiry thou
would be willing to take was the Property thy Own." The goods were not to be
sold for grain unless the price was such that the grain could be freighted to Providence without loss to Almy & Brown. Wilkinson was also asked to hunt up some
suitable person in Hartford to sell yarn for knitting.

A letter of March 26, 1798, to a William Brown (no address) gives some in-
sight into marketing methods. Brown was informed that "We are free to furnish
You with any quantity of yarn you can dispose of either by the Bundle or Pound.
Neither do we intend So long as you give us satisfaction to supply any others on
your Island with the same to sell on Commissions. But should there be application
to Purchase the Yarn of us We expect to sell the same as heretofore."

On May 1, some cotton yarn "Spun by Water," as they were careful to explain, was sent by Almy & Brown to one Jacob Merritt, who with his brothers
Daniel and Isaac, had been recommended by a certain John Barker as "suitable

---

[13]The letters quoted in this section are from the Almy & Brown Papers in the Rhode Island Historical Society, Providence.

persons to sell the same." It seems likely that Merritt was in New York State, as his brothers were, since Almy & Brown stated that since "this was sent only on Tryal it would be most agreeable to you to sell it on Commissions as several others do in Hutson Albaney & elsewhare." The yarn was charged at the "Retale Price," and Merritt was expected "to sell it at that Price & for us (Almy and Brown) to allow thee a Commission of 5 p. cent for doing the Business for us (after paying) & (for us) to pay all expenses attending the Transportation (&c)." The words in parentheses are crossed out in the original copy.

It is evident that Almy & Brown felt that this yarn was a commodity not very familiar to the section of the country in which Merritt lived. Consequently, they carefully explained the different grades and how they were sold. "The yarn," they wrote, "is sold Without any Trouble of Weighing, every skain of which haveing been Weighed to 7 1/2 skains to the Pound, in order to make that easy, the Purchaser has his choice either to take 7 or 8 skain, paying for the 1/2 skain or having it deducted either as is most agreeable." Although the Merritt brothers were strangers to Almy & Brown, still "from recommendation given We hereby entrust you with the yarn," requesting a notification upon its arrival and on the "Prospect of selling the same."

In May 1798, another letter contained a refusal to send further yarn to a client until a settlement of accounts had been made. This letter stated that, in view of the fact that Almy & Brown had to pay for their material and labor regularly, they had to place their yarn where they would be sure of payments at stated times.

A letter of July 26 to Benjamin Chamberlain, Philadelphia, regretted that no whitened yarn was on hand and instructed him to pay Elijah Waring, their agent at Philadelphia, for the yarn already sold. Another letter of October 7, evidently in reply to a letter of inquiry from Stephen Hoyt of Poughkeepsie, gave the terms under which, in this case, they would allow him to sell their yarn, namely at 5 percent commission, Almy & Brown to pay all expenses of transportation, advertising, postage, and so on. Another, December 15, to their Philadelphia agent, Elijah Waring, instructed him to settle with Benjamin Chamberlain, receive the yarn left on his hands, return the yarn not likely to be sold, and put the rest in the hands of Letchwork or some other person "either to sell on our acct. [or?] their own." A letter directing Chamberlain to settle with Waring followed. The impression given is that it had been thought best to sever the connection and that the reason was Almy & Brown's dissatisfaction with the way in which Chamberlain was handling the business.

Apparently by this time their yarn was disposed of easily, as is seen in a letter of December 21, 1798, to Hussey, Faber & Co. This letter acknowledged the receipt of a sum of money and an order for yarn but stated that in the future, the commission would be smaller since we "think that 5 per cent on yarn Sold at whole Saile now a considerable quantity is and probably more will be vended, is rather too high a comishons when the Sales of it was only getting introduced we thought we might give that premium, but now we apprehend that two & half per Ct would be as much as is usually given. . .if that would be agreeable to you to receive the yarn at in future, we shall be glad to furnish you with as good an assortment as we can from time to time." Whether or not Almy & Brown made this reduction effective, it is evident that they felt that their yarn had been firmly established.

By 1801, Almy & Brown were selling to storekeepers in Portland, Newburyport, Marblehead, Salem, Boston, New Bedford, Nantucket, and other coastal cities in Massachusetts, as well as to ports along the Rhode Island and Connecticut shores. They were also shipping a large portion of their product to New York City, Albany, Philadelphia, and Baltimore. The quantities sent to each place continued to be small—only Portland, Boston, and Philadelphia took as much as $1,000 worth—yet the market steadily widened. By 1801, there were even some manufacturers who were buying yarn from Almy & Brown for the purpose of having it put out to be woven or knitted. For ten years, the firm had enjoyed a near-monopoly of machine-made cotton yarn in this country. Imported English woven goods still dominated the market for quality fabrics, but among those customers who could not afford to buy their cloth ready-made, the cotton yarn marketed by Almy & Brown had to compete only with expensive imported yarn or with low-quality domestic yarn that was spun by hand or on jennies.

### Dissension among the Partners

As production increased, Slater appears to have grown restive under the agreement which virtually transferred financial control of the cotton manufacturing business to the firm of Almy & Brown. A letter written by Slater's two partners in 1798 indicates that Slater was beginning to feel himself aggrieved.

Providence 8th *mo.* 21 1798

Respected Friend
Samuel Slater

\* \* \* \* \*

In my reply to thy suggestions, that we do not pay attention to the settlement of our accts with thee, that a long period of time has elapsed since their commencement, that they lies in a precarious situation—and that thou thinks it high time that they were settled, We say that we have always been ready to make a settlement with thee, at any given time since our accts were opened, that we have repeatedly manifested that readiness—and that we are now also ready to close them whenever thou will attend to it. Whence, therefore, this very extraordinary Paragraph in they Letter, that on "Monday next, being the 27th Inst. I *will* stop making rovings, so that all the rovings there are on hand may be spun in the course of a few days, in order to weigh off all the yarn, and stock on hand, so that we may complete our settlement." If, indeed, thou means that after that period thou shalt decline having concern in the mill and withdraw thy personal attention from the business it would be a subject of consideration & discussion how far that would comfort with thy engagements, but if thou means a total stopping and derangement of the business, we now inform thee that we can by no means consent to such a measure. We have not indeed invested in that business our Propperty and exerted our Credit as Extensively to effect the establishment, and continuance of it, to have it put a period to and made a sacrifice of, whenever it may suit the proposed interestet or *Will* of any Individual. There are a variety of ways and means that they may be devised to ascertain the yarn & stock on hand unattended with such unnecessary derangement & loss.

Upon the whole, notwithstanding the terms in which thine is couched, we must suppose, thou meant it as a proposition merely, which having so fully expressed our disapprobation of, we rest, depending that thou will not fulfill so infamous a measure, as it must eventually prove to thyself as well as to us.

We are respectfully fds
Almy & Brown

Dissension was increased the following year when Obadiah Brown, a son of Moses Brown and a new partner in the firm of Almy, Brown & Slater, announced his intention of joining with friends to promote a new cotton mill in Warwick, a few miles southwest of Providence. Obadiah and his associates wished to equip their mills with Slater-type machinery, but Slater refused them the privilege of hiring his trained machinists to supervise the construction. Nevertheless, Brown insisted on his right to the machinery designs owned by Almy, Brown, & Slater and finally exercised the right even at the cost of Slater's friendship.

Slater retaliated in the following year, 1800, by forming a partnership with his father-in-law, Oziel Wilkinson, and his brothers-in-law, Timothy Greene and William Wilkinson, to build and operate the so-called "White Mill" in Rehoboth, Massachusetts. Slater's interest in the new partnership was one half, Oziel's was one fourth, and that of the other two one eighth each. At first Almy & Brown refused Slater permission to erect the mill on a piece of property owned by the Almy, Brown & Slater partnership, but Slater took the matter to court and secured a jury decision to partition the land and the water privileges.

These personal differences did not, however, bring about a dissolution of the Almy, Brown & Slater partnership. By 1806, the partners were planning a joint extension of their manufacturing facilities and the addition to the partnership of Slater's younger brother, John. Slater had induced his brother, who was likewise a skilled mechanic, to leave England in 1803 and to bring with him as extensive a knowledge of the new manufacturing techniques as he could acquire by visiting the textile-producing centers of the country before his departure for the United States.

The new mill, erected in 1806, was built on a water-power site in northern Rhode Island that had been personally selected by John Slater. Around the mill was built a company town to which was given the name of Slatersville. This town is still in existence, but there are no longer active textile mills there.

## Competition

During the years 1806 to 1812, neither the Browns nor the Slaters added to their mill properties, though the period saw a rapid expansion of Slater-type mills, especially along the Blackstone River north of Pawtucket. The embargo acts of 1807–1808 effectively prevented the importation of competing English yarns and

fabrics and led America promoters to undertake the production of domestic ma-
chine-made cottons in competition with Almy, Brown & Slater. In 1806, there
were only 15 cotton mills operating in the United States. By the end of 1809, there
are said to have been 62 cotton mills in operation in the United States and 25 in the
process of being erected.[14]

Most, if not all, of these mills were built by men who had received their training either directly or indirectly under Samuel Slater. The turnover among Slater's
machine builders and repairmen was high, for as soon as a man learned the design
and operation of Slater's machines, he was in a position to sell his services as an
itinerant machine builder. Some of these men came to specialize in the production
of a particular machine and eventually set up shop and went into business for
themselves. From this beginning the textile machinery business of southern New
England took form.

Marketing was a serious problem for Almy, Brown & Slater in those years of
mounting competition from domestic manufacturers. The pioneering work which
they had done had made their yarn favorably known over a considerable area.
The Almy & Brown correspondence with agents in 1803–1804 shows that they
were trying to build up a demand for superior quality and to extend their market
farther south and into the newer West. They were attempting to hold their old customers, but also to add new ones, and particularly to increase direct sales at a discount for cash. In 1803, Obadiah Brown made a trip for Almy, Brown & Slater
through Maryland, Delaware, Pennsylvania, New Jersey, and New York, securing new customers and pushing sales. In a letter of April 8 from New York City, he
mentioned that he had been in Newport, Troy, and Eastown, taking orders for
cotton yarn, stocking yarn, and sewing cotton. In a letter of May 20 from Carlisle,
Pennsylvania, he wrote that he had been traveling about through that state with
Elijah Waring, visiting possible or former customers in Philadelphia, Lancaster,
Carlisle, and Yorktown, and taking orders for cotton yarn, bedticking, and stocking yarn, some to sell on trial and some for cash. At this time, Almy & Brown also
began to encourage hand weaving, extending credit to master weavers.

Almy & Brown wrote to one agent in March 1807: "If thou can dispose of
yarn when your river is open we will send thee an assortment as we are extending
our business in that line, and as others are also getting into the same business, in
consequence of which we shall probably have to extend our sales, we therefore
wish to keep all our old correspondents supplied."

The embargoes brought depression to the commercial ports which had been
Almy, Brown & Slater's best customers. In 1808, new devices were adopted in an
attempt to revive the market. Almy & Brown ordered their agents to advertise and
print handbills announcing the superiority of their yarn. They aggressively sought
new customers. They offered extensive credit. They agreed to accept produce of
various sorts and tried to exchange their goods for other goods to be sold in their
store. They tried to get wholesale agents to sell in small lots. They considered

---

[14]Albert Gallatin, *Report on American Manufactures* (Boston: Farrand, Mallory, 1810).

sending out peddlers but feared the difficulty of securing good men. They even tried to maintain a price agreement among manufacturers. At the same time their agents were writing of generous offers made to them by other mills.

A word might be said on price maintenance. Almy & Brown, who had originally set the price, had made it their policy to maintain price. "As we were the first that undertook the business of spinning cotton yarn in this country," they wrote in 1808, "consequently we were the first that made a price for the article, which price has, as far as we have any knowledge, been adhered to by those who are concerned in the business. Should any vary the price, we should be very much obliged by being informed of it, and the quality of their yarn, conceiving a mutual understanding among the makers and vendors of the article would be mutually beneficial."

One way of increasing the demand for yarn was to encourage hand-loom weavers. At this early period we have no information concerning Slater's relations, if any, with the problem of weaving, but the practices of his partners are indicated in their correspondence. In June 1808, they wrote to John Wintringham, a master weaver of Poughkeepsie:

> We are glad to hear that thou are extending thy business by setting more looms up, as we are desirous to encourage the manufacture of the yarn into cloth, by others rather than by ourselves, wishing to promote the industrious mechanic and manufacturer of cloth. We wish thee to increase thy sales to the full extent of the sales of cloth in the parts of the country where thou lives, having ourselves been obliged to get our yarn wove into blue stripes, etc. in order to sell the same, but if we can sell the yarn to the weaver and be certain of our pay, we shall prefer doing that to manufacturing it ourselves.

It should be noted that the practice of one manufacturer specializing in the spinning of yarn and another in the weaving of cloth was typically English. In this country, however, textile manufacturers brought the spinning and weaving functions under one management at a very early date.

From time to time the partners of Almy, Brown & Slater put out their yarn to household weavers to be converted into cloth at so much per yard. However, the partners disliked the irregularity in quantity and quality inherent in the domestic putting-out system and preferred to sell their yarn to manufacturers who specialized in weaving. In a letter to John Wintringham, January 17, 1808, they wrote: "We have several hundred pieces now out weaving, but a hundred looms in families will not weave so much cloth as ten at least constantly employed under the immediate supervision of a workman." In order to provide such supervision, Slater and other mill owners moved the weavers and their hand looms into central shops near their spinning establishments.

Rather little effort was made at the Slater mill to produce goods in quantities that bore any very close relationship with market demand. The mill produced and the mercantile firm of Almy & Brown disposed of the output as best it could. On one occasion in the spring of 1809, Almy & Brown had accumulated an inventory of 100,000 pounds of unsold yarn, including a three-year supply of one kind. A common way of disposing of such a surplus was to conduct a large-scale auction sale. For years the New England cotton textile industry, divided as it was with the production function under one management and the sales function under another, continued to produce at a steady pace until the markets had become saturated, whereupon an auction was held, followed by a period of complete demoralization of sales and widespread layoffs at the mills.[15]

## Additional Mills (1812–1820)

By 1812, Samuel Slater probably regarded himself as a wealthy man. Besides his half interest in the highly profitable mill owned by Almy, Brown & Slater, he held a half interest (with his in-laws) in the "White Mill" at Rehoboth, and a quarter interest (with Almy, Brown and his brother John) in the mill at Slatersville.

With the outbreak of the War of 1812, Slater saw the opportunity of extending his financial interests by taking advantage of the period when British imports were shut off from American markets. He therefore directed one of his employees, Bela Tiffany, to make a careful survey of mill sites in the region north of Providence. On Tiffany's recommendation, Slater decided to construct at Oxford, Massachusetts (now Webster), a mill known as the "Green Mill," with Tiffany as a minor partner.

According to a letter written by Slater on February 23, 1814, to Elijah Waring of Philadelphia, the "Green Mill" was expected to produce $100,000 worth of yarn annually, most of which Slater hoped to market in Philadelphia. Evidently, too, there was some talk that Slater wanted to have charge not only of the marketing of yarn from his own mills but also of that part which was his rightful share in the production of the mill owned by Almy, Brown & Slater. Although nothing seems to have come of this latter proposal, it is evident that the original partners were still not conducting their business on cordial terms.

Slater's next venture, inspired by the War of 1812, was the establishment in 1815 of a woolen mill, also in Oxford, with an Englishman, Edward Howard, as partner and operating head. The establishment of the second mill at Oxford greatly extended Slater's management responsibilities. Although he could rely on Howard to carry out the day-to-day details, he had to make frequent trips to Oxford to keep in touch with both his cotton and his woolen interests there. In addition, he had the principal management responsibility for the "Old Mill" at Pawtucket, and the "White Mill" at Rehoboth. (The Slatersville mill was under John Slater's management.)

It may have been that Slater was willing to carry this added burden in the thought that his son and namesake would soon be ready to shoulder some of the responsibilities, but in 1818, Samuel Slater, Jr., died. The following year, therefore, Slater sold his interest in the "White Mill" and concentrated his attention on the mills at Providence and Oxford.

---

[15]Much of the above information on marketing comes from Chapter iii of Caroline Ware's *The Early New England Cotton Manufacture* (Cambridge: Riverside Press, 1931).

The postwar years were difficult ones for the young cotton textile industry in the United States. As soon as peace was declared, British merchants dumped on the New York market large quantities of goods that had accumulated during the war. Auctions became common, prices fell, and many poorly financed cotton mills went into bankruptcy. Even the more efficient ones shut down for long periods of time. In 1818, Bela Tiffany asked to be bought out of the "Green Mill," and Slater, whose financial position was strong enough to withstand a period of losses, found himself sole owner of his Oxford cotton manufacturing enterprises.

The 1820s brought a return of prosperity to New England's cotton textile industry, and Slater began again to add to his mill properties. By this time so many mills were in operation that it was possible for Slater to expand his operations by purchase rather than by construction as had formerly been the case. In 1823, he and his brother bought the mills of the Jewett City Cotton Manufacturing Company of Jewett City, Connecticut. In 1826, he bought an interest in the mills of Amoskeag Village (now Manchester), New Hampshire. In 1828, he and several associates pioneered with a new mill in Providence, driven by steam engine rather than by water, which had been the universally used motive force before that time. By 1828, Slater had all his liquid capital tied up in these manufacturing ventures. In addition, he had endorsed notes to enable his many partners to take full advantage of the booming conditions in the textile industry. Consequently, when a sharp recession took place in that year, accompanied by a tight money market, Slater was very nearly driven into bankruptcy.

By 1830, Slater's finances had sufficiently recovered so that he was able to buy the Providence Steam Cotton Mill outright, while he and his brother, John, were able to retrieve their ownership of the mill at Slatersville by buying out William Almy completely. Nevertheless, Slater's rather substantial fortune was severely hit by the depression and had not had time to recover by the date of his death in 1835. At the time he died Slater owned:

1. The Providence Steam Cotton Mill (outright).
2. The "Green Mill" at Oxford (outright).
3. The woolen mill at Oxford (in partnership with his sons).
4. The mill at Slatersville (in partnership with brother).
5. The mill at Wilkinsonville (outright).
6. The mill at Amoskeag (one-fifth ownership).

## Labor in Slater's Mills

As an aid in the study of working conditions in Slater's mills, there exists a time book for Slater's mills at Oxford, beginning in 1813 and continuing into 1836, and a book of accounts between Slater and his employees for 1817–1819.

Scant though it is, the information contained in the earliest time book, beginning February 1813, does tell us a few things. From the names of the workers, it is seen that they were what would be called today "old Americans," "Nordic," or "Anglo-Saxons." The names recorded for the first month were such as Tiffany, Hitchcock, Green, Phettiplace, Holmes, Fuller, Simmons, Munyan, Howland,

Johnson, Hill, Cady, Chase, Worsely, Benson, Learned, Reynolds, Stone, Weaver, Wilmoth, and Sheldon. The Christian names showed that the Puritan leaven was still at work.

By 1831, a change was coming in the nationality of Slater's workers. Contracts were made with at least five men whose names were typically Irish: Coyle, Ryan, Corcoran, Burns, and Callaghan, the last two signing their names with a cross. In 1833, more workers with typically Celtic names—Mooney, Dentt, Callahan—joined the force. In 1834, came Moore and Davit, both literate. But in 1836, the year after Samuel Slater's death, we find contracts with O'Reille, Burke, Davitt, Doyle, and Kelly, each signed with "his X mark." Not until 1837, came the pioneers in the French or French-Canadian invasion, Peter and Oliver Bargue, both "X" men.

There is no definite record of the age situation in 1813, but it was probably not much different from the situation in 1790 when the work was done by boys and girls of from 10 to 15 years. We have a hint of this in the surname groupings of the listed workers. Out of the 36 names listed in February 1813, there were only 21 different family names. Five of these family names covered 20 of the workers. Evidently, the workers were made up chiefly of family groups, which probably consisted largely of minor children. It is difficult to ascertain the extent to which parents worked with the children. There were two Willard Howlands in the February list, possibly father and son.

Fourteen years later when Slater was operating two mills at Oxford, the number of laborers had grown to 144. Of these, 79 were males and 65 females. Family groups were still as conspicuous as they had been in 1813. The 114 workers had only 62 family names, and a little over half of the family names (33) included more than 80 percent (116) of the laborers. Evidently minors still made up the bulk of the laborers. There were eight pairs of males possessing the same name, with the addition of "Jr." or "Sr." Evidently there were at least eight fathers working with their children. This may be compared to the situation in 1814 when there was a minimum of two fathers, out of a total 23 families represented, who were working with their children.

The normal working day was 12 hours, as may be seen from the time book for 1813–1836. Wages varied widely. The heads of families signed in acknowledgment of the receipt of the wages of the members of their families and of their own. The wages of men in 1817 seemed to vary around a normal standard of 6s. per day. The shilling then being worth about 17 cents, $1.00 a day seems to have been the most common wage. (The old colonial shilling continued to be used by New England mills in quoting wage scales until well after 1900.)

Many of the women worked at piecework, but there is no record of how much they could do in a day. Children were apparently always paid by the day, while men in this period were paid by the week. Children received sometimes as little as 3s. a week. Reduced to cents, this could be about 50 cents per week or 6d. (8-⅓ cents) for a day of 12 hours. Wages increased steadily with an increase in age, until the highest-paid minor found in this period received 25s. 6d. per week or 4s. 3d. a day (70 cents), only a little less than the lowest paid adult.

At this time workers in the mill who had no homes in the villages were "boarded-out" to various local families whose members worked there. Apparently Samuel Slater paid for the board of such workers to the heads of the families with whom they boarded at the same time that he paid the family wages to family heads, subtracting these payments from the wages of the boarders when settlement was made with them. The charge for women's board per week in 1817 was 7s. or 8s., about $1.20 to $1.35. Men, on the other hand, were uniformly charged $2.00 per week.

## Delay in Adopting the Power Loom

During the years of postwar depression, Slater missed an opportunity which a few competitors seized to their long-range advantage. In England, a loom had been invented which could be driven by water power instead of by hand. The workings of the power loom were brought to America by Francis Cabot Lowell and by a Scots mechanic named Herrocks. But Slater stood firm against the new invention, partly perhaps because he did not wish to risk the investment during depressed times, but also because he preferred to concentrate on the part of cotton manufacture which he knew best: spinning. Herrocks personally visited the mill and was successful in selling John Slater on the new device, but Samuel remained adamant.

To compete with mills that were offering machine-woven goods along with their yarn output, Slater returned to the practice of subcontracting the weaving operation to domestic weavers in the areas adjacent to his mills. As a result, nearly half the families working in the spinning mills had members who at least occasionally did hand-loom weaving. In some cases, children worked in the mill, and the father and mother—in their spare time or during slack seasons in their ordinary occupations—did hand-loom weaving, assisted perhaps by other children who were not employed in the mill. In hand-loom weaving usually the name of only the family head would appear on the weavers' book, since with him the contract was made, to him the money was paid, and on him lay the responsibility. He might, however, actually do little or none of the work, that being left to his wife and children.

Hand-loom weaving seems to have reached its peak between 1820 and 1825. During that period, 600 weavers were individually receiving yarn from the mills, to say nothing of a large number whose names do not appear on the list; the latter were receiving webs through the medium of subcontractors to whom "the great bulk" of the webs went. The irregularity of the individual weavers was still conspicuous. Of all the weavers during these five years, only 65 returned as many as 25 webs, or an average of 5 per year. This irregularity extended also to the cloth. On the flyleaf of a weaver's book is a list of 33 names with comments: on 23 "good," 1 "middling," 9 "poor," and on individual accounts such notes as "it is desirable that he should weave no more."

By 1823, Slater began to install small spinning machines to take the place of the hand weavers. But only in 1827, when anthracite coal from Pennsylvania first became available for industrial purposes, did Slater and his associates build a large mill at Providence. Powered by steam, it integrated weaving with spinning. Only then was Slater and the other southern New England textile producers able to compete with the large integrated mills built first by Francis Cabot Lowell on the Charles and later by Lowell's associates on the Merrimack River at the new town of Lowell. In the next decades, steam-driven factories in the coastal cities of Providence, Fall River, New Bedford, Boston, Salem, and Portsmouth, to which coal could be shipped easily by water, competed successfully with the large water-driven mills on the Merrimack at Lowell, Lawrence, Nashua, and Manchester, on the Connecticut at Holyoke and Chicopee, and on other major New England rivers.

## The Introduction of the Power Loom, and Origin of Lowell (by Nathan Appleton, originally published in 1858)*

My connection with the Cotton Manufacture takes date from the year 1811, when I met my friend Mr. Francis C. Lowell, at Edinburgh, where he had been passing some time with his family. We had frequent conversations on the subject of the Cotton Manufacture, and he informed me that he had determined, before his return to America, to visit Manchester, for the purpose of obtaining all possible information on the subject, with a view to the introduction of the improved manufacture in the United States. I urged him to do so, and promised him my cooperation. He returned in 1813. He and Mr. Patrick T. Jackson, came to me one day on the Boston exchange, and stated that they had determined to establish a Cotton manufactory, that they had purchased a water power in Waltham, (Bemis's paper mill), and that they had obtained an act of incorporation, and Mr. Jackson had agreed to give up all other business and take the management of the concern.

The capital authorized by the charter was $400,000, but it was only intended to raise $100,000 until the experiment should be fairly tried. Of this sum, Mr. Lowell and Mr. Jackson, with his brothers, subscribed the greater part. They proposed to me that I should take ten thousand of this subscription. I told them, that theoretically, I thought the business ought to succeed, but all which I have seen of its practical operation was unfavorable; I, however, was willing to take $5,000 of the stock, in order to see the experiment fairly tried, as I knew it would be under the management of Mr. Jackson; and I should make no complaint under these circumstances, if it proved a total loss. My proposition was agreed to, and this was the commencement of my interest in the cotton manufacture.

On the organization of the Company I was chosen one of the Directors, and by constant communication with Messrs. Lowell and Jackson, was familiar with the progress of the concern.

---

*This well-known essay has been reprinted in George Rogers Taylor, ed., *The Early Development of the American Cotton Textile Industry* (New York: Harper and Row, 1969).

The first measure was to secure the services of Paul Moody of Amesbury, whose skill as a mechanic was well known, and whose success fully justified the choice.

The power loom was at this time being introduced in England, but its construction was kept very secret, and after many failures, public opinion was not favorable to its success. Mr. Lowell had obtained all the information which was practicable about it, and was determined to perfect it himself. He was for some months experimenting at a store in Broad Street, employing a man to turn a crank. It was not until the new building at Waltham was completed, and other machinery was running, that the first loom was ready for trial. Many little matters were to be overcome or adjusted, before it would work perfectly. Mr. Lowell said to me that he did not wish me to see it until it was complete, of which he would give me notice. At length, the time arrived. He invited me to go out with him to see the loom operate. I well recollect the state of admiration and satisfaction with which we sat by the hour, watching the beautiful movement of this new and wonderful machine, destined as it evidently was, to change the character of all textile industry. This was in the autumn of 1814.

Mr. Lowell's loom was different in several particulars from the English loom, which was afterwards made public. The principal movement was by a cam, revolving with an eccentric motion, which has since given place to the crank motion, now universally used; some other minor improvements have since been introduced, mostly tending to give it increased speed.

The introduction of the power loom made several other changes necessary in the process of weaving. The first was in the dressing, for which Mr. Herrocks of Stockport, had a patent, and of which Mr. Lowell obtained a drawing. On putting it in operation, an essential improvement was made, by which its efficiency was more than doubled. This Waltham dressing machine continues in use, with little change from that time. The stop motion, for winding on the beams for dressing, was original with this company.

The greatest improvement was in the double speeder. The original fly-frame introduced in England, was without any fixed principle for regulating the changing movements necessary in the process of filling a spool. Mr. Lowell undertook to make the numerous mathematical calculations necessary to give accuracy to these complicated movements, which occupied him constantly for more than a week. Mr. Moody carried them into effect by constructing the machinery in conformity. Several trials at law were made under this patent, involving with other questions, one, whether a mathematical calculation could be the subject of a patent. The last great improvements consisted in a more slack spinning on throstle spindles, and the spinning of fulling directly on the cops, without the process of winding. A pleasant anecdote is connected with this last invention. Mr. Shepherd, of Taunton, had a patent for a winding machine, which was considered the best extant. Mr. Lowell was chaffering with him about purchasing the right of using them on a large scale, at some reduction from the price named. Mr. Shepherd refused, saying, "You must have them—you cannot do without them as you know, Mr. Moody." Mr. Moody replied—"I am just thinking that I can spin the cops direct upon the bobbin." "You be hanged," said Mr. Shepherd. "Well, I accept your offer." "No," said Mr. Lowell, "it is too late."

From the first starting of the first power loom, there was no hesitation or doubt about the success of this manufacture. The full capital of $400,000 was soon filled up and expended. An addition of $200,000 was afterwards made, by the purchase of the place below in Watertown.

After the peace in 1815, I formed a new copartnership with Mr. Benjamin C. Ward. I put in the capital for the purpose of importing British goods, with the understanding that I was not to perform any part of the labor of carrying on the business. I was content with a moderate fortune, but not willing to disconnect myself entirely from business. An accidental circumstance occasioned the continuance of this copartnership until 1830.

At the time when the Waltham Company first began to produce cloth, there was but one place in Boston at which domestic goods were sold. This was at a shop in Cornhill kept by Mr. Isaac Bowers, or rather by Mrs. Bowers. As there was at this time only one loom in operation, the quantity accumulating was not very great. However, Mr. Lowell said to me one day that there was one difficulty which he had not apprehended, the goods would not sell. We went together to see Mrs. Bowers. She said everybody praised the goods, and no objection was made to the price, but still they made no sales. I told Mr. Lowell, the next time they sent a parcel of the goods to town, to send them to the store of B.C. Ward & Co., and I would see what could be done. The article first made at Waltham, was precisely the article of which a large portion of the manufacture of the country has continued to consist; a heavy sheeting of No. 14 yarn, 37 inches wide, 44 picks to the inch, and weighing something less than three yards to the pound.

That it was so well suited to the public demand, was a matter of accident. At that time it was supposed no quantity of cottons could be sold without being bleached; and the idea was to imitate the yard wide goods of India, with which the country was then largely supplied. Mr. Lowell informed me that he would be satisfied with 25 cents the yard for the goods, although the nominal price was higher. I soon found a purchaser in Mr. Forsaith, an auctioneer, who sold them at auction at once, at something over 30 cents. We continued to sell them at auction with little variety of the price. This circumstance led to B. C. Ward & Co. becoming permanently the selling agents. In the first instance I found an interesting and agreeable occupation in paying attention to the sales, and made up the first account with a charge of 1 per cent commission, not as an adequate mercantile commission, but satisfactory under the circumstances. This rate of commission was continued, and finally became the established rate, under the great increase of the manufacture. Thus, what was at the commencement rather unreasonably low, became when the amount of annual sale, concentrated in single houses amounted to millions of dollars, a desirable and profitable business.

Under the influence of the War of 1812, the manufacture of cotton had greatly increased, especially in Rhode Island, but in a very imperfect manner. The effect of the peace of 1815 was ruinous to these manufacturers.

In 1816 a new tariff was to be made. The Rhode Island manufacturers were clamorous for a very high specific duty. Mr. Lowell was at Washington, for a considerable time, during the session of Congress. His views on the tariff were much more moderate, and he finally brought Mr. Lowndes and Mr. Calhoun, to support the minimum of 6-1/4 cents the square yard, which was carried.

In June 1816, Mr. Lowell invited me to accompany him in making a visit to Rhode Island, with a veiw of seeing the actual state of the manufacture. I was very happy to accept his proposition. At this time, the success of the power loom, at Waltham, was no longer matter of speculation or opinion: it was a settled fact. We proceeded to Pawtucket. We called on Mr. Wilkinson, the maker of machinery. He took us into his establishment—a large one; all was silent, not a wheel in motion, not a man to be seen. He informed us that there was not a spindle running in Pawtucket, except a few in Slater's old mill, making yarns. All was dead and still. In reply to questions from Mr. Lowell, he stated that during the war, the profits of manufacturing were so great, that the inquiry never was made whether any improvement could be made in machinery, but how soon it could be turned out. We saw several manufacturers; they were all sad and despairing. Mr. Lowell endeavored to assure them that the introduction of the power loom would put a new face upon the manufacture. They were incredulous—it might be so, but they were not disposed to believe it. We proceeded to Providence, and returned by way of Taunton. We saw, at the factory of Mr. Shepherd, an attempt to establish a vertical power loom, which did not promise success.

By degrees, the manufacturers woke up to the fact that the power loom was an instrument which changed the whole character of the manufacture; and that by adopting the other improvements which had been made in machinery, the tariff of 1816 was sufficiently protective.

Mr. Lowell adopted an entirely new arrangement, in order to save labor, in passing from one process to another; and he is unquestionably entitled to the credit of being the first person who arranged all the processes for the conversion of cotton into cloth within the walls of the same building. It is remarkable how few changes have since been made from the arrangements established by him, in the first mill built at Waltham. It is also remarkable, how accurate were his calculations, as to the expense at which goods could be made. He used to say, that the only circumstance which made him distrust his own calculations was that he could bring them to no other result but one which was too favorable to be credible. His calculations, however, did not lead him so far as to imagine that the same goods which were then selling at 30 cents a yard would ever be sold at 6 cents, and without a loss to the manufacture, as has since been done in 1843, when cotton was about 5 or 6 cents a pound. His care was especially devoted to arrangements for the moral character of the operatives employed. He died in 1817, at the early age of 42, beloved and respected by all who knew him. He is entitled to the credit of having introduced the new system in the cotton manufacture, under which it has grown up so rapidly. For although Messrs. Jackson and Moody were men of unsurpassed talent and energy in their way, it was Mr. Lowell who was the informing soul, which gave direction and form to the whole proceeding.

The introduction of the cotton manufacture in this country, on a large scale, was a new idea. What would be its effect on the character of our population was a matter of deep interest. The operatives in the manufacturing cities of Europe were notoriously of the lowest character for intelligence and morals. The question therefore arose, and was deeply considered, whether this degradation was the result of the peculiar occupation, or of other and distinct causes. We could not perceive why this peculiar description of labor should vary in its effects upon character from all other occupations.

There was little demand for female labor, as household manufacture was superseded by the improvements in machinery. Here was in New England a fund of labor, well educated and virtuous. It was not perceived how a profitable employment has any tendency to deteriorate the character. The most efficient guards were adopted in establishing boarding houses, at the cost of the Company, under the charge of respectable women, with every provision for religious worship. Under these circumstances, the daughters of respectable farmers were readily induced to come into these mills for a temporary period.

The contrast in the character of our manufacturing population compared with that of Europe has been the admiration of the most intelligent strangers who have visited us. The effect has been to more than double the wages of that description of labor from what they were before the introduction of this manufacture. This had been, in some measure, counteracted for the last few years, by the free trade policy of the government; a policy which fully carried out, will reduce the value of labor with us, to an equality with that of Europe.

The following are the changes in the price of the article first manufactured at Waltham:

| | |
|---|---|
| 1816 | 30 cents per yard |
| 1819 | 21 cents per yard |
| 1826 | 13 cents per yard |
| 1829 | 8 1/2 cents per yard |
| 1843 | 6 1/2 cents per yard |

From that time, the price has fluctuated with the price of cotton, from 7 to 9 cents per yard.

# The Origin of Lowell

The success of the Waltham Company made me desirous of extending my interest in the same direction. I was of opinion, that the time had arrived, when the manufacture and printing of calicoes might be successfully introduced into this country. In this opinion, Mr. Jackson coincided, and we set about discovering a suitable water power. At the suggestion of Mr. Charles H. Atherton, of Amherst, N.H., we met him at a fall of the Souhegan river, a few miles from its entrance into the Merrimack, but the power was insufficient for our purpose. This was in September 1821. In returning, we passed the Nashua river, without being aware of the existence of the fall, which has since been made the source of so much power by the Nashua Company. We only saw a small grist mill standing near the road, in the meadow, with a dam of some six or seven feet.

Soon after our return, I was at Waltham one day, when I was informed that Mr. Moody had lately been at Salisbury, when Mr. Ezra Worthen, his former partner, said to him, "I hear Messrs. Jackson and Appleton are looking out for water power. Why don't they buy up the Pawtucket Canal? That would give them the whole power of the Merrimack, with a fall of over thirty feet." On the strength of this, Mr. Moody had returned to Waltham by that route, and was satisfied of the extent of the power which might be thus obtained, and that Mr. Jackson was making inquiries on the subject. Mr. Jackson soon after called on me and informed me that he had had a correspondence with Mr. Thomas M. Clark, of Newburyport, the Agent of the Pawtucket Canal Company, and had ascertained that the stock of that Company, and the lands necessary for using the water power, could be purchased at a reasonable rate, and asked me what I thought of taking hold of it. He stated that his engagement at Waltham would not permit him to take the management of a new Company, but he mentioned Mr. Kirk Boott as having expressed a wish to take the management of an active manufacturing concern, and that he had confidence in his possessing the proper talent for it. After a consultation, it was agreed that he should consult Mr. Boott, and that if he would join us we would go on with it. He went at once to see Mr. Boott, and soon returned to inform me that he entered heartily into the projects; and we immediately set about making the purchases. Until these were made, it was necessary to confine all knowledge of the project to our own three bosoms. Mr. Clark was employed to purchase the necessary lands, and such shares in the Canal as were within his reach, whilst Mr. Henry Andrews was employed in purchasing up the shares owned in Boston.

I recollect the first interview with Mr. Clark, at which he exhibited a rough sketch of the Canal, and the adjoining lands, with the prices which he had ascertained they could be purchased for. He was directed to go on and complete the purchases, taking the deed in his own name, in order to prevent the project taking wind prematurely. The purchases were made accordingly, for our joint account, each of us furnishing funds as required by Mr. Boott, who was to keep the accounts.

Our first visit to the spot was in the month of November, 1821, and a slight snow covered the ground. The party consisted of Patrick T. Jackson, Kirk Boott, Warren Dutton, Paul Moody, John W. Boott and myself. We perambulated the grounds, and scanned the capabilities of the place, and the remark was made that some of us might live to see the place contain 20,000 inhabitants. At that time there were, I think, less than a dozen houses on what now constitutes the city of Lowell, or rather the thickly settled parts of it—that of Nathan Tyler, near the corner of Merrimack and Bridge streets, that of Josiah Fletcher, near the Boott Mills, the house and store of Phineas Whitney, near Pawtucket Bridge, the house of Mrs. Warren, near what is now Warren street, the house of Judge Livermore, east of Concord river, then called Belvidere, and a few others.

[Appleton then lists the articles which incorporated the company with a capital stock of $600,000, to be allocated in this manner:]

|  |  |
|---|---:|
| Kirk Boott, Ninety Shares, | 90 |
| John W. Boott, Ninety Shares, | 90 |
| N. Appleton, One hundred and eighty Shares, | 180 |

| | |
|---|---:|
| P.T. Jackson, One hundred and eighty Shares, | 180 |
| Paul Moody, Sixty Shares, | 60 |
| | 600 |

An Act of Incorporation was granted 5th February, 1822. The first meeting of Stockholders took place on the 27th February, at which By-Laws were adopted and Directors chosen, as follows: Warren Dutton, Patrick T. Jackson, Nathan Appleton, William Appleton, Israel Thorndike, Jr., John W. Boott; Kirk Boott, Treasurer and Clerk. An assessment was made of $500 per share, to be called for by the Directors. The shares in the Locks and Canals to be conveyed to the several Directors in trust. At a meeting of the Directors, the same day, Warren Dutton was chosen President. $200 per share was voted to be paid on the 1st of April. Patrick T. Jackson and Nathan Appleton were appointed a committee to settle Mr. Boott's account, which contained $18,339 for lands of Nathan Tyler, Josiah Fletcher, Joseph Fletcher and Moses Cheever, and $30,217 paid for 339 shares in the Locks and Canals.

The Pawtucket Canal belonged to a Company incorporated in 1792, by the name of "the Proprietors of the Locks and Canals on Merrimack River," apparently established originally with the view of making the Merrimack River navigable to Newburyport. This object was, in a great measure, defeated by the incorporation in 1793 of the Middlesex Canal, opening a direct communication with Boston. A canal, of very moderate dimensions was, however, made around Pawtucket Falls, for the passage of rafts of wood and lumber. The income, up to 1820, hardly averaged 3-1/2 per cent per annum, which made the purchase of the stock an easy matter. It consisted of 600 shares, on which $100 had been paid, each.

The enlargement of this canal, and the renewal of the locks, was the first and most important measure to be accomplished by the new Company. It was decided to make it 60 feet wide and 8 feet deep, which, it was estimated, would furnish 50 mill powers. This was commenced with the opening Spring of 1822, and prosecuted with the utmost vigor; but it was soon ascertained that it could not be accomplished in the manner proposed, in one season. Its cost was upwards of $120,000.

It was decided to place the mills of the Merrimack Company where they would use the whole fall of thirty feet. Mr. Moody said he had a fancy for large wheels. In the meantime, a new canal was to be made to the Merrimack River, mills were to be built, a house for Mr. Boott, and boarding houses for the operatives. A contract was made with the Boston Manufacturing Company, or Waltham Company, for machinery for two mills. As it was all important to the Merrimack Company to have the use of the patents of the Waltham Company, and especially to secure the services of Mr. Moody, it was finally arranged to equalise the interest of all the stockholders in both companies, by mutual transfers, at rates agreed upon, so that there was no clashing of interest in any case. This could only be done by a strong feeling of mutual interest in favor of the measure, and a liberal spirit of compromise in carrying it out. Under this arrangement, it was agreed, in August 1823, to pay the Waltham Company $75,000 for all their patterns and patent rights, and to release Mr. Moody from his contract in their service.

In December, 1822, Messrs. Jackson and Boott were appointed a committee to build a suitable church; and in April 1824, it was voted that it should be built of stone, not to exceed a cost of $9,000. This was called St. Anne's church, in which Mr. Boott, being himself an Episcopalian, was desirous of trying to experiment whether that service could be sustained. It was dedicated by Bishop Griswold, but the Directors of the Merrimack Company never intended to divest themselves of the control of it. Liberal grants of land were made for other places of worship, and subscriptions freely made by the stockholders for different religious societies.

The first wheel of the Merrimack Company was set in motion on the first of September, 1823. In 1825, $500 were appropriated for a Library. Three additional mills were built. In 1829, Mr. Dutton, going to Europe, Nathan Appleton was appointed President. The first dividend of $100 per share was made in 1825. They have been regularly continued, with few exceptions, averaging something over 12 per cent per annum, to the present time.

The business of printing calicoes was wholly new in this country. It is true that after it was known that this concern was going into operation for that purpose, two other companies were got up, one at Dover, N.H., the other at Taunton, Mass., in both of which goods were probably printed before they were by the Merrimack Company. The bringing of the business of printing to any degree of perfection was a matter of difficulty and time. Mr. Allan Pollock thought himself competent to manage it, and was employed for some time. Through the good offices of Mr. Timothy Wiggin, Mr. John D. Prince, of Manchester, was induced to come out, with his family, in 1826, to take charge of the concern and continued in the service of the Company until 1855. He was then relieved, by a younger man, from the more active duties. On account of his long service, and the great skill and success with which he had conducted that department, he was by the Directors granted an annuity of $2,000 per annum, for life.

The then recent improvements in printing were of the highest importance. The old process of printing by blocks of wood was in a great measure superseded by the cylinder. The introduction of machines, carrying one or more cylinders, each distributing a different color, was in printing what the invention of Arkwright was in spinning, the source of immense fortunes. Amongst those who availed themselves of it, one of the earliest was the father of the late Sir Robert Peel, who acquired enormous wealth as a printer. It is related of him, that on his London bankers hinting that he was using his credit too freely, he quieted their scruples by revealing to them his secret, that he was coining a guinea on every piece of calico which he printed.

The engraving of these cylinders was the most important part of the process, and Mr. Boott made one voyage to England solely for the purpose of engaging engravers. The art was then kept a very close mystery, and all exportation of machinery was prohibited. Dr. Samuel L. Dana was employed as chemist, and through the superior skill and talent of Messrs. Boott, Prince and Dana, the Company was brought to the highest degree of success.

In 1828 an arrangement was made by which Mr. J. W. Paige came into the selling agency on the retirement on Mr. Ward from the firm; and it is not too much to say, that to his skill and good judgment, the Company is greatly indebted for its success. This office combined with it the preparation of the pattern under a regular designer, and carried with it a commission of 1-1/4 per cent.

Mr. Warren Colburn was for several years superintendent of the mills, and was succeeded by Mr. John Clark, who held the office until 1848, to the great satisfaction of the Directors.

The first printing cloths were made 30 inches wide in the grey, giving them when printed a width of 27 inches, being about two inches above the average of British prints. None other than fast colors were used, whilst a superior durability from the throstle over mule spinning, combined to give them a higher character than attached to any other goods. In the mean time, Mr. Moody was transferred from Waltham to this place, having charge of the manufacture of machinery in the building erected for that purpose. Mr. Worthen had been employed at an early day. He was a man of superior mechanical genius, and his death, in 1817, was deeply regretted.

At the annual meeting at Chelmsford, May 21, 1823, the Directors were authorised to petition for an increase of capital to $1,200,000 and on the 19th of October, 1824, a new subscription of 600 shares was voted, and a committee appointed to consider the expediency of organizing the Canal Company, by selling them all the land and water power not required by the Merrimack Manufacturing Company. This committee reported on the 28th February, 1825, in favor of the measure, which was adopted; and at the same time a subscription was opened, by which 1,200 shares in the Locks and Canals were allotted to the holders of that number of shares in the Merrimack Company, share for share.

The Locks and Canals were thus the owners of all the land and water power in Lowell. They made the necessary new canals to bring it into use. The first sale was to the Hamilton Manufacturing Company, in 1825, with a capital of $600,000, and afterwards increased to $1,200,000. This Company secured the services of Mr. Samuel Batchelder, of New Ipswich, who had shown much skill in manufacturing industry. Under his management the power loom was applied to the weaving of twilled and fancy goods, with great success. The article of cotton drills, since become so important a commodity in our foreign trade, was first made in this establishment. The Appleton Company and the Lowell Company followed, in 1828. In 1829 a violent commercial revulsion took place both in Europe and this country. It was especially felt by the cotton manufacturers in England, and several establishments in this country operating with insufficient capital, were prostrated. The Merrimack Manufacturing Company made no dividend that year. During this period of depression, Messrs. Amos and Abbot Lawrence were induced, by some tempting reduction in the terms made by the Proprietors of the Locks and Canals, to enter largely into the business; the consequence of which was the establishment of the Suffolk, Tremont and Lawrence Companies, in 1830. The Boott followed in 1835, the Massachusetts in 1839. These Companies involved capital amounting to $12 million. They are all joint stock companies,[16] with a treasurer as

---

[16]A joint stock company is an organization the capital of which has been divided into transferable shares among its members who, however, have the personal liability of partners for the debts of the concern.

the responsible agent, and a superintendent or manager of the mills. The principle on which these corporations have been established, has always been, the filling of these important offices with men of the highest character and talent which could be obtained. It has been thought, as has been found to be, the best economy, to pay such salaries as will command the entire services of such men. The Directors properly consist of stockholders most largely interested in the management of their property. They receive nothing for their services. A very important part also depends on the selling agents, who should be well acquainted with the principles of trade. The success of the establishments at Lowell, may be fairly quoted in favor of the system pursued. It is true that during the present revulsion, the most severe within the memory of the oldest merchant, there is a disposition to attribute the depression of the cotton manufacture to the construction of these companies. It is always easy in such a time to find some new ground of cavil. Corporations, like individuals, will succeed or fail, as they are directed by skill and intelligence, or without them.

The prices of Merrimack prints have varied as follows:

| The average price per yard in 1825 was — 23,07 cents. |
|---|
| "      "      "      "      "      " 1830  "  — 16,36  " |
| "      "      "      "      "      " 1835  "  — 16,04  " |
| "      "      "      "      "      " 1840  "  — 12,09  " |
| "      "      "      "      "      " 1845  "  — 10,90  " |
| "      "      "      "      "      " 1850  "  —  9,24  " |
| "      "      "      "      "      " 1855  "  —  9,15  " |

# APPENDIX A

 *Chronology for Slater and Lowell Enterprises*

| | |
|---|---|
| 1768 | Samuel Slater born in Derbyshire, England. |
| 1783–89 | Apprenticed to Jedediah Strutt in cotton spinning, acting as general overseer in the later years. |
| 1789 | Leaves secretly for America. In touch with Moses Brown of Providence. |
| 1790 | Begins building new spinning machinery in Pawtucket mill. Enters partnership with Almy & Brown |
| 1800 | With partners, builds the "White Mill" at Rehoboth. |
| 1803 | Slater's brother John arrives from England. |
| 1806 | William Almy, Obadiah Brown, and the Slaters build a mill at Slatersville. |
| 1812 | Slater erects "Green Mill" at Oxford (Webster) with Bela Tiffany as partner. |
| 1812–15 | Great prosperity in textile industry. |
| 1813 | Francis Cabot Lowell returns from England with plans for a power loom. Forms Boston Manufacturing Company. |
| 1815 | Slater starts a woolen mill at Oxford with Edward Howard, an Englishman. |
| 1816–19 | Depression in textile industry. Slater fails to install power looms. |
| 1817 | Lowell dies in Boston at 42. |
| 1818 | Tiffany retires from the "Green Mill." |
| 1819 | Slater sells out interest in "White Mill" to partners. |
| 1822 | Bostonians form the Merrimack Manufacturing Company, purchase Locks and Canals Company, and found Lowell, Massachusetts. |
| 1823 | Slater purchases cotton mills at what is now North Village, Webster, and at Jewett City, Connecticut. First power loom used. |
| 1826 | In May Slater becomes owner of one-half the mills at Amoskeag Village in New Hampshire. In December conveys all but one fifth to others. |

| 1828 | The first steam mill erected at Providence by Slater and associates. |
| 1830 | Slater becomes proprietor of Providence Steam Cotton Mill and of mills in Wilkinsonville, Massachusetts. |
| 1835 | Slater dies at East Webster. |

# PART TWO

# *Economic Revolution*

## THE REVOLUTION IN TRANSPORTATION AND COMMUNICATION

## THE REVOLUTION IN DISTRIBUTION AND PRODUCTION

# NEW RELATIONS OF MANAGEMENT AND THE WORK FORCE

# CASE 7

# *The Coming of the Railroads** *

## Introduction

The building of the railroad network ranks as one of the most important developments in American history. By the last quarter of the 19th century, the railroad
had penetrated every cranny of the economy and affected every person's interest
as did no other institution. In 1890, to choose a year at random, railroads carried
79.2 billion ton miles of freight over 163,596 miles of track operated by about
750,000 employees. Passenger mileage amounted to 12.5 billion. Total investment in property, plant, and equipment came to over $10 billion. At their peak in
1916, mileage reached 254,037; employment 1,701,000; and total capitalization
$21 billion. In 1891, the Pennsylvania Railroad alone employed over 110,000,
while the total of the nation's armed services was 34,942.

The chief concern of the business historian in studying the railroads is to determine: (1) their legacy to business management, and (2) their impact on other
businesses and industries and on the relationship between government and business enterprise as a whole. These concerns will be explored in depth in succeeding
cases. The purpose of this case is (1) to discuss methods of transportation preced-

---

*This case was prepared by Assistant Professor Richard S. Tedlow as the basis for class discus-
sion rather than to illustrate either effective or ineffective handling of an administrative situation. Most
of the case is based on "Unifying the National Economy: The Railroads," 9-377-230, by Professor Albro Martin.

Harvard Business School case 384-031, rev. 6/84.

ing the railroads, (2) to outline briefly the early growth of the railroads themselves, and (3) to provide data concerning the growth of the United States as a whole.

## Roads

"The 20th century observer," an historian has rightly commented, "is sure to have difficulty grasping the realities of the overland transportation in the age of Jefferson. . . ."[1] Many of the roads, especially in rural areas.

> were hardly more than broad paths through the forests. In wet places, they presented a line of ruts with frequent mud holes, and, where dry, a powdered surface of deep dust. The largest stones and stumps were removed only so far as was absolutely necessary to permit passage. An early act of the Ohio legislature provided that stumps left in the road should not be more than a foot high. In the most swampy places where mud rendered passage impossible, logs were laid side by side . . . to form what were known as corduroy roads. Across the rivers, a few wooden bridges had been built, but for the most part, fords or ferries were the only recourse.[2]

The roads were maintained as community projects. In slack seasons, farmers would gather to clear roads as best they could, given limited resources.

A wide variety of public figures urged that roads be improved. In a famous report in 1808, Albert Gallatin, Jefferson's brilliant Secretary of the Treasury, urged federal funding for a complex of "artificial roads," by which he meant roads that were surveyed to have no more than a 5 percent grade (a rise of about 250 feet in a distance of one mile), that were ditched on the sides and crowned in the center for drainage purposes, and that were finished with crushed rock or gravel. Indeed, during this period, there was a veritable "rage" for turnpike building.

This enthusiasm had been spurred by the Lancaster Turnpike. Completed in 1794, this thoroughfare connected the rich farmland around Lancaster to Philadelphia. Well-maintained and well-travelled, the road invited imitators.

In New England and the Middle Atlantic states, turnpikes tended to be privately financed. In New England alone, about $6.5 million had been invested in the roads by 1840. Most roads were capitalized at under $100,000. In Pennsylvania, the state contributed about $2 million of the $6 million invested in turnpikes by 1822. In certain other cases, the state and even federal government were given a special role to play in road construction. Thus, when Ohio became a state in 1803, Congress provided that 5 percent of the proceeds from public land sales should be devoted to road construction. Of this amount, Congress was to spend 40 percent and the state itself 60 percent.

The most important road built with federal funds during this period was the National (or Cumberland) Road. Authorized by Congress in 1806, construction on this road began from Cumberland, Maryland (which was connected by the

---

[1]Peter D. McClelland, "Transportation," in Glenn Porter, ed., *Encyclopedia of American Economic History* I (New York: Charles Scribner's Sons, 1980), pp. 309–10.

[2]George Rogers Taylor, *The Transportation Revolution* (New York: Harper & Row, 1951), p. 15.

Frederick Turnpike to Baltimore), in 1811. Wheeling was reached in 1818 and Columbus in 1833. The road's terminus in Vandalia, Illinos, was reached around mid-century.

From the financial point of view, the turnpikes were, with some notable exceptions, less than successful. By 1851, the $2.5 million invested in such roads by Kentucky were worth only between $0.25 and $0.30 on the dollar. Performance was not much better in other states west of the mountains.

In New York, more than half the 4,000 miles of turnpikes in operation in 1822 had been abandoned by 1836. In Pennsylvania, the famous Lancaster Turnpike itself never earned more than 2 percent on its stock, for all its traffic. Even in New England, where population density was high and distances were short, performance was disappointing. Turnpikes were being abandoned as early as 1818, and by 1835, more than half the roads in Massachusetts were partially or completely abandoned. Not more than five or six of the region's 230 ventures paid satisfactory dividends.

The federal road was not that much more successful than those of the states. The National Road did carry its share of immigrants to the West, but its contribution to moving their produce in the opposite direction was limited. The road has probably made a greater contribution to interregional trade as Interstate 40 (its modern incarnation) in the age of the internal combustion engine than it did in the antebellum years. Other federal internal improvements were hampered by sectional political problems and perceived constitutional limitations.

Reasons for the disappointing performance of the turnpikes are numerous:

1. They were very expensive to build. The best stone turnpikes cost between $5,000 and $10,000 per mile.
2. They were very expensive to maintain. Weather and heavy use were very hard on the roads, especially upon those on which the builders had economized.
3. The tolls on the turnpikes were easy to evade. Often, toll takers were not on duty after sundown, so teamsters could wait until dark to move past toll stations. Another illustration of the desire of travelers not to part with funds was the fact that paths around the toll booth or "shun pikes" in the jargon of the day, were not uncommon.
4. Even taking toll evasion into account, the movement of freight by wagon was exceedingly—for some commodities, excessively—expensive. Western produce had an unfavorable ratio of weight and bulk to value. In March of 1817, a New York State legislative committee found that the cost of transportation from Buffalo to New York City was three times the market value of wheat in the latter, six times that of corn, and twelve times that of oats. Transportation costs for wagons are presented along with those for other modes of transportation in Exhibit 1.
5. Road travel was also slow. The fastest stage coaches on good roads might average six to eight miles an hour. Heavy freight on poor roads moved at a snail's pace.

# Canals

As was illustrated in the case on "The Rise of New York Port," canal building was an important weapon in urban competition for western trade. The first canal of great length in the United States was the Erie, which proved to be a phenomenally successful example of public entrepreneurship and daring. (When the idea was proposed to Jefferson shortly before his leaving the presidency in 1809, he is said to have observed, "It is a splendid project and may be erected a century hence." In fact, he lived to see it completed.)

The obvious success of the Erie spawned numerous imitators. By 1860, over 4,300 miles of canals had been built at an estimated cost of almost $200 million. Most of the principal canals were constructed in the Northeast and Midwest. Exhibit 1 provides data on shipping costs via canal. Exhibit 2 shows mileage constructed by decade. Exhibit 3 shows expenditures on canals from 1815 through 1860 broken down by public and private sources. Exhibit 4 supplies a map of the principal canal routes.

Far more than the roads, the canals played a vital role in the development of the Midwest. Their reduction of freight rates made commercially feasible the cultivation of a large volume of agricultural produce in the hinterland. The lure of profit which the Erie always held out spurred the nation to greater entrepreneurial effort. Where distances were short and traffic heavy, as was the case with the anthracite-carrying canals in eastern Pennsylvania and those canals that linked one Great Lake to another, financial success was possible.

The problems canals posed were, however, serious. Though many of these may be obvious, it is worthwhile, nonetheless, to review them:

1. Canals were expensive to build. Most required an outlay of perhaps between $20,000 and $30,000 per mile. The upper bound was $80,000.
2. Possible routes for canals were sharply restricted.
3. Canals depended on water. Sometimes, there was too much. "Freshets," sudden rushes of water down a stream caused by heavy rains or melting snow, were a constant problem for some canals, and the result could be very serious financially. A single freshet in 1852 cost the Chesapeake and Ohio Canal Company $100,000 in repairs. Sometimes there was too little water, especially in late summer. And sometimes, unfortunately, water froze, making canals quite useless in the winter.
4. Upkeep was a difficult problem, even without freshets. Banks had to be protected. The channel had to be kept at the proper depth.
5. Canal travel, though faster than that by roads, was slow relative to the railroads. If locks were frequent, it would be slowed still further.

Canal promoters had hailed their enterprises as boons which would free the state which built them from the necessity of taxation because of the revenue they generated. Unfortunately, these promises turned out to be inflated, and a number of states wound up fiscally embarrassed as a result of overextending themselves for internal improvements.

# Steamboats

The United States is blessed with a complex network of navigable inland water-ways (see Exhibit 5). The harnessing of steam for purposes of water travel was of enormous assistance in the exploitation of these natural highways.

Robert Fulton dramatically demonstrated the utility of steamboating by sailing what was supposedly his "folly," the *Clermont*, 150 miles up the Hudson from New York City to Albany in 1807. The superiority of steamboats quickly became obvious to everyone, including the captains of competing sailing vessels which occasionally tried to ram them. Steamboats sharply reduced travel time for downstream trips and reduced it by orders of magnitude upstream. By 1850, for example, the journey from New Orleans to Louisville could be accomplished by the fastest such vessel in five days. By keelboat, the same trip took three to four months.

As important as steamboats had the potential of being in the East, Fulton understood that the greatest opportunities lay in western lakes and rivers. Four years after the *Clermont's* success, he dispatched Nicholas J. Roosevelt to Pittsburgh to supervise the building and launching of the *New Orleans*. This boat's voyage to its namesake city helped establish the feasibility of steam transport in the West.

A steamboat was, obviously, a type of vehicle rather than a right of way. Its advent, rather than displacing canals or roads, actually increased their use. Indeed, steam travel on the Hudson and on the Great Lakes was a major stimulus to the building of the Erie Canal. The steamboat business could be entered with about $20,000 in capital for a medium-sized boat.

Their numerous advantages made steamboats a major contributor to transportation and thus, to trade. They too, however, had their problems.

1. They depended on water. In the North, water froze in the winter. In the West, water levels fluctuated dramatically. At Cincinnati, for example, the spread between high and low water could be as much as 40 feet in a few weeks. In the summer, water levels tended to drop. (As a result, American engineers built boats that could haul as much as 100 tons while displacing only two feet of water. Westerners joked that boatmen had to have the ability "to navigate in a heavy dew.") In the fall and the spring, torrential floods were the problem.

2. In the West especially, service tended to be irregular because of these unpredictable conditions. Tramp steamboats, which could go where there were water and traffic, were the predominant mode.

3. Steamboating was dangerous. Snags and similar obstructions exacted their toll. Boilers often blew up as captains raced one another like hot-rodders. Of western steamboats built before 1849, nearly 30 percent were lost in accidents. The result was the loss of life and property as well as increased insurance rates.

4. Steamboats could only go where the navigable lakes and rivers were. The result was that the trips were needlessly lengthy. By river, the distance from Pittsburgh to Cinninnati was 470 miles, from Pittsburgh to St. Louis

1,164 miles, and from Cincinnati to Nashville 644 miles. These same distances by rail were 316, 612, and 301 miles, respectively.

# Railroads

For all the problems which they too brought with them—the speculation and peculation, the inflated promises, the bankruptcies, the accidents, the aggravation—the railroads provided a number of benefits which their predecessors did not. Railroads could be built to where the business was. They could keep to a schedule. They could operate in all seasons and in all but the very worst weather. And they were fast. (Exhibit 6 provides a graphic illustration of changing rates of travel during the first six decades of the 19th century.) Railroads made the world of the businessperson, as well as that of the private traveler, predictable as had no other innovation. They carried the majority of freight shipped until the second half of the 20th century and accounted for the majority of passenger miles until just after World War II.

To begin to grasp the impact of the railroads, this case will provide a narrative of their development through the Civil War decade. Succeeding cases will explore key changes in the industry through the remainder of the century and their implications.

As early as the 16th century in primitive Alsatian coal mines and somewhat later on a larger scale in England, the heavy product of mines had been trundled short distances in wagons running on some kind of rails and guided along by flanges (protecting rims designed to hold a wheel in place, give it strength, and guide it) on the wheels. Early in the 19th century, the granite for the Bunker Hill Monument was carted from the quarry in Quincy to boats for the trip across the bay by such a "railway."

As for steam power, efforts had been made to harness it to a wheeled vehicle since the latter part of the 18th century. But the only type of land vehicle people had ever known had run on conventional roads, which could not even support a heavy steam car. What was needed was a practical way of using a steam-driven vehicle to provide the motive power for travel on a road of rails.

The combination of rail and steam was first proven feasible in England, where the need and the know-how were the greatest. The nub of the problem was to make the steam engine more compact, lighter, and more efficient than the clumsy stationary engines of previous years. George Stephenson solved this problem by using a tubular boiler. In October of 1829, Stephenson entered his "Rocket" in the famed Rainhill trials, sponsored by the embryonic Liverpool and Manchester Railway to test the performance of locomotives versus stationary steam engines using rope-hauling. Between 10 and 15,000 spectators turned out to see the Rocket prove its superiority. The Rocket was awarded £500 for pulling a 40-ton payload 12 miles in 53 minutes. The Liverpool and Manchester immediately placed an order for seven units. (Lore has it that, in trying to decide how far apart to space the Rocket's wheels, Stephenson settled on the distance between the wheels of a manure cart and thus fastened on the world the too-narrow gauge of 4 feet 8 ½ inches.)

The solution of the motive power conundrum made possible the exploitation of the basic virtue of rail transportation—the fact that the flanged wheel running on a flat-laid rail encountered less friction than other wheeled conveyances. This is, of course, as true today as it was in 1829. A 40-ton boxcar of freight set in motion at 60 miles an hour on level track will coast for over five miles. A 5,000- horsepower locomotive can haul 5,000 tons. A modern semi-trailer truck rig requires 10 times as much power per ton. If the same kind of comparison were made between the primitive railroad train and a typical horse- or ox-drawn wagon on the National Road, or even a similarly powered canal boat, we would have to conclude that the superiority of even the earliest railroads was dramatic.

There was great interest in the railroad idea in America from the beginning. The citizens of Baltimore, in fact, decided in 1828 that a railroad was their only hope to stay in the game of trading with the rapidly expanding interior now that both New York and Philadelphia had, or would soon have, western canals. The first stone of the Baltimore and Ohio was laid in place by the venerable Charles Carroll, who described the act as "among the most important in my life, second only to my signing the Declaration of Independence, if second even to that." Baltimoreans had no sure idea of what kind of motive power they would use—they experimented with sails, and settled for a short time for real horsepower—but their faith in the new system was reaffirmed when news came that Stephenson had removed at Rainhill all doubt that steam could do the job. The B&O became the first American railroad to haul both freight and passengers by steam on a regular schedule.

But the B&O was not quite the first to haul passengers by steam on a regular schedule. That distinction belongs to the aptly named engine, "Best Friend of Charleston," operated by the Charleston & Hamburg Railroad. This railroad may serve as a symbol of the South's shortcomings in the industrial revolution and a movement to an unfortunate figure in the history of its economic development, Robert Y. Hayne. Hayne began early his effort to propel the South into the industrial age. He envisioned a railroad that would run all the way from Charleston, the South's best port, to Memphis; and, for a few years, the Charleston & Hamburg was, in fact, the longest railroad in the country. But nothing could make up for the inferiority of the South's ports, the lack of adequate markets for imports and diversity of exports, and a slave labor system that immobilized its capital resources. With the sudden early death of Hayne, what entrepreneurial spirit there was in the southern railroad-building program declined, and on the eve of the Civil War, it had barely begun to evolve a true system.

The 1830s were the "demonstration decade" in the railroad age, as those who had turned to railroad building in desperation discovered that they had made the best of all possible choices. Like Baltimore, another important seacoast city, Boston, observed developments in England and decided that only a railroad could carry its commerce across the Berkshires to Albany and a connection with the Erie Canal and the railroads that quickly paralleled it. Efforts to make Massachusetts railroads a public works project failed, but private capital, in part with state-guaranteed bonds, got behind three of the most important early railroads in America: the Boston & Worcester, which soon joined the Western Railroad of Massachusetts and enabled New England to divert some of New York's rich western trade; the Boston & Lowell, running northward to serve the booming textile industry and thereby putting the Middlesex Canal out of business; and the Boston & Providence, traversing a route that for years had carried a heavy traffic.

To the south, it was in Pennsylvania that railroads had their most significant beginnings, but not along the "mainline" between Philadelphia and Pittsburgh, where the great false start was underway in the form of the rail/canal/inclined-plane system. It was the anthracite coal producers of eastern Pennsylvania, anxious to ship their coveted fuel to domestic and commercial users in New York and New England, who undertook some of the most successful canals and, then, railroads in American history: the Philadelphia & Reading, the Delaware & Hudson, the Delaware & Lackawanna, and the Lehigh Valley. Meanwhile, the railroad solved the ancient problem of how to haul the great number of travelers between New York and Philadelphia in speed and comfort. A venerable stagecoach line was quickly replaced by the Camden & Amboy Railroad, operating between the New Jersey steamboat pier on Lower New York Bay and the thriving town just across the Delaware River from Philadelphia. Its earliest cars, quaint copies of the stagecoaches, provided a grueling ride, and the monopolistic grasp that the railroad had on business irked most travelers, but it was a vast improvement over what had been available. Shortly thereafter (1838), it was, in effect, extended to the nation's capital via the Philadelphia, Wilmington & Baltimore Railroad, a ferry across the Susquehanna, and the Baltimore & Ohio's branch from Baltimore to Washington.

Railroad building in New York, meanwhile, was slow to begin, as the success of the Erie Canal (and repressive limitation on railroads adopted by canal-biased state legislators) discouraged adoption of the new mode. But in the valley of the Mohawk River between Albany and Buffalo, a group of short railroads was built by such intensely competitive towns as Troy, Schenectady, Rome, Rochester, and Syracuse to haul the passenger traffic that the canal had engendered, but for which the canal was too slow. Soon, travelers arriving by steamboat at Albany were able to transfer to the first of seven railroads that would carry them with comparative speed to Buffalo, and shippers were beginning to discover that even at the high rates the railroads charged, it was advantageous to dispatch their more valuable freight that way, too. By 1840, there were as many miles of railroads in the United States as there were miles of canals.

Then, in the late 1840s, as the nation emerged from a depression, the shift to railroads increased. In New York State, the residents of the "southern tier" of countries, disgruntled at the advantage the Erie Canal gave their upstate neighbors, clamored for and got a railroad through their region between the Hudson River and Lake Erie. The Erie Railroad was the most poorly planned of the antebellum railroads. It began in the wrong place (Piermont, New York, on the west bank of the Hudson opposite Tarrytown, instead of across the river from Manhattan) and ended up in an even more wrong place (the Lake Erie village of Dunkirk, instead of Buffalo). As if to top those mistakes, it selected a broad gauge in the mistaken notion that other railroads would not be able to take its traffic away from it.

But by 1851, when it reached Lake Erie, it was the longest railroad in the country under one management and an important East-West through route.

As Exhibit 7 shows, railroad building increased substantially in the Atlantic Seaboard states during the 1840s. But during the 1850s, with the opening of the trans-Appalachian region to railroad building, the boom increased beyond imagining (see Exhibits 8 a, b, and c). Track in operation increased approximately fourfold. Lines that eventually became some of the most important in the nation suddenly burst westward from Buffalo towards the raw new cities of Cleveland and Toledo, while west of Detroit, the state of Michigan began a blundering effort to build the Michigan Central towards infant Chicago. The merchants of New York City, alarmed by the ease with which Boston was exchanging East-West trade at Albany via its new railroad, overcame their smugness at the success of their wonderful canal. They privately financed a railroad up the east bank of the Hudson to Albany, where passengers (and more and more freight) could be transferred to the lines that continued west. It remained for Commodore Cornelius Vanderbilt to recognize the true potential of the Hudson River Railroad after the Civil War, but without it, New York City would have declined steadily from the 1850s on.

As for Philadelphia, by the mid-1840s, not even the most obscurantist citizen could ignore the fact that its system of canals and inclined planes was a miserable failure. In 1846, a group of private businesspeople, suspecting correctly that they would later be able to buy at a bargain price the usable rail sections of the "mainline works," secured a charter for what came to be called the Pennsylvania Railroad and tackled the awesome task of building a railroad over the Alleghenies to Pittsburgh. They were spurred on by an act of the state legislature that granted the Baltimore & Ohio Railroad a charter to build a branch of its line to Pittsburgh if the Pennsylvania Railroad was not in Pittsburgh within 10 years—a fate too horrible for the merchants to contemplate. They made it with two years to spare, and the remarkable enterprise that they had created made them, and three succeeding generations, prosperous indeed.

There are a number of reasons that the 1850s became the "miraculous decade" in the development of the American railroad system. The volume of railroad building required access to capital. Much of the funds needed came from European investors who were looking for investment opportunities abroad after having been thoroughly frightened by the revolutions of 1848. Furthermore, many Americans felt that political stability had been secured by the Compromise of 1850, and they optimistically assumed that the slavery controversy would cease to act as a brake on national development.

The 1850s were a period not only of further building on an unprecedented scale but also of the beginnings, formal and informal, of consolidation of individual lines into a national system. It was clear that the railroad's role was to be far greater than that of a connecting link between navigable bodies of water: the trains were becoming, in fact, the basic means of transportation, regardless of the distances involved, the difficulty of the terrain, and the existence of water routes. In 1853, Erastus Corning, whose efficiency in providing upstate New York with railroads, had been well motivated by an exclusive contract to sell them iron rails, engineered the merger of numerous short lines into one continuous line between Albany and Buffalo. Christened the New York Central, it ranks as the first great corporate merger in our history. At almost the same moment, the Lake Shore & Michigan Southern Railroad, destined to become one of the world's greatest profit machines, had been completed, and through service from New York City to Chicago had begun. The axis thus created was the chief one around which the commerce of North America would revolve for the next century and more.

The approach of the Pennsylvania Railroad towards Pittsburgh stimulated the construction of extensions toward Chicago and St. Louis, and by 1860, the East-West railroad system had assumed the general form that it has had ever since. But the expansion of railroads in Ohio, Indiana, and Illinois in the 1850s was truly remarkable, especially in view of the defaults and outright repudiations of the state bond issues that had been authorized in the 1840s to build railroads. The ironmasters of England and Wales would not have sold these states a single fishplate on credit, but by 1850, private capital had rushed in and filled the vacuum. Important North-South lines were also built to do the work that it had originally been hoped the canals would be able to accomplish.

At this point, a major shift in federal policy occurred. Nationalistic Democrats like Stephen A. Douglas, convinced that an America preoccupied with the great work of filling a continent would forget its sectional differences, pushed through Congress the first land grant law. The railroad it helped make possible, the Illinois Central, lived up to its expectations and by 1860 had helped draw the Midwest more tightly into the union than ever before.

Reinforcing this development was the rapid extension of railroads westward from Chicago. In 1856, the Rock Island Railroad, after its brilliant attorney, Abraham Lincoln, had defeated the efforts of river boatmen to prevent it, had built the first bridge across the Mississippi River at Rock Island, Illinois, and was heading across the prairies of Iowa. Railroads had reached the east bank of the Mississippi at seven other places from La Crosse, Wisconsin, to St. Louis, and one, a predecessor of the Burlington Railroad, stretched all the way across Missouri to St. Joseph. The impact of the railroads of the North was felt almost immediately on patterns of interregional trade. No one put it better than New York politician Thurlow Weed, on a trip out West in 1854, who wrote this letter to the New York *Tribune:*

> Time is working a phenomenon upon the Mississippi River. In a business point of view, this river is beginning to run upstream! A large share of the products of the Valley of the Mississippi are soon to find a market up instead of down the river. There is a West growing with a rapidity that has no parallel . . . while the railroads that are being constructed from Cincinnati, Toledo, Chicago, &c., to the Mississippi, are to take the corn, pork, beef, &c, &c, to Northern instead of Southern markets.

By 1860, in fact, more than one half of the cotton crop had deserted New Orleans and other Gulf ports and was being speeded north and east to Atlantic ports entirely by rail. When the Civil War finally broke out, these railroads would play an important role in the outcome and provide the basis for the great westward surge that came afterwards. Not even the South's failure to build East-West railroads of its own (with one exception) was as great a blow to her hopes to retain support of the West as was the joining of the Northeast and Midwest by railroads that reached down into southern Illinois and beyond the great river itself.

## Conditions on the Railroads

American railroads in 1860 were primitive even by the standards of the next generation. Although accompanying maps appear to show smooth, integrated systems, many of the routes were, in fact, broken at numerous points. The science of bridge building was still in its infancy, and most river crossings required travelers to take a ferry, although boats that carried passenger and freight cars intact from one bank to the other were widely used. Thus, trains were ferried across the Susquehanna at Havre de Grace on the important Philadelphia-Baltimore line and across the broad Ohio at Cairo, Illinois, between the Illinois Central and its southern connection. The city of St. Louis, lulled by its golden days as the most important steamboat town on the Mississippi, did not bestir itself to build a bridge across the river at that point until the 1870s; but Chicago, with its superb location at the foot of Lake Michigan, would have eclipsed it anyway. There was no bridge on the Thames River at New London, Connecticut, until the 1880s; through traffic between Boston and New York moved by an inland route, and the famous "Shore Line" did not come into its own until the end of the century. Most serious of all was the variation in track guages, especially in the South, which was not finally corrected until the 1880s.

The roadbeds and rails of antebellum lines were almost toylike. Even the best-engineered lines boasted iron rails that weighed barely a third as much per yard as those of the best railroads of today, reflecting the fact that the rails were more expensive in the United States than in England until the use of the Bessemer steel process in the 1870s. Most lines were poorly built, sometimes not with rails at all but iron straps that could pop up, pierce the car floor, and impale the passengers. Speeds of 10 to 15 miles an hour were typical, and speeds of more than 30 miles an hour, virtually unknown. Even so, derailments were frequent and did not so much crush the passengers as cremate them when the pot-bellied stoves (the only source of heat in winter) set the wooden cars afire. Collisions—front-end and rear-end—produced appalling results, even after the telegraph began to be used to dispatch trains in lieu of "running by the book." Travelers found few amenities either in the railroad stations or aboard the trains. Sleeping cars did not come into general use until after the Civil War, and meals for the travelers who did not prudently carry his own meant a mad scramble for "refreshments" at railroad lunch rooms en route. Like the airliner of today, the train was boring and uncomfortable, but far, far faster than any alternative.

As an occupation, railroad work was grueling and dangerous. The automatic air brake, applied simultaneously throughout the entire train by the engineer, would not make its appearance until the last quarter of the century. Meanwhile, men scrambled down the catwalks atop box cars, in all kinds of weather, to twist the handbrake wheels when the engineer whistled, "Down brakes!" In the yards, brakemen stood between cars to couple them by means of links and pins before the automatic coupler was finally invented late in the century.

### Railroad Data

This case includes various exhibits to illuminate further the growth of the railroads. Exhibit 1 shows railroad rates compared to those of other means of transportation. Exhibit 6 shows the rates of travel from New York City for three years. Exhibit 7 shows railroad mileage in operation from 1830 to 1900. Exhibits 8 a, b, and c show the railroad network in 1840 and three decades later. They also show the railroad-building activity from 1849 to 1854.

## Data on National Growth

The railroads both benefited from and helped to make possible the growth of the United States during the 19th century. The subject of economic growth is a large one which is not the central concern of this case or course. Yet some familiarity with major trends is important. Exhibits 9 a and b provides U.S. population from 1810 to 1900. (From 1810 to 1860, these figures are broken down into three regions and from 1870 to 1900, into eight.) Exhibit 10 shows the percentage of farm and nonfarm workers from 1820 to 1900. Exhibit 11 shows the population of urban and rural territory form 1790 to 1930. Exhibit 12 provides data on per-capita national income. Exhibit 13 shows the value of output of four sectors of the economy from 1839 to 1899.

## EXHIBIT 1

**General Pattern of Inland Freight Rates, 1784–1900** (*cents per ton-mile*)

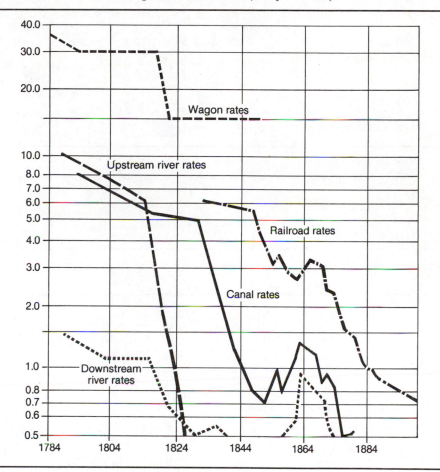

Source: Douglass C. North, *Growth and Welfare in the American Past* (Englewood Cliffs, N. J.: Prentice-Hall, 1966), p. 111.

## EXHIBIT 2

**Development of the Internal Transport Sector, 1820–1860**

|  | *1820* | *1830* | *1840* | *1850* | *1860* |
|---|---|---|---|---|---|
| Canal mileage (1,000) | 0.2* | 1.5 | 3.3 | 3.7 | 4.3 |
| Railroad operating mileage (1,000) | — | — | 2.8 | 9.0 | 30.6 |
| Steamboat (western rivers) operating tonnage (1,000) |  |  |  |  |  |
|     Hunter | 14 | 29 | 84 | 145 | 163 |
|     Haites and Mak | 14 | 25 | 83 | 135 | 195 |

*Data for 1821.

Source: Peter McClelland, "Transportation" in Glenn Porter, ed., *Encyclopedia of American Economic History,* I, p. 314.

## EXHIBIT 3

**Annual Investment in Canals by Region and by Agency of Enterprise, 1815–1860**
(*millions of dollars*)

|  | *United States* | | |
|---|---|---|---|
|  | *Total* | *State* | *Private* |
| *Year* | *(1)* | *(2)* | *(3)* |
| 1815 | a | — | — |
| 1816 | a | — | — |
| 1817 | 0.2 | 0.1 | — |
| 1818 | 0.7 | 0.6 | 0.1 |
| 1819 | 0.8 | 0.6 | 0.2 |
| 1820 | 1.1 | 0.8 | 0.2 |
| 1821 | 1.6 | 1.3 | 0.2 |
| 1822 | 2.7 | 2.3 | 0.3 |
| 1823 | 2.8 | 2.2 | 0.7 |
| 1824 | 2.5 | 1.8 | 0.7 |
| 1825 | 2.7 | 1.5 | 1.2 |
| 1826 | 4.0 | 1.5 | 2.5 |
| 1827 | 5.6 | 2.3 | 3.3 |
| 1828 | 7.8 | 4.0 | 3.7 |
| 1829 | 7.0 | 3.7 | 3.2 |
| 1830 | 7.5 | 5.1 | 2.4 |
| 1831 | 3.7 | 2.2 | 1.5 |
| 1832 | 4.6 | 2.9 | 1.7 |
| 1833 | 5.3 | 2.7 | 2.6 |
| 1834 | 4.4 | 2.8 | 1.6 |
| 1835 | 3.5 | 2.0 | 1.5 |
| 1836 | 4.4 | 1.8 | 2.6 |
| 1837 | 8.2 | 3.9 | 4.3 |
| 1838 | 12.3 | 7.2 | 5.1 |

## EXHIBIT 3 *(concluded)*

| | United States | | |
| | Total | State | Private |
| Year | *(1)* | *(2)* | *(3)* |
|------|-------|-------|---------|
| 1839 | 13.6 | 9.5 | 4.1 |
| 1840 | 14.3 | 11.3 | 3.0 |
| 1841 | 11.7 | 9.8 | 1.9 |
| 1842 | 3.1 | 2.6 | 0.6 |
| 1843 | 1.0 | 0.7 | 0.3 |
| 1844 | 1.0 | 0.7 | 0.3 |
| 1845 | 2.0 | 1.1 | 0.9 |
| 1846 | 1.8 | 0.8 | 1.0 |
| 1847 | 4.7 | 1.1 | 3.6 |
| 1848 | 4.5 | 1.5 | 3.0 |
| 1849 | 3.4 | 1.9 | 1.6 |
| 1850 | 4.9 | 2.3 | 2.5 |
| 1851 | 4.7 | 2.0 | 2.8 |
| 1852 | 3.4 | 1.9 | 1.5 |
| 1853 | 3.8 | 2.4 | 1.4 |
| 1854 | 4.7 | 3.8 | 0.9 |
| 1855 | 5.3 | 4.2 | 1.1 |
| 1856 | 4.2 | 3.2 | 1.0 |
| 1857 | 3.5 | 2.9 | 0.7 |
| 1858 | 2.8 | 1.6 | 1.1 |
| 1859 | 1.9 | 1.4 | 0.5 |
| 1860 | 1.2 | 1.4 | 0.5 |
| | 194.6 | 121.1 | 73.5 |

[a]Less than $50,000.

Detail may not add to totals due to rounding.

Source: H. Jerome Cranmer, "Canal Investment, 1815–1860" in *Trends in the American Economy in the Nineteenth Century* (Princeton: Princeton University Press, 1960), pp. 555–559.

# EXHIBIT 4

## Principal Canals Built by 1860

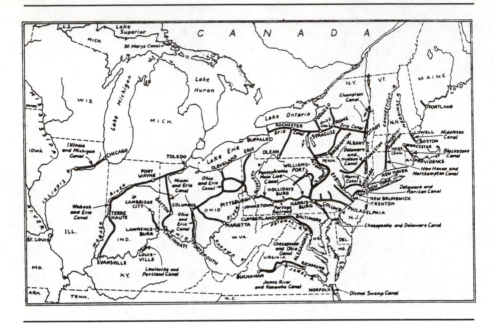

Source: Taylor, *The Transportation Revolution* (New York: Harper & Row, 1968), p. 35.

**EXHIBIT 5**

Navigable Rivers, 1930

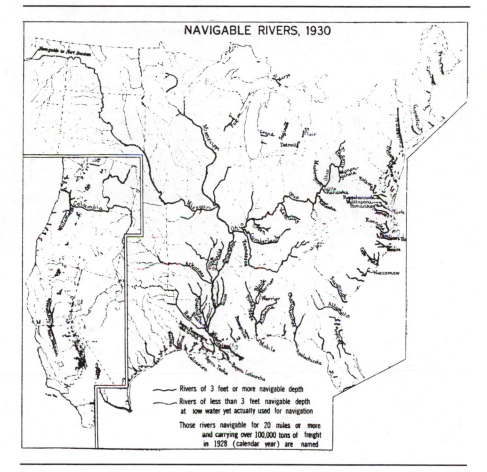

Source: Charles O. Paullin, *Atlas of the Historical Geography of the United States* (Washington, D.C.: Carnegie Institution, 1932), Plate 138F.

## EXHIBIT 6

Rates of Travel from New York

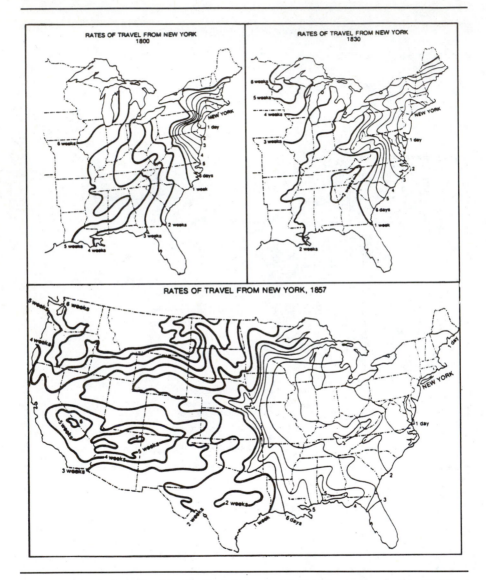

Source: Charles O. Paullin, *Atlas of the Historical Geography of the United States,* as reproduced in Alfred D. Chandler, Jr., *The Visible Hand* (Cambridge: Harvard University Press, 1977).

**EXHIBIT 7**

**Miles of Railroad in Operation by Geographical Sections, 1830–1900**

| Year | New England | Middle Atlantic | South Atlantic | Central Northern | Gulf and Mississippi Valley | North-Western | South-Western | Pacific |
|---|---|---|---|---|---|---|---|---|
| 1830 | 3 | — | — | — | — | — | — | — |
| 1840 | 436 | 1,511 | 994 | 196 | 195 | — | — | — |
| 1850 | 2,423 | 2,596 | 1,478 | 930 | 316 | — | — | — |
| 1860 | 3,660 | 6,353 | 5,463 | 9,583 | 3,727 | 665 | 1,162 | 23 |
| 1870 | 4,494 | 10,577 | 6,481 | 14,701 | 5,106 | 5,004 | 4,625 | 1,934 |
| 1880 | 5,977 | 15,147 | 8,474 | 25,109 | 6,995 | 12,347 | 14,085 | 5,128 |
| 1890 | 6,832 | 20,038 | 17,301 | 36,976 | 13,343 | 27,294 | 32,888 | 12,031 |
| 1900 | 7,513 | 22,361 | 21,917 | 41,138 | 16,211 | 32,165 | 37,530 | 15,486 |

Note: States included in the sections are as follows:
New England: Maine, N.H., Vt., Mass., R.I., Conn.
Middle Atlantic: N.Y., N.J., Pa., Del., Md., D.C.
South Atlantic: Va., W.Va., N.C., S.C., Ga., Fla.
Central Northern: Ohio, Mich., Ind., Ill., Wis.
Gulf and Mississippi Valley: Ala., Miss., Tenn., Ky., La.
Northwestern: Iowa, Minn., Neb., N.D., S.D., Wy., Mont.
Southwestern: Missouri, Ark., Texas, Kan., Colo., N.Mex., Okla. and Indian Terr.
Pacific: Idaho, Ariz., Utah, Nev., Wash., Ore., Calif.

Sources: U.S. Bureau of Statistics, *Statistical Abstract, 1901*, 1901, pp. 390–91 (for 1860–1900); *American Railroad Journal* 23 (July 27,1850), p. 473 (for 1850); 12 (March 1, 1841), p. 157 (for 1840); and, George Rogers Taylor, *The Transportation Revolution*, p. 79.

# EXHIBIT 8 a

Railroads in Operation, December 1840

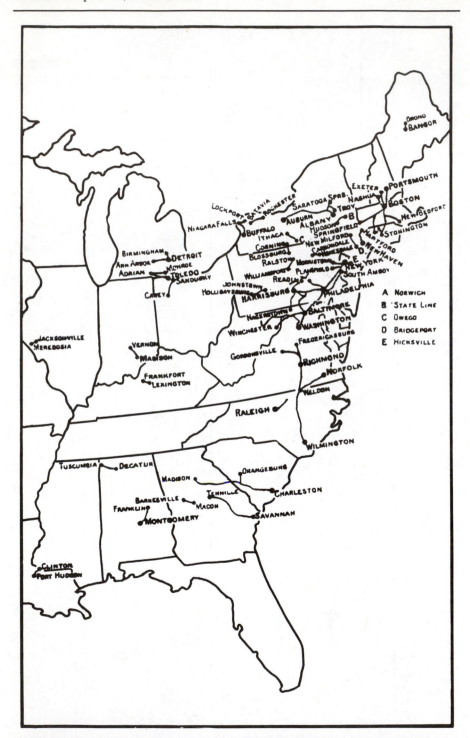

Source: Charles O. Paullin, *Atlas of the Historical Geography of the United States.*

# EXHIBIT 8 b

Railroads, 1870

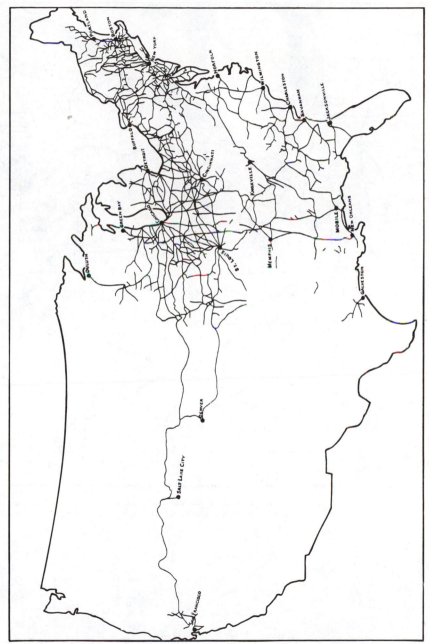

Source: Charles O. Paullin, *Atlas of the Historical Geography of the United States.*

## EXHIBIT 8 c

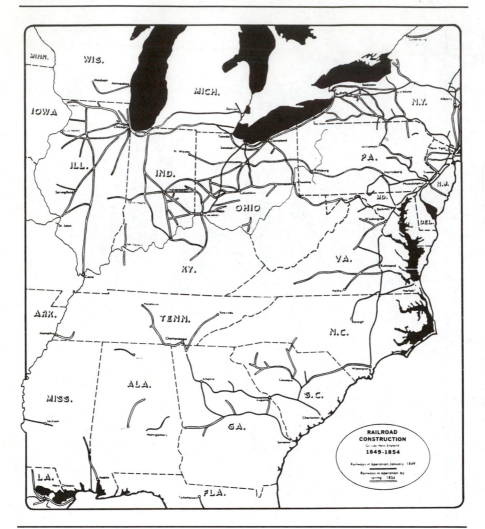

Source: Alfred D. Chandler, Jr., *Henry Varnum Poor* (Cambridge: Harvard University Press, 1956), opposite page 84.

# EXHIBIT 9 a

## United States Population Distribution by Regions 1810–1860

| Year | South* | | West* | | Northeast* | | Total U.S. Population (does not include territories) |
|---|---|---|---|---|---|---|---|
| | Population | % of Total Population | Population | % of Total Population | Population | % of Total Population | |
| 1810 | 2,314,556 | 32.1 | 961,407 | 13.3 | 3,939,895 | 54.6 | 7,215,858 |
| 1820 | 2,918,198 | 30.4 | 1,845,863 | 19.2 | 4,836,722 | 50.4 | 9,600,783 |
| 1830 | 3,774,405 | 29.4 | 2,980,294 | 23.2 | 6,066,169 | 47.3 | 12,820,868 |
| 1840 | 4,749,875 | 27.9 | 4,960,580 | 29.1 | 7,309,186 | 42.9 | 17,019,641 |
| 1850 | 6,271,237 | 27.2 | 7,494,608 | 32.5 | 9,301,417 | 40.3 | 23,067,262 |
| 1860 | 7,993,531 | 25.6 | 11,796,680 | 37.8 | 11,393,533 | 36.5 | 31,183,744 |

*South—Alabama, Arkansas, Florida, Georgia, Louisiana, Mississippi, North Carolina, South Carolina, Texas and Virginia; West—Illinois, Indiana, Iowa, Kansas, Kentucky, Michigan, Minnesota, Missouri, Nebraska, Ohio, Tennessee, Wisconsin, California, Nevada and Oregon; Northeast—Connecticut, Delaware, Maine, Maryland, Massachusetts, New Hampshire, New Jersey, New York, Pennsylvania, Rhode Island, and Vermont.

Source: Douglas C. North, *The Economic Growth of the United States, 1790–1860* (Englewood Cliffs, N.J.: Prentice-Hall, 1961), p. 257.

## EXHIBIT 9 b

**United States Population Distribution by Regions, 1870–1900**

| | Percent of Total | | | |
|---|---|---|---|---|
| *Region* | *1870* | *1880* | *1890* | *1900* |
| New England | 8.8% | 8.0% | 7.5% | 7.4% |
| Middle Atlantic | 24.7 | 23.4 | 22.5 | 22.5 |
| Great Lakes | 22.9 | 22.3 | 21.4 | 21.0 |
| Southeast | 29.1 | 27.3 | 25.5 | 25.1 |
| Plains | 9.7 | 12.3 | 14.2 | 13.6 |
| Southwest | 2.5 | 3.5 | 4.4 | 5.5 |
| Mountain | 0.4 | 0.9 | 1.4 | 1.7 |
| Far West | 1.8 | 2.3 | 3.1 | 3.2 |
| U.S. Total | 39,818,449 | 50,155,783 | 62,947,714 | 75,994,575 |

New England: ME, VT, NH, MA, RI, CT.
Middle Atlantic: NY, NJ, PA, DE, MD.
Great Lakes: OH, MI, IN, IL, WI.
Southeast: VA, WV, KY, NC, SC, TN, GA, AL, MS, AK, LA, FL.
Plains: MN, IA, MO, ND, SD, NE, KS.
Southwest: TX, OK, NM, AZ.
Mountain: MT, ID, WY, CO, UT.
Far West: WA, OR, CA, NV.

Source: Douglass C. North, *Growth and Welfare in the American Past*, p. 257.

**EXHIBIT 10**

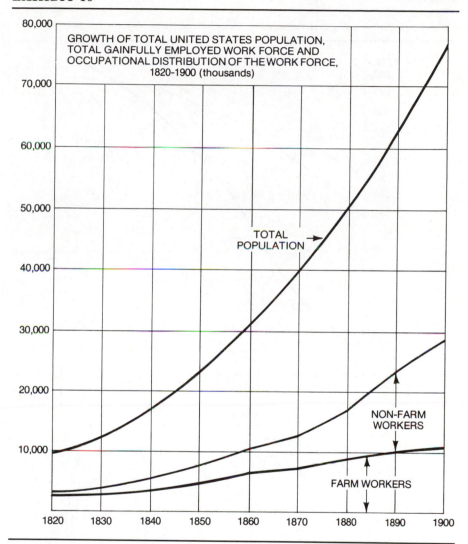

GROWTH OF TOTAL UNITED STATES POPULATION,
TOTAL GAINFULLY EMPLOYED WORK FORCE AND
OCCUPATIONAL DISTRIBUTION OF THE WORK FORCE,
1820–1900 (thousands)

TOTAL POPULATION

NON-FARM WORKERS

FARM WORKERS

Source: Total Population, U.S. Bureau of the Census, *Historical Statistics of the United States, Colonial Times to 1957,* 1960, p. 7. Gainful Workers: *Ibid.*, p. 72.

## EXHIBIT 11

Population in Urban and Rural Territory by Size of Place, 1790–1940 (*in 100,000s*)

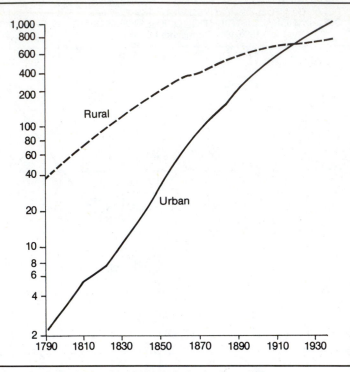

Source: Douglas C. North, *Growth and Welfare in the American Past,* p. 22.

## EXHIBIT 12

**Per Capita Realized National Income**

| | Dollars | | | Indexes, 1929 = 100 | | |
|---|---|---|---|---|---|---|
| Year | Current Income | Income Adjusted by the Cost of Living* | Income Adjusted by the General Price Level† | Current Income | Income Adjusted by the Cost of Living* | Income Adjusted by the General Price Level† |
| 1839 | 98 | 198 | 197 | 15.0 | 29.1 | 31.1 |
| 1849 | 107 | 235 | 241 | 16.4 | 34.5 | 38.6 |
| 1859 | 140 | 296 | 300 | 21.4 | 43.5 | 48.0 |
| 1869 | 180 | 237 | 233 | 27.5 | 34.8 | 37.3 |
| 1879 | 147 | 309 | 315 | 22.5 | 45.4 | 50.4 |
| 1889 | 173 | 383 | 385 | 26.5 | 56.2 | 61.6 |
| 1899 | 205 | 482 | 456 | 31.3 | 70.8 | 73.0 |
| 1900 | 212 | 480 | 459 | 32.4 | 70.5 | 73.4 |

*Cost of Living Index, Federal Reserve Bank of New York and National Industrial Conference Board.

†Price Index, Snyder Index, Federal Reserve Bank of New York and National Industrial Conference Board.

Source: Robert F. Martin, *National Income in the United States, 1799–1938* (New York: National Industrial Conference Board, 1939), p. 6.

## EXHIBIT 13

**Value of Output by Industry in Current Prices, 1839–1899 (*in billions of dollars*)**

| Year | Total | Agriculture | Mining | Manufacturing | Construction |
|---|---|---|---|---|---|
| 1839 | $ 1.04 | $0.71 | $0.01 | $0.24 | $0.08 |
| 1844 | 1.09 | 0.69 | 0.01 | 0.31 | 0.08 |
| 1849 | 1.40 | 0.83 | 0.02 | 0.45 | 0.11 |
| 1854 | 2.39 | 1.46 | 0.03 | 0.66 | 0.23 |
| 1859 | 2.57 | 1.50 | 0.03 | 0.82 | 0.23 |
| 1869 | 4.83 | 2.54 | 0.13 | 1.63 | 0.54 |
| 1874 | 5.40 | 2.53 | 0.15 | 2.07 | 0.65 |
| 1879 | 5.30 | 2.60 | 0.15 | 1.96 | 0.59 |
| 1884 | 7.09 | 2.84 | 0.20 | 3.05 | 1.01 |
| 1889 | 7.87 | 2.77 | 0.28 | 3.73 | 1.10 |
| 1894 | 7.83 | 2.64 | 0.29 | 3.60 | 1.30 |
| 1899 | 10.20 | 3.40 | 0.47 | 5.04 | 1.29 |

Source: Douglas C. North, *Growth and Welfare in the American Past*, p. 19.

# CASE 8

# The Railroads and the Beginnings of Modern Management *

Modern management first appeared in the United States during the second half of the 19th century. Many of the present-day practices and procedures used in the administration of business enterprise were originally devised to meet the requirements of operating the railroads and the factories that grew to unprecedented size. The purpose of this set of readings is to probe more deeply into the nature of the managerial challenges facing railroads specifically and into the solutions they provided.

The first selection on railroad management contains the earliest writings on business administration published in the United States. It is a detailed report of Daniel C. McCallum, general superintendent of the Erie Railroad, to that road's president, which was printed in the Erie's Annual Report for 1855. In it, McCallum outlined the difficulties and problems he faced and the solutions he devised in operating the road, which, completed less than five years earlier, was at that time one of the very largest in the world.

After the construction of the first large American railroads was completed and their original organizational structure put into effect, railroad managers began to concentrate on improving control over operations. Therefore following the 1850s, the emphasis turned from organization building to formulating elaborate systems for costing and control. The best known of such systems is described in the second selection, an excerpt from Albert Fink's famous exposition on cost accounting, published in 1874 in the *Annual Report of the Louisville and Nashville Railroad,* a highly successful railroad company of which Fink was president.

The third selection is a memorandum written in 1885 by Charles E. Perkins, president of the Chicago, Burlington and Quincy Railroad, as he was putting into operation a new organizational structure to manage his road, which in the previous seven years had grown from a line of 500 miles to a system of over 5,000 miles. Following the model of the Pennsylvania Railroad, Perkins had set up a structure similar to the multidivisional form used today by modern industrials. It included four large autonomous geographical divisions, each headed by a general manager who was responsible for operations and profits and whose activities were planned, coordinated, and evaluated by four top managers—a president and three vice presidents—working out of the General Office and assisted by a general staff. Perkins's memorandum is one of the best analyses of the organization of a large railroad system and the needs that brought it into being that is available from contemporary sources.

## Creating a Management Structure

Superintendent's Report[1]
Office General Sup't N.Y. & Erie R.R.
New York, March 25, 1856

Homer Ramsdell, Esq.
President of the New York and Erie Railroad Company:

Sir:

The magnitude of the business of this road, its numerous and important connections, and the large number of employees engaged in operating it, have led many, whose opinions are entitled to respect, to the conclusion, that a proper regard to details, which enter so largely into the elements of success in the management of all railroads, cannot possibly be attained by any plan that contemplates its organization as a whole and in proof of this position, the experience of shorter roads is referred to, the business operations of which have been conducted much more economically.

Theoretically, other things being equal, a long road should be operated for a less cost per mile than a short one. This position is so clearly evident and so generally admitted, that its truth may be assumed without offering any arguments in support of it; and, notwithstanding the reverse, so far as practical results are con-

---

[1]From Daniel C. McCallum, "Superintendent's Report," March 25, 1856, in *Annual Report of the New York and Erie Railroad Company for 1855* (New York, 1856), pp. 33-37, 39-41, 50-51, 57-59.

sidered, has generally been the case, we must look to other causes than the mere difference in length of roads for a solution of the difficulty.

A superintendent of a road 50 miles in length can give its business his personal attention, and may be almost constantly upon the line engaged in the direction of its details; each employee is familiarly known to him and all questions in relation to its business are at once presented and acted upon, and any system, however imperfect, may under such circumstances prove comparatively successful.

In the government of a road 500 miles in length a very different state of things exists. Any system which might be applicable to the business and extent of a short road, would be found entirely inadequate to the wants of a long one: and I am fully convinced, that in the want of a system perfect in its details, properly adapted and vigilantly enforced, lies the true secret of their failure: and that this disparity of cost per mile in operating long and short roads, is not produced by a difference in length, but is in proportion to the perfection of the system adopted.

Entertaining these views, I had the honor, more than a year since, to submit for your consideration and approval, a plan for the more effective organization of this department. The system then proposed, has to some extent been introduced, and experience, so far, affords the strongest assurances that when fully carried out, the most satisfactory results will be obtained.

In my opinion a system of operations, to be efficient and successful, should be such as to give to the principal and responsible head of the running department a complete daily history of details in all their minutiae. Without such supervision, the procurement of a satisfactory annual statement must be regarded as extremely problematical. The fact that dividends are earned without such control, does not disprove the position, as in many cases the extraordinarily remunerative nature of an enterprise may ensure satisfactory returns under the most loose and inefficient management.

It may be proper here to remark, that in consequence of that want of adaptation before alluded to, we cannot avail ourselves to any great extent of the plan of organization of shorter lines in framing one of this, nor have we any precedent or experience upon which we can fully rely in doing so. Under these circumstances, it will scarcely be expected that we can at once adopt any plan of operations which will not require amendment and a reasonable time to prove its worth. A few general principles, however, may be regarded as settled and necessary in its formation, amongst which are:

1. A proper division of responsibilities.
2. Sufficient power conferred to enable the same to be fully carried out, that such responsibilities may be real in their character.
3. The means of knowing whether such responsibilities are faithfully executed.
4. Great promptness in the report of all derelictions of duty, that evils may be at once corrected.
5. Such information, to be obtained through a system of daily reports and checks that will not embarrass principal officers, nor lessen their influence with their subordinates.

6. The adoption of a system, as a whole, which will not only enable the general superintendent to detect errors immediately, but will also point out the delinquent.

## Organization

The following comprises a list of the principal officers acting directly under the general superintendent, with powers and duties arranged with reference to obtaining the results proposed.

1. Division and branch superintendents.
2. Masters of engine and car repairs.
3. Car inspectors.
4. General freight agent.
5. General ticket agent.
6. General wood agent.
7. Superintendent of telegraph.
8. Foreman of bridge repairs.

For the more convenient working of the road it is now separated into divisions as follows:

— The Eastern Division and Union Railroad extending from Jersey City, to Port Jervis in the county of Orange—88 miles.
— The Delaware Division extending from the Port Jervis Station, to Susquehanna Station in the county of Susquehanna, Penn.—104 miles.
— The Susquehanna Division extending from the Susquehanna Station, to Hornellsville in the county of Steuben—139 miles.
— The Western Division extending from Hornellsville, to Dunkirk on Lake Erie—128 miles.
— Newburgh Branch extending from Newburgh, westward, to the intersection with the main line near Chester, in the county of Orange—19 miles.
— Piermont Branch extending from Piermont to Sufferns—18 miles.

The several divisions and branches are in charge of superintendents, who are held responsible for the successful working of their respective divisions, and for the maintenance of proper discipline and conduct of all persons employed thereon, except such as are in the employment of other officers acting under directions from this office, as hereinafter stated. They possess all the powers delegated by the organization to the general superintendent, except in matters pertaining to the duties of general ticket agent, general freight agent, general wood agent, telegraph management, and engine and car repairs.

They have authority to change, by telegraph or otherwise, the movement of trains from the times specified in the tables.

Masters of engine repairs are held responsible for the good condition of the engines and machinery in shops, and the cost of their repairs. It is their duty to make frequent and thorough inspection of the engines so as to guard them from accidents and injuries which may result from the want of seasonable and trifling renewals; also to see that the engines are otherwise in efficient condition for use. They are also required to report to the division superintendents all cases they may discover of abuse or maltreatment of locomotives by engineers or dispatchers.

There are eight engine repair shops on the line. . . . [McCallum identifies the shops and the personnel in charge of them and then outlines the duties of the car inspectors.]

The general freight agent has the supervision of the freight charges. His duties are, with the approval of the president or general superintendent, to make and regulate prices for the transportation of freight; to negotiate contracts and arrangements with individuals and other companies, and to see that such contracts are fairly and equitably complied with. Also, to investigate and examine all claims for damages and losses of freight or baggage, and certify such of them as are found valid, to the general superintendent for approval.

The general ticket agent is required, with the approval of the president or general superintendent, to regulate the prices for transportation of passengers; to negotiate ticket arrangements with other companies, and to supervise all matters connected with the sale of tickets. [McCallum next describes the duties of the general wood agent, the superintendent of telegraph, and the foreman of bridge repairs.]

The above will serve to show the division of the administrative duties upon the line, and the general organization of this department. Each officer possesses all the power necessary to render his position efficient, and has authority, with the approval of the president and general superintendent, to appoint all persons for whose acts he is held responsible, and may dismiss any subordinate when in his judgment the interests of the company will be promoted thereby.

The enforcement of a rigid system of discipline in the government of works of great magnitude is indispensible to success. All subordinates should be accountable to, and be directed by their immediate superiors only; as obedience cannot be enforced where the foreman in immediate charge is interfered with by a superior officer giving orders directly to his subordinates.

It is very important, however, that principal officers should be in possession of all the information necessary to enable them to judge correctly as to the industry and efficiency of subordinates of every grade.

To acquaint themselves in this particular, and remedy imperfections without weakening the influence of subordinate officers, should be the aim of officers of the higher grades.

It would occupy too much space to allude to all the practical purposes to which the telegraph is applied in working the road; and it may suffice to say, that without it, the business could not be conducted with anything like the same degree of economy, safety, regularity, or dispatch. The constantly increasing amount of business to be performed by it, has rendered it necessary to put up an additional wire over the Delaware Division, for through messages: and I have no doubt the increase of traffic will soon compel its extension over every portion of the road.

The minimum amount of service consistent with the largest net revenue, is also an important subject for consideration, the proper regulation of which must mainly depend upon data derived from the actual expenses and earnings of each train, as nearly as can be ascertained.

In the economical management of a freight traffic are involved:

First, the most effective use of motive power.

Second, the regulation and reduction of speed to the lowest standard consistent with the exigencies of business.

Third, the means of controlling the movement of rolling stock, that the greatest amount of service may be derived therefrom.

Fourth, the reduction of dead weight,[2] and a corresponding increase of useful load[3] hauled.

Fifth, the reduction of friction, by which the cost of repairs of rolling stock is diminished, and the facilities for economical transportation are proportionately increased.

By the introduction of a system of reports, and the use of the telegraph, much has been accomplished in obtaining these and other desirable results; and when the telegraphic system shall have become fully matured and carried out, I have the best of reasons for believing that its efficacy will justify the most sanguine expectations.

It would be tasking your patience too much to force the consideration of its details on you at the present time, but as the results of the last year's operations have shown a gratifying reduction in the expenses of the road, and believing as I do, that it is mainly attributable to this cause, I should be doing injustice to my own feelings were I to omit furnishing at least a faint sketch of it.

The powers and duties of the principal officers on the line have been given, and are such as to harmonize in all branches of duty. It will be seen that their subordinates cannot communicate with higher officers, but through them, and can only be communicated with through the same means. There are, however, some exceptions to this rule, as conductors and station agents report, daily, their operations directly to the general superintendent; and it is in a great measure through these means that the business—so far as relates to the movement of trains, the amount of freight carried, and its prompt transmission—is controlled.

## System of Reports and Checks

Hourly reports are received by telegraph, giving the position of all the passenger and the principal freight trains. In all cases where passenger trains are more than 10 minutes, or freight trains more than half an hour behind time, on their arrival at a station the conductors are required to report the cause to the operator, who transmits the same by telegraph to the general superintendent: and the information being entered as fast as received, on a convenient tabular form, shows, at a glance, the position and progress of trains, in both directions, on every division of the road.

---

[2]Weight of cars.

[3]Weight of freight.

The importance of ascertaining the particulars connected with delays cannot be overestimated, as they are frequently the result of mismanagement, are often the primary cause of accidents, and in their history is developed a class of facts and delinquencies which could not be so easily detected in any other way. By these means, the prevailing causes of delays are made known, and an opportunity is given to apply the corrective, where the nature of the case will permit.

The daily reports of passenger conductors give the designating numbers of the engines and cars, the names of the persons employed on the trains, the time of arrival at and departure from the several stations, the particulars in regard to delays, and such other matters of interest as occur on the trip.

The daily reports of freight conductors, in addition to the above, give a general description of the load contained in each car, the place whence taken, where left, and destination as per waybills.

The station agents' daily reports give the time of the arrival and departure of all freight trains at their respective stations; the name of the conductor and number of the engine; the numbers of the cars taken and left, with the tonnage of freight in each; the numbers and kinds of cars remaining at their station, and whether the same be loaded or empty; how many are required for the business of the station, and the nature of that business; and whether any conductor has refused to take cars or freight waybilled to other stations; also, a statement of freight over or short of bills, or damaged or wrongly directed; delays of freight and causes thereof; damaged cars at stations, with particulars as to cause thereof; an accurate daily report of all baggage received and forwarded; from whom received and to whom given; a list of unclaimed baggage remaining on hand at the close of the report; and any other information of interest pertaining to the business of their respective stations.

The division superintendents report monthly the number of miles run, the expense of engineers and firemen, and the quantity and cost of oil, waste, and tallow for each engine on their respective divisions.

The masters of engine repairs report monthly the amount expended for repair on each engine.

The general wood agent reports monthly the number of cords of wood used by each engine, and the cost of the same.

The information thus obtained is embodied in the statistical accounts kept in this office, and from it we deduce the following:

— The speed of the train between the several stations.
— The average load carried in each car.
— The tonnage of useful load carried.
— The tonnage of cars in which it was transported.
— The tonnage of empty returned cars.
— The position or location of the cars.

Each of the above items is given for the different trains over the several divisions.

As relates to engines, we obtain for each:

— Number of miles run.
— Cost per mile run for engineer and fireman.
— Gallons of oil used.
— Miles run to one pint.
— Pounds of waste used.
— Pounds of tallow used.
— Cost for oil, waste, and tallow.
— Cost per mile run for oil, waste, and tallow.
— Cost for repairs.
— Cost per mile run for repairs.
— Cords of fuel used.
— Cost of fuel.
— Cost per mile run for fuel.
— Total cost for all of the above items.
— Cost per ton per mile for the same.

The above reports, with others not now enumerated, furnish to the officer at the head of this department, a fund of information, the judicious use of which materially assists in directing the business of the road to the best advantage: but interesting as this information is, in instituting comparisons between the business performed by the several engines and trains and the cost thereof, it is only in its practical application in pointing out the neglect and mismanagement which prevail, thus enabling us to remedy the defect, that its real value consists.

An experiment referred to in another portion of this report has furnished data for determining the effects of the ruling grades and curvature on each division, and from this data a tabular statement giving the amount of load each engine is capable of moving over the several divisions has been prepared, and we shall be enabled hereafter to observe whether they work up to their capacity. Proper attention to this subject I have no doubt will effect the necessary reform.

The experiment to which I have alluded, furnishes data for determining what ought to be the relative cost of transporting freight over the several divisions, having reference to their grades, alignment and condition; and it is proposed, as soon as the necessary arrangements can be made, to keep division accounts, with the view of ascertaining how far the actual results agree. This comparison will show the officers who conduct their business with the greatest economy, and will indicate, in a manner not to be mistaken, the relative ability and fitness of each for the position he occupies. It will be valuable in pointing out the particulars of excess in the cost of management of one division over another, by a comparison of details; will direct attention to those matters in which sufficient economy is not practiced; and it is believed, will have the effect of exciting an honorable spirit of emulation to excel.

It will be seen that to some extent the operations on the road are conducted under the directions of officers wholly independent of each other; and it may be thought difficult, under such an organization, to preserve that harmony, in all the branches of duty, which is so essential to success. Subject as they all are to one principal officer, who, as the head of the department, prescribes rules for each, no difficulty need be entertained on this subject; and as a precautionary measure, it is provided that, should any difficulty or misunderstanding arise between division or branch superintendents, general freight agent, general ticket agent, masters of engine repairs, general wood agent, car inspectors, superintendent of telegraph, or either of them, as to the performance of their respective duties, or the relative powers of each, or in reference to the acts of any subordinate of either, copies of all correspondence in relation thereto shall be furnished to the general superintendent, in order that all matters in discussion may be at once adjusted.

The foregoing will probably be sufficient to point out the general features of our organization, without descending to the particulars as affecting the officers of lower grades, where the same rigid discipline is maintained, and whose duties are all systematically arranged with the view of enforcing personal accountability. To enter fully into all the details would extend this communication to too great a length. I trust what has been said will be sufficient to show that, under its operations, provision has been made for carrying out those leading principles which are of such vital importance in conducting great and important works.

It seems to have been generally conceded, that railroad companies have not the same means of controlling the various items of earnings and expenditures, as are within the reach of persons managing the same business but acting in an individual capacity; and whilst it is a humiliating circumstance that railroad companies have not, in many particulars, conducted their business with the same economy as would have been done by private enterprise, it by no means proves that they have not the power to do so.

All that is required to render the efforts of railroad companies in every respect equal to that of individuals, is a rigid system of personal accountability through every grade of service.

# Developing Modern Cost Accounting

## Classification of Operating Expenses[4]

Before leaving this subject, attention is called to the classification of accounts in Table 1. It will be observed that the accounts are divided into three classes:

— Maintenance of road, buildings, and general expense, from account 1 to 29.
— Station expenses, from account 30 to 40.
— Movement expenses, from account 41 to 74.

The expenditures of each class bear a distinct character, to which I will now refer more particularly.

---

[4]From Albert Fink, "Classification of Operating Expenses," in Annual Report of the Louisville & Nashville Railroad Company for the year ending June 30, 1874 (Louisville, Ky., 1874), pp. 37–47, 63–64.

Those in the first class are not affected by the amount of business transacted, within certain limits to be referred to hereafter. The roadway must be kept in good order. Cross-ties when decayed must be renewed, bridges kept in repair, and a certain organization of officers and men must be kept up, whether one or more trains are to pass over the road.

This class of expenditure per mile of road will vary on different roads according to the permanency of construction, the number of bridges to be kept in repair, the nature of the soil, the climate, and many other local conditions. They will also vary with the amount of business, but only to the extent to which an increase of business requires more extensive accommodation, such as depot-building, side-tracks, etc., which have to be kept in repair. On a road with an established business, and having suitable accommodation for the same, considerable variation in business may take place without affecting this class of expenditures.

The second class of expenditures are incurred at stations in keeping up an organized force of agents, laborers, etc., for the purpose of receiving and delivering freight, the selling of tickets, etc.

One portion of these expenditures does not vary with the amount of business; another portion does. A certain number of agents have to be employed, whether there is more or less work to be done; but the number of persons employed to handle freight may be varied in proportion to the number of tons of freight to be handled. This whole class of expenditures, however, is entirely uninfluenced by the length that either freight or passengers are hauled, or, in other words, by the work of transportation performed. Freight or passengers may be hauled five or two hundred miles, the station expenses incurred on their account being the same.

In the third class of expenditures have been collected all those that vary with the number of trains run.

On the roads on which there is sufficient freight business to fill all trains that are run from one terminus of the road the amount of freight transported will be nearly in proportion to the number of freight train-miles; and hence on such roads this third class of expenditures will be nearly in proportion to the amount of business. It is this class of expenditures alone which possesses that characteristic.

On roads, however, upon which freight-trains have to be run at stated times, whether fully loaded or not, this class of expenditures does not vary with the business, but very nearly with the number of trains run. The expenditures and amount of freight transported in this case are irrelative, the cost of transporting freight being dependent entirely upon the loads as accidentally offered for transportation.

To the three classes of expenditures just named, and which have been shown separately and in detail in (Table 1), must be added a fourth, not shown (in this table), but which forms a large proportion of the total operating expenses of railroads—viz., the interest on the capital invested.

This class is mainly uninfluenced by the amount of work done. Only so far as an increase of business involves the necessity of additional investments for its accommodation is it influenced by the amount of business.

In the consideration of the subject of the cost of railroad transportation it is of the greatest importance to discriminate between the expenditures which vary with the amount of work performed and those which are entirely independent thereof. The latter form so large a proportion of the total operating expenses of railroads that it becomes impossible to make the amount of work performed a criterion or measure of the cost.

The fixed or inevitable expenses which attach to the operation of railroads, and which are the same whether one or many trains are run over a road, have to be ascertained separately in each individual case. These expenditures are in the nature of a tax upon the business of the road; the smaller the business the larger the tax. What the tax may or should be per ton of freight or per passenger carried in any one case cannot be predetermined by any general rule or law, but can only be ascertained after the two elements on which it depends—(1)the fixed expenditures, and (2) the amount of work done—are actually known. These elements vary on all roads; it would be a singular accident to find them alike on any two.

The disregard of these facts in estimating the cost and the value of railroad transportation with a view of judging of the reasonableness of railroad tariffs has led to many erroneous conclusions, which appear to be now fixed in the public mind. It is of great importance to the owners of railroad property at this present time—more so perhaps than heretofore—to possess correct information upon the subject of the cost of railroad transportation. It may therefore not be considered out of place here to show how the cost of transportation varies upon the various roads operated by the Louisville & Nashville Railroad, and the reasons therefor.

The following Table A shows the percentage of the four classes of expenditure above referred to, of the total operating expenses on the seven roads operated by the Louisville & Nashville Railroad Company.

## TABLE A

|  | M.S. | M.L. | N.&D. | K.B. | B.B. | R.B. | G.B. |
|---|---|---|---|---|---|---|---|
| Movement expenses | 41.367 | 38.589 | 38.594 | 22.428 | 10.490 | 17.634 | 28.761 |
| Station expenses | 18.161 | 12.924 | 12.259 | 4.367 | 6.209 | 5.832 | 5.007 |
| Maintenance on road | 14.453 | 17.179 | 17.554 | 17.964 | 22.505 | 17.295 | 9.361 |
| Interest on investment | 26.019 | 31.308 | 31.593 | 55.241 | 51.796 | 59.239 | 56.871 |
| Total | 100.000 | 100.000 | 100.000 | 100.000 | 100.000 | 100.000 | 100.000 |

From this table will be seen the great diversity existing in the relative proportions of each class of expenditures.

The movement expenses, the cost of conveying freight from one place to another after it is loaded in the cars—the transportation expenses proper—are 41.3 percent on the Main Stem, and only 17.6 on the Richmond Branch, of the total operating expenses. We have therefore in one case 58.7, in the other 82.4 percent of the total operating expenses, which are entirely uninfluenced by the amount of work performed as measured by weight and distance, or ton-miles.

The station expenses vary from 4.3 percent on the Knoxville Branch to 18.1 percent on the Main Stem of the total operating expenses.

The cost of maintenance of road is 9.3 percent on the Glasgow Branch and 22.5 on the Bardstown Branch.

The interest account is 26 percent on the Main Stem, and 59.2 percent on the Richmond Branch.

With such great variations in the constituting elements of the cost of transportation uniformity in the final results cannot be expected.

## Causes of Difference in Cost of Transportation

I will now compare the expenditure of each class per ton-mile on the seven roads, and show more particularly the reasons for the great difference in cost.

The following Table B shows each class of operating expenses per ton-mile on the seven roads operated by the L. & N. R.R. Co.

## TABLE B

**Cost per Ton-Mile** (*in cents*)

|  | M.S. | M.L. | N.&D. | K.B. | B.B. | T.B. | G.B. |
|---|---|---|---|---|---|---|---|
| Movement expenses | .7365 | .8102 | .9787 | .9364 | 1.5039 | 1.6934 | 5.4928 |
| Station expenses | .3233 | .2714 | .3109 | .1823 | .4791 | .5601 | .9563 |
| Maintenance of road | .2573 | .3607 | .4451 | .7499 | 1.7366 | 1.6608 | 1.7877 |
| Total operating exp. | 1.3171 | 1.4423 | 1.7347 | 1.8686 | 3.7196 | 3.9143 | 8.2368 |
| Interest | .4633 | .6574 | .8011 | 2.3061 | 3.9968 | 5.6887 | 10.8615 |
| Total operating expenses & interest | 1.7804 | 2.0997 | 2.5358 | 4.1747 | 7.7164 | 9.6030 | 19.0983 |

Movement expenses (comprised of items 41–73 [Table 1]). It appears that on the first four roads this class of expenditures varies from .73 cents to .97 cents per ton-mile; on the last three named from 1.50 cents to 5.49 cents per ton-mile. The first four roads belong to that class on which fully loaded freight-trains can be started from one terminus of the road; on the last three named trains are started at regular times, regardless of the amount of load that is to be carried. Hence we find greater agreement in the cost of moving one ton one mile on the first four roads than on the latter, on which the cost depends altogether upon accidental causes.

If on the first four roads the grades, curves, and the cost of labor and material were the same, and also the character of the business, then the cost per ton-mile should be the same; but as these elements of cost differ, uniformity in the cost even in the movement expenses cannot be expected.

The character of the business of a road has a great influence upon the cost of transportation.

We find the average trainload carried on the first four roads, and the movement expenses per ton-mile, as follows:

|  | M.S. | M.L. | N.&D. | K.B. |
|---|---|---|---|---|
| Average trainloads (in tons) | 134 | 113 | 96 | 77 |
| Movement expenses per ton (in cents) | 0.73 | 0.81 | 0.97 | 0.93 |

On the Main Stem the average net load carried per train is nearly twice as much as on the Knoxville Branch.

On the first-named road a large amount of freight is carried over its whole length; while on the latter, which is a mere local road, it only passes over a portion of its whole length. The capacity of the locomotive and train cannot therefore be as fully utilized on the latter as on the former road.

On the Main Stem the tonnage in one direction is 73 percent of the tonnage on the other direction, while on the Knoxville branch it is only 21 percent; hence more empty cars have to be run on the latter than on the former road.

The result is that an average of 135 tons of freight is being carried per train on the Main Stem, while only 77 tons can be carried on the Knoxville Branch; yet the same attention is paid on both roads to secure maximum loads to each train.

It is the character of the business peculiar to each road that brings about this great difference, which, of course, influences the cost of transportation.

On the roads on which there is not sufficient business to secure full loads in the movement expenses per ton is found still greater.

The following table shows the average loads carried in the trains of the three branch roads, and the cost per ton-mile for moving the freight.

|  | B.B. | R.B. | G.B. |
|---|---|---|---|
| Average number of tons freight carried on one train | 18.2 | 24.0 | 4.9 |
| Movement expenses per ton-mile (in cents) | 1.5 | 1.7 | 5.5 |

It is on account of the small loads carried on the Glasgow Branch per train (4.9 tons) that the movement expenses are so much larger than on the other branches, on which the trains carry from 18.2 to 24 tons.

Station expenses (items 30–40 [Table 1]). The elements controlling the cost per ton-mile for station expenses are:

**a.** The cost of handling one ton of freight—for loading, unloading, clerking, agents' salaries, depot expenses, switching, etc.
**b.** The length of haul.

Supposing that the cost of handling freight per ton were the same on all roads and at all stations of a road, then the cost per ton-mile of freight would vary according to the length of haul. For each particular length of haul there would be a different cost per ton-mile for this service.

The average cost of station expenses per ton of freight handling on the Main Stem of the road is 23 cents per ton. For freight that passes over the whole length of the line, say between Louisville and Memphis, the cost per ton-mile would be $2 \times 23/377 = 0.12$ cents, and for freight carried only five miles it would be $2 \times 23/5 = 9.2$ cents. We have therefore a difference between the cost per ton-mile from 0.12 to 9.2 cents, although the actual cost of performing the work was the same in both cases; thus showing that the ton-mile is not a proper unit of measure of cost of this service.

But there is even considerable variation in the cost of handling one ton of freight at various stations. . . .

. . .Dividing the number of tons into the number of ton-miles gives the average haul, and dividing this into the cost per ton for handling gives the average cost per ton-mile for handling freight.

For example, take Brooks Station. Number of tons of freight received and forwarded . . . 654: freight to and from Brooks Station was carried 14,335 miles, therefore the average haul $14,333/654 = 21.8$ miles; station expenses per ton at Brooks Station . . . 71 cents; cost per ton-mile $71/21.8 = 3.26$ cents. To this has to be added the expenses at the station from or to which the freight was forwarded.

If both stations are known, the cost per ton-mile for station expenses can be readily ascertained. . . . For example, for freight shipped between Louisville and Brooks Station, distance 9.2 miles:

| | (*in cents*) |
|---|---|
| Station expenses at Brooks Station per ton | 71.0 |
| Station expenses at Louisville per ton | <u>24.3</u> |
| Total cost per ton | 95.3 |

Length of haul, 9.2 miles; cost per ton-mile 10.4 cents.

This example sufficiently illustrates the great variety in cost, and the impossibility of making the ton-mile the measure of cost of or compensation for this service. The ton handled would be a more correct measure, although there is necessarily much variety even in this cost, as we have seen. . . .

It must therefore be evident that it is possible to predetermine the cost per ton-mile of freight for handling without taking into consideration the length of the haul and the conditions under which the station service has to be performed.

**Maintenance of roadway and general expense (items 1–29).**   The two elements that determine the cost per ton-mile for this service are:

**1.** The cost of maintaining one mile of road, etc., during a given time.
**2.** The number of tons of freight passed over it during the same time.

The former differs on each road, and so does the latter; hence uniformity in cost per ton-mile is impossible.

The following table shows the cost of maintenance of roadway and general expense per mile of road on the seven roads operated by the Louisville & Nashville Railroad Company during the last year, and the average number of tons of freight passed over one mile of each road; also the cost per ton-mile:

| | M.S. | M.L. | N.&D. | K.B. | B.B. | R.B. | G.B. |
|---|---|---|---|---|---|---|---|
| Cost of maintenance of road per mile per year (Table 1, item 29) | $1,857.87 | $1,142.25 | $1,243.49 | 906.76 | 436.69 | 436.61 | 262.73 |
| Tons of freight passed over one mile of road | 433,662 | 152,273 | 143,378 | 72,436 | 11,538 | 16,656 | 6,137 |
| Cost per ton-mile (in cents) | 0.26 | 0.36 | 0.44 | 0.75 | 1.74 | 1.66 | 1.78 |

Part of the cost of maintenance of roadway and buildings is chargeable to the passenger traffic. The division of charges between the two classes of traffic has been made in proportion to train-miles. It follows from this that the cost per ton-mile of freight is in a measure affected by the relative use made of a road by the passenger and freight traffic.

From this statement will be noticed the great difference in cost of maintaining one mile of road, buildings, etc. On the Main Stem this cost is $1,857.87, on the Glasgow Branch $262.73 per mile.

An examination of the items from 1 to 28 will show in what particulars these differences occur. A few may be mentioned here. The cost of a mile on the Main Stem and Glasgow Branch is as follows:

| | M.S. | G.B. |
|---|---|---|
| Renewal of ties | $ 368.89 | $32.96 |
| Bridge superstructure | 250.26 | 25.14 |
| Ditching | 69.23 | 26.06 |
| General expense | 346.14 | — |
| Salaries, insurance and taxes | 100.40 | — |
| Total | $1,134.92 | $84.16 |

The difference in cost in these five items on the Main Stem and Glasgow Branch is $1,050.76 per mile of road. Part of this great difference is caused from the fact that on one road greater expenditures were made during this year than was due to the year's business: on the other road less. It will be remembered that the yearly depreciation of crossties on the Main Stem was found to be for 16½ years at the rate of $257.11 per mile, while during the past year there was expended $368.89 on the Main Stem, and on the Glasgow Branch only $32.96 per mile; the first sum more, the latter considerably less than is required to make good a year's depreciation.

There are great differences in other expenses, such as repairs of bridges, on the two roads. On the Main Stem, as has been mentioned before, the cost of bridge repairs during the last year was unusually heavy, while on the Glasgow Branch, with only one small bridge, the cost is very small. The general expenses of administration on the Main Stem are not incurred on the Glasgow Branch, which is also exempt from taxation. Hence the great difference in cost of maintenance of road and buildings and general superintendence between the two roads.

When we examine into the differences existing in regard to the amount of business transacted in one year over one mile of road—the other element named which enters into the cost of one ton per mile—we find the variation still greater. On the Main Stem 433,662 tons, on the Glasgow Branch only 6,137 tons, pass over one mile of road per year. We can therefore not be surprised that the cost on the Main Stem for maintenance of road is only one-fourth of a cent per ton-mile and on the Glasgow Branch 1.8 cents.

**Interest account.**   The original cost of the road and the rate of interest form one element and the amount of business transacted the other which determines the cost per ton-mile.

The cost of roads per mile and the business transacted over the same vary so much that the cost per ton-mile for interest cannot be expected to be the same in any two cases.

It is impossible to predetermine what is a proper charge for interest on any particular road until these elements—viz., the cost of road and the amount of business—are known.

On the Main Stem of the Louisville & Nashville Railroad, dividing the number of ton miles of freight carried into the interest chargeable to the freight business, the cost per ton-mile is 0.46, while on the Richmond Branch it is 10.86 cents, over twenty times as much. On the five other roads the interest charge varies from 0.65 to 5.7 cents per ton-mile. (For further particulars refer to Table B.)

We have not considered the variation in each class of expenditures and the causes therefor per ton-mile. When we find so much variation in the elements which make up the cost of transportation we cannot expect to find uniformity in the total cost.

From Table B it appears that the variation in the total cost per ton-mile is from 1.78 cents on the Main Stem to 19.09 cents on the Glasgow Branch. The work performed—viz., the movement of one ton of freight one mile—is the same on all roads, yet the cost of performing is ten times more on one road than on the other.

Great as this variation is on the seven roads under the same management, the variation of the cost per ton-mile is still greater even on the same road, depending as it does upon the different conditions under which the service has to be performed. It would lead here too far to thoroughly analyze the cost of railroad transportation in all its details, and I will only state that a careful investigation shows that under the ordinary conditions under which transportation service is generally performed the cost per ton-mile in some instances may not exceed one-seventh of a cent and in other will be as high as 73 cents per ton-mile on the same road. The lower cost applies to freight carried in cars that otherwise would return empty; the higher cost to freight in small quantities carried short distances.

It is impossible to predetermine the cost of carrying freight on any one road unless the conditions under which it is to be carried, as far as they affect the cost of transportation, be previously known.

In order to estimate the cost of transportation under the various conditions that occur it is necessary to classify the expenditures, and to separate those that increase with the amount of work done from those that are fixed and independent of it; and to ascertain the ratio of increase of cost with the increase of work. Without such an analysis of the cost it is impossible to solve the question of cost of transportation that arises in the daily practice of railroad operation. A mere knowledge of the average cost per ton-mile of all the expenditures during a whole year's operation is of no value whatever in determining the cost of transporting any particular class of freight, as no freight is ever transported under the average condition under which the whole year's business is transacted. We can therefore not make the average cost per ton-mile the basis for a tariff, if it is to be based upon cost; but we must classify the freight according to the conditions affecting cost of transportation, and ascertain the cost of each class separately.

## TABLE 1

**Heading of Accounts**

|  |  |
|---|---|
| *Maintenance of Roadway and General Superintendence* | 35.   Total per train mile |
| Roads Repairs per Mile of Road | 36.   Stationery & printing |
| 1.   Adjustment of track | 37.   Telegraph expenses |
| 2.   Ballast | 38.   Depot repairs |
| 3.   Ditching | 39.   Total per train mile |
| 4.   Culverts and cattleguards | 40.   Total station expenses per train mile |
| 5.   Extraordinary repairs, slides, etc. | *Movement Expenses per Train Mile* |
| 6.   Repairs of hand and dump cars | 41.   Adjustment of track |
| 7.   Repairs of road tools | 42.   Cost of renewal of rails-value |
| 8.   Road watchmen | 43.   Labor replacing rails |
| 9.   General expense of road dept. | 44.   Train expenses hauling rails |
| 10.   Total | 45.   Joint fastenings |
| 11.   Cross-ties replaced, value | 46.   Switches |
| 12.   Cross-ties, labor replacing | 47.   Total cost of adjustment of track & replacing rails per train mile |
| 13.   Cross-ties, train expenses hauling | 48.   Locomotive repairs |
| 14.   Total cost of cross-ties per mile of road | 49.   Oil & waste used on locomotives |
| 15.   Bridge superstructure repairs | 50.   Watching and cleaning |
| 16.   Bridge watchmen | 51.   Fuel used in engine house |
| 17.   Shop building repairs | 52.   Supervision and general expense in engine house |
| 18.   Water station repairs | 53.   Engineers' and firemen's wages |
| 19.   Section house repairs | 54.   Total engine expenses per train mile |
| 20.   Total cost of bridge and building repairs per mile of road | 55.   Conductors and brakemen |
| 21.   General superintendence and general expense of operating department | 56.   Passenger car repairs |
| 22.   Advertising & soliciting passengers and freight | 57.   Sleeping car repairs |
| 23.   Insurance and taxes | 58.   Freight car repairs |
| 24.   Rent account | 59.   Oil and waste used by cars |
| 25.   Total per mile of road | 60.   Labor oiling & inspecting cars |
|  | 61.   Train expenses |
|  | 62.   Total car expenses per train mile |

**TABLE 1** (*concluded*)

| | | | |
|---|---|---|---|
| 26. | Salaries of general officers | 63. | Fuel used by locomotives |
| 27. | Insurance & taxes, & general expense | 64. | Water supply |
| 28. | Total per mile of road | 65. | Total fuel & water expense per train mile |
| 29. | Total cost per mile of road for mainte-nance of roadway and buildings | 66. | Damage to freight and lost baggage |
| 29½. | Total cost per train mile for mainte-nance of roadway and buildings | 67. | Damage to stock |
| | | 68. | Wrecking account |
| | *Station Expenses per Train Mile* | 69. | Damage to persons |
| 30. | Labor loading & unloading freight | 70. | Gratuity to employees |
| 31. | Agents and clerks | 71. | Fencing burned |
| 32. | General expense of stations, lights, fuel, etc. | 72. | Law expenses |
| 33. | Watchmen and switchmen | 73. | Total per train mile |
| 34. | Expense of switching, engine repairs, engineers' and firemen's wages, ex-pense in engine house | 74. | Total movement expenses per train mile |
| | Supervision & general expense | 75. | *Grand total* for maintenance and move-ment per train mile |
| | Oil and waste | | |
| | Water supply, fuel | | |

**Formula for Ascertaining the Cost of Railroad
Transportation per Ton-Mile**

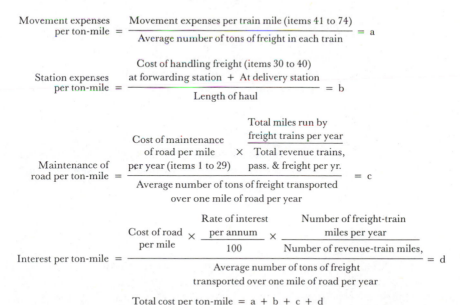

$$\text{Movement expenses per ton-mile} = \frac{\text{Movement expenses per train mile (items 41 to 74)}}{\text{Average number of tons of freight in each train}} = a$$

$$\text{Station expenses per ton-mile} = \frac{\text{Cost of handling freight (items 30 to 40) at forwarding station} + \text{At delivery station}}{\text{Length of haul}} = b$$

$$\text{Maintenance of road per ton-mile} = \frac{\text{Cost of maintenance of road per mile per year (items 1 to 29)} \times \dfrac{\text{Total miles run by freight trains per year}}{\text{Total revenue trains, pass. \& freight per yr.}}}{\text{Average number of tons of freight transported over one mile of road per year}} = c$$

$$\text{Interest per ton-mile} = \frac{\text{Cost of road per mile} \times \dfrac{\text{Rate of interest per annum}}{100} \times \dfrac{\text{Number of freight-train miles per year}}{\text{Number of revenue-train miles,}}}{\text{Average number of tons of freight transported over one mile of road per year}} = d$$

$$\text{Total cost per ton-mile} = a + b + c + d$$

In order to make use of this formula it is necessary to know . . . 58 items of expense (above), all of which vary on different roads, and enter into different com-binations with each other. Some of the items of movement expenses (41 to 74) change with the weight of trains, and have to be ascertained in each individual case. The average cost for the year can be made the basis of the estimate. Besides the items shown (above), the following other items enter into the calculation: the average number of tons of freight in train per mile of the round trip of the train, the average length of haul, the number of miles run over the road with freight and passenger trains per annum, the cost of the road, the rate of interest, and the total number of tons of freight carried during a year over one mile of road. Without these data it is impossible to make a correct estimate of the cost of transportation on railroads.

---

# Administering a Great Railroad System*

## III

In deciding the question of organization it will be necessary to consider two stages, so to speak, of railroad development. The first stage where the volume of traffic is not sufficient to make necessary or to warrant the highest degree of physical efficiency; and the second stage where the volume of traffic is so great as not only to warrant the expenditure, but also to make it economical to maintain the physical efficiency at the highest point.

Ordinarily the second stage will come only with increased mileage and while there are exceptional cases where roads of small fixed mileage acquire a large business by reason of their forming a link in a through line, or being in direct competition with one or more other roads between two commercial centers, they are so rare that it is best in considering the general question of organization to assume that a road in the second stage will be one of 500 miles or more in length. On the other hand, a road of even larger mileage may belong to the first stage.

## IV

*The responsible head of the operations of a road* in the first stage is usually the general superintendent, a general manager only becoming necessary when the road has grown and business has so increased as to make it desirable to confine the general superintendent to the care of the machine alone. In the first stage he can and will himself look closely after his track and rolling stock as well as the traffic. In the second stage with the increase of traffic he will find his time and mind largely occupied with business questions, and also that he can draw the straight line of perfection to work to, and can safely trust to educated experts most of the questions relating to the efficient maintenance of the machine. The proper economical maintenance of a road in the first stage is not an exact science, while that of a road in the second stage is, and scientific methods which would be unnecessary and extravagant on the one may become necessary and economical on the other.

---

*From a memorandum of Charles E. Perkins, "Organization of Railroads," written in 1885, from the personal papers of Charles E. Perkins, president of the Chicago, Burlington and Quincy Railroad, 1881–1901 © 1965 by Richard C. Overton. Printed by permission.

V

An organization for the management of a road in the first stage is comparatively simple. The duties of the president will be to advise the chief financial and accounting officer and the chief operating officer and also the purchasing and supply agents, to supervise and execute all important contracts, to conduct the most important negotiations, to specifically approve all expenditures chargeable to capital account before they are incurred, to supervise and direct the more important purchases of material and equipment, and to watch closely the results by means of reports from the heads of the two great departments of accounts and operations.

One officer as secretary and treasurer will have charge of accounts, finances, archives, titles, etc., or perhaps if the road be a large one it may be necessary to have an auditor also.

Such a road will ordinarily not have miles enough or business enough to require both a general manager and a general superintendent, and if so the general superintendent will take care of the business matters as well as of the track and the equipment. He will need to be a man of ability and energy, and he will attend to all important details himself, including questions of engineering if he has been educated as an engineer. His general freight and passenger agent or agents, if one should be required for each of these two departments, will consult him frequently—and especially as to all departures from established rates or rules. His track master and his train master, or if the road embraces miles enough to be put into divisions, his superintendents of divisions will come to him daily as will also the master mechanic.

He will himself see his road every few days and will decide all questions as to quality and quantity of material—and on all questions of wages, down to individuals, he will himself be the judge. If receipts are falling off he will cut down expenses.

Business being light, he can often safely delay making renewals of track and equipment, because having personal knowledge of the whole situation, and being able to watch it, he can personally judge just how far it is safe to go.

The business questions which he will have to decide will be mostly local and in direct connection with his own road. And his time will not therefore be largely taken up in meeting the managers of other roads to arrange rates, pools, time schedules, etc., but can be devoted closely to his home affairs as above.

VI

An organization for the management of a large road in the second stage is on the other hand more complex. Here the duties of the president will be the same as in the first stage of development, but the amount of expenditure, the number of contracts, negotiations, reports, interviews, new schemes, etc., will have so largely increased that the president may require the aid of one vice president to assist him generally and possibly two or three personal assistants with fixed duties besides.

The departments of accounts and finances will also have grown so that a second vice president may be needed to look after the treasurer, the auditor and the secretary, three offices which in the first stage would be so combined as to be held by one, or at the most two persons.

So of the departments of operation and construction. If the mileage is large it will be found expedient probably to put a third vice president at the head of this great department, which controls so largely the income and outgo. Under him again will be a general manager in direct charge of the daily details and taking the position occupied by the general superintendent in the first stage. The purchasing agent will act under the 3rd vice president and also especially in making large purchases of rails, rolling stock, etc. directly under the president.

## VII

The purchasing agent should buy or regulate the buying of all supplies, acting under the president and 3rd vice president.

The purchasing agent would buy all supplies for operating the road upon order from the general superintendent or others properly authorized by the president or 3rd vice president. All materials and supplies should be turned over *as bought* to the general superintendent or to an officer acting under him and on his staff, called supply agent.

The duty of inspecting and testing supplies and materials would thus be thrown upon the general superintendents as a check upon the purchasing agent.

The supply agent may be authorized by the purchasing agent to make certain purchases of a local character.

## VIII

In the second stage the business questions will be numerous and difficult and the physical questions in many respects different from those arising in the first stage: and if, as is often the case, such a road embraces large mileage, the general manager in command of its operations will find his time so fully occupied with general matters as to make systematic attention to details impossible. So that it will be necessary that he should have under him men of ability, education and experience at the heads of the four chief branches of the service conducted by him, namely:

First. The general superintendent managing the road itself and the rolling stock as a machine.

Second. The chief engineer.

Third. The general freight agent in charge of the freight traffic.

Fourth. The general passenger agent in charge of the passenger traffic.

## IX

The general superintendent should have as his staff an engineer of track, bridges and buildings, a superintendent of motive power and cars, a supply agent and an agent in charge of the daily distribution of cars. This office is distinct from that of the car accountant, who belongs to the audit department, although the two offices may sometimes be held by one man.

The engineer of track, bridges and buildings will act as an inspector of work and supervisor of plans and methods and will also have charge of such other engineering matters as the general superintendent may direct.

The superintendent of motive power and cars will regulate the power in use upon the different divisions, will overlook the assistant superintendents of motive power and cars, and will distribute the motive power as directed by the general superintendent.

Under the general superintendent will be the superintendents of divisions.

The supply agent will have charge of all supplies as soon as purchased, will regulate their inspection and distribution and may purchase certain local supplies like coal, ties, etc., being authorized to do so by the purchasing agent.

## X

The duties of the chief engineer on the staff of the general manager will be of an advisory rather than of an executive character, except as regards the construction of new roads.

He will supervise plans and standards and will advise the general manager, as well as the general superintendent and the superintendents of divisions, the engineer of track, bridges and buildings and the assistant engineer of each division. He should be a man thoroughly educated in the science of engineering rather than in managing men. The direct management of all new work, except the construction of new roads, as well as of maintenance and repairs should be in the hands of the superintendents of divisions. The general manager may deem it expedient in special cases to charge the chief engineer, rather than the general superintendent, with the execution of certain work—but as a rule it is not expedient to do so. The location and construction of new roads or branches to be included in any unit of management would be in charge of the chief engineer acting under the general manager until ready for business when they should be turned over to a general superintendent.

## XI

The duties of the general freight agent and the general passenger agent will be the same here as in the first stage, but the field being larger they will need a number of assistants not only in the general office but also in the different divisions of the road.

The supply agent on the staff of the general superintendent will keep himself and the purchasing agent advised as to the requirements of the service. All requisitions for supplies on the road will go to and be filled by him in accordance with such rules as the general superintendent shall establish.

## XII

The property in the second stage will perhaps consist of a main line belonging clearly to the second stage while many short branches running to and feeding it will belong more properly to the first stage. But as they make a part of the homogeneous whole their management cannot be separated from that of the main stem, the whole making what may be called a unit of management all under one general manager. This unit, under the organization described and operated as one property with the results merged so far as accounts are concerned, should nevertheless be managed with the fact clearly in view that its main line is a road of one kind while its branches are roads of another kind.

## XIII

Remembering this it will be expedient wherever a branch is 100 miles or more in length to make a division or a subdivision of it depending upon circumstances, more especially its geographical relation to other parts of the property, and put over it a division or an assistant superintendent as the case may be, capable of looking after both the track and trains in detail subject to the general superintendent if it is a division, or to a division superintendent, if it is a subdivision.

The traffic of the branch being light it will not be economical to spend money enough upon it to get scientific accuracy in every detail.

The main line with such branches as are too short to be made into separate divisions will then be cut into divisions, each in charge of a superintendent responsible to the general superintendent. Local circumstances will to a certain extent determine the size of a division. It should not exceed 500 miles. The division will again be divided into subdivisions of from 100 to 200 miles in length depending upon the proportion of main line and other circumstances.

## XIV

The superintendent of a division if it is a large one, should have attached to his staff a division engineer of track, bridges and buildings, and a division superintendent of motive power and cars, a division car distributor and a division supply agent. The division engineer of track, bridges and buildings would be the maker of plans and methods and an inspector of work. He would be more an executive officer than the engineer of track, bridges and buildings because nearer to the details on a division there would be more or less new work of such a character as to be carried on by orders direct from the superintendent of division through the division engineer of track, bridges and buildings, and he would also in fact be the division superintendent of track repairs acting under the superintendent of division.

There should also be attached to each larger division a representative of the freight and passenger departments acting under the heads of those departments, but also responsible to the superintendent of division who would be the ranking officer on the spot.

## XV

On the main line when the traffic is heavy it will be found economical to insist upon having the track maintained at the highest point of scientific accuracy. To accomplish this there should be an assistant engineer in charge of each 100 miles of main line track with nothing else to look after, and directly responsible to the assistant superintendent of the subdivision, as well as to the engineer, or division engineer, of tracks, bridges and buildings. This assistant engineer should be a man of scientific education as an engineer and of practical experience as well, and with orders to make and keep a perfect track he can and will do it, and while it will cost what may at first seem a large amount of money the expenditure will pay in the end.

The amount of main line track to be so placed under one man should not exceed 100 miles, because it is important that the assistant engineer should see his road frequently by walking over it. Under him should be two roadmasters one for each 50 miles of road who would have the immediate direction of the section men, the field of each roadmaster being subdivided into sections of about five miles length. . . .

## XVI

Obviously there is a limit to the proper growth of any single unit of management under one general manager. Where the proper limit is will depend upon circumstances.

A road 500 miles long as to its main stem may have 1,500 miles of branches, and the whole may be of such a character as to make it almost necessarily one unit for the purpose of operation. Anywhere from 250 to 2,000 miles may be operated successfully as one unit under a general manager if in the second stage or a general superintendent if in the first.

An important question in the management of a large railroad system is how to get local responsibility on the part of those engaged in operating different arms of the system.

It is obvious that to hold a manager responsible for results it is necessary to give him pretty full power over the property which he must use to produce those results, both as to income and outgo. It is also clear that to get this kind of responsibility it is desirable that the unit of management, so to speak shall not be too large, and that it shall be homogeneous. That is to say one manager with his necessary staff having control of the every day details of business must not have too large a field or too many roads differing in character. On the other hand it is desirable and economical to have uniformity in many things and not to cut the system up into too small pieces locally independent of one another. The unit of management being determined the officer in command should in order to keep himself and his men up to their work be able to know at all times what his road is earning and what he is spending—and he should have the responsibility for a loss of business as well as for an excess of expenditures.

Experience shows that where branches or side lines are operated under the same local management as that for the through, or main line, the inevitable tendency is to do things on the branches in the same way as on the main line, which is often a more expensive way than is really necessary for a branch.

Also as regards wages: on a through line with a large and unsteady volume of business where 1,000 men are employed one month and 800 the next wages are fixed at an average point high enough to attract the best *class* of men to be had under the circumstances for the work to be done. Whereas on small roads where few men are employed and the work is steady and less wearing, and they can be selected by the superintendent himself and are drawn mostly from the fixed population along the line of the road the few required can generally be obtained at lower wages than the average paid by a big road.

It is always difficult however to pay one rate of wages on the main line, and another rate on a branch line, where one management operates both. Theoretically it can be, and sometimes is done to some extent, but the drift is always strong in the direction of pushing up the branch wages to the same level as the main line, when the two are operated as one road. With short branches which are run merely as feeders to the main stem, this evil can hardly be overcome.

A branch too short for a superintendent of its own, is put in charge of the force operating the part of the main line contiguous to it, and men are almost of necessity changed about from the branch to the main line and vice versa, either because trains run through sometimes over the branch and part of the main line, or for other reasons. But when it is practicable to group a sufficiently large mileage of second class or "branch" road to justify it, it is clearly desirable to separate the local management from that of the main line, even if it can be conveniently done, to the extent of making a distinct unit of management.

## XVII

A railroad system owned by one company may therefore embrace one or more units of managements, each under a general manager responsible directly to the president and the 3rd vice president and one or more smaller units of management embracing roads in the first stage, each under a general superintendent also responsible directly to the president and the 3rd vice president. Each unit may also if thought expedient have its own accounting office at the head of which would be a local auditor, and its own money office with a local treasurer in charge, and both of these officers would through the auditor and the treasurer respectively be responsible to the 2nd vice president.

By thus operating the property each unit can receive the kind of management most economical under the circumstances and details will receive an amount of attention from the respective general managers or general superintendents which could not be given if one management were put over the whole and the different heads of departments on the general manager's staff made responsible over so wide a field.

## XVIII

The general idea of the plan of management suggested, is that whatever the size of the unit and however many units may be owned by one company, the general organization would not be changed.

The president assisted by the three vice presidents could take care of an indefinite number of units if they keep clearly before them the necessity of local self-government.

By local self-government is meant the possession of very full powers by each general manager or general superintendent as the case may be.

The accounts of two or more units may with proper system be kept in one place and under one general auditor, but if that is done, they should be kept distinct so that each general manager or general superintendent, may be held responsible for his results independently.

The importance of not letting the unit of management become either too large or too heterogeneous is so great that it may sometimes be found expedient in acquiring a new road to continue to operate it under its own corporate organization.

When the consolidation of railroads began it was supposed and argued that one of the things to be gained by it would be the saving of the necessary cost of maintaining separate corporations and general offices.

This was true within limits—two roads each 100 miles long and each maintaining its corporate organization and staff could with economy in the general offices be put together under one set of officers throughout. But this is not true in the same degree of two roads each 1,000 miles long.

And when one general manager, responsible to those over him for the general results, has been charged with the daily supervision of 2,000 miles of railroad he has reached about the limit of physical ability. The amount of necessary attention to details is enormous. It would generally produce better results to limit one man to about 1,000 miles, but with the growth of the large systems and the complications of the business management it has been found in some cases difficult if not impractical to do this. No line however should be rigidly drawn, as it well can be in almost all cases, at about 2,000 miles, and as much less than that down to 1,000 as the circumstances will admit of.

It is sometimes urged against this division of one great property into units of management, that there constantly arise general questions affecting the whole property—that the different operating units will clash and money will be lost to the company owning the whole by reason of efforts on the part of one general manager to get some advantage over another—that the use of red tape will become too much extended—that car mileage offices and other offices will be unnecessarily multipled, etc. But the simple answer to all this is that the gain by reason of the more efficient attention to details on the part of the man responsible for results will be far greater than any possible loss by the unnecessary use of red tape, etc.

As to general questions about which the general managers cannot agree among themselves, they are easily referred to the president or to his representative the 3rd vice president, or in matters of accounts to the second vice president—and as to the objection that offices are multiplied it needs only to be said that very few more men are employed than if they were all under one general manager, but being directly responsible to some one near at hand they do more work and do it better. Not the least among the advantages to be derived from the division into units of management is the fact that the local population in the country and towns through which the road passes can more readily know and more often see in person the general manager. This is a consideration of importance and is alone a good reason for not making a unit too large. Personal acquaintance promotes good understanding and the people like to see those in authority. Again the president and the vice presidents can under this system bring to bear their judgment upon important local questions affecting any unit more effectively through the one local head than through the heads of a number of different departments far removed often from the scene of action.

# CASE 9

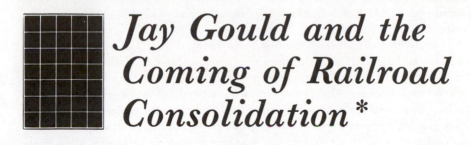

# *Jay Gould and the Coming of Railroad Consolidation* *

## Introduction

Before 1880, few American railroads had grown to great size. The Pennsylvania and the Baltimore & Ohio had built their systems in the 1870s, but other roads had not followed their example. Nearly all railroad men still agreed that a line of over 500 miles was too costly to finance and too complex to manage. Instead of expanding their operations, they preferred to assure a continued flow of traffic over their lines by making alliances with connecting and competing roads. Suddenly early in the 1880s, these men changed their minds. Within a decade the American railroad network became dominated by a relatively few huge railroad systems, each operating several thousand miles of track. The man most responsible for this sudden basic change in the strategy of American railroads was Jay Gould, the most astute of the many notorious speculators of that day. For this reason a review of the role played by Jay Gould, pilloried by contemporaries as the "Mephistopheles of Wall Street," provides an opportunity to analyze the nature of competition and finance and top-level decision making in the nation's first big business.

*This case was prepared by Alfred D. Chandler, Jr. The principal sources are Julius Grodinsky, *Jay Gould: His Business Career* (Philadelphia: University of Pennsylvania Press, 1957) and Alfred D. Chandler, Jr., and Stephen Salsbury, "The Railroads: Innovations in Modern Business Administration" in Bruce Mazlish, ed., *The Railroads and the Space Program* (Cambridge: MIT Press, 1965).

Harvard Business School case 372-301, rev. 6/84.

# The Policy of Alliances

Until the depression of the 1870s, railroad directors and managers were more concerned with building and then learning how to operate their lines than they were with competitive strategy.

The 1850s had witnessed the first great railroad boom, which by 1860 provided the country with over 30,000 miles of track and its basic rail network east of the Mississippi. The Civil War slowed construction, but with the war's end came a railroad building boom that lasted until the onslaught of the depression in 1873. In these same years the volume of traffic rose impressively, particularly along the great east-west routes of trade. During this period of traffic growth, American railroad companies rarely attempted to add new mileage to their lines. As an alternative to a strategy of physical expansion, they joined with connecting and competing lines to make agreements as to traffic movements and rates charged on through traffic.

This policy of alliance was worked out particularly speedily by those roads on the nation's central transportation routes connecting the Mississippi Valley with the Atlantic seaboard. Between 1851 and 1854, the four east-west trunk lines had been completed to their original destinations (Dunkirk, Wheeling, Buffalo, and Pittsburgh), where they made connections to the West—the Erie in 1851, the Baltimore & Ohio and New York Central in 1853 (the latter was a merger of a number of small lines), and the Pennsylvania in 1854. In the autumn of 1854, the presidents and general superintendents of these lines and of other east-west railroads gathered at the St. Nicholas Hotel in New York City. They met, the Pennsylvania's president told his stockholders, "with a view to agreeing upon general principles which should govern railroad companies in competing for the same trade and in preventing ruinous competition. . . ."[1] At this and subsequent meetings at the St. Nicholas Hotel, the roads defined general principles of rate making and freight classification, set rates and classifications, and determined what part of the total through rates each road on that route should receive. Similar agreements were made among roads in New England and among the new roads in the old Northwest. Yet the rates decided upon were rarely maintained. Pressure to cut them was too strong, and the sanctions to maintain them too weak. Then came the Civil War and the postwar boom, which provided for more than a decade almost enough traffic for all, making the need for more formal alliances between competing roads less necessary.

Alliances between connecting lines proved more enduring than those between competing ones. The Pennsylvania was one of the first to strengthen such alliances by taking stock in its connecting roads. As its able president, J. Edgar Thomson, told the road's stockholders in January 1858:

> It has been the policy of this company to aid in the construction of Western Railways designed to facilitate trade to and from its road, and to avoid serious inconveniences and losses to its freighting business from the uncertain character of the navigation of

---

[1] *Eighth Annual Report of the Directors of the Pennsylvania Rail Road Company* (1855), p. 13.

the Ohio River. With this object in view, assistance has been extended to the Pittsburgh, Fort Wayne and Chicago, the Steubenville and Indiana, and the Marietta and Cincinnati Railroad Companies.[2]

This investment, Thomson continued, had already reached over $1,600,000. Begun in 1852, this policy received legal sanction by the Pennsylvania legislature, which passed an act in March 1853, permitting the company "to subscribe capital, or guarantee bonds of other companies, to the extent of 15 percent of its paid up capital." This act, as one of the earliest laws allowing a company to hold the stock of another doing the same business, helped to introduce the holding company, the legal device which became so essential to the growth of the large business enterprise in this country. Besides obtaining allies to the west, the Pennsylvania also made agreements setting rates and providing for mutual use of facilities with roads connecting Philadelphia and other Pennsylvania cities with New York City.

In the East, the Baltimore & Ohio most closely followed the example of the Pennsylvania, making similar investments in and alliances with its connecting lines in the Ohio Valley. The Erie did less, partly because the speculators who had moved on to its board were not interested in the long-term health of the road, and partly because its major connection, the Atlantic and Great Western, was already financed by a wealthy British group and did not need to look to the Erie for financial support. The New York Central relied on another tactic. It purchased stock in the American Express Company and other fast-freight lines and used them to bring traffic to its roads.

In the West the new roads pursued the policy of investing in feeder lines even more extensively than did the Pennsylvania. The Boston investors (headed by John Murray Forbes) who financed the completion of the Michigan Central into Chicago also organized and founded the Chicago, Burlington and Quincy, running west from Chicago to the Mississippi. The New York group that revived the rival Michigan Southern financed the Rock Island to assure their western traffic. Both groups soon were financing the construction of lines across Iowa. In the same manner the Illinois Central and the Chicago and Northwestern supported their connecting lines.

Even though these companies tried to cement their relationships by stock purchases, the alliances rarely remained stable. The younger lines grew large, more prosperous, and increasingly independent. Financial strains in times of recessions, the personal ambitions of their promoters, and a desire to keep alternative traffic routes available often led these allies to threaten to join with other roads.

Nevertheless, railroad managers and directors continued to prefer a policy of alliances to that of purchase and outright control of connecting and competing lines. Consolidation presented complex financial, administrative, and even ideological challenges. The investors on the boards were fearful of the high costs of a policy of consolidation. Operating executives were troubled by the difficulty of managing a road more than 500 miles in length. The president of the Pennsylvania saw still another disadvantage of great size. He told his stockholders that:

---

[2] *Eleventh Annual Report of the Board of Directors of the Pennsylvania Rail Road Company* (1858), p. 14.

Sensible of the prejudice against large corporations since the failure of the United States Bank, the policy of this company was first directed to the procuring of these connections by securing the organization of independent railway companies, and their construction by such pecuniary assistance as was required to effect this business. This course, it was confidently expected, would meet the objects desired without involving this company in the direct management of distant enterprises.[3]

Nevertheless, in 1869 the eastern trunk lines suddenly changed their long-established policies. The Pennsylvania, the Baltimore & Ohio, and the New York Central all began purchasing connecting lines and then began to build giant consolidated systems.

## Jay Gould's Challenge

The man who forced this sudden change was Jay Gould. Gould was still a young man in 1869. Raised on a hardscrabble farm in New York State, he was operating a large tannery before he was 20. In 1859 at the age of 23, he had come to New York to sell leather goods. During the Civil War, he became involved in speculation in securities of small railroads, becoming for a time the chief executive of one. These speculations had drawn him to Daniel Drew, a leading Wall Street operator who had seen the speculative possibilities of the Erie stock in the late 1850s. In 1867, Gould won national notoriety when he joined with Drew and another infamous Wall Street speculator, Big Jim Fisk, to defeat Commodore Cornelius Vanderbilt's attempt to obtain the Erie.

The battle with Vanderbilt came shortly after the Commodore had obtained full control of the New York Central. Vanderbilt, who had made a fortune operating steamboat lines on the Hudson River and Long Island Sound, had decided early in the 1860s to shift his capital and his entrepreneurial energies to railroading. He began by obtaining control, through carefully timed purchases of stock, of the two lines paralleling the Hudson (the Harlem and the Hudson River) from New York City to Albany. He then with comparable care obtained the controlling interest in the New York Central, which meant he controlled the line from Albany to Buffalo, one of the nation's most productive transportation routes.

Vanderbilt moved on to the Erie because he was certain that any treaty made with its managers would not stick. That road, a developmental line constructed through sparsely settled southern counties of New York, had been financed largely through bonds sold to British investors. Although well managed, thanks to the efforts of its innovative superintendent, Daniel C. McCallum, its lack of traffic brought financial difficulties in the depression of 1857. Drew, who provided funds to meet its immediate needs, joined its board and immediately began to use his inside position to manipulate the price of Erie stock on the New York Stock Exchange. Aware of the competitive threat this weak speculative road posed to the New York Central and Hudson River lines, Vanderbilt decided to take over. He

---

[3] *Twenty-Fourth Annual Report of the Board of Directors of the Pennsylvania Rail Road Company* (1871), p. 17.

misjudged, however, the talent of his opponents for financial and legislative chicanery. In a spectacular fight during the first months of 1867, which involved the issuing of millions of dollars worth of fraudulent stock and the wholesale bribing of judges and legislators, Drew, Fisk, and Gould held off Vanderbilt's try for the Erie.

As the smoke of battle cleared, Gould emerged as the leader of the Erie. The last thing Big Jim Fisk wanted to do was to concern himself with railroad management. Drew resigned, commenting, "There ain't nothing more in the Erie."[4] Gould thought otherwise. By building a system around the Erie, he could surely raise the value of Erie stock. In fact, the road might even become a paying proposition if a large flow of traffic were diverted to it. This Gould proposed to do by obtaining complete control of roads that provided it with connections to the West. He quickly leased the Atlantic and Great Western from its British backers, who had become financially distressed.

Gould next embarked on a campaign to obtain control of the western allies of the Pennsylvania. Late in 1868, he began negotiating for the Indiana Central, which connected the Atlantic and Great Western with St. Louis. Thomas A. Scott, the Pennsylvania's executive in charge of external affairs, effectively parried Gould's try for the Indiana Central but only by offering a higher price for it. Gould's attempt to get the Cleveland and Pittsburgh and the Pittsburgh, Ft. Wayne and Chicago, the Pennsylvania's key connections to Cleveland and to Chicago, was more novel. He did so by buying up proxies to be voted at the road's annual meeting. Scott prevented Gould from controlling the meeting by challenging the legality of the proxies in the Ohio courts. He turned aside the threat to the Ft. Wayne by having its charter altered by the Pennsylvania legislature so that only one quarter of the directors could be appointed at each annual meeting. The legislature was sympathetic because its members realized that Gould's control of the Ft. Wayne would divert much of the traffic of the west from Philadelphia to New York City.

Gould's swift and unexpected attack forced the Pennsylvania to adopt a new strategy. "In view of these extraordinary movements, it became evident to your board," Thomson reported to the stockholders, "that this company must depart from the policy that had heretofore governed it, and obtain direct control of its western connections." By July 1, 1869, the Pennsylvania had leased the Fort Wayne and the Cleveland and Pittsburgh on reasonable terms, for their directors far preferred Thomson and Scott as associates to Jay Gould.

Blocked by the Pennsylvania, the Erie's president immediately turned his attention to the lines running along the southern shores of Lake Erie. Early in April he renewed an agreement with the Michigan Southern to obtain access to Chicago. By summer Gould had arranged to merge that line with others along the shore of Lake Erie between Toledo, Ohio, and Erie, Pennsylvania, to form the Lake Shore and Michigan Southern. Here he had the help of Legrand Lockwood, a

---

[4]Quote in Matthew Josephson, *The Robber Barons* (New York: Harcourt Brace Jovanovich, 1934), p. 194.

Wall Street speculator, who had earlier tried to prevent Vanderbilt from obtaining the New York Central. At the same time, Gould began to buy stock in the Toledo, Wabash and Western, a through road connecting Toledo to St. Louis. In August, he was elected to its board. Vanderbilt, who had been echoing the views of the Pennsylvania's executives by saying he had no interest in controlling or managing lines to the West, now suddenly realized he was about to lose these vital western connections to Jay Gould.

It was only Jay Gould's other speculations which permitted Vanderbilt to save the situation by reversing his earlier policies and obtaining control of the Lake Shore. In October 1869, Gould joined Jim Fisk in their most daring speculative coup, the attempt to corner the gold market. In the resulting stock market shake-up that followed the failure of the corner, Lockwood was forced to sell his shares in the Lake Shore. And, as Gould's biographer has pointed out, "It was Vanderbilt, the businessman with funds, not Gould, the speculator without funds, who bought the distressed stock."[5] Besides obtaining control of the Lake Shore, Vanderbilt also picked up blocks of Wabash stock and soon had his representatives on its board, including his son-in-law Horace F. Clark.

## Responses to Gould's Challenge

For all his energy and unscrupulousness, Gould lost his campaign for western outlets. But he did force the other trunk lines to obtain full control of western connections and caused two of them to alter their basic strategies of growth. For the time being Cornelius Vanderbilt did little more than put Horace Clark in charge of the Lake Shore and the Wabash. On the other hand, the senior executives of the Pennsylvania immediately began, in the words of a stockholders' committee, "with grand ideas, [to] form a plan or policy to reach all important points in the West with their lines."[6] In the 1870s, the Baltimore & Ohio and, to a more limited extent, the Erie followed the Pennsylvania's example. In the 1880s, Vanderbilt and railroad men in all parts of the country began to adopt a similar strategy.

In 1869, the Pennsylvania began through lease or purchase to build a vast integrated network of lines joining the major cities of the Midwest to the Atlantic seaboard. It leased or bought control of the major roads connecting Columbus, Cincinnati, Indianapolis, Louisville, Maysville (Kentucky), Cairo (Illinois), and St. Louis. Simultaneously, the Pennsylvania purchased control of lines to the lake ports and the lumber region of Michigan. Then in 1871, it leased for 999 years the "Joint Companies" in New Jersey in order to insure absolute control of the routes from Philadelphia and other Pennsylvania rail centers into New York City.[7] In less

---

[5]Julius Grodinsky, *Jay Gould: His Business Career* (Philadelphia: University of Pennsylvania Press, 1957), p. 65.

[6]*Report of the Investigating Committee of the Pennsylvania Rail Road . . . by Resolution . . . March 10, 1874*, p. 45.

[7]These developments can be followed in the annual reports of the Pennsylvania for the years 1870 to 1874.

than five years, the Pennsylvania had grown from a line of 491 miles of track to one of just under 6,000 miles, which was then 8 percent of the total mileage of railroads operated in the United States. Its capitalization stood at just under $400,000,000, a fraction less than 13 percent of the total capital invested in American railroads. By 1874, its system was much the same as it would be for the next 90 years. By then, too, the total mileage it directly administered equalled that of the railroad network of Prussia. Only two nations in the world, Great Britain and France, had more miles of railroad than did the Pennsylvania system.

In creating a self-contained system, the Pennsylvania carried its strategic planning beyond obtaining its own roads into major cities of the mid-Atlantic and midwestern states. In 1871, it organized the American Steamship Company to run from Philadelphia to Liverpool as a way of lessening its obvious dependence on its New York City outlet and then invested over a million dollars in the International Navigation Company, which ran ships to Antwerp and other continental ports. In the following year, it completed arrangements to purchase full control of one of the major fast freight lines, the Union Railroad and Transportation Company. It also purchased stock in a second such line, the Empire Transportation Company. During the same period, the Pennsylvania even entered mining and manufacturing. In 1872 and 1873, it bought large mining properties in the state's anthracite region. Again it stressed that its motives were defensive. In 1871, Franklin B. Gowen, the newly elected president of the largest of the coal roads, the Philadelphia and Reading, decided, because of increasing competition for coal traffic, "to secure—and attach to the company's railroad—a body of coal-land capable of supplying all the coal-tonnage that can possibly be transported over the road" and thus to have a self-contained enterprise.[8] Inevitably the Pennsylvania and other roads saw their share of the traffic threatened. To prevent such a loss, "and to return some of this traffic for its railroads, the Pennsylvania was compelled," read its annual report for 1873, "to follow the example of the other railroad companies, by securing, in the vicinity of its lines, the control of coal lands that would continue to supply transportation for them." The cost of carrying out this defensive plan came close to $4 million. Shortly thereafter the road spent three quarters of a million to finance the Pennsylvania Steel Works Company to assure it of a steady supply of steel rails produced by the recently invented Bessemer process. Finally, to encourage the cooperation of the supplier of the nation's sleeping and parlor cars, it invested still another million in the Pullman Palace Car Company. Despite this type of growth, the Pennsylvania's holdings in nontransportation enterprises were only a tiny part of its total $400 million worth of assets.

As this strategy of expansion and integration was being executed, Thomson, Scott, and their associates began the legal reorganization of their many properties into a consolidated enterprise by means of the holding company device. The securities or leases of lines running southwest of Pittsburgh were taken over by the Pittsburgh, Cincinnati and St. Louis. The majority of the stock of this company,

---

[8]Quoted from an annual report of the Philadelphia and Reading Railroad in *Dictionary of American Biography* (1946), VII, p. 461.

which became known as the Panhandle Road, was, in turn, held by a new corporation, the Pennsylvania Company, chartered by the Pennsylvania legislature in April, 1870, to become operative twelve months later. The Pennsylvania Company also held the lease of the Fort Wayne and the Indiana Central and the securities and leases of other lines running to the north and west of Pittsburgh. Then the Pennsylvania Company turned over $8,000,000 of its preferred stock out of a total stock issue of $11,360,900 to the Pennsylvania Railroad in exchange for the securities and leases of all those roads which the parent company had originally purchased. The rest of the issue went to the stockholders of the Union Fast-Freight Line to pay for its rolling stock, warehouses, depots, and other properties. In this way the legal ownership of the many companies that made up the Pennsylvania system was placed in the hands of three corporations, the Panhandle, the Pennsylvania Company, and the Pennsylvania Railroad Company, with the last controlling the first two. These two came to administer the companies whose leases or securities they directly held, while the Pennsylvania Railroad Company itself operated those lines running east of Pittsburgh and Erie as well as its coal and express companies and its shipping and steel enterprises.

Legal reorganization was followed by massive administrative reorganization with the creation of three major operating units, each headed by a general manager—the southwest (administered by the Panhandle), the northwest (operated by the Pennsylvania Company), and the eastern (by the Pennsylvania Railroad Company). Managed by general superintendents, each of these was divided into three or four major geographical subdivisions, which were themselves the size of the largest operating railroads in the country during the 1870s. These legal and administrative innovations created by far the biggest business enterprise the world had yet seen (see Exhibits 1 and 2).

Despite pronouncements to the contrary, the Pennsylvania in these same years looked to its connections beyond the Mississippi and south of the Ohio. But outside of "the country which your company thought belonged to them geographically," the executives relied more on the older policy of alliances than on the newer one of direct legal and administrative control.[9] By 1873, the company had purchased securities of railroad corporations connecting Cairo, Illinois, with New Orleans and in roads south of Washington connecting Richmond, Danville, Charlotte, Raleigh, and Atlanta. To the west, the Pennsylvania's interest was more personal than corporate. Tom Scott and probably other senior executives invested their own funds in the Kansas Pacific and in the Union Pacific, and for a year in 1871–1872, Scott was the president of the latter. After retiring from the Union Pacific, he became president of the still-to-be constructed Texas and Pacific.

The coming of the depression of 1873 dampened the expansive mood of the Pennsylvania and its senior executives. They now decided to sell their corporate and most of their personal interests in the roads to the south of the Ohio and west of the Mississippi and to concentrate instead on the more efficient management of

---

[9] *Report of Investigating Committee of the Pennsylvania Rail Road . . . by Resolution . . . March 10, 1874,* p. 75.

the system they directly controlled. As the annual report for the year 1874 announced:

> Your company, having secured lines and extensive terminal facilities at Philadelphia and New York and, through roads controlled by it, at Baltimore and Washington, in the East; the control of roads to Erie, Ashtabula and Toledo, on Lake Erie, with good connecting roads working in harmony to Buffalo; and the control of lines through the lumber regions of Michigan; and in the west having terminae at Chicago, St. Louis, Louisville, Cincinnati, Wheeling and other important commercial centers, with good connections beyond those points; and having also perfected communications with the entire oil region of Pennsylvania, the Connellsville *(sic)* coke region, the city of Cumberland and the Cumberland coal region; and with Frederick and Hagerstown in Maryland, and Martinsburg in West Virginia—your board have concluded to adopt as general policy that no further extension of lines should be made or obligations be assumed by your company, either by lease or otherwise, except to complete the several small branches and extensions now in progress in Pennsylvania and New Jersey. The best energies of your board and its officers will hereafter be devoted to the development of the resources of the lines now controlled. They believe these lines have a great future for the shareholders.[10]

The directors and managers of the Pennsylvania also began to draw back from their steamship, coal, and steel ventures. They had decided that the operation of a self-contained railroad network connecting east to west was about the maximum size transport system they could profitably administer.

Gould's raids on the western allies of the Pennsylvania had had an immediate impact on the Baltimore & Ohio as well as on the Pennsylvania itself. Three years earlier, its president, John W. Garrett, had leased the Central Ohio, a road it had sponsored, running into Columbus. Then in 1869, Garrett quickly purchased control of a line to Lake Erie and another to Pittsburgh. In the same year, the road increased its ownership in the Marietta and Cincinnati and made its vice president, John King, the Marietta's president. Finally, in 1874, Garrett decided he needed his own connection into Chicago and so ordered the construction of 263 miles of new line from the Sandusky road directly to the Illinois metropolis. The Ohio and Mississippi remained a close, though often obstreperous ally, until the Baltimore road obtained the majority of its stock after that western road filed receivership papers in 1876. After the Pennsylvania purchased the Philadelphia, Wilmington and Baltimore in the early 1880s, the Baltimore & Ohio built its own road to Philadelphia but continued thereafter to rely on the Reading and the Central of New Jersey to carry its traffic into New York City.

The Baltimore & Ohio also moved, as had the Pennsylvania, into non-railroad enterprises. It purchased coal properties and in 1872 built and operated a steel rolling mill. After an unsuccessful venture with its own steamship line to continental ports, Garrett turned to an alliance with the powerful North German Lloyd Steamship Company to provide shipping to Britain and the Continent. While the Baltimore & Ohio did not support a large express company, it did devel-

---

[10] *Twenty-eighth Report of the Directors of the Pennsylvania Rail Road Company* (1875), p. 43.

op a chain of hotels along its lines. Moreover, Garrett insisted on building sleeping and parlor cars, even at the cost of a lengthy patent dispute with Pullman and others. As the road's historian has emphasized, Garrett "very much preferred to run the company in every way as a self-contained and highly independent unit."[11]

The Erie, scuttled by Gould in the early 1870s, was financially too weak to carry out a really effective policy of expansion. In 1874, however, it again leased the Atlantic and Great Western, which Gould had sold off at the time of his departure. That road had already obtained a tight, but not complete, control of the Bee Line from Cleveland to Indianapolis. Bankruptcy during the depression postponed its obtaining its own line to Chicago until 1880. Then it did so by building a road 250 miles from the Atlantic and Great Western to Hammond, Indiana, on the outskirts of that key western railroad terminus. This achievement was, however, somewhat soured by the Erie's loss of the Bee Line to Vanderbilt in the following year.

The Vanderbilts had waited for more than a decade after Gould's raid on the Lake Shore before beginning to plan a strategy for building a self-contained, integrated railroad system similar to that of the Pennsylvania, of the smaller Baltimore & Ohio, or even of the Erie. After the unexpected death of his son-in-law and representative, Horace Clark, in 1873, the old Commodore sold the family holdings in the Wabash and in other midwestern roads in which Clark had purchased stock, turned over the management of the Lake Shore to a professional manager, John H. Devereux, and made it clear that he had no intention of enlarging his railroad properties. William Vanderbilt, who took charge of the family interests when his father died in January 1877, was even more cautious and conservative.

The Vanderbilts' caution made good business sense. Their railroad enterprises were the only major ones in the United States based on the personal fortune of a single family. They could only expand their railroad activities by raising large amounts of money or by exchanging the stock of the Central for that of other roads. Either move would dilute their control. Moreover, expansion would require a large increase in the number of professionals in the roads' management and would lessen family control over operating decisions. Julius Grodinsky, who has studied the strategy of railroad expansion with great thoroughness, has suggested the price William Vanderbilt paid for this cautious approach:

> He rarely took the initiative to seize the vantage point from which he could dictate the detailed negotiations; he was almost always on the defensive. In such a position repeated attacks by his opponents forced him into a negative strategy. He was unable to develop mature and well-conceived plans to overcome his opponents so as to make them, and not himself, sue for terms of peace. And when the opposition persisted in its aggressiveness, he frequently sued for peace. He thereby became one of the country's

---

[11]Edward Hungerford, *The Story of the Baltimore & Ohio Railroad Company*, II (New York: G. P. Putnam's Sons, 1927), p. 126. Hungerford's second volume on the Baltimore & Ohio has been used to supplement Grodinsky's *Gould*. Hungerford's *Men of Erie* (New York: Random House, 1946) provided additional information on that road.

greatest business appeasers. In one contest after another, Vanderbilt made the concessions necessary to the termination of a business war.[12]

Nevertheless, Vanderbilt was not as weak and passive as Grodinsky made him out to be. His alternative to expensive consolidation was an eminently reasonable one. It was to join with his competitors in a cartel to set and maintain rates.

In fact, during the 1870s nearly all railroad financiers and managers believed that the formation of formal, regional federations or associations was the most certain way to keep traffic coming over their tracks and to do so at much less the cost of building a large consolidated enterprise in the manner of the Pennsylvania. These men were all too aware of the constant temptation to cheat on posted rates, particularly by the weaker roads who needed income to pay interest on their funded debt to stave off bankruptcy. The more the volume of traffic fell off, the more the necessity increased to put unused equipment and men back to work by rebating or otherwise cutting rates. A rate that little more than covered the out-of-pocket costs was better than one that produced no traffic or income at all. The only way the strong competing roads could meet such price cuts was to make similar ones. Moreover, by going into bankruptcy, a road no longer had to meet interest charges. Its lower fixed costs meant that it could continue to charge lower rates than its competitors. So most railroad men came to believe that the logic of railroad competition was bankruptcy for everyone.

The answer to the problem, they maintained, was a formal association or cartel which pooled through traffic or profits, allocating one or the other according to prearranged percentages. The first such association was formed in 1875 in the South when Albert Fink, the president of the Louisville and Nashville, proposed the setting up of such a cartel and then became its head. Two years later, after a particularly extended and exhausting rate war, the presidents of the great east-west trunk lines asked Fink to come North to set up and manage a similar organization in their area. The initial success of both the Eastern Trunk Line Association and the Southern Railway and Steamship Association quickly led to the formation of several comparable regional ones in other parts of the nation.

All these associations had much the same organization. At annual conventions the traffic managers and presidents of the roads, working with association officials, reviewed and revised the rates and percentages of traffic or profits allocated to each line. The association's executive body then became responsible for seeing that the allocations were made and the rates maintained. In addition, a Board of Arbiters was formed to listen to the complaints concerning administrative action and to settle controversies between the roads as to rates and percentages. (Fink's description of his organization is reproduced as Appendix A.)

Here and elsewhere Fink stressed, and railroad financiers and managers agreed, that such formal federations were the only way to prevent "centralization and absorption of roads under the absolute control of one or a few persons. It makes a separate individual existence of these roads possible, and puts a check on

---

[12]Grodinsky, *Gould,* p. 209.

the consolidation of these roads. . . . It secures all the advantages of consolidation without its disadvantages."

Fink realized that federation was in itself an insufficient answer. The commissioner added, "It must be remarked, however, that the only bond that holds this government together is the intelligence and good faith of the parties composing it." He therefore urged the members of the association and their roads to make concerted efforts to have "the operations of this committee legally binding upon all parties by legislative action, provided that it could be shown, as I believe it can, that its operation is beneficial to the public interests." Yet despite an active campaign before congressional committees, Fink and many other railroad men who supported the proposal failed to get the national legislature to sanction their private federations. And they soon found, to their sorrow, that they could not rely on the intelligence and good faith of railroad executives, particularly speculators such as Jay Gould.

Gould rarely let the Eastern Trunk Line and other associations interfere with his attacks on the traffic and the stocks of other roads. In 1878, the year after the formation of the Trunk Line Association, Gould's aggressive challenges caused Vanderbilt to obtain a majority of the stock of the Michigan Central. To protect this investment, Vanderbilt purchased control of the Canadian Southern, which connected the New York Central with the Michigan Central. These expenditures and his excoriation during the Hepburn Committee hearings helped to convince Vanderbilt of the futility of trying to maintain family control over his properties. So in 1879, he arranged for a rising investment banker, J. Pierpont Morgan, to sell off a portion of his New York Central stock.

Finally in 1881, Gould goaded Vanderbilt into taking the offensive. In that year Gould created, for reasons to be considered shortly, an impressive-looking railroad system reaching from the Rockies to the Atlantic Coast. Then, by sharply cutting rates, he reduced Fink's Eastern Trunk Line Association to shambles. Now convinced that formal federations or associations could not keep the peace, William Vanderbilt decided that he too must have a self-contained system which reached all important commercial centers of the Northeast and the Old Northwest. He moved secretly to obtain control of the Bee Line, hitherto an Erie connection from Cleveland to Indianapolis. The Bee Line only controlled 50 percent of the road from Indianapolis to St. Louis, so he persuaded the Pennsylvania to sell him the remaining 50 percent. Then to forestall the effects of Gould's drive east through the anthracite region, Vanderbilt secured a large, though not controlling, amount of stock in the Reading and built a costly connection between that road and the New York Central.

In 1882, Vanderbilt made two more moves which, while part of his current offensive, were still instigated by the actions of competitors. First he purchased the New York, Chicago and St. Louis, a new road which had just opened, paralleling the Lake Shore from Buffalo to Chicago. Its promoters, Calvin Brice, George I. Seney, and Samuel Thomas, had built the road, which went by the name of Nickel Plate to sell either to Vanderbilt or to Gould. Again Vanderbilt felt forced to buy before Gould did in order to maintain railroad peace. In the same year he leased the Canadian Southern and brought it into the Michigan Central's administrative structure. Here he was responding to the consolidation of the Grand Trunk and Great Western of Canada, who were allies of Gould and who had just completed a branch into Chicago. In 1883, the Central's chief executive set up for the first time an overall structure for the administration of his system and then turned its management over to two of his sons. The resulting organization of the Vanderbilt system, however, remained less sophisticated and rational than that created a decade earlier by the executives of the Pennsylvania.

William's sons, aided by their professional managers, including James H. Rutter and Chauncey Depew, did not round out their system until the end of the decade. By the middle 80s they had strengthened their control over a long-standing ally, the Boston and Albany, by further stock purchases. Soon it was brought more formally into the system. In 1885, Chauncey Depew agreed to buy the West Shore, a road which, completed in that year, paralleled the New York Central. The purchase was part of a negotiation engineered by J. P. Morgan by which the Pennsylvania was to take over the partly built South Pennsylvania, which paralleled its main line, which it was prevented by Pennsylvania law from doing. Finally, at the end of the decade, the New York Central obtained control of the Cleveland, Cincinnati, Chicago and St. Louis in order to have an entrance into Cincinnati and to help maintain the rate structure to its other major termini.

Thus, Gould, and then Brice, Seney, and the promoters of the West Shore, all forced Vanderbilt, much against his better judgment, to build a self-contained system comparable to that of the Pennsylvania and the Baltimore & Ohio. Because Vanderbilt had no real interest in empire building, he did not purchase coal, steel, express, hotel, or ocean steamship enterprises, as the trunk lines to the south had done earlier. But the system he and his sons finally put together was second in assets and size only to the Pennsylvania.

## System Building in the West

The great railroad systems in the West grew in much the same ways and for much the same reasons as did those in the East. The better-located, better-financed, and better-managed roads usually worked for peace through alliances with both connecting and competing roads. Those less advantageously situated and less substantially financed found difficulty in maintaining agreements and in obtaining loyal allies among connecting roads. The latter tended to attract speculators, who then both cut rates and began to buy or build connecting roads. The stronger roads responded first by abandoning their reliance on informal and then formal alliances or cartels and then by obtaining legal and administrative control of lines to major commercial centers in their areas. In the West as in the East, Jay Gould did more than any other individual to stimulate the creation of gigantic railroad enterprises.

There were, however, some differences between the situation facing entrepreneurial groups in the West from that in the East. In the West, the strategy of expansion involved more construction of new roads and less purchasing of existing ones. Since the western roads relied more on outside capital than did those of the East, strategies of construction and competition were often decided by men living far from the line of the road. Many times Wall Street and State Street had the final say as to the direction of growth and ultimate economic destiny of the regions they served. Finally, construction in the West benefited from government subsidies in the form of land grants. This last difference seems, however, to have played a minor role in stimulating the building of railroad systems and encouraging the construction of surplus mileage. Far more track was laid down to assure the formation of integrated, self-contained systems than to meet the time deadlines for the completion of land grants.

Until Jay Gould embarked on his imperial plans in the West at the end of the decade of the 1870s, the roads running northwest, southwest and west of Chicago continued to rely on a policy of alliances through stock purchases to bring traffic over their lines. After the coming of the depression of 1873, they turned to agreements, both informal and formal, with their competitors. The most effective of these was the Iowa Pool, formed in 1870 by the Burlington, the Rock Island, and the Chicago and Northwestern. By 1879, these and others had been replaced by formal cartels based on Fink's Eastern Trunk Line Association. Such agreements had the strongest support of major investors who sat on the boards of these roads, such as John Murray Forbes of the Burlington, William Osborne of the Illinois Central, and David Dows and Peter Geddes of the Northwestern.

On the other hand, a few of the younger professional managers, particularly Charles Perkins of the Burlington and R. R. Cable of the Rock Island, spoke out against the conservative policies of their boards. Perkins and Cable maintained that the then current economic depression provided an opportunity to build their "defenses" by obtaining lines into key cities at low prices. In 1878, in a number of detailed reports, Perkins outlined an explicit strategy. He urged that the Burlington take over its ally in Nebraska, the Burlington and Missouri, and purchase adjoining roads, some of which were still unfinished, to assure it of its own entrance into Kansas City and St. Joseph. "If we do take them now, when they are bankrupt," Perkins wrote Forbes, "and before others awake to the value of that region, we control that country and can extend the roads at our leisure."[13]

Perkins further wanted to gain control of the Hannibal and St. Joseph and so complete an integrated railroad system. For as he told Peter Geddes:

> I have long been of the opinion that sooner or later the railroads of the country would group themselves into systems and that each system would be self-sustaining or, in other words, that any system not self-sustaining would cease to exist and be absorbed by those near at hand and strong enough to live alone. . . . Each line must be its own feeders.[14]

---

[13]Grodinsky, *Gould,* p. 229. Richard C. Overton, *Burlington Route* (New York: Alfred A. Knopf, 1965), pp. 166–70. Thomas C. Cochran, *Railroad Leaders* (Cambridge: Harvard University Press, 1953), p. 307.

[14]Quoted in Cochran, *Railroad Leaders,* p. 433.

But Forbes, Geddes and other directors still believed as they had all through the 1870s that such a consolidated system would become "too large for management" and that expansion was certainly not worth the cost.

And then came Jay Gould. Gould had moved into western railroading by purchasing control of the Union Pacific, the road that with the Central Pacific formed the first transcontinental railroad. Early in the depression of the 1870s, the Union Pacific road was in parlous financial condition, and as a result, its stock was selling at a very low price. Sniffing a good speculation, Gould began to buy, and by the spring of 1875, he had control. At first, Gould concentrated on reorganizing the Union Pacific's finances and management. During this time he became increasingly dissatisfied with the three roads that made up the Iowa Pool and carried his traffic eastward. His first response was to purchase stock in two of these three roads, the Northwestern and the Rock Island. Once on their boards, he attempted in March 1877 to work out with them and the Burlington, an agreement which included joint ownership of the Burlington and Missouri—a proposal that the Burlington's president rejected. Unable to assure himself of eastern connections, Gould then turned as he had done earlier in the East to building a system of his own.

Moving swiftly and relying on his expert skill as a stock market trader, Gould soon put together a system that was for a short moment even more extensive than the Pennsylvania. First, to obtain funds so essential to railroad empire building, he sold his Union Pacific stock in a speculative coup in February 1879. With this money he acquired control of the Kansas Pacific, connecting Denver and Kansas City, and the Denver Pacific, connecting Denver with the Union Pacific at Cheyenne, Wyoming. Then in April 1879, he secretly bought large blocks of stock of the Wabash, running from St. Louis and Hannibal, Missouri, to the Great Lakes at Toledo. Because the Wabash was just out of receivership and because it relied on the more powerful trunk lines for its traffic, its stock was selling at a depressed price. Gould, therefore, captured it at little cost. He next quickly moved to obtain control of roads joining Kansas City to St. Louis. Then Gould outmaneuvered Perkins to get control of the Missouri, Kansas & Texas. By these moves the New Yorker carried off roads Perkins had earlier insisted were essential to assure the Burlington its outlets to the South and West. Finally, Gould closed his campaigns of 1879 by regaining control of the Union Pacific and merging it with the Kansas Pacific and Denver Pacific.

During the following year, he brought the Lackawanna, the Central of New Jersey, and the Erie into his orbit and so created the new trunk line complex which harassed Albert Fink and turned William Vanderbilt to system-building. These bold moves greatly enhanced the value of the securities Gould had purchased. In the same year he expanded his holdings in the Southwest. He also embarked on a broad construction program by building an extension of the Wabash into Chicago, building a line connecting the Wabash to the Lackawanna, building branches of the Union Pacific into Wyoming and Montana, and extending his roads in the Southwest.

By 1881, Gould controlled a railroad empire that was the largest in the nation. It reached Boston, New York, Toledo, Chicago, St. Louis, Kansas City, Omaha, and Denver. He next began a quest for more connections to the Southwest and by 1882 had lines into Fort Worth, Dallas, El Paso, Laredo, Galveston, and New Orleans. He soon owned a total of 15,854 miles of roads or 15 percent of the nation's mileage.[15] But his control proved tenuous and short-lived. He made no attempt to coordinate or efficiently administer the activities of his various properties. Some of his roads actually did not connect with the others, so shipments of through-freight were hampered. Nor did his system, particularly in the East, run over the more favorable transportation routes.

So the Gould empire fell as quickly as it arose. By 1882, he had pulled out of the Union Pacific, using the proceeds to build up the newly acquired network south and west of St. Louis. By 1884, he had disposed of most of his eastern lines. From the mid-1880s on, Gould concentrated on building a regional system in the Southwest.

Short-lived as his empire was, it had a lasting impact on American railroad history. His rapid purchases, his moves into the territories of other lines, his delight in breaking agreements on rates or allocation of traffic forced the directors of western railroads, as well as William Vanderbilt, to create what Perkins had termed "self-sustained" systems. Informal alliances like the Iowa Pool became completely ineffective. Nor did the more formal associations which had grown up in imitation of Fink's trunk-line association prove much more successful. Soon nearly all western railroad men agreed that they must legally control their own lines into the major commercial centers of the regions they served.

On the Burlington and a little later on the Rock Island, the earlier exponents of expansion, Perkins and Cable, became presidents of their roads. Perkins, who wrote Forbes that "Gould moves so rapidly, it is impossible to keep up with him with Boards of Directors," was given a relatively free hand.[16] He merged the Burlington and Missouri in Nebraska for the parent line; he purchased control of an essential if indirect connection with Council Bluffs and Kansas City at a cost that must have shocked many a Boston stockholder. In 1882, in retaliation for the Wabash's move into Iowa, Perkins built his own line to Denver. In the next year he regained full control of the Hannibal and St. Joseph and during this time continued to build into Wyoming, Montana, Colorado, and Nebraska. Finally, in 1885, he financed and had built a road into St. Paul. The Burlington, which operated something over 600 miles in 1870 and was administering 2,772 miles by early 1881, operated close to 5,000 miles by 1887.[17]

In the same first half of the 1880s, the Chicago and Northwestern embarked on a comparable policy of expansion. That road had the benefit of Vanderbilt fi-

---

[15]Grodinsky, *Gould*, p. 354.

[16]Cochran, *Railroad Leaders*, pp. 136–37.

[17]These mileage figures for the Burlington, the Chicago and Northwestern and the St. Paul are from *Poor's Manual of the Railroads of the United States* for 1871–1872, 1888, and 1891.

nancial support, for the New Yorker, anxious to counter Gould, had decided to have the Northwestern as his primary connecting ally west of Chicago. Between 1880 and 1884, its purchases and new construction expanded its mileage from under 1,000 to close to 5,000 in the agricultural region northwest of Chicago.

The St. Paul followed the same strategy. It responded, for example, to Perkins's decisions to build into St. Paul by constructing its own line through Burlington territory to Kansas City. Even before that extension was completed, it had reached the 5,000-mile mark. After the Rock Island directors made Cable president in 1883, that aggressive young officer moved quickly to build up an extensive integrated system that ranged from Chicago to Kansas City, Denver, and Fort Worth. By the mid-1880s, as Grodinsky has emphasized, "Each road suddenly realized that a policy of aggressive invasion was the only safe defense."[18]

In this short stretch of years, similar strategies led to the formation of similar systems in the sparsely settled Far West, the more populous areas of the South, and urban New England. Everywhere, railroad men gave up their faith in informal alliances, lost hope in the effectiveness of more formal federations, and turned to winning their own "self-sustained" systems. Regional variations in this story reflect economic and historical differences. In the West beyond the Missouri and in much of the South where through-traffic was so critically important, consolidation came more quickly than in thickly settled New England, where local traffic provided much more of a road's business.

Except for the Northern Pacific, none of the transcontinentals was initially planned to go from the Mississippi Valley to the Pacific Coast. But during the 1880s, all decided, often against the better judgment of their senior executives, to connect valley to ocean.[19] Under Gould, the Union Pacific had added nearly 1,250 miles of new lines. But his conservative successor, Charles Francis Adams, Jr., purchased and constructed almost twice as much mileage, both to protect his southwest flank from Gould and his eastern one from Perkins. He also built to the northwest to join Henry Villard's Oregon Railway and Navigation Company. By means of trackage and traffic agreements with this road, Adams thus acquired another outlet besides the Central Pacific to the Coast. The Union Pacific, however, quickly found these agreements uncertain and unsatisfactory. So in 1889, Adams, with the assistance of Grenville M. Dodge, obtained control of the Oregon line by a skillful Wall Street maneuver.

To the south the Santa Fe, through a series of defensive strategies, became in 1887 the largest railroad line in the world. In 1880, it had arrived at its original goal by reaching Albuquerque, New Mexico. It then built an extension from Albuquerque to the Southern Pacific at Eming, New Mexico. At that time, Collis P. Huntington's Southern Pacific had still no ambitions outside of California. "Its two objectives were to secure and maintain its control of California business,"

---

[18]Grodinsky, *Gould,* p. 526.

[19]The information on the transcontinentals comes primarily from Robert E. Riegel, *The Story of Western Railroads* (New York: Macmillan, 1926), especially pp. 198–202 and Chapter 12.

noted the foremost historian of the western railroads, Robert Riegel, "and to monopolize the transcontinental entrances into the state."[20]

But both Huntington and William B. Strong, the new president of the Santa Fe, became dissatisfied with relying on one another for connections. To provide an alternate route, the Santa Fe then purchased a half interest in a second road planned to connect Albuquerque to the Coast. Huntington, therefore, then joined forces with Gould to buy, early in 1882, most of the other half of the stock in this second road. The Santa Fe temporarily retreated by agreeing that the new line west of Albuquerque would go no further than the Colorado River, where it could connect with the Southern Pacific. Meanwhile Huntington, even more reluctant to rely on Gould than he was on the Sante Fe, started to construct and purchase his own lines to the growing Texas cities and to New Orleans. In 1884, Huntington and his associate, Charles F. Crocker, combined all these roads and the Central Pacific into a single system headed by a holding and operating concern, the Southern Pacific Company of Kentucky.

In that same year, the directors of the Santa Fe decided that they must have their own line to the Coast. After obtaining full control of the road from Albuquerque to the Colorado River, they purchased lines from the Southern Pacific which, after some additional building, provided them with their own route into Los Angeles and San Diego. Next, Strong decided that he could not rely on Huntington's or Gould's roads as connections to the Southwest. So in 1886, he purchased the connections into Fort Worth and Galveston. Finally in 1887, the Santa Fe decided to obtain, by buying and building, its own road from Kansas City to Chicago. In explaining to their stockholders why they took still another costly step, the directors pointed out that the roads best situated to act as connections into Chicago had "already invaded our territories in Kansas," so any satisfactory agreements would be difficult to arrange.

> A traffic agreement, at best is always uncertain and unsatisfactory, and generally becomes neglected or odious. . . . And it is the history of such contracts that they are effective only so long as it is in the interest of the parties concerned to make them so, and broken as soon as they become burdensome to either party. It is, moreover, more than doubtful if such an agreement could be enforced against the party breaking it, since the law looks with disfavor upon such contracts as contrary to the public interest which demands the utmost freedom on the part of transportation companies.[21]

Such freedom helped to force the Sante Fe to build a system of over 7,000 miles by 1888 and to bring it soon to financial bankruptcy.

To the north of the Union Pacific, the story was much the same. James J. Hill's Manitoba Railroad had no transcontinental ambitions. Until 1883, it was satisfied to serve the wheat region of the Red River Valley of the north. It began to move further west only after the government-subsidized Canadian Pacific made

---

[20]Riegel, *Western Railroads*, p. 179.

[21]*Fifteenth Annual Report of the Board of Directors of the Atchison, Topeka and Santa Fe Railroad Co.* (1887), p. 27.

its decision to build across the Rockies to the Pacific. That same year too, Henry Villard completed the Northern Pacific. Villard had, incidentally, obtained control of the Northern Pacific in 1881 in order to assure that his Oregon Railway and Navigation Company had an outlet to the east.

In the decade of the 1880s, similar systems-building occurred in the South, New England, and the eastern coal regions as well as in the Midwest, Far West, and Southwest. In New England two roads, the Boston and Maine and the New Haven, came to dominate the area. In the South the Louisville and Nashville, the Southern, and the Atlantic Coast Line soon handled the lion's share of the region's traffic; while the Reading, the Chesapeake and Ohio, and the Norfolk and Western became the predominant coal roads. All were created in hopes of developing a self-sustaining system, one that "is its own feeders."

This competitive buying and building during the 1880s led to a large number of financial failures in the 1890s. During the 1880s, 75,000 miles of road were built in the United States, by far the greatest amount of mileage ever built in any decade in any part of the world. During the 1890s, a quarter to a third of all railroad mileage of the United States was in bankruptcy. After the financial and administrative reorganizations of the 1890s, carried out by J. P. Morgan and two or three other leading investment banking houses, some 25 great systems came to operate the greatest share of the railroad mileage in this country. At the turn of the century, these systems secured still greater stability by purchasing large blocks of stock in neighboring ones and so developed what was called a "community of interest" in each major region. Early in the 20th century, 8 to 10 groups controlled the American overland transportation network.

## EXHIBIT 1

Growth of the Pennsylvania Railroad System, 1868–1886

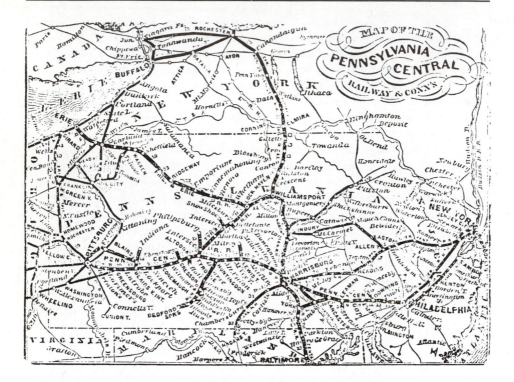

In June 1868, in the map it furnished to the newly founded monthly *Official Railway Guide,* the Pennsylvania Railroad saw itself as a railroad linking Philadelphia to Pittsburgh, with important interests in lines to Baltimore, Erie, and Rochester. (See Exhibit 1.) By 1886, it was an integrated trunkline system, as revealed by the next map from the December 1886 "Investors Supplement" of the *Commercial & Financial Chronicle.* The system was assembled in a few years during the early 1870s by J. Edgar Thomson, president and pioneer builder of the railroad, through acquisitions of lines such as the United Railways of New Jersey, which took the Pennsylvania to New York, or, more accurately, Jersey City, New Jersey; the Pittsburgh, Fort Wayne & Chicago; the Pittsburgh, Chicago & St. Louis; and the St. Louis, Vandalia & Terre Haute. During the presidency of Thomas A. Scott, but actually through the resourcefulness of Alexander J. Cassatt, first vice president, the Pennsylvania outbid the Baltimore & Ohio for the Philadelphia, Wilmington & Baltimore, which, with new construction to Washington, made the system the most important line between New York and Washington and the key link to the railroads of the southeast. (See Exhibit 2.)

EXHIBIT 2

Growth of the Pennsylvania Railroad System, 1868–1886

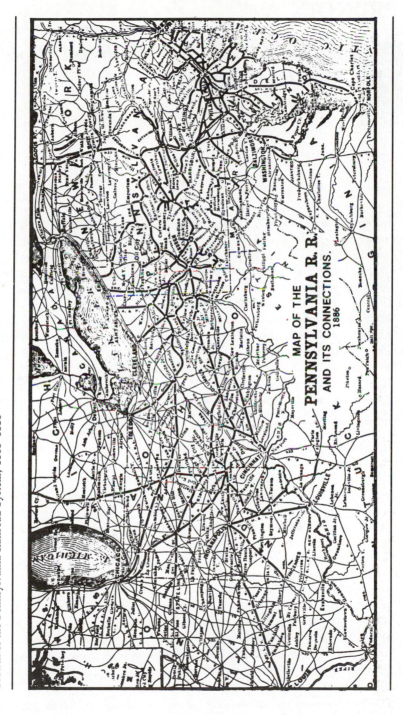

# APPENDIX A

## Albert Fink, "The Railroad Problem and Its Solution"*

The question before this committee, if it desires to deal effectively with the railroad problem, is, therefore: How shall this unity of management be attained in this country, consistent with the public interests, and in accordance with the peculiar institutions and the practical working of this government? That it cannot be obtained through governmental ownership of the railroads is a self-evident proposition.

Before considering this question further, it may be of interest to your committee to know the work that has already been accomplished without the aid of government, by the railroad companies themselves, toward the solution of the railroad problem.

The railroad companies have endeavored to secure unity of action by voluntary cooperation in all matters in which it is absolutely necessary for the proper management of the roads, in the interest of the public, as well as in the interests of the proprietors of the roads. But this cooperation has been most inefficient in all matters relating to the uniformity, equality and permanency of railroad tariffs, although in other respects, as already mentioned, it has been very successful.

It is on account of the great complexity of the tariff problem that this voluntary cooperation has not met with better success, and not for want of effort or desire on the part of the railroad companies to control it, although the public, ignorant of all the difficulties to be overcome, presume to hold each separate road responsible for the working of the whole system. The difficulty, however, has not been so much in agreeing upon the proper tariffs, but in carrying them into practical effects. The necessary means and machinery for that purpose have not been adopted, and there is no authority to enforce such agreements.

The managers of roads meet in convention, and make agreements which are broken before they disperse. Everyone who has paid the least attention to this subject is familiar with these unsuccessful efforts. The press of the country chronicles almost daily some conference held by officers of railroad companies, or some agreement made, and on the following day it chronicles its violation or discontinuance.

---

*Testimony before the Committee on Commerce of the United States House of Representatives January 14, 15, and 16, 1880* (Washington, D.C., 1880), pp. 18–24.

During the last few years, however, some progress has been made toward a closer and more effective cooperation. Associations of railroad companies have been formed, with a proper organization, through which it was made at least possible to control the important tariff question. The first complete organization of this kind, and to which I shall refer hereafter more particularly, and explain fully its object and its methods, was the Southern Railway and Steamship Association, formed in October 1875, and which is still in effective operation.

In 1877 the four Trunk Lines—the New York Central, Erie, Pennsylvania, and Baltimore and Ohio Railroads—entered into a similar compact, by which all the Westbound traffic from the seaboard was managed under one organization. In April, 1878, the Grand Trunk and Vermont Central companies commenced to cooperate with the four other Trunk roads. Through this compact it has been practicable to control the tariffs on the whole of the Westbound traffic from the seaboard to all points West of the termini of the Trunk Lines. Like charges have been made to the public for like service. The tariff has been permanently maintained for a period of two and a half years with only one change during that time—something that has never been accomplished before; thus securing practically to the people the object of the proposed measure now being considered by your committee, viz.: reasonable, just and permanent rates of transportation. I do not mean to say that perfection has been reached in this respect, because much remains to be done; but cases of violation of the tariff rates, as far as the Trunk Lines can exercise their influence, are now the exception, and not, as heretofore, the rule.

Similar efforts at closer and more effective cooperation have been made by the railroads west of Chicago and St. Louis, which have been in a great measure successful.

During the last year the principal roads embraced in the territory east of the Mississippi and the Atlantic seaboard, including the Trunk roads, and the Grand Trunk, have formed an organization known under the name of the Joint Executive Committee, for the purpose of securing uniform and equitable rates on the whole of their Eastbound traffic. This organization is of the same character as that of the Southern Railway and Steamship Association. . . . Acting as chairman of that committee, I beg leave to read an extract of the report which I was able to make at its first annual meeting in Chicago, in December last.

It may not be out of place here to refer briefly to the past operations of this committee, which has now been established one year this day, although its organization was not fully perfected and put into working order until June last. Since then the committee has accomplished, in a great measure, the object for which it was created, namely, to establish reasonable and just tariffs for the competitive traffic, and to permanently maintain such tariffs, securing thereby reasonable compensation to the companies and remedying the great evils that have resulted from want of cooperation between the railroad companies, to the serious injury of their own and the interests of the public.

You have now for the first time established a practical method by which the competitive traffic of your roads can be properly managed and controlled. Heretofore this was impossible; the mere holding of conventions of railroad managers, passing resolutions, and then dispersing and letting things take care of themselves, each party acting as it sees fit, will not accomplish the purpose of intelligent joint management of the

large property under your charge. You have now added to the legislative department—your conventions—also a permanent executive department, the duty of which
is to see that the resolutions passed and agreements made are faithfully carried out. In
addition to this you have also established a judiciary department, consisting of a board
of arbitration, whose duty it is to settle peaceably any question of difference, without
resort to wasteful warfare, with all its injurious consequences. You have thus formed a
complete government over this large competitive traffic over which it has heretofore
been found impracticable to exercise intelligent control.

It must be remarked, however, that the only bond which holds this government together is the intelligence and good faith of the parties composing it. To give greater stability and permanency to the operations of this committee, it would be desirable to
make its operations legally binding upon all parties by legislative action, provided it
can be shown, as I believe it can, that its operation is beneficial to the public interests. I
consider that no other legislative action would be necessary to remedy the evils which
has been attempted unsuccessfully to remedy by State legislation, and which may be
attempted by congressional legislation, I fear, with like results.

The companies composing this association have already, by their voluntary action,
abolished the pernicious system of special contracts, and all shippers are now put upon
an equal footing. Rates for the last few months have been everywhere (in the territory
in which these roads are located) maintained, and the great disparity between the local
rates and the competitive through rates, which has heretofore been so great a source of
trouble and complaint, has ceased to exist. Had such a result been sooner reached, we
would have heard nothing of legislative control of railroads.

I express it as my opinion, the result of the most careful consideration, that the only
legislation required to accomplish the object which the most zealous advocate of the
public interests can desire to accomplish, is to legalize, and even to enforce, the cooperative system of the railroad companies, so far as it is necessary to establish and maintain reasonable rates of transportation upon a uniform and equitable basis, treating
alike all parties situated alike—in other words, to carry out the plan adopted by the
committee, and which has been so successfully practiced during the last few months. I
know that objection will be made by parties not conversant with all the conditions of
limitation and restriction which are enforced upon railroad companies in establishing
their tariffs, that such cooperation or combination, as it is generally called to make it
appear odious, would lead to extortion on the part of the combined railroad companies. The past action of this committee is the best proof that such fears are unfounded.
The committee, during its existence, has established rates lower than they have ever
existed before, and even the highest rates charged have not exceeded those of the last
few years, but have been considerably lower, although the conditions for high rates
have been more favorable this year than they have been for years past.

The only thing which the cooperative system has accomplished, is the maintenance
of the established tariffs and the abolishment of the contract and rebate system. It is
only when agreed rates are maintained, no matter by what means, either by the voluntary action of the railroads or by direct legislative enforcement, that the evils of the
transportation business complained of by the public can be remedied.

If, therefore, our work is to be judged by its fruit, it should recommend itself to
public favor.

From this, it will appear that, in my judgment, the only measure now wanted
in order to give permanency to the operations of these associations, is to recognize
the same as necessary and beneficial, to give legal force to the voluntary agree-

ments that may be made between its members, with the view of carrying out the objects of the association, namely, the establishment and maintenance of reasonable and nondiscriminating transportation tariffs; in fact, the object of your proposed legislation. If Congress would pass a law to this effect, I would consider the whole railroad problem in this country settled, and settled upon truly American principles. It would allow the proprietors of the railroads to manage their own affairs, which they are much better able to do than it could be done under a centralized government, and at the same time it would restrict the operation of each individual road under the legalized cooperative system, to the extent that it is necessary, in order to carry out the intent and spirit of the law which regulates the conduct of common carriers in their capacity as public servants.

I regret that I have not sufficient time to point out at length the great merits and advantages of this American plan of governing the railroads as compared with the European plans, to which I have referred. It accomplishes fully the object contemplated by the centralized government of the railroads in Germany. It brings unity in the management of the roads, as far as that is desirable or necessary; and at the same time, it preserves the individuality of each road, and reserves to it the management of all its local affairs, in which it and the country through which it passes is alone concerned. Cooperation of the roads is only required in so far as the interest of the whole system of roads and the public interest requires it—no further. In this respect, the government of the railroads would be based on the same principle that underlies the government of the United States—the general government taking cognizance only of matters in which the several States are jointly interested, leaving to each individual State—and, in this case, each road—to manage its own local affairs as it thinks best, in accordance with the laws of the State which created it.

Is it necessary to point out the great advantage of such a government as compared with that of a centralized government? Considering the extent of this country and the extent of its railroad system, a government of the railroads, such as is contemplated in Germany, would be utterly impracticable here. Government ownership accomplishes only one purpose—the same as the cooperative plan, it secures unity of management—in other respects the difficulties of the tariff question arise and would have to be dealt with, whether the roads are the property of the State or of private individuals; and State ownership would necessarily bring with it many new difficulties not experienced or even thought of under the management by private owners.

The plan which I propose prevents that very centralization and absorption of the roads under the absolute control of one or few persons. It makes the separate, individual existence of these roads possible, and puts a check upon the consolidation of roads, which is regarded with so much alarm by the people in this country, but which is the natural result of the struggles of the railroad companies: the stronger must at last absorb the weaker. The proposed government of the road secures all the advantages of consolidation, without its disadvantages. Instead of conferring upon and concentrating great power in the hands of a few, it has the contrary effect—it will leave that power distributed among a great many separate corporations.

# APPENDIX B

## *Chronology, 1850–1901*

1850    In Congress, violent sectional debate culminates in Compromise of 1850.
Taylor's death makes Millard Fillmore president.
Nashville convention considers the South's stake in the Union.

1852    Massachusetts adopts first state compulsory education law.
Franklin Pierce elected president.

1853    Upsurge of political nativism, the Know-Nothings.
Gadsden Purchase from Mexico, for $10 million, of 45,000 square miles below Gila River, needed for a railroad route from the South to the Pacific.

1854    Spectacular Know-Nothing election victories signify critical shift in voter loyalties.
Kansas-Nebraska bill rekindles sectional controversy over slavery.
Republican party emerges.
Railroads link New York City with the Mississippi.

1855    Beginning of "Bleeding Kansas."

1856    John Brown's murderous raid at Pottawatomie.
Preston Brook's attack on Senator Charles Sumner.
James Buchanan elected president.

1857    Financial panic and depression.
Dred-Scott decision.
Tariff lowered.
In Kansas, Lecompton constitution ratified as free-state men refuse to vote.
Beginning of great urban religious revival.

1859    A southern commercial convention at Vicksburg calls for reopening African slave trade.
Kansas voters ratify a constitution prohibiting slavery.
John Brown's raid on Harper's Ferry.

Discovery of Comstock lode.

1860    Democratic party, deadlocked at Charleston convention, finally divides along section lines at Baltimore; Constitutional Union Party nominates John Bell; Republicans nominate Abraham Lincoln.

South Carolina secedes from the Union.

1861    Secession of remaining states of deep South (Mississippi, Florida, Alabama, Georgia, Louisiana, and Texas).

Jefferson Davis inaugurated provisional president of the Confederate States of America.

Morrill Tariff Act, first of a series of highly protective tariff acts.

Firing on Fort Sumter precipitates war.

Secession of Virginia, North Carolina, Tennessee, and Arkansas.

1862    Jefferson Davis installed for six-year term as president of Confederacy.

Union forces capture New Orleans.

Union Congress passes Homestead Act, Internal Revenue Act, Morrill Act, creating land-grant colleges, and Pacific Railroad Act, authorizing transcontinental railroad.

Lee's invasion of Maryland halted at Antietam (Sharpsburg), the bloodiest day of the war.

Lincoln issues his preliminary Emancipation Proclamation, promising to free slaves in rebellious region on January 1.

1863    Grant captures Vicksburg.

Lee invades the North but is checked by General George G. Meade at Gettysburg.

Draft riots throughout the North, especially in New York City.

Union Congress passes National Banking Act (strengthened in 1864).

1864    Grant named Union general in chief.

Sherman pushes back Confederates under Joseph E. Johnston and captures Atlanta.

Farragut captures Mobile.

Lincoln reelected president over Democratic candidate McClellan.

Sherman marches from Atlanta to the sea, devastating Georgia.

1865    Cut off from supplies and nearly surrounded, Lee gives up Petersburg and Richmond, and Confederate government flees.

Lee surrenders at Appomattox.

Lincoln assassinated; Andrew Johnson becomes president.

13th Amendment ratified.

1866    Johnson breaks with Republican majority in Congress by vetoing Freedmen's Bureau bill and Civil Rights bill. Latter is passed over his veto.

Congress approves 14th Amendment and submits it to states for ratification.

National Labor Union organized at Baltimore.

Southern whites in Pulaski, Tennessee, organize Ku Klux Klan, which rapidly spreads over the South.

1867    Congress passes Military Reconstruction Act over Johnson's veto.

Annexation of Alaska.

O. H. Kelley founds Patrons of Husbandry (Granger movement).

1868    Former Confederate states hold constitutional conventions, for which former slaves are allowed to vote and adopt new constitutions guaranteeing universal suffrage.

Arkansas, Alabama, Florida, Georgia, Louisiana, North Carolina, and South Carolina readmitted to representation in Congress.

Because of discrimination against Negro officeholders, Georgia representatives are expelled. (State is again admitted in 1870.)

President Johnson impeached. Escapes conviction by one vote.

Grant elected president.

Middle Western states begin passing Granger laws, regulating railroads and grain elevators.

Congress passes 15th Amendment and submits it to states for ratification.

Transcontinental railroad completed.

Public Credit Act affirms government's obligation to pay its debts in gold, not in depreciated paper money.

1870    Incorporation of Standard Oil Company of Ohio.

1871    Knights of Labor formed.

1872    Republicans renominate Grant, who is elected.

Exposure of Credit Mobilier scandal shows prominent Republican politicians tainted by graft.

1873    Coinage Act demonetizes silver in so-called Crime of '73.

Panic of 1873 begins long economic depression.

1874    Greenback Party founded.

1875    Specie Resumption Act provides for return to gold standard by 1879.

1876    Republicans nominate Rutherford B. Hayes for president; Democrats nominate Samuel J. Tilden. Tilden secures majority of popular vote but electoral vote in doubt because of disputed returns from three southern states.

1877    After elaborate political and economic bargaining, Congress creates an electoral commission, which rules that all disputed ballots belong to Hayes, who is inaugurated president.

In *Munn* v. *Illinois,* Supreme Court upholds Granger legislation.

1878    Bland-Allison Act requires United States Treasury to purchase $2 to $4 million of silver each month and coin it, thus slightly inflating the currency but not assuring unlimited coinage as silver interests demanded.

Timber and Stone Act permits inexpensive sale of public lands considered unfit for cultivation.

Miners, lumbermen, and speculators reap huge profits.

1879    As authorized by the 1875 act, Secretary of the Treasury John Sherman begins resumption of specie payments.

Terence V. Powderly elected head of the Knights of Labor, which enters a period of great expansion until by 1886 it has more than 700,000 members.

1880    Garfield elected president.

1881    Charles J. Guiteau assassinates Garfield.

Chester A. Arthur succeeds Garfield as president.

1882    Chinese Exclusion Act restricts immigration of Chinese laborers for 10 years.

In *San Mateo County* v. *Southern Pacific Railroad Company*, Supreme Court accepts Roscoe Conkling's argument that the word *persons* in the 14th Amendment was deliberately chosen to extend protection of due process clause to corporations.

1883    In the civil rights cases, Supreme Court declares unconstitutional 1875 Civil Rights Act because it protected social rather than political rights.

Anticipating Democratic control of Congress, Republicans pass the Tariff of 1883, which nominally makes some reductions in rates but firmly keeps protectionist principle.

In reaction to assassination of Garfield by a disappointed office-seeker, Congress passes Pendleton Act, setting up Civil Service Commission and requiring many future federal appointees to take competitive examinations.

1884    Cleveland narrowly elected, becoming the first Democrat to be elected president since Buchanan.

1886    American Federation of Labor organized; Samuel Gompers, first president.

In *Wabash, St. Louis & Pacific Railroad Company* v. *Illinois,* the Supreme Court invalidates state regulation of railroads when it affects interstate commerce, thus weakening Court's previous ruling in *Munn* v. *Illinois* (the Granger Cases, 1877).

1887    To fill gap in railroad regulation left by Wabash decision, Congress creates Interstate Commerce Commission, first federal regulatory commission in United States history.

1888    In the presidential campaign, Democrats renominate Grover Cleveland and Republicans nominate Benjamin Harrison. Harrison elected president by a majority in the electoral college but receives fewer popular votes than Cleveland.

1889        Department of Agriculture raised to cabinet status.

1890        Sherman Anti-Trust Act passed in attempt to regulate monopolies in restraint of trade.

Sherman Silver Purchase Act passed, resulting in depleted gold reserves.

McKinley Tariff raises duties.

1892        Populists organize in Saint Louis.

Grover Cleveland elected president.

John Muir forms Sierra Club.

Homestead strike in Carnegie steel mills.

1893        Financial panic sends United States economy into four years of depression.

Repeal of Sherman Silver Purchase Act.

Pullman strike begins.

1894        Pullman strike, one of 1,394 strikes in this year, broken by General Managers Association and federal troops.

Henry Demarest Lloyd's, *Wealth against Commonwealth,* exposé of Standard Oil Company.

Wilson-Gorman Tariff lowers some tariffs, makes average rate 39.9 percent.

1895        In *U.S.* v. *E. C. Knight Co.,* government defeated in antitrust suit against sugar monopoly.

*Pollock* v. *Farmers Loan and Trust Co.* invalidates federal income tax.

1896        *Plessy* v. *Ferguson* establishes "separate but equal doctrine." McKinley elected president, defeating Bryan and "Free Silver."

1897        Dingley Tariff raises duties to new high.

1898        Spanish-American War: United States acquires Philippines, Puerto Rico, and Guam, and annexes Hawaii.

1899        Hay's "Open Door" notes to world powers calling for "equal and impartial trade" in China.

Senate ratifies peace treaty with Spain.

1900        McKinley reelected president, defeating Bryan once again.

Robert La Follette elected to his first term as progressive governor of Wisconsin.

National Civic Federation founded by labor leaders and important industrialists.

1901        Theodore Roosevelt becomes president after McKinley assassinated.

Formation of United States Steel Corporation.

Source: Bernard Bailyn *et al., The Great Republic,* pp. 644–45 and 822–24.

# CASE 10

# J. P. Morgan, 1837–1913*

At the beginning of the 20th century J. Pierpont Morgan was perhaps the most powerful man in the American economy. He controlled or had a say in the operations of a large share of America's railroad network. He had just played a major role in reorganizing the American iron and steel, electrical manufacturing, and farm implement industries, among others. The federal government had looked to him for help in the financial crisis of 1895 and would do so again in 1907.

John Pierpont Morgan was born into a well-to-do and influential business family. His father, Junius Spencer Morgan (1813–1890), trained in the mercantile-banking houses of David Welles, Boston, and Morris Ketchum, Morgan & Co., New York, before joining the wholesale dry goods firm of Howe, Mather & Co., Hartford. In 1850, he became a partner in the reorganized firm of Mather, Morgan & Co., but the following year he moved his family to Boston and joined that city's largest wholesale dry goods house—which was renamed J. M. Beebe, Morgan & Co.[1]

---

*This case originally appeared in N.S.B. Gras and Henrietta M. Larson, *Casebook in American Business History* (New York: Appleton-Century-Crofts, 1939) pp. 545–66. This version has been revised by Professor James P. Baughman and Assistant Professor Richard S. Tedlow as a basis for class discussion rather than to illustrate either effective or ineffective handling of an administrative situation.

[1]Among Beebe, Morgan & Co.'s junior partners was Levi P. Morton, who later founded the investment backing houses of Morton, Bliss & Co., New York, and Morton, Rose & Co., London, and who served as a Congressman from New York (1879–1881), as U.S. Minister to France (1881–1885),

Although Beebe, Morgan & Co.'s annual sales were to approach $7 million in 1854, J. S. Morgan resigned from the firm to accept a partnership in George Peabody & Co., merchant-bankers of London. Peabody (1795–1869) was a New Englander who had moved to London in 1837 and had become a major force in Anglo-American trade and finance. His firm of merchant-bankers dealt in foreign exchange and credits, bought and sold commodities and merchandise on both commission and on its own account, and actively dealt in government and corporate securities on its own and joint account. By 1854, Peabody & Co. was supplying iron and short-term capital to American railroads and was offering, on commission, their securities on the London money market. Net income of the firm from these activities stood at £58,081 for the year ending September 30, 1854.

J. S. Morgan was admitted to a 28 percent share in Peabody & Co. on October 1, 1854, and brought his family with him to London. Pierpont was fresh from graduating near the top of his class at Boston's English High as well as from a Grand Tour of Europe. For him, the move meant the finest schools in Switzerland and Germany. At Institut Sillig (1854–1856) and at the University of Gottingen (1856–1857), he studied European history, languages, and literature, chemistry, and mathematics, in which he excelled.

## Morgan Enters Business in New York

Autumn of 1857 found Pierpont "placed" by his father in the office of Duncan, Sherman & Co., American correspondents of Peabody & Co. His previous business experience had been odd jobs in his father's Boston firm and a summer without pay sorting correspondence in the London office of Peabody & Co. In Duncan, Sherman, Morgan began as a junior clerk under an expert accountant, Charles H. Dabney.

Morgan was sent in 1859 to Cuba and Louisiana by his firm to learn sugar and cotton brokerage, but near the end of 1860, he returned to New York and opened his own office. Morgan's work was to collect for the account of his father's firm and to invest for its English clients, but he also traded in foreign exchange on his own and joint account.

Pierpont was soon prominent in the social whirl of Manhattan. He looked up his father's old partners Morris Ketchum and Levi P. Morton, now wealthy and respected New York bankers, and often turned to them for advice and endorsement. Among his younger set were Frank Payson, a classmate from school in Europe who married a daughter of Charles H. Dabney; George S. Bowdoin, who was to marry the daughter of Moses H. Grinnell, New York's most prominent shipping merchant and become Pierpont's partner; George Hale Morgan, a future brother-in-law and partner; Joseph Peabody, nephew of the London banker; Frederick Sturges, a railroad and banking executive and another future brother-

Vice President of the United States (1889–1893), and Governor of New York (1895–1897). The Morgans and the Mortons were life-long friends, and one of Morton's original New York banking partners, Walter H. Burns, married Pierpont Morgan's sister in 1867, joined his father-in-law's London house, and in 1890 became its managing partner.

in-law; and James J. Goodwin, a cousin and confidant who was soon to become a partner.

In 1861, Pierpont married Amelia Sturges, the younger daughter of a founding director of the Illinois Central Railroad. Tragically, his wife suffered from tuberculosis and died on their honeymoon abroad. Morgan plunged again into business and on September 1, 1862, joined his cousin Jim Goodwin in a partnership styled "J. Pierpont Morgan & Co., Bankers." The two young men roomed together until Morgan's marriage in 1865 to Frances Louisa, daughter of Charles Tracy, a leading commercial attorney.

Morgan's initial response to the then-imminent Civil War was typical of many young men of affairs. He paid $300 for a "substitute" to serve in the Union army in his stead. This left him free to immerse himself in the fluctuations and opportunities of the wartime money market. His son-in-law later recalled:

> His firm bought and sold securities, bills of exchange, acceptances drawn against bills of lading, and staple products such as grain, dry goods, and British iron. They were building up a business in foreign exchange, and of course dealing in gold, the most active of all commodities dealt in during the war. He kept himself well informed about the prices current and the trend of the American markets and above all acted as a source of accurate, confidential, detailed information as to events on this side of the water for his father, who had now succeeded to the business of George Peabody & Company. On October 1 (1864), that firm's name was changed to J. S. Morgan & Company.

Morgan himself characterized these days in a letter to his father on September 19, 1862:

> The wear and tear upon me does not arise from deficiency in help the fault is with myself and myself only. It is my nature and I cannot help it. When I have responsibilities laid upon me I cannot throw it upon anyone else however competent the party may be. I am never satisfied unless I either do everything myself or personally superintend everything done even to an entry in the books. This I cannot help. My habit since I have been in business has been so and I cannot learn to do otherwise. I have been pretty well the past week and freer from headaches altho' I do not feel very strong.

One episode in Morgan's Civil War career should suggest his character and business methods. On December 31, 1861, under pressure to conserve its resources for the war effort, the Federal Treasury suspended redemption of its banknotes in gold. Because the rest of the Western world remained on the gold standard, this action increased the sensitivity of gold prices in American and foreign markets to the course of military and diplomatic events. Union reverses threatened the security of customs duties, the collection of taxes, and the payment of interest on the rapidly expanding federal debt—all of which were normally payable in gold. The issuance of short-term Treasury paper and some $400 million in "greenbacks" which were unredeemable in specie until 1879 further muddled the value of gold.

With gold at a fluctuating premium over currency (until the resumption of redemption on January 1, 1879), and since many of the government bond issues sold at par for greenbacks but paid interest in gold, opportunities for arbitrage abounded. And because of their intimacy with domestic and international monetary flows, dealers in exchange normally speculated on the price of gold. Morgan was involved in at least one "gold corner" and was a well-known "bull" on the market. His friendship and cooperation in these dealings with Edward B. Ketchum of Morris Ketchum, Son & Co. brought him guilt by association when young Ketchum was imprisoned for fraud. One can "prove" almost anything on the question of Civil War gold speculation, and the real story of Morgan's participation and profits will never be known; years later, however, he enunciated his philosophy while under oath before a congressional committee:

> Q.:   Would you favor any legislation that would reduce the volume of
>       speculation?
>
> M.:   No.
>
> Q.:   You would let speculation run riot?
>
> M.:   Yes, provided the transactions are legal.
>
> Q.:   Provided they are genuine?
>
> M.:   What you call speculation. You cannot prevent the public buying a
>       thing they think is low, or selling a thing that they think is high.
>
> Q.:   You can prevent them, however, from making fictitious or manipu-
>       lated transactions?
>
> M.:   That is another point.

What is certain about Morgan's Civil War years is that he became quite the man about New York. He was a pillar of fashionable St. George's Church and was admitted to membership in the prestigious Union Club. He reported a taxable income of $55,796 in 1863—compared with Alexander T. Stewart's $1,843,637, William B. Astor's $838,525, and Cornelius Vanderbilt's $680,728.

Morgan's business was growing as fast as his reputation. When Duncan, Sherman & Co. severed its relationship with J. S. Morgan & Co., Pierpont's old friend and mentor, Charles H. Dabney, joined his former pupil. On September 15, 1864, the Morgan-Goodwin firm was expanded into Dabney, Morgan & Co. On January 1, 1867, shortly after his marriage to Pierpont's younger sister, "Cousin" George Hale Morgan brought his experience into the partnership.

# Dabney, Morgan & Co., 1864–1871

International capital flows can be either short-term or long-term funds. The former comprise arbitrage funds, which move rapidly back and forth to take advantage of price differentials, flight capital stimulated by political disruptions, and commercial credits arising from trade. Long-term funds are primarily represented by sales of equity and debt securities and the funds transported by immigrants. By the late 1860s, the Euro-American flow of these funds was guided by European bankers such as the Rothschilds, Baring Brothers, J. S. Morgan & Co. (represented respectively by A. Belmont, S. G. Ward, and Dabney, Morgan & Co., in New York) and young New York houses with strong European connections, particularly Brown Brothers & Co., the Seligmans, Jacob H. Schiff, who joined Kuhn, Loeb & Co. in the 1870s, and Morton, Bliss & Co.

J. S. Morgan and his associate played a particularly important role in domestic and international dealing in government securities. During the years 1861–1865, the federal government issued $1,304,100,000 in long-term bonds and $3,667,700,000 in shorter term, interest- and noninterest-bearing notes and certificates. Flotation of these government issues was initially effected by letting them on competitive bids to small groups of professional bankers and investors. After October, 1862, however, the Philadelphia banking house of Jay Cooke & Co. was retained to sell the securities on commission. Cooke mounted an aggressive sales campaign which reached the man-in-the-street through some 2,500 subagents.

Dabney, Morgan & Co. was an active trader in these Civil War issues on commission and its own account, but it took no part in Cooke's sales campaigns. Its allegiance lay closer to the Mortons and Ketchums of New York and the Drexels of Philadelphia who were Cooke's unsuccessful rivals for government securities contracts.

The Morgans were more active in U.S. governments during the years 1866–1868,when the short-term note and certificate issues of the Civil War were refunded with 6 percent bonds. They made two unsuccessful overtures to Cooke to cooperate in the flotation of the bonds. Subsequently, they did succeed through open-market operations in moving many of these bonds into European hands.

They handled foreign governments as well, including London flotations for Chile and Peru totaling £16,253,620. In 1870, during the Franco-Prussian War, when the French government had been driven from Paris by the Germans, the elder Morgan organized a syndicate which took a 250,000,000 franc loan of the provisional French government at Tours. The success of the loan brought great prestige and some $5 million profit to J. S. Morgan & Co. and its associates.

As American correspondent and agent for J. S. Morgan & Co., Dabney, Morgan & Co. was involved in these international transactions. But its primary business was on its own account in the commercial paper, foreign exchange, and domestic securities markets. Its balance sheet of January 1, 1869, showed a capital investment of $1,200,000 and the personality and standing of the firm are reflected by a confidential report of Dun & Bradstreet:

> J. Pierpont Morgan. . .Is consd. of excellent char., extra ability, shrewd, quick of perception, but oftentimes close & sometimes erratic in minor details which with his peculiar brusqueness of manner has made him & his house unpopular with many. He is the only son. . .of J. S. Morgan of London who is reputed wor. from 8 to $10,000,000, but the greatest part of his present means is the result of his own exertions. He lives well & handsomely, but without great display & is est. wor. from 600 to $700,000. Dabney & Goodwin, the other two prominent partners, are of undoubted char. & standing, the first being always on the cautious side in bus. matters, the latter is of good ability. Have rich & strong bus. friends & relations. Do a conservative, paying bus. & are safe for their engts.

Dabney, Morgan & Co. had a special interest in railroading—an interest which was reenforced and broadened by Morgan's business and social friends. His father had become European fiscal agent for a number of American railroads, including the Baltimore & Ohio, the Illinois Central, and the Louisville & Nashville. Morris Ketchum probably held as many railroad directorships as any of his peers and was a founding partner of the Rogers Locomotive Works. Jonathan Sturges, Pierpont's first father-in-law, served on the Illinois Central board from 1851 to 1875, when he was succeeded by his son (and Pierpont's friend) Frederick. Charles Lanier was Pierpont's age and a close friend; he was also the son of the founder of Winslow, Lanier & Company, a firm which had helped make New York the center of American railroad finance by the 1850s. Samuel Sloan was a Hudson Valley neighbor and commuting crony of Pierpont as well as president of the Delaware, Lackawanna & Western and the Hudson River roads. In 1869, another close friend, Morris Ketchum Jessup, drew Dabney, Morgan & Co. into its first large railroad deal. The Jessup and Morgan firms collaborated as commission agents for the successful public sale of $6,500,000 of first mortgage, 7 percent gold bonds of the Kansas Pacific Railway.

In May 1869, Morgan helped negotiate a $500,000 third mortgage on the Albany & Susquehanna Railroad and became its co-trustee. By fall, this commitment plunged him into a contest with the worst of American railroad manipulators. The contestants were Jay Gould, Jim Fisk, and their followers of the Erie Railroad and Joseph H. Ramsey, president of the Albany & Susquehanna.

The A & S ran between Binghamton and Albany and connected with several older roads running south into the Pennsylvania coalfields which were interested in access to Albany and thence into the New England trade dominated by the New York Central. Gould and Fisk's Erie was the most aggressive and had launched raids on the A & S's equipment and capital stock.

Samuel Sloan, who was strongly anti-Erie, brought Morgan and Ramsey together at the time of the A & S's third mortgage. In September, after further consultation with his father-in-law Charles Tracy and Sloan, Morgan bought his way onto the A & S board and became leader of the Ramsey faction.

Ramsey as president and Morgan as vice president were upheld in their control of the road by a New York Supreme Court decision in December 1869, and in February 1870, Morgan negotiated the lease of the Albany & Susquehanna to the friendly and anti-Gould Delaware & Hudson Canal Co. In the words of the *New York Times* of January 24, 1873, "This contest, waged not only by litigation but by force of arms, made Mr. Morgan universally respected as an able financier."

# Drexel, Morgan & Co., 1871–1895

The partnership constituting Dabney, Morgan & Co. expired under its original limitation of time on June 30, 1871, and was not renewed. Dabney and Goodwin retired and George Hale Morgan moved over into an investment-management partnership with Dabney's sons-in-law E. Heineman and Frank Payson. This left Pierpont free to consider an offer from Drexel & Co. of Philadelphia.

**Drexel-Morgan Partnerships, 1871**

| *Drexel & Co.,*<br>*Philadelphia* | *Drexel, Morgan & Co.,*<br>*New York* | *Drexel, Harjes & Co.,*<br>*Paris* |
|---|---|---|
| Francis A. Drexel | Joseph W. Drexel | Drexel & Co. |
| Anthony J. Drexel | J. Pierpoint Morgan | Drexel, Morgan & Co. |
| James Hood Wright | John Norris Robinson | John H. Harjes |
| Drexel, Morgan & Co. | Drexel & Co. | Eugene Winthrop |
| *Agents & Attorneys for:* | *Agents & Attorneys for:* | |
| London and San Francisco<br>Bank | J. S. Morgan & Co.,<br>London | |
| German Bank of London,<br>Ltd. | | |

Long the most powerful bankers in Philadelphia, the Drexels had invaded New York money markets in the late 1850s—first as Read, Drexel & Co. but after 1863 as Drexel, Winthrop & Co. This firm dealt in governments and gold, made mercantile collections, and handled railroad supplies and securities. When Robert Winthrop retired from the firm, the Drexels approached J. P. Morgan to replace him.

Morgan's initial reaction was negative. While only thirty-four, he was suffering from general fatigue and was seriously considering complete retirement. He decided to accept the Drexels' invitation on the condition he might take a year's leave for travel and recuperation.

The Drexels agreed, and on July 1, 1871, Drexel, Morgan & Co. opened its doors in New York "for the transaction of a General Foreign and Domestic Banking Business." The new firm also served as "Agents and Attorneys for J. S. Morgan & Co., London" and was integrated into the Drexel enterprises through interlocking partnerships.

Morgan returned in 1872 just as his firm was moving into the new seven-story Drexel Building at the corner of Broad and Wall, where it remained until 1914. His role in the large Drexel organization is reflected in a Dun & Bradstreet credit report of 1877:

> The main responsy, rests with the two Drexels who are the principal capitalists of the firm of Drexel & Co. . . . A recent estimate by a party who knows them well sets the Drexels down at between 5 & 6 millions. Mr. Morgan is probably worth $250,000, but being the son of Junius S. Morgan the great London Banker, he would be able to control vry. lgr. facilities if necessary. This young man is smart & is perhaps the most venturesome member of the firm but is kept in check by the Drexels.

Drexel, Morgan & Co. (and its successor J. P. Morgan & Co.) offered a full line of traditional banking services:

> Domestic and Foreign Bankers, Deposits Received Subject to Draft. Securities, Gold, Etc., Bought and Sold on Commission. Interest Allowed on Deposits. Foreign

Exchange, Commercial Credits, Cable Trnsfers. Circular Letters for Travelers available in all parts of the world.

But the major interest of Morgan and the other senior partners soon became the capital requirements of governments and corporations. Among the most important of these men were the New York partners: James Hood Wright, a Drexel partner in Philadelphia since 1865, who succeeded the retiring John Norris Robinson in New York in 1875; Egisto Paulo Fabbri, an Italian immigrant and dry goods merchant, who replaced Joseph W. Drexel on the latter's retirement in 1876; Charles H. Godfrey, Wright's successor in Philadelphia in 1875, who moved over to New York in 1883; and George S. Bowdoin, formerly of Morton, Bliss & Co. and close friend of Morgan.

# J. P. Morgan & Co.

When J. S. Morgan died in 1890, Pierpont became nominal head of the Morgan partnerships, and on January 1, 1895, two years after the death of Anthony J. Drexel, Drexel, Morgan & Co. was reconstituted as J. P. Morgan & Co. His son-in-law characterized the mature Morgan's appearance and nature at this stage of his career.

> . . . [H]is nose always looked inflamed and swollen, and in later years the trouble was very noticeable and gave him much discomfort. He began by degrees to be more sensitive about his appearance, and developed a shyness that he had never known in his early years. This shyness resulted in his often being brusque, a mannerism that was generally misunderstood.
>
> *\*\*\*\*\**
>
> Regular habits suited Pierpont. He liked to know in advance what he was going to do. . . . [His    strengths    were]    truthfulness    and    absolute    fidelity    to his obligations. . .resources and prestige. . .quick, intuitive grasp of a situation, with the details of which he could not have been familiar. . .prompt determination of the question presented. . .bold imaginative and absolute confidence in his own first judgment.
>
> *\*\*\*\*\**
>
> [His desk was] in the thick of it. . .in plain sight of everyone who came in the front door. . . . Anyone who called could speak to him, but anyone who interrupted him unnecessarily or stayed too long was not encouraged to do so again. . . . Occasionally he would go on writing or figuring without looking up and make no answer at all. One could never be sure whether he really heard a question or merely did not want to hear it. . . .[He] was probably the most accessible man (except to reporters!) who ever occupied an important position in the banking world.

Small wonder why, in the words of the New York *Sun* of February 29, 1892, Morgan's movements were "watched more carefully than those of any other man in the financial world."

He was, of course, supported by skilled and hard-working associates. The London house was ably managed by his brother-in-law Walter Burns and by J. P. Morgan, Jr., ("Jack") who had been admitted to partnership in 1892. In New

York, Fabbri had retired in 1885, but his successor, Edward T. Stotesbury (a Philadelphia partner since 1883), and Wright, Bowdoin, and Charles Henry Coster performed admirably. Fabbri and Bowdoin were securities and promotional specialists, Wright was a railroad-management expert, Stotesbury, a general banking partner and coal specialist, and Coster, the railroad genius of the organization—"a white-faced, nervous figure, hurrying from directors' meeting to directors' meeting; at evening carrying home his portfolio of corporation problems." In drafting documents, Coster "had a great clarity of expression and fertility of invention. He continually had to invent forms and devise methods to meet the problems on which Pierpont was working." When he died suddenly in 1900, Coster was a director of 59 corporations.

Morgan also depended heavily upon a small coterie of individuals. These included two personal attorneys, Francis Lynde Stetson, Grover Cleveland's former law partner, and Charles Steele, an Erie Railroad lawyer who became a partner in 1900 following Coster's death and Bowdoin's retirement; Samuel Spencer, a professional railroad consultant; and Robert Bacon, a socially prominent young Bostonian who became a Morgan partner in 1895 following Wright's death.

The general banking side of the business was strengthened by Henry P. Davison, former president of the Liberty National Bank and vice president of the First National Bank of New York, who became a partner in 1909. The most flamboyant of the later partners, however, was George W. Perkins. Perkins was the "boy wonder" of the life insurance business. As officer of the New York Life Insurance Co. and member of its finance committee, he had set up its domestic and foreign agency system and shaped its portfolio of American, British, German, and Russian securities. He was brought to Morgan's attention by James Stillman, president of the National City Bank of which Perkins was a director. Perkins's biographer records the first meeting of Morgan and Perkins:

> He found Morgan in his big, high-ceilinged office separated from his clerks and customers only by an immense glass partition. He was seated at his desk smoking a cigar. Bacon performed the introductions and left them there. Perkins launched at once into his story of the Palisades [Interstate Park Commission], but after a moment or two Morgan interrupted him. "I know all about that. You are the chairman of the Commission. What is it you want?"
>
> "I want to raise $125,000."
>
> "All right, put me down for $25,000. It is a good thing. Is that all?"
>
> Flabbergasted, Perkins asked weakly for suggestions as to who else might contribute. Morgan mentioned John D. Rockefeller, and Perkins mumbled something about calling on Mr. Rockefeller right away. Still stunned by the suddenness of Morgan's offer, he thanked the banker and started to leave.
>
> "I will give you the whole $125,000 if you will do something for me," Morgan said calmly.
>
> "Do something for you," Perkins said. "What?"
>
> Morgan pointed across the room where all Morgan partners worked. "Take that desk over there," he said. . . .
>
> . . ."I have a pretty good desk up at the New York Life," Perkins answered.
>
> But Morgan brushed this reply aside with a word. "No," he said bluntly. "I mean come into the firm. . . . Let me know tomorrow if you can."

During his career as partner (1901–1911), Perkins recalled that "I never went behind the counter or examined into the bookkeeping end of the business. My job was to assist in the physical organization of the great industrial combines which Mr. Morgan was then engaged in financing." Before long the New York *World* reported that "George W. Perkins now does all the talking. . .for the firm of J. P. Morgan and Co. Mr. Perkins has the facility of saying just enough and not too much on any subject." Morgan himself took annual and increasingly prolonged vacations after 1895, arguing "I can do a year's work in nine months, but not in 12."

A division of Morgan's career creates a distortion, for his business was never confined to a single activity. The firms in which he was a partner continued to carry out the several services offered by international banking houses. They handled foreign exchange, letters of credit, and other instruments of financing international trade; and they bought and sold government, railroad, and industrial securities. Nevertheless, the Morgan firms concentrated on certain types of businesses at different periods during the years from 1870 to World War I. The shifts in emphasis in his business reveal much about his role in American finance, the way in which he acquired that role, and the financial requirements of the nation's rapidly industrializing economy.

## Morgan in Government Finance

During the 1870s after he had joined the Drexels, Morgan concentrated on government finance. Here the opportunity came from the decision of the Treasury Department and Congress to refund the Civil War debt. By the Refunding Acts of 1870 and 1871, the $1,304,100,000 worth of 5 percent and 6 percent long bonds issued during the war were to be retired in favor of $1.8 billion worth of 4 percent to 5 percent bonds. Between March and August 1871, refunding bonds were offered by the Treasury Department through some 900 agencies and through representatives in London, Frankfort, Amsterdam, and Paris. Drexel, Morgan & Co. was one of 51 private bankers named as agents in New York City, and J. S. Morgan & Co. was one of six so appointed in London. The amount of bonds sold through their houses in this manner is unknown, but like all agents they were compensated by a commission of 2 percent on sales.

In August 1871, because of poor sales, the Treasury Department modified its bond distribution policy. Thenceforth, most issues were floated through syndicates of bankers, each of which subscribed for stated amounts and assumed all risks of selling. Syndicate members were compensated by their margin on resale of the bonds and by commissions ranging from 0.25 percent to 0.5 percent of sales.

Competition for syndication contracts polarized around two groups: Jay Cooke & Co., fresh from its successful war-bond campaigns and hopeful of entering international banking through an alliance with the Rothschilds; and a faction composed of politician and banker Levi P. Morton, the Drexels, who were Cooke's rivals in Philadelphia, and the Morgans, who were friends of Morton and partners of the Drexels.

Cooke headed the first refunding syndicate (in which Morton, the Drexels, and the Morgans declined participation), but in the second he was forced to accept his rivals as managers. After Cooke's unexpected bankruptcy in September 1873, the next four syndicates were dominated by a New York-London alliance composed of:

| New York | London |
|---|---|
| August Belmont & Co. | N. M. Rothschild & Sons |
| Drexel, Morgan & Co. | J. S. Morgan & Co. |
| J. & W. Seligman & Co. | Seligman Brothers |
| Morton, Bliss & Co. | Morton, Rose & Co. |
| First National Bank | |
| (headed by George F. Baker) | |

The final syndicate did not include the Morgans and was made up mostly of New York and Boston commercial banks.

The role played by the syndicates in refunding is suggested in Table 1. The Morgan firms were second only to the Belmont-Rothschild group in their share of participation (which may have been as high as 10 to 15 percent of the bonds sold).

The completion of refunding ended the Morgan involvement in government finance with two dramatic exceptions: a payroll controversy in 1877 and the gold crisis of 1890–1896.

Because of partisan disagreement over the rate of withdrawal of federal troops from the South, Congress in May 1877 adjourned without appropriating funds to pay the U.S. Army for the fiscal year beginning July 1. Citing his "obvious and sacred duty" to forestall inequity, Morgan volunteered his firm's resources to the War Department. Although the latter could not legally borrow money or guarantee reimbursement, Drexel, Morgan & Co. went ahead on its own account and risk. Morgan's firm met payrolls of $550,000 per month from July 1, 1877, until

## TABLE 1

**Refunding Syndicates, 1871–1879**

| Date Formed | Initial† Pledge | Option | Type of * Bonds | Closing Date | Approximate‡ Total Sales |
|---|---|---|---|---|---|
| 8–14–71 | $ 25 million | $105 million | 5 % | 12–?–71 | $130 million |
| 1–23–73 | 10 | 290 | 5 | 12–1–73 | 50 |
| 8–25–76 | 40 | 260 | 4.5 | 3–4–77 | 200 |
| 6–9–77 | 25 | | 4 | 11–6–77 | 70 |
| 4–11–78 | 10 | 50 | 4.5 | — | 45 |
| 1–21–79 | 10 | 15 | 4 | 6–30–79 | 10 |
| 4–18–79 | 150 | none | 4 | — | 150 |

*The Refunding Acts of 1870–1871 authorized $500 million in 10-year, 5 percent; $300 million in 15-year, 4.5 percent; $1 billion in 30-year, 4 percent bonds.

†The syndicate guaranteed sale of all bonds they took, but took only an initial pledge and then irregular increments of their additional allowed option.

‡Sales can only be approximated as proportions of options actually exercised are not available. The Treasury Department also made sales outside the syndicate through the agency system.

Congress reconvened in November and appropriated funds to pay the army and reimburse Morgan.

The gold crisis was more intricately related to mechanisms of trade. American businesspeople in foreign trade, whose value received from imports of goods and services exceeded the value they received for their exports, incurred obviously a net indebtedness to foreigners. The normal means of canceling these debts was to purchase sterling bills of exchange on London and remit them to one's creditors.

The price of sterling bills of exchange in dollars oscillated around "the par of exchange" of $4.86 ⅔ : £1, depending upon the balance of trade. When trade balances favored the United States, as they did during fiscal 1878–1883, 1885, 1887–1888, and 1897–1899, sterling bills were readily available near par. Adverse trade balances, such as existed during fiscal 1862–1877, 1884, 1886, 1889–1896, and 1900, increased demand and decreased supply for sterling bills in New York and prices rose.

The price of sterling bills of exchange in dollars, however, could not rise above $4.89—the specie export point—that is, the price at which gold itself could be purchased and exported more cheaply than buying a sterling bill of exchange. Whenever sterling bills were unobtainable or their price neared or reached the specie export point, bankers' sterling drafts took over the foreign exchange market. Those seeking sterling funds to remit purchased (in dollars) a sterling draft drawn by a New York banker on his London correspondent.

A banker such as Morgan—who dealt continuously in foreign exchange—had several ways of insuring redemption of his sterling drafts when they were presented abroad. He might cover them by calling claims of his foreign debtors, by drawing against his own foreign deposits, or by borrowing abroad. Normally, however, he converted the check or currency which he received from the purchaser of his draft into gold, which he then shipped abroad. He usually obtained this gold from the reserves of New York banks, but his and their ultimate reservoir was the Federal Treasury. Gold was obtainable from the Treasury by presenting legal-tender currency for redemption.

A decline, between 1890 and 1894, in the net gold reserve of the Treasury from $200 million to $64 million signaled that the normal interrelationships of trade, exchange, and redemption were severely strained.

The decline sprang from many sources. Greenbacks, which had become redeemable in gold in 1879 (after 17 years of irredeemability) and which comprised the bulk of the currency, could not legally be retired from circulation and were endlessly presented for redemption, causing a constant outflow of Treasury gold reserves. The Silver Purchase Act (in effect 1890–1893) worsened matters, for rather than contracting the money supply, it increased it by one-third—in the form of currency redeemable in either silver or gold (but actually only in the latter because of the Secretary of the Treasury's fear of compromising the value of gold).

In addition to these domestic monetary problems, the balance of international gold transfers, which had favored the United States since 1878, turned adverse in 1889 and remained so. The balance of trade deficit was worsened by the abnormal liquidation of American corporate securities held abroad, which followed Baring Brothers' suspension in 1890 and the American Panic of 1893.

By 1890, American demand for sterling bills on London had driven their price in dollars past the gold export price of $4.89. Yet, the gold reserve of New York bankers was soon depleted in covering sterling drafts, and their only recourse was to increase demands on the Federal Treasury's ultimate reserves. In fiscal 1893 alone, a new $87,900,000 in American gold flowed abroad.

The effect of these outflows was worsened by negation of the government's prime means for replenishing its gold reserves—the requirement that customs duties (the bulk of federal income) be paid in gold. After 1890, payment in currency or silver became legal, and the percentage of duties paid in gold declined from 90 percent to below 4 percent by 1892.

Congress favored currency redemption in silver to ease the pressure on gold and check silver depreciation. President Cleveland and Secretary of the Treasury Carlisle, adamant against silver, unable to contract the currency, unwilling to suspend specie payments, and fearing a gold panic, favored public sale of government bonds to replenish the gold supply. The nation's bankers favored private placement of gold bonds.

A first issue in February 1894 of $50 million in 10-year 5 percent bonds was reluctantly taken by a group of New York commercial banks at a minimum price of $117.223, and Treasury gold reserves rose briefly to $107 million. By November, reserves were down to $55 million and a second bond issue of $50 million was floated through Drexel, Morgan & Co. at $117.077. The bankers took these issues at least a point above their resale value and disliked them intensely since by congressional fiat they were payable in either silver or gold. The bankers continually pressured for an issue "specifically payable in gold."

Drexel, Morgan & Co. and A. Belmont & Co. in New York and J. S. Morgan & Co. and N. M. Rothschild & Sons in London repeatedly conferred with federal officials. A dramatic meeting between President Cleveland and Pierpont Morgan, Francis Lynde Stetson, and Robert Bacon produced a new plan. The bankers were convinced that the "public will not take any loan not specifically gold bonds at any price satisfactory to U.S. government." Instead, a bankers' syndicate headed by Morgan agreed to purchase 3,500,000 ounces of gold ($65,116,275 worth) and sell it to the government for $62,314,435 in 30-year, 4 percent bonds. Thus, in effect, the bankers "purchased" the bonds at 104½ and the government was paid 100 percent in gold.

The keys to Cleveland's acceptance of the plan were two guarantees by Morgan: first, that at least one-half the gold would be purchased abroad; second, that the syndicate would "as far as lies in their power, exert all financial influence and will make all legitimate efforts to protect the Treasury of the United States against the withdrawal of gold pending the complete performance of this contract."

Morgan extracted the assent of all leading New York and European banking houses to his plan. He proposed that the New York bankers continue to sell sterling drafts on London but to agree voluntarily not to export any gold to cover their redemption. Rather, they should rely upon calling their claims on foreign debts, drawing against their deposits already abroad; and, if necessary, they should borrow in foreign markets. He proposed that this agreement should last six months and expected that losses could be recouped when the bankers then resold the bonds they had received at such a premium. He also expected that a favorable shift in the balance of payments would occur following this American show of credit strength, thus easing the pressure on American debtors.

A final element in Morgan's plan involved the pricing of sterling drafts: Should they be priced below the gold export point to discourage further exports of specie? He rejected this possibility as too risky for bankers who might later be forced to honor their drafts at higher prices. Confident of his own and his peers' ability to corner the supply of exchange on London and to prevent exports of gold, he chose to price sterling drafts above the gold export point.

He bound his syndicate not to sell drafts below $4.90 and not to export gold. Since there were no bills of exchange on the market and no alternative to the "syndicate price" for sterling drafts, the cost to purchasers was thus $1,500 above the price which they would normally have paid to export gold on every £100,000 of drafts purchased.

The syndicate price held the market from February to June 1895, and even though the adverse balance of trade persisted, almost no gold was exported. In July, however, a New York import house broke the market by selling drafts at $4.89 and covered by exporting gold, which it withdrew from the Federal Treasury. In the last six months of 1895, $65 million flowed abroad and this and domestic redemption brought Treasury reserves to a record low of $50 million by January 1896.

In the meantime, the Morgan-Belmont syndicate had resold the bonds they had received at 103½ for a public subscription price of 112¼. The offer was subscribed six times over and prompted vehement charges of banker profiteering with journalistic estimates as high as $16 million.

When queried in a congressional investigation as to his purposes, Morgan stated, "I had but one aim in the whole matter—to secure the gold that the government needed and to save the panic and widespread disaster that was sure to follow if the gold was not got." When asked why he demanded "exclusive control of the matter," Morgan replied, "Because it was absolutely impossible for more than one party to negotiate—to make the same negotiation for the same lot of gold. It would only have made competition." When asked, "What profit did your house make upon this transaction?" Morgan replied, "That I decline to answer. I wish to state that I am perfectly ready to state to the committee every detail of the negotiation up to the time that the bonds became my property and were paid for. What I did with my own property subsequent to that purchase I decline to state. . . ."

The original books of the Morgan firm reveal that of the $31,157,000 in bonds allotted to the American half of the syndicate, Drexel, Morgan & Co. took less than one tenth and on these made a gross profit (with interest) of $295,652.93. No data are available as to the profits of the European syndicate.

Again in January 1896, Morgan offered to purchase $100 million to $200 million in gold under similar terms, but his plan was rejected in favor of a public Treasury offering of $100 million in 4 percent bonds. Morgan headed a syndicate of his firm, the National City Bank, Harvey Fisk & Son, and the Deutsche Bank which took $38 million of these at 110.6877. Confidence in American obligations was growing and a recovery in trade soon diminished the "crisis."

The firm remained active in foreign government finance as well. In 1899, it participated with three Berlin banks in the purchase and sale of £22,700,000 ($110,095,000) in 5 percent consols of the United States of Mexico. In 1902, Morgan, the Barings, and the Rothschilds took one half of a British issue of £32 million ($155,500,000); and J. P. Morgan & Co., August Belmont & Co., Baring, Magoun & Co., and the National City Bank formed the distribution syndicate for all American sales of an Imperial Russian Government loan of 2,310 million rubles ($1,188,495,000). In 1904, Morgan handled the transfer of $40 million from the U.S. government to France as a part of the Panama Canal transaction, and in 1909, J. P. Morgan & Co. became sole distributor of £2 million ($9,730,000) in bonds of the Argentine Republic.

## Morgan in Railway Finance

The Morgan firms, like all international banking houses, were continuously involved in railroad finance. As the American agents for J. S. Morgan & Co. of London, which continued to be a leading distributor of railroad securities in Britain and on the Continent, Drexel, Morgan and Co. enjoyed a favored position. However, until the completion of the funding operations in 1879, government finance remained the most important part of Morgan's business during the 1870s. Then just as the government business was being phased out, Morgan completed two major negotiations that established his reputation in railroad finance.

The first was the successful sale of 250,000 shares of New York Central stock for William H. Vanderbilt. In 1879, Vanderbilt, under severe attack in the New York State legislature, faced heavy taxation and adverse legislation as the owner of 87 percent of the New York Central's stock outstanding. At the same time his recent purchases of the Michigan Central and Canadian Southern, largely in response to Jay Gould's aggressive tactics, convinced Vanderbilt of the costliness of attempting to maintain personal ownership of his railroad properties. He contacted Morgan, asking that he make the sale privately and quietly so as not to depress the price of the stock or to give the appearance that Vanderbilt or the Central were in financial trouble. Morgan arranged for the sale to a syndicate composed of J. S. Morgan & Co., August Belmont & Co., Morton Bliss & Co., and Jay Gould. The shares, purchased at 120 were sold in London at 130 with no noticeable disturbance in the money markets. Morgan then became a director of the New York Central's board, a position which he held for more than 30 years. Once the news was out, the *Commercial and Financial Chronicle,* New York's leading financial paper, was full of praise for this "grand financial operation."

Morgan's second important coup came in the following year when he carried out what the *Commercial and Financial Chronicle* described as "the largest transaction in railroad bonds ever made in the United States." It involved the sale of $40 million worth of bonds of the Northern Pacific. Chartered in 1864 to run from Lake Superior to Portland, Oregon, the Northern Pacific's financing had been taken over in 1869 by Jay Cooke, whose success in selling Civil War bonds had made him America's foremost financier. Cooke's failure to market the road's securities brought his career as a financier to a disastrous end and the road into bankruptcy.

After a series of reorganizations, mergers, and refundings, the road had by 1879 embarked on a policy of cautious expansion. To finance this growth, a syndicate headed by Drexel, Morgan & Co., and including Winslow, Lanier & Co. and August Belmont & Co., contracted to sell the $40 million issue of 6 percent first-mortgage gold bonds. The syndicate took $10 million at 90 and spread the remainder over the next three-and-a-half years at 92½. In return it received 5 percent commission and placed two directors on the Northern Pacific's board. The syndicate was activated again in October 1883 to take a major portion of a $20 million second-mortgage issue—$15 million at 87½ less 5 percent commission in bonds and a six-month option on $3 million more on the same terms.

These two negotiations, which helped to place Morgan at the center of American railroad finance, provide good examples of his methods. The Vanderbilt sale was one of several in which Morgan sold large blocks of securities on commission for the account of railroad owners or managers. The Northern Pacific transaction was the first of many in which Drexel, Morgan acted as managers of large underwriting syndicates. These syndicates normally agreed to purchase whatever stock, convertible bonds, or convertible notes were not bought in an offering by the corporation's shareholders. Syndicates received a commission of 1 percent to 5 percent on sales. The stock was either marketed for account of the syndicate by the managers or distributed to, and paid for, by the underwriters, who disposed of it or continued to hold it until a market was established. Similarly, Morgan was continually involved in subscription syndicates which subscribed for bonds or notes irrespective of whether the securities, once acquired, were disposed of for syndicate account by the syndicate managers or whether each subscriber was left free to dispose of his proportion of the securities acquired.

A sample of railroad bond and debenture issues for which Morgan acted as syndicate manager before 1897 includes: $10 million for the Allegheny Valley; £900,000 for the Chicago & Alton; $8 million for the Lehigh Valley; $2,500,000 for the Cleveland, Columbus, Cincinnati, & Indiana; £3,600,000 for the Baltimore & Ohio; $5 million for the Illinois & St. Louis Bridge; $2,200,000 for the Pittsburgh & Connellsville; $7,200,000 for the Chicago & Western Indiana; $12,500,000 for the New York Central; $11 million for the Lehigh Valley; $11 million for the Cleveland, Cincinnati, Chicago, & St. Louis; $4,500,000 for the St. Louis Terminal; and $900,000 for the New York & Greenwood Lake.

Between December 31, 1897, and January 22, 1913, J. P. Morgan & Co. was sole underwriter for 11 interstate railroad issues of stock and convertible bonds totaling $62,948,000. The firm managed underwriting syndicates in another four instances totaling $204,364,000. In 122 instances, it acted as initial subscribers for bonds and notes totaling $846,007,000 and in another 61 instances it managed subscription syndicates which placed securities totaling $485,718,000. Morgan was also sole initial subscriber for $10 million in Interborough Rapid Transit bonds and manager of a syndicate which subscribed $22 million in Chicago City & Connecting Railways bonds.

In the 1897–1913 period, the Morgan firm in four instances, totaling $1,223,000, purchased securities for the account of interstate railroad companies.

In 37 cases, it sold securities on account totaling $177,894,000 and 28 times it managed syndicates to do the same totaling $235,001,000, 185 million francs, and £1,400,000. In 6 instances, totaling $24,450,000, J. P. Morgan & Co. loaned money on security collateral to these same railroads.

The Morgan firms were also participants in railroad underwriting and subscription syndicates managed by others. For example, in the 1897–1913 period, they took: one third of four syndicates managed by Lee, Higginson which subscribed $21,400,000 in Kansas City Terminal bonds; one fourth of two syndicates managed by the First National Bank of New York which subscribed $70 million of the bonds of the Chinchow Hukuang railways; and portions of a $20 million Great Northern issue, a $5 million Maine Central issue, and Chesapeake & Ohio issues totaling $7 million managed by the First National Bank, Lee Higginson & Co., and Kuhn, Loeb & Co., respectively.

As syndicate managers, J. P. Morgan & Co. sold all securities for the account of the syndicate—by either public subscription or private placement—for which it received an additional 0.25 percent to 2 percent commission and distributed profits. The pivotal importance of these functions was suggested by Frederick Strauss of J. & W. Seligman in 1917:

> Success in the formation of a syndicate depends to a great extent on the reputation of the syndicate managers for good judgment, fair dealing and success in conducting previous syndicates. In fact, syndicate operations from start to finish are based on faith in character, ability and experience. No syndicate member ever asks for an accounting from the managers to the syndicate participants. The letter announcing the distribution of profits or the apportionment of losses sometimes states that the syndicate accounts are on file for examination by any syndicate member, and such accounts are carefully prepared and kept among the syndicate managers' records, but for any syndicate member to avail himself of the offer contained in the letter of the managers, would be regarded by the latter as an intentional affront and business relations between the managers and the inquisitive syndicate member would terminate as soon as the examination of the accounts was completed.

Morgan himself once told the congressional committee that syndicate managers had additional responsibilities:

> M.:  . . .You must remember that securities that are issued and sold do not always prove good. . .when there is no fiscal agent or person responsible for them who will put their name on them. . . .
>
> Q.:  But the name does not help after the bond is proved bad, does it?
>
> M.:  It does in this way: The house is called upon to protect those bonds, to assist in the reorganization of the road, to make them good in case of a disaster.
>
> Q.:  But what I mean is that the banking house assumes no legal responsibility for the value of the bonds, does it?
>
> M.:  No sir; but it assumes something else that is still more important and that is the moral responsibility which has to be defended as long as you live.

Morgan practiced what he preached. Not only did he, through the reorganization of bankrupt railroads, put them back on their financial feet, he also did his best to prevent the costly cutthroat competition which he considered the basic cause of the railroads' financial difficulties. He strongly supported Albert Fink's Eastern Trunk Line Association and other similar regional traffic cartels in their attempts to maintain rates; and he used his influence to restrain competitive construction.

Morgan's first move as a peacemaker came in 1885 when he arranged a compromise between the two largest railroad systems in the United States, the Pennsylvania and the New York Central, after each had begun to invade the other's territory. The controversy had its beginning after the West Shore, built parallel to the New York Central from New York City to Buffalo, went into receivership in June 1884. The road was built shoddily by promoters, including Jay Gould, who hoped to sell out to Vanderbilt. Vanderbilt, knowing that his well-built, well-run Central would have little difficulty in competing, refused to buy. Then the Pennsylvania began quietly to purchase the bankrupt West Shore's depressed securities. They did so largely because two years earlier Vanderbilt had joined with Andrew Carnegie, who was anxious to break the Pennsylvania's monopoly of transportation out of Pittsburgh, to finance the building of the South Pennsylvania from Reading to Pittsburgh. By late 1884, when the Pennsylvania began openly to improve the West Shore, the construction on the South Pennsylvania was speeded up.

As Morgan was close to Vanderbilt and as the Drexels had long been involved in the financing of the Pennsylvania, the house of Drexel, Morgan & Co. was in a key position to bring peace. Arranging to return from Europe that spring on the same ship as Vanderbilt, Morgan convinced him of the need for compromise. He then invited President George B. Roberts and a senior vice president of the Pennsylvania Railroad to join him and Chauncey Depew, Vanderbilt's top operating executive, for a cruise on Morgan's yacht *Corsair.* By the time the boat had docked, Roberts and his associate agreed to Morgan's compromise proposal.

Drexel, Morgan & Co. managed the transactions necessary to carry out Morgan's proposals. The New York line was purchased at foreclosure by the West Shore Railway Co., which was organized for that purpose. A Morgan partner became its first president, and several men close to Drexel, Morgan & Co. were on its board. The West Shore was then leased to the New York Central with a guarantee of principal and interest on $50 million new bonds. It was agreed that the Pennsylvania should buy its enemy at cost, but under state law direct purchase was impossible. Morgan, therefore, personally bought a 60 percent interest in the road paying for the purchase by means of bonds of another road, which securities were provided and guaranteed by the Pennsylvania.

The *Commercial and Financial Chronicle* of February 20, 1886, and September 10, 1887, expressed the view of the conservative business press:

> since the West Shore settlement we have become so accustomed to peaceable adjustments among the railroads, that we are unprepared for anything else. . . . To railroads, least of all, would our people like to see applied the principle of the survival of the fittest. . . . At this juncture. . .Mr. Morgan conceived the first settlement which was the embryo of them all.

At the end of 1885, Morgan carried his peacemaking activities into another area from which both the Central and the Pennsylvania drew heavy traffic—the anthracite coal region of eastern Pennsylvania. He organized an annual conference of presidents and traffic managers of several anthracite coal carriers including the Philadelphia & Reading, the Delaware, Lackawanna & Western, the Lehigh Valley, and the Delaware & Hudson. Its purpose was indicated by a brief item in the *Commercial and Financial Chronicle* of March 27, 1886:

> *Anthracite Coal Combination*—Representatives of the various coal companies met at the house of Mr. J. Pierpont Morgan this week, and informally decided to limit coal production and maintain prices.

The passage of the Interstate Commerce Act in 1887 enlarged Morgan's role as a railroad peacemaker. That act created a commission to maintain "fair and reasonable rates" and at the same time forbade pooling. Although Albert Fink and the other railroad men who had long advocated legalized pooling were disappointed by the second provision, they still hoped to use the first to maintain rates. Fink's Eastern Trunk Line Association drew up an agreement and a new set of rates. Violations of these rates were to be reported to the new Interstate Commerce Commission. Tonnage would still be allocated, but there would be no traffic or money pools. A railroad with less than its share of an agreed-upon allotment could obtain a discount from the official rate sufficient to recover its agreed-upon share of the traffic. In the words of the *Railroad Gazette:* "The procedure is that if a railroad is actually to be found losing traffic it would be allowed to quote a differential; but if action results in depriving other roads of their traffic, it will not be continued on the same scale." The Southern Railway and Steamship Association followed Fink's example for its region. However, concurrence of the roads west of the Mississippi did not come. There, at least six regional associations attempted to set rate differentials and allocate traffic flows. In that area too, where the pressures for competitive construction were the greatest, a number of roads were unwilling to rely on others to supply them with a steady flow of through traffic.

To help bring peace in the West, Morgan in late 1889 invited key participants to a series of conferences in his New York City home. In attendance were the presidents of all railroads west of Chicago and St. Louis (except the Chicago & Alton, the Southern Pacific, and the Illinois Central); senior partners of the Morgan houses, Brown Brothers & Co., Kidder, Peabody & Co., and Baring Brothers & Co.; and *ex officio* the presidents of the eastern trunkline railroads.

The results included the creation of the Western Freight Association to consolidate three former associations between the Missouri River, Chicago, and Omaha and its combination with the South-Western Railway & Steamship Association, the Trans-Missouri Association, and the Trans-Continental Association into the federated Interstate Railway Association.

This association (later called the Western Traffic Association) bound the western railroad presidents to "strict enforcement of the Interstate Commerce Act of the maintenance of reasonable rates, [and] the principle of arbitration." There was to be a democratic board of managers, which would arbitrate rate conflicts, would allocate traffic, and audit the books of constituents to insure compliance.

Any violations of the Interstate Commerce Act would be promptly reported to federal authorities and any violations of Association rules would incur a fine of $250.

In addition, at the first conference Morgan pledged his word to clamp down on competitive construction. During the discussion President Roberts of the Pennsylvania complained that overbuilding for competitive reasons could be curtailed only if the investment bankers refused to finance such extensions. Morgan replied, "in behalf of the houses represented here," that if the executive committee of the proposed regional association were able to enforce its decisions, these bankers were "prepared to say that they will not negotiate, and will do all in their power to prevent the negotiation, of any securities for the construction of parallel lines, or the extension of lines not unanimously approved by such an executive committee."

Morgan, elated by the success of his efforts, said in a rare statement to the press:

> I am thoroughly satisfied with the results accomplished. The public has not yet appreciated the magnitude of the work. Think of it—all the competitive traffic of the roads west of Chicago and St. Louis placed in the control of about thirty men! It is the most important agreement made by the railroads in a long time, and it is as strong as could be desired.

Nevertheless, several roads—notably the Illinois Central and the Chicago, Burlington and Quincy—declined membership. The arbitration and auditing committees of this and other regional associations were unable to cope with the volume of cases. Throughout the country rate cutting continued, though less openly and vigorously than before. Then in 1897, the federal courts declared all "traffic associations" violations of the Sherman Antitrust Act passed in 1890, and the Western Traffic, the Eastern Trunk Line, and the other associations all closed down permanently.

By the early 1890s, well before the courts' decisions, Morgan had, as most railroad men had done earlier, lost his faith in the formal associations to maintain rates. He agreed that consolidation made more sense than combination, even though the building of consolidated systems in the late 1880s and 1890s was leading to the massive bankruptcies of the mid-1890s. In 1894, for example, the Interstate Commerce Commission reported that over 40,000 miles of road with a capitalization of $2,500 million were in receivership. Morgan now hoped to go one step further beyond consolidation by developing what came to be called "communities of interests" between the new consolidated systems. He used his position as the nation's foremost railroad reorganizer to encourage the creation of such regional alliances.

Morgan's reputation as a railroad reorganizer began in the late 1880s. His firm's first major reorganization, that of the Philadelphia & Reading, came in 1886 and was followed quickly by the reconstruction of the Baltimore & Ohio and the Chesapeake & Ohio. With the onslaught of the depression of the 1890s, the

Morgan firm began a series of reorganizations. The first was that of the roads which became the Southern system. Next Morgan made the notorious Erie financially viable for the first time in 40 years. Then came a second reorganization of the Reading and with it one of the Lehigh Valley. (After the Morgan firm had relinquished control of the Reading following its first reorganization, that road had gone on an expansion binge, which in three years returned it to receivership, thus fully convincing Morgan of the need to maintain control after the completion of a financial reorganization.) Late in 1895, he began working closely with James J. Hill on the refinancing of the Northern Pacific and also on a further reorganization of the Baltimore and Ohio. At this same time the house of Morgan was also involved in the reorganization of the Santa Fe.

In the mid-1890s, Coster, Stetson and Coster's successor, Steele, the railroad specialists among the Morgan partners, perfected the pattern of the firm's railroad reorganizations. It was (1) to raise cash to fund the floating debt and to provide working capital by assessments upon the stockholders (offering warrants on new securities in exchange), by selective liquidation of quick assets, and by the sale of new securities; (2) fixed charges were realigned through exchange of new securities for old; (3) the capitalization and fixed charges of the new corporation were predicated upon its estimated minimum earning capacity; (4) reserves and new securities were programmed to fund future expenses and expansion; (5) a voting trust was created.

These reorganizations were managed by a committee, usually headed by Coster, which drew plans and met expenses until a voting trust could be established. While Morgan and his associates did not invent the voting trust, they were its prime exponents, and as Stuart Dagget has stated, its use increased "in direct relation to the seriousness of the difficulties experienced and to the vividness with which the need for stability was felt."

Voting trust members were appointed by the reorganization committee and vested with full corporate authority by the stockholders. The incidence and tenure of the major railroad voting trusts controlled by Morgan were as follows:

| Railroad | Contractual Tenure | Actual Tenure |
| --- | --- | --- |
| Philadelphia & Reading | 5 years | 5 years (1888–1893) |
| Chesapeake & Ohio | 5 years | 5 years (1889–1894) |
| Richmond Terminal | 5 years or until one dividend of 4% on preferred | 1 year (1893–1894) |
| Southern | same | 20 years (1894–1914) |
| Erie | 5 years or until one dividend of 4% on preferred | 9 years (1895–1904) |
| Reading | 5 years or until two dividends of 4% on preferred | 8 years (1896–1904) |
| Northern Pacific | 5 years | 5 years (1896–1901) |
| Chicago Railways | 5 years | 5 years (1908–1912) |
| Chicago, Great Western | 5 years | 5 years (1909–1914) |

In addition to its control of the reorganization committee and the voting trust, the Morgan firm managed all underwriting, subscription, or loan syndicates demanded by the reorganization. It underwrote all assessments on the stockholders, acted as depository and transfer agent for all securities exchanged, subscribed for all additional securities sold to fund the floating or fixed debts, and met expenses and guaranteed coupon payments on maturing bonds during the course of reorganization.

For loans, the Morgan firm charged 5 percent to 6 percent; as depository and transfer agent, it usually received 0.25 percent commission on the par value of all securities handled; as syndicate manager, it usually received 0.25 percent to 1 percent commission on sales as well as its profit margin on resale; and in addition, it often received cash or blocks of stock in the new corporation for general services rendered, for example, $500,000 in the case of the Erie, $100,000 cash and $750,000 common from the Richmond Terminal.

Some of the results of Morgan's major reorganizations of railroads during the period 1893–1898 are given in Table 2.

In the late 1890s, Morgan used his influence over the roads he financed to rebuild regional "communities of interest." One of the first was in the anthracite coal area of Pennsylvania. As his firm controlled the Reading, the Lehigh Valley, and the Erie and had close connections with the New York Central, which dominated the Delaware and Hudson, and the Lackawanna, Morgan in fact controlled the operations of all the major roads carrying anthracite. He was now able to set price and production schedules far more effectively than had been done through the gentlemen's agreements which he had effected a decade earlier. In 1899, Morgan expanded this community to include other eastern roads. He arranged for the New York Central to invest in the Lehigh Valley, the Erie, and the Lackawanna, while the Pennsylvania purchased blocks of stock in the Baltimore & Ohio, the Chesapeake & Ohio, and the Norfolk & Western; and the Baltimore & Ohio bought into the Reading. In these same years E. H. Harriman and James J. Hill were creating comparable communities of interest in the West. Then in 1901, Morgan arranged to form the Northern Securities Company, which brought the major Hill and Harriman lines—the Great Northern, the Northern Pacific, and the Burlington—under the control of a single holding company.

Although the Supreme Court dissolved the Northern Securities Company in 1904, large systems allied through communities of interest continued to dominate American railroad transportation. By 1906, when the passage of the Hepburn Act gave the Interstate Commerce Commission much stronger powers to set rates, two thirds of American railroad mileage was operated under the surveillance of seven groups: the Vanderbilt roads including the Chicago and Northwestern (22,500 miles); the Pennsylvania group including B&O and the C&O (20,000 miles); the Morgan roads including the Erie, the Reading and other coal roads as well as the southern and allied roads in the South, and the New Haven (which Morgan had financed in the 1890s) totaling just under 20,000 miles; the Gould roads in the Southwest (17,000 miles); the Rock Island group, which came to include the Santa Fe (15,000 miles); the Hill systems (21,000 miles); and the Harriman roads (25,000 miles). The power of the house of Morgan in American rail-

**TABLE 2**

Selected Results of Morgan Railroad Reorganization, 1893–1898

Fixed Charges

| Road | Before | After | *Charges to Income* | *Charges per Mile* | *Total* |
|------|--------|-------|-----------|-----------|-------|
| | | | *Per Cent Decreases* | | |
| Erie | $ 8,637,700 | $8,126,283 | 16.4 | 7.0 | 5.9 |
| Northern Pacific | 13,813,945 | 6,761,960 | 53.0 | 43.0 | 51.0 |
| Reading | 11,422,054 | 9,043,944 | 26.2 | 32.9 | 20.8 |
| Richmond Terminal | 7,498,584 | 4,195,925 | 22.4 | 37.7 | 44.0 |

Types of Securities (%)

| | Before | | | | After | | | |
|------|-------|-----------|--------|-------|-------|-----------|--------|-------|
| Road | Bonds | *Preferred Stock* | *Common Stock* | *Total* | Bonds | *Preferred Stock* | *Common Stock* | *Total* |
| Erie | 58.4 | 4.1 | 37.4 | 100 | 59.0 | 22.1 | 48.1 | 129.2 |
| Northern Pacific | 61.0 | 16.5 | 22.4 | 100 | 71.3 | 34.2 | 36.5 | 142.0 |
| Reading | 80.3 | 0.0 | 19.6 | 100 | 61.2 | 33.2 | 33.2 | 127.6 |
| Southern | 52.2 | 8.8 | 38.6 | 100 | 43.8 | 23.5 | 59.8 | 127.1 |

Aggregate Value of Securities

| Road | *Lowest Quotation of Month 1 Year before Failure* | *Lowest Quotation of Month 1 Year after Reorganization* | *Lowest Quotation December 1906* |
|------|------|------|------|
| Erie | $ 67,190,748 | $ 38,895,077 | $ 82,230,457 |
| Northern Pacific | 157,555,214 | 135,507,699 | 289,557,415 |
| Reading | 88,940,250 | 71,607,223 | 179,190,107 |
| Southern | 45,653,414 | 35,231,356 | 71,411,937 |

roading is emphasized by the fact that besides heading one of the largest groups, it had a prominent influence on the affairs of three of the six others, the Vanderbilt, the Pennsylvania, and the Hill systems.

After 1900, Morgan's continuing interest in railroading lay primarily in rationalizing and occasionally expanding systems in which the firm was already involved, although it did handle a couple of other large reorganizations. In this period, too, the firm made its only major blunder in railroad finance when it gave Charles Mellen of the New Haven, Morgan's handpicked president, a free hand to buy competing interurban trolley and coastal steamship lines. Mellen's extravagant expenditures forced the New Haven into receivership in 1915 two years after Morgan's death.

## Morgan and Industrial Finance

Morgan paid little attention to the financing of industrial enterprises until the 1890s and only seriously moved into industrials at the very end of the decade. His firm did take part earlier in the financing of other transportation ventures besides railroads. In 1878–1879, he subscribed for and marketed the original securities of his friend James Scrymser's Mexican Telegraph Co. In 1880, with J. & W. Seligman & Co. and Winslow, Lanier & Co., Drexel, Morgan & Co. acted as American subscription agents in the worldwide flotation of the 295 million franc stock issue of the French Universal Inter-Oceanic Canal Co. (in Panama). Morgan's firm also attempted, unsuccessfully, in 1902 to form a large steamship combine, the International Mercantile Marine.

After 1900, the house of Morgan became increasingly involved in industrials. For example, it organized and underwrote 145,000 shares preferred and 72,500 shares common of American Bridge, organized under a five-year voting trust and loaned $850,000 working capital to Harper & Brothers, subscribed for 50,000 shares preferred of Associated Merchants Co., underwrote with Kidder, Peabody & Co. the formation of the Hartford Carpet Corp., managed a subscription syndicate for $7 million in notes of the Virginia-Carolina Chemical Co., and reorganized under a 20-year voting trust and subscribed for $5 million in notes of William Cramp & Son's Ship and Engine Building Co.

After 1907, J. P. Morgan & Co. also managed a subscription of $8 million in bonds of United States Rubber Co., purchased 100,000 shares preferred and 22,500 shares common of United Dry Goods Co., took $400,000 of $12 million in issues of American Agricultural Chemical Co., $100,000 of a $4 million issue of Cudahy Packing Co. and some portion of a $4,250,000 issue of United Fruit Co. (all managed by Lee, Higginson & Co.), and subscribed for $1,750,000 in notes of United States Motor Co.

These are only a sampling of the firm's rapidly growing business in industrial securities. It became best known, however, for its roles in the organization of five firms: General Electric, American Telephone and Telegraph, Federal Steel, United States Steel, and International Harvester.

In the case of General Electric, Morgan was a long-time friend of Edison. His partners, Fabbri, Bowdoin, Coster, and Wright, had invested in Edison's original patent company (Edison Electric Co., 1878), in the Edison Electric Illuminating Co. of New York, and in their combination as the Edison Electric Light Co. Morgan was fascinated by Edison, installed electric lights in his home, his office, his church, and his yacht, and was drawn into Edison's firms as an investor. Coster and the other Morgan partners and Henry Villard reorganized the inventor's properties again in 1889 as the Edison General Electric Co. At least half of the relevant underwriting and subscriptions to securities were managed by Drexel, Morgan & Co.

Again in 1891, the Morgan firm participated in the merger of the Edison companies with those of Thomson-Houston, and Morgan and Coster joined the board of the new General Electric Co.

The Morgan firm played an influential role in the development of AT&T without ever participating in a formal reorganization of the company. AT&T, originally the long-distance division of the Boston-based Bell System, had been reorganized in December 1899 as a holding company for all the Bell companies. Expiration of the Bell patents in 1893–1894 had encouraged competing telephone systems. Barred by its Massachusetts charter from expanding its capital to absorb its rivals, AT&T reorganized as a New York corporation and proceeded to acquire the Boston & New York and Erie Telephone & Telegraph companies. The Erie company was in the hands of Thomas J. Coolidge, chairman of Boston's Old Colony Trust Company and a close friend of Morgan's. With his help, AT&T gained complete control over Erie; two months later a block of 50,000 shares of AT&T was sold to George F. Baker and associates on the condition that Baker and John Waterbury of Manhattan Trust Company be elected to the board. These 50,000 shares apparently went into the hands of Baker, Coolidge, Morgan, and Waterbury and mark the beginning of Morgan's direct interest in the firm.

The need of AT&T for fresh capital and the still fragmented nature of the telephone and telegraph industry made for close connections between the company and the bankers. In 1904, Bostonians still dominated the board, and AT&T sold a $20 million bond issue under competitive bidding to Lee, Higginson & Co. and Speyer & Co. This represented the last AT&T bond issue under the competitive bidding system. In 1905, Waterbury proposed a plan to sell $85 million in convertible bonds with an option for $50 million more. The New Englanders on the board opposed the plan but postponed consideration of any alternative. The following year a blanket proposal for issuing $150 million in convertible bonds at the management's discretion was passed despite the protests of many stockholders. Although several firms, including Lee, Higginson, expressed keen interest in the issue, the entire lot was sold without competitive bids to syndicates headed by Morgan & Co. in February 1906 and November 1908.

Morgan & Co. remained active in AT&T finance, particularly in its financing of subsidiary companies: it managed a syndicate subscription of $25 million in notes of the parent, participated in Lee, Higginson & Co.'s subscription of a $5 million issue of Chicago Telephone Co. and of a $6,250,000 issue of Western Electric Co., and took $3,750,000 in Kidder, Peabody & Co.'s subscriptions of $37,500,000 of New York Telephone Co. securities.

The creation of Federal Steel in 1898–1899 sprang from the bitter competition of the steel industry and the pressure exerted on the smaller companies by the Carnegie interests. The objective was to merge several complementary firms— Minnesota Iron Company, the Elgin, Joliet & Eastern Railroad, Illinois Steel Company, and the Lorain Steel Companies of Ohio and Pennsylvania—into one integrated company that could compete with Carnegie more effectively. John Gates, president of Illinois Steel, had tried unsuccessfully to get Morgan to underwrite a proposed merger of wire and nail manufacturers in 1897. The new plan was shaped and organized by Elbert H. Gary, a well-known Chicago corporation lawyer. After perfecting his plan, Gary went to persuade Morgan to underwrite the merger and increase the capital on hand from $10 million to $14 million, part of which would be used to buy the Lorain companies.

Up to this point, Morgan's only interest had been protecting some of his clients' interests in Minnesota Iron. Now, impressed with both Gary and his plan, he agreed to head a syndicate for the needed capital and had the component properties evaluated. The Morgan firm then purchased the three constituent companies and sold them to the newly created holding company, Federal Steel. In effect, Morgan exchanged $100 million in Federal Steel securities for properties with a combined book value of $77 million and cash on hand of $10 million. For the $4,823,373 in cash it provided during the organization, the Morgan syndicate received stock with a total value of $14,123,557 or about 14 percent of Federal's capital stock. Though Gary emphatically denied that the stock had been watered, the Industrial Commission's report in 1900 noted that:

> There can be no doubt that the large amount of stock issued by the Federal Steel Company considerably exceeded a fair market evaluation of the property back of the stock acquired, plus the new cash capital provided, after allowing for the bonded indebtedness. . . . Altogether, the evidence is strong that a considerable portion of the common stock of the Federal Steel Company represented nothing but "water."

After merger, Federal Steel produced about 15 percent of the steel ingots in the country, but its life proved short. In 1901, it became part of another Morgan merger, the formation of United States Steel.

The United States Steel Corp. was incorporated as a New Jersey holding company on February 25, 1901. Within a week Morgan announced the organization of the Steel Corporation and the formation of a syndicate to underwrite new securities. The circular noted that "the entire Plan of Organization and Management of the United States Steel Corporation shall be determined by J. P. Morgan and Company."

The device employed by U.S. Steel for acquiring ownership of most of the constituent companies was to exchange its shares for shares in the subsidiaries. By April 2, 1901, the Steel Corporation had obtained 98 percent of the stock of eight companies: Carnegie Company, Federal Steel Company, National Steel Company, American Steel & Wire Company, American Sheet Steel Company, American Steel Hoop Company, American Tin Plate Company, and National Tube Company. During the remainder of 1901, "Big Steel" also acquired the American Bridge Company, Shelby Steel Tube Company, and Lake Superior Consolidated Iron Mines, as well as the one sixth interest in the Oliver Iron Mining Company and the Pittsburgh Steamship Company not already owned by the Carnegie Company.

U.S. Steel's top management acknowledged that on the basis of the original cost of the properties, the $1,402,846,817 of securities that they issued was excessive. In 1911, the Bureau of Corporations calculated the extent of the overcapitalization. It concluded that the estimated value of the tangible assets acquired by the Steel Corporation amounted to $676 million; the value of the property, tangible and intangible, as measured by the market prices of the securities of all the constituent companies, added up to $793 million.

In explaining the heroic size of the security issues, John Moody, a contemporary student of Wall Street, largely exonerated the promoters. Morgan, Moody stated, "was really the victim of. . .Carnegie" who "held the reins. . .and named the price." The banker accepted the steelman's terms without a quibble. As a biographer has commented: "With. . .Morgan it was not a question of bargaining and saving money when companies were purchased, so much as the elimination of disturbing personalities." The acquisition of the Carnegie interest was the key to the entire merger, and Morgan much preferred to have Carnegie restricted to the sidelines as a creditor rather than as a competitor or as a large and powerful stockholder. Similarly, when Morgan became aware of the importance of acquiring Rockefeller's Lake Superior Consolidated Ore Mines, he paid what some associates considered a prohibitive price. Morgan's reported response to criticism regarding the purchase was the query: "In a business proposition as great as this would you let the matter of $5 million stand in the way of success?"

Morgan & Co.'s syndicate cleared $50 million or a 200 percent return on the amount of funds administered or advanced during this merger. The Morgan firm itself received an additional $12,500,000 in fees. In return, it had created a company which controlled 65.7 percent of steel ingots and castings, 59.8 percent of steel rails, 64.6 percent of plates and sheets, 77.6 percent of wire rods, and 73.0 percent of tin and terne plates. Earnings after interest totaled $61,807,993 for the last nine months of 1901 and $90,306,525 for 1902.

The formation of International Harvester involved the leading firms in the fiercely competitive farm machinery industry. Both McCormick and Deering were family dominated and bitterly distrustful. Increasing costs of raw materials and growing distribution problems suggested merger, but three attempts during 1891–1901 failed because of friction between the two families. In their search for compromise, the McCormicks were directed by their attorney (and Morgan's), Francis Lynde Stetson, to George W. Perkins. Perkins took an immediate interest in the case and gradually drew the somewhat naive McCormicks into his confidence. Since Morgan was abroad at the time, Perkins cabled him for permission to take on the assignment. Morgan expressed some doubt that the firm should become involved. In the end he relied upon Perkins's judgment and approved the final product.

Originally the McCormicks did not want to involve Morgan & Co. financially for several reasons: They needed no outside capital; they strongly opposed any stock watering of the new company; and they feared losing control of the company to Morgan. Gradually Perkins convinced them that Morgan & Co. could serve as a balance of power in the new company to arbitrate differences between the McCormicks and Deerings. This reasoning, together with the growing fear that the Deerings might somehow gain control of the new company, induced the McCormicks to let Perkins take charge. Perkins described his success to Morgan in a letter of July 11, 1902:

> The Deerings are here, the McCormicks are here, the Plano people are here, and we are right down to business, trying to work up a plan by which these concerns can be put together. Already they have agreed that we shall form the new company; that we shall name all the officers and the board of directors; that friends of ours shall constitute a majority of the board of directors without anybody having the right to question any of these matters. This has been a rather delicate thing to bring about.

The final plan formed the International Harvester Company with a capital of $120 million in 6 percent preferred stock deposited in a voting trust until January 1904, when it was divided on the following percentage basis: McCormicks 42.6, Deerings 34.4, Plano 5.2, Champion 3.7, and Morgan 14.0. About 15 percent of this stock was estimated as water: $750,000 was allowed Morgan against his appraisal, legal, and organizational expenses; $3 million was allowed him as a bonus and did not represent any property conveyed or expenses incurred; and the remaining $14 million arose in the overappraisal of tangible property, patents, and good will.

Perkins's view of his firm's role was explicit: "Morgan & Co. would not think of combating the united judgment of McCormick and Deering, but would expect to settle controversies between them. In that sense we would be a third party or the controlling spirit of the new company." Of the 18 directors, five represented the McCormicks, five the Deerings, three the legal advisors for both families, four the banking interests, and the remaining one the required legal resident of New Jersey. Line officers were more or less evenly divided between the families, which resulted in continued friction that threatened to break up the company. In 1906, Perkins and Elbert H. Gary (the Deerings's legal counsel and sometime Morgan attorney) brought about a new compromise that in effect retired the family managers and by 1908 transformed the company into a public corporation listed on the New York Stock Exchange.

# The Height of Morgan's Career, 1900–1913

From 1902 to 1912, J. P. Morgan & Co. was directly responsible for the marketing of interstate corporate issues totaling almost $2 billion. Besides its work in reorganizations and in underwriting and wholesaling securities, it also carried on a large commercial banking business. Some idea of the extent of that business may be gathered from the fact that on November 1, 1912, the New York house had the accounts of over a hundred corporations and had aggregate deposits of $162,491,819.65. Like other banks (and at the same rate), it paid interest on those deposits and was a considerable lender on the stock exchange, keeping a portion of its quick reserves in call loans.

Perhaps the most striking development in Morgan's influence after 1900 was his cooperation with other financial intermediaries. He had been a friend of George F. Baker, president of the First National Bank of New York, and of James Stillman, president and chairman of the National City Bank, since the 1870s and invested in those banks' stocks and sat on their boards. In 1909, Morgan, Baker, and Stillman also purchased a majority stock interest in the Equitable Life Assurance Society. It was this group which formed the Bankers Trust Co. in 1903 and the Guaranty Trust Co. in 1910.

Two emergencies illustrate Morgan's financial strength. Because of his control of coal railroads, he was looked upon as the head of the anthracite industry at the time of the great strike of 1902, though he assented to arbitration after President Roosevelt threatened government operation of the mines. And it was Morgan to whom the banking community of New York looked for leadership during the money panic of 1907. He thoroughly investigated the situation and organized the lending of $18,945,000 by solvent banks to relieve pressure on those institutions endangered.

Like most businessmen of his generation, Morgan considered business simply as private enterprise. His firm's reorganization plans were marvels of bank financial disclosure, but he was slow in acknowledging any need of informing the public about the work of corporations. In 1901, however, he did support the auditing firm of Price, Waterhouse & Company in the contention that consolidated balance sheets should be reported (U.S. Steel was the first firm in America to use this device) and that there should be publication of quarterly statements of earnings and tonnage of United States Steel (considered a doubtful innovation of the time).

Morgan also felt the force of public opposition when he had to testify in the Money Trust Investigation in December 1912. It may have been this experience which led him to say shortly before he died that "American business must henceforth be done in glass pockets." Before the full implications of the investigation were seen, however, Morgan was gone. He died in Rome on March 31, 1913.

# The Money Trust Investigation

The popular fear and criticism of the power of the bankers, which arose early in the century, led to an investigation by the committee on banking and currency, headed by Arsene Pujo, in the House of Representatives in 1912–13. Though there is a difference of opinion as to the validity of some of the conclusions drawn from the findings as published in the reports of the committee, there is no question that the published records of the investigation constitute the most comprehensive source of information on American finance which we have for that time.

From an elaborate table showing the affiliations of 18 leading bankers and banking houses, the report drew the following summaries about various groups.

The table shows that J. P. Morgan & Co., the First National Bank, the National City Bank, the Guaranty Trust Co., and the Bankers' Trust Co. together have—

One hundred and eighteen directorships in 34 banks and trust companies having total resources of $2,679 million and total deposits of $1,983 million.

Thirty directorships in 10 insurance companies having total assets of $2,293 million.

One hundred and five directorships in 32 transportation systems having a total capitalization of $11,784 million and a total mileage (excluding express companies and steamship lines) of 150,200.

Sixty-three directorships in 24 producing and trading corporations having a total capitalization of $3,339 million.

Twenty-five directorships in 12 public utility corporations having a total capitalization of $2,150 million.

In all, 341 directorships in 112 corporations having aggregate resources or capitalization of $22,245 million.

The following excerpts point to the committee's conclusions about concentration:

> Your committee is satisfied from the proofs submitted, even in the absence of data from the banks, that there is an established and well-defined identity and community of interest between a few leaders of finance, created and held together through stock ownership, interlocking directorates, partnership and joint account transactions, and other forms of domination over banks, trust companies, railroads, and public service and industrial corporations, which has resulted in great and rapidly growing concentration of the control of money and credit in the hands of these few men.

*****

> The parties to this combination or understanding or community of interest, by whatever name it may be called, may be conveniently classified, for the purpose of differentiation, into four separate groups.
>
> First. The first, which for convenience of statement we will call the inner group, consists of J. P. Morgan & Co., the recognized leaders, and George F. Baker and James Stillman in their individual capacities and in their joint administration and control of the First National Bank, the National City Bank, the National Bank of Commerce, the Chase National Bank, the Guaranty Trust Co., and the Bankers Trust Co., with total known resources, in these corporations alone, in excess of $1,300 million and of a number of smaller but important financial institutions. This takes no account of the personal fortunes of these gentlemen.
>
> Second. Closely allied with this inner or primary group, and indeed related to them practically as partners in many of their larger financial enterprises, are the powerful international banking houses of Lee, Higginson & Co. and Kidder, Peabody & Co., with three affiliated banks in Boston—the National Shawmut Bank, the First National Bank, and the Old Colony Trust Co.—having at least more than half of the total resources of all the Boston banks; also with interests and representation in other important New England financial institutions.
>
> Third. In New York City the international banking house of Messrs. Kuhn, Loeb & Co., with its large foreign clientele and connections, whilst only qualifiedly allied with the inner group, and only in isolated transactions, yet through its close relations with the National City Bank and the National Bank of Commerce and other financial institutions with which it has recently allied itself has many interests in common, conducting large joint account transactions with them, especially in recent years, and having what virtually amounts to an understanding not to compete, which is defended as a principle of "banking ethics." Together they have with a few exceptions preempted the banking business of the important railways of the country.

*****

> No railroad system or industrial corporation for which either of the houses named has acted as banker could shift its business from one to another. Where one has made an issue of securities for a corporation the other will not bid for subsequent issues of the same corporation. Their frequent and extensive relations in the joint issues of securities has made such a *modus vivendi* inevitable.
>
> This inner group and allies thus have no effective competition, either from others or amongst themselves for these large security issues and are accordingly free to exact their own terms in most cases. Your committee has no evidence that this power is being used oppressively and no means of ascertaining the facts so long as their profits are undisclosed.

The following are selections from the response of J. P. Morgan & Co.:

We ventured to point out to you that such "concentration" as has taken place in New York and other financial centres has been due, not to the purposes and activities of men, but primarily to the operation of our antiquated banking system which automatically compels interior banks to "concentrate" in New York City hundreds of millions of reserve funds; and next, to economic laws which in every country create some one city as the great financial center.

*****

In these tables it is shown that 180 bankers and bank directors serve upon the boards of corporations having resources aggregating 25 billion dollars, and it is implied that this vast aggregate of the country's wealth is at the disposal of these 180 men. But such an implication rests solely upon the untenable theory that these men, living in different parts of the country, in many cases personally unacquainted with each other, and in most cases associated only in occasional transactions, vote always for the same policies and control with united purpose the directorates of the 132 corporations on which they serve. The testimony failed to establish any concerted policy or harmony of action binding these 180 men together, and as a matter of fact no such policy exists. The absurdity of the assumption of such control becomes more apparent when one considers that on the average these directors represent only one quarter of the memberships of their boards. It is preposterous to suppose that every "interlocking" director has full control in every organization with which he is connected, and that the majority of directors who are not "interlocking" are mere figureheads, subject to the will of a small minority of their boards.

Perhaps the greatest harm in the presentation referred to lay in the further unwarranted inference, to which has been given wide publicity, that the vast sum of $25 billion, was in cash or liquid form, subject to the selfish use or abuse of individuals.

*****

These mergers, however, are a development due simply to the demand for larger banking facilities to care for the growth of the country's business. As our cities double and triple in size and importance, as railroads extend and industrial plants expand, not only is it natural, but it is necessary that our banking institutions should grow in order to care for the increased demands put upon them. Perhaps it is not known as well as it should be that in New York City the largest banks are far inferior in size to banks in the commercial capitals of other and much smaller countries. The largest bank in New York City today has resources amounting to only three fifths of the resources of the largest bank in England, to only one fourth of the resources of the largest bank in France, and to less than one fifth of the resources of the largest bank in Germany. As the committee is aware, in New York City there are only three banks with resources in excess of $200 million, while there are ten such institutions in London, five in Berlin and four in Paris.

*****

Since 1907 cooperation has been more active by reason of the lesson which banks in all large cities then learned that, for self-preservation, they could not—as is possible in other countries—rely upon a strong and elastic banking system, but must gain such protection by concurrent action; and second, that such cooperation is simply a further result of the necessity for handling great transactions. . .if transactions of such magnitude are to be carried on, the country obviously requires not only the larger individual banks, but demands also that those banks shall cooperate to perform efficiently the country's business.

*****

Many questions were asked as to the wisdom in having representatives of private banking houses sit upon the boards of corporations, whose securities the same bankers frequently offer for sale. This practice which has been in vogue abroad, ever since the creation of limited companies, has arisen not from a desire on the part of the banker to manage the daily affairs of the corporation or to purchase its securities more cheaply than he otherwise could; but rather because of his moral responsibility as sponsor for the corporation's securities, to keep an eye upon its policies and to protect the interest of investors in the securities of that corporation. For a private banker to sit upon such a directorate is in most instances a duty, not a privilege.

Perhaps the two most widely quoted defenses, however, came from the testimony of two of Morgan's partners. Relentlessly pursued by congressional investigator Samuel Untermeyer, Henry P. Davison blurted out: "I know J. P. Morgan & Co. could do no wrong if their endeavors and the circumstance permitted them to do as they wanted to do." George W. Perkins put it more dramatically:

If J. Pierpont Morgan should make a bond issue from the desert of Sahara and put his name on it, it would be subscribed probably. . .because he has lived an earnest and tremendously strenuous life in the study of these questions for half a century and the people have bought and bought and bought securities that his name has been put to, and have believed that they came out right.

# CASE 11

 *The Railroad Problem and the Solution**

## The Setting

Railroad mileage in 1865 stood at just over 35,000. The roads had proven their strategic importance during the Civil War, and the war's conclusion found the northern rail system functioning well while that of the South was in a shambles. The North took advantage of the South's absence from Congress to push forward the building of rail lines west. The first Pacific Railway bill became law in the summer of 1862. On May 10, 1869, the Union Pacific met the Central Pacific outside of Ogden, Utah, and the first transcontinental rail route was complete. Railroad construction in the trans-Mississippi West boomed during the remainder of the century. Kansas, Minnesota, and Nebraska, to cite three examples, had no railroad mileage in 1860. By 1900, they had 8,719, 6,934, and 5,685 miles, respectively. Total mileage in the latter year stood at about 193,000 and was to increase by more than one quarter in the next decade and a half.

The impact of the rail network was like nothing the United States had ever seen before or indeed has seen since. In the mid-1870s, an estimated 90 percent of all commerce between the West and the East moved by rail. In 1897, the combined value of railway stocks and bonds was estimated to be $10,635 million. The national debt that year was $1,226,794,000.

*This case was prepared by Assistant Professor Richard S. Tedlow as a basis for class discussion rather than to illustrate either effective or ineffective handling of an administrative situation.

Copyright © 1983 by the President and Fellows of Harvard College.

Harvard Business School case 384-032, rev. 6/84.

Great fortunes were made in railroading during these years, both from the benefits of legitimate operation and through chicanery. Corruption took many forms. Owners could reap handsome profits through the manipulation of construction contracts. Financial manipulation was so common that when Edward H. Harriman, ruler of a 25,000 mile rail system, learned of the conservative balance sheet of the Boston and Maine at the turn of the century—no refunding certificates, no second mortgages, no watered stock—he exclaimed, "Great Scott! Is there anything like that left out doors?"[1]

Railroad customers through manipulation of freight rates often made fortunes as well. Favorable rates for Standard Oil and such large Minneapolis millers as Pillsbury meant bonanzas. At the same time, to get the short end of freight rate negotiations could bring bankruptcy for a business and indeed ruin for a community.

It is no wonder that railroads should become the center of controversy.

## The Farmers Complain

The nation's farmers complained about the railroads both as investors and as consumers of the roads' services. Especially in the sparsely settled Midwest, where access to railroads was essential to commercial agriculture, farmers often encouraged local governments to finance them and even invested in them personally. The results were sometimes disappointing. The farmer's stock often proved to be of little value because of "water"; his taxes were high; his property mortgaged; and his transportation costs still excessive. Sometimes the promised roads were not even completed.

Farmers all over the country were infuriated by long-short haul discriminations. The oddities of railroad economics resulted in rates which seemed to fly in the face of common sense. A tub of butter, to select an example out of literally thousands, could be sent from Elgin, Illinois, to New York City for $0.30 while the same item shipped from some points as near to the city as 165 miles cost two and a half times that amount in freight.

In the late 1860s and 1870s, the Granger movement swept the Prairie States and then spread to farmers throughout the nation. Exhibit 1 well sums up Granger attitudes toward the railroads. With the support of the Grangers, legislation was passed in several states designed to fix railroad rates for passengers, freight, and grain storage in road-owned facilities, to see to it that rates were based solely on distance, and to have these measures explored through the establishment of regulatory commissions.

## The Shippers and Merchants Complain

Shippers both of agricultural commodities and manufactured goods complained as bitterly as farmers about the seemingly willful destruction imposed upon them by the crazy quilt of rates. Cities such as St. Louis and Rochester had major industries blighted by the lower rates available to competitors in other cities. Among

---

[1]John F. Stover, *American Railroads* (Chicago: University of Chicago Press, 1961), p. 147.

manufacturers, Andrew Carnegie was a leader in the fight against the rates of the Pennsylvania Railroad, threatening to build a railroad himself in order to bring about lower rates. Others were injured by and protested against differentials for different classes of freight and/or different directions in which freight was shipped. Obnoxious also were the granting of rebates on published rates, or drawbacks, which rewarded favored shippers with a percentage of the rates charged to their competitors and the making of special rates for favored shippers immediately rescinded after the contract was concluded. In the first six months of 1880, the New York Central entered into more than 6,000 such special contracts. Remarked one historian, "[R]ate cutting was universal. The railroads were one big oriental bazaar, with . . . 50 percent of all traffic between New York and the rest of the country moving at special rates."[2]

Perhaps the most vociferous single group objecting to railroad practices were the merchants of New York City. In order to even out traffic and prevent bankruptcy, the Trunk Line Association, a pool consisting of the four great East-West carriers (the New York Central, the Erie, the Baltimore and Ohio, and the Pennsylvania), established a system of east coast port differentials which allowed freight to be shipped more cheaply to Philadelphia and Baltimore than to New York. Much of Gotham's wealth was rooted in its control of the import/export business, and its merchants howled at this practice:

> The changes which have taken place in the dry goods, grocery, hardware, and other leading trades are enormous and [we are] doing business on unsatisfactory margins . . .New York has a prior claim to this trade [importing and interior jobbing], as it first settled and naturally belongs here. The railroads have no right to break up the jobbing trade of this city, and transfer it to the interior of our own or other states.[3]

A leading advocate of the merchants' interest was lawyer Simon Sterne, whose views are presented in a speech (parts of which are reproduced as Exhibit 2).

## The Railroad Executives Complain

Railroad rates declined steadily from the Civil War to the turn of the century. In July of 1866, the Chicago to New York charge for 100 pounds of wheat was $0.65. In 1897, it was $0.20. Similar sharp declines can be discerned not only on commodities but on higher value per weight classifications as well. Part of this decline was the result of the general deflation of the period, but part of it represented productivity increases passed along to the shipper.

Frequent rate wars plagued the carriers, especially during the sharp depressions beginning in 1873 and 1893. Even in the relatively prosperous 1880s, rate wars drove many a railroad executive to distraction. As one of them remarked:

> The point reached since the beginning of 1884 in the prevailing contagion of depression and loss, from the effects of ruinous rates, which were uncontrollable from a lack

---

[2]Albro Martin, "The Troubled Subject of Railroad Regulation in the Gilded Age—A Reappraisal," *Journal of American History* 61, no. 2 (September 1974) p. 349.

[3]Martin, "Railroad Regulation," p. 356.

of adequate protection of railroad interests in the past, is not to be remedied by waiting upon "the survival of the fittest."[4]

Indeed, it seemed that final phrase was particularly annoying because it described precisely the opposite of what the true result of unbridled railway competition would be. "Railroads," commented the leading trade journal of the period, "unfortunately, seem to reverse the rule of the 'survival of the fittest' to the 'survival of the unfittest'. . . when they go into the hands of receivers, they are to be run so long as operating expenses can be paid."[5]

It was due to railroading's version of Gresham's law that the great pools and associations were set up. Albert Fink was the leading proponent of privately operated pools. Yet, even he was not opposed to the principle of government intervention in rate-related issues. He once suggested a law to Congress which featured provisions, including the following:

> Sec. 3. That all competing railroad companies shall jointly establish a tariff for all competing points.

> Sec. 4. That the tariff so established shall be submitted to a commission of experts appointed by the Federal Government, and if they find that the tariff is just and equitable and based upon correct commercial principles, and not in violation of the common laws governing common carriers, then such tariff shall be approved, and shall become the law of the land, until changed in the same manner by the same authority.

> Sec. 5. In cases where railroad companies cannot agree upon such tariffs, or upon any other questions such as might lead to a war of rates between railroad companies, the questions of disagreement shall be settled by arbitration, the decision of the arbitrator to be enforced in the United States Courts.[6]

The problem with pools, as Fink had discovered, was the extreme difficulty of forcing individual roads to keep their word. To be sure, many rail executives looked upon their companies as private property over which the government had no more right to exercise power than it did over any other type of business. But the majority did appear to believe that action by the federal government to help pooling work was to be encouraged.

## The Government Responds

The distinction of creating the first railroad commission belongs to Rhode Island, which established one in 1839 to oversee safety conditions and facilitate interconnections. Connecticut established a similar commission in 1853, and in 1844, New Hampshire established one to deal with problems of eminent domain. By the Civil War, there were four state railway commissions; four decades later that number had increased to 28.

---

[4]Quoted in Gabriel Kolko, *Railroads and Regulation, 1877–1916* (New York: W.W. Norton, 1970), pp. 38–39.

[5]Quoted in Edward C. Kirkland, *Industry Comes of Age* (Chicago: Quadrangle, 1967), p. 79.

[6]D.T. Gilchrist, "Albert Fink and the Pooling System," *Business History Review* 34, no. 1 (Spring 1960), p. 40.

One approach to regulation which became the model in the Northeast was that of Massachusetts. An 1869 statute established a commission which upon its own initiative or receipt of a petition could investigate railroad practices in general or specific grievances. It could then publicly report its findings and suggest action. Observed the first commission chairman, Charles Francis Adams:

> The law could not have been improved. Had it not been a flagrant legislative guess it would have been an inspiration. The only appeal provided was to publicity. The Board of Commissioners was set up as a sort of lens by means of which the otherwise scattered rays of public opinion could be concentrated to a focus and brought to bear upon a given point. The commissioners had to listen and they might investigate and report; they could do little more.[7]

By contrast, regulation in Illinois began with the declaration in the 1870 constitution that "Railways . . . are hereby declared public highways. . . . And the General Assembly shall from time to time, pass laws establishing reasonable maximum rates of charges for the transportation of passengers and freight on the different railroads of this state. . . ." A regulatory act was then passed that set these rates and a board of commissioners established to enforce the legislation and penalize infractions. Many midwestern and southern states adopted this model.

Through the 1870s and 1880s, the adequacy of state regulation was strongly questioned. Objections were raised on many grounds: the commissions were too expensive, too friendly to the railroads, too unfriendly to the railroads, less efficacious than the courts, able to affect only local and not interstate rates, and so forth. Sentiment for national action was growing.

After two decades of petitions and investigation, the Interstate Commerce Act was finally passed. The text of the act is reproduced as Exhibit 3.

## EXHIBIT 1

### *Resolutions of the Second Annual National Congress—a Mid-Western Agrarian Conclave—Indianapolis, 1873*

By committee on the Railway System—Whereas, we recognize the railways of the country as an effectual means of developing its agricultural resources, and as having an interest, common and inseparable, with the country through which they pass; and, whereas, we have in times past fostered and aided them by liberal charters and concessions, made by public and private parties, and still desire to encourage further development of the railway system; therefore,

*Resolved* that a fair degree of reciprocity would suggest that corporations having a common interest and public aid, should, in their turn endeavor to subserve the in-

---

[7]Kirkland, *Industry*, p. 119.

Source: Alfred D. Chandler, Jr., *The Railroads* (New York: Harcourt Brace Jovanovich, 1965), pp. 188–89.

## EXHIBIT 1 (*continued*)

terest of the country through which they pass, by charging fair rates of freights, and by the equitable and just treatment of all localities along their lines.

*Resolved* that, on the contrary, railroad corporations in many instances have been exorbitant in their charges, have discriminated unjustly between localities, and have failed to respond to the generous grants of powers and moneys that have been given them by our national and state governments.

*Resolved* that the system adopted and now practiced in the building of railroads, viz: the soliciting of stock subscriptions from individuals, corporations, and counties, and after receiving these subsidies to depress the value of said stock by forcing it upon the market and depreciating its value to such an extent as to enable a few speculators to secure control of the road, thereby depriving those who aid in its construction of all voice in its management; increasing the cost four or five times above the amount it would have cost if those managing it in the outset had had the foresight to have the funds on hand at the start to build and equip said road; then requiring the producer and shipper to pay dividends upon the fictitious cost by charging excessive freight and passenger tariffs—operates most injuriously to the best interests of the farming class, and calls loudly for reform and restraint by adequate legislation.

*Resolved* that we recommend all farmers to withhold their voices and their aid from railway corporations, unless it be fully conceded and agreed that corporations so aided are subject to regulation by the power incorporating them, and will not, after receiving the advantages conferred by the public authority, claim the immunities of a private corporation.

*Resolved* that we endorse and will support the doctrine promulgated by some of our courts, that a railway corporation in receiving and exercising the state's right of eminent domain, and receiving aid raised by taxation from public authorities has thereby accepted and admitted itself to be a corporation with a public function, and subject to the power from which it has received its charter, in the limitation of its rates.

*Resolved* that a railway being practically a monopoly, controlling the transportation of nearly all the country through which it passes; and that as competition, except as a few points, cannot be relied upon to fix rates, therefore it becomes the duty of the state to fix reasonable maximum rates, affording a fair remuneration to the transporter, and without being an onerous charge to the producer and consumer.

*Resolved* that, inasmuch as Belgium has succeeded in regulating the rates upon railways by government lines, we ask an investigation of the proposition to control the rates upon existing railways by trunk lines built and controlled by the states authorities and run at fixed uniform and cheap rates.

*Resolved* that the consolidation of parallel lines of railway is contrary to public policy, and should be prohibited by law.

## EXHIBIT 1 (*concluded*)

*Resolved* that wherever a railway corporation owns or controls a line or lines in two or more states, it is the right and duty of the general government to regulate the rates of freight and fare upon such lines, under the constitutional power to regulate commerce between the states.

*Resolved* that we commend the thorough organization of the farmers of the country in local, county, and state organizations, for the purpose of reforming the great abuses and dealing out equal and exact justice to all men.

## EXHIBIT 2

### Simon Sterne, "An Address on Interstate Railway Traffic," Delivered to the National Board of Trade in Washington, D.C. (1879)

Why is it that we have a railway problem upon our hands while we have not a breadstuff problem, a petroleum problem, nor, indeed, a problem in reference to any other occupation or private enterprise? The answer is, that we have from the very outset, from the time the railway system took its origin in this country and in England, misunderstood as a people the bearing, the power, and the consequences of giving a public highway into private hands; and we did not suppose— and very naturally we did not suppose—that in granting railway franchises we were in reality not only giving a public highway into private hands but also the exclusive transportation over it. We had nothing to guide us. There had been nothing like it in the history of the world; and it was for the first time that the owner of a road became sole transporter over that road, because all other highways had been built, whether by government or in part by government, and in part or wholly by private enterprise, were built simply for the ownership and control of the highway; and the vehicles that travelled thereon, belonged to private owners and became subjects of private competition, to transport the goods over the highways, so that the analogy of the turnpike did not help us, because the turnpike was simply the ownership of the road, while the goods that were transported over the turnpike went over it in private wagons or vehicles over which the turnpike company had no control except to fix uniform tolls for the use of the road only.

The analogy of the canal gave us no light, because there again the canal company, when it was in private hands, became simply the owner of a canal, while the boats that passed through the canal were provided and propelled by private enterprise, remained private property, and were entirely separate from the canal company. So we, in utter ignorance of the consequences of chartering corporations which would at the same time be the sole transporters over the road, legislated upon the basis or plan as if private carriages could go over the new road, and that

## EXHIBIT 2 (*continued*)

heavy freights never, by any possibility, would be carried over it. You will find, Mr. President, in all the early railroad charters in this country, and in England, provisions incorporated by which the right of a citizen to put his private carriage upon the new roadway was secured, on payment of certain tolls; and you will also find, by a report made in 1833 by four of the then leading engineers in the State of New York to the Legislature of the State, in answer to an inquiry in reference to the future development of this form of highways, these engineers substantially said that they would be exceedingly useful for the carrying of passengers over level plains, but that for the purpose of carrying freight they were not at all to be considered in comparison with the waterways, and that there was, therefore, no necessity for fixing any limit in regard to freight charges which would never be made. It is not to be wondered at, therefore, that our legislators went wrong, and our people went wrong, and that we have now upon our hands a railway problem of the first magnitude. . . .

That the condition of things was not provided against is the fault of our people and our legislation—a fault which is easily explainable by the misapprehension already referred to—that we had nothing to guide us. Our ignorance was, therefore, very naturally taken advantage of by strong and intelligent men, who went into railroading as a business, in which to make as much money as they could, paying no more attention to the public than any man who goes into a private business; and, therefore, the railroad man is not to be blamed for making whatever he could out of his investments. Consequences to the public of the most serious and grave character have flowed from this, and have become aggravated to a degree no longer to be borne; but in legislating upon the subject we must bear in mind that we must be just to the citizens who have, through our own neglect, invested their moneys in these great enterprises upon a different theory than that which will hereafter prevail, and done so at our invitation as a people, to regard it exclusively as a matter of private enterprise. Therefore, the legislation that we want in the first instance is of the most conservative character, because we should avoid the bringing about of any condition of affairs which will permit private interests to say with justice to the public: "We were invited to enter into this business and put our money into it as a private enterprise, and you now put the whole burden upon our shoulders and take the whole benefit to *yourself*. We shall put no more money into enterprises which are subjected to that kind of control." Such was the consequence of some of the Western legislation which decided to embody a hard and fast tariff in the bills creating a board of railroad commissioners, and which attempted to apply the strict rule of a *pro rata* freight toll for the shorter, compared with the longer distance. Now I believe that the adoption of provisions in any bill which would, in the first place, put into the law a hard and fast tariff, not to be changed under any circumstances until the law-makers could again convene and be persuaded, or which would directly apply a *pro rata* freight schedule, without the slightest regard to terminal advantages, or without the slightest regard either to gradients or superior facilities between railroads, or any dangerous legislation, not only to the interests affected, but to the people at large, because it would work so badly as to cause dis-

# EXHIBIT 2 (*continued*)

trust with it and thereby ensure its repeal, thus putting us back again to a condition worse than we were in at the outset, since it will create a feeling that legislation upon that subject is useless.

The reason why the railway question or the railway problem differs from every other problem, and why railroading can never be considered a private business is this: Competition applies in every case where, for the time being, in the individual instances, the supply is larger than the demand. To explain what I mean by this, I will give an example:

> If I want a hat, although all the hats that are wanted by the people, and all the hats the people want, may counterbalance each other (I mean the supply and demand be about equal); yet to each individual man who wants a hat there are practically a million more hats offered to him than he wants, and he therefore is perfectly free to choose. A man who wants a railroad train, or fifty men who want a railroad train from any one point to a given point, have not a million railroad trains to choose from. They generally have but one, which leaves at a stated period of time, and they must take that or none; and, therefore, the supply in that case is the very reverse of what it is in the instance of the demand for a hat. For in the case of the railroad there is but one to supply the want, and a million who want that particular service. In addition to that fact, in almost every other business the conditions are absolutely different. In every private business, the moment that excessive profits can be made, a very limited supply of additional capital drawn from other occupations would tend to create a competition. In a railroad you never can create competition without attempting to raise a sum of money so large as to make it a very serious question whether or not it can be raised, if a railroad to supply such a demand is already in existence; and then, when you have two or three, or even four or five, railroads from any point to another given point, they never can be so multiplied but that the presidents of such railroads can get around a single table and determine upon either a pool or a combination which will fix a rate of freight from one point to another given point, which will pay an interest on all the capital invested in all the railways, thus imposing a burden in addition to that which had been already imposed by the existing railway, four times as great as would otherwise be necessary, simply because additional railways not demanded by the necessities of the case had been built.

Statistics gathered both in this country and in England, show there is not a single line of railway in the world (except those exclusively passenger railways in dense populations, such as the elevated roads in New York, or the underground railways in London), which is operated to a large percentage of its capacity. For instance, the New York Central Railway or the Pennsylvania road—the two roads operated more than any others in this country—are operated not above 15 percent of the actual capacity of the roads for the carriage of trains with safety. Therefore, quite independent of the fact that the roads exercise the right of eminent domain which gives them a *quasi* public nature, the character of their business is such that we cannot expect competition for any long period of time between them, because combination is easy, and combination is more profitable than competition; and there is not the same freedom on the part of the buyer of the commodity of transportation as there is of the seller; consequently, the condition of freedom which lies at the very basis of competition does not exist; and, therefore, quite independently

## EXHIBIT 2 (*continued*)

of the exercise of the right of eminent domain, and of the correlative duties that flow therefrom, the nature of the business requires regulation to secure the freedom which without regulation the past few years, publicly abandoned even the pretense of competition between themselves, and have cast aside the whole basis of American legislation which proceeded on the principle of competition, and was founded upon that idea. Our free railway acts[8] throughout the States, commencing with the State of New York in 1850, copied in all the States of the Union, were based upon the theory that there would be competition in railway management and railway building, precisely as in all other enterprises in this country, and that that competition would result in the most efficient service at the lowest possible prices to the consumer. By a pooling and arbitrary division of the freights to be carried, and agreement as to rates, the twenty-seven leading railways of this country, combined under the management of Mr. Fink, have made a combination as close as though they had for all practical purposes become amalgamated under one board of control. Each railway company has thereby abandoned not only the right to make individually its own traffic rates, but also the right to carry such freights as may be offered to it; so that if I choose to send a particular package by the Erie Railway Company to a western point, whether it shall go to such a particular by the Erie Railway depends not upon my direction, but upon whether that road has already shipped freight to its allotted amount and reached the maximum, when it must send part of its traffic which comes to it under the pooling arrangement to some other road. Therefore, that important part of the whole railway system of this country which runs east and west from St. Louis to the seashore, is combined under one arrangement, which has resulted in an absolute abandonment of competitive traffic by the railways themselves.

This confronts us with a power as great as, and indeed greater than, any of which we have any record; greater by far than has ever been permitted to exist unchecked and uncontrolled by proper legislation. Our secretary, in his annual report, read yesterday, stated that there are now upwards of 80,000 miles of railway in this country, representing a capital of over \$4,500 million, which when aggregated under one head, or a few heads and practically under one management, represents a power so formidable and so above and beyond the power of legislators, either State or national, as they are now organized, that it will break through and defeat any law which we may see fit to make, unless the people in their turn accumulate power to meet power. The railroad has outgrown all State limits and swept (in so far as the railroads are concerned) out of existence, not only by the leasing of parallel lines and the leasing of lines running in conjunction—lines running from Boston, Baltimore, Philadelphia and New York, to St. Louis, Cincinnati, Chicago and Louisville—but by the traffic between them being so controlled by an arrangement as substantially to be equivalent to a pooling of the capital stock; so that in the place of five or six competing lines there is, practically, but one com-

---

[8]Free railway acts, i.e., general incorporation laws.

## EXHIBIT 2 (*concluded*)

pany, having five or six different sets of parallel rails, having different local but the same through traffic; and, therefore, in each one of the states each state finds itself powerless to control anything but a mere section of this vast body of roads. This condition is the basis of an argument that is constantly made, and made by the railroad managers themselves, against legislation in any particular section of the country, that it submits certain portions of a through line to a control which may place it at a disadvantage compared with other through roads; and that, therefore there should be some sort of simultaneous action, so that they shall be treated as a whole; treated as they have practically become, one body.

Source: Alfred D. Chandler, Jr., *The Railroads* (New York: Harcourt Brace Jovanovich, 1965), pp. 188–98.

## EXHIBIT 3

### *The Interstate Commerce Act: An Act to Regulate Commerce, Approved February 4, 1887*

Be it enacted by the Senate and House of Representatives of the United States of America in Congress assembled,

That provisions of this Act shall apply to any common carrier or carriers engaged in the transportation of passengers or property wholly by railroad, or partly by railroad and partly by water when both are used, under a common control, management, or arrangement, for a continuous carriage or shipment, from one State or Territory of the United States, or the District of Columbia, to any other State or Territory of the United States, or the District of Columbia, or from any place in the United States to an adjacent foreign country, or from any place in the United States through a foreign country to any other place in the United States, and also to the transportation in like manner of property shipped from any place in the United States to a foreign country and carried from such place to a port of transshipment, or shipped from a foreign country to any place in the United States and carried to such place from a port of entry either in the United States or an adjacent foreign country: *Provided, however,* That the provisions of this Act shall not apply to the transportation of passengers or property, or to the receiving, delivering, storage, or handling of property, wholly within one State, and not shipped to or from a foreign country from or to any State or Territory as aforesaid.

The term "railroad" as used in this Act shall include all bridges and ferries used or operated in connection with any railroad, and also all the road in use by any corporation operating a railroad, whether owned or operated under a contract, agreement, or lease; and the term "transportation" shall include all instrumentalities of shipment or carriage.

## EXHIBIT 3 *(continued)*

All charges made for any service rendered or to be rendered in the transportation of passengers or property as aforesaid, or in connection therewith, or for the receiving, delivering, storage, or handling of such property, shall be reasonable and just; and every unjust and unreasonable charge for such service is prohibited and declared to be unlawful.

Sec. 2. That if any common carrier subject to the provisions of this Act shall, directly or indirectly, by any special rate, rebate, drawback, or other device, charge, demand, collect, or receive from any person or persons a greater or less compensation for any service property, subject to the provisions of this Act, than it charges, demands, collects, or receives from any other person or persons for doing for him or them a like and contemporaneous service in the transportation of a like kind of traffic under substantially similar circumstances and conditions, such common carrier shall be deemed guilty of unjust discrimination, which is hereby prohibited and declared to be unlawful.

Sec. 3. That it shall be unlawful for any common carrier subject to the provisions of this Act to make or give any undue or unreasonable preference or advantage to any particular person, company, firm, corporation, or locality, or any particular description of traffic, in any respect whatsoever, or to subject any particular person, company, firm, corporation, or locality, or any particular description of traffic, to any undue or unreasonable prejudice or disadvantage in any respect whatsoever.

Every common carrier subject to the provisions of this Act shall, according to their respective powers, afford all reasonable, proper, and equal facilities for the interchange of traffic between their respective lines, and for the receiving, forwarding, and delivering of passengers and property to and from their several lines and those connecting therewith, and shall not discriminate in their rates and charges between such connecting lines; but this shall not be construed as requiring any such common carrier to give the use of its tracks or terminal facilities to another carrier engaged in like business.

Sec. 4. That it shall be unlawful for any common carrier subject to the provisions of this Act to charge or receive any greater compensation in the aggregate for the transportation of passengers or of like kind of property, under substantially similar circumstances and conditions, for a shorter than for a longer distance over the same line, in the same direction, the shorter being included within the longer distance; but this shall not be construed as authorizing any common carrier within the terms of this Act to charge and receive as great compensation for a shorter as for a longer distance: *Provided, however,* That upon application to the Commission appointed under the provisions of this Act, such common carrier may, in special cases, after investigation by the Commission, be authorized to charge less for longer than for shorter distances for transportation of passengers or property; and the Commission may from time to time prescribe the extent to which said designated common carrier may be relieved from the operation of this section of this Act.

## EXHIBIT 3 (*continued*)

Sec. 5. That it shall be unlawful for any common carrier subject to the provisions of this Act to enter into any contract, agreement, or combination with any other common carrier or carriers for the pooling of freights of different and competing railroads, or to divide between them the aggregate or net proceeds of the earnings of such railroads, or any portion thereof; and in any case of an agreement for the pooling of freights as aforesaid, each day of its continuance shall be deemed a separate offense.

Sec. 6. That every common carrier subject to the provisions of this Act shall print and keep for public inspection schedules showing the rates and fares and charges for the transportation of passengers and property which any such common carrier has established and which are in force at the time upon its railroad, as defined by the first section of this Act. The schedules printed as aforesaid by any such common carrier shall plainly state the places upon its railroad between which property and passengers will be carried, and shall contain the classification of freight in force upon such railroad, and shall also state separately the terminal charges and any rules or regulations which in any wise change, affect, or determine any part of the aggregate of such aforesaid rates and fares and charges. Such schedules shall be plainly printed in large type, of at least the size of ordinary pica, and copies for the use of the public shall be kept in every depot or station upon any such railroad, in such places and in such form that they can be conveniently inspected.

Any common carrier subject to the provisions of this Act receiving freight in the United States to be carried through a foreign country to any place in the United States shall also in like manner print and keep for public inspection, at every depot where such freight is received for shipment, schedules showing the through rates established and charged by such common carrier to all points in the United States beyond the foreign country to which it accepts freight for shipment; and any freight shipped from the United States through a foreign country into the United States, the through rate on which shall not have been made public as required by this Act, shall, before it is admitted into the United States from said foreign country, be subject to customs duties as if said freight were of foreign production; and any law in conflict with this section is hereby repealed.

No advance shall be made in the rates, fares, and charges which have been established and published as aforesaid by any common carrier in compliance with the requirements of this section, except after ten days public notice, which shall plainly state the changes proposed to be made in the schedule then in force, and the time when the increased rates, fares, or charges will go into effect; and the proposed changes shall be shown by printing new schedules, or shall be plainly indicated upon the schedules in force at the time and kept for public inspection. Reductions in such published rates, fares, or charges may be made without previous public notice; but whenever any such reduction is made, notice of the same shall immediately be publicly posted and the changes made shall immediately be made public by printing new schedules, or shall immediately be plainly indicated upon the schedules at the time in force and kept for public inspection.

## EXHIBIT 3 (*continued*)

And when any such common carrier shall have established and published its rates, fares, and charges, in compliance with the provisions of this section, it shall be unlawful for such common carrier to charge, demand, collect, or receive from any person or persons a greater or less compensation for the transportation of passengers or property, or for any services in connection therewith, than is specified in such published schedule of rates, fares, and charges as may at the time be in force.

Every common carrier subject to the provisions of this Act shall file with the Commission hereinafter provided for copies of its schedules of rates, fares, and charges which have been established and published in compliance with the requirements of this section, and shall promptly notify said Commission of all changes made in the same. Every such common carrier shall also file with said Commission copies of all contracts, agreements, or arrangements with other common carriers in relation to any traffic affected by the provisions of this Act to which it may be a party. And in cases where passengers and freight pass over continuous lines or routes operated by more than one common carrier, and the several common carriers operating such lines or routes establish joint tariffs of rates or fares or charges for such continuous lines or routes, copies of such joint tariffs shall also, in like manner, be filed with said Commission. Such joint rates, fares, and charges on such continuous lines so filed as aforesaid shall be made public by such common carriers when directed by said Commission, in so far as may, in the judgment of the Commission, be deemed practicable; and said Commission shall from time to time prescribe the measure of publicity which shall be given to such rates, fares, and charges, or to such part of them as it may deem it practicable for such common carriers to publish, and the places in which they shall be published; but no common carrier party to any such joint tariff shall be liable for the failure of any other common carrier party thereto to observe and adhere to the rates, fares, or charges thus made and published.

If any such common carrier shall neglect or refuse to file or publish its schedules or tariffs of rates, fares, and charges as provided in this section, or any part of the same such common carrier shall, in addition to other penalties herein prescribed, be subject to a writ of *mandamus*, to be issued by any Circuit Court of the United States in the judicial district wherein the principal office of said common carrier is situated or wherein such offense may be committed, and if such common carrier be a foreign corporation, in the judicial circuit wherein such common carrier accepts traffic and has an agent to perform such service, to compel compliance with the aforesaid provisions of this section; and such writ shall issue in the name of the People of the United States, at the relation of the Commissioners appointed under the provisions of this Act; and failure to comply with its requirements shall be punishable as and for a contempt; and the said Commissioners, as complainants, may also apply, in any such Circuit Court of the United States, for a writ of injunction against such common carrier, to restrain such common carrier from receiving or transporting property among the several States and Territories of the United States, or between the United States and adjacent foreign countries, or be-

## EXHIBIT 3 (*continued*)

tween ports of transshipment and of entry and the several States and Territories of the United States, as mentioned in the first section of this Act, until such common carrier shall have complied with aforesaid provisions of this section of this Act.

Sec. 7. That it shall be unlawful for any common carrier subject to the provisions of this Act to enter into any combination, contract, or agreement, expressed or implied, to prevent, by change of time schedule, carriage in different cars, or by other means or devices, the carriage of freights from being continuous from the place of shipment to the place of destination; and no break of bulk, stoppage, or interruption made by such common carrier shall prevent the carriage of freights from being and being treated as one continuous carriage from the place of shipment to the place of destination, unless such break, stoppage, or interruption was made in good faith for some necessary purpose, and without any intent to avoid or unnecessarily interrupt such continuous carriage or to evade any of the provisions of this Act.

Sec. 8. That if any common carrier subject to the provisions of this Act shall do, cause to be done, or permit to be done any act, matter, or thing in this Act prohibited or declared to be unlawful, or shall omit to do any act, matter, or thing in this Act required to be done, such common carrier shall be liable to the person or persons injured thereby for the full amount of damages sustained in consequence of any such violation of the provisions of this Act, together with a reasonable counsel or attorney's fee, to be fixed by the court in every case of recovery, which attorney's fee shall be taxed and collected as part of the costs in the case.

Sec. 9. That any person or persons claiming to be damaged by any common carrier subject to the provisions of this Act may either make complaint to the Commission as hereinafter provided for, or may bring suit in his or their own behalf for the recovery of the damages for which such common carrier may be liable under the provisions of this Act in any District or Circuit Court of the United States of competent jurisdiction; but such person or persons shall not have the right to pursue both of said remedies, and must in each case elect which one of the two methods of procedure herein provided for he or they will adopt. In any such action brought for the recovery of damages the court before which the same shall be pending may compel any director, officer, receiver, trustee, or agent of the corporation or company defendant in such suit to attend, appear, and testify in such case, and may compel the production of the books and papers of such corporation or company to any such suit; the claim that any such testimony or evidence may tend to criminate the person giving such evidence shall not excuse such witness from testifying, but such evidence or testimony shall not be used against such person on the trial of any criminal proceeding.

Sec. 10. That any common carrier subject to the provisions of this Act, or, whenever such common carrier is a corporation, any director or officer thereof, or any receiver, trustee, lessee, agent, or person acting for or employed by such corporation, who, alone or with any other corporation, company, person, or party, shall willfully do or cause to be done, or shall willingly suffer or permit to be done,

## EXHIBIT 3 (*continued*)

any act, matter, or thing in this Act prohibited or declared to be unlawful, or who shall aid or abet therein, or shall willfully omit or fail to do any act, matter, or thing in this Act required to be done, or shall cause or willingly suffer or permit any act, matter, or thing so directed or required by this Act to be done not to be so done, or shall aid or abet any such omission or failure, or shall be guilty of any infraction of this Act, or shall aid or abet therein, shall be deemed guilty of a misdemeanor, and shall, upon conviction thereof in any District Court of the United States within the jurisdiction of which such offense was committed, be subject to a fine of not to exceed $5,000 for each offense.

Sec. 11. That a commission is hereby created and established to be known as the Interstate Commerce Commission, which shall be composed of five Commissioners, who shall be appointed by the President, by and with the advice and consent of the Senate. The Commissioners first appointed under this Act shall continue in office for the term of two, three, four, five, and six years, respectively, from the first day of January, Anno Domini eighteen hundred and eighty-eight, the term of each to be designated by the President; but their successors shall be appointed for terms of six years, except that any person chosen to fill a vacancy shall be appointed only for the unexpired time of the Commissioner whom he shall succeed. Any Commissioner may be removed by the President, for inefficiency, neglect of duty, or malfeasance in office. Not more than three of the Commissioners shall be appointed from the same political party. No person in the employ of or holding any official relation to any common carrier subject to the provisions of this Act, or owning stock or bonds thereof, or who is in any manner pecuniarily interested therein, shall enter upon the duties of or hold such office. Said Commissioners shall not engage in any other business, vocation, or employment. No vacancy in the Commission shall impair the right of the remaining Commissioners to exercise all the powers of the Commission.

Sec. 12. That the Commission hereby created shall have authority to inquire into the management of the business of all common carriers subject to the provisions of this Act, and shall keep itself informed as to the manner and method in which the same is conducted, and shall have the right to obtain from such common carriers full and complete information necessary to enable the Commission to perform the duties and carry out the objects for which it was created; and for the purpose of this Act the Commission shall have power to require the attendance and testimony of witnesses and the production of all books, papers, tariffs, contracts, agreements, and documents relating to any matter under investigation, and to that end may invoke the aid of any court of the United States in requiring the attendance and testimony of witnesses and the production of books, papers, and documents under the provisions of this section.

And any of the Circuit Courts of the United States within the jurisdiction of which said inquiry is carried on may, in case of contumacy or refusal to obey a subpoena issued to any common carrier subject to the provisions of this Act, or other person, issue an order requiring such common carrier or other person to appear

## EXHIBIT 3 *(continued)*

before said Commission (and produce books and papers if so ordered) and give evidence touching the matter in question; and any failure to obey such order of the court may be punished by such court as a contempt thereof. The claim that any such testimony or evidence may tend to incriminate the person giving such evidence shall not excuse such witness from testifying; but such evidence or testimony shall not be used against such person on the trial of any criminal proceeding.

Sec. 13. That any person, firm, corporation, or association, or any mercantile, agricultural or manufacturing society, or any body politic or municipal organization complaining of anything done or omitted to be done by any common carrier subject to the provisions of this Act in contravention of the provisions thereof, may apply to said Commission by petition, which shall briefly state the facts; whereupon a statement of the charges thus made shall be forwarded by the Commission to such common carrier who shall be called upon to satisfy the complaint or to answer the same in writing within a reasonable time, to be specified, shall make reparation for the injury alleged to have been done, said carrier shall be relieved of liability to the complainant only for the particular violation of law thus complained of. If such carrier shall not satisfy the complaint within the time specified, or there shall appear to be any reasonable ground for investigating said complaint, it shall be the duty of the Commission to investigate the matters complained of in such manner and by such means as it shall deem proper.

Said Commission shall in like manner investigate any complaint forwarded by the railroad commissioner or railroad commission of any State or Territory at the request of such commissioner or commission, and may institute any inquiry on its own motion in the same manner and to the same effect as though complaint had been made.

No complaint shall at anytime be dismissed because of the absence of direct damage to the complainant.

Sec. 14. That whenever an investigation shall be made by said commission, it shall be its duty to make a report in writing in respect thereto, which shall include the findings of fact upon which the conclusions of the Commission are based, together with its recommendation as to what reparation, if any, should be made by the common carrier to any party or parties who may be found to have been injured; and such findings so made shall thereafter, in all judicial proceedings, be deemed *prima facie* evidence as to each and every fact found.

All reports of investigations made by the Commission shall be entered of record, and a copy thereof shall be furnished to the party who may have complained, and to any common carrier that may have been complained of.

Sec. 15. That in any case in which an investigation shall be made by said Commission it shall be made to appear to the satisfaction of the Commission, either by the testimony of witnesses or other evidence, that any thing has been done or omitted to be done in violation of the provisions of this Act, or of any law cognizable by said commission, by any common carrier, or that any injury or damage has been sustained by the party or parties complaining, or by other par-

## EXHIBIT 3 (*continued*)

ties aggrieved in consequence of any such violation, it shall be the duty of the Commission to forthwith cause a copy of its report in respect thereto to be delivered to such common carrier, together with a notice to said common carrier to cease and desist from such violation, or to make reparation for the inquiry so found to have been done or both, within a reasonable time, to be specified by the Commission; and if, within the time specified, it shall be made to appear to the Commission that such common carrier has ceased from such violation of law, and has made reparation for the injury found to have been done, in compliance with the report and notice of the Commission, or to the satisfaction of the party complaining, a statement to that effect shall be entered of record by the Commission, and the said common carrier shall thereupon be relieved from further liability or penalty for such particular violation of law.

Sec. 16. That whenever any common carrier, as defined in and subject to the provisions of this Act, shall violate or refuse or neglect to obey any lawful order or requirement of the Commission in this Act named, it shall be the duty of the Commission, and lawful for any company or person interested in such order or requirement, to apply, in a summary way, by petition, to the Circuit Court of the United States sitting in equity in the judicial district in which the common carrier complained of has its principal office, or in which the violation or disobedience of such order or requirement shall happen, alleging such violation or disobedience, as the case may be; and the said court shall have power to hear and determine the matter, on such short notice to the common carrier complained of as the court shall deem reasonable; and such notice may be served on such common carrier, his or its officers, agents, or servants, in such manner as the court shall direct; and said court shall proceed to hear and determine the matter speedily as a court of equity, and without the formal pleadings and proceedings applicable to ordinary suits in equity, but in such manner as to do justice in the premises; and to this end such court shall have power, if it think fit, to direct and prosecute, in such mode and by such persons as it may appoint, all such inquiries as the court may think needful to enable it to form a just judgment in the matter of such petition; and on such hearing the report of said Commission shall be *prima facie* evidence of the matters therein stated; and if it be made to appear to such court, on such hearing or on report of any such person or persons, that the lawful order or requirement of said Commission drawn in question has been violated or disobeyed, it shall be lawful for such court to issue a writ of injunction or other proper process, mandatory or otherwise, to restrain such common carrier from further continuing such violation or disobedience of such order or requirement of said Commission, and enjoining obedience to the same; and in case of any disobedience of any such writ of injunction or other proper process, mandatory or otherwise, it shall be lawful for such court to issue writs of attachment, or any other process of said court incident or applicable to writs of injunction or other proper process, mandatory or otherwise, against such common carrier, and if a corporation, against one or more of the directors, officers, or agents of the same, or against any owner, lessee, trust-

## EXHIBIT 3 (*continued*)

ee, receiver, or other person failing to obey such writ of injunction or other proper process, mandatory or otherwise; and said court may, if it shall think fit, make an order directing such common carrier or other persons so disobeying such writ of injunction or other proper process, mandatory or otherwise, to pay such sum of money not exceeding for each carrier or person in default the sum of $500 for every day after a day to be named in the order that such carrier or other person shall fail to obey such injunction or other proper process, mandatory or otherwise; and such moneys shall be payable as the court shall direct, either to the party complaining, or into court to abide the ultimate decision of the court, or into the Treasury; and payment thereof may, without prejudice to any other mode of recovering the same, be enforced by attachment or order in the nature of a writ of execution, in like manner as if the same had been recovered by a final decree in personam and in such court. When the subject in dispute shall be of the value of $2,000 or more, either party to such proceeding before said court may appeal to the Supreme Court of the United States, under the same regulations now provided by law in respect of security for such appeal; but such appeal shall not operate to stay or supersede the order of the court or the execution of any writ or process thereon; and such court may, in every such matter, order the payment of such costs and counsel fees as shall be deemed reasonable. Whenever any such petition shall be filed or presented by the Commission it shall be the duty of the district attorney, under the direction of the Attorney-General of the United States, to prosecute the same; and the costs and expenses of such prosecution shall be paid out of the appropriation for the expenses of the courts of the United States. For the purpose of this Act, excepting its penal provisions, the Circuit Courts of the United States shall be deemed to be always in session.

Sec. 17. That the Commission may conduct its proceedings in such manner as will best conduce to the proper dispatch of business and to the ends of justice. A majority of the Commission shall constitute a quorum for the transaction of business, but no Commissioner shall participate in any hearing or proceeding in which he has any pecuniary interest. Said Commission may, from time to time, make or amend such general rules or orders as may be requisite for the order and regulation of proceedings before it, including forms of notices and the service thereof, which shall conform, as nearly as may be, to those in use in the courts of the United States. Any party may appear before said Commission and be heard, in person or by attorney. Every vote and official act of the Commission shall be entered of record, and its proceedings shall be public upon the request of either party interested. Said Commission shall have an official seal, which shall be judicially noticed. Either of the members of the Commission may administer oaths and affirmations.

Sec. 18. That each Commissioner shall receive an annual salary of $7,500 payable in the same manner as the salaries of judges of the courts of the United States. The Commission shall appoint a secretary, who shall receive an annual salary of $3,500, payable in like manner. The Commission shall have authority to

## EXHIBIT 3 (*continued*)

employ and fix the compensation of such other employees as it may find necessary to the proper performance of its duties, subject to the approval of the Secretary of the Interior.

The Commission shall be furnished by the Secretary of the Interior with suitable offices and all necessary office supplies. Witnesses summoned before the Commission shall be paid the same fees and mileage that are paid witnesses in the courts of the United States. All of the expenses of the Commission, including all necessary expenses for transportation incurred by the Commissioners, or by their employees under their orders, in making any investigation in any other places than in the City of Washington, shall be allowed and paid, on the presentation of itemized vouchers therefor approved by the chairman of the Commission and the Secretary of the Interior.

Sec. 19. That the principal office of the Commission shall be in the City of Washington, where its general sessions shall be held; but whenever the convenience of the public or of the parties may be promoted or delay or expense prevented thereby, the Commission may hold special sessions in any part of the United States. It may, by one or more of the Commissioners, prosecute any inquiry necessary to its duties, in any part of the United States, into any matter or question of fact pertaining to the business of any common carrier subject to the provisions of this Act.

Sec. 20. That the Commission is hereby authorized to require annual reports from all common carriers subject to the provisions of this Act, to fix the time and prescribe the manner in which such reports shall be made, and to require from such carriers specific answers to all questions upon which the Commission may need information. Such annual reports shall show in detail the amount of capital stock issued, the amounts paid therefor, and the manner of payment for the same; the dividends paid, the surplus fund, if any, and the number of stockholders; the funded and floating debts and the interest paid thereon; the cost and value of the carrier's property, franchises, and equipment; the number of employees and the salaries paid each class; the amounts expended for improvements each year, how expended, and the character of such improvements; the earnings and receipts from each branch of business and from all sources; the operating and other expenses; the balance of profit and loss; and a complex exhibit of the financial operations of the carrier each year, including an annual balance sheet. Such reports shall also contain such information in relation to rates or regulations concerning fares or freights or agreements, arrangements, or contracts with other common carriers, as the Commission may require; and the said Commission may, within its discretion, for the purpose of enabling it the better to carry out the purposes of this Act, prescribe (if in the opinion of the Commission it is practicable to prescribe such uniformity and methods of keeping accounts) a period of time within which all common carriers subject to the provisions of this Act shall have, as near as may be, a uniform system of accounts, and the manner in which such accounts shall be kept.

## EXHIBIT 3 (*concluded*)

Sec. 21. That the Commission shall, or or before the first day of December in each year, make a report to the Secretary of the Interior, which shall be by him transmitted to Congress, and copies of which shall be distributed as are the other reports issued from the Interior Department. This report shall contain such information and data collected by the Commission as may be considered of value in the determination of questions connected with the regulation of commerce, together with such recommendations as to additional legislation relating thereto as the Commission may deem necessary.

Sec. 22. That nothing in this Act shall apply to the carriage, storage, or handling of property free or at reduced rates for the United States, State, or municipal governments, or for charitable purposes, or to or from fairs and expositions for exhibition thereat, or the issuance of mileage, excursion, or commutation passenger tickets; nothing in this Act shall be construed to prohibit any common carrier from giving reduced rates to ministers of religion; nothing in this Act shall be construed to prevent railroads from giving free carriage to their own officers and employees, or to prevent the principal officers or any railroad company or companies from exchanging passes or tickets with other railroad companies for their officers and employees; and nothing in this Act contained shall in any way abridge or alter the remedies now existing at common law or by statute, but the provisions of this Act are in addition to such remedies: *Provided*, That no pending litigation shall in any way be affected by this Act.

Sec. 23. That the sum of $100,000 is hereby appropriated for the use and purposes of this Act for the fiscal year ending June thirtieth, Anno Domini eighteen hundred and eighty-eight, and the intervening time anterior thereto.

Sec. 24. That the provisions of sections 11 and 18 of this Act, relating to the appointment and organization of the Commission herein provided for, shall take effect immediately, and the remaining provisions of this Act shall take effect sixty days after its passage.

# CASE 12

# *Nineteenth Century Retailing and the Rise of the Department Store**

## Early Forms: The Generalist and the Specialist

The classic retailing establishment in the first third or so of the 19th century, especially outside of all but the biggest cities, was the general store, and "general" indeed was the merchandise offered for sale. At one rural frontier store, for example, a customer might find tea, sugar, coffee, flour, and liquor among the edibles and "bibibles"; various spices; hardware and leather goods, axes, log chains, kettles, pots, pans, kegs of nails piled in spare spaces (of which there couldn't have been a great many, stores being as small as 400 square feet) or hanging on rafters by cords; and shoes, saddles and harnesses.[1]

Here is a description of the business day at one store in the Missouri Territory in 1818:

|  | *The Widow Wright* |  |
|---|---|---|
| 6 lbs. of coffee | | $3.00 |
| 2 handkerchiefs | | 1.00 |
| 1 comb | | 1.25 |

---

*This case was prepared by Assistant Professor Richard S. Tedlow as a basis for class discussion rather than to illustrate either effective or ineffective handling of an administrative situation.

Copyright © 1983 by the President and Fellows of Harvard College.

Harvard Business School case 384-022, rev. 6/84.

[1]Lewis E. Atherton, "The Pioneer Merchant in Mid- America," *The University of Missouri Studies* 14, no. 2 (April 1, 1939).

| | | |
|---|---|---:|
| 1 damaged sugar bowl | | .25 |
| ¼ lb. Hyson tea | | .75 |
| 1 shawl | | 2.50 |
| 6 yards of gingham | | 3.00 |
| 2 thimbles | | .25 |

**Ezekiel Murray**

| | | |
|---|---|---:|
| 1 pair of trace chains | | 2.50 |

**Customer C**

| | | |
|---|---|---:|
| 4 | lbs. coffee | $4.90 |
| 1 | dozen buckles | .75 |
| 6 | skeins of silk | .75 |
| 3 | yards of plush | 9.00 |
| 5 ½ | yards of cloth | 4.8125 |
| 1 | straw hat | 3.00 |

**Customer D**

| | | |
|---|---|---:|
| 1 | pair shoes | 1.50 |

**Customer E**

| | | |
|---|---|---:|
| 1 | pair shoes | 2.00 |
| 2 | skeins of silk | .25 |

**Customer F**

| | |
|---|---:|
| Ribbon | .50 |

**Customer G**

| | |
|---|---:|
| Ribbon | .33 |

**Customer H**

| | | |
|---|---|---:|
| 1 | handkerchief | .25 |

**Customer I**

| | | |
|---|---|---:|
| ½ | lb. nails | .28 |

Some noteworthy characteristics of early retailing include:

1.  The pace of business was slow. The above description is not atypical of a 14-hour day at many stores.
2.  Transactions were usually not in cash. Credit was granted, sometimes for as long as a year. A shortage of an acceptable circulating medium often led to money-barter, whereby goods would be exchanged for goods with money equivalents used as a standard of value.
3.  Price was a matter of negotiation between storekeeper and customer.
4.  Advertising was usually restricted to the announcement of what goods were available and from where they had been purchased. Prices were not mentioned. Sometimes copy would change no more often than annually.

**5.** The rule of business was *caveat emptor*. "The customers cheated us in their fabrics," recalled a Connecticut storekeeper of the 1820s; "we cheated the customers with our goods. Each party expected to be cheated, if it was possible."[2] Admittedly the man reminiscing is Phineas T. Barnum, but even allowing for possible overstatement, it is not unfair to say that honesty was a rare commodity.

As the urban market developed, retail stores tended to specialize more strictly in the wares they carried. Specialization first developed through four general categories: groceries, dry goods, hardware, and home furnishings. But these general categories quickly broke down as well, so that the major city of 1850 had specialty stores dedicated to tools, boots and shoes, carpeting, china and glassware, cloaks and mantillas, combs and fancy goods, cutlery and hardware, fancy dry goods, feathers and mattresses, furniture, men's furnishings, hats, caps, and furs, hosiery and gloves, India rubber goods, laces and embroideries, millinery, saddles, trunks, and harnesses, silks and ribbons, tea and coffee, tobacco and snuff, upholstery, umbrellas and parasols, butter and cheese, and ready-to-wear clothing for men.

The specialist had a number of noteworthy operational advantages. First, as the industrial revolution progressed, the variety of goods available for sale greatly increased. Thus the maintenance of a "reasonably complete assortment" of, for example, ribbons meant more buying expertise and more working capital in 1860 than it did in 1800. Second, specialization meant greater influence with the supplier. Third, the increase in trading population brought about both by improvements in transportation and by immigration to the cities meant that the retailer did not have to rely on numerous different lines to generate enough business for an acceptable profit.

Not only were retailers specializing by class of trade, they were also specializing by business function. The distribution system had grown thick in the first half of the 19th century with middlemen who financed transactions and physically distributed goods. Dry goods, for example, would pass from the importer (or as the century progressed, the manufacturer), to the wholesaler, and then to the retailer. The great general merchants of the colonial era might handle all these functions (with the exception of manufacturing) themselves. So complete was this specialization in the seaboard cities of the East that a Philadelphia publication remarked in 1855 that "Division of trade into distinct branches appears to be in the natural order of things. . . . The tendency, in all great commercial marts, is to simplification and in many cases only a single class of articles is kept by the merchant as in cotton goods, woolen goods, silk goods."[3]

As these words were being written, however, a movement was under way which would render them inaccurate.

---

[2] Neil Harris, *Humbug* (Boston: Little, Brown, 1973), p. 12.

[3] Ralph M. Hower, *History of Macy's of New York* (Cambridge: Harvard University Press, 1943), pp. 83–84.

# The Department Store

The idea of purchasing a wide variety of goods and services at the same place is not a new one. The fair in the Middle Ages, for example, was a collection of shops at one location. The department store is also a collection of shops at one location, the difference being that, unlike the fair, these shops are under one management.

By 1860, a number of the great names in department store retailing had gotten their starts. These included Macy's, Gimbel's, Jordan Marsh, and Lord and Taylor. Marshall Field, which at the turn of the century was among the largest wholesale and retail distributors in the United States, can be used to illustrate the problems and opportunities of the department store business from 1860 to 1900.[4]

## Potter Palmer and Marshall Field

The story of Marshall Field begins with his predecessor and later partner, Potter Palmer. Palmer arrived in Chicago at the age of 26 with eight years' retail experience behind him and $5,000. The year was 1852, and there were about 35,000 people living in the city. Two decades previously Chicago had been a mere unincorporated crossroads with a population of about a hundred. By 1890, it was one of the great cities in the world, with almost a million and a half inhabitants.

In 1852, the city was still very much on the frontier. "It was only just beginning to emerge from the ooze of the shores of Lake Michigan. The railroad station at the foot of Lake Street . . . was an unroofed shed. The streets were always either deep in mud or sending up choking clouds of dust as horses and wagons rumbled by. Even the largest wagon often became stuck in the bottomless slime. . . . On warm days, garbage, dead rats, and animal excrement fermented together beneath the wooden sidewalks and made walking or shopping something less than a pleasure."[5]

Palmer set out not, as was the custom, to sell everything from codfish to calico. Rather, in his words, "I struck out for a large and distinctive dry goods store." As soon as volume permitted, he hired a full time buyer and sent him east. He specialized in goods of better quality and inaugurated a policy of allowing merchandise to be returned if it "prove[d] unsatisfactory either in price, quality, or style." His advertising was at first of the announcement variety, but he quickly turned to copy with a stronger selling appeal.

By 1860, Palmer had moved the store to spacious quarters and had also inaugurated a wholesale business. His voracity for wholesale customers was as great as that for retail:

> I always hunted for customers. If I learned of a man two hundred miles away in a clearing in the forest, who might buy, I got the name of my establishment to him and invited him in. After he once got acquainted with the store, we rarely lost him.[6]

---

[4]The following discussion is based upon Robert W. Twyman, *History of Marshall Field & Co., 1852–1906* (Philadelphia: University of Pennsylvania Press, 1954).

[5]Twyman, *Field,* p. 1.

[6]Twyman, *Field,* p. 7.

His appeal at both wholesale and retail was price oriented. Low prices were made possible by the low cost position which Palmer achieved through his New York buyer, through establishing direct relations with New England mills, and through making his own buying trips abroad.

Marshall Field arrived in Chicago from Pittsfield, Massachusetts, at the age of 21 in 1855 "determined," as he put it, "not to remain poor." He got a job as a clerk at a retail store at a salary of $400 per year, of which he saved $200. He soon became a wholesale salesman in the hinterland, and despite his conservative manner and mien, he proved quite a success. In fact, the great majority of Field's business experience prior to going into business for himself was in wholesaling rather than the retail trade. He quickly rose to a partnership with his employer. Early in 1865, he and an associate named Levi Leiter formed another partnership, this one with Potter Palmer. The company was capitalized at $750,000, $250,000 of which was supplied by Field, $120,000 by Leiter, $330,000 by Palmer, and the remainder by Palmer's brother. Field concentrated on buying and for a time ran the firm's New York office himself. Leiter was the numbers man who kept a keen eye on the accounts receivable and saw to it also that the firm paid its own bills on time.

In January 1867, Palmer withdrew from the firm, which then became Field, Leiter and Company. But its benefits from association with him continued to be great. First, Field and Leiter adopted Palmer's approach to the market. They guaranteed the quality of their goods and strived to make shopping pleasurable. Second, they continued the dual nature—retail and wholesale—of the company's trade. As Exhibit 1A illustrates, the wholesale business was in fact far greater than retail in terms of sales and profits up to Field's death in 1906. (Exhibit 1B provides data on the annual purchases of the firm. Exhibit 1C gives a comparison of Field sales to business activity in Chicago.) Palmer's reputation and Field's own selling experience helped to solidify the hold of the firm on the trade of the rapidly growing Old Northwest. Field never viewed himself as an innovator. "There were never any great ventures or risks," he once said, "nothing exciting whatever." He followed in Palmer's footsteps. Third, despite the fact that Palmer had withdrawn from the dry goods trade, he was still a force to be reckoned with in Chicago business.

The very year, for example, that Palmer left the Field firm, he decided to move the center of Chicago from Lake Street, the site of Field, Leiter and Company, to State Street. Lake Street was hemmed in at one end by the Chicago River and at the other by the railroad. State Street, on the other hand, presented unimpeded growth opportunities and, what is more, was where the city's southern and western transit lines met. It was not much more than an alley at the time, but Palmer was a man of vision. He secretly bought up run-down properties and cleared a right of way 100 feet wide. He then put up the grand Palmer House Hotel and a six-story marble fronted "dry goods palace." He invited Field and Leiter to become his tenants for the healthy sum of $1,000 per week. They eagerly accepted the offer. Between 1869 and 1871, thirty marble-front buildings arose on the new boulevard. Palmer had spent over $2 million, but as he put it, "There was sense in doing things on a large scale if you could see a return."

The opening of the new Field, Leiter building was an event attended by the "cream of the avenues" ushered in by blue uniformed boys, as spectators looked on. When the patrons entered, they found walnut counters, new gas fixtures, frescoed walls, and carpeting. In addition to the store's standard merchandise offering, exotic satins, silks, and sundry prestige pieces were put on sale especially for the occasion.

Only the first floor and that part of the basement not occupied by machinery were retailing selling space. The second floor was devoted to piece goods, the staple of the dry goods house. On the third floor were displayed woolen goods and bedding. The fourth floor was given over to "notions," more of which momentarily, and the fifth and sixth floors were for storage.

Field's facilities suffered two disasterous fires in the 1870s. The first was the cataclysmic conflagration of October 8, 1871, which gutted a large part of the city. (See Exhibit 2 for the assets of the firm at the time of the fire.) The firm lost $2.5 million in merchandise. Much of this was covered by insurance, but due to bankruptcies among some insurers, the firm wound up suffering a net loss of about three quarters of a million dollars. Field quickly reopened, but from that time forward the retail and wholesale businesses were housed in different structures for insurance purposes.

A second fire on November 14, 1877, gutted the retail building. The retail store had about $1 million in merchandise on hand at the time, four fifths of which was lost. This time insurance had been taken out with firms in various cities, and the loss was covered. On April 9, 1879, the retail store finally occupied again its former location on State Street.

**Merchandise.**  Like Palmer's store before it, Field, Leiter first specialized in dry goods. Indeed, Field and Leiter had declined to purchase Palmer's inventory of carpets. Soon, however, "notions" were added to the offering. This category appeared to have been a catchall, which included soap, umbrellas, ready-to-wear skirts, Parisian cloaks, and men's furnishings. The term "notions" covered a steadily increasing array of products through the 1870s and 1880s.

In 1872, the company reversed an earlier practice and began carrying carpets, rugs, and upholstery. It also started selling furs and a greatly expanded variety of men's furnishings. The offering in ladies' wear expanded in variety as well, as the ready-to-wear garment business grew. Four brands of corsets alone were carried. And a wide array of products for the home—mirrors, drapes, window shades, curtain fixtures, even sewing machine oil—were also added during the great depression of the 1870s.

In the 1880s, in addition to those items already mentioned, the following products were carried: carpet sweepers, baby buggies, dining room tables, tricycles, copper rivets, atomizers, clocks, opera glasses, glue, sporting goods, mattresses, and more.

Under the management of Harry G. Selfridge, who ran the retail end of the business from 1884 to 1904 and then went on to found the large London department store bearing his name, Field finally became a full-line department store after the manner of Macy's in New York, and Wanamaker's in Philadelphia.

There were fewer than 50 departments before Selfridge came and more than 150 at his departure. Selfridge was responsible for the Tea Room and Bargain Basement as well as for shoes, toys, jewelry, and children's clothing departments, and he increased the store's commitment to furniture. Marshall Field himself sometimes objected to this proliferation. As late as 1889, he was still saying, "[W]e're in the dry goods business. Never forget that." But by the time of this declaration, the store appeared to be pursuing a policy of selling everything it could at a profit and putting competing specialty stores out of business in the process.

Selfridge also developed the basement into a more effective tool for disposing of goods at a lower price which the full line retail departments had not been able to move at standard margins. Selfridge at first emphasized the basement's promotional nature, but his price appeal, it was feared, would reflect on the store as a whole. As a result, the appeal was modified to "Less Expensive But Reliable." At the turn of the century, the basement accounted for about a quarter of retail sales.

**Buying.** Field's strategy was to buy in cash, thus securing a 1 to 2 percent discount, and to buy in quantity. From the first, the store sought to eliminate the middleman. This meant going to New York, the wholesale capital of the nation, to New England for dry goods, and abroad for dry goods and specialty goods.

As the store developed, the position of the buyer became key. Everyone, it was said, from the president to the sales clerk worked for him. The buyer selected only such goods purchased by the company's representatives in New York and Europe as he saw fit. He paid 6 to 8 percent to the company for his open-to-buy, and he paid rent for that share of the physical plant he used. He priced and advertised as he wished. If he showed specified results, he would earn a bonus. Retail buying was a bit more complicated than wholesale because departments were more narrowly defined. Retail could buy from wholesale at 6 percent above the latter's cost.

The emphasis in buying was to maintain assortments and to rid the store of surplus stocks. The watchword was that "any surplus in Field's is not stock, it is cash." During the 1870s, Fields began to emphasize this need to buy light and often and to keep stock turning. This, he felt, was more important than "volume of business," which "doesn't make any real difference." Data on stock turn are provided in Exhibit 3.

As the store grew, retail buyers began to operate more independently of the wholesale business. Retail buyers went abroad in increasing numbers, from two in 1875 to 21 in 1906, and like wholesale, retail was having many of its goods made up exclusively by manufacturers.

Indeed, the final step in cutting costs and achieving exclusivity was the development of manufacturing capacity. From the late 1860s, the firm had been served by its own workshops. Not long after the turn of the century, a major commitment was made by the establishment of Fieldcrest Mills.

**Selling.** The selling job was, of course, very different in the wholesale and retail divisions. Marshall Field felt wholesale customers should make periodic trips to Chicago to view in person the store's goods and make their purchases. But as the company's trading area expanded from the Appalachians to the Pacific Coast and as eastern stores began sending traveling men to the hinterland in number, Field realized he had to respond. Field salesmen were divided along the company's product lines, and a single merchant might find himself contacted by a dozen of them in a month. The salesmen might spend as much as a year at a time away from the firm. Their major assets were their firm's merchandise and reputation and whatever personal charm they themselves might possess.

On the retail level, salaries were low, hours long, and supervision close. Nevertheless, morale is said to have been high, because the firm compared well on these dimensions with the competition. The emphasis was on courtesy rather than subservience to customers.

Constant efforts were made to create a pleasant shopping atmosphere. Pressure tactics were discouraged. Efforts were made to see to it that women shoppers were waited on by saleswomen, especially for their apparel needs. And delivery services were provided. The aim in both wholesale and retail was to take the risk out of the purchase. To this end, the firm held strictly to its returns policy. Exhibit 4 shows the increases in retail and wholesale employment.

**Advertising.** As noted earlier, advertising began with the undifferentiated notice but evolved into a more selling-oriented appeal. Price was mentioned less often as time passed. An example of Field advertising is provided in Exhibit 5. For comparative purposes, competitive advertising is reproduced in Exhibit 6. The ratio of advertising to sales and of all other expenses that could be determined to sales are provided in Exhibit 7.

**Competition.** Field was not, of course, the only department store in Chicago. But its dominance is shown by its impact compared to competitors (see Exhibit 8).

In addition to homegrown competitors, eastern firms occasionally tried to enter the Chicago market. The greatest threat was posed by Alexander T. Stewart, the largest dry goods merchant in New York, who opened a Chicago branch in 1876. Stewart immediately slashed prices, and Field responded meeting every cut.

Meetings were held with the new entrant to try to establish prices for staples. But these agreements kept collapsing as Stewart broke ranks. Remarked Field, "The fact will be ascertained by them after a while that at same prices, trade will give us the business . . . and then is when trouble will arise." By 1882, this threat ended as Stewart liquidated its business. When this company's founder died, the organization proved unable to endure.

Another serious threat was represented by the departure of Harry G. Selfridge. Selfridge was instrumental in building the retail side of the Field trade and was a man of undoubted ability. When the firm was incorporated in 1901, Selfridge was given 6,000 of the 60,000 shares issued at a par value of $100. (Field himself held 34,000 shares, while three other partners had 6,666⅔ apiece.)

But Selfridge was anxious to strike out on his own, and fearful that his wholesale counterpart, John C. Shedd, would be chosen Field's successor, he purchased the firm of Schlesinger and Meyer. Selfridge soon found, however, that it was no fun competing against friends. He also learned what difficulties were involved in managing a department store lacking in organizational strength and esprit. "There are a million things to do," he observed soon after taking his new position, "and nobody to do them." He soon sold out (at a profit) to Carson Pirie Scott and left for Britain.

## Marshall Field: The Later Years

The Field, Lieter partnership was terminated in 1881, when Leiter was bought out. He sold his 295/725 interest in the firm for a reported $2,700,000. Field at this point admitted some loyal junior people into the partnership, keeping for himself a 46 ½ percent interest. His power at the firm was never questioned for the rest of his life.

In the 1880s, Field began to take an interest in various other business activities. He started investing in real estate and indeed was the landlord for some competing stores, whose proximity to his own he welcomed. At his death, his real estate holdings were valued at $40 million. He invested in steel and railroads and joined a syndicate headed by John D. Rockefeller to purchase an iron range in Minnesota. For thirty years he sat on the board of the Merchants' Loan and Trust Company, and through control of "his" bank, he was a power in Chicago finance. He was also the largest holder of Pullman Sleeping Car's stock, which company was a major purchaser of bedding from his store. At his death on January 16, 1906, Field's estate was conservatively valued at just under $80 million.

Marshall Field's advice to young people seeking success was, "Be alert and ready to seize opportunities when they present themselves."

## EXHIBIT 1A

**Net Sales of Marshall Field & Co. by Retail and Wholesale, 1865–1905**

| Year | Retail | Wholesale | Total |
|------|--------|-----------|-------|
| 1865 | — | — | $ 8,000,000 |
| 1870 | $ 2,000,000 | $11,000,000 | 13,114,000 |
| 1875 | 3,139,000 | 15,438,000 | 18,577,000 |
| 1880 | 3,676,000 | 20,060,000 | 23,736,000 |
| 1885 | 4,553,000 | 20,454,000 | 25,007,000 |
| 1890 | 6,619,000 | 26,487,000 | 33,106,000 |
| 1895 | 7,622,000 | 24,769,000 | 32,391,000 |
| 1900 | 12,541,000 | 33,853,000 | 46,394,000 |
| 1905 | 24,478,000 | 42,792,000 | 67,270,000 |

**Net Profits of Marshall Field & Co. by Retail and Wholesale, 1865–1905**

| Year | Retail | Wholesale | Total |
|------|--------|-----------|-------|
| 1865 | — | — | $ 240,000 |
| 1870 | — | — | — |
| 1875 | $ 68,000 | $ 1,023,700 | 1,091,700 |
| 1880 | 384,300 | 1,441,500 | 1,825,800 |
| 1885 | 397,600 | 1,270,500 | 1,668,100 |
| 1890 | 740,000 | 1,276,000 | 2,016,000 |
| 1895 | 448,700 | 1,299,100 | 1,747,800 |
| 1900 | 998,300 | 1,496,500 | 2,494,800 |
| 1905 | 1,281,700 | 2,865,300 | 4,147,000 |

Source: Twyman, *Field*, pp. 176–77.

## EXHIBIT 1B

**Annual Purchases of Marshall Field & Co., Wholesale, by Source for 1875–1905**

| Year | New York Purchases | Chicago Purchases | Foreign Purchases |
|------|--------------------|-------------------|-------------------|
| 1875 | $13,334,948 | $ 553,057 | $1,523,035 |
| 1880 | 15,891,862 | 909,825 | 2,036,228 |
| 1885 | 17,147,947 | 896,585 | 2,025,647 |
| 1890 | 20,819,196 | 1,356,869 | 2,755,036 |
| 1895 | 20,740,241 | 1,335,491 | 3,604,236 |
| 1900 | 27,015,829 | 1,661,069 | 4,275,166 |
| 1905 | 40,955,765 | 3,533,841 | 5,317,864 |

Source: Twyman, *Field*, p. 178.

## EXHIBIT 1C

**Relative Rates of Increase: Sales of Marshall Field & Company in Comparison with Total Manufactures and Wholesale Sales of City of Chicago for 1867–1906**

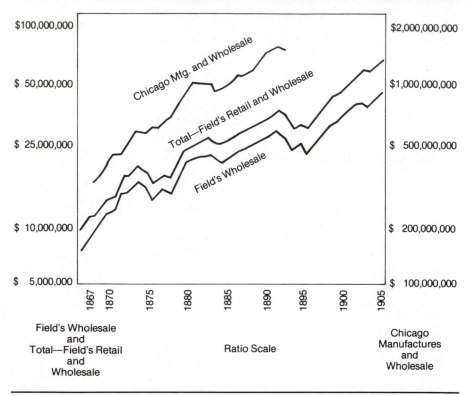

Source: Twyman, *Field*, p. 170.

## EXHIBIT 2

**Assets of Field, Leiter and Company in 1871**

| | |
|---|---:|
| Merchandise (mostly saved from fire or in transit to Chicago at time of fire) | $1,000,000 |
| Money owed to firm | 1,600,000 |
| Cash | 20,000 |
| Real estate | 30,000 |
| Bonds | 120,000 |
| Horses, wagons & harness | 16,000 |
| Collectible insurance | 1,780,000 |
| Total assets | $4,565,000 |

Source: Twyman, *Field,* p. 42.

# EXHIBIT 3

**Average Stock-Turn of Marshall Field & Co. by Retail and Wholesale 1878–1906**

| Year | Dry Goods | Rugs & Carpets | | Upholstery | Retail Average | Wholesale Average |
|------|-----------|------|------|------------|----------------|-------------------|
| | | *Retail* | | | *Total* | |
| 1878 | 5.5 | 4.0 | | 3.5 | 5.3 | 5.9 |
| 1879 | 5.3 | 3.2 | | 3.3 | 5.3 | 5.4 |
| 1880 | 5.0 | 2.4 | | 3.5 | 4.4 | 4.4 |
| 1881 | 5.2 | 3.3 | | 4.0 | 5.1 | 5.2 |
| 1882 | 5.6 | 3.0 | | 4.1 | 5.2 | 5.1 |
| 1883 | 5.7 | 3.3 | | 3.6 | 5.1 | 5.0 |
| 1884 | 5.8 | 2.6 | | 3.1 | 4.7 | 4.7 |
| 1885 | 5.9 | 2.6 | | 3.4 | 4.6 | 4.5 |
| 1886 | 5.2 | 1.8 | 2.4 | 3.2 | 4.1 | 4.1 |
| 1887 | 4.8 | 2.0 | 2.7 | 3.2 | 4.5 | 4.5 |
| 1888 | 6.4 | 2.2 | 3.6 | 2.9 | 4.7 | 4.4 |
| 1889 | 6.3 | 2.1 | 3.1 | 2.9 | 4.8 | 4.6 |
| 1890 | 6.3 | 2.4 | 4.2 | 3.3 | 5.1 | 4.9 |
| 1891 | 5.7 | 3.2 | 2.0 | 4.3 | 4.8 | 4.8 |
| 1892 | 5.9 | 3.7 | 2.0 | 3.7 | 5.4 | 5.4 |
| 1893 | 5.6 | 3.9 | 1.7 | 3.7 | 4.4 | 4.3 |
| 1894 | 5.2 | 4.8 | 1.8 | 3.4 | 5.3 | 5.5 |
| 1895 | 5.8 | 3.7 | 2.2 | 3.7 | 4.9 | 4.8 |
| 1896 | 6.0 | 2.6 | 1.9 | 4.8 | 4.3 | 4.0 |
| 1897 | 6.2 | 3.2 | 1.8 | 4.6 | 4.8 | 4.1 |
| 1898 | 5.8 | 3.8 | 1.6 | 4.1 | 4.6 | 4.4 |
| 1899 | 5.5 | 5.2 | 1.9 | 4.4 | 4.8 | 4.5 |
| 1900 | 5.3 | 3.9 | 2.1 | 4.1 | 4.1 | 3.7 |
| 1901 | 5.7 | 4.8 | 2.3 | 4.5 | 4.8 | 4.6 |
| 1902 | 6.4 | 3.6 | 2.3 | 5.0 | 5.1 | 4.8 |
| 1903 | 7.2 | 4.1 | 2.6 | 5.4 | 5.0 | 4.4 |
| 1904 | 8.2 | 3.8 | 2.7 | 6.5 | 5.3 | 4.5 |
| 1905 | 7.5 | 4.5 | 2.8 | 6.9 | 5.4 | 4.8 |
| 1906 | 6.9 | 3.4 | 2.5 | 7.4 | 5.0 | 4.5 |

Source: Twyman, *Field,* p. 119.

## EXHIBIT 4

**Numbers of Employees of Marshall Field & Co. 1868–1906**

| Year | Retail | Wholesale | Total |
|------|--------|-----------|-------|
| 1868 | 200 | 200 | 400 |
| 1872 | — | — | 1,000 |
| 1875 | — | 500 | — |
| 1877 | 800 | — | — |
| 1882 | 900 | 1,000 | 2,000 |
| 1884 | 1,500 | — | — |
| 1891 | — | 1,700 | — |
| 1894 | 3,000 | 1,800 | — |
| 1902 | 6,800 | — | — |
| 1906 | 6,500 to 9,000* | 3,400 to 3,600* | 12,000 |

*These figures indicate the increase in employees during the Christmas season.

Source: Twyman, *Field,* p. 69.

**EXHIBIT 5**

Advertising of Field

## European Modes.

**State & Washington-sts.,**

Are in receipt of

## "PARISIAN STYLES"

IN

## "Costumes,"
## "Mantles,"
AND
## "Cloaks,"

And will continue to add daily the latest NOVELTIES as they appear in FOREIGN MARKETS.

The Fashions in these Garments are unusually attractive this season.

## Ladies', Misses',
AND
## Children's
## Dresses and Cloaks

Are a special feature with us.

## EXAMINATION INVITED.

Source: Twyman, *Field,* p. 145.

## EXHIBIT 6

**Advertising of a Competitor**

# CHICAGO ELECTRIFIED!

THE **MOST ATTRACTIVE GOODS** FOR **ONE DOLLAR** EVER OFFERED IN THIS CITY.

## TRUTH

### STRANGER THAN FICTION.

I! shall open To-Morrow, at the

## City of Paris

### ONE DOLLAR STORE

The largest display of fine spangled and feathered

## SILK FANS

ever opened in Chicago, the choice for One Dollar. Among the lot are Ivory Fans costing $3 25 to import.

### Fine Lisle Thread Hose,

for Ladies, at one-half the price charged in popular dry goods stores.

Real Oil Paintings, on canvas.

Chromes, and large 10x14 Mirrors, in gilt, rosewood, and walnut frames, for One Dollar, at

---

Stein's City of Paris **ONE DOLLAR STORE,**

### 83 South Clark st.

Lined and Silk Parasols and Sun Umbrellas a la sombrero and a Stradella, for One Dollar, at Stein's.

Bronzed Work Boxes & Bronzed Hdkf. Boxes, something really elegant, for One Dollar.

The largest Glass Vases in the city, not waxed, but fast burned-in flowers. A Vase worth $3 for $1, at

## STEIN'S,

## 83 CLARK STREET.

200 new patterns of articles of bijoutry, among which Bracelets, heretofore retailed at $10 a pair; something truly magnificent, for One Dollar. You come to see them and are conquered.

Last, though not least, Stein continues the sale of Coin Silver Tea-Spoons for One Dollar, at which price all the merchandise in the City of Paris is offered daily to a delighted public.

Having just completed an extensive addition to my Bazaar, I cordially invite those timid persons, whom the large crowds have often deterred from viewing and inspecting the thousand and one great bargains, which the City of Paris is so famous for, and which will be offered in a greater variety, and of a more substantial quality than ever before.

---

Source: Twyman, *Field,* p. 141.

# EXHIBIT 7

**Ratio of Selected Retail and Wholesale Expenses to Retail and Wholesale Sales**

| | Retail | | | | | | Wholesale | | |
| | | | | Returns | | Total Retail | | | Total Wholesale |
| | Advtg. | Delivery | Rent | Cash* | Credit* | Expenses† | Selling | Returns | Expenses† |
|---|---|---|---|---|---|---|---|---|---|
| 1875 | .48% | 1.05% | — | — | — | 15.01% | .02% | — | 5.93% |
| 1880 | .23 | .84 | — | 3.23% | 9.14% | 12.02 | .07 | 2.74 | 6.46 |
| 1885 | .62 | 1.08 | — | 2.89 | 12.43 | 13.72 | .27 | 2.88 | 7.75 |
| 1890 | .56 | 1.24 | 1.66% | 3.75 | 17.81 | 15.31 | .50 | 2.85 | 8.94 |
| 1895 | .82 | 1.71 | 3.12 | 3.75 | 16.67 | 21.09 | .68 | 2.81 | 10.86 |
| 1900 | 1.22 | 2.30 | 2.41 | 4.69 | 21.20 | 19.58 | .91 | 3.24 | 10.80 |
| 1905 | .68 | 2.28 | 2.19 | 5.40 | 24.93 | 22.86 | 1.2 | 3.23 | 11.30 |

*The percentages given here are of cash and credit sales, respectively, rather than of total retail sales.

†These totals include expenses not enumerated here.

Source: Twyman, *Field*, pp. 93, 103–31, 152, 160–61.

## EXHIBIT 8

Value of Dry Goods Imported by Marshall Field & Co. and by Total of All Firms in City of Chicago (*1873–1880*)

| Year | M.F. & Co. | All Chicago | Year | M.F. & Co. | All Chicago |
|------|-----------|-------------|------|-----------|-------------|
| 1873 | $1,212,439 | $1,811,982 | 1877 | $1,058,815 | $1,681,939 |
| 1874 | 1,297,711 | 1,780,915 | 1878 | 1,081,549 | 1,410,285 |
| 1875 | 1,523,035 | 2,074,906 | 1879 | 1,208,568 | 2,033,863 |
| 1876 | 1,099,471 | 1,834,778 | 1880 | 2,036,228 | 2,935,412 |

Source: Twyman, *Field,* p. 28.

# CASE 13

# *The Integration of Mass Production and Mass Distribution* *

The distinctive feature of the modern industrial enterprise is that it is vertically integrated. It combines in a single business firm a number of factories, sales offices, purchasing units, transportation facilities, and sources of raw or semifinished materials. It integrates the processes of mass production with those of mass distribution. This form of business enterprise appeared quite suddenly and simultaneously in a variety of industries during the decade of the 1880s. In all cases, the new enterprises in these industries had the same basic common characteristics. They used continuous, large batch, or interchangeable parts processes of production, and they produced for national and global markets.

## Integration by Users of New Continuous-Process Technologies

The story of James Buchanan Duke provides a revealing example of the rise of a powerful modern industrial corporation. Duke's achievements basically rested on his appreciation of the potential of a cigarette-making machine invented by James Bonsack. Patented in 1882, the Bonsack machine produced, through a continuous-process method, 70,000 cigarettes a day even in its experimental stage. The most

*This case was prepared by Alfred D. Chandler, Jr., as the basis for class discussion. It follows closely his discussion in *The Visible Hand* (Cambridge: Harvard University Press, 1977).

Harvard Business School case 377-031, rev. 6/84.

efficient hand worker could only produce 3,000 a day. Soon the Bonsack machine was spewing out a daily quota of 120,000 cigarettes. In the early 1880s, 15 such machines could supply the entire world demand.

Duke, a manufacturer of smoking tobacco in Durham, North Carolina, decided in 1881, a year before Bonsack invented his machine, to produce cigarettes because he was having difficulty in competing with a well-established neighbor, Blackwell and Company. At that date cigarettes were still a new and exotic product just beginning to find favor in the growing urban markets. Cigarette smoking was only starting to take the place of pipe smoking, chewing tobacco, cigars, or snuff. In 1881, four cigarette firms produced 80 percent of the output, primarily for nearby markets.

As a newcomer, Duke was searching for a way to break into the market. The Bonsack machine looked like a good bet. In 1884, shortly after a sharp reduction in taxes on cigarettes permitted a major price cut to consumers, Duke installed two Bonsack machines. He soon realized that they lived up to the inventor's claim. With such machines, each producing 120,000 cigarettes a day, he could easily saturate the American market. To test the world market, Duke had already sent a close associate, Richard M. Wright, on a 19-month tour overseas. At the same time Duke himself developed machinery to package the first mass-produced tobacco product—packages that announced the brand and its virtues. In June 1885, Duke made his final move. He signed a contract with Bonsack to use the machine exclusively to make all his cigarettes, high quality as well as cheap, in return for a lower leasing charge.

Duke's gamble paid off. Output soared. Selling became the challenge. Even before he had made his basic contract with Bonsack, Duke built a factory in New York, the nation's largest urban market, and set up his administrative offices there. He immediately intensified a national advertising campaign. Not only did Duke rely on advertising agencies, but his own staff distributed vast quantities of cards, circulars, and handbills—all proclaiming the virtues of his brands.

He then began to build extensive sales and buying organizations. Duke followed up the contacts Wright had made on his trip abroad by signing marketing agreements with wholesalers and dealers in all parts of the globe. At the same time, he and one or two other associates established a network of sales offices in the larger American cities. These offices, headed by a salaried manager, became responsible for both the marketing and distributing of the product. The office kept an eye on local advertising. Its salesmen regularly visited tobacco, grocery, drug, and other jobbers and a few large retailers, to obtain orders. Duke's local sales managers worked closely with New York headquarters to assure the effective scheduling of the high-volume flow of cigarettes to jobbers and to a few large retailers.

At the same time that Duke and his close associates were building their sales organization, they were creating an extensive purchasing network in the bright-leaf tobacco region of the southeastern United States. Tobacco, after its annual harvest, was normally dried and cured before being sold to manufacturers. The timing of the process varied from several months to two or three years, according to the leaf and the quality desired. Because the supply of cured tobacco depended both on the size of the crop and the availability of curing facilities, prices fluctuated widely. By building its own buying, storing, and curing facilities, Duke's company was able to purchase directly from the farmers, usually at auctions, and so reduce transaction costs and uncertainties. What counted more was that the company was assured of a steady supply of cured tobacco into its factories in Durham and New York.

By combining mass production with mass distribution, Duke was able to maintain low prices and reap high profits. By 1889, Duke's sales topped $4.5 million, and his profits came to around $400,000 despite heavy advertising costs. To compete, other cigarette manufacturers had little choice but to follow Duke's strategy. They quickly turned to machine production and began to build and enlarge their sales and purchasing organizations. As packages of cigarettes were priced in 5¢ increments—5¢ for the standard package and 10¢ to 25¢ for the better brands—there was little room for price cutting, particularly in the all-important cheaper brands. The manufacturers concentrated on advertising instead. In 1889, Duke's advertising cost rose to $800,000 a year. Here his high volume and resulting cash flow gave him an advantage, for he had a larger cash surplus than the others to spend on advertising. But the cost of these sales campaigns reduced profits.

The desire to control this competition caused Duke and his four competitors to merge in 1890, forming the American Tobacco Company. The oligopoly of cigarettes had become a monopoly. For a brief time the constituent companies continued to operate independently; but after 1893, their functional activities were consolidated into the Duke manufacturing, sales, and leaf (purchasing) departments. As had been the case with railroads and would be again in manufacturing, the largest of the early enterprises became the core organization for continuing growth. The enlarged, centralized, departmentalized company, operating from its New York corporate central office, proved extraordinarily profitable even during the economically depressed years of the 1890s. Profits from cigarettes allowed Duke to install new methods of production and distribution in other branches of the tobacco trade. By 1900, the American Tobacco Company had come to dominate the industry completely, except for the making of cigars.

As Richard Tennant, the most careful student of the modern American tobacco industry, points out: "The struggle for the cigar industry was the one case in which the Trust's methods met with complete defeat." Despite the strongest of marketing efforts, including the creation of an expensive nationwide retailing organization (United Cigar Stores Company with nearly 400 retail stores), and despite the most destructive of price wars, American Tobacco never obtained more than 14 percent of the nation's cigar trade.

Duke's mistake was his failure to appreciate fully that the American Tobacco Company could use little of its existing organization to make and sell cigars. The processes of both production and distribution were different. Plug, smoking tobacco, and snuff all used high-volume continuous processes of manufacturing and packaging. Their leaf came from the same areas in the southeastern United

States, and they were sold to much the same markets and through much the same jobbers as cigarettes. Cigars, on the other hand, were produced by skilled work-men in small batches. Their leaf came from Cuba, Puerto Rico, and scattered areas in the northeastern United States. It was cured quite differently from other types of tobacco. Finally, cigars traditionally had been sold by their makers in small lots to retailers. Like wines, the many different brands had distinctive tastes and flavors. Each appealed to a different type of customer. Cigars were not a prod-uct that could be mass produced and mass distributed, nor could the raw materials be purchased in bulk. Since these processes did not lend themselves to high-volume throughput, administrative coordination did not reduce costs and so raise barriers to entry. Neither massive advertising nor effective organization could bring the dominance of a single firm in the cigar business.

The history of the match industry closely parallels that of the cigarette indus-try except that the development of fully automated machinery for mass produc-tion came more slowly as did packaging and branding. After the Civil War, ma-chines began to replace hand production. By the early 1870s, four machine-using firms accounted for 80 percent of the industry's output. Each had its own special-ized machinery, and each concentrated on a single regional market. After a brief period of competition for the national market, these four combined in 1881 to form the Diamond Match Company.

The leading entrepreneurs in the new firm, E. B. Beecher, William Swift, and Ohio Columbus Barber, then agreed on the strategy of improving the basic machinery by combining the best attributes of the different machines used by the erstwhile competitors. The result was, in the words of the firm's historian, "The beginning of the modern continuous, automatic match machine . . . that revolu-tionized the match industry." At the same time the company developed compara-ble machines for the manufacture of paperboard and strawboard boxes. By the early 1890s, 75 workers could produce two million filled matchboxes a day, an out-put equivalent to that of 500 workers prior to the introduction of the new ma-chines. Production was then consolidated in large plants. In 1880, there were over 30 match factories. By 1900, production was concentrated in one giant plant at Barberville, Ohio, and three smaller ones. By then, Barber, Beecher, and Swift had built a sales organization that, like Duke's, was responsible for establishing and maintaining contact with wholesalers for local advertising and for coordinat-ing the flow of packages to the jobbers and often the retailers. Its buying organiza-tion began to purchase its wood paper and chlorate of potash directly from pro-ducers; the latter material buyers obtained entirely from Europe. Soon the company had its own sawing and woodworking mills in Wisconsin and New Eng-land. In the 1890s, it began to construct the largest match factory in the world in Liverpool. By the end of the decade, it had plants in Germany, Canada, Peru, and Brazil.

New continuous-process methods of production had almost as great an im-pact on the processing and sales of that ancient American industry, milling of grain, as it had on the nation's oldest commercial crop, tobacco. The innovative efforts of Cadwallader Colden Washburn and the Pillsbury Brothers in the development of the automatic all-roller, gradual-reduction mill assured their enterprises leading positions in the industry. So, too, did a comparable mill built in 1882 by the oatmeal producer, Henry P. Crowell. That mill has been described as "the first in the world to maintain under one roof operations to grade, clean, hull, cut, package, and ship oatmeal to interstate markets in a continuous process that in some aspects anticipated the modern assembly line."

These new continuous-process plants had more immediate impact on the structure of the oatmeal than the flour industry. For a while at least, the demand for flour was high enough and the costs reduced enough by the new machinery that the "new process" millers had little difficulty in disposing of their output by selling in bulk to wholesalers. On the other hand, the demand for oatmeal was more limited. A new market had to be found if the great volume of output from the new machines was to be sold. As a result, the modern breakfast cereal industry was invented.

The pioneer in developing this product was Crowell, the builder of the first continuous-process mill. While Ferdinand Schumaker, the largest producer, continued to market in the accepted way of selling in bulk through wholesalers, Crowell packaged and then advertised his brand, Quaker Oats, nationally as a breakfast cereal—a product that was even newer to American tastes than the cigarette. In advertising Quaker Oats, Crowell's staff used, in the manner of Duke, box-top premiums and prizes and added testimonials, scientific endorsements, and the like. The company set up sales offices in the United States and abroad. Its managers were expected, as were Duke's, not only to maintain contact with jobbers but also to schedule flows from the factory to the jobbers. At the same time Crowell built a buying organization that soon came to include "fieldmen" who purchased directly from the farmers in the grain-growing states and buyers who had seats on the Minneapolis and Chicago grain exchanges.

The response of other manufacturers to Crowell's aggressive marketing campaign in oatmeal was similar to that toward Duke's in tobacco. In 1888, after a brief attempt at a cartel, Crowell, Schumaker, and a third large mass producer of oatmeal, Robert Stewart, formed the American Cereal Company. (It became the Quaker Oats Company in 1901.) Despite the determined opposition of Schumaker, who retained his preference for marketing in bulk, the new company took over and expanded Crowell's selling and purchasing organization. Production became concentrated in two giant plants—one at Akron and the other at Cedar Rapids—each using improved continuous-process machinery. After the turn of the century, to make fuller use of its marketing and purchasing facilities, the company added new lines of wheat cereals, farina, hominy, corn meal, specialized baby foods, and animal feed.

In the early 1890s, as the demand for rolled mill flour leveled off, the Minneapolis and other millers began to follow the example of the American Cereal Company. Decline in prices at the beginning of the decade initially brought plans for large-scale mergers. These failed, as the leading companies preferred to remain independent. The Washburn firm was reorganized under the presidency of James S. Bell as the Washburn Crosby Company, and the Pillsbury family continued to operate through what became known as the Pillsbury-Washburn Flour Company. Bell and the Pillsburys quickly turned to the strategy of vertical integration. They began to package their products rather than selling in bulk and to advertise their brands, Gold Medal Flour and Pillsbury, on a national scale. During the 1890s, they created selling and buying networks similar to those of Crowell. From 1889 on, the Pillsburys had a chain of grain elevators in the wheat-growing regions. Because their product, flour, was so widely used and because the supply of wheat was so extensive, a single firm did not come to dominate the industry as in the tobacco, match, and breakfast cereal trades. On the other hand, Washburn Crosby and Pillsbury continued to be the largest American flour millers well into the 20th century.

The first enterprises to utilize fully the "automatic-line" canning factory were those that developed a product line which permitted more than seasonal operations. The most successful of these were H. J. Heinz and Company of Pittsburgh and the Campbell Soup Company of Camden, New Jersey. In 1880, Henry John Heinz, a small processor of pickles, relishes, sauces, and similar products for the local Pittsburgh market, was still recovering from his bankruptcy in 1876. In the early 1880s, he adopted new continuous canning and bottling processes, built a network of sales offices to sell in the national market, extensively advertised his many brands, and created a large buying and storing organization to assure a steady flow of vegetables and other foodstuffs into his factories. By 1888, Heinz had become one of Pittsburgh's most substantial citizens and was completing one of the largest factories in that industrial center. The company has remained to this day one of the largest food processors in the country.

Less is known about the beginning and growth of the Campbell Soup Company; but it appeared at almost the same time and became large in the same way. It has long remained one of the major business enterprises in the Philadelphia area, and the Dorrance family, who had joined with Joseph Campbell to found and operate the firm, has remained one of the city's wealthiest clans.

Other processors who used the large continuous canning plants were those who produced condensed canned milk and canned meats. In 1882, two of the smaller meat packers, Libby, McNeil & Libby and Wilson & Company, began volume production of canned meats in Chicago. At the same time the pioneer in the condensing of milk, the Borden Milk Company, greatly enlarged its operations and expanded and rationalized its marketing and purchasing organizations. It did so partly because of the expanding market but also because foreign enterprises had moved across the sea to exploit the American trade.

In that decade, both the Anglo-Swiss Condensed Milk Company (a forerunner of Nestlé) and the Helvetia Milk Condensing Company (the precursor of two American firms, the Pet Milk Company and the Carnation Milk Company) set up plants and sales organizations in the United States.

Where canning remained seasonal, as was the case for most vegetables, fruit, and fish products, the large canning company did not appear. Instead, canneries came to receive their cans and canning equipment from two large canmaking companies, American Can and Continental Can. American Can, whose first president was Edward Norton, the inventor of the "automatic-line" process, resulted from a merger in 1901. Continental Can was formed in 1906. Only those companies which had early in their history developed products that could be produced year-round continued to remain large and dominant firms. As late as the 1950s, the largest users of cans still included Campbell Soup, H. J. Heinz, Carnation, Borden's, Pet Milk, and Libby, McNeil & Libby. All but the last have made, and some still are making, their own cans.

Yet another industry, soap, adopted continuous-process machinery in the 1880s. Soap production for the commercial market had started as a by-product of the meat-packing industry, with small companies processing animal fats for regional markets. In the late 1870s, mechanical improvements in the mixing and crushing process used in making bar soap greatly expanded output. British firms such as Pears and Pond quickly began to advertise in the American market. In 1879, a small Cincinnati soap maker, Procter & Gamble, developed by accident a soap that floated. It was branded Ivory. By using the new machinery, Procter & Gamble was soon making 200,000 cakes of Ivory soap a day. To sell its volume, the firm began to advertise nationally and then to build a network of branch sales offices. At the same time, it created an extended buying organization to assure itself of a steady supply of perishable raw materials—animal and vegetable oils, fats, and soda ash. By 1885, the company had constructed Ivorydale, a model industrial plant, one of the largest in Cincinnati. To make full and integrated use of its facilities, Procter & Gamble then moved into the production of laundry and other soaps, cottonseed and salad oil, and similar products. During the 1880s, other soap manufacturers, including Colgate & Company, N. K. Fairbanks, B. T. Babbitt, and D. S. Brown, built integrated enterprises similar to Procter & Gamble. These new large enterprises soon found themselves competing with meat packers and cotton-oil producers who had moved into soap production as well as with leading European soap manufacturers who had continued to sell in the American market.

Another major innovation in continuous-process machinery appearing in the 1880s was in the photographic industry. In 1884, George Eastman of Rochester, New York, one of the three largest producers of plate glass photographic equipment, devised continuous-process machinery for making gelatin emulsion film. The new film began to come on the market in 1885. Eastman expected the much cheaper film to replace existing plate glass techniques, and to provide the required volume of photosensitive paper, he invented a similar process for its production. To Eastman's dismay, commercial photographers continued to prefer to use plate glass rather than the less expensive roll film, which was more difficult to handle. To provide a market for his mass-produced film, Eastman concentrated his attention in 1887 on inventing a small, inexpensive hand camera to be operated by amateurs. The new "Kodak" proved an immediate success. To assure a continuing high volume of sales, Eastman then greatly enlarged his marketing organization. He set up branch offices that not only distributed cameras to retail outlets but also handled shipments of customers' exposed and semiperishable film to Rochester for developing and printing. As production of cameras and film soared, Eastman created a network of purchasing offices to buy massive quantities of paper, celluloid, lenses, and other material. Before 1900, Eastman Kodak, the towering giant of the industry, was beginning to manufacture several of these items in its own plants.

Thus, during a very short period in the 1880s, new processes of production and distribution had transformed the organization of a number of major American industries—tobacco, matches, grain milling, canning, soap, and photography. These changes were revolutionary, and they were permanent. The enterprises that pioneered in adopting and integrating the new ways of mass production and mass distribution quickly became nationally known. By 1900, they were household words. Almost a century later the names of American Tobacco, Diamond Match, Quaker Oats, Pillsbury Flour, Campbell Soup, Heinz, Borden's, Carnation, Libby, Procter & Gamble, and Eastman Kodak are still well known.

## Integration by the Processors of Perishable Products

While the mass producers of semiperishable packaged products continued to use the wholesaler to handle the physical distribution of their goods, even after they had taken over that middleman's advertising and scheduling functions, the makers of more perishable products, such as meat and beer, in most cases by-passed the wholesaler altogether. The market for perishable products expanded as the railroad and telegraph networks grew. As early as the 1850s, crude refrigerator cars were used to bring milk, butter, and meat to urban markets. In the 1870s, when the direct movement of cars over long distances became possible, western meat packers began to ship fresh meat to the eastern cities. Then, in 1881, the modern refrigerated car made its appearance. Gustavus F. Swift hired Andrew J. Chase, a leading refrigeration engineer, to design a car to carry Swift's dressed beef from Chicago to Boston. Again, the 1880s were the crucial decade.

The refrigerator car, however, was not the reason why Swift became the innovator in high-volume, year-round production of perishable products. He became the first modern meat packer because he was the first to appreciate the need for a distribution network to store meat and deliver it to the retailers. He was the first to build an integrated enterprise to coordinate the high-volume flow of meat from the purchasing of cattle through the slaughtering or disassembling processes and through distribution to the retailer and ultimate consumer.

When Gustavus Swift, a New England wholesale butcher, moved to Chicago in 1875, nearly all meat went East "on the hoof." Western cattle were shipped alive by rail in cattle cars to local wholesalers who did the butchering and made deliveries to retailers. The economies of slaughtering in the West and shipping the dressed meat East were obvious. Sixty percent of an animal was inedible, and cattle lost weight and often died on the trip east. Moreover, the concentration of butchering in Chicago and other western cities permitted a high-volume, continuous operation, which not only lowered unit cost but also made possible fuller use of by-products.

To carry out his strategy, Swift, who had begun eastern shipments in 1878, not only concentrated on improving the refrigerated car but began to build a network of branch houses, first in the Northeast and then after 1881 in the rest of the country. Each house included refrigerated storage space, a sales office, and a sales staff to sell and deliver the meat to the retail butchers, grocers, and other food shops. Swift soon supplemented this distributing and marketing network with "peddler car routes," which distributed dressed meat in small lots by refrigerator car to small towns and villages.

In executing his plan, Swift met with the most determined opposition. Railroads, startled by the prospect of losing their livestock business, which was an even greater producer of revenue than grain on the route from the West to the East, refused to build refrigerated cars. When Swift began to construct his own, the Eastern Trunk Line Association refused to carry them. Only by using the Grand Trunk, then outside of the association, was Swift able to bring his cars East. At the same time he had to combat boycotts by local wholesalers who, in 1886, formed the National Butchers' Protective Association to fight "the Trust." These butchers attempted to exploit a prejudice against eating fresh meat that had been killed days or even weeks before more than a thousand miles away.

Nevertheless, high quality at low prices soon won out. Though Swift did rely on advertising to counter prejudice against his product, it was clearly the prices and quality made possible by high-volume operations and the speed and careful scheduling of product flow that won the market. Once the market was assured, Swift had to expand his production facilities to keep up with demand. He increased his speed of throughput by subdividing the processes of butchering and by using moving "disassembly" lines. In the 1880s and early 1890s, Swift & Company built new packing plants in six cities along the cattle frontier. The company then bought into adjoining stockyards where men from its purchasing department became experts in buying cattle in volume.

Other packers realized that if they were to compete with Swift in the national market they must quickly follow his lead. By the end of 1882, Philip D. Armour of Chicago and George H. Hammond of Detroit were beginning to build comparable networks of branch houses and to compete with Swift for the best locations along the railroad lines. Nelson Morris of Chicago and the two Cudahy brothers of Omaha constructed similar networks in the mid-1880s. The oligopoly was rounded out when the New York firm of Swartschild and Sulzberger completed a comparable integrated national enterprise in the early 1890s. Except for Hammond, who died in 1886, all these entrepreneurs quickly enlarged their processing facilities, built new packing plants in other western cities, bought into the stockyards, and expanded their fleet of refrigerated cars. Well before the end of the 80s, a small number of very large integrated meat-packing firms dominated the dressed-meat business, and they continued to do so until well into the 20th century.

Improved transportation also encouraged several brewers to enter the national market. In the 1880s, a new pneumatic malting process increased speed and improved control in the process of brewing beer. At the same time the development of temperature-controlled tank cars made it possible to distribute their product nationally. In the 1870s, brewers sold only within a relatively small radius of their plant, relying on traveling salesmen to sell the product by the barrel to wholesalers. In the 1880s, Pabst, Schlitz, and Blatz of Milwaukee, Lamp and Anheuser of St. Louis (the able Adolphus Busch took over Anheuser in 1880), and Moelin of Cincinnati all began to build a nationwide distributing network and to use advertising agencies to reach the national market. For example in early 1879, Pabst had only one branch, in nearby Chicago. That year a second was set up in Kansas City. Between 1881 and 1894, the company built 30 more branches in every part of the country. Although Pabst used wholesalers in some cities, an increasing proportion of sales came to be made through company offices that stored, distributed, marketed, and advertised the Pabst product. In 1887, Pabst went one step further by moving into retailing through purchasing saloons and then renting them to operators. In the same years, Pabst and the other national brewers expanded their purchasing organizations, using them to buy high-quality malt, barley, rice, hops, and other materials in large quantities with precise specifications. They also set up barrel-making plants and purchased timberlands. By the 1890s, these integrated enterprises were, like the meat packers, among the largest businesses in the land.

## Integration by Machinery Makers Requiring Specialized Marketing Services

The other type of manufacturers to by-pass the wholesalers were the makers of recently invented machines which were produced in volume through the fabricating and assembling of interchangeable parts. The sales of these mass-produced machines required marketing services which the existing wholesalers and retailers had difficulty in providing. The history of the production and distribution of sewing machines, the first of this type of machinery to be developed, indicates the nature of these marketing needs. By 1851, sewing machines had been perfected so that they could be sold commercially; but manufacturers were not able to make them in quantity until the legal battle over patents was settled in 1854 and a patent pool formed. The winner of the court trials, Elias Howe, insisted that the pooled patents be released to 24 manufacturers. Nevertheless, the industry became dominated within a very short time by the three firms that first built marketing organizations—Wheeler & Wilson Co., Grover and Baker, and I. M. Singer Company. These manufacturers at first relied on full-time but independent agents who, though receiving a small salary, were paid primarily on a commission basis and were solely responsible for marketing activities within their territories. The manufacturers quickly learned that these agents had little technical knowledge of the machines. They were unable to demonstrate them properly or to service and repair them. Nor were the agents able to provide credit needed if customers were to pay for these relatively expensive goods in installments.

As an alternative, Grover and Baker set up a company-owned and -operated store or branch office to provide such services. By 1856, Grover and Baker had already established such branch offices, as they were called, in 10 cities. In that year Isaac Merritt Singer decided to follow suit. So, almost immediately, did Wheeler

& Wilson. By 1859, Singer had opened 14 branches, each with a female demonstrator, a mechanic to repair and service, and a salesman or canvasser to sell the machine, as well as a manager who supervised the others and handled collections and credits. Nevertheless, because finding and training personnel took time, these three enterprises continued to rely heavily on commission agents to market their goods. The swift selection of these agents and the building of branch stores made it possible for these three firms to dominate the industry. By 1860, they produced three fourths of the industry's output, with Wheeler & Wilson manufacturing 85,000 machines in that year and the other two 55,000 apiece.

After 1860, Singer moved more aggressively than the other two in replacing regional distributors with branch stores supervised by full-time, salaried regional agents. Edward Clark, Singer's partner and the business brains of the partnership, had become even more convinced as time passed of the value of relying on his own sales force. The independent agents had difficulty in supplying the necessary marketing services, and they failed to maintain inventories properly. They waited until their stocks were low and then telegraphed large orders, requesting immediate delivery. They seemed to be always either understocked or overstocked. Moreover, the agents were frustratingly slow in returning payments made on the machines to the central office.

Therefore, Clark was constantly on the lookout for men he could hire as salaried "general agents" or regional managers of geographical districts to supervise existing branch stores and to set up new ones. Where such men could not be found, Clark continued to rely on independent agents; but he insisted that these dealers set up branch offices similar to those in a company-managed district.

When Clark became president in 1876, a year after Singer's death, he decided to eliminate the independent agencies altogether at home and abroad. Singer's central offices in New York and London had as yet little control over the branch stores of the independent distributors and, in fact, relatively little control over their own salaried agents. Little effort had been made to sell in any systematic or standardized way. Little uniformity existed in sales, accounting, credit policies and procedures. The techniques of administrative coordination had not yet been perfected. Moreover, in 1877, the last patents of the 1856 pool were to expire. After that year Singer would have to compete at home, at it had long done abroad, without patent protection.

Working closely with George Ross McKenzie, a Scotsman who helped to build Singer's overseas sales organization and who succeeded him as president, Clark gradually reorganized and rationalized Singer's marketing and distribution network. First, he completed the replacement of the independent distributors with regional offices manned by salaried executives. Then he installed everywhere similar branch offices with teams of canvassers as well as repairmen and accountants. Such offices had proven particularly successful in Great Britain, an area where Singer had never enjoyed patent protection. The network made possible aggressive marketing, reliable service and repair, and careful supervision of credits and collections; it also assured a steady cash flow from the field to the headquarters in London, Hamburg, and New York.

In the period immediately after 1878, Clark and McKenzie perfected the procedures and methods needed to supervise and evaluate this branch office network. In the United States, 15 different regional "general agencies" reported to the central office in New York. In Europe and the other parts of the world, branches were supervised by 26 regional sales offices. The managers in charge of those in Northern and Central Europe reported to headquarters in Hamburg. Those in the rest of Europe, Africa, and the Near East reported to London, while those in Latin America, Canada, and the Far East were supervised by the central New York office.

The expansion and then reformation of the marketing organization resulted in a constant increase in Singer's sales and therefore in the daily output of its factories and the overall size of the enterprise. In 1874, the company built by far the largest sewing machine factory in the world at Elizabethport, New Jersey. During the 1880s, it grew in size; but its capacity was surpassed when the company constructed a plant in 1885 in Kilbowie, Scotland (a suburb of Glasgow). That plant, with a rated capacity of 10,000 machines a week, was constructed to replace a smaller Scottish plant built in 1867. Both plants were constructed to improve coordination between production and distribution. The filling of hundreds and then thousands of orders in Europe from the American factory became more and more difficult. Such delays became the major cause for losing orders. In 1866, for example, the head of Singer's London office complained that the inability to deliver machines had "utterly ruined" the company's business in Britain. All Singer's capital facilities—its two great factories, a small cabinetmaking plant in South Bend, Indiana, and a foundry in Austria—were financed out of current earnings.

Increased demand in these years caused Singer to expand and systematize its purchasing operations. By the 1890s, the company had obtained its own timberlands, an iron mill, and some transportation facilities. These purchases were also paid for from the ample cash flow provided by sale of the machines. Indeed, the company often had a surplus, which it invested in railroad and government bonds and even in other manufacturing firms. Both insiders and outsiders credited Singer's business success to its marketing organization and abilities.

Organization also appears to have been a critical element in the success of the leading manufacturer of the most complex agricultural machine, the mechanical reaper. According to a grandson, who wrote a detailed history of the family enterprise, Cyrus McCormick came to lead the field because he "had at his back the best business organization." During the 1850s, the rapid expansion of the railroads and the telegraph permitted the inventors of reapers, harvesters, and other agricultural machinery to build sizable factories for the first time. In marketing their products, McCormick and his competitors, Obed Hussey, John H. Manny, and Lewis Miller, relied, like the sewing machine makers, on territorial agents or distributors. The agents received a small salary, usually $2 a week, plus a 5–10 percent commission. Fully responsible for all sales activities in their districts, they hired subagents or dealers who made the actual sales, handled service and repair, granted credit, and supervised collections. McCormick differed from his competitors in that he kept a closer surveillance over his distributors through a team of "traveling agents" and through constant correspondence.

The coming of the depression of the 1870s caused McCormick to centralize his sales organization, which had by that time come to include close to 50 distributing agencies. At about the same time that Clark and McKenzie began to phase out the independent distributors at Singer, McCormick decided to replace his regional agents with offices manned by salaried managers and employees. The subagents, who were formerly hired and supervised by the agent, now became franchised dealers. These dealers, usually local livery men, storekeepers, and the like, signed a contract with the company directly. The contract stipulated a dealer's duties in the selling of machines, spare parts, wire, and later, twine for binding. It normally pledged the dealer to handle only McCormick reapers and harvesters but permitted him to market other types of implements made by other manufacturers.

The primary task of the regional office manager was to keep a close watch on the dealers. He also supervised customer credit and collection and handled local advertising. That office had a number of salesmen who assisted the dealers and often made sales on their own account. Finally, the regional office included trained mechanics who assembled the machines when they arrived from the factory, demonstrated their operations, and serviced them when needed. During the harvest season, the factory would normally curtail production and send out skilled men to the branches to assist in the servicing. (In the mid-1880s, the company employed 140 such "field experts.") By creating a regional office network, McCormick pioneered in forming a sales organization to back up franchise dealers, who did the retailing, much as Singer had innovated in developing its network of company-owned and -operated branch retail stores. In the 1880s and 1890s, McCormick began to extend its sales overseas to the wheat-growing regions of Europe, Australia, and New Zealand. For foreign marketing, however, it relied, until the late 1890s, on local independent distributors.

As at Singer, the expansion of the marketing network increased factory output. Between 1880 and 1884, output increased from 20,000 machines to 50,000 machines annually. To assure continuing flow of goods into the factory, the company systematized purchasing. To meet its requirements of 10 million feet a year of ash, hickory, oak, and poplar, the company began in 1885 to buy timber tracts and sawmills in Missouri and Alabama.

In the late 1870s and 1880s, other manufacturers of harvestors and other relatively costly agricultural machinery began to build or expand marketing organizations similar to those of the McCormick company. Walter A. Wood & Co., D. M. Osborne & Co., William Deering & Co., producing the new Appleby Twine Binder, and Warder, Bushnell & Glessner Co., makers of the Champion line, all created national branch office networks. So did the J. I. Case Threshing Company, Inc. and the three leading makers of modern steel plows—John Deere & Company, the Moline Plow Company, both of Moline, Illinois, and the Emerson Brantingham Company of Rockford, Illinois. The three plow makers quickly moved to making other less complex implements, including drills, wagons, mowers, and spreaders, in order to use their sales organizations more fully. All of these firms, like McCormick, began in the 1890s to integrate backward, obtaining hemp and timberlands and, in some cases, even mines.

The integration of mass production and mass distribution of newly invented office machines followed much the same pattern as sewing and agricultural machinery. Scales, letter presses, typewriters, cash registers, adding machines, mimeograph machines, calculators—all required the building of a large marketing organization if the product was to be manufactured in volume. And so the first firms in the field continued long to be the dominant ones.

The experience of the first mass producer of the earliest business machines, E. & T. Fairbanks of St. Johnsbury, Vermont, paralleled McCormick's. Fairbanks, a manufacturer of weighing scales essential to the shipment and sale of goods, began in the 1850s to sell through regional agencies. Like McCormick, "itinerant agents" supervised closely their activities. After the Civil War, the firm built a network of regional branch offices with salaried managers, "scales experts," and canvassers to sell machines, provide consumer credit and continuing service, and also to assure steady flow of goods to and cash from the customers. To make full use of its marketing organization, the company quickly began to develop a full line, selling letter and waybill presses, warehouse trucks, and "money drawers," the predecessors of the cash register.

The pioneering firms in the manufacturing of typewriters and cash registers, which set up their sales forces in the 1880s, relied more heavily on canvassers and small Singer-like branch offices than did Fairbanks. John H. Patterson attributed the swift growth of his innovative enterprise, National Cash Register, after 1884—and with it the expansion of the industry as a whole—to the strength of his canvassing force, the training and competence of his salesmen, and the ability of his marketing organization to provide credit and service.

The Remington experience underlines in a dramatic fashion the necessity of creating an extensive marketing organization to sell a new office machine in volume. As the Civil War came to a close, E. Remington and Sons of Illion, New York, one of the first firms to mass produce the modern breech-loading rifle, began to look for products to use their specialized manufacturing facilities and skills. In 1865, they set up the Remington Brothers Agricultural Works to make mowing machines and cultivators. As they did not attempt to develop the marketing organization, the enterprise failed. Next they were approached by a former Singer executive to produce an improved sewing machine. Again they failed. The machine was excellent, but, in the words of Remington's historian, "To sell it was another matter." They had little success in quickly creating an effective sales organization, and without it, Remington had little chance of competing successfully with Singer and the other established firms.

In 1873, the inventor of the typewriter, Christopher L. Sholes, came to the Remingtons and asked them to manufacture his typewriter at their Illion plant. This time they moved more slowly, selling the product at first through E. & T. Fairbanks. When, in 1881, the typewriter proved a commercial success, the Remingtons hired a small team to build a sales force. Because these men concentrated on the home market, they asked Singer to sell their products abroad. When the Singer company refused, they began to set up their own marketing organization overseas. In 1886, difficulties in the gun business, as well as other activities, brought the Remington Arms Company into bankruptcy. Those men who were developing the typewriter sales organization then bought out the company's typewriter interests and set up a new firm, Remington Typewriter Company. Soon their enterprise was as successful as Singer or National Cash Register. A number of rivals appeared, but only the Underwood Company and the Wagner Typewriter Company, which built similar sales organizations, succeeded in becoming significant competitors.

As the experience of all the new mass-produced machinery companies emphasizes, they could sell in volume only if they created a massive multi-unit marketing organization. All their products were new, all were relatively complicated to operate and maintain, and all relatively costly.

This was even more true for the makers of new, technologically advanced, relatively standardized machinery that was sold to other manufacturers to be used in their production processes. Because such producers' goods were even more complex and more costly, they required specialized installation, as well as closer attention to after-sales service and repair. The sales forces for such manufacturers required more professional training than persons selling light machines in mass markets. Salesmen often had degrees in mechanical engineering. Again, it was the decade of the 1880s when enterprises in these industries began to build or rationalize national and global sales forces.

An excellent example of enterprises producing and marketing in volume for global markets were the makers of recently invented machinery to generate, transmit, and use electricity for power and light. The salesmen at Westinghouse, Thomson-Houston, and Edison General Electric (the last two combined into General Electric in 1892) all knew more about the technical nature of their equipment than did most of their customers. Moreover, few independent distributors could obtain a firm grasp of the rapidly changing new technology. Because of the dangers of electrocution and fire, trained, salaried employees of these companies had to install and service and repair their products.

Moreover, financing involved large sums, often requiring extensive credit, which smaller, nonintegrated producers were unable to provide. Thompson-Houston and Edison Electric and, to a lesser extent, Westinghouse began to finance new local central power stations in order to build the market for their machinery.

In these pioneering years of the electrical equipment business, technology was developing fast, and coordination between the sales, production, and purchasing departments thus involved more than scheduling flows of material. It meant that salesmen, equipment designers, and the manufacturing executives had to be in constant touch to coordinate technological improvements with market needs so that the product could be produced at the lowest possible unit cost. It also meant that independent sales agencies had little chance of acquiring necessary skills to market the product.

Other manufacturers, whose products were based on electricity, developed in these same years similar marketing organizations with worldwide networks of branch offices. Such enterprises included Western Electric, the subsidiary of

American Bell Telephone, which produced telephones and equipment necessary to relay calls, the Johnson Company, which built electric streetcar rails and switches, and the Otis Elevator Company. Otis, established in 1854, began to expand after 1878 when it built its first high-speed hydraulic elevator for commercial buildings. The coming of electricity, a flexible source of power, helped the company expand its market. The branch office network created at Otis in the 1880s permitted it to dominate the business completely abroad as well as at home until well into the 20th century, when Westinghouse became a major competitor.

Other makers of standardized machinery built comparable organizations in the 1880s. One was Babcock & Wilcox, makers of steam boilers and steam machinery, founded in 1881 and financed by Singer Sewing Machine Company profits. Another was the Henry B. Worthington Company, maker of pumps and hydraulic equipment for urban water and sewage systems in all parts of the world. In this same decade Link-Belt Machinery Company, makers of conveying and transmission machinery, and the Norton Company, makers of grinding wheels and grind wheel machinery, set up their widespread sales and buying networks. And there were undoubtedly others.

The makers of new machinery so central to the mechanization of American agriculture, business, and industry created similar integrated enterprises at about the same time and in about the same way. Their organization, operation, and financing of these enterprises manufacturing durable goods was comparable to the firms that pioneered in the mass production and mass distribution of semiperishable and perishable products. Nearly all of these machinery makers either built or perfected their marketing and purchasing organizations in the decade of the 1880s. In nearly all cases, production remained concentrated in a small number of large plants. To manage their multifunctional enterprises, they built similar centralized, functionally departmentalized organizational structures. They differed from the manufacturers of perishable and semiperishable goods in that the purchasing organizations were smaller. The makers of the new sewing machine and agricultural and office machinery integrated backward to control suppliers of raw and semifinished materials, but this was less common among the makers of electrical equipment and other heavy machinery. But like the producers of perishables and semiperishables, these machine companies continued to dominate their industries for decades.

# CASE 14

# The Standard Oil Company— Combination, Consolidation, and Integration *

## Introduction

An understanding of the history of the Standard Oil Company is essential to the understanding of the rise of the large corporation in the American economy. Modern large-scale business organizations appeared in the operation of the major railroads in the 1850s. In the 1870s and 1880s, similar business organizations were formed in the meat packing, sewing machine, harvester, and other industries where the manufacturer was unable to distribute his goods effectively through the existing wholesaler network. The more normal road to size in American manufacturing, however, was the route which Standard Oil took. That road involved horizontal combination followed by legal and administrative consolidation and then vertical integration.

*This case, prepared by Alfred D. Chandler, Jr., is based primarily on: Harold F. Williamson and Arnold F. Daum, *The American Petroleum Industry: The Age of Illumination, 1859–1899* (Evanston, Ill.: Northwestern University Press, 1959); supplemented by Ralph W. Hidy and Muriel E. Hidy, *Pioneering in Big Business, 1882–1911* (New York: Harper & Row, 1955); Allan Nevins, *John D. Rockefeller: The Heroic Age of American Enterprise,* 2 vols. (New York: Scribner's, 1940); Allan Nevins, *Study in Power, John D. Rockefeller, Industrialist and Philanthropist,* 2 vols. (New York: Charles Scribner's Sons, 1953); and Ida Tarbell, *The History of the Standard Oil Company,* 2 vols. (New York: McClure, 1904). It was prepared as a basis for class discussion rather than to illustrate either effective or ineffective handling of an administrative situation. This is a revision of a case originally prepared by S. M. Salsbury under the supervision of A. M. Johnson.

Harvard Business School case 362-001, rev. 6/84.

This pattern of corporate growth became common during the last years of the 19th century. Occasional, short-lived, local combinations had been organized in the 1850s and 1860s as the factory form of production spread over the land. It was not, however, until the severe economic depression of the 1870s that industrialists made a concerted effort to organize nationwide associations to control price and production. In those years, few industries escaped attempts at cartelization. Yet, as was true in the railroad world, these cartels rarely worked. This case suggests why this was so in the early years of the oil industry. And the experience of oil was paralleled in other industries.

The inadequacies of association or federation led to the search for new ways to provide legal control over a large number of individual enterprises. One was the purchase of stock in competing companies or, more often, the exchange of stock between competing companies. More effective was the trust, invented in 1881/1882 by the Standard Oil Company. This legal device made it possible for a single business unit to hold stock in a number of companies in many different states. Still less cumbersome was the holding company, which became the usual form of such control after New Jersey passed, in 1889, a general incorporation law for holding companies.

Legal consolidation permitted administrative centralization. While some managers of the new trusts and holding companies were content to use them as the means to control price and production, others realized the possibility of rationalizing the production facilities under their control. Plants could be modernized and enlarged so as to exploit effectively the economies of scale permitted by the new industrial technology. They could be located to take the best advantage of sources of raw materials and markets. Once production had been rationalized and economies of scale introduced, the managers of the new large enterprises found themselves moving forward into wholesaling and occasionally retailing to assure themselves of direct access to markets and to profit from economies of scale in distribution. They also moved backwards into production of semifinished and raw materials to assure themselves of a constant stock of supplies. The end result was the creation of the large integrated, multifunctional, centrally managed enterprise.

The early history of Standard Oil provides an excellent example of the process of corporate growth via combination, consolidation, and vertical integration, which so many American enterprises followed. Yet, this history is more than just a case study; for Standard Oil was one of the very first to grow and to dominate an industry in this manner. As it was the first to fashion new legal and administrative forms, it pioneered in many of the ways of modern big business. A review of its story thus helps to identify the conditions, motives, and methods that led to the rise of the large, modern corporation in the United States.

# The Early Oil Industry

The oil industry grew from small beginnings. "Rock oil" had been found in Pennsylvania, Kentucky, Ohio, and West Virginia and had been used in the early decades of the 19th century as a cure for an endless list of maladies. However, in the

1850s, petroleum refiners, building upon the technology of the coal oil and natural gas industries, discovered the potentialities of refined petroleum as an illuminant. In 1859 Edwin Drake's drilling success at Titusville, Pennsylvania resulted in a tumultuous rush to the oil fields of western Pennsylvania. Since little capital was required to enter the industry, many would-be millionaires flocked to the oil fields. Farmers became rich overnight, and boom towns mushroomed.

Within ten years after Drake's well opened the new era, the oil industry had grown to great importance. Annual production of crude oil rose from 2,000 barrels in 1859 to 4,800,000 in 1869 and 5,250,000 in 1871. By 1880, oil was the nation's fourth largest export. The basis of this rapid growth lay in the demand of the consuming public for improved illuminants[1] and industrial requirements for more and better lubricants.

In the initial period, a few thousand dollars invested in drilling a well could yield millions, but a gusher that made men wealthy might also suddenly dry up. With minimal capital requirements, high incentive, and ease of entry, something approaching pure competition existed in the producing end of the business. Output was completely unrestrained, failures numerous, and speculation rampant.

Conservation of oil resources simply did not exist. Under the "Rule of Capture,"[2] a well owner could extract as much oil as possible from his well regardless of the effect on the oil pool or the wells of others. This legal sanction encouraged reckless exploitation of the resource.

Instability, therefore, characterized the refining industry. It suffered not only from internal cutthroat competition but from the uncertainties of crude oil production. Both the price and supply of oil fluctuated widely. In 1862, the monthly price per barrel of crude oil ranged between $0.10 and $2.25; in 1864, between $4.00 and $12.13; and in 1871, between $3.83 and $4.83.

These fluctuations in price and supply were, to some extent, mitigated by the ever-increasing markets at home and abroad. Until the mid-1880s, the United States provided most of the world's crude and refined petroleum. It was only after that time that competition from Russia and the Dutch East Indies was of any real significance. Throughout the 19th century, the major market for American refiners remained Europe, which, until 1890, took two-thirds of their output.[3]

Business organizations in the oil industry initially took the form of partnerships, but corporations became more frequent as capital requirements increased. In the early days of the industry, the functions of drilling, producing, transporting, marketing, and refining were in separate hands; refiners often produced only one type of product, such as kerosene, naphtha, or lubricants. Under the impact of competition, however, firms engaged in one operation often attempted to add others. Several efforts at building a variety of combinations both vertical and hori-

---

[1] It should be stressed that during the whole of the 19th century, kerosene was by far the single most important product of the oil industry.

[2] The Rule of Capture, with roots in an English case (*Action* v. *Blundell,* 1843), held that the owner of the soil also owned all that was beneath it. Since oil is fugacious in character, the application of this rule encouraged competitive drilling as the only means of protecting a producer against his neighbors.

[3] See tables in Williamson and Daum, *American Petroleum Industry,* pp. 332, 335, 489, 492, and 660.

zontal were made (usually by means of interlocking partnerships prior to the creation of the Standard Oil group). Nevertheless, most business units in the young oil industry were small and acted individually. As a result, voluntary efforts at cooperation, by such means as informal agreements, fell apart under the pressures of competition.

Transportation had an important place in the industry from its earliest days. Petroleum deposits were found far from existing population and export centers, and the physical problems of moving petroleum were a challenge to early oilmen. Gradually this problem was solved. Small diameter pipelines, called gathering lines, collected oil in the fields and delivered it to railheads, whence it was moved to refineries in tank cars. The rates charged for these services, however, remained at issue long after the physical difficulties of transportation had been overcome.

Under these conditions, the location of refineries with respect to transportation as well as to the market frequently proved to be an important determinant of success. A refinery dependent on one railroad was not in nearly as good a competitive position as one which could choose among several railroads. The railroads themselves were extremely competitive, and large refiners could not only take advantage of rate wars but also demand special concessions and rebates in return for using a specific line.

The petroleum industry as it emerged in the post-Civil War period was thus characterized by numerous small firms competing fiercely in an atmosphere of "anything goes." A wildly fluctuating market, whose unpredictability was based on perennial imbalance between supply and demand, caused both producers and refiners to seek some way of stabilizing their positions. It was John D. Rockefeller and his associates who successfully analyzed and manipulated this complex situation in order to control the competitive climate of the whole industry.

## Rockefeller and the Beginnings of Standard Oil

John D. Rockefeller, whose name is inextricably enmeshed with the development of the petroleum industry and the rise of large-scale enterprise, entered the oil business almost by chance. Born in 1839, he grew up in an unexceptional household, where he was imbued not only with the values of thrift and industry but with a religious piety which was to continue throughout his life. After graduation from high school, he became a bookkeeper in a Cleveland produce commission firm. Three years later in 1859, at the age of 19, he formed his own wholesale grocery business together with Maurice B. Clark. Each partner initially contributed $2,000. About $900 of Rockefeller's share was derived from savings; the remainder he received from his father. The firm of produce merchants did very well, especially during the Civil War when the price of commodities rose sharply.

In 1862, Clark was approached by Samuel Andrews, an old friend and a self-taught chemist, who was seeking help in financing an oil refinery. Though he considered oil as only a "side issue," Rockefeller agreed to join; and in 1863, a new partnership, Andrews, Clark & Company was formed. The refinery began operation under the name of the Excelsior Works. Refining methods were continually improved under the direction of Andrews, and by 1865, the plant was the largest in Cleveland.

The major Midwestern refining centers were Pittsburgh and Cleveland. In the competitive struggle between the two centers, Cleveland had several advantages. It had access to both railroad and water transportation—the Great Lakes for western shipments and the New York canal system for eastern deliveries. In addition, Cleveland businessmen also had a choice of three railroads rather than being entirely dependent upon one, as Pittsburgh was at that time.

In 1865, Rockefeller gave up the produce commission business and began to devote his full efforts to refining. He bought out Clark for $72,000, and the firm continued under the name of Rockefeller and Andrews. The latter was in charge of technical operations. In 1867, William Rockefeller, John's brother, went to New York to handle the firm's eastern and its growing foreign business. The same year the firm added two important men, Henry M. Flagler and Stephen V. Harkness. Flagler, who like Rockefeller had obtained his business experience as a commission merchant, became a partner and took an active role in management. Harkness, who was an uncle of Flagler's wife, had accumulated capital in distilling whiskey. He also invested in the enterprise but did not participate in its management. Together they contributed probably $110,000 to $140,000. In 1869, the various Rockefeller partnerships were consolidated, and in the following year the partnerships were replaced by a corporation.

The Standard Oil Company (Ohio) was capitalized at $1 million. Of the 10,000 shares issued, John D. Rockefeller received 2,667; S. V. Harkness, 1,334; H. M. Flagler, Samuel Andrews, and William Rockefeller, 1,333 each; and the Rockefeller, Andrews and Flagler partnership, 1,000. Nine tenths of the shares were thus held by one silent and four active partners who had previously been concerned with the business. John D. Rockefeller was president, and two of the others were officers.

The years between 1866 and 1869—the critical years for the Rockefeller venture—were ones of rapid growth and expansion. In 1865, the existing refinery was the largest in Cleveland and possibly the largest in the world. Early the next year William Rockefeller set up a sales office in New York to handle the marketing of kerosene, particularly through the all-important export trade. In the same year a second refinery was completed in Cleveland. Between 1866 and 1869, the daily throughput of that refinery complex rose from 500 barrels to 1,500 barrels a day.[4] As of September 30, 1869, the partnership's gross receipts for the previous year were $2,433,689, an income that was reported to be as large as that of the next three largest refineries in Cleveland combined.[5] By 1869, 10 years after oil was discovered in Pennsylvania, the Cleveland works were the largest refining complex in the world, producing one tenth of the nation's output of refined petroleum.

---

[4]Nevins, *Rockefeller*, I, p. 59. The daily charging capacity may have been larger. Rockefeller's estimate for 1869 is for a barrel of refined, while the company bankers estimate in their correspondence was 3,000 barrels of crude capacity. Nevins, *Rockefeller*, I, p. 75.

[5]Nevins, *Rockefeller*, I, p. 74.

It was the first works to reach what the industry's historians have described as an "entirely new scale in plant and still size."[6]

Such scale provided powerful advantages. It permitted the firm to integrate ancillary operations.[7] A large barrel-making works and sulphuric acid plant were built within the complex. The partnership invested in lake shipping and built storage depots in the oil regions as well as tank cars to carry crude from the regions to Cleveland. It also purchased wharfage, warehouses, and lighters in New York Harbor. Scale also permitted a sizable output of by-products, particularly lubricants. Most important of all, the new scale of operations greatly reduced the cost of producing a gallon of kerosene. While unit costs for a refinery with 500 barrel daily throughput was around 6 cents a gallon, those in the refinery with a 1,500 barrel throughput dropped to 3 cents a gallon and probably less.[8] This relationship of scale to costs has remained central to the structure of the oil industry from that date to this. Thus, because Rockefeller's Cleveland refinery complex had become the largest in the industry, it also became its low-cost producer.

Scale provided still more advantages. It made it easy to obtain short-term loans from commercial banks to cover operating expenses if and when necessary, for the Cleveland bankers were fully aware of Rockefeller's prosperity.[9] Increasing profits resulting from the sharply reduced costs provided capital for further expansion in refining and ancillary operations. Finally, the new high volume of output gave Rockefeller and Flagler a far greater leverage with the railroads, particularly those that transported refined oil east, than had their small competitors. Although other Cleveland refiners received concessions from the railroads, obviously Rockefeller's trade was the account railroad traffic managers most cherished. As in all other American industries in the post–Civil War era, railroad competition increased the large shipper's leverage. The intense pressure of their very high fixed costs led railroad managers to grant rebates and other favors in return for guaranteed shipments. Since transportation costs formed a significant part of the total cost of refined products, these railroad practices benefited refiners and other shippers in a position to exploit them.

In 1868, the Rockefeller partnership and two other Cleveland refiners (Clark, Payne and Company and Westlake, Hutchins & Company) attempted to gain additional advantages by acquiring a fourth interest in a gathering pipeline company which possessed an exclusive contract to deliver crude oil to the Atlantic and Great Western Railroad, a subsidiary of the Erie Railroad. The pipeline was receiving drawbacks from the railroad, and the three refiners contracted with the company to receive a portion of those drawbacks. They also received, as a result of their interest in the company, a quarter share of drawbacks received from the ship-

---

[6]Williamson and Daum, *American Petroleum Industry*, p. 273. On pp. 279–86 the authors review the operation and cost of refinery operating at this scale.

[7]Nevins, *Rockefeller, I*, pp. 40–41, 59, 71–74.

[8]Williamson and Daum, *American Petroleum Industry*, pp. 228–30. 283–85, 428–83. As the authors stress, cost data in the early years were crude, but economies of scale were real.

[9]Nevins, *Rockefeller*, I, pp. 74–75.

ments of other firms' oil. By playing railroad against railroad, railroads against water transport, and later, pipelines against pipelines, Ohio Standard strengthened its position in the oil industry.

## The Conquest of Cleveland

Once their enterprise had been incorporated as the Standard Oil Company, Rockefeller, Flagler, and Harkness began a concerted effort to dominate oil refining in Cleveland. Their strategy was to obtain still more favorable rates from the railroads by taking advantage of their large throughput. Sometime in 1870, Flagler proposed to James H. Devereux, the general manager of the Lake Shore Railroad (which had just become a subsidiary of the New York Central), to ship 60 carloads of oil a day, every day if the Lake Shore and the Central would give his company a rate of $1.30 a barrel from Cleveland to New York (the published rate was $2.00 a barrel) and 35 cents a barrel for crude from the Regions to Cleveland.[10] Devereux quickly accepted. As he later testified, the assured regular flow permitted him to run a single train daily made up wholly of oil cars instead of putting oil cars on trains mixed in with other types of freight cars. The improvement in scheduling meant that fewer cars were needed. The resulting lower investment and maintenance costs and the small cost of providing a locomotive and crew for the daily trip meant that the railroad could still make a good profit on the rate. Of course, Devereux knew that if he refused, Flagler could certainly get the same deal from the Erie. When other Cleveland refiners protested after hearing of the rate cut, Devereux claimed these rates were not inequitable because "this arrangement was at all times open to any and all parties who would secure or guarantee the like amount of traffic or an amount to be treated and handled in the same speedy and economical manner. . . ."

Armed with this contract, Flagler and Rockefeller first invited their two major competitors (Clark, Payne and Company and Westlake, Hutchins & Company) to join forces—an invitation the two readily accepted. Then Standard Oil approached the other Cleveland refiners. By the end of 1871, Standard Oil had obtained control of five large and seven small firms, and the conquest of Cleveland was practically complete. At the same time, to strengthen their position in the all-important foreign market, the Standard partners acquired Jabez A. Bostwick & Company of New York, a leading exporting firm with a refinery on Long Island. In Cleveland the larger and more efficient works continued to operate under Standard's control, although the change in command was kept secret. Competent refiners like Payne and Bostwick became senior executives of Standard Oil. On the other hand, smaller refineries not producing specialized products were closed down, and their owners had to find a new business. By 1872, Standard's control in Cleveland gave it control over one quarter of the total daily capacity of the industry.[11]

---

[10]Affidavit of James H. Devereux in the case of *Standard Oil Company* v. *William C. Schofield, et al.*, quoted in Tarbell, *History of the Standard Oil Company,* I, pp. 277–79.

[11]Williamson and Daum, *American Petroleum Industry,* p. 353.

In buying out their Cleveland competitors, Rockefeller and his associates preferred to pay through an exchange of stock rather than in cash. Not only was this method of payment cheaper for Standard Oil, it permitted those competitors who made the exchange to profit from Standard's growth. Many became very wealthy as the value of their Standard shares sharply increased. Whatever the form of payment, Standard Oil appraisers determined the value of the properties purchased. Inevitably the buyer and seller had different views. The sellers thought in terms of the cost of their works; and the buyer, in terms of "use-value" of the plant and equipment to Standard Oil. But most of the sellers felt that they had little choice in the matter. Frank Rockefeller, who had joined one of his brother's competitors, remembers that John had threatened: "If you don't sell your property, it will be valueless because we have advantages of the railroads."[12] Another refiner who did not want to sell, Robert Hanna of a leading Cleveland industrial family, reported that Rockefeller told him, "You can never make money in my judgment. You can't compete with Standard. We have all the large refineries now. If you refuse to sell, it will end in your being crushed."

Late in 1871, as the conquest of Cleveland was drawing to a close, the Standard Oil Company was one of several oil refiners invited by Tom Scott, the vice president in charge of external affairs for the Pennsylvania Railroad, to take part in a railroad pool for oil shipments. The instrument through which the pool was to be carried out was the South Improvement Company, which Scott had had incorporated by the Pennsylvania Legislature. The proposal was to have the South Improvement Company act as an "evener of oil shipments from the interior to the port cities." This meant that the company would administer the allocation of quotas in the oil traffic pool and receive, as a commission, rebates and drawbacks on the shipments. Railroad freight rates were to be increased and stabilized. This move would benefit the railroads. Nonmembers of the South Improvement Company would be charged the full published rates while members would receive rebates. The differential between the rates of members and nonmembers in itself would probably have eliminated nonmembers from effective competition, but in addition to the rebates, members were to receive payments (drawbacks in the form of commissions) on all petroleum shipped by nonmembers. The major share of this money, which it was hopefully estimated would be between $5 and $6 million annually, was to be used to "kill any attempt by rival railroad managers, producers, refiners, speculators, or foreign export agents to break down the contract" between the refiners and the railroads.[13] To give even further advantage to members, the railroads agreed to provide the South Improvement Company with daily reports on all oil shipments, thus giving members inside information on their competitors' business.

The South Improvement Company issued 2,000 shares, of which the Rockefeller group was to have a substantial block. Although it is probable that all refin-

---

[12] This and the following quotation are from Tarbell, *History of the Standard Oil Company,* I, pp. 64, 66–67.

[13] Williamson and Daum, *American Petroleum Industry,* pp. 349–50.

ers were to be invited to join, there was some disagreement regarding the terms on which producers of crude oil would be accepted. It was hoped that producers would agree to limit production of crude oil in return for a guaranteed minimum price. Before this matter could be settled, however, news of the proposal leaked out.

The reaction was devastating; although the South Improvement Company never handled a barrel of oil, angry producers and those refiners who had not been asked to join sought to curb shipments of crude oil to members of the South Improvement Company and conducted a public campaign with the purpose of revoking its charter. Both efforts were effective. The amount of crude oil shipped to the offending refiners dropped sharply. The railroads capitulated first, promising to avoid interference in the relations of producers and refiners and cancelling their contracts with the South Improvement Company. Public opinion sided generally with the producers. Although the "Oil War" ceased when Pennsylvania revoked the company's charter, a legacy of suspicion remained.

The South Improvement episode affected the Standard Oil Company in two quite different ways. It was during the furor over the project in the Regions that knowledge of Standard's conquest of Cleveland, which had been largely carried out in secret, became publicly known. In fact, many oil men believed Rockefeller had used the threat of the South Improvement project to bring the Cleveland companies into line. In subsequent attacks on the oil combination, the memory of that scheme was often revived. The South Improvement proposal also turned Rockefeller and his associates to thinking about stability and control of the refining industry for the nation as a whole. Scott's proposal had aimed at assuring control of all refining output, not just that of one city or region. The senior executives at Standard had decided to try to bring stability to process and output through voluntary methods. But if these failed, then control of output through control of railroad transportation, as Scott had proposed, remained an attractive alternative.

## Voluntary Association as a Means of Stabilization

Control of price and production in the oil industry had been first proposed in 1869 when the producers of crude oil formed their Petroleum Producers Association. Yet, that organization achieved little and by 1872 was defunct. It came to life again, however, when in August 1872, shortly after the collapse of the South Improvement scheme, the refiners formed their National Refiners Association. John D. Rockefeller was named president. Each of the five major oil refining areas (New York, Philadelphia, Pittsburgh, the Oil Regions, and Cleveland) elected three representatives to a 15-man board of directors, which became responsible for general policies. A small permanent board of agents made up of one man from each district was to carry out the policies set by the board as to the buying of crude oil, the allocating of refining quotas, the setting of prices, and the securing of uniform railroad rates for all members. Profits were to be distributed to members on the basis of the value of their properties. Members promised to keep their specific agreements secret. The new association, however, failed to develop any sanctions to enforce its decisions. And not all refiners joined.

The refiners association's first move was to negotiate a contract with the revived producers association. The producers formed a company to purchase all oil produced by its members at a set price and then to sell it to the refiners. Rockefeller, as president of the refiners association, agreed to buy at that price. On December 19, 1872, the two groups signed the "Treaty of Titusville." The price of crude was set at $4.00 a barrel if a gallon of refined sold in New York City at 26 cents a gallon. If the price of refined increased 1 cent a gallon, the price of crude would go up 25 cents a barrel until it reached $5.00 a barrel. But as might have been expected, breakdowns and defections soon developed. The producers simply were unable to prevent increased output and new drilling, and the price of crude dropped again. It soon became apparent that the agreement between the groups could not be fulfilled. Therefore, the contract between them was cancelled.

Nevertheless, the refiners association still attempted to set quotas and divide territories. As a goad for compliance, it added fines for violations. Despite these additional efforts, the group's goal was not achieved. Enforcement proved impossible, nonmember refiners increased output, and prices fell. Within a year of its formation, the association was dissolved. Rockefeller in later years stated: "We proved that producers and refiners associations were ropes of sand."[14]

Failure to achieve stabilization resulted in further overproduction. The amount of crude produced rose rapidly while the prices of both crude and refined products dropped sharply. Output of crude per day rose from 21,000 barrels in 1872 to 33,000 barrels in 1873. The price of crude dropped from $3.75 per barrel in 1872 to $1.80 in 1873.[15] Although the demand for petroleum products continued to grow, it did not keep up with supply. Excess capacity developed. Failures and bankruptcies were frequent.

## The Creation of a National Monopoly

During much of 1872 and early 1873, before the ineffectiveness of the refiners association became clear, Rockefeller and his senior executives concentrated on rationalizing their recently acquired facilities in Cleveland. They consolidated, reorganized, and improved their larger refineries and developed units to handle by-products and auxiliary activities, such as acid restoration, tar manufacture, and lubricating oil. To help assure markets for their increased production, they acquired the Devoe Manufacturing Company, another major exporter with a large refinery on Long Island, and an interest in Chess, Carley & Company, the leading wholesaler in the southeastern United States. By the end of 1873, Standard Oil's expanded Cleveland output and that of its New York refineries accounted for more than third of all the oil refined in the United States. (Before the conquest of Cleveland, Standard's output was about 10 percent.) Yet, in that year, Standard's refineries were only operating at two-thirds capacity.

---

[14]Nevins, *Rockefeller,* I, p. 431.

[15]Williamson and Daum, *American Petroleum Industry,* p. 359.

With the collapse of the National Refiners Association, Rockefeller and his associates decided early in 1874 to bring a large part of the industry directly under Standard's legal control. They proposed to do this by obtaining, preferably through an exchange of stock, a controlling or at least a large minority share of the stock in major companies in the other refining areas besides Cleveland. Such control would permit Standard to have a say in setting price and output of refined petroleum throughout the country. The grinding economic depression that had begun the year before helped to carry out this plan.

Rockefeller decided to use, as he had done in Cleveland, control over transportation and shipping facilities as Standard's primary weapon. In 1872, by obtaining Bostwick, Standard had acquired the lease that that firm had of the New York Central's oil terminal and shipping areas in New York. Then in 1874, Standard leased similar facilities owned by the Erie. This meant that all competitors shipping through New York on the two northern trunklines had to use facilities owned by Standard Oil. In 1874, too, the railroads formed a new oil pool which equalized all rates from the interior to the seaboard. That is, the rates from Cleveland to New York and Philadelphia were the same as those from Pittsburgh and the Regions, even though the distance from Cleveland was a good deal further. Early in 1875, the three trunklines carrying oil also agreed to give Standard and its allies a special extra 10 percent rebate in return for acting as the "evener" of the traffic. In 1874 and 1875, the gathering pipelines that brought oil to the railroad shipping points worked out comparable pools. Because Standard had increased its holding in pipelines, its voice was the most powerful in defining these pooling arrangements.

Standard's executives then used these agreements, as they had earlier ones in Cleveland, to persuade the largest and most efficient refiners to join them. They were careful to offer generous terms in the exchange of stock. In October 1874, the largest refining company in each of three major areas—Philadelphia, Pittsburgh, and New York—entered the Standard Oil alliance by an exchange of stock. With them came some of the most competent executives in the industry.[16] Then in the first months of 1875, the biggest refinery in Parkersburg, West Virginia, and the largest in the Regions also joined the group. These moves were to be kept secret. Each firm was to continue operation under its existing name and to buy up other refiners when the chance appeared.

The Standard Oil combination then revived the old association, naming it the Central Refiners Association. Rockefeller was again named president. But this time, there was a real difference. As Standard Oil controlled the major refineries in the different areas, it controlled a majority of votes on the association's board. Many other refiners did join the new organization whose purpose was, as before,

---

[16]These men included William Warden of the Atlantic Refining Company of Philadelphia; Charles Lockhart, R. J. Waring and William Frew of Lockhart, Frew & Company of Pittsburgh; Charles Pratt and H. H. Rodgers of Charles Pratt & Company of Newtown, N.Y.; J. N. Camden of Camden Consolidated of Parkersburg; and John D. Archbold, the general manager of Porter, Morehouse & Company of Titusville. The last, who was long an implacable foe of Standard Oil, became one of the alliance's most influential executives.

to control all purchases of crude and sales of refined, to make rate agreements with the railroads and pipelines, and to divide profits among its members. To enforce effectively its decision, the association proposed that each refiner would lease his refinery to the association, which would then negotiate transportation contracts for all members. The plan ultimately failed when Pittsburgh refiners, supported by the Pennsylvania Railroad, refused to join.

From then on, members of the Standard Oil combination decided not to work through the association but rather to rely wholly on its economic power resulting from scale and from their power over transportation to obtain control in those firms it wanted through an exchange of stock and to drive those that it felt it did not need out of the business. The strategy was effective. By the end of 1878, the Standard Oil combination controlled over 90 percent of the total refining investment in the United States.

## Challenges to the Standard Oil Combination

As it was achieving its monopoly, Standard Oil faced two vigorous challenges, one from the largest and most powerful corporation in the United States, the other from a combination of producers. Both challengers planned to break the Standard alliance's control over long distance transportation of crude oil. One failed; the other was at least partially successful.

After negotiations for the 1875 pool, the Pennsylvania Railroad became increasingly troubled by Standard's power. The Ohio company already controlled the oil traffic on the two New York trunk lines. The Pennsylvania had to rely largely on independents for shipments. If Standard was not held in check, it could soon dictate to the Pennsylvania the terms of doing business. So in 1876, the railroad supported the proposal of its subsidiary, the Empire Transportation Company (a "fast freight" line that handled the road's oil shipments), to build refineries and to contract extensively for crude to be processed at these new works.

Standard Oil quickly struck back. It withdrew all shipments from the Pennsylvania and cut the price of refined. By mid-1877, those directors and executives of the Pennsylvania not directly concerned with its oil traffic began to question the wisdom of the battle. The road had other pressing problems during this time of continued economic depression. In July came a widespread labor stike of unprecedented violence at Pittsburgh and other points following a general reduction of wages on the road. Burning and rioting resulted in more than $2 million worth of damages. Reeling from this blow, the Pennsylvania decided to give up the fight with Standard. It dissolved the Empire Transportation Company, selling its pipelines and refineries to the Standard alliance; and it meekly accepted the terms of the new pooling arrangements by which Standard received a rebate on all shipments including those of its competitors as payment for acting as the eveners for the railroads.

In September 1877, a few weeks after the Pennsylvania Railroad had capitulated to the Standard combination, the producers once again organized. The new association, the Producers Union, began an attack on Standard on three fronts. It proposed a shutdown of all wells in the Region in the hopes of getting higher prices for crude. It put pressure on the Pennsylvania legislature and the federal Congress to outlaw railroad rate discrimination. Finally, it organized a company to build a pipeline across the Allegheny Mountains to Tidewater.

Only the last had a measure of success. In November 1878, the Tidewater Pipeline Company, Ltd. was incorporated to construct a line from the Bradford fields to the Reading Railroad at Williamsport. Despite a drumfire of legal harassment by the Standard alliance to prevent Tidewater from acquiring its right-of-way, this first long-distance pipeline was completed in May 1879. Tidewater was soon selling its daily delivery capacity of 6,000 barrels to independents in Bayonne, Philadelphia, and Williamsport and in time delivering still larger amounts to its own refinery in Bayonne, which, by 1900, had become the largest refinery in the world.[17]

Predictably, Standard responded with alacrity, for Tidewater had done more than break the combination's grip on the transportation of petroleum from the interior to the seaboard. It had demonstrated that pipelines could carry crude oil over long distances at a far lower cost and in much greater volume than the railroads. Standard immediately embarked on a major program to build a network of long distance pipelines which would, in time, connect all its refineries to the producing Regions. In 1881, these new long distance lines of the oil combination were consolidated in a new enterprise, the National Transit Company. That firm, in turn, took over the stock of the United Pipelines Company, which operated the combination's gathering lines. While building its network, Standard supported the trunk lines in a rate war with Tidewater and the Reading Railroad. The roads quickly found the battle exceedingly costly and so, early in 1880, made an agreement on rates and traffic that would keep the pipeline operating at close to full capacity. Then in 1883, as Standard's long distance pipeline network was being completed, Tidewater and National Transit further stabilized rates by dividing oil transportation from the Regions east at a ratio of 88½ percent for National Transit and 11½ percent for Tidewater Pipeline Company.

While it was meeting the challenges from Tidewater and the Pennsylvania, the Standard Oil combination continued to expand its holdings and membership by lease or exchange of stock. Such lubricating oil and specialty firms as Vacuum Oil Company, the Cheseborough Manufacturing Company, and the Eclipse Lubricating Oil Company, Limited, joined the combination in those years. Minority interest was acquired in the marketing firms of Waters-Pierce Oil Company of St. Louis and the Consolidated Tank Line Company of Cincinnati. In Pittsburgh, Philadelphia, Baltimore, the Oil Regions, and New England, the Standard Oil group enlarged or consolidated its position.

Nevertheless, the number of independent refineries increased rapidly after 1878. The declining costs of various chemical ingredients used in refining contributed to this increase, but perhaps even more important were the opening of huge

---

[17]Williamson and Daum, *American Petroleum Industry,* pp. 443, 465; John Moody, ed., *Moody's Manual of Industrial and Miscellaneous Securities for 1900* (New York: Moody's, 1900), p. 1011.

new oil fields at Bradford, Pennsylvania, and the development of by-products—
especially lubricants. The manufacture of lubricating oils, for which there was a
growing demand, offered a particularly good opportunity to independents who,
by developing specialized products, could appeal to specialized markets. The
Standard Oil combination did not keep pace with this development because its executives felt it more important to complete their pipeline network and reorganize
refineries than to launch immediately into by-product production.

## The Formation of the Standard Oil Trust

In 1881, the Standard Oil alliance completely dominated the American oil industry. It controlled the nation's refining with a capacity to process over 88,000 barrels of crude oil a day. Yet it remained only a combination of legally and administratively independent enterprises located in every major refining region in the
country. The nucleus of the combination was the Standard Oil Company of Ohio.
Five stockholders—John D. Rockefeller, William Rockefeller, Flagler, Harkness,
and Payne—controlled four sevenths of the company's stock. These five and 36
other stockholders held a minority or majority interest in 26 associated companies, interests that had been obtained largely through the exchange of stock.[18]

As a group of legally and operationally independent enterprises held together
only by stock ownership, the Standard Oil alliance faced complex legal and administrative problems. Legal problems arose because at that time the responsibility for chartering and regulating business ventures lay with the states and not the
federal government. There was as yet no way to incorporate to do business on a
national rather than a local scale. The rights of Standard Oil, an Ohio company,
for example, either to own property in other states or to hold stock in other companies had not yet been legally clarified. This weakness was dramatically illustrated in 1881 when Pennsylvania attempted to tax not only the Ohio company's
physical property within the Keystone State but also the corporation's entire capital stock and dividends. For this reason, executives in Standard Oil of Ohio had
from the beginning held the stock that they had exchanged for that of the companies coming into the combination as trustees acting as individuals for the stockholders of the Ohio company. The Standard Oil Company as a legal entity, therefore, did not hold the stock of the members of the combination.

In 1879, this arrangement was formalized in an agreement by which all the
stock of other companies was transferred to three trustees, who then held it in trust
for the 41 shareholders of Standard Oil of Ohio. However, the three trustees had
no specific authority to manage the properties. No arrangement existed for the
election of trustees in case of the death of one of the three nor for the transfer of
ownership certificates.

The combination was even more administratively weak than it was legally
vulnerable. Its executives, through correspondence and occasional meetings,
could decide what prices to charge and how much to produce each year. Execu-

---

[18]Hidy and Hidy, *Pioneering in Big Business,* pp. 44–45.

tives concerned with mutual problems of transportation and sales overseas met relatively regularly to review their problems. But there was no formal place where overall policies could be set, where activities could be coordinated, and where long-term plans could be decided for the combination as a whole. For example, no executives or group of executives had the responsibility of deciding how, where, and when to reorganize refining capacity or expand pipelines.

This weakness became painfully obvious as the coming of long distance pipelines radically altered transportation costs. Not only did the new pipelines carry crude oil far more cheaply than railroads, but they provided excellent storage. Their existence made possible the scheduling of a much greater and steadier refining throughput than was possible using rail shipments. Moreover, because the pipelines could carry crude oil to processing facilities but not refined products, the completion of the long distance lines called for relocation of refinery capacity at centers close to the market, particularly at ports where ships picked up the refined products for the great European markets. To build and manage the long distance pipelines, Standard Oil and its allies had set up the National Transit Company, using that existing catchall Pennsylvania charter, which was capitalized at $30 million. At that time, Standard Oil of Ohio was capitalized at only $3 million. To find a comparable legal vehicle to build, reorganize, and operate refining capacity was a more difficult legal challenge.

The completion of Tidewater's pipeline, by breaking Standard's monopoly over long distance transportation and assuring refiners independent of Standard Oil a cheap, steady source of crude, was certain to increase competition. Indeed, independent refiners, taking advantage of the prevailing favorable profit margins especially in specialized and premium-grade products, trebled their capacity in the four-year period between 1881 and 1884, with the result that Standard's share of the industry's total refining capacity fell from 90 percent to 77 percent.[19] And, as the Standard's managers may have feared, the producers began to look to each other for mutual support.

And, in 1881, Standard faced a challenge potentially even more serious than actions of American competitors or suppliers. At this time, the market for American refined products was still abroad with 70 percent of all kerosene produced in the United States and nearly 80 percent of the output of the Standard combination going to Europe. In 1880, the output of the Baku oilfields on the shore of Russia's Caspian Sea rose sharply. The leading entrepreneurs in opening the Russian fields, the powerful and highly competent Nobel family, had already built an integrated enterprise that was producing, refining, and transporting oil. The Nobels were still concentrating almost wholly on supplying the Russian market. Yet, Rockefeller and his associates were well aware that a railroad was being built from Baku to the Black Sea. On this railroad's completion, the excellent kerosene made from Russian crude would flood the European market. Such a threat could hardly be met by a loose combination of oil refiners whose basic strength was only to control price and production in the United States. The surest way to meet such com-

---

[19] Williamson and Daum, *American Petroleum Industry*, pp. 466, 473.

petition was to improve efficiency and cut costs in the refining and transportation of American petroleum products.

Nevertheless, these competitive threats were still only potential ones. The Baku–Black Sea Railroad would not be completed until 1884. Russian oil could not become competitive in western Europe until 1885. In 1881, the independents were only just beginning to expand capacity. For Rockefeller and his associates, profit opportunities were probably a greater incentive than competitive pressures for physically reorganizing the American oil industry—a restructuring that would require legal consolidation and administrative centralization. The pipeline revolution suddenly made possible an increase in scale and decrease in cost that even over-shadowed the jump from a 500 barrel to a 1,500 barrel throughput a decade earlier. When completed, Tidewater's line had a daily delivery capacity of 6,000 barrels. By 1881, both Tidewater and National Transit lines were pumping 7,000 to 8,000 barrels daily.[20] The cost reductions permitted by building refineries with daily throughput of 6,000 to 7,000 barrels would further enhance Standard's competitive position and increase its profit margins. However, to maintain the greatly increased flow of oil into and through the enlarged refineries and then to the marketing outlets demanded a centralized administrative control that did not yet exist. To grasp the opportunities created by the innovation of the long distance pipeline and to meet potential competitive threats required, therefore, the creation of a central office authorized to build, reorganize, and shut down refineries and then to administer the rationalized network of production, transportation, and marketing facilities. The creation of such an administrative structure, in turn, required the legal consolidation of the many properties of the members of the Standard Oil alliance into a single legally identifiable enterprise.

The legal means to achieve such ends were limited. A holding company was a possible solution, but in 1881 very few states granted charters for this type of organization and then only by a special act of the legislature. Pennsylvania's action to tax all of Ohio Standard's property underscored the need for a system which would allow the Rockefeller associates to set up separate companies in each state with a central legal entity to direct the entire combination.

Such an organization was most easily created through modification of the trusteeship device already used by Ohio Standard to control legally its associated companies. Trusteeship had several outstanding advantages, including the sanction of common law and the assurance of maximum secrecy. Trustees, because they were legally agents for stockholders and not for the corporations involved, could testify truthfully about Standard Oil without revealing information that investigators sought to uncover. This advantage proved particularly useful in obscuring the extent of Standard Oil's holdings in other companies.

The Standard Oil Trust Agreement (January 2, 1882) established a trust to be the sole and central holding agency for all the securities of 41 participating investors in 40 named companies. Rockefeller and his associates put the value of the trust at $70 million, against which they issued 700,000 trust certificates (par value

---

[20]Williamson and Daum, *American Petroleum Industry,* p. 453.

$100) to Ohio Standard's stockholders. Since the net book value of the corporations involved stood at only $55,221,738, the trust's capitalization must have reflected either capitalized earning power, prices paid for properties in excess of market value, or "watered" stock. Actual earnings, however, soon proved the valuation conservative. The nine original trustees (a third of whom were to be elected annually) were John D. Rockefeller, O. H. Payne, William Rockefeller, J. A. Bostwick, H. M. Flagler, W. G. Warden, Charles Pratt, Benjamin Brewster, and John D. Archbold. The agreement vested these men with a wide range of powers and duties, among them an outstanding innovation—fully centralized administrative control. As the Standard Oil Trust Agreement stated:

> It shall be the duty of said Trustees to exercise general supervision over the affairs of said Standard Oil Companies and as far as practicable over the other companies or partnerships, any portion of whose stock is held in said trust. It shall be their duty as stockholders of said companies to elect as directors and officers thereof, faithful and competent men. They may elect themselves to such position when they see fit so to do, and shall endeavor to have the affairs of said companies managed and directed in the manner they may deem most conducive to the best interests of the holders of said Trust Certificates.[21]

The trust agreement thus permitted centralization and systematization of the preexisting combination of firms engaged in the buying, transporting, storing, refining, and marketing of petroleum. The largest stockholders received specific authority as trustees. The whole arrangement facilitated the transfer of holdings and the maintenance of secrecy and in general constituted a major step toward the more efficient administration of a far-flung alliance of refineries and pipelines. The use of the trust as a means of controlling a variety of holdings was an organizational innovation which found a number of imitators.

After the formation of the trust, new subsidiaries were incorporated in different states, the most important of which were the Standard Oil Company of New Jersey and the Standard Oil Company of New York. Once the legal arrangements were completed, Rockefeller and other members of the trust took up their headquarters in New York City at offices on Broadway. In 1884/1885, the trust built a large headquarters building at 26 Broadway that housed the offices of the trustees, of many members of the new administrative committees, and of the staff executives.

## The Reorganization of Refining, 1882-1884

The board of the new trust began the rationalization of its refineries well before the setting up of the Broadway headquarters. The board's basic policy was to concentrate refining in large works in three major marketing and shipping areas. By 1883, 45 percent of Standard's output was located in the New York-New Jersey area and 13 percent more in Philadelphia. Operations in Cleveland, which ser-

---

[21]Williamson and Daum, *American Petroleum Industry*, p. 469.

viced the domestic trade, were further concentrated, while capacity in Pittsburgh and the Regions was shut down. Between 1882 and 1886, the units devoted to producing kerosene were reduced from 53 to 22. A number of the smaller refineries were converted to producing petroleum by-products, such as lubricants, paraffin wax, vaseline, and other specialties. By 1885, three refineries (one in Bayonne, New Jersey, one in Philadelphia, and one in Cleveland) produced nearly two fifths of Standard's total output of 17.7 million barrels of crude oil.[22] These three were the largest refineries in the world, each having an average daily charging capacity of 6,500 barrels. The three produced between one fifth and one quarter of the world's total production of kerosene.

The resulting economies of scale permitted a dramatic lowering of unit costs. Increase in plant size throughout the industry in the 1870s to that of a 1,500 to 2,000 barrel daily charging capacity had cut average costs from 5 cents to 2.5 cents a gallon. By the mid-1880s, the most efficient independent refiners had reduced average costs to 1.5 cents. Standard's records show that the average cost of all its refineries dropped from 0.543 cents a gallon in 1884 to 0.452 cents in 1885, and its profit margin increased from 0.530 cents in 1884 to 1.003 cents in 1885.[23] By running such large units steady and full, Standard maintained and expanded its basic competitive advantage. Its costs remained well below any American competition. They were low enough to compete very effectively with the Nobels for the European markets despite higher transportation and distribution expenses.

## The Expansion of Pipelines and the Centralization of Purchasing, 1882-1884

Critical in the rationalizing of its resources was the continued building of the Trust's pipeline network. Much of this work was left to Daniel O'Day, who headed National Transit and its gathering subsidiary, United Pipelines. Old lines were improved and new ones built for the storage as well as transportation of crude oil. By 1884, O'Day had come close to the goal of having a line to every well and every refinery. By that date, the trust operated 1,300 miles of pipeline and had storage space for 40 million barrels of oil. (In that year the total production of the Appalachian fields was 24 million barrels.)

The Standard Oil Trust used its dominance in pipelines to aid refineries against competitors. Although the costs of shipping by pipeline were far below those of the railroads, Standard's open pipeline rates were maintained at the same level as the rail carriers. Standard refineries, however, paid about half the open rates, while the pipelines still enjoyed a margin of profit. For the trust it was immaterial whether profits were assigned to pipelines or refining. But the few independents who paid the open rate were in effect subsidizing Standard, at least to the ex-

---

[22]Williamson and Daum, *American Petroleum Industry*, p. 475.

[23]Williamson and Daum, *American Petroleum Industry*, pp. 483–484; Hidy and Hidy, *Pioneering in Big Business*, p. 107.

tent of the difference between the open rate and the one charged Standard refineries. In this way the Standard Oil Trust reaped the profits of an innovation in transportation at the expense of its competitors.

Although the transfer of oil shipments from rail to the more efficient pipelines necessarily decreased Standard's dependence upon the railroads, the trust took care to compensate the rail carriers for lost traffic and revenue. In 1884, National Transit agreed to credit the Pennsylvania Railroad with 26 percent of the total transportation revenue for Standard's crude oil shipments to the seaboard—even if the Pennsylvania actually carried no oil at all. The Erie received a direct subsidy. The trust had a strong incentive for this generosity since it needed the Pennsylvania's cooperation in "granting rights of way for pipelines, leasing sites for and laying spur tracks to build distributing plants, carrying raw materials other than petroleum to refineries, hauling coal to pumping stations, and transporting refined oil, naphtha, lubricants, and waxes to market."[24]

Some railroads, however, chafed under Standard's dominance. Although the trust through 1887 continued to demand and get rebates, lines such as the Baltimore & Ohio sought out Standard's competitors and discriminated against the trust in tank car supply. In 1887, when the Interstate Commerce Act banned rebates, the trust ceased taking them. However, by expanding its pipelines, by relocating its refineries, and by using ships for oil movements along the Atlantic Coast, the trust reduced its reliance on rail transportation.

As the trust expanded and tightened its control over transportation, it began to centralize more effectively its purchasing of crude. The Standard Oil Company and its associates had never felt the need to buy or drill their own producing wells. From the beginning, supplies of crude had always been available. And they continued to be so after the formation of the trust. From 1882 through 1885, stock in storage always exceeded the total production of the Appalachian fields. Before 1882, Standard purchased crude, as did nearly all other refiners, in the open market, buying certificates at the oil exchanges or at the wells on the basis of the price of certificates at the exchanges. These certificates were issued to the producer by pipeline operators when the oil was stored. They represented the amount owned by the producers. From the earliest years of the industry, these certificates had been subject to enthusiastic speculation.

In centralizing its purchasing, the trust first began a policy of building up its stocks of crude when the prices of certificates were low and then refraining from buying when the prices rose. In 1884, to assure better control, the trustees placed all its buying in the hands of a wholly owned firm, the Joseph Seep Agency. That agency announced that its "prices would be an average of the daily high and low quotations for certificates on the 'leading oil exchanges.' "[25] The purchasing unit, however, increasingly bought directly from producers. So the transactions on the oil exchanges dwindled. By the early 1890s, the exchanges no longer played a part

---

[24]Hidy and Hidy, *Pioneering in Big Business,* p. 86.

[25]Williamson and Daum, *American Petroleum Industry,* p. 619.

in the sale of crude. In January 1895, in a move which came as no surprise to industry experts, Seep closed the era of the oil exchanges in a famous public circular:

> The small amount of dealing in certificates on the oil exchanges renders the transactions there no longer a reliable indication of the value of the product. . . . Hereafter . . . the price paid will be as high as the markets of the world justify, but will not necessarily be the price bid on the exchanges for certificate oil.[26]

Refiners could no longer buy crude on the open market. Rather they had to contract with producers directly.

## Reorganization of Marketing, 1886–1892

The trust's board only turned its concerted attention to marketing after the refining capacity had been reorganized, pipelines extended, and purchasing centralized. The opportunities for cutting costs were more apparent in these functions. Moreover, as the trust's senior executives had little direct experience with marketing, they tended to give it a lower priority. From the start of the industry, refiners had relied on independent wholesalers to distribute their products. Although an exporter such as Bostwick or Devoe occasionally built a refinery, refiners rarely created their own distributing network. And exporters sold only to large wholesalers in different foreign countries. At home and even more abroad, these wholesalers had contacts with local retailers and other customers and knew local conditions in ways that distant refiners could hardly expect to. To assure themselves of outlets at home, a few refiners had become partners in or taken stock in a distributing company, much as Rockefeller and his associates had done when in 1873 they had purchased a 20 percent interest in Chess, Carley & Company. From 1878 to 1881, the Standard combination for the same reasons had acquired 40 percent of the stock of Waters-Pierce Company, the largest distributor in the Southwest, and comparable interests in other major wholesalers. But even after the formation of the trust, the Standard executives, because they were concentrating on the reorganization of production and purchasing, made little attempt to administer the activities of these marketing affiliates.

By the mid-1880s, several executives at 26 Broadway were beginning to question this hands-off policy. Three different but interrelated reasons suggested a reorganization of marketing. First, markets were changing. At home the demand for illuminating oil as well as lubricants and other products was growing rapidly. Abroad, the Russian threat was becoming a reality. The Nobels and other powerful competitors like the Rothschilds were making a concerted effort to capture the European market. Second, with the increasing pressure to keep its great refineries running full, Standard became more concerned with scheduling and coordinating the flow of its products to the major distributing points. Finally, new methods of bulk shipments were lowering the costs of marketing refined products and promising new economies of scale. At the same time, they were altering the relationships between the refiners and the wholesalers.

---

[26]Williamson and Daum, *American Petroleum Industry,* p. 620.

After 1875, the tank car rapidly replaced the barrel, can, and case for long distance shipments of kerosene and other refined products. A tank car carried twice the volume of an average box car loaded with barrels or cases. Lower handling charges, cheaper rate classification, and smaller losses from evaporation made the tank car still more economical. However, the use of the tank car required distributors to make a large investment in facilities for storage and packaging and in delivery wagons for the retail trade, as well as in fleets of tank cars. The resulting economies gave the larger wholesalers a decisive advantage over their smaller competitors and strengthened their position vis-à-vis the refiner. The wholesaler, rather than the refiner, came to package and brand and to set the quality and price of the product actually sold to the customer. Moreover, Chess, Carley, Waters-Pierce, and other Standard affiliates could and often did buy from independents. In addition, the refiners and wholesalers had conflicting interests. The first wanted large sales to permit the refineries to run full and steady, while the wholesalers were more interested in a large mark-up on each sale. And as the wholesalers' bargaining position improved, they began to act increasingly more independently of the trust.

In 1884, the trust made its first major move into marketing by setting up two wholly-owned companies—the Continental Oil Company and the Standard Oil Company of Iowa—to distribute in the Rocky Mountain and Pacific Coast areas. Then, in 1886, its officers decided to create a centrally controlled marketing organization. They planned to buy out all outside interests in jointly held companies and purchase major independent wholesalers. To execute this plan and to coordinate and control the trust's marketing activities, they formed a Domestic Marketing Committee. That committee, assisted by a new marketing staff housed at 26 Broadway, was to coordinate the distribution, to see that marketing policies as to quality and price were carried out, to collect information on markets, and to eliminate clashes between the different distributing agencies. By 1890, the committee had allocated the trust's marketing activities to eight regionally defined subsidiaries.[27] By that time the trust had obtained full control of all its former marketing affiliates except Waters-Pierce and had bought out 15 independents. By then the Standard Oil Trust had created a centralized marketing organization which distributed at decreasing costs the massive output of Standard's refineries.

In these same years, the Standard Trust was feeling the full impact of the opening of the Russian fields. It soon realized that improved refineries and lower manufacturing and transportation costs were not enough to meet the new threat. The Baku to Black Sea Railroad was completed in May of 1883. Financed by the Rothschilds and other powerful European businessmen, new refineries were set up and tankers were built to carry both crude and refined to southeastern Europe, France, and Spain. The Nobels in the meantime with railroads, pipelines, and new large ocean-going tankers moved into the markets of northern Europe, Germany, and Britain. Exports of Russian kerosene to Europe totaled in 1884 only

---

[27]Indicated on map in Williamson and Daum, *American Petroleum Industry,* p. 689.

2.8 percent of American kerosene exports. By 1889, Russian output had captured close to 20 percent of the European market.[28]

Standard responded by improving its shipping facilities and then by building a more closely controlled marketing organization abroad. By 1888, a new fleet of steam tankers was cutting Standard's trans-Atlantic transportation costs. The new tankers made seven round trips a year, where the older sailing ships which carried their oil cargo in barrels made three.[29] In building its own marketing organization abroad, the trust did not attempt to obtain as full control as it had at home. It seemed better to get experienced nationals to work with resources provided by the trust. The Anglo-American Petroleum Company, set up in 1888, was wholly owned. In Germany, however, the trust joined in 1890 with two leading importers to form the largest enterprise marketing oil in that nation. Similar joint enterprises were created in Holland, Italy, and Denmark. By the early 1890s, then, the Russian threat had been effectively met. During that decade Russian kerosene was never able to increase its share of the critical European market much above 20 percent.[30] By World War I, Standard Oil still accounted for over 75 percent of oil products sold in Europe.

## The Move into Crude Oil Production

Until the mid-1880s, the Standard Oil Trust had an explicit policy of staying out of the production of crude oil. Why invest in oil fields and wells when it could get all the crude it needed at the price it wanted from the many small producers? In the late 1880s, three developments led the board to alter this policy. One minor reason for change was the excellent return the trust was getting on the production of natural gas. Early in the decade, minor executives connected with the trust's pipeline affiliates recognized the profit to be made by supplying natural gas on a large scale to mills and factories. In 1883, the trust authorized National Transit to expand its gas pipelines and to go into production as well. By 1886, National Transit controlled nine natural gas companies representing a total investment of more than $7 million in Pennsylvania, New York, and Ohio. Profits from this venture helped to convince the trust that ownership of oil production was not only feasible but desirable.

Far more influential in convincing the board to move into crude oil production was the opening of new oil fields in northern Ohio and Indiana—the Lima fields—and the simultaneous decline in output of the older Appalachian fields. Discovered in 1886, the output of the Lima fields increased so rapidly that in two years Ohio and Indiana accounted for 35 percent of all crude oil production in the United States. The senior executives of the trust hesitated about using the new fields as a source of supply. To do so required a massive investment in pipelines

---

[28]Williamson and Daum, *American Petroleum Industry,* p. 660.

[29]Williamson and Daum, *American Petroleum Industry,* pp. 642–43.

[30]Williamson and Daum, *American Petroleum Industry,* p. 660; Robert W. Tolf, *The Russian Rockefellers* (Stanford, Calif.: Hoover Institution Press, 1976), p. 185.

and storage facilities. The risk was high, for Lima crude had a high sulphuric content which not only increased refining costs but resulted in a sour-smelling inferior kerosene. So investment in the fields meant development of new markets for that type of crude and new refining processes to convert Lima crude into a high quality illuminating oil at competitive prices.

Still the declining output in Pennsylvania, which threatened existing supplies, made the risk seem worth taking. Moreover, if others were successful in developing transportation and refining the output of the new fields, Standard might have to face new major competitors at home as well as abroad. Therefore, in March 1886, Standard's board authorized the creation of the Buckeye Pipeline Company. This corporation, which received its management and capital from National Transit, rapidly developed a gathering and storage system which ultimately handled 85 percent of the new region's oil.[31] Simultaneously, Standard Oil began extensive purchases of Lima crude, and soon tanks and pipelines virtually overflowed with oil seeking a market.

At the same time, the trust embarked on a major research program to develop new refining techniques. It hired Herman Frasch, the outstanding expert in the field, to find an economic means to remove the sulphur from the oil. Success was hard won—Frasch worked for two years and spent over $200,000 before he found the solution in 1888 and perfected it by 1890. Although other refiners developed alternate means of removing sulphur, the trust's patent monopoly on the Frasch process provided the basis for the high earnings of many Standard units for at least fifteen years.

Meanwhile, the trust attempted to push the sale of Lima oil as an industrial fuel which could replace coke and coal. By 1887, strong promotion and advertising began to develop a substantial market, and in 1888, over three million barrels (nearly a third of the Ohio-Indiana oil produced) were sold as fuel.

Up until 1888, the trust had made no attempt to buy oil-producing properties in the Lima field. It merely repeated what it had done earlier in Pennsylvania, buying from oil well operators and storing the crude, which was then shipped to its refineries. By 1888, however, it was apparent that Frasch had made a breakthrough on developing processes for refining Lima crude. A much more important cause, however, of the change in Standard's policy was the fact that producers in the Pennsylvania regions had, for the first time, carried out a successful shutdown and had done so with the fullest assistance of Standard Oil. On November 1, 1887, the producers agreed to reduce daily production from 60,000 to 42,500 barrels, and Standard agreed to purchase at prices the producers set. Standard joined the agreement partly because it was troubled by the threat of the producers to integrate forward into transportation and refining. It also did not want to have its supplies cut off just as it was doing its best to meet Russian competition. The shutdown helped to raise the price of crude temporarily. Standard was now becoming convinced that it must have supplies of its own.

---

[31]Hidy and Hidy, *Pioneering in Big Business,* pp. 158–59.

In moving into production in the Lima fields, the trust preferred to buy existing units, like the Ohio Oil Company and the Carter Oil Company, than to purchase oil lands on its own. In this way, it obtained the experience and expertise of successful producers. Some of these men were put on the Production Committee, which was formed in 1889 to coordinate and control the activities of this new function. The committee also directed the strategy of expansion which within three years had Standard producing 25 percent of the nation's crude oil. In 1889, the board also decided to set up a new refinery at Whiting, Indiana, outside of Chicago, to process Lima crude. Connected to the fields by a 205-mile trunk pipeline, the Whiting refinery with its 10,000 and ultimately 36,000 barrel daily throughput became and long remained the largest in the world. It was the heart of a new trust subsidiary, Standard Oil of Indiana.

Standard Oil's vast financial resources made possible its decisive moves into the Indiana-Ohio fields. As of December 1891, the trust had expended more than $32 million or an amount equal to three fifths of its net assets in 1882 in the "Ohio Crude Business." Book profits varied from plus 57 percent on the pipelines to minus 144 percent on fuel oil sales. Creating a market for a new product and developing new refining methods had been costly, but the figure of 13.42 percent for overall earnings seemed to justify the risks.[32]

The move was further justified when in the early 1890s the producers in the Pennsylvania fields were able to carry out an earlier threat by constructing a pipeline to the seaboard, building large refineries, and making arrangements with European wholesalers to market abroad. The new enterprise, which in 1895 became the Pure Oil Company, did not, as Tidewater had done earlier, make a deal with Standard on prices and output. Standard's move into production was, therefore, central to its continuing dominance in the American oil industry. This move into production, like those of Tidewater and Pure Oil into refining and marketing, also foreshadowed what was to become the structure of the oil industry all over the world. Competition in the oil industry would be between a few large vertically integrated giant enterprises. It would be oligopolistic rather than monopolistic.

# Evolution of the Trust's Organizational Structure

The most distinctive feature of Standard's organizational structure, the committee form of management, reflected its origins as a federation of legally and administratively separate business enterprises. In the late 1870s, leading executives of different firms in the alliance who dealt with railroads and pipelines met regularly, though informally, as a Transportation Committee. Others concerned with the European wholesalers formed what would become the Export Trade Committee. Then, as discussions were underway in 1881 to work out ways to reorganize refining facilities, a Manufacturing Committee was formed. After the trust's headquarters were set up in New York, a Cooperage and a Case and Can Committee were organized. The Lubricating Oil Committee came into being in 1885, when

---

[32]Hidy and Hidy, *Pioneering in Big Business,* p. 166.

the sale of lubricants was centralized in New York. As the trust moved into new functions, its board quite naturally set up new committees. So the Domestic Trade committee appeared in 1886, and the one for production of crude, in 1889.

After the formation of the Trust in January 1882, the functions of the committees were to set policies and to coordinate and standardize the activities of all Standard Oil units involved in handling one function or specialized product.[33] As the committee members were senior executives or directors of subsidiary firms, they usually had the responsibility for carrying out the decisions agreed upon. The success in executing these decisions depended upon the degree of ownership in the constituent companies, the personalities of the managers, the nature of the decision and its resulting directive, and the exigencies of the moment.

The senior committee of Standard Oil was, of course, the Executive Committee, which consisted of those trustees who were at 26 Broadway on any given day. That committee determined all of Standard Oil's basic policies until 1911. It not only handled "general policies," but also matters of routine, including questions on which subordinates disagreed. The committee passed on recommendations presented to it by other committees and senior executives. Its primary responsibility and its fundamental source of power lay, however, in the allocation of funds to the many operating units. For it had to approve of all appropriations involving $5,000 or over. Another critical task was the appointing, shifting, and rewarding of executive personnel. All salaries over $600 a year had to be approved by a subcommittee of the Executive Committee. Three of its members also voted as a Proxy Committee the shares in all elections of directors of the Standard companies.

Since the trustees were usually presidents or responsible representatives of the associated companies, decisions made by the Executive Committee usually took the form of a suggestion to one or more of its members who headed the company concerned. If local executives protested or opposed a decision of the Executive Committee, its members preferred discussion and compromise to autocratic decrees. The committee normally instituted policies only after careful consideration of the attitudes and opinions of the executives involved. Implementation of decisions took the form of requests, suggestions, and recommendations but rarely orders.

Clearly there were disadvantages to decision by consultation and agreement. It was tedious; opportunities might be missed through delay or the temptation to compromise; and few men had both the patience to preside over interminable discussion and the ability to produce the tactful and effective compromise at the right moment. On the other hand, the method permitted the necessary weighing of evidence advanced by all interested parties—especially the views of the experts and those who would execute the policy. Standard Oil found the conference method essential to unity and cooperation in a business managed by formerly competitive, aggressive individualists.

The creation of an efficient executive organization necessitated staff assistance. In the mid-1880s, an extensive staff was brought together at 26 Broadway.

---

[33]Hidy and Hidy, *Pioneering in Big Business,* pp. 59, 63.

The central administrative units had diverse origins; not all the staff functions were crystallized into departments by 1886. Occasionally, it was necessary to forego some advantages of centralization in order to secure the best work from key men on the lower echelons. By 1886, there were 11 major staff units: Auditing, Legal, Crude Stock (i.e., purchasing), Cooperage, Domestic Trade, Southern and Western Domestic Trade, Chief Oil Inspector, Barrel Preparing, Lubricating Oil and Paraffin Wax, Lubricating Oil and Western Sales, and Foreign Barrel (i.e., foreign shipping and sales).

Accounting particularly demanded the creation of a specialized and efficient staff. With a few exceptions, the trust expected every subsidiary company to show a profit. In order to analyze the trust's financial condition, separate accounts were set up for the numerous departments and companies. Procedures required a semi-annual balance sheet, and accountants carefully computed average costs to four places after the decimal point. Although accounting remained crude—it was little more than bookkeeping—plant superintendents, office managers, and other executives were judged on the basis of their costs and profits.[34]

The Executive Committee and operating companies received valuable information from other units besides the accounting department. The crude stock department, for example, provided the top committee with a daily "crude oil report" which included the latest information on new wells, total production in the United States, stocks in storage, Standard's overall holding of crude, runs from tanks at wells, deliveries to refineries, and new purchases. The Manufacturing Committee forwarded monthly cost and yield statements for each refinery. The beginnings of systematic marketing data started with the monthly Barrelling and Marketing Report, prepared in 1884 by the Cooperage Committee. The three Sales Committees later improved these data. Every sales representative was expected to report his own receipts and those of all competitors in his area. Standard's network of refineries, producing and buying offices, pipelines and shipping points, as well as its marketing offices provided an impressive intelligence network that covered the United States and indeed, most of the world.

It was this committee and staff organization that made the Standard Oil Trust such a powerful business enterprise and so greatly differentiated it from its predecessor, the Standard Oil combination. In the 1890s, the trust's administrative organization still could be improved in many ways. No attempt had been made to forecast demand for its products or to forecast its capital needs. No budget was formulated to aid in the systematic allocation of funds. No staff unit or committee was responsible for coordinating the flow of goods through the enterprise as a whole. Subsidiaries and affiliates often found themselves working at cross purposes. Still the structure that had evolved by the 1890s successfully managed one of the largest and most complex business enterprises in the world.

---

[34]Hidy and Hidy, *Pioneering in Big Business,* p. 71.

# Conclusion

The refining industry by the 1890s was increasingly characterized by vertically integrated firms, although independents did not yet approach Standard Oil's degree of integration. As a result of the trend, entry into the industry was becoming increasingly difficult. A new firm required not only considerable capital for the construction of large refineries, it also had to make costly arrangements to obtain supplies of crude oil and transportation. The discovery of new fields in the Southwest at the turn of the century would justify such investment. Meanwhile, the output of refined oil continued to increase, but this trend was accompanied by a gradual shift in the type of product consumed. As the century came to a close, proportionately less oil was used for illuminating purposes and more for fuel and lubricants. Then in the late 1890s, the greatest threat to Standard's and the oil industry's future appeared with the successful development and rapid spread of Thomas Edison's electric lighting system. The disappearance of the kerosene market was far more than compensated for in the next decade with the coming of the automobile. And over these fundamental shifts in the market, Standard Oil, for all its economic power, had no control whatsoever. As Exhibit 1 indicates, these dramatic changes in the market, as well as changes in supply, brought new firms into the industry. Thus even before the breakup of Standard Oil the Industry had developed into an oligopoly characterized by large integrated firms competing for market share.

Standard Oil, tracing its birth back to a small partnership in the grocery business, grew into a leading refiner in a new industry and then matured into a multimillion dollar integrated industrial enterprise dominating its industry throughout the world. Other firms in other industries followed the same route to great size and power. In the last years of the 19th and the first of the 20th centuries, enterprises in rubber, steel, copper, lead, sugar, salt, whiskey, explosives, and biscuits, to name a few such industries, grew by combination, then consolidation, and then vertical integration. But the history of none of these shows as clearly as does the story of Standard Oil, the first to take this route, the causes for and the process of becoming a modern industrial business corporation.

## EXHIBIT 1

**Petroleum Companies with Assets of $20 Million or More, 1917\***

| *Standard Group* | *Independents before 1911* | *Independents after 1911* |
|---|---|---|
| 2. Standard Oil Co. (N.J.) | 24. Texas Co. | 37. Magnolia Petroleum Co. |
| 14. Standard Oil Co. of N.Y. (no c) [Socony] | 26. Gulf Oil Co. | (no c) [Socony] |
| 34. Standard Oil Co. of Ind. | 45. Pure Oil Co. [Union Oil, 1965] | 56. Sinclair Oil & Refining Corp. |
| 35. Standard Oil Co. of Calif. | 69. Associated Oil Co. [Tide Water] | 64. Pan American Petroleum & Transport Co. [Standard Indiana] |
| 48. Prairie Oil & Gas Co. (c only) [Sinclair] | 71. Union Oil of Calif. | 95. Midwest Refining Co. [Standard Indiana] |
| 61. Ohio Oil Co. (c only) | 124. Tide Water Oil Co. | 110. Cosden & Co. [Sunray-Mid Continent, 1955] |
| 72. Vacuum Oil Co. (no c) [Socony] | 160. Shell Oil of Calif. | 151. California Petroleum Corp. (c only) [Texas Co.] |
| 84. Atlantic Refining Co. | 229. Sun Co. | 162. Texas Pacific Coal & Oil Co. (c only) [Seagrams, 1965] |
| 106. Pierce Oil Corp. (liquidated) | | 168. Houston Oil Co. of Texas (c only) [Atlantic Refining] |
| 205. South Penn Oil Co. (c only) | | 178. General Petroleum Corp. [Socony] |
| 262. Standard Oil Co. (Ohio) (no c) | | 261. Producers and Refiners Corp. (no marketing) [Sinclair] |
| | | 278. Skelly-Sankey Oil Co. (c only) [Getty Oil, 1967] |

\*Numbers indicate rank among the largest 278 industrials in 1917. Unless otherwise indicated, the companies are fully integrated. The letter (c) indicates crude oil operations. Name in brackets is the company into which the firm merged. Dates are given for post-World War II mergers. The current name of Standard Oil (N.J.) is Exxon; Socony Vacuum is Mobil Oil; Ohio Oil is Marathon; and South Penn is Pennzoil United.

Source: Alfred D. Chandler, Jr., *The Visible Hand* (Cambridge: Harvard University Press, 1977), p. 351.

# APPENDIX A

 *Chronology*

| | |
|---|---|
| 1859 | Rockefeller & Clark formed. |
| 1865 | Rockefeller & Andrews formed. |
| 1867 | Rockefeller, Andrews & Flagler formed. |
| 1870 | Standard Oil Company formed. |
| 1870–72 | The conquest of Cleveland. |
| 1871–72 | South Improvement Company project. |
| Aug. 1872 | National Refiners' Association formed. |
| Dec. 19, 1872 | Treaty of Titusville. |
| 1874–76 | Standard Oil Company alliance drives toward monopoly. |
| 1876–77 | Challenge by Empire Transportation Co. |
| 1879–83 | Challenge by Tidewater Pipeline Co. |
| Jan. 2, 1882 | Standard Oil Trust formed. |
| 1882–84 | Reorganization of refining. |
| 1882–84 | Pipeline expansion and centralization of purchasing. |
| 1885 | Headquarters moved to 26 Broadway. |
| 1884–92 | Reorganization of marketing. |
| 1888–91 | Move into crude oil production. |

# CASE 15

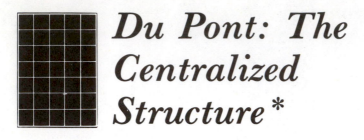 *Du Pont: The Centralized Structure**

The modern Du Pont company, like the Standard Oil Trust, was a product of a merger of many small single-function family firms. However the transformation into a modern integrated enterprise came much more swiftly at Du Pont than it did at Standard Oil. The du Ponts moved quickly from a strategy of horizontal combination to one of vertical integration. They rationalized their production facilities even more speedily than did Standard Oil. And they created a carefully defined, centralized, functionally departmentalized organization. This structure, unlike the one developed at Standard Oil, was widely adopted by American industrials. It remains today the standard form of managing a large enterprise mass-producing a single line of products for national and global markets. One reason for these differences in the strategic planning and organizational structure at Du Pont and Standard Oil was that the Du Pont merger occurred in 1902, 20 years after that in the oil industry. The entrepreneurs at Du Pont, therefore, had the benefit of the experience of many older large industrial corporations. They did not have to pioneer in the new ways but could build on what others had learned.

---

*This case is a revised version of the first part of Chapter 2 in Alfred D. Chandler, Jr., *Strategy and Structure* (Cambridge: MIT Press, 1962). The revisions have been made by Professor Chandler, who is grateful for the suggestions of Professor Derek A. Newton, the Colgate Darden Graduate School of Business Administration, University of Virginia. Reproduced by permission of MIT Press.

# A Change in Command

During the chill winter days of February 1902, the affairs of the venerable E. I. Du Pont de Nemours & Company were drawing to a crisis. Plans for celebrating its 100 years of explosives making were already under way when its president, Eugene du Pont, stricken with pneumonia, suddenly died. The remaining five partners began indecisively to look about for a successor. None of their own group appeared to have the necessary qualifications. Four were either too old or in poor health. The fifth, Alfred I. du Pont, at 37 years of age, seemed too inexperienced and erratic. Perhaps the best thing to do, the elder partners decided, was to sell the company to its ancient and friendly competitor, Laflin & Rand. After all, the Du Pont company owned a sizable amount of its stock, and its president, J. Amory Haskell, trained at the Du Pont-controlled Repauno Chemical Company, had always been close to their interests.

Alfred du Pont disagreed. Young and energetic, he was shocked at the thought of selling the company, his "birthright," to outsiders. If he could get the support of his cousin Coleman du Pont, once his roommate at the Massachusetts Institute of Technology, he would buy it himself. Over long-distance phone, Coleman immediately concurred, but he insisted that they must get Pierre, another cousin, to "handle the finances." A second telephone call brought Pierre's acceptance. The elder du Ponts, on learning of Alfred's allies, were more than willing to sell out to the three cousins at a quickly agreed upon price of $12 million.

Coleman, a tall, broad-shouldered man with a wide grin, had the temperament and training to create business empires. Pierre, quiet and studious, had the rational, analytical outlook of an organization builder. Ironically, Alfred, trained in the powder mills and most happy when he was personally supervising work on the production line, was far less prepared to rebuild and administer a great industrial enterprise.

Coleman was a member of the Kentucky branch of the family and had never been involved in the explosives industry. After graduating from MIT in 1885, he started work in the Kentucky coal mines owned by his uncle, Alfred Victor du Pont. In a short time, he had taken charge of the coal company, making it one of the largest in the region. Then in 1893, he left the coal company to join two of his uncle's protégés, Arthur J. Moxham and Tom L. Johnson, as general manager of their steel mill in Johnstown, Pennsylvania. These two—the latter was soon to become the famous reform mayor of Cleveland—had built with Du Pont financing street railways in a number of American cities. They had put up the steel mill at Johnstown to provide themselves with rails. Shortly after Coleman arrived, they began the construction of a second plant at Lorain, Ohio, one of the largest and most modern of its day.

As Tom Johnson began to turn his attention to politics, Coleman took over more of the management of the new Lorain Steel Company. He quickly showed his empire-building tendencies by erecting shops to make streetcars together with all their parts, including bodies, wheels, and electric motors. (This last item was one of the most technologically complex products of the day.) In 1898, Elbert H.

Gary, backed by J. Pierpont Morgan, persuaded Coleman and his associates to sell the Lorain Steel Company to the Federal Steel Company, which the two financiers had just formed and which three years later was to become the nucleus for the United States Steel Corporation. After the sale, Coleman and Moxham turned their energies back to building electric street railway systems.

Pierre S. du Pont had joined his cousin in Lorain in 1899. Upon graduation from MIT in 1890, he had returned to the family company to take a job at its first smokeless powder works, then being constructed at Carney's Point across the Delaware River from Wilmington. When the close of the Spanish-American War brought a reduction of activity at Carney's Point, Pierre saw little future in Wilmington as long as old men were continuing to manage the family firm in the same old way. So he resigned from the company to join Coleman. At Lorain he helped transfer the properties to Federal Steel Company, managed those which had been retained, and assisted Coleman in his street railway ventures.

## The Strategy of Consolidation

At the time of Eugene du Pont's death, the company and the industry were being managed just as they had been for more than a generation. The Du Pont company itself administered only a few black powder plants and the new smokeless powder works at Carney's Point. Until 1902, it remained a family enterprise. As one du Pont noted: "The business was entirely managed by the senior partner.... The head of the firm was ex officio head of the family." The other partners and nearly all the supervisory force were du Ponts. However, the du Pont family's control ranged well beyond the company. It held stock in other firms, including the Repauno Chemical Company, which was formed in 1880 by Lammot du Pont, Pierre's father, to manufacture a new type of explosive—dynamite. And, through the Gunpowder Trade Association, the Du Pont Company wielded strong influence over the rest of the industry.

The Gunpowder Trade Association had been formed in 1872 when overproduction resulting from an increased output and a surplus of Civil War powder threatened to collapse prices. The association, with each member having a number of votes according to its size, set price and production schedules. After Henry du Pont, the company's president from 1850 to 1889, purchased a controlling interest in more than half a dozen of the larger powder companies during the depression of the 1870s, he held a majority of these votes. To assure compliance with the schedules he set, he worked them out in close cooperation with the executives of the other firms and particularly with Solomon Turck, the president of the industry's second largest company, Laflin & Rand. Because of this close cooperation and because of Henry du Pont's policy of buying a stock interest in most of his major competitors, the Association remained more stable and longer-lived than most combinations in American industry.

Henry du Pont and his successor, Eugene, as presidents of the strongest firm in the combination, had a powerful voice in how much other firms produced and at what price, but they knew almost nothing about how each unit carried on its production and sold its quotas. Nor did they particularly care. Neither the individual companies nor the association paid much attention to costs, to improving processes, or to developing more systematic purchasing and marketing techniques. There was little coordination between the marketing and selling companies. With only a few notable exceptions, the manufacturing firms sold through agents who handled the output of many companies and who apparently also became members of the association. Effective administration was impossible because neither the separate firms nor the combination itself had the information or methods to assure an efficient use of existing resources and so to reduce unit costs and increase output per worker. They did not even have a systematic way of gauging existing or potential demand on which to base their price and production schedules. The lack of administrative control is suggested by the fact that during nearly all of his tenure, Henry du Pont carried on singlehandedly from a one-room office overlooking the powder mills on the Brandywine most of the business of his company and of the association. He wrote nearly all of the business correspondence himself in longhand.

The du Ponts were also involved in the production of the new explosive, dynamite, invented by Alfred Nobel. Because Henry du Pont refused to take on the new product, his cousin, Lammot du Pont (Pierre du Pont's father) and for many years Henry's right-hand man in the black powder business, organized the Repauno Chemical Company. Its works on the Delaware River opposite Chester, Pennsylvania, were completed in 1880. In 1895, the Repauno Company joined with Hercules, Hecla, Sterling, Lake Superior Powder, and Atlantic Dynamite to form the Eastern Dynamite Company. A holding company, Eastern Dynamite had no central office to coordinate flows or allocate resources. It remained merely a more efficient device than a trade association for controlling competition by deciding output, markets, and prices charged by its subsidiaries.

Thus, when the three cousins took over their family inheritance, that inheritance included several small family-controlled firms tied to others in the industry through the Gunpowder Trade Association and the Eastern Dynamite Company. The rather chaotic state of these holdings is indicated by Pierre's comment to his brother Irénée in February 1902 concerning Alfred's proposal to join forces with himself and Coleman.

> I think there is going to be some tall hustling to get everything reorganized. We have not the slightest idea of what we are buying, but we are probably not at a disadvantage as I think the old company had a very slim idea of the property they possess.

To Coleman and Pierre, this hustling meant more than reviving the family birthright. Reorganization provided an opportunity to transform this loose federation of many relatively small firms into a consolidated, integrated, centrally managed industrial enterprise. Methodically the two cousins, supported somewhat hesitantly by Alfred, embarked on the strategy of consolidation and centralization. First came a careful inventory of the properties they had acquired. Next, Coleman concentrated his charms on persuading the stockholders in these and many other explosives concerns to turn over their stockholdings to the du Ponts in return for cash or for stock in the new firm—the E. I. Du Pont de Nemours Powder Company—formed to take over the combined properties.

Then Pierre focused his energies on fashioning a structure to administer them. The legal and financial changes were, in his mind, only necessary preliminaries to the operational and administrative ones. As he stressed later:

> At the time we made the purchase of the properties, we realized that if a good investment was to be made for us, it would necessitate a complete reorganization of the method of doing business; that the administrative end would have to be reorganized, numerous selling organizations, or administrative organizations done away with, and we would have to establish a system of costs in order that an economical manufacture could be installed throughout the business. That was prevented, absolutely, by our lack of control of the properties in which we were interested, and we had no means of establishing a new system of organization in any of these companies.

The formation of the powder company made it possible "to operate the properties in one name, through one set of selling agents, and under one management, or operation." Only in this way could the costly duplication of facilities and personnel be eliminated, the different functions—buying, manufacturing, shipping, and selling—be economically and systematically supervised, and the essential coordination between functions maintained.

As the process of consolidation moved along, the strategy pursued became more precise. The earlier combinations—the trade association and the holding company—had attempted to obtain and retain market power through contractual agreements. During their first months in office, the three cousins became aware of, and indeed often appalled at, the difficulties in maintaining such agreements. Several of the firms in the association had two sets of books, one for themselves and the other for the Association's board. The new strategy—one for obtaining and maintaining market power through administrative efficiency—was first clearly defined by Arthur Moxham in a letter to Coleman du Pont written in June 1903:

> I have been urging upon our people the following arguments. If we could by any measure buy out all competition and have an absolute monopoly in the field, it would not pay us. The essence of manufacture is steady and full product. The demand for the country for powder is variable. If we owned all, therefore when slack time came we would have to curtail product to the extent of diminished demands. If, on the other hand we controlled only 60 percent of it all and made that 60 percent cheaper than others, when slack times came we could still keep *our* capital employed to *the full* and our product to this maximum by taking from the other 40 percent what is needed for this purpose. In other words, you could count upon always running full if you could make cheaply and control only 60 percent, whereas, if you own it all, when slack times came you could only run a curtailed product.

As the reorganizers at Du Pont fully understood, when they were running steady and full, they could produce a keg of black powder at 15 percent less cost than that of their most efficient smaller competitor and could make dynamite, whose production employed a more continuous process, even more cheaply.

In carrying out the strategy of consolidation and in setting up the centralized structure, Pierre and Coleman drew on their experience at Lorain. The customers and competitors of the Lorain Steel Company were among the technologically most advanced and efficiently managed businesses of the day. The improvements in plant layout and manufacturing organization which Henry Clay Frick and Andrew Carnegie had recently completed at their works were incorporated in the new steel plant at Lorain. General Electric and Westinghouse, Lorain's competitors in the making of electrical engines, must have suggested much about ways to put together a large centralized sales and engineering organization.

The cousins also had a successful model nearer home. In 1892, the du Ponts placed two energetic young executives in charge of the dynamite works at Repauno—J. Amory Haskell, who at thirty-one had proved himself an able manager of a coal company, and Hamilton M. Barksdale, a trained civil engineer who had worked with the Baltimore & Ohio Railroad. These two decided to build a sales organization of their own. Dynamite was still a relatively new product and dangerous to use. Agents accustomed to handling black powder often failed to explain to contractors, mining companies, and other customers how the new product should be used. So the new managers appointed Charles L. Patterson, one of the industry's master salesmen, to set up sales offices in different parts of the country. He was also to train a force of salaried men in explosives technique so that they might be able to show customers how to use dynamite efficiently and effectively. As the demand for dynamite grew, Haskell and Barksdale organized production more systematically by forming a manufacturing, an engineering, and a purchasing department.

In 1903, following this model, the three cousins, assisted by Haskell and Barksdale, created much the same type of an administrative organization to knit together the resources of nearly two thirds of the American explosives industry. First they consolidated manufacturing. Production was concentrated in a few of the larger plants, located as advantageously as possible to the major markets. They next set up three administrative departments to coordinate, appraise, and plan the work of the plants—one for each of the company's major products: black powder, high explosives (dynamite), and smokeless powder. Then they formed a nationwide marketing organization with the old Repauno sales department serving as a nucleus. The engineering, traffic, and purchasing units of the new powder company also drew on the older dynamite company's personnel and procedures. Still another unit proposed by Coleman and Pierre was the development department, which was to concentrate on improving product and processes. As it had no predecessor in the explosives industry, the du Ponts may have been inspired by the recently created research organization at General Electric, the first in the United States. Finally, to house the headquarters of these new departments, Coleman ordered the construction of a large many-storied office building in the center of Wilmington.

The six men most active in creating the new company now took over its major executive posts. Coleman, as president, became responsible for broad policy and overall company performance. Alfred, as general manager, was given general supervision of manufacturing activities. Pierre became treasurer. Haskell had full charge of selling. Barksdale headed the largest manufacturing department—high explosive—while Moxham, who had come from Lorain with Coleman and Pierre, was given general oversight of the development department. In carrying out their new duties, these men were not only concerned with assuring effective central office planning, appraisal, and coordination of buying, manufacturing, sales, and other functional activities, but they also saw the need to develop departmental designs for coordinating, appraising, and setting policy for each of the several types of field units. Such a structure was essential, they believed, if the vast resources under their control were to be employed rationally and profitably.

## Creating the Multidepartmental Structure

In the centralized structure, each major department came to have its vice president and its director. The latter was to be responsible for the smooth day-to-day operations of the department; the former was to concentrate more on the long-term planning and appraisal necessary to keep the company alive and growing. Collectively, the vice presidents with the president, acting as the Executive Committee, were to make broad policy for the enterprise as a whole.

Individually, the vice presidents had full responsibility and authority in managing their units. The three manufacturing departments or, as they were then called, the operating departments had been placed under the general supervision of Alfred du Pont as general manager. But Alfred also took the job of vice president in charge of the black powder department and actually continued as de facto plant superintendent at the old Brandywine mills. From their headquarters in the large new office building in Wilmington, Alfred and the vice presidents and directors of the other two operating departments—high explosives and smokeless powder—their assistants and staff officers coordinated, appraised, and planned goals and set procedures for the work carried on at the several plants. These departmental headquarters soon had offices for the recruitment and training of personnel, for the inspection of product and process, for the maintenance of plant, for the improvement of processes, and, for a time, for planning new construction and purchasing supplies other than raw materials and equipment. Before long, however, the engineering and purchasing departments became separate units, reporting directly to Alfred as the general executive in charge of manufacturing.

The lines of communication and authority between departmental headquarters and the plants in the field were defined in terms of line and staff. The new departments closely followed the pattern first fully developed in the United States by the Pennsylvania Railroad. The line of authority ran from the vice president to the department director and his assistants, to the plant or works manager, and then to the supervisors and foremen. The plant executives who handled auxiliary functions such as inspection, personnel, or maintenance were responsible to the works or factory managers for their day-to-day working orders. They looked to their seniors at headquarters only for standards and procedures. Executives at headquarters worked at making more precise the information that flowed through these channels in the form of daily, weekly, and monthly reports and concentrated particularly on deriving more accurate cost figures. Such data not only provided a check on plant performance but, by permitting comparisons between plants and between subdivisions within the plants, made it easier to locate weaknesses and inefficiencies.

To improve communication still further between headquarters and field, each operating department held regular meetings of its plant superintendents and headquarters staff where the managers exchanged information on ways to make their activities more efficient and less costly. Papers read at the regular meetings of Barksdale's high explosives department and circulated to all departmental administrative and supervisory personnel covered such topics as standardization of parts and equipment, new manufacturing procedures, safety measures, customers' complaints, comparative costs and savings made at the different plants, morale, incentives, and other items.

Sales activities were as systematically organized as manufacturing. The sales department's director, Charles L. Patterson, soon instituted a structure comparable, although on a much larger scale, to the one he had fashioned at Repauno. Here the field units included 17 sales offices headed by branch managers in different cities in every part of the country. Each manager, assisted by a small staff, supervised the activities of a corps of field men. Most salesmen specialized in one product—black powder, high explosives, or smokeless powder—although there were a few "general" salesmen. A few also sold small lots of solvents, ether, and other chemicals, the by-products of the making of smokeless powder. The salesmen, who were now company employees, completely replaced the old outside agents or jobbers in marketing the company's products to railroads, mines, contractors, and makers of rifle and shotgun ammunition. In addition to the regional branch officers, there were, at headquarters, one office supervising sales abroad and two for handling large customers. Colonel Edmund G. Buckner's Military Sales Division sold smokeless powder to national governments, while the Contractor's Division sold high explosives and some black powder directly to large contractors.

At sales headquarters, Patterson had three line assistants and three staff officers. The three assistant directors were, at first, responsible for the administration of three geographically defined units—the Eastern, Central, and Western Divisions. Later, each came to handle one of the company's three major products. Patterson continued to train his salesmen, as he had done at Repauno, to become experts in the methods of using industrial explosives so that they could work closely with the customer on his special blasting problems. Such training became the responsibility of the Technical Division, which also worked at enlarging the market for explosives by studying possible new uses and applications for its products. The other staff units were the Advertising and Trade Record Divisions. The latter pioneered in compiling statistics on sales made by the Du Pont company and its competitors. This information became increasingly valuable for making estimates of market demand to be used to set production schedules and then to determine what quantities of raw materials and other supplies must be purchased. These statistics also provided data on the changing share of the market held by the company, which executives at headquarters as well as the branch managers themselves used to check on the performance of each sales office and of the department as a whole. In time, a fourth staff office, the Sales Expense Division, was formed to compile figures on sales costs and to work out methods for reducing these marketing expenses.

Here, as in manufacturing, the relations between headquarters and field were defined on what was essentially a line-and-staff basis. The director, assistant directors, and branch managers had charge of men, while the staff executives at headquarters and in the field were responsible rather for standards and procedures. Advertising was more of a line activity, although the advertising office conferred with the field executives about the nature of their programs. To assist the director and vice president of that department in determining policies and the plans for carrying them out, a Sales Board or Sales Executive Committee, consisting of the assistant directors and the heads of staff offices, met regularly to determine price schedules, to approve of advertising programs, and to decide comparable tactical decisions. Also the sales department appears to have had meetings of headquarters and field officers similar to those in the manufacturing departments.

The five other functional departments reporting directly to the president—essential materials, development, real estate, legal, and treasurer's—were somewhat smaller than sales or operations. The first became responsible for the procurement and transportation of raw materials necessary for production. In 1906, after the new structure was in full operation, Pierre made long-term contracts with nitrate-producing firms in Chile to be assured of supplies of raw materials. In 1911, the company purchased these properties, but they continued to be administered locally, not from Wilmington. The coordination of the flow of supplies from Chile and elsewhere to the Du Pont plants became the job of the essential materials department.

The initial responsibility of the development department was to supervise the two laboratories set up to improve the company's products and the ways of making them. The Eastern Laboratory, founded at Repauno in 1902, concentrated on developments in dynamite, while the Experimental Station, built the following year on the Brandywine, specialized in black powder and the newer smokeless powder. The latter, it might be pointed out, was not an explosive, as was dynamite or black powder, but rather a propellant used for rifle and shotgun shells or, on a much larger scale, for military projectiles. The development department also worked on broad problems concerning markets or sources of supply, usually at the request of the top executives in the central office. It was, for example, on the basis of this department's investigations that Pierre purchased the Chilean nitrate properties.

The treasurer's department provided the central office with even more valuable and more regular information. Beside their routine financial activities—the handling and supervision of the myriad financial transactions involved in any great industrial enterprise—the financial executives concentrated on developing uniform statistics essential to determining overall costs, income, profits, and losses. The department, at first divided into three major units—the treasurer's office and the Accounting and Auditing Divisions—came to have, by the time of World War I, additional units that administered credit and collections, salaries, and forecasts and analyses. The auditing unit gathered information on general external financial and economic conditions as well as on the company's internal performance, while the accounting office continued to develop cost data for production, sales, construction, research, and other activities.

The central office, like that of other sizable industrial enterprises, was comprised of the functional vice presidents and the president, who had one or two assistants. Since the administration of the enterprise as a whole was considered to be the collective task of the senior executives, overall coordination, appraisal, and planning came to be formally carried out in three committees—Finance, Executive, and Administration. The make-up and duties of the Finance and Executive Committees were similar to those in many of the new consolidated industrial firms. The Finance Committee, at first, included the largest stockholders—the three cousins and the older members of the family who had received stock payment for their holdings. The Executive Committee consisted of the men most responsible for fashioning the new organization and then, as time passed, the president and vice presidents in charge of the functional departments.

From the very first, Pierre and Coleman insisted that the Executive Committee should concentrate on long-term planning and appraisal; it must not become involved in making decisions concerning the operating activities of the different departments. Since planning the future use of current facilities and personnel and the development of new resources involved the allocation of funds for both capital and operating expenses, the Executive Committee increasingly took over the financial duties originally assigned to the Finance Committee. Moreover, as the older members of the Finance Committee had little understanding of the new company's operations and policies, the committee's active members soon were only Pierre and Coleman du Pont. For all practical purposes the Finance Committee became temporarily defunct.

The coordination of day-to-day activities of the different departments was left to the Administration or "Operative" Committee made up of departmental directors. Its weekly meetings not only helped to coordinate plans and procedures, but they also provided a place for the interchange of a great deal of information. The members made proposals to the Executive Committee and discussed ways to carry out the strategies and policies that the senior group had agreed upon.

## Structural Modifications, 1903–1919

After its initial shakedown, the structure fashioned in 1903 remained relatively unchanged until after the end of World War I (see Exhibit 1). The modifications which did occur affected the central office rather than the departmental headquarters. These changes were of three sorts. The most important resulted from shifts in the company's top command which in turn reflected the final transformation of the Du Pont company from a family firm to a professionally managed enterprise. A second type of change was the growth of auxiliary departments at the central office, and a third, the improvements made in the informational data used to administer the enterprise as whole.

Of the three cousins who engineered the massive reorganization of the company and the industry, Pierre soon proved himself the most adept in governing it. Alfred preferred to stay close to the black powder operations where he had long worked. Coleman, the empire builder, quickly lost interest in managing the domains he had helped create. Before long, he had a controlling interest in the Equitable Life Assurance Society, and, partly as a result of the changes he encouraged there, he built what was then the largest office building in New York. He turned too to politics, becoming a member of the Republican National Committee in 1908. But Pierre devoted all his energies to the administration of the new Du Pont Company. As its first treasurer, he developed essential statistical data. In 1906, he became the de facto head of the company and in 1909, at Coleman's request, took the title of acting president.

In January 1911, Pierre, with Coleman's support, relieved Alfred of his duties as general manager and as vice president in charge of the black powder department and a member of the Executive Committee. They retained him as a vice president and had him rejoin them on the Finance Committee. Increasing deafness had hindered Alfred's effectiveness. His divorce and remarriage created intense personal and family tensions. But his failure as an administrator was the basic reason for his removal. He was highly competent in personally supervising work in the mills, but he had shown little talent for broader coordination, appraising, and goal setting.

Alfred's removal brought younger men into top management. Barksdale became general manager, and Pierre's brother Irénée, his assistant. The new department heads and members of the Executive Committee—Harry Haskell, the brother of J. Amory Haskell in high explosives; R. R. M. Carpenter, a brother-in-law of Pierre in development; Harry Fletcher Brown in smokeless powder; Frank L. Connable in black powder; and John J. Raskob, Pierre's secretary since the Lorain days, as treasurer—were experienced and loyal administrators.

In the year following these personnel changes came another reorganization. The U.S. District Court, finding that the company had violated the Sherman Antitrust Act, approved a plan to divide its industrial explosives and sporting powder business among three companies—the existing Du Pont company and two new firms, the Hercules Powder Company and the Atlas Powder Company. While this reorganization deprived the Du Pont company of some of its plant and personnel, it had little effect on its basic structure or strategy. These many changes did prove, however, to be too much of a strain on the acting president. After Pierre's health broke, Barksdale became acting president as well as general manager.

Then in 1913, Coleman returned temporarily to oversee the Du Pont company's activities. Pierre, back again in the saddle early in 1914, soon came into conflict with Coleman. At the end of February, shortly after he had received the title of vice president, Pierre removed Barksdale and put Irénée du Pont in the general manager's post and, at the same time, asked for the resignation of Moxham.

The latter, though still active in the Du Pont company management, had been making plans with two of Pierre's brothers-in-law to consolidate several of Du Pont's competitors into a single large firm.

Coleman was apparently disturbed by these changes and other policies that Pierre had instituted, although the evidence available on this controversy is anything but clear. When, in the summer of 1914, Coleman was forced to undergo a serious intestinal operation at the Mayo Clinic in Minnesota, he wrote to Pierre suggesting that the issues be resolved either by letting him buy Pierre out or by having Pierre purchase his shares. Pierre would not hear of the first alternative and hoped to avoid the second. "Before giving further thought to parting, let us take another try at it on the old basis as you suggest," that is, by having Pierre again assume full command. "I will accept the acting presidency, or perhaps it will be better to assume your duties under the title of vice president which I now have." Pierre then suggested changes in the company's top personnel which he hoped Coleman would find satisfactory.

Within a few weeks, Coleman and the board of directors had accepted Pierre's proposals with some modifications. Pierre was again to be acting president and responsible for overall company policy and performance. Irénée, Pierre's brother, became general manager. He was to oversee sales as well as operations and also became chairman of the Executive Committee. Pierre and Irénée would then both be "general" officers responsible for the company as a whole. The rest of the older men in the top command were retired. J. A. Haskell, Barksdale, Moxham, and Patterson (who became a member of the Executive Committee in 1907), relieved of active work, would continue with the company "on salary in advisory capacities" with the title of vice president. The new vice presidents, like those appointed in 1911, were young and loyal to Pierre but also were all experienced and professionally competent.

In carrying out these changes, Pierre deliberately rejected the long-entrenched inherited attitude that the firm was managed for the family and the family was to manage the firm. Alfred and even Coleman or Barksdale (who had married a du Pont) should continue in top positions, Pierre clearly believed, only if they continued to be effective administrators. Pierre did appoint family members (two brothers and a brother-in-law) to senior posts in 1911 and 1914, but only after they had proven themselves managerially competent. From this time on, the criterion for promotion was competence rather than family background—universalistic rather than particularistic.

With the changes in top command completed, Pierre carefully defined the duties of the central office. In so doing, he re-emphasized his strong commitment to the delegation of authority and responsibility and made clear his belief in individual rather than group responsibility for operating administration. The Executive Committee must not interfere with the day-to-day activities of the departments. He insisted that:

> Subject to the Board of Directors and Finance Committee, the Executive Committee have full power in the control of the company's affairs. It is desired that this power be used only with discretion in order to:

(A) Throw responsibility on the heads of departments, where one department alone is interested, and

(B) Throw responsibility on the heads of two or three departments in matters arising which affect but two or three departments.

In the latter case, should the several heads of departments fail to be unanimous, the decision is to be made by the Chairman of the Executive Committee.

Thus it is expected that the Executive Committee should issue final orders only in cases where more than three departments are interested in the decision and on such other matters as the president asks them to decide for him.

The committee's job was to consider only problems and policies of the company as a whole, to set broad goals and policies for the departments, and to coordinate interdepartmental activities in the general interest. Pierre did not expect it to ignore departmental work: "Discussion and criticism of affairs affecting less than four departments is entirely proper," he continued, "so long as discussion and criticism is constructive and given in a spirit to aid the departments interested, but it is not desired that there should be fault-finding where a better solution of a question is not offered."

The Finance Committee, Pierre proposed, was to be returned to "its original position." It would no longer report to the Executive Committee as it had in recent years, but was to be considered equal, and even senior to the latter committee. Still its powers were essentially negative. It would approve the annual and semiannual estimates of appropriations drawn up by the Executive Committee, "thereby authorizing a general financial plan under which the departments may act without further reference to the Finance Committee." Only requests of over $300,000 would be considered in detail. The committee's approval would also be necessary for appropriations of more than $150,000 not included in the annual budget. Finally, it would approve plans for providing funds for future expenditures, and it would recommend dividends. After an exchange of letters, Pierre and Coleman decided the committee should include themselves, Alfred, and William du Pont, the son of Henry du Pont, the company's domineering president of an earlier generation.

In this way, Pierre permitted the major stockholders to retain a say in company affairs without interfering with major policy decisions. They might, if Alfred and William joined with Coleman, reject important proposals made by the Executive Committee for the allocation of funds and other resources, but even here all the data on which they based decisions were those provided by the more professional managers on that committee. Still, they had general oversight of their investment and could make it clear when they disapproved of important policy. The limits to even these powers are suggested by the fact that only a year later Alfred and William were bringing suit against Pierre and other executives over the sale of Coleman's stock.

Just as Pierre was instituting these changes, came the war in Europe and the enormous expansion of the company's munitions business. The existing organizational structure proved admirably suited to meet the needs of the resulting phenomenal growth. Few organizational adjustments had to be made. Black powder operations, which had become of relatively minor importance, were placed in the high explosive department. Plans for postwar product diversification resulted in the creation of a miscellaneous manufacturing department under Lammot du Pont, Pierre's brother.

Of more significance was the growth of the auxiliary or service departments. The Chemical Division came even before the war. It was formed in 1912 to take charge of the research laboratories when the development department turned its energies to devising a strategy of diversification. After 1914, the engineering, purchasing, and traffic departments all grew enormously under the wartime demands. Administratively, these departments became attached to the central office with their directors reporting directly to the president. So too did the Military Sales Division. The relations between the enlarged auxiliary central office departments and the major operating, sales, treasurer's, and essential material departments were not clearly defined until 1919.

The years just before and during the war saw continued advance in the development of statistical data and of the procedures for its use. Pierre and the financial offices refined the methods used for allocating funds systematically. Procedures for the appropriations of capital expenditures included the use of general forecasts of economic conditions and detailed proposals for individual projects. Well before 1918, the forecast and analysis section of the treasurer's department was assisting the functional departments and the Executive Committee to allocate rationally funds and other resources by providing "forecasts of probable financial conditions extended twelve months in advance . . . revised every month." Each specific request for capital appropriations had to include the particulars of cost of, need for, and estimated rate of return on investment for the proposed project.

Among the notable advances made during these years in the working out of information so essential for central office planning, coordination, and appraisal were the techniques that F. Donaldson Brown devised for calculating the rate of return on investment. Brown, trained as an electrical engineer at Virginia Polytechnic Institute and Cornell, had joined the Du Pont sales department in 1908 after serving as general manager of the Baltimore sales office of the Sprague Electric Company. In 1912, he was placed on Barksdale's staff in the general manager's office and, in 1914, became one of Raskob's assistants in the treasurer's department. For Brown, rate of return on equity or even return on capital invested was an inadequate tool for administrative control and strategic planning. As he emphasized, the rate of return on capital invested increased as volume rose and decreased as it fell. The higher the throughput, the greater the rate of return. Brown termed this rate of flow "turnover." He defined it as the dollar volume of sales divided by total investment. Brown then related turnover to earnings as a percentage of sales (then the definition of profit in much of American industry). He did this by multiplying turnover by profit so defined, which gave a figure that accurately reflected the intensity with which the enterprise's resources were being used. This formula devised by Brown (see Exhibit 2) is still the method employed by the Du Pont company and many other American business enterprises to define a rate of return. The significance of this formula was that it provided executives at both central and departmental headquarters with an accurate standard with which to appraise each operating unit's performance, to locate the sources of deficiencies and inadequacies, and to change and adjust present plans and policies.

## Further Centralization, 1919

With the war's end, Pierre became convinced that a new set of executives should take command. Although he was still under fifty, he thought that he and others in top management needed and deserved a rest. More important, new challenges called for young blood and fresh ideas. As Pierre told the board of directors in April 1919: "I am firmly of the opinion that we now have reached another turning point in the conduct of affairs at E. I. Du Pont de Nemours & Company; therefore, it would seem wise to place responsibility for future development and management of the business on the next line of men." Pierre had already consulted Irénée, Raskob, Harry Haskell, and one or two others as to possible replacements for the older men. He now proposed that a subcommittee of the Executive Committee, consisting of Donaldson Brown, who a year earlier had taken Raskob's place as treasurer, Frederick W. Pickard, who, at the same time, had become vice president in charge of sales; Lammot du Pont, chief of the miscellaneous manufacturing department; and Harry Haskell as chairman, study and recommend ways to improve the company's organizatiion.

Haskell was more concerned about structure than personnel, and the changes he favored were essentially those that would strengthen the centralized organization that had worked so admirably during the wartime expansion. As vice president in charge of the high explosives department, he replied to Pierre's proposal for a thorough turnover of top managment by saying:

> I quite agree with the principle of advancing the younger men to positions of executive responsibility, for I believe that one reason the Company has been so successful is that for over twenty years the conduct of its (business) is in the hands of young men and this has served to keep off the dry rot of conservatism that sometimes accompanys [sic] too unchanging management. On the other hand we have sometimes lost by not getting full value out of experienced men—witness Barksdale and J. A. [Haskell]. Perhaps the new plan will be flexible enough not to repeat the mistakes in the latter respect.

Haskell, recalling earlier changes, added: "I have believed in reorganization by evolution rather than the Company's more usual custom by revolution, but I guess it's a good thing to take a little corporate calomel once in a while and if we get rid of the wheat with the tares, why we never quite know whether we are individually wheat or tare and so can comfort ourselves in the belief that maybe it is the other fellow."

Then Haskell turned to the matter of structure, urging Pierre to simplify and to centralize still further the present organization:

> Regarding manufacturing, I feel very strongly that our present method of splitting operations into their parts without any effective means of coordination of effort is inefficient and indefensible. Instead of creating three brand new operating vice presidencies, I would strongly advise one overall manufacturing operations, with a very high

class assistant, the latter on the Executive Committee and as many managers or directors as may be found convenient for the specialized operations of different parts of the manufacture. It may be that it would be better for a few years to carry on the dye business as a separate entity. I think it would because it is a developing, understandardized industry and should merit independent attention just as the Parlin chemical mixtures business was better by itself until standardized—when it was merged with the regular sales and operating departments.

At the end of March, Haskell's subcommittee on organization made its report, which spelled out more explicitly the suggestions and implications of what its chairman had written earlier to Pierre. Its authors thought in terms of organization needs and, in describing them, used organizational concepts that had only recently been developed. Much more than Pierre du Pont, they wholeheartedly endorsed the dictum Barksdale had made years before on the value and importance of organization: "He performs his duty best when he succeeds in working out an organization—a scheme of organization—and then placing in each position to be filled the best available man and then endeavoring to see that in a general way the objects sought for by the organization and by the personnel are achieved."

Many words and ideas in the committee's report indicate its awareness of current ideas concerning large-scale organization. Its members, as concerned with practice as with theory, examined the experience of other companies. Beside talking individually to outside executives, they sent an assistant to study four companies with similar problems—Armour, Wilson and Company (both meat packers), International Harvester, and Westinghouse Electric.

The committee's report began with a careful definition of terms, followed by a lengthy statement of administrative theory. Here the basic points dealt with the purpose of organization:

> The ideal condition is one in which every unit in a group is so coordinated and controlled that each functions to the best advantage with respect to its own work and the work of the whole company.
> The object of organization may be defined as the attainment of maximum of results with a minimum of effort. If we have not enough men of the right sort, maximum results would be impossible. If we have too many men, the results will be obtained at unnecessary expense.

Next can an enunciation of two "principles" based on the company's experience. The first rested on the belief that:

> The most efficient results are obtained at least expense when we coordinate related effort and segregate unrelated effort. For example, purchase of materials is unrelated to the sale of a finished product in a much greater degree than manufacture and sales, or manufacture and purchasing; and legal work is still more unrelated to either of those before mentioned.

This does not mean, the report continued, as "it is so often said, that good organization results from putting like things together." It then gave an example:

> For instance, it is natural to think that all engineers and engineering work should be grouped in one engineering department. Now, surveying a farm, designing and build-

ing a bridge, running a locomotive, or operating a powerhouse, are all "engineering," but it is quite obvious that they are so unrelated that to group them under one head would be uneconomical. On the other hand, the operation of a boiler house at Carney's Point is similar in name and reality to the operation of a boiler house at Haskell, yet one would not think of grouping them under one head in exchange for the authority exercised over each of them by the plant superintendent.

The basic principle was rather "that it is related effort which should be coordinated and not 'like things.' In fact it is often more necessary to combine related efforts which are unlike." For example, the report noted, as had Haskell in his letter, that the present dye-stuff business, like the chemical-mixture business a few years before, was not yet standardized. Therefore it would be wise to have it maintain:

> One individual in control of both production and sales, because the relation of the product and its qualities is so mixed up with the demands of the market for the product that to divorce them and segregate the business into a clearly defined production department and an independent sales department, would be detrimental to the business. Later on when the production of dyes becomes standardized it will no doubt follow the evolution of other portions of the business.

The principle of coordinating "related effort" normally called for placing the different broad functional activities into separate administrative units.

A second underlying principle was that of giving each executive in charge of a set of coordinated or related efforts full authority and responsibility. This was, the committee stressed, the only way to assure flexibility and adjustment in the face of constant change. Here the report repeated and made more explicit the concept of delegation of individual responsibility and authority which Pierre had so often stressed:

> The principle of individual responsibility and undivided authority has been recognized by the Company and consistently followed in the cases of its established divisions. A unit once defined—for example, the Sales Department or the Development Department—is placed in charge of the best available individual, who as head of that department is held responsible for results, and he can in his official capacity arrange every detail of his department according to his best judgment, subject only to the alternative of having someone replace him if his official judgment is not good. The same principle is followed in turn in the case of branch office managers or plant superintendents, who are individually responsible for the conduct of that part of the Company's business over which they have charge, subject only to the business being conducted according to the principles and methods laid down by the authority next higher up. It is to the recognition of this principle that we may in large measure attribute the Company's phenomenally successful performance during the recent abnormal years.

This principle had not been fully effective, however, the report continued, for the Executive Committee had tended to make decisions concerning departmental activities despite Pierre's earlier strictures. The result had been a dangerous trend toward committee management and away from individual responsibility. It must be recognized, the report went on, that:

> We have defeated the principle to a partial extent by allowing the Executive Committee to act for the president as the immediate superior in an executive way to whom the

department heads are held responsible. The interposition of a committee charged with the duty of performing executive acts better done by an individual is, we believe, responsible for most of the minor inefficiencies, inconveniences, wasted effort and unnecessary duplication, which are matters of common knowledge to those engaged in carrying out the daily routine. These are usually small matters with relation to the business as a whole, and for this reason rarely impose themselves on the attention of the higher officers. Nevertheless, in the aggregate they are of no mean importance.

On the basis of these two principles, the committee made its recommendations. First, it suggested that most of the company's activities be segregated into four functional "grand divisions"—the production, sales, development, and treasurer's departments, each headed by a vice president. The production department, for example, would include not only manufacturing activities but also purchasing, engineering, construction, research, chemical process control, and a number of other service functions. The remaining few "joint functions, such as traffic, medical, etc. shall be assigned by or on authority of the first vice president." In other words, the day-to-day administration of all Du Pont activities was to be concentrated in the headquarters of four functional departments. "The objection has been advanced," the report admitted, "that some of the grand divisions are too large and too diversified to be under the control of one individual. The answer is that the controlling individual need not know every detail of the business, but requires only a good mind, sound judgment, and knowledge of general business principles." The committee thus solved the problem of the relations between the auxiliary departments in the central office with the major functional departments by merely incorporating the former into the latter. They would now be staff units at departmental headquarters rather than in the central office.

The central office itself was otherwise little changed. The first vice president (a new position), and not the Executive Committee, was made specifically responsible for appraising and coordinating the work of the major departments and for holding their chiefs accountable for their performance. On this point, Haskell and his colleagues cited the experience of the four—Armour, Wilson, International Harvester, and Westinghouse—"executive control was definitely centralized under a general officer," and "in no cases were divisions or departments responsible to a committee."

The Executive Committee was to be concerned with policy planning and overall appraisal. "The proper function of the Executive Committee," the report read, "is to exercise general supervision over the company's affairs; to decide all questions of policy, and in general to act in the board's stead, and to see that all conduct of business is in accordance with the wishes and policies laid down by the board." The subcommittee on organization thought "it would be better to start with a small Executive Committee, adding one or two members to it later should it appear that some portions of the four grand divisions were not being adequately represented." The committee continued to rely on the departments for information on which it based its decisions. Except for the data provided by the financial offices, the central office had no sources of information outside of the department or ways to check their data. Nor did the central office yet have the responsibility for coordinating the forecasts made by the manufacturing, sales, and purchasing departments even though such coordination was necessary if the movement of product from one department to another was to be smooth and steady.

While the four men signing the report agreed that there should be a Finance Committee, they differed as to its role and make-up. Some, recalling its operations before 1914, thought it again "should be a branch of the Executive Committee." Others held "that matters financial should be segregated from the Company's other activities," and that, as was finally recommended, there continue to be two separate committees. "The opinion was unanimous," the report continued, "on the desirability of having as many members in common as possible on both committees."

The report was then sent to Pierre for study. The president liked its general outlines, but, as he told a special meeting of the board, "the selection of men must to a certain extent precede the choice of form of organization." The structure should be built around men rather than fitting the men into an ideal structure, as Barksdale had earlier suggested. Pierre recommended the promotion of younger executives and proposed that the present Executive Committee members be moved to the Finance Committee, where they would serve in a broad advisory capacity. Actually they were to have more of a semiretired position similar to that of J. A. Haskell, Barksdale, and Patterson after the 1914 changes.

Pierre then listed his choices. He would retire as president, becoming chairman of the board with nominal duties. Irénée would be president, and Lammot, chairman of the Executive Committee. This committee would include, besides Donaldson Brown and Frederick Pickard, six relatively young but experienced managers only one of whom was a du Pont or related to the du Pont family. The Executive Committee and then the board immediately approved Pierre's recommendations.

Within a short time, the new Executive Committee had accepted with some modifications the recommendations of the Haskell report. The major difference was that the purchasing (including traffic), chemical, and engineering departments continued as separate units, although the single production department did have its own large service department made up of the Technical, the Welfare, and the Materials and Products Divisions. This decision left unanswered the nature of the relationship between these more service-like departments and the major operating ones. So the chemical and the engineering as well as the new personnel and the older legal real estate departments now became explicitly advisory staff organizations. They worked to develop standards and procedures for the company as a whole and to advise both the departmental and central officers. But their executives were not to give orders to personnel in the line departments. Purchasing, which now handled the procurement of raw materials and the obtaining of supplies for all the company's facilities, continued to make the major buying decisions and so remained, like production, sales, and finance, a line rather than staff office.

Once the revised structure had been agreed upon, the new Executive Committee members took up their posts as department heads. William C. Spruance became vice president in charge of production; Walter S. Carpenter, Jr., (R. R. M. Carpenter's younger brother) took over the development department;

J. B. D. Edge was put in charge of purchasing; and Brown and Pickard remained the heads of the treasurer's and the sales departments. The staff departments—chemical and engineering—were not represented on a committee. The three remaining Executive Committee members had charge of the major subdivisions of the production department—explosives, cellulose products, and paints and chemicals.

By the summer of 1919, the Du Pont company was ready to meet the postwar world with a new but experienced and seasoned set of top managers and a simplified management structure. Few more rationally planned and thoroughly tested designs existed for coordinating, appraising, and planning the activities of a great vertically integrated industrial enterprise. The departmental directors administered the operational activities in each major function at their headquarters, while the vice presidents in charge of the functional departments and two general officers, meeting collectively as the Executive Committee, made the strategic and entrepreneurial decisions.

## EXHIBIT 1

**Du Pont Structure, circa 1911**

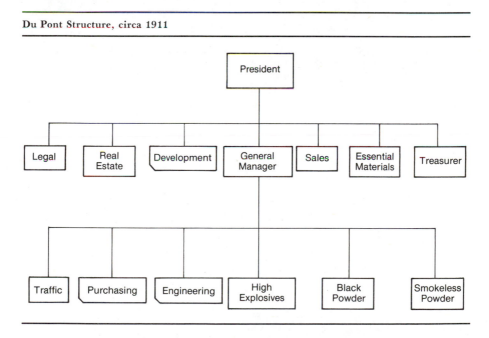

# EXHIBIT 2

**Relationship of Factors Affecting Return on Investment**

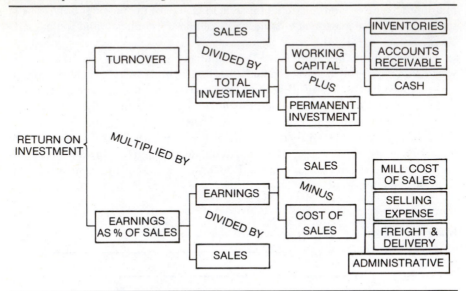

*Also includes small amounts of deferred charges which are not charted.

**EXHIBIT 3A**

Du Pont Structure, 1919–1921

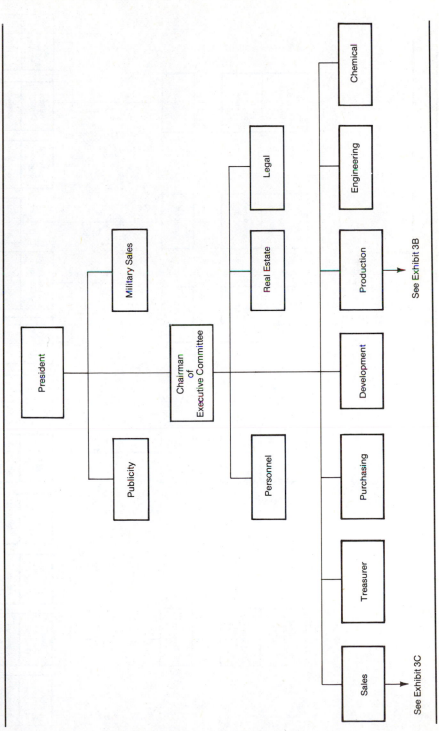

Source: Chandler, *Strategy,* p. 74.

# EXHIBIT 3B

## Du Pont Production Department, 1919–1921

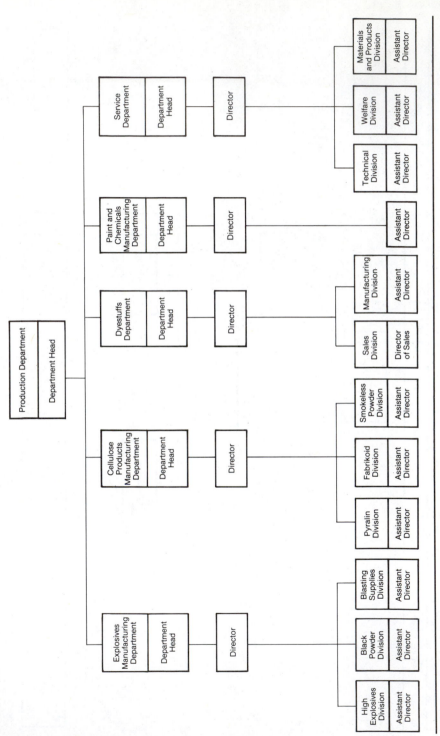

Source: Chandler, *Strategy*, p. 75.

# EXHIBIT 3C

## Du Pont Sales Department, 1919–1921

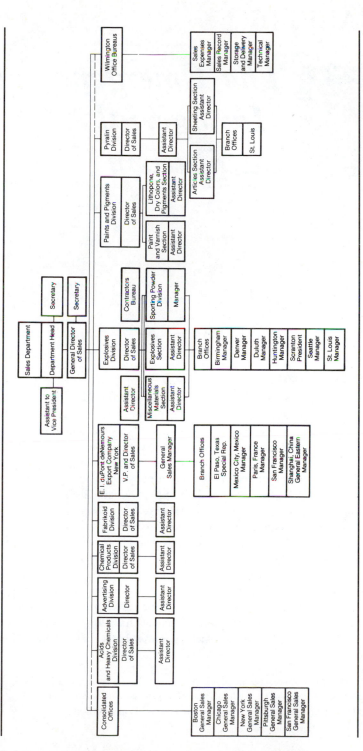

Source: Chandler, *Strategy*, pp. 76–77.

# CASE 16

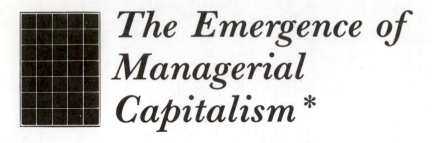

# *The Emergence of Managerial Capitalism* *

## Introduction

This case reviews the emergence of a new type of capitalism in the late 19th and early 20th centuries. What differentiated this new managerial capitalism from traditional personal capitalism was that basic decisions concerning the production and distribution of goods and services were made by teams, or hierarchies, of salaried managers who had little or no equity ownership in the enterprises they operated. Today the major sectors of market economies where the means of production are still privately, rather than state, owned, are operated through such managerial hierarchies. This has not always been the case.

Indeed such managerial hierarchies are entirely modern. As late as the 1840s, with very few exceptions owners managed and managers owned. There were salaried managers before the 19th century, primarily on plantations and estates, but they worked directly with owners. There were no hierarchies of managers comparable to that depicted on Figure 1. By the 1840s personally managed enterprises—those that carried out the processes of production and distribution in market economies—had become specialized, usually handling a single function and a single product. They operated a factory, mine, bank, or trading office. Where the

---

*This case was prepared by Alfred D. Chandler, Jr., as the basis for class discussion rather than to illustrate either effective or ineffective handling of an administrative situation.

Copyright © 1984 by the President and Fellows of Harvard College.

Harvard Business School case 384-081, rev. 6/84.

## FIGURE 1

**Multiunit, Multifunctional Enterprise**

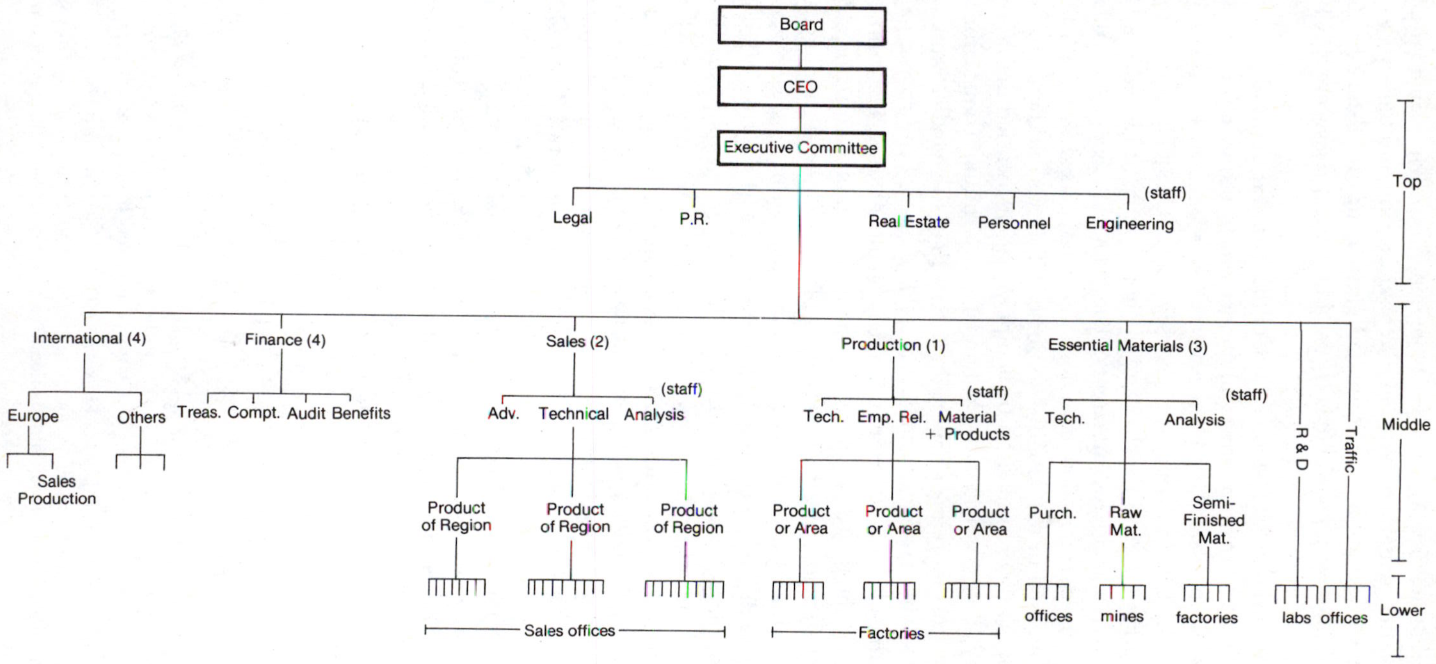

volume of activity was not yet large enough to bring such specialization, merchants often remained involved in manufacturing and banking as they had in the early years of capitalism. Some had partnerships in distant lands. But even the largest and most powerful of early capitalist enterprises were tiny by modern standards.

For example, the Medici Bank of the 15th century and that of the Fuggers in the 16th were far more powerful financial institutions in their day than any of today's giant non-state banks in America, Europe, and Japan are in ours. Yet the Medici Bank in 1470 operated only seven branches. The total number of individuals working in the branches and the home office in Florence was 57. Of these a dozen were considered managers. They, however, were not salaried employees. They were partners, albeit junior ones, who shared in the profits and who had "joint and unlimited liability" for losses.[1] Today's middling-size state banks have as many as 200 branches, 5,000 employees, 300 salaried managers (who have no liability at all); and such banks handle over a million transactions a day. That is, they process more transactions in a week than the Medici Bank processed in the century of its existence. Today, too, small industrial enterprises handle a far greater volume of transactions than did those giants of an earlier capitalism—the Hudson's Bay, the Royal African, or even the East India Company.

What made the difference was, of course, the technological revolution of modern times—an even more profound discontinuity in the history of civilized man than the urban revolution of the 11th to 13th centuries that created the first modern market economies and with them modern capitalism. The enormous increase in the volume of output and transactions was not so much the result of the First Industrial Revolution that began in Britain at the end of the 18th century; that is, it was not the result of the initial application of the new sources of energy—fossil fuel, coal—to the processes of production. It resulted much more from the coming of modern transportation and communication. The railroad, telegraph, steamship, and cable made possible modern mass production and distribution that were the hallmarks of the Second Industrial Revolution of the late 19th and early 20th centuries. These new high-volume technologies could not be effectively exploited unless the massive flows of materials were guided through the process of both production and distribution by teams of salaried managers.

Thus the first such managerial hierarchies appeared during the 1850s and 1860s to coordinate the movements of trains and flow of goods over the new railroad networks and messages over the new telegraph system.[2] They, then, quickly came into use to manage the new mass retailing establishments—the department

---

[1]Raymond de Roover, *The Rise and Decline of the Medici Bank, 1397–1494* (Cambridge: Harvard University Press, 1963), pp. 87, 91. The earlier Peruzzi bank had branches managed by employees (*fattore*). "However, all branches of major importance were managed by partners," p. 80.

[2]Alfred D. Chandler, Jr., *The Visible Hand* (Cambridge: Harvard Univerity Press, 1977), chaps. 3–6, for the coming of such hierarchies to manage railroad and telegraph systems and chap. 7 for their use in the management of mass distribution. Pages 231 and 232 describe the organization of Sears Roebuck.

stores, mail order houses, and chains or multiple shops—whose existence the railroad and the telegraph made possible. For example, by 1905, such an organization permitted Sears, Roebuck in Chicago to fill 100,000 mail orders in a single day—more than the average earlier American merchant filled in a lifetime. These administrative hierarchies grew to still much greater size in industrial enterprises that, again on the basis of modern transportation and communication, integrated mass production and mass distribution within a single business enterprise.

One way to review the emergence of managerial capitalism is, then, to focus on the evolution of this largest and most complex of managerial institutions—the integrated industrial enterprise. These integrated enterprises have had much in common whether they were American, European, or Japanese. They appeared at almost exactly the same moment in history in the United States and Europe and a little later in Japan, only because Japan was later to industrialize. They clustered in much the same types of industries; and finally, they grew in much the same manner. In nearly all cases they became large, first, by integrating forward, that is, investing in marketing and distribution facilities and personnel, by moving backwards into purchasing and control of raw and semi-finished materials, then, though much less often, by investing in research and development. In this way they created the multifunctional organization that is depicted in Figure 1. They soon became multinational by investing abroad, first in marketing and then in production. Finally they continued to expand their activities by investing in product lines related to their existing businesses, thus creating the organization depicted in Figure 2.

## The Similarities

Let us briefly examine these similarities in the location, timing, and processes of growth of this institution. The similarities in the location, as illustrated by Tables 1–5, are particularly striking. Table 1 indicates the location by country and by industries of all industrial corporations in the world which in 1973 employed more than 20,000 workers. (The industries are those defined as 2-digit industrial groups by the U.S. Census Standard Industrial Classification [SIC].) In 1973, 263 (65 percent) of the 401 companies were clustered in food, chemicals, oil, machinery, and primary metals. Just under 30 percent more were in 3-digit categories of other 2-digit groups—subcategories which had the same industrial characteristics as those in which the 65 percent clustered, such as cigarettes in tobacco; tires in rubber; newsprint in paper; plate glass in stone, glass, and clay; cans and razor blades in fabricated metals; and mass-produced cameras in instruments. Only 21 companies (5.2 percent) were in remaining 2-digit categories: apparel, lumber, furniture, leather, publishing and printing, instruments, and miscellaneous.

A second point that Table 1 makes—one that is central to an understanding of the evolution of this institution—is the predominance of American firms among the world's largest industrial corporations. Of the total of 401 companies employing more than 20,000 persons, over a half (212 or 52.6 percent) were American. The United Kingdom followed with 50 (12.5 percent), Germany with 29 (7.29

**FIGURE 2**

The Multidivisional Structure

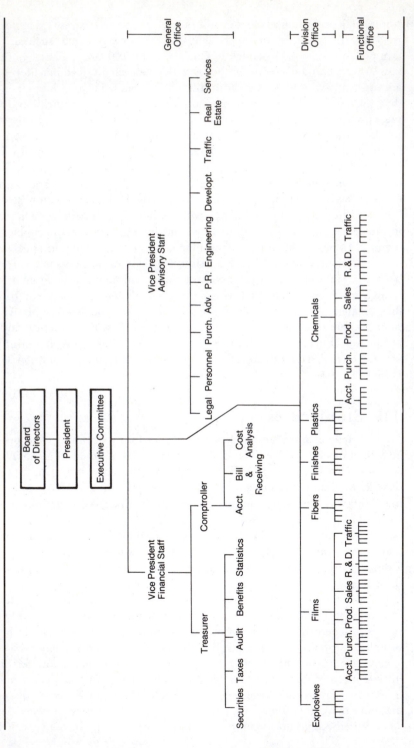

**TABLE 1**

**The Distribution of the Largest Manufacturing Enterprises with More than 20,000 Employees, by Industry and Nationality, 1973**

| S.I.C. | U.S. | Outside of the U.S. | U.K. | Germany | Japan | France | Others | Grand Total |
|---|---|---|---|---|---|---|---|---|
| 20 Food | 22 | 17 | 13 | 0 | 1 | 1 | 2 | 39 |
| 21 Tobacco | 3 | 4 | 3 | 1 | 0 | 0 | 0 | 7 |
| 22 Textiles | 7 | 6 | 3 | 0 | 2 | 1 | 0 | 13 |
| 23 Apparel | 6 | 0 | 0 | 0 | 0 | 0 | 0 | 6 |
| 24 Lumber | 4 | 2 | 0 | 0 | 0 | 0 | 2 | 6 |
| 25 Furniture | 0 | 0 | 0 | 0 | 0 | 0 | 0 | 0 |
| 26 Paper | 7 | 3 | 3 | 0 | 0 | 0 | 0 | 10 |
| 27 Printing and Publishing | 0 | 0 | 0 | 0 | 0 | 0 | 0 | 0 |
| 28 Chemical | 24 | 28 | 4 | 5 | 3 | 6 | 10 | 52 |
| 29 Petroleum | 14 | 12 | 2 | 0 | 0 | 2 | 8 | 26 |
| 30 Rubber | 5 | 5 | 1 | 1 | 1 | 1 | 1 | 10 |
| 31 Leather | 2 | 0 | 0 | 0 | 0 | 0 | 0 | 2 |
| 32 Stone, Clay, and Glass | 7 | 8 | 3 | 0 | 0 | 3 | 2 | 15 |
| 33 Primary Metal | 13 | 35 | 2 | 9 | 5 | 4 | 15 | 48 |
| 34 Fabricated Metal | 8 | 6 | 5 | 1 | 0 | 0 | 0 | 14 |
| 35 Machinery | 22 | 12 | 2 | 3 | 2 | 0 | 5 | 34 |
| 36 Electrical Machinery | 20 | 25 | 4 | 5 | 7 | 2 | 7 | 45 |
| 37 Transportation Equipment | 22 | 23 | 3 | 3 | 7 | 4 | 6 | 45 |
| 38 Measuring Instrument | 4 | 1 | 0 | 0 | 0 | 0 | 0 | 5 |
| 39 Miscellaneous | 2 | 0 | 0 | 0 | 0 | 0 | 0 | 2 |
| Diversified/Conglomerate | 19 | 3 | 2 | 1 | 0 | 0 | 0 | 22 |
| Total | 211 | 190 | 50 | 29 | 28 | 24 | 59 | 401 |

In 1970, the 100 largest industrials accounted for more than a third of net manufacturing output in the United States and over 45 percent in the United Kingdom. In 1930, they accounted for about 25 percent of total net output in both countries.

Source: *Fortune*, May 1974 and August 1974.

percent), Japan with 28 and France with 24. Only in chemicals, metals, and electrical machinery were there as many as four or five more firms outside of the United States than there were within it.

Table 2 shows that large industrial corporations have clustered throughout the 20th century in the United States in the same industries in which they were concentrated in 1973. The pattern depicted in Tables 3, 4, and 5 is much the same for Britain, Germany, and Japan. Other data document what is indicated here, that the American firms were larger, as well as more numerous, than those in other countries. For example, in 1948, only 50 to 55 of the British firms had assets comparable to those of the top 200 in the United States. In 1930, the number was about the same. For Germany and Japan it was smaller. Well before World War II, the United States had many more and many larger managerial hierarchies than did other nations—underlining the fact that managerial capitalism first emerged in that nation.

These tables also suggest (though only barely so) basic differences within the broad pattern of evolution. For example, the large enterprise in the United States was to be found throughout the 20th century in the production of both consumer and industrial goods. Britain had proportionately more large firms in consumer

## TABLE 2

**The Distribution of the 200 Largest Manufacturing Firms in the United States, by Industry***

| S.I.C. | | 1917 | 1930 | 1948 | 1973 |
|---|---|---|---|---|---|
| 20 | Food | 30 | 32 | 26 | 22 |
| 21 | Tobacco | 6 | 5 | 5 | 3 |
| 22 | Textiles | 5 | 3 | 6 | 3 |
| 23 | Apparel | 3 | 0 | 0 | 0 |
| 24 | Lumber | 3 | 4 | 1 | 4 |
| 25 | Furniture | 0 | 1 | 1 | 0 |
| 26 | Paper | 5 | 7 | 6 | 9 |
| 27 | Printing and Publishing | 2 | 3 | 2 | 1 |
| 28 | Chemical | 20 | 18 | 24 | 27 |
| 29 | Petroleum | 22 | 26 | 24 | 22 |
| 30 | Rubber | 5 | 5 | 5 | 5 |
| 31 | Leather | 4 | 2 | 2 | 0 |
| 32 | Stone, Clay, and Glass | 5 | 9 | 5 | 7 |
| 33 | Primary Metal | 29 | 25 | 24 | 19 |
| 34 | Fabricated Metal | 8 | 10 | 7 | 5 |
| 35 | Machinery | 20 | 22 | 24 | 17 |
| 36 | Electrical Machinery | 5 | 5 | 8 | 13 |
| 37 | Transportation Equipment | 26 | 21 | 26 | 19 |
| 38 | Instruments | 1 | 2 | 3 | 4 |
| 39 | Miscellaneous | 1 | 1 | 1 | 1 |
| | Diversified/Conglomerate | 0 | 0 | 0 | 19 |
| Total | | 200 | 200 | 200 | 200 |

*Ranked by assets.

goods than the United States, while the largest industrials in Germany and Japan concentrated much more on producers' goods. Even as late as 1973 (as Table 1 shows), the United Kingdom had 13 of its 50 firms employing more than 20,000 persons in the production and distribution of food and tobacco products; whereas Germany, France, and Japan each had only one. Before World War II, Germany had many more firms in chemicals and heavy machinery than did the British, while Japan, the late industrializer, still had a greater number of textile firms than did the other nations in its top 200. As Japan's economy grew, the number of chemical and machinery enterprises on that list increased substantially.

## Explanation of the Evolutionary Process

Why have these large integrated hierarchial enterprises appeared in some industries but rarely in others? And why did they appear at almost the same historical moment in the United States and Europe? Why did these industrial enterprises in advanced economies grow in the same manner, first, by integrating forward into volume distribution, then taking on other functions, and then becoming multinational and finally multiproduct?

**TABLE 3**

**The Distribution of the 200 Largest Manufacturing Firms in the United Kingdom, by Industry***

| S.I.C. | | *1919* | *1930* | *1948* | *1973* |
|---|---|---|---|---|---|
| 20 | Food | 63 | 64 | 52 | 33 |
| 21 | Tobacco | 3 | 4 | 8 | 4 |
| 22 | Textiles | 26 | 24 | 18 | 10 |
| 23 | Apparel | 1 | 3 | 3 | 0 |
| 24 | Lumber | 0 | 0 | 0 | 2 |
| 25 | Furniture | 0 | 0 | 0 | 0 |
| 26 | Paper | 4 | 5 | 6 | 7 |
| 27 | Printing and Publishing | 5 | 10 | 7 | 7 |
| 28 | Chemical | 11 | 9 | 15 | 21 |
| 29 | Petroleum | 3 | 3 | 3 | 8 |
| 30 | Rubber | 3 | 3 | 2 | 6 |
| 31 | Leather | 0 | 0 | 0 | 3 |
| 32 | Stone, Clay, and Glass | 2 | 6 | 5 | 16 |
| 33 | Primary Metal | 35 | 18 | 28 | 14 |
| 34 | Fabricated Metal | 2 | 7 | 8 | 7 |
| 35 | Machinery | 8 | 7 | 7 | 26 |
| 36 | Electrical Machinery | 11 | 18 | 13 | 14 |
| 37 | Transportation Equipment | 20 | 14 | 22 | 16 |
| 38 | Instruments | 0 | 1 | 4 | 3 |
| 39 | Miscellaneous | 3 | 4 | 3 | 1 |
| | Diversified/Conglomerate | 0 | 0 | 0 | 2 |
| Total | | 200 | 200 | 204 | 200 |

*Ranked by sales for 1973 and by market value of quoted capital for the other years.

Because these enterprises initially grew larger by integrating mass production with volume distribution, answers to these critical questions require a careful look at both these processes. Mass production is an attribute of specific technologies. In some industries the primary way to increase output was to add more workers and machines; in others it was by improving and rearranging the inputs, by improving the machinery, furnaces, stills and other equipment, by reorienting the process of production within the plant, by placing several intermediate processes of production required for a finished product within a single works, and by increasing the application of energy (particularly fossil fuel energy). The first set of industries remained "labor intensive"; the second set became "capital intensive." In this second set of industries, the technology of production permitted much larger economies of scale than were possible in the first. That is, it permitted much greater reduction in cost per unit of output as volume increased. So in these capital-intensive industries with large batch or continuous process technologies, large works operating at minimum efficient scale (scale of operation that brought the lowest unit costs) had a much greater cost advantage over small works than was true with labor-intensive technologies. Conversely, cost per unit rose much more rapidly

## TABLE 4

**The Distribution of the 200 Largest Manufacturing Firms in Germany, by Industry***

| S.I.C. | | 1913 | 1928 | 1953 | 1973 |
|---|---|---|---|---|---|
| 20 | Food | 23 | 28 | 23 | 24 |
| 21 | Tobacco | 1 | 0 | 0 | 6 |
| 22 | Textiles | 13 | 15 | 19 | 4 |
| 23 | Apparel | 0 | 0 | 0 | 0 |
| 24 | Lumber | 1 | 1 | 2 | 0 |
| 25 | Furniture | 0 | 0 | 0 | 0 |
| 26 | Paper | 1 | 2 | 3 | 2 |
| 27 | Printing and Publishing | 0 | 1 | 0 | 6 |
| 28 | Chemical | 26 | 27 | 32 | 30 |
| 29 | Petroleum | 5 | 5 | 3 | 8 |
| 30 | Rubber | 1 | 1 | 3 | 3 |
| 31 | Leather | 2 | 3 | 2 | 1 |
| 32 | Stone, Clay, and Glass | 10 | 9 | 9 | 15 |
| 33 | Primary Metal | 49 | 47 | 45 | 19 |
| 34 | Fabricated Metal | 8 | 7 | 8 | 14 |
| 35 | Machinery | 21 | 19 | 19 | 29 |
| 36 | Electrical Machinery | 18 | 16 | 13 | 21 |
| 37 | Transportation Equipment | 19 | 16 | 14 | 14 |
| 38 | Instruments | 1 | 2 | 4 | 2 |
| 39 | Miscellaneous | 1 | 1 | 1 | 1 |
| | Diversified/Conglomerate | 0 | 0 | 0 | 1 |
| Total | | 200 | 200 | 200 | 200 |

*Ranked by sales for 1973 and by assets for the other three years.

when volume of production fell below minimum efficient scale (of, say, 80 to 90 percent of rated capacity), than was true in labor-intensive industries.

What is of basic importance for an understanding of the coming of the modern managerial industrial enterprise is that the cost advantage of the larger plants cannot be fully realized unless a constant flow of materials through the plant or factory is maintained to assure effective capacity utilization. The decisive figure in determining costs and profits is, then, not rated capacity for a specified time period but rather throughput—that is amount actually processed in that time period. Throughput is thus the proper economic measure of capacity utilization. In the capital-intensive industries, the throughput needed to maintain minimum efficient scale requires not only careful coordination of flow through the processes of production but also the flows of inputs from the suppliers and the flow of outputs to the retailers and final consumers. Such coordination cannot happen automatically. It demands the constant attention of a managerial team, or hierarchy. Thus scale is only a technological characteristic. The economies of scale, measured by throughput, are organizational. Such economies depend on knowledge, skills, and teamwork—on the human organization essential to exploit the potential of technological processes.

## TABLE 5

**The Distribution of the 200 Largest Manufacturing Firms in Japan, by Industry***

| S.I.C. | | 1918 | 1930 | 1954 | 1973 |
|---|---|---|---|---|---|
| 20 | Food | 31 | 30 | 26 | 18 |
| 21 | Tobacco | 1 | 1 | 0 | 0 |
| 22 | Textiles | 54 | 62 | 23 | 11 |
| 23 | Apparel | 2 | 2 | 1 | 0 |
| 24 | Lumber | 3 | 1 | 0 | 1 |
| 25 | Furniture | 0 | 0 | 0 | 0 |
| 26 | Paper | 12 | 6 | 12 | 10 |
| 27 | Printing and Publishing | 1 | 1 | 0 | 2 |
| 28 | Chemical | 23 | 22 | 38 | 34 |
| 29 | Petroleum | 6 | 5 | 11 | 13 |
| 30 | Rubber | 0 | 1 | 1 | 5 |
| 31 | Leather | 4 | 1 | 0 | 0 |
| 32 | Stone, Clay, and Glass | 16 | 14 | 8 | 14 |
| 33 | Primary Metal | 21 | 22 | 28 | 27 |
| 34 | Fabricated Metal | 4 | 3 | 6 | 5 |
| 35 | Machinery | 4 | 4 | 10 | 16 |
| 36 | Electrical Machinery | 7 | 12 | 15 | 18 |
| 37 | Transportation Equipment | 9 | 11 | 18 | 20 |
| 38 | Instruments | 1 | 1 | 3 | 5 |
| 39 | Miscellaneous | 1 | 1 | 0 | 1 |
| | Diversified/Conglomerate | 0 | 0 | 0 | 0 |
| Total | | 200 | 200 | 200 | 200 |

*Ranked by assets.

A well-known example illustrates these generalizations. In 1882, the Standard Oil "alliance" formed the Standard Oil Trust.[3] The purpose was not to obtain control over the industry's output. That alliance, a loose federation of 40 companies each with its own legal and administrative identity but tied to John D. Rockefeller's Standard Oil Company through interchange of stock and other financial devices, already controlled close to 90 percent of the American output of kerosene. Instead, the Trust was formed to provide a legal instrument to rationalize the industry and to exploit more fully economies of scale. The Trust provided the essential legal means to create a corporate or central office that could, first, reorganize the processes of production by shutting down some refineries, reshaping others, and building new ones and, second, coordinate the flow of materials, not only through the several refineries, but from the oil fields to the refineries and from the refineries to the consumers. The resulting rationalization made it possible to concentrate close to a quarter of the world's production of kerosene in three refineries, each with an average daily charging capacity of 6,500 barrels with two thirds of their product going to overseas markets. (At this time the refined petroleum products were by far the nation's largest nonagricultural export.) Imagine the diseconomies of scale—the great increase in unit costs—that would result from placing close to one fourth of the world's production of shoes, or textiles, or lumber into three factories or mills!

This reorganization of the Trust's refining facilities brought a sharp reduction in average cost of production of a gallon of kerosene. It dropped from 1.5 cents a gallon before reorganization to 0.54 cents in 1884 and 0.45 in 1885 (and profits rose from 0.53 cents a gallon to 1.003 cents), with costs at the giant refineries being still lower—costs far below those of any competitor. However, to maintain this cost advantage required that these large refineries have a continuing daily throughput of from 5,000 to 6,500 barrels or a three- to four-fold increase over earlier 1,500 to 2,000 barrels daily flow with concomitant increases in transactions handled and in the complexity of coordinating the flow of materials through the process of production and distribution.

The Standard Oil story was by no means unique. In the 1880s and 1890s, new mass production technologies—those of the Second Industrial Revolution—brought sharp reduction in costs as plants reached minimum efficient scale. In many industries the level of output was so high at that scale that a small number of plants were able to meet existing national and even global demand. The structure of these industries quickly became oligopolistic. Their few large enterprises competed worldwide. In many instances the first enterprises to build a plant with a high minimum efficient scale and to recruit the essential management team have remained until this day leaders in their industries. A brief review of the industries listed in Tables 1–5 in which the large enterprises have always clustered illustrates this close relationship between scale economies, the size of the enterprise, and industrial concentration.

---

[3]Details and documentation are given in "The Standard Oil Company—Combination, Consolidation and Integration," a case written by Alfred D. Chandler, Jr., which appears previously in this volume.

In Groups 20 and 21—food, drink and tobacco—brand-new production processes in the refining of sugar and vegetable oils, in the milling of wheat and oats, and in the making of cigarettes brought rapid reductions in costs. In cigarettes for example, the invention of the Bonsack machine in the early 1880s permitted the first entrepreneurs to adopt the machine—James B. Duke in the United States and the Wills brothers in Britain—to reduce labor costs sharply—in Wills's case from 4 shillings per 1,000 to 0.3 pence per thousand.[4] Understandably Duke and Wills soon dominated and then divided the world market. In addition, most companies in Group 20, and also those producing consumer chemicals, such as soap, cosmetics, paints, and pills, pioneered in the use of new high-volume techniques for packing their products in small units that could be placed directly on retailers' shelves. The most important of these was the "automatic-line" canning process which, invented in the mid-1880s, permitted the filling of 4,000 cans an hour. The names of these pioneers—Campbell Soup, Heinz, Bordens, Carnation, Nestlé, Cadbury, Cross and Blackwell, Lever, Procter & Gamble, Colgate, and others—are still well known today.

In chemicals—Group 28—the new technologies brought even sharper cost reductions in industrial than in packaged consumer products. The mass production of synthetic dyes and synthetic alkalies began in the 1880s. It came a little later in synthetic nitrates, synthetic fibers, plastics, and film. The first three firms to produce the new synthetic blue dye—alizarine—dropped production costs from 200 marks per kilo in the 1870s to 9 marks by 1886; and those three firms—Bayer, BASF and Hochest—are still today, a century later, the three largest German chemical companies.[5]

Rubber production (Group 30), like oil, benefited from scale economies, even more in the production of tires than rubber footwear and clothing. Of the 10 rubber companies listed on the 1973 Table, nine built their first large factory between 1900 and 1908.[6] Since then, the Japanese company, Bridgestone, has been the only major new entrant into the global oligopoly.

In metals (Group 34), the scale economies made possible by maintaining a high volume throughput were also striking. Andrew Carnegie was able to reduce the cost of making steel rails by the new Bessemer steel process from close to $100 a ton in the early 1870s to $12 by the late 1890s.[7] In the refining of nonferrous met-

---

[4]B. W. E. Alford, *W. D. & H. O. Wills and the Development of the U.K. Tobacco Industry* (London: Methuen, 1973), pp. 143–49. Also Chandler, *Visible Hand*, pp. 249–58.

[5]Sachio Kahu, "The Development and Structure of the German Coal-Tar Dyestuffs Firms," Akio Okochi and Hoshimi Uchida, eds., *Development and Diffusion of Technology* (Tokyo: University of Tokyo Press, 1979), p. 78.

[6]This statement is based on a review of histories of and internal reports and pamphlets by the leading rubber companies.

[7]Harold Livesay, *Andrew Carnegie and the Rise of Big Business* (Boston: Little, Brown, 1975), pp. 102–106, 155. When in 1873 Carnegie opened the first works directed entirely to producing rails by the Bessemer process, the cost dropped to $56.64 a ton. By 1859, with increase in sales, the cost fell to $25 a ton.

als, the electrolytic refining process invented in the 1880s brought even more impressive cost reductions, permitting the price of a kilo of aluminum to fall from 87.50 francs in 1888 to 47.50 francs in 1889, with the adoption of the new process, to 19 francs at the end of 1890 to 3.75 francs in 1895.[8]

In the machinery making industries (Groups 35–37), new technologies based on the fabricating and assembling of interchangeable metal parts were perfected in the 1880s. By 1886, for example, Singer Sewing Machine had two plants—one in New Jersey and the other in Glasgow, each producing 8,000 machines a week.[9] To maintain their output, which satisfied three fourths of the world demand, required an even more tightly scheduled coordination of flows of materials into, through, and out of the plant than did the mass production of packaged goods, chemicals, and metals. By the 1890s, a tiny number of enterprises using comparable plants supplied the world demand for typewriters, cash registers, adding machines, and other office equipment, for harvesters, reapers, and other agricultural machinery, and for the newly invented electrical and other volume-produced industrial machinery. The culmination of these processes came with the mass production of the automobile. By installing the moving assembly line in his Highland Park plant in 1913, Henry Ford reduced the labor time used in putting together a Model T chassis from 12 hours and 28 minutes man hours to one hour and 33 minutes.[10] This dramatic increase in throughput permitted Ford to drop the price of the touring car from over $600 in 1913 to $490 in 1914 and to $290 in the 1920s, to pay the highest wages, and to acquire one of the world's largest fortunes in an astonishingly short time.

On the other hand, in the SIC categories of Tables 1–5 where few large firms appear, that is in the older, technologically simple, labor-intensive industries such as apparel, textiles, leather, lumber, and publishing and printing, neither technological nor organizational innovation substantially increase minimum efficient scale. In these industries large plants do not offer significant cost advantages over small ones. In these industries the opportunities for cost reduction through material coordination of high-volume throughput by managerial teams remains limited.

The differentials in potential scale economies of different production technologies indicate not only why the large hierarchical firms appeared in some industries and not in others but also why they appeared suddenly in the last decades of the 19th century. Only with the completion of the modern transportation and communication networks—those of the railroad, telegraph, steamship, and cable—could materials flow into a factory or processing plant and the finished goods move out at a rate of speed and volume required to achieve substantial economies of throughput. Transportation that depended on the power of animals, wind, and

---

[8]L. F. Haber, *The Chemical Industry During the Nineteenth Century* (Oxford: Oxford University Press, 1958), p. 92.

[9]Chandler, *Visible Hand,* pp. 302–14.

[10]Allan Nevins, *Ford: The Times, the Man, the Company* (New York: Charles Scribner's Sons, 1954), chaps. 18–20 (especially pages 473, 489, 511). Alfred D. Chandler, Jr., *Giant Enterprise: Ford, General Motors and the Automobile Industry* (New York: Arno Press, 1980), p. 26.

current was too slow, too irregular, and too uncertain to maintain a level of throughput necessary to achieve modern economies of scale.

However, such scale and throughput economies do not in themselves explain why the new technologies made possible by the new transportation and communication systems caused the new mass producers to integrate forward into mass distribution. Coordination might have been achieved through contractual agreement with intermediaries—both buyers and sellers. Such an explanation requires a more precise understanding of the process of volume distribution, particularly why the wholesaler, retailer, or other commercial intermediaries lost their cost advantage vis-á-vis the volume producer.

The intermediaries' cost advantage lay in exploiting both the economies of scale and what has been termed "the economies of scope." Because they handled the products of many manufacturers, they achieved a greater volume and lower per unit cost (i.e., *scale*) than any one manufacturer in the marking and distribution of a *single* line of products. Moreover, they increased this advantage by the broader *scope* of their operation, that is by handling a number of *related* product lines through a single set of facilities. This was true of the new volume wholesalers in apparel, dry goods, groceries, hardware, and the like and even more true of the new mass retailers—the department store, the mail order house, and the chain or multiple shop enterprise.

The commercial intermediaries lost their cost advantages when manufacturers' output reached a comparable scale. As one economist has pointed out, "The intermediary will have a cost advantage over its customers and suppliers only as long as the volume of transactions in which he engages comes closer to that [minimum efficient] scale than do the transactions volumes of his customers or suppliers."[11] This rarely happened in retailing, except in heavily concentrated urban markets, but it often occurred in wholesaling. In addition, the advantages of scope were sharply reduced when marketing and distribution required specialized, costly product-specific facilities and skills that could not be used to handle other product lines. By investing in such product-specific personnel and facilities, the intermediary not only lost the advantages of scope but also became dependent on what were usually a small number of producers to provide those suppliers.

All these new volume-producing enterprises created their own sales organization to advertise and market their products nationally and often internationally. From the start they preferred to have a sales force of their own to advertise and market their goods. Salesmen of wholesalers and other intermediaries who sold the products of many manufacturers, including those of their competitors, could not be relied upon to concentrate on the single product of a single manufacturer with the intensity needed to attain and maintain market share necessary to keep throughput at minimum efficient scale.

Equally important, mass distribution of these products—many of them quite new—often required extensive investment in specialized product-specific facilities and personnel. Because the existing wholesalers and mass retailers made their

---

[11]Scott J. Moss, *An Economic Theory of Business Strategy* (New York: Wiley, 1981), pp. 110–11.

profits from handling related products of many manufacturers, they had little incentive to make large investments in facilities and personnel that could only be useful for a handful of specialized products processed by a handful of producers on whom they would become dependent for the supplies essential to make this investment pay.

Of all the new mass producers, those making packaged food products and consumer chemical products required the least in the way of product-specific distribution facilities and personnel. However, the new canning and packaging techniques did immediately eliminate one of the major functions of the wholesaler, that of converting large bulk shipments into small packages. Because the manufacturers now packaged, they, not the wholesalers, began to brand and to advertise on a national and global scale. Their sales forces now canvassed the retailers. But because mass sales of these branded, packaged products demanded little in the way of specialized facilities and personnel, their processors continued to use the wholesalers to physically distribute the goods for a fixed mark-up or commission until their, the manufacturers', output became large enough to cancel out the scale advantages of the wholesalers who handled the products of many firms.

All other industrial groupings in which the large firm clustered required major investments in either specialized distribution facilities or specialized personnel or often both. The producers of perishables—meat, beer, and dairy products, particularly those in the United States—made the massive investment required in refrigerated or temperature cars, ships, and warehouses.[12] Gustavus Swift, an inventor of the refrigerator car, realized that effective distribution of fresh meat required the building of a national network of refrigerated storage facilities. When he began to build his branch house network in the mid-1880s, other leading meat packers quickly followed suit, racing Swift for the best sites. By the end of the decade, those packers who had made the investment in refrigerated cars and storage facilities before the end of the decade continued as "The Big Five" to dominate the industry for a half a century. In that decade, neither the railroad nor the wholesale butchers had an incentive to invest in this equipment. Indeed, they had a positive disincentive. The railroads already had a mjor investment in cattle cars to move live animals in what was, next to wheat, their largest traffic generator, while the wholesale butchers were organized specifically to handle the cattle delivered to them by the railroad. Both fought the packers with their new product vigorously but with relatively little success. In this and the next decade, the producers of bananas—primarily United Fruit— and the makers of beer for the national market, including Pabst, Schlitz, and Anheuser-Busch, made comparable investment in refrigerated distribution facilities.

Refined petroleum as well as vegetable or animal oil could be shipped more cheaply in specialized tank cars and ships, stored in local tank farms, and then packaged close to the final markets. Wholesalers hesitated to make such extensive investments as they would be wholly dependent for their continued use and profit-

---

[12]Chandler, *Visible Hand*, pp. 299–302, 391–402.

ability on a small number of high-volume suppliers.[13] When the coming of the automobile required still another new and costly distribution investment in pumps and service stations to provide roadside supplies to motorists, wholesalers were even less enthusiastic about making the necessary investment. On the other hand, the refiners, by making the investment, were not only assured of being able to control the scheduling of throughput necessary to maintain their high minimum efficient scale but were also more certain that the quality of the product was not adulterated, as it might have been if it were packaged by independent wholesalers. In the case of gasoline, in order to avoid the costs of operating the pumps and service stations, most oil companies preferred to lease the equipment they purchased or produced to franchised dealers. A comparable situation occurred in tires, whose mass production benefited from the economies of throughput and whose mass sales required a specialized product-specific distribution network. Again, although tire companies occasionally owned their retail outlets, they preferred to rely on franchised retail dealers.

The mass marketing of new machines which were mass produced through the fabricating and assembling of interchangeable parts required a greater investment in personnel to provide the specialized marketing services than in product-specific plant and equipment.[14] The mass distribution of sewing machines for households and for the production of apparel, typewriters, cash registers, adding machines, mimeograph machines, and other office equipment, harvesters, reapers, and other agricultural machines, and, after 1900, automobiles and the more complex electrical appliances all called for demonstration, after-sales service, and consumer credit. As these machines had been only recently invented, few existing distributors had the necessary training and experience to provide the services or financial resources to provide extensive consumer credit.

On the other hand, the manufacturer had every incentive to do both. The provision of repair and service to help to assure that the product performed as advertised and control of the wholesale organization assured inventory as well as quality control. However, as a great many retailers were needed to cover the national and international markets, the manufacturers preferred to rely, as did the oil and tire companies, on franchised dealers. These retail dealers, who sold their products exclusively, were supported by a branch office network that assured the provision of services, credit, and supplies on schedule. Only the makers of sewing machines, typewriters, and cash registers went so far as to invest in retail stores. They did so primarily in concentrated urban areas where, before the coming of

---

[13]Standard Oil began to make an extensive investment in distribution only after the formation of the Trust and the resulting rationalization of production and with it the great increase in throughput. Harold F. Williamson and Arnold R. Daum, *The American Petroleum Industry, The Age of Illumination, 1859–1899* (Evanston, Ill.: Northwestern University Press, 1959), pp. 687–701. For investment in gasoline pumps and service stations, see Harold F. Williamson et al, *The American Petroleum Industry: The Age of Energy, 1899–1959* (Evanston, Ill.: Northwestern University Press, 1963), pp. 217–230, 466–87, 675–86.

[14]Chandler, *Visible Hand,* pp. 402–11.

the automobile, only such stores were able to provide the necessary services and credit on a neighborhood basis.

The makers of heavier but still standardized machinery for industrial users had to offer their customers much the same market services and even more extensive credit. This was true of manufacturers of shoe machinery, pumps, boilers, elevators, printing presses, telephone equipment, and machinery that generated electric power and light. Manufacturers' agents and other intermediaries had neither the training nor the capital to provide the essential services and credit. For the makers of industrial chemicals, volume distribution demanded investment in product-specific capital equipment as well as salesmen with specialized skills. Dynamite, far more powerful than black powder, required careful education of customers, as well as specialized storage and transportation facilities. So, too, did the new synthetic dyes and synthetic fibers whose use had to be explained to manufacturers and whose application often required new specialized machinery. On the other hand, metals produced by processes with a high minimum efficient scale required less investment in distribution. Even so, to obtain and fill volume orders to precise specifications on precise delivery schedules called for a trained sales force and for close coordination between production and sales managers.

In these ways and for these reasons, the large industrial firm that integrated mass production and mass distribution appeared in industries with two characteristics. The first and most essential was a technology of production in which the realization of potential scale economies and maintenance of quality control demanded close and constant coordination and supervision of materials flows by trained managerial teams. The second was that volume marketing and distribution of their products required investment in specialized product-specific human and physical capital.

Where this was *not* the case, that is in industries where technology did *not* have a potentially high minimum efficient scale, where coordination was *not* technically complex, and where mass distribution did *not* require specialized skills and facilities, there was little incentive for the manufacturer to integrate forward into distribution. In such industries as publishing and printing, lumber, furniture, leather, and apparel and textiles, and specialized instruments and machines, the large integrated firm had few competitive advantages. In these industries, the small single-function firm continued to prosper and to compete vigorously.

Significantly, however, it was in just these industries that the new mass retailers—the department stores, the mail-order houses, and the chain or multiple stores—began to coordinate the flow of goods from the manufacturer to their consumer. In those industries where substantial scale economies did not exist in production, both the economies of scale and those of scope gave the mass retailers their economic advantage. In coordinating these flows, the mass retailers, like the mass producers, reduced unit costs of distribution by increasing the daily flow or throughput within the distribution network. Such efficiency, in turn, further reduced the economic need for the wholesaler as a middleman between the retailer and manufacturer.

In industries where this was the case, that is in those that had the two critical characteristics, the most important entrepreneurial act of the founders of an enterprise was the creation of an administrative organization. That is, it was, first, the recruitment of a team to supervise the process of production, then the building of a national and very often international sales network, and finally the setting up of a corporate office of middle and top managers to integrate and coordinate the two. Only then did the enterprise become multinational. Investment in production abroad followed, almost never preceded, the building of an overseas marketing network. So, too, in the technologically advanced industries, the investment in research and development followed the creation of a marketing network. In these firms, this linkage between trained sales engineers, production engineers, product designers, and the research laboratory became a major impetus to continuing innovation in the industries in which they operated. The result of such growth was an enterprise whose organization is depicted in Chart 1. The continuing growth of the firm rested on the ability of its managers to transfer resources in marketing, research and development, and production (usually those that were not fully utilized) into new and more profitable related product lines, a move that carried the organization shown on Chart 1 to that illustrated by Chart 2. If the first step—that of integrating production and distribution—was not taken, the rest did not follow. The firms remained small, personally managed producing enterprises buying their materials and selling their products through intermediaries.

## The Differences

Thus, in major modern economies, the large managerial enterprise evolved in much the same way in industries with much the same characteristics. However, there were striking differences in the pace, the timing, and the specific industries in which the new institution appeared and continued to grow in each of these economies. These differences reflected differences in technologies and markets available to the industrialists of the different nations, in their entrepreneurial organizational skills, in laws, and in cultural attitudes and values. These dissimilarities can be pinpointed by very briefly reviewing the historical experiences of the 200 largest industrial enterprises in the United States, the United Kingdom, Germany, and Japan.[15]

### The United States

In the United States, the completion of the nation's basic railroad and telegraph network and the perfection of its operating methods in the 1870s and 1880s opened up the largest and fastest growing market in the world. Its population,

---

[15]The analysis of these differences is based on detailed research by the author of available histories, company and government reports, business journals, and internal company documents dealing with these many enterprises.

which already enjoyed the highest per capita income in the world, was equal to that of Britain in 1850, twice that in 1900, and three times that in 1920.[16] American entrepreneurs quickly recruited the managerial teams in production necessary to exploit scale economies and made the investment in distribution necessary to market their volume-produced goods at home and abroad and did so in all the industries in which large industrial firms would cluster for the following century. Most of these firms quickly extended their marketing organizations overseas and then became multinational by investing in production facilities abroad, playing an influential role in a global oligopoly. (See Table 6.) Indeed, in some cases, particularly in mass-produced light machinery, the Americans enjoyed close to global monopoly well before the outbreak of World War I. By that time too, those in the more technologically advanced industries had begun to invest personnel and facilities in research and development.

These large manufacturing enterprises grew by direct investment in nonmanufacturing personnel and facilities. They also expanded by merger and acquisition.[17] Here they began by making the standard response of manufacturers, both the European and American, to excess capacity to which, because of the high minimum efficient scale of their capital-intensive production processes, they were particularly sensitive. American manufacturers first attempted to control competition by forming trade associations to control output and prices and allocating marketing territories. However, because of the existing common law prohibition against combinations in restraint of trade, these associations were unable to enforce their rulings in courts of law. So manufacturers turned to the holding company device. Members of their association exchanged their stock for that of a holding company thus giving a central office legal power to determine output, prices, and marketing areas for the subsidiary firms.

For most American enterprises, the initial incorporation as a holding company took place to control competition. However, for some, like John D. Rockefeller, it became the first step for rationalizing the resources of an enterprise or even an industry in order to exploit fully the potential of scale economies. Even before the enforcement of the Sherman Antitrust Law in the early 20th century made contractual cooperation by means of a holding company legally suspect, a number of American enterprises had been transformed from holding companies to operating ones by consolidating the many factories of their subsidiaries into a single production department, unifying the several sales forces into a single sales department (including an international division) and then, though less often, investing in research and development. In a word, these enterprises were transformed from a loose federation of small operating concerns into a single centralized enterprise as depicted in Figure 1. These firms competed for market share and profits, rarely on price—the largest (and usually the oldest) remained the price leader—but on productive efficiency, on advertising, on the proficiency of

---

[16]W. S. and E. S. Woytinsky, *World Population and Production* (New York: Twentieth Century Fund, 1953), pp. 383–85.

[17]Chandler, *Visible Hand,* chap. 10.

their marketing and distribution services, and on product performance and product improvement.

In such large, complex organizations, decisions both as to current production and distribution and the allocation of resources for future production and distribution came to be made by full-time salaried managers. At the time of World War I, owners who still worked on a full-time basis with their hierarchies continued to have an influence on such decisions. By World War II, growth by diversification into new product lines not only greatly increased the size and complexity of the enterprise but still further scattered stock ownership. By then owners rarely participated in managerial decisions. At best they or their representatives were "outside" directors who met with the inside directors, that is the full-time salaried managers, at the most once a month and usually only four times a year. For these meetings the inside directors set the agenda, provided the information on which decisions were made, and of course were responsible for implementing the decisions. The outside directors still had the veto power, but they had neither the time,

## TABLE 6

**Multinational Companies in 1914 (American companies with two or more plants abroad or one plant and raw material–producing facilities)**

| *Groups 20 & 21: Food and Tobacco* | *Groups 35, 36, & 37: Machinery and Transportation Equipment* |
|---|---|
| American Chicle | American Bicycle |
| American Cotton Oil | American Gramophone |
| Armour | American Radiator |
| Coca-Cola | Crown Cork & Seal |
| H. J. Heinz | Chicago Pneumatic Tool |
| Quaker Oats | Ford |
| Swift | General Electric |
| American Tobacco | International Harvester |
| British American Tobacco | International Steam Pump (Worthington) |
| | Mergenthaler Linotype |
| *Groups 28, 29, & 30: Chemicals & Pharmaceuticals, Oil, and Rubber* | National Cash Register |
| Carborundum | Norton |
| Parke Davis (drug) | Otis Elevator |
| Sherwin-Williams | Singer |
| Sterns & Co. (drug) | Torrington |
| United Drug (drug) | United Shoe Machinery |
| Virginia-Carolina Chemical | Western Electric |
| Du Pont | Westinghouse Air Brake |
| Standard Oil of N.J. | Westinghouse Electric |
| U.S. Rubber | *Others* |
| | Alcoa (33) |
| | Gillette (34) |
| | Eastman Kodak (38) |
| | Diamond Match (39) |

Source: Mira Wilkins, *The Emergence of Multinational Enterprise* (Cambridge: Harvard University Press, 1970), pp. 212–13, 216.

the information nor experience, and rarely even the motivation to propose alternate courses of action. By World War I, managerial capitalism had become firmly entrenched in the major sectors of the American economy.

## The United Kingdom

This was certainly not the case in the United Kingdom. As late as World War II, the large integrated industrial enterprise administered through an extensive managerial hierarchy was still the exception. Nearly all of the 200 leading industrials in Britain had integrated production with distribution, but in a great number of these, owners remained full-time executives. They managed their enterprises with the assistance of a small number of "company servants" who only began to be asked to join boards of directors in the 1930s. In Britain, at the time of World War II, most of the top 200 consisted of two types of enterprises, neither of which existed among the American top 200 at the time of World War I. They were either personally managed enterprises or federations of such enterprises. The exceptions were, of course, Britain's largest and best-known industrial corporations—those that represented Britain in their global oligopolies. However, as late as 1948, these numbered less than 20 percent of the top 200 enterprises.

Large hierarchical enterprises did come when British entrepreneurs responded to the potential of new high-volume technologies by creating management teams for production and invested in distribution and research personnel and facilities. Between the 1880s and World War I, such firms appeared in branded, packaged products like soap, starch, biscuits, and chocolate and in rayon, tires, plate and flat glass, explosives, and synthetic alkalies. For example, Courtaulds, the first to build a plant with a high minimum efficient scale in rayon, became and remained the largest producer of the first synthetic fiber, not only in Britain but also in the United States.

But where British industrialists failed to grasp the opportunity to make the investment and build the hierarchies, they not only lost the world market but the British home market itself. This was particularly striking in machinery, both light and heavy, and in industrial chemicals. The American firms quickly overpowered the British competitors in the production and distribution of light mass-produced machinery, including sewing, office and agricultural machinery, automobiles, household appliances, and the like. The Germans as quickly dominated the synthetic dye business so critical to Britain's huge textile industry, while both the Germans and Americans shared the electrical machinery industry, the new producers of light and of the energy so critical to increased productivity in manufacturing. In 1912, for example, two thirds of the output of the electrical manufacturing industry within Britain was produced by three companies, the subsidiaries of the American General Electric and Westinghouse and the German Siemens.[18] Even those few British firms that achieved and maintained their position in the domestic

---

[18]I. C. R. Byatt, *The British Electrical Industry, 1875–1914* (Oxford: Oxford University Press, 1979), p. 150.

market and the global oligopoly created smaller hierarchies and had more direct owner management than did their American counterparts.

After World War I, a few British firms in such volume-producing industries began to challenge their American and German competition, but they did so only by making the necessary investment in nonmanufacturing personnel and facilities and by recruiting managerial staffs. This was the case for Anglo-Persian Oil Company, for British General Electric and Imperial Chemical Industries in each of their industries, for Metal Box in cans, and for Austin and Morris in automobiles. Nevertheless, the transformation from personal or family management to one of salaried managers came slowly and grudgingly. In even the largest enterprises— those with sizeable hierarchies such as Courtaulds, British Celenese, Pilkington, Metal Box, Reckitts, Cadburys, Ranks, and others—the owners continued to have a much greater say in top management decisions than did their American counterparts.

Why was this the case? The answer is, of course, complex. It lies in Britain's industrial geography and history, in her educational system, in the lack of antitrust legislation, and in a continuing commitment to personal and family management. Because the domestic market was smaller and growing more slowly than the American, British industrialists had less incentive than their American counterparts to exploit scale economies. Moreover, Britain was the only nation to industrialize before the coming of modern transportation and communication. So its industrialists had become attuned to a slower, smaller scale process of industrial production and distribution.

Nevertheless, precisely because it was the first industrial nation, Great Britain also became the world's first consumer society. The quadrangle bounded by London, Cardiff, Glasgow, and Edinburgh remained for almost a century after 1850 the richest and most concentrated consumer market in the world. British entrepreneurs quickly began to mass-produce branded, packaged consumer goods (of all the new industries, these required the least in the way of specialized skills in production and specialized services and facilities in distribution). But in other of the new industries, it was the foreign, not the British, entrepreneur who responded to the new opportunities. Even though that golden quadrangle remained the world's most concentrated market for mass-produced sewing machines, shoe machinery, office equipment, phonographs, batteries, automobiles, appliances, and other consumer durables, as well as electrical and other new heavy machinery and industrial chemicals, Germans and Americans were the first to set up *within Britain* the production teams and to make the investment in the product-specific distribution services and facilities essential to compete in these industries. Apparently British industrialists wanted to manage their own enterprises rather than turn over operating control to nonfamily salaried managers. They seemed to regard their companies as family estates to be nurtured and passed down to their heirs rather than mere moneymaking machines. As a result they and the British economy as a whole failed to harvest many of the fruits of the Second Industrial Revolution.

The commitment to family control was reflected in the nature of British mergers. As in the United States, many British firms grew large by merger and acquisition. As in America, holding companies were formed to control legally the output, price, and marketing arrangements of hitherto small competing enterprises; but in Britain, unlike in the United States, holding companies remained federations of family firms. Until World War I, British industrialists rarely viewed merger as a forerunner to rationalization, consolidation, and centralized administration necessary to exploit the potential scale of economies. Indeed, the very first merger to centralize and rationalize in Britain came in 1920 at Nobel Explosives, the forerunner to I.C.I., which borrowed the necessary organizational techniques directly from its overseas ally, the Du Pont company of Wilmington, Delaware.[19] As late as 1928, Lever Brothers, one of Britain's largest enterprises, had 41 operating subsidiaries and 39 different sales forces. For these reasons, then, the founders of most large British enterprises continued to manage their enterprises directly. Hierarchies remained small and controllable. Sons and grandsons and grandsons-in-law continued to move into the top offices.

Thus Britain continued until World War II to be the bastion of family capitalism. After the Second World War, the rapid decline of the old industries, the end of the cartel system at home and abroad and therefore the increasing need to compete through efficiency, a new emphasis on engineering and business education for managers, and even changes in attitudes about family position and control transformed the large industrial enterprise. Ownership increasingly became separated from management. By the 1970s, the size of the hierarchies, their composition, the organizational structure of the enterprise, the ways of competition and growth were comparable to that of the large American firm 30 years earlier, except that family participation in top management was probably still greater.

## Germany

In Germany, unlike Britain, there were integrated industrial firms that were as large as those in the United States well before the coming of World War I. They were, however, fewer in number and were concentrated in metals and the technologically advanced machinery and chemical industries. Among the top 200 German firms during the interwar years, there were very few producing branded, packaged products, except for the regional breweries. One can only locate two chocolate and confectionery and two drug companies. The remaining few were subsidiaries of Nestlé, Lever Brothers, and the two Dutch margarine makers that joined Lever in 1929 to become Unilever. Nor did the large German firms manufacture light mass-produced machinery in the American manner. Singer Sewing Machine long remained the largest sewing machine maker in Germany. Well before World War I, the factories of National Cash Register and American Radiator and the sales office of International Harvester and Remington Typewriter dominated the German market for their products. In automobiles in 1929, a year when

---

[19]For Nobel, W. J. Reader, *Imperial Chemical Industries: A History,* I (London: Oxford University Press, 1970), pp. 388–394; for Lever Brothers, Charles H. Wilson, *History of Unilever,* II (London: Cassell, 1954), pp. 302, 345.

General Motors produced 1.6 million and Ford 1.5 million cars, only one German car company made more than 10,000, and that firm, Adam Opel, which produced 25,000, was a General Motors subsidiary. Even in standardized industrial machines, American firms such as Mergenthaler Linotype (in printing presses) and Norton (in abrasives and grinding machines) dominated German markets.

The Germans did, like the British, have their one large representative in the rayon, rubber, and oil oligopolies. (The last, EPU, was dismembered during World War I.) It was in complex machinery and chemicals, however, that the Germans made their global mark. In giant production works, German machinery and chemical enterprises produced in quantity a variety of complex machines and chemicals made from the same basic ingredients and processes. Managerial hierarchies even greater in size than those of the production departments of American firms guided the complicated flow of materials from one intermediate process to the next. In the 1880s and 1890s, these enterprises built extended networks of branch offices throughout the world to market products, most of which were technologically new machinery and chemicals, to demonstrate their use, to install them where necessary, to provide continuing after-sales service, and to give customers the financial credit they often needed to make such purchases. Once established abroad, they built and acquired branch factories. Finally, they invested, usually more heavily than the Americans, in research and development.

At home these large integrated enterprises reduced competition by making contractual arrangements for setting price and output and allocating markets. Because such arrangements were in Germany legally enforceable in courts of law, the arrangements became quite formal and elaborate. The I.G., or the community of interest, became the closest legal form to the British and the American holding company. The difference between the British holding company and the German community of interest was that the latter involved large hierarchical firms rather than small family enterprises. Their extensive investment in marketing and distribution and in research and development permitted the large German enterprises to dominate the negotiations setting up cartels, associations, or communities of interest and provided them with the power essential to implement and enforce the contractual arrangements.

Finally, the capital requirements of these capital-intensive producers of industrial products were far greater than those of the American and British makers of branded, packaged products or the American mass producers of light machinery. Because there were no highly developed capital markets in Germany comparable to those of London and New York, German banks became much more involved in the financing of large hierarchical enterprises than was true in Britain and the United States. Although the representatives of banks never sat at the *Vorstand,* the central administrative body of top managers, as did the founder and often full-time family executives, they did become important members of the *Aufsichtsrat* or supervisory board. Because the numbers of large enterprises were small, much smaller than in the United States, and because the major banks were even fewer, the full-time salaried bank managers were probably small enough in number to exchange information. Such outside sources of knowledge about the businesses may have made them less captive to the inside management than the part-time outside directors on American boards. Thus, those sectors where the supervisory board included managers of the leading banks can be said to have been administered through a system of finance capitalism.

Why was it that the large German industrial enterprises were concentrated in metals and complex industrial products rather than branded, packaged goods or light mass-produced machinery? Why did the Germans build large hierarchical organizations when the British did not? Manufacturers in the new German empire of the 1870s, at the time when the transportation and communication revolution was being completed, enjoyed neither the rapidly growing continental market of America nor the concentrated consumer market of Britain. Because per capita income was lower than in the two Anglo-Saxon countries and because Germany was neither a large importer of foodstuffs like the United Kingdom nor an exporter like the United States, there was relatively little entrepreneurial challenge to create large enterprises in packaged and perishable foodstuffs or other consumer products. The challenge to the German entrepreneurs came instead from the demand of industrializing and industrial countries, including Britain and Germany itself, for the new specialized industrial machinery, including electrical equipment and new industrial chemicals, including synthetic dyes. In building their technical sales and research organizations—their basic weapons in international competition—the Germans had the advantage of what had become the world's best technical and scientific educational institutions. Therefore, despite the defeat in two wars, the German strength in international competition still rests on the performance of their science-based industries.

Since World War II, convergence has occurred, as it has in Britain. German industrials successfully moved into the mass production of automobiles, appliances, and other consumer durables as well as into the high-volume production of light machinery. The number of producers of branded, packaged products in foods and consumer chemicals increased. As the number of firms among the top 200 in industries other than machinery and chemicals grew larger and as the firms in those older industries diversified into new product lines, the ability of representatives of banks to bypass the inside managers and therefore to participate in top management decisions lessened. Even so, banks still play a more significant role in German enterprises than they do in American, just as British family members are still more important in top management decisions than those in the United States.

## Japan

The evolution of the large industrial enterprises in Japan differed greatly from those in the West. For Japan was just taking the first steps toward modern industrialization in the same decades that the new transportation and communication revolution was spawning the Second Industrial Revolution in Europe and the United States. Indeed, Japan's first steel mill only went into operation in 1902. Only in the years after World War II was the economy large and strong enough to support modern mass production and mass distribution. Yet even before that war, managerial hierarchies had appeared to exploit new technologies and to reach new markets.

In the early years of this century, Japan's domestic and foreign markets were of a totally different nature. At the time of the Meiji Restoration, Japanese manufacturers enjoyed a highly concentrated domestic market, comparable to Britain's during her early industrialization, with long-established channels for distribution of traditional consumer goods. As a result, only a few Japanese firms (and no foreign companies) began to create marketing networks to distribute branded, packaged products within the country. By World War II, a small number of makers of branded, packaged products such as confectionery, soy sauce, canned sea food, beer, and soap, who advertised nationally and had their own extensive sales force, were listed among the largest 200 Japanese industrial enterprises.

On the other hand, overseas, even in nearby East Asia, the Japanese had had no commercial contact at all for the more than 250 years of the Tokugawa period. Manufacturers using imported processes to produce textiles, fertilizers, and ceramic and metal products sought overseas as well as domestic markets, particularly in the nonindustrialized East and Southeast Asia. Overseas they rarely set up their own branch offices. They had neither the volume nor the distribution needs to require large product-specific investments in distribution. They relied instead on allied trading companies to assure coordination of flow of goods from factories in Japan to customers abroad and also to those at home. These trading companies also supervised the flow of essential materials and equipment from overseas to the producing facilities. These trading companies set up branch offices in Japan and in all parts of the world as well as building a large central office in Tokyo or Osaka. That is, they invested in an extensive marketing and distribution organization that coordinated flows, provided marketing services, and generated information, thus lowering marketing and distribution costs. They became the linchpins of groups of firms of single product manufacturing enterprises, each group having its own banks and trust companies as well as its own trading and warehouse concerns.

The close relationship between the managers of the manufacturing companies and those of the trading firms, either within the giant *zaibatsu* or between cooperating manufacturers in less formal groups, permitted the Japanese to capture an increased share of world trade, particularly in the relatively low-technology industries. However, where marketing and distribution did require product-specific skills, services, and facilities, enterprises did set up their own distributing network and operated outside of the *zaibatsu* and other group enterprises. Before the Second World War, only a small number of such enterprises had appeared, primarily in industrial machinery and particularly in electrical machinery. The latter was especially important, for until the 1950s, Japan relied heavily on hydroelectric power for its energy. Only after the war with the rapid growth of the domestic market did the makers of automobiles, electric appliances, radio, and television build comparable organizations. In the postwar years, these enterprises have been increasingly investing in distribution abroad and have come to operate through extensive managerial hierarchies comparable to those of the West. Like their western counterparts, they began in the 1960s to grow through diversification particularly into appliances, radio, television, and other consumer durables. So by 1970, there were two types of industrial groups in Japan. One was the descendant of the old *zaibatsu,* whose central office had been abolished by the Allied occupational authorities after the war. The other was the maker of machinery, vehicles, and electrical equipment who, after diversifying in the manner of the western companies, often spun off their different product divisions. They remained part of the group but operated as financially independent enterprises, as was not the case for the divisions or subsidiaries of diversified western firms.

## Conclusion

As the Japanese experience illustrates, the vast increase in the numbers and complexity of decisions required to coordinate the activities of a multitude of offices, plants, distribution facilities, research laboratories, and the like in different geographical areas often for several product lines brought a convergence in the type of enterprise and system of capitalism used by all advanced industrial economies for the production and distribution of goods. In Japan the rapid post–World War II growth of a concentrated domestic urban industrial market with a sharply increasing per-capita income provided a base for a large integrated hierarchical enterprise to exploit the potentials of scale economies. Such enterprises quickly took their place in the existing global oligopolies.

In this respect the Japanese challenge to the American and European industrial leadership differs markedly from the earlier challenges of the Americans and Germans to British leadership. The Americans and Germans took over world markets by creating international hierarchical enterprises producing and distributing new products because the British failed to create the organizations required for the development and exploitation of these products. The Japanese, on the other hand, have successfully moved into the international markets by using very similar technological and organizational techniques, often borrowed directly from the Americans and Europeans, and by using them more effectively and efficiently than the first comers.

Thus by the 1970s, in these advanced industrial economies, managers with little or no equity in the enterprises administered made the decisions about present production and distribution and the allocation of resources for future production and distribution. And they did so through much the same basic organizational forms. The type of structure depicted in Figure 2 defines in broad outline the organization of Imperial Chemical Industries, Bayer, Mitsubishi Chemical, and the Du Pont company. Only in rare cases are any of the top 200 in these four leading industrial economies personally managed by their owners. Even the enterprise where owners participate on a full-time basis in the top management decisions of an extensive hierarchy has become the exception.

Nevertheless, variations within this new brand of capitalism are still significant. The differences in the size, number, and location by industry and the systems and styles of management reflect the different routes by which the leading sectors of the different economies reached managerial capitalism—the United States by almost revolutionary changes at the turn of the century, Britain in a much more evolutionary manner that prolonged family capitalism, Germany by way of finance capitalism, and Japan by the development of group enterprise capitalism.

# CASE 17

# *Patterns of Work in Nineteenth Century America**

The following readings are drawn from contemporary documents and describe the work experiences of an itinerant craftsman, of New England textile-mill operatives, and of southern plantation laborers. These original descriptions are supplemented by exhibits which present data concerning the American work force during the 19th century.

In studying the selections and exhibits, the reader should attempt to get an idea of the problems and opportunities which American workers in this era faced.

## Document 1. Memoirs of an Itinerant Worker

The following article was written by Samuel Clough (1824–1905) between the years of 1898 and 1901. Original punctuation, spelling, and grammatical construction have been retained for the most part.

At home, Union Co. Iowa
Post Office, Ellston, Iowa
December 19, 1898

---

*Professor James P. Baughman compiled much of the material in this case. Additions have been made by Professor Alfred D. Chandler, Jr. This case was prepared as a basis for class discussion rather than to illustrate either effective or ineffective handling of an administrative situation.

Copyright © 1972 by the President and Fellows of Harvard College.

Harvard Business School case 372-351, rev. 5/84.

I, Samuel Clough, sit down at the age of 74 to write a few past incidents and memoirs of my life, works, and travels.

My fathers name was Samuel, his fathers name was Jobe Clough. My mothers name was Hannah Clough, her fathers name was John Philbrick.

I was born April 26, 1824 on the farm my father was born on, in the town of Alma, Lincoln Co., State of Maine.

After I was of school age I went to school in summer time for a few weeks until I was 9 years old, when I quit summer school and went to winter school about 2 months in the year until I was 19 years old. When I was 9 years old I began to plow on my fathers farm. I could hold the plow and drive oxen. From then on my principal education consisted in learning how to work the little farm until December 1 before I was 20 years old. December 8, 1843, when I shipped on board the ship *Ontario*. Captain Bearstow from Wiscassett to New Orleans, as a green hand before the mast for $8 per month.

Out of that I paid 20 cents per month tax support the Marine Hospital leaving savings of $7.80 as wages. The ship arrived in New Orleans about the third of January 1844 after a rather pleasant trip. The ship laid there idle until the next summer, as I understood afterward. I stayed with the ship until about the 20th of April. I had received one month pay in advance to fit me with some clothing which I needed, but I got but little money after that. When I left the ship there were some 20 dollars due me, but I could get none and I had no shoes, and I owed one dollar to a man who a few weeks before had loaned me a dollar to pull a bad tooth with which I had suffered with for several weeks.

It had been getting rather dull staying in New Orleans and warm weather coming on and I wanted to be learning Seamanship, so I thought I would find another ship and go to sea again. Freighters were low, times on the sailors were rather hard, wages were low. The only chance I could find was to go to Liverpool in England in the ship *Laura*. Captain Show of Bucksport, Maine, for $7.80 a month, and had to agree to go without any pay in advance. Now I was going to Liverpool, had no shoes, was owing a friend a dollar, but had not so much as one red cent. I had been bare foot for two months, but it was not very cold in that latitude even in February and March but I expected to get up North where I might see ice burgs in April. I expected to get money of Captain Bearstow until within six hours of the time appointed for the ship *Laura* to sail. I worked on the ship *Laura* three days before she was to sail in the evening, about two hours before she was to sail I went to the Captain and told him I wanted one dollar, and if he would let me have two dollars I would be very glad. He put his hand in his pocket and pulled out one dollar and fifty cents and says here take that in such a gruff tone that I dare not say more. So I took it and marched off. I could not pay the dollar and buy the shoes with that, so I decided to go and pay the dollar and went to Europe totally barefoot for want of a dollar to buy a pair of shoes.

It was pretty cold part of the way across the Atlantic Ocean, but I lived through it and quite nicely. That is the last time I was out of money. When I got to Liverpool the first thing I bought was a good pair of English shoes made to order. They done me more service than any other shoes I ever had. They cost me $2.50.

The ship carried cotton and was 43 days on the passage. I remained with the ship until she discharged her cargo of cotton and took a general cargo for Boston, Massachusetts, where she arrived about September 12 as near as I remember.

September 19, 1844, I began to work for the Boston and Maine Railroad Company for Seven and six-pence a day, $1.25, and took board of Clark Durgan on the corner of Canall and Causway Street at $2.50 per week. I continued to work for the R.R. Company until about the first of January, 1845.

Sometime in January, 1845 say about the 10 I went out to the pond and worked for Luther Weith, some six miles from Boston, cutting ice for $1.00 per day at first, but soon he advanced my wages to $1.50 and gave me charge of part of the work. I worked there during the ice season until about the middle of March when I went into Boston. While cutting ice I boarded with a shoemaker and farmer in the neighborhood whose daughter kept house for him.

About the first of April 1845 I began to work for Jeremiah Wetherby and Company to learn to cut stone in Boston, Massachusetts. I worked the first three months for my board that is they paid the price of my board $2.75 per week, at Mr. Burgans. The next three months they paid me $10.00 a month and board, that completed my apprenticeship. From that on until I took this Variloid, they paid me $1.42 per day and I paid my own board. The smallpox got into my boarding house from which I took the Veriloid and was sick about a week. When I got well I went to Methuen and began to work February 13, 1846, to cut stone for John A. Carpenter and Company to build a dam across the Merimac River at Methuen to make water power for manufacturing purposes. I cut some of the first stone put in the dam. I got $1.50 per day all winter, the highest wages paid for cutting stone for the winter.

The stone was quarried and cut in Pellham, New Hampshire, about 7 miles from where the dam was built. The stone was drawn with oxen and horses on wagons. Some sleds were used in the winter. Since that time a very large city had been built called Lawrence.

About April 3, 1847, I went back to Boston and the 9 of April went to work for Wetherby again for $1.75 per day to cut stone. Sometime after this Wetherbys got a portion of the stone work for the Reservoir on Beacon Hill in Boston. He wanted me to go to Cape Ann where the stones was quarried and some of them were cut for his custom in Boston and other towns around, for they done a large business in stone work. They were to pay me $2.00 per day to go to the Cape to cut stone for the Reservoir, and when I got there, Mr. Clifford the foreman and partner thought I could not earn $2 a day as I was only an Apprentice the season before and said he would give me 4 cents per foot and up special measure for cutting bed and build work as it is called. So as by this time I had found out that I was no slouch of a stone cutter. I concluded to take it and went to work, and in about 3 weeks he found out I was making $3.00 a day. Then he wanted me to cut some Cornist stone for a depot. Said he would give $1.75 per foot in length so I cut cornist along side of his old friend.

Flood an old hand, who had worked for the firm several years and was counted an extra hand and was working for $3 a day. Messers Clifford and Flood watched me pretty close until they found I was making $5.00 per day. Flood was mad and Clifford went back on the price and that knocked me out of a job for I would not work for them any more. I demanded a settlement picked up my tools and went to Leadbeaters Island in Penobscot Bay in the State of Maine, and work for Mr. (I have forgotten the name) who was getting out stone to go to Key West in the Gulf of Mexico for a port. I cut by the port and made $3.00 a day until fall. About November 1, 1847 the brigg *Lucy Wotts*, Captain Watly of St. George Maine come to the Island to load with stone for Tay Webb and she wanted a man to go as a sailor. I shiped and went to Key West thence to New Orleans was 33 days on the passage and received $17.95 including unloading at Key West. December 16, 1846 Took board at Mrs. Smith's at $3.50 per week. The 17 began to work for Clark Day and Stoupper for $1.25 per day. They kept a large store of Hardware consisting of iron, tin, lead, farm implements, mechanical tools, oils, boat mill stones, grindstone portable mills, etc. January 8, 1847 began to board with A. Ruth on Jefferson St. New Orleans at $12.00 per month February 14 began to board at Mrs. Hogdens Poidras Street for $3.00 per week. Sold to Mr. Beain of Buffalo, New York, a pair of calfskin boots for $3.50 he paid me $2.00 and that was all I got. He soon went to Buffalo, New York. About April 10, 1847 began to board with Mrs. Verrieges, Phillips St. New Orleans at $3.50 per week. I worked for Clark Day, Stamper and Co. until January 1 when I had $40.00 per month the first of November 1847, then $50.00 per month and I was to have $50.00 a month until January 1, 1848. Then I was to have such wages as they paid their other help which was then about $75.00 per month. But in the Spring of 1847 my father died and it seemed necessary that I should go home to take care of the little farm and my mother, who lived on it at the time. Perhaps I should say here that my fathers farm and home sold under mortgage after I went to sea, and the next spring while I was in Boston learning to cut stone Elbridge Peasley a neighbor of ours in Alma Maine was up to Boston and he called on me and said my fathers farm was sold and nearly past redemption and that if I could redeem it, it would help them. I was a little past 21 years of age but had no money. But my sister Eliza had been working in Boston for a number of years making boots and had $400 or $500 in the Savings Bank, she said she would loan me some money if I could use it to save the place. So I went home and found I could buy the home part of the farm containing the buildings, and the best part of the land by paying $100 dollard down and the balance of the debt against it in a year or so. I went back to Boston, borrowed $100 of Eliza and back to Maine and made the agreements and saved the place, and soon after I finished my trade I began to earn money and paid all the debts off. My father lived on it while he lived, and Mother used it as long as she wanted it free of rent and after that I sold it to Brother Albert.

Sometime in April 1847 Massers Clark Day Stampper and Co. allowed me to go home and paid me up according to our contract so far and kindly sent their team to take my chest and baggage to the ship without charge. When I left for Boston. To save traveling expenses I looked for and found a ship loading for Boston. I said to the Captain that I wanted to go to Boston with him. I would like to work my passage. He said I might go, so I went on board and turned to the same as any sailor and did not expect any wages. But when the Captain paid off his men he paid me as much as any of them, which was $14.00 per month. We were just one month on board. From Boston I went to Maine where I arrived about the first of June as near as I remember.

My brother Albert had planted some corn and some potatoes, and he had gone to Gardiner to learn the carpenter trade and so I hoed the corn and potatoes and cut the hay and shingled the house and made some other repairs and provided for Mother harvested the corn and potatoes for her and left her what hay she wanted for her little stock, and employed Uncle Daniel Clough to bale some of the hay and sell it and rented him the hay ground for the next year and in the fall I went to New Orleans again by way of Boston, Albany, Buffalo, Landusky, Cincinnata, Memphis and on down the Mississippi River. Arrived in New Orleans. Found work in a Whole Sale and Real Estate Drug Store. Soon after the Cholera broke out in New Orleans. I was boarding at Mrs. Smiths and my room mate died with the cholera in about 2 hours after he was taken sick. In a few weeks after that I left New Orleans and come up the Mississippi and Ohio Rivers to Cincinnatti by steam boat on the way up there were 8 deaths on board the boat by cholera and one death by drowning before we reached the mouth of the Ohio River. I think that was the beginning of the year of 1849. The great cholera year. I was sick in New Orleans with the symptoms of cholera and thought it best to leave there. I did not find employment in Cincinnata so I went North to Landusky City. By this time I had got nearly out of money and was obliged to hunt work. I soon fell into cutting ice for Mr. Roosevelt who had just received a lot of tools for cutting ice of Mr. Wyeth of Mass. whom I had worked for cutting ice on fresh pond 6 miles back of Boston a few years before. Mr. Roosevelt had never used those tools before and needed some expert help to cut his ice. I had used the tools and he was glad to have my help and I was glad to get the job. I worked at cutting ice and cribbing until I got money to go to Cleaveland Ohio by stage. I was intending to make my way back to Boston with a view of working at my trade cutting stone again. At Cleveland I found work with the Cleaveland, Columbus and Cincinnatti Railroad Co. who had began to build their R.R. the fall before. I got $25.00 a month helping the Engineers to stake out the line and set grade stakes. I worked there until navagation opened when I took the first boat to Buffalo, New York and thence to Albany by rail. When at Albany I thought I would like to see New York City as I had never been there so I took one of Vanderbilts fine Steamers and run down to New York. The passage cost only 12 1/2 cents or a york shilling as it was called in those days. The United States had began to build a dry dock and engine house of Maine granite in the Navy yard in Brooklin. I applied for work as a stone cutter. They put me to work on trial week and then gave me work at $2.00 per day of 10 hours and I worked all summer. This was in 1849. I had a very pleasant time that summer good wages, nice job in a nice city, good boarding house with Mr. William Bovis and family, corner of Hudson Ave. and High Street. They were a pleasant family to board with. The dry dock was a very nice job of fine cut granite and so was the engine house. There were at one time in the summer when there was near 200 stone cutters at work, and there was a rule that if a man made a mistake in cutting a stone he would be suspended from work for a day or more. I was one of the very few who was not suspended during the seven months I worked there. I was one of the last four stone cutters that was discharged when cold weather come on and the work was stopped for the winter.

While in Brooklin I bought unseen 600 acres of land in Tennessee. December 17, 1849 I started to go and see it. I took maps and charts to sell on the way. I took the cars from New York to Reading Penn. There I began to sell maps and travel on foot in the direction of Cumberland, Md. Thomas Jones a stone cutter went with me as far as Cumberland. We bought maps and charts published by Ensign and Thayer, No. 50 Ann Street, New York. I took $25.25 worth about what I could carry and sold them before I got to Cumberland. I made about $1.00 a day and expenses. Thomas Jones got tired and went back to New York. At Cumberland I fell in with an Englishman and his son. We then footed it over the Allegania Mts. to Brownsville on the Monangahela River, where we took deck passage on a boat down the Monongahala and the Ohio rivers to the mouth of the Cumberland river where my English fellow travelers and I parted company. They went on to St. Louis and I took another boat and went up the Cumberland River to Nashville Tennessee. Here I stopped to see if the land I had bought had been recorded. I found the lands had been deeded by the State to parties who had sold them in New York and deeds recorded all right, so I pushed West on foot some 60 miles to the East Bank of the Tennessee River where my land was supposed to lay. My journey West from Nashville was through a very sparcely settled country for more than 2/3 of the way and many streams to ford. One stream was nearly up to my neck. I took off my clothes and tied them into a bundle and tied them to my valice and held them on my head and waded across. On arriving in the district where my land should have been and on inquiring I found my purchase was a perfect swindle. It came about on this wise. When as the state had sold all the land on a certain District lying on the East side of the Tennessee River that would sell for a very small price it passed a law to grant to any one who would pay the expenses of entering and surveying the remnants of land not sold (and that was a very small part of the land district) it appeared that the then entry taken and the then County Surveyor worked up a plan to make partition entry takers book and in the surveyors book and got deeds for them from the State and they were recorded in the State Capital and the old Quaker of whom I bought in New York told me afterwards that 18,000 acres of those lands had been sold in New York in one winter and the citizens in Tennessee told me that large lots of those Tille had been sold in the large cities in Europe. Those petition entries were located largely on the East Bank of the Tennessee River, where the land was supposed to be good. In 5,000 acre tracts along the bank of the river they were located eleven entrys deep on top of the other. I found this out by refering to the County surveyors book which I had access to 2 weeks when I was there. The former Entry taker had died and the county surveyor had left the county, who had done this work. In order to find where my 600 acres was located I had to begin according to the survey at a point just below. Forms Creek on the East Bank of the Tennessee River. Well after finding out how easily and how badly I had been swindled I concluded to pocket the loss and go back to

New York. So I sold most of my spare clothing, my valice to help pay expenses and lighten my load and walked back to Nashville. There was one stretch of woods and hills and valleys, 12 miles between houses on the way. I am writing this from memory mostly. It is Feb. 1, 1900 and the things I am writing about today happened in the winter of 1849 and 1850 according to an occasional date furnished by some old papers that I had kept. In 50 years I find I have forgotten many things, places, and names which I would like to recall. There are some things that may seem trifling to others that I will put in here because my life had been made up of little lessons and I will relate one of them here. When I got back to Nashville, I was having a very bad cold and sore mouth, my mouth was so sore I could not eat much for several days and I think it was caused in this way. When my English comrad, before mentioned and I had taken deck passage on boat down the river from Brownsville we needed to provide our selves with something to eat on the way. We thought to join in buying provisions and cooking utensils and board together. They wanted to buy coffee pot and dishes, frying pans etc. I though we had better buy cooked food and do without cooking. They couldn't see how to get along without coffee. I said we could live very well for 5 or 6 days on water I finally said I could do without any drink and I concluded to try the experiment so I lived on dry food, such as bread, cheese, smoked fish, etc. without a drop of fluid of any kind for 6 days and I felt no great inconvienience for the time for the want of drink, but I believe it was the cause of my sore mouth a week or two after I rested in Nashville about a week then took deck passage again down the Cumberland river and up to Ohio to Cincinnata where I bought some maps and sold around Cincinnatta until I could order some maps and charts from NewYork, which I received in a few weeks. Then I went up the Ohio River to Bordersville in Virginia where I began to walk toward New York and sell maps on the way. I think it was in March 1850 I put in the following summer selling maps through Virginia, Maryland, Deleware, Penn., New York, New Jersey, and arrived in New York about the beginning of October following as near as I can remember. I sizzaged all the way on foot to within 50 miles of New York City. I struck on my way the Kanacoha River Charlestown the Hawks Nest, Creenbria Co. the Natural Bridge, Lexington, Stanton, Harrisburg, Wood Stock, Winchester, Charleston, Harpers Ferry, Lauden Company, Faerpox Co., Mt. Vernon in Virginia, Baltimore, Philadelphia, New York. A good way to find out how large a state is is to walk over it. It was pretty hard work to sell maps on foot from house to house but I enjoyed the trip very much. I enjoyed the scenery of the country and I liked the people who were generally kind and hospitable. I made my journey and made fair wages and it was a good experience, although my land purchase and land hunt was a failure.

After getting back to New York I called on Arnold Buffern and Co., 11 Park Row, New York, and told him what I found out about my Tenn. land and he paid me back $50.00 of the $75.00 which I paid down and we played quit. Having had success in selling maps I concluded continuing in the business and also concluded to invite my brother Albert to join me in Providence R.I. and we go South and sell. In the meantime I took out maps and went up the Hudson River to Vermont and across the state East by way of Mt. Tabor and Wood Stock to the New Hampshire line all on foot. Then I took the cars for Providence where I met Albert. Thence we went to New York and took out maps and went South into New Jersey and began to sell. After this our cousin Samuel Sevey came out and joined us in the business and we distributed maps, charts, and pictures through the country about Philadelphia, Baltimore, Washington, Northern Virginia, and Maryland. Sevey worked with us some 2 or 3 months then went back to Boston. Albert worked with me some 8 or 9 months and concluded to buy the little farm of me for which he paid me $400 and he went back to Maine and went to farming. I continued map selling until the spring of 1852 when I concluded to go to Iowa by the way of Cumberland and Cincinnata, St. Louis and landed in Keokuk, Iowa, in June 1852. I walked from Keokuk to Fairfield where the United States land Office was. In the next winter I bought 240 acres adjoining my other land. I entered my first land in Henry Co. I think in July 1852. I then looked about the county and sold maps a few weeks, went up to Muscatine from there I went down the Mississippi River by steam boat to Burlington. By this time I had made up my mind to go to work on my land so I ordered a cart made to be used with oxen on the farm. I bought a sythe a rake and pitchfork and walked back to my land and carried my tools about 30 miles and began to mow some hay as I was intending to buy some young cattle which I did the next winter. I paid $6.00 a head for some pretty good spring calves 11 head from Mr. George Ramsey, East of London. I bought other young cattle until I had about 36 head before spring and fed them on the hay I put up. I boarded with James Marting about 2 and 1/2 miles North of my place. This was the nearest house to my place. Mr. Samuel Andrews lived the next nearest about 3 miles North Westerly. The nearest house on the East was Carson and the Jervises about 5 miles along the Virginia Grove. The nearest house South was Mr. Barter about 6 miles. The village of New London was nearly 11 miles South. Mt. Pleasant about 15 miles South West. Mr. Syp was the nearest neighbor in that direction about 10 miles from my place.

This was situated in a beautiful gentle rolling prairie no timber within 5 miles but about 200 acres on Crooked Creek about 1 1/2 miles from where I built my first house, Virginia Grove on the North East 5 miles in sight. All else was prairie grass, thousands of tons of it. How I loved to mow it down, dry it and stack it.

There is a great many things and happenings pleasure and pains all along journeys through life I would like to write about but time will not permit and I will have to content myself with the mention of a very few. I have been very industrious and saving. I was determined to make a home and save some property and have a farm before I married. I have always enjoyed my labor what ever I done. When I went to sea, when I cut stone, when I cut ice, or sold maps or cut hay. I was happy and especially was happy when I secured a thousand acres of as fine land nearly as I ever saw and had it paid for.

I regard labor as one of the greatest blessings that nature bestowed on man kind or any other creature. I have done a great deal of work. I have made 13 farms I have raised thousands of tons of feed and food for man and beast, such as grain, hay, beef, pork, fowels, vegetables, fruit, butter, eggs, honey to supply the wants of my fellow man. Labor has been no punishment for me for partaking of the fruit of knowledge work is pleasure, knowledge is power. Labor and knowledge enable us to make an honest living and be at rest when we die. Now in the fall of 1852 after putting up some hay and buildings a little house 14 feet square I went back to Maine and made a short visit. I went there by finishing my maps came back to Henry Co. Iowa bought a little more land and on the 17 day of April I married Mary F. Clough, Daughter of John and Grace Morley. We moved into our house and began to improve our house and began to improve our land as fast as we could, though it was a slow process when timber was scarce and 6 miles away and our principal market town was Burlington near 30 miles away and our team was made up of young wild steers. In 2 1/2 years we got our timber stone and lumber and built a good substantial house 16 by 18 feet. and with a good cellar under it walled with rock and a chamber (small room above). Then we hauled the first house to within 10 ft. of the new one and built a room between them, then we had a house with 3 rooms, a cellar and chamber. Soon after this a portable circular saw mill come into the neighborhood of my 20 acres of timber in Virginia Grove about 6 miles from home and we went to work cutting logs and hauling them to mill and sawed out a frame for a barn 38 by 44 posts 16 ft. high and brought boards from Burlington and built a most substanial barn. I done nearly all the chopping, hauling, quarrying, and digging for those buildings with my own hands, and with steers to haul. I also fenced ground fast as I could but it was 3 or 4 years before I raised much grain. In the mean time I made good use of the prairie grass and hay. We continued to improve our land and farm and sell a piece of land once in a while for over 11 years when in the summer of 1864 I sold the last 1/2 section (320 a.) and my 30 acres of timber in Virginia Grove for $7500. In the spring of 1863 I began to build a good substanial house 30 by 40 put a good cellar under all with rock wall and was plastering it when I sold so I finished the house and did not move into it. The sales of all the tract of land I had here amounted to $12,000 including my improvements.

In September 1864 I made a sale of personal property and moved to Union County Iowa where I had previously bought of the United States 2 sections and one sixteenth of a section.

We arrived in Union Co. October 1, 1864. We brought 5 children with us to this county and moved into a spare house of Uncle Daniel Clough 5 miles from where we built our home where I now live. The county was very new and scarsely settled. No lumber to be had I went to work dug out rock in the bank of 12 mile creek for a cellar, before the ground froze and hauled them to our place ready to make a cellar in the spring, then to get lumber to build I logged on shares of Uncle John Cloughs land and hauled them to Kentreis and Shepards mill about 1 1/2 miles away and gave 1/2 the logs at the mill. During the winter and spring of that year I got the logs sawed and lumber hauled to my place and soon as the frost was out the ground, dug a cellar and laid up the wall and put the house during the summer and fall and moved in just a year after we arrived in the county. The house was 18 by 24 but substantially built. Shooted and shingled from the ground up all in one room, but not plastered. I filled the cracks with morter and it was quite comfortable. We lived in it about 6 years, by which time built another house

30 by 40 ft. put a cellar under all with rock wall. It will be noticed it took me a whole year to get our first house up including the breaking of about 30 a. of ground and putting up about 10 tons of hay and tending my family. Everything was wide apart from where I built to the timber, and mill was about 6 miles. From the mill to my farm it was 5 miles from where I lived to the quarry then on to my farm was 4 miles. So to complete the circle was about 18 miles more or less and to this I had to cross 5 streams that was unfortable often and in crossing 12 mile creek at one time I got the best horse I ever owned drowned. I paid 15¢ a lb. for nails to build my first stone house in this county. I paid $8.00 a barrel for salt, $6.00 a 100 for flour and went to Winterset in Madison Co. for it. I paid $1.00 a bu. for corn and 50¢ a dozen for sheaf oats of Levi Right. It may be seen that it took money as well as time to make a home in this new county at that time. But we lived through all and enjoyed ourselves nicely.

In the fall of 1865 October 1 we moved into our house and went on to improve our land as fast as we could by fencing and building I bought timber on Grand River some of it 6 and some 3 miles East of our place to fence and build with. I fenced with nails that I made myself, and hauled them mostly with oxen. I fenced 9 farms with rails and 4 with posts and barb wire.

I improved 13 farms in Iowa the smallest 40 acres 2 of them 160 acres. Three of them were 40 acres each the rest were 80 acres each. I build 10 dwelling houses on our land. Two of them were 30 by 40 ft. each they were built on the 160 acre farms. They had good cellars under all with good rock wall. These houses were most substantially built and finished through out. The farm on which I live in Union Co. Iowa has 3 good substantial barns 2 good wagon houses and corn cribs combined and other buildings to the number of 15 good substantial buildings. As I would get my lands inclosed with rails, I would plant hedge inside untill I have made about 7 miles of good Osage hedge fence. Much of the fencing and building material was hauled 10 miles and some of it 13 miles from my timber to the farms. I believe all the hauling of timber, stone and sand to make all of these improvements would average as much as 7 miles. Some sand I hauled 5 miles. Some of the long timbers for barns which were pine I hauled 30 miles. All the fencing was got out of my native timber which I chopped, split and hauled myself. My boys helped me some I hired very little. I have made 5 cellars all walled with rock. I have made 14 good wells on the land all walled with rock which I quarried and hauled myself. I did all the walling of these walls and cellars and did most of the digging myself. Beside this improving of land we have done a lot of farming. We have raised thousands of tons of good things to feed and eat: wheat, corn, oats, and other grains, beef, pork, mutton, poultry, vegetables, fruits, honey, butter, eggs, etc. Besides this work I have done a considerable business in the way of entering land and selling it, paying taxes and loaning money sometimes at a profit sometimes a loss. On the whole I have done moderatly well. On the whole I have enjoyed my labor and been happy and believe I have done some good in the world. We have had 13 children they are all living this 9th day of March 1900. When I look back over our work that my wife and I have done I wonder how we could have done so much and have done it so well.

Having arrived at the age of 75 years and work becoming so hard and my children having all left us but 2 and they are not likely to stay much longer. I concluded to sell our farm and home and stock and tools and go to some small town where we could live comfortably rest from our labors. So we advertised a two day sale on the 17 and 18 days of October 1899. We sold our personal property on the 18 and the farm the 17. The personal property brought about $3,200. The 160 acre farm was bid off by Ed Sherwood but was not taken and was afterward sold to Lew Taylor for $8,000 and we moved March 5, 1900, and we moved to Arispe Union Co., Iowa where we had previously bought a house and lot for $500 where with some addition and repairs we have a good home and not much work to do. This 28 day of October 1901.

---

Source: *Annals of Iowa,* vol. 39 (Spring 1969), pp. 604–619.

## Document 2. The First Official Investigation of Labor Conditions in Massachusetts, 1845

Massachusetts House Document, No. 50, March 1845.

The Special Committee to which was referred sundry petitions relating to the hours of labor, have considered the same and submit the following Report:

The first petition which was referred to your committee, came from the city of Lowell, and was signed by Mr. John Quincy Adams Thayer, and 850 others, "peaceable, industrious, hard working men and women of Lowell." The petitioners declare that they are confined "from 13 to 14 hours per day in unhealthy apartments," and are thereby "hastening through pain, disease and privation, down to a premature grave." They therefore ask the Legislature "to pass a law providing that 10 hours shall constitute a day's work," and that no corporation or private citizen "shall be allowed, except in cases of emergency, to employ one set of hands more than 10 hours per day."

The second petition came from the town of Fall River, and is signed by John Gregory and 488 others. These petitioners ask for the passage of a law to constitute "10 hours a day's work in all corporations created by the Legislature."

The third petition signed by Samuel W. Clark and 500 others, citizens of Andover, is of precisely the same words as the one from Fall River.

The fourth petition is from Lowell, and is signed by James Carle and 300 others. The petitioners ask for the enactment of a law making 10 hours a day's work, where no specific agreement is entered into between the parties.

The whole number of names on the several petitions is 2,139, of which 1,151 are from Lowell. A very large proportion of the Lowell petitioners are females. Nearly one half of the Andover petitioners are females. The petition from Fall River is signed exclusively by males.

In view of the number and respectability of the petitioners who had brought their grievances before the Legislature, the Committee asked for and obtained leave of the House to send for "persons and papers," in order that they might enter into an examination of the matter, and report the result of their examination to the Legislature as a basis for legislative action, should any be deemed necessary.

On the 13th of February, the Committee held a session to hear the petitioners from the city of Lowell. Six of the female and three of the male petitioners were present, and gave in their testimony.

The first petitioner who testified was Eliza R. Hemmingway. She had worked 2 years and 9 months in the Lowell Factories; 2 years in the Middlesex, and 9 months in the Hamilton Corporations. Her employment is weaving—works by the piece. The Hamilton Mill manufactures cotton fabrics. The Middlesex, woollen fabrics. She is now at work in the Middlesex Mills, and attends one loom. Her wages average from $16 to $23 a month exclusive of board. She complained of the hours of labor being too many, and the time for meals too limited. In the summer season, the work commenced at 5 o'clock, A.M., and continued till 7 o'clock, P.M., with half an hour for breakfast and three quarters of an hour for dinner. During eight months of the year, but half an hour is allowed for dinner. The air in the room she considered not to be wholesome. There were 293 small lamps and 61 large lamps lighted in the room in which she worked, when evening work is required. These lamps are also lighted sometimes in the morning. About 130 females, 11 men, and 12 children (between ages 11 and 14) work in the room with her. She thought the children enjoyed about as good health as children generally do. The children worked but 9 months out of 12. The other 3 months they must attend school. Thinks that there is no day when there are less than six of the females out of the mill from sickness. Has known as many as 30. She, herself, is out quite often, on account of sickness. There was more sickness in the Summer, than in the Winter months; though in the Summer, lamps are not lighted. She thought there was a general desire among the females to work but 10 hours, regardless of pay. Most of the girls are from the country, who work in Lowell Mills. The average time which they remain there is about three years. She knew one girl who had worked there 14 years. Her health was poor when she left. Miss Hemmingway said her health is better where she now worked, than it was when she worked on the Hamilton Corporation. She knew of one girl who last winter went into the mill at half past 4 o'clock, A.M., and worked til half past 7 o'clock, P.M. She did so to make more money. She earned from $25 to $30 per month. There is always a large number of girls at the gate wishing to get in before the bell rings. On the Middlesex Corporation one fourth part of the females go into the mill before they are obliged to. They do this to make more wages. A large number come to Lowell to make money to aid their parents who are poor. She knew of many cases where married women came to Lowell and worked in the mills to assist their husbands to pay for their farms. The moral character of the operatives is good. There was only one American female in the room with her who could not write her name.

Miss Sarah G. Bagley said she had worked in the Lowell Mills eight years and a half, six years and a half on the Hamilton Corporation, and two years on the Middlesex. She is a weaver, and works by the piece. She worked in the mills three years before her health began to fail. She is a native of New Hampshire, and went home six weeks during the summer. Last year she was out of the mill a third of the time. She thinks the health of the operatives is not so good as the health of females who do house-work or millinery business. The chief evil, so far as health is concerned, is the shortness of time allowed for meals. The next evil is the length of time employed—not giving them time to cultivate their minds. She spoke of the high moral and intellectual character of the girls. That many were engaged as teachers in the Sunday schools. That many attended the lectures of the Lowell Institute; and she thought, if more time was allowed, that more lectures would be given and more girls attend. She thought that the girls generally were favorable to the 10 hour system. She had presented a petition, same as the one before the Committee, to 132 girls, most of whom said they would prefer to work but 10 hours. In a pecuniary point of view, it would be better, as their health would be improved. They would have more time for sewing. Their intellectual, moral and religious habits would also be benefited by the change. Miss Bagley said, in addition to her labor in the mills, she had kept evening school during the winter months, for four years, and thought that this extra labor must have injured her health.

Miss Judith Payne testified that she came to Lowell 16 years ago, and worked a year and a half at the Merrimack Cotton Mills, left there on account of ill health, and remained out over seven years. She was sick most of the time she was out. Seven years ago she went to work in the Boott Mills, and has remained there ever since; works by the piece. She has lost, during the last seven years, about one year from ill health. She is a weaver, and attends three looms. Last pay-day she drew $14.66 for five weeks work; this was exclusive of board. She was absent during the five weeks but half a day. She says there is a very general feeling of favor of the 10 hour system among the operatives. She attributes her ill health to the long hours of labor, the shortness of time for meals, and the bad air of the mills. She had never spoken to Mr. French, the agent, or to the overseer of her room, in relation to these matters. She could not say that more operatives died in Lowell than other people.

Miss Olive J. Clark is employed on the Lawrence Corporation; has been there five years; makes about $1.62 1/2 per week, exclusive of board. She has been home to New Hampshire to school. Her health never was good. The work is not laborious; can sit down about a quarter of the time. About 50 girls work in the spinning room with her, three of whom signed the petition. She is in favor of the 10 hour system, and thinks that the long hours had an effect upon her health. She is kindly treated by her employers. There is hardly a week in which there is not some one out on account of sickness. Thinks the air is bad, on account of the small particles of cotton which fly about. She has never spoken with the agent or overseer about working only 10 hours.

Miss Cecilia Phillips has worked four years in Lowell. Her testimony is similar to that given by Miss Clark.

Miss Elizabeth Rowe has worked in Lowell 16 months, all the time on the Lawrence Corporation, came from Maine, she is a weaver, works by the piece, runs four looms. "My health," she says, "has been very good indeed since I worked there, averaged $3 a week since I have been there besides my board; have heard very little about the hours of labor being too long." She consented to have her name put on the petition because Miss Phillips asked her to. She would prefer to work only 10 hours. Between 50 and 60 work in the room with her. Her room is better ventilated and more healthy than most others. Girls who wish to attend lectures can go out before the bell rings; my overseer lets them go, also Saturdays they go out before the bell rings. It was her wish to attend four looms. She has a sister who has worked in the mill seven years. Her health is very good. Don't know that she has ever been out on account of sickness. The general health of the operatives is good. Have never spoken to my employers about the work being too hard, or the hours too long. Don't know any one who has been hastened to a premature grave by factory labor. I never attended any of the lectures in Lowell on the 10 hour system. Nearly all the female operatives in Lowell work by the piece; and of the petitioners who appeared before the Committee, Miss Hemmingway, Miss Bagley, Miss Payne, and Miss Rowe work by the piece, and Miss Clark and Miss Phillips by the week.

Mr. Gilman Gale, a member of the city council, and who keeps a provision store, testified that the short time allowed for meals he thought the greatest evil. He spoke highly of the character of the operatives and of the agents; also of the boarding houses and public schools. He had two children in the mills who enjoyed good health. The mills are kept clean and as well ventilated as it is possible for them to be.

Mr. Herman Abbott has worked in the Lawrence Corporation 13 years. Never heard much complaint among the girls about the long hours, never heard the subject spoken of in the mills. Does not think it would be satisfactory to the girls to work only 10 hours, if their wages were to be reduced in proportion. Forty-two girls work in the room with him. The girls often get back to the gate before the bell rings.

Mr. John Quincy Adams Thayer has lived in Lowell for four years, "Works at the physical labor in the summer season, and mental labor in the winter." Has worked in the big machine shop 24 months, on and off; never worked in the cotton or woollen mill; thinks that the mechanics in the machine shop are not so healthy as in other shops; nor so intelligent as the other classes in Lowell. He drafted the petition. Has heard many complain of the long hours.

Mr. S. P. Adams, a member of the House from Lowell, said he worked in the machine shop, and the men were as intelligent as any other class, and enjoyed as good health as any persons who work in-doors. The air in the shop is as good as in any shop. About 350 hands work there, about half a dozen of whom are what is called 10 hour men; they all would be 10 hour men if they could get as good pay.

The only witnesses whom the Committee examined, whose names were not on the petition, were Mr. Adams and Mr. Isaac Cooper, a member of the House from Lowell, and also has worked as an overseer in the Lawrence cotton mills for nine years. His evidence was very full. He gave it as his opinion that the girls in the mills enjoyed the best health, for the reason that they rise early, go to bed early, and have three meals regular. In his room there are 60 girls, and since 1837, has known of only one girl who went home from Lowell and died. He does not find that those who stay the longest in the mill grow sickly and weak. The rooms are heated by steampipes, and the temperature of the rooms is regulated by a thermometer. It is so he believes in all the mills. The heat of the room varies from 62 to 68 degrees.

The above testimony embraces all the important facts which are elicited from the persons who appeared before the Committee.

On Saturday the 1st of March, a portion of the Committee went to Lowell to examine the mills, and to observe the general appearance of the operatives therein employed. They arrived at Lowell after an hour's ride upon the railroad. They first proceeded to the Merrimack Cotton Mills, in which are employed usually 1,200 females and 300 males. They were permitted to visit every part of the works and to make whatever inquiries they pleased of the persons employed. They found every apartment neat and clean, and the girls, so far as personal appearance went, healthy and robust, as girls are in our country towns.

The Committee also visited the Massachusetts and Boott Mills, both of which manufacture cotton goods. The same spirit of thrift and cleanliness, of personal comfort and contentment, prevailed there. The rooms are large and well lighted, the temperature comfortable, and in most of the window sills were numerous shrubs and plants, such as geraniums, roses, and numerous varieties of cactus. These were the pets of the factory girls, and they were to the Committee convincing evidence of the elevated moral tone and refined taste of the operatives.

The Committee also visited the Lowell and the Middlesex mills; in the first of which carpets are manufactured, and in the second, broadcloths, cassimeres, etc. These being woolen mills, the Committee did not expect to find that perfect cleanliness which can be and has been attained in cotton mills. It would, however, be difficult to institute a comparison between the mills on this point, or to suggest an improvement. Not only is the interior of the mills kept in the best order, but great regard has been paid by many of the agents to the arrangement of the enclosed grounds. Grass plats have been laid out, trees have been planted, and fine varieties of flowers in their season, are cultivated within the factory grounds. In short, everything in and about the mills, and the boarding houses appeared, to have for its end, health and comfort. The same remark would apply to the city generally. Your committee returned fully satisfied, that the order, decorum, and general appearance of things in and about the mills, could not be improved by any suggestion of theirs, or by any act of the Legislature.

During our short stay in Lowell, we gathered many facts, which we deem of sufficient importance to the state in this report, and first, in relation to the Hours of Labor.

From Mr. Clark, the agent of the Merrimack Corporation, we obtained the following table of the time which the mills run during the year.

Begin work. From 1st May to 31st August, at 5 o'clock. From 1st September to 30th April, as soon as they can see.

Breakfast. From 1st November to 28th February, before going to work. From 1st March to 31st of March, at 7 1/2 o'clock. From 1st April to 19th September, at seven o'clock. From 20th September to 31st October, at 7 1/2 o'clock. Return in half an hour.

Dinner. Throughout the year at 12 1/2 o'clock. From 1st May to 31st August, return in 45 minutes. From 1st September to 30th April, return in 30 minutes.

Quit work. From 1st May to 31st August, at 7 o'clock. From 1st September to 19th September, at dark. From 20th September to 19th March, at 7 1/2 o'clock. From 20th March to 30th April, at dark.

Lamps are never lighted on Saturday evenings. The above is the time which is kept in all the mills in Lowell, with a slight difference in the machine shop; and it makes the average daily time throughout the year, of running the mills, to be 12 hours and 10 minutes.

There are four days in the year which are observed as holidays, and on which the mills are never put in motion. These are Fast Day, Fourth of July, Thanksgiving Day, and Christmas Day. These make one day more than is usually devoted to pastime in any other place in New England. The following table shows the average hours of work per day throughout the year in the Lowell Mills:

|  | Hours | Minutes |  | Hours | Minutes |
|---|---|---|---|---|---|
| January | 11 | 24 | July | 12 | 45 |
| February | 12 | — | August | 12 | 45 |
| March* | 11 | 52 | September | 12 | 23 |
| April | 13 | 31 | October | 12 | 10 |
| May | 12 | 45 | November | 11 | 56 |
| June | 12 | 45 | December | 11 | 24 |

*The hours of labor on the 1st of March are less than in February, even though the days are a little longer, because 30 minutes are allowed for breakfast from the 1st of March to the 1st of September.

Source: Massachusetts *House Document* No. 50 (March 1845).

# Document 3. The Slave Regime

The next two readings are from a classic description of the antebellum South, Frederick Law Olmsted's *The Cotton Kingdom: A Traveler's Observation on Cotton and Slavery in The American Slave States*, first published in 1861. The first tells of a Georgia rice plantation; the second of a large inland cotton plantation.

### A Georgia Rice Plantation

After passing through tool-rooms, corn-rooms, mule-stables, store-rooms, and a large garden in which vegetables to be distributed among the negroes, as well as for the family, are grown, we walked to the riceland. It is divided by embankments into fields of about 20 acres each, but varying somewhat in size, according to the course of the river. The arrangements are such that each field may be flooded independently of the rest, and they are subdivided by open ditches into rectangular plats of a quarter acre each. We first proceeded to where 20 or 30 women and girls were engaged in raking together, in heaps and winrows, the stubble and rubbish left on the field after the last crop, and burning it. The main object of this operation is to kill all the seeds of weeds, or of rice, on the ground. Ordinarily it is done by tasks—a certain number of the small divisions of the field being given to each hand to burn in a day; but owing to a more than usual amount of rain having fallen lately, and some other causes, making the work harder in some places than others, the women were now working by the day, under the direction of a "driver," a Negro man, who walked about among them, taking care that they left nothing unburned. Mr. X. inspected the ground they had gone over, to see whether the driver had done his duty. It has been sufficiently well burned, but not more than a quarter as much ground had been gone over, he said, as was usually burned in task-work, and he thought they had been very lazy, and reprimanded them. The driver made some little apology, but the women offered no reply, keeping steadily and, it seemed, sullenly, on at their work.

In the next field, 20 men, or boys, for none of them looked as if they were full-grown, were ploughing, each with a single mule, and a light, New-York-made plough. The soil was friable, the ploughing easy, and the mules proceeded at a smart pace; the furrows were straight, regular, and well turned. Their task was nominally an acre and a quarter a day; somewhat less actually, as the measure includes the space occupied by the ditches, which are two to three feet wide, running around each quarter of an acre. The ploughing gang was superintended by a driver, who was provided with a watch; and while we were looking at them he called out that it was 12 o'clock. The mules were immediately taken from the ploughs, and the plough-boys mounting them, leapt the ditches, and cantered off to the stables, to feed them. One or two were ordered to take their ploughs to the blacksmith, for repairs.

The ploughmen got their dinner at this time: those not using horses do not usually dine till they have finished their tasks; but this, I believe, is optional with them. They commence work, I was told, at sunrise, and at about eight o'clock have breakfast brought to them in the field, each hand having left a bucket with the cook for that purpose. All who are working in connection, leave their work together, and gather about a fire, where they generally spend about half an hour. The provisions furnished, consist mainly of meal, rice, and vegetables, with salt and molasses, and occasionally bacon, fish and coffee. The allowance is a peck of meal, or an equivalent quantity of rice per week, to each working hand, old or young, besides small stores. Mr. X. says that he has lately given a less amount of meat than is now usual on plantations, having observed that the general health of the Negroes is not as good as formerly, when no meat at all was customarily given them. (The general impression among planters is, that the Negroes work much better for being supplied with three or four pounds of bacon a week.)

Leaving the rice-land, we went next to some of the upland fields, where we found several other gangs of Negroes at work; one entirely of men engaged in ditching; another of women, and another of boys and girls, "listing" an old cornfield with hoes. All of them were working by task, and were overlooked by Negro drivers. They all laboured with greater rapidity and cheerfulness than any slaves I have before seen; and the women stuck their hoes as if they were strong, and well able to engage in muscular labour. . . . The dress of most was uncouth and cumbrous, dirty and ragged; reefed up, as I had once before described, at the hips, so as to show their heavy legs, wrapped around with a piece of old blanket, in lieu of leggings or stockings. Most of them worked with bare arms, but wore strong shoes on their feet, and hankerchiefs on their heads; some of them were smoking, and each gang had a fire burning on the ground near where they were at work, but which to light their pipes and warm their breakfast. Mr. X. said this was always their custom, even in the summer. To each gang a boy or girl was also attached, whose business it was to bring water for them to drink, and to go for anything required by the driver. The drivers would frequently call back a hand to go over again some piece of his or her task that had not been worked to his satisfaction, and were constantly calling to one or another, with a harsh and peremptory voice, to strike harder, or hoe deeper, and otherwise taking care that the work was well done. Mr. X. asked if Little Sam ("Tom's Sue's Sam") worked yet with the "three-quarter" hands, and learning that he did, ordered him to put with the full hands, observing that though rather short, he was strong and stout, and, being 20 years old, well able to do a man's work.

The field-hands were all divided into four classes, according to their physical capacities. The children beginning as "quarter-hands," advancing to "half-hands," and then to "three-quarter hands"; and, finally, when mature, and able-bodied, healthy, and strong, to "full hands." As they decline in strength, from age, sickness, or other cause, they retrograde in the scale, and proportionately less labour is required of them. Many, of naturally weak frame, never are put among the full hands. Finally, the aged are left out at the annual classification, and no more regular field-work is required of them, although they are generally provided with some light, sedentary occupation. I saw one old woman picking "tailings" of rice out of a heap of chaff, an occupation at which she was probably not earning her salt. Mr. X. told me she was a native African, having been brought when a girl from the Guinea coast. . . .

The field-hands are nearly always worked in gangs, the strength of a gang varying according to the work that engages it; usually it numbers 20 or more, and is directed by a driver. As on most large plantations, whether of rice or cotton, in eastern Georgia and South Carolina, nearly all ordinary and regular work is performed by tasks: that is to say, each hand has his labour for the day marked out before him, and can take his own time to do it in. For instance, in making drains in light, clean meadow land, each man or woman of the full hands is required to dig 1,000 cubic feet; in swamp-land that is being prepared for rice culture, where there are not many stumps, the task for a ditcher is 500 feet: while in a very strong cypress swamp, only 200 feet is required; in hoeing rice, a certain number of rows, equal to one-half or two-thirds of an acre, according to the condition of the land; in sowing rice (strewing in drills), two acres; in reaping rice (if it stands well), three-quarters of an acre; or sometimes a gang will be required to reap, tie in sheaves, and carry to the stack-yard the produce of a certain area, commonly equal to one fourth the number of acres that there are hands working together. Hoeing cotton, corn, or potatoes; one half to one acre. Threshing; 500 to 600 sheaves. In ploughing rice land (light, clean, mellow soil) with a yoke of oxen, one acre a day, including the ground lost in and near the drains—the oxen being changed at noon. A cooper, also, for instance, is required to make barrels at a rate of 18 a week. Drawing staves, 500 a day. Hoop poles, 120. Squaring timber, 100 ft. Laying worm-fence, 50 panels per hand. Post and rail do., posts set 2 1/2 to 3 ft. deep. 9 ft. apart, 9 or 10 panels per hand. In getting fuel from the woods, (pine, to be cut and split,) one cord is the task for a day. In "mauling rails," the taskman selecting the trees (pine) that he judges will split easiest, 100 a day, ends not sharpened.

These are the tasks for first-class able-bodied men; they are lessened by one quarter for three-quarter hands, and proportionately for the lighter classes. In allotting the tasks, the drivers are expected to put the weaker hands where (if there is any choice in the appearance of the ground, as where certain rows in hoeing corn would be less weedy than others), they will be favoured.

These tasks certainly would not be considered excessively hard, by a northern labourer; and, in point of fact, the more industrious and active hands finish them often by two o'clock. I saw one or two leaving the field soon after one o'clock, several about two; and between three and four, I met a dozen women and several men coming home to their cabins having finished their day's work.

Under this "organization of Labour," most of the slaves work rapidly and well. In nearly all ordinary work, custom has settled the extent of the task, and it is difficult to increase it. The driver who marks it out, has to remain on the ground until it is finished, and has no interest in overmeasuring it; and if it should be systematically increased very much, there is danger of a general stampede to the "swamp"—a danger the slave can always hold before his master's cupidity. In fact, it is looked upon in this region as a proscriptive right of the Negroes to have this incitement to diligence offered them; and the man who denied it, or who attempted to lessen it, would, it is said, suffer in his reputation, as well as experience much annoyance from the obstinate "rascality" of his Negroes. Notwithstanding this, I have heard a man assert, boastingly, that he made his Negroes habitually perform double the customary tasks. Thus we get a glimpse again of the black side. If he is allowed the power to do this, what may not a man do?

It is the driver's duty to make the tasked hands do their work well. If, in their haste to finish it, they neglect to do it properly, he "sets them back," so that carelessness will hinder more than it will hasten the completion of their tasks.

In the selection of drivers, regard seems to be had to size and strength—at least, nearly all the drivers I have seen are tall and strong men—but a great deal of judgment, requiring greater capacity of mind than the ordinary slave is often supposed to be possessed of, is certainly needed in them. A good driver is very valuable and usually holds office for life. His authority is not limited to the direction of labour in the field, but extends to the general deportment of the Negroes. He is made to do the duties of policeman, and even of police magistrate. It is his duty, for instance, on Mr. X.'s estate, to keep order in the settlement; and, if two persons, men and women, are fighting, it is his duty to immediately separate them, and then to "whip them both."

Before any field of work is entered upon by a gang, the driver who is to superintend them has to measure and stake off the tasks. To do this at all accurately, in irregular-shape fields, must require considerable powers of calculation. A driver, with a boy to set the stakes, I was told, would accurately lay out 40 acres a day, in half-acre tasks. The only instrument used is a five-foot measuring rod. When the gang comes to the field, he points out to each person his or her duty for the day, and then walks about among them, looking out that each proceeds properly. If, after a hard day's labour, he sees that the gang has been overtasked, owing to a miscalculation of the difficulty of the work, he may excuse the completion of the tasks; but he is not allowed to extend them. In the case of uncompleted tasks, the body of the gang begin new tasks the next day, and only a sufficient number are detailed from it to complete during the day, the unfinished tasks of the day before. The relation of the driver to the working hands seems to be similar to that of the boat-swain to the seamen in the navy, or of the sergeant to the privates in the army.

Having generally had long experience on the plantation, the advice of the drivers is commonly taken in nearly all the administration, and frequently they are, de facto, the managers. Orders on important points of the plantation economy, I have heard given by the proprietor directly to them, without the overseer's being consulted or informed of them; and is often left with them to decide when and how long to flow the rice-ground—the proprietor and overseer deferring to their more experienced judgment. When the drivers are discreet, experienced, and trusty, the overseer is frequently employed merely as a matter of form, to comply with the laws requiring the superintendence or presence of a white man among every body of slaves; and his duty is rather to inspect and report than to govern. Mr. X. considers his overseer an uncommonly efficient and faithful one, but he would not employ him, even during the summer, when he is absent for several months, if the law did not require it. He has sometimes left his plantation in care of one of the drivers for a considerable length of time, after having discharged an overseer; and he thinks it has then been quite as well conducted as ever. His overseer consults the drivers on all important points, and is governed by their advice.

Mr. X. said, that though overseers sometimes punished the negroes severely, and otherwise ill-treated them, it is their more common fault to indulge them foolishly in their disposition to idleness, or in other ways to curry favour with them, so they may not inform the proprietor of their own misconduct or neglect. He has his overseer bound to certain rules, by written contract; and it is stipulated that he can discharge at any moment, without remuneration for his loss of time and inconvenience, if he should at any time be dissatisfied with him. One of the rules is, that he shall never punish a Negro with his own hands, and that corporeal punishment, when necessary, shall be inflicted by the drivers. The advantage of this is, that it secures time for deliberation, and prevents punishment being made in sudden passion. His drivers are not allowed to carry their whips with them on the field; so that if the overseer wishes a hand punished, it is necessary to call a driver, and the driver has then to go to his cabin, which is, perhaps, a mile or two distant, to get his whip, before it can be applied.

I asked how often the necessity of punishment occurred.

"Sometimes, perhaps, not once or two or three weeks; then it will seem as if the devil had got into them all, and there is a good deal of it."

As the Negroes finished the labour required of them by Mr. X., at three or four o'clock in the afternoon, they can employ the remainder of the day in labouring for themselves, if they choose. Each family has a half-acre of land allotted to it, for a garden; besides which there is a large vegetable garden, cultivated by a gardener for the plantation, from which they are supplied, to a greater or less extent. They are at liberty to sell whatever they choose from the products of their own garden, and to make what they can by keeping swine and fowls. Mr. X.'s family have no other supply of poultry and eggs than what is obtained by purchase from his own Negroes; they frequently, also, purchase game from them. The only restriction upon their traffic is a "liquor law." They are not allowed to buy or sell ardent spirits. This prohibition, like liquor laws elsewhere, unfortunately, cannot be enforced; and, of late years, grog-shops, at which stolen goods are bought from the slaves, and poisonous liquors—chiefly the worst whisky, much watered and made stupefying by the infusion of tobacco—are clandestinely sold to them, have become an established evil, and the planters find themselves almost powerless to cope with it. They have, here, lately organized an association for this purpose, and have brought several offenders to trial; but, as it is a penitentiary offence, the culprit spares no pains or expense to avoid conviction—and it is almost impossible, in a community of which so large a proportion is poor and degraded, to have a jury sufficiently honest and intelligent to permit the law to be executed.

## A Large Inland Cotton Plantation

It was a first-rate plantation. On the highest ground stood a large and handsome mansion, but it had not been occupied for several years, and it was more than two years since the overseer had seen the owner. He lived several hundred miles away, and the overseer would not believe that I did not know him, for he was a rich man and an honourable, and several times been where I came from—New York.

The whole plantation, including the swamp land around it, and owned with it, covered several square miles. It was four miles from the settlement to the nearest neighbor's house. There were between 13 and 1,400 acres under cultivation with cotton, corn, and other hoed crops, and 200 hogs running at large in the swamp. It was the intention that corn and pork enough should be raised to keep the slaves and cattle. This year, however, it has been found necessary to purchase largely, and such was probably the case, though the overseer intimated the owner had been displeased, and he "did not mean to be caught so bad again."

There were 135 slaves, big and little, of which 67 went to field regularly—equal, the overseer thought, to fully 60 prime hands. Besides these, there were 3 mechanics (blacksmith, carpenter and wheelwright), 2 seamstresses, 1 cook, 1 stable servant, 1 cattle-tender, 1 hog-tender, 1 teamster, 1 house servant (overseer's cook), and one midwife and nurse. These were all first-class hands; most of them would be worth more, if they were for sale, the overseer said, than the best field-hands. There was also a driver of the hoe-gang who did not labour personally, and a foreman of the plough-gang. These two acted as petty officers in the field and alternately in the quarters.

There was a nursery for sucklings at the quarters, and 20 women at this time who left their work four times each day, for half an hour, to nurse their young ones. These women, the overseer counted as half-hands—that is, expected to do half the day's work of a prime field-hand in ordinary condition.

He had just sold a bad runaway to go to Texas, he happened to remark. He was whipping the fellow, when he turned and tried to stab him—then broke from him and ran away. He had him caught almost immediately with the dogs. After catching him, he kept him in irons till he had a chance to sell him. His niggers did not very often run away, he said, because they had found that he was almost sure to catch them. As soon as he saw that one was gone he put the dogs on, and if rain had not just fallen, they would soon find him. Sometimes they did manage to outwit the dogs, but then they almost always kept in the neighborhood, because they did not like to go where they could not sometimes get back to see their families, and he would soon get wind of where they had been; they would come around their quarters to see their families and to get food, and as soon as he knew it he would find their tracks and put the dogs on again. Two months was the longest time any of them ever kept out. He had dogs trained on purpose to run after niggers, and never let out for anything else.

We found in the field 30 ploughs, moving together, turning the earth from the cotton plants, and from 30 to 40 hoers, the latter mainly women, with a black driver walking about among them with a whip, which he often cracked at time, sometimes allowing the lash to fall lightly upon their shoulders. He was constantly urging them also with his voice. All worked very steadily, and though the presence of a stranger on the plantation must have been a most unusual occurrence, I saw none raise or turn their heads to look at me. Each gang was attended by a "water-toter," that of the hoe-gang being a straight, sprightly, plump little black girl, whose picture, as she stood balancing the bucket upon her head, shading her bright eyes with one hand and holding out a calabash with the other to maintain her poise, would have been a worthy study for Murillo.

I asked at what time they began to work in the morning. "Well," said the overseer, "I do better by my niggers than most. I keep 'em right smart at their work while they do work, but I generally knock 'em off at 8 o'clock in the morning, Saturdays, and give 'em all the rest of the day to themselves, and I always give 'em Sundays, the whole day. Pickin time, and when the crop's bad in grass, I sometimes keep 'em to it till about sunset, Saturdays, but I never work 'em Sundays."

"How early do you start them out in the morning, usually?"

"Well, I don't never start my niggers 'fore daylight, 'less 'tis in pickin' time, then maybe I get 'em out a quarter of an hour before. But I keep 'em right smart to work through the day." He showed an evident pride in the vigilance of his driver, and called my attention to the large area of ground already hoed over that morning; well hoed, too, as he said.

"At what time do they eat?" I asked. They ate "their snacks" in their cabins, he said, before they came out in the morning (that is before daylight—the sun rising at this time at a little before 5, and the day dawning, probably, an hour earlier); then at 12 o'clock their dinner was brought to them in a cart—one cart for the plough-gang and one for the hoe-gang. The hoe-gang ate its dinner in the field, and only stopped work long enough to eat it. The plough-gang drove its teams to the "weather houses"—open sheds erected for the purpose of different parts of the plantation, under which were cisterns filled with rain water, from which the water-toters carried drink to those at work. The mules were fed with as much oats (in straw), corn and fodder as they would eat in two hours; this forage having been brought to the weather houses by another cart. The ploughmen had nothing to do but eat their dinner in all this time. All worked as late as they could see to work well, and had no more food nor rest until they returned to their cabins.[2] At half-past nine o'clock the drivers, each on an alternate night, blew a horn, and at 10 visited every to see that its occupants were at rest, and not lurking about and spending their strength in fooleries, and that the fires were safe—a very unusual precaution; the Negroes were generally at liberty after their day's work is done till they are called in the morning. When washing and patching were done, wood hauled and cut for the fires, corn ground, etc., I did not learn: probably all chores not a daily necessity were reserved for Saturday. Custom varies in this respect. In general, with regard to fuel for the cabins, the Negroes are left to look out for themselves, and they often have to go to "the swamp" for it, or at least if it has been hauled to cut it to a convenient size, after their day's work is done. The allowance of food was a peck of corn and four pounds of pork per week, each. When they could not get "greens" (any vegetables) he generally gave them five pounds of pork. They had gardens, and raised a good deal for themselves; they also had fowls, and usually plenty of eggs. He added, "the man who owns this plantation does more for his niggers than any other man I know. Every Christmas he sends me up a $1,000 or $1,500 (equal to $8 or $10 each) worth of molasses and coffee, tobacco, and calico, and Sunday tricks for 'em. Every family on this plantation gets a barrel of molasses at Christmas."[3]

Beside which, the overseer added, they are able, if they choose, to buy certain comforts for themselves—tobacco for instance—with money earned by Saturday

---

[2]This would give at this season hardly less than 16 hours of plodding labour, relieved by but one short interval of rest, during the daylight, for the hoe-gang. It is not improbable. I was accustomed to rise early and ride late, resting during the heat of the day, while in the cotton district, but I always found the Negroes in the field when I first looked out, and generally had to wait for the Negroes to come from the field to have my horse fed when I stopped for the night. I am told, however, and I believe, that it is usual in the hottest weather, to give a rest of an hour or two to all hands at noon. I never happened to see it done. The legal limit for a slave's day's work in South Carolina is 15 hours.

[3]I was told by a gentleman in North Carolina, that the custom of supplying molasses to Negroes in Mississippi, was usually mentioned to those sold away from his part of the country, to reconcile them to go thither.

and Sunday work. Some of them went into the swamps on Sunday, and made boards (which means slabs worked out with no other instrument than an axe). One man sold last year as much as $50 worth.

This was the only large plantation I had an opportunity of seeing at all closely, over which I was not chiefly conducted by an educated gentleman and slave owner, by whose habitual impressions and sentiments my own were probably somewhat influenced. From what I saw in passing, and from what I heard by chance of others, I suppose it to have been a very favourable specimen of those plantations on which the owners do not reside. A merchant of the vicinity recently in New York tells me that he supposes it to be a fair enough example of plantations of its class. There is nothing remarkable in its management, so far as he had heard. When I asked about the molasses and Christmas presents, he said he reckoned the overseer must have rather stretched that part of his story, but the owner was a very good man. A magistrate of the district, who had often been on the plantation, said in answer to an inquiry from me, that the Negroes were very well treated upon it, though he did not think they were extraordinarily so. His comparison was with plantations in general.[4] He also spoke well of the overseer. He had been a long time on this plantation—I think he said ever since it had begun to be cultivated. This is very rare; it was the only case I met with in which the overseer had kept the same place 10 years, and it was a strong evidence of his comparative excellence, that his employer had been so long satisfied with him. Perhaps it was a stronger evidence that the owner of the Negroes was a man of good temper, systematic and thorough in the management of his property.[5]

The condition of the fences, of the mules and tools, and tillage, which would have been considered admirable in the best farming district of New York—the dress of the Negroes and the neatness and spaciousness of their "quarters," which were superior to those of most of the better class of plantations on which the owners reside, all bore testimony to a very unusually prudent and provident policy.

---

Source: Frederick Law Olmstead, *The Cotton Kingdom: A Traveller's Observations on Cotton and Slavery in the American Slave States*.

---

[4]In *De Bow's Resources of the South*, vol. i., p. 150, a table is furnished by a cotton-planter to show that the expenses of raising cotton are "generally greatly underrated." It is to be inferred that they certainly are not underrated in the table. On "a well improved and properly organized plantation," the expense of feeding 100 Negroes, "as deduced from 15 years' experience" of the writer, is asserted in this table to be $750 per annum, or $7.50 each; in this sum is included, however, the expenses of the "hospital and the overseer's table." This is much less than the expense for the same purposes, if the overseer's account was true, of the plantation above described. Clothing, shoes, bedding, sacks for gathering cotton, and so forth, are estimated by the same authority to cost an equal sum—$7.50 for each slave. I had just paid an account on a day labourer on a farm in New York, his board bill, he being a bachelor living at the house of another Irish labourer with a family. The charge is 21 times as large as that set down for the slave.

[5]"I was informed that some successful planters, who held several estates in this neighbourhood (Natchez) made it a rule to change their overseers every year, on the principle that the two years' service system is sure to spoil them."—Russell's *North American: Its Agriculture, etc.*, p. 258.

"Overseers are changed every year; a few remain four or five years, but the average time they remain on the same plantation does not exceed two years."—*Southern Agriculturist*, vol. IV., p. 351.

## EXHIBIT 1A

**Black Population in U.S., for Regions: 1790–1860**

| | Northeast* | | North Central† | | South‡ | |
|---|---|---|---|---|---|---|
| Year | Total | Slave | Total | Slave§ | Total | Slave |
| 1790 | 67,424 | 40,354 | — | — | 689,784 | 657,327 |
| 1800 | 83,066 | 36,370 | 635 | 135 | 918,336 | 857,097 |
| 1810 | 102,237 | 27,081 | 6,934 | 3,304 | 1,268,637 | 1,160,977 |
| 1820 | 110,724 | 18,001 | 18,260 | 11,329 | 1,642,672 | 1,508,692 |
| 1830 | 125,214 | 2,780 | 41,543 | 25,879 | 2,161,885 | 1,980,384 |
| 1840 | 142,324 | 765 | 89,347 | 58,604 | 2,641,977 | 2,427,986 |
| 1850 | 149,762 | 236 | 135,607 | 87,422 | 3,352,198 | 3,116,629 |
| 1860 | 156,001 | 18 | 184,239 | 114,948 | 4,097,111 | 3,838,765 |

*Maine, New Hampshire, Vermont, Massachusetts, Rhode Island, Connecticut, New York, New Jersey, Pennsylvania.

†Ohio, Indiana, Illinois, Michigan, Wisconsin, Minnesota, Iowa, Missouri, North Dakota, South Dakota, Nebraska, Kansas.

‡Delaware, Maryland, District of Columbia, Virginia, North Carolina, South Carolina, Georgia, Florida, Kentucky, Tennessee, Alabama, Mississippi, Arkansas, Louisiana, Texas.

§Virtually all the slaves in the north central region were living in Missouri, which was admitted to the Union as a slave state in 1820.

# EXHIBIT 1B

## Slaves and Slaveholders, by State: 1860

| States | Number of Slaveholders and Slaves | | | | | | | | | | |
| --- | --- | --- | --- | --- | --- | --- | --- | --- | --- | --- | --- |
| | 1 Slave | 2 Slaves | 3 Slaves | 4 Slaves | 5 Slaves | 6 Slaves | 7 Slaves | 8 Slaves | 9 Slaves | 10 and Under 15 | 15 and Under 20 |
| 1 Alabama | 5,607 | 3,663 | 2,805 | 2,329 | 1,986 | 1,729 | 1,411 | 1,227 | 1,036 | 3,742 | 2,164 |
| 2 Arkansas | 281 | 173 | 117 | 88 | 69 | 70 | 50 | 52 | 41 | 99 | 43 |
| 3 Delaware | 237 | 114 | 74 | 51 | 34 | 19 | 15 | 10 | 8 | 17 | 8 |
| 4 Florida | 863 | 568 | 437 | 365 | 285 | 270 | 225 | 186 | 169 | 627 | 349 |
| 5 Georgia | 6,713 | 4,355 | 3,482 | 2,984 | 2,543 | 2,213 | 1,839 | 1,647 | 1,415 | 4,707 | 2,823 |
| 6 Kansas | 2 | — | — | — | — | — | — | — | — | — | — |
| 7 Kentucky | 9,306 | 5,430 | 4,009 | 3,281 | 2,694 | 2,293 | 1,951 | 1,582 | 1,273 | 3,691 | 1,580 |
| 8 Louisiana | 4,092 | 2,573 | 2,034 | 1,536 | 1,310 | 1,103 | 858 | 771 | 609 | 2,065 | 1,157 |
| 9 Maryland | 4,119 | 1,952 | 1,279 | 1,023 | 815 | 666 | 523 | 446 | 380 | 1,173 | 545 |
| 10 Mississippi | 4,856 | 3,201 | 2,503 | 2,129 | 1,809 | 1,585 | 1,303 | 1,149 | 1,024 | 3,432 | 2,057 |
| 11 Missouri | 6,893 | 3,754 | 2,773 | 2,243 | 1,686 | 1,384 | 1,130 | 877 | 640 | 1,734 | 666 |
| 12 North Carolina | 6,440 | 4,017 | 3,068 | 2,546 | 2,245 | 1,887 | 1,619 | 1,470 | 1,228 | 4,044 | 2,029 |
| 13 South Carolina | 3,763 | 2,533 | 1,990 | 1,731 | 1,541 | 1,366 | 1,207 | 1,095 | 973 | 3,334 | 1,876 |
| 14 Tennessee | 7,820 | 4,738 | 3,609 | 3,012 | 2,536 | 2,066 | 1,783 | 1,565 | 1,260 | 3,779 | 1,744 |
| 15 Texas | 4,593 | 2,874 | 2,093 | 1,782 | 1,439 | 1,125 | 928 | 791 | 667 | 2,237 | 1,186 |
| 16 Virginia | 11,085 | 5,989 | 4,474 | 3,807 | 3,233 | 2,824 | 2,393 | 1,984 | 1,788 | 5,686 | 3,088 |
| Total, States | 76,670 | 45,934 | 34,747 | 28,907 | 24,225 | 20,600 | 17,235 | 14,852 | 12,511 | 40,367 | 21,315 |
| *Territories* | | | | | | | | | | | |
| 1 District of Columbia | 654 | 225 | 112 | 72 | 53 | 31 | 24 | 12 | 11 | 20 | 7 |
| 2 Nebraska | 1 | 4 | — | — | — | 1 | — | — | — | — | — |
| 3 Utah | 8 | 2 | — | — | — | — | 1 | — | — | 1 | — |
| Total, Territories | 663 | 231 | 112 | 72 | 53 | 32 | 25 | 12 | 11 | 21 | 7 |
| Total, States and Territories | 77,333 | 46,165 | 34,859 | 28,979 | 24,278 | 20,632 | 17,260 | 14,864 | 12,522 | 40,388 | 21,322 |

**EXHIBIT 1B** (*continued*)

| States | 20 and Under 30 | 30 and Under 40 | 40 and Under 50 | 50 and Under 70 | 70 and Under 100 | 100 and Under 200 | 200 and Under 300 | 300 and Under 500 | 500 and Under 1,000 | 1,000 and Over | Aggregate Holders of Slaves | Total No. of Slaves |
|---|---|---|---|---|---|---|---|---|---|---|---|---|
| 1 Alabama | 2,323 | 1,253 | 768 | 791 | 550 | 312 | 24 | 10 | — | — | 33,730 | 435,080 |
| 2 Arkansas | 35 | 13 | 8 | 6 | 4 | — | — | — | — | — | 1,149 | 111,115 |
| 3 Delaware | — | — | — | — | — | — | — | — | — | — | 587 | 1,798 |
| 4 Florida | 333 | 171 | 99 | 116 | 42 | 45 | 2 | — | — | — | 5,152 | 61,745 |
| 5 Georgia | 2,910 | 1,400 | 739 | 729 | 373 | 181 | 23 | 7 | 1 | — | 41,084 | 462,198 |
| 6 Kansas | — | — | — | — | — | — | — | — | — | — | 2 | 2 |
| 7 Kentucky | 1,093 | 296 | 96 | 51 | 12 | 6 | 1 | — | — | — | 38,645 | 225,483 |
| 8 Louisiana | 1,241 | 695 | 413 | 560 | 469 | 460 | 63 | 20 | 4 | — | 22,033 | 331,726 |
| 9 Maryland | 487 | 179 | 81 | 75 | 24 | 15 | — | 1 | — | — | 13,783 | 87,189 |
| 10 Mississippi | 2,322 | 1,143 | 755 | 814 | 545 | 279 | 28 | 8 | 1 | — | 30,943 | 436,631 |
| 11 Missouri | 349 | 120 | 33 | 26 | 8 | 4 | — | — | — | — | 24,320 | 114,931 |
| 12 North Carolina | 1,977 | 870 | 474 | 423 | 188 | 118 | 11 | 4 | — | — | 34,658 | 331,059 |
| 13 South Carolina | 1,984 | 1,083 | 579 | 710 | 487 | 363 | 56 | 22 | 7 | 1 | 26,701 | 402,406 |
| 14 Tennessee | 1,623 | 643 | 284 | 219 | 116 | 40 | 6 | 1 | — | — | 36,844 | 275,719 |
| 15 Texas | 1,095 | 491 | 241 | 194 | 88 | 52 | 2 | — | — | — | 21,878 | 182,566 |
| 16 Virginia | 3,017 | 1,291 | 609 | 503 | 243 | 105 | 8 | 1 | — | — | 52,128 | 490,865 |
| Total, States | 20,789 | 9,648 | 5,179 | 5,217 | 3,149 | 1,980 | 224 | 74 | 13 | 1 | 383,637 | 3,950,513 |
| *Territories* | | | | | | | | | | | | |
| 1 District of Columbia | 7 | — | — | 1 | — | — | — | — | — | — | 1,229 | 3,185 |
| 2 Nebraska | — | — | — | — | — | — | — | — | — | — | 6 | 15 |
| 3 Utah | — | — | — | — | — | — | — | — | — | — | 12 | 29 |
| Total, Territories | 7 | — | — | 1 | — | — | — | — | — | — | 1,247 | 3,229 |
| Total, States and Territories | 20,796 | 9,648 | 5,179 | 5,218 | 3,149 | 1,980 | 224 | 74 | 13 | 1 | 384,884 | 3,953,742* |

*Number of Slaveholders and Slaves*

*Exclusive of 18 colored apprentices for life (in the State of New Jersey), by the act to abolish slavery, passed April 18, 1846.
Note: In 1860, the Federal Census also recorded 483,620 free blacks. Also note that in 1860, the number of slave holders was approximately 5% of the total Southern white population.
Source: Harold D. Woodman, *Slavery and the Southern Economy* (New York: Harcourt, Brace and World, 1966), pp. 13–15.

# EXHIBIT 2A

## The Labor Force, 1800–1960* (in Thousands)

| Year | Labor Force (10 & Older) | | | Agriculture (10 and older) | Fishing | Mining | Con-struction | Manufacturing | | | Trade | Transport | | Service | |
| | Total | Free | Slave | | | | | Total Persons Engaged | Cotton Textile Wage Earners | Primary Iron & Steel Wage Earners | | Ocean Vessels | Railway | Teachers | Domestics |
|---|---|---|---|---|---|---|---|---|---|---|---|---|---|---|---|
| 1800 | 1,900 | 1,370 | 530 | 1,400 | 5 | 10 | — | — | 1 | 1 | — | 40 | — | 5 | 40 |
| 1810 | 2,330 | 1,590 | 740 | 1,950 | 6 | 11 | — | 75 | 10 | 5 | — | 60 | — | 12 | 70 |
| 1820 | 3,135 | 2,185 | 950 | 2,470 | 14 | 13 | — | — | 12 | 5 | — | 50 | — | 20 | 110 |
| 1830 | 4,200 | 3,020 | 1,180 | 2,965 | 15 | 22 | — | — | 55 | 20 | — | 70 | — | 30 | 160 |
| 1840 | 5,660 | 4,180 | 1,480 | 3,570 | 24 | 32 | 290 | 500 | 72 | 24 | 350 | 95 | 7 | 45 | 240 |
| 1850 | 8,250 | 6,280 | 1,970 | 4,520 | 30 | 102 | 410 | 1,200 | 92 | 35 | 530 | 135 | 20 | 80 | 350 |
| 1860 | 11,110 | 8,770 | 2,340 | 5,880 | 31 | 176 | 520 | 1,530 | 122 | 43 | 890 | 145 | 80 | 115 | 600 |
| 1870 | 12,930 | — | — | 6,790 | 28 | 180 | 780 | 2,470 | 135 | 78 | 1,310 | 135 | 160 | 170 | 1,000 |
| 1880 | 17,390 | — | — | 8,920 | 41 | 280 | 900 | 3,290 | 175 | 130 | 1,930 | 125 | 416 | 230 | 1,130 |
| 1890 | 23,320 | — | — | 9,960 | 60 | 440 | 1,510 | 4,390 | 222 | 149 | 2,960 | 120 | 750 | 350 | 1,580 |
| 1900 | 29,070 | — | — | 11,680 | 69 | 637 | 1,665 | 5,895 | 303 | 222 | 3,970 | 105 | 1,040 | 436 | 1,800 |
| 1910 | 37,480 | — | — | 11,770 | 68 | 1,068 | 1,949 | 8,332 | 370 | 306 | 5,320 | 150 | 1,855 | 595 | 2,090 |
| 1920 | 41,610 | — | — | 10,790 | 53 | 1,180 | 1,233 | 11,190 | 450 | 460 | 5,845 | 205 | 2,236 | 752 | 1,660 |
| 1930 | 48,830 | — | — | 10,560 | 73 | 1,009 | 1,988 | 9,884 | 372 | 375 | 8,122 | 160 | 1,659 | 1,044 | 2,270 |
| 1940 | 56,290 | — | — | 9,575 | 60 | 925 | 1,876 | 11,309 | 400 | 485 | 9,328 | 150 | 1,160 | 1,086 | 2,300 |
| 1950 | 65,470 | — | — | 7,870 | 77 | 901 | 3,029 | 15,648 | (350) | (550) | 12,152 | 130 | 1,373 | 1,270 | 1,995 |
| 1960 | 74,060 | — | — | 5,970 | 45 | 709 | 3,640 | 17,145 | (300) | (530) | 14,051 | 135 | 883 | 1,850 | 2,489 |

*Persons engaged (employees, self-employed, and unpaid family workers), except as specified. Age 10 and over.

Source: Stanley Lebergott, *Manpower in Economic Growth* (New York: McGraw-Hill, 1964), p. 510.

# EXHIBIT 2B

**The Farm Labor Force, 1800–1960\*** (*in Thousands*)

| Year | Total (Age 10 and Over) | Farmers | | | | Laborers* | | | | Percent of Free to Total in Agriculture |
|------|-------------|-------|--------|---------|-------------------|-------|------|-------|------------------|--------------------|
| | | Total | Owners | Tenants | Percent Owners | Total | Free | Slave | Percent Slave | |
| 1800 | 1,400 | 600 | — | — | — | 800 | 310 | 490 | 61 | 65 |
| 1810 | 1,950 | 830 | — | — | — | 1,120 | 415 | 705 | 63 | 74 |
| 1820 | 2,470 | 1,040 | — | — | — | 1,430 | 515 | 915 | 64 | 63 |
| 1830 | 2,965 | 1,235 | — | — | — | 1,730 | 610 | 1,120 | 65 | 62 |
| 1840 | 3,570 | 1,440 | — | — | — | 2,130 | 720 | 1,410 | 66 | 60 |
| 1850 | 4,520 | 1,800 | — | — | — | 2,720 | 850 | 1,870 | 69 | 59 |
| 1860 | 5,880 | 2,540 | — | — | — | 3,340 | 1,120 | 2,220 | 66 | 62 |
| 1870 | 6,790 | 3,130 | — | — | — | 3,660 | — | — | — | — |
| 1880 | 8,920 | 4,300 | 2,980 | 1,320 | 69 | 4,620 | — | — | — | — |
| 1890 | 9,960 | 4,890 | 3,290 | 1,600 | 67 | 5,070 | — | — | — | — |
| 1900 | 11,680 | 5,830 | 3,710 | 2,120 | 64 | 5,850 | — | — | — | — |
| 1910 | 11,770 | 6,230 | 3,870 | 2,360 | 63 | 5,540 | — | — | — | — |
| 1920 | 10,790 | 6,560 | 4,000 | 2,560 | 62 | 4,230 | — | — | — | — |
| 1930 | 10,560 | 6,150 | 3,490 | 2,660 | 57 | 4,410 | — | — | — | — |
| 1940 | 9,575 | 5,480 | 3,330 | 2,150 | 61 | 4,095 | — | — | — | — |
| 1950 | 7,870 | 4,346 | 3,160 | 1,186 | 73 | 3,521 | — | — | — | — |
| 1960 | 5,970 | 2,802 | 2,210 | 592 | 79 | 3,171 | — | — | — | — |

\*Age 10 and over.
Source: Lebergott, "Manpower," p. 511.

# EXHIBIT 2C

**Farm Laborers, Average Monthly Earnings with Board, 1818–1899**

| Region | 1818 | 1826 | 1830 | 1850 | 1860 | 1870 | 1880 | 1890 | 1899 |
|---|---|---|---|---|---|---|---|---|---|
| United States | $ 9.45 | $ 8.83 | $ 8.85 | $10.85 | $13.66 | $16.57 | $11.70 | $13.93 | $14.56 |
| New England | 11.90 | 11.65 | 11.60 | 12.98 | 14.73 | 19.84 | 13.94 | 17.78 | 18.20 |
| Maine | 12.43 | 12.43 | 12.43 | 13.12 | 14.34 | 19.65 | 12.80 | 17.50 | 18.00 |
| New Hampshire | 10.16 | 10.16 | 11.66 | 12.12 | 14.34 | 16.87 | 13.00 | 17.60 | 18.48 |
| Vermont | 10.00 | 10.00 | 10.00 | 13.00 | 14.14 | 20.98 | 14.33 | 17.35 | 18.74 |
| Massachusetts | 13.50 | 13.50 | 12.00 | 13.55 | 15.34 | 22.24 | 15.44 | 18.50 | 18.32 |
| Rhode Island | 11.93 | 11.93 | 11.93 | 13.52 | 16.04 | 17.98 | 14.00 | 18.00 | 18.35 |
| Connecticut | 13.11 | 11.61 | 11.61 | 12.72 | 15.11 | 17.70 | 13.00 | 17.33 | 17.52 |
| Middle Atlantic | 9.82 | 8.38 | 8.52 | 11.17 | 12.75 | 17.89 | 13.71 | 15.76 | 15.98 |
| New York | 10.00 | 8.00 | 8.00 | 11.50 | 13.19 | 18.39 | 13.81 | 16.65 | 17.52 |
| New Jersey | 8.50 | 8.50 | 8.50 | 10.18 | 11.91 | 17.14 | 12.80 | 16.00 | 15.19 |
| Pennsylvania | 11.00 | 9.00 | 9.50 | 10.82 | 12.24 | 17.30 | 13.80 | 14.60 | 14.32 |
| East North Central | 8.86 | 8.73 | 8.73 | 11.44 | 13.79 | 16.94 | 15.48 | 15.92 | 16.90 |
| Ohio | 9.00 | 9.00 | 9.00 | 11.10 | 13.11 | 15.88 | 14.66 | 15.10 | 15.27 |
| Indiana | 9.00 | 9.00 | 9.00 | 10.50 | 13.71 | 17.31 | 14.52 | 14.78 | 15.45 |
| Illinois | 12.00 | 10.00 | 10.00 | 12.55 | 13.72 | 17.67 | 16.25 | 16.35 | 17.76 |
| Michigan | — | — | — | 12.00 | 15.27 | 16.91 | 16.58 | 16.75 | 16.95 |
| Wisconsin | — | — | — | 12.69 | 13.96 | 16.02 | 15.87 | 16.75 | 19.20 |
| West North Central | 10.15 | 10.15 | 10.15 | 12.00 | 13.76 | 17.10 | 14.88 | 15.84 | 18.04 |
| Minnesota | — | — | — | 17.00 | 14.10 | 18.98 | 16.44 | 16.60 | 19.98 |
| Iowa | — | — | — | 11.80 | 13.18 | 17.23 | 16.38 | 17.00 | 19.32 |
| Missouri | 10.15 | 10.15 | 10.15 | 11.81 | 13.63 | 16.13 | 13.34 | 14.00 | 14.57 |
| North Dakota | — | — | — | — | — | — | 19.55 | 17.10 | 21.82 |
| South Dakota | — | — | — | — | — | — | — | — | 20.41 |
| Nebraska | — | — | — | — | 17.45 | 18.81 | 14.53 | 16.60 | 18.87 |
| Kansas | — | — | — | — | 16.12 | 18.04 | 14.06 | 15.05 | 17.46 |
| South Atlantic | 8.10 | 7.18 | 7.16 | 8.20 | 11.08 | 9.95 | 8.81 | 9.46 | 9.32 |
| Delaware | 6.00 | 6.00 | 6.00 | 8.79 | 10.66 | 12.99 | — | 11.15 | 11.98 |
| Maryland | 12.00 | 10.00 | 10.00 | 7.88 | 9.71 | 10.87 | 10.10 | 11.25 | 11.53 |
| Virginia | 6.00 | 6.00 | 6.00 | 8.43 | 11.43 | 9.32 | 8.43 | 9.47 | 10.43 |
| West Virginia | — | — | — | — | — | 15.14 | 11.71 | 12.95 | 13.55 |
| North Carolina | 6.00 | 6.00 | 6.00 | 7.21 | 10.37 | 8.39 | 8.78 | 8.80 | 8.56 |
| South Carolina | 10.00 | 8.00 | 7.00 | 7.72 | 11.37 | 10.33 | 7.95 | 8.62 | 7.34 |
| Georgia | 11.44 | 9.44 | 9.44 | 9.03 | 11.95 | 10.83 | 8.47 | 8.37 | 8.05 |
| Florida | — | — | — | 10.00 | 14.29 | 9.99 | 9.26 | 12.59 | 11.32 |
| East South Central | 10.36 | 9.39 | 9.37 | 9.60 | 14.06 | 12.78 | 10.16 | 10.58 | 10.72 |
| Kentucky | 11.00 | 10.00 | 10.00 | 10.00 | 13.57 | 14.37 | 11.19 | 11.70 | 12.24 |
| Tennessee | 8.50 | 8.50 | 8.50 | 8.67 | 11.94 | 12.86 | 9.58 | 10.12 | 10.33 |
| Alabama | 11.00 | 9.00 | 9.00 | 9.62 | 12.41 | 10.82 | 9.38 | 9.85 | 8.63 |
| Mississippi | 15.00 | 10.00 | 10.00 | 11.00 | 16.66 | 13.38 | 10.24 | 10.50 | 9.27 |
| West South Central | — | — | — | 11.28 | 15.53 | 14.05 | 12.90 | 12.84 | 11.86 |
| Arkansas | — | — | — | 10.63 | 14.25 | 13.52 | 13.03 | 12.55 | 10.54 |
| Louisiana | — | — | — | 12.80 | 17.00 | 14.34 | 12.26 | 11.79 | 10.30 |
| Texas | — | — | — | 12.00 | 16.02 | 14.05 | 13.31 | 13.30 | 12.94 |
| Mountain | — | — | — | — | — | — | 24.74 | 21.67 | 26.33 |
| New Mexico | — | — | — | 6.00 | 14.54 | — | 21.00 | 17.83 | 18.45 |
| Utah | — | — | — | 22.00 | 23.33 | — | 25.00 | 21.00 | 25.72 |

## EXHIBIT 2C (*concluded*)

### Farm Laborers, Average Monthly Earnings with Board, 1818–1899

| Region | 1818 | 1826 | 1830 | 1850 | 1860 | 1870 | 1880 | 1890 | 1899 |
|---|---|---|---|---|---|---|---|---|---|
| Nevada | — | — | — | — | — | — | 35.00 | 23.00 | 31.76 |
| Pacific | — | — | — | 68.00 | 34.16 | 29.19 | 24.77 | 22.64 | 25.10 |
| Washington | — | — | — | — | 43.00 | — | 24.17 | 24.40 | 25.06 |
| Oregon | — | — | — | 75.00 | — | — | 21.60 | 22.00 | 22.89 |
| California | — | — | — | 60.00 | 33.28 | 29.19 | 25.67 | 22.40 | 25.64 |

Source: Lebergott, "Manpower," p. 539.

## EXHIBIT 2D

### Common Laborers, Average Daily Earnings, 1832–1940

| Region | 1832 (with Board) | 1850 (with Board) | 1850 | 1860 | 1869 | 1880 | 1890 (Hourly) | 1919 (Hourly) | 1929 (Hourly) | 1940 |
|---|---|---|---|---|---|---|---|---|---|---|
| United States | $0.52 | $0.61 | $0.87 | $1.06 | $1.55 | $1.23 | $1.46 | $0.41 | $0.44 | $0.51 |
| New England | 0.68 | 0.77 | 1.01 | 1.03 | 1.56 | 1.28 | 1.49 | 0.38 | 0.48 | 0.51 |
| Maine | 0.74 | 0.76 | 1.00 | 1.05 | 1.54 | 1.25 | 1.33 | 0.35 | — | 0.47 |
| New Hampshire | 0.60 | 0.63 | 0.89 | 0.94 | 1.30 | 1.20 | 1.42 | — | — | 0.50 |
| Vermont | 0.60 | 0.72 | 0.97 | 1.04 | 1.44 | 1.17 | 1.24 | — | — | 0.44 |
| Massachusetts | 0.74 | 0.84 | 1.09 | 1.02 | 1.60 | 1.28 | 1.52 | 0.39 | — | 0.53 |
| Rhode Island | 0.65 | 0.72 | 0.95 | 1.05 | 1.50 | 1.17 | 1.45 | 0.36 | — | 0.53 |
| Connecticut | 0.67 | 0.76 | 0.98 | 1.05 | 1.62 | 1.42 | 1.53 | 0.39 | — | 0.54 |
| Middle Atlantic | 0.71 | 0.60 | 0.90 | 1.06 | 1.58 | 1.27 | 1.45 | 0.45 | 0.46 | 0.55 |
| New York | — | 0.67 | 0.90 | 1.02 | 1.50 | 1.29 | 1.46 | 0.41 | — | 0.53 |
| New Jersey | — | 0.65 | 0.88 | 1.07 | 1.64 | 1.32 | 1.44 | 0.44 | — | 0.55 |
| Pennsylvania | — | 0.51 | 0.80 | 1.11 | 1.65 | 1.25 | 1.45 | 0.49 | — | 0.56 |
| East North Central | 0.48 | 0.58 | 0.87 | 1.01 | 1.58 | 1.30 | 1.51 | 0.42 | 0.48 | 0.57 |
| Ohio | 0.50 | 0.56 | 0.78 | 0.98 | 1.60 | 1.29 | 1.48 | 0.43 | — | 0.58 |
| Indiana | 0.46 | 0.55 | 0.78 | 0.98 | 1.56 | 1.24 | 1.38 | 0.39 | — | 0.57 |
| Illinois | — | 0.62 | 0.85 | 1.05 | 1.60 | 1.40 | 1.62 | 0.46 | — | 0.58 |
| Michigan | — | 0.66 | 0.88 | 1.04 | 1.57 | 1.36 | 1.37 | 0.39 | — | 0.57 |
| Wisconsin | — | 0.71 | 1.00 | 1.05 | 1.54 | 1.21 | 1.37 | 0.40 | — | 0.54 |
| West North Central | 0.52 | 0.56 | 0.77 | 0.98 | 1.55 | 1.43 | 1.48 | 0.41 | 0.42 | 0.53 |
| Minnesota | — | 0.86 | 1.37 | 1.20 | 1.75 | 1.50 | 1.57 | 0.37 | — | 0.56 |
| Iowa | — | 0.61 | 0.83 | 0.99 | 1.69 | — | 1.33 | 0.42 | — | 0.54 |
| Missouri | 0.52 | 0.55 | 0.75 | 0.98 | 1.48 | 1.44 | 1.50 | 0.43 | — | 0.55 |
| Nebraska | — | — | — | 1.37 | 2.13 | 1.50 | 1.62 | — | — | 0.50 |
| Kansas | — | — | — | 1.22 | 1.87 | 1.25 | 1.47 | 0.43 | — | 0.47 |
| South Atlantic | 0.45 | 0.48 | 0.68 | 0.84 | 1.06 | 0.96 | 1.19 | 0.36 | 0.30 | 0.39 |
| Delaware | — | 0.51 | 0.78 | 0.87 | 1.56 | 1.17 | 1.31 | 0.50 | — | 0.48 |
| Maryland | — | 0.49 | 0.69 | 0.84 | 1.54 | 1.08 | 1.23 | 0.45 | — | 0.49 |
| District of Columbia | — | 0.63 | 0.98 | 1.00 | — | — | 1.17 | — | — | — |
| Virginia | — | 0.47 | 0.65 | 0.81 | 1.01 | 1.00 | 1.13 | 0.36 | — | 0.36 |

## EXHIBIT 2D (*concluded*)

**Common Laborers, Average Daily Earnings, 1832–1940**

| Region | 1832 (with Board) | 1850 (with Board) | 1850 | 1860 | 1869 | 1880 | 1890 (Hourly) | 1919 (Hourly) | 1929 (Hourly) | 1940 |
|---|---|---|---|---|---|---|---|---|---|---|
| West Virginia | — | — | — | — | 1.27 | 1.33 | 1.47 | 0.47 | — | 0.55 |
| North Carolina | — | 0.42 | 0.54 | 0.77 | 0.82 | 0.51 | 0.94 | 0.34 | — | 0.31 |
| South Carolina | — | 0.49 | 0.66 | 0.82 | 1.01 | — | 1.00 | 0.30 | — | 0.32 |
| Georgia | 0.54 | 0.50 | 0.72 | 0.89 | 1.09 | 0.89 | 1.05 | 0.29 | — | 0.32 |
| Florida | — | 0.68 | 1.03 | 1.16 | 1.20 | — | 1.00 | 0.26 | — | 0.32 |
| East South Central | 0.49 | 0.49 | 0.68 | 0.92 | 1.28 | 1.10 | 1.32 | 0.31 | 0.27 | 0.37 |
| Kentucky | — | 0.50 | 0.69 | 0.97 | 1.39 | 1.25 | 1.35 | 0.43 | — | 0.44 |
| Tennessee | — | 0.43 | 0.58 | 0.84 | 1.15 | 0.95 | 1.22 | 0.30 | — | 0.34 |
| Alabama | — | 0.49 | 0.70 | 0.96 | 1.21 | 1.06 | 1.37 | 0.29 | — | 0.39 |
| Mississippi | — | 0.69 | 0.95 | 1.26 | 1.45 | — | 0.89 | 0.30 | — | 0.36 |
| West South Central | — | 0.70 | 0.95 | 1.27 | 1.61 | — | 1.44 | 0.33 | 0.36 | 0.36 |
| Arkansas | — | 0.54 | 0.75 | 1.04 | 1.39 | — | 1.06 | 0.27 | — | 0.32 |
| Louisiana | — | 0.73 | 1.04 | 1.39 | 1.70 | — | 1.26 | 0.31 | — | 0.36 |
| Texas | — | 0.75 | 1.00 | 1.25 | 1.27 | 1.00 | 1.68 | 0.36 | — | 0.39 |
| Mountain | — | — | — | 2.00 | 2.71 | — | — | 0.42 | 0.45 | 0.47 |
| Montana | — | — | — | — | 6.00 | — | — | — | — | — |
| Idaho | — | — | — | — | 3.50 | — | — | — | — | — |
| Wyoming | — | — | — | — | — | 2.00 | — | — | — | — |
| Colorado | — | — | — | 2.00 | 2.50 | (1.75) | — | — | — | — |
| New Mexico | — | 0.33 | 0.53 | 1.02 | 1.50 | — | — | — | — | 0.36 |
| Arizona | — | — | — | — | 3.25 | — | — | — | — | — |
| Utah | — | 1.32 | 2.00 | 1.94 | — | — | — | 0.59 | — | 0.49 |
| Nevada | — | — | — | — | 3.00 | — | — | — | — | 0.60 |
| Pacific | — | 4.00 | 5.00 | 2.65 | 2.30 | — | 1.96 | 0.49 | 0.48 | 0.60 |
| Washington | — | — | — | 2.82 | 2.50 | — | — | 0.52 | — | 0.62 |
| Oregon | — | 4.00 | 5.00 | — | 2.12 | (1.50) | — | 0.53 | — | 0.60 |
| California | — | 4.00 | 5.00 | 2.62 | 2.31 | (1.75) | 1.96 | 0.44 | — | 0.59 |

Source: Lebergott, "Manpower," p. 542.

## EXHIBIT 2E

**Domestics, Average Weekly Wage, 1850–1900**

| Region | 1850 | 1860 | 1870 | 1900 |
|---|---|---|---|---|
| United States | $ 1.08 | $1.34 | $2.00 | $3.14 |
| New England | 1.35 | 1.50 | 2.45 | 3.48 |
| Maine | 1.09 | 1.32 | 2.53 | 3.24 |
| New Hampshire | 1.27 | 1.63 | 2.58 | (3.58) |
| Vermont | 1.19 | 1.31 | 2.44 | (3.00) |
| Massachusetts | 1.48 | 1.58 | 2.37 | 3.61 |
| Rhode Island | 1.42 | 1.50 | 2.78 | (3.75) |
| Connecticut | 1.36 | 1.50 | 2.44 | 3.16 |
| Middle Atlantic | .96 | 1.24 | 2.08 | 3.14 |
| New York | 1.05 | 1.25 | 2.22 | 3.09 |
| New Jersey | .97 | 1.23 | 2.05 | 3.55 |
| Pennsylvania | .80 | 1.22 | 1.83 | 3.09 |
| East North Central | 1.06 | 1.33 | 2.14 | 3.06 |
| Ohio | .96 | 1.22 | 1.98 | 2.93 |
| Indiana | .90 | 1.28 | 2.11 | (2.95) |
| Illinois | 1.14 | 1.46 | 2.19 | 3.55 |
| Michigan | 1.10 | 1.40 | 2.30 | 2.89 |
| Wisconsin | 1.27 | 1.30 | 2.05 | 2.50 |
| West North Central | 1.28 | 1.44 | 1.95 | 3.00 |
| Minnesota | 2.25 | 1.58 | 2.08 | 2.94 |
| Iowa | 1.07 | 1.27 | 2.16 | 2.82 |
| Missouri | 1.17 | 1.47 | 1.75 | 3.24 |
| Nebraska | — | 1.72 | 3.36 | 3.19 |
| Kansas | — | 1.82 | 2.20 | (2.62) |
| South Atlantic | .99 | 1.20 | 1.50 | 1.86 |
| Delaware | .84 | .92 | 1.86 | (2.25) |
| Maryland | .89 | 1.17 | 1.82 | (2.22) |
| Virginia | .96 | 1.14 | 1.27 | (2.00) |
| West Virginia | — | — | 1.48 | 3.00 |
| North Carolina | .87 | 1.08 | 1.16 | (1.66) |
| South Carolina | 1.42 | 1.82 | 1.72 | 1.83 |
| Georgia | 1.52 | 1.67 | 1.61 | 1.10 |
| Florida | 1.83 | 2.32 | 1.62 | (2.00) |
| East South Central | 1.18 | 1.63 | 1.88 | 2.78 |
| Kentucky | 1.09 | 1.47 | 1.87 | 2.97 |
| Tennessee | 1.00 | 1.28 | 1.54 | (2.33) |
| Alabama | 1.41 | 2.08 | 1.93 | — |
| Mississippi | 1.52 | 2.25 | 2.42 | — |
| West South Central | 2.30 | 2.95 | 2.22 | 2.60 |
| Arkansas | 1.67 | 1.91 | 2.29 | (2.00) |
| Louisiana | 2.57 | 3.36 | 2.33 | (1.77) |
| Texas | 2.00 | 2.50 | 1.97 | (3.67) |
| Pacific | — | — | — | — |
| California | 13.00 | 7.45 | 6.47 | 4.80 |
| Oregon | 10.00 | 5.40 | — | — |

Source: Lebergott, "Manpower," p. 542.

## EXHIBIT 2F

**Cotton Manufacturing, Average Annual Earnings, Full-Time Equivalent, 1832–1899**

| Region | 1832 | 1849 | 1859 | 1869 | 1879 | 1889 | 1899 |
|---|---|---|---|---|---|---|---|
| United States | $163 | $176 | $201 | $298 | $244 | $302 | $286 |
| New England | 166 | 194 | 206 | 303 | 255 | 325 | 341 |
| Maine | 178 | 188 | 202 | 272 | 250 | 303 | 316 |
| New Hampshire | 172 | 198 | 227 | 318 | 262 | 322 | 330 |
| Vermont | 159 | 165 | 207 | 277 | 225 | 283 | 256 |
| Massachusetts | 169 | 199 | 203 | 312 | 258 | 332 | 351 |
| Rhode Island | 156 | 186 | 202 | 312 | 247 | 318 | 334 |
| Connecticut | 166 | 180 | 194 | 269 | 251 | 321 | 333 |
| Middle Atlantic | 172 | 161 | 184 | 281 | 243 | 331 | 339 |
| New York | 153 | 159 | 183 | 287 | 216 | 294 | 298 |
| New Jersey | 188 | 151 | 185 | 287 | 277 | 352 | 342 |
| Pennsylvania | 175 | 163 | 185 | 275 | 254 | 346 | 360 |
| East North Central | — | 136 | 196 | 238 | 225 | 262 | 229 |
| Ohio | — | 141 | 180 | 246 | 218 | 292 | 263 |
| Indiana | — | 111 | 231 | 225 | 230 | 237 | 228 |
| West North Central | — | — | — | — | — | — | — |
| Missouri | — | 125 | 180 | 333 | 193 | — | — |
| South Atlantic | — | 119 | 168 | 200 | 177 | 202 | 181 |
| Delaware | — | 161 | 198 | 262 | 243 | 317 | 373 |
| Maryland | — | 136 | 217 | 235 | 190 | 248 | 251 |
| Virginia | — | 100 | 181 | 132 | 157 | 188 | 228 |
| North Carolina | — | 92 | 109 | 126 | 136 | 173 | 169 |
| South Carolina | — | 126 | 138 | 229 | 189 | 187 | 168 |
| Georgia | — | 122 | 148 | 215 | 183 | 210 | 195 |
| East South Central | — | 112 | 156 | 210 | 171 | 207 | 187 |
| Kentucky | — | 143 | 168 | 215 | 184 | 209 | 208 |
| Tennessee | — | 96 | 154 | 200 | 159 | 210 | 201 |
| Alabama | — | 117 | 152 | 210 | 166 | 193 | 178 |
| Mississippi | — | 124 | 169 | 233 | 191 | 229 | 203 |

Source: Lebergott, "Manpower," p. 543.

## EXHIBIT 2G

**Woolen Manufacturing, Average Annual Earnings, Full-Time Equivalent, 1832–1899**

| Region | 1832 | 1849 | 1859 | 1869 | 1879 | 1889 | 1899 |
|---|---|---|---|---|---|---|---|
| United States | $183 | $214 | $232 | $335 | $306 | $372 | $361 |
| New England | 199 | 224 | 233 | 360 | 317 | 380 | 385 |
| Maine | — | 205 | 256 | 344 | 336 | 378 | 379 |
| New Hampshire | 211 | 217 | 275 | 361 | 304 | 378 | 389 |
| Vermont | — | 216 | 199 | 345 | 261 | 394 | 389 |
| Massachusetts | 192 | 229 | 234 | 355 | 318 | 382 | 385 |
| Rhode Island | 205 | 219 | 253 | 350 | 305 | 369 | 407 |
| Connecticut | 208 | 226 | 252 | 392 | 339 | 390 | 377 |
| Middle Atlantic | 159 | 197 | 234 | 333 | 309 | 376 | 362 |
| New York | 137 | 204 | 235 | 322 | 316 | 373 | 347 |
| New Jersey | — | 195 | 243 | 306 | 283 | 347 | 344 |
| Pennsylvania | 240 | 189 | 232 | 343 | 308 | 381 | 371 |
| East North Central | — | 218 | 261 | 286 | 246 | 311 | 303 |
| Ohio | — | 214 | 246 | 249 | 196 | 314 | 317 |
| Indiana | — | 231 | 282 | 294 | 266 | 284 | 293 |
| Illinois | — | 229 | 272 | 308 | 285 | 343 | 303 |
| Michigan | — | 211 | 243 | 304 | 219 | 314 | 321 |
| Wisconsin | — | — | 257 | 296 | 254 | 332 | 301 |
| West North Central | — | 233 | 228 | 236 | 195 | 306 | 276 |
| Minnesota | — | — | — | 312 | 201 | 355 | 302 |
| Iowa | — | — | 197 | 248 | 236 | 352 | 252 |
| Missouri | — | 261 | 282 | 191 | 160 | 239 | 267 |
| Kansas | — | — | — | 337 | 210 | — | — |
| South Atlantic | — | 199 | 207 | 220 | 201 | 263 | 234 |
| Delaware | — | 223 | 242 | 289 | 418 | 347 | — |
| Maryland | — | 201 | 226 | 251 | 178 | 324 | 252 |
| Virginia | — | 189 | 216 | 211 | 197 | 263 | 287 |
| West Virginia | — | — | — | 189 | 125 | 216 | 258 |
| North Carolina | — | 150 | 237 | 157 | 124 | 201 | 200 |
| South Carolina | — | — | 124 | 72 | 133 | — | — |
| Georgia | — | 251 | 165 | 217 | 176 | 179 | 173 |
| East South Central | — | 184 | 185 | 202 | 198 | 309 | 252 |
| Kentucky | — | 173 | 236 | 233 | 202 | 298 | 234 |
| Tennessee | — | 195 | 247 | 147 | 167 | 240 | 180 |
| Alabama | — | — | 172 | 119 | 169 | 178 | 139 |
| Mississippi | — | — | 96 | 248 | 243 | 283 | 183 |
| West South Central | — | — | — | — | — | — | — |
| Texas | — | 240 | 179 | 203 | 172 | 387 | 304 |

Source: Lebergott, "Manpower," p. 544.

# EXHIBIT 2H

**Iron and Steel Manufacturing, Average Annual Earnings, Full-Time Equivalent 1832–1899**

| Region | Full Time | | Full-Time Equivalent | | | | |
|---|---|---|---|---|---|---|---|
| | 1832 | 1849 | 1859 | 1869 | 1879 | 1889 | 1899 |
| United States | $313 | $292 | $346 | $524 | $394 | $522 | $543 |
| New England | 311 | 349 | 368 | 594 | 404 | 483 | 549 |
| Maine | 311 | 329 | 414 | 483 | — | — | — |
| New Hampshire | 286 | 392 | 364 | 564 | — | — | — |
| Vermont | 289 | 309 | 389 | 452 | — | — | — |
| Massachusetts | 311 | 365 | 380 | 634 | 396 | 474 | 557 |
| Rhode Island | 311 | 356 | 422 | 552 | — | — | — |
| Connecticut | 311 | 324 | 310 | 587 | 483 | 558 | 525 |
| Middle Atlantic | 314 | 296 | 344 | 529 | 418 | 530 | 553 |
| New York | — | 327 | 385 | 578 | 358 | 482 | 565 |
| New Jersey | 311 | 274 | 373 | 585 | 377 | 495 | 470 |
| Pennsylvania | 314 | 283 | 311 | 486 | 433 | 536 | 558 |
| East North Central | — | 315 | 348 | 506 | 416 | 560 | 579 |
| Ohio | — | 312 | 344 | 506 | 412 | 563 | 586 |
| Indiana | — | 310 | 320 | 554 | 422 | 435 | 560 |
| Illinois | — | 318 | 411 | 556 | 478 | 601 | 579 |
| Michigan | — | 349 | 360 | 500 | 299 | 530 | 477 |
| Wisconsin | — | 329 | 351 | 378 | 467 | 519 | 633 |
| West North Central | — | 268 | 438 | 720 | 234 | 516 | 539 |
| Minnesota | — | — | 481 | 508 | — | — | — |
| Iowa | — | 388 | 373 | 506 | — | — | — |
| Missouri | — | 265 | 443 | 742 | 234 | 516 | 539 |
| Nebraska | — | — | — | 106 | — | — | — |
| Kansas | — | — | — | 629 | — | — | — |
| South Atlantic | — | 233 | 300 | 366 | 315 | 408 | 444 |
| Delaware | — | 280 | 372 | 484 | 397 | 467 | 473 |
| Maryland | — | 273 | 304 | 304 | 328 | 298 | 482 |
| District of Columbia | — | 325 | 360 | 552 | — | — | — |
| Virginia | — | 189 | 271 | 298 | 264 | 371 | 317 |
| West Virginia | — | — | — | 577 | 374 | 462 | 513 |
| North Carolina | — | 156 | 237 | 312 | — | — | — |
| South Carolina | — | 163 | 200 | 437 | — | — | — |
| Georgia | — | 236 | 340 | 404 | 142 | 263 | 249 |
| Florida | — | — | 463 | — | — | — | — |
| East South Central | — | 238 | 303 | 398 | 293 | 411 | 356 |
| Kentucky | — | 283 | 380 | 407 | 328 | 467 | 477 |
| Tennessee | — | 162 | 226 | 380 | 214 | 446 | 273 |
| Alabama | — | 337 | 319 | 444 | 352 | 388 | 339 |
| Mississippi | — | 455 | 535 | 269 | — | — | — |
| West South Central | — | 438 | 453 | 639 | 198 | — | 172 |
| Arkansas | — | — | 171 | 389 | — | — | — |
| Louisiana | — | 427 | 467 | 650 | — | — | — |
| Texas | — | 521 | — | 578 | 198 | — | 172 |
| Pacific | — | — | — | — | — | — | — |
| California | — | 280 | 106 | 598 | 557 | 622 | 590 |

Source: Lebergott, "Manpower," p. 545.

# CASE 18

# *Mass Production and the Beginnings of Scientific Management\**

This case includes three sets of readings. The first tells of the coming of mass production in American industry. The second deals with the beginnings of scientific management as defined and practiced by Frederick W. Taylor and his disciples. The third provides a critique of the Taylor system.

## The Coming of Mass Production

Mass production must be viewed as more than factory production. Mass production techniques are those that permit a factory, or a works, to produce continuously or in large batches. Such methods made possible a fast "throughput" of materials within the plant. High "throughput" was as basic to mass production as high "stockturn" was to mass marketing. The greater the throughput for a given plant and set of equipment, the lower the unit costs and the greater the possibility of increased profits.

---

\*This case was prepared by Alfred D. Chandler, Jr., as a basis for class discussion rather than to illustrate either effective or ineffective handling of an adminstrative situation. The first selection is from Alfred D. Chandler, Jr., "Evolution of Enterprise: The United States" in Peter Mathias and M. M. Postan, eds., *The Cambridge Economic History* VII, Part 2 (Cambridge, England: Cambridge University Press, 1978). The second and third selections were taken partly from a case (9-374-352) compiled by Professor Chandler in 1972 entitled "Modern Management Begins" and partly from BH118 originally prepared by Josepha M. Perry called "Selections on Scientific Management."

Copyright © 1977 by the President and Fellows of Harvard College.

Harvard Business School case 377-223, rev. 6/84.

High throughput could be obtained and then increased in a number of ways. Machinery and equipment could be improved and operated at higher speeds. The amount of energy used could be increased. The organizational design and the administrative procedures could be adapted and improved to assure a continuing steady regular flow of materials from one part of the process of production within the plant to the next and to permit more efficient use of the equipment and the workers who handled it. And finally, both workers and managers could become more skilled at their tasks. Except for this last, all these ways of increasing throughput (and the volume output per unit of inputs) increased the ratio of capital, materials, energy, and managers to the size of the working force. Mass production processes thus became capital intensive, energy intensive, materials intensive, and manager intensive.

The possibility of increasing throughput varied with the technology of the production processes. The potential for expanding the speed and productivity was low in industries where mechanization had resulted in merely the replacement of manual labor by relatively simple machines. This was the case in the making of cloth, wood, apparel, shoes, saddlery, furniture, flooring, and the printing of books, journals, and magazines. Once the basic machinery was perfected, better trained workers and managers could raise the productivity of the plant, but the primary way to increase output was to add more machines and more workers. Industries using such processes of production remained labor intensive (i.e., a high ratio of workers to capital) until well into the 20th century. Theirs continued to be factory production similar to that of the early textile mills of the Merrimack Valley. The one change in organization was that all activities for such manufacturing enterprises came to be centralized under the control of a single person or office.

By contrast, in the refining and distilling industries, modern high-speed, high-volume continuous or large batch mass production techniques came very quickly. By 1869, a decade after the drilling of the first commercial oil well, petroleum refineries had been designed which required almost no manual labor at all. The tasks of the working force were largely in packaging the final product. More intensive use of energy through the development of super-heated steam distillation and "cracking" at high temperatures further increased the speed and volume of output. For example, by 1870, "cracking" permitted as much as 20 percent expansion in the output in yields of kerosene from ordinary distillations. Similar innovations occurred in the refining of sugar, cotton seed oil, linseed oil, the brewing of beer, and in the distilling of whiskey, industrial alcohol, sulphuric acid and other chemicals. Production units in these industries quickly became very capital intensive, energy intensive, materials intensive, and manager intensive. In such industries expansion in the size of the plant made possible much greater economies of scale than in the labor intensive mechanical ones. For example, when the Standard Oil Trust reorganized its refinery capacity in 1883 and concentrated almost two fifths of American refinery production in three huge refineries, the unit cost dropped from 1.5 cents a barrel to 0.5 cents a barrel. A comparable concentration of two fifths of the nation's output of textiles or shoes in three plants would, of course, have been impossible.

In other industries, particularly those processing agricultural products, a comparable rate of throughput was achieved through the invention of continuous-process machinery and the designing of continuous-process plants. In the late 1870s and the early 1880s, such innovations appeared in the making of cigarettes, the milling of flour, oats, and other grains, the canning of soups and milk, and the production of soap and photographic film. These industries quickly became capital, materials, and manager intensive. However, once the machinery and the plant design had been perfected, the potential for still further increases in productivity remained limited. This was also true of the refining and distilling industries.

It was then in the furnace and foundry industries, particularly the metal-making and metalworking ones, that the greatest continuing potential existed for increasing the velocity of volume of throughput by improving equipment, a more intensive use of energy, better organization design, and improved managerial skills. In the metal-making industries, it was the integration of several operations within a single works that provided the greatest opportunity for increased productivity from such methods. In the metalworking ones, it was the subdivision of the processes into more specialized units that created such an opportunity. And it was in these industries that modern American factory or works management was perfected.

In the metal-making industries, the most dramatic example of rapidly increasing productivity came in works that integrated blast furnaces, rolling mills, and finishing mills to make rails, wire, sheets, and structures. The adoption of the Bessemer and open-hearth processes enormously increased the volume of output through the adoption of massive machinery and an intensive use of energy. Moreover, as emphasized by Alexander J. Holley, the engineer who built nearly all of the new Bessemer works in the United States, the larger output of American over British mills came not only from improved converters and other equipment but from the careful layout of plants, which included as many as 70 buildings and 30 miles of internal railway. Holley further noted, "Better organization and more readiness, diligence and technical knowledge on the part of management have been required to run works up to their capacity, as their capacity has become increased by better arrangement and better appliances." As an economic historian, Peter Temin, has recently pointed out concerning the last decades of the century:

> The speed at which steel was made was continually rising, and new innovations were constantly being introduced to speed it further. Steam and later electric power replaced the lifting and carrying action of human muscle, mills were modified to handle steel quickly and with a minimum of strain to the machinery, and people disappeared from the mills. By the turn of the century, there were not a dozen men on the floor of a mill rolling 3,000 tons a day, or as much as a Pittsburgh rolling mill of 1850 rolled in a year.[1]

As the steel and other metal-making works became capital and energy intensive, they also increased the ratio of managers to workers. For the increased speed and

---

[1]Peter Temin, *Iron and Steel in Nineteenth Century America* (Cambridge: Harvard University Press, 1964), pp. 164–65.

volume of materials through the plant intensified the need for supervision and control.

The organizational design and the operating procedures of the new iron and steel enterprises owed much to the railroads. The connection between the railroads and the iron and steel industry had always been close. The first Bessemer rail mills were financed by railroads. The steel industry's foremost entrepreneur, Andrew Carnegie, received his business training as division superintendent of the Pennsylvania's Pittsburgh Division. Leading executives of that road, J. Edgar Thomson and Thomas Scott, joined Carnegie in financing the construction of the largest and the most efficient of the early Bessemer works—the J. Edgar Thomson Works, begun in 1873 near Pittsburgh.

Carnegie brought W. P. Shinn, an experienced professional manager, from the Pennsylvania Railroad to become the general manager of the new works. Shinn introduced and modified railroad accounting and cost techniques, including a voucher system employed in the locomotive shops. His daily cost sheets and other data were used to determine costs and prices and to evaluate departmental performance. No order was accepted until its costs had been carefully estimated. Summarized weekly and monthly reports went to the company's board of managers, made up largely of department heads, and to Carnegie himself. According to one of the company's executives, "the minutest detail of cost of materials appeared from day to day and week to week in the accounts and soon every man in the place was made to realize it. The men felt and often remarked that the eyes of the company were always on them through the books." Furthermore, as Temin points out, Carnegie used his accounts to evaluate the technological innovations introduced to expand output and to lower costs. And where Carnegie pioneered, others quickly followed, not only in the making of iron and steel but in the production of copper, zinc, glass and paper.

It was in the metal*working* industries, however, that improvements in machinery, organizational design, and managerial performance made the most difference to productivity. Metal was more difficult to shape than cloth, wood, or leather, but it could be shaped to much finer tolerances and much more precise specifications than could other materials. Therefore, new and improved machinery permitted a greater increase in the speed and output of metal goods than did the use of machines in shaping wood, cloth, and leather. Between the 1850s and 1880s, major innovations occurred in milling, grinding, and stamping machines, in lathes, and in other equipment for cutting and working metal. Indeed, the history of the American machine tool industry in its most innovative years is largely the story of providing equipment for the metalworking industries. These innovations involved not only machine design but also the development of metal alloys, which improved the cutting edges of tools and, therefore, sped up their operation.

Organizational design and managerial skills were particularly critical for increasing output and productivity in the metalworking industries because their processes of production permitted a greater subdivision of labor than was possible in other industries. Such subdivision, by increasing the number of subdepartments within a works, made more difficult the managerial tasks of maintaining a steady throughput. These managerial tasks became the most difficult in those enterprises which mass-produced machinery and other products through the fabrication and assembling of interchangeable parts. These included firms making firearms, locks, clocks, watches, sewing machines, typewriters, cash registers, harvesters, threshers, and other complex agricultural machinery, electrical machinery, pumps, and other heavy equipment. These enterprises also used a wider variety and a greater number of raw and semifinished materials than did any other type of manufacturer.

During the 1850s and 1860s, the men in charge of these metalworking enterprises concentrated on improving their machinery and plant design. Only after the depression of the 1870s created pressures to cut costs, did they begin to pay close attention to improving organizational design. The innovators in the new systematic or scientific methods of shop and factory management were nearly all mechanical engineers connected with the metalworking industries. In fact the history of the scientific management movement in the United States can best be followed in the *Proceedings* of the meetings of the American Society of Mechanical Engineers founded in 1880. By the middle of the 80s, organizational design had become one of the association's top concerns. At its annual meeting in 1881, Henry R. Towne, its president and also the head of the Yale & Towne Lock Company, in a presidential address entitled "The Engineer as an Economist" urged its members to concentrate on shop management and shop accounting:

> Under the head of Shop Management fall the questions of organization, responsibility, reports, systems of contract and piece work, and all that relate to the executive management of works, mills and factories. Under the head of Shop Accounting fall the questions of time and wage systems, determination of costs, whether piece or day work, methods of booking, distribution of the various expense accounts, the ascertainment of profits, and all that enters into the system of accounts which relates to the manufacturing departments of a business, and to the determination and record of its results.[2]

One technique to improve both shop management and accounting which the society discussed in its early meetings was the "shop-order system" of tickets and cards. This method was first fully developed in sewing machine enterprises which appear to have borrowed it from railroad locomotive shops. It required the plant superintendent to give each order a number and a special set of cards and tickets. The foreman of each shop or subdepartment then recorded the amount of materials and labor used on each order and on each item in that order as it passed through his bailiwick. One copy of the ticket stayed in that shop and a master copy accompanied the order through the remaining departments of the works. The latter provided gross costs for each order from all departments. A compilation of the copies of the former could permit a review of the materials and labor expended by one shop or department over a specific period of time. Such information provided

---

[2]Henry R. Towne, "The Engineer as an Economist," *Transactions, American Society of Mechanical Engineers*, Vol. 7 (1886), pp. 429–30.

accurate data on prime costs (labor and materials) by product and by process. It also made possible controls over the flow of goods through the factory and over inventories of raw and semifinished materials. Finally, such data permitted managers to evaluate the performance of the subunits and of the factory as a whole.

In order to get workers and foremen to accept such new control procedures, Towne, in the late 1880s, proposed a plan by which the employees as well as owners received the benefits of the resulting increases in productivity. By this scheme any reduction in costs through more efficient planning of time, more effective use of materials and machines, and the introduction of better equipment would be shared equally between the company and the workers, with the hands getting 30 to 40 percent of the savings involved and the foreman getting 10 to 20 percent. Modified by another engineer, Frederick Halsey, this plan was adopted in a number of American metalworking plants.

Then Frederick W. Taylor of the Midvale Steel Company, which produced a variety of machined castings and parts, entered the scene. He had earlier instituted at Midvale a shop-order method of control and other systematic ways to raise output. In 1895, he delivered an influential paper before the Society of Mechanical Engineers. In it he explicitly addressed himself to improving the gain-sharing plans of Towne and Halsey. First, he pointed out, such plans erred in basing costs and the resulting savings to be shared on past experience. Instead, they should be based on a standard time and output to be determined "scientifically," through careful job analyses and time and motion studies of the work involved. Secondly, Taylor wanted to add the stick to the carrot. Whereas Towne rewarded workers if they exceeded normal output and cut the costs, Taylor would also punish by reducing a worker's pay if he failed to meet the standards set.

To carry out his plan, Taylor expected to eliminate the shop foreman altogether. He proposed to form a planning department, which would administer the factory as a whole and would do so through a number of highly specialized bosses or "functional foremen." The planning department would handle job analyses and time and motion studies. It would also set standards of output. After reviewing orders received at the plant, it would, on the basis of its analysis and its information, schedule the flow of current orders and set the daily work plan for each operating unit in the factory. In addition, it was to refine the shop-order systems of control and to keep constant check on "costs of all items manufactured with complete expense analysis and complete monthly comparative cost and expense exhibits." Finally, it was to have charge of hiring and firing. Such careful, impersonal overall control would permit each worker to concentrate on doing a single, highly specialized and routine task.

Taylor's goal of extreme internal specialization was rarely achieved in American industry. In the plants reorganized by practitioners of scientific management, the subdepartments continued to be managed by foremen. These foremen remained generalists rather than specialists, stayed on the line of authority from the president through the general manager or superintendent, and remained responsible for the control of throughput in their units. The planning office became the plant manager's staff. The new staff offices included those for personnel, accounting, inspection, power and works engineering, product design, methods, production efficiency, and orders. The last was usually responsible for scheduling the flow of materials through the plant, while the department of production efficiency concerned itself with design, with the movement of men (based on time and motion studies), and with setting wage rates.

After 1900, the most dramatic increases in productivity within the metal-working industries came from improvements in metals used in machine tools and in the increased use of energy applied to the movement of materials through the processes of production. Taylor himself played an important part in intensifying the velocity of production in 1899 when he and an associate developed high-speed steel, an alloy that permitted the cutting of metals at much greater speeds. Such increases in speed, in turn, made possible an even more radical reorganization of shop practices.

# Development of Scientific Management

### Frederick W. Taylor and the "Taylor System"

Frederick W. Taylor (1856-1915) was called the father of scientific management. Having served an apprenticeship as a machinist, Taylor had gone to the Midvale Steel Company as a laborer in 1878 and was shortly promoted to foreman. Convinced from his experience as a machine operator that his fellow-workers "soldiered" on the job to protect themselves from pressure and from rate-cutting, he set out to devise a system of work control that would facilitate maximum output per man and a wage-payment plan that would give men an incentive to work at the maximum speed consistent with health. Low wages, he asserted, were no assurance of low labor cost. The standard of performance on which he wanted to base his wage rate was the output of "a first-class man in favorable conditions."

To produce favorable conditions was management's responsibility. It involved planning the flow of work, determining proper methods and tools of each job, and training workers in these methods. Job analysis was Taylor's first step in eliminating time lost by a machine operator in "nonproductive" work, such as adjusting the machine and going after materials.

"Functional foremanship" was Taylor's means of management control at the production level, carrying the division of labor into the foreman's domain. Taylor divided the elements of shop control into eight functions. Four of these were the responsibility of the planning room: (1) routing and order-of-work plans, (2) instruction and specification cards, (3) time and cost records, and (4) shop discipline and personnel records. In the shop four other functions were represented by (1) the gang boss (machine preparation and setup), (2) the speed boss (technical supervision), (3) the repair boss (maintenance of equipment), and (4) the inspector (quality control). Although Taylor's plan for eight separate foremen with authority over each worker was seldom put into practice, the division of planning and operating functions was of basic importance in organization for control.

To manage these functional foremen, Taylor relied on a planning department. "The shop, and indeed the whole works, should be managed not by managers, superintendents and foremen, but by the planning department," Taylor insisted. As has been pointed out, the planning department was, on the basis of its analysis and information, to schedule the flow of current orders and set the daily work plan for each operating unit and indeed each worker in the factory. Its employment bureau was to have charge of recruitment and laying off of workers. Overall, the planning department was to be responsible for "the maintenance of the entire system, and of standard methods and appliances throughout the establishment, including the planning room itself."

By 1895, Taylor had devised his "differential piece-rate" method of wage payment, which, he believed, coupled with efficient planning, routing, and specialization of jobs, would give maximum output per man and maximum wages to each worker. Taylor's differential piece-rate plan of wage payment was based on a time-study of each job. From data collected by use of a stop watch, the time to be allowed for each operation was calculated. From this, a day's task was set. For completing or exceeding the task, a worker received a condensed piece-rate 50 percent higher than if his output fell short of the designated amount. Since the lower differential figures would allow scarcely an ordinary day's pay, the plan quickly eliminated workers who could not make the task and held the better workers, who under his plan could make higher wages than anywhere else.

## Operation of the Taylor System

An appendix to the Report of the Chief of Ordnance for 1913 discussed the Taylor system at some length. The following comment indicates the procedure of setting up the system:[3]

> The Taylor system of shop management may be roughly divided into two general parts. The first part relates to the systemization of processes of manufacture, so that these processes shall be carried on in a perfectly orderly manner, with better forethought and provision than has ever before been given them, and with more detailed arrangements concerning their relations to each other. To the natural inquiry as to what there is new in this, since everybody has always been striving for system and order in manufacturing operations, the answer must be made that the amount of attention which is given under Mr. Taylor's method to system, as evidenced by the number of personnel engaged and the expense involved—that is, by the amount of administrative energy which is devoted to it—is so different from that which has ever anywhere before this time been devoted to systemization as to be absolutely revolutionary.
>
> The second part relates to the quality of output to be obtained from the workman, and the stimulus required to induce him to cheerfully and earnestly and intelligently strive to give the output. This part rests upon the theory that the best and most expeditious way of doing a piece of work is too difficult to ascertain for the workman who has to do it to have any reasonable chance of arriving at it; and that it must be reached

---

[3]Report of the Chief of Ordnance, U.S. Army, 1913, Appendix I, "The Taylor System of Management at the Watertown Arsenal." (Washington: Government Printing Office, 1913), pp. 60–62.

through painstaking study, by methods prescribed by a highly skilled and expensive specialist, utilizing measurements of the time required by the various elements of a job, and a great deal of knowledge such as the workman does not have and cannot be expected to have. There is the further theory that the current rate of wages, as it exists in any manufacturing community, is not that corresponding to the best directed and most earnest efforts of the employees, but is that corresponding to the class of performance in connection with which the rate has grown up, which is very far from being the best reasonably and agreeably attainable. By expensively finding out the best method of doing a given piece of work, and the time in which it can reasonably be done by following this method, and then by making it very well worth the employee's while to approach, within a given interval, this time, or to improve upon it, means are found to improve the individual output, and to improve the compensation which is paid for it, in a manner profitable and satisfactory to both employer and employee.

\* \* \* \* \*

. . . the process can be described as follows: A workman being employed upon a job for which it is intended to set a rate, the time-study man takes his station near him and, openly and with full knowledge upon the part of all concerned of what he is about, proceeds to study the job by first dividing it into its different component movements and periods. He then times carefully each one of the movements and periods, usually more than once. From the data thus obtained he works out what he considers the best sequence of movements and periods, making, if possible, certain elements simultaneous which before were successive, and arrives at a complete program for performing the job and at an estimate of the time in which, by attentively following the program, the job should be completed. This time is called the "task time." It must be understood that the management has theretofore had no definite idea as to the time in which the job should be done, or that it was being done unnecessarily slowly. Knowledge has been lacking to permit an idea as to this point to be formed. Also, any unnecessary slowness is likely to have been caused as much by unscientific methods as by lack of diligence on the part of the workman. The whole object is to secure an intelligent idea of the best way to do the work and of the right time for it. Upon these two points all hands have been without reliable information.

After the task time has been arrived at; and it must be remembered that no necessity for unpleasant exertion is admitted in fixing the time; some stimulus in the form of increased pay is given to the workman for meeting this time, or for approaching it. The particular scheme of increase is not important, provided always that it gives an adequate reward for good effort. The scheme applied at the Watertown Arsenal is as follows: The workman is informed that his regular pay is not to be affected. He continues to receive that in any event. The task time is then increased by two-thirds, and he is told that for every minute which he saves within this increased time he will be paid, in addition to his regular pay, for half a minute, at his regular rate. From this it follows that if he completes the job in exactly the task time the increase in his pay will amount to 33 1/3 percent. No limit is placed upon the time in which he can do the work or the extra amount which he can thus earn, and it frequently happens that the task time is bettered, and more than 33 1/3 percent extra is earned.

\* \* \* \* \*

It is the object of the management to have as many men as possible working under the premium system, and effort is made to enable each workman to increase his premiums to the fullest extent. There has been introduced a system of rewarding the foreman by premiums which increase with the proportion of their subordinates who are working upon premium jobs and with the amount of premiums which they earn. So that the foremen are stimulated to assign as many men as possible to jobs on which they can increase their pay in this way, and to help each one of them to the greatest possible increase.

## Taylor's View of the Essentials of Scientific Management

In testimony before a special congressional committee in 1911, Taylor defined the essentials of scientific management, according to his view, as follows:[4]

Scientific management is not any efficiency device, not a device of any kind for securing efficiency; nor is it any bunch or group of efficiency devices. It is not a new system of figuring costs; it is not a new scheme of paying men; it is not a piecework system; it is not a bonus system; it is not a premium system; it is no scheme for paying men; it is not holding a stop watch on a man and writing things down about him; it is not time study; it is not motion study nor an analysis of the movement of men; it is not the printing and ruling and unloading of a ton or two of blanks on a set of men and saying, "Here's your system; go use it." It is not divided foremanship or functional foremanship; it is not any of the devices which the average man calls to mind when scientific management is spoken of. The average man thinks of one or more of these things when he hears the words "scientific management" mentioned, but scientific management is not any of these devices. I am not sneering at cost-keeping systems, at time study, at functional foremanship, nor at any new and improved scheme of paying men, nor at any efficiency devices, if they are really devices that make for efficiency. I believe in them, but what I am emphasizing is that these devices in whole or in part are not scientific management; they are useful adjuncts to scientific management, so are they also useful adjuncts of other systems of management.

Now, in its essence, scientific management involves a complete mental revolution on the part of the working man engaged in any particular establishment or industry— a complete mental revolution on the part of these men as to their duties toward their work, toward their fellow man, and toward their employers. And it involves the equally complete mental revolution on the part of those on the management's side—the foreman, the superintendent, the owner of the business, the board of directors—a complete mental revolution on their part as to their duties toward their fellow workers in the management, toward their workmen, and toward all of their daily problems. And without this complete mental revolution on both sides scientific management does not exist.

That is the essence of scientific management, this great mental revolution. . . .

I think it is safe to say that in the past a great part of the thought and interest both of the men, on the sides of the management, and of those on the side of the workmen in manufacturing establishments has been centered upon what may be called the proper division of the surplus resulting from their joint efforts, between the management on

---

[4]U.S. Congress, House Special Committee to Investigate the Taylor and Other Systems of Shop Management (1911), *Hearings*, vol. 3 (Washington: Government Printing Office, 1912), pp. 1386–1389. Under a resolution of August 11, 1911, this special committee was set up to investigate the effects of scientific management plans, especially in government arsenals. Ordnance Department officers, workers, and proponents of scientific management testified at the hearings.

the one hand, and the workmen on the other hand. The management have been looking for as large a profit as possible for themselves, and the workmen have been looking
for as large wages as possible for themselves, and that is what I mean by the division of
the surplus. Now, this question of the division of the surplus is a very plain and simple
one (for I am announcing no great fact in political economy or anything of that sort).
Each article produced in the establishment has its definite selling price. Into the manufacture of this article have gone certain expenses, namely the cost of materials, the expenses connected with selling it, and certain indirect expenses, such as the rent of the
building, taxes, insurance, light and power, maintenance of machinery, interest on the
plant, etc. Now, if we deduct these several expenses from the selling price, what is left
over may be called the surplus. And out of this surplus comes the profit to the manufacturer on the one hand, and the wages of the workmen on the other hand. And it is
largely upon the division of this surplus that the attention of the workmen and of the
management has been centered in the past.

* * * * *

The great revolution that takes place in the mental attitude of the two parties under
scientific management is that both sides take their eyes off the division of the surplus as
the all-important matter, and together turn their attention toward increasing the size
of the surplus until this surplus becomes so large that it is unnecessary to quarrel over
how it shall be divided. They come to see that when they stop pulling against one another, and instead both turn and push shoulder to shoulder in the same direction, the
size of the surplus created by their joint efforts is truly astounding. They both realize
that when they substitute friendly cooperation and mutual helpfulness for antagonism
and strife they are together able to make this surplus so enormously greater than it was
in the past that there is ample room for a large increase in wages for the workmen and
an equally great increase in profits for the manufacturer. This, gentlemen, is the beginning of the great mental revolution which constitutes the first step toward scientific
management. . . .

There is, however, one more change in viewpoint which is absolutely essential to
the existence of scientific management. Both sides must recognize as essential the substitution of exact scientific investigation and knowledge for the old individual judgment or opinion, either of the workman or the boss, in all matters relating to the work
done in the establishment. And this applies both as to the methods to be employed in
doing the work and the time in which each job should be done.

Scientific management cannot be said to exist, then, in any establishment until
after this change has taken place in the mental attitude of both the management and
the men, both as to their duty to cooperate in producing the largest possible surplus
and as to the necessity for substituting exact scientific knowledge for opinions or the
old rule of thumb or individual knowledge.

These are the two absolutely essential elements of scientific management.

## Taylor's Definition of a First-Class Worker

Taylor explained his much debated concept of the first-class worker as follows:

> **Mr. Taylor**:  Now, what I mean by "first-class" men is set before you by what
> I mean by first-class horses. I mean that there are big, powerful men suited
> to heavy work, just as dray horses are suited to the coal wagon, and I would
> not use a man who would be first class for this heavy work to do light work

for which he would be second class, and which could be just as well done by a boy who is first class for this work, and vice versa. What I want to make clear is that each type of man is first class at some kind of work, and if you will hunt far enough you will find some kind of work that is especially suited to him. . . .

Among the first-class big dray horses that are hauling coal wagons you will find a few of them that will balk, a few of them that can haul, but won't haul. You will find a few of these dray horses that are so absolutely lazy that they won't haul a coal wagon. And in the same way among every class of workmen we have some balky workmen—I do not mean men who are unable to do the work, but men who, physically well able to work, are simply lazy and who through no amount of teaching and instructing and through no amount of kindly treatment, can be brought into the first class. That is the man whom I call "second class." They have the physical possibility of being first class, but they obstinately refuse to do so.

**The Chairman**: Scientific management has no place for such men?

**Mr. Taylor**: Scientific management has no place for a bird that can sing and won't sing.

**The Chairman**: We are not in this particular investigation dealing with horses nor singing birds, but we are dealing with men who are a part of society and for whose benefit society is organized; and what I wanted to get at is whether or not your scientific management had any place whatever for a man who was not able to meet your own definition of what constitutes a first-class workman.

**Mr. Taylor**: Exactly. There is no place for a man who can work and won't work.

**The Chairman**: It is not a question of a man who can work and won't work; it is a question of a man who doesn't meet your definition of first-class workmen. What place have you for such men?

**Mr. Taylor**: I believe the only man who does not come under first class as I have defined it, is the man who can work and won't work. I have tried to make it clear that for each type of workman some job can be found at which he is first class, with the exception of those men who are perfectly well able to do the job, but won't do it.

**The Chairman**: Do you mean to tell the committee that society is so well balanced that it just provides the proper number of individuals who are well fitted to a particular line of work to furnish society with the products of that line of work?

**Mr. Taylor**: Certainly not, Mr. Chairman. There is not a fine balance in society. It is sometimes difficult to find jobs right near home for which men are well suited, that is, for which they are first class. There is an immense shortage of men, however, who are needed to do the higher classes of work. There always has been and always will be, an immense shortage near the top. It is not so great down below, but at the top there is an immense shortage of first-class men, so that there is plenty of room for men to move up.

**The Chairman**: If society does not produce an equal balance in all the lines of production of first-class men, must there not of necessity be some men who are not first class in any particular line of work where they can secure employment?

**Mr. Taylor**: I do not think there is any man, so far as I know, who is physically fitted for work, who in this country has to go without work in ordinary times. I do not know of this case except in very dull times.

\* \* \* \* \*

**The Chairman**: Is it not true that today there is a shortage of men, and that there frequently is a shortage of men for the higher skilled trades, while at the same time men who have not acquired that skill are unable to find employment?

**Mr. Taylor**: I think there is a shortage of men for the very high classes of work in the dullest of dull times, but not that same shortage of men in the very elementary kinds of work, in dull times. I think that is right, Mr. Chairman. I think that I catch your point, Mr. Chairman—that working people frequently suffer because they are unable to find the particular kind of work that they want and I agree with you in this. We who are engaged in creative industries—the industries in which you and I have worked during our lives—fail to realize the fact that those men who are in creative industries are a small minority of the whole community. Perhaps 17 percent (I think I am right) of the people of the country are in what may be called creative industries.

Now, there is a very large outside field of work for people to go into, and in this outside field it is an undoubted fact that the selection of workmen and that the training of workmen is not nearly as accurate as it is in the industrial field. You will realize that in domestic employment and in the farm work, and in the ordinary work of sweeping the streets of the cities, for instance, the ordinary work that goes on largely in an isolated way all over the country—that the same careful selection of workmen is not made as occurs in the industrial field. The same study of workmen is not made in those occupations as in the trades at which you and I have worked.

The following passage from *The Principles of Scientific Management* is the famous "Story of Schmidt." Taylor believed that this story was a good illustration of how best to improve worker productivity.

One of the first pieces of work undertaken by us, when the writer started to introduce scientific management into the Bethlehem Steel Company, was to handle pig iron on task work. The opening of the Spanish War found some 80,000 tons of pig iron placed in small piles in an open field adjoining the works. Prices for pig iron had been so low that it could not be sold out of profit, and it therefore had been stored. With the opening of the Spanish War the price of pig iron rose, and this large accumulation of iron was sold. This gave us a good opportunity to show the workmen, as well as the owners and managers of the works, on a fairly large scale the advantages of task work over the old-fashioned day work and piece work, in doing a very elementary class of work.

The Bethlehem Steel Company had five blast furnaces, the product of which had been handled by a pig iron gang for many years. This gang, at this time, consisted of about 75 men. They were good, average pig iron handlers, were under an excellent foreman who himself had been a pig iron handler, and the work was done, on the whole, about as fast and as cheaply as it was anywhere else at that time.

A railroad switch was run out into the field, right along the edge of the piles of pig iron. An inclined plank was placed against the side of a car, and each man picked up from his pile a pig iron weighing about 92 pounds, walked up the inclined plank and dropped it on the end of the car.

We found that this gang were loading on the average about 12 1/2 long tons per man per day. We were surprised to find, after studying the matter (time study), that a first class pig-iron handler ought to handle between 47 and 48 long tons per day, instead of 12 1/2 tons. This task seemed to us so very large that we were obliged to go over our work several times before we were absolutely sure that we were right. Once we were sure, however, that 47 tons was a proper day's work for a first-class pig iron handler, the task which faced us as managers under the modern scientific plan was clearly before us. It was our duty to see that the 80,000 tons of pig iron was loaded on to the cars at the rate of 47 tons per man per day, in place of 12 1/2 tons, at which rate the work was then being done. And it was further our duty to see that this work was done without bringing on a strike among the men, without any quarrel with the men, and to see that the men were happier and better contented when loading at the new rate of 47 tons than they were when loading at the old rate of 12 1/2 tons.

Our first step was the scientific selection of the workman. In dealing with workmen under this type of management, it is an inflexible rule to talk to and deal with only one man at a time, since each workman has his own special abilities and limitations, and since we are not dealing with men in masses, but are trying to develop each individual man to his highest state of efficiency and prosperity. Our first step was to find the proper workman to begin with. We therefore carefully watched and studied these 75 men for three or four days, at the end of which time we had picked out four men who appeared to be physically able to handle pig iron at the rate of 47 tons per day. A careful study was then made of each of these men. We looked up their history as far back as practicable and thorough inquiries were made as to the character, habits, and the ambition of each of them. Finally we selected one from among the four as the most likely man to start with. He was a little Pennsylvania Dutchman who had been observed to trot back home for a mile or so after his work in the evening about as fresh as he was when he came trotting down to work in the morning. We found that upon wages of $1.15 a day he had succeeded in buying a small plot of ground, and that he was engaged in putting up the walls of a little house for himself in the morning before starting to work and at night after leaving. He also had the reputation of being exceedingly "close," that is, of placing a very high value on a dollar. As one man whom we talked to about him said, "A penny looks about the size of a cart wheel to him." This man we will call Schmidt.

The task before us, then, narrowed itself down to getting Schmidt to handle 47 tons of pig iron per day and making him glad to do it. This was done as follows. Schmidt was called out from among the gang of pig iron handlers and talked to somewhat in this way:

Schmidt, are you a high-priced man?

Vell, I don't know vat you mean.

Oh, yes, you do. What I want to know is whether you are a high-priced man or not.

Vell, I don't know vat you mean.

Oh, come now, you answer my questions. What I want to find out is whether you are a high-priced man or one of these cheap fellows here. What I want to find out is whether you want to earn $1.85 a day or you are satisfied with $1.15, just the same as all these cheap fellows are getting.

Did I vant $1.85 a day? Vas dot a high-priced man? Vell, yes I vas a high-priced man.

Oh, you're aggravating me. Of course you want $1.85 a day—every one wants it! You know perfectly well that that has very little to do with your being a high-priced man. For goodness sake answer my questions, and don't waste any more of my time. Now come over here. You see that pile of pig iron?

Yes.

You see that car?

Yes.

Well, if you are a high-priced man, you will load that pig iron on that car tomorrow for $1.85. Now do wake up and answer my question. Tell me whether you are a high-priced man or not.

Vell—did I got $1.85 for loading dot pig iron on dot car tomorrow?

Yes, of course you do, and you get $1.85 for loading a pile like that every day right through the year. That is what a high-priced man does, and you know it just as well as I do.

Vell, dot's all right. I could load dot pig iron on the car tomorrow for $1.85, and I get it every day, don't I?

Certainly you do—certainly you do.

Vell, den, I vas a high-priced man.

Now, hold on, hold on. You know just as well as I do that a high-priced man has to do exactly as he's told from morning till night. You have seen this man here before, haven't you?

No, I never saw him.

Well, if you are a high-priced man, you will do exactly as this man tells you tomorrow, from morning till night. When he tells you to pick up a pig and walk, you pick it up and you walk, and when he tells you to sit down and rest, you sit down, and you don't talk back at him. Now you come on to work here tomorrow morning and I'll know before night whether you are really a high-priced man or not.

This seems to be rather rough talk. And indeed it would be if applied to an educated mechanic or even an intelligent laborer. With a man of the mentally sluggish type of Schmidt it is appropriate and not unkind, since it is effective in fixing his attention on the high wages which he wants and away from what, if it were called to his attention, he probably would consider impossibly hard work.

What would Schmidt's answer be if he were talked to in a manner which is usual under the management of "initiative and incentive?" Say, as follows:

Now, Schmidt, you are a first class pig iron handler and know your business well. You have been handling at the rate of 12 1/2 tons per day. I have given considerable study to handling pig iron, and feel sure that you could do a much larger day's work than you have been doing. Don't you think that if you really tried you could handle 47 tons of pig iron per day, instead of 12 1/2 tons?

What do you think Schmidt's answer would be to this?

Schmidt started to work, and all day long, and at regular intervals, was told by the man who stood over him with a watch, "Now pick up a pig and walk. Now sit down and rest. Now walk, now rest," etc. He worked when he was told to work, and rested when he was told to rest, and at half-past five in the afternoon had his 47 1/2 tons loaded on the car. And he practically never failed to work at this pace and do the task that was set him during the three years that the writer was at Bethlehem. And throughout this time he averaged a little more than $1.85 per day, whereas before he had never received over $1.15 per day, which was the ruling rate of wages at that time in Bethlehem. That is, he received 60 percent higher wages than were paid to other men who were not working on task work. One man after another was picked out and trained to handle pig iron at the rate of 47 1/2 tons per day until all of the pig iron was handled at this rate, and the men were receiving 60 percent more wages than other workmen around them.[5]

## Other Leaders in the Scientific Management Movement

**Henry L. Gantt.** Henry L. Gantt (1861–1919), an associate of Taylor's and a proponent of scientific management, modified Taylor's differential piece-rate in experiments with a task and a bonus plan. Under his plan the employer paid a bonus for work done beyond the task, but instead of a punitive low piece-rate on work below task, he guaranteed a time wage at a low rate. This gave the average worker a sense of security. Gantt, more aware of worker psychology than Taylor, also used as a stimulus a man-record chart which indicated for all to see whether a worker made his task day after day or fell below it.

For the benefit of management, Gantt devised a production chart showing day by day the work schedule on each job order and the work accomplished. Delay in a production schedule thus became evident at a glance and remedies could be applied or delivery dates adjusted accordingly.

**Harrington Emerson.** Harrington Emerson (1853–1931) introduced a modification of the task and bonus wage plan. He proposed to spread the rewards for efficiency over a wider range of accomplishment. In the following selection from his testimony before the United States Commission on Industrial Relations, he summarizes his views:[6]

**The Chairman**: What I asked Mr. Emerson was whether there were any points not mentioned in his written statement which he thought might throw light upon the question of efficiency as applied to labor.

**Mr. Emerson**: I do not know that there is any question of that kind. It has seemed to me this afternoon that on both sides the subject was perhaps not understood, or there seemed to be misconceptions as to what the aims were.

---

[5]Frederick W. Taylor, *The Principles of Scientific Management* (New York: Harper, 1911), pp. 41–47.

[6]U.S. Commission on Industrial Relations, *Final Report and Testimony*, vol. I (Washington: Government Printing Office, 1916), pp. 823–25.

Let us take up the matter of the determination of the standard task. That was one of the matters that was discussed by Mr. Taylor. We feel that the test of a standard lies ultimately absolutely with the worker. If a worker attains a standard without overspeeding and without undue strenuousness, that in itself justifies the standard. There is no penalty whatever imposed on a man who does not attain the standard.

Under the method that I prefer, the man is always guaranteed his day wages. That is fundamental, irrespective of what he accomplishes. The mere fact that he comes and offers his time entitles him to his wage. I consider the management always responsible for anything that goes wrong in a plant. I have never considered the worker responsible. If the worker is not furnished the work, it is the fault of the management, and he should not be made to suffer. That is the reason I am absolutely, wholly opposed to piece-work. I always have been, for the last 10 years. Ten years ago I denounced piece rates, and I have constantly worked and written and struggled against piece rates ever since. Piece rates impose responsibility on the worker, and the worker has only small authority. The responsibility of what is going on rests with the management to an extent to 90 percent.

Under the method I use, we therefore pay a fixed day rate. That rate is properly subject to bargaining, either individual or collective.

The second principle we use as to payment is that there shall be no determined equivalent for a day's work, and that equivalent should be determined by a scientific expert, neither by the management nor by the worker, and yet it should be accepted by both before it becomes valid. As you have it now, there are the two fixed principles of a fixed rate of pay per day, and the equivalent for that rate. In other words, a bushel consists of 60 pounds. You have a definite equivalent for what the day rate is.

Now, men vary very much in their abilities, in their speed, and under our plan there are many men who attain what we would call 80 percent efficiency, and there are other men who attain 120 percent efficiency. Instead of their all attaining exactly 100, they vary. We would expect, as a test of our standard, that there should be some few men as low as 80 percent, and that there would be some few men as high as 120 percent; that is, the bulk of the men would rank somewhere between 90 and 110 percent. We feel that the man who has it in him to deliver 120 percent should receive an individual reward on account of that. We should not, by any possibility, dispense with the man who attains 80 percent, because it is absolutely his right to stay on the 80 percent level. I would even go further; I would allow the man who has 120 percent ability to shorten his hours, if he saw fit. He could work 8 hours a day instead of working 10 hours. That would be at his option. The determination of the standard is, of course, the basis of the fairness of the relations between the employer and the employee. As a rough check on a standard, we make it one-half of what a man can attain by a stunt record, that we call 100 percent. To illustrate what I mean by that, the athletic record for walking is 8 miles in an hour. That is the world's record for walking. We would set 4 miles an hour as a good, stiff performance, and if a man walks more than that he would be paid accordingly. We would not think of discharging a man who walks as little as 2 1/2 miles an hour.

Now, if a man feels for any reason that he is not treated fairly, if we should attempt in any way to cut the standard, we would suffer far more than the man, because if he dropped back from 100 percent to 80 percent, still earning his day rate, the loss to the manager would be far greater than the loss to the workman, so that that stands absolutely as a barrier against any cut in the standard. Moreover, what we do is to check up the actual performances under the standards through a long course of time, as has been done by different men on different occasions, and if we do find that a performance the standard of which has been six and seven-tenths hours a day regularly takes six and nine-tenths hours, we come to be ameliorated, that it ought to be changed, that it ought to be made easier. The one intention is that the standard shall be fair, and when that is understood by both employer and employee—and I have had just as much trouble getting the employer to understand the point of view as the employee—when that relation is established there is very little difficulty in changing the standard one way or the other, in order to be fair.

* * * * *

As to wages, I feel absolutely certain that the law of progress depends on the fact that value increases faster than cost and therefore the endeavor should always be to secure the highest paid man that it is possible to get; that what is coming is that there will be a rivalry and competition for the high-priced man rather than for the low-priced man. I would be perfectly willing in any plant to accept a wage rate of $5 a day and make the costs lower in that plant than on any less sum than that you could mention. I would beat out the man and would feel confident that I would beat out the man who was paying $4 a day or $3 a day or $2 a day.

Now of course, there is a limit. I believe that the man should receive increasing wages for better conditions just as long as the unit price goes down, and no longer, because if you increase the wages when the unit price is going up, you are violating that other fundamental law, that with our increased power over the resources of the universe, costs are coming down. We are getting more than we formerly got. Therefore I give the worker increasing remuneration up to the point of increasing cost, and at that point I stop. I give the public a lower price, just as long as the volume of the product it buys enables me to make a lower cost, and no further. That is the way that I apportion the difference between cost and selling prices.

**Frank B. Gilbreth.** Frank B. Gilbreth (1868–1924) developed his ideas on improved individual efficiency before he met Taylor, but his work came closer to Taylor's when he extended his investigations into methods of general management. Gilbreth utilized motion study as a means of eliminating ineffective expenditure of energy. In addition to the stopwatch, he used a motion picture camera to provide material for analysis of a worker's movements (micromotion study) and fatigue.

The following selection summarizes the Taylor and Gilbreth systems:[7]

In 1912 Gilbreth devised and began to use a technique of work measurement which he called "micromotion study," which employed a motion picture camera to record the performance of a worker on a job, with a clock calibrated in hundredths of a minute placed in viewing range. With this technique, Gilbreth could record the motions, the time, and the conditions surrounding the job. His major objective was the recording, and ultimate simplification and improvement of the motions of the worker. His method permitted him to time both the motions of the worker and the total job, and also provided an opportunity to reproduce the performance of the worker a relatively unlimited number of times. Gilbreth subsequently devised other schemes of recording and tracing worker motions, but he considered micromotion study to be his most important contribution to scientific management.

Work measurement was, of course, one of the most significant aspects of scientific management. The Taylor program was based on the use of stop watch time study, under which the time study technician determined what the "elements" of a particular job were, and took a number of stop watch readings of each of the elements in developing data from which the ultimate time standard for the job would be developed. Taylor, himself, considered time study to be the "foundation of scientific management," and the Taylorites were primarily interested in the timing of the job. While Gilbreth was, of course, vitally interested in establishing a standard time for the job, he was perhaps more interested in analysis of work methods and patterns and in achieving economy of motions and effort, and he therefore viewed the setting of work standards from a different point of view. It is therefore not surprising that when Gilbreth described his new technique to the scientific management leader, the reaction was something less than enthusiastic. "Showed micromotion to Taylor," he noted, "and told him what it would do and told him I was surprised that he did not recognize its meaning. He said it was undoubtedly good where one was investigating the minutia of motions. He acted so that I saw he was hurt and so I changed the subject. . . ."

* * * * *

The Gilbreths characterized time study as unethical, wasteful, and inaccurate, among other things, although they were careful to point out that they were not personally criticizing Frederick Taylor, "the great founder of stop watch time study." (It would, however, have been strange indeed if their audience, and readers of the Taylor Society *Bulletin,* did not construe their strongly adverse criticism of time study to be an attack upon Taylor himself, because the most popular symbol of the latter's program was the stop watch.) The Gilbreths' essential contentions were that time study did not "preserve the best that has been done," employed questionable statistical methodology in arriving at standard times, and was costly because of the inaccurate and useless data it developed. They took pains to point out that motion study was not the same as

---

[7]Milton J. Nadworny, "Frederick Taylor and Frank Gilbreth: Competition in Scientific Management," *Business History Review,* 31, no. 1 (Spring 1957), p. 27.

time study, nor "a part of time study," and denounced the developers and practitioners of time study for failing to "cooperate with motion study."

\* \* \* \*

What has happened in the field of work measurement is that an accommodation
has taken place, and both stop watch time study and motion study and its derivatives
are used, either by individual firms or within the same work measurement program. It
is, in a sense, a triumph for the Gilbreths and particularly Frank Gilbreth, who, long
ago, suggested to Taylor that motion study "should really go with your great invention
of time study." It was not, of course, the kind of economic or intellectual triumph that
Gilbreth might have desired in 1921, but rather a process of gradually increasing
cooperation between the techniques and their representative practitioners, his more
consistently sought goal. No doubt the absence of the leading antagonists and competitors expedited the process of accommodation.

# Critique of Scientific Management

## An Evaluation of Scientific Management by U.S. Commission of Industrial Relations in 1912

**Abuses in its application.**  The report of the Commission on Industrial Relations summarized the shortcomings of scientific management as follows:[8]

To sum up, scientific management in practice generally tends to weaken the competitive power of the individual worker and thwarts the formation of shop groups and
weakens group solidarity; moreover, generally scientific management is lacking in the
arrangements and machinery necessary for the actual voicing of the workers' ideas
and complaints and for the democratic consideration and adjustment of grievances.
Collective bargaining has ordinarily no place in the determination of matters vital to
the workers, and the attitude toward it is usually tolerant only when it is not understood. Finally unionism, where it means a vigorous attempt to enforce the viewpoint
and claims of the workers, is in general looked upon with abhorrence, and unions
which are looked upon with complacency are not the kind which organized labor in
general wants, while the union cooperation which is invited is altogether different
from that which they stand ready to give. In practice scientific management must,
therefore, be declared autocratic in tendency—a reversion to industrial autocracy,
which forces the workers to depend on the employers' conception of fairness and limits
the democratic safeguards of the workers.

The arbitrary will of the employer and the law of economy are two potent special
forces which contribute to the existing diversity, incompleteness, and crudity of scientific management as it is practiced, even where the systematizer is possessed of the
highest intelligence and imbued with the best motives of his group.

But to explain the situation as it exists at present, two other important factors must
be taken into consideration. The first of these is the existence and practice of self-styled

---

[8]U.S. Commission on Industrial Relations of 1912, *Final Report and Testimony*, Vol. I, pp. 136–38.

scientific management systematizers and time study experts who lack in most respects the ideals and the training essential to fit them for the work which they claim to be able to do. Scientific management as a movement is cursed with fakirs. The great rewards which a few leaders in the movement have secured for their services have brought into the field a crowd of industrial "patent medicine men." The way is open to all. No standards or requirements, private or public, have been developed by the application of which the goats can be separated from the sheep. Employers have thus far proved credulous. Almost anyone can show the average manufacturing concern where it can make some improvements in its methods. So the scientific management shingles have gone up all over the country, the fakirs have gone into the shops, and in the name of scientific management have reaped temporary gains to the detriment of both the employers and the workers.

**Possible benefits of scientific management to labor and society.**  From the report of the United States Commission on Industrial Relations:[9]

1. As a system, scientific management presents certain possible benefits to labor and to society:

   a. A close (casual) relation exists between productive efficiency and possible wages. Greater efficiency and output make possible higher wages in general and better conditions of employment and labor. Insofar, then, as scientific management affords opportunities for lower costs and increased production without adding to the burden of the workers in exhaustive effort, long hours, or inferior working conditions, it creates the possibility of very real and substantial benefits to labor and to society.

   b. It is the policy of scientific management, as a preliminary to strictly labor changes, to bring about improvement and standardization of the material equipment and productive organization of the plant, particularly:
   Machinery:  installation, repair, operation.
   Tools:  storage, care, delivery.
   Material equipment:  rearrangement to avoid delays, etc.
   Product:  devices for economical and expeditious handling and routing.
   Processes and methods:  elimination of waste motions, improvement of accessories, etc.
   Reorganization of managerial staff and improvement of managerial efficiency.
   Reorganization of sales and purchasing departments with a view to broadening and stabilizing the market.
   Improvements in methods of storekeeping and regulation of delivery, surplus stock, etc.

   All such improvements are to be commended, and investigation shows that they are not only accepted by labor without opposition but are, in fact, welcomed.

2. Scientific management in its direct relation to labor is not devoid of beneficial aspects, inasmuch as it is to a large extent an attempt at immediate standardization of

---

[9]U.S. Commission on Industrial Relations of 1912, *Final Report and Testimony*, vol. I, pp. 128–29.

labor conditions and relations. It may also serve labor by calling the attention of the employer to the fact that there are other and more effective ways to meet severe competition than by "taking it out of labor."

It is true that scientific management and organized labor are not altogether in harmony in their attitude toward standardization of labor conditions and relations. While both seek to have the conditions of work and pay clearly defined and definitely maintained at any given moment, they differ fundamentally as to the circumstances which may justly cause the substitution of new standards for old ones. Trade-unionism tends to hold to the idea that standards must not be changed in any way to the detriment of the workers.

Scientific management, on the other hand, regards changes as justified and desirable, if they result in increase of efficiency, and has provided methods, such as time study, for the constant suggestion of such changes.

3. The same may be said of many other major claims of scientific management. Whether the ideals advocated are attained or at present attainable, and whether scientific managers are to be found who purposely violate them, scientific management has in these claims and in the methods upon which they are based shown the way along which we may proceed to more advantageous economic results for labor and for society. It may not have succeeded in establishing a practical system of vocational selection and adaptation, but it has emphasized the desirability of it; it may not set the task with due and scientific allowance for fatigue so that the worker is guarded against overspeeding and overexertion, but it has undoubtedly developed materials which make it possible to better prevailing conditions in this respect; it has called attention most forcibly to the evils of favoritism and the rough and arbitrary decisions of foremen and others in authority. If scientific management be shown to have positive objectionable features, from both standpoint of labor and the welfare of society, this constitutes no denial of these beneficial features, but calls rather for intelligent social action to eliminate that which is detrimental and to supplement and control that which is beneficial to all.

## Continuing Objections by Workers As Described by the U.S. Bureau of Labor Statistics in 1942[10]

In the early days of the factory system, piecework was common only in such industries as clothing and textile manufacture. These industries had their beginnings in home work, the worker being paid by the bundle for completed or semicompleted work. When the work was transferred to the factory, it was divided into many operations, making possible a further refinement in the incentive system. In the majority of early industrial establishments, however, piecework was not applied, because the tasks to be performed were extremely varied and required workers of higher all-round skill than was possessed by the more specialized pieceworker.

\* \* \* \* \*

The introduction of complex incentive methods in conjunction with scientific-management techniques was a significant feature of the decade following the

---

[10]U.S. Bureau of Labor Statistics, *Bulletin* No. 717, "Incentive-Wage Plans and Collective Bargaining" (Washington: Government Printing Office, 1942), pp. 2, 6–7.

first World War. The rapid growth of such industries as the manufacture of auto-mobiles and of electrical products, which were characterized by frequent style and model changes and continuous improvement in process and equipment, made necessary more detailed attention to production and efficiency problems. The time-study staff became a regular part of large factory operations. Many compan-ies, both large and small, hired outside engineers, each of whom had developed his own particular type of incentive system.

The installation of some of these plans was accompanied by thorough reorga-nization of factory production along more efficient lines, with the result that the incentive system increased production and earnings without marked increase in work effort on the part of the employees. In other cases, incentive systems were imposed on existing inefficient management methods, and such savings as were made in labor cost resulted only from speeding up the workers. No matter how thorough the original installation, inequities and confusion frequently developed after the engineer departed and the local management was left to carry on a com-plicated system, the essentials of which were only faintly understood in some cases.

* * * * *

In computing workers' pay for their output, the more complex incentive sys-tems make use of formulas that are confusing to most of the workers. The pay is not calculated according to the mere number of pieces produced or the number of hours of work but by means of some special unit such as a "manit" or a "B-hour." Workers claim that the use of a complex formula for wage payment facilitates rate cutting, because actual changes in production standards which affect the unit of measurement may be concealed from them. Whether rate cutting occurs or not, the worker finds it difficult to check the relationship between his pay and his out-put or effort. Thus, while simple piece rates are often accepted by workers as logi-cal and necessary, the more complicated bonus and premium plans, with their mathematical formulas for determining the workers' earnings, are likely to arouse deep suspicion.

A form of automatic rate cutting takes place in the "decreasing earnings curve" which is an essential part of the so-called "gain-sharing" incentive sys-tems. Inherent in the formulas by which earnings are computed under these plans is the principle that the reward shall be in a decreasing ratio for increased output. These incentive systems are referred to as "gain sharing," because a part of the value of the workers' increased production above "task" is retained by manage-ment for efficient supervision and efficient working conditions which theoretically helped make possible the increased output. Naturally enough, workers do not un-derstand the complicated theories behind such sharing of gains between manage-ment and labor for increased output, and often refer to the decreasing earnings curve as the "take-away curve."

Underlying the workers' fear and suspicion of rate cutting is their objection and uneasiness over a purely "scientific" approach to their jobs. Workers claim that almost any job contains elements which cannot be evaluated by the quantitative, stop-watch technique. They point to unpredictable variations in the quality of materials, in working equipment, and in other conditions surrounding their jobs. They know that every time study is adjusted to include "allowances" for delay, fatigue, and personal time which are arbitrarily determined. They are conscious of the fact that each of the job elements measured by the stop watch is evaluated by the time-study expert on the basis of his judgment as to whether the worker being timed is a slow, fast, or average worker.

Basically, the workers' grievances against scientific management, especially as practiced in the early days, are attributable to the tendency of management engineers to consider labor as impersonal and as a part of the machine process. Workers feel that they are being treated as abstract "labor," rather than human beings at work, when engineers break down jobs into repetitive operations, study work methods to discover short cuts and more efficient routines, shorten the cycle of operations which each workman is allowed to perform, and emphasize financial rewards instead of creative workmanship as an incentive towards efficient production.

Workers' objections to "scientific" wage setting may be alleviated or enhanced by management's approach to the time-study problem. In some plants, no one may become a member of the time-study staff who has not had years of working experience on regular production. In many instances, however, time-study "experts" are employed who have no first-hand familiarity with the jobs they are investigating. The "scientific" determination of working methods and standards by such persons is viewed with suspicion and distrust by workers on the job. Moreover, the impersonal treatment which workers resent is likely to be accentuated when an outside engineering firm is engaged to install an incentive plan. Such a firm is not subject to the controls of personal friendship and community interest which may influence a local plant management.

Workers are particularly opposed to the practices, formerly in widespread use, of employing secret or concealed time studies, or of placing "pace setters" in a department temporarily to get fast timings. These are viewed as instances of employer "cheating" on incentive workers, and they increase the hostility of workers toward all time-study methods.

As noted previously, the more complicated the incentive system, the more opposition it arouses in the workers. To many workers, the very "scientific" nature of the job standards under the complex plans appear merely another means of concealing from them the rate cuts and speed-up of which they complain. Although disagreement over piece rate, bonus rate, or production standard may represent simply a difference of opinion as to what constitutes "a fair day's work for a fair day's pay," the question is often complicated by management's conviction that the workers will not accept facts proved by scientific study and by the workers' feeling that, while they are not able to disprove management's technical case, they know their own jobs and believe that "the rates are not right."

# CASE 19

# Organized Labor and the Worker*

## Background

It is not easy to discuss "the worker" prior to large-scale industrialization in the United States, because the very idea that there should be a category of individuals who worked for others and whose purview and interests should be determined by that situation over a lifetime or even an extended period was not universally accepted. An important part of American ideology was that an individual did not have to labor for others, at least not all his life. Further, it was widely believed that relations between those who supplied manual labor and those who provided work were and should be characterized by a "harmony of interests." A well-known lawyer and publicist during the time of Andrew Jackson, for example, explained that "Society . . . is divided into two classes—those who do something for their living and those who do not. All honest men," he held, "belong to one party because they have all pure intentions and a common object—the greatest good of the greatest number."[1] Included in his definition of working men were, among others, Newton, Franklin, Washington, and Shakespeare.

---

*This case was prepared by Assistant Professor Richard S. Tedlow as a basis for class discussion rather than to illustrate either effective or ineffective handling of an administrative situation.

Copyright © 1983 by the President and Fellows of Harvard College.

Harvard Business School case 384–052, rev. 6/84.

[1]Marvin Meyers, *The Jacksonian Persuasion* (Stanford: Stanford University Press, 1960), pp. 215–16.

Ideology, of course, is rarely a precise descriptor of reality (although in this case it does indeed describe an important tendency). Prior to the Civil War, one can delineate a working class with a number of components.

First, of course, were the slaves. There were almost four million living in the United States in 1860. A voluminous literature on this subject demonstrates that it would be a gross distortion to depict masters as unfettered actors and slaves as purely acted upon. It is, however, reasonably accurate to say that at law the slave had virtually no control over the terms of his or her labor or indeed over his domestic living arrangements.

Second, there were in major cities artisans who were organized along lines similar to the guild system of Europe. These artisans included printers, shoemakers, coopers, and others who supplied the needs of urban residents and business people. At their head were the masters who determined who would be admitted to the trade, what product would be produced, and what price would be charged. They were assisted by journeymen who shared in their income and by apprentices who received room and board in exchange for learning the trade.

Third, there were also clustered in major cities casual laborers. These individuals performed unskilled manual labor such as dock work. They were employed irregularly and were often transients.

In the antebellum period, labor organization developed within artisan ranks. By 1830, organizations of shoemakers, printers, and various other craftsmen had been formed in Boston, Baltimore, Philadelphia, New York, and Pittsburgh. These early union-like organizations were restricted to a particular trade or craft and were local. Their aims included the upholding of craft standards, the restriction of hours of work, and, of course, better pay. They also served as benevolent societies which came to the aid of a member in case of unemployment or illness. To achieve their goals, these organizations bound their membership to strict rules and made use of the strike when necessary.

One authority has written:

> Although the early unions sought aims familiar to modern trade unionists, they practiced a singular form of bargaining. Rather than sit across a table from their employers and discuss the terms and conditions of employment, the craftsmen simply drew up a list of their demands, posted it publicly, and waited for the employer to accept or reject it. Acceptance would produce a settlement; rejection, a strike.[2]

The antebellum years witnessed a number of developments which anticipate modern labor organization. First, unions began to take political stands and even founded labor parties as early as 1828 in major cities. Second, they developed national organizations. Third, they made vigorous use of the strike.

The problems unions faced prior to the Civil War were also similar in some respects to those of a later era. First, there was the law. The legality of strikes particularly was questionable because of the doctrine that they constituted conspir-

---

[2]Melvyn Dubofsky, "Labor," in Glenn Porter, ed., *Encyclopedia of American Economic History*, vol. II (New York: Charles Scribner's Sons, 1980), pp. 525–26.

acies in restraint of trade in violation of the common law. Thus the Philadelphia Cordwainers' Conspiracy case held that one shoemaker could withhold his labor, but two or more could not jointly do so. The legality of the strike was not established until *Commonwealth v. Hunt* in 1842.

Second, labor organizations were acutely susceptible to economic conditions. Periodic business panics and depressions often faced workers with the choice of union or job.

Third, domestic geographic mobility and immigration from abroad acted to loosen ties to a local union. Foreign immigration into the United States from 1820 to 1860 totaled:

| | |
|---|---|
| 1820–1829 | 128,452 |
| 1830–1839 | 538,381 |
| 1840–1849 | 1,427,337 |
| 1850–1859 | 2,814,554 |

By 1860, 48 percent of New Yorkers, 50 percent of Chicagoans and Pittsburghers, and 60 percent of St. Louisians were foreign born. Most immigrants were British, Irish, or German.

## The Civil War and Postwar Developments

With the waning of the Panic of 1857, even before the Civil War broke out, the nation saw increased labor organizational activity. In response to cutthroat competition among manufacturers of cast iron stoves in 1859, various local unions combined to form the Iron Molders International Union. Also preceding the war were national (or at least nonlocal) organizations of printers, hat finishers, stone cutters, cigar makers, machinists, and blacksmiths. Many of these organizations were founded before the Panic of 1857. Having proven capable of surviving it, they grew stronger during the war years themselves.

The war generated sharply higher prices with wages lagging behind. However, it also resulted in labor shortages, which led to increased union membership and power. The first of the railway brotherhoods (for locomotive engineers) came into existence in 1863, followed by brotherhoods for the conductors (1868) and firemen (1873). In response to the displacement of skilled workers by the unskilled tending newly introduced machinery, shoemakers formed the Knights of St. Crispin, which by 1870 was the largest national craft union with 50,000 members. By 1870, perhaps as many as 300,000 workers were unionized.

Some of the craft unions appear to have been tightly organized and effectively managed. In the case of the printers, for example,

> Control of the organization became centralized in a general executive board consisting of well-paid national officials with substantial expense accounts and office staffs; the union levied relatively high dues in order to amass strike funds and disburse welfare benefits to its members; in return for strike payments and welfare benefits, local un-

ions surrendered the right to call strikes to national officers. Finally, because the printing trades operated primarily in a local market situation and competition was more common between workers than employers, the union issued traveling cards that promoted craft solidarity and curtailed scabbing.[3]

In 1866, a convention of trade unions and various reform societies met to establish a federation of national unions. The resultant organization, the National Labor Union, welcomed both skilled and unskilled workers. It established a lobby in Washington and agitated for, among other things, the eight-hour day, the granting of lands in the public domain to individuals only (rather than to corporations), and women's rights. It also favored the formation of worker-owned cooperatives, opposed strikes, and supported arbitration.

The NLU's leader, until his death at the age of 41 in 1869, was William Sylvis of the Iron Molders. In 1868, Silvis wrote to Karl Marx on the occasion of the First International:

> Our cause is a common one. . . . Go ahead in the good work you have undertaken, until the most glorious success crowns your efforts . . . moneyed power is fast eating up the substance of the people. We have made war upon it, and we mean to win it. If we can we will win through the ballot box; if not, we will resort to sterner means. A little bloodletting is sometimes necessary in desperate cases.[4]

At its height, the NLU had an estimated 170,000 members. By the early 1870s, it began to concentrate largely on controversial political goals. It backed a candidate in the 1872 presidential election, but he turned his back on it and the result was acute embarrassment. By this time the stronger trade unions had begun to leave the NLU in the hands of various radicals: "labor leaders without organizations, politicians without parties, . . . and cranks, visionaries, and agitators without jobs."[5] The dreadful depression of 1873 wiped out the NLU completely as well as almost all of the more than 30 trade unions founded in the 1860s. Indeed, during the years of the depression, the American union movement virtually ceased to exist.

## The Knights of Labor

Among the organizations that did survive the depression was the Noble Order of the Knights of Labor. The Knights had its beginnings as an organization of garment cutters in Philadelphia. It adopted the ritual paraphernalia often popular amongst fraternal organizations of the day. "To ensure secrecy the order was never referred to by name; it was known as the Five Stars or the Five Asterisks. Its meetings were called by mysterious symbols chalked on fences and sidewalks; its mem-

---

[3]Dubofsky, "Labor Organizations," p. 530.

[4]Quoted in Melvyn Dubofsky, *Industrialism and the American Worker* (New York: Crowell, 1957), p. 53.

[5]Norman Ware, *The Labor Movement in the United States, 1860–1895* (New York: Appleton, 1929), p. 11.

bers were supplied with grips, passwords, and countersigns."[6] At first it was concerned with the usual issues of craft unionism, but with its new Grand Master Workman, Terence V. Powderly, the Knights attempted to transform itself into a national organization. The basic approach was to welcome all regardless of race, sex, or skill (with the exception of selected "parasitic" professions such as liquor dealers, gamblers, stockbrokers, lawyers, and bankers) who were or had ever been victimized by the wage system or who recognized its inherent evils. The goal, in the words of one historian, was "to teach the American wage earner that he was a wage earner first and a bricklayer, carpenter, miner, shoemaker after; that he was a wage earner first and a Catholic, Protestant, Jew, white, black, Democrat, Republican after. . . ."[7] Approximate membership figures were

| 1879 | 9,000 | 1885 | 104,000 |
|------|-------|------|---------|
| 1880 | 20,000 | 1886 | 703,000 |
| 1881 | 28,000 | 1887 | 510,000 |
| 1882 | 19,000 | 1888 | 260,000 |
| 1883 | 42,000 | 1889 | 220,000 |
| 1884 | 52,000 | 1890 | 100,000 |

The reason for the dramatic increase in 1886 was the spectacular success of a strike against a wage cut Jay Gould attempted to impose on the workers on three of the railroads he controlled. The walkout was spontaneous, but confronted with it, the Knights supported it. Gould was in a particularly exposed position at this time and gave into the workers' demands almost immediately. The decline of the Knights can be explained by the complete failure of another strike against Gould, the failure of a strike for the eight-hour day, and the riot at a meeting of radicals at Haymarket Square, which led to widespread antilabor opinion. Exhibit 1 is a speech by Powderly in 1880, and Exhibit 2 is a declaration of aims of the Knights in 1884. Together, these documents provide a summary of the goals and philosophy of the organization.

## The American Federation of Labor

Founded in 1886 from the ashes of the moribund Federation of Organized Trades and Labor Unions of the United States and Canada, the A F of L was destined to become the most important voice for labor for a half century. A leading reason for its success was the man who served as its president (with the exception of one year) from its founding to his death in 1924, Samuel Gompers.

Gompers, a Jew of Dutch descent born in London in 1850, migrated to New York with his family in 1863. He was a cigar maker by trade.

Cigar rolling was quiet work, and the men used this advantage by assigning one of their number as reader, sharing their product with him so that he suffered no loss of in-

---

[6]Joseph G. Rayback, *A History of American Labor* (New York: Free Press, 1966), p. 143.

[7]Norman Ware, *Labor Movement,* p. xviii.

come. The readers roamed far and wide across the esthetic, political, and economic literature of the time and sampled the current newspapers and magazines. After the readings, the workers engaged in lively, sometimes heated discussions contributing significantly to "the fellowship that grew between congenial shopmates which was something that lasted a lifetime." For Sam, "life in the factory," which proved a Hogarthian nightmare for many, remained "one of [his] most pleasant memories."[8]

By 1875, Gompers was a union organizer, knocking on the doors of shops and tenements and writing pamphlets in English and German after working a 10-hour day. The depth of his commitment to his work is indicated by the fact that in his later years he could not remember whether he had had 10 or 12 children. Gompers participated fully in the intellectual ferment that was New York in these years, and he learned a lot from socialists, communists, and the sundry reform movements of the day. His foremost lesson was that in his view such people had no business in the labor movement. He favored "pure and simple" unionism of, by, and for workers themselves. He opposed ideologies, ideologues, and politics. Selected samples of Gompers' views are presented in Exhibit 3. For membership in the A F of L, see Exhibit 7.

By the turn of the century, Gompers had won a seat at the banquet of the mighty as the spokesman for "responsible" organized labor. He was a member of the National Civic Federation, an organization founded in 1900 to promote industrial harmony, and as such hobnobbed with Carnegie, Astor, Belmont, and Hanna. Woodrow Wilson, of whom he was an ardent supporter, appointed him to the Council on National Defense during World War I.

## Industrial Unions

Various organizations sprang up from 1890 to 1920 which rejected the strict craft union/skilled worker bias of the A F of L in favor of "one big union" which would comprehend all workers in an industry regardless of the work they performed. Within the A F of L, one major affiliate had this structure. This was the United Mine Workers. Dispersed in small towns, the miners found the craft approach impractical. Their hardbitten and shrewd leadership masterminded important advances against the mine owners, and their membership grew from about 63,000 in 1899 to about 270,000 in 1907. But Gompers was always rather suspicious of the miners' tactics and felt threatened by the UMW's power within the A F of L. The only year between 1886 and 1924 that he lost the presidency of the Federation was in 1895; the victor was from the UMW.

Eugene Victor Debs was one of the leading industrial union advocates. From a middle-class background, Debs became an official of the Brotherhood of Railway Firemen in the 1870s. He started his career as a conservative, opposing the railway strikes of 1877. But by the early 1890s, he had become convinced that the craft approach was inadequate to cope with the power of big business, and in June of 1893, he founded the American Railway Union along industrial lines with power

---

[8]Harold C. Livesay, *Samuel Gompers and Organized Labor in America* (Boston: Little, Brown, 1978), p. 13.

and control vested in a central organization. Soon thereafter, unorganized workers on the Great Northern struck against a wage cut and appealed to the Debs union for help. The ARU responded and the unexpectedly quick victory brought an onrush of new members. In one year, the ARU had attracted 150,000 members.

In 1894, however, the union was drawn unwillingly into another strike, this one in sympathy with employees of the Pullman Palace Car Company. George Pullman was a tough customer, and he found plentiful support in an organization of railway executives. With the help of federal and state troops and the vigorous use of court injunctions, the strike was completely crushed in July of 1894 after rioting and loss of life. Debs was jailed and during incarceration became a socialist. He was the socialist candidate for president on five occasions, winning about 6 percent of the popular vote (901,000) in 1912, a higher percentage than any other socialist before or since. In 1920, he received over 920,000 votes while in a jail cell for having spoken out against World War I in June of 1918.

Another important industrial union was founded in 1905 by a group of radical leftists committed to organizing the mass of unskilled workers. From 1909 to 1919, the Industrial Workers of the World was at the center of almost a dozen violent industrial conflicts, gaining some notable successes. The IWW was really more than an industrial union. It was a radical cadre which preached seizure of the productive assets of the nation by direct worker action in factory and even farm. The IWW was crushed by business and government soon after World War I.

## EXHIBIT 1

### *Speech by Terence V. Powderly, Grand Master Workman of the Knights of Labor, September 1880*

One of the evils which beset the trades union, and which ever and anon comes to the surface in this organization, is the strike.

Though my views upon this subject are well known to you, since I have plainly stated them through both the public press and The Journal of United Labor; still I think it proper to advise, and, if possible, point out to you some of the errors which many of our Local Assemblies have committed, in the hope that you may, in your deliberations, steer clear of the breakers into which they have dashed only to strike the rocks and go down to destruction by disbanding, or else linger along in a demoralized condition. Many of our Locals have spent a great deal of valuable time in discussing the best means of supporting their Brethren in that most disastrous of all methods of obtaining a redress of grievances, the *Strike*.

Do not, I beg of you, fall into the same error, but endeavor to direct every effort toward the perfection of measures for the destruction of the evils which make strikes a necessity.

We are the willing victims of an outrageous system that envelops us in the midst of the ills of which we complain. We should not war with man for being what *we* make him, but strike a powerful, telling blow at the base of the system which makes the laborer the slave of his master.

## EXHIBIT 1 (*continued*)

So long as the present order of things exist, just so long will the attempt to make peace between the man who sells and the man who buys labor be fruitless.

So long as it is to the interest of one kind of men to purchase labor at the lowest possible figure, and so long as it is to the interest of another kind of men to sell labor to the highest possible bidder, just so long will there exist an antagonism between the two which all the speakers and writers upon labor cannot remove.

So long as a pernicious system leaves one man at the mercy of another, so long will labor and capital be at war, and no strike can hit a blow sufficiently hard to break the hold with which unproductive capital today grasps labor by the throat.

In what direction should we turn to see our way clear to a solution of the difficulty? Far be it from me to say that I can point the way; would to Heaven that I could with certainty do it! I can only offer a suggestion, which comes to me as the result of experience, and that suggestion is to abolish the Wage System.

This is the system which carries with it into the workshop, the mine, and factory, a host of evils, which, to repeat, would completely exhaust the whole vocabulary of murmurings which fill the complaint book of Labor.

This is the system which, serpent-like, pushes itself along wherever those bands of commercial iron and steel are laid, carrying discontent and misery in its train.

This is the system which enables a half a dozen men to sit at their tables in any of our large centres of trade, and, without any thought of the welfare of the country, issue the imperial mandates which direct the movements of the whole industrial population of the United States.

This is the system which makes every railroad superintendent, every factory or mine superintendent, an autocrat, at whose nod or beck the poor unrequited slave who labors must bow the head and bend the knee in humble suppliance.

To point out a way to utterly destroy this system would be a pleasure to me. I can only direct your attention to it, and leave the rest to your wisdom; and I firmly believe that I have pointed out the most vicious of all evils which afflict labor today.

But are we prepared to lay siege to this bulwark of oppression? Remember that for centuries it has been slowly, yet steadily, creeping onward, making each year new and deeper inroads upon labor, until today it stands so well established and powerful that even the staunchest heart in the ranks of Labor's defenders almost sinks in despair at the thought of breaking down the barriers of fear, ignorance, and superstition, to which its existence has given birth.

The wage system, at its inception was but an experiment, and for a time doubts were entertained as to its adoption; but the avaricious eye of the Shylock of labor saw in it a weapon with which he could strike the toiler to the dust, and today that system has so firm a hold upon us that every attempt at shaking off the fetters, by resorting to a strike, only makes it easier for the master to say to his slave, "You must work for less wages."

We must teach our members, then, that the remedy for the redress of the wrongs we complain of does not lie in the suicidal strike: but it lies in thorough, ef-

## EXHIBIT 1 (*concluded*)

fective organization. Without organization we cannot accomplish anything; through it we hope to forever banish that curse of modern civilization—wage slavery.

But how? Surely not by forming an association and remaining a member; not by getting every other worthy man to become a member and remain one; not by paying the dues required of us as they fall due. These are all important factors in the method by which we hope to regain our independence, and are vitally important—they are the elements necessary to a complete organization.

Organization once perfected, what must we do? I answer, study the best means of putting your organization to some practicable use by embarking in a system of cooperation which will eventually make every man his own master, every man his own employer; a system which will give the laborer a fair proportion of the products of his toil. It is to cooperation, then, as the lever of labor's emancipation, that the eyes of the workingmen and women of the world are directed, upon cooperation their hopes are centred, and to it do I now direct your attention. I am deeply sensible of the importance, of the magnitude, of the undertaking in which I invite you to engage. I know that it is human nature to grow cold, apathetic, and finally indifferent, when engaged in that which requires deep study and persistent effort, unattended by excitement; men are apt to believe that physical force is the better way of redressing grievances, being the shorter remedy; but even that requires patience and fortitude as well as strength. I need but point out to you the war of the Revolution, which took nearly eight years of hard fighting and persistent effort upon the part of men who fought for a principle. Had these men fallen into the same error which Labor has so often fallen into, there would be no independence; had they gone to their homes after the battle of Bunker Hill, there would be no Bunker Hill monument erected, even though the result of that battle was encouraging.

To the subject of cooperation, then, do I invite your attention, and I liken it unto the Revolutionary War. If you decide upon carrying it out at this convention, it will be the Bunker Hill of Industrial Independence but you must also bear in mind, though the longest term allotted to man be yours to live, you will not see during that term the complete triumph of your hopes. The war for American Independence had its Bunker Hills and its Washingtons, but it also had its Valley Forges and its Benedict Arnolds. The enthusiasm of the hour will avail us nothing, and cooperation requires every Washington of labor to be up and doing. The laboring man needs education in this great social question, and the best minds of the Order must give their precious thought to this system. There is no good reason why labor cannot, through cooperation, own and operate mines, factories, and railroads.

Source: Harvard Business School case 372–319.

## EXHIBIT 2

### *Preamble and Declaration of Aims of the Knights of Labor*

The alarming development and aggressiveness of great capitalists and corporations, unless checked, will inevitably lead to the pauperization and hopeless degradation of the toiling masses.

It is imperative, if we desire to enjoy the full blessings of life, that a check be placed upon unjust accumulation, and the power for evil of aggregated wealth.

This much-desired object can be accomplished only by the united efforts of those who obey the divine injunction, "In the sweat of thy face shalt thou eat bread."

Therefore we have formed the Order of Knights of Labor, for the purpose of organizing and directing the power of the industrial masses, not as a political party, for it is more—in it are crystallized sentiments and measures for the benefit of the whole people, but it should be borne in mind, when exercising the right of suffrage, that most of the objects herein set forth can only be obtained through legislation, and that it is the duty of all to assist in nominating and supporting with their votes only such candidates as will pledge their support to those measures, regardless of party. But no one shall, however, be compelled to vote with the majority, and calling upon all who believe in securing "the greatest good to the greatest number," to join and assist us, we declare to the world that our aims are:

I. To make industrial and moral worth, not wealth, the true standard of individual and national greatness.

II. To secure to the workers the full enjoyment of the wealth they create, sufficient leisure in which to develop their intellectual, moral and social faculties: all of the benefits, recreation and pleasures of association; in a word, to enable them to share in the gains and honors of advancing civilization.

In order to secure these results, we demand at the hands of the State:

III. The establishment of Bureaus of Labor Statistics, that we may arrive at a correct knowledge of the educational, moral and financial conditions of the laboring masses.

IV. That the public lands, the heritage of the people, be reserved for actual settlers; not another acre for railroads or speculators, and that all lands now held for speculative purposes be taxed to their full value.

V. The abrogation of all laws that do not bear equally upon capital and labor, and the removal of unjust technicalities, delays and discriminations in the administration of justice.

VI. The adoption of measures providing for the health and safety of those engaged in mining, manufacturing and building industries, and for indemnification to those engaged therein for injuries received through lack of necessary safeguards.

# EXHIBIT 2 (*continued*)

**VII.** The recognition, by incorporation, of trades' unions, orders and such other associations as may be organized by the working masses to improve their condition and protect their rights.

**VIII.** The enactment of laws to compel corporations to pay their employees weekly, in lawful money, for the labor of the preceding week, and giving mechanics and laborers a first lien upon the product of their labor to the extent of their full wages.

**IX.** The abolition of the contract system on National, State and Municipal works.

**X.** The enactment of laws providing for arbitration between employers and employed, and to enforce the decision of the arbitrators.

**XI.** The prohibition by laws of the employment of children under 15 years of age in workshops, mines and factories.

**XII.** To prohibit the hiring out of convict labor.

**XIII.** That a graduated income tax be levied.

And we demand at the hands of Congress:

**XIV.** The establishment of a National monetary system, in which a circulating medium in necessary quantity shall issue direct to the people, without the intervention of banks that all the National issue shall be full legal tender in payment of all debts, public and private; and that the Government shall not guarantee or recognize any private banks, or create any banking corporations.

**XV.** That interest-bearing bonds, bills of credit or notes shall never be issued by the Government, but that, when need arises, the emergency shall be met by issue of legal tender, noninterest-bearing money.

**XVI.** That the importation of foreign labor under contract be prohibited.

**XVII.** That, in connection with the post office, the Government shall organize financial exchanges, safe deposits and facilities for deposit of savings of the people in small sums.

**XVIII.** That the Government shall obtain possession, by purchase, under the right of eminent domain, of all telegraphs, telephones and railroads, and that hereafter no charter or license be issued to any corporation for construction or operation of any means of transporting intelligence, passengers or freight.

And while making the foregoing demands upon the State and National Government, we will endeavor to associate our own labors.

**XIX.** To establish cooperative institutions such as will tend to supersede the wage system, by the introduction of a cooperative industrial system.

**XX.** To secure for both sexes equal pay for equal work.

## EXHIBIT 2 (*concluded*)

**XXI.** To shorten the hours of labor by a general refusal to work for more than eight hours.

**XXII.** To persuade employers to agree to arbitrate all differences which may arise between them and their employees, in order that the bonds of sympathy between them may be strengthened and that strikes may be rendered unnecessary.

Source: Harvard Business School case 372–320.

## EXHIBIT 3

### *A Selection of the Views of Samuel Gompers*

#### C.L.F. Charter

Some few months ago the Central Federation of Labor of New York City made an application for a certificate of affiliation. It was accompanied by a list of the organizations attached to that body. At the head of the list was the name of the American Section of the Socialist Labor Party. The matter received my keenest thought and best judgment. I consulted the constitution and saw there clearly defined which organizations were entitled to affiliation with the American Federation of Labor. The Socialist Labor Party or any other party or section of a party is not included among the number. But, apart from any constitutional considerations, I believed then and am convinced now that the Socialist Labor party, *as a party,* is not entitled to representation in a purely trade union organization.

I informed the Central Labor Federation of the above fact, and they declared their determination not to ask the Socialist Labor Party to withdraw and renewed their request for the charter. I reiterated the opinion expressed in my former letter and resolved to refer the entire matter to this convention to decide whether the position I took was correct.

Since this matter was first broached a number of people, glad to clutch at anything that promises something to "talk about" and sow the seeds of dissension, have ascribed to me all sorts of opinions and motives. It has been charged that I am trying to drive the Socialists out of the movement; that I am intolerant of others' opinions, and other insinuations equally ridiculous and untrue and too numerous to mention. I desire to take this opportunity of saying that I have ever held that the trade unions were broad enough and liberal enough to admit of any and all shades of thought upon the economic and social question; but at the same time the conviction is deeply rooted in me that in the trade union movement the first condition requisite is good-standing membership in a trade union, regardless of which party a man might be a member of.

Those who have had any experience in the labor movement will admit the

## EXHIBIT 3 (*continued*)

great work and forbearance, tact and judgment requisite to maintain harmony in organization. The trade unions are no exception to this rule. In the trade union movement I have ever endeavored to attain that much desired end, and recognize that that in itself is of a sufficiently important nature and requirement as to preclude the possibility of jointly acting with organizations based upon different practical workings or policy.

I am willing to subordinate my opinions to the well being, harmony and success of the labor movement; I am willing to sacrifice myself upon the altar of any phase or action it may take for its advancement; I am willing to step aside if that will promote our cause, but I cannot and will not prove false to my convictions that the trade unions pure and simple are the natural organizations of the wage workers to secure their present material and practical improvement and to achieve their final emancipation.

### Strikes

For quite a time a great deal has been said in condemnation of strikes by labor or pseudo labor men, with which, I confess, I have no patience. It is true that no man who has given the question of strikes and the labor movement any thought can look upon strikes with favor; but to be continually condemning them is entirely another thing. To know when to strike, and particularly *when not to strike,* is a science not yet fully understood. To strike upon a falling market, or being insufficiently organized, or if organized, not properly equipped with the ammunition so necessary to a successful strike—funds—is unquestionably the height of ignorance. The story of the strikes that may have failed of their immediate objects yet have prevented reductions in wages and worse conditions will probably never be entirely told. Mounting condemnation of strikes, we find, by experience, does not abolish or even reduce their number. As a consistent opponent of strikes, though, I do find that those organizations of labor which have best provided themselves with the means to strike have continually less occasion to indulge in them. The most potent factor to prevent or reduce the number of strikes is a well organized trade union with a full treasury ready to strike should the necessity arise. It is notable that there were few successful strikes of great significance during the past year. The continual condemnation of them caused a consequent failure to prepare for them. It did not prevent them, it merely defeated them.

### Strike Assistance

Several applications have been made to this office for financial assistance during strikes by local organizations, the members of which went on strike first and applied for assistance afterwards.

In many instances, upon the mere statement of the fact that they were affiliated to the American Federation of Labor, their demands were acceded to; in others, with what assistance we could give them, they were successful, but there were

## EXHIBIT 3 (*continued*)

instances in which the men were so thoroughly unprepared that they were immediately compelled to make application for financial assistance, which we could not give.

Those most persistent in their applications were generally those who had paid nothing but the small per capita tax to the office for the mere running expenses of the organization.

I desire to impress upon the minds of the working people the absolute necessity that they should keep in view that it is not bluster nor ostentation that will win victories for them.

Such organizations of labor may at times win victories from their employers, but they are generally of a transitory character. We must not only be right, but possess the power to enforce that right, and there is no argument so potent with unwilling or unfair employers to grant reasonable demands as a well-organized Trade Union, with a well-filled treasury, to stand them in need should a strike be necessary to enforce the demand.

The payment of fair dues in a union, regularly contributed in times of peace, is much more valuable than assessments enforced during strikes. The workers are then always prepared to meet any attack and give their organizations the character of permanency so essential to success.

### Higher Dues and Their Results

In connection with the subject of taxation and assessments of affiliated Unions to support each other when engaged in trade difficulties to defend their position against the encroachments of their employers, or to make advances to promote and improve their condition, I desire to add what I have often repeated both in my reports to previous Conventions and elsewhere, that those Unions which have a good financial system have ever been on the increase in their membership. That there is no means by which the reductions in wages are prevented and ever keeps onward and forward in its growth, influence and power to maintain and raise the vantage ground of their members than high dues.

It is false economy to suppose that success in a Trade Union results from small initiation fees and low dues. It is idle to imagine and at variance with experience that organizations grow when the initiation fees and dues of Unions are small. It may be true that a Union may be organized and gain a number in its fold upon the cry of low dues, but I am sure the history of the labor movement will demonstrate beyond a doubt that such organizations have been but of a transitory character.

Our Unions should charge a fair initiation fee and high dues. It is likely that they will not receive large accessions of membership spasmodically, but the growth will be steady and continuous. From the large dues paid our Unions should and can be of permanent benefit to their members. Our Trade Unions should contain the benevolent as well as the protective features. They should be the defenders and protectors of the wage workers in every sphere of life. It has been ably said that in all past history it has always been the "remnant" in society that has saved it from

## EXHIBIT 3 (*continued*)

retrogression and barbarism. So with the Trade Unions; they are the "remnant" in the present society that must save the people from retrogression and barbarism. Our Trade Unions are the germs of the future society based upon honesty, fair dealing and a broader conception of human rights.

### Political Action

Many delegates may feel, and I have heard that the matter would be brought to the attention of this convention, the desirability of forming a third, or what is known as an independent, political party; but in view of recent experience, I can only say that such action, for the present at least, would be in the extreme unwise. If we are zealous and earnest in the advocacy of agitation and desire the enforcement of the eight-hour work day, it will require all we can possibly do to muster all our efforts and concentrate our power upon its attainment. The experiences of the past have taught that we may and can obtain great practical results, both political as well as economical, by creating a healthy public opinion if we devote ourselves energetically to our organization, the development and maintenance of our trade unions.

### Shall We Change Our Methods?

Many of our earnest friends in the labor movement, having witnessed the brutal outrages of the monopolistic class and their hirelings upon the toiling masses within the past few months have had their innermost feelings stirred, and impatiently declare that a new path must be struck by the working people in order to overcome defeats and achieve victories. They look upon some of the recent defeats and predict the annihilation of the economic effort of organized labor—or the impotency of the economic organizations, the trade unions—to cope with the great power of concentrated wealth. There are few, if any, who have given our movement any thought, but who have shared the intensity of feeling caused by the brutal exhibitions referred to, but feelings often prompt action which good judgment forbids.

It is not true that the economic effort has been a failure, nor that the usefulness of the economic organizations is at an end. It is true that in several instances they have been defeated; but, though defeated, they are not conquered; the very fact that the monopolistic and capitalist class having assumed the aggressive, and after defeating the toilers in several contests, the wage workers of our country have maintained their organizations is the best proof of the power, influence and permanency of the trade unions. They have not been routed, they have merely retreated, and await a better opportunity to obtain the improved conditions which for the time they were deprived of.

Upon the field of labor, like every other contest in human life, it is a matter principally of intelligence, judgment and foresight.

## EXHIBIT 3 (*continued*)

### Union Organization and Operations

The Cigar Makers' International Union, of which I have the honor of being a member, and have been since 1864, continuously, was at one time an incoherent mass of federated members into a federated number of local unions, each absolutely independent of the other, except that they could, if they chose, accept a member's traveling card and accord him the hand of fellowship. During the early history of the organization it possessed no real merit, until a strike occurred and brought about an understanding among my fellow-craftsmen that there was something more necessary than simply the declaration that one was a union man, and that was that wherever you are a union man you are naturally to observe the same obligations, perform the same duties, and be entitled to the same privileges and benefits. That dawned upon us just after a great strike and just previous to the greater strike of 1877, when there were about 10,000 cigar makers out on strike, after suffering all the miseries that one could imagine. It was at the convention of 1877 that we adopted the first proposition of uniform dues and uniform initiation fees. Previous to that one local union would charge $5 for initiation fee, another one would charge $3, another $1, another, not so fortunately situated, would charge 10 cents, or perhaps accept them without any initiation fee at all, and usually where we charged very low figures they used to run in in swarms. If I could coin a word expressive of the way they ran out, I should be glad to—the way they left the organization. And this was true, too, of the lack of uniformity in dues; lack of uniformity of duties and rights. We gradually introduced a system by which not only the dues were increased, but the funds belonged to the membership in their collective capacity, but were held in the local unions, never at general headquarters. We established a system, too, by which a member was entitled to the same benefits—strike benefit, lockout benefit, victimization benefit, sick benefit, traveling benefit—that is, when a member was out of employment, so that he need not be arrested as a tramp or vagrant his union card entitled him to a loan from the union under whose jurisdiction he was, so that he could travel to the next point, and get 50 cents in addition to the mileage, so as to buy a meal or get a lodging, and from place to place those loans were accorded to him until he could return to work, and then he paid 10 percent of his wages in repaying the organization the loan advanced. It was a loan system, without interest, of course. Then there was the out-of-work benefit—benefit when a man is out of work; that condition for which society makes no provision at all, not even the charitably inclined. Our organization proposed to go to the defense of the member and pay him, not a stipend as a matter of charity, but something in his own right as a contributing member. Then the death benefit, from $50 for the first year of membership to $550 to a member's family or nearest of kin for 15 years' membership. There is a graduated figure or sum between those sums. We pay 30 cents per week as dues for these benefits and we receive in return a larger amount in the shape of benefits, direct benefits, than is paid by any insurance or beneficial association on earth. The

## EXHIBIT 3 (*continued*)

combination makes its administration economical. The percentage of expenditure for administration is very small; and this does not refer to the strike benefit or lock-out benefit, or victimization benefit.

### The Wage System

I know that we are operating under the wage system. As to what system will ever come to take its place I am not prepared to say. I have given this subject much thought; I have read the works of the most advanced economists, competent economists in all schools of thought—the trade unionist, the socialist, the anarchist, the single taxer, the cooperationist, etc. I am not prepared to say, after having read, and with an honest endeavor to arrive at a conclusion—I am not prepared to say that either of their propositions are logical, scientific, or natural. I know that we are living under the wage system, and so long as that lasts, it is our purpose to secure a continually larger share for labor, for the wealth producers. Whether the time shall come, as this constantly increasing share to labor goes on, when profits shall be entirely eliminated, and the full product of labor, the net result of production, go to the laborer, thus abolishing the wage system; or whether, on the other hand, through the theory of the anarchist, there should be an abolition of all title in land other than its occupation and use, the abolition of the monopoly of the private issuance of money, the abolition of the patent system—whether we will return to the first principles; or whether, under the single tax, taxing the land to the full value of it—I am perfectly willing that the future shall determine and work out. I know that as the workers more thoroughly organize, and continually become larger sharers in the product of their toil, they will have the better opportunities for their physical and mental cultivation instilled into them, higher hopes and aspirations, and they will be better prepared to meet the problems that will then confront them. For the present it is our purpose to secure better conditions and instill a larger amount of manhood and independence into the hearts and minds of the workers, and to broaden their mental sphere and the sphere of their affections.

### Capital and Labor

I should regard (the possibility that the interests of capital and labor will someday be identical) upon the same plane as I would the panaceas that are offered by our populists, socialists, anarchists, and single tax friends, as very remote and very far removed, if that time should ever come. I am perfectly satisfied to fight the battles of today, of those here, and those that come tomorrow, so their conditions may be improved, and they may be better prepared to fight in the contests or solve the problems that may be presented to them. The hope for a perfect millenium—well, it don't come every night; it don't come with the twinkling of the eye; it is a matter which we have got to work out, and every step that the workers make or take, ev-

## EXHIBIT 3 (*concluded*)

ery vantage point gained, is a solution in itself. I have often inquired of men who have ready-made patent solutions of this social problem, and I want to say to you, sir, that I have them offered to me on an average of two or three a week, and they are all equally unsatisfactory. I maintain that we are solving the problem every day; we are solving the problems as they confront us. One would imagine by what is often considered as the solution of the problem that it is going to fall among us, that a world cataclysm is going to take place; that there is going to be a social revolution; that we will go to bed one night under the present system and the morrow morning wake up with a revolution in full blast, and the next day organize a Heaven on earth. That is not the way that progress is made; that is not the way the social evolution is brought about; that is not the way the human family are going to have interests advanced. We are solving the problem day after day. As we get an hour's more leisure every day it means millions of golden hours, of opportunities, to the human family. As we get 25 cents a day wages increase it means another solution, another problem solved, and brings us nearer the time when a greater degree of justice and fair dealing will obtain among men.

Source: Harvard Business School case 372–319.

# EXHIBIT 4

## Labor Force and Employment, by Industry: 1800 to 1920 (in Thousands of Persons 10 Years Old and Over)

| | Labor Force | | | | | | | Employment | | | | Transport | | Service | |
| | | | | | | | | Manufacturing | | | | | | | |
| Year | Total | Free | Slave | Agriculture | Fishing | Mining | Construction | Total Persons Engaged | Cotton Textile Wage Earners | Primary Iron and Steel Wage Earners | Trade | Ocean Vessels | Railway | Teachers | Domestics |
|---|---|---|---|---|---|---|---|---|---|---|---|---|---|---|---|
| 1920 | 41,610 | — | — | 10,790 | 53 | 1,180 | 1,233 | 11,190 | 450 | 460 | 5,845 | 205 | 2,236 | 752 | 1,660 |
| 1910 | 37,480 | — | — | 11,770 | 68 | 1,068 | 1,949 | 8,332 | 370 | 306 | 5,320 | 150 | 1,855 | 595 | 2,090 |
| 1900 | 29,070 | — | — | 11,680 | 69 | 637 | 1,665 | 5,895 | 303 | 222 | 3,970 | 105 | 1,040 | 436 | 1,800 |
| 1890 | 23,320 | — | — | 9,960 | 60 | 440 | 1,510 | 4,390 | 222 | 149 | 2,960 | 120 | 750 | 350 | 1,580 |
| 1880 | 17,390 | — | — | 8,920 | 41 | 280 | 900 | 3,290 | 175 | 130 | 1,930 | 125 | 416 | 230 | 1,130 |
| 1870 | 12,930 | — | — | 6,790 | 28 | 180 | 780 | 2,470 | 135 | 78 | 1,310 | 135 | 160 | 170 | 1,000 |
| 1860 | 11,110 | 8,770 | 2,340 | 5,880 | 31 | 176 | 520 | 1,530 | 122 | 43 | 890 | 145 | 80 | 115 | 600 |
| 1850 | 8,250 | 6,280 | 1,970 | 4,520 | 30 | 102 | 410 | 1,200 | 92 | 35 | 530 | 135 | 20 | 80 | 350 |
| 1840 | 5,660 | 4,180 | 1,480 | 3,570 | 24 | 32 | 290 | 500 | 72 | 24 | 350 | 95 | 7 | 45 | 240 |
| 1830 | 4,200 | 3,020 | 1,180 | 2,965 | 15 | 22 | — | NA | 55 | 20 | — | 70 | — | 30 | 160 |
| 1820 | 3,135 | 2,185 | 950 | 2,470 | 14 | 13 | — | NA | 12 | 5 | — | 50 | — | 20 | 110 |
| 1810 | 2,330 | 1,590 | 740 | 1,950 | 6 | 11 | — | 75 | 10 | 5 | — | 60 | — | 12 | 70 |
| 1800 | 1,900 | 1,370 | 530 | 1,400 | 5 | 10 | — | — | 1 | 1 | — | 40 | — | 5 | 40 |

NA = Not available.

Source: *Historical Statistics of the United States: Colonial Times to 1970*, p. 139.

# EXHIBIT 5

Indexes of Employee Output, 1869–1920

| Year | 1958 = 100 | | | | 1958 Dollars | |
|------|------------|--------|---------------|-----------|--------------|-------------|
| | Output per Man-Hour[a] | Nonfarm Output per Man-Hour[b] | Manufacturing Output per Man-Hour | Farm Output per Man-Hour | Output per Employee[c] | Output per Person Engaged[d] |
| 1920 | 38.1 | 43.0 | 32.0 | 31.3 | 3,774 | 3,402 |
| 1919 | 38.4 | 43.1 | 30.2 | 31.9 | 3,713 | 3,388 |
| 1918 | 36.0 | 40.1 | 31.7 | 31.3 | 3,607 | 3,259 |
| 1917 | 33.3 | 35.7 | 31.7 | 33.1 | 3,525 | 3,123 |
| 1916 | 35.1 | 38.6 | 34.1 | 31.2 | 3,676 | 3,308 |
| | | | | | | |
| 1915 | 32.7 | 34.8 | 34.7 | 34.2 | 3,382 | 3,085 |
| 1914 | 31.4 | 33.9 | 30.7 | 31.9 | 3,279 | 3,015 |
| 1913 | 33.6 | 37.1 | 30.6 | 29.9 | 3,482 | 3,238 |
| 1912 | 32.5 | 34.8 | 29.2 | 33.1 | 3,425 | 3,159 |
| 1911 | 31.9 | 35.3 | 25.4 | 28.9 | 3,384 | 3,103 |
| | | | | | | |
| 1910 | 31.3 | 33.9 | 26.6 | 31.0 | 3,317 | 3,051 |
| 1909 | 31.9 | 35.0 | 26.9 | 30.4 | 3,347 | 3,100 |
| 1908 | 29.7 | 32.1 | 23.8 | 31.1 | 3,146 | 2,897 |
| 1907 | 31.2 | 33.9 | 25.5 | 30.7 | 3,316 | 3,094 |
| 1906 | 31.3 | 33.7 | 26.4 | 32.2 | 3,325 | 3,117 |
| | | | | | | |
| 1905 | 29.1 | 31.3 | 26.1 | 30.7 | 3,146 | 2,898 |
| 1904 | 28.4 | 30.6 | 26.0 | 30.5 | 3,041 | 2,820 |
| 1903 | 28.4 | 30.6 | 24.8 | 29.9 | 3,108 | 2,848 |
| 1902 | 27.8 | 30.1 | 25.6 | 29.1 | 3,030 | 2,793 |
| 1901 | 28.9 | 31.6 | 24.4 | 29.5 | 3,093 | 2,890 |
| | | | | | | |
| 1900 | 27.0 | 29.0 | 22.9 | 29.8 | 2,873 | 2,695 |
| 1899 | 26.6 | 28.6 | 23.7 | 29.8 | 2,903 | 2,667 |
| 1898 | 26.1 | 27.9 | 24.6 | 30.0 | 2,890 | 2,585 |
| 1897 | 25.7 | 27.7 | 22.2 | 28.9 | 2,965 | 2,565 |
| 1896 | 24.1 | 25.9 | 21.3 | 27.2 | 2,763 | 2,402 |
| | | | | | | |
| 1895 | 24.6 | 27.4 | 22.5 | 25.5 | 2,858 | 2,469 |
| 1894 | 23.2 | 25.8 | 21.1 | 24.2 | 2,764 | 2,310 |
| 1893 | 23.0 | 25.5 | 20.1 | 23.6 | 2,687 | 2,334 |
| 1892 | 24.0 | 26.7 | 21.4 | 24.4 | 2,636 | 2,447 |
| 1891 | 22.6 | 24.3 | 21.2 | 25.9 | 2,523 | 2,295 |
| | | | | | | |
| 1890 | 22.2 | 23.9 | 21.2 | 25.1 | 2,438 | 2,251 |
| 1889 | 21.2 | 22.2 | 20.5 | 25.8 | — | 2,158 |
| 1884[e] | 21.8 | 23.9 | NA | NA | — | 2,183 |
| 1879 | NA | NA | 16.2 | 23.9 | — | NA |
| 1974[f] | 16.0 | 15.8 | NA | NA | — | 1,613 |
| | | | | | | |
| 1869 | — | — | 14.7 | 20.1 | — | — |

NA = Not available.

[a]For total private domestic economy.

[b]For nonfarm business economy.

[c]Derived by dividing gross national product (in 1958 dollars) by total employment.

[d]Derived by dividing gross private domestic product by persons engaged in the private domestic economy.

[e]Decade average, 1879–1888.

[f]Decade average, 1869–1878.

Source: *Historical Statistics of the United States: Colonial Times to 1970*, p. 162.

# EXHIBIT 6

## Daily Wages of Five Skilled Occupations and of Laborers, Manufacturing Establishments, 1860–1880

| Year | Average Daily Wage* | Skilled Occupations | | | | | Laborers |
| --- | --- | --- | --- | --- | --- | --- | --- |
| | | Blacksmiths | Carpenters | Engineers | Machinists | Painters | |
| 1880 | $2.26 | $2.31 | $2.15 | $2.17 | $2.45 | $2.21 | $1.32 |
| 1879 | 2.16 | 2.21 | 2.05 | 2.08 | 2.35 | 2.08 | 1.27 |
| 1878 | 2.15 | 2.23 | 2.03 | 2.06 | 2.29 | 2.04 | 1.26 |
| 1877 | 2.18 | 2.27 | 2.06 | 2.11 | 2.29 | 2.09 | 1.28 |
| 1876 | 2.24 | 2.32 | 2.12 | 2.17 | 2.34 | 2.20 | 1.33 |
| 1875 | 2.39 | 2.41 | 2.42 | 2.33 | 2.47 | 2.35 | 1.39 |
| 1874 | 2.48 | 2.52 | 2.42 | 2.40 | 2.53 | 2.60 | 1.43 |
| 1873 | 2.62 | 2.70 | 2.52 | 2.50 | 2.73 | 2.68 | 1.52 |
| 1872 | 2.64 | 2.69 | 2.59 | 2.53 | 2.72 | 2.70 | 1.52 |
| 1871 | 2.58 | 2.66 | 2.57 | 2.38 | 2.72 | 2.67 | 1.50 |
| 1870 | 2.61 | 2.68 | 2.64 | 2.47 | 2.67 | 2.67 | 1.52 |
| 1869 | 2.60 | 2.73 | 2.68 | 2.40 | 2.66 | 2.61 | 1.53 |
| 1868 | 2.58 | 2.73 | 2.67 | 2.35 | 2.66 | 2.52 | 1.51 |
| 1867 | 2.59 | 2.69 | 2.75 | 2.38 | 2.73 | 2.47 | 1.53 |
| 1866 | 2.62 | 2.74 | 2.77 | 2.44 | 2.73 | 2.40 | 1.53 |
| 1865 | 2.50 | 2.61 | 2.68 | 2.33 | 2.56 | 2.31 | 1.48 |
| 1864 | 2.33 | 2.42 | 2.58 | 2.19 | 2.28 | 2.25 | 1.39 |
| 1863 | 2.00 | 2.07 | 2.09 | 1.87 | 2.05 | 2.02 | 1.20 |
| 1862 | 1.78 | 1.77 | 1.97 | 1.72 | 1.77 | 1.76 | 1.08 |
| 1861 | 1.67 | 1.65 | 1.80 | 1.65 | 1.66 | 1.64 | 1.04 |
| 1860 | 1.62 | 1.64 | 1.65 | 1.61 | 1.61 | 1.62 | 1.03 |

*Weighted by number of establishments; unweighted within each occupation.

Source: *Historical Statistics of the United States: Colonial Times to 1970*, p. 165.

# EXHIBIT 7

Membership in the American Federation of Labor

| | | | |
|---|---|---|---|
| 1881: | 40,000 | 1901: | 787,000 |
| 1882: | 65,000 | 1902: | 1,024,000 |
| 1883: | 76,000 | 1903: | 1,465,000 |
| 1884: | 105,000 | 1904: | 1,676,000 |
| 1885: | 125,000 | 1905: | 1,494,000 |
| 1886: | 138,000 | 1906: | 1,454,000 |
| 1887: | 160,000 | 1907: | 1,538,000 |
| 1888: | 175,000 | 1908: | 1,586,000 |
| 1889: | 210,000 | 1909: | 1,482,000 |
| 1890: | 225,000 | 1910: | 1,562,000 |
| 1891: | 238,000 | 1911: | 1,761,000 |
| 1892: | 255,000 | 1912: | 1,770,000 |
| 1893: | 260,000 | 1913: | 1,999,000 |
| 1894: | 275,000 | 1914: | 2,020,000 |
| 1895: | 270,000 | 1915: | 1,946,000 |
| 1896: | 265,000 | 1916: | 2,072,000 |
| 1897: | 264,000 | 1917: | 2,371,000 |
| 1898: | 278,000 | 1918: | 2,726,000 |
| 1899: | 349,000 | 1919: | 3,260,000 |
| 1900: | 548,000 | 1920: | 4,078,000 |

Sources: Leo Wolman, *The Growth of American Trade Unions* (New York: National Bureau of Economic Research, 1924), p. 32; Philip Taft, *The A. F. of L. in the Time of Gompers* (New York: Harper & Row, 1957), pp. 233, 362. The statistics for 1881 through 1885 are for the Federation of Organized Trades and Labor Unions, the predecessor of the American Federation of Labor.

# EXHIBIT 8

## Work Stoppages, Workers Involved, and Major Issues, 1881–1920

| Year | Stoppages | | | | Workers Involved (1,000) | | | |
|---|---|---|---|---|---|---|---|---|
| | Total | Major Issues | | | Total | Major Issues | | |
| | | Wages and Hours | Union Organization | Other and Not Reported | | Wages and Hours | Union Organization | Other and Not Reported |
| 1920 | 3,411 | 2,036 | 622 | 751 | — | — | — | — |
| 1919 | 3,630 | 2,036 | 869 | 725 | — | — | — | — |
| 1918 | 3,353 | 1,869 | 584 | 900 | — | — | — | — |
| 1917 | 4,450 | 2,268 | 799 | 1,383 | — | — | — | — |
| 1916 | 3,789 | 2,036 | 721 | 1,032 | — | — | — | — |
| 1915 | 1,593 | 770 | 312 | 511 | — | — | — | — |
| 1914 | 1,204 | 403 | 253 | 518 | — | — | — | — |
| 1906 | — | — | — | — | — | — | — | — |
| 1905 | 2,186 | 942 | 800 | 444 | 302 | 191 | 57 | 54 |
| 1904 | 2,419 | 944 | 964 | 511 | 574 | 272 | 210 | 92 |
| 1903 | 3,648 | 1,773 | 1,200 | 670 | 788 | 396 | 235 | 156 |
| 1902 | 3,240 | 1,604 | 1,051 | 585 | 692 | 279 | 279 | 134 |
| 1901 | 3,012 | 1,413 | 1,016 | 583 | 564 | 288 | 161 | 115 |
| 1900 | 1,839 | 931 | 414 | 494 | 568 | 210 | 282 | 76 |
| 1899 | 1,838 | 1,014 | 471 | 353 | 432 | 288 | 66 | 79 |
| 1898 | 1,098 | 645 | 236 | 217 | 263 | 184 | 30 | 49 |
| 1897 | 1,110 | 680 | 193 | 237 | 416 | 335 | 36 | 45 |
| 1896 | 1,066 | 547 | 297 | 222 | 249 | 160 | 53 | 36 |
| 1895 | 1,255 | 810 | 217 | 228 | 407 | 305 | 51 | 51 |
| 1894 | 1,404 | 865 | 206 | 333 | 690 | 469 | 25 | 196 |
| 1893 | 1,375 | 783 | 257 | 335 | 288 | 162 | 59 | 66 |
| 1892 | 1,359 | 693 | 261 | 405 | 239 | 122 | 59 | 57 |
| 1891 | 1,786 | 867 | 334 | 585 | 330 | 221 | 55 | 54 |

| 1890 | 1,897 | 1,039 | 318 | 540 | 373 | 276 | 32 | 66 |
| 1889 | 1,111 | 662 | 173 | 276 | 260 | 207 | 29 | 24 |
| 1888 | 946 | 540 | 163 | 243 | 163 | 100 | 23 | 41 |
| 1887 | 1,503 | 836 | 299 | 368 | 439 | 249 | 91 | 99 |
| 1886 | 1,573 | 1,073 | 210 | 289 | 610 | 445 | 79 | 87 |
| 1885 | 695 | 486 | 67 | 142 | 258 | 214 | 14 | 30 |
| 1884 | 485 | 341 | 50 | 94 | 165 | 145 | 4 | 16 |
| 1883 | 506 | 372 | 55 | 79 | 170 | 131 | 28 | 12 |
| 1882 | 476 | 353 | 38 | 85 | 159 | 133 | 12 | 14 |
| 1881 | 177 | 382 | 32 | 63 | 130 | 118 | 5 | 7 |

Source: *Historical Statistics of the United States: Colonial Times to 1970*, p. 179.

# EXHIBIT 9

**Price Index** *(1957–1959 = 100)*

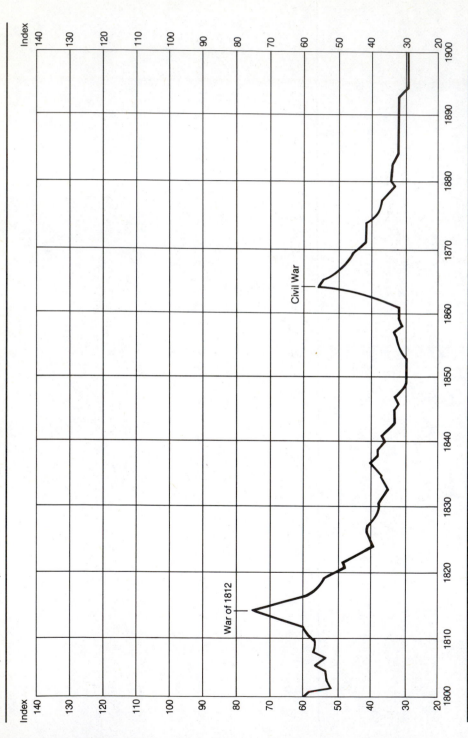

Source: John A. Garraty, *The American Nation* (New York: Harper & Row, 1983), p. 453.
Reproduced by Permission.

# EXHIBIT 10

## Immigration Trends

IMMIGRATION, 1865-1915

——— Northern & Western Europe
—·—·— Southern & Eastern Europe
———— Asia, North & South America

Thousands
of Immigrants

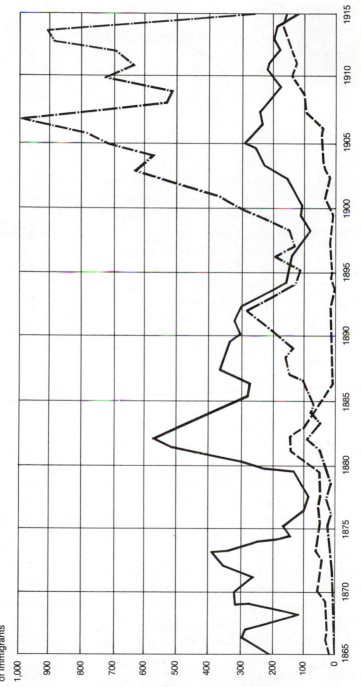

Note the great tide of "new" immigration in the early 1900s.

Source: John A. Garraty, *The American Nation* (New York: Harper & Row, 1983), p. 476. Reproduced by permission.

# APPENDIX A

 *Chronology of Labor Organizations*

1792–  Early trade unions formed by shoemakers, printers, and cabinet makers
1815:  in various cities. Objectives included higher wages, shorter hours, the closed shop, and union control of apprenticeship.

1806:  Cordwainers Conspiracy Case. Strikes found to be conspiracies in restraint of trade, illegal at common law.

1827:  Formation of first city central labor federation (in Philadelphia). By 1836, 13 cities had centrals.

1828:  Foundation of first Workingmen's Party (in Philadelphia). Others followed, but by the mid-1830s they were absorbed by other political organizations. These organizations favored the 10-hour day, abolition of imprisonment for debt, curbs on licensed monopolies, especially banks, and universal education.

1834:  First use of federal troops to intervene in a labor conflict.
Formation of the National Trades Union, an organization of city labor federations. The movement toward national union organizations was checked by the Panic of 1837.

1840:  Ten-hour day established for federal employees by executive order of President Van Buren.

1842:  Massachusetts Chief Justice Lemuel Shaw finds both unions and strikes for a closed shop to be lawful.

1852:  The beginnings of lasting national trade unions with the Typographers (1852), Hat Finishers (1854), Cigar Makers (1856), Iron Molders (1859), and others.

1860:  Successful strike of 20,000 New England shoemakers.

1863:  Emancipation Proclamation
First of the Railway brotherhoods (Locomotive Engineers).

1865:  The 13th Amendment frees the slaves.

1866:  Formation of the National Labor Union, which falls apart in the early 1870s.

1868:  First federal eight-hour law.

1869:   Foundation of Knights of Labor, which collapsed in 1893.

1873:   Beginning of a severe depression.

1875:   Conviction of 24 "Molly Maguires" for coalfield violence; 10 hanged.

1876:   Foundation of the predecessor of the Socialist Labor Party.

1877:   Violent railroad strikes on many lines east of the Mississippi. Nine killed in West Virginia, and 26 in Pittsburgh, which also saw between $5 and $10 million in property damage. Federal troops used.

1879:   Terence V. Powderly becomes Grand National Workman of Knights of Labor.

1881:   Foundation of Organized Trades and Labor Unions, predecessor of American Federation of Labor.

1882:   First Labor Day.

1886:   Haymarket Affair. Death and injury in a riot following a radical meeting in Chicago which had been called in a show of sympathy for a failed strike at McCormick Reaper. Labor movement injured by association with the radicals.

1892:   Strike by Amalgamated Association of Iron and Steel Workers at Carnegie's huge Homestead Works. About a dozen strikers and Pinkertons killed. Strike crushed by Henry Clay Frick.
Martial law declared in the Coeur d'Alene silver mines in Idaho to quell labor violence.

1894:   Pullman strike and labor violence in Chicago. Strike crushed and Eugene V. Debs jailed.

1898:   Erdman Act provides for mediation in railroad disputes.

1901:   Amalgamated Association of Iron, Steel, and Tin Workers defeated in a five-month strike against U.S. Steel.

1902:   Anthracite coal strike leads to presidential intervention. A qualified victory for the unions.

1905:   Formation of Industrial Workers of the World.

1908:   Supreme Court holds the boycott to be an illegal restraint of trade. In another case it upholds a state law regulating hours for women.

1911:   Triangle Shirtwaist Factory fire kills 146 women and leads to the revision of the New York State factory code.
Publication of Frederick W. Taylor's *Principles of Scientific Management.*

1912:   IWW wins wage increases in Lawrence, Mass., textile strike.

1913:   Foundation of U.S. Department of Labor.

1914:   Federal Trade Commission created to regulate business practices.
Clayton Antitrust Act limits use of injunctions in labor disputes.
"Ludlow Massacre" in which National Guard attacks a tent colony of striking Colorado miners and kills 11 women and two children.

1916:   Adamson Act provides eight-hour day on railroads.
Federal Child Labor Law passed (declared unconstitutional two years later).

1919:   General strike in Seattle.
        Police strike in Boston.
        350,000 steelworkers strike for the eight-hour day and the right to orga-
        nize.

# CASE 20

# From Lean Years to Fat Years: The Labor Movement between the Wars *

## Lean Years

As the interwar years began, there were some indications that the American labor movement was looking toward a bright future. Association with business through organizations such as the National Civic Federation had seemingly endowed unionism with a new social acceptability. Labor was able to claim partial credit for the achievements of American industry during the war and also to point with pride to the service of union men in the armed forces. By 1920, union membership had achieved dizzying heights. Over five million workers were organized, representing 20 percent of the labor force. Four fifths of these were affiliated with the A F of L. (For membership statistics, see Exhibit 1.) Tradition had it that prosperous times meant opportunity for organizers. But the 1920s proved quite the reverse.

The reasons for the "leanness" of these lean years are manyfold. First, at the close of World War I, there was a series of particularly disturbing work stoppages. In February 1919, 60,000 workers in Seattle walked off their jobs in support of a strike in the metal trades. The strike lasted less than a week, and essential city ser-

*This case was prepared as the basis for class discussion rather than to illustrate either effective or ineffective handling of an administrative situation. Parts of this case were written by the following individuals: Professor George C. Lodge, Research Associate Audrey T. Sproat under the direction of Professor Bruce R. Scott, and Assistant Professor Richard S. Tedlow.

Harvard Business School case 384–104, rev. 5/84.

vices were maintained, yet Mayor Ole Hanson saw fit to denounce the strikers—in widely circulated remarks—as revolutionaries. That summer, the mayor had a bomb mailed to him as did such other public figures as Attorney General A. Mitchell Palmer and John D. Rockefeller, Jr. In September, the Boston police went out on strike in an effort to raise their wages above prewar levels. The strike failed, with the then governor of Massachusetts, Calvin Coolidge, sending in more state troops than the situation called for. When Samuel Gompers asked Coolidge for help in having the policemen reinstated, he replied that, "There is no right to strike against the public safety, by anybody, anywhere, anytime," which statement helped catapult him to national prominence.

Also in September came the first major effort to organize the steel industry since the Homestead debacle of 1892. Three hundred fifty thousand workers struck the industry, but by February the strike was a dead letter. Company posters printed instructions to the workers in eight languages to return to their jobs.

In all, more than four million workers took part in strikes in 1919. Some of these were characterized by a savagery which spasmodically marked such disruptions. America seemed disoriented. In addition to the labor stoppages, business suffered a sharp downturn in 1920. And radicalism appeared to be on the march. The spectre of Bolshevism haunted America as well as Europe and would continue to do so for the rest of the century. During the winter of 1919–1920, Attorney General of the United States, A. Mitchell Palmer, engineered a series of mass arrests, raids, and deportations of radicals and suspected radicals, which, if anything, increased fear rather than diminishing it.

As the trauma associated with wartime conversion and postwar readjustment waned, however, discontent appeared to abate as well. At any rate, that discontent which persisted seemed to go underground—literally in the case of the bituminous coal industry and figuratively in the case of such other troubled sectors as agriculture and textiles. The nation seemed to be groping toward a "new era" in the management of the economy in general, of specific industries, and of labor relations. Antitrust was under a cloud in the 1920s as were other regulatory schemes designed to have the government impose rules for structure and conduct in industry. The goal of this new drift was never fully articulated. Indeed, it was never accurately named. (Should it be called "war socialism," "war guildism," "associationalism," etc?.)[1] But the general idea seems to have been that through its trade associations, business should seek to establish all kinds of guidelines governing how companies in various trades should conduct themselves. Once an industry settled on reasonable rules of conduct, the government should lend its imprimatur and its aid.

Labor relations were to play a key role in this new regime of industrial cooperation. The nation cherished a memory of industrial relations, doubtless more imagined than real, in which the boss worked down at the shop with the men to

---

[1]See Ellis W. Hawley, "Three Facets of Hooverian Associationalism: Lumber, Aviation and Movies, 1921–1930," in Thomas K. McCraw, ed., *Regulation in Perspective* (Boston: Harvard Business School, 1981).

solve problems together. They called one another by first names, and social intercourse was easy. With the coming of big business to American industry, such relationships proved impractical. Workers were far too numerous to know as individuals. (Over 100,000 worked at the gigantic Ford plant on the River Rouge when it was running at peak capacity in the interwar years.) What was more, there were social, ethnic, and/or racial differences between owner and workers.

Business people developed a variety of responses to the "human problem." One model was sheer brute force: "I have always had one rule," an old-time Carnegie iron master once expostulated, "when a worker sticks up his head, hit it." Though hard-boiled operators like Henry Clay Frick might subscribe to such sentiment, many others remained dissatisfied with it. Some business leaders relied on a version of divine right to justify their opinions. George F. Baer, President of the Reading Railroad, declared during an anthracite strike in 1902, with no sense of irony, that God, in His infinite wisdom, had rightly given control of the nation's property to good, Christian men. And John D. Rockefeller is said to have once declared that God gave him his money.

These approaches were unsatisfactory for a number of reasons. Naked appeals to brute force have no place in American society. They violated the business person's conception of himself as a good citizen and a good person. Appeals to predestination and divine right failed to strike a chord in an increasingly secular and skeptical society. They were disturbingly unscientific. During the 1920s, business began to look to the social sciences for help in industrial relations. That decade saw the real beginnings of systematic industrial relations, of the transformation from people to personnel.

Welfare capitalism was the name given to the effort to convince the labor force that the old dream of a harmony of interests among all those involved in a business could and would be a reality. Measures instituted under the rubric of welfare capitalism included worker housing and education, employee stock ownership plans, old-age pensions (the United States was the only major industrial nation without a social security system), paid vacations (International Harvester, in what one historian has called an "electrifying innovation," announced a two-week annual paid vacation in 1926),[2] and even higher wages. The mechanism for instituting these reforms, for learning what the worker wanted and thought, and for more fully integrating him or her into the system was the Employee Representation Plan or the company union. There were 385 such plans in 1922. That number rose to only 399 by 1928, but the number of employees covered increased from 690,000 in the former year to 1,547,766 by the latter. The company union differed fundamentally from the outside labor organization. It

> lacked authorization to strike, had no funds to finance a stoppage, and was incapable of coordinating its acts with other firms in the industry. Its only sanction, if it may be called that, was persuasion.[3]

---

[2]William E. Leuchtenburg, *The Perils of Prosperity* (Chicago: University of Chicago Press, 1958), p. 178.

[3]Irving Bernstein, *The Lean Years* (Baltimore: Penguin, 1960), p. 173.

Management, indeed, held all the high cards.

What was the place of independently organized labor in this new scheme? Samuel Gompers had long believed that labor management relations had to be characterized by the management of conflict rather than harmony. But Gompers died in 1924 soon after having dragged himself literally at death's door to Texas for one last A F of L convention. His successor was William Green. Green was a good and decent man, but he was neither a leader nor a sparkling intellect. John L. Lewis, who was both, once quipped:

> Explore the mind of Bill Green? Why, Bill and I had offices next door to each other for ten years. . . . I have done a lot of exploring in Bill's mind, and I give you my word, there is nothing there.[4]

Green's lack of creativity was demonstrated by his attitude toward welfare capitalism. The leading historian of labor in these years, Irving Bernstein, has written that under Green, the A F of L "shifted from militancy to respectability. With business supreme, [it] sought to sell itself as a necessary auxiliary."[5]

The problem with this stance was that independently organized labor had no part in the new business synthesis. The labor problem would be managed just as the production problem was or the innovation problem or the export problem: from the top down. And as the 20s progressed, the system did indeed seem to be working. In 1929, the old muckraker Lincoln Steffens wrote, "Big business in America is producing what the Socialists held up as their goal: food, shelter and clothing for all."

# Fat Years

In the 1930s, the Great Depression struck the nation with the force of a physical blow. The American economy fell off a table. By 1932, major business and economic indicators hit depths which three short years previously were simply unimaginable. The nation was utterly unprepared sociologically or psychologically to absorb the punishment the decade meted out. The United States, which had appeared as the world's economic physician in the 1920s, became the patient. In the spring of 1931, natives in the Cameroons sent $3.77 for the relief of the starving masses of New York City. The money was doubtless needed.

In his presidential address to the American Economic Association in December 1932, Professor George E. Barnett declared, "I see no reason to believe that American trade unionism will so revolutionize itself within a short period as to become in the next decade a more potent social influence than it has been in the last decade."[6] When Barnett spoke, there were about 3,200,000 unionized workers in the United States. These workers were organized predominantly on a craft basis,

---

[4]Bernstein, *Lean Years,* p. 96.

[5]Bernstein, *Lean Years,* p. 97.

[6]Quoted in Melvyn Dubofsky, "Labor Organizations," in Glenn Porter, ed., *Encyclopedia of American Economic History,* vol. II (New York: Charles Scribner's Sons, 1980), p. 538.

and the basic industries of steel and automobile manufacture were almost completely open shop.

Within 10 years, union membership more than tripled, steel and autos were organized on an industrial basis, and a new organization had been created to challenge the hegemony of the A F of L. A revolution in labor law, the most important element of which was the Wagner Act, had struck a blow against the intimidation of workers and against company unions and provided mechanisms for independent organizations to gain recognition. A crisis in the sociology of basic industry in America had been reached and passed.

The reasons for these developments are many. It can be said, however, that events would have unfolded significantly differently than they did had it not been for the role played by John L. Lewis.

John Llewellyn Lewis was born into an immigrant Welsh coal mining family in 1880. "Think of me," he once said, "as a coal miner, and you won't make any mistakes."

> The thing that gives me strength is the fact that I am able correctly to interpret the aims of my people. I know the psychology of the coal miner. I know about his dreams and his ideals and trials and tribulations. I have lived with coal miners. I am one of them. My family has been associated with the mining industry for a century and a half and an understanding of the miners' problems is inbred in me.
>
> I have laid down in a mine tunnel with my face in a half- inch of water, and pulled my shirt up over my head, expecting to die the next minute in an explosion I heard coming toward me. And when God performed a miracle and stopped the explosion before I died, I think it gave me some understanding of what men think about and how they suffer when they are waiting to die in a coal mine explosion.[7]

As this passage amply demonstrates, Lewis had a gift for persuasive self-expression. He also had an understanding of the need for decisive and dramatic gestures. At the 1935 convention of the A F of L, where the American labor movement split in two, he not only engaged in debate, excerpts of which are reproduced as Exhibit 2, he also punched his chief adversary, Big Bill Hutcheson of the Carpenters Union, right in the face and sent him sprawling across the convention floor, thus starting a brawl.

Lewis was not bashful when it came to publicizing himself ("He that tooteth not his own horn, the same shall not be tooted," he declared; and a reporter once observed that "Lewis had come to believe that his own birthday should be celebrated instead of Christmas"), and he had an outstanding sense of humor. The story is told that once during the Depression when a busload of tourists paused in front of his Alexandria, Virginia, home, he, with an air of studied insouciance, bent over, as they gaped, to tie a shoelace. "Even the posterior of a great man," he later remarked, "is of interest."[8]

---

[7]Bernstein, *Lean Years,* p. 124.

[8]Melvyn Dubofsky and Warren Van Tine, *John L. Lewis* (New York: Quadrangle, 1977), p. 283.

The potential for radical change in American political and social life was probably greater during the 1930s than it had been since the Civil War. Numerous Communists helped organize the industries under the aegis of the CIO, which Lewis formed when he walked out of the A F of L in 1935. He needed the Communists for their willingness to work long and hard for virtually no pay and for their idealism and courage in the face of terrible danger. Yet Lewis himself, despite his unquestioned empathy with the people he represented, shared none of the Communistic attitude toward class. For Lewis, the working class was something to get out of. He did indeed spend time in the mines but not a great deal; and he never contemplated spending a lifetime there. He quickly rose to important positions in the United Mine Workers, becoming president in 1920 and remaining in that post for four decades. His passport described him as an "executive" rather than a union leader; he sent his children to the most prestigious schools (Bryn Mawr, Princeton); and he loved to associate with the high and mighty. While directing the climactic organizational drives in steel and autos, he was simultaneously expending every effort to gain admission to Washington's exclusive Cosmos Club. Wrote one astute observer:

> Though an exceptional man, Lewis is also a deeply ordinary one. . . . he has a chauffeur in whipcords to drive him about in the 12-cylinder automobile his union bought for him; which is what every ordinary American would like to have. . . . That fine machine and the snappy cap on the chauffeur's head are ordinary symbols, generally craved in America, though rarely attained and which, incidentally, are apt to be an important source of Lewis's power.[9]

As for the Communists, when a fellow trade unionist voiced concerns about their role in the CIO, Lewis replied, "Who gets the bird, the dog or the hunter?"

Lewis's shrewdness, his willingness to gamble, and his understanding of the nature of power in the United States were central factors in the success of the CIO. The climax of CIO success was the victory of the United Automobile Workers in the sit-down strikes in Flint, Michigan, in 1936–1937. It is that strike with which the remainder of this case will concern itself.

## The Flint Strike

At 7:00 A.M. on December 30, 1936, some 50 workers in General Motors' Fisher Body plant No. 2 at Flint, Michigan, sat down in the factory and tied up production. By nightfall the sit-down had spread to the much larger Fisher No. 1 nearby. Together with the strikes that had previously closed other GM body lines in Atlanta, Kansas City, and Cleveland, the strike in Flint would suffice to cripple GM's output even if the conflict spread no further—which it did. From 53,000 a week, GM's car assemblies were to fall to 1,500 by early February. The union had focused its attack on body plants in order to achieve precisely this effect: since bodies were too large to store, GM had no inventory with which to keep on building cars.

---

[9]Quoted in Dubofsky and Van Tine, *Lewis,* p. 291.

The strike against GM was mounted by a relatively small new union, the United Auto Workers (UAW). It had the support of the larger but even newer Congress of Industrial Organizations (CIO), a multiunion grouping to which the UAW belonged.

Several union demands were at issue in the strike, but both sides indicated that the key demand was the UAW's insistence on recognition as the "sole" bargaining agent for all production workers at GM. Hitherto, no company had acceded to such a role for any union. The CIO-UAW hoped to break industry resistance by first cracking resistance at GM; Chrysler Corporation was not quite big enough for a victory to be decisive, and the Ford Motor Company was so hostile as to make a victory unlikely.[10]

GM would be a formidable opponent:

> The corporation that the UAW struck at the end of 1936 was a concern of enormous economic strength. It was not simply "big" but, as *Fortune* remarked, it was "colossal." It had 69 automotive plants in 35 cities and 14 states, and its total assets exceeded $1.5 billion. It produced passenger cars "for every price and purpose" ("Chevrolet for *hoi polloi*, . . . Pontiac . . . for the poor but proud, Oldsmobile for the comfortable but discreet, Buick for the striving, Cadillac for the rich"), commercial vehicles, trucks and trailers, a great variety of parts and accessories, refrigeration, heating, and air-conditioning equipment, lighting equipment, household appliances, airplanes and aviation equipment, locomotives, and power plants, and it had very substantial interests in real estate, finance, and insurance. Its 342,384 shareholders at the end of 1936 received over $200 million in dividends for the year, a record for the corporation. It accounted for 43.12 percent of all new passenger-car registrations and 37.8 percent of new truck registrations in the United States that year, and the more than two million cars and trucks that it sold around the globe constituted 37 percent of the entire world's sales of such vehicles and was 7.3 percent above the corporation's 1929 sales. Its 171,711 hourly employees worked an average of 40.5 hours per week and received an average hourly wage of 75.6 cents which compared very favorably with the average hourly rate of 55.6 cents for production workers in all manufacturing. Eighty-five percent (145,860) of these employees had been on the company payroll for the full year and had earned an average of $1,541 for the year, which was 7 percent above the 1929 figure in current dollars and 29 percent above in real terms and which exceeded by 19.7 percent the average annual earnings for full-time employees in manufacturing as a whole.[11]

GM was so big that a strike against it was bound to spread beyond the confines of the corporation. Flint was a "company town" in the sense that GM employed about half of all its workers; a GM strike in Flint would flatten its economy. Nearby Detroit would also suffer as would the entire state of Michigan when GM's decline hit auto feeder plants and suppliers. According to *Business Week,* the GM strike might even stifle the national economic upturn that was gathering steam in 1936 after five years of severe worldwide depression.[12]

---

[10]Sidney Fine, *Sit-Down* (Ann Arbor: University of Michigan Press, 1969), pp. 134 ff.

[11]Fine, *Sit-Down,* p. 133.

[12]*Business Week,* January 9, 1937, p. 13.

Concern with GM's strike soon spread. Active from the first as would-be mediators were U.S. Secretary of Labor, Frances Perkins, and Michigan Governor, Frank Murphy. Others soon drawn into the fray included Senator Robert M. LaFollette's Congressional Committee on Civil Liberties, the American Federation of Labor, which was a union rival of the CIO, the "Flint Alliance," a back-to-work movement, the Flint police, the Michigan police and National Guard, two Michigan judges who issued injunctions against the strikers, several "law-and-order" state legislators who wanted to impeach the Governor for not acting decisively enough, and—ultimately—the President of the United States, Franklin D. Roosevelt, who, in November 1936, had been elected by a landslide vote to his second term in office.

## General Motors Corporation

General Motors managed the problems of the Depression as well as if not better than any other American corporation. It was one of the few large U.S. firms that never passed a dividend or failed to earn a profit. In his book, *My Years with General Motors,* CEO Alfred P. Sloan, Jr., remarked that even though production dropped 75 percent from 1929 to 1932, GM cut its costs to the point where it was able to earn $248 million and pay shareholders $343 million.

Looking back on his career, Sloan recalled some of his beliefs about GM and about the role of business in general:

> If I have expressed or implied in this book a so-called ideology, it is, I suppose, that I believe in competition as an article of faith, a means of progress, and a way of life. . . . We set out to produce not for the chosen few but for the whole consumer public on the assumption of a continuously rising standard of living.
>
> It is as I see it the strategic aim of a business to earn a return on capital, and if in any particular case the return in the long run is not satisfactory, the deficiency should be corrected or the activity abandoned for a more favorable one.
>
> The measure of the worth of a business enterprise as a *business* . . . is not merely growth in sales or assets but return on the shareholders' investment, since it is their capital that is being risked and it is in their interests first of all that the corporation is supposed to be run in the private-enterprise scheme of things.[13]

## The Impact of Depression on Automotive Labor

Workers had been pouring into Detroit and nearby auto towns ever since that January day in 1914 when Henry Ford had announced that $5.00 would be the daily wage in his factories. By the next morning, despite bitter cold, 12,000 men had lined up outside Ford's employment gate. As reported by the *Detroit News* for January 12, 1914, "The crowd stormed the doors of the plant, hundreds forcing their way through; bricks and other missiles were hurled at the officers and buildings, and the rioters were dispersed only after a drenching with ice-cold water."[14]

---

[13]Alfred P. Sloan, Jr., *My Years with General Motors* (New York: Doubleday, 1964), pp. xxiv, 49, 213.

[14]*Detroit News,* January 12, 1914.

But no firehose could stem the flow. From the backwoods of Arkansas, the cottonfields of Georgia and Alabama, the farms of Kentucky and the mountains of Tennessee, men had come to Detroit by the thousands: immigrants, illiterates, young and old, black and white. By 1929, some 470,000 men were employed in auto plants.

By 1931, however, with the change in the economic climate, some 150,000 people had left the city—either to go back where they came from or to wander. Some 211,000 were on relief.[15] To those still employed, the job might seem hard—but to those out of work conditions seemed much harder. Here is how one auto worker summarized the situation he and his friends faced:

> We used to get out to the employment gates by six in those days and we would build a fire and wait around. If you knew someone inside you stood a better chance of being called in. Foremen used to come out and pick whom they wanted, and seniority didn't mean a thing. My brother was a superintendent, so I used to get some breaks. I felt sorry for the others, but what could you do? When I started to sign fellows up in the union my superintendent warned me I'd get fired and never get another job. He said he couldn't believe I would do anything like that when I had a brother who was a superintendent. One night my brother came over to the house and begged me to quit. He was afraid of losing his job because I was a union man.[16]

## Recent Changes in Labor's Environment

The depths of the Depression were not an easy time to build a labor union. But conditions were changing in 1936. The economy was looking up, and the auto industry was looking forward to a 5-million unit year, its best since 1929.

Since 1933, moreover, the White House had been occupied by Franklin D. Roosevelt, and his administration had pushed through laws the effect of which was to help labor organization. The most important of these was the National Industrial Labor Relations Act, also known as the Wagner Act.

The National Industrial Labor Relations Act of 1935 not only made it illegal for an employer to refuse to bargain collectively, it also forbade company support for company unions, and it substituted majority rule for proportional representation. That is, the representatives selected by the majority of the employees in an appropriate bargaining unit were to be the exclusive representatives of *all* the employees in that unit. The prohibition against company unions and against proportional representation constituted major changes from past practice.

Companies, including GM, looked with disfavor upon the Wagner Act. Pending the testing of the Act by the courts, GM's Sloan indicated that GM would continue to support proportional representation for its workers as sanctioned by the President in 1934.

---

[15]Irving Howe and B.J. Widdick, *The UAW and Walter Reuther* (New York: Random House, 1959), p. 29.

[16]Howe and Widdick, *UAW*, p. 30.

# Evolution of New Unions and the CIO

New laws alone were not enough to pull workers into labor unions. This required effort by the unions themselves.

Up to 1935, the only important, certifiably viable U.S. union grouping was the A F of L. Under the leadership of the A F of L, unionism in the United States had lagged behind that of Western Europe. Unions covered only 13 percent of all U.S. nonagricultural workers in 1932 and only 13.8 percent in 1936. They were especially weak in the large mass-production industries where work was subdivided to the point where skilled craftsmen tended to be only a small minority of the work force. Thus, while unionism was strong in mining, transportation, the needle trades, and construction, it was unimportant before 1935 in rubber, electrical machinery, steel, and automobiles. These fields were known to labor as the "untouchables."

The controversy within the A F of L about the nature of union organization is encapsulated in Exhibit 2. When the issue came to a vote, the Majority Report was upheld by 18,024 to 10,933. Soon thereafter, the CIO was organized within the A F of L by the pro-industrial faction. In November 1935, Lewis resigned as a vice president of the A F of L. At its 1936 convention, the Federation, in turn, suspended all CIO-affiliated unions.

The UAW was one of the unions that followed the CIO out of the A F of L. The precipitating factor was an A F of L order to give up certain workers whom the UAW had recently recruited. As one local leader put it, his people refused to be "parcelled out like fish." Said another, "That is awful; that is not union, that is disunion. . . . Let them go to hell."[17]

The UAW decamped to the CIO in July 1936. In the previous April, it had claimed about 40,000 members, but fewer than 24,000 were "paid-up." Under its President, Homer Martin, the union was conducting a membership drive during the month when the GM strike started, but it gave no public count of its size at that time.[18]

# Evolution of New Tactics for Industrial Warfare

Besides founding a new kind of union, the U.S. labor movement by 1935 had hit upon a set of new tactics. These included striking bottleneck operations rather than trying to pull out all workers, sitting down in the plant rather than just picketing outside it, and targeting attacks at one employer within an industry rather than at all so that the victim would see his competitors growing fat on his lost sales.

Of these new labor tactics the sit-down attracted by far the most attention. Labor's advantages from the sit-down compared with other tactics have been summarized as follows:

> The fear that his job would be taken by a strikebreaker or that production would somehow be maintained without him, a fear that deterred the potential striker or impaired

---

[17]Fine, *Sit-Down,* p. 87.

[18]Fine, *Sit-Down,* pp. 89, 181, 182.

the worker's morale when he was on strike, was removed when the employee sat by his idle machine outside the plant. As a picket outside the plant, moreover, the striker might be attacked by the police or even arrested and sent to jail. The employer, however, would hesitate to employ force to dislodge strikers inside his plant because this cast him in the role of aggressor, because violence might damage his machinery, and because the strikers were capable of putting up a more formidable defense inside the plant than on an exposed picket line. The strike on the inside thus offset the advantages which access to the forces of law and order normally gave the employer.

It was in some ways easier to maintain the morale of participants in a sit-down than in a conventional strike. The strikers were removed from outside pressures and the hostility of the community that their action might have induced. Bad weather did not constitute a problem for sit-downers as it did for the pickets in an outside strike. The strikers inside the plant might even find the experience an enjoyable one in many ways. They became better acquainted with fellow workers and might develop a group feeling, a "consciousness of kind," that they had not heretofore experienced on the job. If the strikers controlled the gates, they could be provided with necessities from the outside without difficulty, they could keep in touch with family and friends, and they could come and go subject to such regulations as governed the conduct of the strike.[19]

Despite these benefits, union leaders were not entirely pleased with the sit-down. It was almost undoubtedly illegal,[20] and it was difficult to control. (In fact, the GM strike of 1936–1937 had not at first been authorized by the UAW leaders, and the CIO had been planning to conserve its efforts for a strike against "Big Steel" before striking autos.)

# Early GM Policies on Labor Relations

Prior to 1933, GM had little experience with unions. Its policy toward its employees was one of "welfare capitalism."[21] That is, beside paying an average hourly wage one-third or more higher than the all-industry average, GM had a housing plan (closed in 1933), an Employees Savings and Investment Plan, a preferred stock subscription plan, several recreational and educational plans, and a group insurance plan, which had been started in 1926 and expanded in 1928.

All this had not changed in 1933, but GM had added some new policies. These included support for company unions and the hiring of Pinkerton detectives to mingle with and report on the workers. According to Senator LaFollette's Congressional Committee on Civil Rights, GM spent almost $1 million on "labor spies" between January 1, 1934, and July 31, 1936.[22]

In addition, during two UAW strikes in 1934 and 1935, GM had announced certain principles bearing on its relationship with unions. One of these was its re-

---

[19]Fine, *Sit-Down*, p. 121.

[20]The illegality of the sit-down was not finally established until 1939 when in the *Fansteel* case the Supreme Court declared it to be "a high-handed proceeding without a shadow of legal right." Fine, *Sit-Down*, p. 176.

[21]Fine, *Sit-Down*, pp. 23 ff.

[22]Fine, *Sit-Down*, p. 38.

sistance to union demands for majority rule rather than proportional representation. Another was local settlement of local disputes, although the company did not go on to say just which issues were local and which were central. A third announced principle was "diversification of plants where union strength is dangerous." Just what this meant emerged after the 1935 strike had closed a bottleneck transmission plant in Toledo, Ohio; when the plant reopened, about half of its equipment was pulled out and sent elsewhere, leading to a local loss of several hundred jobs.[23]

# Position Statements, January 4, 1937

Once the GM strike hit Flint, it became front-page news throughout the country. On January 5, 1937, the *New York Times* published what were in effect position statements by the parties most involved in the strike.

### The UAW Statement

The UAW statement, depicted by *The Times* as an "ultimatum," was a repetition of demands that the union had sent to GM earlier, only to be told that the proper place for their negotiation was at the plant-manager level. The union gave two "basic reasons" why a discussion at the local level could not "meet the problem at hand." First, GM's employees were said to have "encountered widespread discrimination and wholesale discharges . . . at the hands of the plant managers" because of "their mere affiliation with this union." This behavior was said to imply "a nationwide policy" on the part of GM "not to permit the organization of a union"—a policy that was "in absolute violation of the National Labor Relations Act [of 1935] and also in contravention of the accepted principles in the United States today." Second, the presence of "diverse factors among the various plants" of GM was not sufficient reason, as the company had claimed, for treating the union's demands as local issues. GM's "fundamental policies" were said to be "adopted and fixed" by its "national executive officers," and the kinds of issues being posed by the union could only be discussed at the top.

The union statement of January 4, then went on to repeat the eight demands that had been included in an earlier communication. These were (1) a national collective bargaining conference, (2) abolition of all piece-work systems of pay, (3) a 30-hour week, a six-hour day, and time and a half for overtime, (4) a minimum rate of pay "commensurate with American standards of living," (5) a reinstatement of employees who had been "unjustly" dismissed, (6) seniority based on length of service only, (7) recognition of the UAW as the "sole bargaining agency" for GM's workers, and (8) the mutual determination by management and union committees of the speed of production in GM's plants.

Commenting on this list, observers noted that some of the demands were more "serious" than others; most important was recognition of the UAW as the

---

[23]Fine, *Sit-Down*, p. 49.

sole bargaining agent, with the speed-up of the line, an easy-to-monitor system of seniority, and the end of piecework pay also significant for the rank and file.[24]

Why the union attached so much weight to being the "sole" bargaining agent was spelled out more fully in later press releases. Here the union claimed a "long and sad experience" with proportional representation and with management efforts to check outside unions by means of company unions. The UAW was convinced that pluralism led only to "confusion, disruption, and strife." Thus, "unified representation" was the only proper method of collective bargaining, the indispensable prelude to the orderly joint determination of conditions of employment by employer and employee. Those who opposed the idea were really opposed to the idea of collective bargaining itself.[25]

In commenting on the UAW's demand to be a "sole" bargaining agent, observers noted that the UAW criticized GM for alleged "violation of the National Labor Relations Act—but that the union, too, bypassed the Act when it claimed to speak for all of GM's workers without putting this claim to a test via an election as called for by the statute. Neither the union nor the company chose to raise this subject at any time.

### The GM Statement

Although the UAW letter had been addressed to GM's Executive Vice President William S. Knudsen, the answer came from President Sloan. It took the form of a statement sent to every GM employee, posted in every plant, and distributed to the press. The *New York Times* for January 5, 1937, ran its story under the headline, "Sloan Refuses to Deal with 'Labor Dictators' . . . Company Head Declares Management Will Not Surrender Rule."

After some preliminaries on the economic impact of the strike on GM's employees, Sloan began his statement to the workers by turning to the issue of collective bargaining:

> You are being told that you had better join a union. You are being told that to bargain collectively you must be a member of a labor organization. You are being told that the automotive industry is to be run as a closed shop. You are being told that if you do not join now it will be impossible for you to work in any automobile plant when the union wins, unless you pay. In other words, you will be without a job, therefore you must sign up, pay dues; or else.
>
> I want to say to you most frankly, that this is positively not so. Do not be misled. Have no fear that any union or any labor dictator will dominate the plants of General Motors Corporation. No General Motors worker need join any organization to get a job or keep a job.
>
> Neither is it necessary for you to join any organization in order to bargain collectively. General Motors is pledged to collective bargaining on the basis of absolute and uninfluenced freedom of choice on the part of any worker to join any organization without coercion, restraint or intimidation.

---

[24]Fine, *Sit-Down,* pp. 181–82.

[25]Fine, *Sit-Down,* pp. 181–82.

As Sloan saw it, however, "collective bargaining" was not the "real issue" that had brought about the current situation. "The real issue is perfectly clear, and here it is":

> Will a labor organization run the plants of General Motors Corporation or will the management continue to do so? On this issue depends the question as to whether you have to have a union card to hold a job, or whether your job will depend in the future, as it has in the past, upon your own individual merit.
>
> In other words, will you pay tribute to a private group of labor dictators for the privilege of working, or will you have the right to work as you may desire? Wages, working conditions, honest collective bargaining, have little, if anything, to do with the underlying situation. They are simply a smoke screen to cover the real objective.

In his next paragraphs, Sloan turned to "the real purpose" of his message, namely to provide a statement of "General Motors' position":

> 1. General Motors will not recognize any union as the sole bargaining agency for its workers, to the exclusion of all others. General Motors will continue to recognize, for the purpose of collective bargaining, the representatives of its workers, whether union or nonunion.
>
> 2. Work in General Motors plants will continue to depend on the ability and efficiency of the worker—not on the membership or nonmembership in any labor organization whatsoever. . . .
>
> 3. General Motors will continue to pay the highest justifiable wages in the future, as it has in the past, and just as it is doing at present. It believes in high wages. It is justly proud of its record in that respect.
>
> 4. General Motors' standard work week will continue to be 40 hours. Time and a half will be paid for overtime.
>
> 5. Seniority rights will be observed under the rules laid down by the Automobile Labor Board appointed by the President of the United States in March 1934. These rules are recognized as fair and just to all workers and permit no discrimination against any worker on account of any organization membership.

## The Outcome, February 11, 1937

The exchange of January 4 constituted a definitive statement of the differences between the company and the union. While the two parties "continued to trade verbal blows," these later statements "added relatively little to the substance of the debate."[26] Thus, future news about the strike focused on events in the running battle between the two main antagonists, Sloan of GM and John L. Lewis, president of the CIO, and on the efforts of state and federal officials to discover a formula for peace.

---

[26]Fine, *Sit-Down,* p. 183.

Throughout January and into February, the conflict at Flint continued. On February 9, Michigan Governor Murphy, who had already ordered units of the state's national guard to stand by in Flint, called Lewis to his office and told him that he felt it was his duty to "take necessary steps to restore possession of the occupied plants to their rightful owners."

Lewis' reply, as he later reported it, was as follows:

> I do not doubt your ability to call out your soldiers and shoot the members of our union out of those plants, but let me say that when you issue that order I shall leave this conference and I shall enter one of those plants with my own people. . . . And the militia will have the pleasure of shooting me out of the plants with . . . [them].[27]

Governor Murphy backed down and a few days later a settlement was reached.

The business community—or at least the business press—was loud in condemnation of the strikes. *Business Week,* for example, editorialized as follows:

> By means of sit-down strikes, the country has been put at the mercy of thoroughly irresponsible groups which in effect have no leadership, no control, no authority that can restrain them. Great industries, whose operations affect the daily welfare of millions, are confronted with demands to sign contracts with groups which, day by day and hour by hour, demonstrate that they have almost no control over their own people, no conception of the validity or the sanctity of a contract, no respect for property rights or for rights of any sort except their own.[28]

Years later, the comments of GM's Alfred P. Sloan appeared in his autobiography. Looking back on 1936 and 1937 from the vantage point of 1964, he assessed the strike from his current point of view on union scope, management prerogatives, and the appropriate role of government:

> One is inclined to forget that unionization in large industries was not then the custom in the United States. The significance of large-scale unionization was not yet clear to us. We knew that some political radicals regarded unions as instruments for the attainment of power. But even orthodox "business unionism" seemed to us a potential threat to the prerogatives of management. As a business man, I was unaccustomed to the whole idea. Our early experiences with the A F of L unions in the automobile industry were unhappy; the chief issue with these unions became organizational. They demanded that they represent all our workers, even those who did not want to be represented by them. Our initial encounter with the CIO was even more unhappy; for that organization attempted to enforce its demands for exclusive recognition by the most terrible acts of violence, and finally seized our properties in the sit-down strikes of 1937. I have no desire to revive the bitter controversies that arose over these early encounters with labor organizations. I mention them merely to suggest one of the reasons why our initial reaction to unionism was negative.
>
> What made the prospect seem especially grim in those early years was the persistent union attempt to invade basic management prerogatives. Our rights to determine

---

[27]Fine, *Sit-Down,* pp. 298–99.

[28]*Business Week,* April 10, 1937.

production schedules, to set work standards and to discipline workers were all suddenly called into question.[29]

On February 11, 1937, after the union finally had accepted a compromise on its demand to speak for all the workers, GM signed an agreement. This outcome was viewed as a strikers' victory for the following reasons:

> GM had been compelled to sign its first agreement with a union, and it had for the first time agreed to recognize an international union as a party to the collective bargaining process. It had accepted the UAW contention that all the demands set forth in the January 4 letter should be discussed at a general conference, that strikers were employees, and that even strikers guilty of acts of violence should be returned to their jobs without discrimination. Although the company had insisted that the sit-down was illegal, it had agreed nevertheless to secure the dismissal of injunctions directed against the strikers. Above all, the strike had been for organizational purposes, and in this sense too it had been successful. In 17 plants, including the strategically significant Cleveland Fisher Body, Flint Fisher Body No. 1, and Chevrolet No. 4 plants, the UAW was, in effect, given six months to become the majority union, free from any concern that the company might foster a rival organization.[30]

Alfred Sloan saw government support of the UAW as a principal reason for the outcome.

> The UAW was able to enlist the support of the government in any great crisis. The government's attitude went back as far as the 1937 sit-down strikes, when we took the view that we would not negotiate with the union while its agents forcibly held possession of our properties. Sit-down strikes were plainly illegal—a judgment later confirmed by the Supreme Court. Yet President Franklin D. Roosevelt, Secretary of Labor Frances Perkins, and Governor Frank Murphy of Michigan, exerted steady pressure upon the corporation, and upon me personally, to negotiate with the strikers who had seized our property, until finally we felt obliged to do so.[31]

---

[29]Sloan, *General Motors,* pp. 405–406.

[30]Fine, *Sit-Down,* p. 309.

[31]Fine, *Sit-Down,* p. 393.

# EXHIBIT 1

## Labor Union Membership, 1920–1946

| Year | Total Union Membership | A F of L | CIO | Total Labor Force |
|------|------------------------|----------|-----|-------------------|
| 1946 | 14,974 | 7,152 | 6,000 | — |
| 1945 | 14,796 | 6,931 | 6,000 | 66,210 |
| 1944 | 14,621 | 6,807 | 5,935 | 66,320 |
| 1943 | 13,642 | 6,564 | 5,285 | 64,780 |
| 1942 | 10,762 | 5,483 | 4,195 | 60,330 |
| 1941 | 10,489 | 4,569 | 5,000 | 57,720 |
| 1940 | 8,944 | 4,247 | 3,625 | 56,100 |
| 1939 | 8,980 | 4,006 | 4,000 | — |
| 1938 | 8,265 | 3,623 | 4,038 | — |
| 1937* | — | — | — | — |
| 1936* | — | — | — | — |
| 1935* | — | — | — | — |
| 1934 | 3,728 | 3,045 | — | — |
| 1933 | 2,857 | 2,127 | — | — |
| 1932 | 3,226 | 2,532 | — | — |
| 1931 | 3,526 | 2,890 | — | — |
| 1930 | 3,632 | 2,961 | | 47,404 |
| 1929 | 3,625 | 2,934 | | — |
| 1928 | 3,567 | 2,896 | | — |
| 1927 | 3,600 | 2,813 | | — |
| 1926 | 3,592 | 2,804 | | — |
| 1925 | 3,566 | 2,877 | | — |
| 1924 | 3,549 | 2,866 | | — |
| 1923 | 3,629 | 2,926 | | — |
| 1922 | 3,950 | 3,196 | | — |
| 1921 | 4,722 | 3,907 | | — |
| 1920 | 5,034 | 4,079 | | 41,610 |

*The Bureau of Labor Statistics unfortunately does not provide data for these years.

Source: *Historical Statistics of the United States: Colonial Times to 1970,* pp. 131, 139, 177. Membership in the A F of L for 1920 was 4,079,000 according to the Bureau of Labor Statistics. According to Philip Taft, whose A F of L statistics were used in the previous case, the membership that year was 4,078,000. See *The A F of L in the Time of Gompers* (New York: Harper, 1957), p. 362.

## EXHIBIT 2

*Excerpts From the 1935 A F of L Convention*

### Majority Report of the Resolutions Committee on Organization Policies

The Declaration adopted by the convention [in San Francisco] last year was specific upon the question involved. It was recognized that in many industries large numbers of so-called mass production workers were employed. The skill they required being of an entirely different character from that of those who became craftsmen through years of apprenticeship. In many mass production industries, the newly employed workers within a few months become as competent to perform the specialized operation required to do the work, as they ever will be. This is in marked contrast to the skill required of craftsmen who, in addition to their years of apprenticeship, require additional time before they master all of the knowledge required to round out complete mastery of their craft.

The Declaration of the San Francisco Convention [in 1934] provided that the workers classified as "mass production employees" should be granted charters in the mass production industries which would include all of the mass production workers employed in such industries. So that there might be no misunderstanding, and for the purpose of differentiating between craftsmen and mass production workers, the Declaration adopted last year included the following language:

> The American Federation of Labor is desirous of meeting this demand. We consider it our duty to formulate policies which will fully protect the jurisdictional rights of all trade unions organized upon crafts lines and afford them every opportunity for development and accession of those workers engaged upon work over which these organizations exercise jurisdiction. Experience has shown that craft organization is most effective in protecting the welfare and advancing the interests of workers where the nature of the industry is such that the lines of demarcation between crafts are distinguishable.

So that there might be no infringement upon the rights of the National and International Unions affiliated with the American Federation of Labor, provision was made in the Declaration to protect these rights. The final paragraph of the Declaration reading,

> That in order to protect and safeguard the members of such National and International Unions as are chartered, the American Federation of Labor shall for a provisional period direct the policies, administer the business, and designate the administrative and financial officers of the newly organized unions.

The convention could not have done otherwise than reaffirm the rights and the jurisdiction given to the National and International Unions which had been chartered by the American Federation of Labor, many of which had become International Unions before the Civil War and had maintained a continuous existence since that time.

## EXHIBIT 2 (*continued*)

It was principally these great International Unions which had brought the American Federation of Labor into existence. When the American Federation of Labor was organized, and these Unions accepted charters, and when National or International Unions have been organized since 1881, a contract was entered into between the American Federation of Labor and the National and International Unions.

The contract called for loyalty to the purposes and policies of the American Federation of Labor. In return, the National and International Unions were guaranteed two specific things: first, jurisdiction over all workmen doing the work of the specific craft or occupation covered by the organization; secondly, guaranteeing to the National or International Unions complete autonomy over all of its internal affairs.

The American Federation of Labor could not have been organized upon any other basis of relationship between the National and International Unions and the Federation. It is recognized that where a contract is entered into between parties, it cannot be set aside or altered by one party without the consent and approval of the other.

For these valid and vital reasons, your committee recommends nonconcurrence with [the] Resolutions [favoring industrial unionism], and reaffirmation of the Declaration of the San Francisco Convention upon this subject.

Delegate Howard, International Typographical Union: . . . The report of the minority of the committee is presented because the report of the majority of the committee was not acceptable, after hours of debate upon this question. The minority report says:

### Minority Report of the Resolutions Committee on Organization Policies

During the 55 years the American Federation of Labor has existed its declared purpose has been to organize the unorganized industrial workers of the nation. The contributions from its numerous affiliates have been made in the belief that organization would be advanced for the purpose of adding economic strength to the various units and that the organization policies would at all times be molded to accomplish the main purpose of organizing the unorganized workers in the industrial field.

During the existence of the American Federation of Labor and since the date many of the charters were granted to National and International Unions upon craft lines, the changes in industrial methods have been such that the duties of millions of industrial workers are of a nature that did not exist at the time many National and International charters were issued. This makes it apparent that jurisdiction over these new classes of work could not have been anticipated and included in the jurisdictional outlines of charters issued to National and Interna-

## EXHIBIT 2 (*continued*)

tional Unions at a time when the work that is now performed by these millions of industrial workers did not exist.

We refuse to accept existing conditions as evidence that the organization policies of the American Federation of Labor have been successful. The fact that after 55 years of activity and effort we have enrolled under the banner of the American Federation of Labor approximately three and one-half millions of members of the thirty-nine millions of organizable workers is a condition that speaks for itself.

We declare the time has arrived when common sense demands the organization policies of the American Federation of Labor must be molded to meet present day needs. In the great mass production industries and those in which the workers are composite mechanics, specialized and engaged upon classes of work which do not fully qualify them for craft union membership, industrial organization is the only solution. Continuous employment, economic security and the ability to protect the individual worker depends upon organization upon industrial lines.

In those industries where the work performed by a majority of the workers is of such nature that it might fall within the jurisdictional claim of more than one craft union, or no established craft union, it is declared that industrial organization is the only form that will be acceptable to the workers or adequately meet their needs. Jurisdictional claims over small groups of workers in these industries prevent organization by breeding a fear that when once organized the workers in these plants will be separated, unity of action and their economic power destroyed by requiring various groups to transfer to National and International Unions organized upon craft lines.

To successfully organize the workers in industrial establishments where conditions outlined herein obtain there must be a clear declaration by the American Federation of Labor. It must recognize the right of these workers to organize into industrial unions and be granted unrestricted charters which guarantee the right to accept into membership all workers employed in the industry or establishment without fear of being compelled to destroy unity of action through recognition of jurisdictional claims made by National or International Unions.

It is not the intention of this declaration of policy to permit the taking away from National or International craft unions any part of their present membership, or potential membership in establishments where the dominant factor is skilled craftsmen coming under a proper definition of the jurisdiction of such National or International Unions. However, it is the declared purpose to provide for the organization of workers in mass production and other industries upon industrial and plant lines, regardless of claims based upon the question of jurisdiction.

The Executive Council of the American Federation of Labor is expressly directed and instructed to issue unrestricted charters to organizations formed in accordance with the policy herein enunciated. The Executive Council is also instructed to enter upon an aggressive organization campaign in those industries in which the great mass of the workers are not now organized, issue unrestricted charters to workers organized into independent unions, company-dominated un-

# EXHIBIT 2 (*continued*)

ions and those organizations now affiliated with associations not recognized by the American Federation of Labor as bona-fide labor organizations.

Submitted by:  Charles P. Howard,
David Dubinsky,
Frank B. Powers,
John L. Lewis,
A. A. Myrup,
J. L. Lewis.

Delegate Howard: I move you, Mr. Chairman, that the minority report be substituted for the majority report and adopted by this convention.

Conditions as they exist at this time make it more necessary, in my opinion, for effective organization activity than at any time during the life of the American Federation of Labor. In response to the demands of labor there has been adopted by the Federal Congress what is known as the Wagner Act. Many of us understand that the Wagner Act does not give the workers of this country any right or privilege that could not have been exercised under the Constitution of the United States. The one particular difference is that it makes it the duty of the Government to protect the rights of workers engaged in industries devoted to interstate commerce, to bargain collectively, choose their own representatives and form an organization of their own choice.

Now, let me say to you that the workers of this country are going to organize, and if they are not permitted to organize under the banners of the American Federation of Labor they are going to organize under some other leadership or they are going to organize without leadership. And if either of those conditions should eventuate, I submit to you that it would be a far more serious problem for our Government, for the people of this country and for the American Federation of Labor itself than if our organization policies should be so molded that we can organize them and bring them under the leadership of this organization.

I contend that the success of an organization campaign depends upon molding the policies of the American Federation of Labor to meet the desires of those whom we decide to organize, rather than to attempt to mold the desires of the millions of workers who are unorganized to accept the policies that we would impose upon them.

That is one of the principal, fundamental reasons that I am presenting to this convention in a minority report an organization policy which I believe will accomplish that result. I represent in this convention what is usually referred to as strictly a craft union. I cannot be charged with having a personal or organizational interest in this matter other than the general welfare of the workers of my country. I understand, because of contact during the past three or four years, the reasons why we have failed to organize the workers in these mass production industries.

## EXHIBIT 2 (*continued*)

First, there is involved the question of continuous employment. Any one who is familiar with the situation knows that under the system for the operation of these industries the workers are required, perhaps within the limit of one day, to perform work that would come under the jurisdiction of more than one national or international craft union. Now these workers are sufficiently intelligent to know that immediately they are directed to step across jurisdictional lines by their supervisors that there is the possibility of a jurisdictional controversy which will affect their opportunity for continuous employment. I am told by some of those who are employed in the type of craft that we seek to organize that there are times when a worker will be engaged upon work that would come under the jurisdiction of three or four craft unions within a single day. I submit to you that it is not possible to induce those men, with their inexperience, to organize upon craft lines.

I am one of those who are willing, first to organize them, and to organize them with the assurance that their continuous employment is not going to be affected by jurisdictional controversies. And I am willing to believe that their experience in organization in the future will indicate the class of organization that will most effectively protect and advance their interests.

Now there is another condition that interferes with the organization of workers in these plants. And it is not a theoretical fear, it is one that has been experienced in many places and it is one that is real in the minds of these workers. They believe—and not without cause—that if they be organized in a Federal Union without the drawing of jurisdictional lines, that as soon as some national or international union makes a jurisdictional claim for a small block of these workers, that the unity of action will be destroyed and that this group will be forcibly removed from the Federal organization on industrial lines and set over into a craft organization that cannot protect them under the existing conditions.

I was told since I came into this hall where there is a plant that employs about 2,000 workers. Those interested in organization work in that particular city set out upon an organization campaign for the purpose of organizing those employed by this plant. They succeeded to a marked degree and they secured from the American Federation of Labor a charter. And after they secured that charter jurisdictional claims were made by national and international unions for some of those in the group who were organized, with the result that the charter was recalled and in that plant today there is no semblance of an organization. Now that story can be repeated as applying to numerous places in this country.

I ask you if it be the policy of the American Federation of Labor to organize the unorganized workers, where is there common sense in making requirements that cannot be and will not be met? And where is there common sense in continuing to make organizational lines which defeat the very purpose of this organization?

When we go into the practical application of our present organizational policies, what is the condition with which we are confronted? Here is a plant in which

# EXHIBIT 2 (*continued*)

there may be 600 or 6,000 workers. Nobody outside of those who have access to the payroll are fully informed as to the nature of the duties the workers perform, but for some reason or other, because they have read in the public press that the workers have a right to organize, or because they have heard an inspirational address upon the subject of organization, or because they have read something that the President may have said, there is inspired in some of those workers a desire to organize.

Of course they are inexperienced, they know nothing about the process of forming an organization, and perhaps through inquiry they learn that the information could be secured from the American Federation of Labor and they endeavor to seek information as to whether or not a charter could be secured. I say to you that nobody this side of Heaven could answer that question under the present conditions. You have got to know the classification of work, you have got to know the duties these workers are performing, you have got to be able to judge how many of the national and international craft unions might claim jurisdiction, and after you have secured that information any one of the national or international craft unions that is inclined to object to the issuance of a charter to that group can prevent the issuance of a charter. I submit to you that that is not a common sense policy if we desire or intend to organize the unorganized workers in this country.

I don't know, there is no one in this convention knows, and I don't know that there is a man in the United States who knows, how many workers have been organized into independent unions, company unions, unions and associations that may have some affiliation with subversive influences during the past few years. However, I am inclined to believe that the number of members in these classes of organization is far greater than any of us would grant. If that be true, I submit to you that there is a menace rapidly growing, a menace to the American Federation of Labor, because if some one or some agency interested in creating a movement that is dual to the American Federation of Labor, they have a fertile field and a very fine basis upon which to work, and I am sure that that is a condition that no delegate in this convention desires should arise or a condition with which the American Federation of Labor should be confronted at any time in the future.

In discussing the question of organizational policies I have been asked many times as to how they were to be applied. The minority report says it is not the purpose to take from any national or international union any part of their present membership, or any part of their potential membership employed in certain types and plants of industry. Certainly that should be accepted as protecting their craft and national or international unions. I do not believe there should be such a degree of selfishness or organizational interest that would inspire an objection to the issuance of a charter to a large number of workers in a plant simply because one or more organizations might have workers employed in there who would be eligible to membership in our craft unions.

I believe the organization of these workers is far too important to permit ob-

## EXHIBIT 2 (*continued*)

jections of that kind to prevent the issuance of charters to industrial and plant unions in the types of industries which we have referred to.

I heard an address from this platform this morning upon the subject of industrial peace. I bow to no delegate in this convention in the matter of industrial peace. I do not believe that the workers in any line of industry profit as a result of industrial warfare. I submit to you that the only way we can have industrial peace in the industries of this nation is to organize the workers to a sufficient extent that those who manage and operate and own the industries and the tools of production of the country will not dare to invite a conflict of that kind. My interest in this matter is to provide an organization policy that will bring about that condition.

I think no truer words have been said than the statement . . . this morning that it has been the policy of the industrial kings of this country to divide and conquer, and so long as they are permitted to continue that policy they will continue to divide and conquer, and it is my belief that the American Federation of Labor cannot stand still upon a question of this kind, that it should not be wedded to the policies that were made a half a century ago, or even a year ago, but that we must go ahead and perform our full duty in organizing the unorganized workers of this country.

I thank you.

President Green: The Chair recognizes Chairman Woll of the committee.

Vice President Woll: Mr. Chairman, . . . I have carefully listened to the reading of the report as submitted by these six delegates who are members of the committee. I wish that I might reconcile the presentation of Delegate Howard on the subject of organization, the need, the assurance of protection to the various national and international unions when compared with the document presented for adoption by the committee's report. At first it had been my belief until I heard the document read and very carefully viewed it—and frankly I have not yet had the time to carefully analyze all phrases contained in there—that the difference of opinion between the majority and the minority today was not a question of the report adopted at the San Francisco convention upon the unanimous recommendation of all concerned, in a divided report, that it was purely a matter of interpretation of a matter of enforcement. The delegate in one part of his statement practically reaffirmed that point of view. It is difficult, however, to reconcile the report with that. I wish that this might be the clear cut issue, that other extraneous issues might not become involved, but I cannot help, in reading this report of the six delegates, referring to the fact that throughout the report it speaks of industry establishments, plants and industries.

I think a great menace and a great danger is involved in speaking of plant organization, in connection with industrial organization. I don't think the delegates

## EXHIBIT 2 (*continued*)

had in mind endorsing plant organization, but certainly the document throughout gives you that clear cut indication.

Then we read further that,

it is not the intention of this declaration of policy to permit the taking away from national or international craft unions any part of their present membership or potential membership in establishments where the dominant factor is skilled craftsmen coming under a proper definition of the jurisdiction of such national or international union[s]. However, it is the declared purpose to provide for the organization of workers in mass production and other industries upon industrial and plant lines, regardless of claims based upon the question of jurisdiction.

Is that to be the policy of the American Federation of Labor . . . , that our members should be organized, in a more broadly defined term of industry, . . . into one industry? Do we understand likewise that this committee intends that we shall go into a process of plant organization?

Reading further, the final recommendation of the committee:

The Executive Council of The American Federation of Labor is expressly directed and instructed to issue unrestricted charters to organizations formed in accordance with the policies here enunciated. The Executive Council is also instructed to enter upon an aggressive organization campaign in those industries in which the great mass of the workers are not now organized, issue unrestricted charters to workers organized into independent unions, company-dominated unions and those organizations now affiliated with associations not recognized by the American Federation of Labor as bona fide organizations.

What is the implication? What is the meaning? What is the interpretation to be placed upon these directions and instructions where no volition, no discretion, is given to your Executive Council? Is it that the American Federation of Labor, where there is a company union and their organization so decides, shall issue a charter to it? Or here is an independent or dual organization—shall we issue a charter to it? The instructions are clear. The language would imply that. And yet we are asked to adopt declarations of that kind and type and character.

Might I say this question of organization of labor is of the utmost importance to all of us. Delegate Howard has referred to the Industrial Labor Disputes Act. Bear in mind that we now have legislation on our books which does not make us the sole factor in determining the form and character of organization that shall hereafter prevail in the labor movement. That power, to a large degree, has now been lodged in a Federal government agency. Of course it is hoped that in its administration we may not find the full vigor and rigor of this law applied against our respective organizations, industrial or craft, whatever designation we might give to our own particular organization.

That that power has been vested and that it leaves out the question of industrial organization as we understand it is clearly indicated by merely a cursory review

## EXHIBIT 2 (*continued*)

of the Act itself. On the question of organization it means that regardless of what our point of view is, regardless of what difficulties we may have in our convention, it is one of the most important things we must consider. We must not be guided by sentiment but by cold logic and reasoning and by no political preferment or otherwise in reaching conclusions on this matter.

Section 7 of the Act, first of all, gives the employes the right of selecting their own representatives and we know, of course, interpreted rigidly it would mean entirely an employe or plant organization and not groups of organizations within an industry, trade or calling. We have sought to safeguard that by the exception in Section 3 by saying:

> Nothing in this act or in any other Federal statute shall preclude an employer from making an agreement with a labor organization (not established, maintained, or assisted by any action defined in this act as an unfair labor practice) to require as a condition of employment membership therein, if such labor organization is the representative of the employes as provided in Section 9.

While of course we seek to safeguard our collective agreements requiring every member in the industry or craft to belong to our respective organizations, the question of the validity of our organization finally in its right to represent employes rests with the Labor Board—to be determined how? Not as it may please, but as it is prescribed in the law itself.

When we get to Section 9 what does it say:

> Representatives designated or selected for the purposes of collective bargaining by the majority of the employes in a unit appropriate for such purposes, shall be the exclusive representatives of all the employes in such unit for the purposes of collective bargaining in respect to rates of pay, wages, hours of employment or other conditions of employment.

In addition this section provides that the individual employes or groups of employes shall have the right at any time to present grievances to their employers.

Realize that here is the enactment of law—that a majority in the plant may bind all within that plant as to right of representation.

Now Charlie Howard and I might differ as to philosophies of organizations. Better that we come to an understanding and forget our present difficulties and differences of opinion and look more to the greater danger that would seek to disrupt our entire movement.

But then how is the Board to make its decisions: "The Board shall decide in each case whether in order to insure to employes the full benefit of their right to self organization"—we may issue charters all we want, we are not the supreme body in this matter, self-organization is not to be determined in the councils of the American Federation of Labor. We may issue a charter, we may seek to grant the claims of jurisdiction and seek to safeguard those claims from the invasion of any other group of workers, but we are not the ultimate judges. This Board shall be the Judges.

## EXHIBIT 2 (*continued*)

Let me quote again:

> The Board shall decide in each case whether in order to insure to employes the full benefit of their right to self-organization and to collective bargaining and otherwise to effectuate the policies of this Act, the unit appropriate for the purposes of collective bargaining shall be the employer unit, craft unit, plant unit or subdivision thereof.

There is no industrial unit provided for in the law. Can there be any doubt about that? And it is not for us to interpret that, because it is to be interpreted by the Board. Unconsciously, I am sure, this report of the committee in emphasizing plant organization and charters to independent unions and company-dominated unions, regardless of claims of affiliated national and international unions, will be supporting the decisions and enactments of a Board that is confined in the nature and character of its decisions that it is delegated by the Government to render.

So you see throughout this report it was clearly understood that it laid down a policy of organizing the unorganized, of issuing charters of broader jurisdiction in the three specific instances, and then a general delegation of power in miscellaneous trades, with the assurance and understanding had by the convention, regardless of the understanding Delegate Howard might have had as to the language used, that the Executive Council would ultimately be the determining factor in defining the jurisdictions of charters to be granted, so that every organization, craft, trade, or industry might have the opportunity of laying its difficulties or its claims of infraction upon its rights before the Executive Council and thus have its day in court.

This report would now destroy that discretionary power, in addition to the enlargement and the changing of the fundamental character of the issuance of charters in the American Federation of Labor.

I have confidence in the Executive Council, no matter who may be its personnel, whether I am on that Council or not, for it is the only efficient method we have in dealing with problems arising from day to day, yes in the matter of form of organization, and we cannot wait from year to year and merely outline a strict course wherein no discretion is permitted.

Now the fact that that is true and that the report of a year ago was sound is best illustrated in several resolutions which have been presented to your committee and which the committee is not now reporting on, but as stated by the secretary of the committee, will be reported on later on. One of them is an appeal to the convention that the jurisdiction as defined by the Executive Council in the automobile industry shall be enlarged and that limitations placed upon that charter be removed. The question is a valid one in this way: That it does present the opportunity of the organizations and the workmen affected to differ with the Executive Council and to come to a convention of the American Federation of Labor and to indicate to the delegates, if they can, that the Executive Council was in error in its judgment. That is as it should be. . . .

## EXHIBIT 2 (*concluded*)

If we don't trust the Executive Council, if we have no confidence in their judgment, if we feel they are biased, then pray let us change the Executive Council, but let us not adopt a policy of straitjacket judgment and decisions that permit of no flexibility. That, I dare repeat, will lead us into a channel that will strengthen the forces within industry and government that would force labor to submit to its judgment and deprive organized labor of America of its voluntary character, with all of its difficulties, with all of its conflicts, with all of its travail—a self-formed organization, founded upon the basis of volunteerism.

I hope the majority report will be substantiated and approved by this convention.

Delegate Lewis, United Mine Workers: Mr. Chairman and delegates of the convention—I rise to support the minority report as presented to this convention by Delegate Howard. . . .

Then, as now, the American Federation of Labor offered to the workers in these industries a plan of organization into Federal labor unions or local trade unions with the understanding that when organized they would be segregated into the various organizations of their respective crafts. Then, as now, practically every attempt to organize those workers broke upon the same rock that it breaks upon today—the rock of utter futility, the lack of reasonableness in a policy that failed to take into consideration the dreams and requirements of the workers themselves, and failing to take into consideration the recognized power of the adversaries of labor to destroy these feeble organizations in the great modern industries set up in the form of Federal labor unions or craft organizations functioning in a limited sphere.

For 25 years or more the American Federation of Labor has been following this precise policy, and surely in the absence of any other understanding of the question a record of 25 years of constant, unbroken failure should be convincing to those who actually have a desire to increase the prestige of our great labor movement by expanding its membership to permit it to occupy its natural place in the sun.

What is the record? Delegate Howard expressed it when he said that we laid claim to a membership of approximately three and a half million, out of an organizable number of approximately thirty-nine million. There is the answer. If we know nothing else on the question we can at least read the results, and in reading the results we surely understand that our influence is less great, that our activities are more circumscribed, and that our power is more limited to achieve our natural and desirable and virtuous objective than it would be if we had those twenty-five million workers that President Green, in his public address in 1934, talked of organizing. Where are they? Where are those twenty-five million that in a moment of exuberance we were going to organize? Perhaps President Green's arithmetic was wrong and he meant twenty-five thousand, because the total results are nearer the twenty-five thousand than the twenty-five million.

Source: *Proceedings* of the Annual Convention of the American Federation of Labor (1935), pp. 521–30, 533–34.

# EXHIBIT 3

**Labor Force and Employment, by Industry: 1920–1950** *(in thousands of persons 10 years old and over)*

| Year | Labor Force Total | Agriculture | Fishing | Mining | Construction | Employment — Manufacturing | | | Trade | Transport | | Service | |
| | | | | | | Total Persons Engaged | Cotton Textile Wage Earners | Primary Iron and Steel Wage Earners | | Ocean Vessels | Railways | Teachers | Domestics |
| --- | --- | --- | --- | --- | --- | --- | --- | --- | --- | --- | --- | --- | --- |
| 1950 | 65,470 | 7,870 | 77 | 901 | 3,029 | 15,648 | 350 | 550 | 12,152 | 130 | 1,373 | 1,270 | 1,995 |
| 1940 | 56,290 | 9,575 | 60 | 925 | 1,876 | 11,309 | 400 | 485 | 9,328 | 150 | 1,160 | 1,086 | 2,300 |
| 1930 | 48,830 | 10,560 | 73 | 1,009 | 1,988 | 9,884 | 372 | 375 | 8,122 | 160 | 1,659 | 1,044 | 2,270 |
| 1920 | 41,610 | 10,790 | 53 | 1,180 | 1,233 | 11,190 | 450 | 460 | 5,845 | 205 | 2,236 | 752 | 1,660 |

Source: *Historical Statistics of the United States: Colonial Times to 1970,* p. 139.

# EXHIBIT 4

## Work Stoppages, Workers Involved, Man-Days Idle, Major Issues, and Average Duration: 1920 to 1950

| | Work Stoppages and Workers Involved | | Man-Days Idle | | | | | Stoppages* Major Issues | | | Major Issues and Average Duration | | Workers Involved (1,000) Major Issues | | | |
|---|---|---|---|---|---|---|---|---|---|---|---|---|---|---|---|---|
| | Stoppages | Workers Involved | | Man-Days Idle | Percent of Estimated Total Working Time | | | | | | | Average Duration of Stoppages (days) | | | | |
| Year | Total | Number (1,000) | Percent of Total Employed | Number (1,000) | Total Economy | Private Nonfarm | Per Worker Involved | Total | Wages and Hours | Union Organization | Other and Not Reporting | | Total | Wages and Hours | Union Organization | Other and Not Reporting |
| 1950 | 4,843 | 2,410 | 5.1 | 38,800 | .33 | .40 | 16.1 | 4,843 | 2,559 | 919 | 1,365 | 19.2 | 2,410 | 1,460 | 130 | 819 |
| 1949 | 3,606 | 3,030 | 6.7 | 50,500 | .44 | .59 | 16.7 | 3,606 | 1,682 | 781 | 1,143 | 22.5 | 3,030 | 1,540 | 82 | 1,410 |
| 1948 | 3,419 | 1,960 | 4.2 | 34,100 | .28 | .37 | 17.4 | 3,419 | 1,737 | 780 | 902 | 21.8 | 1,960 | 1,210 | 228 | 518 |
| 1947 | 3,693 | 2,170 | 4.7 | 34,600 | .30 | .41 | 15.9 | 3,693 | 1,707 | 1,102 | 884 | 25.6 | 2,170 | 805 | 931 | 431 |
| 1946 | 4,985 | 4,600 | 10.5 | 116,000 | 1.04 | 1.43 | 25.2 | 4,990 | 2,238 | 1,617 | 1,135 | 24.2 | 4,940 | 3,710 | 568 | 663 |
| 1945 | 4,750 | 3,470 | 8.2 | 38,000 | .31 | .47 | 11.0 | 4,616 | 1,956 | 946 | 1,714 | 9.9 | 3,070 | 1,340 | 671 | 1,060 |
| 1944 | 4,956 | 2,120 | 4.8 | 8,720 | .07 | .09 | 4.1 | 4,958 | 2,146 | 808 | 2,004 | 5.6 | 2,130 | 810 | 395 | 922 |
| 1943 | 3,752 | 1,980 | 4.6 | 13,500 | .10 | .15 | 6.8 | 3,734 | 1,906 | 585 | 1,243 | 5.0 | 1,970 | 1,220 | 226 | 523 |
| 1942 | 2,968 | 840 | 1.0 | 4,180 | .04 | .05 | 5.0 | 3,036 | 1,423 | 943 | 670 | 11.7 | 852 | 429 | 191 | 232 |
| 1941 | 4,228 | 2,360 | 6.1 | 23,000 | .23 | .32 | 9.8 | 4,314 | 1,535 | 2,138 | 641 | 18.3 | 2,360 | 1,110 | 744 | 512 |
| 1940 | 2,508 | 577 | 1.7 | 6,700 | .08 | .10 | 11.6 | 2,493 | 753 | 1,243 | 497 | 20.9 | 573 | 235 | 190 | 148 |
| 1939 | 2,613 | 1,170 | 3.5 | 17,800 | .21 | .28 | 15.2 | 2,639 | 699 | 1,411 | 529 | 23.4 | 1,180 | 352 | 641 | 185 |
| 1938 | 2,772 | 688 | 2.8 | 9,150 | — | .15 | 13.3 | 2,772 | 776 | 1,385 | 611 | 23.6 | 688 | 252 | 224 | 211 |
| 1937 | 4,740 | 1,860 | 7.2 | 28,400 | — | .43 | 15.3 | 4,720 | 1,410 | 2,728 | 582 | 20.3 | 1,950 | 436 | 1,160 | 347 |
| 1936 | 2,172 | 789 | 3.1 | 13,900 | — | .21 | 17.6 | 2,156 | 756 | 1,083 | 317 | 23.3 | 710 | 251 | 365 | 94 |
| 1935 | 2,014 | 1,120 | 5.2 | 15,500 | — | .29 | 13.8 | 2,003 | 760 | 945 | 298 | 23.8 | 1,102 | 663 | 288 | 151 |
| 1934 | 1,856 | 1,470 | 7.2 | 19,600 | — | .38 | 13.4 | 1,817 | 717 | 835 | 265 | 19.5 | 1,480 | 346 | 762 | 372 |
| 1933 | 1,695 | 1,170 | 6.3 | 16,900 | — | .36 | 14.4 | 1,672 | 926 | 533 | 213 | 16.9 | 1,144 | 544 | 465 | 135 |
| 1932 | 841 | 324 | 1.8 | 10,500 | — | .23 | 32.4 | 852 | 560 | 162 | 130 | 19.6 | 325 | 234 | 73 | 18 |
| 1931 | 810 | 342 | 1.6 | 6,890 | — | .11 | 20.2 | 796 | 447 | 221 | 128 | 18.8 | 346 | 155 | 115 | 74 |

| Year | | | | | | | | | | | | | | | |
|------|------|-----|--------|---|-----|------|-------|-------|-----|-----|------|-----|-----|-----|----|
| 1930 | 637 | 183 | .8 | 3,320 | — | .05 | 18.1 | 651 | 284 | 207 | 160 | 22.3 | 182 | 73 | 76 | 33 |
| 1929 | 921 | 289 | 1.2 | 5,350 | — | .07 | 18.5 | 924 | 373 | 382 | 169 | 22.6 | 286 | 104 | 102 | 80 |
| 1928 | 604 | 314 | 1.3 | 12,600 | — | .17 | 40.2 | 620 | 222 | 226 | 172 | 27.6 | 323 | 140 | 95 | 88 |
| 1927 | 707 | 330 | 1.4 | 26,200 | — | .37 | 79.5 | 666 | 273 | 240 | 153 | 26.5 | 319 | 232 | 45 | 43 |
| 1926 | — | — | — | — | — | — | — | 1,035 | 478 | 206 | 351 | — | — | — | — | — |
| 1925 | — | — | — | — | — | — | — | 1,301 | 537 | 219 | 545 | — | — | — | — | — |
| 1924 | — | — | — | — | — | — | — | 1,249 | 537 | 244 | 468 | — | — | — | — | — |
| 1923 | — | — | — | — | — | — | — | 1,553 | 721 | 308 | 524 | — | — | — | — | — |
| 1922 | — | — | — | — | — | — | — | 1,112 | 583 | 208 | 321 | — | — | — | — | — |
| 1921 | — | — | — | — | — | — | — | 2,385 | 1,501 | 373 | 511 | — | — | — | — | — |
| 1920 | — | — | — | — | — | — | — | 3,411 | 2,038 | 622 | 751 | — | — | — | — | — |

*For 1920 and 1927, 1947 to 1950, the data are for stoppages beginning in calendar years. For the remaining years, the data are for stoppages ending in calendar years.

Source: *Historical Statistics of the United States: Colonial Times to 1970*, p. 179.

# APPENDIX A

## *Chronology of Labor Relations*

| | |
|---|---|
| 1919 | Record-breaking number of workers involved in numerous strikes during chaotic postwar readjustment. Strikers include civil servants, longshoremen, and steelworkers. |
| 1919–20 | The "Palmer Raids," in which the U.S. Attorney General carries out attacks on radicals and suspected radicals, violating civil liberties. More than 2,500 people taken into custody. |
| 1920 | Wall Street bombing further inflames fear of radicals and communists. |
| | John L. Lewis becomes president of the United Mine Workers of America. |
| 1922 | Herrin Massacre: Miners in Southern Illinois kill 20 guards and strike-breakers. |
| 1924 | Samuel Gompers dies. William Green becomes president of the A F of L. |
| 1926 | Railway Labor Act requires employers to bargain collectively and prohibits discrimination against unionists. |
| 1929 | The Crash. |
| 1932 | The "Bonus Army" marches to Washington to demand liberalized compensation for veterans and is routed by police and army. |
| | Norris-La Guardia Act limits federal injunctions in labor disputes and makes "yellow dog" contracts (contracts that demand that the signatory not join a labor union) unenforceable in federal courts. |
| | Franklin D. Roosevelt elected president. |
| 1933 | Passage of the National Industrial Recovery Act. Section 7(a) guarantees the right of workers "to organize and bargain collectively through representatives of their own choosing." A National Labor Board was created to oversee collective bargaining. One historian calls the NIRA "the spark that |

| | |
|---|---|
| 1933 (cont.) | rekindled unionism within American labor." (Bernstein, *Turbulent Years,* p. 37.) |
| | The United Mine Workers, which had dwindled from half a million members in 1920 to 150,000 in 1932, launches an all-out organizing drive which meets with great success. By 1936, there are 578,000 people in the union. |
| | Sidney Hillman's Amalgamated Clothing Workers Union wins substantial benefits in strikes. Membership in this year climbs from 75,000 to 125,000. |
| | Early in the year, David Dubinsky's International Ladies Garment Workers Union has 40,000 members, less that two fifths the membership in 1920. By May 1934, after successful strikes and organizing drives, membership stands at an all-time high of 200,000. |
| | 50,000 workers in the rubber industry are unionized. |
| | Other unions secure similar gains. |
| | The National Association of Manufacturers begins to propagandize in favor of the Open Shop. |
| 1934 | Numerous major strikes all over the country. |
| 1935 (May) | In *Schecter* v. *U.S.,* the Supreme Court declares the NIRA unconstitutional. |
| (June) | Congress passes Wagner Act (National Labor Relations Act) which grants workers the right to join unions of their own choosing and to bargain collectively. Employers are enjoined from interfering with and coercing workers in the exercise of their rights. |
| (October) | A F of L convention in Atlantic City. Industrial unionism voted down. Lewis slugs Hutcheson. |
| (November 9) | Lewis, Hillman (Men's Clothing), Dubinsky (ILGWU), Zaritsky (Hatters), Howard (Printers), Fremming (Oil Workers), Brown (Mine, Mill and Smelter Workers), and McMahon (Textile Workers) meet to form the Committee of Industrial Organizations, or CIO. The CIO positions itself as the pro-industrial union bloc within the A F of L. |
| (November 23) | Green writes leaders of the CIO to warn them of the dangers of dual unionism. Lewis writes Green resigning his A F of L vice presidency. Not until 1938 does the CIO formally set itself up as an entity separate from the A F of L. |
| 1936 (June 4) | The Steel Workers Organizing Committee, founded and controlled by Lewis, begins its campaign to organize the steel industry. |
| (June 6) | Creation of the La Follette Committee whose Senate hearings generate much publicity concerning the violation of basic rights of workers by large employers. |

| (July 2) | The United Automobile Workers Union affiliates with the CIO. |
| (November 3) | Franklin D. Roosevelt overwhelmingly reelected for a second term in office with the help of enthusiastic labor support. |
| (December 29) | Sit-down strikes at Fisher Body and Chevrolet plants of General Motors begin in Flint, Michigan. |
| 1937 (January 1) | Frank Murphy, a liberal Democrat, becomes Governor of Michigan. |
| (January 2) | A judge issues an injunction ordering the sit-down strikers in Flint to leave the plants. They refuse, and the injunction is discredited when it is revealed that the issuing judge owns more than $200,000 worth of GM stock. |
| (January 9) | Myron Taylor, chief executive officer of United States Steel, and John L. Lewis meet by chance in a crowded Washington restaurant. Negotiations begin soon thereafter. |
| (January 11) | "The Battle of Bulls Run"—organizers win a skirmish at Flint in the first bloodshed in the GM strike. |
| (February 2) | GM obtains another injunction from another judge ordering the evacuation of the plants. The union defies the injunction. |
| (February 11) | It having become apparent that Governor Murphy would not use troops to evict the strikers, GM enters into the preliminary negotiations which result in the unionization of the company. |
| (March 2) | U.S. Steel and the Steel Workers Organizing Committee sign a preliminary agreement. |
| (April 6) | Chrysler recognizes the UAW. |
| (May 26) | Walter Reuther and other UAW leaders are beaten by company thugs from Ford at the "Battle of the Overpass." The UAW fails to organize Ford. |
| (May 30) | Ten marchers killed by police at Republic Steel's South Chicago plant. "Little Steel" resists unionization. The strike fails. |
| 1936–37 | The CIO secures important gains in various other industries such as rubber and electrical work. It also suffers setbacks in autos and steel. |
| 1937–41 | The A F of L launches impressive organizational drives, accepting the principles of industrial unionism. |
| 1938 | Fair Labor Standards Act establishes minimum wages and maximum hours. |

| | |
|---|---|
| 1940 | Lewis repudiates Roosevelt and threatens to resign from the CIO presidency if FDR is elected to a third term. |
| | Roosevelt elected president. Lewis resigns as president of the CIO but remains at the helm of the United Mine Workers. Philip Murray, head of the Steel Workers Organizing Committee, becomes president of the CIO. |
| 1941 | Ford recognizes the UAW. |
| | "Little Steel" organized. |
| 1945–46 | Most massive strike wave in American history including steel, autos, rubber, rail, electrical workers, and miners. Strikes settled with little violence. Workers make substantial economic gains which employers find affordable. |

# PART THREE

# *Twentieth Century Developments*

## THE ROLE OF GOVERNMENT

## BUSINESS MANAGEMENT IN THE MODERN ERA

# A LOOK AHEAD

# CASE 21

# *The Antitrust Movement: Symbolic Politics and Industrial Organization Economics* *

*Once the United States had an antitrust movement without antitrust prosecutions; in our time, there have been antitrust prosecutions without an antitrust movement.*[1]

## The Setting

In the last third of the 19th century, the organization of major industries in the United States underwent a fundamental transformation. At the beginning of this period,

> the major industries serviced an agrarian economy. Except for a few companies equipping the rapidly expanding railroad network, the leading industrial firms processed agricultural products and provided farmers with food and clothing. These firms tended to be small, and bought their raw materials and sold their finished goods locally. Where they manufactured for a market more than a few miles away from the factory, they bought and sold through commissioned agents who handled the business of several other similar firms.

---

*This case was prepared by Assistant Professor Richard S. Tedlow as the basis for class discussion rather than to illustrate either effective or ineffective handling of an administrative situation.

Copyright © 1983 by the President and Fellows of Harvard College.

Harvard Business School case 384–051. rev. 7/84.

[1]Richard Hofstadter, "What Happened to the Antitrust Movement?" in *The Paranoid Style in American Politics* (New York: Vintage, 1967), p. 189.

By the beginning of the 20th century, many more companies were making producers' goods, to be used in industry rather than on the farm or by the ultimate consumer. Most of the major industries had become dominated by a few large enterprises. These great industrial corporations no longer purchased and sold through agents, but had their own nationwide buying and marketing organizations. Many, primarily those in the extractive industries, had come to control their own raw materials.

In the terms of the economist and sociologist, a significant sector of American industry had become bureaucratic, in the sense that business decisions were made within large hierarchical structures.[2]

These changes were both the cause and the result of a number of developments:

— The dramatic growth of the railroad network.
— The development of centralized markets for industrial securities.
— The rapid growth of urbanization.
— The growth of total population from 31,443,321 in 1860 to 75,494,575 in 1900.
— Scientific and technological breakthroughs in electric power, transportation, communication, and basic industrial processes for the transformation of raw materials to finished products.

To appreciate fully the impact of these developments on the consciousness of the average American, one should try to put oneself in the position of a white American male born in an eastern or midwestern state in, say, 1843. Such a man was most likely born on a farm or perhaps in a small town. The rhythm of his life was based on nature. ("God's time" was transformed to "Vanderbilt's time" when the railroads adopted standard time in 1883. Prior to that, there had been 38 local times in Wisconsin alone.) He arose with the sun and ceased his labors when it set. His life vastly differed in accord with the seasons of the year. He was his own boss.

Such a man might have seen four years of action during the Civil War. That conflict was a galvanizing event, setting the terms of important aspects of political and social organization in some respects down to the present day. A major reason for the North's decision to vote the Republicans into power in 1860 and to take up arms when the South refused to accept the electoral verdict was the belief that the great slave owners were involved in a conspiracy to impose, in some sense on the nation as a whole and certainly on the western territories not yet organized into states, a set of values and institutions fundamentally antithetical both to political freedom and economic enterprise. Indeed, this individual would probably have seen an identity between political and economic freedom. The word "employee" does not appear in Civil War Era polemics. Every man either should be or could become his own boss. There was no need to labor for another all one's life.

---

[2]Alfred D. Chandler, "The Beginnings of 'Big Business' in American Industry," *Business History Review* 33, no. 1 (Spring, 1959), p. 4.

The ideal was the independent man, not, it should be pointed out, the individualist. We have been misled by slogans of individualism. Americans have always been motivated by desires for community and an interest in working together. True individualists like Henry David Thoreau, who sought a life in the woods where they would make their own rules and constitute a "majority of one," were outside the mainstream. The independent individual entered into all kinds of associations and organizations but did so on a voluntary basis, not through coercion.

This model of political economy carried the moral freight of the nation. People saw it as a medium not only for material well-being, but for the attainment of whatever was good in life in terms of character. But in the postwar years, our protagonist would have seen the system productive of such values being obliterated by big business with its impersonality and manipulation.

His indignation would have been stirred by the extraordinary outpouring of anti-big business literature. Merely to recite the titles of leading articles and books of the time is to summarize their conclusions: *Wealth Against Commonwealth, Frenzied Finance, The Octupus,* to name only a few. The productive capacity of the nation seemed to be in the process of being engrossed by unworthy men who were pictured as violating the old values of thrift and sobriety. The political influence of the giant corporations seemed everywhere apparent. The Senate was pictured as a millionaires' club run of, by, and for the monopolists. Indeed, big businessmen seemed to flaunt their political manipulations. Testified Jay Gould:

> We had to look after four states: New York: New Jersey, Pennsylvania [and] Ohio and have helped men in all of them; it was the custom when men received nominations to come to me for contributions and I made them and considered them good paying investments for the company; in a Republican district, I was a strong Republican, in a Democratic district I was Democratic, and in doubtful districts I was doubtful; in politics, I was an Erie Railroad man every time. . . .[3]

It was not unreasonable to ask whether such men were above the government.

## The Sherman Act

The need to place the federal government above business which was national in scope was expressed by the passage of the Interstate Commerce Act in 1887. Railroads were widely looked upon as a special case, a "natural monopoly" where competition could not flourish. But many people found bigness in manufacturing and distribution just as dangerous.

There was a long tradition in the Anglo-Saxon common law which held that contracts involving restraints of trade or efforts to monopolize were against public policy and therefore not legally enforceable. Unenforceability did not, however, prevent such contracts from being entered into. And as new and more efficient ways for business to combine appeared in the form of trust arrangements, such as

---

[3]Quoted in Edward C. Kirkland, *Industry Comes of Age* (Chicago: Quadrangle, 1967), pp. 113–14.

that pioneered by Standard Oil in 1881/1882, the sentiment began to spread that a more forceful and explicit statement of public policy with regard to competition and growth was needed. By 1890, 21 states had either enacted antitrust statutes or incorporated clauses into their constitutions aimed at "restoring" competition.

Federal action was called for, however, because the reach of the states was insufficient and because of the general sentiment that a pronouncement that the national government was the most powerful force in the nation was appropriate. (One influential senator said his colleagues were simply looking for "some bill headed: 'A Bill to Punish Trusts' with which to go to the country.") The upshot of this climate of opinion was the Sherman Antitrust Act, produced as Exhibit 1, passed in the summer of 1890 with only one dissenting vote in all of Congress.

For its first decade, the statute was, if not quite a dead letter, not vigorously enforced. Only 18 cases were brought under it, four of which were aimed at labor unions. One of these limited its reach notably.

Certainly, the act failed to inhibit the concentration of American industry. As the deep depression which hit in 1893 waned, mergers and internal business growth took place at an unprecedented rate. In the ten years from 1896, the 100 largest corporations increased their size by a factor of four and gained control over 40 percent of the national industrial capital. By 1900, the average manufacturing plant served an area more than three times as large as that of the average plant in 1882.

The years 1898 to 1902 saw the most intense merger activity in American history. Two thousand six hundred fifty-three firms disappeared with merger capitalizations totaling over $6.3 billion, greater than the total of all the other years prior to 1914 combined.

## The Trust Problem in the Progressive Era

The trust problem was a central concern in both politics and business during the Progressive Era (roughly 1900 to 1917). Theodore Roosevelt resolved to make use of the Sherman Act not only to break up certain large mergers but also to assert the preeminence of the federal government among American institutions. His first case provided all the drama which national political theater so needs.

The Northern Securities Company was a giant holding company for three great northwestern railroads: the Northern Pacific, the Great Northern, and the Chicago, Burlington and Quincy. In the words of one historian, "The company's architects, J. P. Morgan and Company, the Rockefeller interests, James J. Hill, and E. H. Harriman, were the very Sanhedrin of the nation's railroad and financial oligarchy."[4] The government's case was upheld by the Supreme Court in 1904 (two years after it was brought) to the general approval of the informed public but to the disapproval of Wall Street interests. During the course of Roosevelt's

---

[4]George E. Mowry, *The Era of Theodore Roosevelt* (New York: Harper & Row, 1958), p. 131.

tenure in office, from 1901 to 1909, some 44 actions were brought under the Sherman Act, including those against Standard Oil and American Tobacco, which were to result in the breakup of both firms.

Roosevelt's comparative vigor in using the Sherman Act earned him the sobriquet "Teddy the Trust Buster." This nickname was not a fair reflection of his feelings, which ranged at various times from the antitrust pugnacity of Northern Securities on the one hand to efforts on the other to distinguish between good and bad trusts (in the former category he placed International Harvester and United States Steel). In 1908, he bellowed that informed public policy called for "Federal control over all combinations engaged in interstate commerce, instead of relying upon the foolish antitrust law." His feelings in 1911 are set forth in Exhibit 2.

Roosevelt's successor in the White House, William Howard Taft, discarded the distinction between good and bad trusts (U.S. Steel and International Harvester were both targets of his Justice Department). Between 1910 and 1912, the Taft Administration brought 58 antitrust cases, some which had negative political consequences for him. A major development in those years, though not directly a result of Taft's policies, was the breakup of Standard Oil and American Tobacco in May 1911 and the enunciation of the "Rule of Reason" by Chief Justice White. Excerpts from White's opinion and from a dissenting view are reproduced as Exhibit 3. Taft's reaction to these two views is provided in Exhibit 4.

If the imaginary American mentioned at the beginning of this case were to have lived to his biblical three score years and 10, he would have had the opportunity to vote in the election of 1912. In addition to Roosevelt and Taft, candidates for the presidency were Eugene Victor Debs for the Socialist Party and Woodrow Wilson for the Democrats. Debs's views on political economy are expressed in his acceptance speech for his party's nomination (see Exhibit 5). Wilson's opinions are contained in a campaign speech reproduced as Exhibit 6.

Wilson was, of course, elected and assumed the Presidency in 1913. During his first administration, two more statutes were passed which round out the antitrust activity of this period. The first was the Clayton Antitrust Act, passed on June 5, 1914. The Clayton Act, in addition to excusing labor and farm groups from the purview of antitrust enforcement, specified certain practices not enumerated in the Sherman Act to be illegal "where the effect may be to substantially lessen competition or tend to create a monopoly." Included were price discrimination with intent to injure a competitor, exclusive dealing, and corporate stock acquisitions.

The second statute of note was the Federal Trade Commission Act, which became law on September 10, 1914. This act declared "unfair methods of competition in commerce" to be illegal. The unfair methods in question were not specified because, as the bill's floor leader in the Senate noted, "We have the testimony of experts in business that unfair competition is so multiform that if we condemn 20 practices that exist today, 20 more will be invented tomorrow." The idea was for an expert Commission to determine when unfair competitive practices were in use and to prohibit them.

According to antitrust authority and former Solicitor General Robert H. Bork:

> The years 1890 to 1914 witnessed the origin of every major theory that drives and directs the evolution of antitrust doctrine to this day. What the courts, the Congress, and the enforcement agencies have wrought since is little more than the working out of the implications of those early hypotheses.[5]

## EXHIBIT 1

---

### *The Sherman Antitrust Act, July 2, 1890*

*An Act to protect trade and commerce against unlawful restraints and monopolies*

*Be it enacted that*

Sec. 1. Every contract, combination in the form of trust or otherwise, or conspiracy, in restraint of trade or commerce among the several States, or with foreign nations, is hereby declared to be illegal. Every person who shall make any such contract or engage in any such combination or conspiracy, shall be deemed guilty of a misdemeanor, and, on conviction thereof, shall be punished by fine not exceeding $5,000, or by imprisonment not exceeding one year, or by both said punishments, in the discretion of the court.

Sec. 2. Every person who shall monopolize, or attempt to monopolize, or combine or conspire with any other person or persons, to monopolize any part of the trade or commerce among the several States, or with foreign nations, shall be deemed guilty of a misdemeanor, and, on conviction thereof, shall be punished by fine not exceeding $5,000 or by imprisonment not exceeding one year, or by both said punishments, in the discretion of the court.

Sec. 3. Every contract, combination in form of trust or otherwise, or conspiracy, in restraint of trade or commerce in any Territory of the United States or of the District of Columbia, or in restraint of trade or commerce between any such Territory and another, or between any such Territory or Territories and any State or States or the District of Columbia, or with foreign nations, or between the District of Columbia and any State or States or foreign nations, is hereby declared illegal. Every person who shall make any such contract or engage in any such combination or conspiracy, shall be deemed guilty of a misdemeanor, and, on conviction thereof, shall be punished by fine not exceeding $5,000, or by imprisonment not exceeding one year, or by both said punishments in the discretion of the court.

Sec. 4. The several circuit courts of the United States are hereby invested with jurisdiction to prevent and restrain violations of this act; and it shall be the duty of

---

[5]Robert H. Bork, *The Antitrust Paradox* (New York: Basic Books, 1978), p. 15.

## EXHIBIT 1 (*concluded*)

the several district attorneys of the United States, in their respective districts, under the direction of the Attorney-General, to institute proceedings in equity to prevent and restrain such violations. Such proceedings may be by way of petition setting forth the case and praying that such violation shall be enjoined or otherwise prohibited. When the parties complained of shall have been duly notified of such petition, the courts shall proceed, as soon as may be, to the hearing and determination of the case; and pending such petition and before final decrees, the court may at any time make such temporary restraining order or prohibition as shall be deemed just in the premises.

Sec. 5. Whenever it shall appear to the court before which any proceeding under Section four of this act may be pending, that the ends of justice require that other parties should be brought before the court, the court may cause them to be summoned, whether they reside in the district in which the court is held or not; and subpoenas to that end may be served in any district by the marshal thereof.

Sec. 6. Any property owned under any contract or by any combination, or pursuant to any conspiracy (and being the subject thereof) mentioned in Section one of this act, and being in the course of transportation from one State to another, or to a foreign country, shall be forfeited to the United States, and may be seized and condemned by like proceedings as those provided by law for the forfeiture, seizure, and condemnation of property imported into the United States contrary to law.

Sec. 7. Any person who shall be injured in his business or property by any other person or corporation by reason of anything forbidden or declared to be unlawful by this act may sue therefore in any circuit court of the United States in the district in which the defendant resides or is found without respect to the amount in controversy, and shall recover threefold the damages by him sustained, and the costs of suit, including a reasonable attorney's fee.

Sec. 8. That the word "person," or "persons," wherever used in this act shall be deemed to include corporations and associations existing under or authorized by the laws of either the United States, the laws of any of the Territories, the laws of any State, or the laws of any foreign country.

Source: *U.S. Statutes at Large,* vol. XXVI, p. 209.

## EXHIBIT 2

### *Theodore Roosevelt on Big Business*

The suit against the Steel Trust by the Government has brought vividly before our people the need of reducing to order the chaotic Government policy as regards

## EXHIBIT 2 (*continued*)

business. As President,* in Messages to Congress I repeatedly called the attention of that body and of the public to the inadequacy of the Anti-Trust Law by itself to meet business conditions and secure justice to the people, and to the further fact that it might, if left unsupplemented by additional legislation, work mischief, with no compensating advantage; and I urged as strongly as I knew how that the policy followed with relation to railways in connection with the Inter-State Commerce Law should be followed by the National Government as regards all great business concerns; and therefore that, as a first step, the powers of the Bureau of Corporations should be greatly enlarged, or else that there should be created a Governmental board or commission, with powers somewhat similar to those of the Inter-State Commerce Commission, but covering the whole field of inter-State business, exclusive of transportation (which should, by law, be kept wholly separate from ordinary industrial business, all common ownership of the industry and the railway being forbidden). In the end I have always believed that it would also be necessary to give the National Government complete power over the organization and capitalization of all business concerns engaged in inter-State commerce. . . .

When my Administration took office, I found, not only that there had been little real enforcement of the Anti-Trust Law and but little more effective enforcement of the Inter-State Commerce Law, but also that the decisions were so chaotic and the laws themselves so vaguely drawn, or at least interpreted in such widely varying fashions, that the biggest business men tended to treat both laws as dead letters. The series of actions by which we succeeded in making the Inter-State Commerce Law an efficient and most useful instrument in regulating the transportation of the country and exacting justice from the big railways without doing them injustice—while, indeed, on the contrary, securing them against injustice—need not here be related. The Anti-Trust Law it was also necessary to enforce as it has never hitherto been enforced; both because it was on the statute-books and because it was imperative to teach the masters of the biggest corporations in the land that they were not, and would not be permitted to regard themselves as, above the law. Moreover, where the combination has really been guilty of misconduct the law serves a useful purpose, and in such cases as those of the Standard Oil and Tobacco Trusts, if effectively enforced, the law confers a real and great good.

Suits were brought against the most powerful corporations in the land, which we were convinced had clearly and beyond question violated the Anti-Trust Law. These suits were brought with great care, and only where we felt so sure of our facts that we could be fairly certain that there was a likelihood of success. As a matter of fact, in most of the important suits we were successful. It was imperative that these suits should be brought, and very real good was achieved by bringing them, for it was only these suits that made the great masters of corporate capital in

---

*Theodore Roosevelt was President of the United States from 1901 to 1909. This essay was written in 1911, with an eye to the campaign of 1912.

## EXHIBIT 2 (*continued*)

America fully realize that they were the servants and not the masters of the people, that they were subject to the law, and that they would not be permitted to be a law unto themselves; and the corporations against which we proceeded had sinned, not merely by being big (which we did not regard as in itself a sin), but by being guilty of unfair practices towards their competitors and by procuring unfair advantages from the railways. But the resulting situation has made it evident that the Anti-Trust Law is not adequate to meet the situation that has grown up because of modern business conditions and the accompanying tremendous increase in the business use of vast quantities of corporate wealth. As I have said, this was already evident to my mind when I was President, and in communications with Congress I repeatedly stated the facts. But when I made these communications there were still plenty of people who did not believe that we would succeed in the suits that had been instituted against the Standard Oil, the Tobacco, and other corporations, and it was impossible to get the public as a whole to realize what the situation was. Sincere zealots who believed that all combinations could be destroyed and the old-time conditions of unregulated competition restored, insincere politicians who knew better but made believe that they thought whatever their constituents wished them to think, crafty reactionaries who wished to see on the statute-books laws which they believed unenforceable, and the almost solid "Wall Street crowd" or representatives of "big business" who at that time opposed with equal violence both wise and necessary and unwise and improper regulation of business—all fought against the adoption of a sane, effective, and far-reaching policy.

It is a vitally necessary thing to have the persons in control of big trusts of the character of the Standard Oil Trust and Tobacco Trust taught that they are under the law, just as it was a necessary thing to have the Sugar Trust taught the same lesson in drastic fashion by Mr. Henry L. Stimson when he was United States District Attorney in the city of New York. But to attempt to meet the whole problem not by administrative governmental action but by a succession of lawsuits is hopeless from the standpoint of working out a permanently satisfactory solution. Moreover, the results sought to be achieved are achieved only in extremely insufficient and fragmentary measure by breaking up all big corporations, whether they have behaved well or ill, into a number of little corporations which it is perfectly certain will be largely, and perhaps altogether, under the same control. Such action is harsh and mischievous if the corporation is guilty of nothing except its size; and where, as in the case of the Standard Oil, and especially the Tobacco Trusts, the corporation has been guilty of immoral and anti-social practices, there is need for far more drastic and thoroughgoing action than any that has been taken, under the recent decree of the Supreme Court. In the case of the Tobacco Trust, for instance, the settlement in the Circuit Court, in which the representatives of the Government seem inclined to concur, practically leaves all of the companies still substantially under the control of the 29 original defendants. Such a result is lamentable from the standpoint of justice. The decision of the Circuit Court, if allowed to stand, means that the Tobacco Trust has merely been obliged to change

## EXHIBIT 2 (*continued*)

its clothes, that none of the real offenders have received any real punishment, while, as the New York "Times," a protrust paper, says, the tobacco concerns, in their new clothes, are in positions of "ease and luxury," and "immune from prosecution under the law."

Surely, miscarriage of justice is not too strong a term to apply to such a result when considered in connection with what the Supreme Court said of this Trust. That great Court in its decision used language which, in spite of its habitual and severe self-restraint in stigmatizing wrong-doing, yet unhesitatingly condemns the Tobacco Trust for moral turpitude, saying that the case shows an "ever-present manifestation . . . of conscious wrong-doing" by the Trust, whose history is "replete with the doing of acts which it was the obvious purpose of the statute to forbid, . . . demonstrative of the existence from the beginning of a purpose to acquire dominion and control of the tobacco trade, not by the mere exertion of the ordinary right to contract and to trade, but by methods devised in order to monopolize the trade by driving competitors out of business, which were ruthlessly carried out upon the assumption that to work upon the fears or play upon the cupidity of competitors would make success possible." The letters from and to various officials of the Trust, which were put in evidence, show a literally astounding and horrifying indulgence by the Trust in wicked and depraved business methods—such as the "endeavor to cause a strike in their [a rival business firm's] factory," or the "shutting off the market" of an independent tobacco firm by "taking the necessary steps to give them a warm reception," or forcing importers into a price agreement by causing and continuing "a demoralization of the business for such length of time as may be deemed desirable" (I quote from the letters). A Trust guilty of such conduct should be absolutely disbanded, and the only way to prevent the repetition of such conduct is by strict Government supervision, and not merely by lawsuits.

The Anti-Trust Law cannot meet the whole situation, not can any modification of the principle of the Anti-Trust Law avail to meet the whole situation. The fact is that many of the men who have called themselves Progressives, and who certainly believe that they are Progressives, represent in reality in this matter not progress at all but a kind of sincere rural toryism. These men believe that it is possible by strengthening the Anti-Trust Law to restore business to the competitive conditions of the middle of the last century. Any such effort is foredoomed to end in failure, and, if successful, would be mischievous to the last degree. Business cannot be successfully conducted in accordance with the practices and theories of 60 years ago unless we abolish steam, electricity, big cities, and, in short, not only all modern business and modern industrial conditions, but all the modern conditions of our civilization. The effort to restore competition as it was 60 years ago, and to trust for justice solely to this proposed restoration of competition, is just as foolish as if we should go back to the flintlocks of Washington's Continentals as a substitute for modern weapons of precision. The effort to prohibit all combinations, good or bad, is bound to fail, and ought to fail; when made, it merely means

# EXHIBIT 2 (*continued*)

that some of the worst combinations are not checked and that honest business is checked. Our purpose should be, not to strangle business as an incident of strangling combinations, but to regulate big corporations in thoroughgoing and effective fashion, so as to help legitimate business as an incident to thoroughly and completely safeguarding the interests of the people as a whole. Against all such increase of Government regulation the argument is raised that it would amount to a form of Socialism. This argument is familiar; it is precisely the same as that which was raised against the creation of the Inter-State Commerce Commission, and of all the different utilities commissions in the different States, as I myself saw, 30 years ago, when I was a legislator at Albany, and these questions came up in connection with our State Government. Nor can action be effectively taken by any one State. Congress alone has power under the Constitution effectively and thoroughly and at all points to deal with inter-State commerce, and where Congress, as it should do, provides laws that will give the Nation full jurisdiction over the whole field, then that jurisdiction becomes, of necessity, exclusive—although until Congress does act affirmatively and thoroughly it is idle to expect that the States will or ought to rest content with nonaction on the part of both Federal and State authorities. This statement, by the way, applies also to the question of "usurpation" by any one branch of our Government of the rights of another branch. It is contended that in these recent decisions the Supreme Court legislated; so it did; and it had to; because Congress had signally failed to do *its* duty by legislating. For the Supreme Court to nullify an act of the Legislature as unconstitutional except on the clearest grounds is usurpation; to interpret such an act in an obviously wrong sense is usurpation; but where the legislative body persistently leaves open a field which it is absolutely imperative, from the public standpoint to fill, then no possible blame attaches to the official or officials who step in because they have to, and who then do the needed work in the interest of the people. The blame in such cases lies with the body which has been derelict, and not with the body which reluctantly makes good the dereliction.

　　Few will dispute the fact that the present situation is not satisfactory and cannot be put on a permanently satisfactory basis unless we put an end to the period of groping and declare for a fixed policy, a policy which shall clearly define and punish wrongdoing, which shall put a stop to the iniquities done in the name of business, but which shall do strict equity to business. We demand that big business give the people a square deal; in return we must insist that when any one engaged in big business honestly endeavors to do right he shall himself be given a square deal; and the first, and most elementary, kind of square deal is to give him in advance full information as to just what he can, and he cannot, legally and properly do. It is absurd, and much worse than absurd, to treat the deliberate lawbreaker as on an exact par with the man eager to obey the law, whose only desire is to find out from some competent Governmental authority what the law is, and then to live up to it. Moreover, it is absurd to treat the size of a corporation as in itself a crime. As Judge Hook says in his opinion in the Standard Oil Case: "Mag-

## EXHIBIT 2 (*continued*)

nitude of business does not alone constitute a monopoly. . . . the genius and industry of man when kept to ethical standards still have full play, and what he achieves is his . . . success and magnitude of business, the rewards of fair and honorable endeavor [are not forbidden] . . . [the public welfare is threatened only when success is attained] by wrongful or unlawful methods." Size may, and in my opinion does, make a corporation fraught with potential menace to the community; and may, and in my opinion should, therefore make it incumbent upon the community to exercise through its administrative (not merely through its judicial) officers a strict supervision over that corporation in order to see that it does not go wrong; but the size in itself does not signify wrong-doing, and should not be held to signify wrong-doing.

Not only should any huge corporation which has gained its position by unfair methods, and by interference with the rights of others, by demoralizing and corrupt practices, in short, by sheer baseness and wrong-doing, be broken up, but it should be made the business of some administrative governmental body, by constant supervision, to see that it does not come together again, save under such strict control as shall insure the community against all repetition of the bad conduct—and it should never be permitted thus to assemble its parts as long as these parts are under the control of the original offenders, for actual experience has shown that these men are, from the standpoint of the people at large, unfit to be trusted with the power implied in the management of a large corporation. But nothing of importance is gained by breaking up a huge inter-State and international industrial organization *which has not offended otherwise than by its size,* into a number of small concerns without any attempt to regulate the way in which those concerns as a whole shall do business. Nothing is gained by depriving the American Nation of good weapons wherewith to fight in the great field of international industrial competition. Those who would seek to restore the days of unlimited and uncontrolled competition, and who believe that a panacea for our industrial and economic ills is to be found in the mere breaking up of all big corporations, simply because they are big, are attempting not only the impossible, but what, if possible, would be undesirable. They are acting as we should act if we tried to dam the Mississippi, to stop its flow outright. The effort would be certain to result in failure and disaster; we would have attempted the impossible, and so would have achieved nothing, or worse than nothing. But by building levees along the Mississippi, not seeking to dam the stream, but to control it, we are able to achieve our object and to confer inestimable good in the course of so doing.

This Nation should definitely adopt the policy of attacking, not the mere fact of combination, but the evils and wrong-doing which so frequently accompany combination. The fact that a combination is very big is ample reason for exercising a close and jealous supervision over it, because its size renders it potent for mischief; but it should not be punished unless it actually does the mischief; it should merely be so supervised and controlled as to guarantee us, the people, against its doing mischief. We should not strive for a policy of unregulated competition and of the destruction of all big corporations, that is, of all the most efficient,

# EXHIBIT 2 (*concluded*)

business industries in the land. Nor should we persevere in the hopeless experiment of trying to regulate these industries by means only of lawsuits, each lasting several years, and of uncertain result. We should enter upon a course of supervision, control, and regulation of these great corporations—a regulation which we should not fear, if necessary, to bring to the point of control of monopoly prices, just as in exceptional cases railway rates are now regulated. Either the Bureau of Corporations should be authorized, or some other governmental body similar to the Inter-State Commerce Commission should be created, to exercise this supervision, this authoritative control. When once immoral business practices have been eliminated by such control, competition will thereby be again revived as a healthy factor, although not as formerly an all sufficient factor, in keeping the general business situation sound. Wherever immoral business practices still obtain— as they obtained in the cases of the Standard Oil Trust and Tobacco Trust—the Anti-Trust Law can be invoked; and wherever such a prosecution is successful, and the courts declare a corporation to possess a monopolistic character, then that corporation should be completely dissolved, and the parts ought never to be again assembled save on whatever terms and under whatever conditions may be imposed by the governmental body in which is vested the regulatory power. Methods can readily be devised by which corporations sincerely desiring to act fairly and honestly can on their own initiative come under this thoroughgoing administrative control by the Government and thereby be free from the working of the Anti-Trust Law. But the Law will remain to be invoked against wrong-doers; and under such conditions it could be invoked far more vigorously and successfully than at present.

But punishment should not be the only, or indeed the main, end in view. Our aim should be a policy of construction and not one of destruction. Our aim should not be to punish the men who have made a big corporation successful merely because they have made it big and successful, but to exercise such thoroughgoing supervision and control over them as to insure their business skill being exercised in the interest of the public and not against the public interest. Ultimately, I believe that this control should undoubtedly indirectly or directly extend to dealing with all questions connected with their treatment of their employees, including the wages, the hours of labor, and the like. Not only is the proper treatment of a corporation, from the standpoint of the managers, shareholders, and employees, compatible with securing from that corporation the best standard of public service, but when the effort is wisely made it results in benefit to both the corporation and to the public.

The National Government exercises control over inter-State commerce railways and it can in similar fashion, through an appropriate governmental body, exercise control over all industrial organizations engaged in inter-State commerce.

---

Source: "The Trusts, The People, and the Square Deal: Editorial by Theodore Roosevelt," *Outlook*, Nov. 18, 1911, pp. 649, 651–56.

# EXHIBIT 3

*Chief Justice Edward D. White Proposes a Rule of Reason*

Let us consider the language of the first and second sections, guided by the principle that where words are employed in a statute which had at the time a well-known meaning at common law or in the law of this country they are presumed to have been used in that sense unless the context compels to the contrary.

As to the first section, the words to be interpreted are: "Every contract combination in the form of trust or otherwise, or conspiracy in restraint of trade or commerce . . . is hereby declared to be illegal." As there is no room for dispute that the statute was intended to formulate a rule for the regulation of interstate and foreign commerce, the question is what was the rule which it adopted?

In view of the common law and the law in this country as to restraint of trade, which we have reviewed, and the illuminating effect which that history must have under the rule to which we have referred, we think it results: . . . .

**b.**    That in view of the many new forms of contracts and combinations which were being evolved from existing economic conditions, it was deemed essential by an all-embracing enumeration to make sure that no form of contract or combination by which an undue restraint of interstate or foreign commerce was brought about could save such restraint from condemnation. The statute under this view evidenced the intent not to restrain the rights to make and enforce contracts, whether resulting from combintion or otherwise, which did not unduly restrain interstate or foreign commerce, but to protect that commerce from being restrained by methods, whether old or new, which would constitute an interference that is an undue restraint.

**c.**    And as the contracts or acts embraced in the provision were not expressly defined, since the enumeration addressed itself simply to classes of acts, those classes being broad enough to embrace every conceivable contract or combination which could be made concerning trade or commerce or the subjects of such commerce, and thus caused any act done by any of the enumerated methods anywhere in the whole field of human activity to be illegal if in restraint of trade, it inevitably follows that the provision necessarily called for the exercise of judgment which required that some standard should be resorted to for the purpose of determining whether the prohibitions contained in the statute had or had not in any given case been violated. Thus not specifying but indubitably contemplating and requiring a standard, it follows that it was intended that the standard of reasons which had been applied at the common law and in this country in dealing with subjects of the character embraced by the statute, was intended to be the measure used for the purpose of determining whether in a given case a particular act had or had not brought about the wrong against which the statute provided.

And a consideration of the text of the second section serves to establish that it was intended to supplement the first and to make sure that by no possible guise

# EXHIBIT 3 (*continued*)

could the public policy embodied in the first section be frustrated or evaded. The prohibitions of the second embrace "Every person who shall monopolize, or attempt to monopolize, or combine or conspire with any other person or persons, to monopolize any part of the trade or commerce among the several states, or with foreign nations. . . " by reference to the terms of Sec. 8 it is certain that the word person clearly implies a corporation as well as an individual.

[W]hen the second section is thus harmonized with and made as it was intended to be the complement of the first, it becomes obvious that the criteria to be resorted to in any given case for the purpose of ascertaining whether violations of the section have been committed, is the rule of reason guided by the established law and by the plain duty to enforce the prohibitions of the act and thus the public policy which its restrictions were obviously enacted to subserve. And it is worthy of observation, as we have previously remarked concerning the common law, that although the statute by the comprehensiveness of the enumerations embodied in both the first and second sections makes it certain that its purpose was to prevent undue restraints of every kind or nature, nevertheless by the omission of any direct prohibition against monopoly in the concrete it indicates a consciousness that the freedom of the individual right to contract when not unduly or improperly exercised was the most efficient means for the prevention of monopoly, since the operation of the centrifugal and centripetal forces resulting from the right to freely contract was the means by which monopoly would be inevitably prevented if no extraneous or sovereign power imposed it and no right to make unlawful contracts having a monopolistic tendency were permitted. In other words that freedom to contract was the essence of freedom from undue restraint on the right to contract.

## Justice John Marshall Harlan Dissents

But my brethren, in their wisdom, have deemed it best to pursue a different course. They have now said to those who condemn our former decisions and who object to all legislative prohibitions of contracts, combinations and trusts in restraint of interstate commerce, "You may *now* restrain such commerce, provided you are reasonable about it; only take care that the restraint is not undue." The disposition of the case under consideration, according to the views of the defendants, will, it is claimed, quiet and give rest to "the business of the country." On the contrary, I have a strong conviction that it will throw the business of the country into confusion and invite widely extended and harassing litigation, the injurious effects of which will be felt for many years to come. When Congress prohibited *every* contract, combination or monopoly in restraint of commerce, it prescribed a simple, definite rule that all could understand, and which could easily be applied by everyone wishing to obey the law, and not to conduct their business in violation of law. But now, it is to be feared, we are to have, in cases without number, the constantly recurring inquiry—difficult to solve by proof—whether the particular

## EXHIBIT 3 (*concluded*)

contracts, combination or trust involved in each case is or is not an "unreason-able" or "undue" restraint of trade. Congress, in effect, said that there should be *no* restraint of trade, *in any form,* and this court solemnly adjudged many years ago the Congress meant what it thus said in clear and explicit words, and that it *could not* add to the words of the act. But those who condemn the action of Congress are now, in effect, informed that the courts will allow such restraints of interstate commerce as are shown not to be unreasonable or undue.

It remains for me to refer, more fully than I have heretofore done, to another, and, in my judgment—if we look to the future—the most important aspect of this case. That aspect concerns the usurpation by the judicial branch of the Government of the functions of the legislative department. The illustrious men who laid the foundations of our institutions, deemed no part of the National Constitution of more consequence or more essential to the permanency of our form of government than the provisions under which were distributed the powers of Government among three separate, equal and coordinate departments—legislative, executive, and judicial. This was at that time a new feature of governmental regulation among the nations of the earth, and it is deemed by the people of every section of our own country as most vital in the workings of a representative republic whose Constitution was ordained and established in order to accomplish the objects stated in its Preamble by the means, *but only by the means,* provided either expressly or by necessary implication, by the instrument itself. No department of that Government can constitutionally exercise the powers committed strictly to another and separate department.

I said at the outset that the action of the court in this case might well alarm thoughtful men who revered the Constitution. I meant by this that many things are intimated and said in the court's opinion which will not be regarded otherwise than as sanctioning an invasion by the judiciary of the constitutional domain of Congress—an attempt by interpretation to soften or modify what some regard as a harsh public policy. This court, let me repeat, solemnly adjudged many years ago that it could not, except by *"judicial legislation,"* read words into the Anti-Trust Act not put there by Congress, and which, being inserted, give it a meaning which the words of the act, as passed, if properly interpreted, would not justify. The court has decided that it could not thus change a public policy formulated and declared by Congress; that Congress has paramount authority to regulate interstate commerce, and that it alone can change a policy once inaugurated by legislation. The courts have nothing to do with the wisdom or policy of an act of Congress. Their duty is to ascertain the will of Congress, and if the statute embodying the expression of that will is constitutional, the courts must respect it. They have no function to declare a public policy, nor to *amend* legislative enactments.

Source: *Standard Oil Company of New Jersey et al.* v. *The United States of America,* 221 U.S., pp. 59–63; 98–100; 102–105.

## EXHIBIT 4

*The Delivery of the "Rule of Reason" Opinion and President William Howard Taft's Reaction*

The Court acted on May 15, 1911. Ponderously, because he was large in body, Chief Justice White mounted the bench with his colleagues. The spectators in the old Supreme Court chambers may have noted that Associate Justice Harlan, never wholly happy after the elevation of White instead of himself to the highest place on the court, seemed even more irascible than usual. For while he concurred in the illegality of the Standard Oil, he disagreed violently with the reasoning of the other eight jurists. His was to be the dissent from an otherwise unanimous decision. The Chief Justice read the 20,000-word opinion upholding the government and ordering the dissolution of the Standard Oil Company. He traced in detail the history of its growth and the methods it had used to expand. No "disinterested mind," he said, could "survey the period in question without being irresistibly driven to the conclusion that the very genius for commercial development and organization which . . . was manifested from the beginning soon begot an intent and purpose to exclude others which were frequently manifested by acts and dealings wholly inconsistent" with legal business development. The intent had been, he said, "to drive others from the field and to exclude them from their right to trade." The history of the Rockefeller companies and their methods "all lead the mind up to a conviction of purpose and intent which we think is so certain as practically to cause the subject not to be within the domain of *reasonable contention.*"

This "reasonable contention" was one form of the legal conception of reasonableness over which such controversy would rage. The Chief Justice also said, referring to the Sherman act:

> In view of the many new forms of contracts and combinations, which were being evolved from existing economic conditions, it was deemed essential by an all-embracing enumeration to make sure that no form of contract or combination by which an *undue restraint* of interstate or foreign commerce was brought about could save such restraint from condemnation.
>
> The statute under this view evidenced the intent not to restrain the right to make and enforce contracts, whether resulting from combination or otherwise, which did not *unduly restrain* interstate and foreign commerce, but to protect that commerce from being restrained by such methods, whether old or new, which could constitute an interference that is *undue restraint.*

What the Chief Justice was doing, of course, was to base his opinion on the common-law exemption of "reasonable" restraint of trade agreements from attack. It was this theory to which Taft had objected in 1910, although he would now reverse himself and agree with the court. Justice Harlan, however, could not tolerate this limitation of the anti-trust law. The Court, he said, while he angrily pounded the bench in front of him, had put "words into the antitrust act which Congress did not put there." He pictured the confusion which, in his judgment,

## EXHIBIT 4 (*concluded*)

would surely result. He said that many a trust would crawl through this new hole in the law.

But the President—perhaps he was already swinging toward the distaste for dissenting opinions which would mark his career as chief justice—said that this was a "good opinion—the Standard Oil Company will have to dissolve." True, the Court's reasoning "did not take exactly the line of distinction I have drawn, but it certainly approximates it." Taft regretted Harlan's actions, which he called a "nasty, carping and demagogic opinion, directed at the Chief Justice and intended to furnish LaFollette and his crowd as much pabulum as possible."

The Standard Oil decision demanded that the parent concern, the Standard Oil Company of New Jersey, divest itself of its 30 or more subsidiaries within 30 days. All the corporations and their officers were enjoined from conspiring to reestablish the monopoly. Two weeks after the ruling, the court handed down its decision in the prosecution of the Tobacco Trust. This action, against the American Tobacco Company and 28 other companies, had also been started under Roosevelt. The Chief Justice again wrote the opinion and it reiterated the doctrine that "reasonable" restraint was lawful. It was not true, he insisted, that the Sherman law was thereby weakened. On the contrary, no longer would there be any possibility of frustrating the act "by resorting to any disguise or subterfuge of form, since resort to reason rendered it impossible to escape by any indirection the prohibitions of the statute."

The President decided to uphold this interpretation. There was, he insisted, "no conflict between what I have said and what the court says." Instead, "there is a real resemblance between them that makes me proud."

"I was contending throughout for a reasonable construction of the act with a view to the evil aimed at," Taft claimed. "What I was criticizing in the use of the word *reasonable* was when it was proposed to be applied to a monopoly or a partial monopoly or a restraint of trade for the purpose of enhancing prices, and it was supposed to distinguish between restraints of this character and leave it to the court to say that those in which the profits exacted by such means were moderate were lawful, and those in which they were exorbitant were to be condemned."

Taft insisted that the "rule of reason" did not permit the Supreme Court to distinguish between "good" and "bad" trusts and that the Standard Oil and Tobacco Trust cases had strengthened the law rather than the reverse. . . .

Source: Henry F. Pringle, *The Life and Times of William Howard Taft* (New York: Farrar and Rinehart, 1939), Vol. II, p. 664.

# EXHIBIT 5

## *The Acceptance Speech by Eugene Victor Debs for the 1912 Socialist Party Presidential Nomination*

It is with a full sense of the responsibility it imposes and the service it exacts that I accept the nomination for president tendered to me by the Socialist Party of the United States. Personally I did not wish the nomination. It came to me unsought. It came as summons to service and not as a personal honor.

Every true member of the Socialist Party is at the party's service. The confidence of his comrades is to him a sacred trust and their collective will the party's law.

My chief concern as a presidential candidate is that I shall serve well the party, and the class and the cause the party represents.

### Socialist Party Different

The Socialist Party is fundamentally different from all other parties. It came in the process of evolution and grows with the growth of the forces which created it. Its spirit is militant and its aim revolutionary. It expresses in political terms the aspiration of the working class to freedom and to a larger and fuller life than they have yet known.

The world's workers have always been and still are the world's slaves. They have borne all the burdens of the race and built all the monuments along the track of civilization; they have produced all the world's wealth and supported all the world's governments. They have conquered all things but their own freedom. They are still the subject class in every nation on earth and the chief function of every government is to keep them at the mercy of their masters.

The workers in the mills and factories, in the mines and on the farms and railways never had a party of their own until the Socialist Party was organized. They divided their votes between the parties of their masters. They did not realize that they were using their ballots to forge their own fetters.

But the awakening came. It was bound to come. Class rule became more and more oppressive and wage slavery more and more galling. The eyes of the workers began to open. They began to see the cause of the misery they had dumbly suffered so many years. It dawned upon them that society was divided into two classes—capitalists and workers, exploiters and producers; that the capitalists, while comparatively few, owned the nation and controlled the government; that the courts and the soldiers were at their command, and that the workers, while in a great majority, were in slavish subjection.

When they ventured to protest they were discharged and found themselves blacklisted; when they went out on strike they were suppressed by the soldiers and sent to jail.

## EXHIBIT 5 (*continued*)

They looked about them and saw a land of wonderful resources; they saw the productive machinery made by their own hands and the vast wealth produced by their own labor, in the shadow of which their wives and children were perishing in the skeleton clutch of famine.

### Began to Think

The very suffering they were forced to endure quickened their senses. They began to think. A new light dawned upon their dark skies. They rubbed the age-long sleep from their eyes. They had long felt the brutalizing effect of class rule; now they saw the cause of it. Slowly but steadily they became class-conscious. They said, "We are brothers, we are comrades," and they saw themselves multiplied by millions. They caught the prophetic battle-cry of Karl Marx, the world's greatest labor leader, the inspired evangel of working-class emancipation, "Workers of all countries, unite!"

An now, behold! The international Socialist movement spreads out over all the nations of the earth. The world's workers are aroused at last. They are no longer on their knees; their bowed bodies are now erect. Despair has given way to hope, weakness to strength, fear to courage. They no longer cringe and supplicate: they hold up their heads and command. They have ceased to fear their masters and have learned to trust themselves.

And this is how the Socialist Party came to be born. It was quickened into life in the bitter struggle of the world's enslaved workers. It expresses their collective determination to break their fetters and emancipate themselves and the race.

Is it strange that the workers are loyal to such a party, that they proudly stand beneath its blazing banners and fearlessly proclaim its conquering principles? It is the one party of their class, born of their agony and baptized in the blood of their countless brethren who perished in the struggle to give it birth.

Hail to this great party of the toiling millions whose battle cry is heard around the world!

### Doesn't Plead for Votes

We do not plead for votes; the workers give them freely the hour they understand.

But we need to destroy the prejudice that still exists and dispel that darkness that still prevails in the working class world. We need the clear light of sound education and the conquering power of economic and political organization.

Before the unified hosts of labor all the despotic governments on earth are powerless and all resistance vain. Before their onward march all ruling classes disappear and all slavery vanishes forever.

The appeal of the Socialist Party is to all the useful people of the nation, all who work with brain and muscle to produce the nation's wealth and who promote its progress and conserve its civilization.

## EXHIBIT 5 (*continued*)

Only they who bear its burdens may rightfully enjoy the blessings of civilized society.

There are no boundary lines to separate race from race, sex from sex or creed from creed in the Socialist Party. The common rights of all are equally recognized.

Every human being is entitled to sunlight and air, to what his labor produces, and to an equal chance with every other human being to unfold and ripen and give to the world the riches of his mind and soul.

Economic slavery is the world's greatest curse today. Poverty and misery, prostitution, insanity and crime are its inevitable results.

The Socialist Party is the one party which stands squarely and uncompromisingly for the abolition of industrial slavery; the one party pledged in every fibre of its being to the economic freedom of all the people.

So long as the nation's resources and productive and distributive machinery are the private property of a privileged class the masses will be at their mercy, poverty will be their lot and life will be shorn of all that raises it above the brute level.

### New Progressive Party

The infallible test of a political party is the private ownership of the sources of wealth and the means of life. Apply that test to the Republican, Democratic and Progressive parties and upon that basic, fundamental issue you will find them essentially one and the same. They differ according to the conflicting interests of the privileged classes, but at bottom they are alike and stand for capitalist class rule and working class slavery.

The new Progressive Party is a party of progressive capitalism. It is lavishly financed and shrewdly advertised. But it stands for the rule of capitalism all the same.

When the owners of the trusts finance a party to put themselves out of business; when they turn over their wealth to the people from whom they stole it and go to work for a living, it will be time enough to consider the merits of the Roosevelt Progressive Party.

One question is sufficient to determine the true status of all these parties. Do they want the workers to own the tools they work with, control their own jobs and secure to themselves the wealth they produce? Certainly not. That is utterly ridiculous and impossible from their point of view.

The Republican, Democratic and Progressive parties all stand for the private ownership by the capitalists of the productive machinery used by the workers, so that the capitalists can continue to filch the wealth produced by the workers.

The Socialist party is the only party which declares that the tools of labor belong to labor and that the wealth produced by the working class belongs to the working class.

## EXHIBIT 5 (*continued*)

Intelligent workingmen are no longer deceived. They know that the struggle in which the world is engaged today is a class struggle and that in this struggle the workers can never win by giving their votes to capitalist parties. They have tried this for many years and it has always produced the same result to them.

The class of privilege and pelf has had the world by the throat and the working class beneath its iron-shod hoofs long enough. The magic word of freedom is ringing through the nation and the spirit of intelligent revolt is finding expression in every land beneath the sun.

The solidarity of the working class is the salient force in the social transformation of which we behold the signs upon every hand. Nearer and nearer they are being drawn together in the bonds of unionism; clearer and clearer becomes their collective vision; greater and greater the power that throbs within them.

### Hosts of Freedom

They are the twentieth-century hosts of freedom who are to destroy all despotisms, topple over all thrones, seize all sceptres of authority and hold them in their own strong hands, tear up all privilege by the roots, and consecrate the earth and all its fullness to the joy and service of all humanity.

It is vain to hope for material relief upon the prevailing system of capitalism. All the reforms that are proposed by the three capitalist parties, even if carried out in good faith, would still leave the working class in industrial slavery.

The working class will never be emancipated by the grace of the capitalist class, but only by overthrowing that class.

The power to emancipate itself is inherent in the working class, and this power must be developed through sound education and applied through sound organization.

It is foolish and self-destructive for workingmen to turn to Republican, Democratic and Progressive parties on election day as it would be for them to turn to the Manufacturers' Association and the Citizens' Alliance when they are striking against starvation wages.

The capitalist class is organized economically and politically to keep the working class in subjection and perpetuate its power as a ruling class. They do not support a working class union nor a working class party. They are not so foolish. They wisely look out for themselves.

The capitalist class despise a working class party. Why should the working class give their support to a capitalist class party?

Capitalist misrule under which workingmen suffer slavery and the most galling injustice exists only because it has workingmen's support. Withdraw that support and capitalism is dead.

## EXHIBIT 5 (*concluded*)

The capitalists can enslave and rob the workers only by the consent of the workers when they cast their ballots on election day.

Every vote cast for a capitalist party, whatever its name, is a vote for wage-slavery, for poverty and degradation.

Every vote cast for the Socialist Party, the worker's own party, is a vote for emancipation.

We appeal to the workers and to all who sympathize with them to make their power felt in this campaign. Never before has there been so great an opportunity to strike an effective blow for freedom.

### Capitalism Doomed

Capitalism is rushing blindly to its impending doom. All the signs portend the inevitable breakdown of the existing order. Deep-seated discontent has seized upon the masses. They must indeed be deaf who do not hear the mutterings of the approaching storm.

Poverty, high prices, unemployment, child slavery, widespread misery and haggard want in a land bursting with abundance; prostitution and insanity, suicide and crime, these in solemn numbers tell the tragic story of capitalism's saturnalia of blood and tears and shame as its end draws near.

It is to abolish this monstrous system and the misery and crime which flow from it in a direful and threatening stream that the Socialist Party was organized and now makes its appeal to the intelligence and conscience of the people. Social reorganization is the imperative demand of this world-wide revolutionary movement.

The Socialist Party's mission is not only to destroy capitalist despotism but to establish industrial and social democracy. To this end the workers are steadily organizing and fitting themselves for the day when they shall take control of the people's industries and when the right to work shall be as inviolate as the right to breathe the breath of life.

Standing as it does for the emancipation of the working class from wage-slavery, for the equal rights and opportunities of all men and women, for the abolition of child labor and the conservation of all childhood, for social self-rule and the equal freedom of all, the Socialist Party is the party of progress, the party of the future, and its triumph will signalize the birth of a new civilization and the dawn of a happier day for all humanity.

---

Source: Arthur M. Schlesinger, Jr., ed., *Writings and Speeches of Eugene V. Debs* (New York: Hermitage, 1948), pp. 361–66.

# EXHIBIT 6

## *Woodrow Wilson on Big Business*

There was a time when we could indulge in all sorts of pleasantries at each other's expense in politics. But every time I find myself tempted to pleasantry there comes over me a feeling of the critical seriousness of the choice to be made in the year 1912, not the critical seriousness, ladies and gentlemen, of choosing between one man and another man, for there is no indispensable man, but the criticalness of choosing between one policy and another. We are at the parting of the ways. As we determine the direction which we take in 1912 we shall determine the future political development and the future economic development of the United States of America. It looks like a very small difference sometimes when you state it, but you know that where roads come together the separation is small but where they end the separation is not small. Although it may seem that they are choosing just to deviate a little in this direction or a little in that, remember where they are going to lead. Remember where the finger of that road points and make up your mind what the goal is at the other end.

There is one proposition upon which this compaign turns. I have repeated it very often already in other speeches and I am going to repeat it until I am sure everybody's heard it. That proposition is this: this monopoly is inevitable. That is what some of the people who want us to adopt a certain purpose maintain, and that is what I deny. If monopoly is inevitable, then the thing to do is for the government to take hold of monopoly and regulate it. If monopoly is not inevitable, then the thing for law to do is to break it up and prevent its forming again. I believe that monopoly can be broken up. If I didn't believe it, I would know that all the roads of free development were shut in this country.

The reasons I say that this campaign depends upon that proposition is this: I understand the leaders of the third party,* for example, to have a great many attractive things in their program. Nevertheless, they start with this proposition: that the big combinations which now control business in this country are inevitable, and that the best we can do is to establish an industrial commission which will take charge of them and see to it that they are good to us. I deny the fundamental proposition. I deny that these big combinations are inevitable. And I can prove that they were not inevitable by the processes by which they were established.

You know that back of this whole question lies the question of the tariff. And I want you to remember that the tariff question is a very different question in our day from what it was in the day, for example, of Mr. McKinley and Mr. Blaine. They had an argument which it was very difficult, I am frank to admit, to meet successfully; because they said here in the United States you have so enormous an

---

*The "third party" is a reference to the "Progressive Party." This organization was founded by supporters of Theodore Roosevelt and served as a vehicle for his bid for the presidency in 1912, because he had been unable to secure the Republican nomination from the incumbent, William Howard Taft.

# EXHIBIT 6 (*continued*)

area of absolute[ly] free trade and unrestricted competition that there is no danger that these men would control prices and make them intolerably high because within this great continent they compete with others; and their competition with each other, the clash of their brains, the rivalries of their genius, the organizations which contend with one another for supremacy in the domestic market make it certain that there will be a normal level of prices. Some of you men are old enough to remember that argument.

But where is the domestic competition that these gentlemen talked about? The object of these combinations that have been formed in our time is to shut competition out and to get control of the market by seeing to it that there is no successful competition such as will bring prices down. The most conspicuous example of it is the Steel Trust.

There was one particular set of factories, or rather of mills, which the gentlemen who first put their heads together to set up this would-be monopoly found that it was most difficult to deal with. There was one man in the United States who knew how to manufacture steel rails so cheaply and had such a genius for the organization of business upon an economic scale and for its development by the discovery of finer and finer devices for cheapening the production that nobody else in the United States could compete with his brains in that particular line. His name was Andrew Carnegie. When the Steel Trust came to be formed Andrew Carnegie didn't care to come into it. Why should be come into it? He could undersell every man of them. There wasn't any reason why he should wish to come in when the market was his already for the asking. And they had to pay him—I have forgotten how many times—I think it was four times the value of his plant and of his business in order to get him out of the way; and they had to pay a number of other gentlemen, other independent mills and independent businesses in this field, very much more than their business was known to be worth in order to get them to come into the combination. It wasn't worth their while in view of their already established success to come into this combination unless they were paid so much more than their business was worth that they were willing to give the business up.

Then what happened? They made a combination upon which they issued the securities to the amount representing, let's say, four times the value of Mr. Carnegie's business and several times the value of other businesses which they had absorbed. Then they based the new price of steel on the interest they had to pay on those securities, didn't they?

In other words, they are making us pay for steel on the most uneconomic and inefficient basis that can be imagined. And when these gentlemen say that these big combinations are necessary for economy and efficiency, the only answer I can think of that meets the suggestion is: Rats! Go and tell all that to the Marines. Go and tell that to somebody that doesn't even read the daily newspapers. Don't venture to tell it to anybody who knows the circumstances by which these combinations were made and the diligence with which these gentlemen have seen to it that understandings with regard to price should not be broken.

## EXHIBIT 6 (*continued*)

Why would anybody desire to break the understanding because it was possible to sell cheaper and capture the market? And those men were interested in seeing that nobody would sell cheaper and capture the market when it was possible for the man who had brains, exercised economy and ingenuity, and knew how to assemble the parts of his plant at any time he chose, to make steel cheaper and undersell them.

These combinations were not made for efficiency but to control and keep up the price. They were meant to control the domestic market, and just so soon as you make it possible to compete with these gentlemen you'll see a very great change in their business. I don't want to put them out of business. I simply want to make them attend to business. I want to make sure that steel and everything else that illustrates my subject is made as cheaply and as well as possible in America, and that profits and the successes of enterprise are not founded upon anything else but brains and success.

But the gentlemen of the third party say: "You are very much more mistaken. It may be that many inequities were practiced in the establishing of these things, but they were built up. And now they have become a constituted and necessary part of our modern business and the only thing we can do is to regulate them, is to regulate the memberships, is to legalize the thing that ought never to have been done and need never to have been done, and to see to it through a government agency, through a government commission, that they treat us kindly; that they don't impose upon us; that they are gentle in the market; that they don't do anybody any more harm; that they are shot through with the kindliness of Christianity."

Now I don't expect to convert the trust by any special means of evangelization. Moreover, when you have set up a government that has the right to create a commission of that sort, what temptation, I would like to have you tell me, have you added to the present almost overwhelming temptations of politics? If the President of the United States can through a commission guide the business of the United States, soon the businessmen of the United States who are interested in these combinations will put forth greater ingenuity and endeavor than ever to capture the Presidency of the United States. Ah, gentlemen, don't deceive yourselves. If men control business, then business will seek to control men. The only salvation for this country is that law shall control business. Now here is the parting of the ways.

You say, "Well, if we are not going to legalize the trusts and control them, what are we going to do?" Well, haven't you observed how the trusts were built up? You say, "Are you going to return by law to the old-fashioned competition?" I say, "No." It is the old-fashioned competition that enabled these men to build up these combinations, because the old-fashioned competition used in the new way was this: Here is a man with some personal capital, or with some personal credit at the local bank, and he tries to set out in a little business. Here in another city is a great combination of men with millions of money at their back who come there

## EXHIBIT 6 (*continued*)

and say: "You are a mighty little fellow and you can't come into this thing. We don't want any interlopers here. You have got only your little local market. Very well, we will cut into your little local market and sell at a loss, sell at a figure that you can't possibly sell at because everywhere else in the United States we will sell at a profitable figure, meet our losses in your locality, and we will put you out of business." That is not a fictitious hypothetical case. That thing has happened by scores and hundreds of instances all over the United States. Now, that is competition, but what sort of competition is it?

The alternative to regulating monopoly is to regulate competition: to say that to go into a community and sell below cost for no other purpose—for it can't be the purpose of profit—for no other purpose than to squeeze out a competitor shall be an offense against the criminal law of the United States, and anybody who attempts it will have to answer at the bar of a criminal tribunal. It won't make any difference whether he is big or little, he will have to answer at the tribunal; for we have been having trials and investigation by Congress, and we know the processes of unrestricted competition by which these men have accomplished the setting up of their monopolies. If we don't know how to stop them, then the lawyers of this country have lost their ingenuity and their intelligence.

I was saying at one of the way stations where they permitted me to make a short speech this afternoon that it was a very serious thing that if a man became a candidate for office and it was discovered that at any time or place he had been counsel for a great corporation, he would have to spend the rest of the campaign explaining that away; and that after the campaign ended he wouldn't have had time enough to explain it sufficiently to get elected. Now, there is nothing dishonorable in advising a corporation, is there? Any body of men in this country doing their business legitimately is entitled to the advice of counsel and it is not dishonorable to advise them. Why are corporation lawyers therefore excluded from running for office? Because it is thought—sometimes unjustly, but universally thought—that what they have been advising their clients to do is something that has been to the detriment of the business of this country. Can you imagine any other explanation?

I know scores of lawyers who have been the intimate counsel of great corporations have never advised them to do anything illegal, but there are a great many legal things that you can do now that will put the little man out of business. That is the reason that I want to change the law, not the lawyer. I was a lawyer myself once, and you can't change a lawyer. But you can change the law. And then the whole atmosphere will clear. The lawyer will be obliged to say: "Why, my dear sirs, that is a very fine scheme; but if you follow it, you will get into the penitentiary, because you can be found out."

Some very interesting things were found out in the trial of the meat packers. For example, we found out that you didn't have to form a great combination; that all you had to do was to be polite; that all that the meat packers did was to meet together without forming a legal union of any kind and consult together as to what

EXHIBIT 6 (*concluded*)

they would like to have meat sell at. Then a very nice young gentleman whom they employed for the purpose as their secretary and spokesman would write a very prettily phrased letter to all of them suggesting that perhaps it was desirable to quote meat at such and such prices; and they felt bound with the etiquette of perfect gentlemen to observe that price. That is so.

Now, I had been saying, before I knew that, that the price of meat was artificial and excessive; and it turned out that I had a couple of young friends who had been pupils of mine in the university who were connected with the meat business and were very much distressed that I should have said these things, because they thought them unjust. They wrote me some very serious lectures on them. I had lectured them and it was all right for them to lecture me, and I was very impressed.

I said: "Is it possible that I have been mistaken? These are perfectly honest fellows. I know all about them. I know they are not lying to me." But after the meat packers' trial I saw where the trouble was. It was in the method of bookkeeping. Because they charged up all their costs of every kind to the edible part of the animal, to the meat, and everything else was free profit. The hide and the hoof and the head, everything that could be made into glue and into shoes and I don't know what all was clear profit. And the profit on the edible part, on the meat, was very small indeed. But if I can have all the rest that is left over, I can afford to sell the meat at cost—that is to say, at the cost of the business.

We shall be getting on the inside of a lot of the big business of the United States. And I venture to say that with the proper kind of legal advice you and I could easily sit down together and stop these things overnight. That is what I call the regulation of competition, saying: "Oh, yes, up to a certain point you can use your great power, a giant against a pigmy. But let me warn you that if you put that pigmy out of business, the pigmy will prove bigger than you are. He will stay out of the penitentiary and you will go in."

Choose your course then, gentlemen, on the fifth of November. Adopt the great trusts into the family and depend upon your government to make them be good, or else take the course by which it will be impossible for them to live by anything except economy and brains. Let your government patronize them, or else put them on their mettle and let them survive, as all honest business ought to be able to survive, in the open competition of the market.

Source: John Wells Davidson, ed., *A Crossroads of Freedom: The Campaign Speeches of Woodrow Wilson* (New Haven: Yale University Press, 1956), pp. 167–73.

# APPENDIX A

## *A Chronology of Regulatory and Antitrust Activities, 1887–1914*

1887    Congress passes an act to regulate interstate commerce, outlawing rebating, long-, short-haul discrimination, and pooling and establishing the Interstate Commerce Commission.

1890    Congress passes the Sherman Antitrust Act, declaring "Every contract, combination in the form of trust or otherwise, or conspiracy, in restraint of trade or commerce among the several states" to be illegal.

1895    *U.S.* v. *E. C. Knight Co.* The Supreme Court holds that the Sherman Act was inapplicable to intrastate manufacturing combinations, thus placing most monopolies beyond the reach of federal control.

1897    *U.S.* v. *Trans–Missouri Freight Association.* The Supreme Court holds that concerted action by 18 western railroads to uphold published tariffs was in violation of the Sherman Act.

1899    *Addyston Pipe and Steel Co.* v. *U.S.* The Supreme Court states that a market allocation plan constitutes a violation of the Sherman Act, thus restoring some of the power that the statute had lost in E. C. Knight.

1903    Elkins Act strengthens ICC's power to fight rebating by providing for the punishment of shippers and railway officials as well as of railroad corporations.

1904    *Northern Securities Co.* v. *U.S.* The Supreme Court greatly strengthens the Sherman Act by upholding the government's dissolution of a large railroad holding company on antitrust grounds.

1905    *Swift and Co.* v. *U.S.* The Supreme Court approves the government's action against the beef trust and holds that certain local business agreements can be considered integral parts of interstate commerce.

1906    Hepburn Act increases ICC power by providing that the Commission can set specific maximum rates upon a showing that rates were "unreasonable."

Pure Food and Drug Act forbids manufacture or sale of adulterated or fraudulently labelled foods and drugs sold in interstate commerce.

Meat Inspection Act provides for enforcement of sanitary regulations in packing establishments and federal inspection of all companies selling meat in interstate commerce.

1908    *Muller* v. *Oregon.* The Supreme Court upholds an Oregon law limiting maximum working hours for women and denies that the Act impairs 14th Amendment freedom of contract guarantees. Brandeis successfully uses sociological and economic statistical data on the side of the state (Brandeis Brief).

1910    Mann-Elkins Act gives the ICC power to suspend any scheduled rate increase and places burden of proof of reasonableness of proposed rates on the railroads.

1911    *Standard Oil Co. of New Jersey et al.* v. *U.S.* The Supreme Court upholds the dissolution of the company and applies the "rule of reason" to the Sherman Act.

    *U.S.* v. *American Tobacco Co.* The Supreme Court orders reorganization of the tobacco trust under the rule of reason.

1914    The Federal Trade Commission Act is passed, designed to prevent "unfair methods of competition" in commerce. The Federal Trade Commission is established, superseding the Bureau of Corporations, and the five-member, nonpartisan Commission is empowered to investigate the actions of persons and corporations (except banks and common carriers) and to issue cease and desist orders subject to judicial review.

The Clayton Antitrust Act specifies various activities—price discrimination, tying contracts, interlocking directorates, and acquisition of stockholding—as illegal under certain circumstances. Labor and agriculture are specifically exempted from antitrust action.

# CASE 22

# *The Great Depression: Causes and Impact* *

## The American Economy in the 1920s

In the early months of 1929, few Americans questioned the strength and vitality of the American economy. After a decade of impressive economic growth, even better times seemed certain to be in the offing. Such an attitude appeared to be born out by the phenomenal performance of the stock market. In February 1928, stock prices had begun to climb and with only temporary lapses continued to do so for the next year and a half. The number of shares traded on the New York Stock Exchange each day had averaged between two and three million during most of the 20s; but in 1928 and early 1929, six, seven, and eight million share days were not uncommon, and the daily total occasionally topped 12 million. Thousands of Americans were investing for the first time; and the speculative mania was fueled by the easy credit offered by brokerage firms (margin rates were often as low as 10 percent).

While a few skeptical economists warned that the boom could not continue, most Americans saw no end to the prosperity of the previous decade and nodded with approval in August of 1928 when Secretary of Commerce (and Presidential

---

candidate) Herbert Hoover announced, "We in America are nearer to the final triumph over poverty than ever before in the history of any land." In early October of 1929, few took issue with Irving Fisher, the well-known Yale economist, who announced confidently that "stock prices have reached what looks like a permanently high plateau."

The decade of the 1920s began with a brief recession that sharply cut industrial production and investment but had little effect on overall consumption or the GNP. Prices fell rapidly, but after the recovery there was remarkable price stability between 1921 and 1929. After the recovery the GNP grew at an average rate of 4.7 percent per year, and real per capita income for the economy as a whole grew by 28 percent. However, not every segment of American society benefitted equally from this prosperity. Per capita farm income rose only by 10 percent and the total amount of farm mortgage debt increased enormously while the value of farm real estate actually declined. Moreover, the majority of Americans, those whose income was dependent on earnings from blue-collar, nonfarm labor, achieved only minimal gains. (For an economic profile of the 1920s and 1930s see Table 1.)

There were a number of structural weaknesses in the American economy in the 1920s which indicate that the prosperity was not as soundly based as the aver-

## TABLE 1

**Real GNP and Selected Components, 1919–1939** (*billions of 1929 dollars*)

|      | Total Consumption Expenditures | Gross Investment | Construction | Gross National Product |
|------|--------------------------------|------------------|--------------|------------------------|
| 1919 | 50.2 | 10.7 | 4.8 | 74.2 |
| 1920 | 52.7 | 12.8 | 5.0 | 73.3 |
| 1921 | 56.1 | 7.4 | 4.9 | 71.6 |
| 1922 | 58.1 | 10.6 | 7.1 | 75.8 |
| 1923 | 63.4 | 15.6 | 8.2 | 85.8 |
| 1924 | 68.1 | 12.4 | 9.0 | 88.4 |
| 1925 | 66.1 | 16.4 | 10.0 | 90.5 |
| 1926 | 71.5 | 17.1 | 10.7 | 96.4 |
| 1927 | 73.2 | 15.6 | 10.4 | 97.3 |
| 1928 | 74.8 | 14.5 | 9.8 | 98.5 |
| 1929 | 79.0 | 16.2 | 8.7 | 104.4 |
| 1930 | 74.7 | 10.5 | 6.4 | 95.1 |
| 1931 | 72.2 | 6.8 | 4.5 | 89.4 |
| 1932 | 66.0 | .8 | 2.4 | 76.4 |
| 1933 | 64.6 | .3 | 1.9 | 74.2 |
| 1934 | 68.0 | 1.8 | 2.0 | 80.8 |
| 1935 | 72.3 | 8.8 | 2.8 | 91.4 |
| 1936 | 79.7 | 9.3 | 3.9 | 100.9 |
| 1937 | 82.6 | 14.6 | 4.6 | 109.1 |
| 1938 | 81.3 | 6.8 | 4.1 | 103.2 |
| 1939 | 85.9 | 9.9 | 4.9 | 111.0 |

Source: Peter Temin, *Did Monetary Forces Cause the Great Depression?* (New York: W. W. Norton, 1976), p. 4.

age citizen assumed. One is the oft-cited increase in speculative activity by middle-class savers in the last years of the decade. By the late 1920s heavy borrowing had made the financial system as a whole less liquid and more vulnerable to shocks. Secondly, American economic health was increasingly dependent upon foreign trade, particularly with Europe, at a time when the European economy was extraordinarily unstable. The third weakness concerned one particularly unstable component of investment outlays—construction. Real expenditures on construction rose from $5 billion in 1920 (39 percent of gross investment) to a peak of $10.7 billion in 1926 (63 percent of gross investment) and then dropped to $8.7 billion in 1929.

By mid-1929, the United States was unquestionably experiencing a decline in business activity. Auto sales fell from 600,000 to 400,000 from March to September. Overall industrial production peaked in June of that year and fell by 9 percent at year's end. Stock prices continued to rise until mid-September when they peaked at a point 2.16 times the 1926 level. Stock prices began to slip in earnest on October 3, but there was little public concern about the drop in prices until the end of the month.

## The Stock Market Crash

On October 21, the market dipped sharply but then recovered. Two days later the index of industrial prices fell more than 18 points in just a few hours. The following day—the so-called "Black Thursday"—anxiety turned to panic as the bottom began to fall out of the inflated bull market. An effort by J. P. Morgan, Jr., and other New York bankers to shore up the market with the creation of a $240-million fund to purchase stock halted the decline temporarily, but on the following Monday prices again fell sharply. By October 29, "Black Tuesday," all evidence of market confidence had vanished. That day 16 million shares changed hands; the industrial index fell by 43 points; and no relief was in sight. October losses alone totalled $16 billion, and by mid-November the industrial index had fallen from an August high of 380 to 198.7. The average share of common stock had by mid-November fallen 40 percent. In the months that followed, the situation grew even worse, and no one, other than the professional market analysts, expected the situation to improve. By 1930, stocks that had been worth over $87 billion the previous summer were valued at only $18 billion.

Financial institutions were strained, and finally broken, by the economic catastrophe. A wave of bank failures hit the Midwest and border states in October 1930, and one large New York bank, the private Bank of the United States, collapsed in December 1930. In the spring of 1931, a second round of bank failures swept the banking industry, and an even more serious run on the banks occurred in early 1933. Altogether, 9,000 banks suspended operations between 1930 and 1933 with total losses to depositors and shareholders totalling $2.5 billion. Of equal significance was the resulting loss of faith in banks as financial intermediaries by the general public. While the total amount of currency and commercial bank deposits with the Federal Reserve actually grew in these years, M2 (which combines outstanding currency with checking and savings deposits) fell by one third between 1929 and 1932 (see Table 2).

The effects of the Depression were of course not limited to the financial markets. The American Gross National Product declined by 25 percent between 1929 and 1932 (from $104 billion to $76.4 billion). The consumer price index fell by 25 percent and the wholesale price index by 32. Farm prices, which in fact had not benefitted from the general prosperity of the 1920s, plummeted as total farm income slid from $12 billion to $5 billion. Capital investment almost came to a halt as the amount invested to promote capital growth declined from $16.2 billion to a little more than $300 million. As economic activity contracted, industrial unemployment increased, hitting 25 percent in 1932 and averaging 20 percent through the decade of the 1930s. In certain cities in the industrial Northeast and Midwest,

## TABLE 2

**The Money Stock and Related Quantities, 1919–1939** (*billions of dollars*)

|      | $M_1$ | $M_2$ | High-Powered Money | D/R | D/C |
|------|------|------|------|------|------|
| 1919 | 21.7 | 30.8 | 6.6  | 10.2 | 6.7  |
| 1920 | 23.5 | 34.5 | 7.2  | 11.0 | 6.7  |
| 1921 | 21.2 | 32.5 | 6.5  | 11.3 | 7.1  |
| 1922 | 21.5 | 33.6 | 6.3  | 11.4 | 8.2  |
| 1923 | 22.7 | 36.4 | 6.7  | 11.8 | 8.3  |
| 1924 | 23.5 | 38.4 | 6.9  | 11.7 | 8.8  |
| 1925 | 25.5 | 41.8 | 7.0  | 12.3 | 9.6  |
| 1926 | 25.9 | 43.3 | 7.1  | 12.5 | 9.9  |
| 1927 | 25.9 | 44.5 | 7.2  | 12.6 | 10.3 |
| 1928 | 26.2 | 46.1 | 7.1  | 13.0 | 10.9 |
| 1929 | 26.4 | 46.2 | 7.1  | 13.0 | 11.0 |
| 1930 | 25.4 | 45.2 | 6.9  | 12.8 | 11.2 |
| 1931 | 23.6 | 41.7 | 7.3  | 11.8 | 9.2  |
| 1932 | 20.6 | 34.8 | 7.8  | 10.3 | 6.2  |
| 1933 | 19.4 | 30.8 | 8.2  | 8.2  | 5.1  |
| 1934 | 21.5 | 33.3 | 9.1  | 6.4  | 6.3  |
| 1935 | 25.5 | 38.4 | 10.7 | 5.6  | 7.1  |
| 1936 | 29.2 | 42.9 | 12.2 | 5.4  | 7.3  |
| 1937 | 30.3 | 45.0 | 13.4 | 5.0  | 7.1  |
| 1938 | 30.0 | 44.9 | 14.6 | 4.3  | 7.2  |
| 1939 | 33.6 | 48.7 | 17.6 | 3.7  | 7.1  |

Note: All yearly figures are the averages of the respective monthly figures.

$M_1$ = Currency held by the public and (adjusted) demand deposits held in commercial banks.

$M_2$ = Currency held by the public and (adjusted) demand and time deposits held in commercial banks.

High-Powered Money = Currency held by the public plus bank vault cash plus bank deposits at Federal Reserve banks.

D/R = Commercial bank deposits (demand plus time) divided by bank reserves (member bank deposits minus float plus nonmember bank clearing account, seasonally adjusted by Shiskin-Eisenpress method)

D/C = Commercial bank deposits divided by currency held by the public.

Source: Peter Temin, *Did Monetary Forces Cause the Great Depression?* (New York: W. W. Norton, 1976), p. 5.

the situation was much worse. In Ohio, for example, the cities of Cleveland, Akron, and Toledo reported 1932 unemployment rates of 50, 60, and 80 percent respectively. (For the dimensions of the economic collapse see Table 3).

# Causes of the Depression

While the stock market crash was perhaps the most graphic event of the early days of the Great Depression, it was not its cause. It was a sign of the coming crisis, and it contributed in several ways to its severity; but the true beginnings of the Depression predate the crash by many months. Well before October 1929, the two American industries most responsible for the prosperity of the 1920s—construction and automobiles—had begun to display signs of weakness. Construction had passed its peak and was declining rapidly, and the sales of new automobiles were no longer increasing at a rate equal to that of their production. Total business inventories in 1929 were three times those of 1928, and the traditional indicators of the economy's well-being, freight car loadings, industrial production, and wholesale prices, were all declining. To a certain extent, these warning signals were obscured by the artificial successes of the stock market, which had the effect of pumping new money into the economy to offset declining sales.

The question of the cause or causes of the Great Depression has been a source of debate among historians for almost 40 years. There is, however, a general agreement that many factors were involved, the most important of which can be summarized as follows:

1. After the stock market crash of October 1929, no new money was available to counteract the decline in the sales of consumer goods.
2. The crash itself shattered the confidence of many Americans in the stability of their economy, thereby discouraging investors and adding to the general sense of distress.
3. The American economy in the 1920s was dependent on a few basic industries (notably construction and automobiles), and when these industries declined, other sectors of the economy were unable to fill the void.
4. More importantly, purchasing power in the 1920s was maldistributed in a fundamental way. In 1929, only one family in six owned a car; only one in five, a modern bathtub; less than one in four had electric power; and only one in 10 possessed a telephone. Throughout the decade the proportion of profits going to rural Americans, industrial workers, and other potential consumers was too small to create a market for the goods produced by American business. Once capital investments had created sufficient plant space, factories began to produce more goods than consumers could afford to purchase.
5. Government policies also contributed to economic maladies. A disproportionate taxing system had worked to increase, not decrease, the disparity in incomes between the rich and individuals of modest means; lax regulation had permitted egregious abuses and irresponsible speculation on the

## TABLE 3

**New York Stock Prices, 1926–1938**

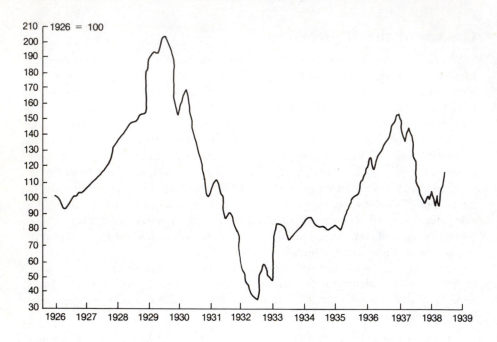

The Standard Statistics Index of New York stock prices shows the magnitude of the market crash. From an index level of 100 in 1926, the market soared to a high of 216 in September 1929 before collapsing to 34 in June 1932.

Source: Charles Kindleberger, *The World in Depression, 1929–39* (University of California, 1973), pp. 110–11.

|      | Jan. | Feb. | Mar. | Apr. | May | June | July | Aug. | Sep. | Oct. | Nov. | Dec. |
|------|------|------|------|------|-----|------|------|------|------|------|------|------|
| 1926 | 102  | 102  | 96   | 93   | 93  | 97   | 100  | 103  | 104  | 102  | 103  | 105  |
| 1927 | 106  | 108  | 109  | 110  | 113 | 114  | 117  | 112  | 129  | 128  | 131  | 136  |
| 1928 | 137  | 135  | 141  | 150  | 155 | 148  | 148  | 153  | 162  | 166  | 179  | 178  |
| 1929 | 193  | 192  | 196  | 193  | 193 | 191  | 203  | 210  | 216  | 194  | 145  | 147  |
| 1930 | 149  | 156  | 167  | 171  | 160 | 143  | 140  | 139  | 139  | 118  | 109  | 102  |
| 1931 | 103  | 110  | 112  | 100  | 81  | 87   | 90   | 89   | 76   | 65   | 68   | 54   |
| 1932 | 54   | 53   | 54   | 42   | 38  | 34   | 36   | 52   | 56   | 48   | 45   | 45   |
| 1933 | 46   | 43   | 42   | 49   | 65  | 77   | 84   | 79   | 81   | 76   | 77   | 79   |
| 1934 | 84   | 88   | 85   | 88   | 80  | 81   | 80   | 77   | 76   | 76   | 80   | 80   |
| 1935 | 81   | 80   | 75   | 79   | 86  | 88   | 92   | 95   | 98   | 100  | 110  | 110  |
| 1936 | 114  | 120  | 124  | 124  | 118 | 119  | 128  | 131  | 133  | 141  | 146  | 144  |
| 1937 | 148  | 154  | 154  | 144  | 138 | 134  | 142  | 144  | 124  | 105  | 96   | 95   |
| 1938 | 100  | 99   | 96   | 86   | 86  | 92   | 106  | 103  | 104  | 114  | 114  | 112  |

Source: League of Nations, *Statistical Yearbook,* to 1934, 1935–1938, Standard Statistics (1934–1936 index converted to 1926 base).

part of American corporations, banks, and the securities industry; high tariffs had restricted foreign trade and what foreign markets that did exist were kept alive by U.S. loans which were regularly going into default.

Dozens of theories have been offered to explain the Great Depression. They range from the Marxist argument that it was the result of internal contradictions in capitalism that lead to increasingly unstable cycles in business activity to the religious fundamentalist belief that it was the product of God's wrath to the conspiracy theorist desire to place responsibility in the hands of a small consortium of Swiss and British bankers.

The more academically respectable explanations are of two basic types— those that see the prime cause of the economic collapse in the reduction of the money supply and those that tie the collapse to a fall in autonomous spending, i.e., capital goods, consumer goods, and exports. Monetarists, inspired by Milton Friedman and Anna Schwartz's *Monetary History of the United States,* pin the blame on the Federal Reserve's failure to save the banks and argue that a sound monetary policy would have speeded recovery. Keynesians and assorted post-Keynesians (represented most prominently by Professor Paul Samuelson of MIT) find fault in the government's failure to fill the shortfall in private spending with government outlays or tax-cut-induced private purchasing power.

## Responses to the Great Depression, Part 1: The Local Response

The public welfare system of the 1920s, administered almost exclusively at the local level, was woefully inadequate to meet the demands made upon it in the years after 1929. In many cities relief efforts simply collapsed under the weight of the demand for public assistance. Even those cities and states which maintained their programs could offer only a pittance. New York City, which had among the highest relief benefits in the United States, could offer families only an average of $2.39 per week. This was almost a fortune, though, compared to the two cents per person per day paid in Toledo. New Orleans simply refused to accept any relief applicants after 1931, and St. Louis arbitrarily cut its relief roles in half that year.

Whenever possible, private charities attempted to supplement the public efforts. However, in spite of near heroic efforts by the Red Cross, the Salvation Army, and various religious groups, private efforts were hardly adequate. In addition to industrial unemployment, the relief efforts had to address the problem of a surplus rural population. Overproduction had plagued American agriculture during the 1920s, and this problem was exacerbated as the domestic market shrank and the international market disappeared altogether. Further complicating the situation was the worst drought in American history, which began in 1930 and made large sections of the American heartland uninhabitable.

Thousands of rural Americans packed their belongings into the family car or truck and left their farms in search of opportunity and a more tolerable climate. Most found work only as migrant farm workers at minimal wages. More than two million men simply took to the roads, often riding freight trains from city to city in search of work. The soup kitchen became a new part of the urban landscape along with bread lines which stretched for blocks and blocks.

As local efforts to combat the effects of unemployment proved inadequate, many looked to state governments to expand their role in the realm of public relief. Few states were willing to act. State budgets were already extremely tight; and with tax revenues declining, most legislatures felt they lacked the wherewithal to respond. Furthermore, state governments were often dominated by men who feared that any permanent welfare system would undermine the moral fiber of its clients. There was no state relief organization in the United States until September 1931, when New York State, at the insistence of Governor Franklin D. Roosevelt, established the Temporary Emergency Relief Administration. There was no state program of unemployment insurance until January of 1932, when Wisconsin established such a system. As the vast economic distress continued unabated, Americans increasingly turned to the federal government for a solution to the crisis.

## Responses to the Great Depression, Part 2: The Hoover Administration

At the time of his inauguration in March of 1929, Herbert Hoover shared the optimism of the middle class in regard to the country's economic prospects. Unlike many of the most enthusiastic disciples of American business, he was not an advocate of laissez-faire. He believed that the government (and the president) ought to play a significant role in ordering and stabilizing the economy. During the first six months of his administration, he attempted to expand the politics he had advocated during his eight years as Secretary of Commerce in the Harding and Coolidge administrations, working to complete what he termed the "American System" of cooperative individualism.

In his efforts to deal with the economic calamities besetting the American economy, Hoover proved to be a more energetic and activist President than any of his predecessors. He devoted his full energies to the problem; he attempted to play an active role in promoting recovery; and he rejected all arguments that the government should not interfere in the affairs of private enterprise. Ultimately though, Hoover's efforts were unsuccessful. His continued commitment to the concept of individual initiative and responsibility, his fiscal conservatism, and his limited view of the role of government all worked to limit his effectiveness. Moreover, beginning in the summer of 1931, Hoover became convinced that it was not the domestic American economy that was to blame for the Depression but the structure of international finance. From this perspective the proper response was not an active social and economic program at home but an effort to restore international stability. While many of his proposals for a revamped international economic order were sound (such as his proposed moratorium on international debts), they had little chance of heading off the financial panic that was sweeping Europe.

Because of his opposition to direct federal relief for the unemployed, Hoover advocated a policy of decentralized work relief. In October 1930, he formulated a relief program that called for federal leadership of a national voluntary effort by agencies operating on a self-help basis in state and local communities. His object was to "preserve the principles of individual and local responsibility." On December 2, he requested a Congressional appropriation of $100 to $150 million for the construction of public works and the following year created a number of national emergency relief organizations. These measures had little effect on unemployment as the total number out of work rose to 10 million by the end of 1931. The failure of his early voluntaristic policy finally forced Hoover to consider new initiatives.

At this point Hoover was willing to take unprecedented action to curb the effects of the Depression. By late 1931, he began to advocate an economic recovery program based upon the assumption that government loans to banks and railroads could check deflation in agriculture and industry and ultimately restore the levels of employment and purchasing power. Toward this end he proposed the creation of a government lending agency with the authority to issue tax-exempt bonds and with wide powers to extend credit. Congress responded quickly, and by February 2, the Reconstruction Finance Corporation (RFC) was in operation under the directorship of Charles G. Dawes.

The RFC was capitalized at $500 million and authorized to borrow up to $2 billion to provide emergency financing for banking institutions, life insurance companies, building and loan societies, railroads, and farm mortgage associations. It was also empowered to subscribe capital for government-owned corporations. Within six months it had authorized a total of $1.2 billion in loans to approximately 5,000 of the first-named institutions above. In July the Relief and Construction Act (RCA) extended the scope and functions of the RFC and authorized it to incur a total indebtedness of $3 billion. The RFC was empowered to provide $1.5 billion in loans for the construction by state and local agencies of public works of a self-liquidating character and to furnish $300 million in temporary loans to states unable to finance the relief of economic distress. The act also broadened the powers of the RFC to assist agriculture.

The same month saw the passage of Hoover's Federal Home Loan Bank Act which created a series of discount banks for home mortgages that would provide financial relief to homeowners. The measure was designed to reduce foreclosures, stimulate residential construction, and encourage home ownership through long-term installment loans. In an effort to shore up farm prices, Hoover proposed (and Congress accepted) the Agricultural Marketing Act, which for the first time established a major government effort to help farmers maintain prices, and the highly protectionist Hawley-Smoot Tariff of 1930. Like most of the efforts of the Hoover administration, the former proved ineffective while the latter was an unqualified disaster as foreign governments responded by enacting retaliatory trade restrictions.

By November 1932, the fortunes of Hoover and the Republican Party had sunk to a new low. Although Hoover was renominated on the first ballot, few Republicans expected to hold on to the presidency after the events of the preceding four years. Heading the Democratic ticket, Governor Franklin D. Roosevelt of New York talked vaguely about the importance of government in assisting business to develop a stable and well-regulated economic system and, from the time of his acceptance speech at the Democratic convention, pledged himself to an as yet undefined "new deal for the American people." To the surprise of no one, Roosevelt won by a landslide. Hoover carried Maine, New Hampshire, Vermont, Connecticut, Pennsylvania, and nothing else. In the popular vote Roosevelt outpolled his opponent 57.4 percent to 39.7 percent, with 2.2 percent going to the Socialist candidate.

In the interim between the presidential election and the inauguration, economic conditions reached critical proportions. From December 1932 to March 1933, the index of industrial production dropped from 64 to an all-time low of 56. The nation's banking system revealed signs of alarming weakness as runs on banks became increasingly frequent and the hoarding of currency set in on a large scale. By the eve of Roosevelt's inauguration, a total of 5,504 banks (with total deposits of $3,432 million) had closed, and by March 4, virtually every bank in the United States had been closed or placed under restriction by state proclamations.

# Responses to the Great Depression, Part 3: The First New Deal

The Democratic Party platform of 1932 advocated a drastic cut in government spending, a balanced budget, a competitive tariff for revenue, unemployment and old-age insurance under state laws, a sound currency, U.S. participation in an international monetary conference, repeal of the Prohibition Amendment, and expanded veterans pensions. It called for the "enactment of every constitutional measure that will aid the farmer to receive for basic farm commodities prices in excess of the cost of production." The platform advocated banking and financial reforms including the federal regulation of holding companies, of exchanges trading in securities and commodities, and of the rates of interstate utility companies. It supported protection of the investing public by requiring full publicity and filing with the government of all offerings of foreign and domestic stocks and bonds.

During the campaign Roosevelt delivered numerous speeches in which he set forth a program of economic nationalism and social reconstruction shaped by him with the aid of a group of assistants known as the "Brain Trust" (the most prominent of which were Rexford G. Tugwell, Raymond Moley, and Adolf A. Berle, Jr.). While Hoover condemned Roosevelt's philosophy of government as a "radical departure" from the American way of life, Roosevelt actually entered office free from any specific ideological commitments, and his proposals for combatting the effects of the Depression, vague as they were, seemed in many ways only extensions of the ideas and programs already advanced by Hoover himself. What Roosevelt was committed to was the importance of decisive action.

Immediately after taking office, Roosevelt summoned the Democratic 73rd Congress to convene in special session. Invoking powers granted by the Trading with the Enemy Act of 1917, he declared a four-day national bank holiday which suspended all transactions in the Federal Reserve and other banks, trust companies, credit unions, and building and loan associations. The proclamation also placed restrictions on the export of gold, silver, and currency. Roosevelt also used this occasion to send to Congress the Emergency Banking Relief Act (which had been drafted by holdovers from the Hoover Administration), which was designed to protect the solvency of larger banks from the weakness of smaller ones. A pliant Congress passed the measure the day it was introduced.

The legislation authorized the Federal Reserve System to issue notes against the assets of the banks (thus increasing liquidity); it allowed the Reconstruction Finance Corporation to provide funds to banks by buying their stock; it forbade the hoarding and exporting of gold; and, more importantly, it provided for Treasury Department inspection of all banks before they would be allowed to reopen. The gamble behind the bank holiday proved successful. Confidence in the soundness of the banking system was restored, and after the bank holiday more than 5,000 banks reopened (including 75 percent of all member banks of the Federal Reserve System). Within two weeks stock prices rose 15 percent, and hoarded currency flowed back into the banking system at a rapid rate.

Once the banking crisis had passed, Roosevelt decided to hold Congress in session to deal with the problems of unemployment and farm relief. What followed came to be known as "The Hundred Days." By the time Congress adjourned on June 16, it had enacted a comprehensive body of legislation affecting banking, industry, agriculture, labor, and unemployment relief. This was the initial phase of the "First New Deal," which lasted until 1935 and which concerned itself with questions of relief and recovery.

The legislation of "The Hundred Days" altered previous thinking concerning the power and responsibility of the federal government. The full complexity of the legislation and the political and ideological battles that went on behind the scene are too complicated to summarize here; but the following list of congressional acts adopted between March 9 and June 16 illustrates the dimension of these developments:

1.  The Economy Act, March 20—sought to balance the federal budget by cuts in the salaries of federal employees, cuts in veterans pensions, and by the reorganization of government agencies. The Act ultimately saved about $243 million.

2.  Civilian Conservation Corps Reforestation Relief Act, March 31—an employment relief measure which established the Civilian Conservation Corps (CCC) and initially created 250,000 public jobs in reforestation, road construction, the prevention of soil erosion, and national park and flood control projects. Eligibility was restricted to unemployed males between the ages of 18 and 25. By 1941, the CCC had employed more than two million men.

3.  The official abandonment of the gold standard for U.S. currency, April 19.
4.  Federal Emergency Relief Act, May 12—created the Federal Emergency Relief Administration, which provided $500 million in outright grants to states and municipalities for the purpose of work relief.
5.  Agricultural Adjustment Act, May 12—designed to restore the purchasing power of farmers. Its chief objectives were the elimination of surplus crops of basic commodities through curtailed production and the establishment of parity prices for enumerated basic commodities. The act also relieved the credit situation by providing for the refinancing of farm mortgages through the agency of the Federal Land Banks.
6.  Tennessee Valley Authority, May 18—the establishment of an independent public corporation charged with the responsibility of the economic and social development of the Tennessee Valley.
7.  Federal Securities Act, May 27—required full disclosure to investors of information relating to new securities issues publicly offered or sold through the mails or in interstate commerce.
8.  National Employment Service Act, June 6—established the U.S. Employment Service and provided matching funds for state appropriations for employment services.
9.  Home Owners Refinancing Act, June 13—provided funds for the reinforcing of home mortgage debts for nonfarm families. More than one million mortgages were covered between 1933 and 1936.
10. Banking Act of 1933 (Glass-Steagall Act), June 16—created the Federal Bank Deposit Insurance Corporation. Individual deposits were guaranteed up to $5,000; the ability of banks to speculate financially was restricted; branch banking was permitted; and the Federal Reserve System was expanded to include savings and industrial banks.
11. Farm Credit Act, June 16—refinanced farm mortgages on long terms at low rates of interest through the Farm Credit Administration.
12. Emergency Railroad Transportation Act, June 16—designed to remove unnecessary duplication of services and facilities, promoted financial reorganization of the carriers, and created the position of Federal Coordinator of Transportation.
13. National Industrial Recovery Act (NIRA), June 16.

The last of these acts, the NIRA, was potentially the most significant piece of legislation of "The Hundred Days." The NIRA was designed to revive industrial and business activity and to reduce unemployment. It was based on the principle of industrial self-regulation, operating under government supervision through a system of fair competition codes. The act created the National Recovery Administration and formalized the fair trade codes that had been used by many industrial and trade associations in the period after World War I. Under the NIRA, fair competition codes drawn up by such associations and approved by the president were enforceable by law. The president was also empowered to prescribe codes for industries and to make agreements or prescribe voluntary agreements. Actions under codes and agreements were exempt from the operations of the antitrust laws, and the courts could issue injunctions against violators. Section 7a of the NIRA guaranteed labor's right "to organize and bargain collectively through a representative of their own choosing," and subsequent to its adoption, the NIRA provided the basis for the first National Labor Board, which was established to enforce the right of collective bargaining.

General Hugh S. Johnson was appointed head of the NRA (i.e., the National Recovery Administration, which was created by the National Industrial Recovery Act), and the agency ultimately affected more than 500 industries and 22 million employees. The NRA's symbolic blue eagle was a common sight in the United States during the first two years of the Roosevelt administration. The NIRA's prescription for recovery went beyond simply encouraging labor, business, and government cooperation. For example, Title II of the act established the Public Works Administration and authorized $3.3 billion for the construction of roads, public buildings, and other public sector projects. The PWA represented at least a temporary commitment to "pump priming" as a way of increasing employment, stimulating business activity, and raising the popular consuming power. All told the PWA spent $4.25 billion on more than 34,000 projects.

From the outset this experiment in economic planning was beset with serious difficulties. While the NRA achieved numerous initial successes, it was soon subject to a barrage of public criticism. Code violations became increasingly frequent, and complaints of cutthroat competition and unfair price fixing became numerous. The NRA's codes regularly favored large businesses over small ones; they often raised prices higher than market forces would have justified; and they enabled many unhealthy businesses to continue operating when they should have been allowed to fail.

Furthermore, the anticipated major economic revival never materialized. In fact, the index of industrial production declined from 101 in July 1933 to 71 in November. The situation was not helped at all by the probusiness attitudes of General Johnson. In 1934, a specially appointed National Recovery Review Board chaired by the famous attorney Clarence Darrow reported that the NRA was encouraging monopoly and cartelization to the detriment of the small businessman. Having lost the support of both the general public and the business community (which opposed the prolabor union portions of the act), the NRA was virtually moribund when the NIRA was declared unconstitutional by the Supreme Court in the 1935 case *Schechter Poultry Corp.* v. *U.S.*

When Congress reconvened in October 1933, the pace of legislation slowed, but the Roosevelt Administration was, nevertheless, able to push through program after program in late 1933 and 1934. Among these were the Commodity Credit Corporation, the Civil Works Administration (the emergency make-work unemployment relief program), the Farm Mortgage Refinancing Program, the Works Progress Administration, the Home Owners Loan Act, the Securities Exchange Act (which established the Securities Exchange Commission), the Communications Act (which established the FCC), the Federal Farm Bankruptcy Act, the National Housing Act (which established the Federal Housing Administration), to name only a few.

The programs advanced by the Roosevelt administration in 1933 and 1934 had the twin goals of relief and economic reform. For most of the New Dealers, relief was assumed to be an emergency function of the federal government. Relief was the primary responsibility of state and local government, and whenever possible, relief funds were channelled to local programs. Roosevelt and most of his advisers viewed relief as a danger to the moral fiber of the nation in all but extraordinary circumstances. Nevertheless, the experience of the New Deal challenged these assumptions, and in spite of their intent, these early relief programs laid the groundwork for the national policy of social welfare which would emerge as a permanent element of American society.

On the question of the proper program for economic recovery, Roosevelt's policies often reflected the substantial disagreement within his own administration. Advisers Raymond Moley and Adolf Berle advocated a program not far removed from the business associationalism of Herbert Hoover by which the government would encourage rational planning of the economy by the business community. Others, like Rex Tugwell, shared this faith in the importance of planning but believed that government itself should be the planner. Still others, like Harvard Law Professor Felix Frankfurter and Supreme Court Justice Louis Brandeis, urged a vigorous program to restore competition in the economy. Roosevelt himself responded by adopting a series of uneasy compromises that, while initially favoring the planners, embodied some aspects of each position.

## Responses to the Great Depression, Part 4: The Second New Deal

Whereas the legislation of 1933 and 1934 had been focused primarily on relief and recovery, the legislative program Roosevelt presented to the 74th Congress was one of social reform. Partly to counter those critics like Huey Long of Louisiana who insisted that the New Deal had not gone far enough, President Roosevelt used his annual message to Congress on January 4 to launch the so-called Second New Deal. In his address and in the months that followed, he presented legislation with three designated goals: security of livelihood through the better use of national resources, security against unemployment, old age, illness, and dependence, and slum clearance and better housing. He also recommended a works program for absorbing the needy unemployed. The tone of the Second New Deal was decidedly more hostile to corporate America and much of the cooperational emphasis which had characterized the early New Deal was abandoned. The primary beneficiaries of the Second New Deal were to be not the middle classes but labor and the smaller farmers.

The new program began in April with the Emergency Relief Appropriation Act, a major piece of legislation which signalled the withdrawal of the federal government from the arena of direct relief, which was left to the states and local communities. Instead it was committed to addressing the larger causes of poverty and economic backwardness. Agencies established under the authority of the Emergency Relief Appropriations Act included the Works Progress Administration (a large scale national works program), the Resettlement Administration, which addressed the problems of impoverished rural families, the Rural Electrification Administration, and the National Youth Administration, a work relief and employment program for persons between the ages of 16 and 25.

A second major accomplishment of the Second New Deal included the National Labor Relations Act (the Wagner Act), which revived the prolabor Section 7a of the now-defunct NRA. The Wagner Act created a new National Labor Relations Board with power to determine appropriate collective bargaining units subject to elections it supervised at the request of the workers, to certify the duly chosen trade union, and to take testimony about unfair employer practices and issue cease and desist orders. In addition to upholding the right of employees to join labor organizations and to bargain collectively through representatives of their own choosing, the act defined unfair labor practices on the employers' part.

Additionally, 1935 saw the passage of the Social Security Act (and with it the establishment of a cooperative federal-state system of unemployment compensation and a national old-age and survivors insurance program), the Banking Act of 1935, which revamped the Federal Reserve System, the antimonopolistic Public Utility Holding Company Act, the Farm Mortgage Moratorium Act, and the Revenue Act of 1935 (the so-called Wealth Tax Act).

During the Second New Deal, just as during the first, Franklin Roosevelt and his associates attempted to keep the federal commitment to relief limited and temporary. Once again, however, they discovered that the nation's needs required a far larger response than they had originally envisioned. And future generations would discover that many programs established as temporary expedients ultimately became, in one form or another, permanent parts of the federal government.

## American Business and the New Deal

During the early years of the New Deal, the Roosevelt administration worked hard to conciliate the business community. Roosevelt's own commitment to fiscal conservatism was evident in the Economy Act of 1933, and corporate leaders themselves had been called upon to help design and operate the National Recovery Administration. In his own mind he believed that he had made every reasonable effort to woo big business into the New Deal coalition. By the end of 1934, however, this effort had clearly failed. The New Deal, of course, retained considerable support from some sectors of the business community, but a large portion of it had become quite hostile.

The disenchantment with Roosevelt was in part a result of structural shortcomings in the NRA programs and in part a reaction to general suspicion of Roosevelt's methods and motives. Critics in the business community denounced the New Deal for its reckless spending, its "socialist" reforms, and its alleged favoritism toward organized labor. Roosevelt himself was accused of provoking "class hatred," turning worker against employer, the poor against the rich, and in undermining the work ethic and traditional American values.

Some of this opposition came from existing organizations, such as the Chamber of Commerce and the National Association of Manufacturers. In August 1934, however, businessmen and political conservatives organized a new association, the American Liberty League, designed specifically to arouse public opposition to the New Deal. A few major industrialists took the lead in organizing the League. The organization campaigned vigorously against Roosevelt's "dictatorial" policies, accusing him of flouting the Constitution, destroying free enterprise, undermining states' rights, and eroding the strength of the "American Plan" for labor-management relations.

While the Liberty League claimed to be open to membership from Americans of all regions, parties, and backgrounds and while it did count among its officers former Democratic presidential candidate Al Smith, it primarily attracted northern industrialists, most of whom were already Republicans. At its peak, League membership numbered only about 125,000. Its real strength lay in the wealth of its constituency, and its large budget guaranteed that it would be heard in the arena of public opinion.

Business hostility toward the New Deal only increased after 1935, when the programs of the Second New Deal were interpreted as embodying a new, hostile attitude toward business. It was true that after 1935 Roosevelt had given up hope of attracting the support of big business and no longer attempted to conciliate financiers and industrialists. In practice, however, the "anti-business" legislation of the Second New Deal (like the Public Utilities Holding Act or the Revenue Act of 1935) were either watered down by amendments that limited their effects or else so full of loop-holes (like the Tax Act) that they sounded much more burdensome than they actually were. In the long run American business easily accommodated itself to the New Deal. While few were astute enough to recognize it at the time, the "broker state" arrangements that emerged out of the 1930s actually worked to assure a continued prominent and powerful role for the American business community.

# The Recovery

By historical standards, the recovery of the American economy between 1933 and 1937 was quite reasonable. During this period the economy grew at an average annual rate of 10 percent with a 6 percent average annual gain in real consumption. The recovery of the banking sector was equally brisk as the nominal money supply (M2) had almost regained its 1929 level by 1937, and since prices were much lower, the aggregate purchasing power was actually much greater.

However, given how far below operating capacity the American economy had fallen, a growth rate of 10 percent was hardly adequate. Private investment in capital plant remained minimal throughout the period even though the labor force grew by as much as 12 percent after the stock market crash. As a consequence, even though output increased 47 percent between 1933 and 1937, 9 percent of the work force remained unemployed with an additional 5 percent on temporary government payrolls.

Even though 7.5 million people remained unemployed and 4.5 million families were still on relief, there were, nevertheless, reasons to be optimistic in 1937. By August, steel producers were operating at 85 percent of capacity and the stock market had slowly climbed back to its 1928 (preboom) level. The GNP, which in 1929 dollars had dropped from $104.4 to $74.2 billion between 1929 and 1933, had risen to $109.1 billion. To Roosevelt and many of his advisers, the time seemed ripe for a drastic retrenchment in government spending. It was time, as Roosevelt put it, for the business community to once again stand on its own two feet. Not coincidentally, it also seemed to be a good time to balance the federal budget, whose mounting deficits had never ceased to trouble the president.

To implement this policy change the Roosevelt Administration raised interest rates and slashed the budgets of one relief program after another. The result of these changes was an apparent disaster. The fragile recovery collapsed, and the private sector was unable to compensate for the decrease in government spending. Steel production slumped to 26 percent of capacity and stock prices dropped 30 percent. Overall production dropped 5.4 percent, and the unemployment rate rose to 19 percent. Fortunately the 1937 recession was just that, a recession, and output reached the 1937 level again in 1939, regaining the moderate rate of recovery of the 1933–1937 period. However, unemployment remained over 10 percent until mid-1941, and it was not until late 1942, under a wartime economy, that full employment was achieved.

The crisis of 1937 forced another reevaluation of New Deal policies. FDR was inclined to blame the recession on the "selfish interests" of the American business community, and between 1938 and 1942, the government committed itself to a more vigorous policy of antitrust enforcement in the hopes of breaking up concentrated wealth and reinstituting healthy competition. Moreover, the advocates of government spending as an antidote to the Depression stood apparently vindicated, and the notion of using government deficits to stimulate the economy—an idea associated with the British economist John Maynard Keynes—had established its first foothold in American public policy. In October 1937, the president asked Congress for an emergency appropriation of $5 billion for public works and relief programs, and government funds soon began pouring into the economy once again.

By 1938, the worst effects of the previous year's recession had come to an end as had, for all practical purposes, the New Deal. High unemployment remained, and it would not be until American entry into World War II that the chronic economic dislocations of the Great Depression were eradicated.

## TABLE 4

**Aggregate Price Indexes, 1919–1939**

|      | Wholesale Price Index (WPI) (1947–1949 = 100) | Consumer Prime Index (CPI) (1947–1949 = 100) | Implicit GNP Price Deflator (1929 = 100) |
|------|-----------------------------------------------|-----------------------------------------------|-------------------------------------------|
| 1919 | 90.1  | 74.0 | 106 |
| 1920 | 100.3 | 85.7 | 121 |
| 1921 | 63.4  | 76.4 | 103 |
| 1922 | 62.8  | 71.6 | 98  |
| 1923 | 65.4  | 72.9 | 100 |
| 1924 | 63.8  | 73.1 | 99  |
| 1925 | 67.3  | 75.0 | 101 |
| 1926 | 65.0  | 75.6 | 101 |
| 1927 | 62.0  | 74.2 | 99  |
| 1928 | 62.9  | 73.3 | 100 |
| 1929 | 61.9  | 73.3 | 100 |
| 1930 | 56.1  | 71.4 | 96  |
| 1931 | 47.4  | 65.0 | 85  |
| 1932 | 42.1  | 58.4 | 77  |
| 1933 | 42.8  | 55.3 | 75  |
| 1934 | 48.7  | 57.2 | 80  |
| 1935 | 52.0  | 58.7 | 79  |
| 1936 | 52.5  | 59.3 | 82  |
| 1937 | 56.1  | 61.4 | 83  |
| 1938 | 51.1  | 60.3 | 83  |
| 1939 | 50.1  | 59.4 | 82  |

Source: Peter Temin, *Did Monetary Forces Cause the Great Depression?* (New York: W. W. Norton, 1976), p. 6.

## TABLE 5

**Unemployment, 1929–1942**

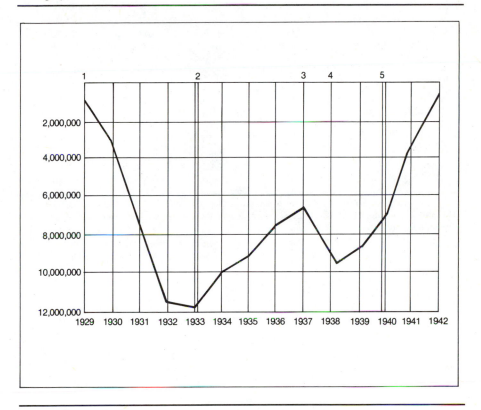

1 Stock Market Crash

2 New Deal Begins

3 New Deal Recovery

4 Recession

5 Outbreak of World War II

## TABLE 6

**An Economic Profile of the 1920s** (*Indexes, with 1929 = 100*)

| Year | Real Consumption | Real GNP | Real Gross Investment | Real Industrial Production | GNP Price* Deflator |
|------|------------------|----------|-----------------------|----------------------------|---------------------|
| 1920 | 66.7 | 70.2 | 79.0 | 65.9 | 121 |
| 1921 | 71.0 | 68.6 | 54.7 | 53.2 | 103 |
| 1922 | 73.5 | 72.6 | 65.4 | 66.9 | 98 |
| 1923 | 80.3 | 82.2 | 96.3 | 76.7 | 100 |
| 1924 | 86.2 | 84.7 | 77.8 | 73.1 | 99 |
| 1925 | 83.7 | 86.7 | 101.2 | 81.3 | 101 |
| 1926 | 90.5 | 92.3 | 105.6 | 86.6 | 101 |
| 1927 | 92.7 | 93.2 | 96.3 | 87.4 | 99 |
| 1928 | 94.7 | 94.3 | 89.5 | 91.2 | 100 |
| 1929 | 100.0 | 100.0 | 100.0 | 100.0 | 100 |

*The GNP Price Deflator is a price index that covers all goods and services in the economy, rather than just wholesale goods or consumer goods. It is the measure most appropriately used in adjusting the effects of price change on national income.

Source: Peter Temin, *Did Monetary Forces Cause the Great Depression?* (New York: W. W. Norton, 1976), p. 4. U.S. Department of Commerce, *Long-term Economic Growth* (Washington, D.C.: Government Printing Office, 1966), p. 169.

# CASE 23

# The Federal
# Government and
# Employment*

As year followed year in the 1930s, as each glimmer of recovery was followed by dreary disappointment, "Americans came to realize that something profound and terrifying had occurred."[1] Their world view, grounded in belief in individual initiative and responsibility, was challenged as never before by the irreconcilable brute fact of a massive breakdown of the system through which they ate and moved and had their being. The Great Depression marked the real end of American innocence.

The symbol of the Depression was the unemployed worker—"the worm that walked like a man" in the phrase of a journalist.[2] As the months turned into years, the unemployed found themselves face to face with the possibility that they might never again be productive, contributing members of society—that they might only hold a government "make work" job if that.

In the early months of the depression, jobless men made the rounds in search of work only to be faced by hastily scrawled signs with the legend "NO HELP WANTED." By the spring of 1934, the legends were painted in gilt letters, as if to make the words more

*This case was prepared by Assistant Professor Richard S. Tedlow as the basis for class discussion rather than to illustrate either effective or ineffective handling of an administrative situation.

Copyright © 1983 by the President and Fellows of Harvard College.

Harvard Business School case 384-125.

[1]Stephen K. Bailey, *Congress Makes a Law* (New York: Columbia University Press, 1950), p. 6.

[2]Irving Bernstein, *Turbulent Years* (Boston: Houghton Mifflin, 1971), p. 131.

enduring. The embarrassed "Sorry, buddy" had given way to the brusque "Can't you read signs?" Men who had once felt certain they could find a job the next day, the next week, the next month, had lost their self-assurance. One worker remarked, "There is something about the anniversary of your layoff which makes you feel more hopeless."

To be unemployed in an industrial society is the equivalent of banishment and ex-communication. A job established a man's identity—not only what other men thought of him but how he viewed himself; the loss of his job shattered his self-esteem and severed one of his most important ties to other men. Engulfed by feelings of inferiority, the jobless man sought out anonymity. He withdrew from the avocations he had had before he lost his job, even tried to escape the company of friends and neighbors whose opinion he respected.[3]

John Kenneth Galbraith doubtless exaggerated when he wrote that in comparison to this, World War II was "an almost casual and pleasant experience for most Americans."[4] Yet it is true that the war, with its sense of purpose and mission and with its offer of the possibility of personal and collective heroism which unemployment denied, came as something of a relief. And as soon as the military situation was brought under control and victory seemed assured, many Americans both in and out of government turned their attention to the problem of a recurrence of depression. An annotated bibliography of books and articles on the employment problem published from 1943 to 1945 came to 56 dense pages of text. By 1944, some 33 federal agencies were planning for postwar reconversion. And a wartime contest sponsored by the Pabst Brewing Company with the employment problem as the subject drew a remarkably high 36,000 responses. In 1944, both major parties featured the avoidance of unemployment in their platforms. Galbraith has labelled the fear of the recurrence of the disaster of the 1930s the "depression psychosis." It is a fear which is with us to this day. No better illustration of its pervasiveness is that the very word *depression* is rarely used publicly. All one hears is its substitute, *recession*.

Federal concern for postwar employment was spearheaded by a very wealthy, very liberal senator from Montana, James E. Murray. He introduced a bill in January of 1945 aimed at establishing "a national policy and program for assuring continuing full employment." (See Exhibit 1.) Between its introduction and the Senate vote on September 28, hearings were held during which some opposition, especially from representatives of business, was voiced. For excerpts from the testimony of a vice president of the Guaranty Trust Company of New York, Mr. William L. Kleitz, see Exhibit 2. On September 28, the Senate approved an amended bill by a vote of 71 to 10.

The bill experienced far heavier sledding in the House. It was there that its opponents, especially from the business community, focused their attention. A greatly changed piece of legislation was approved by the lower chamber in December. The bill which finally became law in February of 1946 is reproduced as Exhibit 3. Exhibit 4 provides selected performance data for the economy.

---

[3]William E. Leuchtenburg, *Franklin D. Roosevelt and the New Deal* (New York, Harper & Row, 1963), pp. 118–19.

[4]John Kenneth Galbraith, *American Capitalism* (Boston: Houghton Mifflin, 1952), p. 69.

# EXHIBIT 1

## *The Full Employment Bill As Originally Introduced, 79th Congress, 1st Session (S.380)*

### IN THE SENATE OF THE UNITED STATES
January 22, 1945

Mr. Murray (for himself, Mr. Wagner, Mr. Thomas of Utah, Mr. O'Mahoney, Mr. Morse, Mr. Tobey, Mr. Aiken, and Mr. Langer) introduced the following bill: which was read twice and referred to the Committee on Banking and Currency

### A BILL

To establish a national policy and program for assuring continuing full employment in a free competitive economy, through the concerted efforts of industry, agriculture, labor, State and local governments, and the Federal Government.

Be it enacted by the Senate and House of Representatives of the United States of America in Congress assembled,

Sec. 1. This Act may be cited as the "Full Employment Act of 1945."

### DECLARATION OF POLICY

Sec. 2. The Congress hereby declares that—

(a) It is the policy of the United States to foster free competitive enterprise and the investment of private capital in trade and commerce and in the development of the natural resources of the United States;

(b) All Americans able to work and seeking work have the right to useful, remunerative, regular, and full-time employment, and it is the policy of the United States to assure the existence at all times of sufficient employment opportunities to enable all Americans who have finished their schooling and who do not have full time housekeeping responsibilities freely to exercise this right;

(c) In order to carry out the policies set forth in subsections (a) and (b) of this section, and in order to (1) promote the general welfare of the Nation; (2) foster and protect the American home and the American family as the foundation of the American way of life; (3) raise the standards of living of the American people; (4) provide adequate employment opportunities for returning veterans; (5) contribute to the full utilization of our natural resources; (6) develop trade and commerce among the several States and with foreign nations; (7) preserve and strengthen competitive private enterprise, particularly small business enterprise; (8) strengthen the national defense and security; and (9) contribute to the establishment and maintenance of lasting peace among nations, it is essential that continuing full employment be maintained in the United States;

(d) In order to assist industry, agriculture, labor and State and local governments in achieving continuing full employment, it is the responsibility of the Fed-

## EXHIBIT 1 (*continued*)

eral Government to pursue such consistent and openly arrived at economic policies and programs as will stimulate and encourage the highest feasible levels of
employment opportunities through private and other non-Federal investment and
expenditure;

(e) To the extent that continuing full employment cannot otherwise be
achieved, it is the further responsibility of the Federal Government to provide
such volume of Federal investment and expenditure as may be needed to assure
continuing full employment; and

(f) Such investment and expenditure by the Federal Government shall be designed to contribute to the national wealth and well-being, and to stimulate increased employment opportunities by private enterprise.

## THE NATIONAL PRODUCTION AND EMPLOYMENT BUDGET

Sec. 3. (a) The President shall transmit to Congress at the beginning of each
regular session the National Production and Employment Budget (hereinafter referred to as the "National Budget"), which shall set forth in summary and detail,
for the ensuing fiscal year or such longer period as the President may deem appropriate—

(1) the established size of the labor force, including the self-employed in industry and agriculture;

(2) the estimated aggregate volume of investment and expenditure by private
enterprises, consumers, State and local governments, and the Federal Government, required to produce such volume of the gross national product, at the expected level of prices, as will be necessary to provide employment opportunities
for such labor force (such dollar volume being hereinafter referred to as the "full
employment volume of production"); and

(3) the estimated aggregate volume of prospective investment and expenditure by private enterprises, consumers, State and local governments, and the Federal Government (not taking into account any increased or decreased investment
or expenditure which might be expected to result from the programs set forth in
such Budget). The estimates and information herein called for shall take account
of such foreign investments and expenditure for exports and imports as affect the
volume of the gross national product.

(b) The extent, if any, by which the estimated aggregate volume of prospective investment and expenditure for any fiscal year or other period, as set forth in
the National Budget in accordance with paragraph (a) (3) of this section, is less
than the estimated aggregate volume of investment and expenditure required to
assure a full employment volume of production, as set forth in the National Budget in accordance with paragraph (a) (2) of this section, shall for the purposes of
this title be regarded as a prospective deficiency in the National Budget. When
there is a prospective deficiency in the National Budget for any fiscal year or other

## EXHIBIT 1 (*continued*)

period, the President shall set forth in such Budget a general program for encouraging such increased non-Federal investment and expenditure, particularly investment and expenditure which will promote increased employment opportunities by private enterprise, as will prevent such deficiency to the greatest possible extent. The President shall also include in such Budget such recommendations for legislation relating to such program as he may deem necessary or desirable. Such program may include, but need not be limited to, current and projected Federal policies and activities with reference to banking and currency, monopoly and competition, wages and working conditions, foreign trade and investment, agriculture, taxation, social security, the development of natural resources, and such other matters as may directly or indirectly affect the level of non-Federal investment and expenditure.

(c) To the extent, if any, that such increased non-Federal investment and expenditure as may be expected to result from actions taken under the program set forth in accordance with subsection (b) of this section are deemed insufficient to provide a full employment volume of production, the President shall transmit a general program for such Federal investment and expenditure as will be sufficient to bring the aggregate volume of investment and expenditure by private business, consumers, State and local government, and the Federal Government, up to the level required to assure a full employment volume of production. Such program shall be designed to contribute to the national wealth and well-being, and to stimulate additional non-Federal investment and expenditure. Any of such programs calling for the construction of public works by the Federal Government shall provide for the performance of the necessary construction work by private concerns under contracts awarded in accordance with applicable laws, except where the performance of such work by some other method is necessary by reason of special circumstances or is authorized by other provisions of law.

(d) If the estimated aggregate volume of prospective investment and expenditure for any fiscal year or other period, as set forth in the National Budget in accordance with paragraph (a) (3) of this section, is more than the estimated aggregate volume of investment and expenditure required to assure a full employment volume of production, as set forth in the National Budget in accordance with paragraph (a) (2) of this section, the President shall set forth in such Budget a general program for preventing inflationary economic dislocations, or diminishing the aggregate volume of investment and expenditure to the level required to assure a full employment volume of production, or both.

(e) The programs referred to in subsections (b), (c), and (d) of this section shall include such measures as may be necessary to assure that monopolistic practices with respect to prices, production, or distribution, or other monopolistic practices, will not interfere with the achievement of the purposes of this Act.

(f) The National Budget shall include a report on the distribution of the national income during the preceding fiscal year, or such longer period as the Presi-

## EXHIBIT 1 (*continued*)

dent may deem appropriate, together with an evaluation of the effect upon the distribution of the national income of the programs set forth in such Budget.

(g) The President may from time to time transmit to Congress such supplemental or revised estimates, information, program, or legislative recommendations as he may deem necessary or desirable in connection with the National Budget.

## PREPARATION OF NATIONAL BUDGET

Sec. 4. (a) The National Budget shall be prepared in the Executive Office of the President under the general direction and supervision of the President, and in consultation with the members of his Cabinet and other heads of departments and establishments.

(b) The President shall transmit to the several departments and establishments such preliminary estimates and other information as will enable them to prepare such plans and programs as may be needed during the ensuing or subsequent fiscal years to help achieve a full employment volume of production.

(c) The President may establish such advisory boards or committees composed of representatives of industry, agriculture, labor, and State and local governments, and others, as he may deem advisable for the purpopse of advising and consulting on methods of achieving the objectives of this Act.

## JOINT COMMITTEE ON THE NATIONAL BUDGET

Sec. 5. (a) There is hereby established a Joint Committee on the National Budget, to be composed of the chairmen and ranking minority members of the Senate Committees on Appropriations, Banking and Currency, Education and Labor, and Finance, and seven additional Members of the Senate, to be appointed by the President of the Senate; and the chairmen and ranking minority members of the House Committees on Appropriations, Banking and Currency, Labor, and Ways and Means, and seven additional Members of the House of Representatives to be appointed by the Speaker of the House of Representatives. The party representation of the Joint Committee shall reflect the relative membership of the majority and minority parties in the Senate and the House of Representatives.

(b) It shall be the function of the Joint Committee—(1) to make a study of the National Budget transmitted to Congress by the President in accordance with section 3 of this Act; and (2) to report to the Senate and the House of Representatives, not later than March 1 of each year, its findings and recommendations with respect to the National Budget, together with a joint resolution setting forth for the ensuing fiscal year a general policy with respect to such National Budget to serve as a guide to the several committees of Congress dealing with legislation relating to such National Budget.

# EXHIBIT 1 (*continued*)

(c) Vacancies in the membership of the Joint Committee shall not affect the power of the remaining members to execute the functions of the committee, and shall be filled in the same manner as in the case of the original selection. The committee shall select a chairman and a vice chairman from among its members.

(d) The Joint Committee, or any duly authorized subcommittee thereof, is authorized to sit and act at such place and times, to require by subpoena or otherwise the attendance of such witnesses and the production of such books, papers, and documents, to administer such oaths, to take such testimony, to procure such printing and binding, and to make such expenditures as it deems advisable. The cost of stenographic services to report such hearings shall not be in excess of 25 cents per hundred words. The provisions of sections 102 to 104, inclusive, of the Revised Statutes shall apply in case of any failure of any witness to comply with any subpoena, or to testify when summoned, under authority of this section.

(e) The Joint Committee is empowered to appoint and fix the compensation of such experts, consultants, technicians, and clerical and stenographic assistance as it deems necessary and advisable, but the compensation so fixed shall not exceed the compensation prescribed under the Classification Act of 1923, as amended, for comparable duties. The committee may utilize such voluntary and uncompensated services as it deems necessary and is authorized to utilize the services, information, facilities, and personnel of the departments and establishments.

(f) The expenses of the Joint Committee shall be paid one-half from the contingent fund of the Senate and one-half from the contingent fund of the House of Representatives upon vouchers signed by the chairman or vice chairman.

## RATE OF EXPENDITURES

Sec. 6. (a) The President shall review quarterly all Federal investment and expenditure for the purpose of ascertaining the extent to which the current and anticipated level of non-Federal investment and expenditure warrants any change in the volume of such Federal investment and expenditure.

(b) Subject to such principles and standards as may be set forth in applicable appropriation Acts and other statutes, the rate of Federal investment and expenditure may be varied to whatever extent and in whatever manner the President may determine to be necessary for the purpose of assisting in assuring continuing full employment, with due consideration being given to current and anticipated variations in savings and in investment and expenditure by private business, consumers, State and local governments, and the Federal Government.

## AID TO COMMITTEES

Sec. 7. The heads of departments and establishments shall, at the request of any committee of either house of Congress, furnish such committee with such aid and information with regard to the National Budget as it may request.

## EXHIBIT 1 (*concluded*)

Sec. 8. Nothing contained herein shall be construed as calling for or authorizing—(a) the operation of plants, factories, or other productive facilities by the Federal Government;

(b) the use of compulsory measures of any type whatsoever in determining the allocation or distribution of manpower;

(c) any change in the existing procedures on appropriations; or

(d) the carrying out of, or any appropriation for, any program set forth in the National Budget, unless such program shall have been authorized by provisions of law other than this Act.

## EXHIBIT 2

### *Testimony of Mr. William L. Kleitz, Vice-President, Guaranty Trust Company of New York, before the Senate Committee on Banking and Currency*

**Mr. Kleitz**: First, I should like to state emphatically that the institution I represent here is in full accord with what we take to be the broad objectives of the bill. Those objectives, as we understand them, are, first, to prevent to the greatest possible extent in the future the hardships that have been associated with unemployment in the past; and, second, to prevent those hardships without sacrificing, but rather by fostering, the system of free competitive enterprise that the vast majority of Americans consider an integral part of our democratic way of life. We offer no objection to any sound and effective measures by the Federal Government to encourage investment, production, and employment in private enterprise, or to regulate the timing of necessary public works in such a way as to smooth out fluctuations in employment, or to organize and systematize the plans of Federal, State, and local governments to prevent the misery and despair that unemployment can cause. On the contrary, we believe these aims to be highly desirable, but we believe that the machinery provided in this bill has three fundamental defects:

1. Responsibility for full employment should not be assumed by the Federal Government, because the implementation of such a policy would inevitably lead to the exercise of powers which would eventually destroy the private enterprise system.

2. The character of the measures that the Federal Government would be obliged to adopt in order to comply with the directives in the bill are such as expe-

## EXHIBIT 2 (*continued*)

rience has shown would result in an impairment of confidence on the part of private industry and a consequent decrease in employment opportunities.

**3.** Such estimates and forecasts as may be obtained to provide a basis for the national production and employment budget as set forth in section 3 subsections (1), (2), and (3) of the bill cannot be sufficiently reliable to form a basis for a concrete program such as would be required by the bill.

> Let me add that it is not our purpose to be critical merely. With your permission, I will place before you very briefly the broad outline of a program which we believe would be more conducive to high levels of production and employment, and much less fraught with danger to our free institutions, than the program provided for in this bill.

> The question that has to be answered is not whether the objectives of the bill are desirable but whether its specific provisions embody the best available means of striving for those objectives. We have to consider to what extent it is possible for government investment and expenditure to provide an adequate substitute for private investment and expenditure in maintaining the volume of employment, and to what extent a program of full employment by Government investment and expenditure is consistent with the bill's avowed aim "to foster free competitive enterprise and the investment of private capital in trade and commerce." In considering the first of these questions, we have some practical experience to go by; in seeking an answer to the second, we have to rely mainly on general principles.

> First, as to the feasibility and adequacy of Government investment and expenditure as a substitute for, or supplement to, private investment and expenditure. Our recent experience bearing on this question may be divided into three main periods: the 1920s, the 1930s, and the war period. During most of the 1920s the United States enjoyed a high level of prosperity, with large production and substantially full employment. In that period—or, more precisely, in the fiscal years from 1922 to 1929, inclusive—the expenditures of the Federal Government ranged between $3.5 and $4 billion annually, and the public debt was reduced by more than $7 billion or at an average rate of nearly 900 million a year.

> The last Federal budgetary surplus was in the fiscal year 1929–30. From 1931 through 1939, Federal expenditures averaged 6¾ billion dollars annually, and the public debt rose at an average rate of about 2⅔ billion a year, more than three times as fast as it had been reduced in the 20s.

**Senator Lucas:** Why was that? What caused that?

**Mr. Kleitz:** The difference was caused principally by a drop, I should say, in the tax revenues, and a substantial increase in expenditures by Govern-

## EXHIBIT 2 (*continued*)

ment designed to meet the Depression or cure the Depression. I could find statistics to support that.

**Senator Lucas**: Why make the comparison? You admit that in such a depression as we had, we had to use these things. You assume that everything has been normal, I take it, from 1931 to 1939.

**Mr. Kleitz**: No. If you will bear with me a moment, I think you will see why I make that point.

**Senator Lucas**: All right.

**Mr. Kleitz**: Contrasting the budgetary surplus with the period of budgetary deficits.

What was the effect on employment? According to the estimate of the American Federation of Labor, the number unemployed declined irregularly from the peak of 15⅔ million in March 1933 to 7½ million in September 1937, and then rose irregularly to more than 11½ million in January 1939. In August 1939, the last month before the outbreak of the war, the total was more than 10 million, or very nearly two thirds of the peak figure more than 6 years earlier.

What are we to infer from these figures? For one thing, that budgetary surpluses do not necessarily inhibit business prosperity and full employment, and that large Government investment and expenditure—particularly deficit spending—does not necessarily produce or maintain full employment. More specifically, we see that Government investment and expenditure in the 30s, at a rate which raised the national debt far above the postwar peak in 1919, did not suffice to take up more than one third of the employment slack.

Of course we must recognize that this evidence is not conclusive. Human society is not an experimental laboratory when phenomena can be isolated and conditions controlled. There were numerous factors making for prosperity in the 20s and numerous factors making for depression in the 30s. The state of the Federal budget, whatever its influence may have been, was only one of many influences. It may be argued that the budgetary surpluses of the 20s helped to bring on the crash of 1929, although I doubt whether many authorities believe that to be the case. It may be argued that the Government spending of the 30s did increase employment and that the only reason it failed to take up the employment slack is that there was not enough of it. On the other hand, it may equally well be argued that the sound condition of Federal finances in the 20s was among the most potent factors bolstering business confidence and thereby stimulating production and employment, and that the series of very large budgetary deficits in the 30s may have destroyed more employment than it created, by shaking the faith of the people in the future of their Government's credit and the soundness of their currency.

This brings us to one point which I think may be insufficiently appreciated not only by the supporters of this bill but also by the advocates of other forms

## EXHIBIT 2 (*continued*)

of economic planning. I refer to the enormous influence of the psychological factor in general business situations, and the fatal incompleteness of any analysis based solely or primarily on statistical totals. Investment and expenditure, production and employment, are not merely items in an economic balance sheet, to be kept in balance by making entries of the proper amounts on the debit or the credit side. They are products of the mental processes of millions of individual businessmen, investors, and consumers. These mental processes go to make up what is commonly termed "confidence." When confidence is impaired, consumers become reluctant to buy, investors hesitate to take risks, and business concerns fear to expand, or even maintain the scale of their operations. Income payments distributed to wage-earners and owners of capital, or retained by the business enterprises that earned them, are not fully translated into effective demand for producers' and consumers' goods and services. Instead they are retained, either in the form of cash or idle bank balances.

From the middle of 1933 to the middle of 1939 the amount of money in circulation increased from $5 ¾ billion to $7 billion, and the amount of demand deposits in banks rose from $15 billion to $29 billion. But meanwhile the annual rate of turnover of deposits, as calculated by the Federal Reserve Bank of New York, dropped from 32.4 to 22.1. Government investment and expenditure had increased the volume of ready purchasing power by large amounts, but the purchasing power had manifestly failed to take its intended place in the income stream. Once the money was spent by the Government and found its way into the banks and safe-deposit boxes, it tended to lie stagnant. Belief in the worth-whileness of business ventures, which is the mainspring of enterprise, was weakened.

Why did this business apathy continue year after year in the face of the truly strenuous efforts of the Government to prime the pump of recovery? I have already suggested that the pump-priming process itself may have been partly responsible, since it resulted in a series of Treasury deficits which, to many if not most of our people, was highly disturbing. But there were other and perhaps even more powerful depressive influences at work. Taxes on business enterprise, particularly on large concerns, and on individuals in the higher income brackets were sharply increased. Corporate earnings distributed as dividends were made subject to double taxation. The issuance of corporate securities was hedged about with rules, restrictions, and liabilities. Wages and hours of labor were regulated, and employers were closely restricted in their dealings with their employees. Some branches of business were subjected to Government competition. Public officials were given broad powers to manipulate credit and currency, and some of those powers were exercised.

These and other drastic and experimental changes in the economic environment, coming in quick succession, led many to believe that there was an undercurrent of antagonism in governmental circles towards business, espe-

## EXHIBIT 2 (*continued*)

cially the large business concerns and the wealthy individuals that supply much of the capital and much of the driving power upon which free competitive enterprise depends. Thus, added to the harmful effects of the specific measures actually adopted was a pervasive fear and uncertainty as to when and where the lightning might strike next.

The result of all this was that the actual and prospective costs and risks of doing business were increased, the opportunities for profit were restricted, business management was deprived of much of its freedom of action, and confidence in public credit and in the future value of the currency was impaired. In short, it became less worthwhile to make business ventures, and hence to create jobs, than it had been before.

**Senator Murray**: Did you oppose those activities on the part of the Government at the time or did you feel they were unwarranted?

**Mr. Kleitz**: As I recall it, at that time we were not invited to express our opinion, sir.

**Senator Murray**: Why do you select this period, the two periods, the 20s and the 30s, to illustrate the points you wish to illustrate here? It seems to me that those were two unusual periods in the history of our country. In the first place, the 20s was a period of inflation brought on by American business. Then the 1930s was another unusual period in the history of the country in which there was an effort to bring back employment in the country. Why couldn't you select some other period in the history of the United States that could illustrate the point that you wish to illustrate here?

**Mr. Kleitz**: Well, if we say the 1920s was a period of inflation, of course an inflation is the hardest thing in the world to define, I am not sure I know what the definition is.

**Senator Murray**: Do you approve the rapid rise in stocks and securities during that period and the manipulations that took place on the stock exchanges of the country which were afterward investigated by the Banking and Currency Committee, shown to be fraudulent and dishonest?

**Mr. Kleitz**: No, sir, I certainly do not condone anything fraudulent or dishonest.

**Senator Murray**: You realize that in the period of the 1920s that the manipulations that were going on were draining the country of its wealth. You were manipulating these stocks and securities, running them up to a fictitious value and getting the people to purchase them, and they were afterward defrauded. Isn't that true?

**Mr. Kleitz**: You say you were doing that?

**Senator Murray**: Well, you represent the banking and financial fraternity down in Wall Street. You are coming here to oppose this bill, and I say you represent them down there and you represent their philosophy.

## EXHIBIT 2 (*continued*)

**Mr. Kleitz**: May I say, with all due respect, that I am coming here because Senator Wagner telegraphed and asked if we would have a representative come to this hearing.

**Senator Murray**: Yes. I am asking you why you could not have selected some other period besides the period that you select to illustrate the points that you wish to illustrate here. They are both very unusual periods in the history of our country and do not represent the general operation of the economic system.

**Mr. Kleitz**: Well, they are the two most recent periods. I cited three periods, the 1920s, the 1930s, and the war period. They are the most recent periods in our country's business and economic history.

**Senator Murray**: And they all have no relation to the operation of our economic system at all. They were unusual periods.

**Mr. Kleitz**: Well, it is hard to say when there was a usual period, when there was a normal period.

**Senator Murray**: Well, I think your statement is true, because in the last 40 or 50 years there has been a tendency to expand monopoly, and the undue concentration of business in this country and the manipulation of stocks and securities have gone on periodically, and we have had periodical depressions and inflations, of course. We had that, but it seems to me that that is a very unusual period for you to select to come here and try to make a point of the failure of the Government, through Government spending, to accomplish a return to full employment.

**Mr. Kleitz**: Well, I assume, sir, that one way by which this bill could be implemented to provide job opportunities by the investment and expenditure of Government funds would be through deficit financing, and occasion. . . .

**Senator Murray**: But that is only the last resort. That is the last thing in the bill to be considered. Everything else is to be done before that provision of the bill is to be resorted to.

**The Chairman**: To help private industry.

**Mr. Kleitz**: Well, as I go along in the statement, I am thoroughly in accord with any legislative or governmental action that stimulates and encourages private industry.

**Senator Murray**: Yes. But are you not opposed to a regulated program of Government expenditures, either, in order to hold back Government spending during periods of prosperity and to let it out during periods of depression or unemployment?

**Mr. Kleitz**: That is quite true. By the same token, the Government expenditures in periods of depression, as in the 20s again, would be at a time of seriously reduced Government revenue through taxation, and thereby would take the route of deficit financing, I assume.

## EXHIBIT 2 (*continued*)

**Senator Murray**: Well, of course, under this bill the Government also undertakes to study the tax problems of the country, and the legislature is expected under this measure to so adjust taxes as to give that incentive to
business.

**Mr. Kleitz**: And I am not . . .

**Senator Murray**: There is no intention under this bill to maintain high
taxes, which have a tendency to prevent business expansion and at the
same time furnish high Government expenditures to offset the effect of the
deflationary tax policies.

**Mr. Kleitz**: It is quite true, and that section of the bill on page 5 which says
that "Such program"—meaning the program that may be suggested by
the President—

Such program may include, but need not be limited to current and projected Federal
policies and activities with reference to banking and currency, monopoly and competition, wages and working conditions, foreign trade and investment, agriculture, taxation, social security, the development of natural resources, and such other matters as
may directly or indirectly affect the level of non-Federal investment and expenditure.

To the extent that such a program encourages private enterprise, I am
certainly not in opposition to that section of the bill or any . . .

**Senator Murray**: Well, what is it that you oppose in the bill?

**Mr. Kleitz**: I oppose primarily the assumption by the Federal Government
of the responsibility—practically a guaranty—of providing full employment because I feel that in order to make that program effective the Government will step by step be led into a program that will be the antithesis of
private industry and a system of private enterprise.

**Senator Murray**: Well, unless the Government does through some means
assure the existence of full employment in this country, don't you think
that we are in danger of having serious conditions develop?

**Mr. Kleitz**: I do not think I am competent to debate the moral or philosophical aspects of it, but I recognize the fact that as a matter of sheer political
necessity, when we do come to a period of substantial unemployment, if we
do, the Federal Government will be obliged to undertake a public-works
program that will relieve the distress at that time.

**Senator Murray**: Do you not think there should be a program in operation
which would prevent that serious development, such as this bill envisages?
This bill undertakes to have the trends studied, and, when a trend of unemployment is developing, to take such action as to stimulate private
enterprise to keep up employment, and also provides under those conditions that the Government take such action as necessary in various fields to
encourage business to maintain the responsibility of supplying employment.

## EXHIBIT 2 (*continued*)

**Mr. Kleitz**: But isn't there a difference between recognizing the necessity of meeting emergency conditions with emergency measures, on the one hand, and adopting by legislative enactment, on the other, a statement that it is the responsibility of the Federal Government to assure full employment?

**Senator Murray**: Well, don't you think that would be a splendid thing for the country if it was made clear to the American people, to business, and enterprise, that the Government was going to assure full employment in this country and that businessmen could go forward with their plans with the feeling that they were not going to encounter a period of depression and unemployment and lack of purchasing power which would upset their plans; and don't you think it could be possible for us to try out this program and see if it didn't accomplish that result?

**Mr. Kleitz**: I suppose the foremost student in the world, and generally considered so, of Government action to relieve unemployment is William Beveridge. Would you agree with that?

**Senator Murray**: Well, we are not following Sir William Beveridge's proposals here in this bill or in this country.

**Mr. Kleitz**: No; but I think this bill takes the first step down that road.

**Senator Murray**: This bill takes the first step down that road?

**Mr. Kleitz**: When it says specifically that it is the responsibility of the Federal Government to assure full employment.

**Senator Murray**: Well, don't you think it should be the responsibility of the Federal Government to assure full employment?

**Mr. Kleitz**: No, sir.

**Senator Murray**: Don't you think our economic system and our political system are endangered if the American people are not going to be protected from the fluctuations which we have had in the past? Don't you think that another unemployment situation such as we have recently passed through would endanger the continuance of our political system?

**Mr. Kleitz**: I think our political and economic system as we know it now would be in great danger from the adoption of the philosophy expressed in this bill.

**Senator Murray**: Why?

**Mr. Kleitz**: Because, as I said in (1) here, I think that the implementation of such a policy—I have no idea that the sponsors of the bill at the present time have in mind the sort of program that might develop—probably would develop—with the implementation of this bill, leading toward an authoritarian form of government.

**Senator Murray**: I cannot see any such danger in this bill; in fact, I can see more of a danger leading toward totalitarian government in this country through the failure of having such a measure as this.

# EXHIBIT 2 (*continued*)

**Senator Lucas**: Well, but you keep indicating that you are for full employment, but you don't want the Government to have much to do with it?

**Mr. Kleitz**: Yes sir, I don't want the Government to assume the responsibility for continuing full employment.

*    *    *    *    *

**Senator Lucas**: You would rather have these depressions and then just let them iron themselves out, as I take it?

**Mr. Kleitz**: I wouldn't rather have them. I think that they are inevitable under the free-enterprise system and that the best we can hope to do is to limit their depth and their duration.

**Senator Lucas**: And isn't that Government's responsibility, to limit their depth and their duration?

**Mr. Kleitz**: Yes, sir; by creating a climate favorable to private enterprise, so that employment opportunities will be created.

**Senator Taylor**: Mr. Chairman.

**The Chairman**: Yes.

**Senator Taylor**: But would you say, Mr. Kleitz, that there was a favorable climate in the Gay Twenties?

**Mr. Kleitz**: Oh, yes; of course there was a favorable climate for business.

**Senator Taylor**: Well, the whole thing went to pot, didn't it?

**Mr. Kleitz**: Yes, but I—Senator Murray asked me if I were an economist. I am not, and probably there is a lot about cyclical depressions, booms, and unemployment that I don't know, but I am firmly convinced from what I do know that no one has yet found the answer to why we have the booms and depressions.

**Senator Taylor**: Do you think there was any danger of violent revolution in 1930 and 1932?

**Mr. Kleitz**: No, sir.

**Senator Taylor**: Where were you at that time?

**Mr. Kleitz**: In New York.

**Senator Taylor**: In the bank?

**Mr. Kleitz**: Yes, sir.

**Senator Taylor**: Well, I wasn't. I was right out among the people, and I frankly believe that they were almost at the limit of their endurance. We know that these depressions have become more pronounced each succeeding one, and if we have another one anything like the one we had in 1929, I think the peaceful revolution we have just witnessed in England among those people whom we have come to look upon as the most conservative

## EXHIBIT 2 (*continued*)

and tradition-worshiping people in the world—I think that peaceful revolution would just be a picnic to what would happen in this country, and I can say for those of us who sponsor this bill that our hope is to take a minimum of measures to prevent a recurrence of such a condition in order to protect our free-enterprise system. If, as you say, the Government should take no hand and just let the depressions come along and then try to work our way out as best we can, I believe we shall have lost our free-enterprise system completely.

**The Chairman**: You remember that a great many still talk that way. They say, "What's the use of talking about this Charter taking care of our international situation and preventing war? You are always going to have war." Well, that is the defeatist. So, I think your attitude is that of a defeatist when you say we are going to have these depressions every little while, and we are not defeatist here. The members of this committee and the introducers of the legislation are going to try their best to avoid any future depressions, and I think we are going to, too.

**Senator Murray**: Mr. Kleitz, don't you think that in the 1920s, if we had had a proper Government interference during that period, that a good deal could have been done to have prevented that depression from mounting like it did?

**Mr. Kleitz**: You mean inflation?

**Senator Murray**: Yes.

**Mr. Kleitz**: As you say, the inflation of the 20s?

**Senator Murray**: Yes.

**Mr. Kleitz**: It is my impression that that period in the 20s was a matter of the psychology of all the people in the country.

**Senator Murray**: Yes. And if we had the whole . . .

**Mr. Kleitz**: Everybody was making a lot of money.

**Senator Murray**: Yes.

**Mr. Kleitz**: Everybody was speculating.

**Senator Murray**: But it was fictitious, though. It was fictitious.

**Mr. Kleitz**: Yes, but I . . .

**Senator Murray**: And the public was sold by newspaper articles and stories that were paid for by those in Wall Street who were seeking to inflate securities. The testimony afterward showed that they were resorting to all sorts of fictitious methods and plans for deceiving the public, and that is what made it necessary for Congress to enact the Securities and Exchange Commission Act.

**Senator Lucas**: I still have a couple of those bonds at 7 ½ percent bonds that some of you boys in New York sold me. I was gullible enough in those days to buy them.

# EXHIBIT 2 (*continued*)

**Senator Murray**: I was ultraconservative in that period myself, and I bought some Chase National Bank in 1929 and found that it wasn't everything that Chase National Bank stock was represented to be.

**Mr. Kleitz**: Well, I'm sorry that Wall Street hasn't a more capable defender at this moment than the man who sits in this chair because I do not feel competent to engage in the defense of Wall Street.

**Senator Murray**: Mr. Aldrich of the Chase National Bank appeared before a subcommittee of the Senate back here in 1938, and he attempted at that time to blame the recession of 1938 on the administration, on the Government and the New Deal, claiming that as a result of the New Deal activities in this country we had brought on a fog of fear and uncertainty in the minds of businessmen and that they were afraid to invest their money and that that was what caused the recession in 1938. But on cross-examination he didn't support that theory and admitted that all of those activities in Wall Street during the 1920s brought on that depression, and that the recession too was largely brought on because of their failure to cooperate with the Government in that period. So that I think you have done pretty well in representing the banking fraternity of New York in opposition to this bill, because that seems to be the general position taken by the conservative elements in American enterprise everywhere.

**Mr. Kleitz**: Of course, Senator Murray, it isn't only the banking fraternity in New York that are opposed to it. The Commerce and Industry Association, for one, has . . .

**Senator Murray**: Well, the small retailers, the representatives of the small retail establishments, small business concerns of the country, don't take that position. We had a man here the other day from Louisville, Ky., the head of a department store down there, who represents an association of retail dealers, and he was just 100 percent for this bill and pointed out that it was absolutely necessary, and pointed out the fact that we were late in having it enacted.

**Mr. Kleitz**: I would be the last to deny that there is room for an honest difference of opinion of this subject. I am merely stating what I know to be the opinion of the institution with which I am associated, and what I conceive to be the opinion of a great many business people that I meet and talk with.
    Shall I proceed, Mr. Chairman?

**Senator Murray**: Yes.

**The Chairman**: Yes.

**Mr. Kleitz**: The crucial danger in all this lies in the grave risk—I am tempted to say the certainty—that the guaranty cannot be made good without destroying free competitive enterprise in the process. Jobs are created by private employers, and the number of jobs available at any time depends on a large and complex set of conditions over which no one in a free society

## EXHIBIT 2 (*concluded*)

has control. As soon as, and to the extent that, such control is undertaken, the society ceases to be free. To make good a guaranty of full employment, a government must have control over the conditions that determine employment, and these conditions include production, consumption, prices, wages, working hours, and other working conditions, savings, investment, and even continuity of political policy itself. An unlimited commitment for full employment requires a government of unlimited powers.

**Senator Lucas**: If your theory is correct, then it would become necessary for this Government not only to continue the wartime controls, but to strengthen them.

**Mr. Kleitz**: I think that is one of the means by which the policy would have to be implemented.

May I say that it is quite apparent to me what I understand by this guaranteed full employment is quite different from what the writers and the sponsors of this bill understand. But I feel that the danger of this bill is the very large number of people in this country that will understand in this bill what I understand in it.

**Senator Lucas**: There may be propaganda along that line, of course, throughout the press and, by the bankers and people who disagree with this bill. That is what I said a while ago, that I do not believe your statement is a fair picture. I think the implication is unfair. I may be wrong. If your statement is correct, it would become necessary, as I see it, for this Government to continue all controls the same as we had in wartime, and not only that, but to strengthen them. On the other hand, we see the President of the United States and his executive departments getting rid of all controls as fast as they possibly can.

**Mr. Kleitz**: Yes; and I refer to that in my statement later on.

**Senator Lucas**: But that is a challenging statement, it seems to me, as far as the administration is concerned and those in charge of this bill. The mere fact that we are obliterating these controls overnight is a challenge to your statement that by the full employment bill we are now seeking to put across we would require more controls than we have at the present time to make it work.

Source: Committee on Banking and Currency. Full Employment Act of 1945: Hearings on S. 380. 79th Cong., 1st Sess., 1945, pp. 521–28, 537–40.

## EXHIBIT 3

### *The Employment Act of 1946*

An act to declare a national policy on employment, production, and purchasing power, and for other purposes.

## EXHIBIT 3 (*continued*)

Be it enacted by the Senate and House of Representatives of the United States of America in Congress assembled. That:

### SHORT TITLE

Sec. 1. This act may be cited as the "Employment Act of 1946."

### DECLARATION OF POLICY

Sec. 2. The Congress hereby declares that it is the continuing policy and responsibility of the Federal Government to use all practicable means consistent with its needs and obligations and other essential considerations of national policy, with the assistance and cooperation of industry, agriculture, labor, and state and local governments, to coordinate and utilize all its plans, functions, and resources for the purpose of creating and maintaining, in a manner calculated to foster and promote free competitive enterprise and the general welfare, conditions under which there will be afforded useful employment opportunities, including self-employment, for those able, willing, and seeking to work, and to promote maximum employment, production, and purchasing power.

### ECONOMIC REPORT OF THE PRESIDENT

Sec. 3. (a) The President shall transmit to the Congress within sixty days after the beginning of each regular session (commencing with the year 1947) an economic report (hereinafter called the "Economic Report") setting forth (1) the levels of employment, production, and purchasing power obtaining in the United States and such levels needed to carry out the policy declared in section 2; (2) current and foreseeable trends in the levels of employment, production, and purchasing power; (3) a review of the economic program of the Federal Government and a review of economic conditions affecting employment in the United States or any considerable portion thereof during the preceding year and of their effect upon employment, production, and purchasing power; and (4) a program for carrying out the policy declared in section 2, together with such recommendations for legislation as he may deem necessary or desirable.

(b) The President may transmit from time to time to the Congress reports supplementary to the Economic Report, each of which shall include such supplementary or revised recommendations as he may deem necessary or desirable to achieve the policy declared in section 2.

(c) The Economic Report, and all supplementary reports transmitted under subsection (b), shall, when transmitted to Congress, be referred to the joint committee created by section 5.

# EXHIBIT 3 (*continued*)

## COUNCIL OF ECONOMIC ADVISERS TO THE PRESIDENT

Sec. 4. (a) There is hereby created in the Executive Office of the President a Council of Economic Advisers (hereinafter called the "Council"). The council shall be composed of three members who shall be appointed by the President, by and with the advice and consent of the Senate, and each of whom shall be a person who, as a result of his training, experience, and attainments, is exceptionally qualified to analyze and interpret economic developments, to appraise programs and activities of the government in the light of the policy declared in section 2, and to formulate and recommend national economic policy to promote employment, production, and purchasing power under free competitive enterprise. Each member of the council shall receive compensation at the rate of $15,000 per annum. The President shall designate one of the members of the council as chairman and one as vice chairman, who shall act as chairman in the absence of the chairman.

(b) The council is authorized to employ, and fix the compensation of, such specialists and other experts as may be necessary for the carrying out of its functions under this Act, without regard to the civil-service laws and the Classification Act of 1923, as amended, and is authorized, subject to the civil-service laws, to employ such other officers and employees as may be necessary for carrying out its functions under this Act, and fix their compensation in accordance with the Classification Act of 1923, as amended.

(c) It shall be the duty and function of the council—(1) to assist and advise the President in the preparation of the Economic Report; (2) to gather timely and authoritative information concerning economic developments and economic trends both current and prospective, to analyze and interpret such information in the light of the policy declared in section 2 for the purpose of determining whether such developments and trends are interfering, or are likely to interfere, with the achievement of such policy, and to compile and submit to the President studies relating to such developments and trends; (3) to appraise the various programs and activities of the Federal Government in the light of the policy declared in section 2 for the purpose of determining the extent to which such programs and activities are contributing, and the extent to which they are not contributing, to the achievement of such policy, and to make recommendations to the President with respect thereto; (4) to develop and recommend to the President national economic policies to foster and promote free competitive enterprise, to avoid economic fluctuations or to diminish the effects thereof, and to maintain employment, production, and purchasing power; (5) to make and furnish such studies, reports thereon, and recommendations with respect to matters of federal economic policy and legislation as the President may request.

(d) The council shall make an annual report to the President in December of each year.

# EXHIBIT 3 (*continued*)

(e) In exercising its powers, functions and duties under this Act—(1) the council may constitute such advisory committees and may consult with such representatives of industry, agriculture, labor, consumers, state and local governments, and other groups, as it deems advisable; (2) the council shall, to the fullest extent possible, utilize the services, facilities, and information (including statistical information) of other government agencies as well as of private research agencies, in order that duplication of effort and expense may be avoided.

(f) To enable the council to exercise its powers, functions, and duties under this Act, there are authorized to be appropriated (except for the salaries of the members and the salaries of officers and employees of the council) such sums as may be necessary. For the salaries of the members and the salaries of officers and employees of the council, there is authorized to be appropriated not exceeding $345,000 in the aggregate for each fiscal year.

## JOINT COMMITTEE ON THE ECONOMIC REPORT

Sec. 5. (a) There is hereby established a Joint Committee on the Economic Report, to be composed of seven Members of the Senate, to be appointed by the President of the Senate, and seven Members of the House of Representatives to be appointed by the Speaker of the House of Representatives. The party representation on the joint committee shall as nearly as may be feasible reflect the relative membership of the majority and minority parties in the Senate and House of Representatives.

(b) It shall be the function of the joint committee—(1) to make a continuing study of matters relating to the Economic Report; (2) to study means of coordinating programs in order to further the policy of this act; and (3) as a guide to the several committees of the Congress dealing with the legislation relating to the Economic Report, not later than May 1 of each year (beginning with the year 1947) to file a report with the Senate and the House of Representatives containing its findings and recommendations with respect to each of the main recommendations made by the President in the Economic Report, and from time to time to make such other reports and recommendations to the Senate and House of Representatives as it deems advisable.

(c) Vacancies in the membership of the joint committee shall not affect the power of the remaining members to execute the functions of the joint committee, and shall be filled in the same manner as in the case of the original selection. The joint committee shall select a chairman and a vice chairman from among its members.

(d) The joint committee, or any duly authorized subcommittee thereof, is authorized to hold such hearings as it deems advisable, and, within the limitations of its appropriations, the joint committee is empowered to appoint and fix the compensation of such experts, consultants, technicians, and clerical and stenographic

## EXHIBIT 3 (*concluded*)

assistants, to procure such printing and binding, and to make such expenditures, as it deems necessary and advisable. The cost of stenographic services, to report hearings of the joint committee, or any subcommittee thereof, shall not exceed 25 cents per hundred words. The joint committee is authorized to utilize the services, information, and facilities of the departments and establishments of the government, and also of private research agencies.

(e) There is hereby authorized to be appropriated for each fiscal year, the sum of $450,000, or so much thereof as may be necessary to carry out the provisions of this section, to be disbursed by the Secretary of the Senate on vouchers signed by the chairman and vice chairman.

Approved February 20, 1946.

## EXHIBIT 4

**Selected Statistics on the U.S. Economy**

|                    | 1929–32  | 1932–39 | 1939–44 | 1944–46 |
|--------------------|----------|---------|---------|---------|
| Real GNP           | (10.9%)  | 5.5%    | 11.5%   | (7.0%)  |
| Government Spending | 3.2     | 5.5     | 38.9    | (48.4)  |
| Export             | (15.6)   | 5.0     | 5.3     | 60.6    |
| Imports            | (13.8)   | 4.0     | 9.0     | (8.6)   |

|                        | 1939   | 1940  | 1941 | 1942  | 1943  | 1944  | 1945  | 1946  |
|------------------------|--------|-------|------|-------|-------|-------|-------|-------|
| Inflation              | (1.5%) | 1.50  | 7.7  | 12.3  | 7.2   | 2.3   | 2.6   | 11.8  |
| Unemployment           | 17.2%  | 14.60 | 9.9  | 4.7   | 1.9   | 1.2   | 1.9   | 3.9   |
| Armed Forces           | .4m    | .54   | 1.6  | 4.0   | 9.0   | 11.4  | 11.4  | 3.5   |
| Labor Force            | 56.0m  | 56.00 | 58.0 | 60.0  | 65.0  | 66.0  | 65.0  | 61.0  |
| Civilian Employment    | 46.0m  | 48.00 | 50.0 | 54.0  | 54.0  | 54.0  | 53.0  | 55.0  |
| Federal Employment     | .9m    | 1.0   | 1.3  | 2.2   | 2.9   | 2.9   | 2.9   | 2.9   |
| 2.2                    |        |       |      |       |       |       |       |       |
| Average Weekly Wage    | $ 57   | $59   | $67  | $ 75  | $ 83  | $ 86  | $ 82  | $ 74  |
| National Debt          | $436   | $45   | $56  | $102  | $154  | $212  | $253  | $230  |

# CASE 24

# *Regulatory Agencies* *

The term *regulatory agencies* is broad enough to encompass the entire range of public and private institutions involved in the regulation of economic activity. In its common meaning, the term pertains chiefly to that group of boards and commissions which in the states regulates public utility enterprises, and in the federal government regulates such industries as transportation and broadcasting, and such general aspects of economic life as competition and product safety.

Despite their extraordinary diversity, most regulatory agencies in the United States exhibit several common characteristics. Most commissions, whether state or federal, are appointed by the executive, are nonpartisan or bipartisan by law, and are supposedly expert in their fields. The typical regulatory statute delegates broad discretionary powers and avoids specific details. Most regulation occurs at the borderlands of politics, law, and economics, and those who have shaped its evolution have come from these three fields. Of the three, the first two have tended to overshadow the third, and considerations of politics and legal process have customarily triumphed over those of economic efficiency. Even so, the single most important context in which regulators have had to operate has been the inherent economic nature of the industries under regulation.

Historically speaking, the onset of regulation usually occurred in response to an identifiable crisis in a particular industry. To be sure, not all crises produced

---

*This case consists of an article by Professor Thomas K. McCraw which originally appeared in Glenn Porter, ed., *Encyclopedia of American Economic History* vol. II (New York: Scribners, 1980), pp. 788–807.

regulation; but regulation practically never emerged in the absence of some severe exigency that injured the industry itself, some other industry, or the consuming public.

The historical epoch during which most such crises occurred ranged roughly from the 1870s through the 1930s, with a second wave of social and environmental regulation beginning in the 1960s. Prior to the first wave, most Americans who thought about the matter probably agreed with Adam Smith that market competition was the natural and best regulator of prices and outputs. But industrialization and the rise of big business in the mid-19th century suddenly made competition inadequate to meet some of the economic needs of the society. For one thing, the great virtue of the Smithian market as regulator—its ability to respond at once to changes in supply or demand—defined it as a short-range mechanism. Unassisted, the market could not promote long-run goals such as the equitable distribution of wealth and income, or the preservation of immeasurable aesthetic or ecological values. More important for the onset of regulation, competition alone could not accommodate certain profound changes in the industrial system, notably the rise of enterprises based on scale economies, with such huge fixed costs that they could not be sensibly risked to the vagaries of the classical market. The new processes of production and marketing gave rise to regulatory mechanisms, particularly in the private sector, as they changed the fundamental structure of the business system itself: thus the emergence of the oligopoly, the trade association, the rate bureau, and the price leadership phenomenon.

In the public sector, regulation first appeared for those industries that seemed distinctly out of the mainstream of the Smithian market system. Some of these industries were social overhead enterprises of critical significance to the economy as a whole, and of such an economic nature as to popularize the term *natural monopoly.* Since it obviously made no sense to have multiple competing railroad lines serving thinly settled areas or numerous systems of electrical power distribution for a single city, late 19th-century contemporaries began to question the efficacy of market competition as a regulator. Of what use was Adam Smith's model of numberless buyers and sellers in regulating industries with only one seller or only a few?

Perceptions of the failure of competition derived more from experience than from theory; the normal process was trial and error. In the early days of the railroad and electric utility industries, state and city governments often attempted to regulate through the granting of charters or franchises to numerous competing groups and occasionally to all comers. In neither industry did this kind of remedy work very well. Throughout the post–Civil War period the railroads showed an inexorable tendency toward consolidation into ever-larger systems. Even the great trunk lines, denied government permission to divide their traffic by pooling, took the alternative route to "certainty" by developing self-contained, integrated networks with exclusive feeder lines branching into the hinterlands of their major routes. Similarly, from the 1880s well into the 20th century, competing gas and electric companies throughout urban America merged into single systems serving entire metropolitan areas, sometimes with higher costs to the consumer but usually with greatly improved service.

The reasons behind the inclination of railroads and utilities toward natural monopoly tended in turn to shape the methods of regulation selected to replace competition. The central characteristics of natural monopoly are decreasing unit costs over the whole range of possible outputs—in other words, virtually unlimited economies of scale—and a very high ratio of fixed costs to variable costs, so that a large initial investment is necessary to enter the market. These traits obviously applied to railroads, which had to purchase and develop rights-of-way, construct and maintain roadbeds and tracks, and acquire expensive locomotives and rolling stock before they could carry a single passenger or a ton of cargo. But once these facilities were in operation, they could transport numerous passengers and very heavy cargos without much additional expense. The same characteristics may be observed for electric utilities, which had to construct generation and distribution facilities, both at tremendous costs, before they could sell a single kilowatt-hour to a customer. The waste involved in building duplicate railroad or electric facilities at very great cost constitutes the core of the natural monopoly concept. It also underlies the unusual situation in which, for certain industries, monopoly is inherently more efficient than competition. For this reason, commission regulation first emerged in part as a surrogate for the lost discipline of a market system that bore little relevance to the railroad and utility industries. At the time, few observers realized that natural monopoly was a static notion that the dynamism of industrial technology might eventually overtake.

As the economic need for regulation became apparent, lawyers searched for a legal foundation on which to base it. They located it in the doctrine of "affectation with a public interest." Derived from ancient English precedent and from 19th-century American riparian law, the doctrine held that such industries as railroads and utilities so impinged on the public welfare that they stood clearly apart from the normal run of enterprise. They were therefore subject to the regulatory powers of the state, even unto the prices they might charge. A corollary was that drafters of legislation often cited the "public interest" doctrine when they wrote regulatory statutes. Such phrases as "the public good" appeared in such laws as that which created the first modern regulatory agency, the Massachusetts Board of Railroad Commissioners, in 1869.

Afterward, the repetition of "public interest" and similar phrases became a distinguishing mark of both the law and the ideology of regulation. Often "public interest" purported to serve as a rudimentary guide for regulators, a general standard for them to observe in the discharge of their quasi-legislative, quasi-executive, quasi-judicial duties. Legislators' heavy reliance on "public interest"—a high-minded but vague and sometimes meaningless basis for decision—together with their avoidance of precise instructions to regulatory agencies, has produced mixed results, as might be expected. Although commissions have enjoyed a helpful freedom of action in setting their policies, they have often failed to develop clear standards of permissible business behavior or precise criteria for some of their own decisions. They have thereby opened themselves to charges of arbitrariness, caprice, and sometimes corruption.

In law the "public interest" doctrine, latitudinarian in aim, grew gradually more restrictive in impact as successive Supreme Court majorities applied it negatively, not to justify the regulation of industries within the category but to prevent the regulation of those outside it. In truth, the doctrine itself could be a semantic trap, as Justice Harlan F. Stone explained in a dissenting opinion of 1927: "To say that only those businesses affected with a public interest may be regulated is but another way of stating that all those businesses which may be regulated are affected with a public interest." Ultimately the Supreme Court overruled the restrictive thrust of the "public interest" doctrine and in effect opened the way for broader affirmative regulation under the commerce clause of the Constitution.

In the meantime "public interest," in its nonlegal but equally ambiguous common usage, continued to undergird the ideology of regulation. In some respects the very basis of public regulation has always depended on the existence of a definable public interest, however elusive the definition. The theoretically perfect regulatory agency is still conceived much as it was more than a century ago: as an apolitical, specialized, expert tribunal devoted to the pursuit of the public interest and concerned with both the complex details and the broad policy questions raised by industrialization and the partial failure of the competitive market. Few commissions, either state or federal, have quite come up to this ideal.

## State Commissions

The first modern regulatory agencies were state commissions created to deal with the multitudinous problems associated with railroads. As organizations, the railroad corporations dwarfed all others in American life, public or private. As the first big business in the nation, they exemplified most of the problems later associated with that institution: corporate arrogance and corruption, the decline of entrepreneurial opportunity, the disproportionate division of wealth and power. Since they took the corporate form from the very beginning and since they wielded the power of eminent domain, the early railroads required charters from the states in which they operated. They therefore were enmeshed in state politics, and from the 1830s until the 1880s regulatory activity centered in the states.

The earliest commissions were formed in New England. The most significant of these agencies was that of Massachusetts, created in 1869 and dominated during its first decade by Charles Francis Adams, Jr., descendant of two presidents and one of the leading rail experts in the nation. Adams explained in 1868, during his campaign for a commission, why a new instrumentality must supplement legislative committees if regulation were to be effective: "Those committees are eternally fluctuating, are not peculiarly well informed, judiciously selected, or free from bias." What was needed, wrote Adams, was a group of detached, apolitical experts organized into specialized agencies:

> Work hitherto badly done, spasmodically done, superficially done, ignorantly done, and too often corruptly done by temporary and irresponsible legislative committees, is

in future to be reduced to order and science by the labors of permanent bureaus, and placed by them before legislatures for intelligent action. The movement springs up everywhere; it is confined to no one country and no one body. . . .[1]

Conscious of the transcendent importance of railroads in the regional and national economies, and of their anomalous position as gigantic intruders into a democratic polity, Adams preached that the interests of the corporations must somehow be harmonized with those of the general public. He especially believed that railroad policy must promote the economic growth of the state of Massachusetts. Implicitly defining the public interest as the maximizing of passenger and freight traffic, Adams sought to induce rail managers to manipulate their rates to promote economic development: low rates for raw materials such as coal and iron, recouped by slightly higher ones on manufactured items that could more easily bear the cost.

Adams consistently played down the exercise of raw power by the commission, in the belief that good sense and informed opinion would better harmonize the interests of the railroads and the public. Accordingly, his major effort went into systematic study of the "railroad problem" in all its aspects, and subsequent publication of his findings. The annual reports of the Board of Railroad Commissioners during Adams' tenure from 1869 to 1879 remain among the clearest, most insightful set of reports ever produced by any state or federal regulatory agency. They reflect his conception of the proper role of regulation: "The board of commissioners was set up as a sort of lens by means of which the otherwise scattered rays of public opinion could be concentrated to a focus and brought to bear upon a given point."

The Massachusetts agency became a national prototype of the "weak" commission, a model for many other states that wished to regulate railroads but, for one reason or another, did not wish to assume the power of setting rates and fares. In one respect the designation "weak" is deceptive, for in Massachusetts the legislature stood behind the orders of the board, took its advice, and shaped state railroad policy in accordance with its recommendations. The commission itself deliberately relied on voluntary compliance, recognizing the inherent indeterminacy and ambivalence of the relationship between the roads and the public. It all added up to a precise reversal of previous state railroad policy, which had produced very strong regulatory statutes that everyone ignored and that therefore constituted an embarrassing impotence. The extraordinary success of the Massachusetts agency may be attributed to Adams' powers as an analyst and publicist, his historically revered name, and the diversity of the economy of the state, which did not encourage simple dichotomies of merchant versus farmer or people versus corporations. Accepting the dysfunctional role of competition as a regulator of railroads, Adams and his colleagues promoted standardization of methods and procedures, accepted consolidation as inevitable, and endeavored to show how monopoly could as easily serve the shipper and passenger as hurt them.

---

[1]Charles Francis Adams, Jr., "Boston," in *North American Review* 106 (Jan. 1868), p. 18.

An alternative to the "weak" commission appeared in the early 1870s, in the states of Illinois, Wisconsin, Minnesota, and Iowa. Beginning in 1871, their legislatures passed statutes directly regulating the rates of roads operating within each state and, in three cases, creating "strong" commissions. These agencies had powers to prescribe maximum rates and to adjust the discriminatory rate structures ordinarily used by railroads. In contradistinction to their popular generic name, these "Granger laws," reflected the ire of bucolic citizens less than they did mercantile rivalries among cities that served as transshipment points for agricultural commodities, and between areas with adequate rail service and those to which the roads had not yet penetrated. More important for the overall evolution of regulatory agencies, they represented a path seriously considered but ultimately abandoned and thus were another way station on the inexorable march toward federal regulation. For various reasons the Granger laws did not prove as effective as their proponents had hoped, and most of them were repealed within a few years of enactment because of political counterattacks by the railroads or because of the depression conditions of the 1870s, which drove down rates throughout the nation faster than regulatory agencies could hope to do, or because of the inflexibility inherent in the performance of the pricing functions of giant interstate corporations by small state agencies. In law the "Granger cases" (1877) established the power of public agencies to regulate, but in practice the Granger commissions failed to surpass the successes of their "weak" counterparts in the East.

The model "weak" commission, that of Massachusetts, continued to enjoy a measure of national prestige even after the departure of Adams in 1879. Such decline as its reputation did suffer occurred over a long period and reflected several tendencies common to state regulatory agencies. For one thing, after the onset of federal railroad regulation in 1887, the focus of state regulatory efforts shifted gradually to public utilities. A second problem of the Massachusetts board was its failure, after the first generation of its existence, to attract the best-quality personnel. This problem had plagued practically all regulatory agencies, and it constitutes the signal failure of the regulatory experience in America.

The shift in focus from railroads to public utilities came more rapidly in Massachusetts than in other states, but the transition there may be taken as a typical institutional evolution. Building on the railroad model of 1869, the state in 1885 created the Board of Gas Commissioners. In 1887, this agency became the Board of Gas and Electric Light Commissioners, with general supervisory powers over the companies under its jurisdiction, but—following the railroad pattern—with no strong authority over rates. In 1909, both the original railroad board and the gas and electric commission received new powers over security issues. Four years later the railroad commission became the Public Service Commission, with additional responsibility for telephone companies, street railways, and steamships. The final step in consolidation occurred in 1919 as the state merged its railroad and utility commissions into one and named the new body the Department of Public Utilities. This agency still exists, having evolved over a century from the original three-member Board of Railroad Commissioners, with its single staff member, to a small bureaucracy of more than one hundred full-time employees housed in a government office building in downtown Boston.

Much the same pattern of institutional growth occurred in state after state as the industrial economy matured. The significant leaders in public utility regulation were New York and Wisconsin, both of which revised their commission laws in 1907 and thereby inaugurated the modern system of "rate-of-return" regulation (explained in detail below). As commissions evolved in the states, they took jurisdiction over new industries such as trucking, telephone communications, and natural gas production. Sometimes an agency created to deal with one problem, such as the Texas Railroad Commission, later spent its energies on quite another, such as the control of output by the oil wells in the state. The names of these commissions, and the industries they regulate, vary from state to state. So does the degree of regulatory authority, which ranges from general supervision to detailed pricing powers. All state commissions now have jurisdiction over gas and electric utilities, the only exceptions being Nebraska, the public power state, and South Dakota, where municipalities grant permits and set rates. The jurisdiction of most state commissions does not extend to publicly owned utilities or to rural cooperatives.

In addition, a number of other industries are regulated by state commissions, including the following:

|  | *Number of States* |
| --- | --- |
| Railroads | 47 |
| Motor buses | 47 |
| Telephone/telegraph | 45 |
| Common carrier trucks | 44 |
| Water supply | 42 |
| Contract carrier trucks | 41 |
| Petroleum pipelines | 24 |
| Steam heating | 23 |
| Taxicabs | 21 |
| Air transport | 18 |
| Sewers | 18 |
| Water carriers | 18 |
| Street railways | 13 |
| Toll roads and bridges | 10 |
| Warehouses | 10 |
| Community antenna television | 10 |

In many states, service on commissions is a virtual sinecure, with light duties and low prestige. In others, seats on regulatory agencies are avidly sought and often go to highly qualified professionals. Most state commissions have three members, but again the range is broad, from one in Oregon to seven in South Carolina. The typical term of office is six years, with terms staggered so as to minimize turnover. In 36 states the governor appoints the members of regulatory agencies. In 12 others they are elected by the voters, and in two they are appointed by the state legislature. In 25 states the governor also appoints the chairperson; in 20 he or she is elected by the commissioners themselves and in the other five is chosen by some alternative means, such as rotation. About half the states require by law or custom that the minority party be represented on their commissions. By a very wide margin, the profession most typical of state commissioners is that of attorney—a fact indicative of the past and present values and preoccupations of regulatory agencies and significant for understanding their devotion to due process, as distinct from their economic performance.

Organizationally the commissions are as varied as the states themselves. Some are set up along functional lines, others along product division lines, and a few both functionally and divisionally (see Figures 1A and B). Some are tiny agencies that could not behave like bureaucracies even if they wished to do so. Others are large, complex organizations with major segments assigned to specialized aspects of the regulatory process.

The New York Public Service Commission, for example, a pioneer in utility regulation shortly after the beginning of the twentieth century, had grown by the 1970s to a sizable bureaucracy employing some seven hundred persons and spending about $15 million annually. The chairman of the New York commission was the highest-paid state or federal regulator in the nation, with a salary in the 1970s in excess of $50,000. The functions of the agency, which in most respects other than scale are typical of state commissions, may be inferred from the following list of its professional staff members:

| | |
|---|---:|
| Inspectors and investigators | 103 |
| Engineers | 57 |
| Auditors | 54 |
| Accountants | 28 |
| Attorneys | 21 |
| Administrative staff | 14 |
| Rate analysts | 13 |
| Hearing examiners (lawyers) | 13 |
| Economists | 8 |

# Rate Regulation

The most important aspects of state public utility regulation have to do with rates. The basic premises of the agencies, almost from the beginning, have been acceptance of the natural monopoly concept and reliance on the "rate-of-return" method. Problems with the method originated in the Supreme Court case of *Smyth* v. *Ames* (1898), in which the Union Pacific Railroad challenged a Nebraska statute that specified the maximum freight rates the corporation could charge. The court ruled that the railroad was entitled to a "reasonable" return on "the fair value of

## FIGURE 1A

The Evolution of Commissions

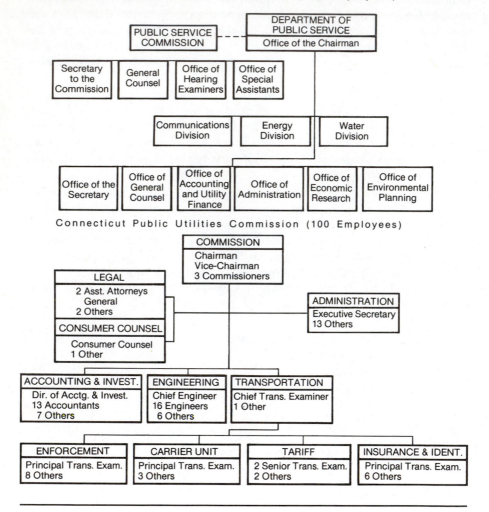

New York Public Service Commission (700 Employees)

Connecticut Public Utilities Commission (100 Employees)

the property being used for the convenience of the public." In enunciating this "fair value" doctrine, the court inadvertently opened a Pandora's box that would plague lawyers, accountants, economists, and commissioners for the next two generations. At various times particular commissions or the Supreme Court have included in "fair value" such considerations as the original cost of the property, less depreciation (the consumer's view in periods of inflation); the cost of reproducing the same property (the view of the corporation in periods of inflation); the

# FIGURE 1B

## The Evolution of Commissions

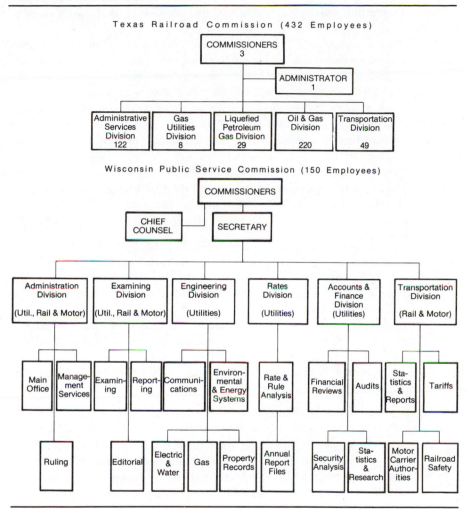

market value of the stocks and bonds of the corporation; and numerous other major and minor factors.

After deciding on the allowable rate base, commissions must specify the rate of return. Historically, state agencies have set allowable rates of return at some figure roughly between 5 and 8 percent of the rate base. In the 1970s, the allowable percentage exceeded 10 percent, in response to rising capital costs and inflation. Although this percentage has been the subject of considerable controversy (should it equal the rate of return on other, nonutility enterprises? the cost of capital to the

utility?), the major problems associated with public utility regulation have clustered around the rate base. If the percentage rate of return is to be multiplied by
the rate base, then clearly the latter is quite as decisive a figure as the former. The
revenue of the utility will depend as much on the rate base as on the percentage of
return.

From the adjudication of *Smyth* v. *Ames* in 1898 until the ameliorating doctrine
in *Federal Power Commission* v. *Hope Natural Gas Co.* (1944), and to some extent even
afterward, utility commissions struggled with the "fair value" question in determining rate bases. No authoritative solution ever met with unanimous acceptance. In truth, courts and commissions might as well have attempted to make the
sun stand still as to make ultimate sense of "fair value." And even if they had, the
rate-of-return method would still have produced considerable mischief. At bottom, "fair return on fair value" is a cost-plus-formula, vulnerable to the many
problems associated with such pricing systems. Some of these problems appeared
early in the history of regulation, and several of them still trouble the state commissions. Such problems include the following:

1. Temptation to pad the rate base
2. Disincentives to cut costs and therefore to efficient operation
3. Temptation to shift diminished performance from raised prices to reduced
   quality of service
4. Creation of a strong prejudice to emphasize capital inputs over others, in
   order to augment the rate base
5. "Regulatory lag," in which the typically tedious deliberations of the commission take so long that they begin to apply more to obsolete situations
   than to present or future requirements
6. The problem of boundaries, in which one part of an enterprise is a natural
   monopoly but another is not.

These problems have promoted the rise of ingenious accounting methods
within regulated industries, all calculated to maximize revenues in the face of limitations on rates of return. At worst, they have made the process of rate regulation
a peculiar type of charade, serving cultural imperatives more than economic efficiency. In practice, even the rate-of-return method has in recent years been applied more or less opposite to the original theory. The procedure varies from state
to state, but in essence it is as follows: the commission determines the total revenue requirements of the utility, then computes the price mix that will yield the required revenue. To do this, the commission selects a "test year," which may be an
average of recent years, a projected typical year in the future, or some combination of hypothetical and actual years. The regulated firm then produces a proposed budget for the test year, showing its actual or anticipated expenses, broken
down into categories required by the standardized accounting procedures of the
commission. After scrutiny by the commission, the budget is adjusted according
to the recommendations of the professional staff of the agency.

Full-scale rate cases are laborious proceedings that do not occur every year. In
general, the regulatory process is less formal, characterized as much by negotia-

tion and compromise as by litigation and other adversary contests. This circumstance has increased the vulnerability of commissions to charges of "capture" by the regulated interests. Historically, it is clear that "capture" has often occurred, but this result derives from other factors besides the informality of the regulatory process, among them the greater resources of the industries vis-á-vis the agencies and above all the importance of the health of the industries to the economy.

# Federal Regulation

State regulation of many industries has continued from its origins down to the present with no abatement of importance or of jurisdictional range. The movement from state to federal regulation, therefore, has been a selective one that has not occurred across the spectrum of regulated industries. As is obvious from the preceding discussion, for example, most public utilities have continued to be regulated principally by the states.

For several other industries, state regulation perforce yielded to federal. Typically the industry grew to such size or geographical extent as to render state boundaries irrelevant to its proper control. This kind of sequence illustrates once more the transcendent point that the inherent nature of an industry is often the decisive context in which regulatory agencies must operate.

As in so many other ways, the railroad industry set the pattern. In the late 19th century, as the "railroad problem" grew to national scope, its nature became more and more complex. In the East the problem sometimes took the form of excessive competition, with too many roads handling too little traffic. In the West and South, by contrast, it could take the form of too little competition. Whole communities complained of monopoly, as they depended on single railroad corporations for their very existence. And in all regions the railroads often exhibited tendencies toward frenzied finance, corporate arrogance, and discriminatory pricing practices that, however logically they might flow from the economics of railroading, nevertheless appeared to violate basic notions of fairness. And underlying the entire "railroad problem" was the political incongruity of a democratic society in the role of handmaiden to one of its industries.

Ultimately the railroad industry grew so powerful and vital to the national economy that continued reliance on state regulation was plainly futile. The final precipitant of federal entry into the situation was the Supreme Court decision in *Wabash, Saint Louis and Pacific Railroad Company* v. *Illinois* (1886). In it the court ruled that commerce originating or ending beyond the boundaries of a state was beyond the power of that state to regulate, even though the federal government had not otherwise provided for its regulation. This doctrine partially overturned the previous rulings of the Supreme Court in the Granger cases, and it made the resort to federal regulation all but inevitable.

In 1883, Senator Shelby M. Cullom, a Republican from Illinois, had introduced a bill that provided for a federal railroad commission that would administer a general and flexible set of guidelines. The *Wabash* decision swung majority support to Cullom's bill, and the Interstate Commerce Commission was created in

1887. By that time a virtual national consensus had developed in favor of federal regulation. Merchants, farmers, passengers, politicians, and even many railroad men had become convinced, after years of trial and error with other methods, that serious federal railroad regulation was essential.

The greatest significance of the Interstate Commerce Act of 1887 lay in its creation of the prototype federal regulatory tribunal. Most of the later federal commissions were more or less patterned on the ICC in appointment and tenure of members and in relationships with the legislative, executive, and judicial branches of government (see Figure 2). It is a measure of the success the ICC had in its first 50 years, or was perceived as having had, that the pattern was so often repeated in the creation of new agencies.

## Federal Regulatory Agencies and Their Functions

The Interstate Commerce Commission (ICC) began life in 1887 with several missions, not all of which were easily consistent with each other or with the inherent nature of the railroad industry. The Interstate Commerce Act forbade pooling, rebating, and—with certain important exceptions—rate discrimination between long-haul and short-haul traffic. The statute insisted that railroad rates be "just and reasonable"; and it provided a new arena, the ICC, in which determinations of reasonableness could occur. The five members of the commission were to be appointed by the president and confirmed by the Senate for staggered terms of six (later seven) years. No more than three of the five could come from one political party, and each commissioner was to receive an annual salary of $7,500, a very large sum for 1887. This salary, greater than that of any federal judge except those on the Supreme Court, was a reflection of the importance Congress attached to the new agency.

After an auspicious beginning under its influential and distinguished first chairman, Thomas M. Cooley, the ICC encountered severe difficulties with the courts. Led by the Supreme Court, the federal judiciary restricted the powers of the agency and reduced it, by the late 1890s, to a mere collector of data. The events of the next several decades constituted a dialectical process of adjustment, involving the commission, the courts, and Congress. In response to continuing problems within the railroad industry and problems between the ICC and the judiciary, Congress steadily added to the authority of the commission and broadened its jurisdiction. The highlights in this long process are listed below.

The Elkins Act (1903) gave teeth to the prohibition on rebating in the original Interstate Commerce Act.

The Hepburn Act (1906), gave the commission power to fix maximum rates, shifted the burden of proof in rate proceedings from the commission to the railroads, and made ICC decisions effective as soon as they were reached. It also gave the commission regulatory powers over petroleum pipelines.

The Mann-Elkins Act (1910) broadened the rate-making authority of the commission, reinforced the long-haul/short-haul rule, and created the Court of Commerce, a short-lived experiment in specialized judicial review.

**FIGURE 2**

Organizational Charts of Six Federal Regulatory Agencies

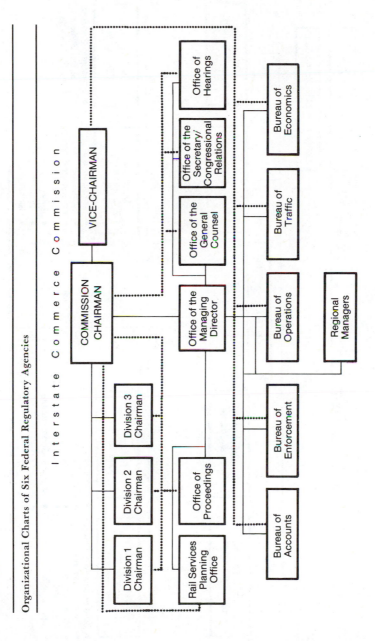

Interstate Commerce Commission

**FIGURE 2** *(continued)*

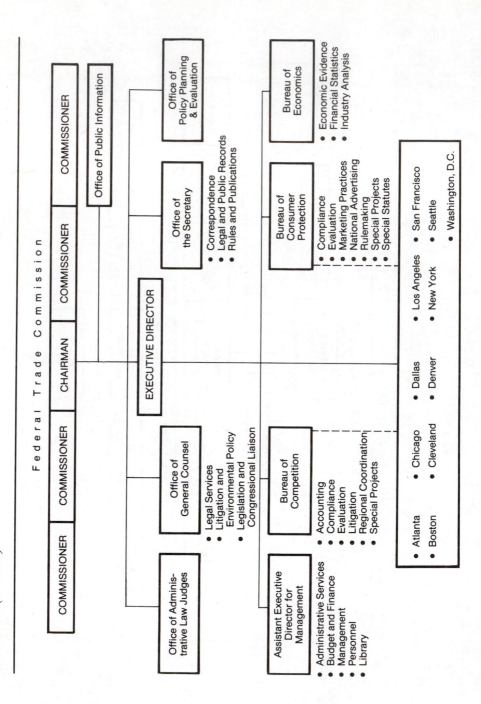

Federal Trade Commission

Federal Power Commission

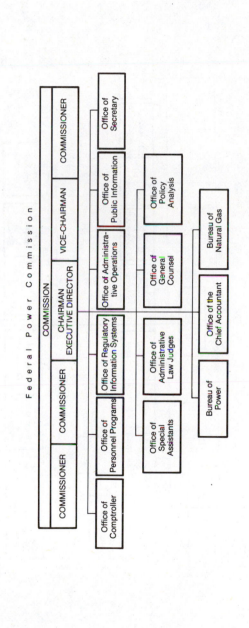

COMMISSION

COMMISSIONER | COMMISSIONER | CHAIRMAN / EXECUTIVE DIRECTOR | VICE-CHAIRMAN | COMMISSIONER

Office of Comptroller

Office of Personnel Programs

Office of Regulatory Information Systems

Office of Administrative Operations

Office of Public Information

Office of Secretary

Office of Special Assistants

Office of Administrative Law Judges

Office of General Counsel

Office of Policy Analysis

Bureau of Power

Office of the Chief Accountant

Bureau of Natural Gas

**FIGURE 2** *(continued)*

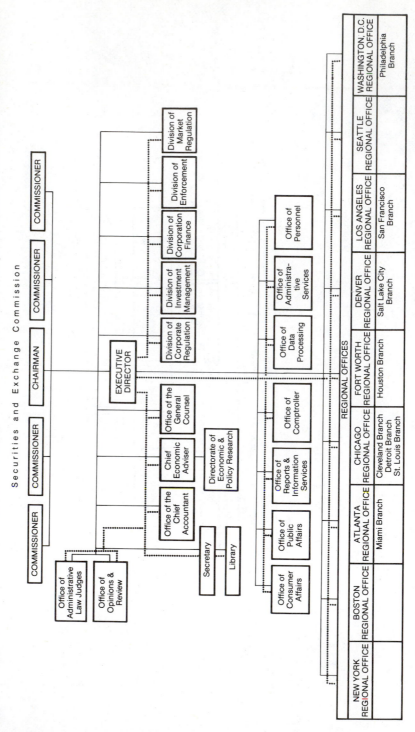

Securities and Exchange Commission

COMMISSIONER | COMMISSIONER | CHAIRMAN | COMMISSIONER | COMMISSIONER

Office of Administrative Law Judges
Office of Opinions & Review
Office of the Chief Accountant
Chief Economic Adviser
Office of the General Counsel
EXECUTIVE DIRECTOR
Directorate of Economic & Policy Research
Secretary
Library

Division of Corporate Regulation
Division of Investment Management
Division of Corporation Finance
Division of Enforcement
Division of Market Regulation

Office of Consumer Affairs
Office of Public Affairs
Office of Reports & Information Services
Office of Comptroller
Office of Data Processing
Office of Administrative Services
Office of Personnel

REGIONAL OFFICES

NEW YORK REGIONAL OFFICE | BOSTON REGIONAL OFFICE | ATLANTA REGIONAL OFFICE | CHICAGO REGIONAL OFFICE | FORT WORTH REGIONAL OFFICE | DENVER REGIONAL OFFICE | LOS ANGELES REGIONAL OFFICE | SEATTLE REGIONAL OFFICE | WASHINGTON, D.C. REGIONAL OFFICE

Miami Branch | Cleveland Branch Detroit Branch St. Louis Branch | Houston Branch | Salt Lake City Branch | San Francisco Branch | Philadelphia Branch

——— LINES OF POLICY AND JUDICIAL AUTHORITY

·········· LINES OF BUDGET AND MANAGEMENT AUTHORITY

Federal Communications Commission

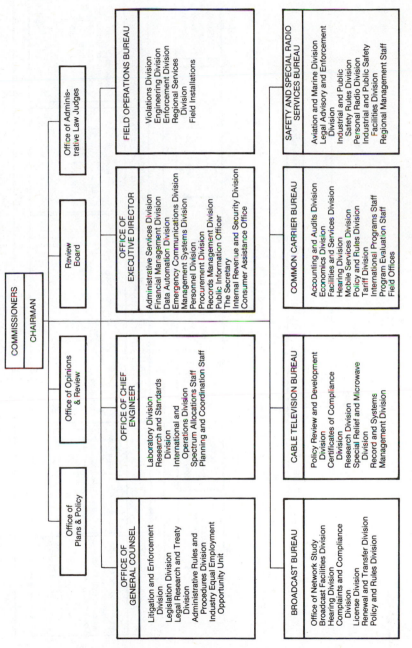

**COMMISSIONERS**

**CHAIRMAN**

Office of Plans & Policy

Office of Opinions & Review

Review Board

Office of Administrative Law Judges

**OFFICE OF GENERAL COUNSEL**

Litigation and Enforcement Division
Legislation Division
Legal Research and Treaty Division
Administrative Rules and Procedures Division
Industry Equal Employment Opportunity Unit

**OFFICE OF CHIEF ENGINEER**

Laboratory Division
Research and Standards Division
International and Operations Division
Spectrum Allocations Staff
Planning and Coordination Staff

**OFFICE OF EXECUTIVE DIRECTOR**

Administrative Services Division
Financial Management Division
Data Automation Division
Emergency Communications Division
Management Systems Division
Personnel Division
Procurement Division
Records Management Division
Public Information Officer
The Secretary
Internal Revenue and Security Division
Consumer Assistance Office

**FIELD OPERATIONS BUREAU**

Violations Division
Engineering Division
Enforcement Division
Regional Services Division
Field Installations

**BROADCAST BUREAU**

Office of Network Study
Broadcast Facilities Division
Hearing Division
Complaints and Compliance Division
License Division
Renewal and Transfer Division
Policy and Rules Division

**CABLE TELEVISION BUREAU**

Policy Review and Development Division
Certificates of Compliance Division
Research Division
Special Relief and Microwave Division
Record and Systems Management Division

**COMMON CARRIER BUREAU**

Accounting and Audits Division
Economics Division
Facilities and Services Division
Hearing Division
Mobile Services Division
Policy and Rules Division
Tariff Division
International Programs Staff
Program Evaluation Staff
Field Offices

**SAFETY AND SPECIAL RADIO SERVICES BUREAU**

Aviation and Marine Division
Legal Advisory and Enforcement Division
Industrial and Public Safety Rules Division
Personal Radio Division
Industrial and Public Safety Facilities Division
Regional Management Staff

**FIGURE 2** (*concluded*)

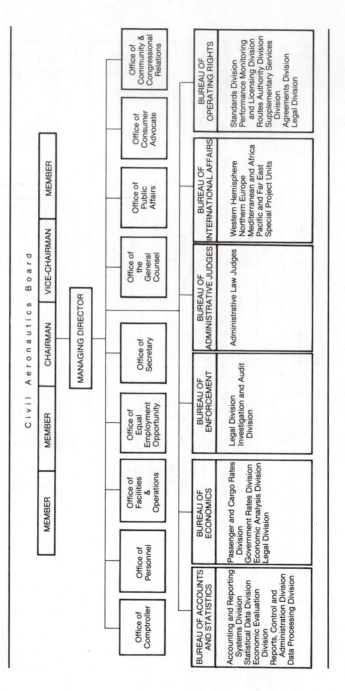

Civil Aeronautics Board

MEMBER | MEMBER | CHAIRMAN | VICE-CHAIRMAN | MEMBER

MANAGING DIRECTOR

Office of Personnel

Office of Facilities & Operations

Office of Equal Employment Opportunity

Office of Secretary

Office of the General Counsel

Office of Public Affairs

Office of Consumer Advocate

Office of Community & Congressional Relations

Office of Comptroller

BUREAU OF ACCOUNTS AND STATISTICS
Accounting and Reporting Systems Division
Statistical Data Division
Economic Evaluation Division
Reports, Control and Administration Division
Data Processing Division

BUREAU OF ECONOMICS
Passenger and Cargo Rates Division
Government Rates Division
Economic Analysis Division
Legal Division

BUREAU OF ENFORCEMENT
Legal Division
Investigation and Audit Division

BUREAU OF ADMINISTRATIVE JUDGES
Administrative Law Judges

BUREAU OF INTERNATIONAL AFFAIRS
Western Hemisphere
Northern Europe
Mediterranean and Africa
Pacific and Far East
Special Project Units

BUREAU OF OPERATING RIGHTS
Standards Division
Performance Monitoring and Licensing Division
Routes Authority Division
Supplementary Services Division
Agreements Division
Legal Division

The Transportation Act (Esch-Cummins Act) of 1920 empowered the commission to set minimum as well as maximum rates, to supervise the issuance of securities by carriers, and to approve the previously forbidden practice of pooling. It also instructed the ICC to undertake comprehensive studies toward a systematic and partially consolidated transportation network.

The Motor Carrier Act (1935) added the regulation of trucking to the missions of the ICC and thereby increased its work load substantially. The reasons for this measure involved the Great Depression and the ill health of the railroad industry, as well as a crisis in trucking. Unlike some common carriers, trucking did not tend toward natural monopoly, but its great flexibility permitted it to take the most profitable freights away from the railroads. The long reliance of the railroads on value-of-service rate making made the matter worse, and depression conditions necessitated action by Congress.

The Transportation Act of 1940 added domestic water carriers to the list of industries under ICC jurisdiction, continuing the trend toward regulation of all interstate transportation.

Throughout its history the ICC has remained controversial. Sometimes, as in the Progressive Era (1901–1920) it has been the target of industry criticism that it infringes on the prerogatives of management and wields pricing authority without responsibility for the consequences. More often, consumer groups have accused it of protecting the carriers at the expense of the general public. Sometimes critics with entirely different viewpoints have joined in blaming the ICC for the almost uninterrupted decline in rail service. But the most damning criticism of the ICC has been on the grounds of economic inefficiency. This line of argument holds that the commission has prevented competitive market forces from automatically selecting the optimal modes of moving different types of freight, and that it has thereby injected an institutional inefficiency into the national system of freight transport, at great cost to society.

The Federal Trade Commission (FTC), created in 1914, exhibits some of the characteristic patterns set by the ICC. Its five members are appointed for staggered terms, and only a bare majority may come from one political party. The commission is supposed to be "independent," that is, outside the three major branches of government but exercising some of the functions of each. On the other hand, the FTC differs from some regulatory agencies in that its jurisdiction stretches across the business establishment and is not confined to a single industry or group of industries. The original legislation was short and simple, and it left a great deal up to the agency itself. The most optimistic early promoters of the commission expected it to be a principal agent for settling the "trust" question in America, and even today the agency shares antitrust responsibilities with the Antitrust Division of the Department of Justice. Its other missions and duties include the investigation of particular industries, the regulation of advertising and branding, and the policing of "unfair methods of competition in commerce." The FTC has no pricing powers, as do state utility commissions and several federal agencies. Of the major federal commissions, it is the one most like a court in function and the one most clearly dominated by lawyers.

The recurring criticisms of the FTC, almost from the beginning, have held it to be unduly industry-minded, insufficiently aggressive in promoting competition, and too ready to expend its small resources on trivia.

The third federal regulatory commission to emerge was the Federal Power Commission (FPC: renamed Federal Energy Regulatory Agency in 1977), created by Congress in 1920 to deal with the waterpower question, a perennial problem of Progressive Era politics and a part of the larger issue of conservation. Unlike the ICC and the FTC, the FPC originally had little real "independence," being composed of three cabinet officers: the secretaries of the interior, war, and agriculture. This odd administrative setup reflected the intragovernmental disputes over jurisdiction that had seemed to make such a commission desirable in the first place. After a decade of unsatisfactory experience, Congress changed the organizational form of the agency to correspond to that of other regulatory bodies; and since then the FPC has shared the characteristics of its counterparts. A reorganizing statute of 1930 also gave the commission substantial authority over interstate rates for electricity, the security issues of electric power companies, and the licensing and valuation of hydroelectric projects. Its functions thus overlap those of the state utility commissions, and the FPC has had to pay close attention to fence-mending operations and administrative coordination.

Historically, the biggest problems of the FPC have come from its extremely heavy work load and from deep cleavages within American society over energy policy. The energy debate focused on electric power and the holding companies in the 1930s and was the subject of considerable New Deal legislation. In the late 1940s, the focus shifted to natural gas. Congress had given the FPC certain powers over this industry through the Natural Gas Act of 1938, but most observers believed that this act did not extend to the regulation of "field prices" for wellhead sales by hundreds of small producers. The commission, Congress, and the courts were each divided over this issue.

The resolution of the issue occurred with the Supreme Court decision in *Phillips Petroleum Company* v. *Wisconsin* (1954). After this ruling the FPC began to control the field prices of natural gas, even though most observers agreed that the industry bore little resemblance to the natural monopolies that are the most usual concerns of regulatory agencies. Economists in particular were critical of this portion of natural gas regulation. They pointed out that it tended to distort national patterns of fuel consumption, especially in periods of marked inflation and that it upset the normal business growth of an important industry.

The Radio Act of 1927 created the Federal Radio Commission, which in 1934 became the Federal Communications Commission (FCC). The Radio Act was a remarkably broad delegation of power, even for a regulatory statute. Behind federal entry into broadcasting lay an almost purely technological reason: the electromagnetic spectrum can accommodate only a finite number of broadcasters, and in the absence of some authority to allocate frequencies, competing users would create electronic chaos. Ranging from local police and citizens' band operators to the affiliates of national television networks, they constitute a heterogeneous mix of applicants. The chief tool of the FCC is the licensing power over stations: it may grant, renew, or deny at its discretion.

Analysts have pointed out that this "either-or" situation hampers effective regulation. Many contend that the denial of a license is too drastic a remedy; that, like the death penalty in criminal law, it is appropriate only in the most extreme cases. For the usual situations, some more moderate means of regulation would be more suitable. The FCC has made use of the "raised eyebrow" method to meet this need, and it has very seldom resorted to the ultimate power of license denial. Indeed, many of its critics think that it has been more cooperative with the broadcasting industry than is either necessary or wise. Economists have argued that FCC restrictions on entry into the business, and particularly the inhospitable stance toward cable television, have kept the industry too small, the offerings of commercial television too narrow, and the viewers' fare too standardized and uncontroversial. The industry itself has complained that the commission has sometimes tended to use its powers of allocation to serve a censorship function not intended by the Radio Act and forbidden by the First Amendment to the Constitution. Still other critics have charged that the FCC has done a lackluster job of regulating the telephone industry, a task it inherited in 1934 from the ICC, which had had jurisdiction since 1910.

In 1934, Congress created the fifth major federal regulatory agency, the Securities and Exchange Commission (SEC). Rightly or wrongly, most Americans blamed Wall Street for the stock market crash of 1929 and the ensuing depression. The Securities Act (1933) and the Securities Exchange Act (1934) responded to this conviction and to the obvious need for regulation of stock exchange practices. Like the FCC, the SEC uses the basic tool of licensing to serve its regulatory purposes. Before a company may issue securities, it must file with the commission a set of thoroughgoing registration forms that disclose information of possible use to investors. If the registration statement is defective or misleading about either the issue or the company, the commission may hold a hearing that could result in a "stop order," which suspends the effective date of the offering. In addition the SEC promulgates numerous rules pertaining to such matters as insider trading, proxy solicitations, and the governance of exchanges. The commission also adminsters parts of the Public Utility Holding Company Act of 1935, the Trust Indenture Act of 1939, and Chapter X of the Bankruptcy Act.

Of all the federal commissions, the SEC has probably achieved the highest reputation for effective performance. If it has not received the least criticism, then the criticism it has received has been the least persuasive. Its personnel, especially in the early years, were a cut above those of most agencies. (Its first four chairmen were Joseph P. Kennedy, James M. Landis, William O. Douglas, and Jerome Frank, an exceptionally distinguished quartet.) Moreover, the unpopularity of the securities industry during and after the Great Depression facilitated aggressive pursuit by the SEC of its mandate. Most attacks on the SEC have held that it sometimes has gone beyond the intent of Congress and involved itself in affairs that are none of its business. This line of criticism intensified after the 1960s, with respect to such matters as the responsibilities of the legal and accounting professions and the business practices abroad of American multinational corporations.

The last created of the six federal "economic" regulatory agencies was the Civil Aeronautics Board (CAB). Its origin in 1938 points up the striking outburst of regulatory legislation during the New Deal, when aviation, securities, public-utility holding companies, natural gas, and trucking all came under federal regulation for the first time.

The principal difference between the functions of the CAB and those of the ICC, its counterpart in surface transportation, is that Congress intended commercial aviation, a struggling infant industry in 1938, to be promoted and subsidized as well as regulated. The CAB thus came into existence with a dual set of missions that sometimes ill accorded with each other. For many years it made or channeled payments to certain airlines in return for mail service or in the form of direct subsidies. At the same time the CAB, like other agencies that focus on a particular industry, wielded extraordinary powers. It controlled entry into the business of air transport, approved rates and routes, and to some extent regulated air safety, although the separate Federal Aviation Administration has principal responsibility there.

In effect the CAB operated a cartel. In so doing, it acquired the reputation of being unduly industry-minded, a result of both its promotional mission and of its historic failure to prevent air fares from rising to unnecessarily high levels.

Economists who have evaluated the performance of the CAB note that its highest priorities have often been the extension of air service to small cities that cannot support it, the promotion of technologically advanced aircraft, and the maximization of the size of the industry instead of its efficiency. These priorities, coupled with rising equipment and fuel costs in the industry, often brought the anomalous situation in which airlines did not usually show high profits and sometimes suffered net losses, but passenger and freight rates were obviously too high. The low rates charged by a few intrastate airlines beyond the reach of CAB regulation stood as a silent indictment of the performance of the board. On the other hand, since the early 1950s, the quality of service in the industry has been much better than that available for other modes of travel, and in 1977 the CAB began to take decisive action to cut airline fares. In 1978, Congress sharply curtailed the CAB's authority and inaugurated an era of deregulation of the airline industry.

## "Social" and "Environmental" Regulation by Federal Commissions

A new wave of federal regulatory legislation began in the 1960s and continued well into the 1970s. The new commissions that emerged from this process bore less resemblance to such older industry-specific agencies as the ICC and CAB than they did to early state agencies for industrial safety and workmen's compensation. Each new commission cut broadly across industry lines and focused on some functional aspect of business practice: equal employment opportunity, environmental impacts, occupational safety and health, and consumer product safety. They originated less in response to some crisis in a particular industry than to changing values in American society.

The designation of this new regulation as "noneconomic" often disguised the heavy economic effects it had on business. Because the new wave of regulation is by no means spent, "social" and "environmental" regulations are clearly the types of greatest concern to business as a whole. Uncertainties are greater, the growth of the agencies is faster (see Table 1), and the potential impact is virtually unlimited. It is therefore important to distinguish this new regulation conceptually from the old and not to misconstrue well-publicized campaigns for deregulation as presaging diminished concern for social justice and a clean environment. Most proposals for deregulation apply to rate regulation by older agencies such as the ICC and CAB, and not to the new commissions.

The first of the new agencies was the Equal Employment Opportunity Commission (EEOC), created to administer Title VII of the Civil Rights Act of 1964. The EEOC encourages and assists voluntary action by employers and unions in developing affirmative action programs. It is a major publisher of data on the employment status of minorities and women. It receives and evaluates written charges of discrimination made against public and private employers, and it also may initiate charges that Title VII has been violated. Ultimately it may sue in federal courts to enforce its mandate but only after due notice and referral to affiliated state and local agencies.

The Environmental Protection Agency (EPA) was the institutional offspring of the congressional consolidation in 1970 of several existing agencies concerned with water and air quality. Its multitudinous activities are evident from the complexity of its organizational chart (see Figure 3), and it has been the fastest-growing regulatory agency in American history. The EPA attempts to abate and control pollution through a combination of programs involving research, monitoring, standard setting, and enforcement. It also tries to coordinate antipollution activities by state and local governments, public and private groups, individuals, and educational institutions.

The Occupational Safety and Health Administration (OSHA) is not technically an "independent" commission, but a division set up within the Department of Labor in 1970. Headed by an assistant secretary of labor, OSHA develops and promulgates standards and regulations, conducts investigations and inspections to determine compliance, and issues citations and proposes penalties for noncompliance. Of all the new agencies, OSHA has confronted the most formidable enforcement tasks, since it would take an army of inspectors to visit the hundreds of thousands of American workplaces even once a year. OSHA has also had the harshest reception (EEOC being a distant second). Critics have lampooned its excessive concern with such matters as the number of rungs for ladders of given lengths and the proximity of toilets to ranch hands.

The Consumer Product Safety Commission (CPSC), established in 1972, promulgates mandatory product safety standards. It also has the authority to ban hazardous consumer products. Upon its emergence it took over responsibility for the administration of existing federal statutes, such as the Flammable Fabrics Act, the Poison Prevention Packaging Act, and the Hazardous Substances Act. The precise role of CPSC in the field of product liability is not yet clear.

The foregoing discussion of ten major agencies—six old and four relatively new—does not by any means exhaust the possible number of federal regulatory bodies that might be mentioned. Many others share some of the same administrative and functional characteristics: the Nuclear Regulatory Commission, the Commodity Futures Trading Commission, the Federal Maritime Commission,

**FIGURE 3**

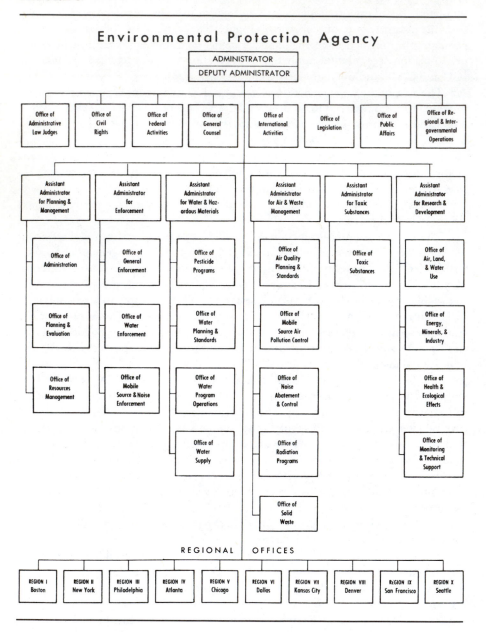

## Environmental Protection Agency

the National Highway Traffic Safety Administration, the Food and Drug Administration, and the National Labor Relations Board. All are regulatory in mission. All mix legislative, executive, and judicial functions. And all follow the administrative procedures characteristic of most commissions.

**TABLE 1**

**The Growth of Federal Regulation in America: Personnel of Selected Agencies, 1935–1977**

| | *"Economic" Regulation Agencies* | | | |
|---|---|---|---|---|
| | *1935* | *1945* | *1960* | *1975* |
| Interstate Commerce Commission (1887) | 1,093 | 1,817 | 2,409 | 2,142 |
| Federal Trade Commission (1914) | 527 | 484 | 756 | 1,569 |
| Federal Power Commission (1920) | 70 | 723 | 850 | 1,320 |
| Federal Communications Commission (1934) | 234 | 1,757 | 1,454 | 2,022 |
| Securities and Exchange Commission (1934) | 153 | 1,249 | 1,000 | 2,150 |
| Civil Aeronautics Board (1938) | — | 385 | 766 | 713 |

| | *"Social" or "Environmental" Regulation Agencies* | | |
|---|---|---|---|
| | *1970* | *1973* | *1977 (Est.)* |
| Equal Employment Opportunity Commission (1964) | 780 | 1,739 | 2,377 |
| Environmental Protection Agency (1970) | 3702 | 8,270 | 9,550 |
| Occupational Safety and Health Administration (1970) | — | 1,285 | 2,306 |
| Consumer Product Safety Commission (1972) | — | 579 | 890 |

Source: *Budget of the U.S. Government* (Washington, D.C., various years).

# An Evaluation and Perspective

On the whole, the evolution of regulatory agencies in America suggests that regulation is an institution adaptable to many different ends and purposes. It is a flexible tool whose handle may be seized by reformers, business executives, bureaucrats, or consumers and may be manipulated quite as easily for the particularistic goals of one of these groups as for the public interest. The functional diversity that has been the hallmark of regulation derives from several variables: the industry involved, the health of the economy, the political climate. Regulation serves not only economic functions but political, legal, and cultural ones as well.

No single theory from any academic discipline will predict without error precisely which industries will be regulated and which will not. Some industries that in other national economies tend toward cartelization are in America regulated—but not all. Some regulated industries have social overhead functions and are obviously "affected with a public interest"—but not all. Some are natural monopolies, with sharply declining costs to scale—but not all. Most of the transportation industry is regulated—but not all of it.

Although most agencies originated within the context of reform politics, particularly in the Progressive and New Deal eras, their subsequent behavior often departed from the reform premises that underlay their creation. More than anything else, the inherent nature of the industries under regulation shaped the diverse experiences that the agencies encountered, the conflicting functions they performed. Some agencies, notably the FTC, sought to maximize competition in an increasingly oligopolistic economy. But others, such as the CAB and the state utility commissions, limited competition in order to promote stabilization and orderly development. That nearly every agency was perceived by the public as ideally devoted to low prices for consumers above all other functions led to numerous misapprehensions on the part of reformers, journalists, and some scholars. This was especially true for those industries in which low prices were a prelude to diminished quality of service, or even to bankruptcy.

Nearly all commissions served one function not readily apparent from the statutes detailing their duties or from the rhetoric of their advocates and opponents. This was the function of legitimization. Capitalist economies, in which the generative force of economic activity is reducible as much to self-interest as to any other single motive, need ameliorating institutions for the peace of mind of the population. In this sense, regulation, a distinctly American institution, may be seen as a bastardized form standing somewhat illogically between the flawed free market and public ownership—especially for social overhead industries like public utilities and transportation. For other industries, such as securities trading, regulation permitted the continuance of an essential element of the capitalist framework that had grown so corrupt and repugnant that it could no longer perform its function of channeling investment capital into enterprise. This too was legitimization.

So was the regulation of price discrimination in the utility and transportation industries, where the nature of the business virtually mandated different prices for different classes of customers or commodities. Without an authoritative public agency overseeing such discriminatory prices, they lacked legitimacy, as the political history of the railroad and electric utility industries shows so well.

In surveying the functional diversity of regulation, one is struck by the inescapability of controversy as the one constant in the regulatory experience. Most of the functions assigned to commissions had to be performed by some institution. But whatever agency accepted the tasks also accepted the intrinsic controversy that had made the tasks necessary in the first place. In this respect the issues common to regulatory agencies can be finally settled only when the American electorate comes to consensus on such matters as the efficacy of competition, the desirability of interindustrial harmony, and the overall worth of industrial and finance capitalism.

# CASE 25

# *The Federal Trade Commission and the Shared Monopoly Case against the Ready-to-Eat Cereal Manufacturers* *

## The Federal Trade Commission: Promise and Performance

The Federal Trade Commission in 1980 was one of more than a dozen independent federal regulatory bodies. It exercised responsibilities in two basic areas: competitive practices and consumer protection. In the former, it acted along with a division of the Justice Department as an antitrust enforcement agency. In the latter, it protected the public from false and misleading advertising and the consumer from fraud. The agency had five commissioners nominated by the president and approved by Congress, which also determined its budget. In 1978, that budget came to about $69,543,000. The commissioners were the final authority in all commission proceedings. They served for terms of seven years, and not more than three could belong to the same political party.

The major remedial weapon at the commission's disposal was the cease and desist order, which prohibited a respondent from continuing to engage in practices the commission had declared illegal. Respondents could litigate a commission complaint within the agency before an administrative law judge. If they lost

*This case was written by Assistant Professor Richard S. Tedlow, under the supervision of Professor Thomas K. McCraw, as the basis for class discussion rather than to illustrate either effective or ineffective handling of an administrative situation.

Copyright © 1984 by the President and Fellows of Harvard College.

Harvard Business School case 384-265.

there, they could appeal to the commissioners themselves and from them to the federal courts. Respondents were subject to fines for violated cease and desist orders which had become final.

The Federal Trade Commission was created by an act of Congress in 1914 to deal with what some historians have seen as the single most important issue in pre-World War I American public life—the problem of bigness in business. In 1890, Congress had passed the Sherman Antitrust Act in an effort to declare illegal by statute monopolistic practices long prohibited at common law. For numerous reasons, however, the act failed to stem the tide of corporate giantism.

Stirred by 2,000 muckraking articles exposing corporate chicanery, real and alleged, the public at the turn of the century began to demand action to curb this trend. Middle-class ideology at this time held that the small trader and yeoman farmer could produce prosperity enough for all and that the economic independence which these individuals embodied was essential in the development of morally upright character. A nation in which the novels of Horatio Alger had enjoyed a readership of 50 million believed that social mobility could make every man the equal of every other. But of what use were "pluck and luck" in a world in which between them J. P. Morgan and Co. and the Rockefeller National City Bank group could, by 1913, name 341 directors to 112 corporations worth over $22.2 billion?

One school of thought held that bigness was inevitable and not unwelcome because it led to a more efficient economy. Those such as Theodore Roosevelt who adhered to this view believed that the way to cope with the problem was not to rage against the rising tide but to build public institutions large and powerful enough to enable the ship of state to navigate on it.

This approach, however, violated too many treasured homilies to gain easy acceptance. Another school believed that what was needed was not "regulated monopoly" but "regulated competition." Woodrow Wilson and his followers asserted that bigness was not the result of efficiency at all. They adopted the convenient view that trusts were created by brute force and that if the collusion and predatory practices which characterized their lust for power could be eliminated, all the benefits of both efficiency and character which small enterprise bestowed could be preserved. The problem for Wilson and his trusted advisor Louis D. Brandeis (author of among other works, *The Curse of Bigness*) was not only to regulate business but to find a way to do it without government growing large in the process. Part of the solution they lit upon was embodied in the Federal Trade Commission Act.

Originally the idea behind the act was specifically to enumerate competitive practices to be enjoined. But Wilson and his advisors found it "extremely difficult to draft definitions that would reach the evil aimed at and only that evil." As a result, the decision was made to give the commission broad general powers. Section Five of the act declared "unfair methods of competition" to be unlawful and empowered the commission to move against such conduct "if it shall appear to [it] that a proceeding by it in respect thereof would be in the interest of the public. . . ." Congress was saying that it couldn't detail what those "unfair methods" were nor could it know what new unfair methods innovative tycoons would come up with in the future. If it had to denominate each one legislatively, it would be bogged down interminably. What it called for was an independent regulatory commission, composed of disinterested, public-spirited men above politics, to make these determinations.

Many of the FTC's subsequent dilemmas were rooted in its ambiguous mandate. Its aim was to preserve competition. But competition was by nature dynamic. Could it be frozen? Was not a stable system of competition a contradiction in terms? Could the FTC protect competition without at the same time protecting inefficient competitors?

Furthermore the FTC's role was fashioned as much out of the needs of ideology as of dispassionate analysis. The keystone of the philosophy behind it was that bigness in business was unnatural and could be prevented if cheating in the competitive arena were eliminated. But what could the commission do when bigness was achieved without collusion or predation?

Philosophy, of course, was far from the FTC's only problem. Its powers were emasculated in the federal courts in the 1920s; it was under-funded; and its appointees seemed more often than not to be at daggers drawn. It was hamstrung by politics. Its case selection was petty enough as to border on the frivolous, and litigation before it seemed to take an eternity.

Various attempts were made to rectify the agency's problems over the years. The Robinson-Patman Act of 1936 gave the commission added power over price discrimination, but that statute has been labelled as retrograde special interest legislation and described by the Supreme Court as "singularly opaque and illusive." In 1938, in part as a response to the small but noisy consumer movement, the Wheeler-Lea Amendments enabled the FTC to move against "unfair or deceptive acts or practices in commerce" even if such conduct did not have anti-competitive overtones. In other words, the commission could act to a degree as a consumer protector and not solely as an antitrust enforcer. In addition, the amendments provided for fines in case of violation of cease and desist orders and gave injunctive power under certain circumstances. The passage of the amendments focused much attention on the commission, especially from the advertising industry, and for a few years after their passage, the commission displayed an unwonted vigor. It seemed, however, incapable of sustaining the excitement, and it soon returned to its prior standards, standards which were to make it a legend in Washington. The case which critics often pointed to in order to illustrate the commission's shortcomings was Carter's Little Liver Pills. In 1943, the commission decided that "Liver" should be deleted from the name of the product because it had no effect on that organ. The commission emerged victorious in this struggle—in 1959, after 16 years of litigation.

Periodically, scholarly reports had been published about the FTC. These had been almost invariably negative in tone, often focusing on the shortcomings of the agency's personnel. Attracting and keeping able people had been a problem from the beginning, but the situation worsened during the New Deal. Franklin Roosevelt failed in an attempt to remove a controversial and recalcitrant chairman and then apparently gave up on the commission as an active participant in the making of public policy. He decided instead to use it for political patronage, and he turned it over to Tennessee Senator Kenneth D. McKellar and Mayor Edward Hull "Boss" Crump of Memphis. Under their stewardship, "The FTC sank into a quagmire of political cronyism." The chairman from 1933 to 1949 was their fellow Tennesseean Ewin L. Davis. It was Davis who in 1939 hired as a trial lawyer University of Tennessee football star Paul Rand Dixon. Dixon became chairman of the commission when the Democrats returned to power in 1961 and served as a commissioner into the 1980s.

To be sure, the commission's record was not unrelievedly bleak. Probably its most outstanding contribution to public welfare was forcing cigarette manufacturers to put health warnings on cigarette packages in 1964 following the Surgeon General's report. And outstanding individuals have served on it. However, in the words of a man who himself was a commissioner from 1961 to 1971, "In general, . . . .excellence at the commission has been fortuitous."

## 1969: Year of Decision

The Federal Trade Commission might have ambled on contentedly were it not for the fact that it stood athwart one of the hottest public issues of the 1960s: consumerism. In the summer of 1968, a group of law students under the supervision of Ralph Nader began a study of the commission. *The Nader Report* on the Federal Trade Commission was published in January of 1969 and created a sensation. In the righteously indignant tone which characterized the work as a whole, Nader wrote in the preface:

> On paper, the FTC was the principal consumer protection agency of the Federal Government. As such, the commission could have been an exciting and creative fomenter of consumer democracy. In reality, the "little old lady on Pennsylvania Avenue" was a self-parody of bureaucracy, fat with cronyism, torpid through an inbreeding unusual even for Washington, manipulated by the agents of commercial predators, impervious to governmental and citizen monitoring.

The "Raiders" concluded that in the absence of reform, "there will be no substantial purpose to be served by [the commission's] continued existence."

During the summer of 1969, the commission found itself the subject of yet another task force study. This one was conducted by the American Bar Association at the request of Richard Nixon. Its report, issued September 15, was couched in the milder language befitting its eminent authors, but it was certainly nonetheless damning. It agreed with Nader about the commission's shortcomings in consumer protection. In its other major enforcement area, antitrust, the agency was not without accomplishment, but even here the record was nothing to be too proud of. "If the measure of the quality of FTC performance in the antitrust area is whether the agency has broken new ground and made new law by resort to its unique administrative resources, it seems clear that the record is one of missed opportunity." Other commentators were not even this kind. The commission, many in the antitrust bar believed, was confined "by political and intellectual limitations" to bring insignificant nuisance cases.

The ABA report offered, as was usual in this genre of literature, various proposals to facilitate managerial efficiency in the agency. But in a "Separate Statement," Richard A. Posner dared think the unthinkable. Fifty years of failure, he said, proved the commission hopeless. Its appropriations should be frozen and it should be granted no new responsibilities until it demonstrated that it could properly discharge its present ones. Without actually quite saying it, Posner made it clear that he felt the nation would be better off without any Federal Trade Commission at all.

# The Commission and Oligopoly

In response to internal demands for more important cases from the consumer point of view, attorney Rufus E. Wilson of the then Bureau of Restraint of Trade (later renamed the Bureau of Competition) submitted a memorandum in July of 1969 calling for action on a relatively untested antitrust theory, one which had been receiving some attention within the commission.

A truly consumer-oriented antitrust program would not focus on the predatory, anti-competitive practices which make the industrial history of late 19th-century America such colorful reading. The modern monopolist does not need such practices, claimed Wilson. He had turned to strategies "more subtle and elusive." By concentrating on conduct, "the law had seized the shadow and missed the substance of the problem at hand."

From a consumer standpoint, the genuinely significant questions concerned structure (concentration, product differentiation, and entry barriers) and performance (especially pricing). Oligopolistic market structure facilitated supracompetitive pricing with resultant impact on the consumer budget and misallocation of resources in the economy as a whole. If the FTC could get a toehold in the battle against noncompetitive industry structure, it would be doing something worthwhile indeed.

What was more, claimed Wilson, an action brought on such grounds would not get bogged down endlessly in debates about the minutiae of corporate conduct "[T]he structural case is inherently much briefer . . . ."

Commentators outside the commission entertained differing opinions about the benefits of such an action, but no one doubted the impact of its successful prosecution. Noted the *Antitrust Law and Economics Review* in 1971:

> If such a case is in fact filed by the FTC, it would be the most important antitrust action in the nation's history, one that, by its mere filing, would amount to nothing less than a challenge to the legality of perhaps a third of the country's manufacturing sector, the third, that, in Professor Galbraith's phrase, constitutes the country's "industrial heartland."

The problem of oligopoly—which Wilson had chosen to attack—was a major conundrum in modern economics. Market theory in cases where there were many competitors and where there were none was well developed. Indeed there were few constructs in the history of thought more powerful than that expounded by Adam Smith. There was, however, a middle term between monopoly and competition. This was the situation in which sellers were few. The theory of oligopoly had been applied to this intermediate range of market structures. Many felt that oligopoly had received insufficient attention from economists.

Oligopoly rather than monopoly became the standard form of concentration in American industry for a variety of historical reasons. In addition to mergers, the three decades before World War I witnessed much vertical integration. Vertical integration led to concentration in capital-intensive, high energy-consuming industries where administrative coordination by professional managers proved more efficient than market coordination. In such situations oligopoly tended to develop in three different ways:

1.  When manufacturers integrated backward, producers of raw materials were often forced to respond strategically by integrating forward. Sometimes marketers moved back into manufacturing.
2.  Two or more enterprises would often integrate forward or backward virtually simultaneously.
3.  Integrated enterprises began to compete against each other by developing by-products or new products as they made further use of their facilities.

Historian of Management Alfred D. Chandler, Jr. has written:

> A final reason for continuing competition between the large integrated firms was public policy. Antitrust legislation and its interpretation by the courts in these years discouraged monopoly but not oligopoly. Yet, it must be remembered that although such legislation was significant, it was only one of several reasons why concentrated industries became and remained oligopolistic rather than monopolistic.

Once those industries which (1) adopted continuous process machinery which dramatically expanded their output and/or (2) needed specialized distribution and marketing services had established themselves, impediments to competition beginning from a standing start were not unimpressive. Wrote Chandler:

> The most important barrier to entry in these industries was the organization the pioneers had built to market and distribute their newly mass-produced products. A competitor who acquired the technology had to create a national and often global organization of managers, buyers, and salesmen if he was to get the business away from the one or two enterprises that already stood astride the major market channels. Moreover, where the pioneer could finance the building of the first of these organizations out of cash flow, generated by high volume, the newcomer had to set up a competing network before high volume output reduced unit costs and created a sizeable cash flow. In this period of building he had to face a competitor whose economies of speed permitted him to set prices low and still maintain a margin of profit. Newcomers, of course, did appear. Kellogg and Postum in breakfast cereals and Colgate and Babbitt in soaps are examples. But all these industries were highly concentrated from the moment mass production methods were adopted. Except for flour milling, the industries

in which these integrated industrial enterprises first appeared immediately became oligopolistic and so remained.[1]

Thus it would appear that not through conspiracy but through parallel incentive one fourth to one third of American business enterprise had developed a structure different from the model of perfect competition. This circumstance has far-reaching implications not only in economics but from the point of view of society as a whole. With seductive simplicity, perfect competition provides an admirable explanation for how goods are distributed to each citizen. It posits a complete decentralization of decision making, which is bound to have a special appeal in a nation which has always claimed to value individual autonomy. "Oligopoly" is something else again.

The fundamental proposition of oligopoly theory is "oligopolistic interdependence." This consists of the assertion that in industries where there are few sellers, each one will understand that its own price and output decisions will have a significant effect on the industry as a whole. To illustrate the different views of perfect competition and oligopoly, let us take the example of

an imaginary widget industry . . . composed of 100 firms of equal size making a uniform product, which is sold to 1,000 well-informed purchasers. Under these conditions . . . no company would have power significantly to affect the market price for widgets because both its output and the variations in its output would be trivial with respect to total industry output. The demand for the output of any individual manufacturer would then be perfectly elastic, which is just a way of saying that any manufacturer who quoted a price above the prevailing market price would make zero sales, since every purchaser would turn to another supplier. Any manufacturer who quoted a price below market would be offered all the business. . . .

Our hypothetical widget manufacturer also lacks short-run control over the costs of making his product. Costs are presented to him as brute facts of life in the prices of labor, raw materials, machinery, electricity, and so forth. His existing method of coordinating these factors of production determines his costs, and he cannot alter costs until he finds a better method of coordination, that is, a better method of production or distribution. He does, however, have power to affect one species of costs, those that vary with his rate of output. By changing his rate of output he can change his marginal cost (the cost, starting at any specified rate of output, of producing one more widget in the period of time under discussion). Thus, if he is producing 5,000 widgets per week, his marginal cost is the additional cost he would incur by increasing the rate to 5,001. This is important to the manufacturer, for though he cannot change market price or basic cost determinants, he can alter his rate of output and so choose the marginal cost associated with the new rate.

The manufacturer may not be completely aware of these facts, but in adjusting his rate of output until he arrives at the profit-maximizing solution, he will, whether he thinks of it that way or not, be working up and down his marginal cost curve. The profit-maximizing solution may be described for all sellers, whether competitors or monopo-

---

[1]Alfred D. Chandler, Jr., *The Visible Hand* (Cambridge: Harvard University Press, 1977).

lists, as the rate of output at which marginal cost is equal to marginal revenue. For the competitor alone, however, marginal revenue is equal to market price. . . .

But the situation is thought by many persons to be different if the industry becomes concentrated. Suppose that in the fragmented widget industry, over time, some firms grow and others decline, many leaving the industry altogether, so that eventually there remain only four firms. One of these has 50 percent of actual sales, another 30, a third 15, and the fourth is struggling somewhat at 5 percent. Almost all economists would describe such an industry as "oligopolistic" or "concentrated," and perhaps most would predict that its structure would cause it to behave noncompetitively. The basis for that prediction is the concept of *oligopolistic interdependence*. Each firm is aware that its price and output decisions are no longer insignificant with respect to total industry price and output. Sellers no longer face an impersonal market price but one they can, to a greater or lesser degree, affect.

This much is true. If the 50 percent firm, which, let us suppose, now makes 12,500,000 widgets annually, expanded its output by 10 percent, perhaps because it lowered its costs, to 13,750,000 widgets per year, the market price would drop initially from $30 to under $28 per widget. If the other firms adjusted by reducing output to equate marginal cost with the new price, the price would rise somewhat above $28 but below $30. The point of all this is that the widget makers would be aware of their power over price and might separately decide to try raising it. The 50 percent firm might begin by announcing a new $35 widget price. If the others did not follow, the higher price would not last long. The theory supposes, however, that the 30 percent firm's management will realize that undercutting the largest firm is short-sighted, since that firm will drop its price and all firms will be back where they began. Why not follow the price up? If the other two firms reason similarly, all will be getting $35, a price above the competitive level, though not at the monopoly level. By such a process the rivals may work themselves up to the monopoly price (and the restricted output necessary to raise the price), jointly maximizing their profits, without ever once meeting surreptitiously at a country club or leaving the telltale evidence of long-distance calls to one another in the telephone company's records.[2]

There was a wide variety of industries which could have been used to test the structural antitrust approach. Rufus Wilson, however, felt that the food industry, a traditional concern of the commission in antitrust, was the place to begin. Food was a highly visible item. The average family shopped for it between two and three times a week and expended 20 percent of its budget on it. Secondly, if the FTC could bring prices down, "the very lowest income groups would be," according to Wilson, "the principal beneficiaries since a disproportionately large portion of their total income (up to 50 percent . . .) is spent on food."

Of food processors, the ready-to-eat cereal manufacturers seemed particularly inviting. In 1966, two economists observed that "if the workability of competition were to be questioned purely on the basis of structured indexes, by far the most likely candidate of all food industries is the ready-to-eat cereal industry."

RTE sales had increased substantially in the three and a half decades prior to the issuance of the complaint from $284,300,000 in 1947 to $953,100,000 in 1970. During the same time, the level of concentration was also increasing. The four

---

[2]Robert Bork, *The Antitrust Paradox* (New York: Basic Books, 1978), pp. 92–93, 102–103.

largest firms accounted for 68 percent of industry sales in 1935, 79 percent in 1947, and 91 percent in 1970. The absolute number of competitors had also declined, from 55 in 1947 to 30 in 1967.

RTE profit performance had been gratifying. Compared to the less concentrated cookies and crackers industry, for example, the 1964 figures were as follows:

**Profits of Manufacturers, 1964**

| | Net Income After Taxes | Breakfast Cereals | Cookies & Crackers | Food & Related Products |
|---|---|---|---|---|
| As % of sales: | | | | |
| Largest 4 companies | | 7.8 | 5.1 | — |
| All companies | | 7.3 | 4.2 | 2.7 |
| As a % of net worth: | | | | |
| Largest 4 companies | | 19.4 | 13.3 | — |
| All companies | | 18.0 | 12.7 | 9.8 |

During the 1960s, Kellogg had averaged a not unimpressive profit rate of more than 20 percent after taxes on stockholders' equity.

By 1970, the industry was dominated by large manufacturers, as the following chart shows:

**Structure of RTE Cereal Industry**

| | Kellogg | General Mills | General Foods | Quaker Oats | Nabisco | Ralston/ Purina |
|---|---|---|---|---|---|---|
| Sales in millions of $ | 614 | 1,000 | 2,000 | 579 | 868 | 1,500 |
| Assets in millions of $ | 347 | 655 | 1,300 | 391 | 503 | 775 |
| *Fortune* 500 ranking | 191 | 116 | 45 | 195 | 140 | 71 |
| Sales of RTE cereals in millions of $ | 300 | 141 | 92 | 56 | 26 | 20 |
| Percent of RTE market | 45 | 21 | 16 | 9 | 4 | 3 |
| Advertising expenditures in millions of $ for RTE cereals | 36 | 19 | 9 | 9 | 3 | 4 |

However, the selection of this industry may have been prompted by more than economics alone. RTE cereal manufacturers did a great deal of television advertising to children which (i.e., the advertisements and the programs on which they appeared) some consumerists found very offensive. In 1968, Peggy Charren formed Action for Children's Television, an organization highly skilled in the arts of publicity, which bombarded federal agencies with protests about "Kid Vid." Most of the FTC's concern with this issue had focused on the Bureau of Consumer Protection, but with this effort the Bureau of Competition became involved as well.

The FTC announced its intention of taking action against the four largest firms—Kellogg, General Mills, General Foods, and Quaker Oats—on January 24, 1972. There followed the normal, 90-day postponement of action the purpose of which was to see if a settlement could be reached without litigation. No such accord was struck.

The complaint itself, a modest eight pages in length, dealt not only with the oligopolistic structure of the industry but with the conduct through which that structure had been attained. Traditional antitrust cases had concentrated on conduct, but in this instance conduct was used primarily to explain how the structure had been attained. So prominently was advertising mentioned that some observers "speculated that the case was being used to test certain economic theories about the anticompetitive effects of advertising. These theories . . . have received widespread attention in the economics and business literature." Indeed as far back as 1937, the then Assistant Attorney General Thurman W. Arnold suggested that intensive advertising could be a monopolistic practice.

The FTC complaint, however, was not aimed directly at changing advertising or other alleged anti-competitive practices. It was aimed at breaking up the industry pure and simple. As Wilson said in his memorandum:

> We would emphasize again . . . that the central thrust of any proceeding here would be oriented primarily toward the structure/performance characteristics of the industry in question and that the role of the relevant conduct described above—the use of a very high advertising/sales ratio—is a secondary one. First, we expect that, should litigation eventually result, perhaps as much as 90 percent of the evidence introduced by complaint counsel would be aimed at developing those noncompetitive features of the industry's structure and performance, a rather modest 10 percent or so to its conduct or behavioral features. Secondly, the "conduct" pattern we expect to find in the industry is not the gravamen of the case in another and even more fundamental sense, namely, it does not necessarily bear a great deal of relation to the kind of relief that we might ultimately want to ask for. For example, an offer from the three dominant firms here to revise their advertising/sales ratio downward—from, say, its present level of 20 percent or more to perhaps a much more modest 2 percent or 3 percent figure—would by no means necessarily constitute a satisfactory resolution of the matter from the consumer's standpoint. If they offered such a "settlement," the reasonable inference would be that they had found some other way to maintain their dominant market shares and their monopoly prices. And these, not their advertising schedules, are our real concern here. Everyone is always interested in eliminating, of course, any and all devices that have proven helpful to the monopolist or the oligopolist in developing and maintaining his power, but we think it important to distinguish carefully between the ends themselves and the particular means of getting there that happen to have been used in the past. It is monopoly the law is concerned with, for example, not advertising; and the fact that a monopoly or an oligopoly happens to have been built or maintained by advertising in a particular instance does not mean that that is the only way it could have been built or maintained in that industry in the past or the only way it can be built or maintained there in the future.

After the preliminary notification, protestations of injured innocence issued forth from the firms. Kellogg charged that the commission was attacking bigness and efficiency and that if the order were accepted, the result would be "a far-reaching devastating effect on many industries." General Mills' chairman was "puzzled as to why we have been singled out" to test the commission's novel theories. General Foods said there was plentiful competition in the RTE industry, while Quaker Oats found it "impossible to see how its 9 percent market share could constitute basis for a monopoly charge."

## The Hearing

Pretrial preparations for the case were laborious, complex, and time consuming. It was not until April 28, 1976, four years after the complaint had originally been issued, that the hearing finally began.

In the interim there had been some noteworthy occurrences. Kellogg diversified through purchase of Mrs. Smith's Pie Company for $50 million. Kellogg had failed to consummate a merger with Tropicana Products in 1974. It tried again at a higher price a few weeks after the hearing began but failed a second time.

In February of 1976, complaint counsel filed their 524-page pretrial brief. It began by declaring:

> The monopolized RTE cereal market is . . . a textbook example of the dangers of concentration and the evils of monopoly. . . . The respondents' "supra-competitive" profitability has resulted from their tacit conspiracy or agreement not to engage in price competition.
>
> "Shared monopoly" [is] the presence of market power in a few firms who use that power to earn monoply profits, to avoid competition, and to exclude entry. . . . The respondents' market power derives from the concentration and the realization of supra-competitive profits. . . . Exclusionary conduct has included brand proliferation, product differentiation, intensive advertising and shelf-space allocation programs.

The use of the term *shared monopoly* instead of oligopoly represented a major antitrust initiative. It also represented a public relations offensive. Oligopoly is not a well-known word, but monopoly has had negative connotations for years. In a sense, the assignment of the commission lawyers was to demonstrate that "shared monopoly" was not what it appeared on its face to be—self-contradictory.

The brief suggested a shift in concern at the commission. The original complaint had never actually used the term *shared monopoly*. It had alleged that the industry's noncompetitive structure had led to poor economic performance (i.e., high prices and profits) and that various marketing practices, especially heavy advertising which was often deceptive to children, had created "barriers to entry."

These elements were present in the pretrial brief but, according to observers, somewhat downplayed in favor of the charge that the behavior of the leading firms constituted "an intricate, tacit conspiracy" in violation of Section I of the Federal Trade Commission Act. It was this tacit conspiracy which had enabled the firms to avoid price competition and encourage activity that barred entry.

The theory in outline proceeded through the following steps:

1. The industry was concentrated.
2. This concentrated structure had made possible a tacit conspiracy to avoid

price competition. This conspiracy had been made possible by use of industry monitoring reports, trade association activity, and the collection of price information by salesmen.

3. The result had been high prices and profits.
4. High profits have not invited competition because of barriers to entry erected by respondents.
5. The following marketing practices made up these barriers:
   brand proliferation
   product differentiation
   intensive advertising
   shelf space control.

The four practices under item 5 were so basic a part of modern marketing that many observers felt the commission "has mounted a fundamental challenge to marketing thought and practice." The commission analysis of these practices deserves some attention.

What the FTC calls "brand proliferation" and what the industry calls "product innovation" constituted the continual introduction of new cereal brands with the object of forestalling the maturity and decline stages of the product life cycle. The introduction of new brands had succeeded in attracting new customers to mature product lines and in cementing the allegiance of older customers.

This strategy had led to the occupation and thus, some have said, to the preemption of virtually every profitable product position. With so many brands competing in each space, the promotional costs of introducing just one new one became very high. Of 80 brands introduced from 1950 to 1972, only two attained a 4 percent share.

Brand proliferation was made possible, charged the commission, by artificial "product differentiation." This consisted of "conduct which draws the consumer's attention to minor variations between products, thereby diverting his attention from a comparison of the basic similarities between them." Practices constituting "artificial" differentiation included product symbols, packaging, trademarks, nutritional claims, and changes in shape, color, texture, flavor, or additives.

The foundation of this edifice was intensive advertising. The commission found this advertising especially noxious in that it allegedly concentrated on misleading children into the belief that there really was something special about a particular brand. The staff charged the respondents with using heavy advertising to (1) Support brand proliferation and product differentiation. (2) Create entrenched consumer preferences in order to dislodge which new entrants must themselves incur heavy promotional expenses. Established brand loyalty also diminished new entrant impact on prices. (3) Indirectly create brand loyalty because retailers tended to stock and prominently display heavily advertised brands. (4) Obtain quantity discounts from media which placed new entrants at a further disadvantage.

And finally, the FTC charged that manufacturers had promoted a retail shelf space allocation program designed by Kellogg which served further to exclude possible new entrants. The plan allocated shelf space in accord with market share and thus reinforced it. It located the favored products advantageously in center aisle, displayed these products in billboard fashion, and grouped cereals by producer (e.g., General Mills) rather than by product type (e.g., corn flakes) thus further impeding consumer comparison.

The commission was unimpressed by the fact that the other companies offered shelf space allocation plans, because it believed these were not vigorously promoted.

The chart on the following page denominates industry practices discussed in the pretrial brief, the FTC and its staff's interpretation of them, and how they have been viewed by modern marketing practitioners.

All the foregoing notwithstanding, the priorities of Rufus Wilson survived the revised charges. Even if the practices alleged did not characterize the industry or, if they did, even if they could not be shown to fall into the category of "unfair or deceptive acts or practices in commerce," the basic facts of the industry's structure constituted evidence sufficient to call for antitrust remedy.

And the remedy proposed in this case was draconian. First, divestiture. Kellogg would lose three of its four plants, General Mills one of five, and General Foods one of two. These would be taken over by five smaller manufacturers or new entrants. According to the pretrial brief:

> The order must strike at the basis of the respondents' conduct—the highly concentrated market structure of the RTE cereal industry in which entry is all but barricaded. Thus, five new cereal firms should be created by "spin offs"—three from Kellogg's assets, one from General Mills' assets and one from General Foods' assets. This will reduce concentration and intensify competition.

Secondly, the respondents would be forced to license on a royalty-free basis their trademarks, product formulae, and package design for selected brands for 20 years. Quoting from the pretrial brief once again:

> To assure the viability of these [new] firms, Kellogg would be ordered to divest the following well-established brands: Rice Krispies for the Memphis plant and Special K for the San Leandro plant. These brands would account for approximately 40 percent

**Concentration and Size**

| Firm | Pre-Divestiture | | Post-Divestiture | | |
| | Market Share | No. of Plants | Market Share | No. of Plants | Loss Market Share |
| --- | --- | --- | --- | --- | --- |
| Kellogg | 45% | 4 | 25% | 1 | 20% |
| General Mills | 21 | 5 | 17 | 4 | 4 |
| General Foods | 16 | 2 | 11 | 1 | 5 |
| Quaker Oats | 9 | 4 | 9 | 4 | 0 |
| Total | 91 | 15 | 62 | 10 | 29 |
| Ratio largest firm (Kellogg) to smallest firm (Ralston) sales | 11.3 to 1 | | | 6.3 to 1 | |

Source: *FTC's Complaint Counsel Trial Brief—In the Matter of Kellogg Company et al.*, Federal Trade Commission, Docket No. 8883, 1976, vol. 11, p. 123.

# A Comparison of Interpretations of the Cereal Companies' Behavior

| *Behaviors* | *FTC Staff's Interpretation* | *Marketing Textbook Interpretation* |
|---|---|---|
| 1. Monitoring of competitors' activities through:<br>a. Salesperson's reports<br>b. Subscriptions to Nielsen, SAMI, etc.<br>c. Participation in a trade association | 1a, b, c. Policing actions designed to ensure compliance with a code of conduct | 1a, b, c. Marketing intelligence gathering |
| 2. Use of pricing policies such as:<br>a. Prior announcement of increases<br>b. Delivered pricing<br>c. Offering "price protection"<br>d. Suggesting retail price<br>e. Making price changes at different times than cost changes<br>f. Keeping high prices for failing brands | 2. Avoiding price competition by:<br>a. Reducing uncertainty<br>b. Keeping wholesale prices uniform geographically (reduces) uncertainty<br>c. Allowing instant retaliation to a price cut<br>d. Keeping retail prices uniform (reduces uncertainty)<br>e. Reducing uncertainty by cutting frequency of changes<br>f. Avoiding price cuts | 2a, b, c, d. Helping a manufacturer establish better relationships with retailers<br><br>e. Demand-oriented pricing<br><br>f. A milking strategy |
| 3. Nonuse of:<br>a. Trade allowances and<br>b. Cents-off deals<br>c. Private labels<br>d. Vitamin fortification (until pressured)<br>e. In-Pack premiums (for 10 yrs.) | 3a, b, c, d, e. Avoiding actions that could stimulate price competition | 3a, b, c, d, e. Avoiding destructive costly forms of competition; also avoiding government accusations of using predatory or discriminatory practices |

| 4. Use of: | 4. Excluding entry by: | 4a. Helping retailers |
|---|---|---|
| a. Promotion of shelf space plans | a. Allowing new firms only poor shelf locations | |
| b. Brand proliferation | b, c. Leaving no profitable positions for new firms | b, c. Serving diverse consumer tastes |
| c. Product differentiation | | |
| d. Intensive advertising | d. Building brand loyalty and setting scale-economy barriers | d. Stimulating primary demand, awareness, and reinforcing purchase decisions |

Source: Paul N. Bloom, "The Cereal Companies: Monopolists or Super Marketers?" *M.S.U. Business Topics* (Summer 1978), p. 43.

and 62 percent of plant capacity respectively which would enable two new firms to produce new cereals, to engage in price competition in order to expand their sales and to produce private label RTE cereal. The third firm [Omaha plant] would be given comparable brands to the brands of the other two firms. Similarly, General Mills would be required to create a new firm which would be given the South Chicago plant and the Wheaties brand which accounts for about 80 percent of the South Chicago plant.

Quaker would be spared the divestiture and licensing provisions, but along with the other respondents, it would be prohibited from making acquisitions for 20 years and from using a shelf space allocation program. The disparity in the treatment of the firms led *Advertising Age* to speculate that if the complaint were successful, Quaker would be strategically positioned to increase its market share.

Quaker was indeed the "joker" in this proceeding. It had managed to increase its market share from 2 percent to 9 percent in the 12 years prior to the complaint. This was the sort of thing which was not supposed to happen in the commission's view. In the process, it had been less profitable, which would also, from the regulatory view, make it apparently less of a miscreant.

Quaker used its eccentric position masterfully and two years into the hearing managed to get the charges against it dropped. The company's strategy was to distinguish itself from the other defendants by emphasizing its "competitive feistiness." Unlike the other firms, which used prestigious outside counsel, Quaker's defense was skillfully conducted by Luther McKenney, who had been a senior partner of a major firm but who took a vice presidency at Quaker and conducted the case as in-house counsel. His questioning of one of the government's chief witnesses elicited the assertion in open court that the case against Quaker should be dropped. Administrative Law Judge Harry R. Hinkes agreed, and his decision was not overturned.

This development seemed a serious blow to the commission's case. Commented *Fortune*:

> If . . . Hinkes is willing to look at the conduct of an individual company apart from the overall industry, then perhaps the spell the FTC is trying to cast—look at the *gestalt* or total picture, not at the participants—may be broken and the FTC's enchanted castle in the air dissolved.

*The Wall Street Journal* enquired whether the three remaining firms were now being accused of constituting three fourths of a "shared monopoly."

But Quaker had always been an anomaly. Despite this setback, officials at the Bureau of Competition felt they were making a very good case. Besides, they had far too much invested to turn back now.

There matters stood when Administrative Law Judge Harry R. Hinkes announced a change in his status.

## The Hinkes Announcement

On September 8, 1979, at the 242nd trial session and after 35,043 pages of testimony had been taken, Harry R. Hinkes made the following statement:

I have decided to retire for personal reasons that make it imperative that I commence my pension at this time. The agency, of course, is anxious to have no interruption to this proceeding; and for that reason, I have agreed with them to devote my time exclusively to this case rather than to the matters that may come my way generally as an Administrative Law Judge for any case that is pending as, for example, my necessary interruption in this case for Nestle matters that I was also engaged in.

In that connection, I will be retained then by the agency on a contract basis for the purpose of completing this case, completing the hearings, receiving the briefs of the parties, and writing a decision at which time my connection with the agency and with this case will terminate.

I don't expect there to be any difference in our course of conduct in this proceeding whatsoever. I will continue to act as I have been acting in this case as the hearing officer; and I trust that the participants in this preceeding will continue to conduct themselves just the same as heretofore.

# The Administrative Law Judge

The administrative law judge (hereinafter ALJ) served two principal purposes. He presided over the making of the hearing record, and he wrote a decision based upon that record. In the hearing, the ALJ functioned not unlike a judge, and indeed he was addressed as "judge" in the hearing room. Like a judge, he was to see to it that the facts were "clearly and fully developed."

Despite this seeming similarity, however, the ALJ did not have the stature of federal judges. The latter were created by Article Three of the Constitution and had a carefully guarded independence. The ALJ was delegated his responsibility because the press of administrative business made it impossible for commissioners to preside over the making of a record for every case brought by their agency.

In delegating this responsibility, however, the agency surrendered no power. In the words of Section 557 of the Administrative Procedure Act, the agency had "all the power which it would have in making the initial decision," including determination of law, fact, policy, and discretion. A leading commentator has written:

> Of course, examiners [the former term for ALJ] are subordinates. The power is in the agencies, not in the examiners. Every decision by an examiner, whether disposing of the merits at the end of a proceeding or whether ruling on an interim question, is subject to reversal by the agency. . . . The agency may substitute judgment for that of the examiner on any and all questions, including even the credibility of the witnesses, whose behavior the examiner observes but the agency can know only from the record.

Another authority has asserted, however, that the examiner's assessment of the credibility of a witness did and should deserve "special weight."

When the presiding officer rendered a decision, that decision became the decision of the agency, according to Section 557 of the Administrative Procedure Act, "unless there is an appeal to, or review on the motion of, the agency within time provided by rule." However, either side could appeal an ALJ's decision to the commission, and the commission could review whatever it chose whether there had been an appeal or not. In a 1964 survey, only about one examiner decision in 10 (leaving aside social security cases) became final without review.

He may not have had the final say, but the ALJ performed an important function and his prestige had been increasing over the years. Early regulatory agency statutes placed examiners in a class with "clerks. . .and other employees." *The Attorney General's Manual on Administrative Procedure* in 1941 sought to increase the power of the examiner because it was believed that with the conduct of the hearing divorced from responsibility the hearing itself degenerated. It recommended that examiners by "men of ability and prestige, [with] a tenure and salary which will give assurance of independent judgment."

The Administrative Procedure Act, passed in 1946, took steps toward this goal by establishing a degree of independence for the presiding officer. He was not to be subject to supervision by anyone "engaged in the performance of investigative or prosecuting functions for an agency." In order to insulate him from reprisal for writing decisions displeasing to the agency, he was to "be assigned to cases in rotation so far as practicable." This would prevent his being stuck with insignificant cases. His pay was to be set by the Civil Service Commission "independently of agency recommendations or ratings," and only the Civil Service Commission, not the agency to which he was assigned, could remove him and then only for cause and after a hearing.

The numbers of ALJs and their salary have been steadily increasing. The salary range was from $8,399 to $12,690 in 1955 and from $25,044 to $31,724 in 1970. In the latter year, the federal government employed about 650; in 1977, that number had increased to 1,002. In 1972, the Civil Service Commission changed the title of "hearing examiner" to "Administrative Law Judge," a change that the Federal Trial Examiner Conference had long urged. Some observers criticized this semantic elevation because they felt it would diminish the prestige of Article Three judges.

Thus, the situation of the ALJ was ambiguous. His determination of no part of the case he heard was binding on the agency for which he worked, not to mention on the federal courts. No determination he made, even on a motion, was necessarily final. Yet he did preside over the hearing and thus helped establish the tone for the first formal proceeding of the agency against the respondent. He did write the initial decision which, while not binding itself, became part of the record to be considered by the commission and later, if appealed, by the federal courts. This decision was often closely analyzed in the trade press. His report, according to some, should be given special attention in matters of demeanor. He could also participate in the drafting of the agency's final report.

In sum, the administrative law judge functioned enough like an Article Three judge for the government to take the special precautions previously noted to separate him from the agency to which he was attached. Otherwise, the agency appeared as judge of its own case, a situation which had been abhorrent to Anglo-Saxon jurisprudence for about 600 years.

# Harry Hinkes Decides to Retire

Harry Hinkes entered the service of the federal government in 1945 and was thus in his 33rd year of employment and eligible for retirement in 1978. He first joined the FTC as a hearing examiner in 1959. Partly through the efforts of commission personnel, he was saved from a reduction in force by being transferred to the National Labor Relations Board in 1965. He returned to the commission in 1972. When he was assigned the RTE case, it was said (although he disputed the claim) that he "made an unequivocal commitment to the Chief Judge that he would follow the matter through to its final conclusion."

There was an established procedure for dealing with situations in which judges became "unavailable" because of retirement, death, or for any other reason. According to *The Attorney General's Manual on Administrative Procedure*, "Where the hearing officer becomes unavailable to the agency, the agency may itself complete the hearing or substitute another hearing officer to do so." This had not been done in this case. Rather, the commission and the sitting ALJ had made an unprecedented arrangement.

# CASE 26

# *The Multidivisional Enterprise* *

In 1919, after the end of World War I, the Du Pont Company perfected the centralized, functionally departmentalized structure that had served it so well during its initial growth and then during the great expansion of World War I. By the 1920s, a large majority of vertically integrated industrial enterprises were using a comparable organizational structure. Nevertheless within two years the senior managers at Du Pont had scrapped the organization that made their explosives company one of the most efficient and profitable enterprises in the nation. To meet changing needs, they created a new form—the multidivisional structure. They were the first to build this type of structure, which became in the years after World War II widely used in the United States and abroad by industrial enterprises operating in more than one major market.

## The Strategy of Diversification

The Du Pont Company had taken some tentative steps toward diversification before World War I. Yet in 1913, only 3 percent of its business was outside of explo-

*This case is a slightly modified version of the first part of Chapter 2 in Alfred D. Chandler, Jr., *Strategy and Structure* (Cambridge: MIT Press, 1962). The modifications have been made by Professor Chandler, who is grateful for suggestions made by Professor Derek A. Newton, The Colgate Darden Graduate School of Business Administration, University of Virginia. This is reproduced by permission of the MIT Press.

sives. The Du Pont Company had rejected an opportunity to diversify shortly after its rebirth in 1902 and 1903, preferring to concentrate on its primary line. At the time of the consolidation, one of the constituent firms, the International Smokeless Powder and Chemical Company of Parlin, New Jersey, was carrying on a small business in solvents, ether, and lacquers, largely as a by-product of its smokeless powder manufacturing. The consolidated company continued this mixed chemical business but looked on it only as a small secondary activity and not as one to be developed into a major new line. As Irénée du Pont later put it: "We made an excellent quality and most attractive material, but the volume was too small to make a good industry out of it."

The first planned move beyond explosives came in 1908 and was initially, like the later developments, a response to a threat of excess capacity. The danger of idle plant and personnel arose when the government temporarily cancelled a major part of its orders for military powder. The 1903 consolidation had given the Du Pont Company a monopoly of the manufacture of military powder, and political protest was not long in coming. In 1906, Congress provided funds for the army to build a small plant as a check on the cost of making powder. Two years later, after the government had instituted an antitrust case against the Du Pont Company, the House and Senate amended a naval appropriations bill to read that "no part of the appropriation could be spent for purchase of powder from any trust or combination in restraint of trade or from any corporation having a monopoly of gunpowder in the United States, except in the event of an extraordinary emergency." The navy then built enlarged facilities at its Indian River plant in Maryland, while the army completed a factory at its Picatinny Arsenal. This construction doubled the country's smokeless powder capacity. In 1908, well before its completion, the Du Pont Company closed down one of its three smokeless powder plants and kept the other two running at reduced volume.

"The likelihood of our having a considerable idle capacity at our smokeless powder plant" led the company's Executive Committee to appoint a subcommittee in December 1908 to investigate and report on "what steps are already being taken, and what additional steps they would recommend, in the direction of developing further uses for guncotton or any of the other productions of our smokeless powder plants." This loss of orders also turned the company's top executives to a more general review of the value of the government business. If unemployed resources might be turned to new uses, possibly even plant and personnel still operating on government work could be shifted to more profitable activities. As Pierre wrote his cousin William du Pont in the following spring: "Reviewing the whole government powder business, it has not paid us to go into it but having gone in we can not let it go. The situation has led us to investigate other lines which might occupy the manufacturing capacity which is now occupied in government business."

Pierre placed his brother Irénée, who had also received his technical training at MIT, in charge of planning the new program by putting him at the head of the Development Department and on the Executive Committee. On the basis of some of the department's superficial earlier surveys, Irénée decided to concentrate his attention on the potentials of the three industries whose products had nitrocellulose as their basic ingredient—artificial leather, artificial silk, and pyroxylin (celluloid-type) products including photographic film. According to the department's reports, the total requirements of these three industries were close to 700,000 pounds of nitrocellulose, or a little more than double the amount normally taken by the army and navy in previous years.

Which of these potential fields, then, offered the broadest opportunity to use the company's existing resources? Pyroxylin products enjoyed a large market, but their manufacturing raised difficulties. Investigation indicated that "it would be necessary to engage in a great amount of detail manufacture to successfully compete with the large companies at present engaged in this business who sell their products largely in finished forms of combs, collars, knickknacks, etc., or in sheets in hundreds of different thicknesses and color." As was still true of the mixed chemical business at Parlin, the volume of each product was too small to be a profitable business. So instead of attempting to compete with the pyroxylin producers, the department recommended that the company continue to investigate the possibility of supplying those companies with raw materials by developing "nitrocellulose from short fibre cotton which would be suitable for celluloid manufacture."

A move into the artificial silk industry presented other types of problems. As nothing in this line had as yet been done in the United States, a real opportunity existed. But it dimmed when the Chardonnet Company, successful manufacturers of artificial silk by the nitrocellulose or pyroxylin method in France and Italy, asked too high a price for their patents. Moreover, the company's leading chemists believed that the recently developed viscose process might soon supersede the pyroxylin method of manufacture.

Artificial leather, on the other hand, not only required less initial capital than did artificial silk, but it also provided a field where the company's technological experience, training, and resources could pay off. Since artificial leather had been manufactured in this country from nitrocellulose for only about a decade, it was still, the Development Department reported, "of poor quality although there exists an unsatisfied demand for the high grade article." The company was in an excellent position to improve process as well as product and also to find technological answers to the industry's major unsolved problem—the efficient recovery of solvents. Moreover, artificial leather, like explosives but unlike pyroxylin articles, was a relatively high-volume undifferentiated product that was sold in bulk to other manufacturers for further processing.

To be more certain "whether a satisfactory artificial leather can be produced at a reasonable cost as well as to determine whether the solvents used in the manufacture can be recovered," the department set up a small pilot plant in the closed-down smokeless powder works in the fall of 1909. The operation proved successful, and on the department's recommendations, the Executive Committee agreed to go into the business. This decision immediately raised another question. Should the company start by building its own artificial leather plant close to the existing nitrocellulose capacity, or should it learn more about the business by purchasing a going concern? Deciding on the second alternative, the company in

1910 purchased for $1,195,000, largely in Du Pont securities, one of the leading firms in the field, the Fabrikoid Company, which had its main plant in Newburgh, New York.

For a short period after 1910, the Executive Committee did little toward further diversification. Naval expansion plus the lack of inhibiting amendments in later appropriations bills again brought large government orders for smokeless powder. Also as the Fabrikoid venture proved profitable, the company expanded its output of artificial leather, transferring some of its smokeless powder facilities and personnel to Newburgh. The Development Department continued to work on enlarging the company's line in this field and soon turned over its initial work in patent leathers and one of two other products to the Operating and Sales Departments for further development. Then, in the summer of 1913, excess capacity again became a problem. Government orders dropped off after Congress reduced military appropriations in 1911 and again in 1912. The Du Pont Executive Committee again asked the Development Department to investigate "uses, other than those with which we are already familiar, that seem susceptible of development into outlets for material quantities of nitrocellulose in addition to our present sales."

The Development Department in 1913 recommended that the company carry out the plans it had started to work on in 1910 for making pyroxylin from nitrocellulose based on short-staple cotton. The department had become most enthusiastic about the prospects for such a product. First, the demands for raw materials, for simifinished pyroxylin products (sheets, rods, and tubes), and for finished products were all increasing rapidly. Second, shipping costs kept out foreign competition and so helped provide a protected market. Finally, the company's large operations in nitrocellulose assured it of lower raw materials costs and of production experience that could be concentrated on finding ways to lower cost and improve quality.

Further investigation, however, showed that the company would have difficulty in supplying the existing pyroxylin companies with their nitrocellulose requirements. Young Walter S. Carpenter, Jr., assisting his brother, R. R. M. Carpenter, recently appointed vice president in charge of development, analyzed the problem in this way. The manufacturing firms would not buy from outsiders because "they would sacrifice the perfect control and supervision of their product throughout its manufacture which they now enjoy." The only way to retain such control would be "to instruct us in the details of manufacture or composition of character of their product." As such information was among their most valuable trade secrets, they would hardly give it out to a potential competitor. In other words, by requiring such close coordination between supplier and manufacturer, this process made a policy of vertical integration a business necessity. If the Du Pont Company was to develop cellulose on a large enough scale to make it profitable, it would have to move into the making and selling of semifinished and, most probably, finished products.

Once the Executive Committee agreed to go into the pyroxylin business, the next question again was whether to do so by building a plant or by buying out a going concern. On the basis of another of Walter Carpenter's reports, the committee this time chose the first alternative. The advantage of purchasing the trade, reputation, and "intimate knowledge of the manufacture" of an existing company was outweighed by the benefits of closer integration with the company's present production facilities, more effective use of company-provided raw materials, and technical know-how that would accrue from the building of a new plant at the Haskell Smokeless Powder Works. This plant could use currently idle equipment and personnel. It would "afford an opportunity for employing to good advantage the technical and manufacturing ability of the smokeless powder organization, thus taking advantage of the facilities and capabilities rendered superfluous by decreasing smokeless powder business." Given its lower cost of raw materials, its "probably greater knowledge of cellulose" which would make possible further continued improvement in product and processes, and its large sales force, the company with its new plant could meet "powerful competition" and still make "a generous return of 20 percent on capital invested," the committee thought.

The outbreak of the war in Europe modified the pyroxylin program, for in the fall of 1914, the Du Pont Company began to receive huge orders for smokeless powder from the Allies. The Executive Committee, as it turned its attention to the new situation, agreed not to abandon plans for a pyroxylin plant but instead to build and operate a small pilot one at the Experimental Station rather than at the Haskell plant. At the same time, the department began its first serious study of the possibilities of a move into photographic film. However, until the late spring of 1915, the company paid little attention to matters other than the construction of the enormous plant and other facilities needed to meet the war orders.

## Intensified Pressure for Diversification

Wartime expansion was to increase greatly the problem of excess capacity in the smokeless powder operations, for the giant European orders were largely for smokeless powder to propel shells, rather than for the high explosives that accounted for the lion's share of the company's normal business. Starting with a capacity of 8,400,000 pounds a year, the three existing plants at Carney's Point, Haskell, and Parlin—all in New Jersey—increased to a production of 200 million pounds a year by the end of 1915. By April 1917, this had reached 450 million pounds a year, or 54 times that of the October 1914 rate. Moreover, in 1915, Major William G. Ramsay and his Engineering Department completed in record time the construction of the largest guncotton plant in the world at Hopewell, Virginia. At the same time, at Repauno and other plants devoted to making high explosives for commercial purposes, there was a smaller but by older standards still extremely rapid expansion in the production of TNT and other explosives based on toluene, tetryl, picric acid, ammonium nitrate, and ammonium picrate. Similarly, the output of special explosives and accessories like caps, fuses, and ignition pellets grew enormously.

Also because of the unexpected increase in volume, the du Ponts began to manufacture more of their raw materials than they had in the past. In these years the company produced vast quantities of sulphuric, nitric, and lactic acids, alchohol, toluene, and such new items as diphenylamine, ammonium picrate, and analine, as well as purifying cotton linters and making ice machinery to recover alcohol and acids. The new demand led the company's research laboratories to concentrate on improving its supplies of acids and semi-raw materials as well as making its processes more efficient. The need for assured supplies demanded increasing vertical integration.

Almost from the beginning, Pierre du Pont, the company's president, was concerned about the impact of this enormous demand and expansion on the future of the Du Pont organization. Writing Coleman shortly after the work on the first war orders had begun, he emphasized:

> We must be careful that our point of view is not entirely warped out of line by this temporary situation. It will take very careful thought and maneuvering to return to former conditions. The Engineering Department has expanded beyond our wildest dream. Those in the Smokeless Operating Department have seized men from other departments in order to quickly meet demands. The other departments all have responded splendidly and have done their utmost to adjust themselves to the new conditions.

Not only did the new demands mean a great expansion in plant capacity, but also in the number of trained personnel and in the amount of capital employed. The total number of men working for Du Pont rose from 5,300 in the fall of 1914 to over 85,000 in the fall of 1918, while the managerial or administrative group (men receiving salaries of $4,200 or more) grew from 94 to 259. The gross capital employed by the company increased from $83.5 million in 1915 to $309 million by the end of 1918. Profits—which grew comparably—provided ample funds for any program developed for the postwar use of this greatly enlarged plant and personnel.

The company began to consider the details of such a program as soon as powder-plant construction was far enough along to assure the filling of military orders. An enlarged Development Department had the responsibility for planning the postwar diversification, but the final strategic decisions on where and when to move were those of the Executive Committee. From the first, all agreed that the department must focus its attention on industries whose processes were based on the science of chemistry. There the company was technologically strong, and the market opportunities particularly inviting. "In mechanical manufactures," the Development Department pointed out, "the United States is far in advance at present of any country in the world. In chemical manufacture, Germany is undoubtedly in advance of any country in the world." And the war had closed the American market to German goods.

The planning of postwar diversification went through two distinct stages. First, the department's new Excess Plant Utilization Division concentrated on finding uses for the greatly enlarged smokeless powder facilities, since "only a portion of the present equipment will be useful after the European wars are settled." Then, in 1917, the department began to consider its resources as more than physical plant and facilities. Its planners began to think about the use of its laboratories, its sales organization, and particularly, its personnel trained in the complex processes of nitrocellulose technology and in the administration of great numbers of men and large amounts of money and materials.

The resulting diversification program into chemical-based industries developed along three lines. First, there was expansion in industries in which the company had already entered—artificial leather (Fabrikoid) and pyroxylin. Growth in the pyroxylin field was hastened when the Arlington Company, maker of Pyralin, a high-grade pyroxylin, approached the du Ponts with an offer to sell. Their management was old and had been troubled by internal dissensions as well as labor and competitive difficulties. The Du Pont Company quickly accepted the offer, for the Arlington firm, one of the largest celluloid producers in the country, was an integrated firm with valuable properties and a well-established name. Its plants at Arlington, New Jersey, Poughkeepsie, New York, and Toronto, Canada were well located for easy coordination with the existing Du Pont operations. Moreover, its paper mill in New York and camphor plantation in Florida assured it of supplies which the European war was making difficult to obtain. In the following year, the Du Pont Company enlarged its Fabrikoid production through the purchase of the Fairfield Rubber Company in Fairfield, Connecticut, a concern whose major product was rubber-coated automobile and carriage tops. In January 1917, to assure itself of adequate supplies, it moved further toward vertical integration by purchasing the Marokene Company of Elizabeth, New Jersey, maker of the "gray goods" base for the Fabrikoid products.

Second, the company entered areas where the European war had caused critical scarcities. Of these, the most important was dyes. The Du Pont Company went into dyemaking hesitantly even though many of its products, such as diphenylamine and anthracene, were used as "intermediates" in dye manufacturing. Despite urgings of the textile industry, the American government, and the Allied powers, the Development Department as late as December 1915 made adverse recommendations. The company at the moment had neither the experience nor plant capacity to go into dye production. Walter Carpenter, as director of development, noted the specific reasons: "First, as all our plant capacity is fully occupied, we would have to build a complete new plant for the production of intermediates. Second, due to the scarcity of crude materials. Third, due to the time of our technical men being fully occupied." Carpenter further commented that Pierre du Pont did not altogether agree with his position. A little later, Pierre and the Executive Committee decided that a start should be made. With the assistance of German dye chemists recruited by the State Department, a dye-manufacturing operation was set up at Deepwater, New Jersey, where several new acid plants had been built. The development of a satisfactory product was slow as was the development of plant and personnel. Dyestuffs continued to be a costly drain on the company's treasury until long after the end of the war.

Third, the Development Department continued to study a variety of new products that could use postwar capacity. At first, it hoped to do this by manufacturing chemicals which the company was "making or could make with very slight expenditure" and which should have a wide market as raw materials in the rubber and chemical industries. Quickly it decided that the demand for these could not employ many of the existing resources.

Then it began to investigate individually the smokeless powder plants in order to determine just what were the specific advantages of each in location, equipment, and personnel. After much study, the Development Department experts suggested that the Hopewell plant was entirely too big. While that plant held possibilities for the production of water-soluble chemicals, fertilizers, or paper and other products using wood and cotton pulp, it was almost impossible to find "any one industry capable of using a plant of this size through a long period of time." In May 1916, the department submitted a detailed report on the future use of the other smokeless powder works. According to this report, the Deepwater works offered the best combination for the new dyestuffs and allied organic chemical products; facilities and personnel at Carney's Point could be turned to the development of castor, linseed, and other vegetable oils to be used as raw materials for Fabrikoid, paint, and varnish production; and Haskell appeared better suited to the manufacturing of more finished products such as Fabrikoid, pyroxylin, and other plastics. Haskell also might be the place to begin work on artificial silk.

The Parlin works, their report on plant utilization continued, could be used to develop varnishes for which there was a wide and growing market. "Varnish of different kinds is used in large quantities by manufacturers of furniture, leather goods, etc., while there is a similar large consumption of varnish by numerous consumers each requiring relatively small amounts. Varnish is handled by every paint store and used by every painter in the country." Both types of varnish—spirit and oil—would use as raw materials the products of other plants and so provide new outlets for production from existing capacity. Moreover, although they would not use exactly the same equipment, the manufacturing process, the machinery used, and the technical skills needed were close enough to those employed in the plant's current operations to permit the use of surplus equipment and trained personnel.

In this report the Development Department noted that:

> Varnish manufacture would give the company a more complete business which would make it easier to meet trade conditions. The present sales organization could undoubtedly handle the varnishes to a large extent by the same salesmen and force in general as in the case of pyroxylin solutions and thereby reducing the selling expense for both.

Parlin's proximity to New York was a "great advantage," a second report pointed out. Moreover, it was a "logical point for a very small package business and tin can company due to the existing production of ether and pyroxylin solutions." Once Parlin had made good in varnish, it could easily move into the manufacturing of paint.

Since the Executive Committee looked with favor on these proposals, particularly those for the Parlin works, the Development Department, during the spring and summer of 1916, concentrated on its investigation of varnish and paint with detailed consideration of various products, processes, output and price trends, and technical developments. Later in the year, the Executive Committee decided on the basis of Development Department studies, to go into the varnish and paint business on a large scale. The move required only a small investment, the committee agreed, because of anticipated "excess plant." The company enjoyed the advantages of vertical integration since it could supply its own alcohol, pigments, resin, and other materials. Produced on a high-volume basis, they could be delivered to the company plants at a lower price than most existing smaller paint firms currently paid for such supplies. These benefits could be increased when the other plants, particularly those included in the plans for the new Deepwater dyestuff operations, developed raw materials for paints, like linseed oil, chemical colors, and organic chemicals. Such advantages should place the company in a good competitive position and assure a satisfactory return on investment.

The Executive Committee accepted the department's recommendation to "acquire by purchase one or more suitable going concerns, if obtainable at figures indicating a profitable return on investment, with a view to transfer of operations to Parlin at the first opportune moment." Partly because of this decision and partly because of the continuing need for basic chemicals and other supplies, the Du Pont Company, late in 1916, bought Harrison Brothers and Company, a large integrated concern with plants in Philadelphia, Newark, and Chicago, which, besides making paints, had a large sulfuric capacity and also controlled bauxite and sulfur mines in the South. However, the need to assure supplies of essential materials, added to desire for diversification, gave Du Pont personnel and facilities in the paint industry that were too extensive to be easily transferred to the smokeless powder works after the war.

# The Final Definition of the Strategy of Diversification

The entry into the paint business helped to bring the Development Department and the Executive Committee to a reappraisal of the objectives of their diversification policies. Up to this time, the emphasis had been on the best use of existing plant capacity. Investigation continued to show the difficulty of finding one product or group of products that could take up the available capacity. Therefore, the department's senior officers, R. R. M. Carpenter and Walter S. Carpenter, decided that the company should investigate businesses which would put to use all types of resources—talents, equipment, and capital—in the whole Du Pont organization rather than primarily the facilities of individual plants. The reasons for the change in policy are best summarized in a resolution which R. R. M. Carpenter recommended and which the Executive Committee passed in February 1917:

> Whereas, the Development Department has, during the past eighteen months, been engaged in the matter of finding industries allied and otherwise to our organization which will be capable of utilizing our military powder plants after the war, and
>
> Whereas, this study develops the fact that there are no industries which will be likely to use more than 25 percent to 30 percent of the value (costs) of these plants, and
>
> Whereas, it has been developed that there are industries which can utilize much more extensively our organization and at the same time offer good returns;
>
> Resolved that it is the sense of the Executive Committee, and that the Development Department be advised as follows:

That from the studies made and reported in detail to this committee, the Executive Committee are of the opinion that the energies of the Development Department should therefore be in the direction of employing our organization to the full and that their efforts be confined, especially as to future action, to the development of the following industries:

1. Dyestuff and allied organic chemicals.
2. Vegetable oil industry.
3. Paint and varnish.
4. Water-soluble chemicals.
5. Industries related to cellulose and cotton purification.

This new definition of the company's policy of diversification led to the continuing purchase of paint firms during the spring of 1917, firms which included the Becton Chemical Company, manufacturer of lithopone, and Cawley, Clark & Company, both of Newark, and the Bridgeport Wood Finishing Company in Connecticut. Despite low profits and actual losses in the paint business, the Development Department in the spring of 1918 recommended the continued building of a full line of paint products; and the Executive Committee approved the purchase of plants in Flint, Michigan, and in Everett, Massachusetts. The first of these concentrated on supplying the automobile trade; the second, like the Bridgeport concern, handled varnishes for interior work. Later in the year, plans for further expansion and consolidation in the paint business were dropped because of increasing marketing difficulties and continuing losses.

Except for expansion in the paint industry, the entry of the United States into the war slowed down the diversification program. Energies were again turned mainly to increasing explosives production. Nevertheless, by November 1917, the Development Department reported some progress in other areas besides paint. The dyestuff operations at Deepwater had been transferred from the Development Department to an operating department. New plant had been added at the Deepwater works. Both the development and the operating departments were concentrating attention on organic chemicals other than those used specifically for dyes. A cream of tartar plant had been set up at Hopewell. Work had begun on water-soluble chemicals and acids at Hopewell, Harrison, and other recently purchased paint plants. The department had decided to concentrate its wood-pulp and paper-product development at Hopewell. Only the vegetable oil group still remained in the investigating stage. The department also continued its study of the possibilities of moving into artificial silk. Negotiations were opened with the American Viscose Company but were dropped because of the "extraordinary price asked for goodwill and business opportunity." For the time being, the company made no effort to look into other chemically based fields for expansion.

In December 1917, the Du Pont company purchased 27.6 percent of available General Motors stock. The suggestion for the purchase of General Motors stock came from John J. Raskob, the company's treasurer, and the treasurer's department. The Development Department, which had played the critical role in determining the direction of the diversification program, had no part in this move and, in fact, appeared to have been strongly averse to it.

At the end of the war and with the rapid contraction of the explosives business, the company continued to move into the new industries outlined in the 1917 resolutions. Because utilization of the Hopewell works continued to present difficulties, the company formed a subsidiary in 1919 to sell its properties there. With that sale, the water-soluble or heavy-chemical program was somewhat curtailed, and the wood-pulp and paper plans dropped. Further investigation indicated that the vegetable oil industry would not provide a good return on investment. So, by the spring of 1919, the Du Pont Company was firmly established in the chemical, paint and varnish, pyroxylin (celluloid), and artificial leather business as well as explosives. Dyestuffs were still in the development stage. Later in the year, the Executive Committee finally decided to take the plunge into the manufacture of artificial silk or rayon.

## Problems Created by the New Strategy

Diversification greatly increased the demands on the company's administrative offices. Now the different departmental headquarters had to coordinate, appraise, and plan policies and procedures for plants or sales offices or purchasing agents or technical laboratories in a number of quite different industries. The development of plans and the appraisal of activities were made harder because executives with experience primarily in explosives were making decisions about paints, varnishes, dyes, chemicals, and plastic products. Coordination became more complicated because different products called for different types of standards, procedures, and policies. For although the technological and administrative needs of the new lines had many fundamental similarities, there were critical dissimilarities.

The central office was even more overwhelmed than the departments by the increased administrative needs resulting from diversification. Broad goals and policies had to be determined for and resources allocated to functional activities, not in one industry but several. Appraisal of departments performing in diverse fields became exceedingly complex. Interdepartmental coordination grew comparably more troublesome. The manufacturing personnel and the marketers tended to lose contact with each other and so failed to work out product improvements and modifications to meet changing demands and competitive developments. Coordinating the schedules of production and purchasing on the basis of market demand was more difficult for several lines than for one, particularly when the statistical offices at Du Pont had no experience in estimating types of markets other than explosives and when little of this sort of analysis had been tried by anyone in the industries Du Pont had entered. Also in 1919, no one in the Du Pont Company had been assigned the overall responsibility for compiling and acting on these forecasts in order to maintain an even and steady use of company facilities by preventing the piling up of excessive inventories in any one department. Each of the three major departments—Purchasing, Manufacturing, and Sales—made its own estimates and set its own schedules.

The poor performance of some of the company's new ventures provided the first warning of these difficulties. Even in the boom year of 1919, many new products had failed to return the expected profits. Paints were actually showing serious losses. In 1917, the company recorded a loss of $108,720 on a gross sale of $1,265,328 in its paint and varnish business. In 1918, the loss was $321,492 on a gross of $2,958,999 and in 1919, the final reckoning was to show a still larger loss on a larger gross—$489,337 on $4,015,769. "The more paint and varnish we sold," one report wryly noted, "the more money we lost."

Such performance was especially disturbing because the du Ponts had assumed that large volume would bring profits through lowering unit costs. This was indeed one reason why they had moved so readily into the paint business. The industry at that time was made up of many small non-integrated, highly competitive firms. Sherwin-Williams was the only large integrated enterprise. Du Pont had anticipated an "opportunity for consolidation and economy in such an industry, as there were no particular secret processes, patents, or other causes which would interfere with a new concern engaging in that business, but that the advantages of careful business management on a large scale would be fully realized." Yet in 1919, when they were losing money, many of the smaller paint companies were enjoying one of their most profitable years.

While the story in other new businesses was less bleak, profits were still well below expectations. Those products which, like paint, were sold in small lots to retailers or ultimate consumers, were turning in the poorest showing. For example, the small return on finished articles helped bring the estimated return on investment in Du Pont's pyroxylin business down from an estimated 21.06 percent in 1916 to 10.95 percent in 1917 and 6.60 percent in 1918.

Selling, nearly all agreed, raised the most difficult problems. The manufacturing of the new lines used many of the same materials and processes as explosives, but there was little similarity in their marketing. Before the end of the summer of 1919, Frederick W. Pickard, the vice president in charge of sales, had already outlined the problem to the Executive Committee. "The expansion of the Du Pont organization into various lines of activity logical from the manufacturing standpoint," Pickard wrote, "has produced a sales condition which compels consideration of a wider variety of products which have no logical sales connection with one another."

The greatest problems had resulted, Pickard believed, from trying to administer different kinds of marketing activities. "The clearest line of demarcation seems to be between merchandising and tonnage distribution," as "entirely different methods of selling are applied to these two general classes of distribution." Before the war, Pickard continued, "95 percent of the business was distributed, whether to consumers, or dealers, on a tonnage basis." With the move into new lines, particularly those of the purchase of the Harrison paint and varnish and the Arlington cellulose products businesses, the company had taken over the selling of a variety of small packaged goods for use by the ultimate consumer. The result of this "forcible introduction to the merchandising game," the Sales Department chief admitted, "to date has been negative rather than positive." The marketing of consumer goods demanded a new and more extensive type of advertising "with a direct appeal to the customer," and the creation of an enlarged national distributing organization including, possibly, even retail outlets.

Product diversification offered the company three marketing alternatives, Pickard reasoned. It could energetically push the "expansion of merchandising effort on a national scale" for the new lines of consumer goods. It might withdraw and sell out these lines to outsiders, or it might retain its present " 'middle of the road' policy, namely, continuing to merchandise those of our lines which are now handled in that way but without extending their scope or endeavoring to develop other lines."

The first course would be expensive. The vice president in charge of sales pointed out that a national advertising campaign alone could run from three to five years at a cost of $3 to $5 million a year. In addition, this alternative would "require a large expenditure for special packing plants, storage warehouses, and distributing facilities. The working capital account of the company would be tremendously increased." The second course, a more conservative one, might keep the company from profitable areas and from making the most of its production facilities, its trained personnel, and other resources. The third alternative, Pickard reasoned, could only be temporary: "Like most compromises it is the easiest way, and my personal feeling is that, except as a temporary expedient, it is unsound economically and, if adopted, should be for the purpose of experiment and observation to enable us to reach more accurate conclusions a year or two hence than we can arrive at now."

To decide among such alternatives proved exceedingly difficult. The executives within the Sales Department had been unable to come to a conclusion on a satisfactory course of action. Moreover, such a decision was of major significance for the future of the company. Pickard therefore urged the Executive Committee to appoint a subcommittee of representatives of the four grand divisions—production, sales, treasurer's, and development—to make a thorough study of the problems and possible solutions.

## The Problems Analyzed

The Executive Committee immediately formed such a subcommittee of the heads of the Sales, Treasurer's, and Development Departments—Pickard, Donaldson Brown, and Walter Carpenter—and A. Felix du Pont, general manager of the Explosive Manufacturing Department. These men, too busy to give the necessary attention to the critical problems, then selected a subcommittee of one able representative from each department plus one of the president's assistants. After six months of fairly intensive work, these five men submitted a report to their seniors on March 16, 1920. First, both the subcommittee and its sub-subcommittee were careful to define just what they meant by merchandise, industrial, and jobbers trade. Then they made a detailed study of outside experience. A Mr. Boyd of the Curtis Publishing Company came to Wilmington to give them "a brief dissertation on advertising and merchandising in general." Next, after examining a list of companies with market activities comparable with their own, the members of the sub-subcommittee decided to study the activities and to interview the managers of eight leading industrial enterprises. These included Armour and International

Harvester, which the Haskell Committee had looked into the previous winter, and also Johns-Manville, Scovill Manufacturing, Aluminum Company of America, Procter & Gamble, Colgate & Company, and United States Tire Company.

The interviews failed to provide much specific data useful for answering the Du Pont Company's immediate problems, for none of these companies had so diversified a product line as Du Pont's. But the survey did furnish some useful general information. "In general, we concluded that each company seems to have its own problem and that in management they tend to follow a single controlling head over their manufacturing and sales departments." The sub-subcommittee members also found that those firms which produced both semifinished and finished goods transferred the bulk goods to the finishing division "either at a fixed profit or at market prices." This question had been raised because diversification had made interdivisional billing a much more complex problem at Du Pont since the divisions making finished products bought many of their raw materials, such as nitrocullulose and chemicals, from other units within the company. Finally, the managers of the visited companies usually stressed the need for "very careful attention to the minutest detail and the exercise of considerable patience and perseverance in following every item."

With its background studied completely, the sub-subcommittee then turned to considering Pickard's alternatives. In determining whether to expand, contract, or continue the company's merchandising business, it decided to look at the different lines individually and to concentrate on pyroxylin, chemicals, paint, and varnishes. Explosives and Fabrikoid products were currently profitable and were sold almost entirely by bulk, while dyes were still not developed enough commercially to make an investigation worthwhile. In its recommendations on the individual lines, this committee decided that a return of 15 percent "on total capital invested" was to be considered an "ideal profit." In determining profit the "transfer of products from bulk to article branches [that is the transfer from raw or semifinished materials to the final manufacturing units] shall be based on the market price with some adjustment." On the basis of the resulting analysis, a number of detailed recommendations were made as to which lines should be maintained, dropped, or expanded.

The more general findings of the committee suggested that, first, cost and other statistics clearly demonstrated the critical differences between tonnage and merchandise sales. Nearly all the semifinished products—pyralin rods and sheets, pyroxylin, pigments, acids and heavy chemicals, and bulk paint shipments—made a reasonable profit, while almost all of the finished packaged products for the ultimate consumer returned less than 15 percent on investment, many of them even showing a heavy net loss. Second, except for celluloid cuffs and collars, these same finished goods businesses—paints, varnishes, celluloid articles, pharmaceuticals, ether and pyralin chemicals, household cement, and solvents—were at this time prosperous. In other words, where Du Pont was losing money, others were making profits.

On the basis of these findings, the sub-subcommittee came to the conclusion early in 1920 that the underlying problem was not one of selling but organization.

In the paint and varnish business and in the making of finished celluloid articles, the company's competitors had "no advantage over us in the purchase of raw materials, and no secret process, no patents preventing us from using the best method of manufacture." Therefore, the sub-subcommittee concluded, "the factor or factors making this great difference between our success in the articles and paint and varnish lines are entirely within ourselves."

"The method of carrying on the business is through its organization," the committee continued in its final report. In the Du Pont Company's paint and articles business it found "an excellent line of responsibility for carrying on each of the functions of the business," but "we have been unable to find the exact responsibility for profits."

> We do not find any competitors who are carrying on these two businesses in the same manner in which we are doing, that is, in no case do we have a divided control, and in all cases have a central control. Are we prepared therefore to say that our method of organization is suitable to these businesses?

In the development within the Du Pont Company of new products like dyes and, in the previous few months, artificial silk, responsibility both for manufacturing and sales had been combined in order to meet new and different problems. Were not the paint and articles lines, "although established businesses, somewhat in the same position in respect to the Du Pont Company? Will not the same treatment, for a time at least, assist in solving the problem?"

## A New Structure Proposed and Rejected

Thereupon, the sub-subcommittee recommended strongly a fundamental change in structure: make product rather than function the basis of the organization; take the offices handling purchasing, manufacturing, marketing, and accounting for paints and varnishes and for pyralin and celluloid articles out of existing offices and place each of the two lines under one executive responsible for all four functions as well as for profit and performance. The committee then drew up an organization chart to indicate how these two divisions could be "practically self-contained" units. In each unit, the managing director would have his own purchasing, accounting, manufacturing, and sales departments. The last two offices the committee sub-divided into merchandising and bulk operations, each headed by an assistant manager.

Under the new plan, the Executive Committee would have general supervision over the managers of the proposed divisions. In these new units the line of authority would run from the president to the division's general manager and then through him and his assistants to the heads of the functional units within the division. The staff departments in the central office would have an advisory relationship to the new division. In the words of the report:

> The managing director of each of the branches will report directly to the Executive Committee in such manner as they may prescribe; and the relations of his company (or division) to the Development, Chemical, Engineering and Service Departments

will be entirely through the managing director and these general departments will be used at the discretion of the managing director. Any additional expenditures for the business, that is, further experimental work or looking well to the future, are general charges and will be handled at the discretion of the committee out of the profits turned in by the particular sub-companies or sub-divisions as the company may be. We would like to see as far as possible a monthly compilation of the standing of each business with respect to its own balance sheet if possible, so that within a week or so after the first of each month the general manager will know the exact condition of his business in respect to the profits for which he is responsible.

Members of both the subcommittee on the marketing problem and the Executive Committee itself had strong objections to these recommendations. One senior member made his views clear in penciled notations on the margin of the report. In this critic's opinion, the proposed structure ran counter to "the theory of our present organization," based as it was on functional specialization. Second, the subcommittee had failed to show exactly "where is the benefit of the reorganization?" A week later he, or another critic said: "The report cites the agency for solving ills (namely, change in organization) though does not cite ills or how [they are] to be cured by a change in organization."

Moreover, this executive was certain that the recent losses were the almost inevitable result of moving into new businesses and that they would be rectified with the development of proper administrative procedures and reliable information. "We have carried excessive stock," he noted, "we have made several unfortunate guesses on the purchase of raw materials," or have been "working against orders rather than setting up appropriate stocks." Selling expenses have been too high; the company has taken too many small orders; and "while our business has been large enough for economical business, we have been scattered over a wide field." Finally, the rationalizing and systematizing of the new manufacturing processes had been expensive and were still not completed. "Our rearrangements, repairs, renewals, and replacements of plants have been high." There were still "miscellaneous shortcomings in factory operations such as poor routing, and inefficient piece-work, pay schedules, short-runs, etc."

The answer was not reorganization but better information and knowledge. It was not the development of new offices and new lines of authority and responsibility but rather the fashioning of more effective inventory controls, of more accurate volumes, sales, and market figures, and of other data to flow through the existing lines of communication. Such information would help prevent unnecessary purchasing and make it possible to find just where the high manufacturing and selling expenses were located. Because of these views, the subcommittee's senior members deleted all of the sub-subcommittee's analyses and recommendations on organization when it forwarded the report to the Executive Committee.

Nevertheless, the suggestions made by the more junior men were discussed among the company's executives, and within a few weeks the Executive Committee appointed another special committee, made up of Donaldson Brown, William S. Spruance—the vice president in charge of production—and Pickard to study the whole question of organization. By June, these three senior executives had come to substantially the same position as had the sub-subcommittee. On July 8, 1920, they recommended an extension of the early proposals for the paint and pyroxylin businesses to all of the company's lines. Related products in one industry were to be gathered together into self-contained segregated units each under a single general manager who had the authority for all operations and was responsible for profits. This form of organization not only would provide the essential coordination between purchasing, production, and sales, but, as the committee stressed, "affords more direct and logical control of the investment of Working Capital," which could now be separated for each of the major lines.

The new committee on organization also spelled out in more detail the relations between the proposed product divisions and the auxiliary department at headquarters. While the executives in the staff departments were to have no direct authority over divisional activities, they were still to have a part in the administration of the new divisions:

> Directors of staff should be able to establish and maintain general policies, procedures and correlation of the functional activities of like-named units of the departmental organizations to a degree sufficient to insure proper uniformity and efficiency. . . . It is assumed that advisory functional staff officials will employ periodical and special meetings of appropriate officials of the line departments to establish and maintain general policies and procedures . . . . and [will] discuss and advise regarding special major problems.

President Irénée du Pont raised objections to the findings in this report. He disliked abandoning the proven "principle of specialization." The steady growth of the company's efficiency had resulted, he maintained, from "having specialists in charge of the various departments." So he turned the report back to the committee for further study. When that body resubmitted an enlarged report with substantially the same proposals in November 1920, the president, traditionally having the final say on organizational matters, again vetoed them.

## A Compromise Structure Adopted

Faced with such skepticism about the radical new plan, Pickard and other executives began to seek ways to administer more effectively the activities of those units that handled the same line of products in the different functional departments. During the fall, Pickard and Walter Carpenter had encouraged three men—one from the Sales Department, another from the Manufacturing, and a third from the Development Department—to meet "unofficially and without portfolio" to consider ways of improving the company's performance in the paint business. One of the three, Frank S. MacGregor, had been the Development Department's representative and chairman of the sub-subcommittee that had made the initial proposals for reorganization. This informal "council," as the three called themselves, had worked up some detailed plans by November 1920. Then, at the Executive Committee meeting of the 23rd of that month, four days after Irénée had turned down for the second time the organization committee's recommendations, Pickard suggested that the Executive Committee agree to formalization of this paint "council." On December 10, Pickard forwarded the report of the group to the Executive Committee.

The council's report was titled "A Plan to Make 10 Percent on Our Paint and Varnish Net Sales." The report began by pointing out that in 1919 the company had "lost nearly $500,000 in actual cash in addition to an expected return on investment of nearly $500,000 which made a total loss of income to the company of nearly a million" and that most of these losses were on over-the-counter merchandising sales. The performance for the current year was little better, and the forecast for 1921 indicated a probable loss of $800,000. The council then suggested a number of specific ways by which to turn this loss into a profit. It provided excellent detailed figures on the costs of raw materials and production and selling expenses, and indicated just how these might be cut. Such action, however, would require that "the responsibility of profits and the control of the business be in [the] same place," and this place should be "a council composed of the plant sales director, the paint production assistant director, and a neutral member."

The Executive Committee, apparently impressed by the specific nature of the suggestions, approved the plan. The same men who had written the report were appointed to a new council or, as it came to be called, the Paint Steering Committee. MacGregor, as its chairman, was given full responsibility for Du Pont's performance in the paint and varnish business.

Only a week after the Paint Steering Committee had been approved, Pickard and his associate on the subcommittee on organization, William Spruance, broadened the council idea to include most of the company's activities. They made their recommendations in a report on statistical controls. That October (1920), Treasurer Donaldson Brown, the third member of the subcommittee on organization, had pointed out that the growing postwar recession was showing deficiencies in current statistical methods. These had, after all, been developed to meet the requirements of the explosives industry, not those of the new businesses. Inventory control based on three-month forecasts had failed to prevent losses from overbuying of gray goods for Fabrikoid production and from similar overstocking of both raw materials and finished goods in other products. Moreover, several executives had been insisting that the company's present need was for better information rather than for a new organization. At Brown's urging, Spruance and Pickard were assigned to study the existing statistical controls. Brown did not join these men in their final report to the Executive Committee on December 22, for he was then preparing to leave the company to join Pierre du Pont, who three weeks earlier had taken over the presidency of General Motors. As their colleagues undoubtedly expected, Pickard and Spruance insisted that the real problem was not statistics but organization.

The current data were adequate enough, but were not properly utilized. The channels for the flow of this information for the different product lines were not yet clearly defined. This was primarily because each major functional department developed its own statistics.

The statistical scheme, so far as quarterly forecasts are concerned, rests upon three independent series of calculations, i.e., the sales forecast, the forecast of the manufacturing program, and the estimated cost of materials which will be consumed in carrying out the manufacturing program. These calculations are furnished respectively by the Sales, Production, and Purchasing Departments. Your committee feels that in the absence of any formal and recognized procedure for the consideration of these calculations jointly by the three interested departments there has been, and there is likely to be, a failure on the part of management to forecast or to carry out a unified business program, as well as to take advantage properly of changes in the business situation as they affect the program of one or more of our industries.

Also under the 1919 plan, the Manufacturing Department had been given full responsibility for inventory control, but such control, the report pointed out, must be the joint responsibility of all three departments. Therefore, in order to "obtain the maximum benefit from the statistical scheme," the two men proposed the creation of "industry councils" for each major product similar to the one already started in paints. Each related line of goods would be managed by a Divisional Council that would include the executive in the Sales, Manufacturing, and Purchasing Departments most concerned with that line:

> These Divisional Councils by uniform, proper, and definite delegation of authority by the heads of these departments respectively, and without in any way interfering with the functional responsibility or authority of the departments in their own spheres of action, can exercise the necessary joint control of the business program which is embodied in the quarterly forecasts and harmoniously and effectively carry it out.

To check on the Divisional Councils' work and to resolve any issues arising among the junior executives, Pickard and Spruance further proposed similar councils of department directors and vice presidents.

The plan for Divisional Councils was thus another attempt to redefine the channels of authority and communication in order to assure more effective administration of the company's diversified product lines. Pickard and Spruance proposed that:

> Sufficient authority be delegated to the members of the Divisional Councils to permit them, when there is complete agreement, to settle problems concerning the immediate control of the particular industry. In reaching a conclusion it would be their duty to call upon appropriate individuals in other functional departments of the company, such as the assistant treasurer (Forecast and Analysis), the economic statistician, the assistant director of Materials and Product Division of the Service Department, or the Development, Chemical, or Engineering Department's representatives when these representatives were needed.

Where the members disagreed, after consulting the staff executives, the matter was to go to the departmental and, if necessary, to the vice presidential councils. In this way the councils, in much the same way as the divisions proposed earlier by the sub-subcommittee on marketing problems, were to assure coordination of the different functional activities for each "industry" or major product line. They were to be responsible, for example, for the coordination of product flow through the departments by deciding the level of inventories and volume of orders within each functional department's headquarters.

The councils were to develop and apply standards of controls over capital expenditures, apply budget systems for controlling operating expenses, outline plans for chemical and engineering experimental work, and devise "additional plans for expansion of the business." In fact, Pickard and Spruance believed the interfunctional product committees could administer all the company's operational activities and make most of its tactical decisions. These committees could handle "nearly all the routine matters concerning immediate control of each industry, with the minimum of delayed decisions or failures to agree on action," and would further "ensure the desirable degree of exchange of ideas and information of mutual direct and indirect interests."

The three members of each Divisional Council were to meet frequently, in fact daily, if possible. A permanent secretary would keep a record of the meetings and make brief monthly reports to the Executive Committee on important decisions taken during the previous months, on general current conditions, and on the outlook for the future. The councils differed from the Paint Steering Committee and from the divisions proposed earlier in that no departmental representative was made chairman or general manager of the council, and in that the members were under the supervision of their seniors rather than given full autonomy. The councils, indeed, would create a type of committee government for most of the Du Pont Company's activities.

The Executive Committee immediately accepted the Pickard and Spruance proposals. As 1921 opened, the Du Pont Company was beginning to move toward a de facto structure based on product divisions rather than functional departments. The senior executives soon came to consider the new Divisional Councils (High Explosives, Blasting Powder, Blasting Supplies, Commercial Smokeless, Colors and Pigments, Pyralin, Acids and Chemicals, Pyralin Chemicals, and Fabrikoid), the Paint and Varnish Steering Committee, and the Dyestuff Department as similar units. For example, in March 1921, all of these groups were asked to submit the same type of uniform monthly reports.

Of the new coordinating committees, the Paint and Varnish was the most active, and this was because one man alone had full responsibility for its work. MacGregor began by making a number of organization changes—eliminating and combining offices in the sections dealing with paints in the Sales, Production, and Purchasing Departments. Under this control, the paint and varnish business began to improve. At least, the losses lessened. Nevertheless, no one suggested during the winter and spring of 1921 that the example of the paint unit be followed by giving a single executive full responsibility for any one of the nine councils. In fact, the subcommittee on organization agreed in May that the new council system was working well, and on its recommendation the Executive Committee voted to continue the current scheme for at least a year.

# Crisis and the Acceptance of the Multidivisional Structure

This compromise structure lasted, however, only until September. The company's financial statement for the first half of 1921 provided the shock that finally precipitated a major reorganization. In those six months, as the postwar recession became increasingly severe, the company had lost money on every product except explosives. At the end of the first six months, the profits from explosives had been close to $2,500,000, but the losses for the other products had been over $3,800,000. The largest deficit, over a million, came from the Dyestuff Department. Paints added a loss of $717,356, cellulose products $746,360, and Fabrikoid $863,904. When other items, such as interest, were taken into account, the total net loss for the six-month period was $2,433,491.

The Executive Committee's regular review of the semiannual operating statistics brought home to it the need for changes. The six-month performance had been one of the worst in the company's long history. Pickard's opening remarks at the Executive Committee meeting of August 2 revealed a sense of crisis. He urged the appointment of a "dictator." He had long been advocating a new long-term scheme of reorganization, the senior sales executive reminded the committee, but this was no time to make such a complicated change. Rather, the company needed a single man with "absolute jurisdiction over personnel" and with full authority to do what he could to meet the crisis. "What is needed," he insisted, "is decision and action and that you get from an individual and not from an organization of talent such as is seated around this table." The other members agreed. Even Spruance, who felt that the council system should be given more of a trial, felt that while "it had improved matters, it had fallen short of what should be accomplished by other means." The committee discussed the alternatives for some time, then decided to take no action until its next regular meeting when the president, who was out of town, would be back in Wilmington.

Before that meeting, however, H. Fletcher Brown, manager of the Smokeless Powder Department from 1911, had written a letter based on his second thoughts and probably those of some of his colleagues. His letter, clearly outlining the situation and the alternatives, became a guide for the top committee's major decisions in the following weeks. After going over the company's financial position, Brown emphasized that: "The trouble with the company is right here in Wilmington, and the failure is the failure of administration for which we, as directors, are responsible." Du Pont had had little trouble until it began to diversify. After the war it "made money for a year because of a temporary spurt in business. It is now losing money very fast, partly on account of inventory losses which still continue, partly on account of our inexperience in the dyestuffs business, and partly because of the failure of our organization to adjust itself to present conditions." The adjustment, Brown continued, called for two remedies. The centralized functionally departmentalized organization structure should be completely replaced by the one recommended in the previous year. Second, the Executive Committee should not be made up of operating executives.

The Executive Committee was weak, Brown believed, largely because it could not be objectively critical and analytical and because its members were unable to get an overall picture of the company's needs and problems:

> The Executive Committee has failed and will continue to fail because, although it is held responsible for results, it is not properly constituted and it lacks authority. With the exception of the chairman, all members of the Executive Committee are heads of departments, and in accordance with custom the members usually refrain from discussing in their meetings the affairs of any one department. The committee member at the head of any one department is moreover in no position to investigate or criticize the work of another department. It has never been found practicable for this committee to discuss and control the conduct of affairs of any one department. Furthermore it is unreasonable to expect that a majority of the members will be able to subject their own departments to such self-examination and criticism so that the company as a whole will operate efficiently. The various departments of the company lack an adequate directing and coordinating force at the present time, without which success is impossible. The Executive Committee furthermore lacks authority. Its careful study of our organization last year resulted in a well thought out plan for managing the various industries. The plan was vetoed by our president who, according to our custom, exercises the prerogative of deciding all questions of organization. The Executive Committee may find itself unable to produce satisfactory results under such conditions and limitations.
>
> We have handed over the details of management of this business to the third-line men who form our divisional councils. They have come up against the stone wall of excessive cost and extravagance and have appealed to us for help.

The present emergency, Brown concluded, demanded the abolition of the present Finance and Executive Committees and the appointment of a new small combined top committee. This committee should be of five men, "no one [of] whom shall be the head of any department in this company." In this way the department head would be able to "give his undivided attention to the details of his own department," and "the Executive Committee will direct and control the operations of the company as a whole."

On August 22, 1921, nearly all the senior executives in the company met at a joint meeting of the Executive and Finance Committees. Even Pierre du Pont and Raskob left their busy General Motors affairs to attend. The group quickly agreed on Fletcher Brown's suggestions and then asked him to draw up, with Pickard and Spruance, members of the old subcommittee on organization, plans for a structural reorganization. The three immediately brought forth from the subcommittee's files the earlier proposals for dividing the company into five product or industrial departments of eight staff or auxiliary departments plus the Treasurer's Department. The only additional change proposed was to reshape the Executive Committee in the way Brown had outlined (see Exhibit 1).

Their final report fully described the functions of the proposed divisions and the new general office. The report did not follow Brown's suggestion of uniting the Finance and Executive Committees, but rather specifically recommended that they remain separated. This was probably because Pierre, and other Du Pont officials and large stockholders no longer actively connected with day-to-day affairs of the company, still wanted to have a place to check on its activities and performance. No department head or other executive with operating responsibilities was to sit on the new Executive Committee for the very reasons Brown had proffered. Nor was any member, except for its chairman, to sit on the Finance Committee. The Executive Committee was to concentrate on the administration of the company as a whole and was to be responsible for its ultimate performance.

While the members of the new committee, with no direct operating duties, were to concentrate on overall planning, appraisal, and coordination, each was also to help oversee one set of functional activities in all five of the new product divisions. In carrying out these last duties, the committee members were to act only in an advisory way. In the report's words:

> It is our opinion, furthermore, that no member of the Executive Committee should have the direct individual authority or responsibility which he would if he was in charge of one or more functional activities of the company. His relations to such functions should be advisory only. For example, our plan provides that one member of the Executive Committee, who may be best fitted by experience for his duty, will coordinate the sales function by holding regular meetings with appropriate representatives of the five industrial departments. At these meetings, sales policies will be discussed and coordinated, subject to the Executive Committee as the final authority.

Besides a member of sales, there would be a second one for purchasing, a third for manufacturing, and a fourth for both chemical and engineering development work. The Executive Committee would therefore take over some of the coordination of functional activities which earlier recommendations had proposed should be given to the staff departments.

The report next took up the duties of the general managers of the new departments:

> According to this plan, the head of each industrial department will have full authority and responsibility for the operation of his industry, subject only to the authority of the Executive Committee as a whole. He will have under him men who will exercise all the line functions necessary for a complete industry, including routine and special purchasing, manufacture, sales, minor construction, normal and logical chemical and engineer operative and experimental laboratory activities, work supplies, cost-keeping routines and analysis, finished products standards and complaints, orders, work planning, routine traffic, trade records and sales expense.

A general manager was to report to the Executive Committee which, on a regular schedule, would analyze departmental reports and discuss them with the manager and his assistants. The manager's work was to be evaluated on the basis of financial performance in terms of return on investment as defined by Donaldson Brown's formula. Therefore, interdivisional billing appears to have been based on current market prices as first proposed in the sub-subcommittee's report on "Merchandising versus Tonnage Sales."

With the general managers handling day-to-day administration and the Executive Committee charged with overall coordination, appraisal, and policy planning, the duties of the eight more specialized functional departments now became wholly the provision of advice and services, to both the divisional and general offices. The eight departments included legal, purchasing, development, engineering, chemical, service, traffic, and advertising:

> The eight Auxiliary Departments will act as consultants and will also perform staff and service functions for the company as a whole for other departments, and in addition will conduct within their departments such activities as may, with the consent of the industrial department heads of the Executive Committee, be so handled in the interest of economy and efficiency. The Executive Committee shall secure proper coordination and avoid an unjustifiable degree of specialization in the technical, service, and other functions within the industrial Departments. Each Auxiliary Department reports individually to the Executive Committee.

Only the Treasurer's Department continued to have some line authority. It would set overall accounting practices and prescribe the forms for statistical and other regular reports. However, the details of cost accounting were to be left to the general managers.

The discussion on this report focused on the role of the two departments that could still carry out more than simply service functions—treasury and purchasing—and especially on the make-up of the new top committee. In the discussion over the Executive Committee, there was early agreement that the president and treasurer, as officers in a general view, should be added to it. The latter, who would still report to the Finance Committee, could supply the statistical and financial information necessary for any major policy decision.

Throughout these meetings in late August and early September 1921, Irénée du Pont remained skeptical about the underlying concept of the committee. He disliked the abandoning of administration by functional specialists, and he was unhappy about the prospect of group management at the top. "No man on the Executive Committee," he said at one meeting, was "to have individual responsibility." This lack of responsibility would cause difficulties, he felt. Despite this, in deference to the strong opinion of the majority of his colleagues, he voted at the same meeting to institute the new committee. Possibly Irénée's protest encouraged the appointment of the president to the Executive Committee, for the president continued to be the individual entrusted with the final responsibility and authority for the company's affairs.

Once the role of the committee and the Treasurer's Department was decided, the one other point at issue was purchasing. Irénée, Lammot, and most of the other members of the existing top committees agreed that the general managers should have "full control" over their purchasing. Only Edge, the vice president in charge of purchasing and traffic, made a strong plea for continuing centralized purchasing through the existing organization. During a week between meetings on the new plan, he had one of his assistants study the purchasing practices of 11 large companies as well as those of New York City and the federal government. All the institutions investigated, Edge reported, had or were about to institute centralized purchasing. Edge's arguments convinced the committee, and the Purchasing Department was made a separate unit somewhat similar to the Treasurer's Department. However, it was to "close no contract affecting any department except with the approval of the general manager and/or the assistant general manager." If the department head was certain he could buy to better advantage and was unable to convince the Purchasing Department, then the question would go to the Executive Committee for decision.

Since there was general agreement on all matters except purchasing, the new plan was quickly adopted. The Executive Committee approved it on September 8 and then voted the men for the new posts. Two weeks later, the board of directors approved all changes. In September 1921, the Du Pont Company put into effect this new structure of autonomous, multidepartmental divisions and a general office with staff specialists and general executives. Each division had its functional departments and its own central office to administer the several departments.

Unencumbered by operating duties, the senior executives at the general office now had the time, information, and more of a psychological commitment to carry on the entrepreneurial activities and make the strategic decisions necessary to keep the overall enterprise alive and growing and to coordinate, appraise, and plan for the work of the divisions. As the Executive Committee noted in their report to the board of directors on the proposed changes, the members of the new committee could "give all their time and efforts to the business of the company as a whole. Being connected with no . . . . [division], they will be able to consider all questions or problems without bias or prejudice."

If the general officers were better equipped to handle overall strategic decisions, the division managers had full authority and the necessary facilities to make the day-to-day tactical ones. As each controlled the functional activities needed for making and selling one major line of products, each could determine, within the framework set and funds allotted by the Executive Committee, the most efficient ways to use the resources at his command. "This type of reorganization fixes responsibility," the final report to the board continued. "When a man is made responsible for results, his interest is stimulated—hard and effective work follows, which brings success. We believe that the adoption of this plan will bring a tremendous improvement in the morale of the Du Pont employees."

**EXHIBIT 1**

First Proposal of a Decentralized Structure in Report of Subcommittee, March 16, 1920

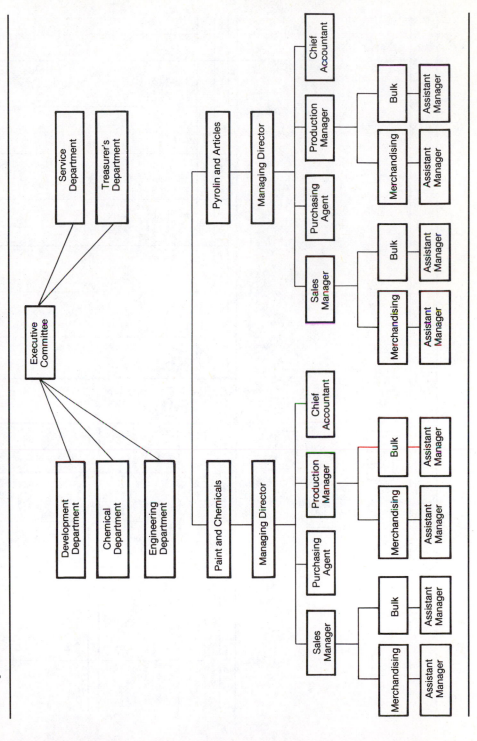

# EXHIBIT 2

## Proposed Organization for the Du Pont Company, August 31, 1921

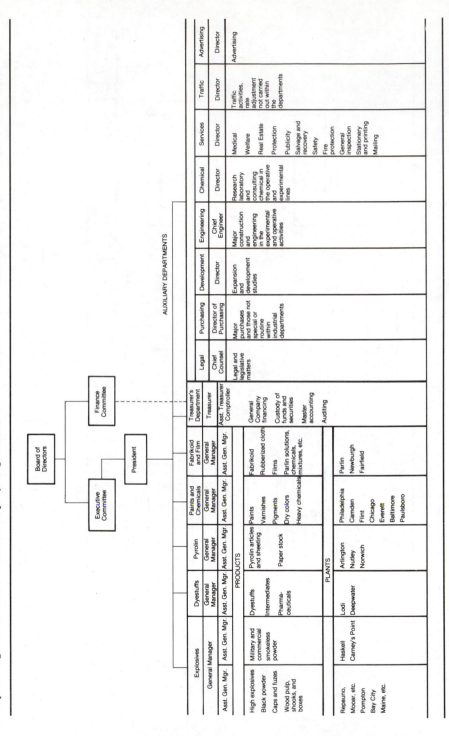

# APPENDIX A

 *Statistics on the Spread of Multiindustry, Multidivisional Enterprise since World War II*

The creation of the multidivisional structure (the M-form as it has been identified by Oliver Williamson and other economists) at General Motors and Du Pont made possible the effective management of complex and diverse activities. It also encouraged the adoption of a continuing strategy of diversification into new products and into new markets. On the basis of this technical or marketing know-how, the enterprise was able through its research and development department to develop and test the commercial value of new products. The executives in the general office, freed from all day-to-day operating decisions, determined whether the new product used enough of the company's present resources or made a sufficient contribution to the development of new ones to warrant its production and sale. If it did, and the potential market was similar to that of the current line, then its production and sale were handled through an existing division. If the market was quite different, a new division was formed. In this way, then, the M-form institutionalized the strategy of diversification in many large American corporations.

The use of the new strategy and the new structure spread slowly before World War II. The Depression, by causing a decline in demand and an increase of unused and excess capacity, increased pressure to diversify into new markets and to build a multidivisional structure. World War II, with its requirements for vastly increased plant and productive capacity and the development of new complex technologies, led many enterprises to accumulate new resources and skills that would have to be employed in the postwar world. A large number of American companies thus found themselves in 1945 in precisely the same position that the Du Pont company had been in in 1917. So with the reconversion from war to peacetime businesses many firms embarked on a strategy of diversification. This note provides data which illustrate aspects of the changing strategy and structure of large American firms.

Tables 1 through 4 summarize a detailed study by Richard Rumelt, *Strategy, Structure and Economic Performance* (Boston: Harvard Business School, 1974). To un-

This Appendix was prepared by Professor Alfred D. Chandler, Jr.

## TABLE 1

**Evolution of Strategy and Structure of the *Fortune* 500, 1949–1969**

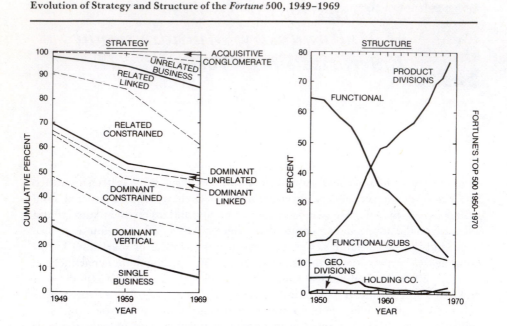

Source: Richard Rumelt, *Strategy, Structure and Economic Performance* (Boston: Harvard Business School, 1974), p. 52. Reproduced by permission.

## TABLE 2

**Financial Characteristics of the Major Strategic Categories,* 1950–1970**

|  | *Single* | *Dominant* | *Related* | *Unrelated* | *Average* |
|---|---|---|---|---|---|
| Growth in sales | 7.17 | 8.03 | 9.14 | 14.24 | 9.01 |
| Growth in earnings | 4.81 | 7.95 | 9.39 | 13.86 | 8.72 |
| Growth in earnings per share | 3.92 | 5.99 | 7.64 | 7.92 | 6.57 |
| Price/Earnings | 14.60 | 15.74 | 19.21 | 15.75 | 17.02 |
| Return on capital | 10.81 | 9.64 | 11.49 | 9.49 | 10.52 |
| Return on equity | 13.20 | 11.64 | 13.55 | 11.92 | 12.64 |

*All estimated values expressed as percentages except for Price/Earnings, which is expressed as a ratio.

Source: Richard Rumelt, *Strategy, Structure and Economic Performance* (Boston: Harvard Business School, 1974), p. 91.

derstand Rumelt's tables, it is necessary to be aware of his definition. First consider his primary categories. For Rumelt a *single business* enterprise is one which manufactures and distributes a single product, a single line of products with variations in size or style, or a set of closely related products where the relationship is due to

## TABLE 3

**Financial Characteristics of the Strategic Categories,\*1950–1970**

| | | Dominant | | | Related | | Unrelated | | |
| --- | --- | --- | --- | --- | --- | --- | --- | --- | --- |
| | Single | Vertically Integrated | Con-strained | Other | Con-strained | Linked | Passive | Acquisitive Conglomerate | Average |
| Growth in sales | 7.17 | 7.42 | 9.48 | 6.93 | 9.62 | 8.06 | 6.10 | 20.64 | 9.01 |
| Growth in earnings | 4.81 | 7.34 | 9.08 | 8.10 | 10.39 | 7.15 | 7.78 | 18.64 | 8.72 |
| Growth in earnings per share | 3.92 | 5.14 | 7.60 | 6.11 | 8.56 | 5.57 | 5.96 | 9.46 | 6.57 |
| Price/Earnings | 14.60 | 15.68 | 15.92 | 15.41 | 19.19 | 19.27 | 13.77 | 17.43 | 17.02 |
| Return on capital | 10.81 | 8.24 | 12.71 | 8.69 | 11.97 | 10.43 | 9.40 | 9.56 | 10.52 |
| Return on equity | 13.20 | 10.18 | 14.91 | 10.28 | 14.11 | 12.28 | 10.38 | 13.13 | 12.64 |

*All estimated values expressed as percentages except for Price/Earnings, which is expressed as a ratio.

Source: Richard Rumelt, *Stragegy, Structure and Economic Performance* (Boston: Harvard Business School, 1974), p. 92.

## TABLE 4

**Financial Characteristics of the Structure Categories,\* 1950–1970**

| | Functional | Functional with Subsidiaries | Product Divisions | Average |
| --- | --- | --- | --- | --- |
| Growth in sales | 8.55 | 6.49 | 9.77 | 8.98 |
| Growth in earnings | 6.76 | 9.57 | 10.66 | 9.17 |
| Growth in earnings per share | 5.08 | 8.32 | 8.63 | 7.37 |
| Price/Earnings | 14.86 | 16.60 | 18.73 | 17.21 |
| Return on capital | 10.28 | 9.49 | 10.75 | 10.43 |
| Return on equity | 12.28 | 11.09 | 12.90 | 12.45 |

*All estimated values expressed as percentages except for Price/Earnings, which is expressed as a ratio.

Source: Richard Rumelt, *Strategy, Structure and Economic Performance* (Boston: Harvard Business School, 1974), p. 93.

the imperatives of manufacturing technology or market structures or both. Such a firm does at least 95 percent of its sales volume in this business. A *dominant business* firm is one which derives 70 to 95 percent of sales from a single business or from a vertically integrated chain of businesses. A *related business* enterprise is one that has diversified in related areas where no business accounts for as much as 70 percent of sales. Finally, an enterprise in *unrelated businesses* is one which has diversified without relating new businesses to old where no single business accounts for as much as 70 percent of sales.

Within these categories Rumelt found important distinctions. First were firms within the related and dominant categories whose product lines were either "linked" or "constrained." For Rumelt the *constrained* strategy was one that "reflects a managerial decision to undertake only those business activities that relate to and can draw on strengths from some product, skill, or market characteristic that is common to all." Firms in the *linked* category "were those which had related new activities to old in such a way that they were eventually active in businesses which, considered by themselves, are virtually unrelated." Rumelt points out that the enterprises using the constrained strategy had the most successful financial performance. However, the reason the constrained strategy was abandoned or departed from was that in many industries, markets and technologies no longer assured a continuing high rate of return. "Therefore, controlled diversity is probably not the *cause* of high performance; it is rather that high performance eliminates the need for greater diversification."

In the dominant category (i.e., those enterprises with only from 5 to 30 percent of sales outside of their primary one) Rumelt found a third subcategory in addition to those of constrained and linked. Here he placed the enterprises that grew through a strategy of vertical integration. Such a strategy normally resulted in a high concentration of assets in raw material, processing, and production.

One problem with Rumelt's analysis is that it fails to indicate those industries in which the large enterprise successfully adopted the strategy of diversification and those in which it did not. The second set of tables gives some indication of the extent of vertical integration and product diversification carried out by the largest American manufacturing enterprises in 1909 and 1960. These firms are listed by 2-digit industrial groups as defined by the government's 1957 *Standard Industrial Classification Manual*. The tables were compiled by Glenn Porter and Harold C. Livesay and appear on pp. 282–289 of the *Business History Review*, Autumn 1969. The data for these tables were taken from lists of the 100 top firms (by total assets) in A. D. H. Kaplan, *Big Enterprise in a Competitive System* (Washington: Brookings Institution, 1964). Real estate, transportation, retailing, and other firms not primarily in manufacturing were deleted. The Standard & Poor's 425 Industrial Average and the Moody's 125 Industrial Average were checked to determine the number of 4-digit industries in which each firm manufactured.

An enterprise with products in more than one 4-digit industry has probably embarked on a strategy of vertical integration. (An exception would be the oil companies, where all the products of an integrated firm fall into one S.I.C. 4-digit category.) An enterprise with products in more than five industries has probably started on a strategy of diversification. Those with products in more than ten 4-digit industries have become full-fledged diversified enterprises.

Table 7 is from Alfred D. Chandler, Jr.'s, *Strategy and Structure*. It places the 70 largest industrials in 1959 into three groups. The first lists those in industries where firms rarely adopted the new strategy and its accompanying structure. The second gives those in industries where there was by the late 1950s a strong trend toward their adoption. The third group are the industries in which by 1959 all the enterprises had adopted the new strategy and structure.

# TABLE 5

**Number of Products of Large American Manufacturers, 1909–1960\***

*1909*

| Industrial Group | Number of Industries | Industrial Group | Number of Industries |
|---|---|---|---|
| Group 20: | | Group 29 (*continued*): | |
| American Cotton Oil | 4 | Mexican Petroleum | — |
| American Ice | 1 | Standard New Jersey | 1 |
| American Malting | 1 | Texas Co. | 1 |
| American Sugar | 2 | Tide Water Oil | 1 |
| Armour | 5 | Union Oil of California | 2 |
| Borden | 1 | | |
| Corn Products | 3 | Group 30: | |
| Cudahy | 1 | Goodrich | 3 |
| Distillers Securities | 2 | Intercontinental Rubber | 1 |
| Morris | 1 | U.S. Rubber | 2 |
| Sulzberger & Sons | 2 | | |
| National Biscuit | 3 | Group 31: | |
| Swift | 1 | American Hide & Leather | 2 |
| United Fruit | 1 | Central Leather | 2 |
| Group 21: | | Group 32: | |
| American Tobacco | 6 | Harbison-Walker | |
| United Cigar | 1 | Refractories | 1 |
| Group 22: | | Group 33: | |
| American Woolen | − 2 | American Smelting & Refg. | 5 |
| | | American Steel Foundries | 7 |
| Group 23: | | Anaconda | 6 |
| None | | Bethlehem Steel | 5 |
| | | Calumet & Hecla | 2 |
| Group 24: | | Cambria Steel | 9 |
| None | | Colorado Fuel & Iron | 2 |
| | | Copper Range Consolidated | 2 |
| Group 25: | | Crucible Steel | 3 |
| None | | Devel. Co. of America | 2 |
| | | Goldfield Consolidated | 2 |
| Group 26: | | International Nickel | 3 |
| American Writing Paper | 1 | Jones & Laughlin | 1 |
| International Paper | 3 | Lackawanna Steel | 2 |
| Union Bag and Paper | 4 | Lake Superior Corp. | 1 |
| | | National Lead | 6 |
| Group 27: | | Pennsylvania Steel | 3 |
| None | | Phelps-Dodge | 2 |
| | | Republic Steel | 4 |
| Group 28: | | United Copper | 2 |
| American Agricultural | | United Cast Iron Pipe | |
| Chemical | 4 | & Foundry | 2 |
| American Linseed | 1 | U.S. Smelting, Refg., | |
| Du Pont | 1 | & Mining | 4 |
| General Chemical | 3 | U.S. Steel | 10 + |
| International Salt | 1 | | |
| Virginia-Carolina | — | Group 34: | |
| | | American Can | 3 |
| Group 29: | | National Enameling and | |
| Associated Oil | 1 | Stamp. | 4 |
| General Asphalt | 5 | | |
| Houston Oil of Texas | 1 | | |

## TABLE 5 (*continued*)

### 1909

| Industrial Group | Number of Industries | Industrial Group | Number of Industries |
|---|---|---|---|
| Group 35: | | Group 37: | |
| Allis-Chalmers | 5 | American Car & Foundry | 6 |
| Deere & Co. | 1 | American Locomotive | 5 |
| International Harvester | 3 | Baldwin Locomotive | 2 |
| International Steam Pump | 4 | Pressed Steel Car | 2 |
| Singer | 1 | Pullman | 1 |
| Union Typewriter | 1 | Railway Steel Spring | 1 |
| United Shoe Machinery | 1 | Group 38: | |
| Group 36: | | Eastman Kodak | 1 |
| General Electric | 10 + | Group 39: | |
| Westinghouse | 10 + | None | |

### 1960

| Industrial Group | Number of Industries | Industrial Group | Number of Industries |
|---|---|---|---|
| Group 20: | | Group 27: | |
| Armour | 10 + | None | |
| Bordens | 10 + | Group 28 | |
| Coca-Cola | 2 | Allied Chemical & Dye | 10 + |
| Corn Products Refg. | 10 + | American Cyanamid | 10 + |
| Distillers Corp— | | Dow | 10 + |
| Seagrams | 2 | Du Pont | 10 + |
| General Foods | 10 + | Grace, W.R. | 10 + |
| National Dairy | 10 + | Monsanto | 10 + |
| National Dist. & | | Olin-Mathieson | 10 + |
| Chemical | 10 | Procter & Gamble | 8 |
| Schenley Industries | 8 | Union Carbide & Carbon | 10 + |
| Swift | 10 + | Group 29: | |
| Group 21: | | Atlantic Refining | 1 |
| American Tobacco | 4 | Cities Services | 2 |
| Reynolds | 6 | Continental Oil | 3 |
| Group 22: | | DX-Sunray Oil | 2 |
| Burlington Industries | 10 + | Gulf | 3 |
| Group 23: | | Ohio Oil | 1 |
| None | | Phillips Petroleum | 7 |
| Group 24: | | Pure Oil | 1 |
| Weyerhaeuser | 9 | Richfield | 2 |
| Group 25: | | Shell | 2 |
| None | | Sinclair | 3 |
| Group 26: | | Socony Vacuum | 2 |
| International Paper | 8 | Standard California | 4 |
| Minnesota Mining & Mfg. | 10 + | Standard Indiana | 4 |
| St Regis Paper | 10 + | Standard New Jersey | 9 |
| Crown-Zellerbach | 5 | Sun Oil | 2 |
| | | Texas Co. | 5 |

**TABLE 5** (*continued*)

|  | 1960 | | |
|---|---|---|---|
| *Industrial Group* | *Number of Industries* | *Industrial Group* | *Number of Industries* |
| Group 29 (*continued*): | | Group 34: | |
| Tidewater Associated Oil | 1 | American Can | 6 |
| Union Oil of California | 3 | Continental Can | 8 |
| Group 30: | | Group 35: | |
| Firestone | 10+ | Allis-Chalmers | 10+ |
| Goodrich | 10+ | Caterpillar Tractor | 4 |
| Goodyear | 10+ | Deere & Co. | 4 |
| U.S. Rubber | 10+ | International Business | |
| | | Machine | 5 |
| Group 31: | | International Harvester | 9 |
| None | | Sperry-Rand | 7 |
| Group 32: | | Group 36: | |
| Owens-Illinois | 10+ | General Electric | 1+ |
| Pittsburgh Plate Glass | 10+ | General Telegraph & | |
| | | Electronics | 10+ |
| Group 33: | | Radio Corp. of America | 10+ |
| Aluminum Co. of America | 9 | Westinghouse | 10+ |
| Armco Steel | 6 | Group 37: | |
| American Smelting & Refg. | 7 | Boeing | 6 |
| Anaconda | 10+ | Borg-Warner | 10+ |
| Bethlehem Steel | 9 | Chrysler | 7 |
| Inland Steel | 5 | Douglas Aircraft | 5 |
| International Nickel | 7 | Ford | 8 |
| Jones & Laughlin | 7 | General Dynamics | 10+ |
| Kaiser Aluminum | 8 | General Motors | 10+ |
| Kaiser Steel | 5 | Lockheed | 10+ |
| Kennecott | 8 | United Aircraft | 6 |
| National Steel | 4 | Group 38: | |
| Phelps-Dodge | 9 | Eastman-Kodak | 8 |
| Republic Steel | 3 | Group 39: | |
| Reynolds Metals | 5 | Brunswick Corp. | 6 |
| U.S. Steel | 10+ | | |
| Youngstown Sheet & Tube | 6 | | |

*The twenty SIC manufacturing groups employed above are as follows:*

Group 20—Food and kindred products
Group 21—Tobacco manufacturers
Group 22—Textile mill products
Group 23—Apparel and other
    finished fabric products
Group 24—Lumber and lumber mill
    products
Group 25—Furniture fixtures
Group 26—Paper and similar products
Group 27—Printing and publishing
Group 28—Chemicals

Group 29—Petroleum refining and
    related products
Group 30—Rubber and miscellaneous
    plastic products
Group 31—Leather and leather products
Group 32—Stone, clay, and glass products
Group 33—Primary metal industries
Group 34—Fabricated metal products
    except ordnance, machinery
    and transportation machinery
    except ordnance, machinery

**TABLE 5** (*concluded*)

---

*The twenty SIC manufacturing groups* (continued)

Group 35—Machinery except electrical
Group 36—Electrical machinery
Group 37—Transportation equipment

Group 38—Optical goods, instruments,
    photographic apparatus and
    supplies
Group 39—Miscellaneous manufacturing

---

*"Industrial Group" refers to the two-digit and "Industrial Product" to four-digit classification used in the 1957 Standard Industrial Classification Manual.

Source: P. Glenn Porter and Harold C. Livesay, "Oligopolists in American Manufacturing and Their Products, 1909–1963" (Appendix to Alfred D. Chandler, Jr., "The Structure of American Industry in the Twentieth Century"), *Business History Review* 43, no. 3 (Autumn, 1969), pp. 290–91, 297–98.

# TABLE 6

## Seventy Large Industrials, 1948 and 1959

### I. None of these firms have the M-form:

| 1948 | Steel | 1959 |
|---|---|---|
| 3 | U.S.Steel | 3 |
| 12 | Bethlehem Steel | 12 |
| 29 | Republic Steel | 16 |
| 35 | Jones & Laughlin | 42 |
| 43 | National Steel | 33 |
| 49 | Armco Steel | 27 |
| 50 | Youngstown | 55 |
| 53 | Inland Steel | 43 |

| 1948 | Nonferrous | 1959 |
|---|---|---|
| 20 | Anaconda | 25 |
| 14 | Kennecott Copper | 47 |
| 28 | Aluminum Company of America | 22 |
| 44 | International Nickel | — |
| 45 | International Paper | 30 |
| 54 | American Smelting and Refining | 86 |
| 57 | American Can | 36 |
| 58 | Phelps Dodge | 89 |
| 70 | Pittsburgh Plate Glass | 61 |

| 1959 | 1948 | Mass Merchandising |
|---|---|---|
| 28 | 13 | Sears, Roebuck |
| 57 | 23 | Montgomery Ward |
| 39 | 36 | A. & P. |
| 66 | 40 | F. W. Woolworth |
|  | 60 | J. C. Penney |

### II. Some of these firms have the M-form; others do not:

| 1948 | Agricultural Processing | 1959 |
|---|---|---|
| 18 | American Tobacco | 46 |
| 26 | R. J. Reynolds | 40 |
| 17 | Swift | 68 |
| 30 | Armour | 92 |
| 31 | Liggett & Myers | 91 |
| 38 | Distillers-Seagrams | 85 |
| 41 | Schenley Industries | 77 |
| 46 | United Fruit | — |
| 47 | National Dairy Products | 58 |
| 48 | Procter & Gamble | 35 |
| 73 | General Foods | 80 |
| 67 | Borden | 101 |
|  | [General Mills] |  |

| 1959 | 1948 | Oil |
|---|---|---|
| 1 | 1 | Standard Oil (NJ) |
| 9 | 4 | Standard Oil (IN) |
| 7 | 5 | Socony-Vacuum |
| 6 | 6 | Texaco |
| 5 | 7 | Gulf Oil |
| 10 | 11 | Standard Oil (CA) |
| 18 | 16 | Sinclair Oil |
| 14 | 21 | Shell Oil |
| 16 | 22 | Phillips Petroleum |
| 45 | 34 | Atlantic Refining |
| 48 | 61 | Continental Oil |
| 90 | 69 | Standard Oil (Ohio) |

| 1948 | Rubber | 1959 |
|---|---|---|
| 32 | Goodyear | 1 |
| 37 | U.S. Rubber | 9 |
| 39 | Firestone | 7 |
| 62 | B. F. Goodrich | 6 |

**TABLE 6** (*concluded*)

III. All of these firms have the M-form:

| 1948 | Electrical and Electronics | 1959 |
|---|---|---|
| 9 | General Electric | 11 |
| 17 | Westinghouse Electric | 17 |
| 66 | RCA | 44 |
| 68 | IBM | 20 |

| 1948 | Auto and Power Machinery | 1959 |
|---|---|---|
| 2 | General Motors | 2 |
| 10 | Ford Motor | 4 |
| 19 | International Harvester | 24 |
| 25 | Chrysler | 21 |
| 63 | Deere | 60 |
| 65 | Allis-Chalmers | 72 |

| 1948 | Chemical | 1959 |
|---|---|---|
| 8 | Du Pont | 8 |
| 15 | Union Carbide | 15 |
| 33 | Eastman Kodak | 32 |
| 42 | Allied Chemical & Dye | 50 |
| 52 | Dow Chemical | 37 |
| 64 | Celanese | 93 |
| 71 | American Viscose | 129 |
| 86 | Monsanto Chemical [Hercules] | 54 |

Numbers indicate relative size according to 1948 and 1959 assets. Data for 1948 adapted from A. D. H. Kaplan, *Big Enterprise in a Competitive System* (Washington: Brookings Institution, 1964), and data for 1959 from *Fortune's* "Directory of the 500 Largest Industrial Corporations."

Source: Alfred D. Chandler, J., *Strategy and Structure* (Cambridge: MIT Press, 1962), pp. 5–6.

# CASE 27

# *The Multinational Enterprise**

The large diversified multidivisional enterprise grew rapidly after World War II by developing new products for new markets. In the 1950s, it further expanded its activities by moving into new regions. As most large firms already covered the national market, this meant expansion overseas. A number of large enterprises had, of course, been operating in foreign countries for a half a century or more. Many of these early American multinationals went abroad to capture the large markets available for their products in foreign countries. After establishing international marketing organizations, some such firms later invested in manufacturing facilities to service these markets more efficiently. The second major reason for early foreign investment was the need to secure supplies of scarce raw materials, such as rubber, bauxite, and nitrates. Of course these two purposes were not mutually exclusive.

The first period of overseas expansion for the large American firm came to an end with the outbreak of World War I in 1914. With the exception of a few years during the 1920s and with the general exception of the oil companies, such direct investment abroad remained small until World War II.

After the war, the firms that led the overseas expansion were those based on the new technologies, particularly those of chemistry and electronics. Because

---

*This case was prepared by Professor Alfred D. Chandler, Jr., as a basis for class discussion rather than to illustrate either effective or ineffective handling of an administrative situation.

Copyright © 1973 by the President and Fellows of Harvard College.

Harvard Business School case 373-369, rev. 6/84.

such high-technology enterprises had relatively little need for massive supplies of raw materials and because their technology gave them competitive advantages in sophisticated markets, these firms made their investments largely in the high-income, advanced economies of Western Europe rather than in the less developed countries of Asia and Africa. This market became particularly attractive after the signing of the Treaty of Rome in March 1957 created the European Economic Community and so presaged the rapid reduction of internal trade barriers on the European Continent.

In the 1960s, this "American challenge" brought major changes in the activities and form of the large European enterprises. The natural response for European companies was to adopt strategies and structures similar to those earlier put into practice by the American firms. In the 1960s, the European firms with the necessary market and technological know-how began to move from a single line of business for a single market into new and diversified product lines and also began to seek markets in other countries. For many, the original line remained the dominant one, accounting for more than 70 percent of total sales; but others developed a variety of related product lines, none of which accounted for more than 70 percent of sales.

Changes in structure followed those in strategy. In the mid- and late-1960s, the multidivisional form began to take the place of functionally departmentalized structures in operating companies and in even more cases of loosely federated holding companies. For in Europe, the holding company was used far more widely and for a much longer period than in the United States.

The relatively quick response of the European enterprise to the American challenge in turn hastened changes in the internal structure of the large American multinational enterprise. Soon after they made their first direct investment overseas, most American firms set up an international division to supervise foreign activities. With further growth abroad and increased competition from foreign firms, the international division proved cumbersome. It had difficulties in meeting rapidly changing market and technological needs and opportunities, in assuring an effective coordination of steady and regular product and cash flows through its far-flung organization (and therefore in attaining the maximum economies of scale), in evaluating operating performance in many parts of the world, and, finally, in allocating resources efficiently. In multidivisional enterprises operating in a number of related businesses, overseas activities were often turned over to the existing product divisions which now became worldwide in their activities. In a dominant or single business enterprise, such as oil or aluminum, the international division tended to be replaced by geographical divisions covering large parts of the world. Some firms compromised. The international division continued to supervise some activities, and product or area divisions, others. And a very few began to develop a grid structure with complex relationships as to reporting and profit responsibilities between the overseas operating units, the area and product divisions, and the general office in the United States.

The following charts and tables illustrate and document these trends in the strategy and structure of multinational enterprise. The first set of tables and explanatory text comes from Lawrence E. Fouraker and John M. Stopford, "Organizational Structure and the Multi-National Strategy," *Administrative Science Quarterly* (June 1968). It indicates that for large American enterprises, there was a close correlation between the intensity of research and development, the adoption of the multidivisional structure, and the building of a multinational organization. In this piece, Type II refers to the centralized functionally departmentalized structure, and Type III to the multidivisional structure. Economists, following Oliver Williamson's example, have labelled the first the U form—U for unitary—and the second the M Form.

The second set of charts and tables indicates the changing internal structure of the American multinational enterprise as it became more involved in foreign operations and had to compete with reorganized and managerially improved European companies. They are taken from John M. Stopford and Louis T. Wells, *Managing the Multinational Enterprise* (New York: Basic Books, 1972). Here, "domestic stage 2" refers to the centralized functionally departmentalized structure or U form and "domestic stage 3" refers to the M form. Table 1 lists the organizational structure of 162 American multinationals. The charts that follow outline the types of organizational structure used for each of the categories listed in Table 1.

The final selection included here is an article by Christopher A. Bartlett. Professor Bartlett's essay illustrates some of the difficulties encountered by major multinationals as they try to create organizations which best serve their strategies and approaches which mitigate these difficulties.

# "Organizational Structure and the Multinational Strategy"*

Chandler classifies the 70 largest American industrial companies in 1959 into three categories: (1) industries consisting of companies that tended to remain as Type II organizations (steel and nonferrous metal); (2) industries partially accepting the Type III structure: argicultural processing, oil, rubber, and mass merchandising; and (3) industries consisting of firms that had generally adopted the Type III structure: electrical, automobile (transportation), power machinery, and chemicals.

The last four industries have clearly played a prominent role in the economic process that we have been discussing. They are quite diversified, supporting Chandler's thesis that diversification leads to the adoption of the Type III structure. They are leaders in research and development activity, supporting the Burns and Stalker propositions. They are the source of most of the U.S. export strength, as indicated by Gruber and others. And they are among the leaders in foreign direct investment in plant and equipment.

A crude measure of aggregate diversification is the number of manufacturing employees outside the primary industrial activity in which the firm has been classified. Of the 17 manufacturing industries of interest, the five leaders are shown in Table 1. It

---

*Excerpted from Lawrence A. Fouraker and John M. Stopford, "Organizational Structure and the Multi-National Strategy," *Administrative Science Quarterly*, 110–13 (June 1968).

should be noted that this is a measure of domestic diversification, and that Chandler's four industries are among the five leaders.

Table 1 also shows an aggregate measure of research and development activity provided by total employment figures for people placed in these categories by their employers. Chandler's Type III industries dominate the research and development activity of U.S. manufacturing establishments. The leading manufacturing contributors to the U.S. trade balance are also identified. Eight of the 17 manufacturing industries had export surpluses on an industry basis; nine had deficits. Chandler's four represented 96.4 percent of the total export surplus by industry category of the United States in 1964. This is consistent with the Vernon position, as is the evidence that these same industries tend to follow their trade advantage with direct foreign investment as shown in Table 1.

The evidence is summarized in Table 2, which relates the four industries Chandler identified as having generally accepted the Type III structure and the four activities under discussion. The numbers in the body of the table indicate the rank of the organizations in these activities among the 17 industries.

From these two tables, it seems evident that the American manufacturing company with extensive international interests is likely to be: (1) diversified in its domestic business activities; (2) Type III in organizational structure; (3) a leader in research and development; and, (4) a major exporter from the United States. These propositions can be investigated in greater detail by using relative measures and data on individual companies.

Chandler distributed the 70 largest industrial companies (1959) in his three categories. Joan Curhan, under the direction of Raymond Vernon, compiled a list of 170 companies that were in the 1964 or the 1965 *Fortune* classifications and that had manufacturing subsidiaries in six or more foreign countries at the end of 1963 where the parent company owned 25 percent or more of the subsidiaries. The Curhan list represents most of the American controlled manufacturing activity abroad.

## TABLE 1

**Employment outside Primary Industry and in Research and Development; Export Surplus and Direct Foreign Investment for Major Industries**

| Industry (and SIC Number) | Number of Employees | | Export Surplus 1958–1964 (millions of dollars)† | Direct Foreign Investments 1959–1966 (millions of dollars)‡ |
|---|---|---|---|---|
| | Outside Primary Industry 1958* | For Research and Development 1958* | | |
| Transportation (37) | 474,095 | 27,094 | + 493.6 | 4,870 |
| Primary and fabricated metals (33–34) | 342,284 | — | — | 1,962 |
| Electrical (36) | 265,473 | 36,305 | + 486.3 | 1,401 |
| Machinery (35) | 254,160 | 4,526 | + 2,063.0 | 2,698 |
| Chemicals (28) | 170,875 | 14,667 | + 752.7 | 4,130 |

*U.S. Bureau of the Census, *Enterprise Statistics 1958* (Washington, D.C.: Government Printing Office, 1963).

†Trade Relations Council of the U.S., *Employment, Output, and Foreign Trade of U.S. Manufacturing Industries, 1958–1964/65* (New York, 1966).

‡U.S. Department of Commerce, *Survey of Current Business* (Washington, D.C.: Government Printing Office, various dates).

Comparison of the Chandler and the Curhan lists shows that only 35 percent of Chandler's first group (predominantly Type II organizations) were also on the Curhan list. The only steel company on both lists was the most decentralized of the steel companies. In Chandler's mixed second group, 45 percent of the companies were also on the Curhan list (54 percent if merchandising was excluded from Chandler's group, as it was from the Curhan list). Chandler's third group of companies were all on the Curhan list except for one company which had gone out of existence through merger.

## TABLE 2

**Rank of Chandler Type III Industries (out of 17) as to Diversification, Research and Development, Export Surplus, and Foreign Investment**

|  | *Chemical* | *Machinery* | *Electrical* | *Transportation* |
|---|---|---|---|---|
| Diversification | 5 | 4 | 3 | 1 |
| Research and development | 3 | 4 | 1 | 2 |
| Export surplus | 2 | 1 | 4 | 3 |
| Foreign investment | 2 | 3 | 5 | 1 |

## TABLE 3

**Structural Classification of Companies by Industry**

|  |  |  | *Structure* | |
|---|---|---|---|---|
| *Industry\* SIC Number* | *Number of Companies in Sample* | *Stage II* | *Stage III with International Division* | *Stage III with Other Forms of International Structure* |
| 20 | 28 | 5 | 16 | 7 |
| 21 | 1 | — | 1 | — |
| 22 | 2 | — | 2 | — |
| 25 | 1 | — | 1 | — |
| 26 | 5 | 1 | 3 | 1 |
| 27 | 1 | — | 1 | — |
| 28 | 41 | 1 | 21 | 19 |
| 29 | 8 | — | 2 | 6 |
| 30 | 5 | — | 5 | — |
| 31 | 1 | — | 1 | — |
| 32 | 7 | 1 | 5 | 1 |
| 33 | 8 | 4 | 2 | 2 |
| 34 | 8 | 1 | 4 | 3 |
| 35 | 19 | 4 | 9 | 6 |
| 36 | 17 | 1 | 8 | 8 |
| 37 | 11 | — | 4 | 7 |
| 38 | 5 | — | 4 | 1 |
| 39 | 2 | — | 1 | 1 |
| Total | 170 | 18 | 90 | 62 |

*For the industry represented by each number, see pp. 703–704 of the Appendix to the previous case. This table is referred to in the text on p. 712.

The mechanism by which this relationship is maintained was examined in more detail. The 170 companies of the Curhan list were sorted into the following categories: (1) Type II organizations, (2) Type III with an international division, and (3) Type III with the other forms of organized international activity that were described earlier. This sorting was done on the basis of annual reports, interviews and secondary sources.

Each company was also classified by the two-digit Standard Industrial Classification number of its largest product line. The result of these classifications is summarized in Table 3 which shows that only 18 of the 170 companies in the sample have Type II structures. This finding immediately suggests that foreign investment is dominated by Type III organizations, which is the thesis of this paper.

# Managing the Multinational Enterprise*

In their study, Stopford and Wells developed "stage theories" to describe the changing patterns of multinational corporate strategy and structure. While these models are not absolutely predictive of the organizational structure any particular enterprise will adopt as it moves into the global marketplace, they do effectively outline the major patterns of growth and change for each important strategy. In this way they reveal the importance of the demands that the three key variables of multinational enterprise—product, function, and area—play in determining a successful organizational structure.

The Stopford and Wells sample is composed of 187 firms, chosen for two reasons: (1) They were listed among the Fortune 500 in 1963 or 1964, and (2) they owned at least 25 percent of a major manufacturing facility in at least six countries. These multinationals comprise an impressively diverse and resourceful group. The median firm had worldwide sales of nearly a half billion dollars, operated in 10 different countries, and manufactured products in 10 different industries. As a group, they were more advertising or R&D intensive than were their domestic counterparts.

As we review several of the important organizational patterns that these firms adopted to meet their particular international strategies, it is necessary to keep the authors' basic stage scheme in mind. "Stage 1" organizations are relatively small firms administered by a single individual, usually the founder or owner. This corresponds with Chandler's owner-operated or family firm, in which there is little or no delegation of management responsibilities and certainly no modern managerial hierarchies. "Stage 2" firms are large, functionally organized companies designed to handle higher volumes of business which would have overwhelmed the Stage 1 organization. This functional form is typically used by single-product, single-country firms. Department heads generally report directly to the president, and strategic planning and general management are limited. Finally, "Stage 3" is the divisional structure. It is created to meet the need for new internal information flows and administrative coordination as the firm diversified. The central chal-

---

*This section is based upon John M. Stopford and Louis T. Wells, *Managing the Multinational Enterprise* (New York: Basic Books, 1972).

lenge of the Stage 3 firm is, according to the authors, "to strike a balance between central coordination and the independence of each subsystem." Difficult enough for the domestic multidivisional enterprise, this task becomes even more challenging when corporations begin marketing and manufacturing in foreign environments.

Stopford and Wells have described what they view as the characteristic three-step scenario of foreign expansion. First, direct ties with foreign subsidiaries are established. Next, an international division is established which is administered separately from the domestic divisions. Finally, closer administrative links are established with the international division as the needs for reintegration with central planning are recognized. Figure 1 is an example of a Stage 3 structure with an international division. This is not to say that firms typically became multidivisional after they became multinational. Rather, the overwhelming pattern was that Stage 2 firms became involved abroad and then established a domestic Stage 3 structure before their international division (foreign Stage 3).

Beyond the international division, a number of multinationals found it expedient, because of the particular requirements of their products, functions, and

## FIGURE 1

**The Stage-3 Structure with an International Division**

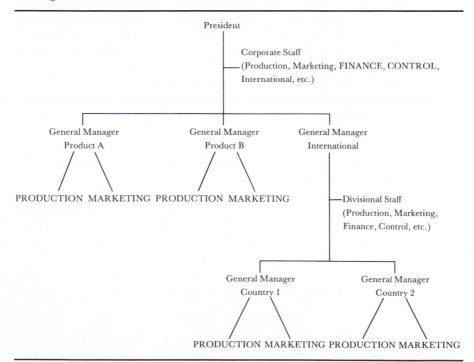

Note: The functions in capital letters indicate operating responsibility; those in lowercase letters indicate advisory and coordinating roles.

areas, to develop true "global" organizational structures to better coordinate the flows of information, materials, and products. These four types of structure are (1) Worldwide Product Divisions, (2) Area Divisions, (3) Mixed, and (4) Grid. In the first type, product diversification abroad moves from an international division to a global structure in which "each domestic product division is assigned responsibility for the worldwide activities in its product line" (see Figure 2). Here product coordination takes precedence over area coordination. The purpose of this reorganization is, again, to "increase the integration between domestic and foreign activities in the enterprise."

Less common were the firms that developed area divisions as a global strategy (see Figure 3). As shown in Table 1, these enterprises were typically single-product firms which operated over a wide area. This is because area divisions were not well suited to multiple product lines. By adding an extra level of senior general managers, such firms created organizational microcosms at the regional level. In a few cases, uniform marketing practices were achieved despite the varying national environments. In others, the highly standardized nature of products permitted the rationalization of separate plants. The advantage of area divisions was, however, that they "can be tailored to meet the conflicting requirements for centralized production and decentralized marketing."

In the "mixed" structure, elements of both the area and product divisional forms are combined (see Figure 4). Several factors can explain the appearance of this complex structure. The fact that all of the mixed enterprises spent over 1 percent of sales on R&D indicates that technological innovation is critical to these organizations. Some were the result of mergers and acquisitions. "The foreign subsidiaries of the acquired firms were never attached to the international division, so that the international division did not have to face the problems of managing a diverse product line." In other instances, the mixed organization served as a convenient transitional form in the conversion from international division to worldwide product divisions. The international division was simply dismantled one piece at a time, making the transition of each product to worldwide division status a less drastic transition for the entire firm.

The most complex organizational response to the demands of international manufacturing and marketing is the "grid" structure (see Figure 5).[1] Here, solutions to the underlying orgainzational tensions between product and region and between central coordination and divisional autonomy are sought through formal institutional channels. Whatever form these grid structures take, and there are many, they all "have the common characteristics of responsibility being shared among divisions, and of managers having multiple reporting relationships." Thus, both divisional and area managers report to top management with roughly equivalent authority, making this form of management as much contractual as hierarchical.

---

[1]As the authors warn, "Any chart of a grid structure is bound to be somewhat misleading, because there is no effective way of representing the full extent of the important informal relationships and communications patterns."

# FIGURE 2

**Worldwide Product Divisions**

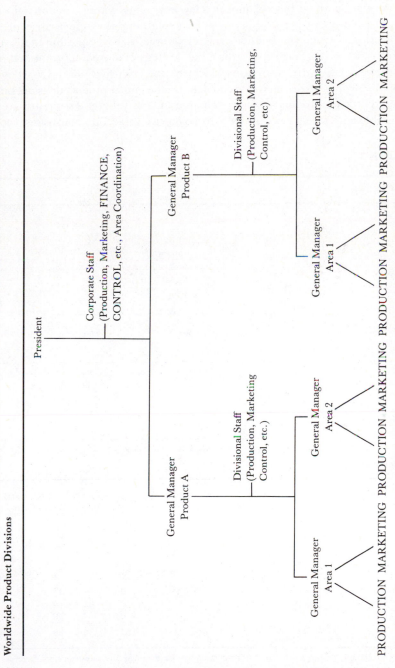

President

Corporate Staff
(Production, Marketing, FINANCE,
CONTROL, etc., Area Coordination)

General Manager
Product A

General Manager
Product B

Divisional Staff
(Production, Marketing
Control, etc.)

Divisional Staff
(Production, Marketing,
Control, etc)

General Manager
Area 1

General Manager
Area 2

General Manager
Area 1

General Manager
Area 2

PRODUCTION  MARKETING  PRODUCTION  MARKETING  PRODUCTION  MARKETING  PRODUCTION  MARKETING

Note: The functions shown in capital letters indicate operating responsibility; those in lowercase letters indicate mainly advisory and coordinating roles.

The Stopford and Wells evidence is a significant contribution to our understanding of the relationship between strategy and structure in multinational enterprise. With this "stage theory" model, a few key points emerge. For one, the absolute size of an enterprise is critical in explaining the appearance of some organizational structures, but not all. For example, size is important in the transition from Stage 1 to Stage 2 structure, but strategy is more important in the shift from Stage 2 to Stage 3. Also, firms which created area divisions did so when their international division threatened to equal in size the largest product division, but size mattered little for product division companies. Clearly, Stage 2 structures were incompatible with foreign expansion. Moreover, as Table 1 demonstrates, the level

## FIGURE 3

---

**Area Divisions**

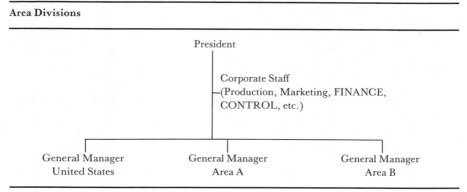

Note: The functions in capital letters indicate operating responsibility; those in lowercase letters indicate advisory and coordinating roles.

## TABLE 1

---

**Multinational Enterprises, Classified by Structure and by Foreign Product Diversity, for 162 American Multinationals**

| Structure | Total Number of Firms | Number of Firms, Classified by Foreign Product Diversity* | | |
|---|---|---|---|---|
| | | *None* | *Low* | *High* |
| International Divisions With: | | | | |
| Domestic Stage 2 (U form) | 8 | 7 | 1 | 0 |
| Domestic Stage 3 (M form) | 82 | 39 | 39 | 4 |
| Area divisions | 17 | 11 | 4 | 2 |
| Worldwide product divisions | 30 | 0 | 11 | 19 |
| Mixed | 22 | 0 | 13 | 9 |
| Grid | 3 | 0 | 0 | 3 |
| Total | 162 | 57 | 68 | 37 |

*"None" indicates that a firm has all its products in a single two-digit SIC industry. "Low" indicates that a firm has products in more than one industry but that one product line is of dominating importance. "High" indicates that a firm has products in many industries and no dominant product line.

Sources: *News Front*, November 1965, January 1966, and February 1966, and annual reports of the firms.

**FIGURE 4**

The Mixed Structure

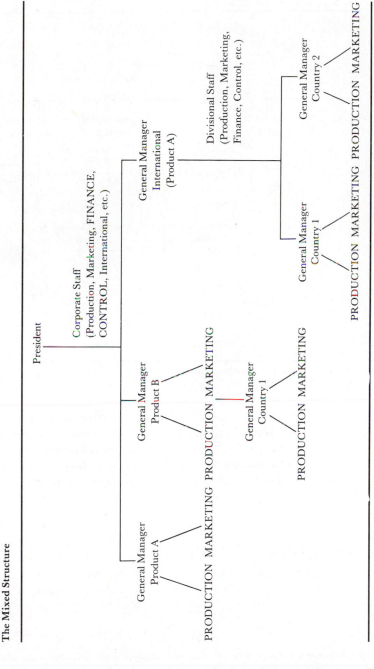

Note: The functions shown in capital letters indicate operating responsibility; those in lowercase letters indicate advisory and coordinating roles.

**FIGURE 5**

**A Grid Structure** *(Partial organizational chart)*

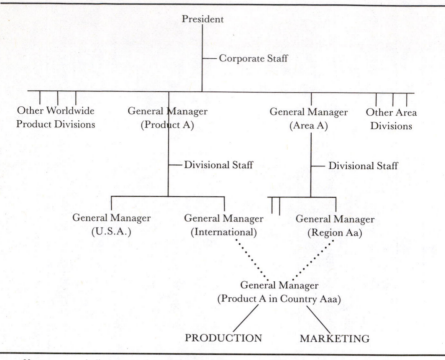

Note:_____ indicates reporting relationships where responsibility is not shared. ...... indicates reporting relationships where responsibility is shared.

of a firm's product diversity was one of the key ingredients determining its appropriate structure. In short, what determined the kind of structure a multinational enterprise adopted was the strategy its managers formulated (usually after some time lag) to meet the firm's special combination of products, functions, and areas. And while an imperfect match of structure with strategy did not necessarily spell disaster, the most well-matched firms did appear to be the most successful.

# How Multinational Organizations Evolve*

*When companies grow and expand overseas, they often experience such organizational problems as classic conflict between line and staff and between country and functional managers. Often, the companies that succeed are those that take a*

---

*Source: Christopher A. Bartlett, "How Multinational Organizations Evolve," *Journal of Business Strategy* 1, no. 3 (Summer, 1982), pp. 20–32.

*gradual and adaptive approach rather than engaging in a series of abrupt and traumatic reorganizations.*

For most of this century, Westinghouse's international activities were managed through Westinghouse Electric International, a separate organization based in New York and maintaining only limited contact and interaction with the rest of the company.[1] In the 1960s, Westinghouse tried to build its overseas strength by acquiring strong national firms and linking them to the U.S. parent through its international division. Difficulties arose not only in obtaining suitable companies (de Gaulle personally vetoed one key acquisition), but also in integrating them into Westinghouse. Thus, in 1971 the separate international organization was disbanded and the company's 125 division managers were given worldwide responsibility for the businesses they had been managing in the domestic U.S. market.

By 1978, however, top management was concerned that the company was gaining a reputation abroad for being internally disorganized with a total lack of coordination between divisions. Several of its overseas companies were in difficulty and had to be sold off. Furthermore, foreign customers and governments were complaining that the company was difficult to do business with because of its insensitivity to local situations and its inability to coordinate various businesses in a given country.

In early 1979, the vicechairman's response was to reorganize once again. He gave one of his key executives 90 days to analyze Westinghouse's international operations and make recommendations for the organizational change required. The report recommended that the company supplement its worldwide product organization with a network of geographic managers reporting to a strong international chief. By July 1979, Westinghouse had begun installing a formal global matrix organization structure by overlaying the existing product organization with the new geographic organization. Newly appointed country managers reported to four regional presidents who, in turn, reported to an international president with a seat on the powerful corporate management committee. This reorganization, the company believed, would help it achieve the global integration it needed to remain efficient and competitive and the sensitivity to national environments it required to be effective locally.

Westinghouse's situation provides a good illustration not only of the multiple strategic pressures that have confronted most companies as they have expanded abroad, but also of the typical structural responses in U.S.-based multinational corporations (MNCs).

Like Westinghouse, many MNCs found themselves confronted by multiple, and often conflicting, strategic demands as they grew internationally. Most became aware quite early of the need to develop an understanding of the diverse characteristics of the various national environments in which they operated. However, as foreign operations grew, they began to recognize the opportunity and the need to rationalize these diverse worldwide operations to capitalize on their poten-

---

[1]This account of Westinghouse's growth abroad is based largely on the article "Westinghouse Takes Aim at the World," *Fortune*, January 14, 1980, pp. 48–53.

tial global efficiencies. As global competition intensified and, at the same time, pressures from host countries grew, managers of MNCs were confronted with the simultaneous need to be globally competitive and nationally responsive.[2] Responding consistently and appropriately to the variety of diverse, changing, and often conflicting demands has provided, for many companies, the major administrative challenge of the past decade. Their decision processes had to adapt to the challenge of becoming multidimensional—able to respond simultaneously to the global and the national strategic imperatives.

For many companies, the need for the decision-making process to respond to these diverse and growing pressures led to a series of reorganizations similar to those undertaken by Westinghouse. So familiar did the pattern become that various "stages theories" of organizational development became widely recognized.[3] Some academics, consultants, and managers began to think of this series of reorganizations in normative rather than descriptive terms, and for some MNCs it seemed that organizational structure followed fashion as much as it related to strategy.[4] Reorganizations from international divisions to global product or area organizations, or from global structures to matrix forms, became widespread. This, after all, was the classic organizational sequence described in the "stages theories."

Yet many companies that had expected such changes to provide them with the strategy-structure "fit" to meet the new pressures were disappointed. Developing a multidimensional decision-making process that was able to balance the conflicting global and national needs was a subtle and time-consuming process not necessarily achieved by redrawing the lines on a chart. Examples of failed or abandoned multinational organizations abound.[5]

While there were many companies, like Westinghouse, that appeared to concentrate largely on changes in the formal organizational structure as a means to achieve the desired changes in their administrative processes, there were others that appeared to have developed successful multidimensional decision-making processes without resorting to major changes in their formal organizations. Most notable was the substantial number of companies that had built large, complex,

---

[2]Yves Doz has written extensively on the nature of these demands. See, e.g., "Strategic Management in Multinational Companies," *Sloan Management Review*.

[3]Perhaps the best known of the "stages theories" of multinational organization development was developed by John Stopford. See, e.g., John M. Stopford and Louis T. Wells, *Managing the Multinational Enterprise* (New York: Basic Books, 1972).

[4]Richard Rumelt noted a tendency for strategy to follow fashion in his study of *Fortune* 500 companies. See Richard P. Rumelt, *Strategy, Structure, and Economic Performance* (Boston: Division of Research, Harvard Business School, 1974), p. 149.

[5]Perhaps the two most widely cited examples of multidimensional matrix organizations apparently have pulled back from their original structure. Davis and Lawrence describe the demise of Dow Chemical's global matrix but point to the emergence of a more recent multinational matrix success: Citibank. Stanley M. Davis and Paul R. Lawrence, *Matrix* (Reading, Mass.: Addison-Wesley, 1977), pp. 206–22. Recent reports indicate that Citibank has now abandoned its global matrix. See "It's a Stronger Bank That David Rockefeller is Passing to His Successor," *Fortune*, January 14, 1980, p. 44.

and successful foreign operations while retaining their supposedly embryonic international division structures.[6] If these companies had been successful in achieving a strategy-structure fit, they had done so without resorting to the sequence of traumatic reorganizations as described in the stages theories and as experienced by Westinghouse.

To understand why this substantial group of MNCs had not followed the stages model of organizational change, a detailed clinical study of nine of these companies was undertaken.[7] It was hypothesized that either the parameters of the generally accepted stages models were inappropriate or there were alternative means of structural response that were not revealed in a simple classification of formal organization.

The companies studied were selected from two industries with diverse strategic characteristics: four from the food processing industry and five from the health care industry. In trying to understand why these companies did not evolve through the series of reorganizations described in the stages models, two quite different explanations emerged.

The companies in the food processing industry had retained their international division structure for a very simple reason: The key strategic demands of their operations were perceived as being unidimensional. The nature of the business resulted in the key tasks being focused at the national level, with little longterm advantage to be gained by global operations. Product development, manufacturing, and marketing were all national rather than global tasks for a variety of cultural as well as economic reasons.[8] The conclusion reached was that increasing size and complexity did not cause these companies to abandon the "federal" organization structure needed to manage this business.

This article concentrates on the findings relating to the five companies in the health care industry (ethical and proprietary drugs, hospital supplies). The administrative challenges confronting managers in these companies were more interesting since they clearly did face the diversity of global and national demands and environmental conditions that had forced many other companies to follow the traditional stages of reorganization into global and then matrix forms of organization. The companies studied, however, seemed to achieve their state of strategy-structure fit by a different process. Rather than focusing on "anatomical" changes, these companies seemed to spend more time modifying the "physiological" and even the "psychological" characteristics of their organizations. They seemed to view the required change from unidimensional to multidimensional organizations

---

[6]A follow-up study of the original Stopford sample of companies is planned. A preliminary estimate indicates that well over 30 percent of the companies classified as having international divisions in 1967 retained them 12 years later despite their growth and the changing environmental demands.

[7]See Christopher A. Bartlett, *Multinational Structural Evolution: The Changing Decision Environment in International Divisions*, unpublished doctoral dissertation, Harvard University Graduate School of Business Administration, 1979.

[8]For a full exploration of the strategic demands in the food industry, see Ulrich E. Wiechmann, *Marketing Management in Multinational Firms* (New York: Praeger, 1976).

as an adaptive, evolutionary process rather than as a series of powerful, yet perhaps traumatic, reorganizations. In contrast to companies such as Westinghouse and others which followed the "strategic crisis-structural reorganization" route, these companies developed, adjusted, and integrated the required new skills, structures, and processes gradually but continuously. It is this alternative process of adaptation from unidimensional to multidimensional organization that will be described in the remainder of this article.

## Strategic Demand: Handling Multidimensional Tasks

Before describing the structural and administrative changes made by the various companies, it may be helpful to have an understanding of the overall task demands that provoked the changes. What were the strategic issues facing companies in the health care industry that prevented them from retaining the simply unidimensional "federal" organization structure that proved adequate for the food processing companies?

The task complexity facing the health care companies could be described briefly along three dimensions: the need to be simultaneously responsive at the national level, yet efficient globally; the need to develop multiple functional expertise at multiple organization levels; the need to be flexible in the way all of these demands were managed. Each will be described briefly.

**1.** As they expanded abroad, these companies needed to understand and respond to the variety of local national demands that affected their success in each national market. They had to understand the structure and operation of national health delivery systems, the nature of government product registration processes, the formal and informal demands for local sourcing of critical products, and a variety of other such national pressures. However, they also had to recognize that if they were to be effective global competitors, their research efforts, manufacturing capacity, product policy, and a variety of other tasks had to be coordinated and perhaps integrated on a worldwide basis. In short, they were faced with the challenge of being simultaneously responsive and flexible at the national level while maintaining the competitive efficiency that comes from global coordination.

**2.** Unlike the food processing industry, where the marketing function was the dominant success factor, in the health care industry the marketing, research, and manufacturing functions were all regarded as key success factors. Furthermore, in the food industry all the key tasks were concentrated at the national level (e.g., products developed to meet national tastes, local manufacturing due to freshness and transportation limitations, etc.). Key tasks in the drug industry, however, needed to be managed at multiple organizational levels (e.g., for economic and quality-control reasons, active ingredients for most drugs were prepared centrally, while tablet and capsule plants could be operated efficiently on a regional or national basis; basic research obviously needed global coordination, yet product development was often handled on a regional basis, and local clinical trials were needed for national product registration).

**3.** Unlike the food processing industry, where the markets, the technology, and the products were typically mature, the health care industry tended to present a much more dynamic operating environment. Particularly in the areas of new product development and government controls and regulations, changes were occurring at a very rapid rate in the 1960s and 1970s. Furthermore, the state of maturity and rate of change varied substantially by market.

## The Multidimensional Organization: How Companies Responded

Clearly, companies could not hope to manage this set of complex, diverse, and changing demands through their simple unidimensional "federal" organizational structures. They were faced with the major challenge of developing complex multidimensional "global" organizations. As stated previously, in the companies studied, such organizational structures were developed not through the series of reorganizations described by the stages theories, but through a more gradual evolutionary process. This process appeared to involve three distinct yet closely interrelated changes, and although there was considerable overlap, these changes tended to occur sequentially. First, new management skills and perspectives were gradually developed to reflect and respond to the growing range of task demands facing these companies; next, subtle modifications were made to the organizational structures and systems to allow better interaction between the newly developed range of management perspectives; finally, conscious efforts were made to change the organizational "climate" in an attempt to institutionalize the relationships required in an effective decision-making process in a complex and uncertain multidimensional organizational environment.

The purpose of these changes in the formal and informal structures and systems was to allow the organization's decision-making process to evolve from a unidimensional to a multidimensional focus. Associated with each stage of the structural development was a change in what can be termed the predominant "management mode." Substantive decision management by senior management in the first phase tended to evolve toward a temporary coalition management mode, which in turn gave way to decision context management in the final phase. Each will be explained and illustrated in the following sections.

The nature of these structural developments and the changes in the decision-making process that accompanied them will provide the focus for the remainder of this article. Only one additional note needs to be added at this stage. Although each company studied had made adaptations to skills, structure, and "climate," it was also clear that they were not at all the same stage of development in creating their multidimensional organizational structures and management processes. One had concentrated mainly on developing the range of management skills and perspectives required to respond to the diversity of task demands it faced and continued to utilize the substantive decision management mode. Others had supplemented such changes with varying degrees of change in their structures, systems, and basic administrative processes and had broadened their repertoire of "management modes" in decision making. To illustrate the description of each of these modes, however, examples are provided from the companies that most closely correspond to the phase of multidimensional development being described. It should be recognized, however, that none of the companies fit neatly into such convenient categories: in effect, there were as many structural and administrative solutions as there were companies studied.

# Developing New Management Perspectives: Substantive Decision Management

### Changing the Organization

In their early stages of overseas expansion, all five of the health care companies studied had developed networks of strong, independent country subsidiaries. The key strategic tasks were perceived as being, first, to develop an understanding of the various national operating environments and, second, to use that knowledge to build strong, initial market positions. Thus, country subsidiary managers with local expertise were granted considerable autonomy and independence to perform these tasks.

The organizational structure that resulted could best be described as a "federal" structure in which the country managers' knowledge of their national operating environments gave them a dominant role in key decisions. Their power was formally recognized by the fact that geographic managers were line managers in organizations in which line authority was rarely challenged. Product and functional managers filled staff roles that were primarily defined as support functions for the country managers. Headquarters intervention into subsidiary operations was limited and infrequent, and the country managers' view dominated the strategic decision process.

As a consequence, even decisions with global implications were frequently made on the largely unchallenged recommendation of country subsidiary managers. For example, in each of the companies studied, this early period of development was marked by the proliferation of manufacturing operations worldwide as country managers argued that a local plant was essential for the success of the national subsidiary. There was little resistance to such demands for two reasons: first, nobody in the organization had sufficient knowledge of the various national environments to challenge country managers' claims of customer demands or government pressures; second, little if any analysis was being done to determine the global costs and efficiency of this multiple plant "strategy."

Although this "federal system" proved adequate for the early stages of establishing foreign subsidiaries, it became clear that a company's global strategy could not be defined by the simple sum of its various national strategies. Geographically based demands had to be supplemented with product and functional views;

national perspectives had to be counterbalanced by regional and global perspectives.

The major impediment to the goal of adding new perspectives to the decision process was that the product and functional managers who should have been able to provide such input were unable to do so. The dominance of the geographic perspective in the past had resulted in the development of product and functional managers whose major task was to service the needs of country subsidiary managers and act as headquarters links and information conduits. They had neither the expertise nor the organizational credibility to counter the country managers' proposals with arguments that took a more integrated global viewpoint. The first challenge in building a more multidimensional organization, therefore, was to develop managers who could represent these additional perspectives.

In all five health care companies, the process of developing the broader product and functional management skills and viewpoints followed a remarkably similar pattern. It began with the growth of a regional office and culminated with the establishment of management groups at the divisional level that had a substantial input to all major strategic decisions.

Ironically, it was the demands of the geographic line managers for more support at the regional level that gave product and functional managers an opportunity to develop their information access, their control role, and their coordination responsibilities. Through these changes their power and influence in the ongoing decision process increased substantially. In response to subsidiary criticism that the staff groups at division headquarters were too distant and often of too little experience to provide the required level of support, regional offices were established in all five companies studied. By working closer to the various markets, product and functional managers made important developmental advances as they gained greater understanding of and credibility in the subsidiary operations.

The next critical phase in the development of the product and functional managers occurred during the control period that tended to follow the initial rapid growth abroad. As foreign sales and overseas investment levels grew to a level of corporate importance, senior management began demanding better information about and control over the largely autonomous subsidiaries. The product and functional management groups, with their closer contact with operations, began to be seen as appropriate sources of information and means of control. Increasingly, their visits to subsidiaries were at the instruction of top management to report on a problem rather than at the request of the country manager to provide technical information or support.

With increased knowledge, access to regular, current, reliable data, and power gained through their new control responsibility, it was inevitable that the product and functional managers eventually would move to the third important phase in their development within the organization. In each of the companies observed, these more sophisticated, more powerful management groups began to recognize opportunities to coordinate and integrate activities being managed separately by the various country operations. While initial projects tended to concentrate on the provision of regional services to subsidiaries (e.g., EDP systems and facilities, intercompany payments netting), as soon as their credibility was established, these managers often began to take on major coordination and integration responsibilities such as regional manufacturing rationalization or regional product management coordination.

The increased credibility that grew out of their greater access to operations, the new influence that derived from their control role, and the upgraded power that flowed from their new coordination responsibilities all provided the regional product and functional managers with considerably greater impact on the decision process. Their increasing importance and power was symbolized by the growth of the regional office that took place during this period in each of the companies observed. Country managers were particularly conscious of this change in influence of product and functional managers, and in numerous instances tensions and even open conflict developed between staff and line.

Nevertheless, senior management found the additional information, services, and advice helpful in counterbalancing the previously unidimensional analyses and recommendations they had been receiving. To develop better global perspectives and to obtain improved access to the newly developed expertise, senior management typically began to build the product and functional management groups at the division headquarters level. Many of the stronger managers developed at the regional level were transferred to the division level as part of this process.

This development resulted in the power and influence of product and functional managers being developed even more. First, their proximity to senior management enhanced their access to and influence in key decision-making processes. Equally important, however, was the role these managers began to play in linking the international division to the rest of the corporation. Their product or functional expertise gave them credibility in other parts of the organization, while their greatly improved understanding of country-level operations made them knowledgeable spokesmen on international issues. Typically, these managers became international representatives to corporate bodies responsible for product policy, research priorities, capacity decisions, and other such global issues.

In all five health care companies studied, the development of strong credible product and functional management groups appeared to be the first major step in supplementing the country-level, geographically dominated decision process. The pattern of building a strong regional office and then developing strong division-level management groups was remarkably consistent. This process seemed to provide a means to educate and legitimize the product and functional managers close to country-level questions before bringing them to headquarters where they could input more directly into major decisions.

## Changing Management Process

Prior to the development of managers who could represent the global product and functional perspectives, country managers' analyses and proposals to senior managers went largely unchallenged. Even if a staff manager did question the country manager's views, his protests often went unheeded due to his low status and credibility in the organization. Clearly in these companies, decision influence was dominated by the geographic line managers.

As the new management skills and prespectives were developed, however, the decision process on key issues became more complex. Arguments for national responsiveness faced strong counterproposals for global integration, and the only means of resolving the inherent conflict was to elevate it to the senior management level. This mode of management can be termed "substantive decision management" because senior management's key role is as arbitrator on the merits of issues in dispute.

This process arose largely due to the lack of any other organizational means to resolve the inevitable differences in opinions and recommendations. However, it was also a process that seemed to suit senior management, at least temporarily. By retaining the integrator and arbitrator role, these managers were able to develop a fuller understanding of the global issues being raised by the newly developed product and functional groups and to appreciate the nature and extent of the trade-offs required between national and global perspectives.

All of the sample companies found the substantive decision management mode a convenient and simple way to integrate new perspectives into the management process in their early stages of multidimensional development. Not only did it provide a means for the newly developed global skills and perspectives to be integrated into the decision process, it also represented a process of education for senior management, allowing them to form judgments on the relative importance of the various perspectives on different issues. Eventually, however, most of them found it a cumbersome administrative system to maintain as the prime decision-making process.

There were three major classes of problems that these companies seemed to encounter after using this management process over a period of time. The first related to the reliability of the inputs to key decisions. By having advocacy groups take frequently opposing positions on issues, the analysis and recommendations being fed to senior management risked being less than objective. Analyses were often based on incomplete, conflicting, or even biased data, and decisions frequently had to be made from the limited and sometimes extreme set of alternatives generated.

The second type of problem encountered in this decision mode related to top management overload. As the only source of integration and resolution, senior management soon became overburdened. The inevitable slowdown in the decision-making process that followed had the effect of dampening the generation of proposals from within the organization or of leading middle managers to short-circuit the system by making decisions without referral to others.

The third problem area was related to implementation. Disputed issues resolved by senior management often had to be implemented by managers who had fought hard for an opposite outcome. Without the uncompromising support of those responsible, implementation effectiveness often suffered.

While these problems caused most companies eventually to abandon the substantive decision management mode, one of the sample group retained this as a key part of its decision-making process. Having developed extremely strong functional management to counterbalance its geographic line managers, Merck and Company had used a substantive decision management style for many years and continued to use it as its dominant decision process in 1979.

The main reason for the continued use of this management mode appeared to be that such a process was neither unfamiliar nor uncomfortable in a company with an historical origin rooted in the fine chemicals business. Since this industry was characterized by large-scale centralized manufacturing and research and a few big customers, centralized decision making was the norm, and Merck followed the pattern.

The acquisition of Sharp and Dohme took Merck into the international pharmaceutical business, and while its traditional management style did not appear to restrict the growth of foreign subsidiaries with substantial autonomy, senior management at Merck recognized very early the need to control its activities and counterbalance its strong national perspectives with more integrated global views. The division level functional staffs that were developed in this company were substantially larger than equivalent groups in similar companies studied. The international division marketing staff, for example, numbered over 100, and its manufacturing staff, over 74, ten times the size of other similar-sized drug companies studied.

These functionally organized division staff groups quickly established credibility with senior management and began to act as a filter and a control on subsidiary proposals, elevating those with which they did not agree for arbitration. A weekly international executive committee meeting, consisting of the division president and his geographic and functional vice presidents, was the center of major decisions. From the different perspectives presented on key issues, senior management felt it was able to obtain a broader appreciation of implications than any of the middle managers alone. They felt this put them in a better position to resolve differences in opinions. The strength of their division staff groups allowed extensive analyses to be made at senior management's request to help reach final decisions.

Yet despite its strong tradition of centralized decision making, even Merck seemed to be moving away from the substantive decision management mode as its primary administrative process. The senior vice president responsible for Europe said: "We centralize many more decisions than we should. Personally, I am trying to change this practice, primarily through my emphasis on grass roots profit planning." His expectations were that alternative structures and systems would be developed to allow more views to be integrated and trade-offs to be made below the senior management level. This certainly had been the path followed by the other companies in the sample.

# Developing New Structures and Systems: Temporary Coalition Management

### More Organizational Change

The process of developing appropriate and credible new management skills and perspectives clearly had implications for and impact on existing organizational structures and systems. Regional offices were established, division level staff groups were strengthened in both quality and size, and management information and control systems became more sophisticated. These changes to the formal organizational structure and systems provided the means by which the newly developed staff groups could enter the existing strategy decision-making process. The regional and division offices gave them the legitimate power base, and the new systems provided them with the information flow and the communication channels they required to exercise their new skills and perspectives.

While these changes in formal structure increased the new product and functional managers' access to and credibility with senior management, the existing organizational structure and decision processes ensured that "geographic" managers retained the power implicit in their line positions. Thus, although the new formal structures allowed the product and functional managers to influence the decision process, it required them to do so through the existing formal hierarchy. While most senior managements found this process helpful in educating themselves to the new perspectives being developed, in many stiuations the administrative burden of consolidating and resolving the conflicts generated by an evolving multidimensional organization created difficulties.

Most of the companies studied tried to alleviate some of these problems by developing additional structures and systems that would allow the required integration of divergent points of view to take place within the organization, rather than at the senior management level. Through the use of temporary structures and systems, many of them were able to bring together managers with different perspectives to review complex issues before automatically elevating any problems or conflicts for resolution.

As senior management became more familiar with the implications of the multiple management perspectives, they became more willing to delegate the responsibility of resolving the implicit conflict. Rather than asking a product manager to critique a subsidiary manager's proposal, for example, a product subsidiary project team might be created to make a joint recommendation on the particular issue. Ongoing decisions that required continued balancing of input were often passed through a standing committee that incorporated managers representing the various relevant points of view.

In four of the companies observed, there was a proliferation of such temporary structures and ad hoc groups soon after the newly established management perspectives were in place in the organization. It was through such task forces, joint teams, and committees that the variety of management perspectives could be engaged selectively into various decision processes. The key attribute of all of the devices used was that they were flexible, allowing management to continually shift the composition of the inputs to various decisions and issues.

In the global recession of 1974/1975, Baxter Travenol used a series of task forces to reorient subsidiary managers from their traditional focus on the income statement (and particularly on sales volume) to a greater concern for the balance sheet. Corporate or regional finance managers worked with subsidiary managers to set targets for current asset levels, developed plans to achieve those targets, and often assisted in the implementation. The new status of these staff managers was reinforced by the power they derived by being appointed to this high-visibility task force by senior management. Their influence and achievements were very impressive, and senior management was, for example, relieved of the task of continually resolving arguments about the impact inventory reduction would have on budgeted sales levels.

Bristol-Myers' senior management found itself getting involved in product development disputes between country managers, with priorities and modifications derived from their various market situations, and division product staff, whose priorities usually derived from existing corporate expertise and other constraints. A pharmaceutical council was formed with senior geographic line managers and business development staff managers as members. Debate in this forum allowed a jointly agreed set of priorities to be developed.

New plant capacity decisions were inevitably difficult ones in all companies, with various management perspectives justifying vastly different manufacturing configurations. For example, country managers typically promoted the need for local plants, finance managers argued to maximize the use of tax-sheltered operations, and manufacturing staff groups pushed for large specialized plants as regional or global sources. Warner-Lambert found that one useful solution was to create a joint task force of regional geographic managers, together with manufacturing, finance, materials, and marketing staff representatives to develop recommendations on worldwide capacity needs.

## Forging Coalitions

Through the use of such teams, task forces and committees, senior management was able to ensure that the diverse recommendations generated by the development of multiple management skills and perspectives were reconciled or, at least, more focused before being escalated. As such devices began to be used more extensively, managers with different perspectives on the same problem developed an ability to work together to find solutions. Senior management found itself having to intervene directly in the substance of key decisions far less frequently. Yet its control of the decision process remained strong. By being able to decide the agenda, the focus, the composition, the leadership, and the power of the particular overlaid structure, senior management could not only ensure that a particular issue was dealt with from a miltidimensional perspective, but could also influence the direction of the resulting analysis, recommendations, or decisions. This mode of management can be termed "temporary coalition management."

The development of a variety of integrative structures and systems was a necessary phase for most of the sample companies in assimilating the new skills and perspectives that had been established. The use of such means of integration had an important impact on the interactions between managers with different perspectives and responsibilities. If the interventionist style of the "substantive decision management" phase served to raise senior management's awareness and understanding of key issues from a variety of viewpoints, the "temporary coalition management" phase tended to broaden the perspectives of the middle-management group. Not only was this phase important to exposing managers throughout the organization to the complex trade-offs required in most decisions, but it also served to develop the interrelationships and communications necessary in a multi-dimensional decision-making process.

Of the sample companies, Bristol-Myers and Warner-Lambert seemed to have evolved to this stage. Not only had they developed managers with the skills and perspectives necessary to supplement and counterbalance the predominantly local national view, but they had supplemented the traditional structure with a variety of temporarily overlaid devices that allowed these new perspectives to be integrated into the decision process lower in the organization. In effect, these companies had increased their decision-making repertoire by supplementing the substantive resolution made with a coalition management approach.

In both companies, the increased use of task force teams and committees provided the vehicles by which product and functional managers could become involved in the decision process at an earlier stage. Yet as the use of those temporary structures increased, country managers felt that corporate-level understanding of local needs was being increasingly threatened. Their concern derived not only from the fact that product and functional groups were being upgraded in size and status, but also because they were positioned organizationally to leverage their point of view. On the latter point, two factors were important. First, they had the substantial advantage of physical proximity to senior management; second, they had strong well-established product and functional counterparts elsewhere in the organization with whom they could form powerful alliances. The country managers expressed the concern that because they were so distant from corporate headquarters and because they had no geographic counterparts there to defend their point of view the proposals for global coordination and integration presented by the product and functional managers could easily swamp their arguments for local flexibility and responsiveness.

Senior management at both Bristol-Myers and Warner-Lambert were conscious that such concerns could be well founded. Therefore, while the product and functional managers were given greater access to the decision-making process through their appointment to task forces and committees, simultaneous efforts were made to reassert the role and power of the country manager and to ensure that his point of view was not overwhelmed by these changes.

Although the reality clearly was that there was a narrowing power and influence gap between product and functional staff managers and geographic line managers, in both companies a vigorous defense of the key role of the country manager was undertaken. At Bristol-Myers, management continually emphasized that the country manager was "king in his country" and that the growing product and functional staff influence was to help him supplement his entrepreneurial skills with technical and administrative capabilities. Warner-Lambert's senior management also talked about the increasing role of staff managers as being "to help build rounded managers at the country level."

In the two companies that were using the temporary coalition mode to supplement their substantive decision management process, senior management seemed to concentrate on two key tasks: maintaining the legitimacy of the groups and individuals representing each of the decision perspectives and ensuring the appropriate influence of each of these perspectives in key decisions. The achievement of the first objective led senior management in Bristol-Myers and Warner-Lambert to spend considerable time supporting and emphasizing the continuing key role of country managers, while simultaneously creating the temporary structures that allowed product and functional staff to input to important issues. In both companies, all groups of managers felt their influence and responsibility had increased— an impression that was probably well founded given their prior roles in a more "substantive decision management" process. It was this widespread sense of legitimacy and influence in the decision process that appeared to be a prerequisite for the successful operations of the temporary coalition mode of management. In the words of the Bristol-Myers International president, "As all managers began to be perceived as having legitimate points of view and viable influence on decisions the absolute distinction that has historically been drawn between line and staff managers is starting to have less meaning."

The second prerequisite of this mode of management was to ensure that the various management perspectives were appropriately represented in each of the many key decisions. It was here that companies experienced the greatest difficulty.

Despite the clear advantages the "coalition management" process offered over the "substantive decision intervention" stage, demands on senior management were still substantial in forming, restructuring, and dissolving coalitions to manage the growing number of multidimensional problems. Furthermore, the mere creation of various coalitions did not ensure that the resulting decision process would be cooperative, and stress and divisiveness seemed an inevitable part of the operation of many teams and committees. In some cases the result was paralysis, as opposing views became locked in impasse; in other instances decision making deteriorated to "horse trading" rather than the open interchange of views that was expected.

Thus, while task forces, teams, and committees often did provide useful means by which solutions to multidimensional issues could be found without continual intervention by senior management, they were limited when they degenerated into forced alliances between reluctant colleagues. Some companies that had perceived the coalition management mode as being the solution to the bottleneck problems of their earlier substantive decision management process began to recognize the need for further organizational adaptation. The open communication, cooperation, and understanding that is required between managers in multidimensional decisions could not be legislated by changes in the formal organization alone.

# Developing a New Organizational "Climate": Decision Context Management

Just as they had recognized the difficulty of having senior management intervening in the content of key decisions, some companies began to recognize that to have them continually involved in structuring and controlling a large number of complex, variable decision-making processes was also very limiting. In the judgment of many managers, a process that often depended on forced alliances between reluctant colleagues, each protective of his turf, probably would not be effective in the long run.

Having developed the appropriate management perspectives and created viable structures and systems through which they could interact, the next major challenge for the developing multidimensional organization was to build an appropriate decision-making environment. The goal was to create an organizational climate in which flexible, constructive, and cooperative interaction between managers with different perspectives was institutionalized. Rather than having individual decisions being arbitrated or regulated from above, the objective was to achieve a more self-regulating decision process in which managers themselves could negotiate the appropriate balance of views in multidimensional decisions.

In order to achieve this kind of environment, the managers had to supplement their ability and willingness to represent a particular viewpoint with an overall understanding of the corporation's broad objectives and a willingness to adapt, cooperate, and compromise to achieve those larger goals. Such changes could not be achieved overnight and required top management to focus on three major tasks:

—To broaden managers' perspectives and open multiple channels of communication through the creative use and control of manager movement and interaction within the organization.
—To change formal systems so as to facilitate and reinforce the desired cooperative and flexible decision-making climate.
—To create a value system that provided the organizational security required to encourage managers to take the risks involved in such flexible, broad-perspective decision making.

Of the companies studied, Eli Lilly and Baxter Travenol appeared to be the most conscious of creating this type of flexible, cooperative decision environment. Examples of the changes made will be drawn from these companies.

Managements of both companies seemed to realize that flexible cooperative interactions would be difficult to develop solely through the limited channels and hierarchical relationships provided by the formal organization. Management's considerable control over individuals' movements and interactions in the organization gave it a powerful tool to impact two separate aspects of the decision environment. First, managers' understanding and appreciation of different organizational issues could be influenced; second, interpersonal relationships and informal communications channels could be developed. For example, a subsidiary marketing manager transferred to a headquarters staff is likely to develop a far greater appreciation for both the local and the global issues involved in key marketing decisions. Furthermore, the personal relationships he develops in each assignment facilitate communications and cooperation on issues involving national and global marketing input.

Eli Lilly had a well-established career development system in which managers were transferred throughout their careers from line positions to staff, from country operations to headquarters, from product to functional or geographic responsibility. Several managers attributed the good contacts and cooperative working relationships that were the norm at Lilly largely to this strongly institutionalized career development track. While less well developed, Baxter had also consciously begun to engage in a similar use of temporary assignments and long-term transfers.

Both companies also created forums in which multidimensional issues could be explored openly, without the pressures or competitiveness that often existed in task forces. Baxter, for instance, modified its annual country general managers' meeting to become a senior management conference to which staff and line managers were invited. For one week each year, common management problems were confronted by the entire group and joint recommendations and action plans agreed to. The president explained that his objectives were twofold: to broaden the identification of his top management from their parochial, geographic, or functional views to a companywide perspective, and to create an environment in which they could cooperate on key multidimensional problems.

By consciously focusing on transfers, assignments, career paths, forums, and meetings, senior management was shifting its means of influence from the formal to the informal organizational structures and systems.

This conscious subtle use of transfers, assignments, and meetings provided senior management with a means of influencing the organization's informal structure and systems rather than the formal channels that had previously been their main focus. Their ability to influence the informal structure was strengthened by the fact that in a multinational corporation there were considerable barriers of distance, language, and culture that tended to limit contacts and interactions between individuals. Management's control of the nature, frequency, and composition of interpersonal interactions therefore could have a very strong influence on the development of an informal structure.

In both Lilly and Baxter, senior management was conscious of this important influence and used it continuously. It also recognized that the behaviors and relationships that could be developed through the informal systems needed to be reinforced through the formal organization. Existing management systems had to be changed to recognize the need for cooperative flexible decision-making behavior.

In Eli Lilly, for example, the formal evaluation process was changed so that a manager would be evaluated not only by his immediate line superior, but also by managers in other parts of the company with whom he had regular working relationships. Baxter also began broadening its evaluation process to allow product and functional managers to input into the evaluation of country managers and vice versa.

At Lilly, career path management had become highly formalized. There were personnel directors for each major function, product, and geographic area who met frequently with senior management to review all actual and potential openings and all possible candidates. Managers were counseled on the importance of developing contacts and expertise in multiple responsibilities, and the broad career development histories of the senior management provided models for younger managers.

However, the process of influencing the informal system to develop cooperation and mutual understanding and realigning formal systems to reinforce such behavior could only be successful if undertaken in an operating environment that was extremely supportive. Asking a manager to abandon the simple certainty of defending his clear point of view from his defined position of organizational responsibility is asking him to take substantive personal and organizational risk. To foster the desired flexible compromising decision-making process, an organization needs a strong, well-established value system that provides the stability and security to allow an individual to take such risks.

Eli Lilly had an internal value system that not only had its roots in the founders' objectives, but also was continually reinforced by current management. In the words of the late Mr. Eli Lilly, "Values are, quite simply, the core of both men and institutions. By combining our thoughts and helping one another, we are able to merge the parts of the corporation into a rational, workable management system." The values he spoke of were also referred to frequently in the organization and included openness, honesty in dealings with others, and the need for mutual trust. With strongly held corporate values such as these, the development of the desired cooperative, flexible interaction between managers was more easily achieved.

Although Baxter's corporate value system had tended to be more competitive and less supportive over a number of years, the international division president had been working to modify some of the accepted organizational norms. At every gathering of managers, his speeches and private remarks emphasized the need for cooperation and joint action between managers. He tried to make his own behavior and management style a model for the organization. He publicly applauded appropriate cooperative problem solving and decision making among management groups with diverse interests and perspectives. Gradually the adversary relationships that existed between country managers and headquarters staff gave way to a cooperative mutual respect.

There was a noticeable cumulative effect of helping to build a network of cooperative informal relationships, reinforcing such cooperation through the formal systems, and institutionalizing the resulting decision-making behavior in a set of organizational values that strongly supported a flexible and cooperative management style. The companies that consciously worked on these changes began to develop an organizational climate in which managers recognized the broad corporate goals and worked cooperatively to help achieve them, even when this meant compromising some more parochial concerns. This management mode can be labeled "decision context management."

Senior management's role in this mode was twofold: to support the organizational values, the informal structure, and the formal systems that created the cooperative flexible decision process, and to communicate clearly and frequently the broad corporate objectives toward which such decisions should be directed. This represented a subtle and a delicate task, but less all consuming than an involvement with individual decision outcomes or even with coalition building and management.

In the decision context management mode, the middle-management level showed a much greater willingness to take a multidimensional approach on key issues. In Baxter, for example, when the general manager of the Brazilian subsidiary wanted to build a local plant, he first discussed the matter at length with both the manufacturing manager and the product marketing manager at division headquarters and with the corporate financial staff. When all views had been fully discussed, a mutually agreed-upon set of alternatives and a recommended approach were submitted to top management.

It should be noted again that decision making in companies that pursued the decision context management mode was not all so easily self-regulated. On sensitive issues, senior management still had to intervene either by defining the coalition that was to make the analysis, recommendation, or decision or by actually resolving specific issues where resolution by cooperation and compromise had not been possible. Like the other modes, this one simply broadened the repertoire of decision processes available to help resolve complex multidimensional issues.

## Conclusion

The strategic challenges faced by the five health care companies are typical of the situations confronting many MNCs. Increasing pressure from host governments and global competitors increasingly force companies to develop and integrate their management capabilities at the local *and* the global levels; accelerating change in both arenas requires that these multiple skills and perspectives interact flexibly.

While change in the formal organization has been thought of by many managers as the principal means of adapting the decision processes, the subtlety and complexity of a flexible multidimensional decision-making process appears difficult to achieve solely (or even primarily) through formal organizational change. By retaining their simple international division structures, the five companies observed maintained a stability in their formal organization that allowed gradual changes in people, relationships, and processes to be introduced through more informal and less traumatic means. Rather than focusing their attention on the structure per se, managers of these companies seemed to be more concerned with the nature of decision process that the change was designed to achieve.

While their formal organizational structures seemed to belie the fact, each of these companies had developed the flexible multidimensional decision process that its strategic environment demanded. Westinghouse's hope was that its newly installed matrix structure might take five years "to force product managers to interact with geographic specialists." Managers in the health care companies studied believed that their evolutionary approach achieved the same ends with less trauma.

# CASE 28

# The Conglomerates and the Merger Movement of the 1960s *

The mid-1960s have been referred to as the "go-go" years in the history of American finance.[1] The great bull market, powered by such glamor stocks as IBM, Xerox, Polaroid, Kodak, and Control Data, resulted in record prices. In January of 1966, the Dow Jones Industrial Average breached the psychologically important 1,000 mark for the first time.

An important component of these "go-go" years was intensive merger and acquisition activity. This activity was different from the two previous merger waves (at the turn of the century and in the 1920s). In the 1960s, a new kind of business enterprise played a key role in mergers and acquisitions. This was the conglomerate. Eleven of the top 25 acquiring companies in the 1960s were classified as conglomerates.[2] These 11 firms acquired over 500 companies between 1961 and 1968. And these acquired companies represented over 92 percent of the acquired firms' assets by the latter year.

---

*The readings and tables which constitute this case were collected and assembled by Professor Alfred D. Chandler, Jr., as the basis for class discussion rather than to illustrate either effective or ineffective handling of an administrative situation.

Harvard Business School case 373-250, rev. 6/84.

[1]See John Brooks, *The Go-Go Years* (New York: Ballantine, 1973).

[2]Eight were petroleum companies, and six were classified as "other." Federal Trade Commission, *Economic Report on Corporate Mergers,* 1969.

The defining characteristic of the conglomerate—that trait which differentiated it from the diversified company—was said to be that it made its acquisitions in unrelated industries. The wide variety of conglomerate investments is illustrated by Table 2 of the Diversification Tables in this case. It should be noted, however, that it is not at all clear where the definitional line should be drawn between a conglomerate and a diversified firm. Table 1 shows that some diversified firms do business in a wide variety of industries. This is especially striking when Table 1 is compared to Table 3, which shows the lack of diversity of the product lines of the largest Japanese manufacturers.

Nevertheless, it can be said that the classic conglomerates—firms like ITT, Litton, Textron, and Ling-Temco-Vought—approached diversity in a way different from that of the typical diversified. They developed a new administrative structure to manage their holdings.

Because the individual companies which comprised the conglomerate produced such diverse products, many functions could not be supervised at the level of the central office. While the related-diversified firm had advisory staffs for such critical functions as R&D and marketing for its various divisions, the conglomerate did not. Typically, therefore, central offices of conglomerates were small. Often those with sales of over $1 billion had fewer than 100 people above the operating level. The primary functions of the central office included finance, acquisitions, control, and some minor staff functions. Legal and planning responsibilities were sometimes also included. Clearly, the first two activities—finance and acquisitions— predominated and, in fact, characterized the conglomerate. This left purchasing, production, R&D, and marketing to the separate divisions (i.e., the former firms). In fact, the supervisory role of the central office consisted to a large extent in setting quotas for the various units—of management by objectives—and judging performance on a quantitative basis.

Critics of the conglomerate have attacked both its strategy and structure. Of the former, they have claimed that through complex financial manipulations, hostile takeovers, frequent reorganizations, and the like, the conglomerates attempt to create value where none should exist. At best, they say, this amounts to concentrating on paper profits instead of investing in plant and equipment. Others have claimed that by commanding massive resources in scores of different industries, the strongest conglomerates present a threat to the marketplace that is beyond the reach of antitrust law. Still others have pointed to the highly opportunistic and performance-oriented nature of conglomerate management. This approach is said to saddle their subsidiaries with short time horizons which are antithetical to stability and long-term economic growth.

The central criticism of the conglomerate structure is that it fosters underadministration and the wasteful duplication of functions. Curiously, the unique "top light" structure of the conglomerate managerial hierarchy has been used to explain both higher and lower levels of efficiency as compared with the "concentric" (related-diversified) multidivisional firm. Some believe that centralizing finance and acquisition functions at the top level creates legitimate synergies. However, others believe that efficiencies in the more critical areas of production and R&D

are lost, resulting in overall poor performance. Some experts believe that the most important defect of the conglomerate is that the monitoring of current performance and the allocation of resources for future efforts are perforce the responsibility of executives whose knowledge of the businesses they are overseeing has to be very limited. The result is that they are forced to manage by the numbers. Quantitative indicators are of course essential to all managers, but the problem in the conglomerate is the extent to which the managers will be able to understand what the numbers really mean.

Despite these problems, the conglomerate corporations were widely heralded in the 1960s as an important new innovation. Their executives received plentiful favorable publicity and most impressive was their performance on Wall Street.

But it was on Wall Street that the doubts which existed about conglomerates made themselves felt toward the end of the decade. Litton stock fell 50 percent in two months in 1968, proving to be a harbinger of more general conglomerate troubles soon to come. The reasons for the dramatic decline of conglomerate market values by the end of the decade were complex. Fears of government action against them, stricter accounting procedures, a torpid stock market, reports of poor conglomerate performance, and questions about their abilities to continue high rates of growth all played a part. As conglomerates fell from the position they would never regain and the financial limelight turned elsewhere, government oversight not only quieted but soon took on an almost conciliatory tone. In 1972, an FTC report on conglomerate mergers was released, stating that "From a competitive standpoint, the effects of conglomerate diversification . . . appear to be neutral."[3]

This case is composed of two articles and a set of tables. The first article by Neil H. Jacoby on "The Conglomerate Corporation," published in *The Center Magazine* of July 1969, focuses on the environment that brought into being the merger movement of the late 1960s—a movement highlighted by the creation of many of the best known of today's conglomerates. Jacoby proposes a Conjuncture Hypothesis to explain this merger movement as well as the two earlier ones that have occurred in the United States. The peaking of mergers came, he suggests, when two conditions occurred. The first was when business people perceived new profit opportunities that could be exploited through mergers. The second condition was the existence of an exuberant capital market enjoying a strong demand for new securities. Jacoby then outlines the changes in the larger environment that created opportunities that might be realized through mergers at the time when the capital market became buoyant in the mid-1960s. He concludes by evaluating the possibilities for both private and social gains accruing from the new conglomerates that were created in the resulting merger movement and by analyzing the impact these mergers had on concentration and competition.

---

[3]Stanley E. Boyle and Phillip W. Jaynes, *Economic Report to the Federal Trade Commission—Conglomerate Merger Performance: An Empirical Analysis of Nine Corporations,* National Technical Informational Services, U.S. Department of Commerce, November 1972, p. 127.

The second reading is Norman Berg's study of the "Corporate Role in Diversified Companies," a working paper prepared at the Harvard Business School. Berg compares and contrasts the organizational structure of the new conglomerate with that of the older diversified enterprise or, as Berg calls them, "the diversified majors." Of particular importance are Berg's findings on the differences between the corporate staff of the two types of enterprises. He suggests that these differences in structure reflect the views of their general executives as to the role and function of the general office and the goals of the enterprise as a whole.

Lastly, the case presents a set of tables which illustrate the extent of diversification of the largest corporations in the United States and Japan.

* * * * *

# The Conglomerate Corporation*

This decade has witnessed the third great wave of corporate mergers in the American economy during the present century. Its dominant feature has been the burgeoning of the conglomerate corporation. During 1968, more than 4,400 companies disappeared by mergers (including combinations and acquisitions) involving an estimated $43 billion worth of securities—an all-time record. In this tidal wave of mergers, which may now have crested and begun to recede, conglomerate firms accounted for a substantial or a preponderant fraction of all firms and assets involved, depending upon the definition of "conglomerate."

Why did a third merger wave peak in the 1960s and emphasize conglomeration? Is the conglomerate a stable and efficient form of business, the heir apparent to American corporate power? Or is it a financial fad, a source of monopoly, a threat to small business? Does it pose any new problems of public regulation? Is it monster or model of the future?

# The Conglomerate Defined

"Conglomerate" is used herein to mean a business corporation producing products or services of several industries that are unrelated with respect to raw material sources, product development, production technology, or marketing channels. A "conglomerate merger" brings together two or more such enterprises engaged in unrelated lines of business. It is a particular mode of enterprise growth in which the firm penetrates industries outside its current operations.

Many managers of diversified firms avoid use of the word, believing that it denotes lack of any inner logic and has a pejorative ring. They prefer to describe their companies as "multimarket" or "multiindustry" firms. However, "conglomerate" has gained too wide a currency to be discarded, and it is a special kind of multiindustry firm.

---

*Reproduced by permission from *The Center Magazine,* a publication of the Center for the Study of Democratic Institutions, Spring 1969. The author is Neil H. Jacoby.

Modes of enterprise expansion may be classified as follows:

1. Vertical
   a. Backward (toward raw material sources)
   b. Forward (toward consumers of final products)
2. Horizontal (market extension within the same industry)
3. Product extension (into additional industries)
   a. Producing related products (concentric)
   b. Producing unrelated products (conglomerate)

Merger is a minor method of growth of American business corporations, the predominant source being internally generated funds. Up to recent years most mergers have been of the vertical or horizontal types, in which the surviving firms acquired other firms within the same industries or industrial groups. During the 1960s, however, most large mergers involved firms operating in different industries. Some encompassed firms producing products that were *related* with respect to sources of raw materials, production technology, or marketing channels. These have been aptly termed "concentric" companies. Others involved *unrelated* enterprises—the true conglomerates.

Product relationships are, of course, a matter of degree, and opinions may differ on whether those within a diversified company are significant. Spokesmen for multiindustry firms often offer tenuous theories of centrality to avoid the brand of conglomerate. Are such traditional giants as General Motors (diesel locomotives, refrigerators, and air conditioners as well as motor vehicles) and General Electric (jet engines and metallurgical chemicals as well as hundreds of electrical products) conglomerates or concentrics? Should Transamerica be classed as a concentric because its avowed field is "services"? Norton Simon, Inc. because it "serves the needs of the individual as a consumer, homemaker, and person"? Bendix because it is committed to "growth through technology"? Or Occidental Petroleum Corportion, which describes itself as a "producer and processor of natural resources"? Occidental, for example, rejects the conglomerate label because common technologies are used in exploring for and producing oil, natural gas, coal, sulphur, and phosphates, and all of these raw materials enter into fuels, fertilizers, industrial chemicals, and plastics, its major products.

On the other hand, there are many huge corporations whose activities are so disparate that their managements do not even attempt to formulate a theory of centrality. Among them are Litton Industries, which makes office equipment, builds ships, operates restaurants, sells packaged foods, and operates national development plans, among many other activities. Ling-Temco-Vought, International Telephone and Telegraph Company, Gulf & Western Industries, and Tenneco, Inc., are other conglomerates whose manifold products clearly lack common raw materials, production technology, or marketing channels. Even the names of some conglomerates imply an all-encompassing generality, such as National Environment, Commonwealth United, or National General.

Although concentric companies are sometimes grouped with conglomerates, it is preferable to adopt a strict definition, which focuses attention upon the managerial and financial economies that distinguish the true conglomerate corporation. The conglomerate has managerial and financial control over products so diverse that negligible economies of scale can be realized in performing the functions of product development, purchasing, production, or marketing. Thus it differs from multiplant, or multiproduct, or multiindustry firms that do achieve these economies. It differs, on the other hand, from the investment company, which does acquire ownership interests in firms producing unrelated products but does *not* have management and financial responsibility for them.

## Lessons from the Past

We may more confidently assess the meaning of the current wave of conglomerations, predict its duration, and forecast the economic effects and public regulations it may produce by examining the course of past merger activity in the United States. Economic historians generally agree that the American economy has experienced three major business merger episodes since the 1890s.

The first wave, in which activity rose markedly above its long-term trend during the five-year period of 1897 to 1902, peaked in 1899. In the peak year approximately twelve hundred mining and manufacturing corporations with total capitalizations of $2.3 billion (about ten billion in 1968 dollars) were involved. The major thrust of this wave was the joining of local and regional railroads into national systems and of one-plant manufacturing companies into national multiplant entities. U.S. Steel Corporation, U.S. Rubber Company, and American Can Company were born in this epoch.

The second episode, marked by a high level of activity during 1924–30, reached its peak in 1929. In that year some 1,250 mergers were reported, apparently involving securities of much larger total value than in 1899. Vertical and horizontal combinations of manufacturing, public utilities, and merchandising companies were prominent in this wave.

The third period of hyperactivity began about 1965, when the graph of annual mergers broke sharply upward from its long-term trend line. Mergers continued to rise through 1968 when some 2,500 mining and manufacturing companies were acquired with around $20 billion worth of securities. The most prominent actors in this wave were the conglomerates.

The long-term curve of merger activity displays much kurtosis. A four- or five-year buildup to a peak year of activity has been followed by a year or two of swift decline. In view of the anti-inflationary policies of the Nixon Administration and consequent leveling of stock prices, this pattern suggests that 1968 may turn out to mark the high point of the current wave, and that merger activity will subside during the next year or two to a "normal" level. If so, 39 years would separate the second and third peaks, while 30 years separated the first and second peaks. Over the past 75 years, merger activity has risen at a rate of under 4 per cent per year. Because this has been little more than the rate of growth of real GNP, merger activity does not appear to have become relatively more important over the long term.

Although measures of merger activity are incomplete and one may not generalize upon a basis of two or three waves, the evidence supports a conjecture that the hectic merger activity in 1968 will not be matched again for a number of years. The economy is probably not moving up an accelerating secular trend of business concentration through merger, and conglomeration should not be viewed in apocalyptic terms. The 4,400 business corporations that disappeared by merger during 1968 were a small number compared with the 12,000 that disappeared by failure or the 207,000 new corporations formed. Even the $43 billion in securities exchange mergers that year was less than 4 per cent of the market value of corporate securities.

## Merger Episodes: An Hypothesis

Why has American merger activity taken the historical form of a strong wave at long time intervals? We know that merger peaks have not corresponded closely with peaks in production, commodity prices, or overall business activity. Of all economic indicators, merger activity has been most closely related to movements in industrial stock prices. A booming stock market has been present at the crest of all merger waves. Yet a high level of mergers has not accompanied all stock market peaks.

In the extensive literature on mergers, three theories have been advanced to explain their motivation and economic effects. Many observers have seen in business combinations only the elimination of competitors, so that surviving firms can reap monopoly profits. Others have stressed the dominance of promoters and bankers, who engineered mergers in order to sell securities to the public at inflated prices. Still others have viewed mergers as a natural response of businessmen to new opportunities to reduce costs and expand sales and profits in a competitive environment. We may call these the "monopoly," the "stock promotion," and the "efficiency" theories.

None, taken by itself, provides a satisfactory explanation of the long periods of time that have separated peaks of merger activity. There is no reason why the quest of businessmen for monopoly power should mount to a climax every 30 or 40 years. Stock market cycles have been much shorter than a decade in their duration. Population growth and technological changes, which father business opportunities, take place more or less continuously.

The conjecture is made that *long-term merger waves in the United States are explained by the infrequent conjuncture of two preconditions:* (1) an accumulation of perceived and unexploited profit-making preconditions for enlarging the scale of enterprises, arising from basic technological and social changes, and (2) a buoyant capital market with strong demand for new securities.

This Conjuncture Hypothesis, which is put forth as an interesting conjecture and not as a scientific theory, combines elements of the "efficiency" and "stock promotion" theories. It asserts that, before merger hyperactivity can occur, there must be present both an unusually large number of opportunities for enlarging profits by combining independent firms, and strong public demand for the new securities created in the merger process. Because these two preconditions do not often coincide in time, merger hyperactivity is much less frequent than stock market peaks.

The Conjuncture Hypothesis reasons that the predominant motives for mergers are the drive of businessmen to realize larger profits by capitalizing upon newly perceived economies of scale, and the ability of bankers to sell new securities to the public on profitable terms. It rejects the notion that monopoly power has been an important motive for corporate mergers during the past half century. The quest for monopoly power apparently did play a role in the first merger wave that peaked in 1899, because antimonopoly laws were then not vigorously enforced. Since World War I, however, the Sherman Act, the Federal Trade Commission Act, and state antimonopoly laws have generally forbidden combinations that threatened to create undue market power. The Conjuncture Hypothesis does not, of course, imply that substantial advantages of larger scale are necessarily present in all mergers. History demonstrates that in the hyperenthusiasm of a stock market boom many mergers are launched that later founder on the rocks of reality.

Why does a combination of a large number of perceived opportunities for profits from enlarging firms and buoyant capital markets occur infrequently? The idea that change is the only constant in modern society is by now a cliché. Less well understood is the distinction between tactical (small, superficial) and strategic (salient, structural) changes. Most tactical changes cancel or offset each other through time. A few cumulate into strategic shifts in the structure of technology and society. Not only do strategic changes take many years to accomplish but there is a time lag between their occurrence and their general perception by people. Many strategic changes create opportunities for profit by enlarging enterprises. In the pervasive optimism of a stock market boom, once-overlooked opportunities, or known opportunities previously not financiable, are acted upon. Given the rapidity of communication in financial markets, such perceptions multiply and build up to a climax. Wall Street goes through a phase of "merger madness."

Later, the pool of profit-making opportunities for business combinations is drained. Concurrently, financial expectations deteriorate. Merger activity falls off as quickly as it previously mounted. Many years pass before structural changes in technology and society create a new pool of perceived chances for gains from enlarging the scale of corporate operations. When a new reservoir of opportunities has been filled, and this knowledge permeates the business and financial communities, the conjuncture of a boom in equity security prices will trigger another merger wave.

Let us consider merger waves of the past. Certain structural changes set the stage for the first peak in 1899. One was the creation of a national railway network during the 1880s by the connection of hundreds of local and regional lines and the building of tens of thousands of miles of new lines. The same era witnessed the completion of national telegraphic and telephone communications. These facilities enormously reduced the cost and increased the speed of transportation and communication. National markets became a reality. By 1895, opportunities for profit by combining firms into larger units and reaping the benefits of lower costs through economies of scale in production had grown immensely. Meanwhile, the nation had developed a national capital market. By 1895, rising security prices had met the other necessary condition, and the first merger wave rolled on. That stock promotion gains may have played a significant role in this merger wave is suggested by the fact that a large number of the combinations made in that era subsequently failed.

The structural changes that undergirded the second merger peak in the 1920s also took place in transportation and communication. With the development of reliable mass-produced motor vehicles and the completion of national network of all-weather roads, the U.S. economy was motorized after World War II. Autos and trucks gave people and goods unparalleled mobility, enlarging markets, destroying local monopolies, and creating new economies of scale. Concurrently the home radio receiver made national advertising cheap and effective, built the value of national brand names, and enhanced the advantages of national marketing. Single-unit distribution was doomed. By the mid-20s, businessmen generally perceived the astonishing opportunities for larger firms opened up by these changes. The booming stock market of 1921–29 satisfied the other precondition, and the second great merger episode was under way. Its economic rationale focused upon economies of scale in marketing, although it also exploited production economies.

## Structural Foundations of the Conglomerate Merger Wave of the 1960s

The Conjuncture Hypothesis is consistent with the main facts about the great merger wave still under way. Structural changes in the United States since World War II had by the early 1960s created a pool of perceived opportunities for profits by enlarging the scale and diversifying corporate operations. The buoyant capital market that emerged in the last half of the decade triggered the merger boom that began about 1965 by making it easy to sell new securities to the public. Most fundamental and powerful of the underlying structural changes was a revolution in management science. Other contributory factors were the postwar research-and-development explosion, the rise of the service economy, a quantum increase in taxation, and a doubling of the price of capital.

### Management Science and Computers

Radical changes occurred in the science of enterprise management after World War II. These changes had their roots in the wartime efforts of mathematicians to solve complex logistical and military problems by "operations research." Concepts and methods were then developed that were later found to be equally powerful in dealing with the management problems of a civilian economy. Intuitive judgment has been progressively superseded by rational decision-making processes. Such problems as evaluation of investment projects, choice of financing plans, locating facilities, scheduling production and controlling inventories are now solved by mathematical and statistical methods.

The concurrent phenomenal development of electronic computers has promoted and facilitated the expansion of management science. The computer not only does routine accounting with fantastic speed but performs that great volume of calculations involved in solving management problems. In 1950 only a few computers were operating in businesses; at the end of 1968 there were more than 20,000.

This fundamental development has created opportunities for profits through mergers that remove assets from the inefficient control of old-fashioned managers and placed them under men schooled in the new management science. Managers are able to control effectively a larger set of activities. Being of general applicability to business operations, management science makes possible reductions in financial and managerial costs and risks through acquisitions of firms in *diverse* industries. These gains differ markedly from the familiar economies of scale in production, purchasing, or marketing that normally accrue from mergers of firms with *related* products. Thus the new management science is the primary force behind conglomeration.

## Research and Development Explosion

In the postwar era outlays on scientific research and development have grown nearly 14 per cent a year, from $1.5 billion in 1946 to nearly $24 billion in 1968. This dramatic increase in the national commitment to applied science and technology is a seminal factor in the evolution of the U.S. economy. By the 1960s it had created whole new industries—lasers, cryogenics, oceanography, electrooptics, xerography, and so on. It had generated thousands of new products in established industries—plastics, synthetic fibers, aircraft, electronic equipment, among others. Most important, it had evolved a proven method for deliberately creating commercially needed products through research.

Research and development is now an established function of corporate business. Its economics call for organizations of considerable scale and specialization, which, in turn, require large sales volumes to keep down costs per unit. Also, research produces unexpected findings, and leads enterprises into diverse industries and product lines. These are powerful motives behind mergers of the conglomerate type.

## Rise of the Service Economy

During the past quarter of a century, the United States has been transformed from a "commodity" to a "service" economy. Most working Americans now produce services rather than tangible commodities. White-collar jobs outnumber blue-collar jobs. As real incomes have risen, and leisure time has expanded, a larger part of income is spent on personal and professional services, transportation, education, and recreation; a smaller part on food, clothing and shelter. Established ser-

.vice industries like insurance, banking, consumer finance, medical care, air transport, television, motion pictures, and education have enormously enlarged their dimensions. Whole new service industries have come into being, such as computer leasing, auto rental, credit card and travel agencies. Data generation and processing aspects of service industries—which by definition serve masses of people— are especially large. Service industries have generally been in the forefront in computerizing their operations and using advanced management controls. It is no accident, therefore, that some of the largest conglomerates have specialized in services, including Transamerica, International Telephone and Telegraph, and National General.

## Quantum Leap in Taxation

A fourth factor underlying the current merger wave is the steep rise in the load of corporate-income taxation since World War II. In 1940 the effective federal corporate income-tax rate was 27 percent; in 1968 it was 53 percent, including the 10 percent surtax. Rates of state and local taxes on business incomes have risen commensurately.

The manifold impacts of heavy income taxation on corporate policies can scarcely be exaggerated. They are a prime move behind mergers. International oil and minerals companies with unused foreign tax credits acquire companies whose incomes can be "sheltered" by those credits. American petroleum producers with large drilling expenses acquire high-profit firms for the same reason. Companies with profits merge with those having losses carried over from previous years that can be used to offset the profits. Many railroads found that diversification enabled them to use their past losses to reduce the tax liabilities of the companies they acquired. A central motive behind Container Corporation's union with Montgomery Ward to form Marcor was to defer payment for several years of more than $60 million a year of federal income taxes by taking fuller advantage of Ward's ability to defer taxes on profits arising from installment credit sales.

Equity securities of companies acquired in a merger are often replaced by convertible debentures of the surviving company, resulting in the replacement of taxable income paid out as dividends by tax-deductible interest. Also, debenture holders have been able to defer income taxes on their profits until the debentures are paid off. Tax avoidance is a powerful private motive for merger that puts a premium on conglomeration vis-a-vis vertical or horizontal combinations.

## Doubled Price of Capital

Since World War II the price of capital—the going rate of return to investors—has more than doubled. Medium-grade industrial bonds that yielded 3.3 percent in 1945 returned 7.2 percent in late 1968. Home mortgage loan rates went from 4 percent to 8 percent in the same span of time. The dominant cause of the doubled price of capital can be expressed as a vast expansion of demand for investment funds in relation to the available supply. Expanding American research and development activities, the reconstruction and modernization of European economies, and the demands of less-developed countries have combined to open up unprecedented demands for investment funds. Demand has tended to outrun available supply. Europe felt the sharpest impact of this imbalance and long offered higher returns to investment than did the United States. During the mid-60s the difference began to shrink by a marked rise in U.S. interest rates. Today, prices of capital are about equal in the world's major money markets.

The higher price of capital has had many consequences. Corporations have tried to use their capital more efficiently. Cash management programs have proliferated. Investment projects have been screened more rigorously. The finance officer has moved to the top of the corporate hierarchy. Aggressive managements have looked for merger partners laden with cash or liquifiable assets. Banks, insurance, and finance companies have been especially sought after as acquisitions by industrial companies, because of their steady inflows of deposits, premiums, or loan repayments. Yet any company with liquifiable and low-earning assets has been a target. Thus, the pervasive quest for financial resources has been the motive behind many a conglomerate merger.

# Private and Social Gains from Conglomeration

An exploration of the principal structural changes in the U.S. economy that have fostered conglomerate mergers helps to identify the gains that may accrue from this kind of corporate diversification. A critical distinction should be drawn between social gains and private gains. Public policies should encourage, or at least permit, those mergers that have the potentiality of yielding net gains to society. It should not encourage those that result only in transfers of wealth or income among individuals.

The two principal kinds of private gain from mergers are promotional profits and reductions in tax liability. While these private gains may or may not be accompanied by social benefits, it is probable that both result from most conglomerate mergers.

Consider the extreme case of a merger whose sole purpose and effect is to generate profits for promoters and bankers, who take advantage of the optimism of the public during a stock market boom. The standard gambit is to have a "growth" company, whose stock is selling at a high multiple of its annual earnings, acquire another company whose stock is evaluated at a low multiple of earnings, in the expectation that after a pooling of interests that market will value the equity of the expanded survivor at the higher multiple. In the atmosphere of a boom this expectation is often realized. Earnings per share of the acquiring firm will increase as a result of the merger. The market will apply the high multiplier and bid up the price of the stock. This makes further acquisitions through exchange of stock attractive. They are the basis of a further expansion in reported earnings per share and further inflation of the market price of the stock.

The game can continue until the public recognizes that there is no growth in the operating earnings of the acquired companies. The price of the conglomerate's stock then plummets to a point where the price/earnings ratio is normal. At this much lower price, further acquisitions are unattractive and cease. Meanwhile, promoters will probably have unloaded their shares on less sophisticated investors, and bankers will have pocketed their commissions. By assumption the mergers produce no social benefits, so that all that happens is a transfer of capital values from one to another set of individuals. Such "stock promotion" mergers have tended to take the form of conglomeration in recent years, because court decisions have made other larger mergers difficult.

Public policy can do little to prevent such mergers, beyond enforcing Securities and Exchange Commission regulations requiring full disclosure of all material facts. If speculators ignore the rule *caveat emptor,* they suffer the consequences. A good number of the mergers during past waves have subsequently failed, implying a want of real social gains. Of course, their promoters may have sincerely believed that real gains were possible, but their hopes were disappointed. Given the dynamism and complexity of business life, predictions of social gains are inevitably hazardous, and there is no feasible means of distinguishing promoters with honest intentions from others. The public is best protected by education and full disclosure.

The second type of private gain from mergers is reduction of tax liability. If a company with carried-over losses is merged into a profitable company, reducing the taxes of the survivor, government may be obliged to impose heavier taxes upon other firms in order to restore the preexisting level of revenues. There is a shift of tax burden from stockholders of the merged companies to those of the other firms. Society will be unaffected, except for a possible deterioration in the equity of the tax system.

Public policy can do little to inhibit mergers arranged solely to cut taxes, given the high tax rates. Opportunities for reducing taxes by merger could be curtailed by radical simplification of the structure of federal taxation of corporate income. This structure is now highly differentiated and shot through with special treatment of particular industries.

Several types of gains from mergers are, at least potentially, of value to society.

**1.** *Reduction of the risk/reward ratio.* By definition, the conglomerate firm combines operations unrelated in respect to raw materials, technologies, or markets. The annual sales or profits of its different operations will be negatively correlated. In the aggregate they will produce a more stable return through time. For any given rate of return on investment, risk will be less; for any given risk, expected reward will be higher. The standard gain from portfolio diversification will be realized. This benefits society as well as the conglomerate's stockholders, because the reduction in the premium for risk is equivalent to a cut in the company's costs and, via market competition, in the prices of its products.

**2.** *Lower capital costs and avoidance of "Gambler's ruin."* Closely related to the gains of diversification are the advantages reaped by the conglomerate of lower capital costs and avoidance of "Gambler's Ruin." The conglomerate can raise funds on either a debt or equity basis at lower cost than could its constituents.

In addition, having a "long purse," it is in a position to finance temporary operating losses of a subsidiary that would bankrupt the latter if it were an independent firm. The conglomerate is in a position to "out-spend, out-dare, and out-wait" smaller and financially less secure firms in its effort to win a market. This is socially beneficial, provided that the conglomerate continues to face adequate competition in its several markets—a subject to which we shall return. Of course, this same argument can apply to any large corporation—whether conglomerate or not.

**3.** *Economies of scale in performing general management functions.* Acquisitions can enable the conglomerate firm to apply over a wider sales base the talents of a skilled general management team. General management functions are involved, and include those of planning, organizing, staffing, budgeting, and controlling—generic functions in all kinds of enterprises. While organizational structures of conglomerates differ, the central corporate management commonly delegates wide authority to each divisional management, and holds the latter accountable for a "target" rate of return on the investment in its division. The central corporate officers enforce a planning and controlling discipline upon all divisional managers. They make the major decisions on capital allocation. Characteristically, they also provide a kind of "inside" management consulting service to the entire organization.

**4.** *Acquisition of highly specialized management talent.* Closely related to the third factor is the possibility that the conglomerate, with its larger and more diverse activities, can utilize efficiently specialized experts in operations analysis, computer science, behavioral science, incentive systems, international business, and so on. The scale of operations of the smaller firms it acquires is often too small to justify their cost.

**5.** *Transfer of assets to more efficient management.* A real social gain occurs when the assets of an enterprise are transferred via merger into the control of a superior management. Striking advances in management science, combined with great inequalities among firms in its application, have opened up extensive opportunities for gains from such transfers. Through more informed decisions and better information systems, resources can be deployed with greater efficiency, resulting in lower costs and product prices. While this kind of social gain can flow from any kind of merger, it is most likely in conglomeration. The reason is that market competition generally compresses differences in the quality of management of firms in the same industry to a smaller dimension than is present among firms in different industries. Hence the frequency and size of such gains from conglomerate mergers is probably greater.

In what proportion of conglomerate mergers are social gains realized, and how large are those gains? Regrettably, these questions cannot be answered in the present state of knowledge. Answers would require intensive, elongated case studies of the costs, prices, profits, and managements of conglomerates and their constituents, before and after merger. Most conglomerate corporations have had too recent a life history to permit confident conclusions. Professor J. F. Weston analyzed the financial performance of 58 multiindustry firms over the 9-year period 1958–66. As might be expected, their sales grew at an annual compound rate of 17.8 percent a year, double that of all U.S. manufacturing firms. Earnings per share grew 10 percent a year versus 6.7 percent for all firms in the Standard and Poor's stock index. Stock prices at each year's high point rose 10.5 percent a year, against 5.4 percent for the Dow-Jones Industrial Average. In 1967 conglomerates earned 12.6 percent on their net worth compared with 11.9 percent for all manufacturing firms.

Prima facie, the conglomerates gave a superior performance. Yet, these figures do not prove that they managed assets more effectively than other corporations. Many of the firms in the Weston study were concentrics rather than true conglomerates. His study did not take into account the heavier leveraging of equity capital by conglomerate managements—a strategem that is profitable during strong business expansion, but which can backfire under adversity. Also, conglomerate managers not infrequently introduced new accounting practices that inflated their earnings. Empirical proof of the frequency and size of gains from conglomeration thus remains to be produced.

## Conglomeration, Concentration, and Competition

The most important issue of public policy raised by conglomeration is its effect upon the vigor of competition. Traditionally, business mergers have been identified with tendencies to monopoly. This is understandable, because most mergers in past years have been of the horizontal or vertical types. Many have increased industrial concentration—the percentage of the total sales or output of an industry accounted for by its leading four or eight firms. Economists generally agree that there is a positive but loose correlation between the level of concentration of an industry and the probability of noncompetitive or oligopolistic behavior by its leading firms. When the preponderance of all output of an industry is produced by three or four leading corporations, collusion among them is easier, or there may be a tacit mutual recognition that all can profit from higher than competitive prices. As the level of industrial concentration drops, the chances of noncompetitive behavior diminish and become negligible when the number of competing firms is more than 20. Proposed mergers of important members of the same industry are therefore properly scrutinized by the antitrust authorities for anticompetitive consequences, and are generally frowned upon. This is not to deny that there is vigorous competition in many highly concentrated industries (i.e., automobiles), and that mergers of several weak firms in such industries may sometimes create a strong enterprise able to offer sharper competition to its rivals than did its components.

A conglomerate merger involves a union of firms in different industries. It necessarily leaves the ratios of concentration of all industries unchanged. Conglomeration does replace two or more smaller firms with one larger enterprise, and thus may increase macroeconomic concentration—the percentage of total industrial activity in the economy accounted for by the leading 100 or 200 nonfinancial corporations. Indeed, conglomeration by large firms appears to have held industrial concentration in the economy about constant, while increasing macroeconomic concentration since World War II.

Manifestly, it is *industrial* concentration that is directly related to the vigor of competition. Macroeconomic concentration need not be of concern as long as the number of giant diversified corporations is large enough to preclude overt or tacit collusion among them. Because it takes more than 100 corporate giants to account for even a half of all manufacturing assets in the nation, we are far from the possibility of noncompetitive behavior because of inadequate numbers.

In general, conglomerate mergers are likely to invigorate competition. By strengthening the managerial and financial support available to each of its constituents, the conglomerate is able to make each a more energetic competitor in the industry in which it operates. Each entity can draw upon the conglomerate's pool of specialized managerial talent, utilize its management science, obtain financial assistance, and assume a more innovative and risk-taking posture than it could as an independent firm. Conglomeration can thus transform simple competition into multiple competition.

Beyond this, the conglomerate is more likely to possess the financial and other resources needed to enter additional industries, theretofore closed to its smaller constituents. Established firms in those industries will, as a result, tend to behave more competitively than before in pricing their products in the hope of deterring the potential competition of the conglomerate. It has been aptly said that the conglomerate "sits on the edge of any and all markets," ready to enter, and thus keeps the Establishment on its toes. Indeed, a German economist has interpreted the conglomerate merger as a self-correcting force in American capitalism, making it more competitive and denying the Marxian prophecy of increasing monopoly. Certainly, enhanced potential as well as actual competition can be an important social gain.

While conceding the probability that conglomeration energizes competition, many observers contend that large diversified corporations may engage in predatory or other kinds of conduct prejudicial to small firms. Several arguments are advanced.

It is said that the large conglomerate can engage in cut-throat or predatory pricing in one of its lines of business, subsidizing temporary losses from profits earned in other lines until its smaller competitors are driven from the field. In practice, instances of cross-subsidization are rare. Not only does it violate federal and state antimonopoly laws but it flies in the face of accepted principles of management. In a multiindustry company, it is not feasible to force the manager of one division or subsidiary to operate unprofitably when this requires abandonment of established targets and management incentive plans. Also, unless barriers to entry of new firms are very high, the subsidized division cannot reap monopoly profits once its competition has been eliminated, because its efforts to raise prices will attract new competitors and deny it an opportunity to recoup its losses.

Somewhat related to the cross-subsidization argument is the idea that the large financial resources of the conglomerate (its "deep pocket") enable it to engage in nonpredatory but temporarily losing activities, such as expensive product development or large-scale advertising that smaller competitors are unable to finance, which ultimately give it the competitive edge in the market. While there may be truth to the contention, the advantage of the larger firm arises from superior resources and not from conglomeration. Unless one believes that public policy should protect smaller firms at any cost, one cannot object to product and market development activities which are in the consumers' interest, even though they are open only to enterprises with ample financial means.

Yet another standard objection to large firms, whether or not conglomerate in nature, is that they achieve such important advantages of scale that they raise the barriers to entry into an industry. Here again there is truth in the argument. Conglomeration as well as other modes of business diversification can enable the surviving firm to benefit from reductions in risks or costs through enlargement of operations. By increasing the stakes in the industrial game they make it harder for poor players to survive. If these economies are real, society benefits—provided that competition remains effective and obliges the conglomerate to pass the economies along to the public via lower prices or product improvements. Few will defend the perpetuation of inefficient small-scale firms at heavy cost to the public. What is important is that a sufficient number of firms remains in each industry to discipline each other.

The possibility that the conglomerate firm will cause its constituents to practice commercial reciprocity, to the disadvantage of its small competitors, is usually mentioned in assessing the effects of mergers upon competition. If intradivisional sales are made on competitive terms, there can be no complaint. Is it realistic, however, to expect the manager of one division of a conglomerate to do business with another division on unfavorable terms, counting upon recouping the loss by selling the other division some of his own product at higher than competitive prices? The answer is negative because, as previously noted, it violates basic principles of management.

Business reciprocity can also be practiced in purchases and sales among different companies in such subtle ways as to escape detection by antitrust authorities. However, there is no clear evidence that conglomerates are more culpable than other large firms. Corporate systems of incentive and control normally delegate to divisional managers the authority to buy and sell in the cheapest market.

Finally, there is concern that conglomeration may be a new route to dangerous aggregations of economic and political power in American society. A competitive democratic order manifestly requires an adequate dispersion of power. Citizens and lawmakers must remain vigilant to stop undue concentrations of all kinds. It has frequently been noted that over the 16-year period of 1947–63 the top 200 corporations expanded their share of total value added in American manufacturing from 30 to 41 percent, and that by 1963 the 100 largest firms had a greater share than was held by the 200 largest in 1947. There are, nevertheless, reasons for believing that macroeconomic concentration is not at a dangerous level. Although reduced, the number of large manufacturing corporations remains so large as to preclude the possibility of oligopolistic behavior. Levels of industrial concentration have not risen, and they are the relevant criteria for judging competition, as the 1964 guidelines published by the Attorney General recognized.

American courts have consistently held that large size is not, per se, an offense against the antitrust laws. If corporate giantism were antisocial the government should long ago have proceeded to break up the larger nonconglomerate giants. In a ranking of 130 members of the "billion dollar club" in descending order of their 1968 sales revenues, the five largest conglomerates were International Telephone and Telegraph, 14th; Ling-Temco-Vought, 30th; Tenneco, 45th; Litton, 48th; and Textron, 59th. If public policy required a dismantling of these largest conglomerates, some 54 other giants should first be broken up. Only eight conglomerates ranked among the two hundred largest manufacturing corporations.

Conglomeration helps to keep down industrial concentration in manufacturing and mining, in the face of rising macroeconomic concentration. For any assumed level of macroeconomic concentration, a population of conglomerate firms will produce lower average industrial concentration than would a population of single-industry or concentric firms. This is shown by a simple hypothetical example: American manufacturing is classified by the Census Bureau upon a basis of product line into 470 "industries," which are aggregated into 21 "major manufacturing groups." Let us arbitrarily—but not entirely unrealistically—assume that "industries" define competitive markets in the sale of products and that each "major manufacturing group" embraces "related" products as the word is used herein. Assume further that macroeconomic concentration rises greatly to the point that *all* manufacturing activity is carried on by 500 giant corporations. What kind of corporate structure will minimize industrial concentration and maximize the probability of effective competition at the industrial level? There are three major alternatives:

1. A single-industry structure, under which there would be on the average about one firm in each of the 470 industries.
2. A concentric firm structure, under which there would be on the average about 24 firms in each of the 21 major manufacturing groups and 470 industries.
3. A conglomerate firm structure, under which all 500 firms could conceivably compete in every one of the 470 industries.

Under the assumed high level of macroeconomic concentration, a single-industry structure would result in widespread monopoly. Even a concentric firm structure might leave some industries highly concentrated. Only a conglomerate firm structure would provide high assurance of effective competition.

# Other Potential Effects

Corporate conglomeration can have, at least potentially, important effects upon the role of internal financing of business, upon investment policies, upon the relationship of banking to industry, and upon the process of allocating investment among industries.

Conglomeration tends to increase the role of internal financing of business enterprises by reducing the firm's reliance for funds upon external sources. In an industrially diversified firm, some divisions may be throwing off cash. The aggregate demand for external funds by the conglomerate will fluctuate less through time than will the demand of an equally large but more highly specialized firm. Other things being equal, conglomerates will have less recourse upon the commercial banking system for short-term financing.

Another likely, but still largely potential, consequence of conglomeration is a restructuring of investment portfolios. If a rising proportion of publicly owned corporations conglomerate, each incorporating the principle of portfolio diversification, managers of mutual funds, trust officers, and individual investors will find it less necessary to diversify their portfolios. Thus an investor might achieve the same protection against extreme fluctuations in the value of and income from his holdings by buying $1 million worth of stock in International Everything, Inc., as by buying $50,000 dollars' worth of stock of companies in each of 20 industries.

Another potential effect of conglomeration is to bring commercial banks and industrial corporations under common control. Already, several industrial conglomerates have acquired commercial banks. The more popular route, however, is use of the "one-bank holding company" to acquire financial and industrial enterprises. A one-bank holding company is created when a sponsoring commercial bank issues stock of a new holding company to its shareholders in exchange for their present shares. The primary motive is to acquire a corporate vehicle able to diversify into financial services not open to commercial banks, such as computer leasing, credit cards, mortgage banking, or sale of mutual investment shares. Up to the end of 1968, some 34 of the nation's largest banks holding over one hundred billion dollars of deposits had formed such holding companies. Unlike chains or groups of banks controlled by bank holding companies, which are prohibited by the Bank Holding Company Act of 1951 from acquiring nonfinancial enterprises, one-bank holding companies are unregulated and able to enter nonbanking activities.

A serious potential consequence of conglomeration could be a worsening of resource allocation in the economy as a result of less accurate knowledge of returns to investment in different industries. Most conglomerates report their sales and net profits in the aggregate; they do not publish for investors the financial results of their operations in each industry or industrial group. The relative profitability of different lines being unknown, investors are unable to allocate their funds among industries with as much knowledge as they would possess in a nonconglomerate world. More and larger errors are likely to be made. Society will lose from a less efficient use of scarce capital.

\* \* \* \* \*

# Corporate Role in Diversified Companies*

The field research for this study was undertaken . . . in the effort to determine whether the very different organizational approaches of the two large diversified companies in which the researcher had had the opportunity to do clinical research were representative of broader classes of companies or simply "one of a kind" situations. Since these two companies were excellent examples of two broadly different strategies of diversification which have been followed in American industry, it seemed appropriate to construct groups of companies with similar administrative histories, with possible similarities and differences in the approaches to corporate organization to be determined. The hope was to include in each category companies which had "stabilized" at a certain approach to organization, and not companies that were still making the transition from the extremes of either a holding company or a functionally organized pattern of operation.

Companies chosen for inclusion in the group called "diversified majors" were selected because they had become diversified largely by the means described by Chandler:

1. As part of a long-term trend, starting in the 1920s,
2. With a characteristic pattern of
   a. Initial expansion and accumulation of resources in a single business,
   b. Rationalization in the use of resources,
   c. Expansion into new (often related) markets and lines to help assure the continuing full use of resources, and
   d. Development of new administrative structures to deal with the new management problems.

Companies selected for inclusion in the "conglomerate" group were chosen because they had become diversified in a different manner, as well as much more recently, than the diversified majors. It was intended that companies in this group would generally have

1. Achieved most of their growth and diversification within the last 5–15 years,
2. Followed a characteristic pattern of expansion
   a. Largely by a series of acquisitions, rather than internally generated diversification,
   b. Often into widely unrelated areas,
   c. Often by means of aggressive financial policies rather than with excess resources, and
3. Shown serious interest in contributing to the operating performance of their acquisitions, even though there was considerable variation in the financial and acquisition policies of the companies in the sample.

---

*Norman Berg, "Corporate Role in Diversified Companies," Harvard Business School Working Paper #71–2BP2.

In addition, it was hoped that companies in both groups would be primarily manufacturing oriented, with the bulk of their business in the United States, and would be between about $500 million and $2 billion in size.

A total of 18 companies were contacted with regard to assisting in the project. Three declined, and in another the illness of the president made the request inconvenient. Data from four companies were not used. One company that was thought to be in the diversified major category proved to be too strongly influenced by its relatively recent emergence from being primarily a chemically based company. Data from three companies that were clearly in the conglomerate category were not used because, as the project developed, their size and age characteristics made them less suitable for inclusion in the conglomerate group, as they were in the $100–$300 million category and were less than five years old.

The companies from which usable data were obtained, along with a brief statistical summary of each of the companies, are shown in Table 1.

In terms of overall characteristics of the two groups, then, the important points for our purposes are:

1. All of the companies (except "Y," which is not included in the averages) were in the $500 million to approximately $2 billion sales range.
2. The average size in the conglomerate group was about $1.4 billion, or about 40 percent larger than the approximately $1 billion for the diversified major group.
3. Companies in the conglomerate group were much more diversified than their counterparts, with an average of 70 4-digit SIC numbers as compared to 30 for the diversified majors.

## Summary of Findings

The results of the field research are shown on pages 758 through 760 in numerical form (Table 2) and in simple graphic form (Figure 1). The most striking conclusion to be drawn directly from the data is the substantial similarity within groups and differences between groups with regard to the emphasis accorded R&D, marketing, manufacturing, and purchasing functions at the corporate level. None of these functions (with one exception in the case of purchasing) were represented at all at the corporate level in the conglomerates; in only three cases were any of these four functions *not* represented at the corporate level in the diversified majors. The greatest difference was in terms of numbers in the R&D function, with an average of 151 in the diversified majors and 0 in the conglomerates.

The diversified majors had, on the average, more than three times as many people at the corporate level as the conglomerates. Part of this difference was represented by the great disparity in the emphasis accorded R&D, marketing, manufacturing, and purchasing, as pointed out above, but the average number of professionals in the other six categories listed was, without exception, lower for the conglomerates. Not only did the conglomerates refrain completely from undertak-

# TABLE 1

## Statistical Data on Companies

*Statistical Data*

| *Companies* | 1969 | | | | | | *Approx. #<br>Acquis.<br>1959–69* | 1959 | |
|---|---|---|---|---|---|---|---|---|---|
| | *Sales<br>(Million $)* | *Fortune<br>Rank* | *Assets<br>(Million $)* | *Employees<br>(Thousands)* | *Number of<br>Divisions* | *4-Digit<br>SIC #* | | *Sales<br>(Million $)* | *Fortune<br>Rank* |
| **Diversified Majors** | | | | | | | | | |
| Bendix | $1,468 | 72 | $ 980 | 63.5 | 53 | 30 | 16 | $684 | 62 |
| Borg-Warner | 1,087 | 108 | 949 | 41.6 | 35 | 25 | 3 | 650 | 68 |
| Ingersoll-Rand | 711 | 160 | 690 | 33.7 | 27 | 31 | 11 | 162 | 269 |
| Company "X" | About 500 | — | — | — | — | About 35 | NA | — | — |
| Average | About $1,000 | — | — | — | — | About 30 | — | — | — |
| Company "Y" | See text for comments | | | | | About 50 | NA | — | — |
| **Conglomerates** | | | | | | | | | |
| Gulf & Western | $1,564 | 64 | $2,172 | 85.0 | 37 | 89 | 45 | — | — |
| Kidde (W.J.) | 786 | 143 | 775 | 35.7 | 55 | NA | 74<br>('64–69) | $ 41 | — |
| Lear-Siegler | 587 | 186 | 319 | 26.6 | 56 | 40 | 50 | 87 | 431 |
| Litton | 2,177 | 39 | 1,580 | 116.0 | 70 | 64 | 80 | 126 | 322 |
| Textron | 1,682 | 57 | 895 | 70.0 | 32 | 85 | 55 | 308 | 146 |
| Average | $1,359 | 98 | $1,148 | 66.6 | 50 | 70 | 61 | — | — |

NA = not available.

Source: *Fortune* 500 Survey, plus company data on divisions, SIC codes, and acquisition.

**TABLE 2**

Organizational Data on Companies

| Companies | Diversified Majors | | | | | | | Conglomerates | | | | | | |
|---|---|---|---|---|---|---|---|---|---|---|---|---|---|---|
| | Company | | | | Four Cos: | | | Company | | | | | Five Cos: | |
| Functions | A | B | C | X | Total | Avg. | "Y" | F | G | H | I | J | Total | Avg. |
| General Executives | 5 | 5 | 4 | 2 | 16 | 4 | 23 | 4 | 1 | 4 | 3 | 14 | 26 | 5 |
| Finance | 28 | 61 | 101 | 144 | 334 | 84 | 582 | 8 | 22 | 29 | 91 | 106 | 256 | 51 |
| (of which Control) | (10) | (36) | (78) | (107) | (231) | (58) | (424) | (6) | (12) | (8) | (38) | (49) | (113) | (23) |
| Legal-Secretarial | 4 | 10 | 22 | 42 | 78 | 20 | 92 | 1 | 7 | 5 | 6 | 66 | 85 | 17 |
| Personnel Adm. | 11 | 6 | 20 | 25 | 62 | 16 | 90 | 1 | 2 | 3 | 10 | 20 | 36 | 7 |
| Research & Dev. | 54 | 130 | 139 | 232 | 555 | 139 | 1012 | 0 | 0 | 0 | 0 | 0 | 0 | 0 |
| Marketing | 5 | 0 | 34 | 0 | 39 | 10 | 101 | 0 | 0 | 0 | 0 | 0 | 0 | 0 |
| Manufacturing | 5 | 1 | 0 | 5 | 11 | 3 | 190 | 0 | 0 | 0 | 0 | 0 | 0 | 0 |
| Public Relations | 1 | 6 | 9 | 16 | 32 | 8 | 45 | 5 | 3 | 5 | 6 | 9 | 28 | 6 |
| Purchasing & Traffic | 10 | 1 | 33 | 4 | 48 | 12 | 30 | 5 | 0 | 0 | 2 | 0 | 2 | 0 |
| Corporate Planning | 3 | 3 | 2 | 6 | 14 | 5 | 8 | 5 | 4 | 1 | 7 | 9 | 26 | 5 |
| Totals | 126 | 223 | 364 | 476 | 1,189 | 297 | 2173 | 24 | 39 | 47 | 125 | 224 | 459 | 92 |

Note: Numbers shown indicate professional personnel in corporate functions as determined from field research.

## FIGURE 1

**Corporate Personnel versus Sales**

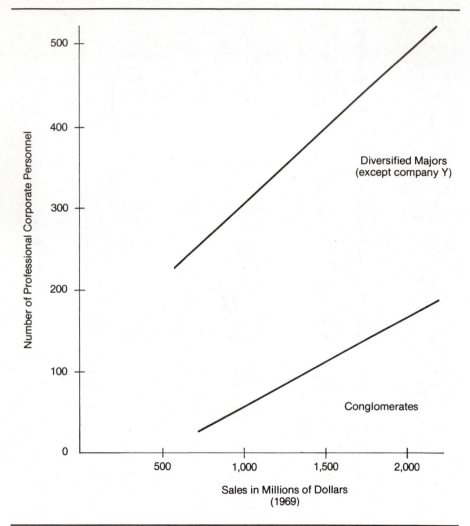

Source: Tables 1 and 2. Points are not shown in order to avoid identifying companies. Straight lines were fitted to the data by means of the method of least squares.

ing four major activities at the corporate level, then, they were also more thinly staffed than the diversified majors in all of the remaining activities.

Both the finance and control functions represented a significantly larger proportion of the total corporate effort in the conglomerates (56 percent and 25 percent, respectively) than in the diversified majors (28 percent and 19 percent). In terms of the average number of people involved, however, the conglomerates had only about 60 percent as many as the diversified majors.

These contrasts are heightened by the facts that the sales for the average company in the conglomerate group were 40 percent larger than for the average diversified major, and that the conglomerates were both more diversified and had more divisions than the diversified majors. In addition, the group averages were based on the five companies in the conglomerate group but for only the four companies named in the diversified major group. The effect of including Company "Y" in the group averages, as shown in the last column of Table 2, would be to more than double these averages for almost every organizational category, accentuating in a dramatic but perhaps misleading way the contrast between these two groups of companies.

It is important to note that the figures by no means include the total corporate effort in any one of the areas listed, as they do not include activities at the group or division level. Neither do they allow for variations in the amount of outside services purchased. It was originally hoped that a way could be found to summarize the functions and people at the group levels as well, thereby getting a more accurate picture of the total of the functions and people within the company but "above" the level of the division manager. The complexity and variation in practices at the group level dictated a deferral of this effort, however, even though much of the data was collected.

## Comments on Companies

Although detailed comments on individual companies which would tend to identify the companies would not be in order, a number of observations can nevertheless be made.

In the conglomerate group, Company H seemed to have the clearest strategy with regard to the types of businesses they were interested in and the organizational approach they would follow in order to make each division as effective as possible as an individual unit. Executives had often expressed their preference for acquiring and operating divisions which could function effectively as individual units, and not as customers of, suppliers to, or collaborators with other divisions. Perhaps as a consequence of the above, they had the most straightforward organization of all the companies visited in either group. If a single companay were to be selected to typify the "conglomerate approach to organization," H would serve the purpose well.

The president often had stated his views on the importance of having as few levels and people as possible between himself and the operating divisions. He was also determined to avoid building up staff units and assistants to line executives in order to make it more likely that important issues could be identified and resolved quickly by the line organization. He, and his predecessors, had very consciously avoided building up existing corporate staff units, "assistant to" positions, or functional areas such as R&D, marketing, or manufacturing. Even the audit and control area was relatively small because, as he put it, "We have always preferred to take our chances in the direction of too much rather than too little trust of the operating units with regard to keeping us informed of their problems."

This company had no staff at all at the group level; even the recently appointed group controllers reported to the corporate controller rather than the group officers. The principal reasons were to make it as unlikely as possible that "issues or problems would get lost or side-tracked," and to provide some independent check on the group officers as well as the divisions.

Company J was perhaps the most interesting of the conglomerates, however, because it departed farthest from the averages for the conglomerate group as a whole. They had chosen to build up their staff very considerably in selected areas: They had by far the most general executives, and they had significantly more people in the Finance area, the Legal section (there was virtually no legal work done outside or in the divisions), and the Personnel and Administration areas. In addition, they were above the averages for the diversified majors in each of these areas.

In the areas of R&D, Marketing, Manufacturing, and Purchasing and Traffic, however, the pattern was consistent with the other conglomerates again, and clearly different than the diversified majors. A director of the company commented that "We decided on Day 1 that we would never have any corporate staff in these areas, and so far nothing has happened to make us change our thinking." One could argue, then, that this company had gone farther than any of the other conglomerates in building up a corporate staff effort similar to the diversified majors, *except* in the critical areas of R&D, Marketing, Manufacturing, and Purchasing and Traffic. They seemed to be very consciously mixing the two approaches, and the evolution of this company should be most interesting to observe.

More variation in both the strategy of diversification and the organizational approach adopted to deal with it was found in the diversified majors, and summary statements are more difficult to make about this group. The organizational functions were more complex and difficult to explain to an outsider. It is tempting to use the evolutionary analogy of a later and more highly developed organism, but this seems more misleading than helpful with regard to understanding the present differences or making any predictions about the future development of these organizations.

In terms of the history of diversification, for example, one of the companies had gone through a considerable acquisition phase some 30–40 years ago, had continued to diversify but had operated with a very small corporate staff for a long period of time, and was still in the process of building up functions and people at the corporate level. The president commented:

> When we were formed back in the late 20s, we ran largely as a holding company for a while. We added financial controls first but didn't begin building up in other areas until much more recently. I don't anticipate anything in the marketing or manufacturing areas, but we are currently engaged in a study just like you are doing to find out how some other companies are approaching these corporate organizational questions. At present, we are especially interested in defining our role with regard to EDP, Financial Analysis, and Strategic Planning.
>
> My approach is influenced, of course, by how I have defined my job as well as my own preferences and "style." I think my job is to do all I can to insure that we are making the right decisions as a corporation on the businesses that we get into and get out

of, and that our divisions are doing the best possible job in the business they are in. My personal preferences are to have the fewest but best people possible at the corporate level.

Another of the diversified majors, however, was still in the process of cutting down on their headquarters staff. A vice president commented:

We really started to move away from our 50-year-old functional approach about five years ago. Out total for headquarters personnel has declined from 1,000 to 400 in the last several years, even though the number of plants we operate has increased more than six times. Our most recent changes have been to break up and move the accounting, credit, and marketing functions out to the divisions.

The unique administrative history of each company, and especially the diversified majors, is clearly of major importance in understanding the reasons for the present approach to organization. In spite of this factor, however, the differences between the two board groups of companies are great. We will turn next to a discussion of these differences between the groups.

## Comments on Group Differences

The data show clearly that there are considerable similarities within groups and differences between groups with regard to the functions undertaken and the emphasis accorded those functions at the corporate level. Before turning to the implications of this for research and administration, we will explore a few of the possible reasons for the differences. Since the conglomerates represent a more recent development than the diversified majors, it will be useful to describe the differences primarily in terms of why the conglomerates differ from the diversified majors.

Companies in the conglomerate group have, by definition, recently acquired independent businesses; the diversified majors more often developed their divisions internally. In the one case the division manager or entrepreneur and his staff already existed; in the other they had to be created as the functions were taken away from the existing corporate staff. Simply following the path of least resistance in each case would lead in the direction indicated by the data, especially in those cases where a "strong" manager came with the acquisition.

Although the differing histories are clearly important, it does not seem likely that it is the sole factor, or perhaps even the major factor, responsible for the differences. A number of the conglomerates have been of significant size for 5 or 10 years, and have had the opportunity to build staff if they thought it advantageous. No systematic attempt was made to obtain comparable detailed historical figures, as generally they were not readily available. Without exception the executives providing the information had intimate knowledge of the general development of the corporate organization over a number of years, though, and although all reported some modest increases in staff, none felt that drastic changes had occurred in the recent past.

In addition, none of the conglomerates foresaw much of a build-up in any area, and several were very explicit about *not* taking on any of the major functions they were not now performing. One of the older and larger of the conglomerates, for example, was at the time of this research engaged in planning their corporate office space requirements for a number of years in the future due to the scheduled move to a new office building shortly. Their corporate organization had changed very little in terms of functions or numbers for at least the last five years, and they were projecting less than a 10 percent increase in numbers and no addition in functions at the corporate level. Another, which had had a net increase of only two people at the corporate level in the preceding two years, during which the sales had increased by about 50 percent, had no plans for increasing their staff. A third thought that they might actually reduce the number at the corporate level as "we rationalize our operations and develop more professional managers in the divisions."

It is true, of course, that the skills and interests of the one or two top men in many conglomerates have been more financial than operating. This could easily have resulted in a low priority given to the establishment of those corporate functions more concerned with operations than finance, as many observers have noted. In addition, during most of the 1960s, a variety of factors combined to make acquisitions a much faster and easier path to growth than improvement of operations,[4] which could make efforts devoted to managing the divisions seem relatively less rewarding.

Another important reason for the differences is in the philosophy and background of the top managers in the conglomerates.[5] They have written and spoken at great length about the virtues of their "lean" organizations and the emphasis they place on seeing to it that their divisions are well managed rather than in taking an active part in their management. Many have been very explicit about seeing their role with regard to the divisions as providing a greater financial resource for the newly acquired company; relieving the manager of "corporate" tasks such as dealing with the SEC, the financial community, and stockholders, thereby freeing the division manger to concentrate on the design, production and marketing of his products; recognizing the need for and providing some help in installing "modern management methods" in basic areas such as financial controls and manufacturing policies; and finally providing an organizational framework, planning format, and system of incentives that can both motivate and prod the divisions' management into doing an effective operating job.

Many conglomerate managers seem to believe their approach is more effective, and attracts better managers, than the more "bureaucratic" approach of the diversified majors. They see their lean staff as a virtue to be retained as long as possible, not a weakness to be overcome as they become more "mature."

The importance of creating a climate which entrepreneurs will find attractive at the division level is constantly emphasized, and the avoidance of a large corpo-

---

[4]Neil Jacoby, "The Conglomerate Corporation," *The Center* (for the Study of Democratic Institutions) *Magazine* II, no. 4, July 1969.

[5]See, for example, Dan Carroll, "What Future for Conglomerates," *Harvard Business Review*, May–June 1969.

rate staff is seen as essential in creating such a climate. Since the theme is so often emphasized, and is supported by the data collected, it seems reasonable to at least consider that it may be an explanatory variable of some importance. It is not just the fact that conglomerates acquired companies with complete staffs that is significant, then, but also the fact that conglomerate managers appear to believe *and* behave as though it is important to leave much of the staff effort at the division level.

Another important explanation for the differences found is surely in the nature of the businesses the particular diversified companies are engaged in. "Comparable size and diversity" can be a deceptively misleading term with regard to the management approaches appropriate for specific companies. Although the administrative history and management philosophy are likely to be important, there is no doubt more opportunity or need for centralized staff services for some businesses and combinations of businesses than others. To the extent that the diversified majors as a group tend to be in businesses that are more closely related to each other in terms of the customers served and the manufacturing skills and technologies involved, for example, than those of the conglomerates, regardless of quantitative measures of diversity, there will likely be more opportunity to apply corporate-wide the efforts of a larger and more expensive corporate organization.

\* \* \* \* \*

# Diversification Tables

## TABLE 1

**Product Lines of the 200 Largest Manufacturing Firms in the United States, 1973**

| SIC 20: *Food and Kindred Products* | | *Herfindahl Index\** | | |
|---|---|---|---|---|
| *Rank* | *Firm* | *1960* | *1965* | *1965* |
| | | *3 dig.* | *3 dig.* | *2 dig.* |
| 74 | General Foods, 20:88% *204*† | .7904 | .7752 | .2735 |
| | *202, 203, 205, 206, 208, 283, 284, 289,* | | | |
| | *514, 518* | | | |
| 90 | Borden 20:61%; 28:22% *202* | .3627 | .7307 | .3659 |
| | *203, 205, 206, 208, 209, 204, 282, 284,* | | | |
| | *285, 286, 289, 514, 581* | | | |
| 98 | Coca-Cola *2086* | .2180 | .4853 | .0000 |
| | *203, 209, 358, 514* | | | |

\*The Herfindahl Index is a measure used by economists to illustrate the extent to which a company is diversified. An index reading of .0000 is an undiversified company. A reading of .999 is maximally diversified.

†The numbers which appear along with the names of the corporation in these Diversification Tables provide an indication of the variety of products which the corporation in question markets. The two-digit groups (such as, for example, 20—Food and Kindred Products or 28—Chemicals and Allied Products) are the most general manufacturing aggregation. Three-digit numbers indicate subsectors of the two-digit groups. Four-digit numbers are subsectors of three-digit groups, etc. Thus, as noted, major group 20 is comprised of Food and Kindred Products. Three-digit subgroup 202 is Dairy Products. Four-digit industry 2021 is Creamery Butter.

## TABLE 1 *(continued)*

| *SIC 20: Food and Kindred Products* | | *Herfindahl Index** | | |
|---|---|---|---|---|
| *Rank* | *Firm* | *1960* | *1965* | *1965* |
| | | *3 dig.* | *3 dig.* | *2 dig.* |
| 99 | Kraftco 20:97% *202* | .5248 | .6073 | .0838 |
| | 201, 203, 207, 209, 265, 289, 307, | | | |
| | 322, 342, 363, 374, 514 | | | |
| 107 | Joseph E. Seagram & Sons *2085* | .5893 | .2325 | .2277 |
| | 208, 291, 518 | | | |
| 109 | United Brands *017* | | | |
| | 201, 203, 204, 282, 286, 307, 514 | | | |
| 112 | CPC International 20:69% *204* | .4410 | .5704 | .0563 |
| | 203, 205, 206, 207, 209, 284, 287, 289, | | | |
| | 514, 581 | | | |
| 118 | PepsiCo 20:77%; 39:10% *2086* | .0581 | .0000 | .0000 |
| | 204, 394, 411, 514, 751 | | | |
| 122 | Ralston Purina 20: almost 100% *204* | .3050 | .6325 | .1908 |
| | 207, 209, 282, 287, 514 | | | |
| 124 | Norton Simon 20:57%; 28:16% 207 | | | |
| | 201, 203, 208, 284, 272, 275, 322, 341, 355, | | | |
| | 365, 399, 483, 512, 781 | | | |
| 125 | Esmark 20:89%; 28:6% *201* | .5075 | .4656 | .2611 |
| | 202, 204, 207, 209, 281, 284, 287, 291 | | | |
| | 311, 514 | | | |
| 126 | Beatrice Foods *202* | .3832 | .5953 | .0441 |
| | 201, 203, 205, 206, 208, 209, 22, 23, 251 | | | |
| | 285, 286, 316, 355, 363, 3714, 375, 422 | | | |
| | 504, 508, 514, 516, 021, 125 | | | |
| 134 | National Distillers & Chemical | | | |
| | 20:48%; 28:21% *2085* | .6906 | .8165 | .7462 |
| | 204, 281, 282, 286, 222, 228, 514, 518 | | | |
| 136 | Consolidated Foods 20:60% *203* | | | |
| | 201, 205, 206, 208, 209, 232, 233, 238, 251, | | | |
| | 264, 275, 277, 284, 306, 354, 363, 394, 399, | | | |
| | 502, 533, 514, 541, 581, 734 | | | |
| 150 | General Mills 20:75%; 23:10%; 39:10%; | | | |
| | 28:4% *204* | .6126 | .6419 | .2674 |
| | 201, 205, 206, 209, 233, 394, 396, 283, 286, | | | |
| | 514, 581, 596 | | | |
| 151 | Nabisco *205* | .2701 | .3855 | .0960 |
| | 202, 204, 206, 284, 283, 394, 514 | | | |
| 155 | H. J. Heinz 20:100% *203* | .5347 | .5810 | .0000 |
| | 201, 205, 209 | | | |
| 164 | Standard Brands 20: almost 100% *209* | .8089 | .8081 | .2580 |
| | 201, 203, 204, 206, 207, 208, 306, 329, | | | |
| | 514, 518 | | | |
| 168 | Carnation *202* | .6131 | .6447 | .1617 |
| | 203, 201, 204, 341, 024, 514 | | | |
| 189 | Anheuser-Busch 20: almost 100% *2082* | .7692 | .7350 | .4537 |
| | 201, 204, 209, 518, 799 | | | |
| 177 | Campbell Soup 20:100% *203* | .3750 | .5121 | .0000 |
| | 201, 204, 205, 206, 209, 514, 581, 599 | | | |
| 197 | Quaker Oats 20:72% *204* | .4130 | .6674 | .2169 |
| | 201, 205, 206, 209, 222, 223, 286, 394, 514 | | | |

**TABLE 1** *(continued)*

| *SIC 28: Chemicals and Allied Products* | | *Herfindahl Index\** | | |
|---|---|---|---|---|
| | | *1960* | *1965* | *1965* |
| *Rank* | *Firm* | *3 dig.* | *3 dig.* | *2 dig.* |
| 18 | E.I. Du Pont de Nemours 28 more than 80% *286* 281, 282, 283, 284, 285, 287, 289, 306, 307, 369, 516 | .7788 | .7808 | .3355 |
| 22 | Union Carbide 28:79% *281* 282, 286, 287, 289, 307, 333, 392, 516 | .8794 | .8595 | .7546 |
| 24 | Dow Chemical *281* 282, 284, 286, 287, 307, 333, 335, 516 | .6520 | .9200 | .8189 |
| 35 | Procter and Gamble 28:70%; 20:23% *284* 204, 207, 209, 264, 516 | .7330 | .7496 | .6303 |
| 40 | Monsanto 28:86% *286* 281, 282, 283, 284, 287, 291, 307, 358, 516 | .8253 | .8181 | .5699 |
| 55 | W. R. Grace 28:48%; 20:21% *286* 282, 283, 287, 203, 205, 206, 209, 262, 291, 307, 314, 3714, 384, 102, 103, 441, 516, 581, 594 | .8243 | .8928 | .7105 |
| 69 | Allied Chemical 28:78%; 29:15% *281* 282, 286, 287, 291, 222, 307, 331, 3714, 121, 131, 516 | .4567 | .7746 | .5776 |
| 72 | Celanese 28 c.a. 85% *282* 283, 285, 286, 289, 261, 307, 347, 349, 356, 364, 329, 516 | .4518 | .6567 | .2981 |
| 92 | American Cyanamid *287* 281, 283, 284, 286, 289, 251, 307, 327, 384, 152, 154, 651, 655, 516 | .8488 | .8415 | .4142 |
| 97 | Prizer 28 almost 100% *283* 281, 284, 287, 384, 516, 512, 516 | .5667 | .541 | .2862 |
| 100 | Warner-Lambert *283* 284, 206, 342, 358, 383, 384, 516, 512, 516 | .8247 | .7249 | .5392 |
| 114 | Olin 28:30%; 34:22%; 26:19% *281* 282, 286, 287, 343, 344, 346, 262, 263, 264, 265, 152, 154, 516 | .8873 | .9142 | .7252 |
| 117 | Colgate-Palmolive 28 c.a. 90% *284* 283, 287, 239, 264, 307, 384, 394, 221, 516 | .2975 | .3200 | .0000 |
| 123 | American Home Products 28 c.a. 70%; 20:21% *284* 284, 285, 287, 206, 209, 342, 514, 516, 512 | .6321 | .6675 | .5294 |
| 130 | Hercules 28 c.a. 70% *286* 281, 282, 284, 285, 287, 289, 209, 262, 307, 355, 364, 376, 516 | .7316 | .7686 | .3154 |
| 133 | Eli Lilly *283* 284, 287, 307, 512, 516 | .1247 | .2027 | .2027 |
| 140 | NL Industries 28:39%; 33:32% 34:24% *281* 282, 285, 286, 333, 343, 345, 346, 516 | .8578 | .8467 | .6337 |
| 141 | Merck *283* 281, 284, 286, 287, 289, 207, 358, 516, 512 | .5335 | .4477 | .0130 |
| 142 | Williams Companies 287:45%; 33:18% *287* 331, 461, 51, 53 | | | |
| 144 | Squibb 28:83% *283* 284, 201, 206, 516, 581, 512 | | | |

## TABLE 1 *(continued)*

| SIC 28: *Chemicals and Allied Products* | | Herfindahl Index* | | |
|---|---|---|---|---|
| Rank | Firm | 1960 | 1965 | 1965 |
| | | 3 dig. | 3 dig. | 2 dig. |
| 146 | Bristol-Myers 28 almost 100% *284* | .4081 | .5247 | .0641 |
| | 283, 399, 516 | | | |
| 159 | Rohm and Haas 28 almost 100% *282* | .6763 | .7475 | .0799 |
| | 283, 286, 287, 307, 516 | | | |
| 163 | Diamond Shamrock 28:65%; 29:24%; | | | |
| | 10÷3:10% *281* | .5184 | .7427 | .5298 |
| | 282, 283, 286, 291, 299, 101, 102, 121, | | | |
| | 131, 204, 307, 516 | | | |
| 167 | Texasgulf *281* | | | |
| | 287, 193, 147, 241, 242, 243, 291, 333, 516 | | | |
| 178 | Foremost-McKesson 28:49%;20:48% *283* (40%) | .4932 | .4352 | .0000 |
| | 284, 202, 512, 514, 516, 518, 591, 651, 655 | | | |
| 182 | Avon Products *284* (almost 100%) | | | |
| | 891 | | | |
| 186 | Ethyl 38:50%; 30:21%; 26:15%; 33:14% *286* | | | |
| | 281, 282, 289, 307, 262, 333, 385, 516 | | | |
| 189 | Abbott Laboratories 28: almost 100% *283* | .5625 | .7312 | .6639 |
| | 284, 287, 306, 307, 384, 385, 516, 512 | | | |
| 198 | Stauffer Chemical 28: almost 100% *281* | .5191 | .5383 | .2516 |
| | 282, 286, 287, 355, 516 | | | |
| 199 | GAF 28:35%; 38:26%; 32:18% *286* | .8047 | .8153 | .6602 |
| | 281, 282, 386, 327, 329, 229, 276, 357, | | | |
| | 369, 3714, 516 | | | |
| SIC 35: *Machinery, Except Electrical* | | | | |
| 5 | International Business Machines *357* | .5375 | .4990 | .4783 |
| | 276, 369, 508, 651, 655, 737, 739, 154 | | | |
| 30 | Xerox *357* | | | |
| | 271, 272, 273, 276, 366, 369, 508, 737,739 | | | |
| 34 | International Harvester 35:95% *352* (83%) | .8237 | .7904 | .6431 |
| | 351, 353, 229, 331, 371, 372, 376, 508, 614, | | | |
| | 631 | | | |
| 39 | Honeywell *357* | .8502 | .8599 | .7305 |
| | 358, 348, 349, 361/2, 364, 366, 369, 372, | | | |
| | 376, 381, 382, 383, 384, 386, 171, 173, 508, | | | |
| | 506, 737, 739, 762, 769, 891 | | | |
| 47 | Caterpillar Tractor *352* | .4225 | .5747 | .0000 |
| | 351, 353, 354, 356, 362 | | | |
| 61 | Singer *3636* | .7455 | .8672 | .6912 |
| | 354, 355, 357, 366, 251, 382, 508, 394, 829 | | | |
| 64 | Sperry Rand 35:70% *357* | .8758 | .8666 | .7450 |
| | 352, 356, 358, 363, 366, 369, 382, 508, 737 | | | |
| 65 | NCR 35: almost 100% *357* | .6763 | .6914 | .6883 |
| | 276, 355, 508, 737 | | | |
| 68 | Control Data *357* | | | |
| | 276, 508, 615, 641, 737, 739 | | | |
| 70 | Deere 35: almost 100% *352* (c.a. 75%) | .5188 | .4962 | .1740 |
| | 351, 353, 379, 508, 614 | | | |
| 77 | Burroughs *357* | .3141 | .1892 | .1863 |
| | 355, 276, 367, 395, 508, 737 | | | |

**TABLE 1** *(continued)*

| | | | Herfindahl Index* | |
|---|---|---|---|---|
| Rank | Firm | 1960<br>3 dig. | 1965<br>3 dig. | 1965<br>2 dig. |

*SIC 35: Machinery, Except Electrical*

| Rank | Firm | 1960 3 dig. | 1965 3 dig. | 1965 2 dig. |
|---|---|---|---|---|
| 101 | FMC 35:45%; 28:44%; 34:11% *355*<br>351, 352, 353, 356, 358, 281, 284, 287,<br>332, 348, 349, 371, 373, 374, 501, 508 | .8264 | .8743 | .7165 |
| 111 | Teledyne *355*<br>354, 356, 358, 333, 335, 346, 363, 366, 372,<br>382, 384, 394, 508, 631, 632, 633, 739, 891 | | | |
| 135 | Ingersoll-Rand 35 almost 100% 353 (68%)<br>351, 354, 355, 356, 342, 346 | .8148 | .8185 | .2778 |
| 137 | Studebaker-Worthington—Studebaker-<br>Worthington<br>*356*, 351, 352, 354, 358, 284, 289, 291,<br>304, 307, 329, 344, 361/2, 363, 364, 3714,<br>372, 376, 374, 382, 508, 615, 981 | .8045<br>.8108 | .7724<br>.8654 | .5559<br>.6568 |
| 149 | Allis-Chalmers 35:80%; 36:20% *353*<br>351, 352, 355, 356, 358, 361/2, 379,<br>506, 508, 615 | .8394 | .8561 | .5840 |
| 157 | Babcock & Wilcox *351*<br>356, 358, 325, 331, 329, 343, 344, 346, 349,<br>361/2, 365, 3714, 508 | .8346 | .8844 | .7801 |
| 160 | Combustion Engineering 35:56% *358*<br>353, 355, 356, 241, 321, 323, 329, 325,<br>332, 244, 346, 349, 361/2, 382, 508, 739, 891 | .7200 | .6834 | .3698 |
| 162 | Dresser Industries *353*<br>351, 354, 355, 356, 358, 325, 329, 332,<br>355, 349, 361, 381, 382, 103, 138, 145,<br>147, 508 | .8368 | .8731 | .6840 |
| 165 | Clark Equipment 35: c.a. 85% *353*<br>352, 355, 356, 358, 254, 332, 344, 367, 3714,<br>501, 508, 614, 615 | .6053 | .6976 | .5697 |
| 174 | Carrier *358*<br>354, 356, 344, 372, 508 | .6267 | .4623 | .3126 |
| 192 | Otis Elevator 35: almost 100% *353*<br>366, 375, 508 | .0000 | .0000 | .0000 |

*SIC 36: Electric and Electronic Equipment*

| Rank | Firm | 1960 3 dig. | 1965 3 dig. | 1965 2 dig. |
|---|---|---|---|---|
| 6 | General Telephone & Electronics *481/366*<br>361/2, 364, 365, 367, 274, 307, 382, 506,<br>737 | .8132 | .8527 | .4507 |
| 11 | General Electric *361/2*<br>363, 3-4, 365, 366, 367, 369, 351, 372,<br>376, 374, 506, 614, 615 | .9211. | .9325 | .6214 |
| 19 | Western Electric *366*<br>334 | .5692 | .5397 | .3427 |
| 20 | Westinghouse Electric *261/2*<br>363, 364, 273, 274, 281, 286, 344, 351, 358,<br>374, 382, 376, 152, 154, 483, 506, 651, 655 | .9361 | .9349 | .6662 |
| 29 | RCA *365*<br>366, 227, 229, 273, 376, 482, 483, 506, 751 | .6904 | .7663 | .4598 |
| 139 | Motorola *366*<br>365, 367, 376, 506, 781, 782 | .6641 | .7193 | .1723 |

## TABLE 1 *(continued)*

| SIC 36: Electric and Electronic Equipment | Herfindahl Index* | | |
|---|---|---|---|
| Rank    Firm | 1960 | 1965 | 1965 |
| | 3 dig. | 3 dig. | 2 dig. |
| 158    Texas Instruments *367* | .8416 | .8846 | .7391 |
| 366, 357, 376, 382, 506 | | | |
| 170    Whirlpool 36: c.a. 90% *363* | .4986 | .5054 | .5054 |
| 365, 358, 393, 506 | | | |
| 183    Raytheon 36:71% *367* | .6813 | .7858 | .5411 |
| 363, 366, 369, 273, 353, 355, 358, | | | |
| 376, 506, 739 | | | |
| 201    Emerson Electric *361:2* | .8618 | .8156 | .6149 |
| 363, 364, 365, 367, 354, 358, 372, | | | |
| 376, 506 | | | |
| *SIC 37: Transportation Equipment* | | | |
| 2    General Motors *3711/13* | .7784 | .753 | .6674 |
| 3714, 372, 373, 374, 376, 379, 332, 351, | | | |
| 358, 363, 365, 501, 508, 551, 614, 615, | | | |
| 631, 632, 633 | | | |
| 4    Ford Motor *3711/13* | .6168 | .6216 | .6033 |
| 3714, 3715, 321, 352, 356, 363, 366, 152, | | | |
| 154, 591, 508, 551, 614, 615, 632 | | | |
| 14    Chrysler *3711/13* | .4700 | .5049 | .4796 |
| 3714, 372, 373, 376, 379, 307, 348, 351, | | | |
| 358, 171, 501, 507, 551, 614, 752 | | | |
| 41    McDonnell Douglas 37:100%—McDonnell | .8333 | .8000 | .7500 |
| Douglas *372* | .2960 | .3445 | .3445 |
| 376, 737 | | | |
| 54    Rockwell International 37:56% *372* | .6375 | .8174 | .8083 |
| (28%) 3714 (28%), 376, 354, 356, 358, 365, | | | |
| 366, 367, 382, 501, 508 | | | |
| 63    Lockheed Aircraft 37: almost 100% *372* | .8003 | .7011 | .6596 |
| 373, 376, 366, 508 | | | |
| 79    Boeing 37: 100% *372* (76%) | .3692 | .4654 | .4654 |
| 376 (21%), 373, 508 | | | |
| 91    TRW 37:49% *3714* | | | |
| 371, 376, 351, 354, 355, 358, 366, 367, 363, | | | |
| 362, 361, 382, 396, 501, 737, 891 | | | |
| 95    Bendix *372* | .9268 | .9317 | .8199 |
| 3714, 372, 376, 379, 243, 244, 245, 354, | | | |
| 356, 358, 359, 365, 366, 382, 501, 508 | | | |
| 96    Avco *372* | .8598 | .9038 | .8261 |
| 3714, 376, 379, 273, 351, 352, 356, 359, 331, | | | |
| 365, 366, 382, 483, 501, 508, 614, 615, 651, | | | |
| 739, 781, 782, 891 | | | |
| 101    Signal Companies *3713* | .7376 | .6033 | .5506 |
| 3714, 372, 376, 307, 336, 351, 355, 382, | | | |
| 152, 154, 501, 508, 655 | | | |
| 106    United Aircraft 37: almost 100% *372* | .3872 | .2640 | .2640 |
| 376, 351, 358, 361:2, 366, 367, 508 | | | |
| 116    Borg-Warner *3714* | .8843 | .8898 | .7862 |
| 251, 282, 285, 286, 307, 343, 344, 351, 355, | | | |
| 356, 358, 362, 365, 382, 501, 508, 614, 615 | | | |

**TABLE 1** *(concluded)*

| SIC 37: Transportation Equipment | | Herfindahl Index* | | |
|---|---|---|---|---|
| | | *1960* | *1965* | *1965* |
| *Rank* | *Firm* | *3 dig.* | *3 dig.* | *2 dig.* |
| 121 | Eaton *3714* | .6534 | .8500 | .7230 |
| | 3713, 301, 332, 242, 345, 346, 349, 352, | | | |
| | 353, 355, 356, 358, 359, 362, 504, 508 | | | |
| 136 | General Dynamics 37:65% *372* | .8053 | .8879 | .8648 |
| | 373, 376, 325, 327, 329, 344, 357, 365, 366, | | | |
| | 367, 382, 111, 121, 508 | | | |
| 152 | Fruehaur *3715* | .0861 | .6091 | .0938 |
| | 3713, 3714, 372, 373, 376, 341, 344, 501, 551, | | | |
| | 614, 615 | | | |
| 166 | AMF *375* | .9241 | .9337 | .8519 |
| | 3714, 373, 3719, 232, 245, 343, 347, 352, | | | |
| | 353, 356, 358, 361, 362, 366, 367, 379, 382, | | | |
| | 387, 394, 501, 508 | | | |
| 181 | American Motors 37N almost 100% *3711* | .2534 | .2339 | .2339 |
| | 3713, 3714, 307, 501, 551, 553 | | | |
| 194 | White Motor 37:66% *3713* | .2292 | .7335 | .6054 |
| | 3714, 352, 353, 501, 508 | | | |
| 195 | Dana *3714* | .6822 | .8310 | .6962 |
| | 373, 329, 346, 356, 359, 501 | | | |

*SIC 38: Instruments and Related Products*
- 21  Eastman Kodak
- 45  Minnesota Mining & Mfg.
- 113  Johnson & Johnson
- 172  Polaroid

*SIC 39: Miscellaneous Manufacturing Industries*
- 193  Armstrong Cork

## TABLE 2

**Business Activities of Conglomerate Firms in the United States in 1979** *(SIC 2-digit industries)*

| | *Conglomerate Firms* | No. of Industries | |
|---|---|---|---|
| *Rank* | *Firm* | *Mfg.* | *Nonmfg.* |
| 8 | International Tel. & Tel. | 14 | 24 |
| | 20, 24, 25, 26, 27, 28, 30, 32, 33, 34, 35, 36, 37, 38, 01, 12, 13, 14, 15, 16, 17, 41, 42, 44, 47, 48, 50, 51, 54, 55, 59, 61, 63, 67, 70, 73, 76, 89 | | |
| 15 | Tenneco | 13 | 15 |
| | 20, 22, 24, 26, 28, 29, 30, 31, 32, 33, 34, 35, 37, 01, 07, 13, 15, 42 | | |
| 42 | Gulf & Western Industries | 19 | 22 |
| | 33, 34, 35, 36, 37, 38, 39, 10, 12, 14, 17, 42, 50, 51, 52, 53, 56, 58, 61, 62, 63, 64, 65, 67, 70, 73, 78, 79, 89 | | |
| 51 | Litton Industries | 11 | 8 |
| | 25, 26, 27, 28, 33, 34, 35, 36, 37, 38, 39, 13, 15, 44, 50, 51, 73, 76, 89 | | |
| 66 | LTV | 8 | 10 |
| | 20, 30, 32, 33, 34, 35, 36, 37, 40, 44, 47, 50, 51, 60, 67, 10, 12, 13 | | |
| 73 | Illinois Central Industries | 11 | 15 |
| | 20, 24, 25, 27, 30, 32, 33, 34, 35, 36, 37, 40, 42, 45, 47, 50, 51, 54, 55, 57, 58, 59, 63, 65, 70, 73 | | |
| 103 | Textron | 14 | 2 |
| | 20, 22, 26, 27, 28, 30, 32, 33, 34, 35, 56, 37, 38, 39, 42, 73 | | |
| 104 | Greyhound | 7 | 12 |
| | 20, 22, 28, 35, 37, 38, 39, 41, 42, 47, 50, 51, 56, 58, 59, 60, 67, 73, 89 | | |
| 128 | Martin Marietta | 8 | 6 |
| | 24, 25, 28, 32, 33, 34, 36, 37, 14, 15, 50, 51, 73, 75 | | |
| 131 | Dart Industries | 12 | 6 |
| | 20, 23, 24, 28, 30, 32, 33, 34, 35, 36, 38, 39, 42, 50, 51, 59, 73, 89 | | |
| 132 | U.S. Industries | 17 | 7 |
| | 22, 23, 24, 25, 26, 27, 28, 30, 31, 32, 33, 34, 35, 36, 37, 38, 39, 14, 17, 50, 51, 59, 61, 79 | | |
| 143 | Northwest Industries | 11 | 7 |
| | 20, 22, 23, 25, 28, 30, 31, 32, 34, 35, 36, 10, 42, 50, 51, 54, 55, 59 | | |
| 173 | Walter Kidde | 12 | 10 |
| | 24, 25, 27, 30, 31, 32, 33, 34, 36, 37, 38, 39, 14, 16, 17, 42, 50, 51, 59, 73, 79, 89 | | |
| 180 | Ogden | 5 | 8 |
| | 20, 33, 34, 35, 37, 42, 44, 45, 47, 50, 51, 59, 79 | | |
| 188 | Colt Industries | 6 | 3 |
| | 32, 33, 34, 35, 36, 37, 42, 50, 67 | | |

**TABLE 3**

Product Lines of the 200 Largest Manufacturing Firms in Japan in 1973

| | | *Japan 1973* | *Major* | *Others* |
|---|---|---|---|---|
| 33 | 20 | Kirin Brewery | 2082 | 2086 |
| 63 | 20 | Taiyo Fishery | 209 | n.a. |
| 76 | 20 | Santory | 2085 | |
| 86 | 20 | Ajinomoto | 2099 | 2075, 2048 |
| 98 | 20 | Nichiro Gyogyo | 2092 | 2091, 204 |
| 100 | 20 | Nippon Suisan | 2092 | 2091, 44 |
| 101 | 20 | Snow Brand Milk | 202 | 2079 |
| 111 | 20 | Sapporo Breweries | 2082 | 2086 |
| 116 | 20 | Asahi Breweries | 2082 | 2086 |
| 125 | 20 | Meiji Seika | 2065 | 2052, 283, 203, 2066, 2099 |
| 135 | 20 | Morinaga Milk Ind. | 202 | |
| 143 | 20 | Meiji Milk Product | 202 | |
| 149 | 20 | Nisshin Flour Mill | 204 | 47, 422 |
| 152 | 20 | Nippon Reizo | 2092 | 2097, 514 |
| 162 | 20 | Morinaga | 2065 | 2052, 203, 65 |
| 178 | 20 | Kikkoman Shoyu | 2099 | 2085 |
| 190 | 20 | Nihon Nosan Kogyo | 204 | |
| 192 | 20 | Nisshin Oil Mills | 2075 | 287 |
| 201 | 20 | Nippon Oils & Fats | 207 | 284 |
| 18 | 28 | Mitsubishi Chem. Ind. | 286 | 282, 287, 333, 299 |
| 21 | 28 | Asahi Chemical Ind. | 282 | 222, 286, 307, 283, 20, 32 |
| 22 | 28 | Toray Industries | 282 | 222, 286, 307 |
| 23 | 28 | Sumitomo Chemical | 286 | 282, 333, 281, 287, 283 |
| 29 | 28 | Showa Denko | 286 | 333, 281, 2895 |
| 30 | 28 | Teijin | 282 | 222 |
| 37 | 28 | Mitsui Toatsu Chem. | 286 | 282, 307, 287, 281, 283 |
| 43 | 28 | Takeda Chemical Ind. | 283 | 287, 281, 286, 20 |
| 48 | 28 | Mitsubishi Petrochem. | 286 | 282 |
| 51 | 28 | Mitsubishi Rayon | 282 | 222, 307, 228 |
| 66 | 28 | Kuraray | 282 | 222, 307, 228 |
| 73 | 28 | Kainippon Ink Chem. | 282 | 289, 284 |
| 74 | 28 | Mitsui Petrochemical | 286 | |
| 85 | 28 | Sekisui Chemical | 282 | 307 |
| 89 | 28 | Electro Chemical Inc. | 281 | 287, 2869, 282 |
| 92 | 28 | Mitsubishi Gas Chem. | 286 | 282, 307 |
| 103 | 28 | Shiseido | 284 | |
| 105 | 28 | Toyo Soda Mfg. | 282 | 327, 281 |
| 112 | 28 | Kanegafuchi Chem. Inc. | 282 | 207, 222, 333, 286, 208, 283 |
| 119 | 28 | Sankyo | 283 | 287, 20 |
| 121 | 28 | Kyowa Hakko Kogyo | 286 | 2099, 283, 2085, 287 |
| 122 | 28 | Nissan Chem. Inc. | | |
| 133 | 28 | Shinetsu Chem. Inc. | 282 | 307, 367, 286, 331, 281 |
| 146 | 28 | Chisso | 286 | 287, 282, 281 |
| 147 | 28 | Shionogi | 283 | |
| 148 | 28 | Daicel | 282 | 307 |
| 150 | 82 | Nippon Soda | 281 | 286 |
| 151 | 28 | Nippon Sanso | 281 | 354, 286 |
| 156 | 28 | Tanabe Seiyaku | 283 | |
| 161 | 28 | Kureha Chem. Ind. | 282 | 307, 286, 281, 287 |

**TABLE 3** *(continued)*

| | | Japan 1973 | Major | Others |
|---|---|---|---|---|
| 174 | 28 | Fujisawa Pharmaceut. | 283 | |
| 183 | 28 | Kao Soap | 284 | n.a. |
| 193 | 28 | Banyu Pharmaceutical | 283 | |
| 195 | 28 | Toyo Ink Mfg. | 289 | 282, 307 |
| 199 | 28 | Nippon Kayaku | | |
| 200 | 28 | Mitsubishi Plastics | 282 | 307 |
| 19 | 35 | Komatsu | 353 | 355, 356, 332 |
| 26 | 35 | Sumitomo Shipbldg. | 353 | 373 |
| 32 | 35 | Kubota | 351 | 344, 346, 332, 356 |
| 40 | 35 | Fujitsu | 3573 | 366, 367 |
| 79 | 35 | Japan Steel Works | 355 | 332, 331, 348 |
| 81 | 35 | Niigata Engineering | 351 | 355, 356, 373, 353, 355, 374 |
| 94 | 35 | Koyo Seiko | 3562 | |
| 118 | 35 | Nippon Seiko | 3562 | |
| 124 | 35 | NTN Toyo Bearing | 3562 | |
| 126 | 35 | Kaikin Kogyo | 3585 | 3569, 355, 2819, 307 |
| 131 | 35 | Toyoda Auto Loom | 3552 | 3714, 353 |
| 132 | 35 | Ebara Mfg. | 358 | |
| 138 | 35 | Ricoh | 357 | 2648, 3861 |
| 169 | 35 | Fujikoshi | 3562 | |
| 184 | 35 | Toyo Umpanki | 353 | |
| 196 | 35 | Kato Works | 353 | |
| 202 | 35 | Riccar | 3636 | n.a. |
| 205 | 35 | Janome Sewing Mach. | 3636 | n.a. |
| 4 | 36 | Hitachi | 361/2 | 363, 364, 365, 366, 358, 374 |
| 9 | 36 | Tokyo Shibaura Elec. | 361/2 | 363, 364, 365, 366, 367 |
| 12 | 36 | Matsushita Elec. Ind. | 366 | 363, 367, 364, 365, 3692, 361/2 |
| 13 | 36 | Mitsubishi Electric | 361/2 | 366, 358, 363, 364, 365 |
| 20 | 36 | Nippon Electric | 366 | 367 |
| 46 | 36 | Fuji Electric | 361/2 | 358, 362, 363, 364, 365 |
| 49 | 36 | Sony | 3651 | 3652, 366, 367 |
| 52 | 86 | Sanyo Electric | 366 | 367, 363, 364, 365 |
| 72 | 36 | Sharp | 3651 | 363, 364, 367 |
| 96 | 36 | Oki Electric Ind | 3661 | construction |
| 123 | 36 | Matsushita Electron. | 367 | |
| 144 | 36 | Yasukawa Elec. Mfg. | 361/2 | |
| 159 | 36 | Shinko Electric | 361/2 | 356, 353, 361, 3728, 357 |
| 160 | 36 | Meidensha Elec. Mfg. | 361/2 | 353, construction |
| 187 | 36 | Omron Tateishi Elect. | 3661 | construction |
| 2 | 37 | Mitsubishi Heavy Ind. | 373 | 356, 344, 351, 358, 384, 353, 3721 |
| 5 | 37 | Ishikawajima Harima | 373 | 3728, 355, 356, 353, 344 |
| 7 | 37 | Nissan Motor | 3711 | 3713, 3714, 3552, 372 |
| 11 | 37 | Toyota Motor | 3711 | 3713 |
| 14 | 37 | Kawasaki Heavy Ind. | 373 | 353, 356, 358, 351, 372, 344, 374 |
| 16 | 37 | Hitachi Shipbldg. | 373 | 344, 353, 356, 358, 332 |
| 17 | 37 | Toyo Kogyo | 3711 | 3713, 3714, 3532, 354 |

**TABLE 3** *(concluded)*

| | | Japan 1973 | Major | Others |
|---|---|---|---|---|
| 24 | 37 | Mitsui Shipbldg. Eng. | 373 | 355, 353, 351 |
| 34 | 37 | Isuzu Motor | 3713 | 3711, 3714 |
| 35 | 37 | Honda Motor | 375 | 3711, 3711 |
| 53 | 37 | Hino Motors | 3713 | 3711, 3714 |
| 70 | 37 | Sasebo Heavy Ind. | 373 | 344, 348, 35 |
| 78 | 37 | Fuji Heavy Industries | 3711 | 3721, 374, 3713, 35 |
| 87 | 37 | Suzuki Motor | 3711 | 375, 3714 |
| 88 | 37 | Hakodate Dock | 373 | construction |
| 90 | 37 | Nippon Denso | 3714 | |
| 110 | 37 | Daihatsu Kogyo | 3711 | 3714 |
| 140 | 37 | Aishin Seiki | 3714 | |
| 153 | 37 | Sanoysasu Dockyard | 373 | 344, construction |
| 167 | 37 | Nippon Sharyo Seizo | 374 | |
| 75 | 38 | Fuji Photo Film | | |
| 155 | 38 | Shimazu Seisakusho | | |
| 177 | 38 | Konishiroku Photo | | |
| 191 | 38 | Nippon, Kogaku | | |
| 197 | 38 | Canon | | |
| 129 | 39 | Nippon Gakki | | |

# CASE 29

# *General Electric, Strategic Position— 1981\**

On December 21, 1980, the General Electric Company announced that John F. Welch, Jr., 45, would become chairman and chief executive officer effective April 1, 1981. Welch had spent 20 years in GE's operating organization—first in the plastics business, later in consumer products, and then as vice chairman. He would be replacing the retiring Reginald H. Jones, a man described by some as a "legend." Indeed, *The Wall Street Journal* reported that GE had "decided to replace a legend with a live wire."

The company that Jack Welch would be leading was the 10th largest industrial corporation in the United States and the only firm among *Fortune's* 10 largest that could be characterized as diversified. Its financial performance was solid—AAA bond rating, 19.5 percent return on equity, and $2.2 billion in cash and marketable securities. In addition, GE's management systems and in particular its strategic planning system were most highly regarded; the following comments were typical.

> Probably no single company has made such a singular contribution to the arts and wiles, the viewpoints and the techniques of large-scale corporate management as GE. . . .
> Today the technique uppermost in the minds of GE top management is planning—a

---

*Professor Francis J. Aguilar and Associate Professor Richard Hamermesch prepared this case as the basis for class discussion rather than to illustrate either effective or ineffective handling of an administrative situation.

Copyright © 1981 by the President and Fellows of Harvard College.

Harvard Business School case 381-174.

776

preoccupation in which GE is again an acknowledged master and innovator among corporate giants.

*Management Today,* August 1978

Shortly after I took this job, I visited some people at the Defense Department because I had heard that they had just finished an exhaustive survey of industrial planning systems. They told me I was probably inheriting the world's most effective strategic planning system and that Number Two was pretty far behind.

Daniel J. Fink, Senior V.P., Corporate Planning
and Development, General Electric

When Japanese managers come to visit us, they don't ask to see our research centers or manufacturing facilities. All they want to know about is our management system.

a General Electric executive

GE's excellent performance and reputation were not guarantee of future success. Jack Welch would be challenged to meet the company's long-term objective of increasing earnings per share 25 percent faster than the growth in GNP in the face of tougher foreign competition and a continued slowdown in the growth of GE's traditional businesses. To meet this challenge, he would have to decide how to stimulate and promote growth and what role GE's famed planning system would play in the years ahead.

# Origins of Strategic Planning

As the decade of the 1960s was nearing a close, a number of circumstances came together which led to a major reexamination of the way General Electric was being managed. One of the more salient of these was the company's profitless growth (see Exhibit 1 for financial information). While sales in 1968 of $8.4 billion were 91 percent higher than in 1960, net income had increased only 63 percent and return on total assets had fallen from 7.4 percent to 6.2 percent. This lackluster profit performance came at the same time that three major ventures—commercial jet engines, mainframe computers, and nuclear power systems—were demanding more and more of the company's financial resources. Pressure on corporate management was mounting: GE's "sacred Triple A bond rating" was in jeopardy.

Improving this financial situation was no easy task. In 1968, GE was widely diversified, competing in 23 of the 26 two-digit SIC industry categories, and was decentralized into 10 groups, 46 divisions, and over 190 departments. Indeed, diversification and decentralization had been the major strategic and organizational thrusts of GE's two prior CEOs—Ralph Cordiner, 1950 to 1963, and Fred Borch, 1963 to 1972. Under decentralization, GE's departments became organizational building blocks, each with its own product-market scope and its own marketing, finance, engineering, manufacturing, and employee-relations functions. One GE executive noted:

In the 1950s, Cordiner led a massive decentralization of the company. This was absolutely necessary. GE had been highly centralized in the 1930s and 1940s. Cordiner broke the company down into departments that, as he used to say, "were a size that a man could get his arms around." And that the company would say after giving a man his department was, "Here, take this $50 million department and grow it into $125 million." Then the department would be split into two departments, like an amoeba.

In addition to decentralization, Cordiner pushed for expansion of GE's businesses and product lines. With growth and diversity, however, came problems of control:

> The case for Cordiner lies in his improvement of GE's numerators and in his creation of a truly remarkable "can-do" organization. He was the champion of volume and diversity and of make rather than buy. He built a company unmatched in American business history in the capacity to pursue those objectives. In the sense of home grown know-how, GE *could* do almost anything; and, in the sense of in-house capacity, GE could do a lot of a lot of things, simultaneously.
>
> But the very expansiveness and evangelism that were Cordiner's strengths were flawed by permissiveness and lack of proportion. "We can do it" too often became "we should do it." For example, massive investments with long payback periods were undertaken simultaneously in nuclear power, aerospace, and computers, with a blithe self-confidence in GE's ability to "do-it-ourselves." A sort of "marketing macropia" persisted in which previously constrained market segmentations and product definitions were escalated beyond experience or prudence.[1]

As Fred Borch faced the challenges of leading General Electric in the mid-1960s, internal studies of the company's problems began to proliferate. One such study set out to give management a tool for evaluating business plans by delineating the key factors associated with profitable results.[2] Another study undertaken by GE's Growth Council tried to determine how the company would properly position itself to meet its long-time goal of growing faster than the GNP. Despite these and other staff studies, however, profitless growth continued.

Reg Jones assessed the company's situation at the time:

> Our performance reflected poor planning and a poor understanding of the businesses. A major reason for this weakness was the way we were organized. Under the existing structure with functional staff units at the corporate level, business plans only received functional reviews. They were not given a *business* evaluation.
>
> True, we had a corporate planning department, but they were more concerned with econometric models and environmental forecasting than with hard-headed business plan evaluation. Fortunately, Fred Borch was able to recognize the problem.

In 1969 Borch commissioned McKinsey & Co. to study the effectiveness of GE's corporate staff and of the planning done at the operating level. He commented on McKinsey's study:

> They were totally amazed at how the company ran as well as it did with the planning that was being done or not being done at various operating levels. But they saw some

---

[1] James P. Baughman, "Problems and Performance of the Role of Chief Executive in the General Electric Company, 1892–1974," mimeographed discussion paper, July 15, 1974.

[2] This approach eventually led to the PIMS model that has been made available to industry at large by the Strategic Planning Institute.

tremendous opportunities for moving the company ahead if we devoted the necessary competence and time to facing up to these, as they saw it, very critical problems.

In their report, they made two specific recommendations. One was that we recognize that our departments were not really businesses. We had been saying that they were the basic building blocks of the company for many years, but they weren't. They were fractionated and they were parts of larger businesses. The thrust of the recommendation was that we reorganize the company from an operations standpoint and create what they call Strategic Business Units—the terminology stolen from a study we made back in 1957. They gave certain criteria for these and in brief what this amounted to were reasonably self-sufficient businesses that did not meet head-on with other strategic business units in making the major management decisions necessary.[3] They also recommended as part of this that the 33 or 35 or 40 strategic business units report directly to the CEO regardless of the size of the business or the present level in the organization.

Their second recommendation was that we face up to the fact that we were never going to get the longer-range work done necessary to progress the company through the 70s, unless we made a radical change in our staff components. The thrust of their recommendation was to separate out the on-going work necessary to keep General Electric going from the work required to posture the company for the future.

## Introduction of Strategic Planning

In reporting the results of the McKinsey study to GE's management in May 1970, Fred Borch noted: "We decided that their recommendations on both the operating front and the staff front conceptually were very sound. They hit right at the nut of the problem, but the implementation that they recommended just wouldn't fly as far as General Electric was concerned. We accepted about 100 percent of their conceptual contribution and virtually none of their implementation recommendations."

To develop an approach for implementing the McKinsey recommendations in a way suitable for GE, Borch had set up a task force headed by Group Vice President W. D. Dance. This group spent two intensive months preparing alternatives and recommendations for consideration by the corporate executive office.

As a result of these efforts, a decision was made to restructure GE's corporate staff into two parts. The existing staff units, which provided ongoing services to the CEO[4] and to the operating units, were grouped as the corporate administrative staff reporting to a senior vice president. The administrative staff would deal with functional, operational matters. As a counterpart, a corporate executive staff was created to help the CEO plan the future of the company. It comprised four staff components—finance, strategic planning, technology, legal and governance—each headed by a senior vice president.

---

[3]The general characteristics of an SBU were defined as follows: a unique set of competitors, a unique business mission, a competitor in external markets (as opposed to internal supplier), the ability to accomplish integrated strategic planning, and the ability to "call the shots" on the variables crucial to the success of the business.

[4]The CEO here refers to the corporate executive office, which included the chairman and chief executive officer and the vice chairmen. GE usually had two or three vice chairmen.

### Establishing Strategic Business Units

The task force anticipated several problems in implementing McKinsey's recommendation to create strategic business units reporting directly to the CEO. One problem had to do with GE's existing line reporting structure of groups, divisions, and departments. McKinsey's proposal had been to abandon GE's current organizational structure and to reorganize on the basis of SBUs. The task force was concerned that such a change might seriously jeopardize the successful functioning of GE's operational control system. To avoid this risk, management decided to superimpose the SBU structure on the existing line reporting structure. For ongoing operations, managers would report according to the group-division-department structure. However, only units designated SBUs would prepare strategic plans.

As shown in Figure A, a group, division, or department could be designated an SBU. This overlay of a strategic planning structure on the operating structure resulted in a variety of reporting relationships. When a department was named an SBU, for example, the department manager would report directly to the CEO for planning purposes, but to a division manager for operating purposes. GE managers expressed the opinion that this approach provided the company with the best of both worlds—tight operational control on a comprehensive basis and planning at the relevant levels. One manager commented:

> In theory, the intervening layers of management were supposed to be transparent for planning purposes and opaque for control purposes. In practice, they were translucent

## FIGURE A

**SBU Overlay on Existing Organization**

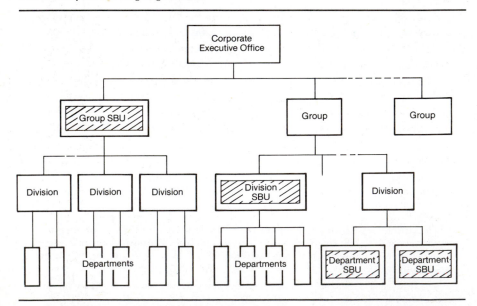

for both. Even though the department or division SBU managers were to report directly to the CEO for planning, they would normally review their plans with the group executive. In a sense, we loosened the SBU structure to allow personal influence and power to shape the important strategic decisions.

The designation of SBUs posed a second problem for the task force. According to GE executives, about 80 percent of the SBU designations could be readily agreed upon. The remaining 20 percent required considerable judgment whether the appropriate SBU level was the department, division, or group. In these cases Fred Borch would make the final judgment, often based on his "comfort index" with the business and with the manager running the business. Not until the end of 1972 were all of the SBU designations completed. Of the 43 SBUs, 4 were groups, 21 were divisions, and 18 were departments. Two other problems on the task force's agenda concerned the kind of information to be contained in a SBU plan and the numbers and kinds of people to staff the planning effort.

## Defining a Business Plan

Even with the reduction in the number of business plans from 190 departments to 43 SBUs, the CEO faced a formidable task of review. One GE manager noted that "Borch had a sense that he wasn't looking for lots of data on each business unit, but really wanted 15 terribly important and significant pages of data and analysis."

To deal with this problem, three of the group vice presidents were asked to work with three different consulting companies (Arthur D. Little, Boston Consulting Group, and McKinsey & Co.) to find a way to compress all of the strategic planning data into as effective a presentation as possible. For example, GE's collaborative effort with McKinsey led to the development of the 9-block summary of business and investment strategy shown in Figure B.[5] One GE executive commented that "the 9-block summary had tremendous appeal to us not only because it compressed a lot of data, but also because it contained enough subjective evaluation to appeal to the thinking of GE management."

The only instructions for the SBU manager on the content of a business plan was a listing of the topics to be covered. Over time, new topics were added and some were deleted. But the corporate office never specified how each topic should be treated. The following list contains the topics specified for the 1973 SBU plans:

1. Identification and formulation of environmental assumptions of strategic importance.
2. Identification and in-depth analysis of competitors, including assumptions about their probable strategies.
3. Analysis of the SBU's own resources.
4. Development and evaluation of strategy alternatives.

---

[5]See Exhibit 2 for a description of GE's 1980 criteria for assessing industry attractiveness and business position.

## FIGURE B

Investment Priority Screen

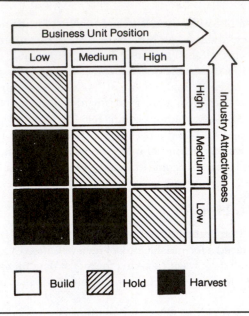

5. Preparation of the SBU strategic plan, including estimates of capital spending for the next five years.
6. Preparation of the SBU operating plan, which detailed the next year of the SBU strategic plan.

Reg Jones, who became GE's chairman and chief executive officer in December 1972, added a proviso on how the plans were to be presented:

> At our general management conference in January 1973, I stirred up quite a few members of that audience when I said that I expected every SBU manager to be able to stand before a peer group and, without benefit of visual aids, give a clear and concise statement of his strategic plan. And that every manager reporting to him should fully understand that statement and be able to explain it to his troops. I meant it. When that happens, then you can say that planning has become a way of life.

### Staffing the Planning Effort

With the new SBU planning approach in place, the question remained of how to staff the effort. Here, two important actions were taken. First, each SBU manager was required to hire an SBU strategic planner. Because of the limited number of experienced strategic planners in the company at that time, many of the people filling these posts were hired from outside the company, an unusual practice for GE.[6]

Second, both the SBU general managers and strategic planners were required to attend special strategic planning seminars set up at GE's Management Development Center in Crotonville, New York. Each department and division general manager (over 240 in number) was also given a metal suitcase with a slide and tape show to present to subordinates after taking the course.

## Acceptance of Planning: 1972–1977

In the 1950s and 1960s, a characteristic of GE was the belief that the company could succeed in all of the businesses in which it competed. A frequently voiced reaction to strategic planning and particularly to the 9-block analysis, on the other hand, was that it legitimized exiting from certain businesses. According to *Fortune,* "GE stopped making vacuum cleaners, fans, phonographs, heart pacemakers, an industrial X-ray system, and numerous other products that failed to deliver the returns Jones demanded." During Jones's entire tenure as CEO, a total of 73 product lines were exited.

GE's successful exit from the mainframe computer business in May 1970 also played a pivotal role in legitimizing divestitures; as one manager commented:

> While the sale of GE's computer business actually preceded the adoption of strategic planning, somehow people began to connect the two. From then on it became fashionable to prune businesses. And Jones's subsequent promotion gave even more credibility to those managers who were willing to face up to the fact that certain businesses had to be exited.
>
> The planning system was just another tool which enabled a manager to face up to certain inevitabilities. Prior to this, we had really operated with a "floating J curve." In other words, businesses would forecast two or three years of flat or declining profitability, but then all of the numbers would point upwards. What Jones was able to do with the computer business and what strategic planning revealed was that the floating J curve was a fantasy.

### Impact on the Business Mix

As shown in Table A one impact of strategic planning was a shift in GE's mix of businesses. Reg Jones commented:

> Another source of confidence for us is the continued development of a strategic planning system that provides a strong discipline for differentiating the allocation of resources—that is, investing most heavily in areas of business that we identify as offering the greatest leverage for earnings growth, while minimizing our investments in sectors we see as growing more slowly or remaining static. [1973 annual report]

---

[6]Over time, many of the SBUs developed planning staffs and the planning positions were filled internally. By 1980 there were approximately 200 senior level planners in GE. About half of these were career planners, while the others rotated through the position as part of their career development.

## TABLE A

**GE's Business Mix (%)**

|  | Sales | | Earnings | |
|---|---|---|---|---|
|  | 1970 | 1977 | 1970 | 1977 |
| Consumer products and services | 22.8 | 23.5 | 29.6 | 29.6 |
| Power systems | 21.5 | 18.0 | 26.5 | 6.9 |
| Industrial components and systems | 23.1 | 20.6 | 28.4 | 17.6 |
| Technical systems and materials | 28.5 | 23.1 | 9.1 | 22.7 |
| Natural resources | 0.0 | 5.4 | 0.0 | 18.0 |
| International | 15.9 | 14.3 | 20.1 | 6.5 |
| Corporate eliminations | (11.8) | (4.9) | (13.7) | (1.3) |

Source: General Electric 10-K reports for 1970 (recast for organizational changes) and 1977.

Comparing the company today with the General Electric of only a few years ago shows that, in selectively allocating our resources to the growth opportunities identified through strategic planning, we have developed decidedly different sources of earnings and a different mix of businesses, whose potentials for profitable growth exceed those of our historic product lines. [1976 annual report]

As Table A illustrates, a major contributor to the shift in GE's business mix was the acquisition in 1976 of Utah International, a billion dollar mining company with substantial holdings of metallurgical coal.[7] Many saw in Utah a potential hedge against inflation and numerous opportunities for synergy with GE's other businesses. While not denying these benefits, *Fortune* reported:

Jones wanted to make a lasting imprint on his corporation by providing a new source of earnings growth and creating what he likes to call "the new GE." Utah provided him with a means to make that concept credible. When the opportunity arose, he relied not on his hallowed planning staff, but rather seized the chance to personally lead his company into its biggest move in many years. As Jones himself now acknowledges: "Nothing in our strategic planning said that we should acquire Utah International."[8]

Internal developments also contributed to the shift in business mix, as described by one of GE's senior executives: "Much of the recent growth has come from the internal development of businesses brand new to GE. For example, engineered materials didn't even exist as a business in 1960. It was just a bunch of research projects. Now, it will have sales of $2 billion, it will make $200 million net,

---

[7]General Electric's 1976 annual report related a pooling-of-interest exchange of 41 million shares of GE common stock for all outstanding shares of Utah International, effective December 20, 1976. Utah International's 1976 earnings were $181 million and sales were $1,001 million. The company's principal operations included the mining of coking coal, steam coal, uranium, iron ore, and copper. By far the most important contribution to 1976 earnings came from Australian coking coal supplied under long-term contracts to Japanese and European steel producers.

[8]"General Electric's Very Personal Merger," *Fortune,* August 1977.

with a ROI of 18 percent, and it will have plants all over the world. The company's experiences with aircraft engines, information services, and several other businesses have been much the same."

## Impact on Management Systems

By 1977, the impact of strategic planning was being felt by GE's other management systems. For example, manpower evaluation and selection had been keyed to the strategic plans. A manager in the executive manpower department noted: "The strategic plans gave us, for the first time, a means by which we could evaluate if a manager really delivered on what he said he would do. All we have to do is check the previous plans. This also helps when there are job changes. We can now determine what current problems are caused by earlier mistakes, so the wrong person doesn't get blamed."

In the area of incentive compensation, performance screens were developed that separated financial and nonfinancial objectives for the business. This was intended to provide greater emphasis on longer-term considerations and it did to some extent, but as one manager noted, "It's a great theory, but in a crunch it's the financial results that matter."

In terms of GE's organization structure, only one major change was apparent. This was the dissolution of the corporate executive staff and the return to a number of separate functional staff components. Reg Jones explained: "The corporate executive staff was originally set up with two major objectives: to straighten out the venture messes and to devise a planning system to prevent those troubles in the future. By 1974 the venture problems were solved, and we had a planning staff that was managing the new strategic planning process. By 1975, we dissolved the [corporate executive] staff."

## Assessment of Strategic Planning

By 1977, strategic planning had won widespread management support for a variety of reasons. GE executives commented as follows:

> "In the views of some managers, there was more planning being done in the mid-1960s than today. There was lots of futurism, scenario writing, contingency planning, and model building. But those efforts were not related to the problems of our ongoing businesses as is the SBU analysis."
>
> "Not specifying the precise format of a strategic plan turned out to be very useful. For one thing, it enabled the SBUs to avoid spending time on issues that weren't important to them. More important, it provided room for some creativity and originality in the writing of the plans."
>
> "Since strategic planning was implemented, our real growth businesses have been funded, even when we were cash short in 1974 and 1975. The key is for the guy who is running a growth business that requires resources to gain the confidence of the people at the top of the organization. Strategic planning can help to get that confidence."

An internal audit of strategic planning, completed in December 1974, reported that "the overwhelming feeling is that strategic planning has become ingrained in General Electric: 80 percent felt there would be no slippage and 16 percent only minor slippage if corporate requirements for SP [strategic planning] were removed."

Not surprisingly, complaints of shortcomings in GE's strategic planning were also voiced. Some of the complaints reported in the audit had to do with the excessive effort devoted to cosmetics and upward merchandising of strategic plans. Another set of complaints had to do with a perceived ineffective review of SBU plans. The audit reported, "One issue is clear: The operations managers feel that corporate-level reviewers do not understand their businesses well enough to be competent reviewers."

The earlier review of strategic plans at the division and group levels was also considered by many managers as ineffective. The reason for this failing was attributed to the fact that managers at these levels typically "were really participants in generating the plans and thus were not objective reviewers." At the CEO level, on the other hand, the review of all 43 SBU strategic plans was requiring an inordinate amount of time and effort.

Pressures for current earnings were also cited as undermining the strategic planning process. One executive, quoted in the audit, commented: "Strategic planning process won't work in General Electric, at least not in the context in which we are trying to make it work. The company needs to project an attractive financial and cash-flow image. The pressure to provide a steady profit growth and a sustained P/E ratio results in short-term demands on operations which disrupt long-term programs."

## A Single General Electric and Value Added

The problem corporate management had in evaluating 43 SBU strategic plans was coupled with a growing concern about a lack of integration and cohesiveness among the many business initiatives under way. By the mid-1970s, SBU planning, while helping to strengthen GE's competitive positions and to improve profits, was also leading to a balkanization of the company. GE appeared to be moving in the direction of becoming a holding company.

This development ran directly counter to a basic GE management tenet. As early as 1973, Jones addressed management about the need to work "with the grain" rather than against it in reshaping the company. Prominent among the "abiding characteristics of General Electric," according to Jones, was "a strong preference for a single General Electric identity, despite our broad diversification." The world-famous GE monogram symbolized this core identity.

Coupled with the concept of a single GE identity was the notion of "value added." The recurrent attacks on big business, aimed at dismantling U.S. industry giants in the interest of increased competition, posed a serious potential threat to GE. As one senior GE executive explained: "The whole has got to be significantly greater than the sum of its parts. We have nothing to defend (against increasing external pressures to break up or, at a minimum, harass very large companies) unless we have a very effective, productive corporate level." Given top management's strong preference for a cohesive General Electric, SBU strategic planning, good as it was, was not adequate for GE's needs. Something more was needed.

# Integrating Strategic Planning: 1977–1980

At the general management conference in January 1977, Reg Jones announced his intention "to revise GE's strategic planning system and to establish a 'sector' organization structure as the pivotal concept for the redesign effort." The proposed changes aimed to improve the strategic planning review process and to develop a cohesive plan for GE as a single, integrated entity.

### Improving the Strategic Planning Review Process

In Jones's mind, corporate review of SBU plans suffered from overload. He explained:

> Right from the start of SBU planning in 1972, the vice chairmen and I tried to review each plan in great detail. This effort took untold hours and placed a tremendous burden on the corporate executive office. After awhile I began to realize that no matter how hard we would work, we could not achieve the necessary in-depth understanding of the 40-odd SBU plans. Somehow, the review burden had to be carried on more shoulders.

Creating the sector structure was Jones's way of spreading the review load. The sector was defined as a new level of management which represented a macro-business or industry area.[9] The sector executive would serve as the GE spokesperson for that industry and would be responsible for providing management direction to the member SBUs and for integrating the SBU strategies into a sector strategic plan. The sector strategic plan would focus heavily on development opportunities transcending SBU lines but still within the scope of the sector. The corporate executive office would thereafter focus its review on the strategic plans of the six sectors.

Below the sector, the SBU continued to be the basic business entity. To permit greater competitiveness (and visibility) for important strategic businesses within certain SBUs, however, GE introduced the concept of business segments. For example, the Audio Department became a business segment within the Housewares and Audio SBU because it was a unique business that could operate more effectively within the SBU than on its own.

The new organizational line structure is depicted in Figure C. The dual organization in use since 1971—SBUs for planning; group, divisions, and depart-

---

[9]Robert Frederick, the executive who had been assigned the tasks of introducing the sector structure and making it work, explained the new nomenclature: "We picked the word *sector* because no one knew what it meant. In that way there would be no preconceived notions of what the sectors would do."

## FIGURE C

Sector-SBU Structure

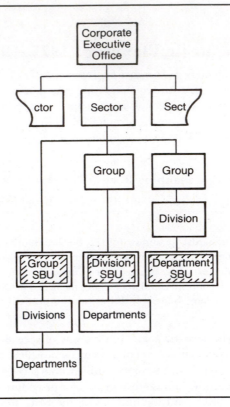

ments for operations—was supplemented by the sector-SBU structure. The earlier designations of group, division, and department were retained to indicate the relative size of an SBU.

Along with improved review, the new sector structure was also seen as clarifying the responsibilities for business development in GE. According to a senior corporate strategic planning staff executive: "Conceptually, SBUs are expected to develop new business opportunities by extending into contiguous product-market areas. Sectors are expected to develop new SBUs by diversifying within their macroindustry scopes. And corporate is expected to develop new sectors by diversifying into unserved macroindustries."

Improving strategy review and business development were two visible reasons for the new sector structure. (Figure D is an organization chart showing the new sector structure and management assignments.) Jones also had a private reason for this organizational change:

I had a personal road map of the future and knew when I wanted to retire. Time was moving on, and I could see a need to put the key candidates for my job under a spotlight for the board to view. The sector executive positions would provide the visibility.

The men were assigned to sectors with businesses different from their past experience. I did this not only to broaden these individuals but also to leaven the businesses by introducing new bosses who had different perspectives. For example, major appliances had long been run by managers who had grown up in the business. I put Welch, whose previous experience had been with high-technology plastics, in charge to see if he could introduce new approaches.

## Strategic Integration and Corporate Challenges

Along with improving strategic review, Jones saw a need to develop a cohesive plan for GE as a single, integrated entity. His concern reflected two problems that appeared to be growing in parallel with SBU planning itself:

> Over the years, we were discovering serious discontinuities among the SBU plans. At the operating level, we were suffering unnecessary costs from duplication and from uncoordinated actions.
>
> At the strategic level, we seemed to be moving in all directions with no sense of focus on what I saw as major opportunities and threats for the 1980s. For example, I saw a need to push forward on the international front, a need to move from our electromechanical technology to electronics, and a need to respond to the problems of productivity. We needed a way to challenge our managers to respond to these pressing issues in an integrated fashion.

To provide corporate direction and impetus on such issues, GE introduced the concept of corporate planning challenges. As shown in Figure E the planning challenges set the stage for the annual strategic planning cycle. Each year the CEO would issue a number of specific challenges that had to be addressed in the strategic plans of the SBUs and the sectors. For example, a 1980 corporate challenge called for SBUs and sectors to plan for a productivity improvement appropriate for their industry to counter worldwide competitive threats. The productivity target for GE as a whole was set for 6 percent.

The selection of challenges was seen by Jones as a vital function of the chief executive officer:

> It's the job of the CEO to look ahead. Planning can be helpful, but it is really our job to look at the decade ahead. You look at the environment and couple that with your knowledge of the operations. You begin to see gaps that are beyond the plans. You have studies made to examine the possible shortcomings.
>
> For example, as a defrocked bookkeeper, I have always had a concern about technology. In 1976, I commissioned a company-wide study of our strengths, weaknesses, and needs in technology. The findings—16 volumes of them—triggered a technological renaissance in GE. We stepped up our R&D budgets, built up our electronic capabilities, and reoriented our recruiting and training activities. Now every SBU has a firm technological strategy integrated with its business strategy.

# FIGURE D

Organization Chart, June 1, 1978

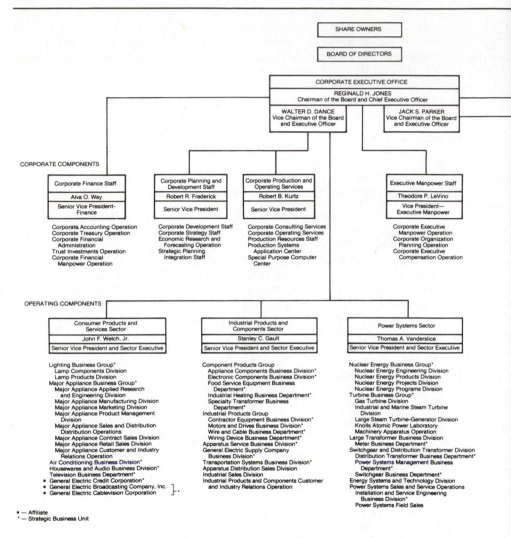

In addition to the CEO as a source of challenges, the restructured management system included two new approaches for generating planning challenges. One element aimed at fostering GE's international activities, the other at integrating GE's planning for critical resources.

**International sector.**   To increase the importance and the visibility of international operations in GE, Jones set it up as a sector. It was, however, to play a

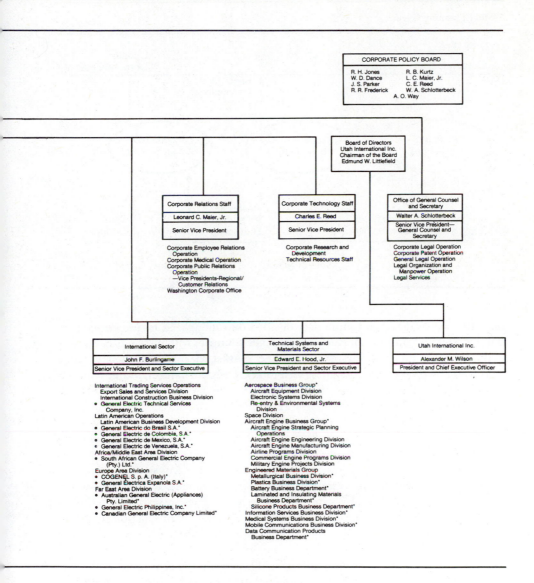

CORPORATE POLICY BOARD

R. H. Jones      R. B. Kurtz
W. D. Dance      L. C. Maier, Jr.
J. S. Parker     C. E. Reed
R. R. Frederick  W. A. Schlotterbeck
        A. O. Way

Board of Directors
Utah International Inc.
Chairman of the Board
Edmund W. Littlefield

Corporate Relations Staff
Leonard C. Maier, Jr.
Senior Vice President

Corporate Employee Relations
  Operation
Corporate Medical Operation
Corporate Public Relations
  Operation
  —Vice Presidents–Regional/
    Customer Relations
Washington Corporate Office

Corporate Technology Staff
Charles E. Reed
Senior Vice President

Corporate Research and
  Development
Technical Resources Staff

Office of General Counsel
and Secretary
Walter A. Schlotterbeck
Senior Vice President—
  General Counsel and
  Secretary

Corporate Legal Operation
Corporate Patent Operation
General Legal Operation
Legal Organization and
  Manpower Operation
Legal Services

International Sector
John F. Burlingame
Senior Vice President and Sector Executive

International Trading Services Operations
  Export Sales and Services Division
  International Construction Business Division
  • General Electric Technical Services
    Company, Inc.
Latin American Operations
  Latin American Business Development Division
  • General Electric do Brasil S.A.*
  • General Electric de Colombia, S.A.*
  • General Electric de Mexico, S.A.*
  • General Electric de Venezuela, S.A.*
Africa/Middle East Area Division
  • South African General Electric Company
    (Pty.) Ltd.*
Europe Area Division
  • COGENEL S. p. A. (Italy)*
  • General Electrica Expanola S.A.*
Far East Area Division
  • Australian General Electric (Appliances)
    Pty. Limited*
  • General Electric Philippines, Inc.*
  • Canadian General Electric Company Limited*

Technical Systems and
Materials Sector
Edward E. Hood, Jr.
Senior Vice President and Sector Executive

Aerospace Business Group*
  Aircraft Equipment Division
  Electronic Systems Division
  Re-entry & Environmental Systems
    Division
Space Division
Aircraft Engine Business Group*
  Aircraft Engine Strategic Planning
    Operations
  Aircraft Engine Engineering Division
  Aircraft Engine Manufacturing Division
  Airline Programs Division
  Commercial Engine Programs Division
  Military Engine Projects Division
Engineered Materials Group
  Metallurgical Business Division*
  Plastics Business Division*
  Battery Business Department*
  Laminated and Insulating Materials
    Business Department*
  Silicone Products Business Department*
Information Services Business Division*
Medical Systems Business Division*
Mobile Communications Business Division*
Data Communication Products
  Business Department*

Utah International Inc.
Alexander M. Wilson
President and Chief Executive Officer

special role among sectors. In addition to preparing a sector plan for GE's overseas affiliates, the international sector was also given responsibility for fostering and integrating international business for General Electric as a whole.

A subsequent effort to integrate electric iron manufacturing on a worldwide basis illustrates one of the roles that the international sector was intended to play. The SBU responsible for irons had developed a newly designed iron which it planned for production in a single small country. At international sector urging,

## FIGURE E

**Annual Planning Cycle**

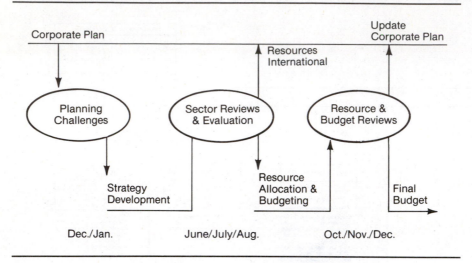

the SBU reconsidered and ultimately decided on rationalized multicountry production in three countries, including two larger countries with international sector affiliates. This approach improved cost and market share potentials in affiliate countries as well as cost effectiveness on a total GE system basis. This intervention led to an internal joint venture for irons between the international sector and the SBU to share risks and rewards on a worldwide basis.

**Resource planning.** Corporate management's concerns with GE's handling of critical resources were to be dealt with through another companywide integrating mechanism. For this purpose, senior corporate staff executives were given responsibility "for an objective assessment of key resources and the identification of issues impacting the company's strategic strengths." These assessments of financial resources, human resources, technology resources, and production resources would lead to planning challenges to the sectors and SBUs wherever practices needed to be improved.

Planning for human resources illustrated how this approach was to work. The vice president in charge of this planning described two of the issues he had subsequently raised for management consideration:

> One of the major human resources issues GE has had to face had to do with the potential impact of transferring work and jobs to overseas locations. This practice has important implications for the company, for the employees, and for the communities involved which had to be thought through beforehand. Another important issue had to do with GE's image as it related to recruiting college graduates. In the next few years GE has to hire some 2,800 scientists and engineers, competing with some glamorous firms for the good people.

## Implementing the New Structure

In characteristic fashion, GE management recognized the need to allow time for the new structure to take root. As the initiating report stated: "The objective of integrated levels of planning is just that—an objective. It may take two or three cycles to accomplish."

True to this schedule, Jones made the following assessment three years later: "The sector approach has turned out to be very successful. It even exceeded my expectations. Now I can look at six planning books and understand them well enough to ask the right questions. I could not do that before. The sectors also gave the board and me an excellent means for deciding on my successor. By 1979 the competition had been narrowed down to Burlingame, Hood, and Welch, and these men were moved up to vice chairman positions." Exhibit 3 contains biographical data on Jones, Welch, Burlingame, and Hood.)

Jones was also pleased with the progress GE had made in responding to a number of corporate challenges. He pointed with particular pride to the "technological renaissance" that had been launched at GE:

> These past few years, we have pressed hard the challenge to change the company's basic technology from electromechanical to electronics. Today we have a true company-wide effort to apply the new microelectronics and the related information-based technologies to every possible product, service, and process in GE.
>
> The proposed purchase of Calma, a leading producer of interactive graphics equipment, and the acquisition of Intersil, a maker of advanced microelectronic chips, give evidence to this commitment.[10] Perhaps our commitment to broad-based innovation is best expressed by our rising investment in research and development. Since 1977, we have increased GE-funded R&D expenditures 85 percent to $760 million. Total R&D, including external funding, reached $1.6 billion in 1980.

# GE in 1980: A Call for Growth

In a presentation to the financial community at the Hotel Pierre in New York City on December 11, 1979, Jones pointed to how GE was "positioned to achieve the objective of sustained earnings growth, faster than the growth of the U.S. economy, in the 1980s." He added: "General Electric is embarked on a course of large-scale innovation, productivity improvement, and business development for the 1980s, and we have built up the financial resources to bring that bold and entrepreneurial strategy to a successful conclusion."

## Challenging Static Forecasts

This public promise of rapid growth carried major implications for strategic planning. At the annual general management conference at Belleair held a month

---

[10]According to GE's 1980 annual report, Intersil was acquired for $235 million. The Calma acquisition was cleared by the Federal Trade Commission in early 1981. The purchase agreement called for an initial payment of $100 million, and additional payments of up to $70 million with the exact amount determined by Calma's sales over the next four years.

later, Daniel Fink, the newly appointed senior vice president for corporate planning and development (development had been added to stress the growth objective), questioned the adequacy of the existing strategic plans to meet Jones's growth challenge. He began by reviewing the recent and projected changes in business mix. The relative earnings figures are summarized in Table B. (See Exhibits 4 and 5 for more detailed financial statements.) Armed with these figures, Fink then argued:

> Our implied strategy seems to be one of slowing, or even halting, the aggressive and successful diversification of the past decade. The vision of GE in 1984 that we get from the long-range forecasts is very much like GE in 1979—same product mix, same international mix, same strategy of leveraging earnings over sales growth.
>
> How can that be? And—more important—do you believe it? Do you believe we'll really have the same product mix in view of even the most obvious technological changes we can see ahead? Do you really think that international mix will hold, despite the faster growth of many world markets? And that we can have the same strategy of leveraging earnings over sales, just as if that last 10th of a point was as easy to achieve as the first?
>
> It's that contradiction of a steady-state GE and a rapidly changing world that gives us, I think, the key strategic issue as we enter the 80s. How do we attain the vision now to reject that static forecast and then take the strategic actions that will move us forward in the 80s, just as we did in the 70s?

Fink next disputed the basis on which the existing strategic plans had projected growth:

> Back in 68 we earned 4½ percent on sales, by 74 it was 5 percent, 6 percent in 78, and the LRFs [long-range forecasts] say 7 percent in 1984, but it doesn't follow that just because the company went from 5 percent to 6 percent in the 70s, it will easily move up to 7 percent in the 80s.
>
> There are several reasons for caution. First, most of our SBUs, urged on by last year's business development challenge, carry the expense burden of major investment plans. And finally, we'll be twice as dependent on productivity, rather than price, for inflation recovery. So, under these circumstances, we certainly must consider the 7 percent at risk.

## TABLE B

**GE's Business Mix (%)**

|  | 1968 | 1979 | 1984 | Projected Change |
|---|---|---|---|---|
| Electrical equipment | 80 | 47 | 44 | − 3 |
| Materials | 6 | 27 | 27 | 0 |
| Services | 10 | 16 | 19 | + 3 |
| Transportation | 4 | 10 | 10 | 0 |
| International | − 16 | 40 | 43 | + 3 |

Just suppose we hold our ROS at the current 6 percent level. The difference in 84 would be almost $400 million of net income and widening each year. To compensate for that shortfall, we would have to add something like $6–$7 billion of sales. That's another sector.

These are big increments. They aren't going to be achieved by simple extensions of our current businesses. They do demand a period of unprecedented business development in the 80s. Unprecedented business development. Consider what that has to mean to a company that has already made the largest acquisition in U.S. business history; that has produced more patentable inventions than any other company in the world; and that already is the largest diversified corporation on *Fortune* 500 list.

## Realigning GE's Resources

The first step to generating unprecedented business growth in the 1980s was to select the target areas with the greatest potential for GE. In-depth corporate planning staff analysis led to the definition of six broad business areas. These areas, called *arenas,* were identified as follows:

- Energy
- Communication, information, and sensing
- Energy applications-productivity
- Materials and resources
- Transportation and propulsion
- Pervasive services (nonproduct-related services such as financial, distribution, and construction)

A common charcteristic of the arenas was that they cut across sector organizational lines. Fink described the dilemma and indicated a need for new approaches:

How are we going to tackle these new opportunities which cut across organization lines? Sometimes the solution is to reorganize and collect those synergistic businesses under single management. But there are too many opportunities out there. We'd have to reorganize every three days just to keep up with them.

How many times have you heard customers, or even competitors, say, "If you guys could only get your act together!" Well, we're going to have to get our act together if we're to tackle some of these new opportunities. We're going to have to develop coventuring techniques, motivation and measurement techniques that have thus far eluded us. It won't come easy; it's nontraditional. It's not traditional for those of us who learned to manage at the John Wayne school of rugged individualism.

To get GE's "act together," the CEO issued explicit arena-related challenges to launch the 1981 planning cycle. Each challenge listed the specific sectors and corporate staff units to be involved and designated the sector responsible to lead the effort. One of the specific challenges related to the energy applications-productivity arena, for example, was to develop a strategic business plan to exploit the growing opportunities associated with factory automation and robotics. The industrial products and components sector, which was already heavily involved with factory automation, was given lead responsibility for this factory of the future challenge.

Support roles were assigned to the information and communications systems group (a unit in the technical systems and materials sector) because of its experience with mobile communications, and to the corporate production and operating services staff unit because of its responsibility for improving productivity within GE itself.

Just how this cross-organizational business development would function still had to be worked out. Jones clearly viewed this approach as preliminary and evolving: "I don't want operating managers worrying about arenas for a while. At this point in time, arenas are for our use at the corporate level. They help to give us another view of the company." The provisional nature of the arena approach was also indicated in the following comment by a senior executive: "The success or failure of the arena concept will depend to a great extent on how hard corporate management pushes it."

### The Next Steps

The General Electric Jack Welch was preparing to lead in 1981 was in the midst of actively probing a panoply of new technology businesses. Lively discussions were being held in offices throughout the company on what GE should do about the factory of the future, the office of the future, the house of the future, the electric car, synthetic fuel, and the like. The list of opportunities seemed endless. Clearly, GE would have to make some hard choices. In this connection, Welch was reported to have said: "My biggest challenge will be to put enough money on the right gambles and to put no money on the wrong ones. But I don't want to sprinkle money over everything."[11]

What kind of management system would he need to meet this challenge? Jack Welch had used SBU and sector planning to build businesses and later had a hand in shaping GE's approach to strategic management. He laid to rest any idea of dismantling the apparatus in place: "GE was a well-run company before anyone ever heard of John Welch. Most of the corporate revolutions you hear about are when a guy moves from company X to company Y and tips it upside down. Sometimes it works and sometimes it doesn't. That won't happen here."

Despite this commitment, Welch was inheriting a management system undergoing major changes. Crossroad choices would have to be made here as well. The 1981 management audit indicated numerous important management system issues for attention:

- Can the sectors as presently defined accommodate the size and diversity of company operations in 1985? In 1990? Alternatives?
- The 1981 corporate strategy was developed through an arena segmentation which is deliberately different from the GE sector segmentation. Is this useful to the CEO in developing a vision for the company? Will it be a workable approach that leads to truly integrated strategies?

---

[11]*Business Week,* March 16, 1981.

- Is there a better way than our international integration process to determine and pursue company international objectives?

How these management system issues were handled would be influenced by the broad substantive issues GE faced. While opinions differed as to priorities, senior managers agreed on several key challenges. Reg Jones put dealing with inflation at the top of his list. Increasing productivity and increasing international business were also high on his and everyone else's list of major issues. For many senior executives, increasing entrepreneurship and new ventures in GE were also a major challenge in view of the company's ambitious growth goals.

The list of issues—both those having to do with substance and those having to do with management systems—was long, far too long for all to be dealt with in depth. Management would have to be selective in choosing areas for attention. One executive neatly summed up his views of the situation with the comment: "GE is going to be a very exciting company these next few years. You can just feel the electricity in the air."

# EXHIBIT 1

## Ten-Year Statistical Summary, 1961–1970 ($ millions, except per share amounts)

| | 1970 | 1969 | 1968 | 1967 | 1966 | 1965 | 1964 | 1963 | 1962 | 1961 |
|---|---|---|---|---|---|---|---|---|---|---|
| Sales of products and services | $8,726.7 | $8,448.0 | $8,381.6 | $7,741.2 | $7,177.3 | $6,213.6 | $5,319.2 | $5,177.0 | $4,986.1 | $4,666.6 |
| Net earnings | 328.5 | 278.0 | 357.1 | 361.4 | 338.9 | 355.1 | 219.6 | 272.2 | 256.5 | 238.4 |
| Earnings per common share | 3.63 | 3.07 | 3.95 | 4.01 | 3.75 | 3.93 | 2.44 | 3.05 | 2.89 | 2.70 |
| Earnings as a percentage of sales | 3.8% | 3.3% | 4.3% | 4.7% | 4.7% | 5.7% | 4.1% | 5.3% | 5.1% | 5.1% |
| Earned on share owners' equity | 12.6% | 11.0% | 14.8% | 15.9% | 15.7% | 17.5% | 11.5% | 14.9% | 15.0% | 14.8% |
| Cash dividends declared | $235.4 | $235.2 | $234.8 | $234.2 | $234.6 | $216.7 | $197.7 | $183.1 | $177.5 | $176.4 |
| Dividends declared per common share | 2.60 | 2.60 | 2.60 | 2.60 | 2.60 | 2.40 | 2.20 | 2.05 | 2.00 | 2.00 |
| Market price range per share | 94½ – 60¼ | 98¼ – 74⅛ | 100⅜ – 80¼ | 115⅞ – 82½ | 120 – 80 | 120¼ – 91 | 93⅝ – 78¾ | 87½ – 71¾ | 78½ – 54¼ | 80¾ – 60½ |
| Current assets | $3,334.8 | $3,287.8 | $3,311.1 | $3,207.6 | $3,013.0 | $2,842.4 | $2,543.8 | $2,321.0 | $2,024.6 | $1,859.7 |
| Current liabilities | 2,650.3 | 2,366.7 | 2,104.3 | 1,977.4 | 1,883.2 | 1,566.8 | 1,338.9 | 1,181.9 | 1,168.7 | 1,086.6 |
| Total assets | 6,309.9 | 6,007.5 | 5,743.8 | 5,347.2 | 4,851.7 | 4,300.4 | 3,856.0 | 3,502.5 | 3,349.9 | 3,143.4 |
| Total share owners' equity | 2,665.1 | 2,540.0 | 2,493.4 | 2,342.2 | 2,211.7 | 2,107.0 | 1,944.2 | 1,889.2 | 1,764.3 | 1,654.6 |
| Plant and equipment additions | 581.4 | 530.6 | 514.7 | 561.7 | 484.9 | 332.9 | 237.7 | 149.2 | 173.2 | 179.7 |
| Depreciation | 334.7 | 351.3 | 300.1 | 280.4 | 233.6 | 188.4 | 170.3 | 149.4 | 146.0 | 131.6 |
| Total taxes and renegotiation | 309.4 | 313.2 | 390.5 | 390.1 | 409.1 | 403.8 | 277.3 | 331.4 | 298.7 | 289.9 |
| Provision for income taxes | 220.6 | 231.5 | 312.3 | 320.5 | 347.4 | 352.2 | 233.8 | 286.7 | 254.0 | 248.9 |
| Employees—average worldwide | 396,583 | 410,126 | 395,691 | 384,864 | 375,852 | 332,991 | 308,233 | 297,726 | 290,682 | 279,547 |
| Gross national product (current $ billions) | 982 | 936 | 869 | 796 | 753 | 688 | 636 | 595 | 564 | 523 |

Source: General Electric annual reports; *Business Statistics*, U.S. Department of Commerce, p. 245, for GNP.

**EXHIBIT 2**

**GE's 1980 Criteria for Investment Priority Screen**

| *Criterion* | *Measure* |
|---|---|
| **Industry Attractiveness** | |
| 1. Market size | • 3-year average served industry market dollars |
| 2. Market growth | • 10-year constant dollar average annual market growth rate |
| 3. Industry profitability | 3-year average ROS, SBU, and "Big Three" competitors<br>• Nominal<br>• Inflation adjusted |
| 4. Cyclicality | • Average annual percent variation of sales from trend |
| 5. Inflation recovery | • 5-year average ratio of combined selling price and productivity change to change in cost due to inflation |
| 6. Importance of non-U.S. markets | • 10-year average ratio of international to total market |

| *Criterion* | *Measure* |
|---|---|
| **Business Position** | |
| 1. Market position | • 3-year average market share (total market)<br>• 3-year average international market share<br>• 2-year average relative market share (SBU/"Big Three" competitors) |
| 2. Competitive position | Superior, equal, or inferior to competition in 1980:<br>• Product quality<br>• Technological leadership<br>• Manufacturing/cost leadership<br>• Distribution/marketing leadership |
| 3. Relative profitability | 3-year SBU's ROS, less average ROS, "Big Three" competitors<br>• Nominal<br>• Inflation adjusted |

Note: Box indicates measure used for the first time in 1980.

## EXHIBIT 3

**Biographical Data**

**Reginald Harold Jones:** born Stoke-on-Trent, Staffordshire, England, 1917. B.S. in Economics, University of Pennsylvania, 1939. Joined the General Electric Company in 1939 as a business trainee and traveling auditor, 1939–1950; assistant to controller, Apparatus Department, 1950–1956; general manager, Air Conditioning Division, 1956–1958; general manager, Supply Company Division, 1958–1961; vice president, General Electric, 1961; general manager, Construction Industries Division, 1964–1967; group executive, 1967–1968; vice president finance, 1968–1970; senior vice president, 1970–1972; vice chairman, 1972; president, 1972–1973; chairman of the board and chief executive officer, 1973–1981.

**John F. Welch, Jr.:** born Massachusetts, 1935. BSCHE, University of Massachusetts, 1957; MSCHE, University of Illinois, 1958; Ph.D., 1960. Joined the General Electric Company in 1960 as a process development specialist for chemical development operations; process development group leader, 1962; manager-manufacturing polymer products and chemical development operations, 1963; general manager, Plastics Department, 1968; general manager, Chemical Division, then Chemical and Metallurgical Division, 1971; vice president and general manager, Chemical and Metallurgical Division, 1972; vice president and group executive, Components and Materials Group, 1973; senior vice president and executive, Consumer Products and Services Sector, 1977; vice chairman and executive officer, 1979; chairman of the board and chief executive officer, 1981.

**John Francis Burlingame:** born Massachusetts, 1922. B.S., Tufts University, 1942. Joined GE in 1946; vice president and general manager, Computer Systems Division, 1969–1971; vice president-employee relations, 1971–1973; vice president and group executive, International, 1973–1977; senior vice president, International sector, 1977–1979; vice chairman, 1979–.

**Edward Exum Hood, Jr.:** born North Carolina, 1930. M.S., Nuclear Engineering, North Carolina State University, 1953. Joined GE in 1957 as a powerplant design engineer; vice president and general manager, Commercial Engine Division, 1968–1972; vice president and group executive, International, 1972–1973; vice president and group executive, Power Generation, 1973–1977; senior vice president and sector executive, Technical System and Materials, 1977–1979; vice chairman, 1979–.

## EXHIBIT 4

**Ten-Year Statistical Summary, 1971–1980** (*$ millions, except per share amounts*)

| | *1980* | *1979* | *1978* | *1977* | *1976* | *1975* | *1974* | *1973* | *1972* | *1971 (2-for-1 Stock Split)* |
|---|---|---|---|---|---|---|---|---|---|---|
| Summary of operations | | | | | | | | | | |
| Sales of products and services to customers | $24,959 | $22,461 | $19,654 | $17,519 | $15,697 | $14,105 | $13,918 | $11,945 | $10,474 | $9,557 |
| Operating margin | 2,243 | 2,130 | 1,958 | 1,698 | 1,528 | 1,187 | 1,171 | 1,070 | 877 | 772 |
| Earnings before income taxes and minority interest | $2,493 | $2,391 | $2,153 | $1,889 | $1,627 | $1,174 | $1,181 | $1,130 | $963 | $847 |
| Taxes | 958 | 953 | 894 | 773 | 668 | 460 | 458 | 457 | 385 | 333 |
| Net earnings | $1,514 | $1,409 | $1,230 | $1,088 | $931 | $688 | $705 | $661 | $573 | $510 |
| Earnings per common share | $6.65 | $6.20 | $5.39 | $4.79 | $4.12 | $3.07 | $3.16 | $2.97 | $2.57 | $2.30 |
| Dividends declared per common share | $2.95 | $2.75 | $2.50 | $2.10 | $1.70 | $1.60 | $1.60 | $1.50 | $1.40 | $1.38 |
| Earnings as a percentage of sales | 6.1% | 6.3% | 6.3% | 6.2% | 5.9% | 4.9% | 5.1% | 5.5% | 5.5% | 5.3% |
| Earned on average share owners' equity | 19.5% | 20.2% | 19.6% | 19.4% | 18.9% | 15.7% | 17.8% | 18.4% | 17.5% | 17.2% |
| Dividends | $670 | $624 | $570 | $477 | $333 | $293 | $291 | $273 | $255 | $250 |
| Market price range per share | 63–44 | 55⅛–45 | 57⅝–43⅝ | 57¼–47⅜ | 59¼–46 | 52⅞–32⅜ | 65–30 | 75⅞–55 | 73–58¼ | 66½–46½ |

# EXHIBIT 4 *(concluded)*

| | 1980 | 1979 | 1978 | 1977 | 1976 | 1975 | 1974 | 1973 | 1972 | 1971 (2-for-1 Stock Split) |
|---|---|---|---|---|---|---|---|---|---|---|
| Price/earnings ratio range | 9–7 | 9–7 | 11–8 | 12–10 | 14–11 | 17–10 | 19–9 | 24–17 | 25–20 | 26–18 |
| Current assets | $9,883 | $9,384 | $8,755 | $7,865 | $6,685 | $5,750 | $5,334 | $4,597 | $4,057 | $3,700 |
| Current liabilities | 7,592 | 6,872 | 6,175 | 5,417 | 4,605 | 4,163 | 4,032 | 3,588 | 2,921 | 2,894 |
| Share owners' equity | 8,200 | 7,362 | 6,587 | 5,943 | 5,253 | 4,617 | 4,172 | 3,774 | 3,420 | 3,106 |
| Total capital invested | 10,447 | 9,332 | 8,692 | 8,131 | 7,305 | 6,628 | 6,317 | 5,679 | 5,118 | 4,754 |
| Earned on average total capital invested | 17.3% | 17.6% | 16.3% | 15.8% | 15.1% | 12.5% | 13.4% | 13.7% | 12.7% | 12.3% |
| Total assets | $18,511 | $16,644 | $15,036 | $13,697 | $12,050 | $10,741 | $10,220 | $9,089 | $8,051 | $7,472 |
| Property, plant and equipment additions | $1,948 | $1,262 | $1,055 | $823 | $740 | $588 | $813 | $735 | $501 | $711 |
| Employees—average worldwide | 402,000 | 405,000 | 401,000 | 384,000 | 380,000 | 380,000 | 409,000 | 392,000 | 373,000 | 366,000 |
| Gross national product (current $ billions) | 2,626 | 2,414 | 2,128 | 1,900 | 1,702 | 1,529 | 1,413 | 1,307 | 1,171 | 1,063 |
| Common stock performance | | | | | | | | | | |
| General Electric common share price | $44–63 | | | | | | | | | $47–67 |
| Dow Jones Industrial Index | 759–1000 | | | | | | | | | 798–950 |
| Standard & Poor's Industrial Index | 111–161 | | | | | | | | | 99–116 |

Source: General Electric annual report, 1980; U.S. Department of Commerce for GNP; Moody's.

# EXHIBIT 5

## Financial Statements, 1979 and 1980 ($ millions)

### Balance Sheets*

| | 1980 | 1979 |
|---|---|---|
| **Assets** | | |
| Cash | $ 1,601 | $ 1,904 |
| Marketable securities | 600 | 672 |
| Current receivables | 4,339 | 3,647 |
| Inventories | 3,343 | 3,161 |
| Current assets | 9,883 | 9,384 |
| Property, plant and equipment | 5,780 | 4,613 |
| Investments | 1,820 | 1,691 |
| Other assets | 1,028 | 956 |
| Total assets | $18,511 | $16,644 |
| **Liabilities and Equity** | | |
| Short-term borrowings | $ 1,093 | $ 871 |
| Accounts payable | 1,671 | 1,477 |
| Progress collections and price adjustments accrued | 2,084 | 1,957 |
| Dividends payable | 170 | 159 |
| Taxes accrued | 628 | 655 |
| Other costs and expenses accrued | 1,946 | 1,753 |
| Current liabilities | 7,592 | 6,872 |
| Long-term borrowings | 1,000 | 947 |
| Other liabilities | 1,565 | 1,311 |
| Total liabilities | $10,157 | $ 9,130 |

### Income Statements

| | 1980 | 1979 |
|---|---|---|
| **Sales** | | |
| Sales of products and services to customers | $24,959 | $22,461 |
| **Operating costs** | | |
| Cost of goods sold | 17,751 | 15,991 |
| Selling, general and administrative expense | 4,258 | 3,716 |
| Depreciation, depletion and amortization | 707 | 624 |
| Operating costs | $22,716 | $20,331 |
| Operating margin | 2,243 | 2,130 |
| Other income | 564 | 519 |
| Interest and other financial charges | (314) | (258) |
| **Earnings** | | |
| Earnings before income taxes and minority interest | 2,493 | 2,391 |
| Provision for income taxes | (958) | (953) |
| Minority interest in earnings of consolidated affiliates | (21) | (29) |
| Net earnings applicable to common stock | $ 1,514 | $ 1,409 |
| Earnings per common share (in dollars) | $6.65 | $6.20 |
| Dividends declared per common share (in dollars) | $2.95 | $2.75 |
| Operating margin as a percentage of sales | 9.0% | 9.5% |
| Net earnings as a percentage of sales | 6.1% | 6.3% |

*Balance sheet information is continued on the following page.

# EXHIBIT 5 (concluded)

*Balance Sheets*

| | 1980 | 1979 |
|---|---|---|
| **Liabilities and Equity** (*continued*) | | |
| Minority interest in equity of consolidated affiliates | 154 | 152 |
| Common stock | 579 | 579 |
| Amounts received for stock in excess of par value | 659 | 656 |
| Retained earnings | 7,151 | 6,307 |
| | $ 8,389 | $ 7,542 |
| Deduct common stock held in treasury | (189) | (190) |
| Total share owners' equity | 8,200 | 7,362 |
| Total liabilities and equity | $18,511 | $16,644 |

# CASE 30

# The Challenge Ahead: Economic Growth, Global Interdependence, and the New Competition*

The search for sustainable growth will continue to shape the managerial challenge in the final decades of the 20th century. That challenge, however, now must be framed within the context of global interdependence and diminishing economic hegemony. The proliferation of the transnational enterprise and the international mobility of both capital and production technologies have transformed the boundaries of the domestic economy. Foreign markets have become an integral extension of domestic markets while domestic markets are increasingly shared with foreign producers. It is no longer useful to think of the U.S. economy as a closed system. The ability of managers and the workforce to rapidly and effectively adjust to market dislocations in a global arena characterized by a dense network of interdependencies, and therefore by an increased vulnerability to external disruption, is the factor most likely to determine our relative international competitiveness and overall standard of living in the future.

From a position of clear dominance in the world economy at the end of World War II, the United States enjoyed unprecedented prosperity for two, indeed nearly three, decades as international markets expanded along with aggregate output. The lauded American system of industrial production and administrative coordi-

*This case was prepared by Katherine Hughes as a basis for class discussion rather than to illustrate either effective or ineffective handling of an administrative situation. The author wishes to acknowledge the helpful suggestions of Alfred D. Chandler, Jr. in the preparation of this case.

nation embodied in the integrated, diversified, transnational corporation repeatedly demonstrated flexibility and adaptability in response to the swift pace of technological and economic change. Our extraordinary postwar economic power allowed us to construct the institutional framework needed to support an open, international trading system. The International Monetary Fund (IMF) and the General Agreement on Tariff and Trade (GATT) were established under American sponsorship in 1945 and 1947 respectively. Over time, these international agreements fostered world-wide capital mobility and the progressive reduction of international trade barriers. Manufacturing, marketing, finance, and employment have taken on a supranational perspective. Managers have learned to evaluate their prospects in terms of where in the world they can most cheaply raise a new loan, build a new plant, or launch a new product.

In response to growing markets at home and abroad, U.S. manufacturers invested heavily in new capacity during the 1950s and 1960s. The slower growth in demand that resulted from the worldwide economic slowdown in the 1970s impelled producers to increase their exports and extend their operations abroad in pursuit of growth through lower unit costs. In the main, the perception that U.S. competitiveness in international markets was beginning to lag behind that of some other nations first became newsworthy during the 1970s as domestic producers faced excess capacity (the loss of scale economies), high interest rates, and increasing import penetration. The economic impact of successive oil-price increases and the loss of world market shares along with massive layoffs in the highly visible auto and steel industries intensified the perception. Yet, there is considerable evidence that the decline in the U.S. international competitive position actually began in the mid-1960s with a slowdown in productivity growth and a drop in the U.S. merchandise trade balance. In the mid-1960s, there were growing trade surpluses in capital goods, chemicals, and agricultural products, but deficits in consumer goods and nonagricultural industrial supplies and materials. Trade in automotive products switched from surplus to deficit in 1968.[1]

At one time we may have been able to dismiss worries about the steady decline of the U.S. share of total world production and the declining ratio of U.S. exports to foreign imports as predictable trends, the result of postwar rebuilding and the expansion of industrial capacity in the lesser developed countries. For several decades after World War II, the pattern of U.S. trade was distorted by the fact that industrial capacity had been significantly reduced in Europe and Japan. Given comparable levels of education of their populations and comparable access to raw materials and fuels in an open trading system, the continuation of overwhelming American dominance in world trade would have been surprising and anomalous. However, slower growth and the severe economic disturbances of the 1970s made adjustment to the dislocations of market change more difficult than during the earlier postwar decades of rapid economic growth and market expansion. By the

---

[1]William H. Branson, "Trends in United States International Trade and Investment Since World War II," in Martin Feldstein, ed., *The American Economy in Transition* (Chicago: University of Chicago Press, 1980), p. 207.

1980s, economic analysts could no longer assuage their concern for the declining U.S. competitive position with the knowledge that some decline in the U.S. trade position was inevitable.

It is difficult to precisely determine what part of the relative deterioration of U.S. competitiveness in international markets can be attributed to postwar adjustment trends; what part has resulted from domestic fiscal and monetary policies that, perhaps inadvertently, exhibited an anti-industrial bias during the 1970s; what part has resulted from a failure to adjust to the new conditions of international competition; and, finally, what part can actually be attributed to a fundamental loss of growth dynamism in the U.S. economy (alone or in concert with the North Atlantic industrial countries). Analysis is complicated by the interactive consequences of persistent inflation and unemployment, our large domestic debt burden (both public and private), our increased vulnerability to world trade cycles, and the policies of promotion, subsidy, and market protection adopted by our major trading partners. While there is a general consensus among economists that a decline in the international competitiveness of the U.S. economy has occurred, there is considerable disagreement over its cause, measurement, and duration. The concept of "competitiveness" itself is quite elusive. For instance, there may be a large difference between the international competitiveness of an individual U.S. firm, even an entire industrial sector, and the competitiveness of the U.S. economy as a whole. Transnational firms may remain competitive by shifting capital, production, and employment from one country to another, while producers confined to the domestic arena may be uncompetitive in either domestic or export markets, sometimes both. Furthermore, structural change does not only take place between industries, but also within industries and within individual firms. Even when market share remains constant for an industry or firm, certain subactivities may be in absolute decline while others gain ground. And, in declining sectors there are normally a number of firms which are profitable. Is competitiveness, then, to be defined by the ability of American plants employing American workers at average manufacturing wages to market their output competitively in world markets without protection or subsidy, or simply by the ability of U.S.-based firms to operate profitably in international markets?

Moreover, there is a problem in defining a norm against which American competitiveness can be assessed. During the 1950s and early 1960s, the United States was completely dominant in both its share of world exports and the share of innovative products brought to market. Even with the establishment of the European Economic Community and the rapid development of the East Asian economies, the question of "deterioration compared to what?" is difficult to address in terms of the world's largest single economy. In addition, there is considerable argument concerning the appropriate measures to be used in assessing international competitiveness. Economists disagree over which are the more appropriate statistical data as well as over the significance of any change in those measures. Some argue that the traditional measures of economic activity that were developed for an expanding industrial economy should be revised to reflect the increased importance of service-sector output. Others believe that traditional measures fail to cap-

ture the complexities of transnational production, thus confounding their interpretation. Nor should it be ignored that identical statistics have been used in the
service of opposing analyses.

Bruce Scott of the Harvard Business School believes that national competitiveness should be analyzed like corporate competitiveness, in terms of market
share and profitability.[2] He argues that it is not so much the U.S. trade deficit in
manufactures as the steady decline of world market share for many industrial exports that signifies the loss of American competitiveness. Scott found that only 10
of the 26 industrial groupings he studied gained world market share during the
1965–1980 period. Gains were experienced in the aircraft, office machines, and
agricultural chemicals categories. The most significant losses were in the motor
vehicles, fuels, animal and vegetable oils and fats, and the electrical equipment
categories. Scott's data also indicate that while high-technology sectors have
gained ground in the overall mix of U.S. exports, seven of the top 10 high-technology industries actually lost world market share between 1965 and 1980. Engines
and turbines, professional and scientific instruments, electrical equipment and
components, optical and medical instruments, drugs and medicines, plastics and
synthetic materials, and industrial chemicals lost market share. Of the high-technology group, only agricultural chemicals made a significant gain during the
1965–1980 period. Scott cites the declining profitability of U.S.-based firms from
the mid-1960s as a second telling indicator. The U.S. Department of Commerce
reports that total manufacturing profits increased at a rate of only 0.2 percent between 1974 and 1982. Profits per unit of output decreased at a rate of −0.7 percent.[3]

Others rely on the more traditional trade balance, productivity, investment,
import penetration, and disposable income data to indicate declining U.S. competitiveness. They also point to indirect symptoms such as the perceived decline in
product quality in sectors such as automobiles, the decline in government support
for nondefense basic research, the growing problem of underemployment, and the
extreme antagonism that characterizes many labor-management negotiations.
Some cite more eclectic data that indicate we may tend to understate both the extent and the velocity of change in the U.S. competitive position when using aggregate data and traditional measures. For example, U.S. machine tool manufacturers lost 42 percent of the domestic market to imports in 1982, up from 25 percent
in 1980.[4] Although American machine tools are comparable in quality to those of
other countries (principally West Germany and Japan), they are frequently higher
priced. In 1983, the Japanese took more than 75 percent of the U.S. market for
the new advanced "machining centers" (numerically controlled).[5] Our exports of

---

[2]Bruce R. Scott, "National Strategy for Stronger U.S. Competitiveness," *Harvard Business Review*, March/April 1984, pp. 77–91.

[3]U.S. Department of Commerce, Bureau of Industrial Economics, *U.S. Industrial Outlook, 1984*
(Washington, D.C.: January 1984), p. 34.

[4]National Machine Tool Builders Association estimate. Seymour Melman, "How the Yankees
Lost Their Know-How," *Technology Review*, October 1983, pp. 58–59.

[5]"A U.S. Toolmaker Cozies Up to Its Former Foe," *Business Week*, April 16, 1984, p. 66.

steel are now less than one tenth of Japan's. Our exports of automobiles are over-balanced five to one by our imports. Japanese cars, not Fords, are second in the American market. Japan, not the United States, is first in the world auto market.[6] Japan is the world's largest shipbuilder, South Korea the second largest.

Japanese manufacturers succeeded in capturing 70 percent of the world market for 64K Random Access Memory chips (RAMs) within two years, and they appear to be ahead of U.S. manufacturers in the process of bringing the next generation of computer-microchip technology (256K RAMs) to market. Most Japanese circuits are now assembled with automated equipment. In contrast, most circuits sold by U.S. firms are assembled manually in developing countries.[7] In addition, the Japanese are aggressively involved in the race to develop new technologies such as fifth generation computers, robotics, and biotechnology. In 1983, the U.S. imported $43 billion worth of goods from Japan, overwhelmingly industrial products, and exported $25 billion worth, the largest items of which were agricultural products. Similar trade imbalances in industrial goods characterize our relations with Taiwan, South Korea, Hong Kong, and Singapore.[8] In 1980, for the first time the volume of business between the U.S. and the 21 trading nations of the Pacific Rim outstripped trans-Atlantic trade. Although our balance of trade with Western Europe remained positive during the 1980s, it has become increasingly negative with our Pacific Rim trading partners. In 1983, the U.S. merchandise trade deficit with the Pacific Rim countries was $34 billion, over half of the $61.1 billion total.[9]

When it comes to assessing the reasons behind the relative decline of U.S. competitiveness in international markets, there are essentially two schools of thought. The first, composed of many mainstream economists, including President Reagan's Council of Economic Advisers, concludes that it is the overvalued U.S. dollar and the global economic slowdown (declining demand) that lie behind the competitiveness problem.[10] They do not believe that merchandise trade deficits should cause undue alarm. They point out that investment income continues to rise, reflecting earnings on foreign direct investment and foreign loans, and that net service income and high-technology exports, areas of relative strength, represent an increasingly large share of the U.S. current account balance (a broader measure of U.S. trade that includes services and financial payments as well as manufactured goods). They also point to the lively U.S. venture capital

---

[6]Robert Heilbroner, "Economic Prospects," *The New Yorker,* August 29, 1983, p. 72.

[7]Semiconductor Industry Association (SIA), *The Effect of Government Targeting on World Semiconductor Competition* (Cupertino, Calif.: SIA, 1983), p. 39; Charles H. Ferguson, "The Microelectronic Industry in Distress," *Technology Review,* August/September 1983, pp. 24–37.

[8]Ezra F. Vogel, "The Advent of the Pacific Century," *Harvard International Review,* March 1984, p. 14.

[9]Stuart Auerbach, "A Historic Shift in U.S. Trade Patterns," *The Washington Post National Weekly Edition,* May 7, 1984, p. 19.

[10]See Council of Economic Advisers (CEA), *Economic Report of the President* (Washington, D.C.: USGPO, February 1983), pp. 51–76; CEA, *Economic Report of the President* (February 1984), pp. 87–110.

market as evidence that the United States retains technological leadership. Some argue that during periods of recession, U.S. producers tend to cut production and hold prices, while many of our major foreign competitors tend to cut prices in order to sustain jobs and market shares.[11] The assumption is that lagging U.S. competitiveness is more a cyclical than a structural problem. In general, this group predicts that economic recovery will spur competitiveness across the board, except perhaps in the troubled auto and steel industries where structural adjustment is required. The view here is that market mechanisms are not only adequate but indeed the most effective means of adjusting to the dislocations that result from market change.

Their critics agree that the overvalued U.S. dollar has made a major contribution to recent trade deficits; however, they note that the dollar floated downward between 1973 and 1979, years when the trade deficit increased along trend. They also note that the relatively undervalued Western European currencies have done little to help those economies avoid stagnation and postwar records of unemployment. Many doubt that economic recovery will sufficiently address the problems of lagging competitiveness which they believe are more closely related to enduring structural changes in international trade and production (worldwide sourcing, direct overseas production, rapid technology diffusion, and government policies to promote and protect national industries).

This second group of analysts tend to advocate sector- or firm-specific adjustment incentives and technology-specific market promotion policies as the preferred means of improving the U.S. position.[12] They assert that structural adjustment through market mechanisms is an inadequate policy response when foreign competitors are supported by government targeting policies that distort markets and often impose unacceptable adjustment costs on the U.S. economy. Recent interest in a national industrial policy stems in part from the desire to rationalize the output of declining sectors most affected by excess capacity and technological obsolescence while promoting investment in the growing high-technology sectors most affected by the targeting policies of foreign governments.

Most analysts in the structural school argue that the failure to utilize targeted adjustment policies will result in the continued relative decline of U.S. competitiveness in international markets. But some doubt that business and political leaders will be able to muster the broad-based political support required to implement sectoral restructuring, market promotion, even supportive macroeconomic policies, with sufficient speed to effectively address our competitive problems. Thus, they predict a continuation of the slow growth trend and argue that coping with its ramifications will demand profound changes in our ways of thinking, our habits

---

[11]Richard C. Cooper, "U.S. International Competitiveness: Is There Another Problem?" a presentation at the Arco Forum of Public Affairs, Kennedy School of Government, Harvard University (unpublished, December 1983).

[12]See Ira C. Magaziner and Robert B. Reich, *Minding America's Business* (New York: Harcourt Brace Jovanovich, 1982); John Zysman and Laura Tyson, eds., *American Industry in International Competition: Government Policies and Corporate Strategies* (Ithaca, New York: Cornell University Press, 1983); and Organization for Economic Co-operation and Development, *Positive Adjustment Policies: Managing Structural Change* (Paris: OECD, 1983).

and standards of decision making, and our political, social, and economic institutions.[13]

The following discussion describes with more detail the terms of the debate over the symptoms, causes, and measurement of the decline of U.S. competitiveness in international markets. As the debate continues over appropriate policy approaches to the interactive problems of structural adjustment, slower growth, and global interdependence, it is essential that business and government leaders develop a sense of context in order to better evaluate the evolving issues. Despite tremendous improvements in our analytical methods, we are little better at predicting even the short-term future of the economy than we were 35 years ago at the beginning of the postwar period. Indeed, the economy itself becomes ever more complex even as we improve our ability to understand it. This complexity in large part results from global interdependence. Increasing complexity is also related to the second-, third-, and even fourth-order effects of change in interdependent, open systems. Thus, it is not merely the long litany of woes but the complex interaction of cause and effect that tend to overwhelm analysis. However, business managers have little choice but to grapple with these problems. They are in a position to influence and to help build a national capacity for coherent strategy—that is the challenge.

# The Loss of Growth Dynamism

What are the factors that have led analysts to conclude that the U.S. economy has lost its growth dynamism? Slower growth can be identified in both gross domestic product (GDP) and share of world export measures. Causation is most often linked to the structural shift in output and employment toward the service sector and to reduced productivity growth. Over the long term, many mainstream economists consider declining productivity to be our most significant economic problem.[14] However, the causes of the productivity slowdown are complex and widely debated. In addition, the loss of growth dynamism is linked to the persistent inflation and high unemployment that we have experienced over the last decade. These factors have slowed the economic adjustment process and thus have contributed to slower growth.

## Exports, Production, and the Shift to the Service Sector

At the end of World War II, the United States was the dominant industrial producer in the world. With industrial capacity destroyed in most of Europe, the United Kingdom, and in Japan, the United States produced approximately 60

---

[13]Compare Mancur Olson, *The Rise and Decline of Nations: Economic Growth, Stagflation, and Social Rigidities* (New Haven: Yale University Press, 1982); Bruce R. Scott, "Can Industry Survive the Welfare State?" *Harvard Business Review,* September/October 1982, pp. 70–84; and Samuel Bowles, David M. Gordon and Thomas E. Weisskopf, *Beyond the Waste Land: A Democratic Alternative to Economic Decline* (Garden City, New York: Anchor Press, 1983).

[14]CEA, *Economic Report of the President* (1983), p. 83.

percent of the world output of manufactures in the late 1940s.[15] This, of course, was a transitory situation. During the 1950s, the European economies recovered and rebuilt capacity. Western Europe (especially West Germany), the centrally planned economies, and Japan gained ground in the world trade of manufactures. During the 1960s, Japan's share increased even more rapidly, while growth in Western Europe slowed, and the centrally planned economies actually lost market shares. In the 1970s, the newly industrializing Asian countries experienced rapid growth, and, while Japan's share continued to increase, it did so at a slower rate. Concurrently, the U.S. share of world exports of manufactures dropped from 29 percent in 1953 to 17 percent in 1963 and then stabilized around 13 percent during the 1970s (despite a 40 percent depreciation of the U.S. dollar between 1970 and 1978). (See Exhibit 1.) With manufacturing capacity and output growing relatively rapidly in Europe, Japan, and the newly industrializing countries, a significant improvement in U.S. competitiveness would have been required to hold the U.S. share of world markets. In general during the 1950–1978 period, U.S. costs relative to those of its competitors for world markets, adjusted for exchange rates, did not decline. The result was a shrinking U.S. share of world trade in manufactured goods.

As for total output, the U.S. economy grew at a slower rate along trend during the postwar years than did the recovering economies of Western Europe and Japan. Exhibit 2 shows index numbers for real GDP growth between 1950 and 1978 for seven major industrial countries, including the United States, Canada, Japan, France, Germany, Italy, and the United Kingdom. Among those countries, only the United Kingdom trailed the United States in the rate of increase of real output. United States real GDP increased at a 3.5 percent annual rate during the 1950–1966 period and then declined to a 2.3 percent annual increase between 1967–1978.[16]

The relatively faster growth of exports of manufactures and GDP in Western Europe and Japan during the postwar recovery period reflects an acceleration in the shift of economic resources from agriculture to the more productive goods-producing sectors of their economies. The statistics also reflect the movement into mass-production industries as domestic markets generated sufficient demand to provide a base for the development of scale economies (in many industries for the first time). The attainment of scale economies, in turn, permitted Western European and Japanese manufacturers to move into international markets with the newest plant and equipment. Both factors contributed to the closing of aggregate

---

[15]Branson, "Trends in U.S. International Trade," p. 183. The immediately following trend analysis and the world output of manufacturers and gross domestic product data are drawn from Branson, pp. 183–203. Note that there are many problems involved in making comparisons between different industries and countries as underlying definitions and measures are seldom directly comparable. The least distorted figures come from manufacturing where output is most easily measured.

[16]It is the slower growth in the latter period that most troubles analysts concerned with the competitive position of the United States in the global economy.

productivity differentials between those nations and the United States.[17] For the East Asian newly industrializing countries, growth in the export of manufacturers from the mid-1960s reflects rapid postwar movement into modern mass-production consumer economies. After 1960 in Japan, and during the 1970s in the newly industrializing countries, increasing rates of growth also reflect a shifting of economic resources across industrial activities toward higher value-added output for export.

In the United States on the other hand, while the 1983 total value of output had increased nearly three times over the 1950 level (from $534.8 billion to $1,534.8 billion in constant dollars), the provision of services had displaced the production of goods as the nation's principal economic activity.[18] The structural shift toward the service sector meant not only changes in the distribution of the labor force, but also that an increasing share of total output was generated by the "marginally" less-productive service sector.[19] Most of the structural shift toward the service sector took place in the United States during the three postwar decades. In 1929, 45 percent of the working population was employed in the production of goods. Nearly 20 years later, in 1948, the goods-producing sector of the U.S. economy still employed 44 percent of the working population; but, by 1977, that figure was only 32 percent. Employment in the service sector therefore increased from 56 percent of the working population in 1948 to 68 percent in 1977. The gross-national-product (GNP) statistics in both current and constant dollars exhibited the same shift from goods to services. In 1948, the goods-producing sector accounted for 46 percent of GNP; by 1978, that figure was 34 percent. Service-sector GNP increased from 54 percent to 66 percent over the same period. By 1977–1978, 66 percent of GNP was produced by 68 percent of the working population employed in the service sector.[20]

---

[17]In the United States, the agriculture-to-industry transition was completed in large part during the depression decade of the 1930s, and our large domestic market has been able to support the development of scale economies from the 1860s.

[18]CEA, *Economic Report of the President* (1984), Table B-2, p. 222.

[19]The convention of national accounting allocates to the service sector all output that does not come from the four goods-producing sectors: agriculture, mining, manufacturing, and construction. The service sector thus embraces distribution, transportation, and utilities services; producer services such as accounting, legal, marketing, banking, engineering, and management consulting; consumer services; and nonprofit and government services such as education, health, national defense, and the courts. See Eli Ginzberg and George J. Vojta, "The Service Sector and the U.S. Economy," *Scientific American*, March 1981, pp. 48–55.

[20]Ginzberg and Vojta, "Service Sector," p. 48. The pattern of structural shift in the U.S. economy has come to characterize other industrial economies as well. The World Bank estimates that by 1976, service-sector output made up 52 percent of the overall GDP of industrial countries; manufacturing output contributed 41 percent, and agriculture 6 percent. The Economist, *The World Economy* (New York: Cambridge University Press, 1979), p. 2.

## Productivity Conundrums

Productivity began to falter during the mid-1960s in the United States. The aggregate data show that the slowdown was particularly dramatic after 1973.[21] (See Exhibit 3.) Although productivity experts agree there has been some impact, the extent to which the slower growth of GDP results from the shift in employment toward the "marginally" less productive service sector is difficult to assess with precision within the neoclassical productivity paradigm. In the analysis of productivity, economists hypothesize a technical linkage between trends in output and input, namely the production function. The model of economic activity derived from this hypothesis, however, has not proven particularly useful in generating explanations as to the origins or the macroeconomic significance of the productivity slowdown. Most important, it is not entirely clear whether the productivity slowdown is essentially the cause or only one of the effects of slower economic growth.

There also exist a considerable number of conceptual problems associated with quantifying the contribution of each factor of production to output growth. Quantification difficulties cast doubt on the productivity statistics themselves as well as on any inferences drawn from changes in the data. Often measures are drawn from phenomena only loosely connected by a logical structure of cause and effect. In the multifactor productivity framework, the "residual" (that portion of output unexplained by changes in labor and capital inputs) is equated with "advances in knowledge" and used as a measure of the contribution of technological innovation to economic growth. A more useful statistic, the contribution of research and development expenditures to economic growth, can only be derived from the "residual" measure and then only by making some extremely rough assumptions about the nature of the technological diffusion process. The use of the age-sex proportion of all employees to capture the effect of less experienced and, presumably, less productive new workers requires making broad and perhaps unjustified assumptions about the quality of labor. The measurement of aggregate capital remains a nettlesome problem as does the quantification of nonmarket output.[22]

---

[21]The concept of productivity relates outputs to inputs to obtain a measure of efficiency, the efficiency with which resources are employed in production. Labor productivity relates output to hours of all persons involved in the production process; capital productivity relates output to capital inputs; and multifactor productivity relates output to inputs of labor and capital. The U.S. Bureau of Labor Statistics' labor productivity index is the most familiar and widely cited. Between 1948 and 1967, the growth rate of labor productivity in the private business economy was 3.1 percent, compared to 2.3 percent between 1967 and 1973 and only 0.8 percent between 1973 and 1981. CEA, *Economic Report of the President* (1983), p. 83.

[22]For a review of the conceptual and measurement problems associated with productivity measures, see Richard R. Nelson, "Research on Productivity Growth and Productivity Differences: Dead Ends and New Departures," *Journal of Economic Literature*, September 1981, pp. 1029–1064; Paul S. Adler, "The Productivity Puzzle: Numbers Alone Won't Solve It," *Monthly Labor Review*, October 1982, pp. 15–21. As examples of recent proposals for productivity-measure revisions, see Jerome A. Mark and William H. Waldorf, "Multifactor Productivity: A New BLS Measure," *Monthly Labor Review*, December 1983, pp. 3–15; Samuel Bowles, David M. Gordon and Thomas E. Weisskopf, "A Social Model for U.S. Productivity Growth," *Challenge*, March/April 1984, pp. 41–48.

The rapid development of the service sector in the United States has not led to significant progress in the measurement of service-sector output. Good output measures have not been devised for health, education, banking, legal, or social services where no clearly defined product is involved. The value of government output is estimated solely in terms of wages and salaries. Most analysts agree that service-sector output is less amenable to the application of the machine-based technologies and scale economies that have increased labor productivity in manufacturing and large-scale agriculture over the past century. Many anticipate that the productivity "differential" will diminish, perhaps even disappear, as computerized information-handling technologies are applied to a broader range of service-sector activities. Others argue that we both mismeasure and underestimate service output. They call for revision of output measures that were designed for an earlier industrial era and fail to account for the unique characteristics of information resources that are neither reduced nor diminished by wide distribution and use. Logically extended, this argument can lead to the conclusion that there has been no serious productivity lag.

However, beyond the conceptual and measurement difficulties, most productivity experts agree that there has been a real productivity slowdown. In the manufacturing sector, and in particular in those industries where measurement problems have been the least troublesome, there seems to have been a significant decline. The deceleration is sufficiently important in a large enough range of indicators at both aggregate and industry levels to overcome most skepticism. In addition to a continuation of the postwar shift toward the service sector, the factors widely considered to have exerted a downward pull on productivity growth in the United States since the mid-1960s include: the changing composition of the labor force, rising energy prices, government regulation, excess capacity, lagging capital investment, a slowing of innovation and technology diffusion, and just plain bad management. There is, however, considerable disagreement among experts as to which factors have had the greatest effect in the past and which can be more readily ameliorated in the future. It should be noted that experts disagree in their analyses of the extent to which each of the above factors have actually retarded growth. Blame tends to be more closely specified and villains more readily identified in explanations that reflect an ideological viewpoint.

In brief, the aging of the postwar "baby boom" generation, the increasing number of working women (from 39 percent of the total labor force in 1965 to 53 percent in 1983), and the rapid increase in illegal immigration are the demographic trends most closely identified with the changing composition of the labor force since the mid-1960s when productivity rates first began to fall. Experts argue that the larger share of youthful and inexperienced workers in the labor force effectively reduced the average skill-level of labor. In addition, the increase in low-wage female and immigrant labor is thought to have undercut productivity gains by slowing the substitution of capital for labor. Productivity levels, however, have not much improved now that the baby-boom and new-female-worker bulges in the labor force can be characterized as "experienced." In addition, economists have begun to argue that low-wage labor increases American competitiveness in labor-intensive production and that it is preferable, for the economy as a whole, to employ low-wage labor at home rather than overseas. Thus, it seems unlikely that the demographics of the labor force can be responsible for more than a small share of the decline in aggregate productivity measures.

Estimates vary, but the energy-price explosions of the 1970s are blamed for as much as half of the post-1973 productivity slowdown. The fact that higher energy costs encouraged managers to adopt production technologies that were more energy efficient but sometimes less productive is put forth as explanation for the duration of the decline. Government mandated pollution-control and worker-safety expenditures are considered the cause of perhaps another 10 percent of the post-1973 decline. The commitment to cleaner air and water has had a disproportionately large effect on the costs and profitability of particular sectors, most notably the steel and auto industries. It should be noted, however, that other industrial countries shared similar costs with less dramatic declines in aggregate productivity growth.

**Excess capacity.**  The slower growth of aggregate output itself is considered by some analysts to have negatively affected productivity. As economist Lester Thurow of MIT argues, it seems that strong productivity growth tends to push GNP growth, and strong GNP growth feeds productivity. An expanding economy opens up opportunities for investment, stimulates innovation and the diffusion of technology, and encourages scale economies as output rises toward capacity. There is, of course, a close relationship between the uninterrupted operation of manufacturing facilities at minimum-efficient scale and productivity gains. Thurow asserts there is no significant evidence of a slowdown in productivity in the manufacturing sector of the economy once a correction for idle capacity is computed.[23]

Thurow argues that real productivity growth is a function of the pace at which new technology becomes feasible for use by industry and the rate at which the economy is discarding low-productivity activities. The elimination of a low-productivity plant raises aggregate productivity just as much as opening a high-productivity plant. Thurow suggests that the main failure of U.S. economic policy during the 1970s was in the area of disinvestment. Regardless of changing technology and demand factors, government and private-sector decision makers were reluctant to shut down inefficient or underutilized capacity because of the economic and social dislocations that accompany disinvestment (lower stock market values, smaller organizations, unemployment, political protest). According to Thurow, this reluctance translated into higher relative costs and declining productivity growth rates.

**Capital formation and interest rates.**  The lagging rate of capital formation relative to major industrial competitors is often pointed to as a cause of the productivity slowdown in the United States. (See Exhibit 4.) Over the last decade, the share of GNP going to capital investment has remained remarkably stable, but as GNP

---

[23]Lester C. Thurow, *The Zero Sum Society* (New York: Basic Books, 1980), p. 91.

growth has slowed, so has capital formation. While there is generally a positive relationship between capital investment and productivity in goods-producing industries, that relationship is less clear for knowledge-intensive and labor-intensive
industries in the service sector. It can be argued that a declining rate of capital formation is appropriate for an economy dominated by the service sector. Moreover,
given the variation in competitive environments and differing rates of technological change, capital-formation and industrial-investment statistics fail to reveal the
extent to which investment is rational for a specific sector, industry, or firm. (See
Exhibit 5). Efficient capital allocation is essential for addressing our slow-growth
problems, but it is the rationality and velocity of investment, not its aggregate level, that most affects productivity and relative competitiveness.

Other data indicate that the price of capital services sharply accelerated during the 1970s.[24] Higher interest rates on borrowed capital may have acted as a
brake to slow the substitution of capital for labor. There is also evidence that the
United States has been less successful than its industrial competitors in financing
the second stage of the "product cycle."[25] The venture capital market in combination with the entrepreneurial small-business sector in the United States has been
highly efficient in getting major innovations to market. But, once the competition
shifts toward the second stage of product development where the incremental improvements that reduce costs and improve reliability and standardization become
important, the advantage tends to shift to firms which can mobilize investment
rapidly to expand production and marketing. The Japanese have tended to excel
at the second stage of the product cycle when the ability to borrow aggressively at
low interest rates becomes an advantage. The argument is that the American competitive situation has been twice injured: once, by higher than average capital
costs that make production intrinsically more expensive; then again, by the overvalued American dollar (an indirect reflection of higher interest rates operating
through the exchange rate) that inflates export prices in world markets.

**Innovation and the diffusion of technology.**   Another candidate for blame
is the perceived slowdown in the rate of innovation and technological diffusion.
This slowdown is related to the fact that between World War II and the mid-1960s
federal R&D support increased annually from 10 to 15 percent in real terms. But,
beginning in 1967, federal support leveled off and, after a dip in the 1970s, returned to the mid-1960s funding level in the 1980s. The share of federal support

---

[24]It is estimated that the cost of capital was three times higher in the United States than in Japan
during the mid-1970s. The after-tax cost of industrial capital for fixed investment in Japan was 7.8 percent in 1980 whereas in the U.S. it was 20.8 percent. Otto Eckstein, Christopher Caton, Roger Brin-
ner and Peter Duprey, *U.S. Manufacturing Industries* (Cambridge: Data Resources, Inc., 1984), pp. 33–
42. Also see Julian Gresser, "High Technology and Japanese Industrial Policy: A Strategy for U.S.
Policy Makers," a report submitted to the assistant secretary for East Asian and Pacific Affairs, U.S.
Department of State (unpublished, 1980), pp. 56–9; SIA, *Government Targeting on Semiconductor Competition,* pp. 63–8.

[25]See Raymond Vernon, "International Investment and International Trade in the Product Cycle," *Quarterly Journal of Economics,* May 1966, pp. 190–207.

for overall R&D dropped from over 65 percent in the early 1960s to 46 percent in 1983, largely reflecting the reduced share of gross national product devoted to military expenditure. During the decade of flat federal expenditure (1970s), there was modest relative growth in private-sector R&D expenditures.[26] Some analysts view this expenditure pattern with alarm as traditionally more than 70 percent of industrial R&D funds have been allocated to development, less than 5 percent to basic research (considered the impetus of major technological innovation). Others laud the trend in expenditures in the belief that private-sector R&D expenditures (particularly development expenditures) are more immediately linked to economic performance indicators.[27] However, such analyses are undercut at the industry level where the majority of R&D expenditures occur in only five industries, each with a notably different pattern of funding and expenditure. (See Exhibit 6.)

Research carried out by economist Edwin Mansfield of the University of Pennsylvania has indicated that it is the composition, as well as the size, of an industry's or firm's R&D expenditures that affect its rate of productivity increase. Mansfield found that the rate of productivity increase is significantly and directly related to the extent to which R&D is long term (a proxy measure for "basic" research).[28] Subsequent to recent debate over the question of whether industrial managers were in fact beginning to devote substantially smaller shares of their R&D expenditures to basic research, long-term projects, or "risky" and ambitious projects, Mansfield obtained information from 119 firms concerning the changes that occurred in their R&D budgets between 1967 and 1977. Each firm included in his sample spent over $10 million on R&D in 1976, and together they accounted for about one half of the total industrial R&D expenditures in that year. He found that basic research declined in practically every industry.

In the aerospace, metals, electrical equipment, office equipment and computer, chemical, drug, and rubber industries, the proportion of overall R&D devoted to basic research dropped substantially. In the sample as a whole, the proportion fell about one fourth, from 5.6 percent in 1967 to 4.1 percent in 1977. In four fifths of the sample, the proportion of R&D expenditures devoted to relatively risky projects also declined. In some industries, like metals, chemicals, aircraft, drugs, and rubber, this reduction was rather large. The reason most frequently given by

---

[26]Harvey Brooks, "The Changing Structure of the U.S. Research System, Overview: A Historical Perspective on the Current Situation and Future Issues and Prospects" (unpublished, 1984), p. 1; Willis H. Shapely, Albert H. Teich and Jill P. Weinberg, *American Association for the Advancement of Science Report VIII: Research and Development, FY 1984* (Washington, D.C.: AAAS, 1983), p. 133.

[27]The national R&D distribution by character of work is 66 percent to development, 22 percent to applied research, and 12 percent to basic research. For industrial R&D the figures are 72 percent, 23 percent, and 5 percent respectively. See National Science Foundation, *Science and Technology Data Book* (Washington, D.C.: NSF: Division of Science Resources Studies, October 1983), p. 5; Shapely, *AAAS Report,* p. 135.

[28]Edwin Mansfield, "Technological Change and Economic Growth," a paper presented to the National Academy of Sciences Conference on Science Policy (unpublished, January 1983), pp. 23–25. For more detail see Edwin Mansfield, Anthony Romeo, Mark Swartz, David Teece, Samuel Wagner and Peter Brach *Technology Transfer, Productivity, and Economic Policy* (New York: W. W. Norton, 1982).

managers to Mansfield for cutbacks in basic research and risky projects was the increase in government regulations which they believed reduced the profitability of such projects. This reason was advanced most often by chemical and drug firms. Another reason put forth was that innovation had become more costly and difficult to achieve in the fields of knowledge most thoroughly worked over by scientists in the past. Still another reason was the increased uncertainty that complicates the planning of R&D projects during inflationary periods.

The overall magnitude of the U.S. R&D effort (estimated at $88 billion in 1983) and the large pool of technical manpower (an estimated 3.3 million scientists and engineers in 1982) are elements of strength for the U.S. economy. Nonetheless, there is some concern that these advantages have declined in relative terms. U.S. R&D expenditures as a share of GNP declined slightly during the 1970s, while other industrial nations (beginning from a smaller base, of course) continued to register increases in the rate of growth of R&D spending. Nondefense R&D as a share of U.S. GNP remained essentially stable over the 1968–1980 period while such expenditures increased somewhat in West Germany and Japan.[29] (See Exhibit 7.)

It is difficult to know whether R&D/GNP ratios or absolute expenditure figures are the more significant statistics in assessing relative competitiveness. If one assumes that technological diffusion is slow and remains within national borders, then the R&D/GNP ratio is the more important statistic. If, on the contrary, one assumes that technology diffusion is rapid and easily transferred beyond national borders, then it is the absolute R&D expenditure figures that are the more important. The problem remains, however, whether it is the industrial, the nondefense, or the total R&D expenditure level that is most telling. Observers such as Harvey Brooks of Harvard University assert that during the 1980s it will be the rate at which a national economy appropriates and integrates new technology that will most affect productivity, competitiveness, and economic growth. Here, rapid access to relatively inexpensive capital, the general educational level of the work force, and the state of labor-management relations may be more important indicators of relative competitive strength than R&D expenditure data.

There seems to be considerable agreement that the U.S. productivity slowdown can be only marginally attributed to R&D funding and expenditure patterns. It is doubtful that either the mid-1960s slowdown or the significant post-1973 drop in the "residual" can be wholly explained by a breakdown in "advances of knowledge" or the rate of technological innovation and diffusion. The very healthy U.S. venture capital market signifies otherwise. Nevertheless, advocates of product- or process-specific targeting policies for industrial R&D abound. Advocates argue that the semiconductor and biotechnology industries in particular require additional government R&D support if they are to remain, or become, competitive in international markets when our competitors have preferential access to relatively low-cost capital for the support of long-term or risky R&D projects.

---

[29]NSF, *Science and Technology Data Book,* pp. 7, 25.

**Management failure.** Critics charge that corporate executives deserve a great deal of blame for the deterioration of U.S. competitive vigor. They decry large executive salaries and the time and economic resources given to takeover battles. They argue that American managers have been preoccupied with the management of assets, when the management of technology was more relevant to their problems. They accuse corporate executives of exporting investment capital and of being unwilling to modernize American industry without profit guarantees or tax subsidies. They maintain that productivity, innovation, worker satisfaction and the consideration of other long-term goals have been sacrificed to short-term cost reduction. They note the culpability of the nation's business schools in failing to educate future managers in practical methods of evaluating corporate performance on the basis of productivity as well as the bottom line. Many conclude that U.S. competitiveness in international markets has faltered because industrial managers have failed to give systematic attention to the basics: product design, process innovation, and all-around plant efficiency.

According to Robert Hayes and the late William Abernathy of the Harvard Business School, gradual changes in the emphasis of management theory and technique over the last 30 years have resulted in a preoccupation with near-term results.[30] Hayes and Abernathy argue that the unfortunate by-product of the trend toward the decentralized structuring of large firms has been the development of performance evaluation techniques that rely on quantifiable short-term criteria. As independent profit centers and strategic business units have become the primary units of managerial responsibility, top-level executives have tended to give up "hands-on" management for a continuous flow of financial reports designed to measure performance-to-date against quarterly or year-end goals.

Hayes and Abernathy maintain that the most negative impact of depersonalized management, or "management by numbers," has been the development of corporate environments that penalize risk taking and discourage innovative activity. They note that reliance on formularized approaches to investment decision making that stress quantitative, short-term criteria, tend to penalize unduly even a quarterly dip in profits. When failure carries too high a price, innovation suffers. They report that top-level executives have become increasingly hesitant to invest in new ideas and processes that do not offer a near-term payoff. They assert that innovation suffers when individuals know their entire management team will be penalized if a project they recommend should fail to deliver the specified investment-return.

Professors Hayes and Abernathy go on to charge that American industry has lost its leadership position in mature industries because the preoccupation with short-term results has worked to undermine technical superiority. They note a reluctance on the part of industrial managers to invest in the development of new process technologies. In contrast, they describe Western European and Japanese management as being more committed to the internal development of advanced

---

[30]Robert H. Hayes and William J. Abernathy, "Managing Our Way to Economic Decline," *Harvard Business Review,* July/August 1980, pp. 67–77.

process technologies with the goal of increasing market share over the long term with higher quality and, eventually, lower-cost products. Hayes and Abernathy also see a reluctance on the part of American managers to support the development of truly innovative products that present uncertainty in terms of market acceptance and economic return or that tend to make obsolete existing investment in manufacturing facilities and marketing organizations.[31]

Other critics concentrate on what they argue has been the inefficient utilization of limited investment capital.[32] The speculative investments now so popular among corporate financial managers (real estate, foreign currency contracts, commodity and financial futures) have created profits but not productive capability. In addition, they argue that too much of the available investment capital has been directed toward the rearrangement of ownership of industrial assets through mergers, acquisitions, sell-offs, and leveraged buyouts. Despite claims of "synergy," there is little evidence to suggest that the average merger has enhanced either the productivity or the profitability of the merging firms. The consequences of the current merger movement are difficult to predict. The most recent flurry of sell-off and acquisition activity may make American industry more efficient if scale economies in production, marketing, or R&D are obtained. But it is also possible, particularly in instances of unrelated-product or conglomerate mergers, that the shuffling of assets will only camouflage inefficient productive capacity.

**Comparative productivity measures.**  So much for factors that have contributed to the domestic productivity slowdown. How does domestic productivity compare with that of other advanced industrial nations? Labor productivity in manufacturing has increased in all industrial nations since 1960, but it has increased more slowly in the United States than in Western Europe or Japan. Between 1960 and 1977, labor productivity increased by 279 percent in Japan, 151 percent in France, 150 percent in West Germany, 95 percent in Canada, 64 percent in the United Kingdom, and 60 percent in the United States.[33] The U.S. Department of Labor has made productivity and cost comparisons for the major industrial economies in order to assess their mutual competitive positions, particularly with respect to foreign trade.[34] (See Exhibit 8.) Rates of change in productivity were confined to the manufacturing sector and measured in domestic currency units. The most striking thing about these comparisons is the pervasive-

---

[31]For a detailed study of the U.S. auto industry in this regard, see William J. Abernathy, Kim B. Clark and Alan M. Kantrow, *Industrial Renaissance: Producing a Competitive Future for America* (New York: Basic Books, 1983).

[32]See Robert B. Reich, *The Next American Frontier* (New York: Times Books, 1983), pp. 140–172.

[33]Edwin Mansfield, "The Competitive Position of U.S. Technology," paper presented at the Conference on U.S. Competitiveness, sponsored by the New York Stock Exchange, the U.S. Senate Subcommittee on International Trade, and Harvard University (unpublished, April 1980), pp. 3–4. This pattern in the comparative rates of productivity growth held through 1982. See "The Revival of Productivity," *Business Week,* February 13, 1984, p. 95.

[34]See Patricia Capdevielle, Donato Alvarez and Brian Cooper, "International Trends in Productivity and Labor Costs," *Monthly Labor Review,* December 1982, pp. 3–14.

ness of the world productivity slowdown. In every country examined, the growth rate of productivity fell significantly after 1973, even in Japan. Competitiveness, however, depends on more than productivity; it depends on costs, profit margins, and exchange rates. At the international level, most studies have been concerned with labor productivity. At that level of investigation, the appropriate cost item is the wage rate. Comparative growth rates in unit labor costs, measured in U.S. dollars, are included in Exhibit 8. It is evident from these figures that the productivity slowdown is compounded by an increase in unit labor costs. High wage costs, together with poor productivity growth, contribute jointly to declining competitiveness. A profit margin estimate is needed to translate these figures into the final prices charged that would determine the ultimate degree of competitiveness.

At the industry level, economist Lawrence R. Klein of the University of Pennsylvania has computed comparative indexes for the 1975–1980 period for the auto, electrical machinery and electronics, chemical, textile, and the paper and allied products industries.[35] (See Exhibit 9.) In this period the relatively strong growth performance of Japan stands out (even the exchange appreciation of the yen against the dollar does not wipe out the gains when unit labor cost is computed in U.S. dollar units). Both wage and price changes were also restrained in Japan in comparison with other countries. On the negative side, the United Kingdom performed relatively poorly on both a productivity and a competitiveness standard. The U.S. performance was neither the worst nor the best in these comparisons. Klein concludes from his data that if a cyclical recovery in productivity growth could be attained with wage and price restraint, the United States could become fully competitive in foreign trade markets again.

## Stagflation

"Stagflation," the simultaneous occurrence of rapid inflation with unusually high levels of unemployment, began to plague the global economy after the first oil-price shocks in 1973–1974. Though stagflation and the slower growth of output and productivity are quite different phenomena (and each factor had established a trend prior to 1973), the dramatic escalation in the annual rates of inflation and unemployment in the United States after 1973 correspond with the big drop in productivity and the continuation of the relatively slower growth of aggregate output. The adoption of tight monetary policies beginning in October of 1979 progressively reduced the rate of inflation, and recovery from the business cycle in 1983–1984 has reduced unemployment. But, in a climate of worsening business cycles and lower national growth, the expectation that stagflation will resurface remains.[36] It is not so much the evidence that higher residual rates of inflation and unemployment remain after successive postwar recessions as it is the widely held belief that inflation will escalate as the economy absorbs the unemployed, utilizes

---

[35]Lawrence R. Klein, "International Productivity Comparisons (A Review)," *Proceedings of the National Academy of Sciences, U.S.A.* (July 1983), pp. 4561–4568.

[36]For a discussion of worsening business cycles (more frequent, more severe) and their effect on the U.S. manufacturing sector, see Eckstein, *U.S. Manufacturing Industries,* pp. 17–20.

more capacity, and expands debt that causes concern over our ability to escape the inflation-unemployment spiral over the long term.

But, exactly how poorly has the U.S. economy performed relative to other advanced industrial economies that have faced the same, or at least very similar, economic disturbances and business cycles during the 1970s? Exhibits 10 and 11 present comparative industrial production, inflation, and unemployment data for the United States, Canada, Japan, and the European Economic Community of nations over the 1960–1983 period. The most striking feature of the exhibits is the more favorable performance of the Japanese economy (again, in part reflecting Japan's more recent development as a modern mass-production consumer economy). The United States, Canada, and the European nations appear rather similar in their less favorable performance. Irrespective of the similarities in the United States and Western European record, however, unemployment data mask a significant difference. The U.S. economy, whatever its other difficulties, provided employment for a rapidly growing labor force. During the 1970s, the U.S. labor force increased by over 24 million, while the economy generated 21 million additional jobs.[37] In Europe, by contrast, employment has remained virtually stationary over the last decade, and unemployment levels have steadily increased. Estimates place the number of unemployed persons in the industrial countries of Western Europe at about 18 million—a figure that illustrates the magnitude of the task of restoring labor market health.

Nonetheless, there are serious employment problems in the United States. During 1982, a year when the unemployment rate increased from 8.8 percent to 10.8 percent, 11.3 million Americans were officially counted as unemployed. Another 1.5 million wanted jobs but had given up looking for work, and 5.5 million workers seeking full-time employment had been forced to settle for part-time jobs. If these workers had been included in the official count, the unemployment rate would have exceeded 17 percent.[38] The economic recovery of 1983–1984 has reduced the official unemployment rate to under 8 percent of the work force, but that figure represents the highest postrecession residual in the postwar era. In addition, the structure of unemployment remains a problem. The official rate for black and other nonwhite workers regularly exceeds 17 percent; the rate for nonwhite youths exceeds 45 percent.[39]

# Global Interdependence

Along with slower economic growth and the loss of economic hegemony, the progressive internationalization of finance and trade is the force that has most transformed the U.S. economy over the last 20 years. The reasons for the rapid inter-

[37]Janet L. Norwood, "Labor Market Contrasts: United States and Europe," *Monthly Labor Review,* August 1983, pp. 3–7.

[38]Each percentage point of official unemployment costs the U.S. Treasury between $25 and $30 billion annually in lost tax revenues and transfer payments. Sar A. Levitan and Clifford M. Johnson, "The Politics of Unemployment," *The New Republic,* September 1982, pp. 22–27.

[39]See CEA, *Economic Report of the President* (1984), Tables B-33, B-34, B-35, pp. 259–261.

nationalization of finance and trade are complex and varied. Briefly, the more important factors include the free-trade philosophy espoused by the United States at the Bretton Woods Conference in 1944 that shaped the international trade laws set up under GATT, the international monetary system set up under the IMF, and the beginnings of an international approach to development aid under the International Bank for Reconstruction and Development (World Bank). Initially the World Bank financed Europe's postwar reconstruction; thereafter, it began to concentrate on loans to developing countries. Within this supranational framework, world trade has expanded at a faster rate than total world output. Between 1965 and 1978, the exports of developed market economies grew about 80 percent faster than their industrial production and nearly twice as fast as their gross national product.[40]

A second factor contributing to the rapid growth and internationalization of trade was the growth dynamism of the West German and Japanese economies after reconstruction (from the mid-1950s to the mid-1970s). Their rapidly expanding exports stimulated world trade as a whole. A third factor lay in the formation of the European Economic Community in the late 1950s, which stimulated both internal and international trade among its members. A fourth factor was the expansion of exports from the mid-1960s by East Asian and other middle-income developing countries.

The growth of the transnational corporation is a final important factor that has significantly contributed to the international flow of trade. Not only has the proportion of world output accounted for by these corporations expanded, but increasingly their operations have become integrated on a global scale. Finished products are often assembled in one country from components manufactured in several other countries; they are then marketed around the world. Thus the growth of international trade *within* individual transnational corporations also has been an important feature of postwar trade expansion. Precise calculation is difficult, but it is estimated that transnationals market over half of total world trade and as much as four fifths of world trade when the output of the centrally planned economies is excluded from the total.[41]

In a study completed for the United Nations, economists John Cavanagh and Frederick Clairmonte found that the world's 200 largest transnational corporations increased their share of world GDP (excluding the centrally planned economies) from 18 to 29 percent between 1960 and 1980.[42] (See Exhibit 12.) Their revenues increased tenfold, from around $200 billion to over $2 trillion. But amidst this overall growth, the position of U.S.-based firms declined. In 1960, of the top 200 transnational companies, 127 were U.S.-based; these companies accounted for 72.7 percent of the group's revenues. By 1980, however, only 91 of the top 200

---

[40]Michael Stewart, *The Age of Interdependence* (Cambridge: MIT Press, 1984), p. 20.

[41]John Cavanagh and Frederick Clairmonte, "The Transnational Economy," *Trade and Development: An United Nations Conference on Trade and Development Review,* Winter 1982, p. 8.

[42]Cavanagh and Clairmonte, "Transnational Economy," pp. 10–11.

were U.S. firms, and their share of total revenue had fallen to 50.1 percent. As U.S.-based firms lost their commanding lead, French and Japanese firms in particular gained ground. The number of France's transnationals in the top 200 jumped from 7 to 15, and their sales increased from 1.8 percent to 7.5 percent of total sales. No less dramatic is Japan's ascent, with 20 companies now in the top 200, as opposed to only 5 in 1960. Revenues of the Japanese companies increased from 1.5 percent of the total in 1960 to 7.2 percent in 1980.[43]

The internationalization of output, finance, and commerce in the postwar period both supported and encouraged the ascendancy of the transnational corporation. Technical innovations in containerized shipping (which made dispersal of production facilities profitable), communications networks, and computerized data processing were instrumental in developing the planning and control techniques vital to maximization of global profits and market shares. Data that show the extent of the penetration of foreign markets by U.S.-based transnational firms give an indication of the breadth of global market integration and international economic interdependence. Exhibit 13 shows that, in a listing of the 100 largest U.S.-based transnationals, foreign income comprised more than half the total revenues for firms in the banking and transportation sectors.[44] At the other end of the spectrum, retailing transnationals received only 15 percent of their total revenues from foreign operations. Transnational integration is by no means the sole prerogative of U.S.-based corporations. Rather, it has become a common feature of large corporations in industrial and industrializing economies throughout the world.

## Financial Interdependence

The story of the postwar growth of international finance is a complex one. Here we can only briefly focus on aspects of the story that have particular relevance to the issues of slower growth, economic interdependence, and trade. Like the transnational corporations, the world's transnational banks have played a major role in the growth of nation-state interdependence and international trade. Increasingly they have come to finance both development loans and the internal growth of the world's transnational corporations via merger and acquisition.

A perusal of data compiled by Cavanagh and Clairmonte on the assets, profits, and location of the world's top 100 banks is instructive. In 1981, their combined assets of $4.4 trillion were the equivalent of more than half of global GDP and more than double the combined sales of the top 200 industrial corporations.[45] (See Exhibit 14.) The big Japanese and United States banks alone controlled two

---

[43]The figures for the Japanese companies exclude Japan's general trading companies, the Sogo Shoshas. Led by Mitsui and Mitsubishi, there are nine giant Sogo Shoshas. Their aggregate revenues exceeded $357 billion in 1981. See Cavanagh and Clairmonte, "Transnational Economy," p. 20.

[44]Cavanagh and Clairmonte, "Transnational Economy," pp. 12–13.

[45]Cavanagh and Clairmonte, "Transnational Economy," pp. 10–12.

fifths of the top 100's total assets, with 24 Japanese banks accounting for over a quarter of total assets. This financial leverage has been crucial in the Sogo Sho-shas' conquest of external markets.

Worldwide capital mobility has also been facilitated by the development of the Eurocurrency markets. The original Eurodollars were dollars held outside the United States and recycled by offshore banks like any other currency. The Euro-dollar market grew rapidly during the 1960s in part because of the outflow of U.S. dollars to finance the Vietnam War and in part because banks and transnational corporations wanted to hold, lend, and borrow dollars in countries free from American banking controls. Freedom from state control allows the Euromarkets to pay higher rates for short-term deposits and to lend more cheaply than domestic banks. The 1970s saw a further expansion of the Eurocurrency markets as off-shore markets developed in sterling, Deutchmarks, yen, and a number of other currencies. By the early 1980s, there were approximately one trillion Eurodollars available for commercial use and capable of being moved around as their owners wished.[46]

The rise of the Eurocurrencies has made banking the most supranational of all businesses. Very large sums of money can very quickly be switched from one country or currency to another in response to actual or anticipated changes in in-terest rates, exchange rates, or economic conditions. Transaction costs in financial markets and government-imposed barriers to the flow of capital across national boundaries are today very low among most of the larger industrialized countries. The high international mobility of capital means that the foreign exchange market is now dominated by capital transactions, not by trade transactions.[47] When fixed exchange rates were abandoned for floating rates in 1973, it meant that currency transactions in the Euromarkets could affect the foreign exchange market. In or-der to maintain currency stability and prevent the misalignment of national cur-rencies, governments must intervene in the financial markets by buying or selling their own currency in the short term and by adjusting fiscal and monetary policies over the longer term.

The management of money and credit by a national government affects not only its own currency valuation and domestic trade balances, but the domestic in-vestment, trade balances, employment, and inflation experienced by trading partners as well. When the American-supported system of floating exchange rates was first adopted, it was assumed that national governments would eagerly inter-vene in international financial markets to adjust currency values as market condi-tions changed because overvalued currencies reduce export competitiveness, and undervalued currencies create inflationary pressure. National governments, how-ever, have been slow to take remedial action. The Japanese have been accused of maintaining an undervalued currency in order to deliver cheaper imports to for-

---

[46]The total value of deposits in commercial banks in the United States amounts to approximately $240 billion. It is increasingly difficult to quarantine the U.S. money supply from that located over-seas. Heilbroner, "Economic Prospects," pp. 66–72.

[47]CEA, *Economic Report of the President* (1984), pp. 50–51.

eign markets. U.S. officials, on the other hand, have been charged with boosting the value of the dollar through restrictive monetary policies (meant to inhibit inflation) and high interest rates (the result of massive budget deficits). The appreciation of the dollar has made it more difficult for U.S. firms to compete in world markets.

In addition, higher U.S. interest rates have effectively dampened economic expansion, undercut growth in the volume of world trade, and caused foreign governments to adjust their own fiscal and monetary policies. In an interdependent, open economic system, a change in one unit means adjustment for all. Higher U.S. interest rates also have had a negative effect on the indebted developing countries, where stagnant world trade and falling commodity prices have left many short of the foreign exchange required to meet the interest payments on their $800 billion development-loan debt. It is estimated that with every 1 percent increase in U.S. interest rates, an additional $3.5 billion in interest is required to service the existing debt. Default threatens not only to disrupt international financial markets but to bankrupt the commercial banks that now provide more than 50 percent of the loans to developing countries. Of the $89 billion owed to external debtors by Mexico, for example, 38.2 percent is owed to U.S.-based banks; of Argentina's $43.6 billion debt, 34.5 percent is owed to U.S. banks; and for Brazil's $93 billion debt, the figure is 33.7 percent.[48] The rapid ascent of private commercial finance over the past 10 years, in good part the result of the need to recycle the billions of dollars of savings that OPEC countries could not absorb in the short run, has placed the transnational banks in conflict, at times, with the transnational corporations. Although the relationship between the two is generally harmonious in periods of growth, global recession has caused tensions.

The transnational corporations have depended upon bank loans to provide developing countries with the foreign exchange to buy Western goods. As the banks have decelerated their lending in response to the threat of default, the transnational firms have suffered from the slowing of world trade. During the 1970s, developing countries absorbed more than one third of the total U.S. exports and more than 40 percent of the exports of the Western industrial countries. Commercial banks will have to reschedule their loans and reduce interest charges if the heavily indebted developing countries are to regain their ability to import our goods.

An additional interdependence problem is related to the fact that the advanced industrial countries have adopted policies to protect certain domestic markets from further import penetration. These trade barriers have undercut the ability of the debt-ridden developing countries to acquire the export earnings required to service the interest on external debt. Many have been caught in a real economic bind. Their export earnings have been hampered by foreign protectionism while they have been forced to limit their imports because of external debt. Brazil presents a good example. Brazil needs approximately $12 billion a year to cover the

---

[48]Clyde H. Farnsworth, "The Third World Trade Conflict," *The New York Times,* April 26, 1984, p. D1.

interest on its $93 billion external debt. In 1983, Brazil planned to export $25 billion (mostly steel, textiles, and footwear). Imports were held to $16 billion, mostly oil, food, technology, and spare parts. Brazil's imports and interest payments exceeded the value of its exports by $3 billion.[49] Thus, it would appear that Brazil could not help but go deeper in debt during 1983. In 1984, Brazil will face new barriers to its steel and footwear exports in U.S. markets. At the same time it will be expected to cut imports in order to service its larger debt. The negative ramifications of a Brazilian default would be felt throughout the interdependent, international financial system. A default would also have negative consequences for the exports, GNP, jobs, and interest rates of Brazil's major trading partners.

### Trade Interdependence and the Domestic Economy

Americans have been slow to reach the conclusion that effective trade performance is an important determinant of aggregate growth. Our legacy of resource abundance, technological acuity, and, from 1890, the world's largest domestic market has encouraged a focus on the home economy. Economists have tended to regard the U.S. economy as a self-contained whole, influenced almost exclusively by domestic actions. The structure of international markets and the conditions of international trade have long been of importance to U.S.-based agricultural and mining interests. And from the 1870s, integrated industrials have established operations abroad in order to profit more fully from their technological skills and scale advantages. Nevertheless, because foreign markets have remained only a small part of the total demand for domestic output, foreign trade has had scant relevance to most American workers and little impact on the American standard of living.

However, in the postwar period as international trade accelerated faster than total world output, foreign trade became increasingly important to the U.S. economy. Between 1950 and 1980, the value of exports (goods and services) as a share of GNP doubled (from 5 percent of GNP in 1950 to 12.9 percent in 1980). During the same period, the value of imports as a share of GNP nearly tripled (from 4.3 percent of GNP in 1950 to 11.9 percent in 1980).[50] U.S. Commerce Department data show the growing importance of international trade for the manufacturing sector alone. Between 1974 and 1982, exports of manufactured products increased at an annual rate of 10.6 percent, while imports increased at an annual rate of 11.1 percent. A substantial portion of the growth in the value of both exports and imports was attributable to price increases during this period. However, there was also an increase in real exports and imports. The constant-dollar value

---

[49]Farnsworth, "Third World Trade."

[50]CEA, *Economic Report of the President* (1983), Table B-1, p. 163. Although the underlying data are not directly comparable, Cavanagh and Clairmonte report that in 1980 the value of exports comprised a 23 percent share of GNP in the Federal Republic of Germany; that figure was 22.2 percent in the United Kingdom, 17.8 percent in France, and 12.5 percent in Japan. Cavanagh and Clairmonte, "The Transnational Economy," p. 5.

of exports increased at an annual rate of 6 percent between 1974 and 1982; for imports the constant-dollar annual rate of increase was about 3.4 percent. Between 1974 and 1981, the exports to total shipments ratio in the manufacturing sector increased from 8.0 to 9.5 percent, while the import penetration ratio rose from 7.7 to 9.1 percent.[51]

**Import penetration.** Beginning in the 1950s with simple textiles, products as diverse as aircraft engines, tires, motorcycles, petrochemicals, apparel, footwear, and leather goods have encountered intense foreign competition. The Commerce Department reports that in 1983, 77 percent of U.S. industries faced import competition (that is, 450 of the 580 industries at the four-digit standard-industrial classification system level).[52] The United States now imports 17 percent of its motor vehicles, 22 percent of its steel, 42 percent of its textile machinery, 22 percent of its food-products machinery, 39 percent of its machine tools, and 56 percent of its televisions, radios, tape recorders, and phonographs.[53] In addition, producers of farm and construction equipment have been required to reduce capacity and work forces because of declining export demand.

In the aggregate, the U.S. merchandise trade balance, which last showed a surplus in 1975, turned dramatically downward in 1968 and remained negative during most of the 1970s. The trade deficit totalled $61.1 billion in 1983 and is expected to exceed $100 billion in 1984. The U.S. current account balance showed a $41.3 billion deficit in 1983.[54] Data Resources, Inc., reports that nonelectrical machinery, chemicals, electrical machinery, tobacco, and instruments maintained large positive trade balances between 1970 and 1982. Motor vehicles and parts, petroleum products, steel mill products, other primary metals, apparel, and food and food products maintained large negative trade balances in the same period.[55] (See Exhibit 15.) The President's Council of Economic Advisers argues that a merchandise trade deficit is "normal" in that such deficits are expected and are generally offset by surpluses in exports of services. They blame the larger than normal deficits of the 1980s on the appreciation of the dollar, the substantial loss in net exports to debt-troubled countries, and the fact that the United States has recovered from the business cycle ahead of the European and Japanese economies (therefore we can afford to import at higher levels).[56] Nonetheless, the trade deficit does indicate that industrial jobs are being lost to competitors. John Young, president of Hewlett-Packard and head of a presidential commission on national com-

---

[51]Department of Commerce, *Industrial Outlook 1984,* pp. 34–38.

[52]Department of Commerce, *Industrial Outlook 1984,* industry profile data (various pages).

[53]Department of Commerce, *Industrial Outlook 1984,* pp. 31:5, 18:4, 23:10, 23:9, 20:5, 43:8. The Commerce Department computes import penetration as the percentage of "apparent consumption," or the sum of product shipments plus imports less exports.

[54]CEA, *Economic Report of the President* (1984) Table B–99, p. 332. The 1983 data are revised Department of Commerce, Bureau of Economic Analysis estimates (June 1984).

[55]Eckstein, *U.S. Manufacturing Industries,* p. 84.

[56]CEA, *Economic Report of the President* (1984), p. 43.

petitiveness, estimates that every billion dollars' worth of exports creates 25,000 new jobs. But the opposite is also true. Every billion dollars' worth of imports eliminates something on the order of 25,000 U.S. jobs.[57]

**Adjustment.** Those U.S. industries that have been adversely affected by international competition and slower growth have turned to consolidation, joint ventures, and protectionism to cushion the adjustment process. In recent years, major firms like Chrysler, International Harvester, Kennecott Copper, Admiral, and Weirton Steel have avoided bankruptcy through subsidy, debt restructuring, merger, or employee takeover. In an effort to regain competitive advantage, others like General Motors, American Motors, and Motorola have undertaken joint ventures with, or invited direct investment from, their foreign competitors (Toyota, Renault, and Matsushita, respectively). In the high-technology sector, linkage strategies are proliferating. Corning Glass has joined with Germany's Siemans to manufacture fiber-optic cable, Honeywell with Sweden's L. M. Ericsson to develop and market PBX-switching technology, Hercules with Italy's Montedison to produce polypropylene resin, General Motors with Japan's Fanuc to develop industrial robots, Houdaille Industries with Japan's Okuma to manufacture computer-controlled lathes, and United Technologies with Britain's Rolls-Royce to manufacture aircraft engines. The partners in these technology-sharing joint ventures hope to share risks and more easily gain access to their partners' domestic markets.

Surplus world capacity has curtailed operation at minimum-efficient scale in the domestic oil and steel industries. Here, consolidation and restructuring are seen as the primary means of adjustment for the large, integrated producers. In oil, where declining domestic demand has caused a substantial underutilization of the industry's refining, distribution, and retailing capacities, the consolidation of capacity is expected to improve the efficiency of operating equipment and use of the industry's domestic resource base. With the prospect of heightened foreign competition from the new OPEC export refineries, industry analysts applaud recent mergers: Texaco's acquisition of Getty Oil, DuPont's acquisition of Conoco, Occidental Petroleum's acquisition of Cities Service, and the Socal-Gulf and Mobil-Superior mergers.

In steel, where imports now account for one fifth of the domestic market (up from 2.3 percent in the 1950s, 9.9 percent in the 1960s, and about 15 percent in the 1970s) and domestic minimills (nonintegrated, usually specialty steelmakers) have taken another 25 to 30 percent, surplus capacity has become a significant problem.[58] Representatives of the integrated domestic firms argue that consolidations like the Jones & Laughlin–Republic Steel merger, the Nippon Kokan acquisition of National Steel, and the Wheeling Pittsburgh–Nisshin Steel joint venture in a new plant in the Ohio Valley will help the industry cut costs and obsolete capacity as it fights to regain markets. However, even the lower unit costs obtainable

---

[57]Peter Behr, "Has the American Economy Lost Its Competitive Edge?" *The Washington Post National Weekly Edition,* May 7, 1984, p. 17.

[58]David M. Roderick, "U.S. Steelmakers Fight Back," *Challenge,* January/February 1984, p. 51.

through the steady throughput of rationalized production may not prove sufficient to maintain market share when foreign competitors are state-subsidized and new producers glut international markets. The press toward consolidation in the oil and steel industries may improve productivity if capacity is well matched to demand, innovation takes place, and economies of scale and scope are realized. But consolidation in itself is not a panacea. Not entirely confident themselves that restructuring will sufficiently enhance competitiveness in the near term, steel industry representatives have also lobbied Congress for increased import protection. Major steel producers have joined forces with labor to petition for legislation that would limit steel imports in all categories to a 15 percent share of domestic consumption.

In recent years, the United States has relied on Orderly Marketing Agreements (OMAs) as the primary instrument of protectionist policy.[59] OMAs have been negotiated with major trading partners to protect domestic steel, auto, motorcycle, textile, apparel, footwear, and consumer electronics markets. Because OMAs are restricted and temporary, they are often regarded as the preferred way to reconcile immediate demands for protection with a commitment to free trade. However, OMAs tend to encourage unrestricted new competitors to enter U.S. markets. The OMA signed between the United States and the European Economic Community to curb specialty steel imports, for example, only seemed to encourage the expansion of domestic minimills and to increase specialty steel imports from new producers located in South Korea, Brazil, Mexico, Spain, Rumania, and South Africa. Recent experience with OMAs for the apparel and auto markets has shown that with quantity restrictions, foreign producers tend to move into higher-value goods in order to achieve the largest possible value per unit. By forcing our foreign competitors to do the adjusting, OMAs can accentuate the long-run competitive problems of the domestic industries they are designed to protect. When it is our foreign competitors who adjust more quickly to the dislocations of market change, both initially and after an OMA is in place, it is likely that the domestic industry under protection lacks the flexibility and responsiveness required to maintain a competitive edge in international markets.

## The New Competition

There are several aspects of the new patterns and conditions of competition in international markets that are of central importance to the national industrial policy debate. The first has to do with the quickened pace at which technologies of production have become susceptible to reorganizing innovations in the second stage

---

[59]Quantitative import restrictions limit physical number, or quantity by weight. The most common form was once the quota, a unilateral restriction by one country on the quantity of imports it would accept, either from some other country or from the world. A second type, the Orderly Marketing Agreement, has become popular because of the trade rules established in 1947 under GATT. GATT requires that all member nations get the same tariff treatment (the "most favored nation" doctrine) and that tariffs, in theory, are the only permissible form of barrier: no subsidies, selling below cost (dumping), tax preferences, cheap loans to home industries, no quotas, preferential procurement, or inspection gimmicks designed to exclude foreign goods. However, because OMAs are "voluntary" and bilateral, they are not explicitly prohibited under GATT.

of the product cycle. New products and processes generally require not only high-income markets to recoup development costs, but also the use of skilled labor, capital, and the supportive infrastructures most readily available in developed countries. Once innovative products or processes have been translated into growth industries, however, production technologies tend to become standardized and less dependent on highly developed infrastructures. At this stage in the product life cycle, products and processes that cannot be made more capital- or skill-intensive tend to move to low-wage locations, where, typically, there are still unsaturated markets. Examples from recent experience are the shifts in the global pattern of steel production, shipbuilding, consumer electronics, and basic chemicals.

As policy analyst Robert Reich of Harvard's Kennedy School of Government has argued, whatever the final product, those parts of the production process requiring standardized, high-volume machinery and unsophisticated workers can be accomplished more cheaply in developing nations.[60] Reich maintains that U.S. producers must move from the lowest-value-added products and the most labor-intensive processes into higher-value-added products and skill-intensive processes. He believes that the United States can retain competitive advantage (and jobs) only where precision, custom-tailored, or technology-driven products are produced that require a skilled labor force capable of rapid adjustment to technological advances and changing market conditions. Along with a growing number of analysts, Reich believes "flexible systems" of production to be the new frontier of industrial development for the advanced industrial economies.[61]

But, not every product can be profitably produced in a low-wage area. Most processing industries and some of the new production technologies (computer-aided design/computer-aided manufacturing for example) tend to diminish the role of labor, skilled or unskilled, as a factor of production and, consequently, as a component of total costs. As wage costs become less important, the competitive advantage enjoyed by the low-wage countries necessarily recedes. In the case of fully automated installations, it becomes nil. Production of textiles, particularly simple textiles, shifted in the past from the developed to the low-wage, less developed countries; but there are signs that, with the introduction of highly automated equipment, this process has been arrested and is even being reversed. In addition, many of the smaller trading nations lack a domestic market of sufficient size to support domestic manufacturers while they expand production to the point of attaining world-scale economies. Automobile production presents the most obvious example here. Furthermore, many developing nations lack both the public services and the educational infrastructure needed to support knowledge-intensive industries such as telecommunications.

The second important aspect of the new competition relates to the policies of promotion, subsidy, and market protection pursued by the governments of our

---

[60]Reich, *Next American Frontier,* pp. 117–39.

[61]For a lucid explanation of "flexible" manufacturing systems, i.e., computer-aided design/computer-aided manufacturing, and their potential for stimulating radical change in corporate strategy, see Joel D. Goldhar and Mariann Jelinek, "Plan for Economies of Scope," *Harvard Business Review,* November/December 1983, pp. 141–48.

trading partners. As economist Robert Heilbroner of the New School for Social Research has argued, the nationalized firm and state-led competition are becoming the modern means by which national governments provide supportive infrastructures for economic growth (not unlike road building or education).[62] Some observers believe that these policies amount to "unfair competition" because they distort markets and often impose unacceptable adjustment costs on major trading partners. Others fear their major threat lies in the possibility, even probability, that trading partners will gain technological superiority over U.S. producers either in the developmental or the secondary stages of the product cycle. As Heilbroner argues, it seems evident that we face a critical choice: Shall the United States continue to exert its influence for a more open international trading system, or shall we join most of our trading partners in restricting access to domestic markets while subsidizing selected exports?

Here recommendations for policy fall into two camps. One group of analysts advocates continued pressure on our trading partners to open markets and eschew protectionism. This group generally looks to the use of macroeconomic policies to stimulate the U.S. competitive stance. They advocate tax credits for R&D, accelerated depreciation, incentives to saving, simplification or relaxation of regulation, and revisions of patent and antitrust policies. The second group is less sanguine about the potential for structural adjustment within the free-trade, open-market framework. They assert that it is unlikely that the United States will be able to persuade its trading partners to forego the benefits of "positive" adjustment policies because such policies are the inevitable political consequence, at the national level, of the instabilities and disruptions that emanate from the supranational realm of finance and trade. They argue that buffered trade is often the best means of sharing the costs of industrial change. In addition to supportive macroeconomic policies, the second group advocates a more activist role for government in facilitating structural adjustment of the economy and the labor force when market dislocations require particularly rapid or large-scale disinvestment. They also advocate government subsidy to foster the more rapid development and marketing of emerging products or processes identified as important for national competitiveness (microelectronics and biotechnology are examples).

Regardless of which policy group gains ascendancy, and it is likely that both will continue to shape national policies, it is essential that American industry does in fact adjust to the new patterns and conditions of international competition. The alternative is a weakened national position and chronic stagflation. The larger challenge is to harness our proven capacity for change to the task of reconciling national interests and political purpose with the demands of the supranational realm of finance and production. The complexity of the challenge is immense. There are no simplistic or single-focus answers. As the world's largest single economy, there is much still in our favor, but there is also much work to be done—work that will require serious, concentrated thought and action.

---

[62]Robert L. Heilbroner, "The Coming Invasion," *The New York Review*, December 8, 1983, pp. 23–25.

# EXHIBIT 1

**Distribution of Exports of Manufactures**

| Country | 1953 | 1956 | 1959 | 1962 | 1965 | 1968 | 1971 | 1974 | 1976 |
|---|---|---|---|---|---|---|---|---|---|
| Total ($ millions) | 37,738 | 51,721 | 61,400 | 79,330 | 109,730 | 150,070 | 226,670 | 483,070 | 585,260 |
| | | | | *Percentage of Total* | | | | | |
| Developed[1]: | 88.0 | 83.5 | 82.1 | 81.6 | 82.0 | 83.1 | 83.9 | 83.7 | 83.1 |
| LDCs[2] | 7.0 | 6.6 | 5.3 | 5.3 | 5.8 | 5.8 | 5.5 | 7.8 | 8.0 |
| CPEs[3] | 5.0 | 9.9 | 12.6 | 13.1 | 12.1 | 11.0 | 10.4 | 8.4 | 8.9 |
| Developed: | | | | | | | | | |
| Western Europe | 49.0 | 50.1 | 53.7 | 54.4 | 54.7 | 53.0 | 54.7 | 54.9 | 54.0 |
| EEC | — | — | 31.9 | 33.5 | 34.4 | 34.4 | 35.8 | 44.9* | 44.0 |
| EFTA | — | — | 20.3 | 19.2 | 18.4 | 17.2 | 17.2 | 8.2* | 8.0 |
| Germany | 9.7 | 12.2 | 15.6 | 14.8 | 15.4 | 14.8 | 15.4 | 16.3 | 15.5 |
| United States | 29.4 | 23.0 | 18.7 | 17.6 | 15.8 | 15.8 | 13.4 | 13.2 | 13.2 |
| Canada | 5.0 | 4.3 | 3.9 | 3.5 | 3.7 | 4.9 | 4.6 | 3.4 | 3.5 |
| Japan | 2.8 | 4.2 | 4.9 | 5.5 | 7.1 | 8.1 | 10.0 | 10.9 | 10.9 |
| Other | 1.9 | 2.0 | 1.2 | 0.6 | 0.8 | 1.4 | 1.3 | 1.4 | 1.5 |
| LDC: | | | | | | | | | |
| Africa[4] | 1.6 | 1.4 | 1.3 | 1.2 | 1.3 | 1.3 | 0.9 | 0.9 | 0.6 |
| Latin America | 1.6 | 1.6 | 1.2 | 1.1 | 1.2 | 1.6 | 1.4 | 1.9 | 1.6 |
| Middle East | 0.3 | 0.4 | 0.4 | 0.3 | 0.4 | 0.2 | 0.2 | 0.5 | 0.4 |
| Asia[5] | 3.5 | 3.2 | 2.4 | 2.6 | 2.8 | 2.7 | 2.9 | 4.5 | 5.4 |
| NIC3[6] | 0.9 | 0.9 | 0.8 | 0.9 | 1.2 | 1.5 | 1.8 | 2.4 | 3.0 |

*Reflects admission of the United Kingdom, Ireland, and Denmark to the EEC and their departure from the EFTA.

[1]Developed market economies: United States, Canada, Japan, Western Europe, Australia, New Zealand, and South Africa.

[2]All countries excluding developed countries and CPEs.

[3]Eastern Europe, USSR, People's Republic of China, Mongolia, North Korea, North Vietnam.

[4]Excludes South Africa and Rhodesia.

[5]Excludes developed countries and CPEs.

[6]Republic of Korea, Hong Kong, Singapore (data for Taiwan were not available for the entire period).

Source: William H. Branson, "Trends in United States International Trade and Investment Since World War II," in Martin Feldstein, ed., *The American Economy in Transition* (Chicago: University of Chicago Press, 1980), p. 196.

## EXHIBIT 2

**Index of Real Gross Domestic Product, Own Country Price** (*weights 1967 = 100*)

| Year | United States | Canada | Japan | France | Germany | Italy | United Kingdom |
|------|------|------|------|------|------|------|------|
| 1950 | 53.0 | 43.6 | 21.3 | 44.0 | 33.6 | 39.4 | 62.0 |
| 1955 | 65.1 | 56.3 | 33.0 | 53.8 | 52.7 | 52.6 | 72.2 |
| 1960 | 73.2 | 68.5 | 49.7 | 68.6 | 76.7 | 68.8 | 81.5 |
| 1965 | 91.8 | 90.3 | 80.2 | 90.8 | 97.7 | 88.3 | 95.4 |
| 1966 | 97.4 | 96.7 | 88.9 | 95.5 | 100.2 | 93.4 | 97.5 |
| 1967 | 100.0 | 100.0 | 100.0 | 100.0 | 100.0 | 100.0 | 100.0 |
| 1968 | 104.4 | 105.6 | 114.1 | 104.3 | 106.3 | 106.3 | 103.6 |
| 1969 | 107.1 | 111.1 | 128.0 | 111.5 | 114.6 | 112.3 | 105.3 |
| 1970 | 106.8 | 114.0 | 142.8 | 117.9 | 121.5 | 118.0 | 107.7 |
| 1971 | 109.8 | 121.9 | 150.2 | 124.3 | 125.4 | 119.8 | 110.4 |
| 1972 | 116.2 | 129.0 | 164.3 | 131.7 | 130.0 | 123.6 | 112.7 |
| 1973 | 122.5 | 138.8 | 180.6 | 138.7 | 136.3 | 132.1 | 121.8 |
| 1974 | 120.9 | 143.7 | 180.0 | 143.2 | 137.1 | 137.8 | 119.8 |
| 1975 | 119.5 | 145.5 | 182.5 | 143.7 | 134.4 | 133.0 | 117.8 |
| 1976 | 126.4 | 153.9 | 194.1 | 150.3 | 141.1 | 140.5 | 121.9 |
| 1977 | 133.0 | 158.3 | 204.2 | 154.9 | 144.9 | 143.4 | 123.6 |
| 1978 | 138.4 | 163.8 | 216.0 | 159.6 | 149.4 | 146.9 | 127.9 |

Source: William H. Branson, "Trends in United States International Trade Since World War II," in Martin Feldstein, ed., *The American Economy in Transition* (Chicago: University of Chicago Press, 1980), p. 187.

# EXHIBIT 3

## U.S. Annual Indexes of Productivity, Hourly Compensation, Unit Costs, and Prices (Selected years: 1950–1982)

| Item | 1950 | 1955 | 1960 | 1965 | 1970 | 1975 | 1976 | 1977 | 1978 | 1979 | 1980 | 1981 | 1982 |
|---|---|---|---|---|---|---|---|---|---|---|---|---|---|
| **Business sector:** | | | | | | | | | | | | | |
| Output per hour of all persons | 50.4 | 58.3 | 65.2 | 78.3 | 86.2 | 94.5 | 97.6 | 100.0 | 100.6 | 99.4 | 98.9 | 101.3 | 101.2 |
| Compensation per hour | 20.0 | 26.4 | 33.9 | 41.7 | 58.2 | 85.5 | 92.9 | 100.0 | 108.6 | 118.7 | 131.2 | 143.9 | 155.1 |
| Real compensation per hour | 50.5 | 59.6 | 69.5 | 80.1 | 90.8 | 96.3 | 98.9 | 100.0 | 100.9 | 99.1 | 96.5 | 95.9 | 97.4 |
| Unit labor costs | 39.8 | 45.2 | 52.1 | 53.3 | 67.5 | 90.5 | 95.1 | 100.0 | 108.0 | 119.5 | 132.7 | 142.1 | 153.3 |
| Unit nonlabor payments | 43.4 | 47.6 | 50.6 | 57.6 | 63.2 | 90.4 | 94.0 | 100.0 | 106.7 | 112.8 | 119.0 | 136.2 | 136.9 |
| Implicit price deflator | 41.0 | 46.0 | 51.6 | 54.7 | 66.0 | 90.4 | 94.7 | 100.0 | 107.5 | 117.2 | 128.1 | 140.1 | 147.7 |
| **Nonfarm business sector:** | | | | | | | | | | | | | |
| Output per hour of all persons | 56.3 | 62.7 | 68.3 | 80.5 | 86.8 | 94.7 | 97.8 | 100.0 | 100.6 | 99.1 | 98.4 | 100.3 | 100.2 |
| Compensation per hour | 21.8 | 28.3 | 35.7 | 42.8 | 58.7 | 86.0 | 93.0 | 100.0 | 108.6 | 118.4 | 130.7 | 143.5 | 154.7 |
| Real compensation per hour | 55.0 | 64.0 | 73.0 | 82.2 | 91.5 | 96.8 | 99.0 | 100.0 | 100.9 | 98.9 | 96.1 | 95.6 | 97.1 |
| Unit labor costs | 38.8 | 45.1 | 52.3 | 53.2 | 67.6 | 90.8 | 95.1 | 100.0 | 108.0 | 119.5 | 132.8 | 143.0 | 154.4 |
| Unit nonlabor payments | 42.7 | 47.8 | 50.4 | 58.0 | 63.8 | 88.5 | 93.5 | 100.0 | 105.3 | 110.4 | 118.5 | 135.0 | 137.0 |
| Implicit price deflator | 40.1 | 46.0 | 51.6 | 54.8 | 66.3 | 90.0 | 94.6 | 100.0 | 107.1 | 116.5 | 128.1 | 140.4 | 148.6 |
| **Nonfinance corporations:** | | | | | | | | | | | | | |
| Output per hour of all persons | (¹) | (¹) | 68.0 | 81.9 | 87.4 | 95.5 | 98.2 | 100.0 | 100.9 | 100.7 | 99.8 | 102.3 | 102.8 |
| Compensation per hour | (¹) | (¹) | 37.0 | 43.9 | 59.4 | 86.1 | 92.9 | 100.0 | 108.5 | 118.7 | 130.9 | 143.6 | 154.8 |
| Real compensation per hour | (¹) | (¹) | 75.8 | 84.3 | 92.7 | 96.9 | 98.9 | 100.0 | 100.7 | 99.1 | 96.3 | 95.7 | 97.2 |
| Unit labor costs | (¹) | (¹) | 54.4 | 53.5 | 68.0 | 90.2 | 94.6 | 100.0 | 107.5 | 117.8 | 131.2 | 140.3 | 150.6 |
| Unit nonlabor payments | (¹) | (¹) | 54.6 | 60.8 | 63.1 | 90.8 | 95.0 | 100.0 | 104.2 | 106.9 | 117.4 | 134.4 | 137.6 |
| Implicit price deflator | (¹) | (¹) | 54.5 | 56.1 | 66.3 | 90.4 | 94.7 | 100.0 | 106.4 | 114.1 | 126.4 | 138.3 | 146.1 |
| **Manufacturing:** | | | | | | | | | | | | | |
| Output per hour of all persons | r49.9 | r56.8 | r60.3 | r74.7 | 79.1 | r93.3 | 97.5 | 100.0 | 100.8 | 101.5 | 101.7 | 105.3 | 106.5 |
| Compensation per hour | 21.5 | 28.8 | 36.7 | 42.8 | 57.6 | 85.4 | 92.3 | 100.0 | 108.3 | 118.8 | 132.7 | 145.8 | 158.2 |
| Real compensation per hour | 54.0 | 65.1 | 75.1 | 82.3 | 89.8 | 96.2 | 98.3 | 100.0 | 100.6 | 99.2 | 97.6 | 97.2 | 99.3 |
| Unit labor costs | r43.0 | r50.7 | r60.8 | r57.4 | r72.8 | 91.5 | r94.7 | 100.0 | 107.4 | 117.0 | 130.5 | 138.5 | 148.5 |
| Unit nonlabor payments | r54.9 | r59.0 | r61.9 | r69.1 | r65.2 | 87.3 | 93.7 | 100.0 | 102.5 | 99.9 | 97.7 | 110.2 | 109.2 |
| Implicit price deflator | 46.6 | 53.2 | 61.1 | 61.0 | 70.5 | 90.3 | 94.4 | 100.0 | 106.0 | 112.0 | 120.9 | 130.2 | 137.0 |

Productivity Data are compiled by the Bureau of Labor Statistics from establishment data and from estimates of compensation and output supplied by the U.S. Department of Commerce and the Federal Reserve Board.

## Definitions

**Output** is the constant dollar gross domestic product produced in a given period. Indexes of **output per hour of labor input**, or labor productivity, measure the value of goods and services produced per hour of labor. **Compensation per hour** includes wages and salaries of employees plus employers' contributions for social insurance and private benefit plans. The data also include an estimate of wages, salaries, and supplementary payments for the self-employed, except for nonfinancial corporations, in which there are no self-employed. **Real compensation per hour** is compensation per hour adjusted by the Consumer Price Index for All Urban Consumers.

**Unit labor cost** measures the labor compensation cost required to produce one unit of output and is derived by dividing compensation by output. **Unit nonlabor payments** include profits, depreciation, interest, and indirect taxes per unit of output. They are computed by subtracting compensation of all persons from the current dollar gross domestic product and dividing by output. In these tables, **unit nonlabor costs** contain all the components of unit nonlabor

payments except unit profits. **Unit profits** include corporate profits and inventory valuation adjustments per unit of output.

The **implicit price deflator** is derived by dividing the current dollar estimate of gross product by the constant dollar estimate, making the deflator, in effect, a price index for gross product of the sector reported.

**Hours of all persons** describes the labor input of payroll workers, self-employed persons, and unpaid family workers. **Output per all employee hour** describes labor productivity in nonfinancial corporations where there are no self-employed.

## Notes on the data

In the business sector and the nonfarm business sector, the basis for the output measure employed in the computation of output per hour is Gross Domestic Product rather than Gross National Product. Computation of hours includes estimates of nonfarm and farm proprietor hours.

Output data are supplied by the Bureau of Economic Analysis, U.S. Department of Commerce, and the Federal Reserve Board. Quarterly manufacturing output indexes are adjusted by the Bureau of Labor Statistics to annual estimates of output (gross product originating) from the Bureau of Economic Analysis. Compensation and hours data are from the Bureau of Economic Analysis and the Bureau of Labor Statistics.

Notes: 'not available
    r = revised
    1977 = 100

Source: *Monthly Labor Review*, December 1983, p. 92.

## EXHIBIT 4

**U.S. Ratio of Gross Fixed Capital Formation to GNP**

| | | | | | | | | |
|---|---|---|---|---|---|---|---|---|
| | | | | *Percent* | | | | |
| *Period* | *United States* | *France* | *F.R. Germany* | *Italy* | *Nether-lands* | *United Kingdom* | *Japan* | *Canada* |
| 1970 | 17.4 | 23.3 | 25.5 | 23.1 | ( ) | 18.3 | 35.6 | 21.0 |
| 1977 | 18.2 | 21.2 | 20.8 | 19.6 | 21.0 | 17.9 | 30.5 | 23.0 |
| 1978 | 19.3 | 21.4 | 20.7 | 18.7 | 21.3 | 17.9 | 30.8 | 22.6 |
| 1979 | 19.5 | 21.4 | 21.8 | 18.8 | 21.1 | 17.9 | 32.1 | 23.1 |
| 1980 | 18.3 | 21.7 | 22.8 | 19.8 | 21.1 | 17.3 | 32.0 | 23.3 |
| 1981 | 17.8 | 21.1 | 22.0 | 20.3 | 19.4 | 15.5 | 31.1 | 24.2 |
| 1982 | 16.5 | 20.5 | 20.5 | 19.2 | 18.3 | 15.3 | 29.6 | 21.8 |

Data cover gross national product at market prices, except for France, Italy, and the United Kingdom, which relate to gross domestic product. Gross fixed capital formation covers private and government sectors except military. Ratios of gross fixed capital formation to gross national product or gross domestic product are measured in current prices.

Source: U.S. Department of Commerce, Trade Administration, *International Economic Indicators,* December 1983, p. 15.

# EXHIBIT 5

U.S. Capital Investment Levels and Trade Performance

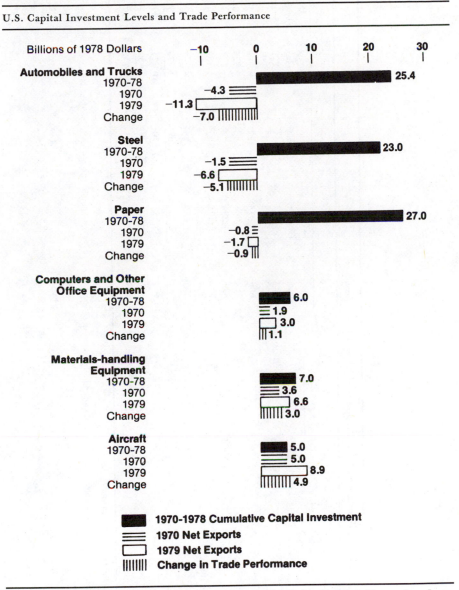

Source: Ira C. Magaziner and Robert B. Reich, *Minding America's Business* (New York: Harcourt Brace Jovanovich, 1982), p. 50.

# EXHIBIT 6

## U.S. Industry Expenditures for R&D by Selected SIC Groupings, 1980 and 1981 (*in millions*)

| Industry | Total R&D Funds | | 1981 R&D Funds | | | | |
| --- | --- | --- | --- | --- | --- | --- | --- |
| | 1980 | 1981 | Federal | Company | Basic Research | Applied Research | Development |
| Chemicals and allied products | $ 4,636 | $ 5,326 | $   383 | $ 4,943 | $   544 | $ 2,272 | $ 2,509 |
| Petroleum refining | 1,552 | 1,917 | 139 | 1,778 | 137 | 791 | 989 |
| Machinery | 5,911 | 6,762 | 689 | 6,073 | 127 | 1,268 | 5,417 |
| Electrical equipment | 9,175 | 10,570 | 3,962 | 6,608 | 288 | 1,774 | 8,553 |
| Motor vehicles | 4,955 | 4,929 | 634 | 4,295 | * | * | * |
| Aircraft and missiles | 9,198 | 11,702 | 8,501 | 3,201 | 135 | 1,487 | 10,080 |
| Professional and scientific instruments | 3,009 | 3,677 | 638 | 3,038 | * | * | * |
| Nonmanufacturing industries | 1,803 | 2,060 | 875 | 1,185 | 115 | * | * |
| All other industries | 4,357 | 5,064 | 644 | 4,421 | 262 | 1,479 | 3,206 |
| Total | 44,596 | 52,007 | 16,465 | 35,542 | 1,670 | 10,771 | 39,566 |
| Discrepancy | – 91 | – 177 | + 3 | – 180 | – 29 | – 59 | – 89 |
| Total | $44,505 | $51,830 | $16,468 | $35,362 | $1,641 | $10,712 | $39,477 |

* = Not separately available but included in totals.

Source: American Association for the Advancement of Science, *AAAS Report VIII: Research & Development, FY 1984* (Washington, D.C.: AAAS, 1983), p. 149.

## EXHIBIT 7

**Scientists and Engineers Engaged in R&D per 10,000 Labor Force by Country**

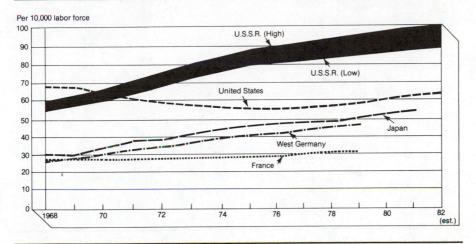

Note: A range has been provided for the U.S.S.R. because of the difficulties inherent in comparing Soviet scientific personnel data.

**R&D/GNP Ratios by Country**

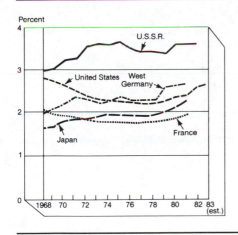

**Nondefense R&D/GNP Ratios by Country***

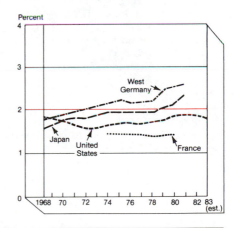

*Separate data for nondefense R&D in the U.S.S.R. are not available.

Source: National Science Foundation, *Science and Technology Data Book* (Washington, D.C.: NSF, Division of Science Resources Studies, October 1983), pp. 43–44.

## EXHIBIT 8

**Changes in Manufacturing Productivity**

| | Output per Hour | |
|---|---|---|
| | *1960–1973* | *1973–1981* |
| United States | 3.0 | 1.7 |
| Canada | 4.5 | 1.4 |
| Japan | 10.7 | 6.8 |
| France | 6.0 | 4.6 |
| Fed. Rep. of Germany | 5.5 | 4.5 |
| Italy | 6.9 | 3.7 |
| United Kingdom | 4.3 | 2.2 |
| Belgium | 7.0 | 6.2 |
| Denmark | 6.4 | 4.1 |
| Netherlands | 7.6 | 5.1 |
| Sweden | 6.7 | 2.2 |

**Changes in Unit Labor Costs in Manufacturing**

| | U.S. Dollars | |
|---|---|---|
| | *1960–1973* | *1973–1981* |
| United States | 1.9 | 7.7 |
| Canada | 1.9 | 6.5 |
| Japan | 4.9 | 7.2 |
| France | 2.8 | 9.4 |
| Fed. Rep. of Germany | 6.1 | 9.1 |
| Italy | 5.4 | 8.1 |
| United Kingdom | 2.6 | 15.0 |
| Belgium | 4.6 | 8.6 |
| Denmark | 5.0 | 7.7 |
| Netherlands | 6.1 | 8.0 |
| Sweden | 4.2 | 9.6 |

Results are expressed as percent change.

Source: Lawrence R. Klein, "International Productivity Comparisons (A Review)," *Proceedings of the National Academy of Sciences, U.S.A.* (July 1983), p. 4565.

# EXHIBIT 9

## Productivity, Unit Labor Cost, and Price, 1975–1980

### Motor Vehicle Industry:

| | Productivity | Unit Labor Cost | | Producer Price |
| --- | --- | --- | --- | --- |
| | | Local Currency | U.S. Dollars | |
| Canada | -2.1 | 14.3 | 10.9 | 9.0 |
| France | 3.1 | 10.7 | 11.0 | — |
| Fed. Rep. of Germany | 0.1 | 7.8 | 14.5 | 3.7 |
| Japan | 10.5 | 2.2 | 3.3 | 0.3 |
| United Kingdom | -1.3 | 12.7 | 13.7 | 15.7 |
| United States | 2.3 | 9.0 | 9.0 | 7.6 |

### Iron and Steel Industry:

| | Productivity | Unit Labor Cost | | Producer Price |
| --- | --- | --- | --- | --- |
| | | Local Currency | U.S. Dollars | |
| Canada | 1.9 | 10.2 | 7.2 | 10.1 |
| France | 7.8 | 4.6 | 4.9 | 7.6 |
| Fed. Rep. of Germany | 4.9 | 2.2 | 8.6 | 1.4 |
| Japan | 8.2 | -1.3 | 4.3 | 6.3 |
| Sweden | 2.1 | 9.3 | 8.9 | 6.9 |
| United Kingdom | -2.2 | 13.6 | 19.8 | 12.9 |
| United States | 0.9 | 10.3 | 10.3 | 8.7 |

### Paper and Allied Products:

| | Productivity | Unit Labor Cost | | Producer Price |
| --- | --- | --- | --- | --- |
| | | Local Currency | U.S. Dollars | |
| Canada | 3.5 | 7.1 | 4.2 | 9.2 |
| France | 6.1 | 7.7 | 8.1 | 5.8 |
| Fed. Rep. of Germany | 5.5 | 2.6 | 9.0 | 2.9 |
| Japan | 5.9 | 0.2 | 5.8 | 6.1 |
| Netherlands | 5.5 | 1.7 | 6.7 | — |
| Sweden | 3.0 | 9.8 | 9.3 | 7.1 |
| United Kingdom | 2.5 | 10.7 | 20.9 | 13.5 |
| United States | 2.6 | 7.4 | 7.4 | 7.9 |

### Electrical Machinery and Electronics Industry:

| | Productivity | Unit Labor Cost | | Producer Price |
| --- | --- | --- | --- | --- |
| | | Local Currency | U.S. Dollars | |
| Canada | 3.3 | 6.8 | 3.8 | 7.2 |
| France | 5.5 | 9.2 | 9.6 | — |
| Fed. Rep. of Germany | 5.0 | 3.0 | 9.5 | 2.0 |
| Japan | 14.1 | -6.7 | -1.5 | 0.4 |
| Netherlands | 7.8 | 1.5 | 6.5 | 1.6 |
| Sweden | 0.6 | 11.5 | 11.1 | 8.3 |
| United Kingdom | 1.8 | 19.9 | 21.0 | 13.4 |
| United States | 4.0 | 5.0 | 5.0 | 7.5 |

**EXHIBIT 9** (*concluded*)

**Textile Industry:**

| | | Unit Labor Cost | | Producer |
|---|---|---|---|---|
| | Productivity | Local Currency | U.S. Dollars | Price |
| Canada | 3.6 | 7.0 | 4.0 | 9.0 |
| Denmark | 3.4 | 7.3 | 7.7 | 6.8 |
| France | 3.2 | 10.6 | 10.9 | 3.4 |
| Fed. Rep. of Germany | 3.6 | 3.7 | 10.2 | 2.6 |
| Japan | 4.2 | 4.1 | 9.9 | 4.2 |
| Netherlands | 7.9 | −0.3 | 4.6 | 3.9 |
| Sweden | 0.3 | 12.4 | 11.9 | 8.6 |
| Switzerland | 5.8 | −0.8 | 6.9 | 0.5 |
| United Kingdom | −0.1 | 15.7 | 16.7 | 12.9 |
| United States | 3.0 | 6.1 | 6.1 | 5.9 |

**Chemicals Industry:**

| | | Unit Labor Cost | | Producer |
|---|---|---|---|---|
| | Productivity | Local Currency | U.S. Dollars | Price |
| Canada | 3.2 | 6.7 | 3.8 | 10.5 |
| France | 4.8 | 10.0 | 10.3 | 9.5 |
| Fed. Rep. of Germany | 3.5 | 3.3 | 10.4 | 2.9 |
| Japan | 9.7 | −1.0 | 4.6 | 9.3 |
| Netherlands | 6.9 | 0.8 | 5.7 | — |
| Sweden | 0.7 | 11.8 | 11.4 | 11.8 |
| Switzerland | 6.9 | −3.0 | 5.8 | −0.6 |
| United Kingdom | 2.6 | 20.5 | 21.6 | 16.3 |
| United States | 4.4 | 5.3 | 5.3 | 9.4 |

Results are expressed as percent change.

Source: Lawrence R. Klein, "International Productivity Comparisons (A Review)," *Proceedings of the National Academy of Sciences*, U.S.A. (July 1983), pp. 4565–4566.

## EXHIBIT 10

### Industrial Production and Consumer Prices, Major Industrial Countries, 1960–1983 (1967 = 100)

| Year or Quarter | United States | Canada | Japan | European Community* | France | West Germany | Italy | United Kingdom |
|---|---|---|---|---|---|---|---|---|
| | | | | Industrial production† | | | | |
| 1960 | 66.2 | 63.1 | 43.0 | 74.7 | 70 | 78.4 | 59.2 | 83.9 |
| 1961 | 66.7 | 65.6 | 51.2 | 78.1 | 73 | 82.8 | 65.5 | 84.2 |
| 1962 | 72.2 | 71.2 | 55.4 | 81.3 | 78 | 86.1 | 71.9 | 85.0 |
| 1963 | 76.5 | 75.7 | 61.7 | 84.8 | 86 | 88.9 | 78.4 | 87.8 |
| 1964 | 81.7 | 82.6 | 71.4 | 91.0 | 90 | 96.6 | 79.2 | 95.0 |
| 1965 | 89.8 | 89.7 | 74.2 | 94.7 | 93 | 102.1 | 82.8 | 97.8 |
| 1966 | 97.8 | 96.2 | 83.8 | 98.4 | 98 | 103.0 | 93.3 | 99.3 |
| 1967 | 100.0 | 100.0 | 100.0 | 100.0 | 100 | 100.0 | 100.0 | 100.0 |
| 1968 | 106.3 | 106.4 | 115.2 | 107.4 | 104 | 109.2 | 106.4 | 107.6 |
| 1969 | 111.1 | 113.7 | 133.4 | 117.6 | 114 | 123.2 | 110.5 | 111.3 |
| 1970 | 107.8 | 115.3 | 151.8 | 123.3 | 120 | 131.1 | 117.6 | 111.8 |
| 1971 | 109.6 | 121.5 | 155.7 | 126.1 | 128 | 133.6 | 117.5 | 111.2 |
| 1972 | 119.7 | 130.7 | 167.0 | 131.7 | 135 | 138.7 | 122.7 | 113.2 |
| 1973 | 129.8 | 144.6 | 190.5 | 141.4 | 145 | 147.7 | 134.6 | 123.3 |
| 1974 | 129.3 | 149.2 | 183.1 | 142.3 | 148 | 145.1 | 140.6 | 120.8 |
| 1975 | 117.8 | 140.3 | 163.9 | 132.8 | 139 | 137.1 | 127.6 | 114.4 |
| 1976 | 130.5 | 148.5 | 182.0 | 142.6 | 149 | 149.1 | 143.5 | 118.1 |
| 1977 | 138.2 | 152.7 | 189.7 | 145.9 | 152 | 152.0 | 145.1 | 124.2 |
| 1978 | 146.1 | 157.8 | 201.1 | 149.7 | 155 | 154.1 | 147.9 | 127.8 |
| 1979 | 152.5 | 167.6 | 215.3 | 156.8 | 163 | 161.8 | 157.6 | 132.8 |
| 1980 | 147.0 | 165.1 | 225.2 | 155.5 | 161 | 162.3 | 166.5 | 124.1 |
| 1981 | 151.0 | 166.6 | 227.5 | 152.1 | 160 | 159.9 | 162.7 | 119.2 |
| 1982 | 138.6 | 148.8 | 228.4 | 149.9 | 158 | 156.2 | 159.1 | 121.7 |
| 1983P | 147.7 | . . . . | . . . . | . . . . | . . . . | . . . . | . . . . | . . . . |

**EXHIBIT 10** (*concluded*)

| Year or Quarter | United States | Canada | Japan | European Community* | France | West Germany | Italy | United Kingdom |
|---|---|---|---|---|---|---|---|---|
| | | | | Industrial production | | | | |
| **1982:** | | | | | | | | |
| I | 141.8 | 155.5 | 230.5 | 151.8 | 159 | 161 | 161.0 | 120.5 |
| II | 139.4 | 150.5 | 227.9 | 151.5 | 159 | 160 | 158.6 | 121.6 |
| III | 138.2 | 146.8 | 228.9 | 149.5 | 155 | 154 | 146.6 | 122.6 |
| IV | 135.3 | 142.1 | 226.3 | 146.7 | 158 | 152 | 149.8 | 122.0 |
| **1983:** | | | | | | | | |
| I | 138.5 | 149.5 | 228.2 | 147.9 | 159 | 154 | 149.0 | 123.6 |
| II | 144.5 | 153.9 | 231.7 | 148.7 | 155 | 157 | 145.0 | 123.0 |
| III | 151.8 | 160.9 | 239.0 | 150.7 | 159 | 157 | 144.1 | 125.3 |
| IV$^P$ | 156.0 | ... | ... | ... | | | ... | ... |
| | | | | Consumer prices | | | | |
| 1960 | 88.7 | 85.9 | 68.3 | 77.0 | 78.0‡ | 82.9 | 74.1 | 79.0 |
| 1961 | 89.6 | 86.7 | 71.8 | 81.1 | 80.6‡ | 84.8 | 75.7 | 81.6 |
| 1962 | 90.6 | 87.7 | 76.7 | 84.5 | 85.4 | 87.4 | 79.2 | 85.1 |
| 1963 | 91.7 | 89.2 | 82.5 | 87.6 | 89.5 | 89.9 | 85.1 | 86.8 |
| 1964 | 92.9 | 90.9 | 85.8 | 90.8 | 92.5 | 92.0 | 90.1 | 89.6 |
| 1965 | 94.5 | 93.1 | 91.6 | 94.2 | 94.8 | 95.0 | 94.2 | 93.9 |
| 1966 | 97.2 | 96.5 | 96.3 | 97.5 | 97.4 | 98.4 | 96.4 | 97.6 |
| 1967 | 100.0 | 100.0 | 100.0 | 100.0 | 100.0 | 100.0 | 100.0 | 100.0 |
| 1968 | 104.2 | 104.0 | 105.3 | 103.7 | 104.5 | 101.6 | 101.4 | 104.8 |
| 1969 | 109.8 | 108.8 | 110.9 | 108.0 | 111.3 | 103.5 | 104.1 | 110.3 |
| 1970 | 116.3 | 112.4 | 119.3 | 113.3 | 117.1 | 107.1 | 109.2 | 117.4 |
| 1971 | 121.3 | 115.6 | 126.5 | 120.3 | 123.5 | 112.7 | 114.4 | 128.5 |

| | | | | | | | | |
|---|---|---|---|---|---|---|---|---|
| 1972 | 125.3 | 121.2 | 132.3 | 127.6 | 131.1 | 119.0 | 121.0 | 137.7 |
| 1973 | 133.1 | 130.3 | 147.9 | 138.3 | 140.7 | 127.2 | 134.0 | 150.2 |
| 1974 | 147.7 | 144.5 | 184.0 | 156.4 | 160.0 | 136.1 | 159.7 | 174.3 |
| 1975 | 161.2 | 160.1 | 205.8 | 176.7 | 178.9 | 144.2 | 186.8 | 216.5 |
| 1976 | 170.5 | 172.1 | 224.9 | 195.2 | 196.1 | 150.4 | 218.1 | 252.4 |
| 1977 | 181.5 | 185.9 | 243.0 | 214.7 | 214.5 | 155.9 | 255.2 | 292.4 |
| 1978 | 195.4 | 202.5 | 252.3 | 229.9 | 233.9 | 160.2 | 286.2 | 316.6 |
| 1979 | 217.4 | 221.0 | 261.3 | 250.7 | 259.1 | 166.8 | 328.5 | 359.0 |
| 1980 | 246.8 | 243.5 | 282.2 | 281.4 | 294.2 | 175.9 | 398.0 | 423.6 |
| 1981 | 272.4 | 273.9 | 296.2 | 313.4 | 332.7 | 186.3 | 472.4 | 473.9 |
| 1982 | 289.1 | 303.5 | 304.1 | 344.3 | 373.1 | 196.2 | 549.4 | 514.7 |
| 1983ᴾ | 298.4 | 321.0 | | | | | | |
| 1982: | | | | | | | | |
| I | 283.0 | 292.2 | 300.3 | 333.4 | 359.8 | 192.7 | 523.7 | 500.5 |
| II | 287.3 | 301.2 | 303.4 | 342.0 | 371.0 | 195.4 | 539.6 | 516.6 |
| III | 292.8 | 307.6 | 304.8 | 347.5 | 376.0 | 197.6 | 562.7 | 518.9 |
| IV | 293.4 | 312.6 | 307.5 | 353.7 | 383.0 | 198.9 | 589.1 | 522.7 |
| 1983: | | | | | | | | |
| I | 293.2 | 314.5 | 306.5 | 359.5 | 393.2 | 199.9 | 609.7 | 525.3 |
| II | 296.9 | 318.8 | 310.1 | 366.6 | 404.4 | 201.1 | 627.5 | 536.1 |
| III | 300.5 | 324.0 | 309.0 | 372.6 | 413.1 | 203.1 | 643.0 | 543.0 |
| IVᴾ | 303.1 | 326.8 | | | | | | |

*Consists of Belgium-Luxembourg, Denmark, France, Greece, Ireland, Italy, Netherlands, United Kingdom, and West Germany. Industrial production prior to July 1981 excludes data for Greece, which joined the EC in 1981.

†All data exclude construction. Quarterly data are seasonally adjusted.

‡Data for 1960 and 1961 are for Paris only.

ᴾPreliminary.

Source: Council of Economic Advisers, *Economic Report of the President* (February 1984) p. 342.

## EXHIBIT 11

**Civilian Unemployment Rate, Major Industrial Countries, 1960–1983** *[Quarterly data seasonally adjusted]*

| Year or Quarter | United States | Canada | Japan | France | West Germany | Italy | United Kingdom |
|---|---|---|---|---|---|---|---|
| | Civilian unemployment rate (percent)* | | | | | | |
| 1960 | 5.5 | 6.5 | 1.7 | 1.6 | 1.1 | 3.2 | 2.1 |
| 1961 | 6.7 | 6.7 | 1.5 | 1.4 | .6 | 2.8 | 1.9 |
| 1962 | 5.5 | 5.5 | 1.3 | 1.3 | .6 | 2.5 | 2.7 |
| 1963 | 5.7 | 5.2 | 1.3 | 1.2 | .5 | 2.1 | 3.3 |
| 1964 | 5.2 | 4.4 | 1.2 | 1.3 | .4 | 2.4 | 2.4 |
| 1965 | 4.5 | 3.6 | 1.2 | 1.4 | .3 | 3.0 | 2.1 |
| 1966 | 3.8 | 3.4 | 1.4 | 1.7 | .3 | 3.3 | 2.2 |
| 1967 | 3.8 | 3.8 | 1.3 | 1.8 | 1.3 | 3.0 | 3.2 |
| 1968 | 3.6 | 4.5 | 1.2 | 2.4 | 1.1 | 3.1 | 3.2 |
| 1969 | 3.5 | 4.4 | 1.1 | 2.2 | .6 | 3.1 | 3.0 |
| 1970 | 4.9 | 5.7 | 1.2 | 2.4 | .5 | 2.8 | 3.1 |
| 1971 | 5.9 | 6.2 | 1.3 | 2.7 | .6 | 2.9 | 3.9 |
| 1972 | 5.6 | 6.2 | 1.4 | 2.8 | .7 | 3.4 | 4.2 |
| 1973 | 4.9 | 5.5 | 1.3 | 2.7 | .7 | 3.2 | 3.2 |
| 1974 | 5.6 | 5.3 | 1.4 | 2.9 | 1.6 | 2.8 | 3.1 |
| 1975 | 8.5 | 6.9 | 1.9 | 4.2 | 3.4 | 3.2 | 4.6 |
| 1976 | 7.7 | 7.1 | 2.0 | 4.6 | 3.4 | 3.6 | 6.0 |
| 1977 | 7.1 | 8.1 | 2.0 | 5.0 | 3.5 | 3.6 | 6.3 |
| 1978 | 6.1 | 8.4 | 2.3 | 5.4 | 3.4 | 3.7 | 6.2 |
| 1979 | 5.8 | 7.5 | 2.1 | 6.1 | 3.0 | 3.9 | 5.6 |
| 1980 | 7.1 | 7.5 | 2.0 | 6.5 | 2.9 | 3.9 | 7.0 |
| 1981 | 7.6 | 7.6 | 2.2 | 7.7 | 4.1 | 4.3 | 10.6 |
| 1982 | 9.7 | 11.0 | 2.4 | 8.7 | 5.9 | 4.8 | 12.3 |
| 1983 | 9.6 | 11.9 | 2.7 | .... | 7.3 | 5.1 | .... |

*Civilian unemployment rates, approximating U.S. concepts. Data for United Kingdom exclude Northern Ireland. Quarterly data for France, West Germany, and United Kingdom should be viewed as less precise indicators of unemployment under U.S. concepts than the annual data. Beginning 1977, changes in the Italian survey resulted in a large increase in persons enumerated as unemployed. However, many also reported that they had not actively sought work in the past 30 days. Such persons have been provisionally excluded for comparability with U.S. concepts; their inclusion would more than double the rates shown for Italy.

Source: Council of Economic Advisers, *Economic Report of the President* (February 1984), p. 343.

# EXHIBIT 12

## Changing Profile of the Top 200 Industrial Corporations 1960–1980

| Country | Number | | | Sales (billions of U.S. dollars) | | | Percent of Sales | | |
|---|---|---|---|---|---|---|---|---|---|
| | 1960 | 1970 | 1980 | 1960 | 1970 | 1980 | 1960 | 1970 | 1980 |
| USA | 127 | 123 | 91 | 144.6 | 313.5 | 1080.4 | 72.7 | 66.0 | 50.1 |
| Germany, Fed. Rep. of | 20 | 15 | 21 | 13.4 | 34.6 | 209.0 | 6.8 | 7.3 | 9.7 |
| UK | 24 | 17 | 16½ᵃ | 19.6 | 39.2 | 199.5 | 9.9 | 8.2 | 9.2 |
| France | 7 | 13 | 15 | 3.5 | 19.8 | 161.0 | 1.8 | 4.2 | 7.5 |
| Japan | 5 | 13 | 20 | 2.9 | 28.1 | 155.2 | 1.5 | 5.9 | 7.2 |
| Netherlands | 3 | 3 | 5 | 6.4 | 15.0 | 89.6 | 3.2 | 3.2 | 4.2 |
| Italy | 3 | 5 | 4½ᵃ | 1.9 | 9.6 | 69.5 | 0.9 | 2.0 | 3.2 |
| Canada | 5 | 2 | 5 | 2.6 | 2.4 | 32.5 | 1.3 | 0.5 | 1.5 |
| Switzerland | 2 | 4 | 4 | 2.0 | 6.4 | 31.9 | 1.0 | 1.3 | 1.5 |
| Belgium | 1 | 1 | 2 | 0.5 | 1.3 | 14.5 | 0.2 | 0.3 | 0.7 |
| Sweden | 1 | 1 | 2 | 0.4 | 1.0 | 11.0 | 0.2 | 0.2 | 0.5 |
| Rep. of Korea | — | — | 2 | — | — | 10.0 | — | — | 0.5 |
| Others | 2 | 3 | 12 | 1.1 | 4.4 | 91.1 | 0.5 | 0.9 | 4.2 |
| Total (excl. USA) | 73 | 77 | 109 | 54.4 | 161.7 | 1074.8 | 27.3 | 34.0 | 49.9 |
| Total | 200 | 200 | 200 | 199.0 | 475.2 | 2155.2 | 100.0 | 100.0 | 100.0 |
| World GDPᵇ | | | | 1126.2 | 2489.0 | 7548.0 | | | |
| Top 200 as percent of GDP | | | | 17.7 | 19.1 | 28.6 | | | |

Note: Countries were selected with more than one corporation in the top 200 in 1980, and ranked according to 1980 sales.

ᵃCorporations owned by interests in two countries are counted as one half.

ᵇExcluding socialist countries.

Source: John Cavanagh and Frederick Clairmonte, "The Transnational Economy," *Trade and Development: An United Nations Conference on Trade & Development Review,* Winter 1982, p. 11. Calculated from *Fortune*'s listings of leading industrial corporations.

# EXHIBIT 13

## Foreign Revenues of Top 100 U.S.-Based Transnational Corporations and Transnational Banks, 1981[a]

| Rank[b] | Company | Total Revenues ($ billion) | Foreign Revenue as Percent of Total |
|---|---|---|---|
| **Banks and nonbank financial:** | | | |
| 13 | Chase Manhattan | 10.7 | 65.0 |
| 19 | J. P. Morgan | 6.8 | 63.3 |
| 9 | Citicorp | 18.3 | 62.0 |
| 83 | Irving Bank | 2.4 | 57.1 |
| 65 | First National Boston | 2.9 | 56.7 |
| 39 | Bankers Trust New York | 4.7 | 55.0 |
| 8 | Phibro-Salomon | 25.1 | 53.3 |
| 22 | Manufacturers Hanover | 7.5 | 53.3 |
| 12 | Bank America | 15.1 | 52.7 |
| 49 | First Chicago | 4.3 | 48.3 |
| 97 | Marine Midland Banks | 2.5 | 47.9 |
| 35 | Chemical New York | 5.7 | 47.2 |
| 41 | Continental Illinois | 6.3 | 37.8 |
| 56 | American Express | 7.2 | 26.9 |
| *Sector average* | | | *53.5* |
| **Transportation:** | | | |
| 36 | Pan Am World Airways | 3.8 | 70.0 |
| 58 | Trans World | 5.3 | 35.8 |
| *Sector average* | | | *50.5* |

| Rank[b] | Company | Total revenues ($ billion) | Foreign revenue as per cent of total |
|---|---|---|---|
| **Automotive[c]:** | | | |
| 5 | Ford Motor | 38.2 | 48.4 |
| 26 | Goodyear | 9.2 | 41.0 |
| 71 | Firestone | 4.4 | 34.9 |
| 46 | International Harvester | 7.0 | 30.3 |
| 87 | Bendix | 4.4 | 29.6 |
| 6 | General Motors | 62.7 | 25.0 |
| 45 | Chrysler | 10.8 | 20.2 |
| *Sector average* | | | *32.9* |
| **Food and beverage:** | | | |
| 34 | CPC International | 4.3 | 64.4 |
| 38 | Coca-Cola | 5.9 | 45.0 |
| 76 | H. J. Heinz | 3.6 | 39.9 |
| 55 | Nabisco Brands | 5.8 | 34.1 |
| 52 | General Foods | 6.6 | 30.9 |
| 32 | Dart & Kraft | 10.2 | 28.5 |
| 75 | Consolidated Foods | 5.6 | 25.6 |
| 91 | Ralston Purina | 5.2 | 24.0 |
| 50 | Beatrice Foods | 9.0 | 23.1 |
| 66 | PepsiCo | 7.0 | 22.7 |
| *Sector average* | | | *31.8* |

**Natural resources (fuel and related):**

| | | | |
|---|---|---|---|
| 43 | Atlantic Richfield | 27.8 | 83.9 |
| 1 | Exxon | 108.1 | 70.1 |
| 3 | Texaco | 57.6 | 67.0 |
| 2 | Mobil | 65.4 | 62.9 |
| 4 | Standard Oil California | 44.2 | 53.9 |
| 11 | Gulf Oil | 28.2 | 36.7 |
| 18 | Occidental Petroleum | 15.3 | 31.7 |
| 21 | Sun Co. | 16.0 | 25.6 |
| 48 | Halliburton | 8.5 | 24.7 |
| 27 | Phillips Petroleum | 16.0 | 21.3 |
| 44 | Getty Oil | 12.9 | 17.8 |
| 60 | Union Oil California | 10.9 | 16.8 |
| 17 | Standard Oil Indiana | 30.4 | 16.4 |
| | *Sector average* | | *48.8* |

**Office equipment and computers:**

| | | | |
|---|---|---|---|
| 62 | NCR | 3.4 | 52.1 |
| 63 | Hewlett-Packard | 3.6 | 48.2 |
| 7 | IBM | 29.1 | 48.1 |
| 24 | Xerox | 8.7 | 44.5 |
| 81 | Burroughs | 3.4 | 40.2 |
| 47 | Sperry | 5.4 | 39.3 |
| 92 | Digital Equipment | 3.2 | 39.1 |
| 68 | Honeywell | 5.4 | 29.0 |
| | *Sector average* | | *44.7* |

**Conglomerates:**

| | | | |
|---|---|---|---|
| 10 | Intl. Tel & Tel | 23.2 | 47.3 |
| 96 | Litton Industries | 4.9 | 24.5 |
| 89 | TRW | 5.3 | 23.9 |
| 33 | Tenneco | 15.5 | 18.8 |
| 80 | Gulf & Western Inds. | 7.4 | 18.6 |
| | *Sector average* | | *31.6* |

**Miscellaneous:**

| | | | |
|---|---|---|---|
| 30 | Colgate-Palmolive | 5.3 | 58.7 |
| 85 | Gillette | 2.3 | 57.3 |
| 69 | American Intl. Group | 3.2 | 48.9 |
| 93 | Avon Products | 2.6 | 47.9 |
| 99 | Singer | 2.8 | 40.6 |
| 61 | American Brands | 4.5 | 40.0 |
| 40 | Minn. Mining & Mfg. | 6.5 | 39.3 |
| 23 | Eastman Kodak | 10.3 | 38.0 |
| 86 | Scott Paper | 3.6 | 36.6 |
| 100 | Ingersoll-Rand | 3.4 | 34.0 |
| 25 | Procter & Gamble | 11.4 | 32.8 |
| 57 | Fluor | 6.1 | 31.6 |
| 70 | Deere | 5.4 | 28.2 |
| 37 | R. J. Reynolds | 9.8 | 27.2 |
| 73 | Continental Group | 5.8 | 25.1 |
| 31 | United Technologies | 13.7 | 22.1 |
| 64 | Caterpillar Tractor | 9.2 | 18.6 |
| 53 | General Tel. & Elec. | 11.0 | 18.4 |
| 98 | Philip Morris | 8.3 | 14.0 |
| | *Sector average* | | *30.7* |

**EXHIBIT 13** *(concluded)*

| Rank[b] | Company | Total Revenues ($ billion) | Foreign Revenue as Percent of Total |
|---|---|---|---|
| | **Chemicals and drugs:** | | |
| 59 | Pfizer | 3.3 | 56.8 |
| 16 | Dow Chemical | 11.9 | 47.9 |
| 82 | Merck | 2.9 | 46.7 |
| 42 | Johnson & Johnson | 5.4 | 44.0 |
| 74 | Warner-Lambert | 3.4 | 42.6 |
| 90 | Bristol-Myers | 3.5 | 36.0 |
| 88 | American Cyanamid | 3.6 | 35.0 |
| 79 | American Home Products | 4.1 | 33.6 |
| 29 | Union Carbide | 10.2 | 31.4 |
| 51 | Monsanto | 6.9 | 29.9 |
| 14 | E. I. Du Pont de Nemours | 22.8 | 29.5 |
| 67 | Allied Corp | 6.4 | 24.4 |
| 78 | W. R. Grace | 6.5 | 21.3 |
| | *Sector average* | | *34.9* |

| Rank[b] | Company | Total revenues ($ billion) | Foreign revenue as per cent of total |
|---|---|---|---|
| | **Electrical, electronics:** | | |
| 95 | Motorola | 3.3 | 36.4 |
| 84 | Texas Instruments | 4.2 | 31.9 |
| 15 | General Electric | 27.9 | 20.9 |
| 77 | RCA | 9.0 | 15.7 |
| 94 | Westinghouse Electric | 9.4 | 13.0 |
| | *Sector average* | | *20.3* |
| | **Retailing (food and non-food):** | | |
| 28 | F. W. Woolworth | 8.3 | 40.9 |
| 20 | Safeway Stores | 16.6 | 24.7 |
| 72 | K. Mart | 17.4 | 8.7 |
| 54 | Sears Roebuck | 29.3 | 6.9 |
| | *Sector average* | | *15.4* |

Note: Calculated from data in *Forbes*, July 5, 1982.
[a]Ranked by foreign as percent to total revenues.
[b]Ranking based on foreign revenues in *Forbes'* 100 largest multinationals.
[c]Including rubber and tire corporations.

Source: John Cavanagh and Frederick Clairmonte, "The Transnational Economy," *Trade and Development: United Nations Conference on Trade and Development Review*, Winter 1982, pp. 14-15.

# EXHIBIT 14

**Profile of Top 100 Banks, 1981**

| Country/Territory[a] | Number of banks | Assets ($ billion) | Percent of Total Assets | Profits ($ billion) | Percent of Total Profits |
|---|---|---|---|---|---|
| Japan | 24 | 1,097.6 | 25.1 | 88.4 | 20.8 |
| USA | 12 | 650.7 | 14.9 | 91.2 | 21.4 |
| France | 8 | 509.2 | 11.6 | 35.8 | 8.4 |
| Germany, Fed. Rep. of. | 11 | 464.3 | 10.6 | 45.9 | 10.8 |
| UK | 5 | 344.5 | 7.9 | 42.1 | 9.9 |
| Italy | 8 | 258.1 | 5.9 | 28.6 | 6.7 |
| Canada | 5 | 240.6 | 5.5 | 34.5 | 8.1 |
| Netherlands | 4 | 160.4 | 3.7 | 2.5 | 0.6 |
| Switzerland | 3 | 141.9 | 3.2 | 12.8 | 3.0 |
| Belgium | 4 | 100.2 | 2.3 | 12.2 | 2.9 |
| Spain | 3 | 67.5 | 1.5 | 6.7 | 1.6 |
| Brazil | 1 | 65.1 | 1.5 | 5.3 | 1.2 |
| Sweden | 3 | 64.6 | 1.5 | 3.1 | 0.7 |
| Australia | 3 | 60.0 | 1.4 | 7.1 | 1.7 |
| Hong Kong | 1 | 52.1 | 1.2 | . . | . . |
| Islamic Rep. of Iran | 1 | 23.9 | 0.6 | 1.1 | 0.3 |
| India | 1 | 20.5 | 0.5 | 1.9 | 0.5 |
| Israel | 1 | 19.2 | 0.4 | 4.2 | 1.0 |
| Mexico | 1 | 18.4 | 0.4 | . . | . . |
| Austria | 1 | 18.2 | 0.4 | 1.7 | 0.4 |
| | 100 | 4,377.0 | 100.0 | 425.1[b] | 100.0 |

Source: Computed from *The Banker,* June 1982.

[a]Countries ranked by banks' assets.

[b]Profit figures not provided for banks in the case of : France (3), Hong Kong (1), Netherlands (2), Japan (1), Italy (1), UK (1), Sweden (1), Mexico (1).

Source: John Cavanagh and Frederick Clairmonte, "The Transnational Economy," *Trade and Development: An United Nations Conference on Trade and Development Review,* Winter 1982, p. 12.

## EXHIBIT 15

**Trade Balances by Industry** (*Millions of dollars*)

|  | Average 1970–1979 | Average 1980–1982 |
|---|---|---|
| Total Manufacturing | 11,084.2 | 27,371.7 |
| Food and Products | − 2,513.7 | − 1,086.9 |
| Tobacco Manufactures | 1,056.8 | 2,045.2 |
| Textile Mill Products | 14.7 | 1,030.0 |
| Apparel | − 2,378.5 | − 6,142.1 |
| Lumber and Wood Products | − 268.9 | 222.6 |
| Furniture and Fixtures | 84.3 | 436.1 |
| Paper and Products | − 659.6 | − 620.5 |
| Printing and Publishing | 304.1 | 675.7 |
| Chemicals | 5,437.8 | 13,948.3 |
| Petroleum Products | − 4,765.0 | − 10,131.8 |
| Rubber and Products | − 611.7 | − 1,046.6 |
| Leather Products | − 716.5 | − 1,559.6 |
| Stone, Clay, and Glass | − 158.1 | − 452.0 |
| Primary Metals | − 4,765.0 | − 8,659.6 |
| Steel Mill Products | − 4,540.0 | − 8,572.6 |
| Fabricated Metals | − 177.9 | − 473.2 |
| Nonelectrical Machinery | 14,479.2 | 33,448.1 |
| Electrical Machinery | 4,321.6 | 8,138.1 |
| Transportation Equipment | 1,500.3 | − 3,165.6 |
| Motor Vehicles and Parts | − 3,869.3 | − 13,511.4 |
| Instruments | 1,396.9 | 2,033.6 |
| Miscellaneous Manufacturing | − 496.5 | − 1,268.2 |

Source: Otto Eckstein, *et al., U.S. Manufacturing Industries* (Cambridge: Data Resources, Inc., 1984), p. 84.

# Permissions

Permission has been granted from the following authors and/or publishers to use material from the works cited. References to specific page numbers can be found where these works are used throughout the text.

Albion, Robert G. "New York Port and Its Disappointed Rivals." *Journal of Economic and Business History*, Vol. 3, Cambridge, Mass.: Harvard Univ. Press, 1931.

Albion, Robert G. *The Rise of New York Port*. Copyright © 1939 by Charles Scribner's Sons. Copyright renewed © 1967. Reprinted with the permission of Charles Scribner's Sons.

American Association for the Advancement of Science. *AAAS Report VII: Research and Development*, FY 1984. ©1983 by the American Association for the Advancement of Science.

Bailyn, Bernard et al. *The Great Republic*, 2d ed. © 1977 by D. C. Heath and Company. Reprinted by permission of the publisher.

Bartlett, Christopher. "How Multinational Organizations Evolve." In *The Management of Headquarters: Subsidiary Relationships in Multinational Corporations* by Lars Otterbeck. © 1981 by Lars Otterbeck and reprinted by permission of St. Martin's Press, Inc.

Bloom, Paul N. "The Cereal Companies: Monopolists or Super Marketers?" *M.S.U. Business Topics*, Summer 1978. Division of Research, Michigan State University Graduate School of Business Administration.

Bork, Robert. *The Antitrust Paradox*, New York: Basic Books, 1978.

Branson, William H. "Trends in United States International Trade and Investment Since World War II." In *The American Economy in Transistion*, ed. Martin Feldstein, Chicago: University of Chicago Press, 1980.

Bruchey, Stuart. *Cotton and the Growth of the American Economy*, New York: Harcourt Brace Jovanovich, 1967. Reprinted with permission of the author.

Bruchey, Stuart. *Robert Oliver, Merchant of Baltimore*, Baltimore: The Johns Hopkins University Press, 1956. Reprinted by permission of the author.

Cavanaugh, John, and Frederick Clairmonte. "The Transnational Economy," *Trade and Development: An United Nations Conference on Trade and Development Review*, Winter 1982.

Clough, Samuel. *Memoirs, Edited by* Mrs. E. B. Troxell. *Annals of Iowa 39*, Spring 1969.

Cranmer, H. Jerome. "Canal Investment, 1815-1860." In *Trends in the American Economy in the Nineteenth Century*. Princeton, N.J.: Princeton University Press, 1960.

Davidson, John Wells. *A Crossroads of Freedom: The Campaign Speeches of Woodrow Wilson*. New Haven: Yale University Press, 1956. Reprinted with permission of the author.

Eckstein, Otto, et al. *U.S. Manufacturing Industries*. Cambridge, Mass.: Data Resources, Inc., 1984.

Fine, Sidney. *Sit-Down*. Ann Arbor: The University of Michigan Press, 1969. © 1969 by The University of Michigan Press.

Fouraker, Lawrence A., and John M. Stopford. "Organizational Structure and the Multinational Strategy." *Administrative Science Quarterly*, June 1968.

Garraty, John A. *The American Nation*. Copyright © 1968, 1971, 1975, 1979, 1983 by Harper & Row by permission of the publisher.

Kindleberger, Charles. *The World in Depression*. Berkeley: The University of California Press.

Klein, Lawrence R. "International Productivity Comparisons (A Review)." *Proceedings of the National Academy of Science USA*, July 1983.

Labaree, Leonard et al., eds. *The Autobiography of Benjamin Franklin*. New Haven, Conn.: The Yale University Press, 1975. Copyright 1975 by The Yale University Press.

Lebergott, Stanley. *Manpower in Economic Growth*. New York: McGraw-Hill, 1964. Copyright 1964 by McGraw-Hill Book Company. Reprinted with permission of the publisher.

Magaziner, Ira C., and Robert B. Reich. *Minding America's Business*. New York: Harcourt Brace Jovanovich, 1982.

Martin, Robert F. *National Income in the United States, 1799-1938*. New York: National Industrial Conference Board, 1939.

McClelland, Peter. "Transportation." In *Encyclopedia of American Economic History*, Vol. I, ed. Glenn Porter, New York: Charles Scribner's Sons, 1980. ©1980 by Charles Scribner's Sons.

McCraw, Thomas K. "Regulatory Agencies," In *Encyclopedia of American Economic History*, Vol. II, ed. Glen Porter. New York: Charles Scribner's Sons, 1980. © 1980 by Charles Scribner's Sons.

Morris, Richard B. *Encyclopedia of American History*. New York: Harper & Row, 1976.

North, Douglass C. *The Economic Growth of the United States 1790 to 1860*. Englewood Cliffs, N.J.: Prentice-Hall, 1961. Copyright © 1961 by Prentice-Hall. Reprinted by permission of the publisher.

North, Douglas C. *Growth and Welfare in the American Past*. Englewood Cliffs, N.J.: Prentice-Hall, 1966. Reprinted by permission of the author.

National Science Foundation, *Science and Technology Data Book*. Washington, D.C.: NSF, Division of Science Resources Studies, October 1983.

Paullin, Charles O. *Atlas of the Historical Geography of the United States*. Washington, D.C.: Carnegie Institution of Washington, 1932.

Porter, Kenneth Wiggins. *John Jacob Astor, Businessman*. Cambridge, Mass.: Harvard University Press, 1931. Copyright renewed © 1959 by Kenneth Wiggins Porter.

Pringle, Henry F. *The Life and Times of William Howard Taft*. New York: Farrar and Rinehart, 1939. Copyright 1939 by Henry F. Pringle. Copyright © 1967 by Catherine D. Massell. Reprinted by permission of Holt, Rinehart & Winston Publishers.

Rumelt, Richard P. Strategy, Structure and Economic Performance. Harvard Business School thesis, 1974. Reprinted by permission of the author.

Stopford, John M., and Louis T. Wells. *Managing the Multinational Enterprise*. New York: Basic Books, 1972. Reprinted by permission of Basic Books.

Taylor, George Rogers. *The Transportation Revolution 1815-1860*. New York: Harper & Row, 1951. Reprinted with the permission of the estate of George Rogers Taylor, Debora T. Davis, executrix.

Temin, Peter. *Did Monetary Forces Cause the Great Depression?* New York: W. W. Norton, 1976.

Temin, Peter. *The Jacksonian Economy*. New York: W.W. Norton, 1969.

Wilkins, Mira. *The Emergence of Multinational Enterprise*. Cambridge, Mass.: Harvard University Press, 1970.

Woodman, Harold D. *Slavery and the Southern Economy*. New York: Harcourt Brace Jovanovich, 1966. Reprinted by permission of the author.

# Index

*This book has been set on the Compugraphic 8600, in 10 point Baskerville, leaded 2 points. Part numbers are 30 point Baskerville and part titles are 36 point Baskerville bold italic. Case numbers are 24 point Baskerville and case titles are 30 point Baskerville bold italic. The size of the type page is 28 by 48½ picas.*